Jimmy Swaggart Bible Commentary

Philippians

JIMMY SWAGGART BIBLE COMMENTARY

- Genesis (639 pages) (11-201)
- Exodus (639 pages) (11-202)
- Leviticus (435 pages) (11-203)
- Numbers
  Deuteronomy (493 pages) (11-204)
- Joshua
  Judges
  Ruth (329 pages) (11-205)
- I Samuel
  II Samuel (528 pages) (11-206)
- I Kings
  II Kings (560 pages) (11-207)
- I Chronicles
  II Chronicles (528 pages) (11-226)
- Ezra
  Nehemiah
  Esther (288 pages) (11-208)
- Job (320 pages) (11-225)
- Psalms (688 pages) (11-216)
- Proverbs (320 pages) (11-227)
- Ecclesiastes
  Song Of Solomon (245 pages) (11-228)
- Isaiah (688 pages) (11-220)
- Jeremiah
  Lamentations (688 pages) (11-070)
- Ezekiel (508 pages) (11-223)
- Daniel (403 pages) (11-224)
- Hosea
  Joel
  Amos (496 pages) (11-229)
- Obadiah
  Jonah
  Micah
  Naham
  Habakkuk
  Zephaniah *(will be ready Spring 2013)* (11-230)
- Matthew (625 pages) (11-073)
- Mark (606 pages) (11-074)
- Luke (626 pages) (11-075)
- John (532 pages) (11-076)
- Acts (697 pages) (11-077)
- Romans (536 pages) (11-078)
- I Corinthians (632 pages) (11-079)
- II Corinthians (589 pages) (11-080)
- Galatians (478 pages) (11-081)
- Ephesians (550 pages) (11-082)
- Philippians (476 pages) (11-083)
- Colossians (374 pages) (11-084)
- I Thessalonians
  II Thessalonians (498 pages) (11-085)
- I Timothy
  II Timothy
  Titus
  Philemon (687 pages) (11-086)
- Hebrews (831 pages) (11-087)
- James
  I Peter
  II Peter (730 pages) (11-088)
- I John
  II John
  III John
  Jude (377 pages) (11-089)
- Revelation (602 pages) (11-090)

**OBADIAH
JONAH
MICAH
NAHAM
HABAKKUK
ZEPHANIAH**

For prices and information please call: 1-800-288-8350
Baton Rouge residents please call: (225) 768-7000
Website: www.jsm.org • Email: info@jsm.org

JIMMY SWAGGART BIBLE COMMENTARY

Philippians

WORLD EVANGELISM PRESS

ISBN 978-1-934655-14-6
11-083 • COPYRIGHT © 2000 World Evangelism Press®
P.O. Box 262550 • Baton Rouge, Louisiana 70826-2550
Website: www.jsm.org • Email: info@jsm.org • (225) 768-8300
13 14 15 16 17 18 19 20 21 22 23 24 25 26 27 28 / RRD / 18 17 16 15 14 13 12 11 10 9 8 7 6 5 4 3
All rights reserved. Printed and bound in U.S.A.
No part of this publication may be reproduced in any form or by any means
without the publisher's prior written permission.

TABLE OF CONTENTS

1. Introduction v
2. Philippians 1
3. Index 473

INTRODUCTION

THE INTRODUCTION OF THE EPISTLE OF PAUL THE APOSTLE TO THE PHILIPPIANS

The Apostle's entrance into Philippi and the founding of the Church there would remain more firmly etched in his memory than possibly most other episodes of his colorful Ministry. It was Paul's first experience on European soil, and had a tremendous bearing on all that which we presently refer to now as *"Western Civilization."* In fact, one might say that the Apostle Paul was the founder, or at least the one who planted the seeds which would later grow into the form of government and freedom which Christians possess presently, and especially in the western world. However, do not mistake that statement as claiming that Paul strongly preached a *"western Gospel,"* for such was not the case at all. The Gospel of Jesus Christ is for the entirety of the world, and that's the Message that Paul preached; however, whereas it was ultimately accepted in the West, it was by and large rejected in the East.

Paul's introduction to this Macedonian city of Philippi came after what was obviously an unmistakable evidence of Divine Guidance before leaving the mainland of Asia.

As recorded in the 16th Chapter of Acts, Paul and Silas admitted Timothy into the Missionary Work at Lystra in Central Asia Minor. However, they felt a definite check from the Lord about going into the provinces of Asia and of Bithynia at that time. At Troas, on the Aegean Sea, a Vision given to Paul by the Lord, directed them to come to Macedonia, which was, as stated, Paul's first presentation of the Gospel in Europe.

THE CITY OF PHILIPPI

After landing in Neapolis, they were soon at Philippi, a *"chief city"* of Macedonia (modern day Greece).

The city of Philippi was located 10 miles inland from Neapolis on the main highway between the East and the West. It was on the site of an ancient town known as *"Krenides"* because of the numerous springs in the area. This site had been chosen because it commanded a strategic pass near Mt. Pangaeum, and because of its proximity to rich gold mines, which long since had been depleted. Philippi also had some important pagan shrines nearby.

Because of its strategic location, dominating as it did the main road between Europe and Asia, the town was enlarged and its name changed to honor Philip of Macedon.

Also because of its strategic location, the destiny of the Roman Empire was settled here in 42 B.C., by the great conflict between the armies of Octavius on one side and Brutus and Cassius on the other. After this battle Octavius (Augustus) retired many of his soldiers and settled them here in a Roman enlargement. In addition, he made Philippi a Roman Colony.

Its special privileges included exemption from oversight of the Provincial Governor, immunity from poll and property taxes, and rights to property according to Roman law. As a result, the character of the city was predominantly Roman; its inhabitants gave their chief allegiance to Rome.

This explains how Paul could remind the Philippian Christians that they were a colony of Heaven, a little outpost in a darkened world (Phil. 2:15).

As well, it explains the change in attitude on the part of the Magistrates after learning that Paul was a Roman citizen (Acts 16:37-39), and also the lack of a Jewish Synagogue in this place and of the readiness with which the inhabitants were ready to condemn Paul and Silas simply because they were Jews (Acts 16:20-21).

WHEN THIS EPISTLE WAS WRITTEN

The Epistle to the Philippians was written about 30 years after the Ascension, about 10 years after the first preaching of the Gospel by Paul at Philippi. This would have put the date in the early 60's.

Christianity was young in all the freshness of its first youth. It had come suddenly into the world.

By contrast, the world seemed to be growing old: the old religions had lost whatever power that they once possessed; the old philosophies were worn out; the energies of political life had been weakened or suppressed by the all-pervading despotism of Rome. Avarice, uncleanness, cruelty, were rampant in the Earth. There was little Faith in God, in goodness, in immortality, for the simple reason, that the people knew nothing about God.

"What is truth?" was the despairing question of the age. At this time, the Gospel flashed upon the scene of moral confusion like, what it is in Truth, a Revelation from Heaven. It brought before the eyes of men a Life and a Person.

The world saw for the first time a perfect life; not a mere ideal, but a real life that had been really lived upon the Earth; a life that stands alone, separate from all other lives; unique in its solitary majesty, in its unearthly loveliness, in its absolute purity, in its entire unselfishness. The world saw for the first time the beauty of complete self-sacrifice. And this life was not merely a thing past and gone. It was still living, and is still living in the Church. This Life of Christ is lived in His Saints.

IT WAS OBVIOUS!

They felt it: *"Not I, but Christ liveth in me."* They could tell others the blessed realities of their own spiritual experience. They were in earnest; they were plain: they had nothing to gain in the world. Paul especially had renounced a career most tempting to Hebrew ambition, for a life of unceasing labor — a life full of hardships, persecutions, dangerous, and evidently destined to end in a violent death. So, we see in this how valuable this Life in Christ actually is.

This man Paul, was consumed with an untiring zeal; despite many personal disadvantages, much natural timidity it seems, the constraining Love of Christ urged him to spend and to be spent in his Saviour's work.

THE CHURCH AT PHILIPPI

After arriving in Philippi, Paul and Silas on the Sabbath searched for the Jewish Synagogue. They found only women gathered for prayer by the river bank, a clear indication that no Synagogue existed, and testifying to the fact that few Jews were living there.

The first convert was an Asiatic businesswoman named Lydia. She and her household were baptized as the first converts on European soil.

Quite possibly the second convert was a Greek slave girl possessed with a spirit of divination. To the superstitious people a girl believed to have such powers would have considerable influence. Consequently, at Philippi, as at Ephesus, the motivation for persecution of Paul and his party, was the loss of income which resulted from people giving their hearts to Christ and ceasing their activity which had been in the realm of darkness.

The third convert may have been the Roman jailer.

If, in fact, that is the case regarding the order of the conversions, it is very significant that the first three converts in Macedonia were representative of the peoples to whom the Gospel was now making its appeal. They represented in order Asia, Greece, and Rome, symbolic of the sequence of the Gospel's progress.

There were also representative in that they included women, slaves, and government officials. To women and slaves especially the Gospel had a great appeal because it offered them freedom — freedom of their spirit.

LATER CONTACTS AT PHILIPPI

The chagrin of the Roman Magistrates at the humiliation of a Roman citizen did not last very long. There is evidence that the converts who remained behind in Philippi suffered persecution as at Corinth (II Cor. 8:2; Phil. 1:28-30).

It is possible that the fires of persecution experienced by the converts at Philippi help explain the relative purity of their Faith and the warmth of their affection for Paul.

Apparently Paul visited Philippi about five years after his original founding of the Church. During this period it seemed that he had frequent communications with Philippi, and it was this Church in particular that distinguished itself by contributing toward Paul's need (Phil. 4:15-16).

In addition to supplying Paul's needs, or at least helping toward this purpose, the Macedonian Churches also responded generously to his appeal for help to the impoverished Brethren in Judea, even though they were nearly impoverished themselves (II Cor. 8:1-5).

It apparently was not until the Fall of A.D. 57 that Paul visited the city again on his third missionary journey (Acts 19:21; 21:1-3; I Cor. 16:5-6; II Cor. 1:15-17). It was here that the Apostle observed the Passover with his friends before departing for Jerusalem where he hoped to observe Pentecost (Acts 20:5-6, 16).

It was probably from Philippi that Paul wrote to the Galatians and may also have penned his second letter to the Corinthians (II Cor. 2:13; 7:5; 8:1; 9:2, 4).

Apparently we have no evidence of any further communication between Paul and the people of Philippi until about five years later, when they heard of his presence in Rome under arrest. This, no doubt, was a shock to them and they took means to demonstrate once again their affection for the Apostle by sending Epaphroditus with a gift of money, and possibly other things (Phil. 4:18).

THE OCCASION FOR THIS LETTER

This Epistle was written during Paul's first imprisonment in Rome after he had written to the Colossians and the Ephesians. The letter was designed to do five things:

1. It was to acknowledge with deep gratitude their generous gifts sent to him in his necessity (Phil. 4:18).

2. It was designed to reassure the people of the Church of Philippi that Paul's imprisonment was not an unmitigated tragedy.

3. It was designed to commend the bearer Epaphroditus and convey Paul's personal greetings, assuring them of his prayers.

4. It was designed to alert the Philippians to the later arrival of Timothy (Phil. 2:19).

5. It gave an occasion to warn the Church of false teachers, which no doubt was and is its most important contribution (Turner).

THE STYLE OF THE EPISTLE

Of all the Letters Paul wrote to Churches, perhaps this one to the Philippians stands out as being the most personal. No sharp rebukes of the congregation mar its joyful spirit: no disturbing problems threatened the progress of the Church. The warnings are of a cautionary and preventive nature that are always in order.

The frequent emphasis on Christ explains the underlying relationship of Paul to his readers. The Names Jesus Christ, Christ Jesus, Lord Jesus Christ, Lord Jesus, Jesus, Christ, Lord, and Saviour, occur some 51 times in the 104 Verses of this Epistle. Consequently, Christ is the central theme of this Epistle, and more particularly, and as always with Paul's writings, *"Christ Crucified,"* portrayed in his denunciation of the *"enemies of the Cross of Christ"* (Phil. 3:18).

Paul wrote four Epistles during his first Roman imprisonment — to the Philippians, Colossians, Ephesians, and to Philemon. The last three were evidently written about the same time. The Epistle to the Philippians has been commonly regarded as the last of the four.

Even though the Apostle is writing this Letter primarily to acknowledge the gracious gift sent by the Philippians, still, the whole Epistle is interpenetrated with Christian Doctrine.

The great doctrinal passage in the Second Chapter asserts most of the distinctive articles of the Christian Creed. Paul insists upon the Divinity of Christ, His preexistence, His equality with God the Father, His Incarnation, His perfect humanity, His precious Death upon the Cross, His glorious Exaltation.

In the Third Chapter we have His Resurrection, His Second Advent, His Divine Power. In that Chapter we have also a full statement of the Doctrines of Justification by Faith, of the transitory character of the Mosaic Law, and of the Church as the City of God. Doctrine, then, is here, as elsewhere, the basis of Paul's teaching; but here, as elsewhere, he enforces doctrine as bearing upon holiness of life.

In the practical portion of the Epistle, the Graces on which the Apostle most insists are, especially and above all others, Christian Joy; then unity; and, as conducive to unity, unselfishness and humility. He also urges the duty of thankfulness, constant prayer, contentment, and the due ordering of the thoughts in that Fourth Chapter, which without a doubt give the greatest teaching on freedom from worry and dependence upon the Lord, and how it is brought about, found anywhere in the Bible.

A PERSONAL NOTE

It is May 10, 1999, as I begin the Commentary on this beautiful and yet basic Epistle of Paul to the Philippians. I do so with great joy, believing that the Lord will help us in this endeavor, and if so, that it will be a Blessing to you the Reader and Student of the Word of God. As I've said many times, *"the Bible is the only revealed Truth in the world today, and in fact ever has been."* As a result, we should do all we can to master its Sacred contents. Of course, to exhaust its body of teaching is absolutely impossible, for the Word of God is absolutely inexhaustible.

Once again I express my great appreciation to Frances for taking over many of the duties of the Ministry in order to afford me more time in this particular effort. I can say the same for Donnie, who takes much of the load of the Church off my shoulders, so once again, I can apply myself to this task.

I am not a Scholar, even as an elementary perusal of this Volume will portray; however, I am definitely a dedicated Student of the Word.

I began studying the Word of God when I was eight years old, the Lord having saved me at that young age. I carried a New Testament with me even from that time, everywhere I went, and would take every opportunity to study its contents. Every Victory, every Revelation, every advancement from the Lord, have always without exception, come through the Word of God. In other words, the Holy Spirit would open up to me the Word as it addressed itself to a particular need in my life. So, from experience, I know that the Word of God holds the answer to every need of fallen man, and that it alone holds those answers.

In 1997, even after several years of seeking His Face, the Lord began to open up to me the Revelation on the Cross and the Resurrection of Christ, which has revolutionized my thinking and even my life. As a Christian, it has been the greatest thing that's ever happened to me. Consequently, my commentary will be flavored as it regards this Volume with that particular Revelation. However, it will be written in this fashion, because I believe that's the way the Holy Spirit has positioned the Word of God. I dare not go beyond the Word, but I definitely dare go to the extent of the Word.

THE THRUST OF THE EVANGELIST

In these Volumes we do our very best to properly explain the Word of God as it is given by the writers. We do everything within our power not to take away from its meaning or add to its meaning. But at the same time, we also attempt to give what we believe is the present application of this which the Holy Spirit has given. Sometimes that angers people, because they do not expect such in a Commentary. Nevertheless, I believe that's what the Lord has told us to do; consequently, even though we attempt to be as diplomatic as possible, at times the words may bite, sting, and even burn, but I think, you will have little difficulty in understanding what we have said.

But isn't that the way of the Gospel? Wasn't that the manner of Paul and Peter and others, in the first place? Above all, wasn't that the manner of Christ?

A Gospel which is remiss in pointing the way, is in reality no Gospel at all! By the help of God, I do my best to point the way and in no uncertain terms. One day I will answer, even as you, for every word I have spoken or written; consequently, I want to stand at the Judgment Seat of Christ, knowing that I did the very best I could do in handling this treasure of all treasures, the Bible, the Word of God.

THE BOOK OF PHILIPPIANS

(1) "PAUL AND TIMOTHEUS, THE SERVANTS OF JESUS CHRIST, TO ALL THE SAINTS IN CHRIST JESUS WHICH ARE AT PHILIPPI, WITH THE BISHOPS AND DEACONS:"

"Paul and Timothy" are associated in the greeting, not because they were coauthors of the Letter, but because Timothy was a well-known Christian leader, especially at Philippi, and was now with Paul. It is certain that Paul alone was the author, in view of the singular verb and pronouns in Philippians 1:3-4, as well as the discussion in Philippians 2:19-23. Timothy had been present at the founding of the Church at Philippi (Acts 16:1-12) and it seems on several subsequent occasions (Acts 19:22; 20:3-6).

Paul does not use his title *"Apostle"* perhaps because he is not stressing his authority but is rather making a personal appeal. The circumstances may be compared to those in the very short Epistle to Philemon, where Paul also does not mention his Apostleship. In marked contrast is the Epistle to the Galatians, where Paul definitely stresses his authority.

Both Paul and Timothy are designated as *"servants of Christ Jesus."* This description emphasizes submission and dependence on their Lord. It is not a technical reference to a specific office, but characterizes their willing service of Christ, their Divine Master. The same designation appears in the Epistles of James, II Peter, and Jude.

Those to whom he writes are named as *"all the Saints in Christ Jesus"* who resided in the Macedonian city of Philippi. Paul places no special emphasis on *"all,"* as though he were counteracting some viewpoint that would exclude some in the Church. Paul frequently employed *"all"* in addressing the various Churches to where he wrote (Rom. 1:7; I Cor. 1:2; II Cor. 1:1; I Thess. 1:2). All Believers are *"Saints"* through their spiritual union with Christ, a fact Paul often expressed by the phrase *"in Christ Jesus"* (Rom. 8:1-2; Eph. 2:6, 10, 13; 3:6), or *"in Christs"* (Rom. 12:5; II Cor. 5:17). This use of the term *"Saint"* emphasizes not personal holiness, though the Believer's conduct should correspond increasingly to his standing, but the objective status each Believer possesses because the merits of Christ are imputed to him. Nor does it refer to a condition after death, as taught by the Catholics, for these *"Saints"* were very much alive at Philippi.

Though *"Bishops and Deacons"* were the two orders of Officers in the local New Testament Churches (I Tim. 3:1-3), Philippians is the only Epistle to mention them in its greeting. Why Paul includes them here is nowhere stated, but several observations suggest themselves.

It is clear that the Church at Philippi was organized and that Paul was not by-passing its local order. Consequently, the Epistle would have been delivered first to the Church Offices for reading to the congregation. Because Epaphroditus had previously been sent with a monetary gift (Phil. 2:25), the Bishops (Pastors) as well as the Deacons may have been particularly involved in the project of aiding Paul (Phil. 4:14-16) (Kent).

PAUL AND TIMOTHEUS

The phrase, *"Paul and Timotheus"* presents the Apostle uniting Timothy with him, even as he did others in some of his other Epistles (I Cor. 1:1; I Thess. 1:1; II Thess. 1:1).

However, Timothy was included more than all, six times other than the two Epistles written to him. It is clear, from this, that Timothy was with Paul at Rome. Why he was there is unknown. It is evident that he was not there as a prisoner with the Apostle; and the probability is, that he was one of the friends who had gone to Rome with a view to help Paul any way he could as it regarded this particular situation, his imprisonment.

There was a special situation in the fact that Timothy was joined with the Apostle in the Greetings regarding this Epistle, for he was with him when this Church was founded, and doubtless felt a deep interest in its welfare (Acts Chpt. 16).

Timothy was won to Christ by Paul on his first Missionary trip (Acts 14:6-7; I Tim. 1:2). He was part Jew and part Greek.

The Apostle was strongly attracted to the young man and although he had only recently replaced Barnabas with Silas as his traveling companion, he added Timothy to his party, perhaps as a substitute for John Mark whom he had refused to take (Acts 15:36).

He was first entrusted with a special commission to Thessalonica to encourage the persecuted Christians. He is associated with Paul and Silas in the greetings of both Epistles directed to that Church, and was present with Paul during at least some of his time at Corinth (II Cor. 1:19).

He is next heard of during the Apostle's Ephesian Ministry, when he was sent with Erastus on another important mission to Macedonia, whence he was to proceed to Corinth (I Cor. 4:17).

From the situation which resulted in Corinth, Timothy's mission it seems was not successful, and it is significant that, although his name was associated with Paul's in the greeting regarding this Epistle, it is Titus and not Timothy who has become the Apostolic delegate. He accompanied Paul on his next visit to Corinth, for he was with him as a fellow-worker when the Epistle to the Romans was written (Rom. 16:21).

When the Apostle was released from his imprisonment and engaged in further activity in the East, as the Pastoral Epistles indicate, it would seem that Paul left Timothy at Ephesus (I Tim. 1:3) as its Pastor at least for a time, and commissioned him to deal with false teachers and supervise public worship and the appointment of Church officials.

Although Paul evidently hoped to rejoin the young man, the fear that he might be delayed occasioned the writing of the first Letter to him, and this was followed by another when Paul was not only rearrested but on trial for his life. Timothy was urged to hasten to him, but whether he arrived in time cannot be ascertained.

There are some who think, that Hebrews 13:23 shows that Timothy himself became a prisoner, but no details are given, and of his subsequent history nothing definite is known.

SERVANTS

The phrase *"The servants of Jesus Christ,"* refers to both men being bound to Jesus Christ by the bands of a constraining love. The word *"servant"* in the Greek is *"doulos,"* and actually means *"slave."* It refers to one born into slavery.

Paul was born into slavery to sin by his first birth, and into the position of a loving bond slave of the Lord Jesus by his new birth. It refers to one who is in a relation to another which only death can break.

Conversely, Paul's relation to Satan was broken by his identification with Christ in His Death (Rom. 6:3-5). He now is in a relation to Jesus Christ which will last forever, since Christ can never die again, and Paul's life is Christ. It refers to one whose will is swallowed up in the will of another. Paul's will was at one time swallowed up in the will of Satan, as are all unconverted. Now his will is swallowed up in the sweet Will of God. It refers to one who serves another even to the disregard of his own interests. Paul originally served Satan to the detriment of his own interests. Now he serves the Lord Jesus with a reckless abandon, not regarding his own interests (Wuest).

A SLAVE OF CHRIST

Being slaves of Christ presents the Christian's true relationship to Christ. We are Christ's property, body, and soul, at His complete and continuous disposal. We are not our *"own"* (I Cor. 6:20) because we have been bought *"by the Precious Blood of Christ"*

(I Pet. 1:18-19). Even as Jesus' *"meat"* was to do the Will of His Father in Heaven (Jn. 4:34), or as a slave exists to do the will of his earthly master, so we exist to do the Will of Christ. Christ is our absolute and common Master. We are His *"love-slaves"* (Ex. 21:1-6), who have freely accepted His Sovereignty.

To be the slave of Christ is to be *free* from sin (Rom. 6:16-18, 20, 22), which is a Blessing of unparalleled proportions.

The intimacy of Paul and Timothy is based not so much on their past experiences together, as on their common commitment to Christ and emancipation from unrighteousness.

SAINTS

The phrase, *"To all the Saints in Christ Jesus which are at Philippi,"* refers to those who are *"set apart"* unto Christ. Saints are Believers set apart from sin to holiness, set apart from Satan to God, thus being consecrated for God's sacred fellowship and service.

The word *"Saint"* as a designation of the Christian, brings at once to our attention the duty of every Believer, that of living a separated life. Actually, the words, *"Saint, Sanctify, Holy,"* are all translations of this same Greek root. They all speak of the absolute separation from evil and dedication to God, that must always be true of the Christian Believer (Wuest).

Paul uses the word *"all"* because he wishes to put those Philippians who had not sent to his support, on a level to those who had. There were some divisions among the Philippians, and Paul set himself above these.

CHRIST JESUS

The name *"Christ"* is the English spelling of the Greek word *"Christos,"* which in turn is the translation of the Hebrew word meaning *"Messiah."* The word *"Christ"* means *"The Anointed One."*

The name *"Jesus"* is the English spelling of the Greek *"Iesous,"* which is in turn the Greek spelling of the Hebrew word *"Jehoshua"* which means *"Jehovah saves."*

We have, therefore, in these two names, the Messianic Office of our Lord, His Deity, and His Substitutionary Atonement.

The phrase, *"In Christ Jesus"* was necessary in defining just who these Saints were. In fact, the Greek word *"Saint"* was used in Philippi as a name for individual worshipers in the pagan Greek religions. Paul wished to differentiate the Saints of God from the Saints in the Greek mystery religions.

The word *"in"* is used as it regards the location or sphere. These Saints were Saints in the sphere of Christ. That is, Christ is the sphere in which the Believer has his new life and all his interests and activities. The Believer's new existence is circumscribed by Christ.

The actual meaning is, that being *"in Christ"* separates the Believer from all else, or at least it is supposed to (Wuest).

IS IT POSSIBLE FOR A SAINT BECAUSE OF SIN TO CEASE BEING A SAINT?

Yes! However, explanation is needed.

The very purpose of the Born-Again experience, is to make one different from the old life. In other words, the Lord does not save in sin but rather from sin. And yet at times, there is quite a struggle which ensues from us going from point A (our conversion) to point B (victory over all sin). However, most of the struggle is caused by the Saint not properly understanding God's prescribed order of victory, which is Faith in the Cross and the Resurrection, and our part and place in that great Work. We will deal with that.

The first thing the Believer must understand, is that we are saved not because of certain things we do or don't do, but solely and completely by our Faith in Christ (Jn. 3:16; Rom. 10:9-10, 13; Eph. 2:8-9; Rev. 22:17). In other words, the Christian does not go in and out of Salvation according to particular problems in their lives over which they are attempting to obtain Victory.

However, it must be quickly stated, that a Believer cannot have sin and Salvation at the same time. By that we mean this:

Some so-called Christians want to live any way they want to live as it regards sin, and then at the same time claim Salvation, by claiming that they *"trust Christ,"* etc. The Truth is, these people have never truly been saved to begin with, which is probably the case with almost all in that category. But yet, there definitely are some few who have truly been saved, but are now entertaining sin in some manner, and are making no effort to obtain

Victory in the Lord. The Scripture is replete with warnings to these individuals (II Cor. 6:14-18; II Tim. 3:1-5; Heb. 6:4-6; 10:26-31; II Pet. 2:20-22; Rev. 3:15-22). The warning is clear, a Christian can experience the loss of his soul if he continues in that capacity.

THE FINISHED WORK OF CHRIST

The greatest reason of all that Christians have a problem with sin in their lives, is because they do not properly understand their place and position in Christ. While the Bible does not teach sinless perfection, it definitely does teach victory over sin in every capacity (Rom. 6:14).

When the believing sinner comes to Christ, Satan immediately sets about to drag the Believer back into the old sins of his past, or sins of any nature. When and if the Believer fails, and I should say *"when,"* because there has never been a Believer who hasn't failed in one way or the other, the Believer then sets about to try to ensure that the failure does not happen again. Almost always, he attempts to do this by efforts of the flesh, i.e., *"through his own ability, strength or willpower."* He will fail every single time in this manner, and as well, despite all of his efforts to the contrary, the situation will not only not be corrected, but will actually get worse. It is because he is not properly trusting Christ, but rather himself, whether he understands that or not.

The problem is, Believers do not really understand that they are trusting self, for the simple reason that if they did understand, they would not do such. That particular direction is engaged because they do not properly understand their place and position in Christ.

WHAT IS THE BELIEVER'S POSITION IN CHRIST?

There are several things the Believer must understand. I will be brief, because at times, brevity is the greatest explanation of all.

Read carefully the following:

1. Everything the Believer needs is in what Jesus did at the Cross and the Resurrection (I Cor. 1:18).

2. When Jesus died on the Cross, He did all of this for us, and not at all for Himself. In other words, that's why He came (Mat. 16:21).

3. When Jesus died on the Cross, He atoned for all sin, past, present, and future, at least for those who will believe. He satisfied the claims of Heavenly Justice and the claims of the broken Law. The Law stated that the soul that sinned must die (Rom. 6:23). That includes all of humanity, because all have sinned (Rom. 3:10:18). Jesus died in our place, so He satisfied the Law in every respect.

As well, in doing this, He defeated Satan and all the powers of darkness, simply because Satan's hold on humanity is *"sin."* When the sin has been atoned for, he has no more hold.

So, every single thing that God demanded, and was needed to liberate and redeem fallen humanity, Jesus did it at the Cross and the Resurrection.

4. Jesus Christ was and is our Substitute. Our Identification with Him, guarantees us all the great Victory which He has purchased with His Own Blood.

5. When the believing sinner puts his Faith in what Christ did on the Cross, in the Mind of God the believing sinner was and is actually in Christ when all of this happened (Rom. 6:3-5). That's what we mean by being properly *"in Christ,"* and understanding our *"place and position in Him."*

6. The Believer is to understand, that the Cross and the Resurrection of Christ, not only has to do with one's initial Salvation experience, but also with our everyday Victory and walk before the Lord.

7. The Believer is to place his Faith in this which Christ has done at the Cross, keep his Faith there, which will guarantee the help of the Holy Spirit, which ensures Satan's continued defeat regarding you as a Believer.

8. If you the Believer are fully trusting in what Christ did at the Cross and the Resurrection, you are doing exactly what the Lord wants you to do, and at the same time, you are not trusting in yourself. This trust in Christ, which speaks of what He did at the Cross and the Resurrection, is the basis for all Salvation and Victory. We are to constantly trust in that, which as stated, ensures the help of the Holy Spirit (Rom. 8:1-2).

With your Faith anchored in this Finished Work of Christ, no sin will ever have dominion over you, and you will walk victorious in Christ all the days of your life, which the Lord intends, especially considering that He paid such a price for our Victory.

Victory is what the Lord intends, and Victory will be yours in totality, if you'll only follow the prescribed way of the Cross.

BISHOPS AND DEACONS

The phrase, *"With the Bishops and Deacons,"* actually refers to Pastors and Deacons of the local Church.

This is the first Letter of the Apostle which mentions Bishops and Deacons, and which addresses them separately. At that time there were several Bishops (Pastors) in one Church, now there are many Churches under one Bishop. Departure from, and corruption of, Truth early manifested itself in Christendom (Williams).

Actually, the words *"Bishops," "Pastors," "Elders," "Presbyters," "Shepherds,"* are all used interchangeably, meaning *"Pastor,"* and *"Pastor"* or *"Pastors"* of a local Church.

The designation of *"Bishops,"* referring to one individual being over a district or a number of Churches, is not Biblical, and was instituted into the Church in the Second Century, even as it began to apostatize.

THE RISE OF MONARCHICAL EPISCOPACY

There is no trace in the New Testament of Government by a single Bishop; the position of James at Jerusalem (Acts 15:13; 21:18; Gal. 2:9, 12) was quite exceptional, and the result of his personal relationship to Christ; but influence is a different thing from office. Among the Apostolic Fathers, Ignatius is the only one who insisted on Monarchical Episcopacy, and even he never states that this is of Divine institution — an argument which would have been decisive, if it had been available for him to use.

Jerome, commenting on Titus 1:5, remarks that the supremacy of a single Bishop arose *"by custom rather than by the Lord's actual appointment,"* as a means of preventing schisms in the Church, in which it probably had the very opposite effect.

The Word of God is to be the criteria for all things. In regard to that we see several things as it relates to Church Government. Some are as follows:

FELLOWSHIP OF CHURCHES

The Book of Acts and the New Testament teach a fellowship of Churches rather than Denominations, etc. These Churches had like doctrine or worship, or at least were supposed to.

We must understand, that had the Holy Spirit wanted anything different this would have been the time to have portrayed such. He could easily have designated the Jerusalem Church as the Headquarters Church, demanding that all other Churches follow their lead. But there is no hint of such a thing. As well, He could easily have placed the original Twelve Apostles in places and position of ultimate authority, but He didn't do that either. Instead, He designated through actual practice, a fellowship of Churches, which He intended to continue and for many reasons.

EACH CHURCH AUTONOMOUS

He made each Church independent unto itself. In other words, even though it was part of a fellowship, it governed itself under particular guidelines which we will address in a moment. All authority began and ended with that particular local Church. This meant that no outside authority of any nature was to have any dictatorial powers over that particular Church. It was autonomous within its own structure.

LEADERSHIP OF APOSTLES

Apostles were designated by the Holy Spirit to serve in positions of leadership, which should continue unto this hour. In other words, as we look at the situation in the Book of Acts and the Epistles, we see the Holy Spirit giving Apostles leading and direction for the Church and the Work of God in general. Primary among these Apostles was the Apostle Paul, but others definitely figured in as well.

However, even Apostles did not have dictatorial authority over any Church. They could suggest, recommend, and proclaim, but that's as far as it went. Even Paul exerted no authority over the Churches he had founded. He suggested and did so strongly at times, but he could not force the local Church to obey. They had to do that of their own volition. This was God's Way then, and it is God's Way now, that is, if the Church truly wants to be Biblical.

CHRIST IS THE HEAD

All of this was done in this manner, simply because Christ was the actual Head of the Church. The moment that men begin to exert dictatorial authority, which means that they formulate religious government which is not Biblical, it always abrogates the Headship of Christ. In the manner of a *"fellowship of Churches,"* with the local Church always maintaining autonomy, and with the responsibility of doctrinal leading being given to Apostles, the Headship of Christ is maintained, and the Will of God is carried out. Under this system of Government, the Church grew and the greatest Missionary effort was carried out, with much of the Roman Empire being evangelized by the end of the First Century. If we do things God's Way, we receive His Blessings. Otherwise, the Holy Spirit is grieved, and the work suffers.

CORRECT BIBLICAL GOVERNMENT

All of this we have stated, which has as its Scriptural reference the entirety of the Book of Acts and the Epistles, does not forbid the forming of Denominations, etc. Ideally a religions Denomination is merely a tool to help carry out the Work of God. As well, Preachers elected by popular ballot to respective offices in these Denominations isn't unscriptural either, at least as long as it is understood that the Denomination within itself carries no spiritual authority, and neither do its elected offices. If these things are done, leaving the government of the Church in its correct Scriptural position, great things can be accomplished for Christ. It is only when men seek to usurp authority over that which is laid down by the Holy Spirit, in effect, formulating their own type of government, that the harm begins.

Everything that the Christian does, that Preachers attempt to carry out, must always be done on the basis of the Word of God serving as the criteria. The question must always be, *"Is it Scriptural?"* Every effort must be made, repeatedly asking the Lord for the help, leading, and guidance of the Holy Spirit, that we make our efforts as Scriptural as possible. To do otherwise, is to fail and to fail miserably!

DEACONS

This is the first time the name *"Deacon"* is used, unless, indeed, as is probable, it is applied to Phebe in Romans 16:1. However, the Office of the Seven, in Acts 6:1-7, is undoubtedly the germ of the Office of Deacon, yet the actual title of *"Deacons"* is nowhere given to them at that time.

The word *"Deacon"* literally means, *"those who serve."* Someone has said, that Bishops (Pastors) were assigned by God to handle the spiritual affairs of the congregation, whereas *"Deacons"* were assigned by God to handle the physical affairs of the congregation (Acts 6:1-4). As long as this distinction is honored, and as long as Christ is honored as operating Head, Assemblies will function Scripturally. The qualities that Deacons should have or work toward, are listed in I Timothy 3:8-13. And yes, and to which we have already alluded concerning Phebe, women can serve as Deacons (Rom. 16:1).

(2) "GRACE BE UNTO YOU, AND PEACE, FROM GOD OUR FATHER, AND FROM THE LORD JESUS CHRIST."

The familiar Blessing, *"Grace and Peace,"* combines Greek and Hebrew expressions, and also transforms them into a thoroughly Christian greeting. Exactly the same wording was used by Paul in six other Epistles (Rom. Chpt. 1; II Cor.; Gal.; Eph.; Phile.).

God's *"Grace"* is His favor, needed by men in countless ways and bestowed without regard to merit, upon Faith.

Here, *"Peace"* is a reference, not to the cessation of hostilities between sinners and God (Rom. 5:1), but to the inner assurance and tranquility that God ministers to the hearts of Believers and that keeps them spiritually confident even in the midst of turmoil (Phil. 4:7).

The Source of these Blessings is *"God our Father and The Lord Jesus Christ."* Paul understands that Jesus the Messiah is the Divine Lord, ascended to the Father's Right Hand and equal to Him in authority and honor. Just as Christ and the Father joined in the sending of the Holy Spirit (Jn. 14:26; 15:26), so They will jointly convey these Blessings (Kent).

GRACE

The phrase, *"Grace be unto you,"* presents the fact that it is hardly too much to say that

God has in no word uttered Himself and all that is in His Heart more distinctly than in this (Trench-Wuest).

When this word is used in the New Testament, it refers to that favor which God did at Calvary when He stepped down from His Judgment Throne to take upon Himself the guilt and penalty of human sin.

The word *"Grace"* had its origin in the Greek language; however, in the case of the Greek, the favor was done to a friend, never an enemy. In the case of God it was an enemy, the sinner, bitter in his hatred of God, for whom the favor was done. God has no strings tied to the Salvation He procured for man at the Cross. Salvation is given the believing sinner out of the pure generosity of God's Heart. What a description of that which took place at the Cross!

The Grace spoken of here is Sanctifying Grace, that part of Salvation given the Saint in which God causes him to grow in Christlikeness through the Ministry of the Holy Spirit, which functions upon the Faith of the Saint registered in the Cross (II Pet. 3:18).

GRACE AND THE CROSS

The Believer must ever understand that the Grace of God, which is the most wonderful and blessed thing that any person could ever know, is all centered in the Cross of Christ (Gal. 2:20-21). Consequently, even as the believing sinner's Faith must be in the Cross in order to be saved, which guarantees the Grace of God, likewise, the believing Christian's Faith must remain in the Cross in order to have Victory in one's everyday walk before God.

The Grace of God is not possible of attainment other than through the Cross. This means that the Believer must understand that Grace is not only undeserved favor, but he must understand as well its source. This means that Grace is not automatic as many believe!

In order to obtain Grace, God as is understood requires Faith, but more particularly, He requires Faith in the Cross, with the understanding that this is the means by which He is able to grant such Grace. It has always worked on this premise and this premise alone.

The Sacrifice of Christ on the Cross satisfied the sin debt, as well as the curse of the broken Law; consequently, the sin debt was forever paid, at least for all who will believe. This made it possible for God to extend this unmerited favor to man, requiring only Faith; however, it must be Faith in that Sacrifice or Grace will not be forthcoming, simply because Grace under any other circumstances cannot be forthcoming. If the Grace of God is predicated on the Cross of Christ which it definitely is, then it follows that the Believer, whether the sinner attempting to be saved or the Christian attempting to have victory, must place their Faith in that Finished Work of Christ, and for it to there remain.

I think most Christians do not properly understand this facet of Grace. As stated, they somehow think it's automatic, not realizing that it comes solely through the Sacrifice of Christ on the Cross, and our Faith in that Sacrifice. In fact, not understanding this, which means to leave the Cross out of our thinking, which leaves it out of our Faith, *"frustrates the Grace of God"* (Gal. 2:21). The sad truth is, most Christians do just that, they frustrate the Grace of God.

HOW DO WE FRUSTRATE THE GRACE OF GOD?

We frustrate God's Grace by depending on anything other than the Finished Work of Christ. That means we are to depend upon the Sacrifice of Christ for anything, everything, and all things that we need, be it economical, physical, mental, or spiritual.

So, if the Believer attempts to use anything such as *"fasting,"* or even *"prayer,"* to obtain Victory over the world, the flesh, and the Devil, we will succeed only in turning these spiritual attributes into works, which frustrates the Grace of God. Don't misunderstand, *"fasting"* and *"prayer"* are two of the greatest attributes of the Child of God, and especially prayer. In fact, we have two prayer meetings a day at the Ministry (10 a.m. and 6:30 p.m.). However, if we attempt to use prayer or anything of that nature, as important as it may be in its own right, as a vehicle with which to overcome sin and Satan, victory will not be the result, but the very opposite.

This which I have just said will probably startle many Christians. Prayer is one of the greatest qualities in which any Christian can engage, and in fact, no Christian can be what he or she ought to be without a proper prayer life. However, prayer must be used in its right way, and not in an attempt to be an overcomer. Also, untold numbers of Christians are running all over the world attempting to find some Preacher to lay hands on them, in order that they receive the *"blessing"* of some sort. While that's certainly not wrong in itself, with the laying on of hands certainly being Scriptural, and the desire of the Saint being legitimate; still, the Victory they seek will not be found in this manner. Stop and think a moment!

THE FINISHED WORK OF CHRIST

If any of these things we have mentioned were required, and many things we haven't mentioned, then that would mean that Jesus did not finish the work at the Cross and something else is needed. We may not think of it in those terms, but that's exactly what we are doing, which in effect, insults Christ.

Our victory over the world, the flesh, and the Devil, comes not at all in all of these good things that we might do, as helpful as they might be in other ways, but rather through our Faith in what Christ has already done. Regrettably, most Christians little understand this, hence their attempting to find what they need through avenues that will never give them what they seek. Actually, when we do these things attempting to bring about Victory, and to be sure all of us have done them at one time or the other, the only thing we succeed in doing is to *"frustrate the Grace of God,"* which is deadly!

Every Christian can walk in Victory and do so totally and completely, if they will only place their Faith in what Jesus did at the Cross and in the Resurrection, and depend exclusively upon that. When this is done, the Holy Spirit guarantees all the benefits of the Cross, which means that the Victory which Christ paid for with His Own Blood, is ours. We don't have to do anything for this Victory, except have Faith in that which Christ did, which was complete and needs nothing added, and was actually, totally and completely for us.

Untold numbers of Saints are seeking Victory, when in reality we *already have* Victory. We are seeking to be an overcomer, when in reality we *already are* an overcomer. We are

NOTES

this because of what Christ did in His great Sacrifice. Faith in that, guarantees that for which He purchased with His Own Blood. Grace then flows to the Child of God in an unending stream and is guaranteed by the Holy Spirit (Rom. 8:2).

Considering this, we should not want to do anything to hinder that flow of Grace, and Faith in anything else other than the Finished Work of Christ, will not merely hinder the flow but actually stop it dead in its tracks.

GRACE, THE BELIEVER,
AND THE CROSS

Whenever the Believer thinks of *"Grace,"* which all of us desperately need and continually, he should at the same time think of the *"Cross."* The two should be synonymous in his mind and thinking. If we divorce one from the other — either one — we forfeit the Grace of God in any case.

In the Commentary on Ephesians, we made the following statement over and over again, and actually will continue to do so, because it is so very significant.

In the last nearly 50 years, the Church has had so little preaching and teaching on the Cross, that it little knows anymore or understands the veracity of this foundational Truth of the great Plan of Redemption. Consequently, it walks in defeat, and in fact, if our understanding of the Cross is skewed, everything else will be colored as well.

This particular generation in the Church has basically been taught nothing but Faith. On the surface, that would seem to be right, and it would be right, were it Faith placed in the correct objective; however, any teaching on Faith that does not place this all-important quality in the Cross, i.e., the Finished Work of Christ, is a misplaced Faith, and will receive nothing from the Lord. Such Faith taught, even though it claims to be based on the Word of God, has by and large *"self"* as its object. Consequently, it is little different than the world's faith which is mostly centered in motivation, despite the fact that Preachers cover such teaching with Scripture.

Everything in the Word of God points toward the Cross of Christ. It is the central theme of the Bible, the foundation of the Faith, everything toward which history strains.

So, that being the case, if the Cross is moved away from square center, in other words from the position from where all things flow pertaining to God, then everything is off course. And that's pretty much the state of the modern Church.

PEACE

The phrase, *"And Peace,"* as stated, speaks of Sanctifying Peace.

As we have explained several times in other of our Volumes, there are actually two types of *"Peace."* There is what is referred to as *"Justifying Peace,"* which is that which comes to the sinner upon accepting Christ. In other words, the enmity is removed between God and man, as that person accepts Christ and what Christ has done on the Cross and the Resurrection as it regards their Redemption. At the moment of their acceptance of Christ, peace with God instantly comes. The great barrier of sin between man and God has been removed. And the only way it can be removed, is by the Precious Blood of Jesus Christ, and our Faith in that Atoning Work. Peace is the result. That is *"Justifying Peace."* This type of *"Peace"* never wavers, remaining steadfast and anchored in our Justification.

The *"Peace"* which Paul mentions here, however, is not Justifying Peace, simply because the Apostle is speaking to Believers, in other words, people who are already saved. So, *"Justifying Peace"* does not have to be proposed for them, that having already been established within their hearts and lives.

Inasmuch as the Apostle is addressing Believers, he is speaking to them of *"Sanctifying Peace."* This type of Peace is not anchored quite like Justifying Peace. In fact, it is up and down according to circumstances and most of all, because of improper Faith in Christ.

SANCTIFYING PEACE

Exactly as Grace, Sanctifying Peace is developed in the heart and life of the Believer, which addresses itself to serenity and well-being, in exactly the same manner, our Faith in the Cross. As Justifying Peace came to the sinner upon Faith in the Finished Work of Christ, likewise, *"Sanctifying Peace"* comes to the Believer in the same manner.

The Believer is to anchor his Faith in the Cross, understanding that all things stream from that Sacrifice.

The idea is, Jesus addressed in the Atonement every single thing that was lost in the Fall. While it is true that we do not now have everything for which the Atonement provides, and in fact, will not have it all until the coming Rapture of the Church; still, Sanctifying Peace is definitely one of the qualities the Believer can now have and have constantly.

As stated, a lack of this type of Peace, which every Believer faces occasionally, is brought about because of improper Faith in the Lord. In facing the circumstances of life which at times are adverse, it is so easy to get our eyes off Him and to get it on circumstances. When we do this, which we all have done, our Sanctifying Peace is weakened, thereby bringing about consternation.

The idea is this: If Jesus suffered as He did, dying on the Cross in order to bring us Redemption, and especially considering that He did this while we were yet sinners, how much more does He love us now after we have accepted Him, making Him the Lord and Saviour of our lives. Once again, it all stems from the Cross, and proper Faith placed there will bring about the Sanctifying Peace and keep it steadfast within our hearts and lives.

GOD OUR FATHER

The phrase, *"From God our Father,"* presents all of this coming from the Father through Christ (Rom. 3:24).

The manner in which the Holy Spirit through Paul proclaims these titles, tells us of the working of the Trinity as it regards our Salvation. We have a reference here to two separate Divine Persons in the Godhead, and considering that the Holy Spirit is the One Who inspired Paul to say these words, we have here the entirety of the Trinity — all working in the capacity of our Salvation.

This *"Grace"* and *"Peace"* come from both ***"God our Father, and from the Lord Jesus Christ,"*** and even though it doesn't say so here, is made real to us through the Person, Office, Ministry, and Work of the Holy Spirit. In fact, it is the Holy Spirit Who executes all the Plans of the Godhead (Rom. 8:26-30).

THE LORD JESUS CHRIST

The phrase, *"And from the Lord Jesus Christ,"* refers to the One Who actually purchased these qualities, and did so by His Own Precious Blood.

Paul also said, *"And that He* (Jesus) *might reconcile both* (Jews and Gentiles) *unto God in one Body* (the Church), *by the Cross, having slain the enmity thereby:*

"And came and preached Peace to you (Gentiles) *which were afar off, and to them that were nigh* (the Jews)."

He then said, *"For through Him* (Jesus) *we both have access by one Spirit* (the Holy Spirit) *unto the Father"* (Eph. 2:16-18).

Which by now is obvious, still, knowing that God did all of this by Jesus, we must ask the question, *"How did He bring about Grace and Peace by Jesus Christ?"*

We are plainly told in Ephesians 2:16, the Scripture just quoted, that Jesus did this *"by the Cross."*

Once again, we see clearly how everything is centered in the Cross of Christ, and surely by now we understand, if we are moved away from that position, the position of the Cross, spiritual error and even spiritual wreckage are guaranteed to be the result.

THE UNDERSTANDING OF THE BELIEVER

What we have said thus far, would be agreed to by almost all Christians; however, the understanding of most Christians places all of this in their initial Salvation experience, little realizing that they must maintain Faith in the Cross ever after, in order to have the great benefits which Christ purchased there with His Own Blood. That's what Jesus was speaking about when He demanded that we take up our Cross daily and follow Him (Lk. 9:23-24).

Bearing the Cross is not *"suffering"* as most Christians have been led to believe. It is actually looking to that Finished Work which Christ suffered to bring about, that we may have these great benefits. That's what He meant by taking up the Cross daily. It is to be done constantly, ever looking to that Finished Work, that all-consummate Sacrifice, that great Work of Redemption.

So, we must ever understand, that everything we receive from God, comes to us because of what Jesus did at the Cross and in His Resurrection. That is to be ever before us, ever understanding the veracity of this Sacrifice, knowing that through that alone, and our Faith in that on a constant basis, do we have daily Victory.

TITLES

"Lord" literally means, *"Master,"* and was used in the Old Testament to translate the word for Jehovah. Though the title is occasionally used in the New Testament as a title of honor (Mat. 13:27), in the Epistles it is constantly employed of Christ. Thus, *"Lord"* as used by Paul indicates full Deity. That Jesus was Divine was the Faith of the New Testament Church, as expressed in its earliest Christian creed, *"Jesus is Lord"* (I Cor. 12:3; Phil. 2:6, 9-11).

As we have stated, *"Jesus"* means *"Saviour"* (Mat. 1:21). He is the Lord, the Master of Paul and Timothy, and the Philippians, and us as well, because He is our Saviour, and Deliverer.

Contrast the experience of the damsel possessed with a spirit of divination at Philippi. She was the slave of those who could not be her savior, while Paul and Silas were *"servants* (literally slaves) *of the Most High God"* (Acts 16:16-17).

"Christ" is a proper title meaning *"Anointed One"* or *"Messiah"* (Isa. 61:1). The Anointed One was the Appointed One, God's Vice-Regent on Earth, the officially accredited Messenger from Heaven to Earth (Mat. 17:5).

The Holy Spirit is not mentioned here because this Grace and Peace is that which the Holy Spirit makes real to us, revealing to us the Father, and bringing to our remembrance the teaching of the Son, from Whom He comes.

The meaning of the salutation is clear: *"No Peace without Grace... No Grace and Peace but from God our Father... No Grace and Peace from God our Father, but in and through the Lord Jesus Christ... No Grace and Peace through the Lord Jesus Christ, unless our Faith is properly placed in what He did at the Cross and the Resurrection."*

(3) "I THANK MY GOD UPON EVERY REMEMBRANCE OF YOU,"

Paul begins his Letter by thanking God for his readers. He follows this pattern in all his Epistles except Galatians, where the absence of such sentiment forebodes this serious discussion to follow.

With the Philippians Paul had a warm relationship, and this tone is established at the outset of the Letter. By stating his thanks to *"My God,"* the author reveals his personal devotion. This was no stereotyped formula, but the natural outflow from the heart of a deeply spiritual man.

The thanksgiving was prompted by the joyous memory Paul had of his Philippian friends. It was not that every single memory caused him to thank God, but that his whole remembrance of them was good (Kent).

THANKS

The phrase, *"I thank my God,"* proclaims by the use of the words *"My God,"* a deep feeling of gratitude in the heart of Paul, that involved him personally.

He is actually saying that the conduct of the Philippians was a proof of the favor of God to him; that is, he regarded their consecration as one of the tokens of the favor of God to his own soul — for in producing that consecration, the instrument used to do so was Paul.

This is the fruit of correct doctrine, of proper relationship with Christ, of a proper Ministry. Such fruit as was in the Philippians, cannot be produced by false doctrine or false apostles. It can only be produced by that which is clearly the Word of God, and the Word of God moved upon and anointed by the Holy Spirit.

AS THE BELIEVER LOOKS AT THIS

Every Believer should ask himself or herself a question. Is what you are hearing from behind the pulpit where you attend Church producing in you Righteousness and Holiness, or something else? If the Holy Spirit is properly present and properly working, as He definitely will do upon the Word of God being properly and clearly preached and taught, the twins of Righteousness and Holiness will be the primary fruit developed in the lives of those who hear such preaching and teaching. It doesn't mean that everyone under such Preaching, whether in their local Church or listening by Radio or Television, will develop this fruit, for many won't, irrespective of what is done. But some definitely will!

If Satan can divert us to other things, and I speak of anything else other than Righteousness and Holiness, he will move Heaven and Earth to do so. And to be sure, Churches are full of spurious doctrines, which do not properly develop the Child of God, but rather do the very opposite. I will be frank:

If the Church where you attend is not properly proclaiming the Cross of Christ as the fountainhead of all things that comes from God to the Believer, they are not properly preaching the Gospel. While it certainly may be true that they are preaching all the Light they have, and thus far so good. But still, if the entirety of the Message of the Cross is not proclaimed properly, the Christian will suffer the consequences, which will always be negative.

And by the Message of the Cross, in simplistic terms, I mean that the Christian must understand four things:

1. The Cross was absolutely necessary for our initial Salvation experience, and it is absolutely necessary as it regards our everyday Victory in the Lord as well.

2. Understanding that, we must know and believe that the Cross and the Resurrection are where all Victory is found. At the same time, we are stating that there must be a proper understanding of that Finished Work, which is outlined in Romans Chapters 6, 7, and 8.

3. We must also understand, that we must put our Faith in the Cross and the Resurrection, and leave our Faith there, knowing and realizing that this is absolutely necessary. That is what Jesus meant by taking up the Cross daily and following Him (Lk. 9:23-24).

4. We must also know, that once our Faith is placed properly in the Cross, and remains in the Cross, for the simple reason that it was here that Satan was defeated and all sin atoned for, then the Holy Spirit will help us with His great Power, which guarantees all that the Atonement has brought about (Rom. 8:1-13).

REMEMBRANCE

The phrase, *"Upon every remembrance of you,"* does not refer to disconnected recollections, but for his total past experience with the Philippians. This unbroken remembrance resulted in unbroken thanksgiving and joy.

It has been said that memory is the fine art of forgetting. Paul is the recipient of this noble gift. He has been granted the power to forget the harsh experiences of imprisonment and suffering at Philippi, save as they enriched his relationship to God and to the Philippians. He remembers with gratitude their conversion (Acts Chpt. 16) and subsequent thoughtfulness on several occasions, even quite recently (Phil. 4:15-18).

Also, this shows to us that even as Paul was a shepherd of souls, a fisher of men, his eagerness at winning converts was matched by his concern for their establishment in Grace. Paul was as strong on follow-up as he was on initial conversion.

(4) "ALWAYS IN EVERY PRAYER OF MINE FOR YOU ALL MAKING REQUEST WITH JOY,"

These Churches Paul planted according to instructions given by the Holy Spirit, actually presented the foundation of the Church as a whole. In fact, these presentations by Paul were the beginnings of the proclamation of the New Covenant, toward which the Old Covenant had been straining from the very beginning. In other words, everything in the past had functioned in order to bring about this glorious moment of the present and the future, the Gospel of Jesus Christ. The Church at Philippi was one of these Churches, and one it seems, with which Paul had the least trouble.

PRAYER

The phrase, *"Always in every prayer of mine for you all,"* proclaims the Apostle continually praying for these people, even as he prayed for all the other Churches. Even though he was now a long way from Philippi, they were still in his prayers, and actually would ever be until the Lord called him home. This love for them is expressed in genuine intercession to God for their welfare. He does not pray from a sense of duty, nor out of an attempt to forget his own circumstances. His prayers are intercessory.

The word *"prayer"* translated here is *"deesei,"* and indicates an intense request for a necessary gift (James 5:16).

NOTES

His prayer is for *"all"* the congregation, because the welfare of each affects all.

HOW IMPORTANT IS INTERCESSION?

We should see from this example just how important it actually is. The Lord has given the Church an amazing amount of responsibility regarding the carrying out of His Work and Plan on the Earth. In other words, if the Church doesn't conduct itself properly, the Work of God simply will not be accomplished. So, what we do or don't do, has great significance. If we properly follow the Lord, the Work of God flourishes. If we do not properly follow the Lord, the Work of God suffers.

Unfortunately, many, if not most, Christians have the erroneous idea, that whatever God is going to do, He just simply does it because He is God, etc. Nothing could be further from the Truth.

Of course, God is able to do anything He desires. But He has purposely given the responsibility of a great part of His Plan and Work to the Church, i.e., *"the Body of Christ."* When we say *"Church"* or *"Body of Christ,"* we are *not* speaking of the institutionalized Church or organizations, but rather those who are truly Born-Again, whatever Church with which they may be associated.

I think that we Christians do not understand this as we should, thereby taking too much for granted, leaving it all to the Lord, with us doing little or nothing. There are three basic ways in which we must function in this capacity. They are as follows:

EVERY BELIEVER HAS A MINISTRY

Every Believer is assigned a particular Ministry by the Holy Spirit. We must find out what that Ministry is, and we definitely can know if we will only seek the Lord, and then ask God's help relative to carrying out this mission that God has given us. Unfortunately, many Christians do not understand this, thinking that it's only Preachers who are assigned particular Ministries. To be sure, every single Believer is supposed to fit in the place assigned for him by the Lord, and carry out that task. Unfortunately, most Christians don't have the slightest idea as to what that place and position for their own personal lives is. Consequently, the Work of God suffers (Rom. 12:1-16).

GIVING

The giving of our time and resources such as money, is the second thing the Believer is called upon by the Lord to do. While the Gospel is free, the taking of the Gospel costs money, as should be obvious. Consequently, the giving of every Child of God is very important. In fact, the giving of the Believer actually tells *what* that Believer is and *where* that Believer is in Christ.

It is regrettable, that Christians too often support that which not only is not of God, even though it loudly purports to be, but is actually working against God. How terrible it is to support something in that category. But yet that's where many Christians actually are. They have such little spirituality, that they don't know the real from the false, the false from the real.

This is why giving is so important. It reveals what a Christian actually is (II Cor. 8:6-7).

PRAYER

Prayer, even as we are discussing here, is the third thing that every Believer must do. Again, it is unfortunate that many Christians do not pray at all; consequently, they have little or no relationship at all with the Lord, for such can come about only by and through a proper prayer life.

If one has a proper prayer life, one will also have a proper attitude toward the Word of God regarding the study of its contents. The two go together, actually being indivisible. If there is little Bible, there will be little prayer. If there is much Bible, there will be much prayer!

Without prayer, there is no way the Believer can have direction, leading, guidance, or as stated, relationship.

If the Believer is proficient in the three things just mentioned, the Believer will be what God wants him to be (Lk. 11:1-3).

REQUEST WITH JOY

The phrase, *"Making request with joy,"* proclaims two factors:

1. Paul was not interceding for this Church because of problems there, but rather

NOTES

for continued blessing. As stated, there were few Churches then that fell into this category. So, the intercession of the Apostle is totally different here than it had been, for instance, for Corinth.

2. Every request he made was done so with joy. This means, as stated, that there was no major problem there, and as well, he felt assured of an answer.

If the Apostle was interceding for my Church or your Church, would his intercession be in the same spirit as it was for Philippi, or would it of necessity be different?

(5) "FOR YOUR FELLOWSHIP IN THE GOSPEL FROM THE FIRST DAY UNTIL NOW;"

There was a deep satisfaction in the heart of Paul for the Philippians' partnership in the Gospel. Two things are brought into focus here:

1. The Philippians had sent a gift of money to help him, which was desperately needed. This was not new to them, having done this before. He had received gifts sent him when at Thessalonica (Phil. 4:16) and at Corinth (II Cor. 11:9). These gifts were a great help.

2. While the gift was one expression of their partnership, Paul was grateful and filled with joy over the frequent evidences of the Philippians sharing in the responsibility of helping take the Gospel to others. Their giving was a reflection of their burden.

FELLOWSHIP IN THE GOSPEL

The phrase, *"For your fellowship in the Gospel,"* refers to *"a joint-participation in a common interest and activity, in this case, the Gospel of Jesus Christ."* The idea is, the Philippians supported Paul with their prayers and finances while he went about his missionary labors. This is basically that for which he was thanking God. This joint-participation in the work of propagating the Gospel had gone on from the first day when Lydia had opened her home to the preaching of the Word (Acts 16:15), until the moment when Paul was writing this Letter. Paul was grateful to God for all their help. He was thanking them for it.

The Greek Expositors tell us that there is a most delicate touch here that cannot be properly brought out in any English translation, since the English language does not have the particular idiom in question.

In the Greek there is a definite article before the adverb *"now,"* actually saying *"the now."*

Putting it in this manner, which as stated does not properly carry over in the English, proclaims the Apostle in essence telling the Philippians that their gift at the present time was very much needed. While he is thanking them for all their gifts, he is proclaiming by the manner in which he phrases himself, that this last gift is, in effect, an answer to prayer.

Exactly what arrangements Paul had in Rome we are not exactly told. We know he was chained to a Roman soldier at least part of the day, and quite possibly 24 hours of each day. We also know, that at this particular time he was not really in a prison, but rather his own *"hired house"* (Acts 28:30).

This probably meant that he was allowed, even though under the eye of a Roman guard, to rent his own quarters. That being the case, he would have had to pay the rent himself, and probably was responsible for his own food, etc. Having no way to earn any money, and thereby, totally dependent on what the Lord sent in by others, one can well understand how the gift from Philippi would have been very much needed.

OUR GIVING

Even though we have just mentioned this, it is so important, I think that we should address it a little more fully, and I speak of support for the Work of God. As stated, to what and to whom a Christian gives, actually serves as a spiritual barometer for that particular person. Let's use Paul as an example:

I think it would be obvious as to how important it was for people to give to Paul's Ministry. The Holy Spirit sanctions His approval here of such by having this account placed in the Sacred Text.

Anything given to Paul, or anyone like Paul, would have been of great service to the Work of God, and definitely would have been in the Will of God, which should be overly obvious. Consequently, every Believer ought to support such a Ministry. Above even that, they should be spiritual enough to know what type of Ministry presently is in the same flavor of Paul of so long ago. The work is the same now as then and the purpose is the same now as then.

Paul was totally controlled by the Holy Spirit, which means totally led by the Spirit. His Ministry had the proper fruit of souls being saved, lives being changed, Believers being Baptized with the Holy Spirit, sick bodies being truly healed, and bondages of darkness being broken. That was the fruit, and that is to be the fruit in all Ministries in one form or the other.

If the Gospel is truly preached and taught, it will have at least some of the fruit mentioned here, if not all. Consequently, that is for what each Believer should look.

OPPOSITION

Let's continue to use Paul by addressing ourselves to the Judaizers, who constantly caused Paul problems, by going to the Churches he had founded after he had left, attempting to turn the Saints toward legalism. In their attempts to propagate this false message, they always denigrated Paul, attempting to tear him down in the eyes of the people, even the people he had brought to the Lord. This was the purpose of his Epistles to the Church at Corinth, and the Churches in Galatia.

Some of the Christians in these particular places were giving these Judaizers money, and quite large sums it seems. Now let's look at that a moment (II Cor. 11:18-20).

The actual truth about these preachers was, that they were *"Satan's ministers"* (II Cor. 11:13-15). So, the giving of money to these people was actually aiding the cause of Satan and not Christ. But yet, this is exactly what these Corinthians were doing.

It is an awful thing not to give to God at all, but worse still to give to those who are not really preaching the Gospel, but rather have their own agenda in mind, which actually means that those who give to such so-called Ministries are actually furthering the work of Satan.

It should be understood, that false apostles and the false message are always dressed up in the proper religious garb. In other words, it looks right and sounds right, so much so in fact, that it fools many Christians, even as it did the Corinthians and others. Therefore, the

Believer must be very sure about what he does as it regards these matters. If not, he can find himself supporting Satan, which regrettably, is actually what is being done in most cases.

Satan doesn't care how much money is poured into Preachers and Ministries of this type. In fact, he aids the process as should be obvious. Conversely, he will do everything within his power to stop the support of those who are truly preaching the Gospel.

REALITY

The Truth is, for every true Preacher of the Gospel, there are at least 20 or 30, or even more, who are not of the Lord, despite their claims. So, how is the Believer to sort through all of this?

If Believers take their cue from other Believers or Preachers, more than likely they are not taking their cue from the Lord. Unfortunately, most Christians little seek the Lord as it regards their giving, but rather give to that which shines the brightest, whatever it might be. They don't check the fruit (Mat. 7:15-20), or else they accept inflated reports which have, in fact, no validity.

Many Christians are fooled by glitter, glamour, big crowds, or manifestations which little fall out to the proper fruit, if at all! In fact, *"manifestations"* are the biggest cause presently for most giving. The bigger rabbit pulled out of the biggest hat, gets the biggest check.

These people never seem to stop and think, or ask themselves the question, if these *"manifestations"* are resulting in proper fruit of souls being saved, lives being changed, sick bodies being truly healed, or bondages being broken, etc.

Manifestations may be of God, or they may not be of God. Within themselves they are not proper fruit. If they fall out to the Salvation of souls and lives being changed, then that is proper fruit. Otherwise it isn't!

TO WHOM ARE YOU GIVING, PAUL OR THE JUDAIZERS?

That is the question!

I'll go back to what I said in the beginning. The giving of the Believer serves as a barometer of our spiritual experience more so than anything else. It tells what we actually are. So, what does your giving say about you?

Are you giving to Paul, or are you supporting the Judaizers?

That was the question then, and it is the question now.

CONSTANT SUPPORT

The phrase, *"From the first day until now,"* refers to the faithfulness of these Philippians. When one considers that the Holy Spirit placed this in the Sacred Text where it will stand for all eternity, lets us know how important all of this is.

The Holy Spirit noted their generosity, their faithfulness, their love for lost souls, their love for the Apostle Paul, and their desire to do all they could do to take the Gospel to the world. Once again, this tells us how important this is, especially considering how the Holy Spirit caused it to be recorded.

If the Holy Spirit was writing here about me or you, what would He say? Would we have the same report as had the Philippians? Or would we have to be placed in the category of the Corinthians who supported the Judaizers, i.e., *"Satan's ministers"* (II Cor. 11:13-15).

If a Believer properly seeks the Lord concerning his or her giving, the Lord will lead and direct.

A PERSONAL EXAMPLE

In the early 1990's, we were on Television in Moscow, over what was referred to then as *"T.V. 1."* This had been the major government Channel which carried Communist propaganda to all 15 republics of the Soviet Union, before the fall of that empire, etc. We were able to get on this Channel, and preach the Gospel for approximately two years.

The Lord used it in a powerful way. I had a Pastor to call me once, a man with whom I was not too well acquainted, telling me of his experience in Moscow.

He went on to relate as to how that he and several other Preachers went to Moscow during those years at least once a year, and would bring in Russian Preachers from all over the Soviet Union, where they would teach them the Word of God intensely for several days and nights. They would pay for the expenses of these Preachers in order that they could come.

On this particular trip he told me how that during one of the sessions, he had matter-of-factly asked each Preacher to stand and tell how he had come to Christ.

He said, *"Brother Swaggart, to my pleasant surprise, over two-thirds of these Preachers, some of them now pastoring large Churches, testified that they had been saved through your Television Ministry."*

During that two years we were on that particular Channel, it was so hard to raise the money to keep the Program airing each week, that we brought the Ministry to the brink of bankruptcy several times, attempting to fund this effort, which I actually think was one of the greatest Works of God in this 20th Century.

Also, I would be remiss if I did not give Jim Woolsey the proper credit for persevering until we were able to secure time on this particular Channel. Had it not been for him, this thing would not have been done.

During this time, one of our supporters wrote me a note, telling me the following:

Some so-called Christians at that particular time, were telling him how foolish he was supporting our Ministry. They told him that we were lying about being on Television in Russia and he was throwing away his money, etc.

To be frank, we have had this problem to such an extent that it beggars description. It has seriously hurt the Work of God. Unfortunately, many Christians believe what they hear and act accordingly.

For several months, this Brother ceased his giving, believing what these people were saying. However, in his heart of hearts he did not feel right about the decision he had made. Consequently, he began to seek the Lord, asking the Lord for direction, and that He would show him what he ought to do.

After seeking the Lord in that fashion, the very next day he was reading the local newspaper. They had reprinted an article from the Washington Post, one of the most prestigious newspapers in the world. It was an account of one of their reporters in Russia making a tour of that particular country.

Down in the body of the text, she made the statement, *"And by the way, I couldn't get away from Jimmy Swaggart wherever I went. He was on Television in every city that I visited."*

NOTES

When he read those words, his heart came up into his throat. Here was proof from an unimpeachable source, in fact, undeniable proof. He immediately started back his support.

But yet, untold thousands of Christians would hear our pleas for help, but turn a deaf ear, because their Denomination told them they couldn't help, or their Pastor, or whoever. My question is, *"What will these people say when they stand before the Lord at the Judgment Seat of Christ?"* Let me give another example:

THE PREACHER

During that time, we had one particular individual who was actually a Russian, who had immigrated to Canada many years before, who called the Brother who was our interpreter (the actual voice in the translation from English to Russian which we did with all the Telecasts), who was also a Russian, attempting to get him to stop interpreting for us. I did not know the man, actually had never met him. But yet he had very harsh things to say about me and our Ministry, but thankfully, our interpreter did not heed this ungodly effort.

At any rate, this man went on a three-month tour (I believe it was) of Russia, going from city to city and town to town preaching meetings, etc. When he came back, he called our interpreter and asked his forgiveness. He said, *"Everywhere I went there was a Move of God already taking place, and almost invariably it was caused by Brother Swaggart's Telecast."*

He then said, *"I was wrong in what I was thinking and what I was doing, please keep interpreting for this Ministry, because it's carrying out a great work for God."*

Thankfully, this Brother did have the Grace to admit he was wrong and to try to make amends, which I very much appreciated. But most, continue on in the wrong direction.

HOW SERIOUS IS IT?

How serious is it to seek to hinder the true Work of God? How serious is it to not only refuse to support Paul, but instead support the Judaizers who were seeking to destroy the Ministry of Paul?

I think the answer to these questions is very obvious. And yet I'm afraid that many Christians find themselves on that side of the fence — the side of hindering the Work of God instead of helping.

Every Christian should always remember this: Satan is a master at getting Believers to believe that which is truly of God, isn't, and that which isn't of God, is. He does this work so well, that he succeeds in many cases.

Why is he so successful?

PERCEPTION?

Many Believers believe as they do, because they perceive something to be what they think it is because of outward circumstances. In other words, they base their decision on perception rather than on what actually is.

What something is perceived to be, may not at all be what it actually is. Due to circumstances and events, something may appear to be the very opposite of what it actually is. And if Christians make judgments based on what they perceive things to be because of outward circumstances, they will almost always go in the wrong direction. But yet that's what most Christians do.

Others parent their Denomination, whatever that Denomination says and does. And one must remember this, it has seldom been the case that religious Denominations, and whatever the stripe, did not oppose true Apostles of the Lord.

Most Christians don't realize, that Satan will not oppose at all that which is not of God, actually making the way clear and open for them to support such, while he will greatly oppose that which is truly of God, using every device at his disposal to get the Christian to lose confidence in the one truly Called of God. Regrettably, he usually succeeds!

Once again, I come back to the question, *"Are you supporting Paul, or those who oppose Paul?"*

(6) "BEING CONFIDENT OF THIS VERY THING, THAT HE WHICH HATH BEGUN A GOOD WORK IN YOU WILL PERFORM IT UNTIL THE DAY OF JESUS CHRIST:"

Of course, it was God Who had produced their transformed lives by the work of Regeneration. So Paul was confident that God would continue this work. Even though he rejoiced in the Philippians' generous gift and their evidences of spiritual growth, his confidence did not rest ultimately on the Philippians themselves, but on God Who would preserve them and enable them to reach the desired goal.

The *"good work"* refers to the Salvation begun at their conversion. To see it as a direct and limited reference to their monetary gift is unwarranted.

God not only initiates Salvation, but continues it and guarantees its consummation. The Apostle's thought relates not to the end of life, but to the Glorious Coming of Jesus Christ that will vindicate both the Lord and His people. So Paul is asserting that God will bring his work to completion. Nothing in this life or after death will prevent the successful accomplishment of God's good work in every Christian, at least those who will believe Him.

"The Day of Christ Jesus" is a phrase occurring with only slight variation six times in the New Testament, three of them in Philippians (I Cor. 1:8; 5:5; II Cor. 1:14; Phil. 1:6, 10; 2:16). The expression is similar to the *"Day of the Lord"* (I Thess. 5:2) and the Old Testament *"Day of Jehovah"* (Amos 5:18-20).

However, in contrast to the Old Testament emphasis on judgment, the *"Day of Christ Jesus"* is mentioned in all cases with reference to the New Testament Church. It will be the time when Christ returns for His Church, which we refer to as the Rapture, when the Believers' works will be examined at the Judgment Seat of Christ and the Believer rewarded (Kent).

CONFIDENT

The phrase, *"Being confident of this very thing,"* refers to both their growth in Christ and their continued financial support.

Paul is using strong language here. It means to be fully and firmly persuaded or convinced. Paul was entirely convinced of the truth of what he said. It is the language of a man who had no doubt on the subject.

This doesn't mean that the Saints in Philippi were perfect or that there was not room for continued growth. Actually, Paul's statements lend credence to the fact that more work by the Holy Spirit was needed, even as the next phrase will portray; however, his confidence lay in the fact that the Philippians would cooperate with the Lord in this continued growth. He knew these people, and had great confidence in them.

A GOOD WORK

The phrase, *"That He which hath begun a good work in you will perform it,"* refers to God, but which work will be carried out by the Holy Spirit, as it is in all Believers.

This *"good work"* did refer in part to the cooperation of the Philippians with the Apostle, as we've already stated, but it cannot be restricted to this meaning. The Holy Spirit was carrying out a far more detailed work in these hearts and lives than that which pertained to their giving. However, even as we've already stated, *"giving"* as it pertains to a Christian is extremely important. It is of far greater consequence than the mere exchange of money. We must not forget that it serves as a spiritual barometer. This speaks of how much we give, how much we have left, to whom it is given, why it is given, and where it is given.

RIGHTEOUSNESS AND HOLINESS

While the Holy Spirit carries out His Work in our hearts and lives in every capacity, still the greatest thrust, which should be obvious, pertains to the Christlikeness of Righteousness and Holiness. This is the *"good work"* toward which He strains. He is successful according to our cooperation with Him. This is a sober thought.

How much are we actually cooperating with Him, in this most important task?

The greatest privilege an individual can have is to know and understand that the Holy Spirit, the Third Person of the Godhead, actually abides within our heart. This is a privilege of unparalleled proportions, and of course, cannot take place until one is Born-Again. As well, the door is opened further, much further, upon one's Baptism with the Holy Spirit (Mat. 3:11). Consequently, we should take advantage of this tremendous privilege, by cooperating with Him in every capacity. The more we do so, the quicker and better this work can be carried out, and the more wholesome and fulfilling will be our lives.

THE DAY OF JESUS CHRIST

The phrase, *"Until the Day of Jesus Christ,"* tells us several things:

1. This particular day speaks of the coming Resurrection, when all the sainted dead will be raised, and all the Saints at that time who will be alive, will be changed gloriously and wondrously. This will be the time when the Saints will put on the *"glorified body"* (I Cor. 15:51-57; I Thess. 4:13-18).

2. This phrase, *"The Day of Jesus Christ,"* refers to a period of time that is definitely going to come. It will mark the beginning of the end for Satan.

The Rapture (Resurrection) of the Church, will be followed by the Great Tribulation period, when the Judgment of God will be poured out on the Earth as never before. That seven year period, called *"the time of Jacob's trouble"* (Jer. 30:7), will conclude with the Second Coming of Christ, with Him then ruling and reigning Personally from Jerusalem.

The world will then enter into a thousand years of peace with Satan locked away in the bottomless pit, along with all his demons and fallen angels, which the Prophets of old predicted (Rev. 20:1-6).

At the end of that particular period, Satan will be loosed out of the bottomless pit, and allowed one more short excursion on the Earth, which will be short-lived. He will then be cast into the Lake of Fire, along with all of his followers, which will include every unsaved person who has ever lived (Rev. 20:7-15). The Lord will then cleanse the Earth by fire (II Pet. 3:10-13).

At that time, the Lord will transfer His Headquarters from Heaven to Earth, as is described in Revelation Chapters 21 and 22.

Then as Paul also stated, *"God will be all in all"* (I Cor. 15:28), exactly as He was before the revolution by Satan, even before the creation of man.

As well, one must not draw from this 6th Verse, any hard and fast doctrine of eternal security. In fact, Paul later admonishes the Philippians in this very Epistle, lest his work among them be *"in vain"* (Phil. 2:14-16; Col. 1:19-23).

3. Paul's statement, *"Until the Day of Jesus Christ,"* does not necessarily picture the Apostle expecting the Rapture at that particular time, as some Expositors claim. Actually, II Thessalonians Chapter 2, proclaims the opposite. The Apostle there is saying that the Rapture cannot take place at that particular time, with certain things that must be carried

out first. He said, *"That ye be not soon shaken in mind, or be troubled, neither by spirit, nor by word, nor by letter as from us, as that the Day of Christ is at hand"* (II Thess. 2:2).

He stated then that first of all there must come a *"falling away,"* which refers to a departure from Truth, the great Apostasy, during which time the Rapture will take place, which will be followed by the Advent of the Antichrist (I Thess. 4:13-18; II Thess. 2:3-4).

Unfortunately for the lukewarm of the Church, and fortunately for the Church that is ready, we are now living in this time predicted by Paul, referred to as the *"falling away."* As stated, it means *"falling away from Truth,"* which perfectly characterizes the modern Church. This means that the Rapture could take place at any moment!

Unfortunately again, much of the modern Church knows nothing about the Rapture, with a great segment, even those who claim to be Spirit-filled, openly repudiating this cardinal doctrine of the New Testament (Lk. 21:34; Jn. 14:1-3; I Cor. 15:51-56; II Cor. 5:1-9; Eph. 5:25-27; Phil. 3:11, 20-21; Col. 3:4; I Thess. 4:13-18; II Thess. 2:1, 7-8; James 5:7-8; I Pet. 5:4; I Jn. 2:28; 3:2).

(7) "EVEN AS IT IS MEET FOR ME TO THINK THIS OF YOU ALL, BECAUSE I HAVE YOU IN MY HEART; INASMUCH AS BOTH IN MY BONDS, AND IN THE DEFENCE AND CONFIRMATION OF THE GOSPEL, YE ALL ARE PARTAKERS OF MY GRACE."

Paul was right in regarding the Philippians so highly, because in a sense they had become partners in his imprisonment and his current legal difficulties. To say they were in his *"heart"* was to use a figure denoting not mere emotions or sentiment, but the essence of consciousness and personality.

The reference to his imprisonment (*"I am in chains"*) belongs with the following rather than the preceding words, as giving evidence of the Philippians' partnership in God's Grace. Even when it might have been dangerous to identify themselves openly with Paul, they had treated his misfortunes as their own and had come to his assistance with their gifts.

"Defending and confirming the Gospel" could be understood as negative and positive aspects of Paul's Preaching Ministry — i.e., defending the Gospel from attacks and proclaiming its Message with proofs. In other words, the Philippians had become one with Paul in this great work of both defending the Gospel and establishing the Gospel.

THE RIGHT THING

The phrase, *"Even as it is meet for me to think this of you all,"* means that it was just and right for Paul to think this of the Philippians, considering their consecration to the Lord.

At least part or the Apostle's feelings toward these people are because of their unflagging support of him, as stated, both prayerfully and financially. In other words they did more than just wish him well, they stood with him respecting finances, which is generally the telltale sign. They put proof to their words.

However, the thing I wish to emphasize is, *"their financial support of him was linked to their spiritual consecration."*

CONSECRATION TO PAUL WAS CONSECRATION TO THE LORD

As we have repeatedly stated, where and how and to whom one gives as it regards the Lord's Work, or that which purports to be His Work, shouts loud as a spiritual barometer.

The giving to Paul by these Philippians, showed far more than a mere handing over of money. It showed that they had a proper burden; it showed that they had a correct understanding of the Gospel of Jesus Christ; it showed that they understood God's Plan regarding His Apostle; and, it showed a tremendous knowledge of the Work of God in general.

As well, and as we shall see, whereas many others were ashamed of Paul because of his imprisonment, even turning away from him, these Philippians pressed in all the more, not caring what anyone thought, standing up for Paul because they knew this was right.

May I be allowed here to be bold also!

Before God, for He sees everything that I write, I can say as well that this Ministry is of God. I speak of Jimmy Swaggart Ministries. In my mind and heart, I can do no less than Paul, by putting those who support us in a category of Godliness. I feel I must, and because of the very reasons given concerning the Philippians.

As well, even though the Apostle does not say anything out front here regarding his detractors, still, what he doesn't say screams in every word he does say. Also, I can do no less!

I do not see how anyone could have fought Paul and at the same time be of God.

Of course, in no way do I even remotely put myself in the shadow of the great Paul, but still, the same Holy Spirit Who lived in his heart, lives in mine. As God called him, He as well, has called me.

I know the burden of my heart, the cry of my soul. I know what the Lord has done for me, and I know the Hand of the Lord upon me for World Evangelism. If I denied that, I would be denying the Lord. Consequently, those who oppose me in this great task of World Evangelism, and in the defense of the Gospel even as Paul, I cannot at the same time, see how these people can be of God. The Lord does not oppose Himself. It is just not possible to oppose Paul and at the same time be right with the Lord. Likewise, I have to feel the same about my own Ministry.

When it comes to those who have stood with me, have stood by my side, even in the face of ridicule and sarcasm, I have to think of these people exactly as Paul thought of the Philippians. It is *"just"* and *"right"* for me to do so, just as it was *"just"* and *"right"* for him to do so!

MY HEART

The phrase, *"Because I have you in my heart,"* according to the Expositors, could have been translated, *"Because you have me in your heart."* Actually, they say this is more so the rendering of the Greek in accord with the context.

The Philippians had a large place in their hearts for Paul, and at this time especially with reference to the two particulars mentioned here, first, with reference to his defense of the Gospel, and second, in his confirmation and proclamation of the same.

However, other Expositors claim that the King James rendition is correct, *"I have you in my heart."*

It really doesn't matter, as it is correct in either case.

BONDS

The phrase, *"Inasmuch as both in my bonds,"* refers to the Apostle's imprisonment in Rome. As well, he was literally chained to a Roman soldier for at least part of the time, and perhaps all of the time.

Every evidence is, that some Christians were embarrassed concerning Paul's situation. He said as much in II Timothy 1:16. Even though he was speaking there of his second imprisonment, which led to his death, still, I'm sure this problem prevailed in the first imprisonment as well.

The Judaizers undoubtedly claimed that were Paul really what he said he was, an Apostle of Jesus Christ, surely the Lord would not allow him to be placed in prison. Others probably claimed that he did not have proper Faith, or he would not be there. And then some, no doubt, claimed that there was hidden sin in the life of the Apostle, hence the Lord *"locking him up."*

Of course, none of that is true, but it doesn't stop the tongues from wagging. Unfortunately, even as now, all the professing Christians of that time were not consecrated to the Lord. We find constantly, that Satan raised up some of the greatest opposition to Paul from inside the Church. In fact, this has always been the case!

There is no record that the Lord ever actually told Paul as to why he allowed him to be placed *"in bonds."* At any rate, the Apostle came to terms with the situation, knowing that God had a purpose in all of this, hence him referring to himself as *"a prisoner of Jesus Christ,"* which meant that he did not consider himself a prisoner of Nero (Phile. vs. 1).

If we have to have an answer from the Lord concerning all things, this shows that we do not properly trust. The Lord did not give Paul a reason for this imprisonment, at least if He did, the Apostle did not record it in any of his Epistles. So, from this we learn that even the great Apostle had to undergo certain things and for particular reasons. No one is exempt from these lessons, and some of us need greater lessons than others.

I suspect that one who is used by the Lord extensively so, even as Paul, can expect greater training, and this is exactly the way the Apostle looked at this situation, even as we shall see.

DEFENSE

The phrase, *"And in the defence,"* refers to the defense of the Gospel.

Actually, Paul is not on trial; the Gospel is on trial.

The word *"defence"* is a Greek judicial term referring to an attorney talking his client off from a charge, thus presenting a verbal defense. Paul was defending the Faith before the tribunal of the world, Nero's throne.

HOW DOES ONE DEFEND THE GOSPEL?

First of all, the Gospel of the New Covenant was given to Paul. To be sure, Satan used every tactic at his disposal to weaken, hinder, and even destroy this Gospel, and adding insult to injury, he used the Church to attempt this more so than anything else.

The greatest thrust during the time of Paul, was the attempt by the Judaizers to add Law to Grace, which of course, was an impossibility. Following this effort, came Gnosticism, which had begun to rear its ugly head toward the close of Paul's Ministry, which he addressed briefly in his Epistle to the Colossians.

In all of this he had to stand foursquare in defense of the Gospel and did so by proclaiming its truths, and pointing out the errors propagated by others (Rom. 6:1-2).

Of course, whenever error is pointed out, it generally arouses great anger toward the one doing the correcting. This was no less true against Paul. Actually, in the propagating of these false doctrines, almost invariably, the individuals concerned attempted to turn Believers against Paul, even some of his own converts.

This is one of the reasons that error is seldom addressed. Most Preachers don't want the heat which always follows. They don't want to be called a *"troublemaker,"* or a *"destroyer of unity,"* or a few other names we could list. So, they compromise, and the Gospel of Jesus Christ is greatly hindered.

Some claim that error should never be opposed, only that Truth should be proclaimed, which will accomplish the task within itself. That sounds good, but unfortunately it's untrue.

The human being is so constructed, that one has to literally put one's finger on the error, calling it what it is in no uncertain terms, before the majority will figure out what is actually happening. To be sure, Jesus strongly attacked error, even going so far as to attack those who propagated such, namely the Pharisees (Mat.

NOTES

Chpt. 23). Paul did the same thing, calling the Judaizers *"fools"* (II Cor. 11:19).

Yes, the Truth must be preached, as certainly should be obvious, but as well, it is necessary that error be pointed out also. In fact, the word *"confirmation"* in the next phrase, proclaims the proclamation of Truth.

CONFIRMATION

The phrase, *"And confirmation of the Gospel,"* refers to the proclamation and establishment of the Gospel.

"Confirmation" in the Greek is *"bebaiosis,"* meaning *"making fast or sure; establishing."* It is a legal term for a guarantee. One might say it this way, *"Confirmation is the obligation under which the seller gives to the buyer a guarantee against all claims to what he has purchased."* In other words, he guarantees the validity of the deed or title. Paul's defense then is a guarantee of the Gospel.

The idea is, the Gospel of Jesus Christ works. It sets captives free. It changes men. The reason is, it is not a mere philosophy, as that made up by men, but is the Word of God, and backed up by the Power of God. In effect, the Power is in the Cross (I Cor. 1:18). However, that Power comes about through the Holy Spirit.

What Jesus did at the Cross and the Resurrection, gives a legal right to the Holy Spirit to do certain things for the Child of God, at least upon continued Faith in the Finished Work of Christ.

As we've already stated, before the Cross, the Holy Spirit could not even come into the hearts and lives of Believers to abide (Jn. 14:17). The reason pointed to the sin debt which hung over the heads of men, even ardent Believers, because the blood of bulls and goats could not really take away sin (Heb. 10:4). However, the Death of Christ on the Cross took away all sin, for those who will believe, making it possible for the Holy Spirit to come into the heart and life of the Believer (Jn. 1:29).

As well, the Believer being *"in Christ,"* and understanding that this is the source of all of his Victory, the Holy Spirit acts upon the Faith of the Believer, guaranteeing all the benefits of the Cross and the Resurrection (Rom. 8:1-2).

When the believing sinner exhibits Faith in Christ and what the Lord did by dying on the Cross, even though he understands very little about this great activity, still, his Faith is rewarded with Salvation. The Holy Spirit has convicted him of sin, as the Word of God is presented in some manner, and has literally brought him to Christ. The consequence is Salvation.

Likewise, after the individual comes to Christ, he is to ever keep his Faith in the Cross and the Resurrection, understanding that it was there that Jesus paid it all, and that his Faith in the Cross, placed him *"in Christ, and keeps him in Christ,"* which consequence is Victory over all sin. As stated, the Holy Spirit guarantees that (Rom. 8:2).

This is the Power of the Gospel of Jesus Christ, its actual confirmation, and which must be defended at all costs. Satan will do everything he can to push the Church away from the True Gospel, which is always in the Cross, knowing that in doing so, he will keep the Christian from Victory, and because Victory can be obtained in no other manner.

PARTAKERS OF GRACE

The phrase, *"Ye all are partakers of my Grace,"* has a twofold meaning:

1. It refers to the time that Paul preached the Gospel unto them, even when they were pagans, and they accepted and received the Grace of God, actually the same Grace that Paul had received from the Lord, even as all receive who accept Christ.

2. Inasmuch as they were now co-sharers in the Grace of God, they were also joint-participants with Paul in telling others of this great Grace of God. This is the way of the Gospel. We receive, and we want others to receive.

The structure of this phrase, tells us that Paul does not write as from a superior to an inferior, but simply as a fellow Christian. The phrase would have probably been better translated as *"Ye all are partakers with me of Grace."*

As we have previously stated, the Grace of God is not a commodity or substance as such, it is simply the favor of God bestowed upon human beings, who do not deserve such favor, in fact, cannot deserve such favor, and can do nothing to earn such favor. In fact, if we try to earn it in any way, we frustrate the Grace or rather nullify it. We receive this favor from God simply by having Faith in what Jesus did at the Cross and the Resurrection. Constant Faith in that guarantees a continued supply of the Grace of God. The moment we insert *"works"* of any kind into the mix, attempting to make those works a reason or cause of our Salvation or Victory, and irrespective as to how holy or noble those works may be, or even Scriptural in their own right, in the doing of that, we automatically frustrate the Grace of God, which means that it stops, and which means we are in big trouble (Gal. 2:21).

In all of these explanations, we do not want to lose sight of the main thrust of Paul's statement, of him thanking these Philippians profusely for standing with him as it regards the Gospel of Christ. They have not allowed his imprisonment to hinder them or to deter them in any way. Their love for him, their gratitude for him, and their loyalty to him, have never wavered. As we've already stated, all of this carries a far greater weight than the mere giving of money as it regards their gift to him at this time, telling us of their actual spirituality.

(8) "FOR GOD IS MY RECORD, HOW GREATLY I LONG AFTER YOU ALL IN THE BOWELS OF JESUS CHRIST."

Only God could truly vouch for Paul's feelings about his Philippian friends, because they ran so deep. This was not an oath but a statement of fact.

Paul's yearnings for this Church were not merely the human longing to be with friends, but were prompted to be the very *"affection of Christ Jesus,"* with Whom Paul was in vital union. It was the indwelling Christ Who was producing the fruit of love in Paul by the Holy Spirit and Who thus enabled him to yearn for their welfare with the compassion of his Lord (Kent).

MY WITNESS

The phrase, *"For God is my record,"* actually means *"one who bears testimony."*

Paul is not making this statement because he felt the Philippians distrusted him in some way, but simply because he lacks words to express his earnest disposition toward them. So all he can do is *"call God to record."*

Countless times I have attempted to compose a letter, expressing my deep appreciation to someone who has been kind and gracious to the Ministry, most of the time exactly as it was here with Paul. They had given a sum of money which we so desperately needed. Every time vocabulary fails me, and I feel that I'm not expressing myself at least to the fullest extent of what I feel in my heart. Consequently, all I can do is relate to them that the Lord will greatly and grandly repay them, of which I am unable to properly express.

LOVE

The phrase, *"How greatly I long after you all,"* means to desire earnestly, to have a strong affection for.

Not only does Paul have an intense desire or longing for the Philippians, but he longs over them. What a miracle of Divine Grace for this heretofore proud Pharisee to have tender heart-longings for these pagan Greeks! (Wuest).

This within itself, is a confirmation of the Gospel. As stated, it changes men and does so dramatically and wondrously. In fact, it is the only power on Earth, but which actually came from Heaven, that can perform these types of miracles. This is the need of humanity, the only answer for the evil hearts of men.

Congress passes laws attempting to address these problems, but law can never change the hearts of men. Racism, prejudice, bias, hatred, all of these evil things, will continue to exist, irrespective of psychological counseling, governmental programs, change of environment, etc., unless Christ Jesus comes into the heart. That is the only solution.

When this happens, the black man loves the white man, and the white man loves the black man. The idea then of *"ethnic cleansing"* becomes preposterous. The Believer in Christ realizes and knows, that all men everywhere are precious in the sight of God, and that none are better than others. However, this devilish racism, this evil supposed ethnic superiority, this *"black is beautiful"* or *"white is right"* all fall by the wayside in Christ.

Before meeting Christ, Paul was a hate-filled Pharisee. He literally hated all who did not measure up to his standards, and above all he hated Gentiles, who all Pharisees referred to as *"dogs."* But now there is a love in his heart for these same Gentiles, a love I might quickly add which is genuine, sincere, and real and not something feigned or contrived.

This and this alone, and I speak of the entrance of Christ into one's heart and life, stops hatred, stops war, stops prejudice, etc., and because the person is changed inside, i.e., *"the heart."* Any other type of proposed solution, is about the same as putting a Band-Aid over a cancer. It is doomed to failure.

THE PRESENT PROBLEM

As the nation sat in shocked, stunned silence, viewing the account by Television of the massacre in Littleton, Colorado, in the Spring of 1999, the questions began to fly thick and fast, *"What can we do to stop this?"*

The answer is that man can do absolutely nothing. If in fact he could to something, then Jesus Christ would not have had to come down here and die on a Cross. The Lord is the only One Who can change such a situation. However, the majority of the world has always rejected that solution, even as they continue to reject that solution. So, the idea that the world is gradually going to be saved, is refuted by the very happenings taking place all around us.

To be sure, it will be saved, but only when Jesus Christ Personally comes back, which He shall, during which time some particular steps are going to be taken to rectify the situation.

First of all, even as we have previously stated, Satan and all of his demon spirits and fallen angels, are going to locked away in the bottomless pit. That will take place immediately at the Second Coming (Rev. 20:1-3).

Then, Jesus is going to set up a Government of Righteousness with Himself as its Head (Isa. 2:1-4; 9:6-7; 11:1-10). Only then will things be as they ought to be. The key totally and completely, is Jesus Christ.

THE HEART OR COMPASSION OF CHRIST

The phrase, *"In the bowels of Jesus Christ,"* refers to the compassion of Christ.

The Ancients regarded the intestines as being the compassion of the individual. Consequently, when they (Gentiles) would offer up an animal in sacrifice, they would take out its intestines and other organs, and then hold the whole bloody mass over their heads, calling it, *"the compassion."* Thus, when Paul uses this symbol, it presents a powerful metaphor describing perfect union with Christ. Combined with the genuine human affection toward the Philippians is Divine Love. Christ is the Source of Paul's life, the Heart of his love. Christ's Heart has become his, so that he can love the Philippians with the very love of Christ.

The Believer is to have no yearnings apart from his Lord; his pulse beats with the very pulse of Christ; his heart throbs with the heart of Christ (Rom. 12:10).

Could the transforming power of the Gospel be more striking revealed than in the union or fellowship of these two unlikely parties, a former devotee of Pharisaism on the one hand, and on the other a group whose total life had been formed by the proud atmosphere of a Roman colony! This is what Jesus Christ can do!

(9) "AND THIS I PRAY, THAT YOUR LOVE MAY ABOUND, YET MORE AND MORE IN KNOWLEDGE AND IN ALL JUDGMENT;"

Concern for others should express itself first in prayer, as one recognizes the importance of the Divine factor in any lasting spiritual growth. The basic petition of Paul's prayer is that his reader's love might abound more and more. Love is a Fruit of the Spirit (Gal. 5:22) that enables all other spiritual virtues to be exercised properly (I Cor. 13:1-3). Without it no Christian is spiritually complete (Col. 3:14).

Love must be intelligent and morally discerning, that is, if it would be truly the Love of God. In fact, love never reaches a saturation point.

What is encouraged here is not a heedless sentiment, but love based on knowledge, the intellectual perception that has recognized Jesus Christ as the Head, and as well recognized the principles of the Word of God as illuminated by the Holy Spirit. In other words, that the Bible is the Word of God, and in fact, the only Revealed Truth in the world today.

Spiritual knowledge, gained from an understanding of Divine Revelation, enables the Believer to love what God commands and in the way He reveals.

The joining of the expression *"depth of insight"* to *"knowledge"* stresses moral perception and the practical application of knowledge to the myriad circumstances of life. Spiritual knowledge is thus no abstraction but is intended to be applied to life. In this instance it will serve to deliver the Believer's love into avenues both Biblically proper and pure (Kent).

THIS I PRAY

The phrase, *"And this I pray,"* presents that which is directed consciously to God, and with a definite aim.

As Paul prayed, he was actually praying in the Spirit, and, therefore, had a definite consciousness of the Presence of God, and that he was actually speaking, not into mere space, but to a Person, and that Person was listening, giving attention to what he was saying (Wuest).

I think it should be understandable by now, that Paul prayed about everything. As well, this should be the principle of every Child of God.

The privilege of taking everything to the Lord, is a privilege unparalleled, especially when we know and understand that He hears what we say, and will do great and mighty things. As well, the greater principle of prayer is not really petition, but rather fellowship with the Lord, where He leads us and guides us into His Way. If we think of prayer only as petition, then we miss the point altogether. While the Lord definitely does implore us to petition Him for the things we need, we should not stop there, but allow the Holy Spirit to deal with our hearts in communion, bringing us into that which the Lord desires.

GROWTH

Let this first be noted, that Paul's prayer as it regards the Philippians is for spiritual growth. All that Grace has wrought in these Believers, everything in their state that filled his heart with thankfulness, he regards as the beginning of something better still. For this he longed; and, therefore, his heart is set on progress. So we find it in all his Epistles. *"As ye have received how ye ought to walk and to please God — so abound more"* (I Thess. 4:1).

This means that the spiritual prosperity of Believers should be measured not so much by the point they have reached, but by the fact and measure of the progress they are making. Progress in likeness to Christ, progress in following Him; progress in understanding His mind and learning His lesson; progress ever from the performance and the failures of yesterday to the new discipline of today, — this is Paul's Christianity. In this world our condition is such that the business of every Believer is to go forward in Christ.

For any Christians, at any stage of attainment, to presume to stand still is perilous and sinful. A beginner in Christ that is pressing forward is a happier and a more helpful Christian than he who has come to a standstill, though the latter may seem to be on the borders of the land of Beulah.

The first may have his life marred by much darkness and many mistakes; but the second is for the present practically denying the Christian Truth and the Christian Call, as these bear on himself. It is impossible to exhaust the Word of God, the Ways of the Lord, or the Lord Himself; consequently, there is no end to the potential of Christian growth, that is, if the Believer will continue to press forward.

THE REVELATION THE LORD HAS GIVEN ME

As previously mentioned, I speak of that which the Lord began to give me in 1997 concerning the Cross and the Resurrection. Even though this was given in stages, the moment the first light began to come, I knew that this was the answer to the pleadings and even travail before the Lord concerning particular questions. It had a powerful effect in my life immediately, but I also knew that this was just the beginning.

In prayer, sensing that I had only scratched the surface, I asked the Lord, which I have continued to do, that He would continue to open up these Truths to me, knowing that it's literally impossible to exhaust the potential of the Atonement, i.e., *"what Jesus did at the Cross and the Resurrection."*

The Lord heard that petition, and has not ceased to open up Truth after Truth, even unto this very hour. I literally exult with anticipation at times, wondering how far the Lord will take me into this which is actually the great Foundation Truth of Redemption.

We have a 90-minute Radio Program each morning five days a week, over our network of Stations. For the last two years I have been teaching on this subject, and the Lord just keeps opening up the Word to Truth after Truth regarding the Cross. It is the most revolutionary thing I have ever known or experienced. As stated, it has literally changed every part of my life. As well, the Testimonies we are receiving from others who have caught this Truth from hearing us over Radio, Television, or in the Church (Family Worship Center), tell me that it's having an effect on others in the same manner, as of course it will. The Words of the Master are clear, *"And ye shall know the Truth, and the Truth shall make you free"* (Jn. 8:32).

THE LOVE OF WHICH PAUL SPEAKS

The Love spoken of here in this phrase is the Love that God is (I Jn. 4:16), produced in the heart of the yielded Believer by the Holy Spirit (Rom. 5:5). Its chief ingredient is self-sacrifice for the benefit of the one who is loved (Jn. 3:16), and its constituent elements analyzed for us is found in I Corinthians Chapter 13.

"Abound" is from a Greek word which means *"to exceed a fixed number or measure, to exist in superfluity."*

This Divine Love as an exotic flower from Heaven, planted in the foreign soil of the Believer's heart (I Jn. 3:1), was existing in superabundance in the hearts of these Greeks who had been saved out of gross paganism, and was overflowing into the hearts of others. Even though it is already there in superabundance, Paul prays that it might continue to increase.

This is the wonder of all that God has and is. It simply cannot be exhausted, and it is the desire of the Holy Spirit that irrespective as to the abundance of the degree of that which the Lord has already given us, that it continue to increase. Nothing could be more wonderful than that.

KNOWLEDGE

The phrase, *"In knowledge,"* speaks of knowledge gained by experience, as contrasted to intuitive knowledge, which is from another Greek word.

The idea is this. This great volume given by the Lord respecting love, needed to be brought within guiding limitations lest it work harm rather than bring Blessing. There was an eager and enthusiastic spirit among these new converts, but a lack of a deep understanding of the Truth, and also a lack of sensitive moral perception and tact. So Paul prays that this love may overflow more and more, but that its outflow and application might be brought within the guiding limitations of knowledge and judgment.

In the Greek, the idea is *"full knowledge."* The full knowledge which these Philippians could only gain by experience was a better understanding of God's Word as translated into their experience, and a clearer vision of the Lord Jesus in all the beauty and fragrance of His Person.

A Christian can have an *"understanding knowledge"* of the Word, that is, be able to explain its meaning to others, without having an experiential knowledge of the same. But when that Christian has put the Word of God into practice in his life, then he has what Paul is talking about here. This is the difference between a young convert and a matured Believer.

The former has not had time to live long enough to live out the Word in his life, the latter has. The former, if his life is wholly yielded, is a delight to look upon in his Christian life, as one would enjoy the vigor and sparkle of youth.

The latter, in his mellowed, well-rounded, matured, and fully-developed Christian experience, his life full of tender reminiscences of his years of companionship with the Lord Jesus, has the fragrance of heavenly things about him.

This was what the Philippian Saints needed, but it would take time for this to be brought about (Wuest).

THE CHURCH

This of which Paul speaks presents the great need. Not only is love needed, of course it is needed; however, love without proper knowledge can fall out to harm rather than help. That's the reason that the grey heads who have the knowledge of experience are so very much needed in the Church. The Church is very foolish if it does not recognize that. Zeal is great, but zeal without knowledge, creates great problems as well.

While as stated, this knowledge can only be gained by experience, the experience can be speeded up by proper study of the Word, and a conscious effort to learn more about the Lord Jesus Christ (Mat. 11:28-30).

Even though this knowledge covers every aspect of the Christian experience, I think I would be remiss if I did not state the following:

KNOWLEDGE AND THE CROSS

If the knowledge of the Cross is not the foundation of all knowledge, I personally feel that whatever is learned will not be exactly as it should be. The Believer, irrespective as to whether he is a Preacher or otherwise, must understand the rudiments of the Atonement, which of course, is the Finished Work of Christ. He should understand what the Holy Spirit is saying through Paul in Romans, Chapters 6, 7, and 8. This is the Magna Carta of the Christian experience, hence Paul referring to knowledge some nine times in those three Chapters (Rom. 6:3, 6, 9, 16; 7:1, 14, 18; 8:22, 28). So I think the Holy Spirit intends for us to know these things, which constitute the very foundation of our Faith.

The point I am attempting to make, is, that the knowledge of the Believer must be built squarely on the Atonement, what Jesus did for us at the Cross and the Resurrection, what it means to the sinner coming to Christ, and what it means to the Believer as it regards his everyday living and above all his Victory over the world, the flesh, and the Devil. If he has proper knowledge there, everything else will fall into place. Otherwise, nothing will fall into place.

JUDGMENT

The phrase, *"And in all Judgment,"* refers to being able to judge a situation quickly and with sensitivity. How often we Saints mean to be loving to others, but rather say the wrong words or do the wrong thing. We lack that delicate sensibility, that ability to express ourselves correctly, that gentile, wise, discriminating touch which would convey the love we have in our hearts to the lives of others.

But this can be ours if we but live in close companionship with the One Who always exhibited that sense of delicate tactfulness in His life (Wuest).

The idea is this: Irrespective as to who the person is, if they will allow the Holy Spirit the latitude that He desires, earnestly seeking to know all they can about the Lord and ever attempting to grow closer to Him, and there are ways which we have stated in which this can be done, the Holy Spirit will literally transform the worst nature or disposition. He Alone can do this, and He will do it if we will only give Him the latitude to do so.

SELF HELP

In fact, this of which we are speaking is one of the most practiced efforts in the secular world. People are ever trying to improve themselves; however, to be frank, in the natural, and irrespective of the efforts made, such is impossible. There are too many quirks, idiosyncrasies, and foul dispositions in human nature, for man to be able to change himself. It is a fruitless task, irrespective of the amount of money paid for a particular self-development course. However, the Spirit of God can do this thing, but He does it in Christ, Who and Which, are not available to the world.

In fact, that's one of the basic Ministries of the Holy Spirit to the Believer. He wants to give you sensitivity. He wants to make you tactful. He wants to give you the right word at the right time. He wants to help you with sensitive graces, that you might be what you ought to be, and be a blessing to other people instead of the opposite. I emphasize it again and again, the Holy Spirit Alone can do these things, and for Him to do this, we must cooperate with Him.

I speak to the Believer! Start with the Cross and go forward, and watch everything change for the better.

DISCERNMENT

One of the meanings of this word *"judgment"* is *"discernment,"* which is a spiritual and moral sense or feeling.

"All judgment" can mean *"all discernment,"* and, therefore, refers to all kinds of discernment.

Even though discernment is greatly needed in everything as it regards life, probably more than all it is needed as it regards the Moving and Operation of the Holy Spirit. Regrettably, many modern Christians have so little spiritual discernment that they hardly know what is of God and what isn't. If the Preacher can pull a rabbit out of the hat, they automatically think it's of God.

At least one of the reasons for such poor discernment, is because of a serious lack of knowledge as it regards the Word of God, and the Person of Christ. Once again we go back to the Cross. If the person's knowledge there is faulty, and regrettably, because there has been so little preaching and teaching on the Cross in the last nearly half century, most knowledge in this respect is faulty. Hence, all other knowledge is flawed, and especially proper *"judgment,"* i.e., *"discernment."*

The foundation of Christianity is the Cross. If the foundation is ignored or misunderstood, as it is as it regards most Believers, everything else is going to be skewed as well! That is quite a statement but it is true. Let me give an example:

Thousands of Preachers are faced constantly by individuals needing help in certain areas of their lives, and the Pastor little knows what to tell them to do, and many times doesn't even really have victory in his own heart and life. These words are not meant to be critical, but are meant to be truthful.

If the Preacher has pretty much lost Faith in the Word of God, he will recommend a Psychologist, which is worse than nothing. There is no help there! If he loves the Lord and believes the Word of God, he will tell the individual in question, *"You must trust God more"* or *"Get in the Altars,"* etc. While this advice is good, it really does not go far enough at all, even as we have previously stated.

To be frank, most Preachers really do not know what to tell anyone as it regards problems of any nature. The reason is, they have little knowledge of the Cross themselves, over and above the sinner coming to Christ. They have almost no knowledge as to the part the Cross pays in the lives of Believers. How it affects our Victory, our everyday walk, our *"more abundant life,"* exactly as Jesus promised (Jn. 10:10). If they don't know, and most don't know, they don't know what to tell the person who needs help. And that's where the modern Church basically finds itself presently.

As stated, start with the Cross and go forward, and one will then find the Holy Spirit working graciously and abundantly within one's heart and life. The progress will be amazing, and even in all of these great qualities which Paul mentions, i.e., *"Love, Knowledge, Judgment, Fruits of Righteousness,"* etc.

(10) "THAT YE MAY APPROVE THINGS THAT ARE EXCELLENT; THAT YE MAY BE SINCERE AND WITHOUT OFFENCE TILL THE DAY OF CHRIST;"

Paul continues to speak of discernment. The discerning atmosphere in which our love should operate will require us continually *"to discern what is best."* Some things are clearly good or bad. In others the demarcation is not so readily visible. Regarding Christian conduct in the exercise of love, such factors as one's influence on others, as well as the effect on oneself, must be considered (I Cor. 10:32). The question should not only be *"Is it harmful?"* but *"Is it helpful?"* or better yet, *"Is this the Will of God?"* (I Cor. 10:23).

The goal in view is the Day of Christ (the Judgment Seat of Christ), in which every Believer must stand before his Lord and give an account of his deeds (II Cor. 5:10). This sobering and joyous prospect for the Believer should have a purifying effect on one's life (I Jn. 3:3) (Kent).

APPROVAL

The phrase, *"That ye may approve things that are excellent,"* refers to the act of testing something for the purpose of approving it, thus *"to approve by testing."*

The word (approve) refers to the ability of the Saints to sift or test a certain thing and thus to recognize its worth and put their stamp of approval upon it, that is if it passes the test.

EXCELLENT

The word *"excellent"* in the Greek comes from a word that means *"to carry two ways,"* thus *"to carry different ways,"* thus *"to differ."* It refers here to those moral and spiritual concepts and actions which involve delicate and keen distinctions, those that require a deep and keen discernment to recognize. This does not refer, to the ordinary, everyday, easily-understood spiritual obligations, but the finer points of Christian conduct which are in the Apostle's mind.

NOTES

Only the person who is close to the Lord, who knows and understands the Word, which means that he or she is keen to know the Will of God and to follow that Will. Regrettably, out of all the multitudes who profess Christianity, only a few fall into this particular category.

Were there more of this type of discernment, many things that go under the guise of Christendom would not be tolerated for a moment. I speak of much of the *"music"* which passes for *"Christian."* I speak of those who claim an abundance of miracles, when in reality there are no miracles. Yes, God still performs miracles, but not on cue! Millions of dollars given to worthless projects, worthless efforts, all a house of cards built on sand, but believed by gullible Christians who have no discernment.

It is a terrible thing to deny something which is truly of God, or conversely to accept something as of God, when it really isn't!

This is the age of apostasy in which we are now living. In fact, it is the last day apostasy, and will, therefore, be the worst. In fact, the rise of the Antichrist along with the false prophet, will be *"with all power and signs and lying wonders"* (II Thess. 2:9).

So, even miracles are no proof! The criteria has ever been, and the criteria must ever be, the Word of God. Is what is happening *"Biblical"*? Does it match up in every respect with the Bible?

No matter how good it looks, and no matter how many are singing its praises, if it doesn't meet this criteria, it must be rejected out of hand.

SINCERITY

The phrase, *"That ye may be sincere,"* means that which is *"distinct, unmixed, pure, unsullied."* There is no hypocrisy about such a Saint. His life is open like a book waiting to be read.

That which is *"sincere"* is that which may be examined in the clearest and strongest light, without a single flaw or imperfection being revealed. Paul's language here comes from the practice of holding up cloth against the Sun to see if there be any fault. Sincerity is perfect openness to God, and is thus as a strong a word as perfection itself. *"The soul that is sincere is the soul that is without sin."* The word properly means that which is *"judged of in Sunshine,"* and then that which is clear and manifest. It is that over which there are no clouds, so to speak. It is not doubtful and dark, but rather pure and bright.

The word *"sincere"* actually means, literally, *"without wax,"* that is, honey which is pure and transparent. Applied to Christian character, it means that which is not deceitful, ambiguous, hypocritical; that which is not mingled with error, worldliness, and sin; that which does not proceed from selfish and interested motives, and where there is nothing disguised. In fact, there is no more desirable appellation that can be given to a man, than to say that he is *"sincere."* As well, there is nothing more lovely in the character of a Christian than *"sincerity."* It means several things:

1. That he has truly converted to Christ — that he has not assumed Christianity as a mask.

2. That his motives are disinterested and pure.

3. That his conduct is free from double-dealing, trick, and cunning.

4. That his words express the real sentiments of his heart.

5. That he is true to his word, and faithful to his promises.

6. That he is always what he professes to be.

A sincere Christian would bear to have the light let in upon him always; to have the emotions of his heart seen; to be scanned everywhere, and at all times, by men, by Angels, and by God.

PURE

Sincerity signifies purity and simplicity of purpose, and singleness of heart in following out that purpose.

Sincere Christians cherish in their hearts no views, no principles, adverse to the Christian Faith. The test of this sincerity is that a man shall be honestly willing to let light shine through him, to evince the true character of his principles and motives. Such a man is on the road to the final, victorious, and eternal sincerity.

For the present there may be within him too much of that which hinders him, and mars his life. But if he is set on dispelling this and welcomes the light which exposes it, in order that he may expel it, then he has a real, present sincerity, and his course is brightening towards the perfect day (Rainy).

WITHOUT OFFENCE

The phrase, *"And without offence,"* refers to not having anything in one's life that would give cause to stumble, or to cause others to stumble (Acts 24:16; I Cor. 10:32; I Pet. 1:17).

This has been called *"a negative virtue,"* which is so contrary to the spirit of the world, that it is actually despised by the world.

The spirit of the world is, that man will climb the ladder of success and do so over the destruction of other men who get in his way. The spirit of the world uses up men and then discards them whenever they have nothing else to give. This is the opposite of true Christianity.

The true Child of God, who is *"without offence,"* injures no one; that neither by example, nor opinions, nor conversation, he leads them astray; that he never does injustice to their motives, and never impedes their influence; that he never wounds their feelings, or gives occasion for hard thought; and that he so lives that all may see that his is a blameless life.

As should be obvious, this is the true Christlike spirit.

THE SPIRIT OF THE WORLD IN THE CHURCH

All too often, the spirit of the world which characterizes ungodly ambition, which places self foremost, which will hurt fellow brothers and sisters in the Lord in order to have one's way, is prevalent in the Church. Christians who tear down the character of another, in order to make themselves look better, can only carry out such tactics among those with a similar spirit. Christians far too often ask the Lord to help them with some certain things, and then after prayer immediately begin to attempt to manipulate the situation. What do we mean by that?

Instead of placing our petition before the Lord, and then letting Him carry out the answer in His Own Way, we immediately set about to manipulate circumstances, situations, and people, in order to bring about the answer in our own way, which is actually of the flesh. This is never of God, as should be obvious. It is, as stated, the spirit of the world, which is the very opposite here of that of which Paul speaks.

Regrettably and sadly, in my many years of preaching this Gospel of Jesus Christ, I have found that there are as much politics in the Church, or even more, than in the world. This is a sad commentary! I speak of Preachers manipulating situations in order to gain the favor of other Preachers, or to be elected to a particular religious office, etc. One will look in vain in the Book of Acts for such an attitude and spirit, at least among the Apostles. Actually, such a spirit is portrayed in the attitude of Simon the Sorcerer, when he offered the Apostles money that they would *"give me also this power, that on whomsoever I lay hands, he may receive the Holy Spirit."*

The answer from Peter was quick in coming, *"Thy money perish with thee, because thou hast thought that the Gift of God may be purchased with money."*

He then said, *"Thou hast neither part nor lot in this matter: for thy heart is not right in the Sight of God"* (Acts 8:18-23).

I'm afraid that the spirit of the Church is too often and too much like that of Simon the Sorcerer, instead of that of Simon Peter.

He who would be a prosperous Christian has not only to watch against duplicity in the heart: he must give diligence also to deal wisely with the various outward influences which strike into our lives, which seem often to do so cruelly and unreasonably, and which wear some false guise that we had not foreseen.

Paul knew this in his own case; and, therefore, he *"studied to keep a conscience void of offence."* We may have wisdom enough for our own practice as to do this, for if Paul had to be very careful in this area, certainly we should follow suit.

THE DAY OF CHRIST

The phrase, *"Till the Day of Christ,"* actually refers to the Rapture of the Church.

Even though the Rapture was not going to take place then, even as the Apostle brought out in the 2nd Chapter of II Thessalonians, and because of certain things which then must be done, such as the establishment of the Church; still, the Apostle ever placed this event in the vision of the Saint. In other words, he in effect, or rather the Holy Spirit through him, is telling us to live every minute as if Christ would come the next. However, I might quickly add, that all of these things which Paul enumerated in II Thessalonians Chapter 2 which were then future, and which are already now in fulfillment means that this admonition given by him is even more apropos presently than then. The total idea is this:

When the Believer dies his work is ended; consequently, everything is then waiting for the Trump of God (I Thess. 4:13-18). So, whether we live or die, everything in our very being, all of our actions, even the very thoughts we think, should ever strain toward the coming *"Day of Christ."* That *"Day"* will be when all the tests are graded, when account will be given, in fact, when every Believer will stand at the *"Judgment Seat of Christ."* It really doesn't matter when the Rapture takes place, whether in the next hour or many years from now, the Believer is to always conduct himself as if the *"Day of Christ"* is at hand.

ANSWER TO CHRIST

The entire structure of Paul's statement in glaring detail, tells us that each Believer is one day going to answer personally to Christ. This is the idea behind all of that of which the Apostle addresses himself.

In fact, Jesus illustrated this perfectly in His *"Parable of the Marriage Feast,"* and the *"Parable of the Ten Virgins,"* along with the *"Parable of the Talents"* (Mat. 22:1-14; 25:1-30). (Please see our Commentary on Matthew.)

Unfortunately, the modern Church, at least for the most part, is so taken up with the *"here and now,"* that it pays scant attention to the *"there and then."* In other words, its desires are not heavenly but rather earthly! Such a spirit is terribly destructive to the Church, but which probably characterizes it presently more than ever before in history.

The modern *"Prosperity Gospel,"* has helped to further this, as well as the *"Kingdom Now"* error.

The spirit of this particular error, pretty much conducts itself the very opposite of the Words of the Master, by attempting to lay up treasure here rather than there (Mat. 6:19-21).

One cannot at the same time have the spirit of the world, and be looking forward to the *"Day of Christ."* Either one cancels out the other.

(11) "BEING FILLED WITH THE FRUITS OF RIGHTEOUSNESS, WHICH ARE BY JESUS CHRIST, UNTO THE GLORY AND PRAISE OF GOD."

The conduct that will receive Christ's commendation must be characterized by *"the Fruit of Righteousness."* Transformed lives are the demonstration that God works in Believers. We must never forget that!

Paul desires that when his readers stand before Christ, their lives will have been filled with the right kind of Fruit. He is not talking about mere human uprightness measured by outward conformity to Law. He is rather speaking of the spiritual Fruit which comes from Jesus Christ, produced by the Holy Spirit Who has been sent by Christ (Gal. 5:22). Consequently, all the Glory and Praise belong not to Believers but to God, for He has redeemed us by the work of His Son and has implanted within us His Spirit to produce the Fruit of Righteousness.

The thought is similar to that in Ephesians 1:6, 12, 14, where Paul says that the entire Plan of Redemption should result in Praise of God's Glory (Kent).

FRUITS OF RIGHTEOUSNESS

The phrase, *"Being filled with the Fruits of Righteousness,"* probably should have been translated *"Fruit of Righteousness,"* in that the oldest manuscripts read *"Fruit"* in the singular.

The idea here is, that Righteousness is by Jesus Christ, in contrast to the Righteousness which is by the Law (Phil. 3:9). Without this Righteousness which is in Christ, no Fruit is possible (Jn. 15:4). Verses 9 through 11 tell us what this *"Fruit"* actually is:

1. Verse 9 says that it is a love that is abounding and informed.

2. Verse 10 says it is a capacity for making proper moral distinctions.

3. Verse 11 says it is a motivation which seeks the Glory of God.

THE HOLY SPIRIT

We must remind the Reader, that even though all of this is made possible by what Jesus did at the Cross and the Resurrection, to which we will address ourselves more broadly momentarily, it is the Holy Spirit Who actually carries out this work within our hearts and lives. These are really the *"Fruit of the Spirit"* (Gal. 5:22-23). But yet, for Him to bring about this *"Fruit"* within our lives, He must have our cooperation at all times. In fact, He does nothing arbitrarily, which means without our conscious help, cooperation, and surrender to Him. Even though He is present at all times in the heart of every single Believer, whether the Believer is weak or strong, still, He must have cooperation on our part if He is to do the things which only He can do.

BY JESUS CHRIST

The phrase, *"Which are by Jesus Christ,"* refers to what He did at the Cross and the Resurrection.

Before His satisfying the sin debt by His Death on the Cross, the Holy Spirit could not even come to abide in the hearts and lives of Believers (Jn. 14:17). The blood of bulls and goats, which pertain to the sacrifices of the Old Testament times, could not take away sin, therefore, even though Believers then were just as saved as we are now, which is all brought about by Faith in the Redeemer, still, until the death of Christ on the Cross, the sin debt remained.

To be sure, in those days the Law which was given to Moses by God, definitely contained Righteousness; however, it was a Righteousness which could only be attained by performance on the part of man, which was impossible. In other words, man, even believing man, simply could not perform that which was demanded, and even though it may come as a shock to most, believing man even presently cannot attain to the Righteousness of the Law within himself. In fact, if he attempts to do so, which all of us have at one time or the other, there will be no *"Fruit of Righteousness,"* simply because we frustrate the Grace of God by such efforts, which stops the Work of the Holy Spirit (Gal. 2:21).

What do we mean by all of this?

THE DESIRE FOR THE FRUIT OF RIGHTEOUSNESS

We will take it for granted that all Believers desire this *"Fruit."* If one is truly Born-Again, thereby having a proper relationship with Christ, this desire is ingrained, in effect, automatic. Upon receiving Christ, the Divine nature automatically comes into the Believer, which refers to the tremendous change afforded by Redemption (II Cor. 5:17-19).

Can you the Reader remember when you first came to Christ? There was a hunger and thirst for the Word of God, with you devouring the pages of the Bible. You couldn't get enough of that Book, and neither could you get enough of Church. You looked for Revivals that you could attend. Everything was brand-new, which is characteristic of the Christ-filled life.

And now I should ask the question, *"Do you still have that same diligence, that same hunger and thirst, that same love that pertains to the things of the Lord?"*

With some of you, *"Yes,"* but with most of you, most likely the answer would have to be *"No!"*

Why?

WRONG DIRECTION

Hungering for this *"Fruit of Righteousness,"* many Believers at this time embark upon a course of *"Law."* The Truth is, they don't know this is what they're doing, but most of the time because of what they hear in their Churches, what they see others do, this is the course they take. They don't know that it's Law, but that's actually what it is. In fact, most Christians don't know the Truth concerning this, even after living for the Lord for many, many years. In other words, they're still on a course of *"Law,"* which means that there is very little *"Fruit of Righteousness"* within their hearts and lives.

What do we mean by Law?

Most Christians on reading this, would automatically think of the *"Law of Moses,"* and just as quickly dismiss it, knowing and understanding that this was for Old Testament times, and does not pertain to the present.

That is partially true, but what the Saint oftentimes begins to do, is the same as attempting to keep the Law of Moses, whether they realize it or not. The idea is this:

Somehow in our thinking, we tend to think we can bring about this *"Fruit of Righteousness"* by being *"holy,"* or doing certain things, etc. Almost all the time, the things we attempt to do are proper and right within themselves, but were never meant to make one holy, etc. But yet, that's all that most Christians know, simply because that's what their Church teaches.

In view of this, we tend to think that certain things bring about this *"Fruit,"* such as giving money to the Church, having a prayer life, engaging in soul winning, being faithful to the Church, trying to live a good, upright, moral life, etc. In fact, all of these things are noble, good, and correct within their own way, but will *not*, and I emphasize, will *not* bring about the *"Fruit of Righteousness"* of which Paul speaks here.

The idea is, that the Fruit of Righteousness produce these things instead of us attempting to produce the Fruit of Righteousness by the doing of these things. In other words, we get it backwards.

In effect, we make *"Laws"* out of all of these things, plus many other things I have not named, by which we attempt to attain to Righteousness. As I've said, most Christians do not understand this, in other words, they don't understand that they are reverting to *"Law"*; however, that's exactly what they are doing, which will produce no proper *"Fruit."*

FRUSTRATION

In all of this, the Believer oftentimes becomes frustrated sensing that something is wrong, but not understanding why, for the simple reason that oftentimes they are trying so hard. In fact, despite their efforts, the situation (sin or whatever) not only does not improve, but rather gets worse. In other words, they are at the most running fast on a treadmill, which means they're going nowhere, and at the worst, they give up altogether, which I'm afraid characterizes all too many.

Paul plainly said, *"I do not frustrate the Grace of God: for if Righteousness come by the Law* (come by me attempting to gain such by various laws of my own making), *then Christ is dead in vain* (the Lord didn't have to die on the Cross, if in fact, I could bring about this Righteousness by my own machinations)" (Gal. 2:21).

In view of all of this, Churches are filled with Saints, who have tried and tried hard to bring about this *"Fruit,"* have not succeeded in doing so, and if anything the situation has gone backwards, so in spirit they have just quit. No, they have not quit Church, in fact, continuing to come and profess Christ. But the Truth is, many Christians have little prayer life, do little for the Lord, sort of living in a spiritual limbo or twilight zone.

Of course, only God knows the reason for this as it regards each and all of these individuals, but I am persuaded that for many of them, they are in this state because of taking a wrong direction in the beginning. To be sure, there are a few Saints in each Church (prayerfully), who work tirelessly for the Lord, and are actually the backbone of the Church, and who have a happy, victorious, overcoming Christian life. These are they who function from a position of Righteousness afforded by Christ, and not themselves, understanding their place and position in Christ. But this number, to be sure, is few.

The others, I think for the most part, are spiritually lukewarm because of frustration. They went about the whole thing in the wrong way, with no Fruit forthcoming. They know that Christianity is real, but they simply don't know what else to do because of not having been properly taught, so they've come to the place that they by and large do nothing.

There is another side to this scenario, with some Christians who, in fact, do not give up but even increase their Law-keeping, which leads them deeper and deeper in legalism. These loudly denounce all who do not follow their rules and prescriptions, which they increase more and more, even on a daily basis. It may sound a little humorous, but these individuals are not very pleasant to say the least. They have perfected their brand of holiness, which is all wrapped up in rules, regulations, and laws. Like the Pharisees of old, the more the better. They are the bane of the Church, and are actually very miserable respecting their own existence.

Are they saved?

Yes, they are saved; however, there is no enjoyment in their Salvation, and for the simple reason that they constantly *"labor"* and are *"heavy laden"* (Mat. 11:28-30). Unfortunately, in their attempt to address the situation, they just add more burden and load on that which they already have, insisting that all others carry the same load.

THE WAY OF THE CROSS

If it is to be noted, Paul said, *"Being filled with the Fruits of Righteousness, which are by Jesus Christ."* What did Paul mean by the words, *"By Jesus Christ"*?

To give the answer immediately, Paul was speaking of what Jesus did at the Cross and in the Resurrection. He is speaking of His Finished Work, the Atonement, that which was done in order to redeem mankind, in which we are to totally trust.

The idea is, man could not do it for himself, therefore, Jesus became our Substitute.

Most Christians understand that as it regards sinners. In other words, they know that a sinner cannot save himself, and must depend totally upon Christ. Unfortunately, after coming to Christ, we too often leave the Cross, attempting to bring about this Fruit by our own means, which we have been addressing. That's not the way, as should be obvious.

Man unable to come by Righteousness according to his own machinations, can only have Righteousness as it is freely imputed by Christ, which automatically comes once the believing sinner trusts Christ. The simple Truth is, that this *"Trust"* must continue in the heart and life of the Believer all the rest of his days. The Believer must understand that the effect of the Cross does not pertain merely to his initial Salvation experience, but pertains to his continued living for the Lord, and will do so forever. In other words, the same Faith that the sinner exhibited in what Jesus did for him by dying on the Cross in order that he might be saved, must continue in the same vein in order that the Holy Spirit may develop within us this beautiful *"Fruit of Righteousness."* As the sinner trusts what Christ did on the Cross for Salvation, the Believer is to trust what Christ did on the Cross as it regards our Sanctification. It is identical in both cases.

THIS IS WHAT I MUST UNDERSTAND:

As a sinner I could not attain to any Righteousness on my own, and as a Believer I fall into the same category. It makes no difference that I am Baptized with the Holy Spirit, speak with other Tongues, even have Gifts of the Spirit, even evidencing great Faith, I still cannot bring about any Righteousness, or *"Fruit"* on my own. I must understand, that Jesus did all of this at the Cross, and all I must do, and in fact, all I can do, is to trust what He has already done, and rest in that (Mat. 11:28-30), which will allow the Holy Spirit to then develop *"Fruit."* It is all in the Cross and the Resurrection. He did it all there, and I rest in that, and in my resting in that, which means I have Faith in what He did, and continue to have Faith in what He did, then the Holy Spirit can develop this Fruit within my life.

Satan will do everything within his power to push the Church, even the individual Believer, away from the Cross. Sadly, he has succeeded to a great extent in these last several decades. In fact, the modern Church has heard so little Preaching and Teaching as it regards the Cross in the last few years, that it actually has little understanding as to the very foundation of the Faith. So, it resorts to Psychology, to the latest fad, to works and laws of its own making, to its own machinations, to its own efforts, which gain no positive results, and in fact, have the very opposite effect. So, we have a Church running all over the world, looking for some Preacher to lay hands on them, so they can get the *"Blessing,"* which may be perfectly legitimate and helpful in its own way, but will not bring about this of which we speak — Fruit of Righteousness. As someone has well said, *"The Church does not need a touch nearly as much as it needs the Truth."*

I don't have this *"Fruit of Righteousness"* merely because of Who Jesus is, or even where He is, but rather because of what He has done.

THE WORLD AND THE CHURCH

The world will accept Jesus as a great Teacher, as a great Preacher, even as a great Prophet. They will accept Him as well as a Miracle-Worker, a Healer, etc.; however, *"Jesus Christ and Him Crucified"* (I Cor. 2:2), is anathema to them. Unfortunately, most of the Church falls into the same category.

The Cross of Christ tells us how bad that man actually is, unable to save himself, unable to afford his own Redemption, irrespective of what he may do. That grates against man. He keeps wanting to think he can effect his own Salvation, which began almost immediately after the Fall, with Cain offering to the Lord the *"fruit of the ground,"* instead of that demanded by God, *"the firstlings of his flock,"* i.e., *"the Fruit of Righteousness"* (Gen. 4:3-5). The problem is, the Church too often attempts to continue in the same capacity — *"fruit of the ground,"* i.e., *"fruit of our own efforts."*

Why is it hard for the Christian to simply trust Christ?

First of all, this built-in problem of self-sufficiency doesn't entirely leave us when we come to Christ. In fact, it remains with us, which Paul referred to over and over again as *"the flesh"* (Rom. 8:1). So, this tends to be a constant struggle with the Child of God. Somehow, we want to earn our way, make our own way, bring about our own Righteousness and Holiness. Inasmuch as we cover these *"good works"* with Scriptures, we fool ourselves into thinking that we are trusting Christ, when all along, we are really trusting *"self."* That road, which most Christians travel, cannot help but lead to failure. There has never been a winner on that road, and there never will be.

But again, I personally think this spirit of self-sufficiency, has fertile ground in which to germinate, simply because most Christians do not know or understand the proper way which is *"by Jesus Christ."* It is not taught behind most pulpits, actually denigrated behind thousands of Charismatic pulpits. This means that the Cross plays little or no part at all in their Christian experience; consequently, they are doomed to failure just as sure as their name is what it is.

Even with the proper teaching on the Cross, and the Saint of God attempting to exhibit Faith in that Finished Work at all times, the struggle with the flesh is unending. That's why Paul dealt with this subject to such an extent (Rom. Chpt. 8).

THE HOLY SPIRIT

As we've already stated, it is the Holy Spirit Who brings about all of these things within our hearts and lives (Rom. Chpt. 8). But the question is, how does the Holy Spirit do such?

Upon reading this question, most Christians would not really have an answer. It would probably be, *"He just does it!"*

If that in fact is the case, why don't we more often see the results of what He does?

The Truth is, most Christians do not know how the Holy Spirit works, why He works, when He works, and on what ground He works. Not knowing this, they provide very little cooperation with Him, in fact, doing the very thing most of the time which frustrates the Grace of God (Gal. 2:21), which frustrates the Holy Spirit as well.

The Believer must have his Faith anchored squarely in the Cross and the Resurrection, or else the Holy Spirit simply will not work. He works totally and completely within the parameters of the Finished Work of Christ. In other words, the things which Jesus did at the Cross and the Resurrection, provide the parameters from which the Holy Spirit works.

What did Jesus do there?

He satisfied the sin debt which was owed to God, a debt in fact, which man could not pay. He as well, suffered the curse of the broken Law, of which all men were guilty, and did so by paying its penalty by dying (Rom. 6:23).

Satan's hold upon humanity is through sin and transgression. This gives him a legal right to do the things he does, which is to hold mankind in captivity, knowing that if they remain in this capacity, they will ultimately be put in Hell forever. He hates man because man is made in the Image of God.

Whenever Jesus satisfied this debt and paid its penalty, Satan then lost his hold and claim on humanity. Unfortunately, most sinners do not know this, and in their deception continue on as servants of Satan which leads to death. More tragic yet, most Christians do not properly understand this as well!

As a Believer, I am victorious not because I do or don't do certain things, but simply because of what Jesus did at the Cross and the Resurrection. I simply have to have Faith in that, and always remember that my Faith must remain in that Finished Work. Faith in the Finished Work means I am having Faith not at all in myself, but totally in what Christ did, which causes Satan to lose all his grip. In this posture, sin will not have dominion over me (Rom. 6:14).

This is the type of Faith, that which is anchored in the Cross and the Resurrection, which gives the Holy Spirit the latitude to do whatever is needed to guarantee us this Victory, etc. That is the way the Holy Spirit works and the means by which He works.

He does not work on our behalf on the mere fact that Jesus is the Son of God, that He was born of the Virgin Mary, that He performed Miracles and cast out Devils, etc. All of that is viable, necessary, and right. But that alone, gives the Holy Spirit no latitude.

What Jesus did at the Cross and the Resurrection, is that which opened up everything. It is that alone on which the Holy Spirit works (Rom. 8:2), and only that on which He works. So what do we mean by that?

DOMINATION BY SIN

Every Christian faces difficulties, in which Satan attempts to bring us back to the place to where we are dominated by sin of some capacity. The Truth is, there are far more Christians being dominated by sin, than those who aren't. In fact, the number of the latter is very small.

Now that's a travesty of the greatest proportions. A Christian who is dominated by sin. And yet, that's where most Christians find themselves.

They don't want to be dominated by sin, in fact, making great efforts to not be dominated by sin, but the fact is, they are dominated by such, or Paul would not have referred to this subject as he did. He said, *"For sin shall not have dominion over you: for you are not under the Law, but under Grace"* (Rom. 6:14). He said it in this way, because sin definitely can dominate the Christian. In fact, if the Christian does not understand the Cross and the Resurrection as it refers to his everyday victorious life, he will find himself definitely being dominated by sin.

This happens because the Believer is attempting to oppose this effort by Satan in all the wrong ways. The harder he tries, even to which we have already alluded, the worse the situation becomes, which greatly frustrates the Christian. Considering that he's trying so hard, he does not understand his predicament.

As we've already stated several times, he is in this predicament because he is reverting to Law, which means his own self-efforts. He may think he is trusting in Christ, but he really isn't. The answer is very simple. If he is truly trusting in Christ, sin will not have dominion over him. If he is not, and despite all the religious works, and good works he may attempt, domination by sin will be the result.

The Holy Spirit will not help us in our self-efforts in this capacity, even though He remains in our hearts and lives. He will only help us, work with us, guarantee this Victory, as we place our Faith in what Christ did at the Cross and the Resurrection, and leave our Faith there. The Christian is to never get the idea that he outgrows the Cross. Such thinking is not only foolish, but catastrophic! The Finished Work of Christ, which is the Cross and the Resurrection, is not possible of exhaustion. In fact, a trillion years from today in the portals of Glory, the benefits of the Cross and the Resurrection will continue to expand within our hearts and lives.

So, when Paul said *"By Jesus Christ,"* that's exactly what he meant.

THE GLORY AND PRAISE OF GOD

The phrase, *"Unto the Glory and Praise of God,"* means simply that when we place our trust in what Christ has done for us at the Cross and the Resurrection, it brings *"Glory and Praise to God."* When we try to bring about this thing in our own efforts, the Praise and Glory goes to self and not to God, as should be obvious.

Before the Reader continues, think about that for just a moment.

When the Church fills itself with rules and regulations, thinking somehow that all of these things will bring about Holiness, the Glory and Praise does not go to God, but always to man. We may not think of it in that capacity, but that's the only place it can go. God will not accept any Glory and Praise as it regards our own pitiful efforts, as ought to be obvious. The Holy Spirit through Paul plainly said, *"So then they that are in the flesh cannot please God"* (Rom. 8:8). And to be sure, all rules and regulations made up by men in order to bring about Holiness, are definitely works of the flesh, whether we realize it or not. And yet too many Churches are filled with such.

EXAMPLES

Let me give an example of that of which I speak. In fact, there are many examples, but we'll deal with that which the carnal mind thinks is very right, but in fact, is very wrong.

In the Constitution and Bylaws of the Assemblies of God and Church of God, the two largest Pentecostal Denominations in the world, they have rulings in some capacity which states, that if any of their Preachers have a sin problem of any nature, they cannot preach for two years. They also have several more rulings added to that.

Now to the world that sounds very right, and in fact, to carnal minds in the Church it sounds right as well. If a person does something wrong, they should pay for that wrong, which is the thinking of most Christians.

I wonder if they have ever stopped to realize, that first of all there is nothing man can do to pay for any wrongdoing he has committed, irrespective as to what he might do. So the very idea of such is an insult to what Christ did at the Cross.

Also, Jesus has already paid it all at the Cross, and for anyone, even a major Denomination, and especially a major Denomination which ought to know better, which seeks to add to what He has already done, in effect, says that He did not pay it all, and other punishment must be added.

Whether we realize it or not, all of this is an insult to Christ of the highest proportions. We may think that it presents a front as to how hard we are on sin, but in fact, it does the very opposite. It makes a mockery out of that which Christ has already done, in effect, saying that His Sacrifice was not enough, and we need to offer up another. How ludicrous can we be! But yet, that's the position of most Religious Denominations!

WHAT HAPPENS TO THESE PREACHERS?

Preachers who have a sin problem of some kind, and that needs to be addressed a little further, if they submit themselves to such an unscriptural direction, it will not have the effect of Redemption, but rather the very opposite. In other words, it will destroy them. The reasons are simple.

First of all, what we have here are sinful men attempting to punish sinful men, and that within itself, is a gross travesty. Does the Reader understand what I'm trying to say?

Much of the time, in fact, if not all the time, the religious officials in these Denominations who are carrying out punishment on fellow Preachers, who have experienced some type of failure, are in worse spiritual condition than the one they are punishing.

How can I say that?

I can say it simply because, they wouldn't be doing such a thing, if they were truly following the Lord themselves. They would first of all realize how unworthy they are to punish anyone else. The Holy Spirit through James dealt with this very succinctly when he said, *"There is One Lawgiver* (the Lord) *Who is able to save and to destroy: who art thou that judgest another?"* (James 4:12).

In plain English he is saying, *"Who do you think you are, thinking you are morally qualified to pass judgment on someone else?"* The Truth is, and as should be overly obvious, no human being is morally qualified to do such a thing. Only God can do such, and for us to attempt such an unscriptural act, only portrays our ignorance of the Word of God, and really as to who and what we are as well.

So, sinful men attempting to punish sinful men, is a travesty indeed!

As well, the Scriptural Way for these things to be addressed is, *"Brethren, if a man be overtaken in a fault, ye which are spiritual, restore such an one in the spirit of meekness; considering thyself, lest thou also be tempted"* (Gal. 6:1).

The word *"spiritual"* refers to those who properly understand their place and position in Christ. They had to learn themselves the Way of the Cross, even as Paul had to learn it, and are now equipped to help others.

The idea is, that the one who is spiritual, should relate to the individual who has failed the reason why he has failed, which almost certainly is because he has tried to bring about Victory within his own strength, instead of trusting in Christ. In other words, whether he realized it or not, he was reverting to Law instead of the Finished Work of Christ.

The one who is spiritual is to patiently and kindly explain this to the one who has failed, showing him why he failed, and how he can stop the failure.

He is to do this in the *"spirit of meekness,"* understanding that he has been in the same place and position, which means that he has failed the Lord previously, just as all Christians have, and had to learn the Way of Victory, as stated, even as Paul had to learn this Way (Rom. Chpt. 7). What I'm trying to say is this:

Every single Christian in the world has failed the Lord at one time or the other, and in fact, many times. We don't like to say that, or even think that. But our denying such does not change the facts. There are no exceptions to this fact.

To those of us who have Victory, we know and understand that it is because of what Jesus did, and our coming to learn and understand that. Before we understood it, we failed as well, which means we don't have any right to judge anyone else. That's what I mean by the statement, *"Sinful men judging sinful men."*

MY OWN PERSONAL EXPERIENCE

As I dictate these words, I can honestly say before the Lord, that sin does not have dominion over me. I say that not with any joy reflected toward myself, but all toward Christ, and more particularly what He did for me at the Cross and the Resurrection. I had to learn this the hard way, even as many have to learn it the hard way. Consequently, I am giving you the great Truths that the Lord has given to me, so that you will not have to suffer as I suffered, and even as Paul suffered (Rom. Chpt. 7).

In all of this, when I meet one who has failed, I do not look at that person as beneath me. I do not think of them as beneath me. Such a thing never crosses my mind. I know that this man or woman who loves the Lord but yet has failed, has more than likely done so simply because they have not known the Way of Victory. They have attempted to bring about an overcoming life within their own self-efforts, which are doomed to failure. I know that, because I've been there myself.

So, when I deal with them, it is never from a place of superiority, but always from the position of having walked where they walked, but yet understanding now what Christ has done for me, and eagerly desiring to show them this glorious way, this Way of the Cross, that they may overcome this failure, and sin shall no longer dominate them as well. That is the Bible Way, not some foolishness devised by men, calling ourselves punishing somebody else, of which we ought to be grossly ashamed.

Again, I wish to emphasize, that there is no Christian who has ever lived who has not failed at one time or the other. To deny such is to deny reality. Understanding that, that gives us no room to judge anyone else. So why do these religious officials think they have the right to punish others?

I do not know what is in their hearts, so I do not judge them. More than likely, it is because they do not know the right way of Christ, or else, they simply no longer have any Faith in God's Way, thus devising their own.

If, in fact, that is the case, and I speak of unbelief, then we have a serious situation indeed!

God's Way is the only Way, and if we veer from that Way, we bring to ourselves untold troubles and difficulties. If we adhere to that Way, that Glorious Way of the Cross, we reap the benefits of all that Jesus has done, which are glorious indeed, and which bring *"Glory and Praise to God."*

(12) "BUT I WOULD YE SHOULD UNDERSTAND, BRETHREN, THAT THE THINGS WHICH HAPPENED UNTO ME HAVE FALLEN OUT RATHER UNTO THE FURTHERANCE OF THE GOSPEL;"

"I want you to know" is a variation of a common statement in Paul's Letters. It invariably introduces an important assertion and may imply that misunderstanding has arisen over the matter, or that inquiry has been made regarding it. In this instance, the significance of Paul's immediate circumstances was the important matter.

On the assumption that the Epistle was written from a Roman imprisonment, Paul is saying that his recent circumstances had not been detrimental but advantageous to the Gospel.

Paul does not imply that his case has been settled, nor that any official action favoring Christianity had been taken. Nevertheless, his immediate circumstances were to be viewed as a plus for the Gospel, not a disaster, as some were probably proclaiming.

THE HOLY SPIRIT WOULD HAVE US UNDERSTAND

The phrase, *"But I would ye should understand, Brethren,"* tells us several things:

NOTES

1. First of all, Paul, as is obvious here by using the word *"Brethren,"* is speaking to Believers. Consequently, the information given can only be understood by Believers. As well, it was a Message not only for the Believers of Paul's time, but also for all Believers for all time, inasmuch as we may learn from this experience.

2. There was a twofold situation here. Those who loved Paul were very much concerned that this situation would hurt the spread of the Gospel, while his detractors, of which there seemed to be many, were no doubt, claiming many things about this situation.

First of all, they could very well have been claiming that were Paul a true Apostle as he claimed, the Lord would not have allowed this to happen to him. Or possibly others may have been saying that Paul was in prison because of a lack of Faith, or perhaps hidden sin in his life; therefore, God had removed him from the scene of action. Others were probably claiming that he was preaching a false message as it regarded Grace, and others were saying, no doubt, that his imprisonment was because of his opposition to the continuance of the Law of Moses.

The word *"would"* as Paul uses it, lends credence to all of these thoughts, and speaks of a desire that has purpose and intention back of it. It is *"will"* with determination. The desire came after mature consideration. The Apostle will quell the fears of those who loved him, and answer the charges of his detractors at the same time.

3. The word *"understand"* is from the Greek word meaning *"to acquire knowledge by experience."* The Philippian Saints, as well as all others and for all time, he desired, should learn something from his experience.

4. If the Saint is in the Will of God, as Paul certainly was, then *"all things* (must) *work together for good to them who love God, to them who are the called according to His Purpose"* (Rom. 8:28).

I'm sure that Paul would have rather been out preaching the Gospel and founding Churches; however, he knew that the Lord wanted him here, but for what purpose he is not exactly certain, although he does have some idea.

We are to live close enough to the Lord, that irrespective as to what happens, we trust

Him, knowing that He has our good at heart at all times, and will do nothing negative to us, or allow anything to happen to us, but that it will ultimately fall out to our good, even though at the outset it may seem to be somewhat grievous.

Everything which happens to the Saint, and of course I speak of those in the Will of God, is either caused by God or allowed by God, for the furtherance of His Work, and the betterment of the Saint, even though at the outset, all of these positive things may not be obvious. As Paul, however, the Saint is to trust God and not allow a question to hinder their spiritual progress.

THINGS WHICH HAPPEN TO US

The phrase, *"That the things which happened unto me,"* pertains as is obvious, to his imprisonment, which had now gone on for several years. The Apostle spent a little above two years imprisoned at Caesarea, and then was transferred to Rome where he also spent about two years imprisoned before being released (Acts 24:17; 28:30). During this time, Paul never speaks of himself as being a prisoner of Nero, or any other potentate, but always as a *"prisoner of Christ Jesus"* (Phile. 1:9; Eph. 3:1; 4:1; II Tim. 1:8). This means two things:

1. He suffered imprisonment for the sake of Christ.

2. He suffered imprisonment because Christ desired that he do so, with reasons known only to the Lord.

Such an attitude that Paul possessed, spoke of submission and obedience to Christ in all things, which should be an example to all Believers.

The phrase, *"The things which happened unto me,"* are literally, *"The things dominating me."* The idea is, that *"nothing ever just happens to the Saint."* Things either come directly from God or they reach us from another source by His permissive Will.

To be sure, Paul was not in prison because he had broken any law, or done anything wrong for that matter. While there definitely were civil leaders who played a part in all of this, still, the Lord could easily have changed the situation at any time He so desired. He allowed this regarding Paul for specific reasons — reasons which He never did fully explain to the Apostle, or else if He did, it is not recorded.

PAUL THE MAN

In view of the great significance of this entire setting, perhaps it would help us to look at this situation a little more closely.

The Apostle's affairs had seemed to be full of trial to himself, all the more that they bore so discouraging an aspect towards the cause to which he was devoted. He had been for years a prisoner.

The work of preaching to the Gentiles the unsearchable riches of Christ had been stopped, except as the narrow opportunities of a prisoner's life offered scant outlets for it. He had, no doubt, his own share of experiences tending to depress and embitter: for in his day prisons were notoriously bad.

Still more depressing to an eager soul was the discipline of delay: the slow, monotonous months passing on, consuming the remainder of his life, while the great harvest he longed to reap lay outside, uncared for, with few to bring it in.

Meanwhile even the work done in Christ's Name was largely taking a wrong direction: many of those under the Christian Name preached another gospel, and perverted the Gospel of Christ, and worse yet even had a freer hand to do their malicious work. Paul, at least in the last several years, had no longer the power to cross their path. Ground on which he might have worked, minds which he might have approached, seemed to be falling under their perverting influence.

All this seemed adverse — adverse to Paul, and adverse to the cause for which he lived — fitted, therefore, to awaken legitimate concern: fitted to raise the question why God's Providence should thus depress the heart and waste the life of an agent so carefully prepared and so incomparably efficient?

A TESTING OF FAITH

Most likely these things had tried the Faith of Paul himself, and they might distress and perplex his friends at Philippi and elsewhere as well. Consequently, it was very difficult to see the positive in all of this which was so negative. But yet, Faith did see that positive, did trust God, did put all of this in His Hands, believing that it would all fall out to the good, which it did.

If the Saint desires to ask questions, then questions abound, for the simple reason that the ground is always fertile for such rumination. However, such questions generally only gender strife (II Tim. 2:23).

CLOSE TO HOME

The words I have just written concerning the great Apostle strike so close to home. How so much it has hurt these last few years to see our efforts curtained to such an extent, when the burden burns as bright as ever as it regards World Evangelism. No, lest the Reader misunderstand, I in no way place myself even in the shadow of the great Apostle. But yet, God Who called him also called me. The Holy Spirit Who led him, also leads me.

Correspondingly, if in these last few years I had allowed the questions to grow, even that which is so similar to Paul, there is no way I could have survived; however, irrespective as to what others may think, I know my heart, at least as far as a poor human being can know such. As Paul, I have had to commit the situation to the Lord, trust explicitly in Him, knowing that He does all things well. The frustrations have been many, even to the point of exasperation. Also, the questions have loomed large; however, if one allows questions to grow as one is prone to do, such can only gender strife (II Tim. 2:23).

Of course, the Church world is quick to retort, *"Well it's your fault!"* My answer is, *"That is correct!"* But at the same time, it is not nearly as simple as it seems. Trying so hard but not succeeding, I did not understand at all, until the Lord showed me the meaning of Romans Chapter 7, which illustrates Paul's personal experience. He also showed me the meaning of Romans Chapters 6 and 8, which proclaim the path of Victory as given by the Lord to Paul, which I previously did not know.

This tells us that Faith in the Cross is the only answer as it regards Salvation for the sinner, and Victory for the Christian. After seeking the Lord for some five years, the Lord gave me this revelation, which has completely revolutionized my thinking and my life, for which I will ever be eternally grateful.

To be sure, I bring up this very distasteful subject, only with the desire to help other Believers, which I know the Lord would have me do.

But at the same time, irrespective of what happens to an individual, irrespective as to how much culpability is on his part, that does not excuse wrongdoing on the part of others toward him. Unfortunately, many Christians think, even as they did with Paul, that if one has done something wrong, or else they think he has done something wrong (Paul had done nothing wrong), this gives them the license to do any negative thing to that person they so desire. This is cruelty at its worst. But yet, many Christians, sadly, fall into this category.

As I've often said, *"When one is down and can do nothing to defend himself, and anyone can do any negative thing to him they so desire, and not be reprimanded at all but rather applauded, then one finds out how many true Christians there actually are."*

There aren't many! Nevertheless, thank the Lord for the few who do exemplify Christ.

THE FURTHERANCE OF THE GOSPEL

The phrase, *"Have fallen out rather unto the furtherance of the Gospel,"* proclaims that which actually happened, and was sanctioned by the Holy Spirit.

The word *"furtherance"* is from a Greek word which is thought to have been used in the First Century to refer to a company of woodcutters preceding the progress of an army, cutting a road through the forest so that it might advance.

Paul says that his circumstances are Divine woodcutters, cutting away through the opposition so that the Gospel might be advanced. What were these circumstances?

His liberty was gone. He was chained to a Roman soldier, possibly both night and day. God had literally built a fence around the Apostle. He had put limitations about him. He had placed handicaps upon him. But Paul says that they are God's woodcutters making a road for the advancement of the Gospel

SO, WHAT WAS ACTUALLY HAPPENING HERE?

The Gospel was now being proclaimed from the pulpit of the Roman Empire. The

Praetorian Guard of 10,000 picked Roman soldiers was hearing it from the soldiers chained to Paul. The jealous Brethren in Rome were announcing Christ more energetically, out of envy of course, but yet announcing Christ. The friendly Brethren out of love for Paul were more zealous in their preaching.

And so it is in every Christian's life. The things that hedge us in, the things that handicap us, the tests that we go through and the temptations that assail us, are all Divinely-appointed woodcutters used by God to hew out a path for our proclamation of the Gospel. It may be that our fondest hopes are not realized. We are in difficult circumstances. Illness may be our lot.

Yet if we are in the center of God's Will, all these are contributing to the progress of the Gospel. They draw us closer to the Lord so that the testimony of our lives will count more for God, and thus we become more efficient in proclaiming the Gospel. So, in effect, Paul was thanking God for the handicaps and the testings. They are blessings in disguise.

When we have limitations imposed upon us we do our best work for the Lord, for then we are most dependent upon Him. Paul consequently said, *"Most gladly therefore will I rather glory in my infirmities, that the Power of Christ may rest upon me"* (II Cor. 12:9). Paul had come to this knowledge the hard way, for to be sure, he had plenty of *"infirmities"* (Wuest).

THE RAPID SPREAD OF THE GOSPEL

Adolph M. Harnack, in his day, it is said, was one of the keenest students of the early Church. He listed several reasons for the rapid spread of the Gospel in the first three centuries. They are as follows:

1. The Christian's hope of life after death, which answered questions that pagan philosophy could not even begin to approach. In fact, that which was given to the Apostle Paul by the Holy Spirit as recorded in I Corinthians Chapter 15, is so wide-sweeping, so conclusive, as to leave little to the imagination. As stated, it was so far ahead of pagan philosophy, which of course was filled with vapid superstition, that there was no contest.

2. Christian love and benevolence put an entirely different complexion on man's dealings with his fellowman, which again was so different from the pagan way.

3. The righteous living of Christians so stood out above the pagans and their ways, that it could not help but leave a marked testimony.

4. Still another was the progress of the Gospel among the soldiers. Large numbers of the members of the Roman Legion, upon coming in contact with the Gospel during their travels, were converted and would carry the Good News with them, both to other troops and to relatives back home.

It is not certain whether the Praetorian Guard refers to a place or to persons. According to Lightfoot, the term referred primarily not to a place but to the soldiers guarding the Emperor.

The Praetorian Guard numbered 10,000, to which we have already alluded, all of Italian birth. Under Tiberius they were assembled at Rome in a fortified camp. They were given double pay and special privileges, their term of service being 12 to 16 years.

They had the same rank as Centurions in the regular legions. Later they became a powerful political body until disbanded by Severus, and then permanently suppressed by Constantine.

At any rate, it was probably members of the Praetorian Guard who guarded Paul, with no doubt a number of these men coming to Christ.

THE ASSURANCE OF THE APOSTLE

Paul assures the Philippian Saints that his circumstances have not only failed to curtail his Missionary work, but they have advanced it, and not only that, they have brought about a pioneer advance in regions where otherwise it could not have gone. It is so in our lives as well.

Our God-ordained or God-permitted circumstances are used of God to provide for a pioneer advance of the Gospel in our Christian Service. We may not be able to see it immediately, but to be sure, it will fall out ultimately to this conclusion. It takes Faith to understand this, and patience.

(13) "SO THAT MY BONDS IN CHRIST ARE MANIFEST IN ALL THE PALACE, AND IN ALL OTHER PLACES;"

There were at least two ways in which the Gospel had been advanced through Paul's circumstances. The first was that it had been made clear throughout the whole Palace Guard that Paul's imprisonment was *"for Christ."* As the Guards were assigned in succession to Paul, it soon became clear to them that he was no ordinary captive. The words *"for Christ"* are connected with *"clear"* in the Greek Text. Thus, Paul was not merely describing his imprisonment as being in the Service of Christ (*"my chains for Christ"*), but was claiming that his relationship to Christ had been made clear to his Guards.

The idea is, instead of falling into self-pity, he took every opportunity to make the Gospel known.

BONDS

The phrase, *"So that my bonds in Christ,"* actually has a double meaning:

1. The *"bonds"* referred to Paul being a prisoner of the Roman Empire, at least as looked at by the world.

2. He was a prisoner because of his relationship to Christ.

The next question would be, *"Who is Christ?"* and the Gospel story would be told. It became known and understood that Paul was in prison because he preached the Gospel of Christ.

Satan's efforts to hinder the Gospel often further it. Not only the members of the Praetorian Guard who had custody of Paul, but the whole Praetorium itself, with all its judges and officials and courtiers, are to be understood as included in this Verse.

MANIFEST

The phrase, *"Are manifest in all the Palace, and in all other places,"* refers to an immense affair, i.e., *"a conglomerate of buildings."*

First of all, Rome was a military system, with much of the business of the Empire being conducted at this place. Consequently, soldiers and officers of the Guard formed an important part of the household. That household, however, as stated, was an immense affair, including hundreds or even thousands of persons — mostly freedmen or slaves, along with the Praetorian Guard as well as Judges and officials, etc., performing all sorts of functions.

Paul, then, coming in contact with individuals belonging to the various reliefs which successively had him in custody, was spoken of as one reserved to the judgment of the Emperor himself. Consequently, he became known throughout the quarters of the Guard, and to persons of the household of every rank and class. In point of fact we know and can prove from evidence external to the Bible that a few years later than this, there were members of the household who were Christians.

Before the end of the century, which would have been 35 or 36 years after this particular time of Paul, a branch of the Imperial Family which then occupied the Imperial Throne seems to have become Christians, perhaps through the influence it is believed, of a Christian nurse, who is commemorated in an inscription still preserved.

THE BONDS AND CHRIST

But how did His bonds *"become manifest in Christ"*?

The words, no doubt, mean that Paul became known extensively as a man whose bonds, whose imprisonment, was for his adherence to the Name and Doctrine of Jesus Christ. Let us consider how this would come about.

There might, at first, be universal indifference with reference to the cause of this prisoner's confinement. When his character and statements led to some curiosity about him, men might find it difficult to understand what the real nature of this mysterious case could be. For while the charge, whatever form it took, was not yet a common one, we may be very sure that the man struck people as profoundly different from ordinary prisoners.

For ordinary prisoners the one thing desirable was release; and they employed every effort, and exhausted every form of influence and intrigue, and were prepared to sacrifice every scruple, if only they could get free.

Here was a man instead, who pleaded for Truth; his own freedom seemed to be quite secondary and subordinate. So at last men came to an understanding, more or less, of the real cause of his bonds. They were bonds for Christ, i.e., *"for Paul's relationship to Christ."* They were the result of his adherence to the Faith of Christ's Crucifixion and Resurrection, and to the truths which that great event sealed. They were connected with a testifying for Christ which had brought him into collision with the authorities of his own nation, which had set on Jews *"everywhere"* to *"speak against him"* (Acts 28:22).

And in his imprisonment he did not lay down his testimony, but preached with all his heart to every man who would hear him. This state of things dawned upon men's minds, so far as they thought about him at all; it became here; it was *"manifest in the Praetorium, and to all the others."*

INFLUENTIAL JEWS

One influence was at work which would at least direct attention to the case. There were certain Jews in the household of the Imperial Palace; there were also Jews in Rome who made it their business, for their worldly interests, to establish connections in the household of the Emperor; and about this time Jewish influence rose to the person nearest to Nero himself, his mistress, Poppaea Sabina. According to Tacitus, she was as ambitious as she was unprincipled, and endowed with every gift of nature except an *"honorable mind."*

Poppaea was favorable to Judaism and had certainly enough influence over Nero, to give Jews an advantage. Actually, she was regarded by them as a proselyte to Judaism. Considering that these particular Jews were so opposed to Paul, with actually their element being responsible for his imprisonment, it is most likely that the influence of Jewish religious authorities would be exerted to produce an unfavorable opinion of the Apostle. It would be felt desirable that the Jews of the household should think of Paul as no loyal Jew, as a seditious person, and of his opinions as not legitimately pertaining to Jewish religion — actually as a belief and practice which Judaism repudiated and denounced.

Thus, while Paul's case might begin to influence the Guard, because members of it were personally in contact with him, in the rest of the household there was a class of persons who would feel an interest in discussing his case, although in a negative way. One way or another, some impression as to the peculiar character of it was acquired.

ABOUT CHRIST

Now think how much was done when some view of the real nature of Paul's bonds had been lodged in the minds of these men. Think what an event it was in the mental history of some of these heathens of the old world. Paul was, in the first place, a man very unlike the ordinary type of movers of sedition.

It seemed that his offence stood only in spiritual opinions or persuasions; and that itself, precisely in Nero's day, was somewhat thin as the ground of political imprisonment. He was persecuted and endangered for his Faith, and he neither denied nor disguised that Faith, but spent all possible pains in proclaiming it. This was new.

He had a Faith, resting professedly on recent facts, which he proclaimed as indispensably necessary to be received by all men. This was new. He seriously told men, any man and every man, that their welfare must be attained through their being individually transformed to a type of character of the unworldliest type; he stressed the fact that this could only be done in Christ Who died on the Cross in order for men to be saved and then rose from the dead on the third day. He could press that alike on sordid Jews and young officers. This was new.

He was a man who in place of the ordinary anxieties and importunities of a prisoner, was ever ready to speak and plead on behalf of Christ, this particular Jew Who had died about 30 years before, but Whom Paul affirmed to be alive. And in all this, however it might strike one as foolish or odd, there were tokens of an honesty, a sanity, and a purity that could not be explained away.

All this struck men who stood near the center of a world falling many ways into moral ruin, as something strange and new. Paul's own explanation of it was in the one word *"Christ."* So his bonds were manifest in Christ.

PAUL AND HIS TESTIMONY

A few of these soldiers and officials might have heard previously of Christianity as a new and a malignant superstition. But another conception of it reached them through the bonds of Paul.

This imprisoned man was a fact to be accounted for, and a problem to be solved. In him was an influence not wholly to be escaped, an instance that needed a new interpretation. Many of them did not obey the truth, some did; but at least something had become manifest that could not easily be gotten rid of again — the beginning, in their case, of that manifestation which was eventually to revolutionize the thinking and feeling of the world.

Remember also that most of these were men to whom Paul at liberty, speaking in Synagogues and the like, would have found no access, nor would he have come near the circles to which their influence extended. But now, being imprisoned, his bonds became manifest in Christ.

Thus, does it often come to pass that what seems adverse proves to be the opposite. Fruit is not always borne most freely when the visible opportunities of laboring are most plentiful.

Rather the question is, how the opportunities given are employed, and how far the life of the laborer bears witness of the Presence and Power of Christ (Rainy).

(14) "AND MANY OF THE BRETHREN IN THE LORD, WAXING CONFIDENT BY MY BONDS, ARE MUCH MORE BOLD TO SPEAK THE WORD WITHOUT FEAR."

The second way the Gospel had been advanced was that Paul's circumstances had emboldened other Christians in Rome. One might suppose that his imprisonment would have dampened any evangelizing efforts and have caused the Believers in Rome to *"go underground,"* but exactly the opposite was true.

They drew courage from Paul's example and laid their fears aside.

The literal rendering of the phrase in the latter part of Verse 14 is *"to a much greater degree they are daring to speak the Word of God without fear."* That it was *"daring"* indicates no lessening of the danger but a new infusion of courage.

The present tense shows it was no momentary enthusiasm that quickly passed but that it was still the situation as Paul wrote his Letter. The Apostle's own attitude to his chains must have been largely responsible for these results.

If he had become depressed by developments, the effect on others would have been far different. It was Paul's use of the change in his circumstances as a fresh opportunity to spread the Word of God that encouraged the Christians in Rome to do likewise (Kent).

BRETHREN

The phrase, *"And many of the Brethren in the Lord,"* refers to an increase of Preaching in the city of Rome itself.

The word *"many"* is literally, *"the most."* Most of the Christian Brethren were preaching now, the implication being that a few still held back.

Besides the direct impression on those who were of Caesar's household, Paul's imprisonment, became the means of stimulating and reinforcing the labors of other Christians. It is not hard to see how this might be.

From Paul's bonds, and from the manner and spirit in which they were borne, these Brethren received a new impression as to what should be done and what should be borne in the Service of Christ.

In other words, they were infected with the contagion of Paul's heroism. The sources of Paul's consecration and of his comfort became more real to them; and no discouragement arising from pain or danger could hold its ground against these forces. So they waxed confident.

CONFIDENT

The phrase, *"Waxing confident by my bonds,"* comes from a word which means *"to persuade."* These Christians had been persuaded by the brave and fearless example of Paul in prison, and had come to a state of settled confidence in the Lord.

While dangers that threaten Christians are still only impending, are still only looming out of the unknown future, men are apt to tremble at them, to look with a shrinking eye, to approach with a reluctant step.

Now here in the midst of those Roman Christians was Paul, in whom were embodied the trouble accepted and the danger defied. At once Christian hearts became inspired with a greater confidence.

BOLDNESS

The phrase, *"Are much more bold to speak the Word without fear,"* refers to the tendency toward silence as being actually overcome.

It is not that they had not been speaking at all about the Lord, but that they are now given new and greater boldness to declare God's Word without fear. Their conquest of fear is not based on the probability of Paul's release, for this is by no means certain, but rather on his triumphant spirit and his evident success in witnessing. It is his courage that has given new heart to the timid Romans, who, possibly through persecutions, had grown discouraged. After all, they were in the very mouth of the lion; however, the Gospel of Jesus Christ was bigger, much bigger, than the lion, i.e., *"Nero."*

The idea is, that the Apostle's heroic sufferings made them think that their danger was small in contrast. By suffering more than his share, others were emboldened to take greater risks than they would have otherwise. Thus, Paul's imprisonment proved to be a catalytic agent that brought things out into the open and had the overall effect of presenting a greater impact upon the City of Rome.

THAT WHICH WAS ACTUALLY HAPPENING

One can almost hear the conversation among these Roman Christians. Some of their own were coming back from visiting Paul, and were relating to all who would listen, how that the Apostle was boldly witnessing about Christ, even right in front of the Praetorian Guards. Beside that, he pulled no punches, trimmed his Message not at all, proclaiming Christ boldly in every capacity.

Upon hearing this, that the Apostle had not backed down, but was rather spending 18 hours a day (more than likely) fearlessly and plainly telling all about Christ who came into his presence, one can well imagine how all of this affected the thinking of these reticent Preachers.

The idea would have been, and instantly, *"If Paul is not fearful of boldly proclaiming Christ right under the nose of Nero, even to the Emperor's personal guard, and doing so continuously, day by day, without let up, surely they could take courage wherever the Lord now opened the door."*

It is not that they had not been previously speaking for the Lord, but that now they are given new and greater boldness to declare God's Word without fear. Their conquest of fear is not based on the probability of Paul's release, for this is by no means certain, but

NOTES

on his triumphant spirit and his evident success in witnessing. It is his courage that has given new heart to the timid Romans who, possibly through persecutions, had grown discouraged.

(15) "SOME INDEED PREACH CHRIST EVEN OF ENVY AND STRIFE; AND SOME ALSO OF GOOD WILL:"

Not all the *"Preachers"* in Rome, however, were responding with the highest of motives. Some were proclaiming the Message of Christ *"out of envy and rivalry."* In the light of Philippians 1:16-17, it is clear that their wrong spirit was directed against Paul.

Who were these disappointing Preachers?

Some have identified these as the Judaizers of Philippians 3:1-16, Paul's old enemies. But it is difficult to imagine that Paul would commend such people for speaking *"the Word of God,"* even as he did in Verses 14 and 15, and then denounce them as *"dogs,"* doers of *"evil,"* and *"mutilators of the flesh,"* even as he did in Philippians 3:2. In Paul's view, Judaizers preached another gospel (Gal. 1:6-9).

It is ventured and is probably the case, that he was referring to a part of the group mentioned in Philippians 1:14. They were doctrinally orthodox, but at the same time mean and selfish, using the occasion of Paul's confinement to promote themselves. Because they were envious of Paul, they stirred up discord within the Christian community, hoping to gain a larger following for themselves.

Others, to their credit, were moved by feelings of good will for Paul. Their renewed vigor in proclaiming Christ was a true joining with Paul in the great enterprise of the Gospel (Kent).

PREACHING CHRIST OF ENVY AND STRIFE

The phrase, *"Some indeed preach Christ even of envy and strife,"* proclaims according to the next Verse that these Preachers, whomever they may have been, were attempting to hurt Paul. One does not have to read very long in the New Testament to discover that everyone was not pleased with Paul. Third-rate Preachers took advantage of Paul's eclipse in prison and gratified their jealousy of him by pressing to the front; and others were hostile, when preaching Christ denounced the

Apostle as a heretic and imposter. But this mighty man was indifferent to it all. Christ filled all the vision of his great soul, and he was quite satisfied and happy that the servant should be denounced and the Master announced, even as we shall see.

WHY DID THESE PREACHERS FEEL THE WAY THEY DID ABOUT PAUL?

Paul had been chosen by the Lord as the Masterbuilder of the Church (I Cor. 3:10). He had also been given by the Lord the New Covenant, this Great Gospel of Grace (Gal. 1:6-12).

In view of this, there were many who were no doubt very jealous of Paul's position. They evidently did not at all see the suffering and infirmities that accompanied this great Calling, but only what they imagined to be authority and power, etc. That is, I think, at least one of the reasons that the Apostle enumerated this extremely negative side of his Ministry (II Cor. 11:23-33).

Jealousy in the Ministry, even unto this hour, is far more pronounced than one would ever dare think. The reason is manyfold; however, it can be wrapped up I think in the following:

Preachers who are jealous of other Preachers, have forsaken that which the Lord has intended for them. In other words, what the Lord does with others is really none of my business. It is my business to know what Ministry He desires for me, and then to attempt to carry out that which He has designed. I am to want and desire only what He wants and desires; consequently, that does not pertain at all to what He does with other Preachers, or what they do on their own.

In that type of atmosphere, in which many Preachers participate, the Ministry is more so an occupation than a Calling. Jealous Preachers are not looking to the Lord for leading and guidance, but rather for promotion, which they will attempt to bring about in any way possible.

Second, Paul strongly defended the Gospel of Jesus Christ, which impacted those who would seek to compromise that Gospel, by adding other particulars such as the Law of Moses, etc. To be sure, this created many enemies along the way. To preach the Truth and at the same time, denounce that which is untrue, does not set well, especially with those who are propagating the error.

Paul would not back down one inch, would not give over to any compromise whatsoever, as it referred to the Gospel of Jesus Christ; consequently, the individuals propagating these false messages detested the Apostle strongly!

This is the reason that the greatest hindrance to the True Gospel of Jesus Christ always comes from inside the Church, and seldom from without. This is where Satan does his best work.

GOOD WILL

The phrase, *"And some also of good will,"* refers to himself. In other words, they were not attempting to preach something that would slam at the Apostle, but rather that which recognized his Calling and did so with respect.

HOW CAN WE FIT ALL OF THIS INTO THE EARLY CHURCH?

It is the idea of some, that perfection ruled at that particular time. The Truth is, ever since the Gospel began to be preached, unworthy motives have combined with worthier in the administration and professed service of it. Mixture of motive has haunted the work even of those who strove to keep their motives pure. And men in whom lower motive and worst motive had a strong influence have struck into the work alongside of the nobler and purer laborers.

So it has pleased God to permit; that even in this sacred field men might be tried and manifested before the judgment of the great day; and that it might be the more plain that the effectual blessing and the true increase come from God Alone.

There were, as we all know, in the Church of those days, powerful sections of professed Believers, who contested Paul's Apostleship, questioned his teaching, and wholly disliked the effects of his work. Among others, as stated, these were the Judaizers.

They were men who looked to Jesus Christ as the Messiah, who owned the authority of His Teaching, and claimed interest in His Promises. But they insisted linking Christianity to Jewish forms, and rules, and conditions of Law-keeping, which were on various grounds dear and sacred to them.

They apprehended feebly the spirituality and Divineness of Christ; and what they did apprehend they wished to enslave for themselves and others, in a carnal system of rules and ritual that tended to stifle and bury the truth. With this went a feeling towards Paul of wrath, fear, and antipathy. Such men were in Rome.

A PRESENT PROBLEM AS WELL

This very same spirit, this poor and questionable zeal for Christ, still works, and does so plentifully. Unfortunately, jealousy still exists and false doctrine is just as plentiful as ever.

As it regards others, we may, in special cases, see the working of such motives clearly enough, as Paul saw them at Rome. But usually we shall do well, when we can, to impute the work of others to the better side of their character: and we may do so reasonably; for as Christian work is far from being all of it so pure and high as we might desire, even on our own part, on the other hand, the lowly and loving temper of Christ's true followers is very often present and operative when it is not easy for us to see it. Let us believe it, because we believe in Him Who worketh all in all. In other words, let's try to find the best in others, if it is at all possible to do so.

(16) "THE ONE PREACH CHRIST OF CONTENTION, NOT SINCERELY, SUPPOSING TO ADD AFFLICTION TO MY BONDS:"

The former group of Preachers spoken of in the first part of Verse 15 were guilty of insincerity, particularly toward Paul. That they *"preach Christ"* and that Paul found no fault with the content of their message shows that their problem was not primarily doctrinal but personal. They were not unbelievers or perverters of Christian Truth. They were self-seeking opportunists, promoting themselves at Paul's expense.

Perhaps they had previously enjoyed some prominence in the Church before he arrived, but had been eclipsed since he came to the city. By taking advantage of Paul's imprisonment, they may have hoped to recover their former popularity.

They may have supposed that he would bitterly resent their success (just as they did his) and his imprisonment would become all the more galling to him. If so, they fail to reckon with the greatness of the man.

PREACHING CHRIST OF CONTENTION

The phrase, *"The one preach Christ of contention, not sincerely,"* presents a class of Preachers unfortunately, which continue unto this present hour.

"Contention" in the Greek is *"eritheia,"* and means *"to stimulate to anger, to provoke."*

The idea is, they have an agenda which is not of God. The motive of the Preacher should be according to the following:

Of course, the primary factor is hearing from Heaven, and then delivering what the Lord has given, not adding to or taking away. However, in this context, and in fact if such is done, several things will happen.

People will be saved, Believers will be Baptized with the Holy Spirit, sick bodies will be healed, people will be delivered from the bondages of darkness, and Believers will grow in Grace and the Knowledge of the Lord. In other words, Christ will be lifted up, will be glorified, will be put forth as the answer and the only answer for the ills of man.

Unfortunately, this is not the case with many Preachers, with them having another motive altogether. Their building, their Denomination, or preaching something that's not Biblical, or attempting to move the people to a particular Doctrine which, in effect, replaces Christ, are their motives. Or they promote themselves, or attempt to wheedle money out of people, with the entirety of the message leaning in that direction.

"Sincerely" in the Greek is *"hagnos,"* and means *"clean, innocent, modest, chaste, pure."*

It refers to exactly what we've been saying, motives which are not exactly of the Lord, but rather in other directions.

The idea is, that these Preachers were not speaking the whole Truth, but only that which served their purpose. Their motives are mixed, corrupted with selfishness (James 3:14). These, therefore, are not preaching in the truest sense. They are making known the facts of the Gospel, perhaps of Jesus' Life, Death, and Resurrection, but they are doing so out of jealousy or other unworthy motives. Quite possibly they may be orthodox, but have no real heart for that of which they are preaching.

These Preachers were individuals who had no real regard for the welfare of the Church or the honor of the great Salvation experience in Christ, but rather another agenda altogether.

TO ADD AFFLICTION

The phrase, *"Supposing to add affliction to my bonds,"* presents something so shameful as to defy description. How could anyone who claims Christ be so heartless, as to desire to add to the difficulties that Paul was already experiencing?

These Preachers were seeking to make Paul's imprisonment a galling experience, even worse than it already was. As stated, these are not Judaizers I think, for Paul in other places declares that they subvert the Gospel; here he does not do so. Some have suggested that these were Preachers who were envious of the wide popularity of Paul. Whether that be true, it is characteristic of human nature that jealousy usually arises within one's own class or profession: doctors are jealous of doctors, Ministers of Ministers, etc. In any case, their actions stem from something personal against Paul. Their preaching, so they assume, will make Paul's imprisonment even worse than it already is.

Some have even suggested, that these individuals, whomever they may have been, attempted to preach in such a way as to excite the rulers against Paul, and, therefore, to produce increased severity in his punishment.

CRUELTY

As stated, it is difficult to imagine Preachers doing such a thing, especially against someone such as Paul, but yet that's exactly what happened.

As we have previously stated, Satan does his best work inside the Church. To be frank, I think that one would have to label these Preachers as *"Satan's ministers"* (II Cor. 11:12-15).

Were these Preachers saved?

I think that question would have to be answered in this fashion.

Let's assume first of all, these Preachers had definitely given their hearts to the Lord at some place in time. While that may not have been true with all, it was probably true

NOTES

concerning most. Through self-will, and a personal agenda, these individuals had gradually come to this place of open rebellion against that which the Lord is doing. To be sure, their spiritual declension did not begin with Paul, but rather with self-will. But due to that, they now find themselves opposing one of the greatest men of God who ever lived.

Even in this state the Lord will deal kindly with these individuals, attempting to move them back to the right position; however, if they refuse to hear the warnings of the Holy Spirit, there will come a time, they will lose their way completely, and then in fact are unsaved. Only the Lord knows that particular time, but the direction points to that which is obvious.

One cannot continue to fight the Lord, which is exactly what these men were doing, which means going against the Holy Spirit, attempting to tear down everything that He is doing, and everything continue to be well. If they are to continue with the Lord, they will ultimately have to come God's Way, which would mean apologizing to Paul, seeking his forgiveness, but first of all doing this with the Lord. If they refuse to heed the admonitions of the Holy Spirit, the Word that the Lord gave a long time ago is still apropos, *"My Spirit shall not always strive with man"* (Gen. 6:3).

RELIGION

The greatest atrocities in the world have taken place in the realm of religion. When men leave God, which means to leave His Way, they then become lifted up in their own self-righteousness, and they justify anything and everything they do, irrespective as to how cruel it might be. That's how the Pharisees and the Sadducees, the religious leaders of Israel, could crucify the Lord in the Name of the Lord. We keep saying, Satan does his best work inside the Church.

To sum up, the only conclusion I can arrive at regarding these Preachers who opposed Paul so strongly, is, if they continue down this path refusing to repent, they will ultimately be lost. I cannot see how it could be any other way. How can one fight and oppose the Lord, and continue to do so refusing to go His Way, which guarantees that the situation will increasingly worsen, and at the same time come out at the conclusion with Salvation? To claim that those who would do such a thing refusing to repent, are still at the same time saved, militates against everything in the Word of God as it refers to Salvation.

It is certainly possible and actually happens all the time, that Believers whether Preachers or otherwise, at times get off course. One could probably say without fear of contradiction that this has happened to every Believer at one time or the other; however, when this happens the Holy Spirit begins to work strongly to bring that person back to the right way. But if they continue in their rebellion and stubbornness, which means they increasingly become worse, for that's the only thing that can happen if rebellion continues, there is no way that individual can remain in Salvation. It is impossible to continue to trust Christ for Salvation, while at the same time opposing Him and His Way. The situation has to ultimately be rectified or else there is a complete rupture. This goes for Preachers or the Laity, in fact, applicable to all (II Pet. 2:20-22).

(17) "BUT THE OTHER OF LOVE, KNOWING THAT I AM SET FOR THE DEFENCE OF THE GOSPEL."

These nobler Preachers recognize the Apostle's sincerity and unselfishness, plus the Call of God on his life. They realized that his present circumstances were part of a larger Divine program and that he had never deviated from it. He had been *"put here,"* and I speak of his prison experience, not by his own miscalculations, nor by chance, but by the operation of God's Sovereignty. God had brought him to this place and time *"for the defence of the Gospel."*

By ways that could never have been foreseen by man alone, God had accomplished within the short space of 30 years the spreading of the Gospel of Jesus Christ from its humble beginnings in obscure Judea to its defence before Caesar at the center of the Empire. No doubt, it was with some sense of awe that Paul evaluated his situation with the comment, *"I am put here."*

Recognition of the nature of Paul's imprisonment caused many stalwart Christians to respond out of love for him and for the cause he represented. They stepped into the breach and took their stand with him, eager to insure that the Gospel did not fail to be proclaimed while Paul was in prison.

LOVE

The phrase, *"But the other of love,"* proclaims the criteria for true Christianity. In other words, by Paul pointing to these particular Preachers whose hearts were filled with love, he at the same time was saying that the other Preachers of the previous Verse did not have love.

Those in the 17th Verse, first of all had a great love for Christ, which at the same time caused them to have a great love for the Apostle of Christ. One cannot have a personal agenda and at the same time have proper love for Christ. One or the other must go.

As well, if there is proper love for Christ in one's heart, this will at the same time bring about a proper discerning spirit in one's heart and life. In other words, individuals cannot properly discern what is right or wrong, or who is of God or not of God, if there is not proper love for Christ in their heart. So, what we are told here, is a very significant thing.

There is no way that one can properly love the Lord and at the same time, oppose that which is of the Lord. The two don't mix. People oppose that which is of God, simply because they do not have the proper love for Christ within their hearts and lives. In other words, God's Will is not their will, and God's Way is not their way. It all comes back to self-will versus the Will of God. Self-will automatically cancels out love for God, which cancels out proper discernment, which cancels out God's Way, which will ultimately cancel out one's Salvation if they remain on that particular course.

THE DEFENCE OF THE GOSPEL

The phrase, *"Knowing that I am set for the defence of the Gospel,"* literally means *"one appointed."* The idea is, that Paul was appointed by the Lord to be a defender of the Gospel, and in fact, this applies to all Preachers, at least those who desire to preach the Truth and defend the Truth.

First of all, what is the Gospel?

Of course, we know that the very word *"Gospel"* means *"Good News."*

What type of Good News?

Man is lost without God and with no way to save himself. Jesus Christ became our Substitute, died on the Cross in our place, thereby taking the full penalty for sin upon Himself, actually becoming a Sin-Offering, which satisfied the claims of Heavenly Justice. He atoned for all sin, past, present, and future, at least for those who will believe (Jn. 3:16).

All this that Christ did on the Cross and as it regards His Resurrection, was totally and completely for sinners. In other words, none of this was for Himself, or Heaven or any part of Heaven, as stated, all for sinners.

Simple Faith in this which Christ has done, guarantees Salvation for any and all sinners, irrespective as to how wicked they may have been. This means that all sin is washed away from the believing sinner, which means that guilt and condemnation is gone, with the person becoming a new creation in Christ Jesus. In this they receive Eternal Life, and become a *"joint-heir with Christ"* (Rom. 8:17).

This also means that their name is written down in the Lamb's Book of Life, which means they will not be confined to an eternal Hell forever and forever (Rev. 20:11-15).

If all of this of which we said, is not *"Good News,"* then I don't know what *"Good News"* actually is!

JESUS CHRIST AND HIM CRUCIFIED

The key to all of this of which we have said, is *"Jesus Christ and Him Crucified"* (I Cor. 2:2). Christ had to die for lost humanity before man could be saved. Consequently, our Salvation is wrapped up totally and completely in what is referred to as *"The Finished Work of Christ."* Everything in the Christian experience must center up on the Cross, which at the same time presupposes the Resurrection. This is what Paul was defending, *"The Message of the Cross."* That is why he said, which we will address later in a more detailed way, *"For many walk, of whom I have told you often, and now tell you even weeping, that they are the enemies of the Cross of Christ."*

Of these, he then said, *"Whose end is destruction"* (Phil. 3:18-19).

Satan fights the Message of the Cross more so than anything else. He knows that if he can push the Church away from the Cross, which he has by and large succeeded in doing in the last several decades, then he can destroy the Source of all Victory for the Child of God. Of course, if our understanding of the Cross is perverted, it also stops sinners from being saved. For the only way that a person can come to Christ, is by believing what Christ did at the Cross (Jn. 3:16; Rom. 10:9-10, 13; Eph. 2:8-9; Rev. 22:17).

This is the Gospel which Paul defended, which the Holy Spirit demanded that he defend, and which all other Preachers must defend as well.

The foray of the modern Church into humanistic psychology, is but another departure from the Cross. As well, the so-called modern Faith Ministry falls into this same category, but in another way. Many in this latter belief system teach the *"Jesus died spiritually doctrine,"* which in effect, bypasses the Cross as it refers to our Salvation. Let me explain:

WHAT IS THE *"JESUS DIED SPIRITUALLY DOCTRINE"*?

Basically, this doctrine teaches that Jesus became a sinner on the Cross exactly like all other sinners, thereby, He had to die and go to Hell, as do all sinners when they die without God. They then teach that He was *"Born-Again"* in Hell, and when we say *"Hell,"* we are speaking of the burning side of the pit.

This is believed by many in the so-called Faith Teaching and is actually a terrible attack against the Atonement, which is serious indeed. Let's examine this:

THE QUESTION

The question being asked is, *"Did Jesus become sin at Calvary and experience spiritual death? Did He become sin on the Cross, as this particular doctrine teaches, or was He a Sin-Offering?"*

We teach and believe that Jesus was a Sin-Offering. We also teach that He was holy and pure just as the Old Testament foreshadowed, actually without sin in any capacity.

Jesus did not go to Hell for three days to redeem mankind from the terrible ravages of sin. Rather, He went to be with His Heavenly Father, because He Himself said, *"Father, into Thy Hands I commend My Spirit"* (Lk. 23:46).

Immediately before Jesus died on Calvary, He uttered the words, *"It is finished"* (Jn. 19:30).

What was finished?

The work Christ came to do. As of that moment, man's Salvation was complete, at least for those who will believe (Jn. 3:16). Nothing else was needed. Nothing else could be done that would aid or abet the Finished Work at Calvary. So these three words stand as a permanent rebuke to the doctrine that Jesus had to go to Hell and die spiritually to redeem man, and whatever else this spurious doctrine claims.

This particular false doctrine also teaches that the sinless Son of God became unregenerate and died as a lost sinner at Calvary, and that He had to be Born-Again and justified from sin. The pitiful thing about this whole line of thinking is that He was somehow, they claim, Born-Again in, of all places, Hell!

Now if perchance this were true, it would have been necessary for someone to die for the Lord Jesus Christ to redeem Him from His unregenerate state and provide for His Justification. Of course, we know this is all utter foolishness, because Jesus did *not* become unregenerate on the Cross or any other time, which means that He did not die a lost sinner.

HIS BLOOD

Some time ago one of the leading proponents of this heresy (and heresy it is) stated, *"When His Blood poured out, it did not atone. It only did away with the handwriting of the ordinances that were against us."*

He went on to say that Jesus redeemed man, not on the Cross but in Hell. Hopefully, the proponents of this doctrine do not know what they are doing, for they are actually denying the Blood Atonement of Jesus Christ, which was the entire purpose of the Incarnation and the Redemption of mankind. It seems they do not understand that they have negated the Power of Jesus' Blood to cleanse from sin by their teaching that Jesus became an unholy Sacrifice on the Cross. This is heresy, and it is dangerous, very dangerous!

IDENTIFICATION OR SUBSTITUTION?

This heresy appears to teach that Jesus identified with the sinner on the Cross, while it seems to ignore the fact that Jesus became a Substitute for sinners — confusing the identification of Jesus with the human race at His Birth with His Substitution for sinners on the Cross.

If Jesus had become literal sin and had become lost and unregenerate, as they teach, while He hung on the Cross of Calvary, then He would have been an unacceptable Sacrificial Offering for the sins of others. Whereas if He indeed remained pure and holy as the Scriptures prove, then God could accept Him as a Substitute on behalf of sinners. It was only in this way that He could fulfill the Old Testament, whereby the animal for the Sin-Offering had to be spotless and *"without blemish"* (Lev. 4:2-3). If you remember, the Sin-Offering was regarded most holy even after its death.

Someone may ask, *"What difference does that make?"*

It makes all the difference in the world because according to the Word of God our Eternal Salvation rests upon what we personally believe concerning the Blood Atonement of Jesus Christ. It is here, at the Cross, that a person's Salvation either stands or falls. The doctrine of Jesus dying spiritually on the Cross and going to Hell, and His having to be Born-Again as a sinner, is heresy of the most serious kind — its seriousness stemming from the fact that if a person believes this perverted doctrine, he will find that in the end he has been robbed of the Blood Atonement on his behalf.

The Bible is emphatic on this matter: one sinner cannot redeem another sinner. Only one who is guiltless could ever act as a Substitute and suffer the punishment for the guilty party, thereby saving the guilty party. Even Jesus could not have done this if He had become guilty Himself, as this particular doctrine contends. The central thrust of the entire Old Testament sacrificial system is that Jesus was the guiltless Substitute Who, like the Old Testament Type, remained pure and holy both on the Cross and after His Death.

THE BASIC TEACHING

This doctrine generally follows something like this.

Jesus became sin on the Cross when He yielded Himself to Satan. He swallowed up the evil nature of Satan, thus becoming one in nature with the adversary, taking upon Himself the diabolical nature of Satan. At that time He became a lost Man crying, *"My God, My God, Why hast Thou forsaken Me?"* (Mat. 27:46; Ps. 22:1). He had now died spiritually (according to this spurious teaching, that is).

Jesus was then taken to the pit of Hell where He was chained with the fetters of sin, wickedness, disease, and all other evils of Satan. The Devil stood before the darkness crying, *"We have conquered the Son of God."* There followed (they claim) a gala celebration down in the pit. Satan believed he had finally triumphed over God.

Jesus consequently suffered agonies beyond description in the pit for three days as all the hosts of Hell were upon Him. Then suddenly Jesus was justified, they say! From His Throne in Heaven Almighty God arose and put His Hands to His Mouth and screamed, *"It is finished; it is enough."* Jesus was now Born-Again and made spiritually alive once more.

Hell itself was shaken. Jesus shook off His chains of sin, sickness, and evil. He walked over to the Devil, grabbed him, and threw him to the ground. As the Devil cowered and trembled on the floor of the pit, Jesus put His Foot on top of him and took the keys of death, Hell, and the grave from Satan.

At this time the Holy Spirit kicked open the gates of Hell and raised Jesus from death. He then ascended to the Father and announced, *"I have paid the price. The prison is now open."* He was now a Born-Again Man who had defeated Satan. Jesus was the firstborn from the spiritually dead. Thus, it was at the time Jesus was made alive down in the pit that the Believer was also made alive. The Church, they say, had its origin in the pit of Hell when Jesus was begotten from the dead as the *"First-born among many Brethren"* (Rom. 8:29).

At first glance it appears to be cause for rejoicing. However, if you think about it for a moment, you have never read anything of this nature on the pages of your Bible — because it's not in the Bible! It is fiction from beginning to end.

The Truth is, "(He) *blotted out the handwriting of ordinances that was against us, which was contrary to us, and took it out of the way, nailing it to His Cross; and having spoiled principalities and powers, He made a show of them openly, triumphing over them in it"* (Col. 2:14-15).

"Nailing it to His Cross . . . triumphing over them in it" means that Jesus' great victory was won on the Cross, and not in Hell as the teachers of the error claim!

THE OLD TESTAMENT SACRIFICES

The Old Testament animal type (a type of Jesus), which was to die as a substitute for the sinner, had to be, as we have stated, without spot or blemish (Deut. 15:21; Lev. 4:3, 27-30; 9:3-4) to teach Israel (and the Church) that a substitute acceptable to God had to be holy and guiltless in order to bear the punishment for the guilt of the sinner, for God would accept nothing less.

This ritual, carried out again and again in the Old Testament, was realized in Jesus Christ as the Lamb of God, Who *"offered Himself without spot to God"* (Heb. 9:14). How much clearer can it be! If Jesus had become a sinner on the Cross, as these false teachers proclaim, He would not have been *"without spot to God,"* and would, therefore, have been unacceptable.

When these teachers teach that Jesus literally became sin with the inherent need to become Born-Again, they expose the basic flaw in their doctrine, which stems from apparent ignorance of the nature of the Old Testament Sacrifices, especially the Sin-Offering. They conveniently forget (if indeed they ever knew) that the Old Testament clearly teaches that at no point does the Sin-Offering become an unholy sacrifice, either before or after its death.

SIN OR SIN-OFFERING?

The Apostle Paul said, *"For He hath made Him to be sin for us, Who knew no sin"* (II Cor. 5:21).

In the Hebrew language the term *"chetta't"* is the same word used for both *"sin"* and *"Sin-Offering."* A single Hebrew term translates both words. *"Sin"* and *"Sin-Offering,"* then, are one and the same, at least as it regards the Hebrew word. It was the context in which the term was used that expressed whether a person was speaking of *"Sin-Offering"* or *"sin."*

For example, if it was a matter concerning Sacrifices, *"chetta't"* was understood to mean a *"Sin-Offering."* If the matter was one of offense, the same word would be used; but the people involved would understand the meaning by the usage, the tenor of it.

We as Gentiles may confuse the word, but no Jewish Christian would ever, confuse *"sin"* with the *"Sin-Offering,"* even though the two thoughts are both expressed by the same Hebrew term.

It is the same with the terms *"trespass"* and *"Trespass-Offering."* The same Hebrew word is used, *"asham,"* meaning that Jesus' Death on the Cross is to be regarded also as a *"Trespass-Offering"* for sinners and not that He Himself became a *"trespass"* or *"sin"* or that He ever Personally *"trespassed"* or *"sinned."*

THE SERPENT (SATAN) AND CHRIST

This erroneous doctrine contends on the basis of Numbers Chapter 21 (which presents the account of the lifting up of the brazen serpent in the wilderness for the healing of those bitten) that Jesus was also lifted up as a serpent when He was made sin on the Cross, and at that time took on the evil nature of Satan. They quote, *"And as Moses lifted up the serpent in the wilderness, even so must the Son of Man be lifted up"* (Jn. 3:14). From this they take it that Jesus became one with the serpent, Satan, and died spiritually.

However, the account in Numbers Chapter 21 does not support this fantasy. God did send fiery serpents as punishment against the rebellious Israelites. As a result of the intercession of Moses, God directed him to make a figure of a serpent in brass, to be elevated on a pole so that it could be seen from all quarters in the camp. All who looked in Faith in its direction were healed.

Naturally, we understand that the brazen serpent did not produce healing; it was merely an emblem of their sin and signified the nature of Divine Judgment. Their Faith in God's Promise to heal brought deliverance through their obedience. To look upon an inanimate object (in this case, a serpent of brass) in itself could never produce healing.

By analogy, if Jesus became a serpent in nature as this erroneous teaching contends, then healing was provided by Satan, the serpent (Num. 21:4-9), not God.

What was being spoken of here was the manner in which Jesus would die, not a change in His Nature. As that serpent was lifted up on a pole, Jesus would also be lifted up on a pole, the Cross, bearing the penalty for every sin that has ever been committed and would ever be committed, at least for those who will believe. It signified that He would defeat Satan, by atoning for all sin. Satan's hold on humanity, which produces guilt and death, is sin. When the sin is removed, which it was by the Atonement of Christ on the Cross, Satan, the serpent, loses his hold, which gives him no more claim on believing sinners. It was all done at the Cross, of which this *"pole"* was a type.

JESUS, A SINNER?

First of all, we know that all men are the children of wrath (Rom. 3:9; 5:12; Eph. 2:3). But we also know that Jesus lived without committing any act of sin (Jn. 14:30; II Cor. 5:21; Heb. 4:15).

The *"Jesus died spiritually"* teachers say that Jesus did not Personally sin, but He was made by God to be Sin, that He took upon Himself the sinfulness of the human race and became evil with Satan's nature.

Of course, this is impossible. Sin is a personal act of disobedience to the Will of God, and Jesus never once disobeyed His Father, and certainly not when He hung on the Cross.

Sin is not something tangible like a coat of black paint that God could drape over His Son, nor is it some type of inoculation of germs that Scientists could inject into the bloodstream as the Nazis did to some of their victims in World War II. Sin is an act (whether deed, word, or thought) that a person must personally commit. This fact alone rules out any possibility that Jesus could be made sin.

In the study of Biblical Theology, the Scriptural Doctrine of imputation shows that sin or Righteousness can be imputed or charged to another's account in a legal sense. Applied to Jesus and His Sacrifice as a Sin-Offering, this indicates that He did not become sin, but remained sinless that He might be able to bear the punishment for our guilt that was imputed to Him. In other words, Jesus did not bear the wickedness and the filth of our sinful nature, but He did bear the terrible punishment that should have been poured out on us. In other words, although innocent, He suffered the penalty for the sin we should have suffered.

Our punishment was imputed to Him. Our sins, in regard to their moral character, are our own. They could not by imputation, other than a legal way, become someone else's. However, Jesus Christ could take upon Himself the punishment for the guilt of our sins, which has reference to the legal liabilities that Christ assumed on our behalf.

So the transfer of our sins to Jesus Christ was not a transfer of the actual transgressions themselves — that is not possible — but Christ made Himself liable to endure the penalty for our sins. On the Cross and in His Death, Christ was a holy, spotless Sin-Offering. To have been anything otherwise would have violated the Old Testament Type and would have disqualified Him as an acceptable Substitute to God.

JESUS, JUSTIFIED IN HELL?

These teachers conclude from the phrase, *"Justified in the Spirit"* (I Tim. 3:16) that Jesus Himself had to be justified, that He had to be made sin and possess an evil, Satanic nature. Thus, it is said, He had to be made Righteous once more, justified and Born-Again, but according to the Greek *"to justify"* is *"to declare Righteous"* or *"to show to be Righteous."* Jesus was evinced to be Righteous as to His Spiritual Nature.

The Bible, in this Passage, was not saying that Jesus was being made Righteous but that His Righteousness was being announced. Jesus never ceased to be Righteous, He never ceased to be just.

Without any Scriptural support whatsoever, these teachers declare, *"Suddenly God justified Jesus in the pit* (Hell) *and He was Born-Again."*

God did not arbitrarily wave His Hand over Christ and say, *"Be Thou cleansed,"* and suddenly Jesus was justified (made Righteous, Born-Again, and restored to Sonship with the Father). There is no Scriptural basis for this doctrine. In fact, it is made up out of whole cloth.

JESUS, ABANDONED BY GOD?

Was Jesus abandoned by God at Calvary? No! Jesus was God's Own Sacrifice, chosen by Him (Isa. Chpt. 53; Jn. 1:29; 3:16), and never out of Divine favor for one moment. He was called *"An Offering and a Sacrifice to God for a Sweetsmelling Savour"* (Eph. 5:2). This is in perfect harmony with the Old Testament teaching that the Sin-Offering was most holy to God (Lev. Chpt. 6).

First of all, it is impossible to separate the Godhead — Father, Son, and Holy Spirit. *"For in Him* (Jesus) *dwelleth all the fullness of the Godhead bodily"* (Col. 2:9). If Jesus had died spiritually, then at the Cross — by His being lost — He would have divided the Godhead, or at the least had made the entire Godhead sinful and in need of the New Birth.

The idea of dividing up the Godhead for three days by sending the Son of God to Hell as a lost sinner, totally abandoned by God the Father and God the Holy Spirit, is totally ridiculous. This spurious teaching even goes so far as to say that God was no longer the Father of Jesus while He was in Hell.

When Jesus uttered the words on the Cross, *"My God, My God, Why hast Thou forsaken Me?"* Jesus was quoting from a prophetic Passage (Ps. 22:1). He also said, *"I thirst"* (Jn. 19:28), an utterance based upon another Old Testament Prophecy (Ps. 69:21). When He uttered these words, *"My God, My God,"* the religious leaders and the people around the Cross misinterpreted what He said, by saying *"This Man calleth for Elias* (Elijah)*"* (Mat. 27:47).

With these words Jesus consciously identified Himself as the One of Whom the Old Testament Prophecies spoke. It is even believed by some Scholars that Jesus recited all of Psalm 22 as well as other Prophecies concerning Him while He hung on the Cross for several hours. We do know, of course, that not everything Jesus did was recorded. Only a small portion was recorded (Jn. 21:25).

Was Jesus forsaken by God? No, He was not. God had temporarily *"turned His Face aside,"* in that Jesus was suffering the penalty for all sin which was death, and that instead of delivering His Son from death, which He did on several occasions (Jn. 7:30), the Father instead, delivered Him up unto death, in that He became a Sin-Offering for others; but this was not abandonment. Jesus Himself said, *"Behold, the hour cometh, yea, is now come, that ye shall be scattered, every man to his own, and shall leave Me alone: and yet I am not alone, because the Father is with Me"* (Jn. 16:32). He could say this because *"God was in Christ, reconciling the world unto Himself"* (II Cor. 5:19).

JESUS, PHYSICAL OR SPIRITUAL DEATH?

The Bible states again and again that Jesus offered up His *"Body"* as a Sacrifice for our sins, that He was put to death *"in the flesh."* In other words, Jesus died physically but not spiritually. Nowhere in the Word of God does it tell us that Jesus died in His Spirit. It does say, however, that... *"Christ... His Own Self bare our sins in His Own Body on the Tree"* (I Pet. 2:21-24).

"Christ... (was) put to death in the flesh, but quickened by the Spirit" (I Pet. 3:18).

"Christ hath suffered for us in the flesh" (I Pet. 4:1).

"He reconciled (us) *in the Body of His flesh through death"* (Col. 1:21-22).

"We are sanctified through the Offering of the Body of Jesus Christ once for all" (Heb. 10:10).

"(He) abolished in His flesh the enmity, even the Law of Commandments" (Eph. 2:15).

So while the Scriptures repeatedly stress that Jesus offered up His Body and His Flesh as a Sacrifice for sin, not once do they say He died in His Spirit.

In fact, God could not die spiritually. Else why would the Son of God need a Body of flesh? He took on flesh so that He could die physically on behalf of sinners, as had the Old Testament Type.

The erroneous teaching, of the Jesus Died Spiritually Doctrine, is that the shedding of Jesus' Blood was insignificant. The following are some of the ridiculous theories of this doctrine:

1. When His Blood was poured out, it did not atone. (How silly can we be?)

2. Jesus bled only a few drops, and when people sing about the Blood of Jesus, they do not know what they are talking about.

3. Jesus' Death on the Cross was relatively insignificant, in that this was just a part of all that He did, with Redemption actually being accomplished when He was Born-Again in Hell.

NOTES

To comment on these would be a foolish waste of time. The efficacy of the Atonement did not depend on how much Blood was shed on the Cross, or how much time was involved in the process of dying. The validity of the Atonement depended on the fact that the Son of God shed His spotless Blood and died on our behalf.

JESUS, BORN-AGAIN?

This false teaching also claims that:

1. Jesus was Born-Again in the pit of Hell as the first Man to be Born-Again under the New Covenant. The proponents of this doctrine apparently are referring to the Verse that says, *"God... hath raised up Jesus again; as it is also written in the Second Psalm, 'Thou art My Son, this day have I begotten Thee'"* (Acts 13:33).

2. He was the first begotten from spiritual death, citing, *"Jesus Christ, Who is the faithful witness, and the first begotten of the dead"* (Rev. 1:5).

3. Jesus started the Church in Hell when He was Born-Again in the pit, citing, *"(Jesus became) the Firstborn among many Brethren"* (Rom. 8:29).

4. He was Righteous while on Earth, on the Cross became unrighteous, went to Hell, then in the pit was made Righteous once more.

That seems strange when the Bible says He is unchangeable (Mal. 3:6; Heb. 13:8).

The first thing we must make clear is that two different English terms were used by the King James translators to translate the same Greek word. *"Firstborn"* and *"First Begotten"* are both taken from the Greek word *"prototokos."* *"First Begotten"* (Heb. 1:6; Rev. 1:5) is *"Firstborn."* *"Begotten"* (Acts 13:33), a different Greek word altogether refers to the physical Resurrection of Jesus and completely rules out the fanciful notion that Jesus was Born-Again in Hell.

In the preceding Verses (Acts 13:16-32) Paul spoke of Christ's physical Death and the Burial of His Body in a sepulcher. Verses 30-33 speak of His physical Resurrection from the dead. The Resurrection of Jesus in the Bible always has reference to the Resurrection of His Body and not His Spirit, since His Spirit did not die (Lk. 24:36-46; I Cor. 15:20-23).

The term *"Firstborn"* in Scripture is used not only to refer to the physical birth of the first child into a family, but also to speak of position and inheritance rights. So the term refers not merely to birth, but also to birthright as well as to position or status. The Firstborn always held a special position in God's Sight, possessing special rights and privileges.

In this same sense Jesus Christ is called the *"Firstborn"* (Rom. 8:29; Col. 1:15; Heb. 1:6). The term in such Passages speaks of position, rank, legal rights, and special privileges. It never has any reference to the New Birth (being Born-Again).

JESUS, IN HELL?

Jesus did go down into Paradise, which was a part of Hell, where the Righteous souls — such as Abraham, Isaac, Jacob, David, and other Old Testament Saints — were kept against their will. These souls were not in the burning part of the pit, but rather in the place commonly referred to as *"Abraham's bosom"* or *"Paradise."* This is the place to which Jesus was referring when He said to the dying thief, *"Today shalt thou be with Me in Paradise"* (Lk. 23:43). He was speaking of that place in the heart of the Earth where He would go. The other thief would go to the punishment side of Hell where the rich man was (Lk. 16:19-31).

After Jesus died on the Cross, He went down into Paradise. Then the Bible says, *"When He ascended up on high, He led captivity captive"* (Eph. 4:8). In other words, those Righteous souls who were kept against their will in the side of Hell called Paradise were led by Jesus to Heaven (like an earthly conqueror). That is what Scripture means when it says Christ descended first into Hell, the lower parts of the Earth (Ps. 16:10; Acts 2:27; Eph. 4:8-10). He captured the Righteous souls from Satan, who had actually been held captive by Satan, who hoped eventually to get them over into the burning side of the pit, but was defeated by Jesus Christ on the Cross, with Christ leading these individuals captive to Heaven when He ascended on high. This fulfilled Psalms 68:18.

Prior to this, all Righteous souls went into *"Hades"* or *"Sheol,"* along with the souls of the wicked who went to another compartment. These two compartments had a great gulf between them (Lk. 16:19-31). Satan could take all the Old Testament Saints down there and hold them captive against their will, simply because the sin debt had not yet been paid. To be sure, they were saved, that is if Jesus actually satisfied the sin debt on the Cross by dying, which paid all the wages of that monster, which He did (Rom. 6:23).

Now, due to what Jesus did at the Cross and the Resurrection, the souls of the Righteous no longer go into the heart of the Earth at death to be held captive against their will. They go immediately to Heaven at physical death to await the Resurrection of the body (II Cor. 5:8; Phil. 1:21-24; Heb. 2:20; Rev. 6:9-11).

The wicked will continue to go unto the torment compartment of *"hades"* or *"sheol"* until the end of the Millennium. Then death and *"hades"* will deliver up the wicked souls, which will be reunited with their body and resurrected to be sentenced to the Lake of Fire forever (Rev. 20:11-15).

In this context a person could say that Jesus went to Hell, but it in no way means that He went down into the burning flames into the pit as a sinner. Nor was He molested by Satan, triumphed over by the powers of darkness, and then suddenly justified by God and Born-Again as the *"Firstborn among many Brethren"* (Rom. 8:29). This is an erroneous teaching that does not understand the Scripture sense of the Atonement and the vicarious Sacrifice paid by Jesus Christ at Calvary's Cross as a Sin-Offering.

No, Jesus, as this false teaching claims, did *not* die as a sinner on the Cross. He did *not* go to the burning (punishment) side of Hell. He was *not* placed under Satan's domain. He was *not* subject to the evil one. He *was* the Perfect Sacrifice as our Substitute, given up as a Sin-Offering. He died physically on our behalf, suffering the penalty of the broken law in our stead, taking the punishment we should have taken, thereby satisfying the terrible sin debt. He did *not* die spiritually, only physically.

(18) "WHAT THEN? NOTWITHSTANDING, EVERY WAY, WHETHER IN PRETENCE, OR IN TRUTH, CHRIST IS PREACHED; AND I THEREIN DO REJOICE, YEA, AND WILL REJOICE."

Paul's conclusion, in effect, *"But what does it matter?..."* reveals his sense of values. The importance of the Gospel and its proclamation so outweighed any personal considerations that he would not cloud the issue by insisting on settling personal grievances.

He was convinced that *"Christ is preached"* even by these Preachers whose motives were suspect. They must have been faithful to the basic Message of Christ. This means, they could not have been Judaizers, at least not in the usual sense of that designation. With Paul, to preach *"Christ"* meant to proclaim the good news of Salvation provided freely by God's Grace through the Redemptive Work of Christ and received by men through Faith without *"works of righteousness"* of any kind. It is inconceivable that any Judaizing message with its insistence on performance of Jewish rites would be characterized by Paul as preaching *"Christ."*

As long as the antagonism was only personal, Paul could rejoice that the greater purpose of disseminating the Gospel was being served. Even when some of the preaching was actually a pretext utilized to camouflage attacks on Paul, the Apostle took the magnanimous view that affronts to himself could be ignored, provided that the Truth of the Gospel of Christ was proclaimed in some way. He rejoiced in this and intended to maintain this wholesome magnanimity, which rose above all personal feelings (Kent).

WHAT SHOULD PAUL DO?

The question, *"What then?"* does not mean that Paul condoned the activities of these Preachers or their motives, who constantly opposed him. He just did not allow it to bother him. What they were doing was wrong, terribly wrong! And to be sure, they would answer to God; however, if in some way Jesus was lifted up, this at least was better than nothing. The motives of these Preachers may not be good, but the result in some way just might be good; the Gospel facts are made more widely known, not only by those who preach sincerely, but even by means of those who strive to promote their own agenda under the pretense of preaching Christ.

CHRIST IS PREACHED

The phrase, *"Notwithstanding, every way, whether in pretence, or in Truth, Christ is preached,"* proclaims the Message as the most important thing of all, not our feelings.

Once again we emphasize, that it seems as if these Preachers, whomever they may have been, were preaching the Truth, but rather out of pretense. We are not actually told what their doctrine was; nor does Paul imply that it was erroneous; it was their motives only which were censored. Had it been essentially unsound, we cannot suppose that he would have *"rejoiced."*

Consequently, that they were of the Judaizing faction, with its *"other gospel,"* seems hardly possible.

They apparently used Paul's imprisonment as an occasion to embarrass him. They may have been his rivals motivated by jealousy. They apparently sought to convince their hearers that the fact that Paul was a prisoner of Rome was a disgrace to the Gospel.

Paul did not worry about any personal disgrace, if by this *"embarrassment"* people would become better acquainted with Christ. The Apostle was sufficiently mature that he rejoiced if attention was called to Christ even from the most unworthy of motives.

He believed that the advertisement designed to discredit the Gospel, or more particularly himself, would lead to investigation. He was convinced that investigation whetted by curiosity would, in many cases, lead to conversion.

REJOICE

The phrase, *"And I therein do rejoice, yea, and will rejoice,"* presents the possibility that at least people will get some knowledge of Christ, which is better than nothing. Consequently, the Apostle would rejoice, and continue rejoicing. So, the efforts of these individuals, whomever they may have been, had the very opposite effect upon the Apostle.

The all-absorbing passion of his life is the *"furtherance of the Gospel."* Consequently, he dwells on the good that is being accomplished — Christ is being announced — not on the bad motives of these particular Preachers. Attention to the essential spares him from any bitterness of soul.

The Truth of the Gospel has captured his love; thus he will endure any blow to himself, rather than allow it to hinder the Message.

There are great lessons we can learn from the attitude of the great Apostle. Some of them are as follows:

1. If we are laid aside from preaching by sickness, or any other means, we should rejoice that others are in health, and are able to make the Saviour known, though we are forgotten.

2. When we are unpopular and unsuccessful, we should rejoice that others are more popular and successful — for Christ is preached.

3. When we have rivals, who have better plans than we for doing good, and whose labors seems to be crowned with success, we should not be envious or jealous — for Christ is preached.

4. When Ministers preach what we regard as error, and their preaching becomes popular, and is attended with success, we can still find occasion to rejoice — for they preach Christ at least in some fashion.

In the error we should not, we cannot rejoice; but in the fact that the great Truth is held up that Christ died for men, we can always find abundant occasion for joy. Mingled as it may be with error, it may be nevertheless the means of saving souls; and though we should rejoice more if the Truth were preached without any admixture of error, yet the very fact that Christ is made known lays the foundation for gratitude and rejoicing.

CAN CHRIST BE LIFTED UP, OR EVEN SOULS BE SAVED, IF THE PREACHING CONTAINS A MIXTURE OF ERROR AND TRUTH?

Most definitely Christ can be glorified, and souls can be saved under such circumstances. The Truth that is preached, despite the error, will bring forth its reward. To be sure, there are very few Preachers, if any, who have never preached anything but Truth. All of our learning is a process, which means that when we are Born-Again, and even some called to preach, that we do not immediately know all the Gospel or understand all of its great Truths. While it is incumbent upon the Preacher to walk in all the Light he has, all Preachers can certainly have more Light added, which means more Truth added, which means that they had been previously preaching some error, or else what Truth they were preaching was incomplete. This goes not only for Light, but as well for motives.

The Truth is, ever since the Gospel began to be preached, unworthy motives have combined with worthier in the administration and professed service of it. Mixture of motive has haunted the work even of those who strive to keep their motives pure. In other words, there are no perfect Preachers. So this means that the Lord always has imperfect vessels through which to work, and I think even Paul would include himself in that mix, which makes it even the more plain that the effectual blessing and the true increase come from the Lord and not men.

Now the Apostle, looking at this, is glad of it. He is not glad that any men, professing Christ, give way to evil and unchristian tempers. But he is glad that Christ is preached, even under less than the best circumstances.

In fact, there were cases in which he vehemently contended with such persons — when they strove to poison and pervert Christians who had learned the better way. But now he is thinking of the outside world; and it was good that the making known of Christ should gather strength, volume, and extension.

And the Apostle knew that the Lord could bless His Own Message, imperfectly delivered perhaps, to bring thirsty souls to Himself, and would not fail in His unsearchable wisdom to care for those who came, and to lead them in the ways He knew best. Let Christ be preached.

The converts do not belong to the Denominations, but first of all to Christ. Neither is it appointed that religious Denominations shall permanently hold those whom they bring in; but Christ can hold them, and can order their future in ways we cannot foretell.

THE PREACHING OF CHRIST

It is not true that the preaching of Christ serves no purpose and yields no fruits, in cases where it is not carried on in the right or the best spirit. Indeed, God honors the pure, loving, lowly hearts, which He has Himself cleansed; they are appropriate agents for His work, and often receive a special blessing in connection with it. But God is not tied up to give no success at all to men acting under wrong motives: at least, if we are to say that He gives some success to them, yet in connection with them He is well able to take success to Himself. Through strange channels He can send blessings to souls, whatever He gives or denies to the unworthy workmen.

But perhaps the success which attends such Preachers is not remarkable nor very long continued. Souls truly gathered in will soon get beyond their teaching. At any rate, it is a poor business to be serving Christ upon the Devil's principles. It cannot be good for us — whatever good may sometimes come thereby to others. Consequently, let us purge ourselves from such filthiness of the flesh and of the spirit.

So, what we have said is never to commend wrong motives or wrong doctrine, but only that God is not limited to perfection. Were that the case, He could use no one.

WHAT MIGHT CHRIST BE FOR MEN?

"Christ is preached." How glad the Apostle was to think of it! How he longed to see more of it, and rejoiced in all of it that he saw! One wonders how far the thoughts and feelings associated with these words in Paul's mind find any echo in ours. Christ is preached.

The meaning for men of that Message, as Paul conceived it, grew out of the anguish and the wonder of those early days at Damascus, and had been growing ever since. What might Christ be for men? — Christ their Righteousness, Christ their life, Christ their hope; God in Christ, Peace in Christ, inheritance in Christ; a new creature, a new world; joy, victory — above all, the Love of Christ, the Love which passes knowledge and fills us with the fullness of God.

Therefore, this was also the burning conviction in Paul's soul — that Christ must be preached; by all means, on all accounts, Christ must be preached. The unsearchable riches of Christ must be proclaimed. Certainly, whoever might do or not do, he must do it. He was to live for nothing else. *"I Paul am made a Minister of the Gospel. Woe is unto me if I preach not the Gospel."*

THE APOSTASY OF THE LAST DAYS

There may be, and in fact is I think, an exception to these things which I have said.

NOTES

Paul also said, *"Now the Spirit speaketh expressly, that in the latter times* (this present day in which we now live) *some shall depart from the Faith, giving heed to seducing spirits, and doctrines of Devils; speaking lies in hypocrisy; having their conscience seared with a hot iron"* (I Tim. 4:1-2).

He also said, and which are some of the last words he wrote, *"For the time will come* (that time is now) *when they will not endure sound doctrine; but after their own lusts shall they heap to themselves teachers, having itching ears; and they shall turn away their ears from the Truth, and shall be turned unto fables"* (II Tim. 4:3-4).

These Preachers and Teachers will come as *"angels of light"* (II Cor. 11:14). They will look like God, act like God, talk like God, and will so much resemble the ways of the Lord, that millions will be deceived. In fact, only those who truly know the Word of God and thereby walk close to the Lord, will be able to tell the difference.

The shocking word is, this time of which Paul spoke has already come. In other words, this of which I say is upon us. It's the time of great apostasy, which means a departure from Truth. It will be and is different, from error as error is known, but will be and is a diabolical effort by Satan to deceive the Church, and, in effect, present *"another Jesus,"* and *"another spirit,"* and *"another gospel"* (II Cor. 11:4). In fact, this has always been, even as it was in Paul's day, but it will be taken to a new level in these last days.

The point I'm making is this: no good at all will come of this proclamation of *"another Jesus,"* but only harm, and great harm at that. In fact, millions will be, and in fact, are being led astray. The end result will be eternal damnation. I do not want to leave the impression that no one at this particular time is preaching the Gospel. In fact, there are men and women of God who are touched by the Lord, anointed by the Lord, and are preaching the Word straight and true. However, that number is few and will become less and less all the time.

There was a day that one knew pretty much what was taught as it regarded the name of the Church on the door; however, that day has long since passed. In other words, it is virtually impossible to tell what is preached behind a pulpit according to the name of the Denomination, etc. Consequently, if the individual is looking to a Denomination to lead them, most will be led astray. Every Believer is going to have to make his personal Calling and Election sure. He is going to have to weigh very carefully what he hears, matching it up with the Word of God. In fact, if he does not know the Word of God as he should, he will be led astray. It's just that simple!

This situation of apostasy is not going to get better but rather worse. In fact, the Bible does not really teach a *"Revival"* for the last days, even though it *does* teach an outpouring of the Holy Spirit (Acts 2:17-21). Instead of Revival, it actually teaches a *"falling away,"* which means a departure from Truth (II Thess. 2:3-12).

The pouring out of the Holy Spirit refers to those who truly want to live for God and are attempting with all their heart, soul, and spirit, to live for Him and serve Him. The Holy Spirit will move mightily upon these individuals, whomever they might be; however, as it regards last day Revival, which refers to the Church being revived, meaning that it will go back to the Standards of Righteousness, which are all wrapped up in the Cross of Christ, this the Bible does not necessarily teach.

So, Preachers and Teachers who function in this apostasy, and there will be many even the majority, will not have anything good for anybody. In other words, what they teach is wholly wrong, and will, therefore, bring about its intended result, which is destruction.

(19) "FOR I KNOW THAT THIS SHALL TURN TO MY SALVATION THROUGH YOUR PRAYER, AND THE SUPPLY OF THE SPIRIT OF JESUS CHRIST,"

There is a difference of opinion among Scholars as to what Paul is speaking about in this particular Passage, whether Salvation in general or deliverance from prison, etc. I think the following statements hopefully will make it clear as to what the Apostle is saying here.

DELIVERANCE

The phrase, *"For I know that this shall turn to my Salvation through your prayer,"* should have been translated *"deliverance,"* for the Greek word is *"soteria,"* speaking of the latter.

He is importuning the Philippians as well as all other of the Churches to pray for him as it regards this all-important aspect of his Ministry. As he will say in the following Passages, he has no personal desire in the situation, wanting only what the Lord wants. But it seems that the Holy Spirit has informed him that he will soon be set free. His Ministry is not finished yet as it regards the Churches, therefore, the Lord will grant his release.

This tells us that Caesar or no other man, dominates things, but rather the Lord. To which we have already alluded, the Church has been given the tremendous privilege of entering into the great Work and Plan of God and helping to bring things to pass. Consequently, whenever Believers begin to pray about certain things, as they have Faith in this respect, certain things take place in the spirit world, with Satan then being defeated.

Satan, no doubt, wanted Paul dead, but of course that would not happen until his work had been finished. From the way the Apostle describes the situation, even though tremendous good had been accomplished for the Cause of Christ during his imprisonment, with doors being opened which would not have been opened otherwise, that now being finished, the Lord desires to move Paul back into the arena of the Churches.

The manner in which Paul uses this particular phrase, *"For I know that this shall turn to my Deliverance,"* is very similar to a quotation from Job 13:16. As well, Philippians 2:12-15 is very close to the final injunctions of Moses to the Israelites (Deut. Chpt. 31), and may indicate a comparison with Moses also. If such speculation is justifiable, Paul is encouraging himself in the Lord (I Sam. 30:6) by considering this similar lot of the Saints of whom he has read in the Old Testament Scriptures. In so doing he is able to see the uses of adversity (Knight).

THE SUPPLY OF THE SPIRIT

The phrase, *"And the supply of the Spirit of Jesus Christ,"* refers to the Holy Spirit, Who proceeds from both the Father and the Son (Acts 16:7; Rom. 8:9; Gal. 4:6).

"Supply" in the Greek is "epichoregis," and means "bountiful supply." The idea is, that Paul's deliverance will be affected by the "resources of the Spirit," Who will "furnish all that is necessary." He will not only initially supply Grace, but will continue to dispense sufficient Grace as the need arises. The expression "Spirit of Jesus" is found only here in the New Testament. As stated, similar expressions make it clear that the reference is to the Holy Spirit (Acts 5:9; 16:7; Rom. 8:9; I Cor. 12:4; II Cor. 3:17; Gal. 4:6).

Whether the Spirit is the supply or brings the supply makes little difference. Lightfoot is probably right in saying, *"The 'Spirit of Jesus,' i.e., the Holy Spirit, is both the Giver and Gift,"* but through Jesus and what He did.

It is clear that the basis of the triumph is through the prayers of the Philippians and *"the supply of the Spirit of Jesus Christ."* The indication is that both are necessary. In the Greek Text there is only one preposition which ties together *"prayer"* and *"supply."* As their prayers go up, the supply of the Spirit comes down. Their prayers and God's Grace are like *"two buckets in a well; while one ascends the other descends."*

WHY DOES PAUL USE THE PHRASE "THE SPIRIT OF JESUS CHRIST," INASMUCH AS HE IS REFERRING TO THE HOLY SPIRIT?

The Name of Christ used in any capacity always has some specialty of emphasis. Thus here, the whole conception of the Passage is of Christ, hence the use of this special and comparatively rare name of the Holy Spirit.

It is used in this manner first of all because this is the way the Holy Spirit desired that it be used. Everything that the Believer has from God, and in whatever capacity, is given to us through and by the Holy Spirit. He Alone carries out the Plan of the Godhead on Earth. However, the following is the important point:

Everything He does, all the work He performs, every blessing He brings, all the work of Salvation, the infilling of the Spirit, Divine Healing, Victory in our everyday walk, leading and guidance in every capacity — all and without exception, are brought to us through the Atoning Work of Christ on the Cross. It is what Jesus did at the Cross and the Resurrection which makes possible all the work of the Holy Spirit on our behalf. In fact, He does nothing for us or to us, other than through the Finished Work of Christ (Rom. 8:2). This must never be forgotten, hence Paul giving us this Name of the Holy Spirit in this fashion.

While it is certainly true, even as we have already stated, that the Holy Spirit proceeds from both the Father and the Son, still, far more is said here in the Name used by Paul, than a matter of mere procession.

HOW THIS AFFECTS THE BELIEVER

Consequently, it is extremely important that the Believer understand these things of which we say. In fact, if the Believer does not understand that the secret of his victory, his life, and in fact, all that he has from God, is found entirely in the Atonement, and his Faith in that great work — if that is not understood, and understood properly, even though the Believer may be Baptized with the Holy Spirit, the Third Person of the Godhead will be able to do relatively little in the Believer's life. In other words, our Faith must always be in that which Christ did at the Cross and the Resurrection. Our Faith must not stray from that Finished Work; our Faith must anchor itself there and remain there, that is if we are to experience the Work of the Holy Spirit in our hearts and lives.

THE HOLY SPIRIT IS THE ONE WHO MAKES REAL THE BENEFITS OF THE ATONEMENT

As we've already stated, the Spirit of God is the One Who brings to us all the great things of the Godhead, which basically refers to all that which Jesus has done at the Cross. He Alone guarantees the benefits of the Finished Work, the resources of the Atonement, in fact, all that for which Jesus died. Let the Reader always understand, that all that of which Jesus did on our behalf, in effect, intending that we have that for which He paid such a price, is brought to us and guaranteed to us by the Holy Spirit (Rom. 8:2). However, He functions and works only according to our Faith being rightly and Scripturally placed in the Finished Work of Christ.

Most Believers think that the Work of the Spirit is automatic. In other words, He just does what He's going to do, irrespective, once the Believer is baptized with the Spirit. Nothing could be further from the Truth.

In fact, most Spirit-filled Christians receive very little of what He can actually do within their lives. The reason is, our Faith is misplaced, which actually means that we are depending on *"self,"* whether we realize it or not, in which the Holy Spirit will not work, and in fact cannot work.

WHY IS FAITH PROPERLY PLACED SO IMPORTANT?

To be sure it is very important, actually the single most important thing there is. Let's look at it in this manner:

If the sinner's Faith is misplaced, in other words, he is trusting in anything else other than what Jesus did on the Cross as it regards his Salvation, he simply cannot be saved. It doesn't matter what he does, how many Churches he joins, or how many good works he performs, he cannot be saved unless his Faith is solely in Christ and more particularly what Christ did on the Cross (Jn. 3:16). To be sure, he may not understand much about it, and in fact, does not understand much about it, but God does demand that his Faith, as little as it might be, be placed in the fact that Jesus died for him. It is imperative that the sinner believe this if he is to be saved (Rom. 10:9-10, 13; Eph. 2:8-9; Rev. 22:17).

Most Christians will agree with that which we have just said. However, what they don't seem to realize is that this same Faith must be carried over into the Believer's life as well, and we speak of Faith being squarely in the Cross. This is the only road to victory over the world, the flesh, and the Devil. The Holy Spirit, according to what Paul said in Romans Chapter 8, will work on no other premise.

Why?

Anything that the sinner attempts to do to bring about his Salvation other than having Faith in the Finished Work of Christ, aborts Salvation, for the simple reason that the sinner cannot save himself. As well, he cannot contribute anything toward his Salvation. Furthermore, he doesn't need to, because Jesus paid it all.

NOTES

Likewise, when the Christian attempts to bring about Victory within his life through his own efforts in any capacity, he is, in effect, doing the same thing that the sinner does in trying to be saved through good works, etc. In other words, he is trying to effect his Victory through his own machinations, his own efforts, his own ability, which are impossible. He cannot make himself victorious by his own efforts, anymore than the sinner can save himself.

Furthermore, he doesn't need to, because again, Jesus paid it all. The Work that He did was not partial but complete. He is today *"sat down"* at the Throne of God, meaning that His Work is total and complete (Eph. 2:6; Heb. 1:3; 10:12).

When Jesus died on the Cross, He atoned for every sin, defeated every demon and Satan himself, satisfied every demand of God, in other words, totally and absolutely completed the work of Redemption. Consequently, for us to try to add to that work, for that's exactly what we're doing, when we attempt to bring about things from God by our own efforts, in effect, says that Jesus didn't do it all, and we must add to that which He has done. Consequently, we are insulting Christ whether we realize it or not.

WHAT EXACTLY IS THE BELIEVER TO DO?

The only thing the Believer is to do, as it regards anything he needs from the Lord, is to simply exercise Faith in that which Christ has already done. We are to furnish a *"willing mind"* (Rev. 22:17), and an *"obedient heart"* (II Cor. 10:5; Heb. 5:8; I Pet. 1:2).

The Believer must *"will"* to have the things of God, and at the same time must be *"obedient,"* which means to place our Faith in the Finished Work of Christ, and to leave our Faith there.

The Reader may think that I stress these great Truths too much and too often, especially in our Commentary on Ephesians and this Epistle; however, if something is out of balance, then greater pressure must be applied to bring things into proper balance. The Church is out of balance in that it has had almost no Preaching and Teaching on the Cross in the last several decades. As a result, the Church has pretty much lost its moorings. The Devil has been very successful in having

Believers place their Faith in that other than the Cross, which he knows will bring about no positive spiritual results. In fact, he doesn't care how much we evidence Faith in other directions, as long as it's not in the Finished Work of Christ. The Truth is, we're not going to receive anything worthwhile in other directions, and he knows that. So, he will fight the Cross, fight our dependence on the Cross, fight our Faith in the Cross, as he opposes nothing else.

I believe the Lord has given me this Revelation as it regards the Cross and the Resurrection not only for my own personal benefit, but as well, for the benefit of the entirety of the Body of Christ. To be sure, this is not a new Revelation, actually being the very foundation of the Church. But the Church, sadly and regrettably, has been moved away from its proper foundation.

Since about 1970, the Church has heard more about Faith than perhaps all the other centuries put together; however, for the most part, in fact almost altogether, it's been Faith in that other than the Finished Work of Christ. Consequently, as ought to be obvious, it has not led people closer to the Lord, but actually further away from the Lord. While some small amount of this teaching has been good the greater part has been altogether the opposite.

The reason?

FAITH IN THE CROSS

As stated, the reason is because it's not Faith properly placed in the Cross, and thereby holds no validity, irrespective of the claims that it is Faith in the Word. The Truth is, it is Faith in the Word of God pulled out of its proper context. Everything must evolve around and center upon the Cross of Christ. If it doesn't, it's not legitimate, irrespective of the claims. To be a little blunt, it is what one might call *"a bastard faith!"*

I believe that's at least one of the reasons why these Commentaries are so very important. No, I do not mean important as far as I am concerned, or my efforts, but rather the great Truths contained as given by the Holy Spirit.

In November of 1991 (I believe it was), the Lord graphically spoke to my heart. It was a Sunday Morning Service at Family Worship Center. This is what He said to me:

"This sickness is not unto death, but for the Glory of God, that the Son of God might be glorified thereby" (Jn. 11:4).

I had no doubt that it was the Lord speaking to me, and in fact, at that moment I didn't even really know if this was Scripture, but found out that it was when I looked it up after the Service.

I will not go into any detail as it regards the statement except to say the following:

The Lord never gets any glory out of sin, but He definitely does get glory out of victory over sin. In this context, this which the Lord has shown me as it regards the Source of Victory and the Way of Victory, which is the Cross, will bring great Glory to the Lord as this great Truth is given to the Body of Christ. Again I emphasize, this is not new, but rather the basic foundation of Christianity, but yet a foundation which the majority of the Church has presently lost.

If that is in fact the case, then all the suffering I have gone through, all the deep and bitter humiliation, for which I blame no one but myself, will not have been in vain. In other words, the Lord will get, even as He is getting, great praise and glory out of this Victory that He has brought about.

WILL THE CHURCH ACCEPT IT?

Some will!

However, that's not my basic concern. My task is to do everything I can do to get this word to every Believer in the whole world. I believe the Lord is going to help us to do this, in fact, He has already begun.

The Truth is, many will deny these things I say, claiming that it is only an excuse for failure. In fact, such accusations have already begun; however, that is not my problem but rather theirs. My task, as stated, is to proclaim the great Truth of the Word of God as it regards the Cross of Christ. Some will hear, even many! As a result, their lives will be eternally changed and a thousand times for the better. They will finally experience what Jesus was talking about when He said that we would have *"more abundant life"* (Jn. 10:10). I prefer to dwell on those individuals, the ones who are seeking Victory, and will find it in that which the Lord so graciously did nearly 2,000 years ago. This and this alone is *"the supply of the Spirit of Jesus Christ,"* and what a *"supply"* it is!

(20) "ACCORDING TO MY EARNEST EXPECTATION AND MY HOPE, THAT IN NOTHING I SHALL BE ASHAMED, BUT THAT WITH ALL BOLDNESS, AS ALWAYS, SO NOW ALSO CHRIST SHALL BE MAGNIFIED IN MY BODY, WHETHER IT BE BY LIFE, OR BY DEATH."

In this time of waiting for the settlement of his case, Paul had a well-founded hope that he would *"in no way be ashamed."* This is a broad statement referring first to his appearance before the authorities for the final disposition of his case. There may also be overtones of his ultimate appearance before Christ, because he speaks of the possibility of death and of the advantage of being with Christ. He has the confident hope that he will continue to maintain the sort of courage characteristic of his ministry in the past. The Apostle was not relying on his own courage, but on the action of the Holy Spirit Who would produce this result in response to his own prayers and those of the Philippians on his behalf.

As stated, I do not think that these statements given in this Verse should serve as a foundation for indecisiveness on the part of Paul regarding his future. While it is certainly possible that he at this time did not know what the outcome would be, still, I personally feel from what he says in the 25th Verse, that the Lord had told him that he would be released shortly.

EARNEST EXPECTATION

The phrase, *"According to my earnest expectation and my hope,"* describes a person with head erect and outstretched, whose attention is turned away from all other objects and riveted upon just one.

The word is used in the Greek classics of the watchman who peered into the darkness, eagerly looking for the first gleam of the distant beacon which would announce the capture of Troy. It is that concentrated, intense hope which ignores other interests and strains forward as with outstretched head, that was Paul's attitude of heart.

Once again, not intimating at all that Paul was fearful of dying, which this very Scripture proclaims the opposite, still, the words *"earnest expectation"* and *"hope,"* point toward his release. Most expositors deny this; however, Verses 19, 25 and 26 bear this out, I think.

As would be overly obvious, all of this was extremely important. Due to the fact that the Lord had allowed the Apostle to be locked up for several years, may have caused him to surmise that quite possibly his work was finished. But yet in his heart, according to that which he will say in later Verses, he doesn't think so. I have every confidence that he sought the Lord earnestly about this, as would anyone. I also feel that the Holy Spirit answered his prayers, telling him that his work was not yet finished, and that he would be restored to the Church.

Most think that Paul continued for another approximate six years after this, of which we have little record. Second Timothy is the last Epistle he wrote shortly before his death. He had been arrested again, and this time placed in the Mammertine Prison in Rome, which was notorious to say the least. In fact, tradition says that his cell was actually a cell beneath a cell. In other words, to be taken out of this particular cell, which he was when he was executed, a rope had to be lowered down through a trap door in the ceiling, fastened about him, and then him pulled up. Thus, did the great Apostle then go home to be with the Lord. But now, he will be released.

NO SHAME

The phrase, *"That in nothing I shall be ashamed,"* refers to the fact that in case he is wrong about that which he feels the Lord has spoken to his heart, namely his release, and in fact, that he will be executed, that at that time, he will conduct himself exactly as he should. He is confident that he will.

In this, we are allowed to see into the heart of the great Apostle. He doesn't take the Lord or himself for granted, for that matter! He feels that he knows what the Lord has in store for him; but irrespective as to which way it goes, he must hold up Christ unto the end, and do so in dignity and power. This is all that matters. Other things are of no consequence. It is only Christ! Only Christ! Only Christ!

BOLDNESS

The phrase, *"But that with all boldness,"* refers to the fact of lifting up Christ, irrespective of the circumstances or the outcome. He wanted to make certain that his voice would be strong in any case, his determination as resolute as ever, his proclamation of Christ unwavering.

It also has to do with his possible appearance before Nero, that is if such actually took place, and there is some evidence that it did. Paul later said, *"Notwithstanding the Lord stood with me, and strengthened me; that by me the preaching might be fully known, and that all the Gentiles might hear: and I was delivered out of the mouth of the lion"* (II Tim. 4:17).

Many scholars think the statement, *"mouth of the lion"* referred to Nero!

At any rate, he wanted to be bold as it regarded Christ and his testimony of the Saviour, whatever the situation might be.

CHRIST IS MAGNIFIED

The phrase, *"So now also Christ shall be magnified in my body, whether it be by life, or by death,"* proclaims the fact of Paul's desire that the Lord Jesus might be seen in his life in all His beauty, that He might be conspicuous, that He might get glory and praise to Himself through the Apostle.

If it is to be noticed, Paul does *not* say, *"I shall magnify Christ,"* but *"Christ shall be magnified."* His body will be the *"theater in which Christ's glory is displayed"* (Rom. 12:1; 6:13).

Paul uses the word *"body,"* simply because it is this part of the human being where all desires, i.e., *"faith or fear"* are carried out. The body and the five senses are the vehicles. It is the part of the human being through which Satan carries out his schemes, and as well, that through which the Lord works, even as proclaimed here by Paul. For the Christian the *"body"* is to be a *"living Sacrifice, holy, acceptable unto God, which is our reasonable service"* (Rom. 12:1). In effect, it could be a *"living Sacrifice,"* which is evidenced by *"life,"* or it could be an *"offered Sacrifice,"* which is referred to here by Paul as *"death."* Either way, it was to be a *"Sacrifice!"*

NOTES

(21) "FOR TO ME TO LIVE IS CHRIST, AND TO DIE IS GAIN."

"For to me" is placed in the emphatic position, stressing the fact that Paul's own Faith was unshaken, regardless of the circumstances. No adverse decision from the Court nor the alarm of his friends could alter his firm belief about his present or his future.

The very essence of Paul's present life was Christ and all that this entailed. From the theological fact that Paul was identified with Christ in a vital spiritual union (Gal. 2:20) issued far-reaching practical implications. Christ had become for him the Motive of his actions, the Goal of his life and ministry, the Source of his strength.

"To die" after such a life could only mean *"gain."* Not only would Paul's state after death bring gain, inasmuch as he would be with Christ, but the act itself of dying at the hands of Rome was no tragedy in Paul's eyes. Such a death would bear added witness to the Gospel; it would confirm that Paul's Faith was steadfast to the end, and it would serve as the gateway to Christ's Presence (Kent).

TO LIVE IS CHRIST

The phrase, *"For to me to live is Christ,"* is proclaimed more fully in Colossians 3:4, *"Christ, our Life."*

Christ is Paul's life in that He is that Eternal Life which Paul received at Salvation, a life which is ethical in its content, and which operates in Paul as a motivating, energizing, pulsating principle of existence that transforms Paul's life, a Divine Person living His life in and through the Apostle. All of Paul's activities, all of his interests, the entire round of his existence is ensphered within that circumference which is Christ.

THE WORK OF CHRIST

As well, the statement refers to the Work of Christ. The idea is, which is obvious, Paul could be of more service to Christ regarding the Church if he were alive than otherwise. He could continue to preach Christ, uphold Christ, and proclaim Christ as the answer to the ills of humanity.

Paul's aim was not honor, learning, gold, pleasure, etc.; it was to glorify the Lord Jesus. This was the single purpose of his soul — a purpose to which he devoted himself with as much singleness and ardor as ever did a miser in the pursuit of gold, or a devotee of pleasure to amusement, or an aspirant for fame to ambition. All of this implied the following things:

1. A purpose to know as much of Christ as it was possible to know — to become as fully acquainted as he could with His Rank, His Character, His Plans, with the relations which He sustained to the Father, and with the claims and influences of His Salvation (Jn. 17:3; Eph. 3:19; Phil. 3:10).

2. A purpose to imitate Christ — to make Him the model of his life. It was a design that His Spirit should reign in his heart, that this same temper should actuate him, and that the same great end should be constantly had in view.

3. A purpose to make the Salvation of Christ known, as far as possible, among mankind. To this Paul seriously gave his life, and devoted his great talents. His aim was to see on how many minds he could impress the sentiments of Christ; to see to how many of the human family he could make Christ known, to whom He was unknown before.

Never was there a man who gave himself with more ardor to any enterprise, than Paul did to this; and never was one more successful, in any undertaking, than he was in this.

4. It was his purpose as well to enjoy Christ. He drew his comforts from Him. His happiness he found in communion with Him. It was not in the works of art; not in the pursuits of elegant literature; not in the fashionable world; but it was in communion with the Saviour, and in endeavoring to please Him.

THE RESULTS

Paul never had occasion, as we see from his words here, to regret this course. It produced no sadness when he looked over his life. He never felt that he had an unworthy aim of living; he did not wish that his purpose had been different when he came to die.

Thus, if it was Paul's duty to live, it is no less that of every Christian. What was there in his case that made it his duty to *"live unto Christ,"* which does not exist in the case of every sincere Christian on Earth? No Believer, when he comes to die, will regret that he has lived unto Christ; but how many, alas, regret that this has not been the aim and purpose of their souls!

DEATH

The phrase, *"And to die is gain,"* should have been translated *"To have died."* The tense denotes, not the act of dying, but the consequences of dying, the state after death.

Death itself would not be a gain to Paul, as it is not really a gain to anyone, but to be in the Presence of His Lord in Glory, that would be gain. This is what the Apostle means!

How is this transition a gain?

"Gain" in the Greek is used to describe interest on money. Thus, to the Christian to die is to cash in both principal and interest and to have more of Christ than when living.

Maclaren comments beautifully on this Passage: *"It matters very little to the servant whether he is out in the cold and wet 'ploughing and tending cattle,' or whether he is waiting on his master at the table. It is service all the same, only it is warmer and lighter in the house than in the field, and it is promotion to be made 'an indoor servant.'"*

At death, the Child of God is made *"an indoor servant."*

No right-thinking Christian wants to die, and neither is that the wish of Paul as well. In fact, death is an enemy. It was not in the original Plan of God, and one day will be eliminated forever (I Cor. 15:54-55). Nevertheless, death holds no terror or fear for the true Christian. In fact, the only real reason for living for the Christian, even as Paul will say, is to carry out the Work of God on Earth. Of course, and as would be obvious, this is extremely important. That's the reason the Scripture says, *"Precious in the sight of the Lord is the death of His Saints"* (Ps. 116:15).

"Precious" in the Hebrew means *"costly!"* In other words, due to the fact that the only light in this world is that of the Saints, costly is their death (Mat. 5:13-16).

SO, WHAT ARE THE ADVANTAGES?

1. At death, the Child of God is freed from all possibility of sin. Here, it is the source of perpetual humiliation and sorrow; in Heaven, we will sin no more, neither will it be possible to sin.

2. With Christ, we will be *"free from all doubts"* in any and every capacity. Here, the best are liable to doubts about their personal consecration, and often experience anxious hours in reference to this point; in Heaven, doubt will be known no more.

3. We will be free from all temptation. Here, no one knows when he may be tempted, nor how powerful the temptation may be; in Heaven, there will be no allurement to lead one astray; no artful, cunning, and skillful votaries of pleasure to place inducements before the Believer to sin; and no heart to yield to them, if there were.

4. The Child of God will then be delivered from all his enemies — from the slanderer, the calumniator, the persecutor. Here, the Christian is constantly liable to have his motives called in question, or to be met with detraction and slander; there, there will be none to do him injustice; all will rejoice in the belief that he is pure.

5. He will be delivered from all suffering. Here, the Christian is constantly liable to it; his health fails, his friends die, his mind is sad. There, there shall be no separation of friends, no sickness, and no tears.

6. There, and we speak of Heaven, will be no death. Here, death is ever nigh — dreadful, alarming, terrible to our nature. As stated, it is an enemy. There, death will be known no more. No face will ever turn pale, and no knees tremble at his approach; in all Heaven there will never be seen a funeral procession, nor will the soil there ever open its bosom to furnish a grave.

7. To all this may be added the fact, that the Christian will be with Christ, and that is the greatest gift of all! To be in His Very Presence, to look upon His Face, to enjoy the overflowing life that proceeds from Him constantly, is the greatest of all Blessings, the most wondrous of all Blessings!

Everything we have named will be wonderful, plus a thousand things we have not named; however, all the other Blessings, the other things of grandness and glory, will all pale into insignificance up beside the Presence of Christ. *"To be with Christ,"* as Paul will say, *"is far better."* That is the *"gain!"*

(22) "BUT IF I LIVE IN THE FLESH, THIS IS THE FRUIT OF MY LABOUR: YET WHAT I SHALL CHOOSE I WOT NOT."

NOTES

Nevertheless, if he should continue to live as a result of a favorable disposition of his case in Rome, which he feels he shall, this would provide continued opportunity for him to labor fruitfully in the Cause of Christ.

For Paul this never meant an easy life. His labors in establishing Churches and nurturing them toward maturity were characterized by frequent opposition, physical hardships, and much spiritual anguish. Yet he looked on his Apostolic Ministry as a challenge to be grasped and as a fruit to be harvested.

The evidence is, that Paul was so positively committed to the Will of God that both life and death held certain attractions. If the choice were left to him, he would not know what to decide. How fortunate that God does not force us to make such choices!

TO LIVE IN THE FLESH

The phrase, *"But if I live in the flesh,"* refers to the idea that if he is right about what he thinks the Lord has told him as it regards being released from imprisonment, then his Ministry will continue, which in fact it did. As stated, it is believed that he was given about six more years of ministry among the Churches before he was finally executed by Nero.

The phrase, *"In the flesh,"* is interesting, in that it proclaims the very opposite of that which is in Heaven.

The physical body, which was originally created by God to live forever, suffered a terrible debilitation at the Fall. As a result, that which was intended to live forever, ultimately ages and dies. The moment the Saint of God dies, the soul and the spirit instantly go to be with the Lord Jesus in Heaven, there to await the coming Resurrection, where the soul and the spirit will be united with a glorified body. Paul explained all of this in I Corinthians Chapter 15.

The soul and the spirit are referred to in the Bible as the *"inner man"* (Eph. 3:16). If one were to see the form of the soul and the spirit at this present time as it resides in Glory, the person would be recognizable, just as Moses was recognizable to Peter, James, and John, when he appeared with Elijah on the Mount of Transfiguration (Mat. 17:1-3). (Strangely enough, Elijah was still in his physical body, for he had never died, having been originally translated, II Ki. 2:11.) Both Moses and Elijah were recognizable, even though the physical body of Moses had by that time been dead for about 1500 years, and Elijah had been translated about 900 years before. (Both men had been in Paradise.)

And yet, neither man will be complete until the Resurrection, when both, as well as every other Believer who has ever lived, will receive a glorified body. Paul likened this state of coming glorification as being as much improved over the present state, as an adult over a little child as it regards intellect and knowledge, etc. (I Cor. 13:8-12).

So when Paul speaks of continuing to *"live in the flesh,"* he has in mind the entire scope of all that Jesus has done as it regards Eternal Life, and more particularly, that which is to come. At the present time, Believers only enjoy part of the fruits of the Atonement. At the Resurrection all of that which Jesus purchased by His Death on the Cross will be given to the Child of God (Rom. 8:19-25).

FRUIT OF MY LABOR

The phrase, *"This is the fruit of my labour,"* refers to the fact that Paul's continued ministry, will result in being most fruitful for the Philippian Saints, and for all Believers for that matter.

Paul's labor for the Lord was the only thing that mattered. It should be the only thing that matters for us as well.

The layman makes a great mistake if he or she thinks that such consecration involves itself only with Preachers, etc. The truth is, every single Believer, and irrespective as to whom that Believer might be, should understand that while he might do certain things to make a living for his family, above all, his life must be spent in the Cause of Christ. Jesus must come first. God's Work must come first.

If God blesses the person with large sums of money, that money should be used to take the Gospel to the world. If God has given talents to a particular person, those talents should be used to further the Cause of Christ. Once again, if we as Christians devote all of our time and attention to temporal things, giving our thoughts to God only in a limited way, we are greatly shortchanging ourselves.

NOTES

This life is very temporal while the one to come is eternal. Consequently, we should make no efforts to *"lay up for ourselves treasures upon earth, where moth and rust doth corrupt, and where thieves break through and steal."*

But rather, we must *"lay up for ourselves treasures in Heaven, where neither moth nor rust doth corrupt, and where thieves do not break through nor steal."*

Then Jesus said, *"For where your treasure is, there will your heart be also"* (Mat. 6:19-21).

And finally, *"No man can serve two masters"* (Mat. 6:24).

That's the problem with Christians, we attempt to serve two masters. We must first of all *"seek the Kingdom of God and His Righteousness,"* and then we don't have to worry. The Lord plainly said if this is done, *"all these* (other) *things shall be added unto you"* (Mat. 6:33).

WHAT IS THE FRUIT OF OUR LABOR?

For that question to properly be answered, we have to ask as to what actually is our *"labor."*

I don't want to leave the impression that I'm saying it's wrong for a Christian to be blessed financially or even to be rich. One should not seek riches (I Tim. 6:11), but if God sees fit to bestow such on one, there is nothing wrong with that. However, the individual in such a case, should seek first the Kingdom of God. The Lord's Work must be on his or her mind at all times. We should labor in that respect.

Every Believer must understand, that when we stand at the Judgment Seat of Christ, which every Believer will do, we are going to have to give an account for our lives, our money, our motives, our consecration or the lack thereof, in other words, our stewardship. Just what was our labor? Was it for God or was it for *"mammon"*?

It grieves me when I see Christian businessmen devote all their time and attention to these temporal things, which might seem to be very important at the present, but when compared with eternity, lose their lustre. Of course, time and attention have to be paid to earthly pursuits. That is understandable. In fact, the Lord will give us the proper wisdom to do all the things we need to do if we will only seek His Face accordingly. The idea is, that God always be first in everything. And that means not merely in word, but in action and deed also.

LET ME GIVE A PERSONAL EXAMPLE

A few months ago (at the beginning of 1999), the Lord spoke to my heart concerning the spread of the Gospel in the U.S.A. by Radio. I'm not speaking of a particular Radio program which we had many years ago, but rather individual stations airing the Gospel from Family Worship Center 24 hours a day, seven days a week. We have tapes of all the Services, which include all the Messages and Worship, etc. In fact, these tapes go back several years.

The Lord instructed me to place this on our Stations instead of the programming we presently had, which we immediately began to do. The results have been, and are, phenomenal. As well, the Lord told me to fill the nation with this of which I have just described.

We immediately set about to secure translator Stations from the F.C.C. These are small F.M. Stations which cover a radius of approximately 20 miles, ten miles in any direction. Some are a little more than that and some are a little less.

As well, we have begun (at this writing) to attempt to secure A.M. Stations as well, which we can purchase considerably cheaper than regular commercial F.M. Stations.

As I dictate these notes, we have just begun this endeavor, which I know the Lord is going to greatly bless. Of course this is in conjunction with our Telecast that is presently aired in about 30 countries of the world, actually translated into several languages.

The Radio Programming is extremely significant in its own right for the simple reason that it's 24 hours a day. As well, it is one particular Ministry which carries the same spirit and the same doctrine which is far less confusing to people. In other words, not only is sound doctrine put into the homes of Believers or unbelievers for that matter, but as well the Moving and Operation of the Holy Spirit accompanies this which is a great blessing to the people. So it serves several purposes:

Gospel preaching under the anointing of the Holy Spirit brings people to Christ. In other words, sinners get saved. As well, Believers are also given an opportunity to be baptized with the Holy Spirit, as those particular type Messages are preached as well. Of course I'm speaking of those who have not yet been filled.

Also, teaching goes forth constantly from the Word of God which grounds Believers in the Faith, which is extremely important, considering that this is the age of apostasy, which refers to a departure from Truth.

As well, the worship that the music provides is absolutely phenomenal, and I can say that because I'm not extolling our efforts, but rather the Moving and Operation of the Holy Spirit.

Unfortunately, in all of this, there is a constant struggle to find the finances to get all of this done. And yet, there are many Christians whom the Lord has greatly blessed with abundant financial resources, but many of them are loathe to part with very much of those resources, even for the Work of God. Thank God for the few who are generous, but sadly, most aren't, and despite the fact, that the Lord has been so good to them.

The point is, there is plenty of money to do the Work of God many times over all around the world; however, Satan has been very successful in causing many Christians who have these funds, to be very miserly with their giving. As well, he has deceived many Christians into supporting that which is really not doing the Work of God, but in reality the very opposite. In that case their money is wasted. In fact, he not only does not hinder those efforts, but actually aids and abets them; however, and to be sure, he opposes in the strongest way possible that which is truly of God, and which truly reaps results for the Kingdom of God. Unfortunately, not all Christians are able to properly discern that of which I speak.

Treasures are laid up in Heaven only in the capacity of that which is truly of God. God can never bless that which may look like Him, and even act like Him, but in reality is not Him. I speak of that which masquerades as an *"Angel of Light,"* but in reality is the Devil (II Cor. 11:12-15).

Once again I ask the question, *"What is the fruit of your labor?"*

If that *"fruit"* is not souls saved, Believers baptized with the Holy Spirit, bondages of darkness broken, and the development of Christian hearts and lives, then it's the wrong kind of fruit.

THE CHOICE

The phrase, *"Yet what I shall choose I wot not,"* actually means, that if he had his choice, he is not certain which he would choose — to remain here longer, or to go on to be with Christ, even as he will say in the next Verse.

The idea is, that the true Christian, one who is truly sold out to the Lord, can hesitate only in the choice of blessings; disappointed in either case, he cannot be. Isn't that beautiful!

Emotionally, Paul was strained between two poles. His love for Christ was such that he longed to be in His Presence, the sooner the better. At the same time, his sense of mission, and his concern for the Church and for the furtherance of the Gospel made him feel that his work was not yet done.

With a hope of rendering further help to the cause, he wanted to stay and be permitted to labor on. This is one of the most intimate pictures we have of the inner struggles of the great Apostle. Paul could stare death in the face and be unperturbed. After further reflection, however, he came to the conclusion that it would be best for all concerned for him to remain in the flesh for a few years longer.

"Choose" in the Greek is *"haireomai,"* and means *"to take for oneself, to prefer."*

Paul is not speaking here of the Will of God, but only in the matter of personal preference. However, anything and everything he did, as far as the final choice was concerned, was always and without exception, predicated on the Will of God. He is speaking here of himself and his personal likes and dislikes. He is in essence saying, *"If I had to make a choice right now as to what to do, I'm not sure exactly what that choice would be. There are great pluses on both sides."* The idea is this:

With a firm foundation of this nature, with both feet planted solidly on that particular foundation, there is really nothing Satan can do to such a person that will greatly hinder them. Death holds no terror, actually only a promotion. So, what can Satan actually do to such a person! Consequently, this is the greatest life that one could ever live, this life in Christ, this life of Christ, and this life for Christ!

(23) "FOR I AM IN A STRAIT BETWIXT TWO, HAVING A DESIRE TO DEPART, AND TO BE WITH CHRIST; WHICH IS FAR BETTER:"

Incidentally, Paul does not mention here soul-sleep while awaiting the Resurrection, nor Purgatory, as taught by some. As he had already explained to the Corinthians, absence from the body means for the Believer to be immediately present with the Lord (II Cor. 5:8).

Regarding the choices on a personal basis, there was no question in Paul's mind as to the ultimate superiority of this. It was *"better by far,"* because it would bring him to the goal of his Christian life. It would bring rest from his laborers and joy of eternal fellowship in the very Presence of the Lord Whom he loved so much.

A STRAIT BETWEEN TWO

The phrase, *"For I am in a strait betwixt two,"* refers to equal pressure being exerted from both sides. It was the desire for continued life and ministry and the desire to be with Christ.

The word *"strait"* is a strong word, actually meaning *"to be pressed on or constrained, so as not to know what to do."* The actual idea is this:

The Apostle even as he will say in the last phrase of this Verse, actually wanted to go on and be with Christ; however, he knew how much he was needed as it regarded the Churches and the Work of God in general. No, it was not a matter of conceit. That's not the idea at all. It was a simple fact, as should be overly obvious.

The life of the Apostle was not easy, to say the least. It was a constant struggle, a constant battle with the powers of darkness, as it concerned his work for the Lord. I am not speaking of his personal life, which was that of perpetual victory. That's not where the struggle fastened itself, but rather, in his efforts for the Lord to take the Gospel to the world.

He alluded to this graphically so in the 11th Chapter of II Corinthians, even as we have previously stated. Of course, the Lord could have stopped all of these things very easily, but knew that they were necessary in the life of the great Apostle, in order that he might remain humble before the Lord, may always understand that his help and strength came totally from the Lord, and not at all of himself. In other words, even Paul suffered the constant danger of worldly pride and self-will. Consequently, these other things were necessary in order to keep those dangers under control. If that were true of him, and it definitely was, how much more does the Reader think that such is true of us also?

The beatings, stonings, shipwreck, hunger, thirst, etc., were never-ending problems. And then for the last several years, he has been chained to a Roman soldier, most probably, day and night. However, those things, as severe as they were, were not really the reason for Paul's thinking. It was strictly a love for Christ, a desire to be with Christ and all that pertained to Christ.

Paul's conversion had been one of the most startling, dramatic, and miraculous in history. The One Who he had fought so hard, he found to be the True Lord of Glory. I know that Paul never stopped thinking about the Grace of God in that the Lord appeared to him on that road to Damascus, which totally changed his life. He knew that it was the Love of God, the Grace of God, the actual Compassion of the Lord, which did all of this. Had that not happened, Paul would have lived and died and thereby would have gone to an eternal Hell. So his love for Christ, I personally think, was greater than most could begin to imagine, transcending all barriers and personal ambition.

TO BE WITH CHRIST

The phrase, *"Having a desire to depart, and to be with Christ; which is far better,"* adequately explains the true attitude and nature of the heart of the Apostle.

It was not the case of dying. As stated, even as Paul had stated, death is an enemy. It wasn't this life as well, because despite the hardships, the Apostle loved life. I think that is obvious from all his writings.

The centerpiece of all of this is Christ. If one draws any other conclusions, one misses the point entirely. It was his strong love for Christ; his anxious wish to be with Him; his firm belief that in His Presence was *"fullness of joy."*

Paul knew that the soul of the Christian immediately goes to be with the Saviour at death. Of course, this completely debunks the erroneous theory of soul-sleep, or even Purgatory, as stated, with neither of these things actually existing. The soul does not sleep at death. It immediately goes to be with Jesus.

Trying to explain all of this, when the Apostle used the phrase, *"Which is far better,"* the original Greek seems to portray the idea that the Apostle is laboring for the proper terminology to fully convey his idea.

In actuality, Paul was not really speaking of death or even being willing to die. The idea is, that being with Christ is a condition greatly to be preferred to remaining on Earth. This is the true feeling of the true Christian; and, having this feeling, death to us holds no terrors.

"A desire" in the Greek is actually *"the desire,"* suggesting that this is *not* just one among many desires, but rather the primary desire.

"Depart" is a metaphor drawn from the loosing of tent stakes and ropes for breaking camp (II Cor. 5:1; II Tim. 4:6). Such a metaphor provides an appropriate way for Paul, a tentmaker by trade, to describe the departure from this side.

Sometimes it was used to describe the pulling up of anchors and setting sail. Adam Clarke suggests that it was a metaphor drawn from the commander of a vessel, in a foreign port, who wants to set sail for his country, but has not yet had orders from his owner to do so.

Barclay points out that it is also the word used for solving problems. The state that follows death will bring solutions to life's deep riddles (I Cor. 13:12).

As well, the words *"To depart, and to be with Christ,"* are simultaneous. That is, the dead come immediately into the Presence of the Lord. For the Christian, to be absent from the body is to be present with the Lord (Jn. 14:3; II Cor. 5:8).

(Incidentally, the Scriptures which some use to teach soul-sleep actually refer to the body, which alone, sees corruption and goes to the grave. This is clear from an examination of all Passages that speak of the dead knowing nothing in the grave. According to James 2:26, it is the body only that dies; and, therefore, this is the only thing that is put in the grave. The souls of men at death go to either one of two places.)

The soul of all Believers instantly at death go to be with the Lord Jesus Christ (II Cor. 5:8), while the souls of all unbelievers at death instantly go into Hell (Lk. 16:19-31).

(24) "NEVERTHELESS TO ABIDE IN THE FLESH IS MORE NEEDFUL FOR YOU."

Of all people, Paul knew the dangers the Church would face without his presence. Of course, irrespective as to how long the Lord would leave him here, he knew that day would come when he would be taken. Having a great concern for the Church, as would be obvious, he knew how important his Ministry was, especially considering that he was the masterbuilder of the Church under Christ.

NEVERTHELESS

The word *"nevertheless"* tells us that Paul certainly knows that no man lives unto himself. Paul must think of the welfare of his friends at Philippi, plus, of course, all of the Churches. He is willing to forego eternal bliss for earthly service. This is actually the *"Mind of Christ"* which has always characterized the life of the Apostle, at least since his conversion (Rom. 9:3; I Cor. 10:33).

No truer picture of the Christian's understanding of the relation of this world to the other world, of reward and service, could be drawn. Paul's longing is not for death, but for Christ. Death will simply be a doorway into a fuller relationship with Him. In no sense does he consider it an escape from the responsibilities of temporal existence.

The charge that the Christian is so otherworldly as to be concerned only with *"pie in the sky bye and bye"* is a caricature based on a misunderstanding of the Christian Faith. The good of others must always come first, ahead of any personal desires.

TO ABIDE IN THE FLESH

The phrase, *"To abide in the flesh,"* refers to this present earthly life. Once again the Apostle uses the word *"flesh,"* signifying the lesser state of what is ultimately to come.

NOTES

While in a sense, the physical body of the Believer will always be flesh, still, at the coming Resurrection it will be glorified, which will put it into a different state altogether, actually an eternal state.

Presently, the physical body, being but flesh, and unglorified, is dying. In a sense, it is dying from the moment the child is born, i.e., *"The seed of death is in the physical body from birth."* So, now is the lesser state of the Believer, with the coming state, the Resurrection, being as advanced over the present state, as stated, as an adult is over a little child.

MORE NEEDFUL FOR YOU

The phrase, *"Is more needful for you,"* expresses the concern the Apostle had for the Philippians, and all other Believers at that time for that matter. As stated, it is the spirit that should characterize every Child of God. It must always be *"others!"*

I think I can say without fear of exaggeration, that there is nothing more important to this world (even though the world little understands such), or to the Church, than God-called Preachers of the Gospel, who walk close to the Lord as Paul (Eph. 4:11). They are the ones who point to Glory and show the way from the Word of God. Nothing could be more important than that.

However, appreciation as it ought to be is seldom given, even as it was in the case of Paul. While there certainly were many who loved him dearly, there were also others who did not fall into that category, and of course, I speak of Christians. It is very difficult to understand how such could be, but it was, even as it is presently.

Even though there are many Preachers, there aren't many who are really close to God. What few there are, often are unrecognized, or rather I should say are little understood as to their true worth. Nevertheless, personal popularity is never the desire of the God-called man or woman of God. It is to please the Lord in all things that is the uppermost goal.

However, the point I attempt to make is, that the statements made by Paul should awaken us to the value of those who are truly God-called. We should not underestimate that or take it lightly. When Paul was ultimately called home, as well as the other great

Apostles of that time, the loss to be sure was keenly felt.

For those who fall into that category presently, whomever they may be, the loss is no less, even though their ministry is finished.

(25) "AND HAVING THIS CONFIDENCE, I KNOW THAT I SHALL ABIDE AND CONTINUE WITH YOU ALL FOR YOUR FURTHERANCE AND JOY OF FAITH;"

Paul was confident that his situation was in the Lord's Hands and that what occurred would bring glory to God, regardless of the specific turn it might take. Furthermore, his confidence now prompted him to say, *"I know that I will remain."*

What was the basis of this confidence?

There is no hint of a new legal development which had given fresh information to Paul. The idea is, that the Lord, I think, had revealed to him that he would be set free.

Some have attempted to say that the word *"know"* should not be pressed into the idea of infallible knowledge; however, I think it definitely does apply to a revelation from the Lord.

CONFIDENCE

The phrase, *"And having this confidence,"* refers to the fact that the Apostle had heard from the Lord, consequently having confidence that he would soon be released. As a result, he would not be very long in seeing the Philippians. In this, the Apostle is at the same time stating the fact that *"The servant of the Lord is immortal until his work is done."*

I KNOW

The phrase, *"I know that I shall abide and continue with you,"* is said in this manner from a settled conviction. As stated, the Lord has spoken to the Apostle as it regards this situation.

One commentator stated that Paul's assurance did not rest on direct inspiration, but rather on a calculation of probabilities. That is basely incorrect.

His knowledge *was* definitely based on revelation. Unfortunately, much of the modern Church does not believe that God hears and answers prayer at this particular time, or that the Holy Spirit leads and guides according to the supplication of the Saint. In fact, there are entire Denominations who claim to be fundamentalist in belief, which means to believe all the Bible, but yet do not believe in revelation from the Lord. With them, Faith is a cold, hard proposition, that is completely devoid of any Moving and Operation of the Holy Spirit.

I maintain that such Faith is really no Faith at all. God does hear and answer prayer at this time, even as He always has. In fact, anything that is done, without the direct leading of the Holy Spirit, at least as it refers to the Work of God, has as the only alternative that of the flesh. Such is disastrous!

WHY DOES MUCH OF THE CHURCH WORLD FALL INTO THIS CATEGORY OF UNBELIEF?

Of course, only the Lord knows the answer in totality to that question; however, I greatly suspect that it is because of an improper approach to the Holy Spirit.

I mentioned a moment ago entire Denominations not believing that God speaks to people presently. These Denominations fall into the category of not believing in the Baptism with the Holy Spirit, with the evidence of speaking with other Tongues (Acts 2:4). They claim that everything is received at Salvation, etc. Consequently, the Holy Spirit has little access to these people, for the simple reason that they really do not believe in much of anything that He does.

Regrettably, many in the Pentecostal ranks fall into the same category of unbelief. These Denominations (Pentecostal), which were raised up on the very foundation of the Moving and Operation of the Holy Spirit, have now to a great extent, abandoned this which actually serves as their foundation. In fact, I am told that less than half of the members of Assemblies of God and Churches of God, anymore, even claim to be baptized with the Holy Spirit. If in fact that is the case, these particular Denominations cannot even legitimately refer to themselves presently as *"Pentecostal."*

If the Believer has an improper understanding of the Holy Spirit whether in the realm of Baptism or Leading, then the Ministry of the Holy Spirit is greatly curtailed in the heart and life of that particular person.

THE BOOK OF ACTS SHOULD BE THE CRITERIA

Unfortunately, that is too often the case in most Christians.

There are many in the old-line Denominations who claim that the Book of Acts is not to be used as an example. As well, some of the Pentecostal Leaders, foolishly proclaim that we have better methods now than they did during the times of the Book of Acts. To be frank, I don't know which statement is more ludicrous, that of the old-line people or the so-called Pentecostal Leaders.

In the first place, the account of things as recorded in the Book of Acts is that which was done by the Holy Spirit. Anyone who thinks they can improve upon the Holy Spirit is foolish indeed. As well, if we're not going to take the Book of Acts as an example of how the Church ought to be, then what do we use as an example?

No, those foolish statements are made simply because of unbelief. The first group does not believe in the Holy Spirit irrespective as to what they might say, and the second group, does not believe in His Leading. Either way, it is a road to disaster regarding those directions.

The Holy Spirit is the Power of the Church. The Truth is, He is to do the leading and guidance in all things as it pertains to the Work of God. To be frank, I want Him to lead me in everything I do, irrespective as to what it might be (Jn. 16:7-15).

However, for such leading to take place, there must be a close walk with the Lord, a sincere consecration, and a singleness of heart respecting a desire for the things of God. The Truth is, if the Holy Spirit doesn't give birth to the idea and then bring it to pass, that simply means that whatever is done is not of God. Tragically, most of that which is done today in the realm of religion, comes out of committee meetings, with little or no leading whatsoever of the Holy Spirit. Consequently, we have all types of religious machinery making all kind of noise and involving itself in all type of activity, but with very little, if anything, being truly done for the Lord.

Yes, Paul walked close to God, and was led by the Lord graphically so.

DOES THE LORD LEAD IN THE SAME MANNER TODAY AS HE DID THEN?

Why not?

To be frank, there is nothing in the Word of God that says anything different, with everything pointing toward the direction that the Lord changes not. The Truth is, the Lord is still setting *"Apostles, Prophets, Evangelists, Pastors and Teachers"* in the Church presently, even as He always has (Eph. 4:11). Yes, there are Apostles now, and they are the same as were Apostles then. The same is true for the other designations.

There is absolutely nothing in the Word of God that limits the working of the Holy Spirit to New Testament Times, with all such activity ending at the end of the First Century. Such thinking is foolish, with absolutely nothing in the Word of God to substantiate such foolishness.

Again, all such attitudes come from unbelief. Whatever it is that the Lord has done in the past, He will do presently, providing it is His Will. He is not going to now open the Red Sea on the whim of some Preacher or anyone else for that matter. But if such a thing were needed presently, even as it was when the Lord did perform this miracle, He definitely would do it again.

The Lord healed in Old Testament Times and in New Testament Times. As well, He heals now, for the Scripture says, *"Jesus Christ the same yesterday, and to day, and for ever"* (Heb. 13:8).

The idea that the days of miracles are over, stems totally from unbelief. Men don't believe God simply because they really don't know God. In fact, it is my belief that many of these people have never really been saved, despite their claims.

Paul could say *"I know,"* simply because he actually did know. It was not guesswork or speculation.

JOY OF FAITH

The phrase, *"All for your furtherance and joy of Faith,"* actually speaks of growth as it regards Faith, which is the greatest thing that can happen to a Christian, and which always brings great joy.

For there to be proper Faith, and even a continued growth in Faith, the foundation must be proper. And what do we mean by that?

One must know what is the object of one's Faith. Far too many Christians have a nebulous idea when it comes to Faith. They speak of *"having Faith in God,"* or *"trusting the Lord,"* or *"trusting Jesus,"* all which is right and correct as far as it goes, but which in actuality does not really say very much.

To have Faith in God, in His Word, in Christ, for that Faith to be what it ought to be, there must be a correct object of Faith. And what do we mean by that?

Everything in the Word of God, whether the Old or New Testaments, strains toward one fixed purpose, and that is the Crucifixion and Resurrection of Christ. The entirety of the Word of God, which means the entirety of the Promises, and the entirety of all things done, strains toward this purpose. It is the Cross and the Resurrection. So, our Faith must be anchored squarely in this great Sacrifice of Christ, and must never leave the Sacrifice of Christ. It is from that from which we receive all things from God. In other words, Jesus paid for it at the Cross, and our Faith in that Finished Work, guarantees us the great benefits for which He paid.

So, when we say that we have *"Faith in the Word,"* we should understand exactly what we're talking about. Attempting to pull salient Scriptures out of context, will never be honored by the Lord.

WHAT DOES PULLING SCRIPTURES OUT OF CONTEXT ACTUALLY MEAN?

If a Christian says that he is *"standing on the Word,"* or *"placing his Faith in the Word,"* most Believers accept that as face value. However, it is not always correct. In fact, it is seldom correct.

If the Christian doesn't understand that every single Promise in the Word of God strains toward the Cross and from the Cross, then he doesn't properly understand the Word. Every Promise in the Word of God is attached to the Finished Work of Christ. In other words, none of the Word is applicable to any Believer unless it's anchored in the Sacrifice of Christ. Everything is predicated on that premise. That is proven by the Sacrifices of the Old Testament, which within themselves could not save anyone, but which were meant to symbolize the One Who was to come, namely Christ, Who could save. The Word of God is wrapped totally around that.

As the Lord gave the New Covenant to Paul, as well, that Covenant which in fact is perfect, and will never be replaced, if one is to notice, it is anchored squarely in the Cross of Christ. This is symbolized totally and completely by the Sacred Ordinance we refer to as *"The Lord's Supper"* (I Cor. 11:23-30). In fact, even the other great Ordinance of the Church, *"Water Baptism,"* is as well, a symbol of the Cross and the Resurrection. That's the reason that Paul said, *"I determined to know nothing among you save Christ and Him Crucified"* (I Cor. 2:2).

So, whenever Christians look at Mark 11:24, or any other similar Passage, and attempt to use these Passages to bring things to pass, if they do not understand that all of these great Promises are anchored in the Cross and the Resurrection, then they will be guilty of basically doing the same identical thing which Satan tempted Jesus to do, which was to twist the Word of God away from its rightful foundation (Mat. 4:1-11).

Faith must be anchored in the Word, but the Word must be anchored in the Cross, which it always is, but must be as well in the hearts and minds of Believers. The great Promises of God are not magic. They are given to us, and their great benefits brought to pass, because of the tremendous price that was paid by the Lord of Glory as it regards the Cross and the Resurrection. He paid for all of this with His Precious Shed Blood. If we forget that, we do so at our peril (Eph. 2:8-9, 13).

MY OWN PERSONAL EXPERIENCE

When the Lord began to open up to me the great Revelation of the Cross and the Resurrection in 1997, several things began to happen.

First of all, that Revelation has continued to expand even unto this hour. As well, and exactly as Paul states here, there was a *"joy"* which accompanied my Faith such as I had never had before. For the first time in my Christian life, my Faith was properly anchored in the Cross and the Resurrection as it pertained to my everyday walk before God. I had always understood the Cross as it referred to the initial Salvation experience; however, I did not understand at all, even as most presently do not understand, that the Cross and the Resurrection figures just as prominently in our everyday walk before God, even as it does in our initial Salvation experience.

For any Believer to foolishly think that they outgrow the Cross, is foolishness indeed! Such is not possible. It's about the same as one going to the Pacific Ocean and dipping down into it with a cup, bringing out the cup filled with water, and then turning away claiming that he has pulled all the water out of that vast Ocean. The very thoughts of such are ludicrous. And yet, that's exactly what we do as it regards the benefits of the Cross and the Resurrection.

To be frank, a trillion years from today, the benefits of what Jesus did at the Cross and the Resurrection, will continue to unfold for the Saints of God. In fact, His Sacrifice is inexhaustible, with its benefits never ending. So, for one to think that one can outgrow the Cross, is unscriptural to say the least, and foolish at its worst!

Once the Lord revealed to me the manner in which the Saint of God is to have victory, and perpetual victory at that, a joy filled my heart that has been absolutely glorious from then until now. In fact, it only increases!

As I've said scores of times in the last couple of Volumes of our Commentaries, the Lord showed me that all of our Victory is in the Cross (Rom. 6:3-14). Consequently, our Faith must be in the Cross and must remain in the Cross. He then showed me that this is the manner in which the Holy Spirit works (Rom. 8:2).

In other words, and as we have repeatedly said, the Holy Spirit will not help us attempt to do that which in fact Christ has already done.

Once the Believer knows this and understands this and acts upon this, the Holy Spirit is then constantly helping the Believer, which provides a joy unspeakable and full of glory.

(26) "THAT YOUR REJOICING MAY BE MORE ABUNDANT IN JESUS CHRIST FOR ME BY MY COMING TO YOU AGAIN."

NOTES

The idea of all of this is, that Paul would be able to teach the Philippians and the other Churches as well, greater Truths concerning Jesus Christ which would of consequence increase their Faith, and nothing could be greater than that for the Child of God. It would provide a joy unexcelled.

REJOICING

The phrase, *"That your rejoicing may be more abundant in Jesus Christ for me,"* presents Paul as the human instrument through which this teaching would come as it referred to Jesus Christ.

The progress which the Saints would make in their trust in the Lord Jesus, which progressive trust would result in growth in their Christian experience and the joy that would be theirs in their enjoyment of this repose of their Faith in their Saviour, would in turn result in their more abundant rejoicing in the Lord Jesus.

Christ Jesus is the sphere in which these Blessings are enjoyed, the sphere in the sense that He made them possible through the Blood of His Cross, and in the sense that He is the joy of the Believer's life, the One Who completely satisfies. As stated, Paul is the human instrument through whom God works, at least in this case, to bring these joys to the Philippians by means of his personal presence with them again (Wuest).

"Rejoicing" in the Greek is *"kauchaomai,"* and means *"glorying."* It may be used in both a false and a legitimate sense (Rom. 15:17; Eph. 2:9). Thus, the Philippians' *"glorying"* must be in Christ.

Fletcher says *"The latter is a 'glorying' or 'rejoicing' upon personally fulfilling the Law of Faith. This rejoicing is what Paul calls the 'witness of the Spirit' or 'the testimony of a good conscience' which, next to the witness of the Word and Spirit concerning God's Mercy and Christ's Blood, is the ground of a Christian's conscience."*

To understand all of this, we go back to the sphere in which all of this is made possible, which is what Jesus did through the Blood of His Cross. In other words, the Saint is to always understand this as the Source. If the Cross is not the Source, then the Faith is spurious, and it is that which the Lord can never honor.

COMING AGAIN

The phrase, *"By my coming to you again,"* contains even in its brevity a startling Truth. Even though we have already alluded to this once, due to its great significance, we should deal with it a little more directly.

Without Paul, this advance in the Faith, this growth in Christ, this greater knowledge of Christ, would probably not be brought about. In fact, at this particular time, there was no one on Earth who knew and understood the New Covenant, which of course, was rooted and grounded in the great Sacrifice of Christ, as did the Apostle Paul. Considering that he was the one to whom the New Covenant was given, this would be obvious. The idea is, even though his associates such as Silas or Timothy may explain these great Truths in a grand manner, still, I think it would be safe to say that no one could equal Paul. Even the original Twelve Apostles, did not exactly enjoy this great knowledge. Peter himself said, *"And account that the longsuffering of our Lord is Salvation; even as our beloved brother Paul also according to the wisdom given unto him hath written unto you."*

He then said, *"As also in all his Epistles, speaking in them of these things; in which are some things hard to be understood"* (II Pet. 3:15-16).

THIS GREAT TRUTH AS REVEALED UNTO US

Every morning from 7 a.m. to 8:30 a.m., we teach the Word of God over our network of Radio Stations. For the last some two years up unto this moment (5/28/99), we have been teaching almost exclusively *"The Message of the Cross,"* and will continue for some time yet. Actually, this is the central core Message of Christianity, *"Jesus and Him Crucified"* (I Cor. 2:2; Rom. 6:3-5). Even though we have spent hundreds of hours on this subject, it basically can be summed up in three short phrases:

1. The Cross which represents what Jesus did for lost humanity, and which presupposes the Resurrection, is the source of all Salvation for the sinner and of all Victory for the Saint of God.

2. We must place our Faith in the Cross, which refers to the Atonement and all that Jesus did there for lost humanity, and keep our Faith there. We must understand what Jesus did there and then by Faith appropriate it to ourselves.

3. When our Faith is properly placed in the Cross and the Resurrection, the Holy Spirit will then work on our behalf, which guarantees us all the benefits of the Finished Work of Christ. This is what Paul meant by walking after the Spirit instead of the flesh (Rom. 8:1). It is also *"The Law of the Spirit of Life in Christ Jesus, which makes us free from the Law of sin and death"* (Rom. 8:2).

Unless we follow this prescribed course that's given to us in the Word of God, we as Christians will not walk in Victory, and in fact, cannot walk in Victory. If we substitute anything else other than God's prescribed method, by taking away or adding to, as A. W. Tozer rightly said, *"We clip the wings of the Holy Spirit."*

In fact, thousands of Preachers preach and teach what a person ought to be as it respects walking in Victory, but they really do not tell people how to do it, and for the simple reason that most don't know how themselves.

AN EXAMPLE

Just yesterday a dear lady called me and was relating to me the teaching of a particular Preacher on Romans Chapter 6 which she had found on the Internet. She read it to me and basically what he was saying was correct, at least as far as he went. He was extolling the virtue and power of the Cross, which is more than most do, but then his statements were, *"We must defeat the flesh and allow the Spirit to have His Way,"* or words to that effect.

While that is certainly true, he did not tell the people how to defeat the flesh or how to allow the Spirit of God to have His Way within their lives. Consequently, the people are left hanging, basically agreeing with what is said, but not knowing how to put it into practice. The Truth is, he really did not know either.

First of all, the flesh is defeated by the Believer putting total Faith and Confidence in the Cross of Christ and what took place there as it regards the Finished Work, and the Believer not depending on himself whatsoever. Actually, the *"flesh"* constitutes any and all efforts made by any Believer, irrespective as to how Scriptural those efforts may be in their own right, which is other than our dependence on the Finished Work of Christ. In other words, while *"fasting"* is definitely Scriptural, and will definitely bless and help the Saint, that is if done in the right way, the Truth is, if we attempt to use fasting, or anything else of similar nature, to give us victory over sin, whether we realize it or not, we have just turned these otherwise Scriptural attributes into *"works,"* which God cannot accept and which means, the Holy Spirit cannot work. That's what Paul means by *"walking after the flesh"* (Rom. 8:1).

All of this fools us simply because many of these things we do in order to bring about Victory within our lives are Scriptural in their own right. Consequently, we don't think of them as being of the *"flesh,"* when in actuality they really are, at least when used in this fashion. The facts are, millions of Christians at this very moment are attempting to use good and legitimate things such as fasting, prayer, faithfulness to Church, giving of money to the Lord's Work, the winning of souls, etc., in order to bring victory within their lives. To be sure, these things ought to be done, but as a *result* of the Victory we already have in Christ, and never as a means to obtain Victory. When done in the latter fashion, God can place them in no category except that of *"flesh."*

When we place our Faith exclusively in the Cross, attempting to add nothing to the Finished Work of Christ, then the Holy Spirit can do for us everything that needs to be done, in effect, guaranteeing the Finished Work of Christ within our lives.

In brief, that's the manner in which the flesh is defeated, and the Holy Spirit is allowed His Way, which always spells Victory. The idea is, we are *"in Christ,"* which position guarantees Victory, that is if we understand those implications, and continue to exercise Faith in the Great Sacrifice of Christ (Rom. 6:3-14).

MY ORIGINAL QUESTION

I should think the Reader would surely understand how important this type of teaching is as it regards the Word of God. In fact, there is nothing more important for the Christian, exactly as there is nothing more important than the Salvation Message for the sinner. But yet, I am concerned that most Christians do not really understand the vast significance of what is being said here.

Understanding human nature somewhat, I wonder as well, if the people at Philippi really understood the tremendous significance of Paul being allowed to remain for several more years, even visiting their Church again? I would hope they did not take it for granted and that somehow, they were made aware of how important all of this really was.

God gave the New Covenant to Paul, which of course, is that for which Jesus died. In other words, the New Covenant, which could not be brought about without the Work of Christ on the Cross, is the single most important Work that humanity has ever known. Consequently, Paul labored extensively that nothing add to this great Covenant or take from it, which Satan over and over again attempted to do, and still does. To be sure, he lived this thing day and night, with it literally burning within his spirit, as should be obvious.

As it regards the Revelation that the Lord has given me on the Cross and the Resurrection, which in effect, is that which was given to Paul, it as well burns within my heart 24 hours a day. Even though what I have been given is definitely not new, actually being the foundation of the Faith, but still being so very important, because it has been all but lost in the last nearly half century, as Satan has been very successful at pushing the Church away from the Cross.

As Paul, everything burns within me to get this Word, this Message, this Truth, to every single Believer, because I know therein is the embodiment of all Victory in Christ.

Regrettably, the Church in straying from the Cross has run toward the ways of the world, which speaks of humanistic psychology. Sadly, there is no help from this source whatsoever, actually only hurt. Also, the Church experiences one fad after the other, with Christians running after manifestations, thinking this will bring the relief they seek. It won't! While it may be a momentary blessing, it will not provide what the Saint seeks. The reason is simple, Believers do not really need a touch, they need the Truth (Jn. 8:32).

Don't misunderstand, I'm not demeaning the *"touch,"* for all of us need a touch occasionally, the more the better. I am saying, that will not solve the problem in the life of the Believer, that being brought about only by the Truth. As well, the Truth is that which we have given you as it concerns the Cross and the Resurrection and the Victory contained therein (Rom. 6:3-14).

(27) "ONLY LET YOUR CONVERSATION BE AS IT BECOMETH THE GOSPEL OF CHRIST: THAT WHETHER I COME AND SEE YOU, OR ELSE BE ABSENT, I MAY HEAR OF YOUR AFFAIRS, THAT YE STAND FAST IN ONE SPIRIT, WITH ONE MIND STRIVING TOGETHER FOR THE FAITH OF THE GOSPEL."

As citizens of a spiritual realm, the Philippians should stand firm in one spirit. They should be true, whatever happens, to Paul, for the responsibility for their spiritual growth rested ultimately with them and their appropriation of the riches of Christ.

Whether Paul would be released and thus enabled to visit them in person, or be forced to remain away from them and learn of their progress through the reports of others, his exhortation was the same. They must conduct their lives in a manner appropriate to the Gospel of Christ.

CONVERSATION

The phrase, *"Only let your conversation be as it becometh the Gospel of Christ,"* refers to their behavior. They were to conduct themselves worthy of the Gospel.

Actually, the balance of this Epistle has to do with the spiritual needs of these Saints. As we study these exhortations, we discover what things were lacking in their lives and what things needed to be corrected. It will suffice for us as well!

"Conversation" in the Greek is *"politeuo,"* and means *"manner of life, behavior."* But yet, it means much more than that.

From it we get such words as *"politic, political."* It referred to the public duties devolving upon a man as a member of a body.

Paul uses it in Acts 23:1, where he answers the charge of having violated the laws and customs of the Jewish people and so subverting the theocratic constitution. He says, *"I have lived in all good conscience before God until this day."*

The words *"Have lived"* are the translation of this word, *"conversation."* In effect, by the use of this word, Paul said, *"I have fulfilled all the duties devolving upon me as a member of the nation of Israel in its relation to God."*

In fact, the word *"conversation"* is also the translation of another Greek word *"anastrepho,"* which also means *"manner of life, behavior"* (II Cor. 1:12; Eph. 2:3). However, Paul uses a different word (*"politeuo"*), which even though meaning *"manner of life, behavior,"* the same as the other Greek word, as well, speaks of one's manner of life seen as a duty to a body or group of which one is a member, and to the head of that group to whom he is responsible. As is obvious, it is a more inclusive word (Wuest).

THE REASON PAUL USED THIS WORD

The use of this word has to do with the fact that the city of Philippi was a Roman colony. It was a miniature likeness of the Roman people, with the political atmosphere of the place being wholly Roman. Consequently, the pride and privilege of Roman citizenship confronted all at every turn. This is the sentiment which stimulated the blind loyalty of the people to Rome.

In effect, Paul is using this, which was very familiar to the Philippian Saints, as an apt symbol of the higher privileges of their heavenly calling. In other words, as these Roman citizens in Philippi attempted to ape Rome in every manner, likewise the Believer is to do all he and she can do to ape Heaven, so to speak.

Actually, Paul uses the same Greek word in its noun form in Philippians 3:20 where he says, *"For our conversation* (citizenship) *is in Heaven,"* or as one could more fully translate, *"For the commonwealth of which we are citizens has its fixed location in Heaven"* (Wuest).

A HEAVENLY ATMOSPHERE

The use of this specialized word colors the entire Epistle, and gives to it a heavenly atmosphere. It teaches us that Christians are citizens of Heaven, having a heavenly origin, and a heavenly destiny, with the responsibility of living a heavenly life on this Earth in the midst of ungodly people and surroundings, telling sinners of a Saviour in Heaven Who will save them from their sins if they will but trust Him.

In fact, the ethics in this Epistle are invested with heavenly standards. The Saints are reminded that as a colony of Heaven, they are to live heavenly lives on Earth, representing their Sovereign by a life which reflects Him. They are taught that obedience to the ethics of the Pauline Epistles is not merely obedience to ethics as such, but involves a duty to which they are responsible to discharge as citizens of a Heavenly Kingdom, and as subjects of a Heavenly King.

BEHAVE AS CITIZENS OF HEAVEN

The expression *"Let your conversation be as it becometh the Gospel of Christ,"* could be variously translated, *"Behave as heavenly citizens. Live as heavenly citizens. Perform your duties as heavenly citizens."*

The Philippian Saints are exhorted to always recognize their duties with respect to their heavenly citizenship, and hold themselves to those duties. Actually, the manner in which Paul uses this phrase, places it in a category of being a stronger exhortation than merely that of commanding someone to do something.

In the normal kind of exhortation, the person obeys the one who exhorts. But in the form in which Paul gives the exhortation, the person exhorted is to recognize his position as a citizen of a Heavenly Kingdom, and while enjoying the exhortation as a matter of obligation to God, yet at the same time realize his responsibility to obey it because of the privileged position he occupies, and literally exhort or charge himself to do the same. Therefore, one could translate: *"Only see to it that you recognize your responsibility as a citizen of Heaven and put yourself to the absolute necessity of performing the duties incumbent upon you in that position"* (Wuest).

THE GOSPEL OF CHRIST

That which Paul is saying here, has a far greater meaning than meets the eye. It has to do not only with that which we believe, but the manner in which we conduct ourselves. In other words, our lives must be shaped by the Gospel in every conceivable manner. Perhaps the following will be of some help:

1. The rules of the Gospel are to be applied to all our conduct — to our conversation, business transactions, modes of dress, style of living, entertainments, etc. There is nothing which we do, or say, or purpose, that is to be excepted from those principles.

2. There is a way of living which is appropriate to the Gospel, or which is such as the Gospel requires. There is something which the Gospel would secure as its proper fruit in all our conduct, and by which our lives should be regulated.

It would distinguish us from those who seek honor and wealth as their supreme object. If all Christians were under the influence of the Gospel, there would be something in our dress, conversation, and aims which will always distinguish us from others.

3. It is very important that Christians should frame their lives by the principles of the Gospel — and, to this end, should study them and know what they are. Of course, the Gospel is the Word of God, and the Word of God is the Gospel, one might say. If men live as *"becometh the Gospel,"* they live well. It is just that simple.

One might say that the foundation of the Gospel was laid in the Old Testament, introduced by Christ in the four Gospels, consummated by Christ on the Cross and by His Resurrection, and given to Paul in that which we refer to as the *"New Covenant."* As the word *"Gospel"* means *"Good News,"* it is truly the greatest news the world has ever known and by any comparison.

In fact, the word *"Gospel"* was quite a common word in Greek usage before the Early Church. It meant *"good news"* in any form, or what was considered to be *"good news."*

However, as the Word of this truly Good News began to be disseminated, little by little the word *"Gospel,"* came to mean only the Message of Jesus Christ. The reasons should be obvious.

Any other so-called good news pales into insignificance in comparison to this great Message; consequently, whenever the word

"Gospel" is now used, it is pretty much understood anywhere and in most languages, that it is referring to the *"Gospel of Jesus Christ,"* i.e., *"The Good News of Jesus Christ."*

WEIGHT

The Greek word translated *"becometh"* is most interesting. It means *"having the weight of* (weighing as much as) *another thing."* It means, *"of like value, worth as much."* Other meanings are *"befitting, congruous, corresponding."*

The Saints are to see to it that their manner of life weighs as much as the Gospel they profess to believe, or their words will not have weight. That which gives weight to a Christian's words, is the fact that his manner of life befits, is congruous to, corresponds with the Gospel he preaches (Wuest).

IN ONE SPIRIT

The phrase, *"That whether I come and see you, or else be absent, I may hear of your affairs, that ye stand fast in one spirit, with one mind,"* refers to standing firm and holding one's ground.

The implication is clear that when one holds one's ground, he does it in the face of enemy opposition. We are to stand fast in *"one spirit."*

The word *"spirit"* refers here to the unity of spirit in which the Church should be fused and blended. The Greek word *"spirit"* is used at times of the disposition or influence which fills and governs the soul of anyone. It is so used here. This unity of spirit when present among members of a local Church, is produced by the Holy Spirit.

"Spirit" has been interpreted as the Holy Spirit by some and as the human spirit by others. Although it is probable that Paul is speaking of the human spirit, still, it is clear that a genuine *"common spirit"* is not a possibility apart from the Holy Spirit.

In fact, the human spirit of the Believer is to be so intertwined, so connected, even so filled and possessed by the Holy Spirit, that they are almost one and the same. In fact, the word *"baptize"* as it is used in *"baptized with the Holy Spirit"* (Acts 1:5), even though speaking of the entirety of the person, definitely includes the human spirit, and in fact, the human spirit more than all. The actual meaning of the word *"baptize"* is: that which is being baptized is filled with that with which it is baptized and vice versa. In the case of the Holy Spirit, it would be that the individual is filled or possessed by the Holy Spirit, with the Holy Spirit also being possessed by the individual. An apt illustration is a ship which has sunk beneath the surface of the Ocean. The ship is filled with and surrounded by the Ocean, and the Ocean fills and surrounds the ship.

As it relates to the Holy Spirit, the word *"filled"* is probably not the best usage. The best word to explain this baptism would probably be *"control"* or better yet *"possessed."*

ONE MIND

The word *"mind"* here is the translation of the Greek word *"soul."* The soul is that part of man which on the one hand receives impressions from the human spirit, and on the other hand, from the outer world. It is the sphere of the emotions, feelings, and passion.

The following is the manner in which God created man and the manner in which man functions:

1. With the physical body, man deals with the world, in essence fellow human beings.

2. With the soul man deals with self and with his spirit. The soul also reaches out to the spirit world, whether to God or to evil spirits.

3. The spirit of man deals with the soul, and as well, with God or even the world of evil spirits. Even though the soul of man is definitely involved in seeking the Lord, it is rather the spirit of man which is the greater contact, hence Jesus saying, *"God is a Spirit; and they that worship Him must worship Him in spirit* (the human spirit) *and in Truth"* (Jn. 4:24).

The soul and the spirit of the human being are immortal and, therefore, eternal. This is the inner man which will never die. The body is the only part of the human being which dies, but even then, at the coming Resurrection of Life, a glorified body will be given to every Saint of God who has ever lived. This glorified body will be identical to the Body that Jesus had after His Resurrection. If one studies that enough, it is obvious that it has amazing qualities. It can appear and disappear at will, go through walls or any substance, but yet has the feel and texture of flesh, but contains no blood (Lk. 24:39). Whereas the life of the flesh is now the blood, then it seems that it will be in the Spirit of God.

The Resurrection of Life as it regards the sainted dead will take place first (I Cor. 15:51-58; I Thess. 4:13-18; Rev. 20:6), and is very near as I dictate these words. The Second Resurrection of Damnation, which will include all the unbelieving dead, will take place a thousand years after the Resurrection of Life (Rev. 20:5). The unbelieving billions will also be given indestructible bodies to join their souls and spirits, where they will be cast into the Lake of Fire forever and forever (Rev. 20:11-15). Conversely, the Saints of all ages will live with Christ forever and forever (Rev. 20:6).

THE FAITH OF THE GOSPEL

The phrase, *"Striving together for the Faith of the Gospel,"* proclaims the first intimation in this Epistle that there were some divisions in the Church. Paul had somehow gotten out of a possibly reluctant Epaphroditus, that there were some problems which needed addressing.

"Striving" is the translation of a Greek word used of an athletic contest. We get our words *"athlete"* and *"athletics"* from it. It refers to an athletic contest in which a group of athletes cooperates as a team against another team, working in perfect coordination against a common opposition. Paul is exhorting the members of the Philippian Church to work together in perfect coordination just like a team of Greek athletes. To be sure, this illustration was no doubt not lost upon the Greek readers of Paul's Epistle (Wuest).

"Faith" as it is used here, is not to be personified as though one were to strive either *"with"* or *"for"* it in an objective sense. Nor does it mean merely a body of teaching.

Rather, it refers to the trust and commitment which come as a result of hearing the Gospel. The entire expression suggests the maintenance of a right relationship to the Gospel and thus to Christ.

The Philippians are to keep themselves in such a spirit of love as to be able to fight *"side by side like one man for the Faith of the Gospel"* (Moffatt).

NOTES

This statement *"Faith of the Gospel"* is extremely important. In fact, there could be nothing more important.

To which we have alluded, it refers to the very foundation of all that we believe as it pertains to Christ. If one is to notice it is not merely Faith, but rather *"The Faith."*

THE FAITH

That of which the Holy Spirit speaks through Paul refers totally and completely to Jesus Christ, but more particularly, to what He did at the Cross and the Resurrection. *"The Faith"* is the *"Finished Work of Christ, the Atonement, the Great Sacrifice of Himself on the Tree."* This means that all we do in Christ, all we are in Christ, all we receive from Christ, and in every capacity, must flow directly from that Finished Work. If this is weakened, hindered, curtailed, or given a lesser position for any reason, we have just tampered with *"The Faith,"* and whatever it is we then have, whatever it might be, is not the *"Gospel,"* but rather *"another gospel"* (II Cor. 11:4).

If one is to notice, the Greek article is also in front of the word *"Gospel"* dogmatically stating, *"The Gospel."* This spells out everything that God is to humanity through Jesus Christ, which pertains to what He did at the Cross and the Resurrection.

When one says *"The Gospel,"* if he is not referring to what Jesus did at the Cross and the Resurrection, and that all things flow from that Finished Work, he is not really speaking of the Gospel of Jesus Christ, irrespective of how much of the Bible is used or the claims made.

The two are hand in hand *"The Faith," "The Gospel." "The Faith"* demands *"the Gospel,"* and *"the Gospel"* demands *"the Faith."*

THE PRESENT SITUATION

To show the Reader how successful that Satan has been in corrupting the whole of the Church, exactly as Jesus said would happen in the last days (Mat. 13:33), one only has to look at the present situation.

The Early Church recorded in the Book of Acts touched the world. However, beginning in the Second Century, and gradually regressing thereafter, it began to apostatize, until ultimately becoming what is known as the Catholic Church. To be brief, there is no dependence whatsoever in those ranks on the Shed Blood of Jesus Christ at the Cross of Calvary, rather depending on Mary and the Church itself. Consequently, there is no proper *"Faith"* in that system.

The Church of Christ teaches that the water saves, referring to Water Baptism, which means they are not trusting Christ and what He did at the Cross, but rather Ordinances, etc.

Most of the Baptists and Methodists have rejected the Holy Spirit, which has left them basically with no more than a *"form of Godliness,"* from which Paul said we must turn away (II Tim. 3:1-5).

The Pentecostal Denominations such as the Assemblies of God and Church of God, have mostly forsaken the Way of the Cross and the Holy Spirit, rather opting for the ways of the world, i.e., *"humanistic psychology,"* etc. To be frank, all Denominations, at least as far as I know, have pretty much gone in that direction, at least as it refers to the United States and Canada.

In some of these Denominations there are still Godly Preachers and Godly people; nevertheless, that number gets less almost by the day, with the slide downward accelerating at an ever faster pace.

The Charismatic world, which is very large, for the most part, has followed the same course, but has added a further evil, that which is referred to as the *"Prosperity Message."* In other words, a person's Faith is judged by the model car they drive, cost of their clothing, type of house in which they live, etc.

Whatever the direction, Satan could care less, just as long as they forsake the Cross and the Resurrection, which is exactly what has happened. The modern Church, with some few exceptions, is not a *"Cross and Resurrection Church,"* but rather something else altogether. To be sure, this move in the opposite direction is very subtle. Lip service is paid to the Cross, but one can tell by the emphasis where the Denomination or Church actually is. If the emphasis is not on the Cross, it will soon become very obvious as to where the emphasis actually is. Conversely, if it's on the Cross, that will be obvious very shortly as well. For the most part,

NOTES

the emphasis of the modern Church is on everything but the Cross, which, in effect, means that what they are promoting is not *"The Gospel,"* and whatever they evidence is definitely not *"The Faith."*

Regrettably, this situation is not going to get better but rather worse. These are the last days, and the Church has already entered into the last great apostasy.

THE OUTPOURING OF THE SPIRIT

However, at the same time, those who do correctly interpret and believe *"The Gospel,"* thereby having *"The Faith,"* are going to see great and mighty things done for the Lord. While it will be a time of terrible spiritual declension for most, it will be a time of tremendous spiritual victories for others.

I pray that I'm not the only one, certainly believing that the Lord has given or is giving this Revelation of the Cross to others around the world; nevertheless, I know what He has given me, and I'm going to do my very best to proclaim this Word of Victory, to the whole of the Church, for that's exactly what it is. I, as well, believe that the Lord is going to give me the means to do so.

Whether they accept or not is not my responsibility; however, at whatever cost, they must know.

They must realize how they have drifted from the true Foundation of the Gospel, which is the Cross and the Resurrection, and thereby return. Some I definitely believe will do exactly that.

(28) "AND IN NOTHING TERRIFIED BY YOUR ADVERSARIES: WHICH IS TO THEM AN EVIDENT TOKEN OF PERDITION, BUT TO YOU OF SALVATION, AND THAT OF GOD."

From this Passage it seems that the Philippian Church was undergoing persecution; consequently, Paul does not want them to be terrified in any respect by these adversaries, whomever they may have been. The noble character of their cause and the recognition that Christ is on their side, should cause Believers to avoid the unreasoning terror that prevents our effort for Christ.

Who were these opponents?

Some have insisted that the reference could not have been to Jews because the Jewish population of Philippi was too small. That is probably correct.

What is virtually certain is that these were external foes, not false teachers within the Church. Whether Jewish or pagan, however, they usually employed the same tactics, and the need for unity and courage among the Believers was always crucial.

ADVERSARIES

The phrase, *"And in nothing terrified by your adversaries,"* probably referred to the pagan Greeks at Philippi who were idolaters. These would oppose a Faith which forbade idolatry.

Someone has said, *"A Salvation from God is evidenced by persecution; and persecution is to be recognized as a gift granted to those who are Christ's true followers."*

Satan is going to oppose the true Christian, of that one can be certain. He will use various means to do so, whether from inside the Church or from outside, which the latter seems to be the case here. Irrespective, the Christian is not to be cowed into submission by persecution or the threat of it. He is to be unswayed by danger. Paul continues to drive home this point by adding that persecution is an occupational hazard of every Christian.

What I'm about to say I think is not too much accepted presently; nevertheless, I think I can say without fear of contradiction that it is Gospel.

Paul, as did James and Peter, seeks to persuade the Philippians that suffering is not only something to be endured but even to be welcomed. To suffer for the Cause of Christ brings one closer to the Master. It is regarded a privilege to suffer for Christ's sake. Jesus emphasized this in the Sermon on the Mount, and the Apostles repeatedly experienced in their lives the joy that comes from being *"baptized with the baptism wherewith He is baptized,"* a baptism, to be sure, in the fires of testing (Mat. 5:10-12; 20:22).

AN EVIDENT TOKEN

The phrase, *"Which is to them an evident token of perdition, but to you of Salvation, and that of God,"* presents a twofold proof:

1. The persecution by the pagans was a clear evidence that these Philippians truly knew the Lord, for Satan does not bother to persecute those who are not truly followers of Christ, as should be obvious.

2. The very fact that these people were persecuting the Christians was *"an evident token"* that they were *not* of God, did not know God, and in fact, because of this stand would one day be judged by God. Consequently, in this which the Holy Spirit says through the Apostle, we have judgment on one hand for the pagans and Salvation on the other for Believers, with the phrase *"That of God,"* guaranteeing both.

"Perdition" in the Greek is *"apoleia,"* and means *"ruin or loss, destruction, perish."*

Those who oppose the people of God, unless they repent, have nothing to look forward to ultimately but the Lake of Fire. This is what is meant by *"perdition."* To be sure, God keeps score. In fact, He is concerned about all things; however, He is concerned more than all about those who follow Him, who name His Name, whom He refers to as *"the salt of the earth"* and *"the light of the world"* (Mat. 5:13-14). He also said, *"But whoso shall offend one of these little ones* (the least Christian) *which believe in Me, it were better for him that a millstone were hanged about his neck, and that he were drowned in the depth of the Sea."*

And then, *"Woe unto the world because of offenses! for it must needs be that offenses come; but woe to that man by whom the offence cometh!"* (Mat. 18:6-7).

ANOTHER THOUGHT

As well, the Lord will not brook or tolerate even Christians persecuting other Christians. If anything, I know I can say that He is more disturbed by Christians acting this way, and I speak of one Christian attempting to punish or hurt another Christian, even than he is those of the world. Those of the world do not know God and are not held as accountable. Consequently, if He has pronounced dire judgment on the unsaved for these offenses, how much more will He pronounce such on those who claim to be Christian, but yet engage in such tactics. This is a sober thought, and we should heed these words very carefully.

The Truth is, every single Believer is bought with a price, and that price is the Shed

Blood of the Son of God on the Cross of Calvary. In other words, the Lord paid a terrible price for each and every Believer. As a result, we really do not anymore belong to ourselves but rather to God. So, as a Believer we should be very careful as to how we treat God's property, i.e., *"other Believers."*

Why do I give this warning as it concerns Christians?

I do so, because somehow many Christians have the idea, that they are justified in their adverse actions toward another Christian. Nothing could be further from the truth!

We must be very careful what we say about other Believers, how we conduct ourselves toward them, what action we take toward them, and in fact, everything we do toward them. We must always keep in mind that we are dealing with property (so to speak) which belongs to the Lord, for Whom He died, and for Whom He paid such a great price.

This is where Denominations sometimes run aground. Their leaders far too often feel they are qualified to punish those whom they do not like, or to take measures against them to hurt and hinder their Ministries, in fact, to even destroy their Ministries. Regrettably, this is not an isolated situation but actually quite common.

Such action strikes at the very tenor of the Word of God. In other words, there is absolutely nothing in the Bible to validate such actions, but rather everything to militate against such. They justify themselves, because they equate their particular Denomination with God, and in their minds, they are protecting the Denomination, i.e., *"God."*

First of all, the Lord is able to protect that which is truly His. The last I heard, He does not own any Denominations, for the simple reason that He did not die for such. He died for human beings, for men and women, for boys and girls. He didn't die for organizations, as should be overly obvious.

We see in the Book of Acts and the Epistles, that the Holy Spirit cautioned the Apostles to take special care as to how they dealt with individuals in each Church. This is especially obvious in the Ministry of Paul who was the actual masterbuilder of the Church. He never threatened or forced, but only requested, even pleaded (I Cor. 1:10).

NOTES

(29) "FOR UNTO YOU IT IS GIVEN IN THE BEHALF OF CHRIST, NOT ONLY TO BELIEVE ON HIM, BUT ALSO TO SUFFER FOR HIS SAKE;"

The whole situation was part of God's gracious provision for those enlisted in the Cause of Christ. The privileges enjoyed by Christians included the ability to not only believe in Christ initially at Regeneration and subsequently throughout the Christian life, but also to suffer for Him.

If we question the propriety of referring to suffering or opposition as a privilege and a *"gracious gift,"* we must remember that the New Testament regards suffering as God's means of achieving His gracious purposes both in His Own Son (Heb. 2:10) and in all Believers (James 1:3-4; I Pet. 1:6-7).

IN THE BEHALF OF CHRIST

The phrase, *"For unto you it is given in the behalf of Christ,"* in effect, pertains to suffering for His sake.

This is not something that is a possibility, but rather that which will definitely happen, and irrespective as to whom the Believer might be, or where the Believer might be. Admittedly, those of us who live in the United States and Canada, as well as certain other countries in the world, are not as subject to persecution as those who live in certain other places. Nevertheless, this of which the Holy Spirit speaks through the Apostle, covers a wide area.

First of all, the world in its entirety, and irrespective as to its location is opposed to Christ. While God may be thought of in abstract terms, and, therefore, not so very much opposed, it is different with the Lord Jesus Christ. He is the One through Whom the individual must go if he is to reach God, and more particularly through what He did at the Cross and the Resurrection.

The Perfection of Righteousness as it pertains to Christ is an offence to a sinful, wicked world. It is an offence as well, that God would have to become man and die on a Cross for man, in order that man might be saved. This offends man simply because he does not admit that he is so spiritually depraved that he needs such a Redeemer. On the other side of the coin, the death of Christ on the Cross tells man that he is not nearly as good as he thinks he is.

Also, every unsaved person is the child of transgression and sin, which means a child of Satan. That is a strong term but it is definitely true, hence the need for mankind to be *"born again"* (Jn. 3:3).

Considering that unconverted man has an evil nature within him, he automatically strikes out in one way or the other at those who have accepted Christ, which is the very opposite of this evil nature. Admittedly, some strike out more than others, but the opposition is in the heart of all who are unsaved. And to be sure, the worst opposition of all is from those who claim Christ but really do not know Him.

CHRIST AND THE CROSS

If Christ could be divorced from the Cross, there would probably be very little opposition. But of course, He cannot be divorced from the Cross, therefore, the opposition remains.

In actuality, it is really the Cross which offends the world. The world can accept Christ the Healer, Christ the Miracle-Worker, Christ the great Prophet, Christ the great King, Christ the great Preacher, but they cannot accept *"Christ and Him Crucified"* (I Cor. 1:18). As stated, the Cross tells the world how evil it is which at the same time, tells the world that it's not nearly as good as it thinks it is, in fact, not good at all! So, it's really the Cross which offends the world and arouses hostility toward the Child of God.

The world as well as the apostate Church, is willing to accept Christ in just about any capacity except in the form of Crucifixion and Resurrection. This is the barrier. However, belief in that which Jesus did regarding the Cross, is the only way to Salvation. There is no other, and that Truth offends the world greatly.

So, when we speak of suffering for Christ, if one could get through all the layers of supposed reasons, one would find at the bottom of it all and the cause of it all, the Cross of Christ. The Cross is the dividing point in every capacity, that which deals life and as well, that which deals death. Acceptance brings life while rejection brings death.

TO BELIEVE ON HIM

The phrase, *"Not only to believe on Him,"* presents the first part of our life in Christ which is Faith. The second part concerns suffering which we will address momentarily.

When Paul speaks of *"believing on Christ,"* exactly what does he mean?

Is it to believe that He is Virgin Born? Is it to believe that He is the Son of God? Is it to believe that He is a Healer and mighty Miracle-Worker? Is it to believe that He is a Prophet? a Priest? a King?

Most certainly it is to include that and even things we have not said; however, the basic object of one's Faith, that which guarantees Salvation, that which guarantees Victory over the powers of darkness, that which gives one Eternal Life making them a new creation, that which guarantees Redemption, is Faith in what Jesus did at the Cross. To be sure, all the other things are of extreme significance. It is absolutely necessary that a Believer understand and believe *all* the rudiments of Christ; however, the basic foundation of Faith, the object of one's Faith, that in which our Faith must be centered and anchored, must at all times be the Cross of Christ. As we have stated, all of these other things are necessary, but as necessary as they were, and even as much as they contributed toward the great Sacrifice of the Cross, within themselves, and I speak of His Incarnation, Virgin Birth, Healings, and Miracles, etc., none of that, as glorious and wonderful as it was and is, could save anyone. So, when we speak of *"believing on Him"* or *"believing in Him,"* the primary objective of such Faith must always be the Cross. And of course, when we say *"The Cross,"* we are at the same time presupposing the *"Resurrection."*

DO WE REALLY KNOW THAT?

The things I've just said, the things I have just attempted to enumerate, most Christians would automatically retort by saying *"I know that!"* However, do we really know that?

After a fashion I am certain that we do; however, in totality, in its total depth, in the capacity of what it all means, I think most of us really don't know this of which we have said. And I'll tell you why I say that.

In thinking of the Cross, that is if Christians think of it at all, they automatically place it in their initial Salvation experience and that alone. One must believe in what Jesus did at the Cross in order to be saved, or something to that effect. That's about as far as it goes with most.

While what Jesus did at the Cross definitely has everything to do with our initial Salvation experience, for without that sacrificial act, no one could be saved; still, we make the biggest mistake of our Christian experience if we leave the Cross at that point. The Truth is, just as the sinner cannot be saved without believing in some way, even as weak as his Faith might be, in what Jesus did at the Cross, neither can the Christian walk in victory without his Faith continuing to be in the Cross. Most Christians don't know that.

It is not my desire to repeat this Truth to the place of tedious boredom, but knowing how far the Church has drifted from the Cross, knowing how mixed up that most of the Church is as it regards the Finished Work of Christ, knowing that most Christians have been led to believe error as it addresses itself to this all-important Truth, I feel compelled in my heart to repeat this Truth in every way that I know, from every direction that I know, in order that the Light may begin to shine in the heart of the Reader. This I know:

Once this great Truth of which I speak begins to make itself felt in the heart and life of any Believer, the glory of Christ will open up in such a way as the Believer has never known before. The *"more abundant life"* of which Jesus spoke (Jn. 10:10), will finally be realized. The glorious *"rest"* that He promised, will now become a reality (Mat. 11:28-30). In other words, the Christianity that Jesus promised, and that which the Holy Spirit stands ready to deliver, will now be made a reality. It is the most glorious life there is, but only when we function according to God's prescribed Order. And His Order is the Finished Work of Christ, the Substitutionary Sacrifice, the Vicarious, Efficacious Offering, the Cross and the Resurrection.

THE BIG MISTAKE MADE BY THE CHRISTIAN

In thinking of this great Redemption process, this great Salvation afforded by Christ, we make a grand mistake if we place the Cross in the mix as merely one of the things that Jesus did. While everything He did was of great significance, as should be obvious, the very purpose, however, for which He came, the very extent of His Incarnation, the very prediction of the Prophecies, in other words the central core of God's Plan for the Redemption of man, always was the Cross and the Resurrection. Although in a very negative sense, this was the very first Promise given by God, which was done immediately after the Fall in the Garden of Eden, when God told Satan through the Serpent, *"And I will put enmity* (hatred) *between thee* (Satan) *and the woman, and between thy seed* (mankind in general) *and her Seed* (The Lord Jesus Christ)*; it* (He) *shall bruise thy head* (defeat you and all the powers of darkness at the Cross and the Resurrection), *and thou shall bruise His heel* (the suffering of the Crucifixion)*"* (Gen. 3:15).

So, the Believer must always make the Cross and the Resurrection the central focus of all that he believes, all that he is, understanding that the Salvation he has, and the Victory he has on a daily basis over the powers of darkness, are all brought about because of what Jesus did at the Cross, and our Faith in that Finished Work, which guarantees the help of the Holy Spirit in every capacity (Rom. 8:1-2).

SUFFERING FOR HIS SAKE

The phrase, *"But also to suffer for His sake,"* actually proclaims in the phrase we have just addressed, as to *why* we *"suffer for His sake."*

What I have just said may seem like a contradiction, and I speak of the *"more abundant life"* which I have just mentioned, which comes about, and can only come about as a result of our proper Faith in the Cross, with Paul now mentioning *"suffering for His sake."* No, it is not a contradiction.

In fact, the suffering comes because of the Cross. As we've already stated, the world hates the Cross, and in fact, the Christ of the Cross. As we've said over and over again, they can accept the Miracle-working Jesus, etc., but it is rather the Cross which is the great intersection of humanity. Because of the Cross, there is a great opposition in the hearts of unredeemed men toward those who have placed their Faith in the Finished Work of Christ, as it regards Salvation. If one's Faith is properly placed in the Cross, which guarantees Victory over every power of darkness, the world will oppose that, even hate that, and with a passion, and regrettably, so will much of the Church.

The idea is this: Through the Cross of Christ the Believer has total Victory, total Joy, total Abundant Life, etc. Because of the Cross, the Believer suffers persecution, suffers antagonism, suffers opposition, all from the world, the flesh, and the Devil, and regrettably a part of the Church even as Paul mentions in Philippians 3:18.

This of which I am saying, I want to make abundantly clear. One can certainly say that Christ is the ideal. He lived a perfect life, enjoying perfect communion with God. He also suffered opposition by the world, and more particularly the world of religion, as is overly obvious. He plainly told all His followers that it would be the same with them. He said:

"If the world hate you, ye know that it hated Me before it hated you.

"If ye were of the world, the world would love his own: but because ye are not of the world, but I have chosen you out of the world, therefore the world hateth you."

He then said, *"Remember the word that I said unto you, The servant is not greater than his lord. If they have persecuted Me, they will also persecute you; if they have kept My saying (persecuted Me), they will keep yours also* (persecute you as well)."

"But all these things will they do unto you for My Name's sake, because they know not Him Who sent Me" (Jn. 15:18-21).

Actually, this is what Paul was talking about when he used the phrase, *"But also to suffer for His sake."*

LET ME GIVE A PERSONAL EXAMPLE

I have lived the experience of Romans Chapter 7, exactly as Paul did. To be frank, so has every other Believer, whether they understand it or not.

At that time, I was like most every other Christian. I believed that the Cross, and my Faith in that, had to do only with my initial Salvation experience, and that's all. I believed that strongly and preached it strongly, and saw untold thousands brought to a saving knowledge of Jesus Christ. But as Paul in Romans Chapter 7, I did not know or understand, that my Victory as it regards my everyday walk before God, has just as much to do with the Cross, even as much as my initial Salvation experience. Not knowing that, my Faith was improperly placed, and no matter how hard I tried, and please believe me I tried to the place of total exhaustion, there was no victory. At that time, I did not understand that I was frustrating the Grace of God, even as Paul mentioned in Galatians 2:21. Consequently, irrespective of how hard one tries, how hard one works, how hard one engages in labor in order to overcome, there will be no victory in that direction. The Holy Spirit simply *will not* function in that capacity, simply because He *cannot* function in that capacity. And please believe me, irrespective that the Believer is Born-Again, is a new creation in Christ, still, without the help of the Holy Spirit an overcoming life simply cannot be lived (Rom. 8:1-5).

In that capacity, the Believer (and there are untold millions in this condition at this very moment) will say as Paul once said, *"O wretched man that I am! who shall deliver me from the body of this death?"* (Rom. 7:24).

BEFORE THE WHOLE WORLD

Even in the face of glaring failure, I still knew that the world held no answer, and that the answer had to be in the Lord. Yet, I was frustrated! I did not understand what was happening to me, especially considering that I was trying with all that was within me to walk as close to God as I knew how. In those circumstances, it's not very pleasant to hear thousands of Preachers refer to one's person in a sarcastic manner, with the barb, *"He wanted to do that!"* or words to that effect. And then considering, that you have become a joke before the entirety of the world, the Church included, such is not very pleasant. Regrettably, most of the Church joined in with the world, in their efforts to steal, kill, and destroy.

No, in no way do I blame others for my own situation; however, the blame for their reaction is definitely laid at their feet.

If a Believer is not opposing the powers of darkness with his Faith in the Cross, which guarantees the help of the Holy Spirit, that Believer is going to fail, I don't care how hard he tries to do otherwise. That's what Romans Chapter 7 is all about. Unfortunately, much of the Church world has attempted to make Romans Chapter 7 a part of Paul's experience before his conversion. To be frank, such Scriptural interpretation is ridiculous. Even an elementary investigation of this Chapter will glaringly portray what was really happening.

Paul had been saved, baptized with the Holy Spirit, and then thought he could surely live the kind of life he wanted to live, which was a life of Victory in Christ. He found he couldn't, and despite how hard he tried. In other words, Satan overrode his willpower, which is about as obvious as anything could ever be (Rom. 7:18). To be frank, Satan is overriding the will of untold millions of Christians even at this very moment. In other words, they are trying with all their strength to not fail, but they are failing anyway. In fact, there are millions, and I think I exaggerate not, who once lived for God, but no longer make any effort to do so, and if one questions them closely, they will say, *"I tried to live it, but I just couldn't do it."*

The sickening truth is, in the manner in which they were attempting to live this life, they in fact could not do such, even as no one can. The Believer can only live this life, can only walk in Victory, as he places his Faith in the Cross, leaves his Faith in the Cross, which pertains to the Finished Work of Christ, which then guarantees the help of the Holy Spirit, which then guarantees Victory (Rom. 8:1-2).

FAILURE

The Christian will fail, irrespective as to whom he or she is, or how much God is using them, if they don't know the Source of Victory. And to add insult upon injury, they will *continue* to fail. It cannot be otherwise. It doesn't matter how hard they try, how much effort they make, how dedicated and sincere they are, even how much they pray or fast, which of course is included in the trying, they will fail.

The sadness is, the Church has moved so far away from the Cross, that it little more knows its source of Victory. While most of the Church (I trust that the word *"most"* applies), still believes in the Cross as it refers to Salvation, it knows almost nothing about the Finished Work of Christ as it refers to one's everyday walk before God. Consequently, the Church is doomed to failure.

At this present time, the Church by and large *is* living in failure. Of course, there are exceptions, but those exceptions are few. The reason is, it simply does not know the way of Victory.

It tries to find it through confession, through prayer, through laying on of hands with the Power of God falling resulting in manifestations, rebuking demons, fasting, and a hundred other things that one might name. While some, or all, of these things are helpful and right in their proper place, these things, plus others we have not named, will not bring about Victory in one's life.

The Christian should stop and think a moment. If any of these things could guarantee Salvation, or Victory in one's life, then Jesus died in vain (Gal. 2:21). In other words, He didn't have to come down here, and bleed and suffer and die on a Cross, if anything else that could be done could bring about that which man desperately needs — Redemption and Victory. However, there is only one thing that can bring about that for which man seeks, and that is what Christ did on the Cross and in His Resurrection.

THE STATE OF THE CHURCH

If I'm right in what I am saying, that there is no victory, and I mean none at all, outside of the Finished Work of Christ, and our continued Faith in that Work, then that means that most of the Church is living in a state of failure. Because the Truth is, most of the Church doesn't have the foggiest idea as to the Source of one's Victory which is the Cross. I know what I'm talking about. I've talked with too many Preachers, and I know my own personal experience which I'm afraid is indicative of most in one way or the other.

Many in the Church have the mistaken idea that if they're not guilty of what I humorously refer to as the big five — cigarettes, alcohol, drugs, immorality, gambling — then they're walking in victory. I remind the Reader, that there are many more sins other than those things just mentioned.

Jesus gave a glaring example of this by giving us the Parable of the prodigal son and the elder brother. Everyone knows the story of the prodigal, and how he wasted his substance with riotous living, but few know the story of the elder brother.

To be brief, the prodigal made it back, because he humbled himself before his Father, etc. He was gloriously and wondrously restored. However, the elder brother, although never leaving the family inheritance, never wasting his substance in riotous living, as far as we know, died and went to Hell. He was mean, unforgiving, sarcastic, self-righteous, spiteful, hateful, arrogant, disobedient, and rebellious. The sadness is, most would have looked at him and thought that everything was perfect. But everything was anything but perfect.

Regrettably, many Christians are in the same state as the elder brother. They are in the Church, participants in the things of the Church, very religious, but in fact, self-righteous and lacking in all the true Graces which speak of true Christianity. In other words, despite not being guilty of the *"big five,"* they are still in a terrible condition, living in victory not at all. They are trusting in themselves instead of the Cross. Satan doesn't care how he snares the Believer, just so he snares him. And to be sure, it is much easier to bring the prodigal back than it is the elder brother. And that's the condition that much of the modern Church is in presently.

In fact, much of the Church is in a state of denial. They compare themselves with others, and they can always find somebody else who they think is beneath them, so they make themselves feel righteous by doing this. However, such righteousness is self-righteousness, which God can never accept (II Cor. 10:12).

WHAT WAS I TO DO?

In a state of brokenness, totally crushed, not knowing what to do, still as stated, I knew the world held no answers, only the Lord. Regrettably, I was not advised too much in that direction. In fact, I was told in essence, that if I trusted the Lord I would be blacklisted, i.e., *"banned, refused, rejected."*

Satan had sprung the trap very carefully. Those who did not believe what I preached, and they were many, took this opportunity to demand their pound of flesh. The upshot of it all, and irrespective as to the statements made, they all wanted to stop me from Preaching, and would use any method at their disposal to do so. When I say *"they,"* I'm speaking of the Denomination with which I was associated, as well as almost the entirety of the Church world. In other words, despite the fact that hundreds of thousands were being brought to a saving knowledge of Jesus Christ, which was obvious for all to see, in other words the fruit was very visible, they still wanted to silence my voice, and as stated, would do anything to bring this about. Let me tell you why.

There was great jealousy involved because of my then large following. And as well, I very much opposed and said so strongly, many things which were then taking place in the Church, and continue unto this hour. I speak of the embracing of humanistic psychology as the answer to the ills of man, which completely repudiates the Cross. I speak of the *"Prosperity Message"* which makes the dollar bill, the end result of one's Faith, instead of Righteousness and Holiness. I speak of the music of the world, which had become the music of the Church. To be frank, I can continue, but I think the Reader gets the idea.

Not wanting my voice to be heard, and irrespective of repentance and crying to God, irrespective of the Anointing of the Holy Spirit which always remained and rightly so, irrespective of the Grace of God, all of this was and is ignored, actually rejected. Doors were and are closed everywhere, but for the most part, doors which are of little consequence anyway. In other words, they are not really doors that one desires to go through, meaning that they lead to nowhere.

However, irrespective of the excuses made or the reasons so-called given, the real reason is that for which we stand and that which we preach (Jude vs. 3). Again, regarding failure, I blame no one but myself, but regarding the reaction of most, I am not to blame.

THERE WERE FEW TO POINT THE WAY

As we have stated, the Church in the last nearly half century, has been moved so far away from the Cross, that it little knows anymore the true source of Victory. Please allow me to repeat myself, in that the Church still believes after a fashion in the Cross of Calvary as it refers to Salvation, but as a whole it knows almost nothing as it concerns this great Finished Work respecting the Christian's continued walk before the Lord, which in fact, is graphically outlined in Romans Chapters 6, 7, and 8.

There was no one to tell me the way, no one to show me the path to Victory, and because I personally believe, almost none knew that way themselves. This means they were living in some way, in some manner, in failure also. So, in actuality they could not function in the capacity of Galatians 6:1.

During those days, I remember speaking with two of the most famous Charismatic Preachers in the world. These were men I had known for a long time, actually household names. I found out that they did not at all know the way of Victory either. I am not demeaning them, because I did not myself know as well. That which they proposed, which I will not now reiterate, I knew was unscriptural. But even though I knew that, I still did not know the right way.

SEEK THE LORD

There was only one thing I could do, and that was to seek the Lord, which I did incessantly. Actually, the Lord told me to begin two prayer meetings a day, which we did, beginning in October of 1991.

He plainly told me that these prayer meetings were to be carried out not so much in the capacity of seeking Him for what He could do, but rather for Who He is. I was to get to know Him, to learn of Him, to understand Him, to commune with Him, at least as far as is possible to do so by the Power of the Holy Spirit.

For some five years I sought the Lord earnestly with tears. At times I related to Him, that if He did not show me the way to Victory, how that the Christian could live a perpetual life of Victory, overcoming every power of darkness, then I simply did not want to live. I was that desperate before Him.

I do not know why it took so long. But thank God the answer did come. I will never forget the moment, that the Light first begin to shine. The Lord took me to Romans Chapter 6. He then showed me the meaning of Chapters 7 and 8 as well.

When He first began to deal with my heart, Victory came immediately. But yet I realized that I had only scratched the surface; consequently, I implored Him to continue the Revelation, which He has unto this hour, and I pray shall ever continue to do so. The Truth is, it is impossible for one to exhaust the potential of the Finished Work of Christ. A million years, even a trillion years into eternity, we will still be learning of that which Jesus did in the Atonement. To be frank, I can sense the Presence of God even as I relate these words. This great Finished Work is so all-inclusive, so exceptional, so powerful, so great, grand and glorious, so sweeping in its embodiment, so consuming in its totality, that it is not possible for a human being to exhaust its resources.

Even though I have said it again and again, please allow me to repeat this, and it will not be the last time:

He showed me that all Victory was found in the Cross, just as all Salvation is found in the Cross.

He showed me that my Faith must be in the Cross, must remain in the Cross, because this is where the great Victory was purchased by Christ.

He then showed me, that once my Faith is properly placed, the Holy Spirit, even as Paul outlined in Romans Chapter 8, will then guarantee all the benefits of the great Sacrifice of Christ (Rom. 8:1-5). This is what is meant by *"walking after the Spirit."*

That is the road to Victory for the Christian and the only road to Victory. There is no other, because there doesn't need to be another. The Believer is *"in Christ,"* by virtue of the Crucifixion and the Resurrection, and one's Faith in that. The secret is to stay *"in Christ,"* which one does by continued Faith in that *"Finished Work."*

WHY IS IT THAT MANY CHRISTIANS ARE TRYING TO GO BEYOND THE CROSS?

While the Cross is being ignored by most Pentecostals, it is being outright denied by many Charismatics. In countless Charismatic Churches, some very large running thousands in attendance, no songs about the Blood are sung in their so-called worship, and nothing about the Cross is mentioned. If it is mentioned at all, it is spoken of as the *"worst defeat of the ages."*

To be frank, any worship that has its origin in anything other than the Cross and the Resurrection (and the two cannot be separated), is not really worship, at least that which God will recognize.

Whenever the Priests under the old economy of God, which draws the blueprint of that which would be, went into the Holy Place of the Tabernacle or Temple, with their Censors, which spoke of worship, the fire they carried in their Censors, and above all the Coals they placed on the Altar of Incense, all must come from the Brazen Altar, which was a type of the Cross. If they went in with any other type of fire, they could be executed on the spot (Lev. 10:1-7).

As well, when the High Priest went into the Holy of Holies once a year to make Atonement for the people, he could not go in without the blood of an innocent victim (clean animal) being placed upon the Mercy Seat. Had he done so, he as well, would have been stricken dead. Of course, this spoke of the great Sacrifice of Christ which would take place in the future, of which this was but a symbol (Lev. 16:14; 23:27; Heb. 9:7; 10:19-23).

This means that any worship based on anything except the Cross, or any type of Atonement based on anything except the Cross, cannot be accepted by God, is flatly refused by God, and in fact, is judged by God, even as it must be judged. God honors only the Sacrifice of Christ.

So, for Preachers to claim that the Cross was incidental, or that it was a place of weakness, and is not to be mentioned or addressed in any fashion whether by songs or by worship, etc., those Preachers are blaspheming. There is no greater sin than that.

Now you see why many Preachers do not like Jimmy Swaggart.

The entirety of the Old Testament is but a symbolism of what the Lord would do in the Redemption of mankind. Everything points toward the Cross, all the Sacrifices, all the Feast Days, even the Sabbath — all pointed to the Cross. Considering how obvious all of this is in the Old Testament, which points toward the New, proclaiming as to what will come, which is the Great Sacrifice of Christ, to ignore this, one has to be spiritually blind or spiritually deaf, or both!

HEBREWS CHAPTER 6

Paul said in Hebrews 6:1 (and I believe Paul wrote Hebrews), *"Therefore leaving the principles of the Doctrine of Christ, let us go on unto perfection."*

It would have been better translated from the original Greek, *"Therefore building upon the principles of the Doctrine of Christ, let us go on unto perfection."*

Even though the word *"leaving"* is correct, it does not come over into the English as it should. (Due to this, many have misinterpreted this Verse.)

The basic idea is: the foundation for the great Work of God and the Redemption of mankind was laid in the Old Testament as is obvious. However, that was only the foundation, and certainly not the Finished Work, which could only be brought about by Christ. Consequently, the Believer is to build on that foundation which structure is the great Sacrifice of Christ on the Cross, which finishes the house one might say, totally and completely, leaving nothing to be desired.

While the proper foundation of a house or a structure of any type is an absolute necessity, if one stops at the foundation, one really does not have anything. The structure must be built upon that proper foundation, for the whole to be complete.

The Old Testament was the foundation, while the New Covenant is the structure built upon that originally given. It is all in Christ, the foundation and the structure.

Does anyone seriously think, that we are to abandon or throw away *"the principles of the Doctrine of Christ,"* at least as such is claimed in many circles? Such is ridiculous! Christ is everything. He is the foundation, the structure, the past, the present, and the future. Everything is in Christ, and for anyone to think that Christ is to be left behind, or that we have now outgrown Christ, is patently absurd!

PERFECTION OR MATURITY

The word *"perfection"* as it is used in Hebrews 6:1, refers to the Finished Work of

Christ. Paul is telling the Jews that they must not stop at the Sacrifices, or the Old Covenant in any capacity, but rather go on (leaving) those particular things which were good and right in their time, but now have served their purpose. Once again, if an individual thinks of the foundation of a house, he will get the picture. While that is necessary, if that's all he has, he really has nothing. While the apparatus is in place, it is not finished as is overly obvious. The builder is to construct on the foundation, finishing the house or whatever structure is desired, which Christ did in His Finished Work regarding the Cross and the Resurrection, which of course, includes the Exaltation as well (Rom. 6:3-14; Eph. 2:6).

The Jews and all others for that matter, are told not to try to *"lay again the foundation of repentance from dead works,"* which refers to the Old Testament practices, and Faith toward God as it regards *those* practices. They were right then, but having served their purpose, which referred to types and shadows, they are no longer of necessity, because the reality has come, namely Christ.

This as well speaks of what Paul said in Hebrews 6:2, *"Of the doctrine of Baptisms* (the many washings which had to do with the Jewish purification processes), *and of laying on of hands* (which pertained to the person laying his hands on the head of the lamb about to be offered and confessing his sins), *and of resurrection of the dead* (of which knowledge was very limited), *and of eternal judgment* (of which knowledge was also very limited under the Old Covenant)."

Paul is saying that all of these things under the Old Covenant have now been replaced with the New. However, the people who claim that Verse 1 pertains to leaving the Cross of Christ, do not claim that Water Baptism, or *"laying on of hands,"* or the *"Resurrection"* are to be left as well. Of course, they don't! However, if one is to interpret Verse 1 in that fashion, one also has to interpret Verse 2 in the same manner, for they both mean the same thing.

No, there is nothing in the Word of God that even remotely hints that the Cross is to be laid aside at conversion, in other words that we go beyond the Cross. Anyone who goes beyond the Cross loses his way, because the Cross alone is the way.

NOTES

So, the suffering which Paul mentions here, has to do with the entire spectrum of true Christianity, but more particularly it refers to the Cross of Christ. Paul plainly said, *"For the preaching of the Cross is to them that perish foolishness"* (I Cor. 1:18). He also mentioned *"the offence of the Cross"* (Gal. 5:11).

If it could all be summed up, the persecution, the opposition, the animosity, whether from the world or the Church, are all because of the Cross. Whenever the Believer says, *"I'm going to trust what Jesus has done for me at the Cross,"* it arouses an animosity in unconverted hearts, and even converted hearts which are going in a wrong direction, for the simple reason that man's ways are rejected, and man, even redeemed man, loves his ways.

(30) "HAVING THE SAME CONFLICT WHICH YE SAW IN ME, AND NOW HEAR TO BE IN ME."

In this matter of suffering, the Philippians were experiencing the same sort of struggle Paul had endured throughout his Ministry. They had seen some of Paul's sufferings when he had been in Philippi (Acts 16:19-24). They had heard of others he had undergone more recently in Rome (perhaps from reports of travellers or other messengers, including those who conveyed the information about Epaphroditus, Philippians 2:26).

THE SAME CONFLICT

The phrase, *"Having the same conflict which ye saw in me,"* in essence speaks of the Christian struggle.

The word *"conflict"* is the translation of a Greek word used of an athletic contest. Our word *"agony"* comes from it. In essence one might say that *"life is in reality a spiritual Olympic festival. We are God's athletes to whom He has given an opportunity of showing what stuff we are made of."*

The word was used in later Greek of an inward struggle. Paul uses it to describe his own life in the midst of his untiring work for the Lord Jesus (Wuest).

In this Chapter we have a beautiful illustration of the true spirit of a Christian, even in circumstances exceedingly trying. The Apostle was in a situation where his true experience with the Lord would show itself, that is if there were such in his heart, which there certainly was. As well, this type of pressure will also bring out the bad passions of our nature, if in fact those are present.

The Apostle was a prisoner. He had been unjustly accused. He was about to be put on trial for his life. He was surrounded with enemies, and there were not a few false friends and rivals who took advantage of his imprisonment to diminish his influence, and to extend their own.

In this situation, he exhibited some of the tenderest and purest feelings that could ever exist in the heart of man — the genuine fruit of Christlikeness.

HIS CONDITION

Looking upon his own condition, he said that the trials which had happened to him, great as they were, had been overruled to the furtherance of the Gospel. The Gospel had become known even in the Imperial Palace. And though it had been preached by some with no good will towards him, and with much error, yet he cherished no hard feelings. He sought no revenge; he rejoiced that in any way, and from any motives, the great Truth had been made known that a Saviour had died, and Faith in His Death would bring Salvation. Even in its weakest form, that was better than nothing.

Looking toward the possibility that his trial before the Emperor might terminate in his death, that is before the Lord spoke to him about his impending release, he calmly anticipated such a result, and looked at it with composure.

He says that, in reference to the great purpose of his life, it would make no difference whether he lived or died, for he was assured that Christ would be honored whatever was the result. To him personally it would be gain to die; and, as an individual, he longed for the hour when he might be with Christ. This feeling is true Salvation, and this is produced only by the hope of Eternal Life through the Redeemer.

An impenitent sinner never expresses such feelings as these; nor does any other form of religion. Only Christianity enables a man to look upon death in this manner. It is not often that a man is even willing to die — and then this state of mind is produced, if in fact it is there, not by the hope of Heaven, but by disgust at the world; by disappointed ambition; by painful sickness, when the sufferer feels that any change would be for the better.

But Paul had none of these feelings. His desire to depart was not produced by a hatred of life; nor by the greatness of his suffering; nor by disgust at the world. It was the noble, elevated, and pure wish to be with Christ — to see Him Whom he supremely loved, Whom he had so long and so faithfully served, and with Whom he was to dwell forever. Consequently, the only reason why he would be content to remain here was, that he might be a little longer useful to his fellow man. As stated, this is real Christianity!

DEADNESS TO THE WORLD

Yet such deadness to the world may be produced — as it was in the case of Paul; such deadness to the world should exist in the heart of every sincere Christian. Where it does exist, death loses its terror, and the heir can look calmly on the bed where he will lie down to die; can think calmly of the moment when he will give the parting hand to his loved ones; can look peacefully on the spot where he will turn back to dust, and in view of all can triumphantly say, *"Come, Lord Jesus, come quickly"* (Barnes).

WHAT TYPE OF CONFLICT?

Paul had been given by the Lord the way of the victorious, overcoming Christian life. He gave us that in Romans Chapters 6, 7, and 8.

This doesn't mean that Satan will never attack us again personally, for he constantly does; however, it does mean if the Believer understands that the Cross is the site and scene of all Victory, and places his Faith in that Atoning Work of Christ, and leaves his Faith in that Atoning Work, that the Holy Spirit will then give power, thereby guaranteeing all the benefits of the Finished Work of Christ. Understanding that and acting upon that, the Christian need not fail.

In fact, this is the only pattern for victory given in the Word of God. There is no other, and any other manner that Christian man may choose, is doomed to failure.

So, when Paul speaks here of *"conflict,"* he's really not speaking of himself bogged down in a struggle with the evil one regarding sin in his own life. That had been conquered a long time before.

The conflict of which he speaks is rather outward conflict. It's the animosity of which we have already spoken, which festers in the heart of the world, against the Child of God. As stated, it is because of the Cross, and more particularly, the Believer's Faith in that great Sacrificial Work of Christ.

Actually, those in the world would not really even understand that, having little knowledge of the Cross, if any at all. Nevertheless, if one were able to go to the germ of all opposition against the Child of God by the world, he would find this as the cause.

Unfortunately, it's not only the opposition of the world that will raise itself against the true Child of God, but regrettably, even much of the Church follows suit. As we have stated, the Cross is an offence to those who would seek to find a way within their own abilities and efforts, which includes many Christians as well.

So, the conflict of which Paul speaks, is not him struggling with inward sin, but rather with outward forces.

THAT WHICH THEY HEARD

The phrase, *"And now hear to be in me,"* refers to his present incarceration in Rome.

It is ironical! Paul had felt strongly in his spirit for some length of time that the Lord had wanted him to minister in Rome, with him, no doubt, working toward this end. (Please see our Commentary on Acts.)

What he felt in his heart concerning the Imperial City was definitely from the Lord, and the unction in his heart to pray about this thing which he no doubt had, was encouraged by the Holy Spirit as well; however, Paul little dreamed of the manner in which all of this would be carried out. He would go to Rome, but as a prisoner of the Roman Empire. He would preach in Rome, but as a prisoner shackled to a Roman soldier.

Nevertheless, he went, and irrespective of the strangeness of the manner, this was what the Holy Spirit wanted and desired. Consequently, he writes to his beloved Philippians from a position of house arrest, with his ears constantly hearing the clank of the chain.

THE CHRISTIAN LIFE

Some of the modern Gospel have tried to make a Heaven on Earth. It is not to be! The purpose of the Holy Spirit is something else entirely.

He is attempting to bring about Holiness and Righteousness within our lives, in other words, to make us Christlike. He is successful more or less, according to our cooperation with Him. However, it will help us greatly to know what He is really trying to do. Unfortunately, millions of Christians (and I exaggerate not), are going in an entirely different direction, the direction of worldly wealth, or at least this dangling carrot which they suppose they will get. The Truth is, they won't receive anything, simply because none of it is of God.

That which the Holy Spirit truly wants to develop within our hearts and lives, at times is not brought about easily or quickly. One would never think that a person of the spiritual stature of Paul would need the clank of the chain. But the Holy Spirit knew he did, and Paul's submission to this is overly obvious in this great Epistle. To be frank, if this is all we learn from this Epistle, it will have been well worth our time spent in its study many times over.

I want to be what the Lord wants me to be. I want the Holy Spirit to carry out within my life that which He has been sent to do. I don't want to stand at the Judgment Seat of Christ, and hear the Lord tell me that if I had only cooperated a little more with the Holy Spirit, things would have been a lot different.

I have made enough mistakes in the past, that I do not want to make them again. If it takes the house arrest, then that's what I want! If it takes the Roman soldier and the clank of the chain, then that's what I want! Nothing matters but Christlikeness! Nothing matters but yielding to the direction the Holy Spirit desires.

I've had enough of self-will and self-effort. From bitter experience I know where that road leads, and I want no more of that. I want only that which the Lord desires, only that which He wants, only that which is His Will. Nothing else will suffice, as nothing else can suffice.

"There will never be a sweeter story,
"Story of the Saviour's Love Divine;

*"Love that bro't Him from the realms
   of Glory,
"Just to save a sinful soul like mine."*

*"Boundless as the universe around me,
"Reaching to the farthest soul away;
"Saving, keeping love it was that found
   me,
"That is why my heart can truly say."*

*"Love beyond our human
   comprehending,
"Love of God in Christ how can it be!
"This will be my theme and never
   ending,
"Great redeeming love of Calvary."*

CHAPTER 2

(1) "IF THERE BE THEREFORE ANY CONSOLATION IN CHRIST, IF ANY COMFORT OF LOVE, IF ANY FELLOWSHIP OF THE SPIRIT, IF ANY BOWELS AND MERCIES,"

The focus now turns to problems within the Church. To encourage the fulfillment of this injunction, Paul lists four incentives. All begin in this Verse with the little word *"if,"* but the condition is assumed to be true.

Thus, the sense of the first phrase is *"If there are any grounds for exhortation because you are in Christ, as indeed there are...."* As Christians, they were in a vital union with Christ and this placed obvious obligations on them. They were responsible to heed the orders of Christ as issued by Him either directly during His Ministry or through His Apostles.

Second, the comfort and encouragement provided by love should prompt the Philippians to join hands in common action. Their love for Christ and for their fellow Believers (including Paul) ought to impel them to desist from divisiveness in any form.

Third, the fellowship produced by the Holy Spirit should stimulate the practical exercise of unity. They have been made one by the Spirit (I Cor. 12:13) and thus are partners with Him and with each other.

Fourth, the existence of tenderness and compassion among them would make the unity that was being called for the normal and expected thing.

NOTES

CONSOLATION

The phrase, *"If there be therefore any consolation in Christ,"* could have been translated, and in fact should have been translated, *"Sense there is . . ."* or *"In view of the fact that there is. . . ."* In the Greek the word *"if"* translated here is actually a *"fulfilled condition,"* and so should not have been translated *"if."* The four things mentioned in this Verse are not hypothetical in their nature. They are facts.

"Consolation" in the Greek is *"imploration, supplication, entreaty, exhortation, admonition, encouragement, comfort, solace."* In fact, this word has several different meanings as is obvious. The meaning is to be used in any particular case being determined by the context in which the word is used.

What these Philippians needed right here was not really consolation but *"exhortation,"* in view of the possible lack of unity among them.

The idea is, that Christ's wonderful life should be an admonition, exhortation, and encouragement to the Philippians to live in a state of harmony among themselves. Paul uses this as a basis for his exhortation to them. In other words, they are exhorted to live Christlike.

If the Presence of Christ, if Communion with Christ, has power to stir the heart, to stimulate the emotions, to constrain the will, then it has the power also to make one Christlike, which will automatically solve the problem of dissension between Brethren. Such disunity should not be, and if Christ be allowed to have His Way, such will not be.

The problem of a lack of unity in the Church at Philippi, which we will address in greater detail later, was all caused by self-will, as all such problems are always caused by self-will.

HOW CAN THE BELIEVER BE CHRISTLIKE?

To be sure, the exhortation given in this Verse is that we must be Christlike. Any true Christian desires this, but how can such be?

If instructions are given in this vein, most of the time it centers up on a person doing something, being faithful to Church, being faithful with their giving, developing a prayer life, winning souls, etc.

All of these things are extremely important, but if we attempt to be Christlike by doing these things, the end result will not be what we think. In fact, we should do these things very heartedly, but because we <u>are</u> Christlike, not to become Christlike. So, that type of consecration, although commendable, will not achieve the desired results. In other words, one cannot become Christlike by *"doing!"*

FAITH

Being Christlike is a matter of Faith just as much as Salvation is a matter of Faith, or our victorious walk with the Lord is a matter of Faith. So, that being the case, what does it mean?

As we've already stated, self-will is the problem in all of these things, and is the opposite of Christlikeness, i.e., *"God's will."* So, the real question is, how do I conquer self-will?

Jesus addressed this question very succinctly when He said, *"If any man will come after Me, let him deny himself, take up his Cross daily, and follow Me."*

He then said, *"For whosoever will save his life shall lose it: but whosoever will lose his life for My sake, the same shall save it"* (Lk. 9:23-24).

In these two Passages, we find the answer to our question.

SELF-DENIAL

Jesus said that if any man, and that means all, would follow Him, the first thing that must be done is for one to *"deny himself."* What did Jesus mean by that?

Most people read this all wrong, thinking that Jesus is demanding that we deny ourselves any pleasure of any nature, living a spartan life, etc.

No! That's not what He is speaking about.

When he speaks of self-denial, He is actually talking about a total lack of dependence on self in any capacity, with total dependence on the Lord. In other words, we stop all of our efforts of *"doing,"* trying to bring about the desired results of Righteousness and Holiness, etc. We quit depending on self, which means to stop all dependence on our own efforts, our own abilities, our own works, ad infinitum. He is not speaking of suffering, or the denial of any type of pleasure, etc., but rather the denial of self as it regards personal effort.

The truth is, this addresses the entirety of the world. One could say I think without fear of exaggeration, that just about everyone in some way is attempting to better themselves, to improve themselves by their own efforts. In fact, self-improvement is one of the great industries in the world. Everybody wants to improve themselves for a variety of reasons, mostly selfish. Consequently, the world introduces all types of self-betterment programs, which are guaranteed, at least in their words, to bring about the intended result.

The Truth is, self-improvement is impossible, at least within one's self. How can corrupt, degraded, demeaned, insufficient, sinful self, improve self? That's like a leopard attempting to change his spots, or an Ethiopian changing his skin. The Bible plainly tells us that such cannot be done (Jer. 13:23). But yet man keeps trying. And perhaps Christians try harder than all.

There is a way that self can be changed, and only one way, this of which Jesus has said, which alone will produce Christlikeness.

THE CROSS

If one is to notice, Jesus said that His followers, and that means all, must take up the Cross in their following Him. What did He mean by that?

When one speaks of taking up the Cross, most think of terrible suffering or terrible privation or want; consequently, most Christians read very hurriedly past these Verses. Torture is not exactly what the human heart desires, so there aren't many takers respecting this of which Jesus demands. Consequently, Satan has been very successful in blinding Christians to what Jesus was really speaking about here.

No, taking up the Cross is not suffering, or privation, or want, or undergoing some terrible trial, or being sent to Siberia, etc. In fact, this of which Jesus demands here, is the most glorious, wonderful, miraculous, fulfilling life that one could ever lead. In fact, it is the only answer to *"more abundant life,"* and the *"rest"* of which Jesus promised (Jn. 10:10; Mat. 11:28-30). And yet most Christians have been blinded to this fact.

Taking up the Cross simply means that one trusts in all the things which were carried out at the Cross. In fact, Jesus suffered so that we won't have to suffer. He suffered that we might enjoy *"more abundant life."* So, He's not asking us to suffer.

He is asking that we place our total dependence on what He did at the Cross and the Resurrection. There He purchased our Redemption, satisfied the claims of Heavenly Justice, atoned for all sin, thereby breaking Satan's grip on the human race, at least for those who will believe. In the Atonement, which is the Finished Work of Christ, the great package of the New Covenant was fulfilled and completed, in order that all may have this *"life, and have it more abundantly"* (Jn. 10:10).

The Cross is where Jesus paid the price for all of this, where He purchased our Salvation and our victorious overcoming power, all with His Precious Blood. Therein lies all Salvation, Redemption, abundant life, overcoming power, Divine Healing, prosperity in every capacity, in other words, everything that the human heart could ever desire. That's what He did at the Cross, hence him telling us to take up that Cross daily and follow Him.

Why did He use the words *"take up"* as it refers to the Cross?

"Take up" in the Greek is *"airo,"* and literally means *"to take up in order to remove."* Having Faith in the Cross, which means having Faith in what it provides, actually refers to removing all things which are harmful to the Child of God. It removes all sin from the believing sinner, and the terrible problem of self-will as it regards the Christian. In fact, this is the only way that these things can be removed.

DAILY

Faith in the Cross is to be exhibited on a *"daily"* basis, exactly as Jesus says here. In fact, that's the way in which the Lord has designed Faith in every capacity.

The Faith I had for yesterday, while an excellent provision for that particular time, will not suffice for today. As stated, it is designed in this fashion. The Lord wants us to appropriate Faith even on a daily basis. Consequently, we are to have Faith in the Atonement, the Finished Work of Christ on a *"daily"* basis, meaning that we *never stop* looking to the Finished Work, which develops trust in Christ on a continuing basis.

Unfortunately, and even as we have said many times, most Christians leave the Cross at their initial Salvation experience. In other words, they do not know or realize the part the Cross plays in their *"daily walk before God."* The truth is, just as important as the Cross is in the initial Salvation experience, just as important is it in our daily living. That's what Jesus is speaking about.

I am to believe this day that what Jesus did at the Cross and the Resurrection, totally and completely set me free. I am to act upon that. If Jesus is victorious, and He definitely is, then I am victorious, and that means I am victorious today right now.

So, the little word *"daily"* is very significant, even as is now obvious.

FOLLOW JESUS

He then said, *"Follow Me,"* and what did He mean by that?

No, He is not telling us to follow Him to the Cross, at least as it regards getting back on that wooden beam, and paying some type of price. That's not the idea at all.

He wants us to follow Him regarding all that which He has done as it pertains to our Salvation, our Victory, and our prosperity.

We are to follow Him to the Cross, as it regards the benefits of the Cross. We are to follow Him in His burial, even as it refers to all our past being buried with its sinfulness and wickedness. We are to follow Him in the Resurrection, which guaranteed us newness of life (Rom. 6:3-5). We are to also follow Him in His Exaltation, which means that He is now exalted, actually seated by the right Hand of the Father. In fact, we are seated there with Him (Eph. 2:6).

Satan has been very successful in getting Christians to believe that taking up the Cross daily meant terrible suffering on their part. Consequently, we don't have many takers, and rightly so.

No, that's not what Jesus meant. To follow Him, is the most glorious, wonderful thing there could ever be.

Why do you think He came down here?

If we could suffer our way into Salvation or Victory, then Jesus would not have had to come and die on the Cross. In fact, if suffering would do it, then almost all the world should have whatever it is that suffering is supposed to provide, because most of the world suffers terribly so.

As long as the Christian believes such foolishness, he will never receive all the benefits the Cross affords.

Yes, Jesus suffered terribly so, but He suffered that we might not have to suffer. He took the penalty for my sins, that I might not have to suffer that penalty. He satisfied the claims of Heavenly Justice, because I could not do so. He paid a debt that I could never have hoped to pay. In fact, He did it all for me. In fact, He came to this very world for that very purpose — to die on a Cross, suffering in my place, that I might have this *"more abundant life."*

Oh! How I sense His Presence even as I say these words. How much my heart fills up with joy when I realize what He has done for me, and for you. Considering the terrible price that He has paid, it is a shame, in fact, the crime of the ages, that we do not enjoy all that He has done for us, once again, considering the price He paid for all this.

LOSING AND SAVING ONE'S LIFE

What did He mean by the statement, *"For whosoever will save his life shall lose it"*?

He simply meant that if we attempt to do all of these things which we need by our own efforts and abilities, such as Salvation from sin, victory over sin as a Believer, victory over Satan in every capacity, improving our own life, etc., we will not get the desired results, but rather the very opposite. Instead of saving our life we will actually lose it.

So, He said *"But whosoever* (and that means all) *will lose his life for My sake, the same shall save it."* He means that we should put our lives totally in Him, which refers to what He did at the Cross and the Resurrection, leaving ourselves there, believing totally in what He did, which will guarantee us life, which means we will save our life. That's what Paul kept talking about when he said over and over again, *"In Christ"* (Rom. 8:1; Eph. 1:3-5, 7, 10).

In fact, this is what Jesus was talking about in John Chapter 10, when He said, *"Verily, verily, I say unto you, he that entereth not by the door into the sheepfold, but climbeth up some other way, the same is a thief and a robber"* (Jn. 10:1). This is the same as saying, that if we try to find our life any other way than in Jesus, we will lose it. God cannot accept us in that fashion, in fact, looking at us as *"a thief and a robber."*

Conversely, if we follow Him, He will *"lead us out,"* i.e., *"out into excellent pasture,"* i.e., *"life"* (Jn. 10:2-3).

All of this is for *"His sake,"* meaning, that God gives us all of these good things, all wonderful things, glorious things, *"for Christ's sake."* He doesn't do these wonderful things on our merit, but rather on His, i.e., *"For His sake!"*

COMFORT OF LOVE

The phrase, *"If any comfort of love,"* refers to coming to the side of one to stimulate or comfort him. It speaks of persuasive address.

The word *"love"* as it is used here, is the Greek word for God's Love.

The realization of the Divine Love which reached down and saved these Philippians, and all of us as well, should urge them to live in a spirit of unity with one another.

In addition to that, this Divine Love produced in the hearts of the Philippian Saints by the Holy Spirit, should cause them to so love each other with a love that impels one to sacrifice one's self for the one loved, that their little differences will be ironed out, and they will live in unity with one another.

So, in the first admonition we have Christlikeness, and in the second we have Love.

In the statement, *"If any comfort of love,"* Paul is actually saying, *"Having the same love."* If in fact that is the case, and it definitely is for those who truly are serving the Lord, though we might have different opinions on certain things, yet we will be united in love. In fact, it cannot be any other way. If the same love is in the hearts of both Christians, and in fact, there is no other type of love, then it should not be difficult at all to love each other.

The harm is, that self-will takes over many Believers, literally rooting out the Love of God, with it no longer having sway. The question is, *"is the Saint ruled by the Love of God, or by self-will?"*

If we are ruled by the Love of God, it will provide a tender comfort at all times, which we will be quick to extend to our brother in the Lord. Conversely, if we are ruled by self-will, as are many, if not most, Christians, then the end result will be the ways of the world. That's the reason the will, i.e., *"self,"* must be hidden in Christ. If it is hidden in Christ, only love will flow from such a heart.

If self-will is the case, the individual will use the ways of the world, which speaks of selfishness, greed, temper, anger, ambition, covetousness, which means the individual becomes manipulative and political. In other words, he ceases altogether to be spiritual!

FELLOWSHIP OF THE SPIRIT

The phrase, *"If any fellowship of the Spirit"* refers to a common interest and a mutual and active participation in the things of God, in which the Believer and the Holy Spirit are joint-participants. This is the result of the Spirit's work of regeneration and His control over the Saint who is definitely to be subjected to Him.

Paul appeals to the Philippians to be likeminded in view of the fact that each of them participates with the Holy Spirit in a common interest and activity, and, therefore, if each Saint is interested in the things of the Spirit, and thus in the same things, there should naturally follow a unity among the Philippians. The Holy Spirit by thus controlling each Saint, produces this unity and accord among them.

One might ask here, *"If each Saint is indwelt by the Spirit, why is there not that unity among all Saints, of which Paul speaks?"*

The answer is, that this joint-participation and interest and a mutual and active participation in the things of God is produced by the Spirit, not by virtue of His indwelling but by virtue of His *control* over the Believer. The trouble in the Philippian Church, and every other Church as well, was that all the Saints were not living Spirit-controlled lives. If they had been, there would have been unity.

Paul's exhortation for unity among the Philippian Saints was, therefore, given upon a reasonable and workable basis. There can be unity if they would all live Spirit-controlled lives (Wuest).

Spirit-control is the key! While the Holy Spirit indwells every Believer, whether weak in the Lord or strong, the mere fact of indwelling does not guarantee many things. All the great and wonderful things He can do, and wants to do, and in fact has been sent to do, cannot be done, unless He has our cooperation.

HOW DO WE COOPERATE WITH HIM?

First of all we must ardently desire Him to have His total and complete way within our hearts and lives. We should also ardently seek the Lord in prayer, making our wishes known to Him, actively *seeking* His control in all things.

We must know and understand, that the Holy Spirit is God, and as such, He can do anything. We must also know, that He has been sent to perform a mission within our lives, and that mission is the Will of God and not our self-will (Rom. 8:27).

In fact, there can be no *"fellowship of the Spirit,"* if we do not have His Mind, but rather our mind. We must want what He wants, and desire what He desires. If in fact we don't want that, we must earnestly seek the Lord that He would mold our will into His will, and certainly desire that He use whatever means He needs to get this done, irrespective as to what it might be. In other words, if I'm not willing, I'm willing to be made willing.

The truth is, many Believers are actually scared of the Will of God. Satan has made them believe a lie in this capacity, exactly as they have believed the lie about the Cross.

They think if they seek the Will of God, that God will want them to do some terrible thing that they don't want to do, in fact, would almost rather be dead than try to do it.

No, the Lord will never do anything of that nature. In fact, He does the very opposite. He seeks only our good, our welfare, our happiness, our joy, our fulfillment, and our development. He has come that we might have *"life and have it more abundantly,"* and that doesn't mean living a life of dreary existence.

So, a Saint having the Will of God is the single most important thing, the single most glorious thing, the single most rewarding thing there could ever be. In fact, it is the only thing that will bring the Saint joy and happiness.

All of this is a matter of surrendering to the Will of God, to the Ways of God, which is hard for the Saint. It shouldn't be, but it is.

Man and even redeemed man, loves his own efforts, his own abilities, his own way. Never mind that his *"way,"* which seems right to him, but in fact is so wrong, has gotten him into all types of problems and difficulties. He still loves this *"fair show of the flesh."* As Abraham was loathe to give us Ishmael, and because Ishmael was a product of Abraham's own efforts; likewise, modern Believers have the same struggle.

BOWELS AND MERCIES

The phrase, *"If any bowels and mercies,"* refers to being tenderhearted, and to have compassionate yearnings and actions.

These Graces present in the lives of the Philippian Saints would move them to live at peace with one another. Little differences (and little they are) would be patched up. Estrangements would be healed. Bickering would cease (Wuest).

"Bowels (compassion)*"* and *"Mercies* (tenderheartedness),*"* should be characteristic of all Christians. The Holy Spirit through the Apostle is saying here that such will be the case, if Christlikeness is paramount, which will always produce *"love,"* which gives the Holy Spirit latitude.

In this one Verse, Paul gives the fourfold basis of Christian unity. Consequently, I think it should be overly obvious as to how important all of this really is. Let's look at it further:

THE FOURFOLD BASIS OF CHRISTIAN UNITY

The exhortations in the Pauline Epistles grew out of the conditions found in the Churches to which they were addressed. Because fallen human nature has not changed in 2,000 years, conditions that prevailed during Paul's time are existent in the Churches of today as well.

There were minor divisions in the Philippian Church, that Church incidently which in such a marked way helped in Paul's support as a Missionary. Two of these divisions possibly centered about two women in the Church who were capable and prominent leaders in its work, especially taking leadership in supporting Paul. These women headed two factions which were at variance with one another. To bring them together would be to heal the breach, not only between them, but between those who followed them.

The exhortation in Philippians 4:2-3, is not abrupt. Paul had prepared the way by laying a groundwork for it in Philippians 2:1-4, where we have detailed exhortation, and Philippians 2:5-8, where we have the great Example portrayed Who in His Life exemplified the one outstanding thing that will heal all such divisions in the local Church, namely a Christlike humility.

In Philippians 2:1, Paul presents four things which constitute the basis for unity among the Saints. These demand careful treatment in the original, which we have attempted, at least in part to do. In brief, the four are as follows:

CHRISTLIKENESS

This produces Humility. Christ's beautiful life is itself the exhortation to unity which these Saints needed. His humility as spoken of in Philippians 2:5-8, is the very thing that would lead to unity, hence the basis of these divisions was pride. His life, therefore, was the ground of appeal which Paul used. *"In view of the fact that there is a certain ground of appeal in Christ which exhorts you ... be likeminded."*

If all the Saints would keep their eyes on the Lord Jesus, and walk in His footsteps of humility, divisions in a local Church would cease.

LOVE

The incentive to unity is produced by love. That is, that love which the Holy Spirit produces in the heart of the Saint, causes and enables that Saint to love his fellow-Saint, and where Divine Love is, there is unity.

Thus, love produces the incentive to unity. If the Saints in a local Church would love each other with the self-sacrificial love of John 3:16, and the love as analyzed for us in I Corinthians Chapter 13, divisions would cease, and unity would prevail.

The secret of the possession of this love is found in a desire for the fullness of the Holy Spirit, and a trust in the Lord Jesus for that fullness (Jn. 7:37-38).

FELLOWSHIP OF THE SPIRIT

This does not mean that there is a fellowship between the Saint and the Holy Spirit. The fellowship of the Saint is with the Father and with His Son Jesus Christ (I Jn. 1:3; Eph. 3:16-17) made possible through the Ministry of the Holy Spirit.

The word *"fellowship"* is from a Greek word which refers to a relation between individuals which involves a common interest and a mutual, active participation in that interest. Here, as stated, it refers to the Ministry of the Spirit in the life of the Saint, and the cooperation of the Saint with the Spirit in His Work causing Him to grow in Grace, this cooperation consisting of the Saint's yieldingness to the Spirit and the act of his freewill in choosing the right and doing it. If followed, this Ministry of the Spirit enables the Saint to live in unity with his fellow-Saints.

BOWELS AND MERCIES

This is Compassion and Grace. As the Lord has had compassion on us, we must have compassion on our fellow-Saints. As well, as the Lord has shown us Mercy, we are to likewise show Mercy to fellow-Saints who have wronged us, etc.

As always, that which the Lord has done for us, we are to make every attempt to carry out the same toward others. While of course, we fall far short, in being unable to do many things, simply because they lie beyond the possible; still, we can show the spirit and the principle of all these things He has done for us, to others.

(2) "FULFIL YE MY JOY, THAT YE BE LIKEMINDED, HAVING THE SAME LOVE, BEING OF ONE ACCORD, OF ONE MIND."

This is another plea by Paul for unity among the people in the Church at Philippi. They were to be *"likeminded,"* that is, being of one mind as it regarded Doctrine, etc.

The enjoinder to maintain unity in their thought and action is elaborated on in four participial phrases. By complying with these instructions, the Readers would create a climate where true unity would flourish:

1. They should be possessing a mutual love. Inasmuch as it is assumed that all were Believers indwelt by the same Spirit, the love that is the fruit of the Spirit (Gal. 5:22) ought to be demonstrated in every life.

2. They should be setting their minds on unity with oneness of soul. This phrase repeats the thought appearing earlier in the Verse and reinforces the conclusion that there was a problem of disharmony within the congregation. It may be unfair to center the problem on Euodias and Syntyche (Phil. 4:2), but they were at least involved, if not primary, in the situation.

3. They should avoid selfish ambition and conceit and consider others above themselves. This is in Verse 3, and we will deal with that regarding commentary on that Verse.

4. They should be looking not only to their own interests but also to those of others. This is in Verse 4, which we will address at that time.

JOY

The phrase, *"Fulfill ye my joy,"* refers to the Philippians going on further in Christ, thereby growing in Grace and in the Knowledge of the Lord. In this case, this would be done by their union, zeal, and humility.

Concerning Paul's statement, Lightfoot says, *"Fill my cup of gladness to overflowing."* This fervent appeal by the Apostle has been called a *"continuing of earnestness."* The idea is, what would complete his joy and love, which would be to heed his admonition, would also be for their good.

The Apostle not only saw the tremendous spiritual growth which these Philippians had experienced, which brought great joy to his heart, he also saw the temptations to rivalry and discord which were working at Philippi. This is not to say that this problem was far advanced, but one could see a risk that it definitely might go further, hence the admonition of the Apostle. He has it in his heart to expel this evil, by promoting the principles and dispositions that are opposed to it.

To be frank, the problems which Paul addresses in this particular Church, were problems in all Churches, and at the same time continue unto this hour in modern Churches. In other words, in all ages and conditions of the Church these dangers are nigh at hand. Self-seeking and self-exaltation are forms in which sin works most easily, and out of these come rivalry and discord by the very nature of the case. Eager grasping at our own objects leads to disregard of the rights and interests of others; and then comes conflict. Danger in this direction was visible to the Apostle.

SELF-WILL

It may be asked how this should be, if the Philippians were genuine and hearty Christians, such as the Apostle's commendations bespeak them? Here a principle comes to light which deserves to be considered.

Even those who have cordially embraced Christianity, and who have loyally given effect to it in some of its outstanding applications, are wonderfully prone to stop short. They do not foresee, or they do not care to realize, the bearing of the same principles, which they have already embraced, upon whole regions of human life and human character; in other words, they leave some parts of their life, their self-will unattended, in effect, ignoring the warnings of the Holy Spirit in these departments.

They are pleased to have won so much ground, and do not think about the Canaanites, so to speak, who still hold a ground in their lives. So, in whole regions of life, the carnal mind is allowed to work on, undetected and practically unopposed.

This tendency is aided by the facility we have in disguising from ourselves the true character of dispositions and actions, when these do not quite plainly affront Christian rules. Self-assertion and bad temper, for example, can put on the character of honest firmness and hearty zeal, when they are actually not that at all.

More particularly, when spiritual principles have led us into certain lines of action, we are apt to take for granted that all is right which we do on those particular lines, when that just might not be the case.

The Philippians, and we as well, might be generally a company of sincerely Christian people. And yet the character of some of them might disclose sad tokens of selfishness and bitterness. Therefore, they must be called (and we ourselves) to give heed to the principles and motives that expel those sins.

CHRISTIAN PRACTICE

One of our problems as a Christian is that we make excuses or allowances for things in our life which are not pleasing to the Lord, but which we have made ourselves believe are not too very important. However, Paul saw this tendency in the Philippians even though they did not seem to see it themselves.

This pertains to the practice of Christianity, in other words, how it plays out in our everyday lives, as we deal with our Brothers and Sisters in the Lord. The idea is, that if proper practice is not heeded and quickened, then Salvation ceases to be real, the Promises wither unfulfilled, in effect, Christ has failed.

The Kingdom of God within us must exist in a light and love for which goodness is a necessity, and evil a grief and heartbreak. But if it is not so with us, where do we stand?

The Philippians knew how Paul had at heart their true welfare and their true spiritual dignity. That which, if it came to pass, would so gladden him, must at the same time be something great and good for them.

Someone has well said, *"The loving solicitude of a keener-sighted and a more simple-hearted Christian, the solicitude which makes his heart throb and his voice tremble as he speaks, has often startled slumbering Brethren into a consciousness of their own insensibility, and awakened them to worthier outlooks."*

LIKEMINDED

The phrase, *"That ye be likeminded,"* refers from the original Greek word, *"phroneo,"* to *"entertain or have a sentiment or opinion."* It does not necessarily refer to all believing exactly in the same manner about every single point of doctrine, but it does mean that if there is disagreement that it be done agreeably, without ill-will, temper, or an attitude of self-will.

Unity of mind and of heart is the thing inculcated. Under the influence of the great objects of Faith and of the motive forces of Christianity this was to be expected. Their ways of thinking and their ways of feeling, however different, should be so molded in Christ as to reach full mutual understanding and a full mutual affection. Nor should they rest contented when either of these fail; for that would be contentment with defeat; but Christ's followers are to always aim at victory.

It is obvious to say here that cases might arise in which turbulent or contentious persons might make it impossible for the rest of the Church, however well disposed, to secure either one accord or one mind. When such occurs, there are Christian ways of dealing with it.

Still more obviously one might say that conscientious differences of opinion, and that even on matters of the moment, must inevitably occur sooner or later; and a general admonition to be of one mind does not meet such a case. Perhaps it may be said in reply that the Church and the Christians have hardly conceived how much might be attained in the way of agreement if our Christianity were sincere enough, thorough enough, and affectionate enough. In that case there might be wonderful attainment in finding agreement, and in dismissing questions on which it is not needful to agree.

But if we are not to soar so high as this, it may at least be said that, while conscientious diversities of judgment are not to be disguised, they may be dealt with, among Believers, in a Christian way, with due emphasizing of the truth agreed upon, with a prevailing determination to speak truth in love.

THE SAME LOVE

The phrase, *"Having the same love,"* presents the Apostle multiplying the admonition, piling one phrase upon another, all meaning essentially the same thing. In effect, Paul taxes the resources of language to make emphatic his urgent demand for unity. However, let us quickly say, the unity of which he proclaims here is not identical with uniformity nor with union.

This short phrase concerning love tells us several things:

1. First of all every Believer as we've already stated, has the same identical love — the God kind of Love. In view of this, accord should not be difficult.

2. This love that God has given to Believers has come forth preparing at great cost and with great pains a new destiny for men. Love had brought Paul and the other Believers, one by one, into this higher region. And it proved to be a region in which love was the ground on which they stood, and love the Heaven over their heads, and loved the air they breathed. And here love was coming to be their own new nature, love responsive to the love of Father, Son, and Spirit, and love going out from those who have been so blessed to bless and gladden others. This was the true, the eternal goodness, the eternal blessedness; and it was theirs. This was what Faith embraced in Christ *"Who loved me and gave Himself for me."* This was what Faith claimed right to be and do. If this was not so, Christianity was reduced to nothing. If a man have not love, he is nothing (I Cor. Chpt. 13).

3. Love is to be the basis on which Christianity works, and this speaks of both the spiritual and practical sides. That means it does not function from the position of intellectualism, place and position, race or color, superiority or inferiority. If it does, it's not functioning from true Christianity.

The world functions on all manner of things, but not at all on love, for it's impossible for the world to have the God kind of love. It does have a type of love, but it nowhere resembles that which is of God. Consequently, it is impossible for those who do not know the Lord to function in the manner which is possible only for true Christians. Therefore, if we do not function in this manner, this manner of love, then we have slipped away from the very foundation of our moorings, and are, in effect, operating in the same manner in which the world operates.

In fact, this is the cause of all fusses, squabbles, fights, and disagreements which lead to splits, anger, malice, sarcasm, etc. Of course, I'm speaking of that which happens in the Church between Christians. It means that one or both of the parties are not operating in love but rather by the ways of the world.

ONE ACCORD

The phrase, *"Being of one accord, of one mind,"* presents a spiritual truth. Several times in the Book of Acts it is stated by the Holy Spirit that the Disciples were *"of one accord."* This was the condition of Pentecost and of the many answers to prayer following it. In fact, this was the condition that led to the proclamation of the Jerusalem Decree (Acts Chpt. 15). Nothing less than this is adequate, urges the veteran Apostle.

The idea in all of this is, that difficulties, whatever they might have been, were such as could be gotten over. There was no good reason why the Philippians should not in their Church life exhibit harmony; it would be so, if Christian influences were cordially admitted into minds and hearts, and if they made a fit estimate of the supreme importance of unity in Christ.

The same thing may be said of the innumerable cases in later times in which Christians have divided and contended. It is right to say, however, that these considerations are not to be applied without qualification to all kinds and degrees of separation between Christians. It is a cause for sorrow that denominational divisions are so many; and they have often been both cause and consequence of unchristian feeling.

Yet when men part peaceably to follow out their deliberate convictions, to which they cannot give ground, and when in doing so they do not unchurch or condemn one another, there may be less offense against Christian charity than in cases where a communion, professedly won, is the scene of bitterness and strife.

As stated, it is one thing to disagree, but quite something else altogether to disagree disagreeably. I can disagree with my Brother or Sister concerning doctrine or practical applications if such arise, while at the same time doing so agreeably, continuing to love them, which is the manner in which it should be done, and in fact, can be done if there is Christlikeness in our hearts and lives.

(3) "LET NOTHING BE DONE THROUGH STRIFE OR VAINGLORY; BUT IN LOWLINESS OF MIND LET EACH ESTEEM OTHER BETTER THAN THEMSELVES."

Paul had experienced adverse affects from this sort of selfish ambition among some unworthy preachers at Rome (Phil. 1:17), and no doubt, from many others in other places through the years. Persons who seek to advance themselves usually enjoy glorying in their success, but all such glory is *"vain conceit."* The Christian attitude should reveal itself in *"humility."*

As it regards this exercise (humility), Paul instructed his readers to *"consider others better than themselves."* This does not mean that we must have false or unrealistic views of our own gifts as compared with those of others. Moral superiority is not in view here. What Paul means is that our consideration for others must precede concern for ourselves (Rom. 12:10). This would go far toward removing disharmony.

STRIFE AND VAINGLORY

The phrase, *"Let nothing be done through strife or vainglory,"* refers to particular factions in the Philippian Church, as this exhortation infers. The prohibitions in the Pauline Epistles are an indication of what is wrong in the situation which the Apostle wishes to correct.

"Strife" in the Greek is *"eritheia,"* and means *"factions or contention."* It contains the idea of taking an argument to the place of disruption, to the extent of forming sides. In other words, *"I'm going to have my way whatever the cost."*

"Vainglory" in the Greek means *"empty pride."*

"Party spirit" in the Church is one of the greatest dangers in running the Christian race. Love is the characteristic of Christian Grace; party spirit and vainglory too often lead professing Christians to break the law of love.

"Strife" contains the idea not only of contention but of rivalry, so a person who practices this approach does things at the expense of other people in order to elevate self.

"Vainglory" contains the word for *"glory,"* but Paul amplified it by adding the word for *"empty"* or *"vain,"* implying that this kind of activity brings a kind of glory that has no substance and, therefore, is meaningless.

LOWLINESS OF MIND

The phrase, *"But in lowliness of mind let each esteem other better than themselves,"* actually means that this estimation rests, not upon feelings or sentiment, but upon a due consideration of facts.

This is no plea for an abject servility, which is often the mask of a false humility. Rather, it is a call for genuine self-appraisal which acknowledges that one has shortcomings unknown to others, and that others possess obvious virtues which one himself does not demonstrate.

The idea is, that *"self"* is not to be foremost; selfishness is not to be the motive.

Probably there is no command in the Bible which has a wider sweep than this, or would touch on more points of human conduct, if fairly applied. Who is there who passes a single day without, in some respects, desiring to display himself?

What Minister of the Gospel, when preaching, has never had a wish to exhibit his talents, eloquence, or learning? How few make a gesture, but with some wish to display the grace or power with which it is done!

The best and only true correction of these faults is humility. This virtue consists in estimating ourselves according to Truth. It is a willingness to take the place which we ought to take in the sight of God and man; and having the low estimate of our own importance and character, which the truth about our insignificance as creatures and vileness as sinners would produce, it would lead us to a willingness to perform lowly and humble offices that we may benefit others.

THE CROSS AND HUMILITY

I think the greatest reason that Paul exhibited the great trait of humility possibly more than others, despite his great power and authority, was because of his correct viewpoint of the Cross. With all of our discussions about humility, how that such is obtained, which of course is the most astute Christlikeness, I think we will find that the Cross is the starting place. If we do not begin at the Cross, I think humility is impossible of attainment.

When we look at the great example given in the following Verses concerning Christ, which is referred to as the *"kenosis of Christ (the self-emptying of Christ),"* we will find that the key to what He was and Who He was, is found in the Passage, *"He humbled Himself, and became obedient unto death, even the death of the Cross"* (Phil. 2:8).

Regarding Christ, the humility had to come before the Cross was reached, but the very idea that the Cross was the objective, brought about, I think, this perfect humility. As it was with Him, so must it be with us.

If the Believer has a correct viewpoint of the Cross, meaning that we must take up the Cross daily in our following of Jesus, then we will be on the correct road. Other than that, there can be no humility.

Taking this particular direction, the direction of the Cross, two things take place, which nurtures humility, and which alone nurtures humility in the Believer. They are as follows:

THE ABSOLUTE DEPRAVITY OF THE PERSON

The Cross tells us that man was and is so wicked, so evil, so unable to help himself, that God would have to do this thing for him. The Cross also tells us just how bad this depravity was, considering that it took the extent of the Cross for man's Salvation to be affected. In other words, if God could have done this any other way, I'm certain that He would have done so.

Whenever the Believer understands that, knowing that he is saved, not through anything he has done, but altogether through what the Lord has done, and considering the great price He had to pay, this has a tendency within itself to humble one.

THE BENEFITS OF THE CROSS ARE RECEIVED BY GRACE THROUGH FAITH

What Jesus did at the Cross, is of such magnitude, such moment, with such wide-sweeping effects, in fact such eternal effects, that Believers will be forever enjoying its benefits.

And yet, these benefits are given to us strictly by Grace, meaning that we do not earn them, and in fact, cannot earn them, which has a great tendency to humble us. It is all the gift of God which means *"by the Grace of God,"* Grace being the favor of God extended to those who do not deserve such, but who have simple Faith in Him.

All of this breeds humility, and this alone breeds humility. That means if we attempt to secure anything from the Lord in any other fashion, except through that which He did at the Cross, self-righteousness will be the result, which is pride and arrogance.

As stated, a proper viewpoint of the Cross guarantees humility, and in fact, this is the only way that humility can be obtained. To have an incorrect view of the Cross, always leads to self-righteousness, i.e., *"pride, arrogance, self-will, etc."*

There are three words which are closely related to one another, and which should be the hallmark of Christians. These words are *"humility, meekness, and gentleness."* Let's look briefly at each one.

HUMILITY

"Humility" in the Greek is *"tapeinophrosune,"* and means exactly what the King James translators said, *"lowliness of mind."*

Trench says of this word: *"The work for which Christ's Gospel came into the world was no less than to put down the mighty from their seat, and to exalt the humble and meek."*

This very Greek word *"tapeinophrosune"* although in the Greek language, was employed by no Greek writer before the Christian Era, nor, apart from the influence of Christian writers after. It is really a fruit of the Gospel.

The word usually used by pagan writers for *"humility"* was *"tapeinos."* However, this word did not have the meaning of Christian humility, but rather spoke of a *"groveling, slavish, and meanspirited attitude."*

Aristotle, the great Greek Philosopher, confessed how hard it is for a man to be truly great-souled, for such a man will not allow any great-soulness which does not rest on corresponding realities of goodness and moral greatness. Aristotle went on to observe, *"that to think humbly of one's self, where that humble estimate is the true one,"* presents the Philosopher coming close to a definition of Christian humility.

Thankfully, the Christian has in his Lord a standard of perfect righteousness before his eyes, which of course portrays perfect humility. Without that example, to be sure, true humility would be lost altogether.

CHRIST?

But it may be objected, how does this account of Christian humility, as springing out of and resting on the sense of unworthiness, agree with the fact that the sinless Lord laid claim to this Grace, saying, *"I am meek and lowly in heart"*? (Mat. 11:29).

The answer is, that for the sinner true humility involves the confession of sin, inasmuch as it involves the confession of his true condition; while yet for Christ Who is unfallen, this Grace truly exists in Him, involving for such the acknowledgement not of sinfulness, which He of course did not have, but rather of *"creatureliness,"* which

NOTES

speaks of absolute dependence, of having nothing, but receiving all things from God.

In His human nature our Lord must be the pattern of all humility, of all creaturely dependence; and it is only as *"a man"* that Christ thus claims to be humble: His human life was a constant living on the fullness of His Father's love; He evermore, as man, took the place which beseemed the creature in the Presence of its Creator.

Cremer said, *"Humility is the disposition of the man who esteems himself as small before God and men, and takes a low estimate of himself."* He went on to say, *"It means to habitually do the just and righteous things in a quiet way unnoticed by others."* Then he adds, *"But it must not be overlooked that this subdued stillness of feeling was no more than a part of humility, and the expression by no means obtained or sufficed for the Biblical conception, especially as denoting humility manifested before God, which arises from the perception of sin, or is at least inseparably connected therewith."*

In all of this we can well understand why the Greeks had no proper conception of humility. True humility is a product of the Holy Spirit in the yielded Believer, which has its foundation in the Cross of Christ.

Actually, the only self-description that ever fell from our Lord's lips was, *"I am meek and lowly"* (Mat. 11:29). Paul singles out this Grace of humility as the keynote that explains the mind of Christ (Phil. 2:5).

Peter speaks of humility as that particular virtue which makes all the other Christian graces what they should be (I Pet. 5:5).

To give a more developed meaning of Humility, we could say that it means *"to make low, bring low, to bring into an humble condition, to abase, to assign a lower rank or place to, to humble or abase one's self, to be ranked below others who are honored or rewarded, to have a modest opinion of one's self, to behave in an unassuming manner."*

MEEKNESS

"Meekness" in the Greek is *"praotes,"* and means *"gentleness and humility."* As stated, these words are very similar in meaning.

Scriptural meekness is not in a man's outward behavior only; nor yet in his relations to his fellowmen; as little in his mere natural disposition. Rather is it an inwrought Grace of the soul; and the exercises of it are first and chiefly towards God (Mat. 11:29; James 1:21).

Meekness is that temper of spirit in which we accept God's dealings with us as good, and, therefore, without disputing or resisting; and it is closely linked with humility as stated, and follows directly upon it (Zeph. 3:12; Eph. 4:2; Col. 3:12). It is only the humble heart which is also the meek; and which, as such, does not fight against God, or more or less struggle and contend with Him.

This meekness, however, being first of all a meekness before God, is also such in the face of men, even of evil men, out of a sense that these with the insults and injuries which they may inflict, are permitted and employed by Him for the chastening and purifying of His elect. This was the root of David's meekness, when Shimei cursed and flung stones at him — the consideration, namely, that the Lord had bidden him (II Sam. 16:11), that it was just for him (David) to suffer these things, however, unjustly the other might inflict them; and out of like convictions all true Christian meekness must spring. He that is meek will indeed know himself as most unworthy among the unworthy. And the knowledge of such unworthiness will teach one to endure meekly the provocations with which others may provoke him, and not to withdraw himself from the burdens which their sin may impose upon him (II Tim. 2:25; Titus 3:2).

PAUL

I think all of this even as we have attempted to explain it, fits perfectly the Apostle Paul. He did not chaff against those who had brought upon him his imprisonment, whether of the Jews or the Romans. He knew that despite the awfulness of their sin against him, for which they would most surely answer, still, in some manner God allowed this thing, and as a result, he would have accepted as chastening from the Lord, and seek to learn thereby from these things allowed by the One Who knows all things. In other words, and as stated, it was just for Paul to suffer these things however unjustly the other might inflict them.

What a lesson for us!

Of course the question would follow quickly, as to why Paul would need chastening.

The truth is, all Believers need chastening for the Scripture says, *"For whom the Lord loveth He chasteneth, and scourgeth every son whom He receiveth"* (Heb. 12:6).

He then said, *"But if ye be without chastisement, whereof all are partakers, then are ye bastards, and not sons"* (Heb. 12:8).

Someone referred to me sometime ago a particular Preacher who was obviously wrong, but seemingly suffering no chastisement from the Lord. They asked *"Why?"*

My answer, uttered very quickly, was very more true than not, *"Perhaps he's not a son, but rather a bastard."*

The idea is, that such a one, if in fact that was the case about this individual, does not really know the Lord as his own personal Saviour. In other words, he does not belong to the Lord, so he suffers no chastisement from the Lord.

GENTLENESS

"Gentleness" in the Greek is *"epieikeia,"* and means *"mildness, gentleness, fairness, sweet reasonableness"* (Acts 24:4; II Cor. 10:1).

Trench says concerning this word, that gentleness and humility *"are in their meanings too far apart to be fit subjects of sameness; but meekness, which stands between, holds on to both."*

Gentleness never urges its own rights to the uttermost, but, going back in part or in the whole from these, rectifies and redresses the injustices of justice.

The archetype and pattern of this grace is found in God. All His goings-back from the strictness of His rights as against men; all His allowance of their imperfect righteousness, and giving of a value to that which, rigorously estimated, would have none; all His refusals to exact extreme penalties . . . all His keeping in mind whereof we are made, and measuring His dealings with us thereby; all of these we may contemplate as *"gentleness"* upon His part; even as they demand in return the same, one toward another, upon ours.

Peter, when himself restored, must strengthen his Brethren (Lk. 22:32). The greatly forgiven servant in the Parable (Mat. 18:23), having known the *"gentleness"* of his lord and king, is justly expected to show the same to his fellow servant.

We now offer a brief summary of the treatment of the three words *"humility," "meekness,"* and *"gentleness,"* pointing out their meanings and the distinctions that exist between them.

HUMILITY, MEEKNESS, AND GENTLENESS, IN SUMMARY

"Humility" is not mere modesty or absence of pretension, nor is it a self-made grace such as making ourselves small when we are great, but it is the esteeming of ourselves small, inasmuch as we are so, the thinking truly, and because truly, therefore, lowly of ourselves.

"Meekness" is that temper of spirit in which we accept God's dealings with us as good, without disputing or resisting them. The meek man will not fight against God, and more or less struggle or contend with Him.

Meekness is also shown towards our fellowman who mistreats us, insults us, treats us with injustice, and that the one who is being injured endures patiently and without any spirit of retaliation the provocations that are imposed upon him. The meek man will not withdraw himself from the burdens which other men's sins may impose upon him.

"Gentleness" is that temper of spirit which expresses exactly that moderation which recognizes the impossibility cleaving to all formal law, of anticipating and providing for all cases that will emerge and present themselves for decisions; which with this, recognizes the danger that ever waits upon the assertion of legal rights, lest they should be pushed into moral wrongs, which, therefore, urges not its own rights to the uttermost, but going back in part or in the whole from these, rectifies and redresses the injustices as much as possible. Gentleness exhibits itself in the act of treating others with mildness, fairness, and sweet reasonableness.

"Humility" has to do with one's estimate of one's self, *"meekness"* with one's attitude toward the dealings of God and man with respect to one's self, and *"gentleness"* with one's treatment of others (Wuest).

(4) "LOOK NOT EVERY MAN ON HIS OWN THINGS, BUT EVERY MAN ALSO ON THE THINGS OF OTHERS."

NOTES

The self-centeredness that considers only one's own rights, plans, and interests must be replaced by a broader outlook that includes the interests of one's fellows.

"But also" indicates that our own affairs need not be totally ignored, but that the interest of others must also form a part of our concern. The Believer of course, should not neglect the welfare of himself and his family (I Tim. 5:8) in order to involve himself in the good of others. What Paul is calling for is a Christian concern that is wide enough to include others in its scope. When each member of the Christian community exercises this mutual concern, problems of disunity quickly disappear (Kent).

PERSONAL THINGS

The phrase, *"Look not every man on his own things,"* means to *only* look at one's own things.

The spirit of the world cares only for its own, with no regard for others, and in fact, will hinder or even destroy others in one's personal quest for preeminence. Selfishness is what is being spoken of here.

This is not to be the attitude, spirit, drive, or attitude of the Christian. The example of Christ is the greatest example of all, which Paul portrays in the next Verses. Jesus Christ gave up everything in order to help the world that was fallen and dying. This is the greatest example of all to say the least, when one considers that this world did not love Him at all. In other words, He gave His life for those who hated Him. So, one can see the power of such an example.

OTHERS

The phrase, *"But every man also on the things of others,"* contains the idea by the word *"also,"* that we are not to neglect our own affairs, but that we are to have an interest in the affairs of others as well concerning their betterment.

This admonition by the Holy Spirit through Paul could contain the following:

1. We are to feel that the spiritual interests of everyone in the Church is, in a certain sense, our own interests. The Church is one. It is confederated together for a common object. Each person is intrusted with a portion

of the honor of the whole, and the conduct of one member affects the character of all. We are, therefore, to promote, in every way possible, the welfare of every other member of the Church.

If they go astray, we are to admonish and entreat them; if they are in error, we are to instruct them; if they are in trouble, we are to aid them.

In fact, every member of the Church has a claim on the sympathy of his Brethren, and should be certain of always finding it when his circumstances are such as to demand it.

2. There are circumstances where it is proper to look with special interests on the temporal concerns of others. It is when the poor, the fatherless, and the afflicted must be *"sought out"* in order to be aided and relieved. They are possibly too retiring and modest to press their situation on the attention of others, and they need that others should manifest a generous care in their welfare in order to relieve them. This is not improper interference in their concerns, nor will it be so regarded.

3. For a similar reason, we should seek the welfare of all others in a spiritual sense. We should seek to arouse the sinner, and lead him to the Saviour. He is blind, and will not come himself; unconcerned, and will not seek Salvation; filled with the love of this world, and will not seek a better; devoted to pursuits that will lead him to ruin, and he ought to be apprised of it. It is no more an improper interference and his concerns to apprise him of his condition, and to attempt to lead him to the Saviour, than it is to warn a man in a dark night, who walks on the verge of a precipice, of his peril; or to arouse one from sleep who's house is in flames.

Anyone does a man a favor who tells him that he has a Redeemer, and that there is a Heaven to which he may rise; he does his neighbor the greatest possible kindness who apprises him that there is a world of infinite woe, and tells him of an easy way by which he may escape it. In fact, this is the greatest care and concern of all regarding others, the concern over the welfare of their soul.

(5) "LET THIS MIND BE IN YOU, WHICH WAS ALSO IN CHRIST JESUS:"

The great example of humility is Christ Jesus. Although Verses 5 to 11 contain one of the outstanding portrayals of the Incarnation in the New Testament, they were actually written to illustrate the point of humility and selflessness. Another instance where Paul makes a sublime statement about Christ, almost incidentally, in illustrating a practical point is Ephesians 5:25-27.

Believers, of course, cannot duplicate the precise Ministry of Jesus but they can display the same attitude.

THIS MIND

The phrase, *"Let this mind be in you,"* refers to the self-emptying of Christ which is to be in Believers as well.

After exhorting the Philippian Saints in Philippians 2:2-4 to think the same thing, to have the same love, to be in heart agreement, and in lowliness of mind to consider one another as excelling themselves, Paul says, *"Let this mind be in you which was also in Christ Jesus."*

This exhortation reaches back to Philippians 2:2-4 for its definition and ahead to Philippians 2:6-8 for its illustration. The Apostle does not give all that is in the Mind of Christ in these Verses. He selects those qualities of our Lord which fit the needs of the Philippians at that moment. That which Paul speaks of as being in the Mind of Christ and which the Philippians were to include in their own spiritual lives consisted of a spirit of humility and of self-abnegation and an interest in the welfare of others. These Graces were illustrated in our Lord's act of becoming Incarnate in the human race and becoming the substitutionary Atonement for sin.

This lack of unity among the Philippian Saints became the occasion for perhaps the greatest Christological Passage in the New Testament as it regards the Incarnation. Among Scholars it is known as the Kenosis Passage, speaking of the self-emptying of the Son of God as He became incarnate in humanity, the word *"kenosis"* being the Greek word meaning *"to empty"* (Wuest).

THE VIRTUES OF CHRIST

The expression *"this mind"* could be translated in a number of ways, each of which while holding the main idea, yet brings out a slightly different shade of meaning.

For instance: *"Be constantly thinking this in yourselves; be having this mind in you; reflecting your own minds, the mind of Christ Jesus; let the same purpose inspire you as was in Christ Jesus."*

The sum total of the thought in the exhortation seems to be that of urging the Philippians to emulate in their own lives, the distinctive virtues of the Lord Jesus spoken of in Philippians 2:2-4. It is the habitual direction of our Lord's mind with reference to self that is in the Apostle's thinking, and an attitude of humility and self-abnegation for the benefit of others, which should be true also of the Philippians. This gives us the key to unlock the rich treasures of the great doctrinal portion of the Letter we are now to study.

CHRIST JESUS

The phrase, *"Which was also in Christ Jesus,"* portrays Christ as the supreme example.

Of course, all of this was for one purpose, and we speak of the Incarnation of our Lord, to affect the Redemption of humanity by going to the Cross. We will find out in these Passages, that this involved far more than appears on the surface. Irrespective, all that was done, all of its great magnitude, the mystery of the Incarnation, what it all means, was but for one purpose, the Redemption of mankind, which necessitated the Cross with all its horror, pain, suffering, and humiliation. Consequently, to say that this is an example, even the supreme example, is perhaps the most gross understatement that has ever been uttered. In fact, it is beyond the pale of understanding regarding the human mind.

Whatever particular shades of meaning one may find in these Passages, Paul's essential message (identical with the thought expressed in II Corinthians 8:9) is not difficult to discover if it be remembered that his primary purpose is practical in nature. He is dealing with a problem which threatens to dissolve the unity of the Believers at Philippi. Over against the mood of some to assert themselves selfishly, Paul sets the Spirit of Christ as the supreme example of obedience.

NOTES

The words, *"In Christ Jesus,"* show that the corresponding words, *"in you,"* cannot mean *"among you,"* but in yourselves, in your heart. The Apostle refers us to the supreme example of unselfishness and humility, the Lord Jesus Christ.

He bids us to mind the things which the Lord Jesus minded, to love what He loved, to hate what He hated; the thoughts, the desires, motives of the Christian should be the same thoughts, desires, motives which fill the sacred heart of Jesus Christ, our Lord. We must strive to imitate Him, to reproduce His image, not only in the outward, but even in the inner life. Especially here we are bidden to follow His unselfishness and humility (Caffin).

HOW THIS CAN BE DONE?

Even though we've already dealt with this and will not go through the subject again, nevertheless to remind the Reader, we must again state that the only way this can be carried out in the life of the Believer, and I speak of Christlikeness in this manner and in every other manner, is that we have a correct interpretation of the Cross, which refers to what Jesus did in that great Sacrifice, understanding our part in that and why it was done, placing all our trust in this Finished Work. If the Cross is that to which He came, and that's exactly why He came, then it is the Cross in which the need of humanity was met. That must be the starting place and the stopping place for all Believers. Actually, the word *"stop,"* probably is not the better word to use, it being literally impossible to exhaust the potential of the Finished Work of Christ.

The Reader must ever understand, that everything in pre-Christ history strains toward the Cross, while everything now strains from the Cross. If the Believer does not base everything on the Cross and in the capacity of the Cross, and we mean everything, denied a proper foundation, all else believed will be skewed as well!

(6) "WHO, BEING IN THE FORM OF GOD, THOUGHT IT NOT ROBBERY TO BE EQUAL WITH GOD:"

Two assertions are made here: Jesus previously existed in the form of God and He did not regard His existing in a manner of equality with God as a prize to be grasped or held on to. *"Being in the very nature God"* is, literally, *"existing in the form of God."* To say that He was existing in the essential form of God is tantamount to saying that He possessed the nature of God; however, this does not need to be regarded as precisely the same as *"the form of God,"* for one's essential nature can remain unchanged, though the manner in which that nature is expressed can vary greatly through changing times and circumstances.

The Sixth Verse has been variously interpreted. Does it mean something that has ceased, or something to be ceased? This uncertainty has led to three possibilities:

1. The preincarnate Christ already possessed equality with the Father and resolved not to cling to it.

2. Christ has no need to grasp at equality with God, for He already possessed it.

3. Christ did not reach for His crowning prematurely, as Adam did, but was willing to wait till after His suffering.

Point #1 seems to be the correct answer.

THE *FORM* OF GOD

The phrase, *"Who, being in the form of God,"* refers to Deity which Christ always was.

"Form" in the Greek is *"morpha,"* and means *"shape or nature."* However, the Greek word has no reference to the shape of any physical object. Actually, it was a Greek philosophical term.

Consequently, Vincent said, *"We must here dismiss from our minds the idea of shape, at least as we normally think of such. The word is used here in its philosophical sense to denote that expression of being which carries in itself the distinctive nature and character of the being to whom it pertains, and is thus permanently identified with that nature and character."*

He then said, *"As applied to God, the word is intended to describe that mode in which the essential Being of God expresses itself."*

In English we actually have no word which can properly convey this meaning, nor is it possible for us to formulate the reality. *"Form"* inevitably carries with it to us the idea of *"shape."* It is conceivable that the essential personality of God may express itself in a mode apprehensible by the perception of pure spiritual intelligences; but the mode itself is neither apprehensible nor conceivable by human minds.

AN EXTENDED MEANING

This mode of expression, *"the Form of God,"* might be said to be the *"setting"* of the Divine Essence. One might say that Jesus is not identical with the Essence itself, Him being God in His Own right, but is identified with this Essence as its natural and appropriate expression, answering to it in every particular. One might say, that Jesus before the Incarnation was a perfect expression of a perfect Essence. This means, that it is not something imposed from without, but something which proceeds from the very depth of the Perfect Being, and into which that Being unfolds, as light from fire.

(Essence is the properties or attributes by means of which something can be placed in its proper class or identified as being what it is.)

Thus, the Greek word for *"form"* refers to that outward expression which a person gives of his inmost nature. This expression is not assumed from the outside, but proceeds directly from within.

Before the Incarnation, our Lord was in the form of God. The word *"God"* is without the definite article in the Greek Text (The God), and, therefore, refers to the Divine Essence. Once again, this means that He was God in His Own right, that is, if it's proper to use such terminology. There is only one God, which means the Godhead cannot be separated as it regards Deity, but yet is manifested in Three Persons, *"God the Father, God the Son, and God the Holy Spirit."*

Thus, our Lord's outward expression of His Inmost Being was as to its nature the expression of the Divine Essence of Deity. Since that outward expression which this word *"form"* speaks of, comes from and is truly representative of the Inward Being, follows that our Lord as to His nature is the Possessor of the Divine Essence of Deity, and being that, it also necessarily follows that He was and is absolute Deity Himself, a co-participant with God the Father and God the Holy Spirit in that Divine Essence which constitutes God, as God.

THE TIME OF WHICH THIS SPEAKS

The time at which the Apostle says our Lord gave expression to His essential nature, that of Deity, was previous to His coming to Earth to become Incarnate as the Man Christ Jesus. But Paul, by the use of the Greek word translated *"being,"* informs his Greek readers that our Lord's possession of the Divine Essence did not cease to be a fact when He came to Earth to assume human form. The Greek word translated *"being"* is not the simple verb of being, but a word that speaks of a previous condition protracted into the present. That is, our Lord gave expression to the Essence of Deity which He possesses, not only before He became Man, but also after becoming Man, for He was doing so at the time this Philippian Epistle was being written.

To give expression to the Essence of Deity implies the possession of Deity, for this expression, according to the definition of our word *"form,"* comes from one's inmost nature.

In fact, this word alone (form) is enough to refute the claim of Modernism that our Lord emptied Himself of His Deity when He became Man.

THE ANGELS

This expression of the Essence of His Deity which our Lord gave in His preincarnate state, was given through a spiritual medium to spiritual intelligences, the Angels. Human beings in our present state of being cannot receive such impressions, since we are not equipped with the spiritual sense of perception which the Angels have.

What Peter, James, and John saw on the Mount of Transfiguration, was an outward expression of the Essence of Deity, but given through a medium by which the physical senses of the Disciples could receive the expression given.

However, when we Believers receive our bodies of glory, we will be equipped then to receive the expression of Deity which the Angels already receive, and through a like spiritual medium. In other words, in the coming Resurrection, the Saints with glorified bodies, will then have the ability to properly receive and understand the expression of Deity. To be frank, if man, even the Godliest man, presently saw God in his undiluted Divine Essence, man could not stand it in any capacity.

One might say that Paul in this statement given in Verse 6, is that God and Jesus Christ are *"of one substance."*

EXACTLY WHAT DOES GOD LOOK LIKE?

In the words of Albert Barnes, *"What was the 'form' Jesus had before His Incarnation? What is meant by His having been then in the Form of God?"* To these questions perhaps no satisfactory answer can be given.

He Himself speaks (Jn. 17:5) of *"the Glory which He had with the Father before the world was"*; and the language naturally conveys the idea that there was then a manifestation of the Divine nature through Him, which in some measure ceased when He became Incarnate; and there was some visible splendor and majesty which were then laid aside, although He continued to be God. What manifestation of His Glory God may make in the heavenly world, of course we as human beings, as stated, cannot know nor understand. Nothing forbids us, however, to suppose that there is some such visible manifestation; some splendor and magnificence of God in the view of the Angelic beings such as becomes the great Sovereign of the universe — for He *"dwells in Light which no man can approach unto"* (I Tim. 6:16).

That *"glory,"* visible manifestation, or splendor, indicating the nature of God, it is said here that the Lord Jesus possessed before His Incarnation.

I merely ask the question, *"Is it possible that God has a spirit body, whatever that might mean?"* (Jn. 4:24).

EQUAL WITH GOD

The phrase, *"Thought it not robbery to be equal with God,"* refers to a judgment based upon facts.

The word *"God"* is used again without the article — *"the God."* Had the article preceded it, the meaning would be *"equal with God the Father."* The word *"God"* here refers to Deity, not seen in the Three Persons of the Godhead, but to Deity seen in its Essence. Equality with God does not refer here to the equality of the Lord Jesus with the other Persons of the Trinity. Nor does it refer to His quality with them in the *"possession"* of the Divine Essence. Possession of the Divine Essence is not spoken of here, but the *"expression"* of the Divine Essence is referred to, although *"possession"* is implied by the *"expression."* Equality with God refers here to our Lord's co-participation with the other Members of the Trinity in the expression of the Divine Essence. This is a very important point, for when we come to consider the fact that our Lord laid aside something, we will see that it was not the *"possession"* but rather the *"expression"* of the Divine Essence.

ROBBERY

The Greek word *"robbery"* has two distinct meanings, *"a thing unlawfully seized,"* or *"a treasure to be clutched and retained at all hazards."*

When a Greek word has more than one meaning, the rule of interpretation is to take the one which agrees with the context in which it is found. The Passage which we are studying is the illustration of the virtues mentioned in Philippians 2:2-4, namely, humility, and self-abnegation for the benefit of others.

If our Lord did not consider it a thing to be unlawfully seized to be equal with God in the expression of the Divine Essence, then He would be asserting His rights to that expression. He would be declaring His rightful ownership of that prerogative.

But to assert one's right to a thing does not partake of an attitude of humility and self-abnegation. Therefore, this meaning of the word will not do here. If our Lord did not consider the expression of His Divine Essence such a treasure that it should be retained at all hazards, that would mean that He was willing to waive His rights to that expression if the necessity arose.

This is the essence of humility and of self-abnegation. Thus, our second meaning is the one to be used here (Wuest).

EQUALITY

The Greek words *"isos,"* which mean *"equal,"* and *"isotes,"* which mean *"equality,"* appear seldom in the New Testament. Yet they represent extremely important concepts that were woven into Greek thought.

At first, equality was simply a numerical concept. But it developed into a philosophical and political concept. The Greeks came to believe that all citizens should enjoy equal standing in society and be treated impartially under the law. The New Testament teaching that Believers are fellow citizens of Heaven and are members of a body in which there is an essential unity despite differences and function (I Cor. 12:4-26) would have been well understood especially in the Greek Churches of that time.

Two Passages that use the concept of equality bear on the issue of Who Jesus is. John Chapter 5 reports Jesus' defense of His Miracles. He identified them as the work of His Father. The Jews understood His meaning. Jesus was claiming equality of will and nature with God. *"For this reason the Jews tried all the harder to kill Him; not only was He breaking the Sabbath* (they said), *but He was even calling God His Own Father, making Himself equal with God"* (Jn. 5:18; 8:48-59).

Philippians 2:6, the Passage of our study, views the Incarnation in relation to prehistory. It reveals Christ Jesus as *"being in very nature God"* and becoming a human being. It explains that He *"did not consider equality with God something to be grasped or clung to."*

In becoming a human being, Jesus did not surrender His nature as God, but He did abandon the Glory, the rights, and the worship that are the prerogatives of the Lord Alone (Richards).

THE EXAMPLE OF CHRIST

It seems reasonable to assume that Christ, being the Revelation of God, might have claimed His right to be recognized as equal with God. But contrary to the accusation of His enemies (Jn. 5:17-18), this is precisely what He refused to do — insist upon His Own rights, or usurp the place of God. He refused to seek self-enrichment or self-gratification. Paul may have had in mind the contrast between the first Adam, who selfishly desired to be *"as gods"* (Gen. 3:5), and Christ, the Second Adam, Who unselfishly looked on the *"things of others."*

In reference to this, Paul seeks to promote unity by urging his readers to contemplate

Christ. Christ did not seek to exploit His advantages; even Christ pleased not Himself (Rom. 15:3).

In fact, this great kenosis (self-emptying) of Christ is one of the most revealing Passages in the New Testament. Nowhere else is the effect of the Incarnation more eloquently described. It is Paul's clearest statement concerning the Incarnation.

This thought is paralleled only in Hebrews and in John (Heb. 2:5; Jn. 1:14). To have the *"mind of Christ"* means to have the same disposition that Jesus had.

While a Christian cannot suffer for the sins of others as did Jesus, He at least can have the Master's attitude and disposition. He can be moved by the same motives and subject to the same discipline of the Spirit.

What is it about Jesus' self-emptying that one through Grace can emulate?

HUMILITY

The Christian should be willing to relinquish his status if the occasion warrants. Jesus did not think that being on an equality with God was a thing to be grasped, clutched, or retained.

Jesus' status was unchallenged and secure but He did not jealously cling to it. He was not afraid to divest Himself of it, at least temporarily.

He did not stand upon His Own rights. He did more than the call of duty demanded. He emptied Himself; that is, He divested Himself of many Divine prerogatives that He had as God, although never ceasing to be God. These included *"Omnipresence, Omniscience, and Omnipotence."*

SERVICE

From the inner likeness or nature of God, Jesus now assumed the inner nature or form of a slave.

It is not surprising that Paul was not hesitant about calling Himself a slave when he believed that Jesus also became a slave.

Slaves were very numerous in the Roman Empire. The possession of a slave was a status symbol. Sometimes the slaves were more virtuous and more intelligent even than their masters. Being a slave, therefore, did not so much denote intrinsic inferiority (the actual worth) as it did relative inferiority or inferiority of status and privilege.

This was unforgettably illustrated when Jesus took a towel and girded Himself and performed the duties of a slave by washing the feet of His disciples (Jn. Chpt. 13). By this gesture Jesus acted contrary to all human canons of propriety. He had to resort to something drastic to compel a revision of the Disciples' attitude toward what constitutes greatness. In so doing He removed the stigma of bondservice and made service a virtue.

HUMAN NATURE

Another step in Jesus' humiliation was that He was made in the outward form of a man. His inner nature remained Divine. His outward, temporary form, however, was different, changed to that of a man.

Jesus was, in fact, God become man; the Incarnation was not a phantom; His humanity was real.

In other words, He was not 50% God and 50% man. He was very God, meaning *"total God,"* although freely giving up some of the expressions of Deity, and Very Man, i.e., *"total man."*

DEATH

The fourth step in Jesus' humiliation was death. It was the most shameful death, a type of execution reserved only for slaves and inferior classes of the populace of the Roman Empire.

Roman citizens were never subjected to this humiliating form of execution. In other words, Jesus went the whole way in the Incarnation. He tasted to the full the penalty that man merits because of his sin.

However, it should be understood, that the death that Jesus died was strictly voluntary on His part. Concerning His life, He said *"No man taketh it from Me, but I lay it down of Myself. I have power to lay it down, and I have power to take it again. This Commandment have I received of My Father"* (Jn. 10:18).

This means that He did not die on the Cross simply because He ran afoul of Roman or Jewish law. Even though both Rome and Israel were guilty of putting Him on the Cross, still, they could only do so because He allowed such.

So, the death He died, the most ignominious even as we have stated, was of His Own choosing, and in fact, was necessary in order that man could be redeemed.

EXALTATION

Paul never dwells long upon the Crucifixion without mentioning the Resurrection. He keeps the balance between life and death. He writes here in the conviction that the time is coming when the kings of this world will acknowledge the Lordship of Christ (Phil. 2:9-11). This is in line with the great affirmation of the Book of Revelation:

"The Kingdoms of this world shall become the Kingdoms of our Lord and of His Christ" (Rev. 11:15).

The language was especially meaningful in an age when kings and kingdoms abounded and when the Emperor was called *"King of Kings."*

EQUAL WITH GOD

To make it easier to understand, the phrase *"thought it not robbery to be equal with God,"* I think can be explained according to the following:

1. Jesus is God. In fact, He had always been God, and despite the Incarnation was still God. Despite the fact of Him becoming human, even with all its limitations, in no way took from Him the possession of His Deity. Also, despite becoming fully man, He in no way felt it was an insult to the Godhead to continue to declare His essential Essence of Deity.

2. He became a man, fully man, total man, absolute man, *"The Man Christ Jesus."* However, even though He willingly laid aside His expression of Deity, He never laid aside His possession of Deity. He was just as much God while man, as He had been God before becoming man. His Essence never changed, despite the fact that He no longer used the power of His Deity, at least during His earthly life of some 33 and a half years.

(7) "BUT MADE HIMSELF OF NO REPUTATION, AND TOOK UPON HIM THE FORM OF A SERVANT, AND WAS MADE IN THE LIKENESS OF MEN:"

The description now moves to Christ's Incarnate state. Two phrases carry the main thoughts: *"(He) made Himself nothing"* and *"He humbled Himself,"* found in the next Verse.

The first phrase is literally *"but Himself He emptied"*; it uses a verb that has lent its name to the so-called *"kenosis"* theories that probe the nature of Christ's *"emptying Himself."* Although the Text does not directly state that Christ emptied Himself *"of something,"* such would be the natural understanding when this verb is used. Furthermore, the context has most assuredly prepared the reader for understanding that Christ divested Himself of something. What it was the following phrase implies.

The One Who was existing in the form of God took on the form of a servant. The word *"taking"* does not imply an exchange, but rather an addition. The *"form of God"* could not be relinquished, for God cannot cease to be God; but our Lord could and did take on the very form of a lowly servant when He entered human life by the Incarnation.

It is sometimes suggested that the term *"servant"* refers to the exalted Servant of Jehovah, but this Passage seems intended to emphasize His condescension and humble station. Consequently, what an example our Lord provides concerning the spirit of humility! Inasmuch as Angels also are servants, the statement makes it clear that Christ became part of humanity: *"Being made in human likeness."*

Thus, by Paul using this word *"likeness,"* it is implied that even though Christ became a genuine man, there were certain respects in which He was not absolutely like other men. Paul may have had in mind the unique union of the Divine and human natures in Jesus, or the absence of a sin nature.

In summation, Christ did not empty Himself of the form of God (His Deity), but of the manner of existence as equal to God. He did not lay aside the Divine attributes, but *"the insignia of majesty."*

Christ's action has been described as the laying aside during the Incarnation of the independent use of His Divine Attributes.

NO REPUTATION

The phrase, *"But made himself of no reputation,"* literally means *"He emptied Himself."*

Instead of asserting His rights to the expression of the Essence of Deity, our Lord waived His rights to that expression, being willing to relinquish it if necessary, which He did. He did not consider the exercise of that expression such a treasure that it would keep Him from setting that expression aside, and making Himself of no reputation. So, on behalf of fallen humanity, he willingly and freely *"emptied Himself."*

The Divine majesty of which He emptied Himself was His Own, His Own rightful prerogative; and His humiliation was His Own voluntary act.

Alford says, *"He used His equality with God as an opportunity, not for self-exaltation, but for self-abasement."*

In fact, Christ's self-humiliation proved His Deity, for this renunciation would have had no value if Christ were not God. He became man; but in contrast with the first man He did not grasp at equality with God by robbery, on the contrary He emptied Himself of all His outward glory of the Form of God, and revealed Himself to the world in the form of a slave.

Adam, by robbery, sought to exalt Himself to the dishonoring of God; the Second Adam humbled Himself to the honoring of God. The first Adam exalted Himself and was humbled; the Second Adam humbled Himself and was exalted.

OF WHAT DID HE EMPTY HIMSELF?

Christ subsisting in the Form of God, i.e., the visible glories shinning forth from His Divine Essence as God, is here set in contrast with His assuming *"the form of a servant,"* which in its turn declares the existence of His human nature. Thus, the *"form of God"* declares His Deity, and the *"form of a servant,"* His humanity.

He did not hold fast and bring down to Earth the visible demonstration of His Deity — for such is the import of the word *"robbery"* — although it was shown out for a moment on the Mount of Transfiguration — but emptied Himself of that outward glory in order to become man and by His death on the Tree, secure the eternal advantage of those who would except His Sacrifice. He fought not on His Own glory but on the glory of others.

NOTES

The question here is not between His being on an equality with God and His emptying Himself — for He never emptied Himself of His Godhead — but the contrast is between His being in the form of God and in the form of a servant. Equality with God declares His Being; the Form of God expresses the manifestations of that Being. It was of the outward demonstrations of His Deity that He emptied Himself.

THE SEVEN STEPS

The seven downward steps of His great renunciation are followed here by the seven upward steps of His Glorious Ascension (vss. 9-11). They are as follows:

1. His renunciation (vs. 6).
2. Emptied Himself.
3. Servant's form.
4. Became in man's likeness.
5. Humbled Himself.
6. Bowed to death.
7. And what a death! The death of the Cross!

The seven upward steps of His Exaltation are:

1. God highly exalted Him.
2. Granted Him the Name which is above every name.
3. Universal dominion.
4. Over Beings in Heaven.
5. Over Beings on Earth.
6. Over Beings under the Earth.
7. Divine Glory. All tongues will confess by and by that Jesus of Nazareth is Jehovah; and such confession will honor and not dishonor God.

THE FORM OF A SERVANT

He took the form of a servant at the time when He assumed humanity, as it is said *"being made in the likeness of men."* It is as follows:

1. His subjection to the Law (Lk. 2:21; Gal. 5:4).
2. His subjection to His parents (Lk. 2:5).
3. His position as a carpenter (Mk. 6:3).
4. His sale for the price of a slave (Ex. 21:32).
5. His death, the death of a slave, and His dependence as a Servant on God, all illustrate His form as a servant (Isa. 49:3, 7).

This proves:

1. He was in the form of a servant directly when He became man.

2. He was in the Form of God before He was in the form of a servant.

3. He as truly subsisted in the Divine nature as in human nature, for He was as much in the Form of God as in the Form of a servant, and was so truly in the Form of God as to be on an equality with God. He, therefore, could have been none other than God (Isa. 46:5; Zech. 13:7) (Williams).

HIMSELF

So, we continue to come to the question, *"Of what did Christ empty Himself?"*

His Deity? His Nature? His Divine prerogative? His equality? Paul simply says that Christ emptied Himself.

The verb used here simply means *"to pour out,"* with Christ Himself as the object. Thus, Christ emptied Himself of Himself.

At no time did He allow selfish considerations to dominate His spotless life.

The words *"made Himself"* means *"to make empty, to make vain or void."* The word does not occur elsewhere in the New Testament except in the Passage before us. The essential idea is that of bringing to emptiness, or nothingness; and hence it is applied to a case where one lays aside his rank and dignity and becomes, in respect to that, *"as nothing."* That is, he assumes a far less rank and station.

As someone has said, when the Sun is obscured by a cloud, or in an eclipse, there is no real change of its glory, nor are its beams extinguished, nor is the Sun itself in any measure changed. It's luster is only for a time obscured. So it might have been in regard to the manifestation of the Glory of the Son of God.

OF FAR GREATER WEIGHT

This one thing is certain, whatever the phrase means, *"But made Himself of no reputation,"* it is far more than the mind of man can even begin to grasp. The reason should be obvious.

Where it is possible for us to see what He became, it is in fact impossible, for us to know in totality what He was before His self-emptying. As a creature, we cannot really even

NOTES

begin to grasp the glory and the grandeur of the Creator, and He was the Creator (Jn. 1:1-3). To be frank, even if shown such, we do not presently have the capabilities of grasping that which we would be shown, even if that were possible. Actually, when we're given a glimpse into the spirit world of the Glory of God, we are as much at a loss to comprehend it, even as the Prophets were in trying to explain it.

If the Reader doubts my words, let him look again at the First Chapter of Ezekiel, or Chapters 4 and 5 of Revelation concerning what John saw. Paul didn't even bother to attempt to explain his *"Visions and Revelations."* He just said that he saw things *"and heard unspeakable words which it is not lawful for a man to utter"* (II Cor. 12:1-4).

Even as I dictate these words I sense the Presence of God.

WHAT DO WE GET OUT OF THIS SELF-EMPTYING OF CHRIST?

If we see only greatness and glory, I think we miss the point. It is *"love"* we must see! It was love that did all of this, a love that is beyond the comprehension of man.

A fallen race was doomed — doomed to die eternally lost. Having forfeited that which was given to them by God, man found himself in a position from which he could not be extricated, at least by his own machinations. So, if he is to be saved, God will have to do the deed Himself.

In His greatness and glory, God could easily have regenerated man without the sin question being addressed; however, His Nature and Holiness could not allow such. The sin question had to be addressed and answered. There was no other way.

This could be done in one of two ways:

1. God could simply have allowed man to die in his lostness, which of necessity would demand his spending eternity in the Lake of Fire. That would have satisfied the sin debt on an individual basis regarding each human being. The wages of sin is death, which means separation from God, and eternal separation from God would have paid the penalty.

2. However, love could not allow such to happen. It must be understood, that man

was not created by God as a result of need. God does not need anything. He created man from a position totally and completely of love.

Some have claimed that God created man because He wanted or needed fellowship. Once again, God has never needed anything, much less fellowship. No! He created man simply and totally from a position of love, and as such He would *"crown him with glory and honor"* (Ps. 8:5). So, if love created Him, then love must rescue Him.

However, to rescue man, even though God had spoken all of creation into existence (Heb. 11:3), He could not speak Redemption into existence. A debt had been incurred, a terrible debt of sin, and that debt must be paid. The only way it could be paid was by death, for that was the penalty (Gen. 2:15-17; Ezek. 18:4; Rom. 6:23). As stated, man could not redeem himself, because he had no sacrifice which would serve the purpose. He could not give himself, because he was sullied, corrupt, and totally depraved, therefore, unsuitable as a sacrifice, that which God could not accept.

There was only one way, God would become man and accomplish what the first man Adam failed to do.

As a man He would face the onslaughts of Satan, never one time using His Deity, but definitely using the Power of the Holy Spirit (Jn. 1:32-34). However, that is not as clear cut as it at first seems.

For the Holy Spirit to function in the manner He must function, that is if the Ministry of Christ was to be what it should be, our Lord would have to perfectly yield in every manner and way to the Spirit and to the Father.

Christian man, even the most consecrated, yields imperfectly even at our best, whereas Jesus yielded perfectly at all times.

WAS JESUS DIFFERENT FROM US?

I think one would have to say, essentially no! While He was not born with a sin nature, as are all other human beings, still, that should not have made a difference. He had to be a man like all other men, or else His Work and Function would be to no avail. That's why the Holy Spirit through Paul referred to Him as *"the last Adam"* (I Cor. 15:45).

Some Scholars argue that Jesus could not have sinned. In other words, it would not have been possible for Him to have sinned.

That is basely incorrect! Had it been impossible for Him to have sinned, the whole thing would have been a farce. While God certainly cannot sin, it definitely is possible for man to sin. Therefore, the possibility had to be there with Christ as well.

Emptying Himself of the expression of His Deity, thereby becoming a man, subjected Him to all that which is possible with man. Hence, He would say *"I thirst,"* when of course, God cannot thirst (Jn. 19:28). As well, He grew hungry, and God cannot hunger (Mat. 4:2). Also, Jesus grew tired, and God cannot tire, at least in that fashion (Jn. 4:6).

Yes, it would have been possible for Jesus to have sinned, but He did not sin, and that despite every effort by Satan to make Him fail.

Had He failed even one time, in thought, word or deed, we could not have been saved. He kept the Law perfectly in every respect, the only Man Who ever did such a thing. Consequently, when He came to the conclusion of His earthly Life and Ministry, He could say, *"For the prince of this world cometh* (Satan), *and hath nothing in Me"* (Jn. 14:30).

He had no relationship with Satan or sin whatsoever, had nothing of Satan in Him. He was not subject to death because He had not sinned.

In the Fall, Satan gained a pseudo sovereignty over man on the principle of possession and consent of a responsible agent, or government by consent of the governed. In fact, God recognized this and permitted Satan to defeat himself by causing him to kill an innocent victim (Jesus) over Whom he had no claim.

When he inflicted death on Christ, he forfeited all his claims, rights and pseudo authority and his right to liberty itself. As well, he lost the right to inflict death on all others who became the property of Christ by virtue of His Redemption of them.

So, what Jesus did regarding His Incarnation, His Life, His Ministry, and more particularly, His Death on the Cross and Resurrection, all as a man, are beyond comprehension.

THE FORM OF A SERVANT

The phrase, *"And took upon Him the form of a servant,"* is actually the translation of the word *"servant"* which Paul used in Philippians 1:1 to describe himself, a bond slave.

The manner in which the Greek phrase is structured, means that our Lord took upon Himself the form of a servant or slave which was the cause of the emptying. Consequently, the translation so far could read, *"emptied Himself, having taken the form of a bond slave."*

The word *"form"* as we have previously stated, refers to the outward expression one gives of his inward being. The words *"form of a bond slave,"* therefore, mean that our Lord gave outward expression to His inmost nature, the outward expression being that of a bond slave. When expressing Himself as a bond slave come to serve, He necessarily exchanged one form of expression for another. In Verse 6 He was in His preincarnate state expressing Himself as Deity. In Verse 7 He expresses Himself in Incarnation as a bond slave. This is the direct opposite of what took place at the Transfiguration.

This *"form,"* not being identical with the Divine essence, but dependent upon it, and necessarily implying it, can be parted with or laid aside. Since Christ is one with God, and, therefore, pure being, absolute existence, He can exist without the form. This form of God, Christ laid aside in His Incarnation.

AN ILLUSTRATION OF THE SERVANT

An illustration of this self-emptying of the Son of God is found in John 13:1-17. Our Lord seated at the table, the Master and Lord of the Disciples, is illustrative of Him in His preincarnate glory, giving outward expression of the glory of His Deity to the Angels.

Our Lord, girded with a towel, and washing the feet of the Disciples, is illustrative of His taking the outward expression of a servant in His Incarnation. His outer garments laid aside for the time being, point to His setting aside the outward expression of His preincarnate glory while He expressed Himself as a bond slave.

The fact that He was still their Master and Lord while kneeling on the floor doing the work of an Oriental slave, speaks of the fact that our Lord's assumption of humanity did not mean that He relinquished His Deity. He was just as much God while on Earth in His humiliation, as He was before He came and as He is now. His act of taking His outer garments again, tells of the resumption of the expression of His Glory after the Resurrection (Wuest).

The word *"servant"* does not mean that Jesus became an actual slave of any single man — though His service was expressed to individual men (Lk. 22:27) — but was the actual *"servant"* of mankind in general.

The phrase *"form of a servant"* should be allowed to explain the phrase *"form of God"* in Verse 6. The form of a servant is that which indicates a condition of a servant, in contradistinction from one of higher rank. It means, to appear as a servant, to perform the offices of a servant, and to be regarded as such. He was made like a servant in the lowly condition which He assumed.

HUMILIATION

There are some who have interpreted this statement as given by Paul as meaning that He became the servant or minister of God; and that in doing it, it was necessary that He should become a man. But the objection to this is obvious.

It greatly weakens the force of the Apostle's argument. His object is to state the depth of humiliation to which Christ descended; and this was best done by saying that He descended to the lowest condition of humanity, and appeared in the most humble garb. The idea of being a *"servant or minister of God"* would not express that, for this is a term which might be applied to the highest Angel in Heaven. Though the Lord Jesus was not literally a servant or slave, yet what is affirmed here was true of Him in the following respects:

1. He occupied a most lowly condition in life.

2. He condescended to perform such acts as are appropriate only to those who are servants. *"I am among you as he that serveth"* (Lk. 22:27).

3. His demeanor was that of a servant, and in every respect. Actually, this was one of the reasons that the religious leaders of Israel so totally rejected Him. He was not at all of the

aristocracy, not at all of the upper class, but in fact, was looked at as a *"Peasant."*

THE LIKENESS OF MEN

The phrase, *"And was made in the likeness of men,"* presents the Lord entering into a new state of being when He became Man. But His becoming Man did not exclude His position of Deity. He was and is today a person with two natures, that of absolute Deity and that of humanity.

"Likeness" in the Greek Text refers to *"that which is made like something else."* Our Lord's humanity was a real likeness, not a phantom, nor an incomplete copy of humanity. But this likeness did not express the whole of Christ's Being.

His mode of manifestation resembled what men are. But His humanity was not all that there was of Him. He was also Deity. He was not a man merely as such, but the Son of God manifest in the flesh and nature of man (Wuest).

The phrase, *"The likeness of men,"* has reference to the humanity of Jesus, which had a beginning in time, and should be taken in the sense of Galatians 4:4: *"God sent forth His Son, born of a woman."*

Baillie said, *"The Church has never taught that the human element in Jesus, His Manhood, was or is coeternal with God, but that it is exactly like ourselves and belongs to the order of created things."* In other words, Jesus was not always man, even though He was always God. He became a man at a point in time.

However, none of this can be taken to be anything less than man. Christ's humanity was no mere mask or disguise. He was *"really like men, as He was truly Man"*; but *"He was also more than man, without which fact there would be no resemblance but mere identity."* Jesus Christ was truly Man, but it was in and through Him that the Revelation of God came. This makes Him unique and distinct from man — He is *"very Man and very God."* The only way Paul can express this truth is to speak of His likeness to man. Christ took upon Himself not merely the fact of a human person, but as well, a human nature. So one could say, even as we have said, that He is one person in two natures.

NOTES

Lightfoot says, *"Christ, as the Second Adam, represents, not the individual man, but the human race."*

HUMAN LIMITATION

In attempting to explain the Deity and the humanity of Christ, we must be very careful that we not weaken the great testimony of His humanity. Certainly it fixes our thoughts on this, at least, that our Lord, by becoming man, had for His, truly for His, the experience the human limitation, human weakness and impoverishment, human dependence, human subjection, singularly contrasting with the glory of the Form of God. This, this humanity, became His.

It was so emphatically real, it became at the Incarnation so emphatically the form of existence on which He entered, that it is the thing eminently to be regarded, reverently to be dwelt upon. This emptiness, as the Holy Spirit through the Apostle proclaims it, instead of His fullness, is to draw and fix our regard. Instead of the Form of God, there arises before us this true human history, this lowly manhood — and it took place by His emptying Himself.

Various persons and schools have thought it right to go further. The word used here, *"in the likeness of men,"* has appeared to them to suggest that if the Son of God did not renounce His Godhead, yet the Divine nature in Him must have bereaved itself of the Divine attributes, or withheld itself from the use and exercise of them; so that the all-fullness no longer was at His disposal. In this line they have gone on to describe or assign the mode of self-emptying which the Incarnation should imply.

THE DIVINE MYSTERY

However, it does not appear to me that one can lay down positions as to the internal privations of One Whose nature is owned to be essentially Divine, without falling into confusion and darkening of counsel. But perhaps we may do well to cherish the impression that this self-emptying on the part of the eternal Son of God, for our Salvation, involves realities which we cannot conceive or put in any words. There was more in this emptying of Himself than we can think or say.

He emptied Himself when He became man. Here we have the eminent example of a Divine mystery, which, being revealed, remains a mystery never to be adequately explained, and which yet proves full of meaning and full of power.

The Word was made flesh. He through Whom all worlds took being, was seen in Judea in the lowliness of that practical historical manhood. We are hard put to explain this. But if we believe it, all things become new for us: the meaning it proves to have for human history is inexhaustible.

He emptied Himself, *"taking the form of a servant,"* or bond slave. For the creature is in absolute subjection alike to God's authority and to His providence; and so Christ came to be. He entered on a discipline of subjection and obedience. In particular He was made after the likeness of men. He was born as other children are, even though He Alone experienced a unique conception. He grew as other children grow; body and mind took shape for Him under human conditions (Rainy).

(8) "AND BEING FOUND IN FASHION AS A MAN, HE HUMBLED HIMSELF, AND BECAME OBEDIENT UNTO DEATH, EVEN THE DEATH OF THE CROSS."

After describing the fact of the Incarnation, Paul turns to the consideration of the depths of humiliation to which Christ went: *"He humbled Himself"* and went to *"death on a Cross."*

The concluding phrase in Philippians 2:7 states what Christ actually was; the opening phrase of Philippians 2:8 looks at Him from the standpoint of how He appeared in the estimation of men.

He was *"found"* by them, as far as His external appearance was concerned as a mere man. Outwardly considered, He was no different from other men. Even this was great condescension for One Who possessed the form of God, but Christ's incomparable act did not end here. He further humbled Himself by *"becoming obedient to death."* He was so committed to the Father's Plan that He obeyed it even as far as death (Heb. 5:8). Nor was this all, for it was not ordinary death, but the disgraceful death by crucifixion, a death not allowed for Roman citizens, and to Jews indicative of the Curse of God (Deut. 21:23; Gal. 3:13).

NOTES

The mention of the *"Cross"* connoted probably the cruelest form of capital punishment. Crucifixion had been practiced by the Phoenicians and Persians and was taken over by the Romans. In Rome it was a punishment reserved for slaves and foreigners, but yet, the type of death which God commanded of His Son the Lord Jesus Christ, that is if mankind was to be redeemed. Actually, the process was twofold:

1. It had to be a Cross, actually demanded by God, which we will deal with momentarily.

2. There had to be a certain type of Sacrifice which only the Son of God could fill. So, the act of crucifixion itself, although necessary, could not save anyone. The total Plan of Redemption demanded not only death by crucifixion, but as well, a perfect Sacrifice, which no human being other than Christ could fulfill.

FOUND IN FASHION

The phrase, *"And being found in fashion as a man,"* presents the word *"fashion"* as the translation of a Greek word that refers to an outward expression that is assumed from the outside and does not come from within. The Greek word for *"form"* as we saw, refers to an outward expression that came from one's inner nature, thereby describing His Deity. That means that our Lord's expression of His Deity was not assumed from the outside, but came from His inmost nature. Likewise, His outward expression as a bond slave came from His inmost nature.

But His expression of His humanity came, not from His inmost nature as God, but was assumed in the Incarnation.

The contrast here is between what He was in Himself, God, and what He appeared in the eyes of men. The word *"fashion,"* therefore, referred to that which is purely outward, and appeals to the senses.

Our Lord's humanity was real. He was really a Man, but He was not a real man in the sense that He was like others of the human race, only a man. He was always in His Incarnation, more than man. There was always that single personality with a dual nature.

His Deity did not make Him more nor less than a Man, and His humanity did not make Him less than absolute Deity. He became in the likeness of man, and He was found in fashion as a man.

"Likeness" states the fact of His real resemblance to men in mode of existence, and *"fashion"* defines the outward mode and form as He *appeared* in the eyes of men. But He was not found in fashion as a man, but rather *"man."*

The indefinite article (a) should not be in the translation. He was found in outward guise as *"man,"* not *"a man."* He was actually *"the Man,"* and because He was also *"God,"* even though He had assumed human nature but yet without its sin.

A DIVINE MIRACLE

"Fashion" denotes the way Christ appeared in men's eyes. His contemporaries saw Jesus as they saw other men, subject to human drives and suffering (Heb. 4:15).

Isaiah said of Him, *"He hath no form nor comeliness; and when we shall see Him, there is no beauty that we should desire Him"* (Isa. 53:2).

In fact, one could say that a Divine Miracle is required to see God in this servant. Faith that He is the full and true Revelation of God comes *"not of blood, nor of the will of the flesh, nor of the will of man, but of God"* (Jn. 1:13).

The confession that He is the Christ springs from a Revelation of the *"Father which is in Heaven"* (Mat. 16:16-17).

Paul puts it elsewhere, *"No man can say that Jesus is the Lord, but by the Holy Spirit"* (I Cor. 12:3).

PAUL'S DESCRIPTION

And so He was *"found in fashion as man."* Could words express more strongly how wonderful it is in the Apostle's eyes, that He should so be found? He lived His Life and made His Mark in the world in human fashion — His Form, His Speech, His Acts, His Way of Life declared Him Man.

But being so, He humbled Himself to a strange and great obedience. Subjection, and in that subjection obedience, is the part of every creature. But the obedience that Christ was called to learn was special. A heavy task was laid upon Him.

He was made under the Law; and bearing the burden of human sin, He wrought Redemption. In doing so many great interests fell to Him to be cared for; and this was done by Him, not in the manner of Godhead which speaks and it is done, but with the pains and labor of a faithful servant.

"I have a Commandment," He said, as He faced the Jews, who would have had His Messianic work otherwise ordered (Jn. 12:49).

THE HUMILITY OF CHRIST

The phrase, *"He humbled Himself,"* means to, *"to be made low or to bring low, but yet to do so willingly."* What a description of the Son of God.

However, this self-humbling does not refer to the self-emptying of Verse 7. That was a self-humbling in His character as God. Here the self-humbling is the act of our Lord as the Son of Man. As we shall see, it was the humiliation of the death of the Cross. This we must consider, if it was humiliating to our Lord in His humanity, now much more was it so in His Deity. In fact, humiliation was characteristic of Him as a man. He did not aspire to high honor; He did not affect pomp and parade; He did not demand the service of a train of menials; but He condescended to the lowest conditions of life (Lk. 22:27).

The words here are very carefully chosen by the Holy Spirit as given by the Apostle. In the former case (vs. 7), when He became a man, He *"emptied Himself,"* or laid aside the symbols of His Glory; now, when a man, He further humbled Himself. That is, though He was God appearing in the form of man — a Divine Person on Earth — yet He did not assume and assert the dignity and prerogatives appropriate to a Divine Being, or even an honored human being, but put Himself voluntarily in a condition of obedience. For such a Being to obey law implied voluntary humiliation; and the greatness of His humiliation was shown by His becoming entirely obedient, as stated, even till He died on the Cross.

THE PARTICULAR TIMES IN WHICH HE LIVED

The world at the time of Christ functioned on the basis of pomp, ceremony, dignity, station, and status. About a third of the population of the Roman Empire at that time were slaves. So, the very spirit of the age pointed toward catering to those of rank and station.

In fact, Roman citizens were divided into three classes, Senatorial, Equestrian, and Plebeian, and the whole system of government harmonized with this triple division.

The Senatorial class was composed of descendants of Senators and those upon whom the Emperors conferred the privilege of wearing the tunic with broad purple border, the sign of membership in this order.

The Equestrian class was made up of those of lesser rank, but yet who were wealthy. These had the privilege of wearing the narrow purple band on the tunic. The Plebeians, which consisted of the general Roman public, wore no band of any nature on their garments.

This spirit of the age had also greatly infected Israel.

THE PHARISEES AND SADDUCEES

Within Israel at the time of Christ, there were found two major parties, one strict and the other lax in the observance of Mosaic Law. The leaders of the former were the highly popular Pharisees, who, according to their name, were the *"Separatists,"* separated from the common and lawless masses, at least according to their interpretation. They tried to surpass each other in their zeal for the traditional ordinances and pious observances. However, among them it was also possible to find at times real piety, although in the New Testament records, where they are described as taking a hostile attitude toward the higher and the highest form of Divine Revelation, and I speak of Christ Himself, they appear at their worst.

Their rivals, the Sadducees, were less fanatical in their observance of the demands of the Law and more willing to compromise with the spirit of the times. To this party belonged many of the more prominent Priests.

Out of this mix came the Jewish Sanhedrin, the highest tribunal of some 71 members, and also of the lower tribunals of 23 members, of which Jerusalem had two. It constituted the ruling hierarchy of Israel. It was made up of both Pharisees and Sadducees, but more so by the Pharisees. It is said that in the time of Salome they were so powerful that *"the Queen ruled only in name, but the Pharisees in reality."*

So in the time of Christ, the Sanhedrin was formerly led by the Sadducean High Priest, but practically ruled by the Pharisees. Most, if not all, of its members were extremely wealthy. Consequently, the status or station in Israel went down from this ruling body through the ranks of these two parties, which, in effect, separated themselves from the *"common masses"* as they were called. In fact, the religious leaders of Israel during the time of Christ, actually consisting of these of which we have mentioned, held themselves aloof from the common people. They would not think of mixing with them, much less personally giving spiritual instruction. Worse yet, they had no real spiritual instruction to give, inasmuch as they really did not know God.

JESUS

Into this status conscious hierarchy of Israel came Christ. He was a Peasant, the son of a carpenter, at least as such was thought. As such, He had no contact whatsoever with this ruling hierarchy, consequently, not at all a product of its schools, etc. As a result, He was looked at by the ruling hierarchy of Israel, as an unlettered, untutored, therefore, ignorant product of the masses. He held no station, no status, no place or position. Consequently, He is automatically labeled as *"one of no consequence."*

Worse yet, He was brought up in the despised village of Nazareth, prompting the reply of Nathanael, *"Can there any good thing come out of Nazareth?"* (Jn. 1:45-46).

Nazareth lay close to several main trade routes for easy contact with the outside world. In fact, it is believed that a Roman garrison was stationed nearby as well. Due to this outside influence, and worst of all of the Roman, if in fact a Roman garrison indeed was stationed nearby, the place was scorned by strict Jews. Even though born in Bethlehem, Jesus spent nearly 30 years in this place (Lk. 2:39).

The schooling that Jesus formerly had, was that of the ordinary village child, which means he was taught to read and write (Lk. 4:17; Jn. 8:6-8). However, on the commencing of His Ministry, even His Own townsfolk would not receive Him.

After the beginning of His Ministry, when He first ministered to them, they already having heard reports of great things done elsewhere, at first listened to Him with admiration. Then, as the magnitude of the claims He was making became apparent to His audience, a very different spirit took possession of them.

"Who was this that spoke this? Was it not Joseph's son?" (Lk. 4:22). There seemed to be disappointment as well, that Jesus showed no disposition to gratify them by working before them any of the miracles of which they had heard so much (Lk. 4:23). Consequently, He told His hearers He had not expected any better reception, and in reply to their reproach that He had wrought miracles elsewhere, but had wrought none among them, quoted examples of Prophets who had done the same thing, Elijah and Elisha (Lk. 4:24-28).

This completed the exasperation of the Nazarenes, who, springing forward, dragged Him to the brow of the hill on which their city was built, and would have thrown Him down, had something in the aspect of Jesus not restrained them.

HIS TEACHING AND PREACHING

The Scripture says, *"He taught them as having authority, and not as the Scribes"* (Mk. 1:22).

The Scribes gave forth nothing of their own. They but repeated the statements of the so-called great authorities of the past. Consequently, it was a surprise to the people to find in Jesus One Whose wisdom, like waters from a clear fountain, came fresh and sparkling from His Own Lips. The authority also with which Jesus spoke commanded attention. He sought support in the opinion of no others, but gave forth His statements with firmness, decision, dignity, and emphasis.

This as well angered the Pharisees and Sadducees, who in fact He ignored, seeking not at all their approval or advice. Consequently, He clashed with them more and more, as they sought to find means to oppose and accuse Him, accepting Him not at all. In fact, they *"took counsel to destroy Him"* (Mk. 3:6).

At the beginning of His Ministry He attracted great crowds of people, with untold numbers being healed of every manner of disease, with even the dead being raised. This gained Him a wide popularity, at least at first. However, as the opposition increased, the last year of His Ministry saw the crowds diminishing somewhat, with Him more and more privately teaching His Disciples.

The Scriptures plainly say, *"They hated Me without a cause"* (Ps. 35:19; 69:4; 109:3; 119:161; Jn. 15:25).

Even though we have only touched the surface, perhaps we can still see somewhat the magnitude of the humiliation He suffered, not only becoming man, but rather a man most humiliated.

OBEDIENCE

The phrase, *"Became obedient unto death,"* does not mean that He became obedient to death. He was always the Master of death. In fact, He died as no other individual ever died or ever will die. He died of His Own volition. He actually dismissed His human spirit.

The word *"unto"* is the translation of a Greek word which means *"up to the point of."* Our Lord was obedient to the Father up to the point of dying. In fact, He said, *"Lo, I come to do Thy Will, O God"* (Heb. 10:9) (Wuest).

Yet Christ subjected Himself to death *"That through death He might destroy him that had the power of death, that is, the Devil; and deliver them who through fear of death were all their lifetime subject to bondage"* (Heb. 2:14-15). It must be emphasized that Christ's acts of self-humiliation and obedience to death were voluntary — of Himself, as stated, He laid down His Life (Jn. 10:17-18) — while at the same time such were in accord with the Will of the Father.

Should it be said that if He was God Himself He must have been Himself the Lawgiver we may reply, that this rendered His obedience the more wonderful and the more meritorious. If a Monarch should, for an important purpose, place himself in a position to obey his own laws, nothing could show in a more striking manner their importance in his view.

The highest honor that has been shown to the Law of God on Earth was, that it was perfectly observed by Him Who made the Law — the great Mediator. In fact, He obeyed even when obedience terminated in death.

In the case of Jesus all of this was wholly voluntary. He placed Himself in the condition of a servant to do the Will of God, and then never shrank from what that condition involved.

THE DEATH OF THE CROSS

The phrase, *"Even the death of the Cross,"* presents the character of His Death. It was the death of a Cross, its nature, one of ignominy and degradation. It was the kind of death meted out to criminals, and only to those who were not citizens of the Roman Empire. *"The death of the Cross"* indicates the climax of Christ's self-abasement, for it was the most ignominious, as stated, of all the modes of death then known. In fact, the Law of Moses had spoken a curse against such a death (Deut. 21:23). Thus, the Cross was surrounded by the deepest shame (Heb. 12:2).

But by His obedience even unto *"the death of the Cross,"* Christ *"hath abolished death, and hath brought life and immortality to light through the Gospel"* (II Tim. 1:10). Consequently, *"The Cross of Christ has come to be His Crown of Glory"* (Rom. 5:19).

WAS SUCH A DEATH NECESSARY?

Yes it was!

If it is to be noticed, Paul did not say *"The death on the Cross,"* but rather, *"The death of the* (a) *Cross."* The idea is, He came to die on the Cross. That was the purpose of His Incarnation, the very purpose of His Coming, the very purpose of it all.

As we have previously said, His Death by crucifixion was not an execution in the truest sense of the word. In other words, He did not run afoul of Roman or Jewish Law, thereby suffering this ignominious death. While they definitely played their part in this travesty, still, it was the Will of God for Him to die accordingly. Jesus said of this situation, *"Woe unto the world because of offences! For it must needs be that offences come; but woe to that man by whom the offence cometh!"* (Mat. 18:7).

If the Church misunderstands the Sacrificial, Atoning Death of Christ in any manner, negative results will always follow. The purpose of the Great Plan of God as it regarded the Redemption of fallen humanity, was always the *"Cross"* (Gen. 3:15; I Pet. 1:19-20; Rev. 13:8). All the predictions of the Prophets, whether directly or indirectly, pointed toward the *"Cross"* (Isa. Chpt. 53). The Incarnation of Christ (God becoming man) was all for the purpose of the *"Cross"* (Mat. 20:28; Mk. 10:45; I Tim. 2:6). Even though He performed Miracles and healed the sick, still, His major purpose was always the *"Cross"* (Mat. 16:21-25).

WHY WAS THE CROSS NECESSARY?

Death is the signature of failure and disgrace. Even with sinless creatures it seems so. Their beauty and their use are past, their worth is measured and exhausted; they die. More emphatically in a nature like ours, which aims at fellowship with God and immortality, death is significant this way, and bears the character of doom.

So we are taught to think that death entered by sin. But the violent death of crucifixion, inflicted for the worst crimes, is most significant this way. What it comprehended for our Lord, although necessary, we cannot measure. We know that He looked to it with the most solemn expectation; and when it came the experience was overwhelming (Lk. 22:39-45). He submitted to the doom and blight of death, and through death He made Atonement and finished transgression.

The Incarnation was the way in which our Lord bound Himself to our woeful fortunes, and carried to us the benefits with which He would enrich us; and His Death was for our sins, endured that we might live.

This type of death was necessary for several reasons:

1. First of all, death was mandated for all who broke the Law (the Law of Moses, i.e., *"Law of God,"*) and all had broken that Law (Rom. 3:10; 6:23).

2. The crime of the breaking of the Law of God is the worse crime that one could begin to imagine. Sin strikes at the very Holiness and Righteousness of God and is destructive of all things (Jn. 10:10). Consequently, the death of Christ on the Cross, the worst form of death, showed the awfulness of that monster called sin (Deut. 21:22-23; Gal. 3:13), all which showed the necessity of the worst type of punishment, a punishment incidentally which should have been ours.

In view of the tremendous significance of this, which in fact, is the most important thing in the history of man, perhaps it would help us to look at this great Sacrifice of Christ more closely.

ATONEMENT

Considering that Jesus atoned for all sin by His Death on the Cross, past, present, and future, perhaps the word *"Atonement"* explains best all the rudiments of Redemption.

The word *"Atonement"* is one of the few theological terms which derive basically from Anglo-Saxon. It means *"a making at one,"* and points to a process of bringing those who are estranged into a unity. The word is used frequently in the Old Testament, but is found only once in the New Testament, and would perhaps even then have been better translated *"reconciliation."*

Its use in theology is to denote the Work of Christ in dealing with the problem posed by the sin of man, and in bringing sinners into right relation with God.

THE NEED FOR ATONEMENT

The need for Atonement is brought about by three things:
1. The universality of sin.
2. The seriousness of sin.
3. Man's inability to deal with sin.

The first point is attested in many places: *"There is no man who does not sin"* (I Ki. 8:46); *"There is none that does good, no, not one"* (Ps. 14:3); *"There is not a righteous man on earth who does good and never sins"* (Eccl. 7:20). Jesus told the rich young ruler, *"No one is good but God Alone"* (Mk. 10:18), and Paul writes, *"All have sinned and fall short of the Glory of God"* (Rom. 3:23). Much more could be cited.

The seriousness of sin is seen in Passages which show God's aversion to it. Habakkuk prays, *"Thou Who art of purer eyes than to behold evil and canst not look on wrong"* (Hab. 1:13).

Sin separates from God (Prov. 15:29; Isa. 59:2). Jesus said of one sin, blasphemy against the Holy Spirit, that it will never be forgiven (Mk. 3:29), and of Judas He said, *"It would have been better for that man if he had not been born"* (Mk. 14:21). Before being saved men are *"estranged and hostile in mind, doing evil deeds"* (Col. 1:21). There awaits the unrepentant sinner only *"a fearful prospect of judgment, and a fury of fire that will consume the adversaries"* (Heb. 10:27).

And man cannot deal with the situation. He is not able to keep his sin hidden (Num. 32:23), and he cannot cleanse himself of it (Prov. 20:9).

No deeds of Law will ever enable man to stand before God justified (Rom. 3:20; Gal. 2:16). If he must depend on himself, then man will never be saved. Perhaps the most important evidence of this is the very fact of the Atonement. If the Son of God came to Earth to save men, then men were sinners and their plight serious indeed.

ATONEMENT IN THE OLD TESTAMENT

God and man, are hopelessly estranged by man's sin, and there is no way back from man's side. But God provides the way.

In the Old Testament Atonement is usually said to be obtained by the Sacrifices, but it must never be forgotten that God says of atoning blood, *"I have given it for you upon the Altar to make Atonement for your souls"* (Lev. 17:11). Atonement is secured, not by any value inherent in the Sacrificial victim, but because Sacrifice is the Divinely-appointed way of securing Atonement. In effect, Atonement was secured by Faith in the coming One the Sacrifices represented, namely Christ.

The Sacrifices point us to certain truths concerning Atonement. Thus, the victim must always be unblemished, which indicates the necessity for perfection. The victims cost something, for Atonement is not cheap, and sin is never to be taken lightly.

BLOOD

The death of the victim was the important thing. This is brought out partly in the allusions to *"blood,"* partly in the general character of the rite itself and partly in other references to Atonement.

There are several allusions to Atonement, either affected or contemplated by means other than the rite itself, and where these bear on the problem they point to death as the way. Thus, in Exodus 32:30-32 Moses seeks to make an Atonement for the sin of the people, and he does so by asking God to blot him out of the Book which he has written. Phinehas made an Atonement by slaying certain transgressors (Num. 25:6-8, 13). Other Passages might be cited.

It is clear that in the Old Testament it was recognized that death was the penalty for sin (Ezek. 18:20), but that God graciously permitted the death of a sacrificial victim to substitute for the death of the sinner. So clear is the connection that the writer of the Epistle to the Hebrews can sum it up by saying *"Without the shedding of Blood there is no forgiveness of sins"* (Heb. 9:22).

ATONEMENT IN THE NEW TESTAMENT

The New Testament takes the line that the Sacrifices of old were not the root cause of the putting away of sins. Redemption is to be obtained even *"from the transgressions under the First Covenant"* only by the Death of Christ (Heb. 9:15). This means that the Sacrifices only pointed to the One Who was to come, thereby symbolic of His Death. Salvation demanded Faith in Christ, rather than the Sacrifice of the animal itself.

Consequently, the Cross is absolutely central to the New Testament, and, indeed, to the whole Bible. All before leads up to it. All after looks back to it.

Since it occupies the critical place, it is not surprising that there is a vast volume of teaching about it. The New Testament writers, writing from different standpoints, and with different emphases, give us a number of facets of the Atonement. There is no repetition of a stereotyped line of teaching. Each writes as he sees.

Some saw more and more deeply than others. But they did not see something different. And what follows we shall consider first of all what might be termed the common, basic teaching about the Atonement, and then some of the information that we owe to one or other of the New Testament Theologians.

THE ATONEMENT REVEALS
GOD'S LOVE FOR MEN

All are agreed that the Atonement proceeds from the Love of God. It is not something wrung from a stern and unwilling Father, perfectly just, but perfectly inflexible, by a loving Son. The Atonement shows us the love of the Father just as it does the love of the Son. Paul gives us the classic exposition of this when he says, *"God shows His Love for us in that while we were yet sinners Christ died for us"* (Rom 5:8).

In the best known Text in the Bible we find that *"God so loved the world that He gave His only Begotten Son . . ."* (Jn. 3:16). In the Gospels of Matthew, Mark, and Luke, it is emphasized that the Son of Man *"must suffer"* (Mk. 8:31). That is to say, the death of Christ was no accident: it was rooted in a compelling Divine necessity.

This we see also in our Lord's Prayer in Gethsemane that the Will of the Father be done (Mat. 26:42). Similarly, in Hebrews we read that it was *"by the Grace of God"* that Christ tasted death for us all (Heb. 2:9).

This thought is found throughout the New Testament, and we must bear it well in mind when we reflect on the manner of the Atonement.

THE SACRIFICIAL ASPECT
OF CHRIST'S DEATH

Another thought that is widespread is that the death of Christ is a death for sin. It is not simply that certain wicked men rose up against Him. It is not that His enemies conspired against Him and that He was not able to resist them. He *"was put to death for our trespasses"* (Rom. 4:25). In other words, no one actually took the life of Jesus from Him, in fact, He gave it up willingly (Jn. 10:18). He came specifically to die for our sins. His Blood was shed *"for many for the forgiveness of sins"* (Mat. 26:28).

He *"made purification for sins"* (Heb. 1:3). He *"bore our sins in His Body on the tree"* (I Pet. 2:24). He is *"the propitiation for our sins"* (I Jn. 2:2). In fact, the Cross of Christ will never be understood unless it is seen that thereon the Saviour was dealing with the sins of all mankind.

In doing this He fulfilled all that the old sacrifices had foreshadowed, and the New Testament writers love to think of His Death as a Sacrifice, which it definitely was. Jesus Himself referred to His Blood as *"Blood of the Covenant"* (Mk. 14:24), which points us to the sacrificial rites for its understanding.

Indeed, much of the language used in the institution of the Holy Communion is sacrificial, pointing to the Sacrifice to be accomplished on the Cross.

THE LAMB OF GOD

Paul tells us that Christ *"loved us and gave Himself up for us, a fragrant Offering and Sacrifice to God"* (Eph. 5:2). On occasion he can refer, not to sacrifice in general, but a specific Sacrifice, as in I Corinthians 5:7, *"For Christ our Paschal Lamb* (Passover Lamb) *has been sacrificed."* Peter speaks of *"the precious Blood of Christ, like that of a lamb without blemish or spot"* (I Pet. 1:19), which indicates that in one aspect Christ's Death was a Sacrifice. And in John's Gospel we read the words of John the Baptist, *"Behold the Lamb of God, Who takes away the sin of the world"* (Jn. 1:29).

Sacrifice was practically the universal religious rite of the First Century. Wherever men were and whatever their background, they would discern a sacrificial allusion. The New Testament writers made use of this, and employed sacrificial terminology to bring out what Christ had done for men. All that to which the Sacrifices pointed, and more, He fully accomplished by His Death.

THE REPRESENTATIVE NATURE OF CHRIST'S DEATH

It is agreed by most students that Christ's death was vicarious (substitutionary). If in one sense He died *"for sin,"* in another He died *"for us."* But *"vicarious"* is a term which may mean much or little. It is better to be more precise.

Most Scholars today accept the view that the death of Christ is representative. That is to say, it is not that Christ died and somehow the benefits of that death become available to men. It is rather that He died specifically for us. He was our Representative as He hung on the Cross. This is expressed succinctly in II Corinthians 5:14, *"One died for all; therefore all have died."*

The death of the Representative counts as the death of those He represents. When Christ is spoken of as our *"Advocate with the Father"* (I Jn. 2:1) there is the plain thought of representation, and as the Passage immediately goes on to deal with His death for sin it is relevant to our purpose.

The Epistle to the Hebrews has as one of its major themes that of Christ as our great High Priest. The thought is repeated over and over. Now whatever else may be said about a High Priest, he represents men. Thus, the thought of representation may be said to be very strong in Hebrews.

SUBSTITUTION TAUGHT IN THE NEW TESTAMENT

However, we can say more.

Whereas representation is definitely taught in the New Testament, Substitution is as well, and graphically so, which, in effect, goes a step further than representation.

In the three Gospels, Matthew, Mark, and Luke, there is the great ransom saying, *"The Son of Man also came not to be served but to serve, and to give His Life as a ransom for many"* (Mk. 10:45).

The same Truth is indicated by Passages which speak of Christ as the suffering Servant of Isaiah Chapter 53, for of Him it is said, *"He was wounded for our transgressions, He was bruised for our iniquities; upon Him was the chastisement that made us whole, and with His stripes we are healed... The Lord has laid on Him the iniquity of us all"* (Isa. 53:5-6).

The shrinking of Christ in Gethsemane points in the same direction. He was courageous, and many far less worthy than He have faced death calmly. The agony seems to be inexplicable other than on the grounds disclosed by Paul, that for our sake God *"made Him to be sin* (a Sin-Offering), *Who knew no sin"* (II Cor. 5:21).

In His Death He took our place, and His holy soul shrank from this identification with sinners. And it seems that no less than this gives meaning to the cry of dereliction, *"My God, My God, Why hast Thou forsaken Me?"* (Mk. 15:34).

The general thought of all of this is, that men should die, but Christ dies instead, which of course, is substitution.

WHAT THE CROSS TELLS US

Paul tells us that Christ *"redeemed us from the Curse of the Law, having become a*

Curse for us" (Gal. 3:13). He bore our curse, which is but another way of *"substitution."*

The same thought lies behind Romans 3:21-26, where the Apostle develops the thought that God's justice is manifested in the process whereby sin is forgiven, i.e., *"the Cross."* He is not saying, as some have thought, that God's Righteousness is shown in the fact that sin is forgiven, but that it is shown in the *way* in which sin is forgiven. Atonement is not a matter of passing over sin as had been done previously (Rom. 3:25). The Cross shows that God is just, at the same time as it shows Him justifying Believers.

This must mean that God's Justice is vindicated in the way sin is dealt with. And this seems another way of saying that Christ bore the penalty of men's sin. This is also the thought in Passages dealing with sin-bearing as Hebrews 9:28; I Peter 2:24. The meaning of bearing sin is made clear by a number of Old Testament Passages where the context shows that the bearing of penalty is meant.

For example, in Ezekiel 18:20 we read, *"The soul that sins shall die. The son shall not suffer for ('bear' in the Hebrew) the iniquity of the father..."* and in Numbers 14:34 the wilderness wanderings are described as a bearing of iniquities. Christ's bearing of our sin, then means that He bore our penalty.

This is extremely important, in that some are teaching that Christ actually became a sinner on the Cross by taking on the nature of Satan, which of course, is ludicrous.

THE PRICE OF REDEMPTION

Substitutionalized behind the statement in I Timothy 2:6 is that Christ gave Himself *"a ransom for all."* The word *"ransom"* given here in the Greek is *"antilytron,"* and is a strong compound meaning *"substitute-ransom."*

It is that which is given in exchange for another as the price of his redemption. Actually, it is impossible to empty the word of substitutionary associations.

A similar thought lies behind John's recording of the cynical prophecy of Caiaphas, *"It is expedient for you that one man should die for the people, and that the whole nation should not perish"* (Jn. 11:50). For Caiaphas the words were sheer political expediency, but John sees in them a prophecy that Christ should die instead of the people.

This is a formidable body of evidence proving the fact of substitution on the part of Christ, but is in no way exhausted. In other words, the Word of God teaches emphatically that Jesus Christ was our Substitute. In the fact of all this, it seems impossible to deny that substitution is one strand in the New Testament understanding of the Work of Christ.

DELIVERANCE

There are many truths set forth concerning the Atonement, with the Holy Spirit, in effect, addressing this all-important subject in so many ways, that it should not be possible for the Bible Student to misunderstand what is being said. In fact, and as should be overly obvious, the Atonement, which of course, signifies what Jesus did at the Cross and the Resurrection as it regards the great Salvation experience, is the foundation, the very bedrock of the Christian Faith. If men are mixed-up concerning the Atonement, in other words if they have something wrong concerning this firm foundation as it regards their interpretation or thinking, everything else will be somewhat wrong as well.

In fact, I personally believe that much error begins with this — an improper interpretation of the Atonement; consequently, this must be corrected first of all before anything else can be properly addressed.

Paul sees in the Cross the way of deliverance, in fact, the only way. This means not only deliverance for the unsaved soul coming to Christ, to which it most certainly does refer, but as well for the Christian. And this is where many Christians miss it. They understand the Atonement as it regards their initial Salvation experience, but have little idea as to how it affects their everyday walk before God, thereby attempting to sanctify themselves by methods of their own devising, or the devising of other individuals, etc. Irrespective, any way other than God's prescribed order, which is the Finished Work of Christ, which of course is the Atonement, is doomed to failure.

Men naturally are enslaved to sin (Rom. 6:17; 7:14). But *"in Christ"* and only *"in Christ"* are men free, and that applies to the

Christian just as well as it applies to the unsaved soul coming to Christ (Rom. 6:14-22).

Along with being free in Christ which takes place at conversion, similarly, through Christ Believers are delivered from the flesh. They have *"crucified the flesh"* (Gal. 5:24).

WHAT DOES CRUCIFYING THE FLESH MEAN?

Let's see first what it doesn't mean.

Believers have been attempting to do this from day one. They (and I should say *"we"*) have tried to do this using every method imaginable.

First of all, what is the flesh?

Paul uses the word *"flesh"* in many ways. It can refer to the physical man. As well, it can refer to the sin nature. It also can refer to the efforts of individuals to sanctify themselves by their own ability, etc. So, it is used in a variety of ways.

However, the word *"flesh"* as Paul uses it in Galatians 5:24, refers to the physical man, which constitutes the physical body and more particularly, the five senses. In fact, this is the battleground. This is the part of man which Satan uses to carry out his evil designs, or at least to attempt to do so. As well, this is what Paul was speaking about when he also said, *"Let not sin therefore reign in your mortal body, that ye should obey it and the lusts thereof."*

He then went on to say, *"Neither yield ye your members* (members of your physical body) *as instruments of unrighteousness unto sin: but yield yourselves unto God, as those that are alive from the dead* (have the Life of Christ), *and your members as instruments of Righteousness unto God"* (Rom. 6:12-13).

An elementary investigation of these Scriptures shows us that the physical body, the flesh as Paul uses it in Galatians 5:24, is actually neutral. However, due to the fact that it is the battleground, the area where Satan tries to carry out his evil designs, sometimes we tend to think that the flesh within itself is evil. It isn't! It can be used, exactly as Paul says here, as an instrument of Righteousness or unrighteousness. So, trying to punish the flesh is not going to solve the problem, because that's not where the problem

NOTES

actually is, at least as Paul uses the word *"flesh"* in this case.

So, what does Paul mean when he, in effect, tells us that we must *"crucify the flesh with the affections and lusts"*? (Gal. 5:24).

He tells us how in Galatians 5:25, *"If we live in the Spirit, let us also walk in the Spirit."*

What does he mean by that?

HOW DO WE WALK IN THE SPIRIT?

Many Pentecostals and Charismatics think that just because they have been Baptized with the Holy Spirit with the evidence of speaking with other Tongues, that this means they are automatically walking *"in the Spirit."*

It means no such thing!

In fact, I think I can say without fear of exaggeration, that millions, even most Spirit-filled Believers are not walking in the Spirit.

We can walk in the Spirit, which means to order our everyday lives according to the Power of the Holy Spirit Which and Who gives us victory, only if we follow God's prescribed order. It definitely is not an automatic process. In fact, millions of Christians at this very moment are living in frustration, simply because they are definitely Spirit-filled, but despite all their efforts they are not walking in the Spirit, which means they are experiencing failure. While they may not be mixed up in what I humorously refer to as the big five (cigarettes, alcohol, drugs, gambling, immorality), nevertheless, there is something else that dominates them such as uncontrollable temper, malice, unforgiveness, self-righteousness, greed, covetousness, depression, etc. In effect, one or more of these things dominate them, which is the exact opposite as to what ought to be (Rom. 6:14).

The Believer can *"walk in the Spirit,"* which gives us victory over the flesh in every capacity, only by placing his Faith in the Finished Work of Christ. The Believer must understand that not only did his Salvation experience originate at the Cross and the Resurrection, but as well, this great Finished Work is the source also of one's everyday victory in the Lord, i.e., *"walking in the Spirit,"* i.e., *"crucifying the flesh."*

The Believer is to understand that his victory is in the Cross. This is where Jesus paid the price, satisfied the Heavenly Courts of Justice, took upon Himself the curse of the broken law, incidentally all on our behalf exactly as we are studying, all which made Redemption and Victory possible. The Believer must understand that his Victory is here and at no other place. If the Believer attempts to go beyond the Cross, which at the same time presupposes the Resurrection, the Believer every single time will lose his way.

It is not possible from a Scriptural standpoint to go beyond the Cross. If it is, where in the Bible is such an account?

Some may argue that we are now Resurrection people, actually seated with Christ in heavenly places, which is exactly correct (Eph. 2:6); however, the Resurrection life which the Believer has, which means he is actually seated with Christ in heavenly places victorious over all the world, the flesh, and the Devil, is all a part of the Finished Work of Christ. In other words, all of this is made possible by the Cross, and the Cross alone. In essence, we should not separate the three, the Cross, the Resurrection, and the Exaltation. Even though they are three definite works, they are all a part of the great one work of the Atonement.

CRUCIFIED FLESH

Getting back to our original question, *"How does one crucify the flesh?"*, let us say first of all that actually it is already crucified. Let me explain.

The words *"in Christ"* actually explain it all (Rom. 8:1). But yet it goes back to Romans 6:3-6.

When Jesus died on the Cross, He died as our Representative Man, in effect, our Substitute, exactly as we are studying here as it regards the meaning of the Atonement. Whenever the believing sinner exhibits Faith in that, and we speak of the Cross, even though he understands very little about this great Work, at least at the outset, he is instantly saved (Jn. 3:16; Eph. 2:8-9; Rev. 22:17). But in the Mind of God that sinner, which includes every Believer who has ever lived, was actually *"in Christ"* when all of this happened. That's why Paul said, *"Know ye not, that so many of us as were baptized into Jesus Christ were baptized into His Death?"* (Rom. 6:3).

NOTES

No, Paul is not speaking here of Water Baptism, but rather the Crucifixion of Christ.

At this time, everything about the believing sinner was crucified, in essence one might say by proxy through Christ. This means all the *"affections and lusts of the flesh."*

However, the Believer is to understand that this not only took place at his initial Salvation experience, but it remains so ever after. We are to have Faith everyday as it regards what Christ did at the Cross and the Resurrection, which keeps the flesh crucified. Whenever we have Faith alone in that, which is the Finished Work of Christ, i.e., *"the Atonement,"* then the Holy Spirit works on our behalf to guarantee us all the benefits of the Cross and the Resurrection, which explains what Paul means by *"walking in the Spirit"* (Gal. 5:25). The Holy Spirit as stated, can only work, and will only work, in the parameters of the Atonement, or the Finished Work of Christ. In other words, it is our Faith in that Work, and our continued Faith in that work I might quickly add, which gives us the help of the Holy Spirit, which actually means to *"walk in the Spirit."* If we try to do this in any other manner, by good works, or even by things which are Scriptural such as prayer, fasting, etc., we will fail. While these other things are great and wonderful, and should definitely be engaged in constantly by Christians, they should never be turned into works, which God can never honor. Our Victory, which speaks of our everyday walk before the Lord, is obtained and continued only by our Faith in the Cross of Christ.

As well, one might quickly add, not only were we crucified with Christ, but we were also buried with Him and raised with Him in *"newness of life"* (Rom. 6:4-5).

Paul then said, which clenches the argument, *"Knowing this, that our old man is crucified with Him, that the body of sin might be destroyed, that henceforth we should not serve sin"* (Rom. 6:6).

That's the only way that the flesh can be crucified. In fact, as we've already stated, it has already been crucified. The problem is, most Christians do not know how it was done, where it was done, when it was done, and what that which was done actually means. Consequently, they walk in failure instead of victory.

Let the Christian always understand, that there is no Victory outside of the Finished Work of Christ. Also, any Faith placed in anything other than that Finished Work, i.e., *"the Atonement,"* is not proper Faith, but rather misplaced Faith, which God can never honor. Unfortunately, *"misplaced Faith"* is probably the greatest problem of the Child of God.

WHAT IS MISPLACED FAITH?

Misplaced Faith is Faith we have in anything, and I mean anything, other than the Finished Work of Christ. Let's explain further.

If the Christian believes that the Cross has to do only with his initial Salvation experience, and does not refer to his everyday walk before God, that means His Faith is wrongly placed, i.e., *"placed in something other than the Cross and the Resurrection."*

Millions of Christians are taught to have Faith in themselves, Faith in their Faith, with the greatest statement being *"Faith in the Word."* However, if the so-called Faith in the Word doesn't place the Word on the foundation of the Cross and the Resurrection, such constitutes a perverted Word, which God will not honor. Regrettably, that's where most Christians are. Let's use this as an example.

Millions of Christians have Faith in the Holy Spirit to give them victory. While this certainly is right at least as far as it goes, it just does not go far enough. And a journey half completed is not a journey finished.

To have proper Faith in the Holy Spirit to do the work in our lives which needs to be done, we must know on what parameters that He works. He does not work automatically, even as we have already stated. He functions only on our Faith as it is anchored in the Cross and the Resurrection. That's what Paul meant when he said, *"For the Law of the Spirit* (the Law by which He works) *of Life* (the Life which He imparts to us) *in Christ Jesus* (the great Work that Jesus did at the Cross and the Resurrection) *hath made me free from the Law of sin and death"* (Rom. 8:2).

THE LAW OF THE SPIRIT

In other words, it is *"the Law of the Spirit"* which means it cannot be broken, at least it will not be broken by Him. If we go outside of that *"Law"* we will not get any favorable results. The tragedy is, most Christians function outside of that Law, which denies them the help of the Holy Spirit, even though they are filled with the Spirit, etc. When this is done, it means the Faith of the individual is misplaced, i.e., *"placed in things other than the Work of Christ."*

There has probably been more teaching on Faith in the last 50 years than all the rest of the centuries of the Church put together. Some small amount of this teaching has been excellent; however, most of it has been very wrong, simply because it does not have as its foundation the great Sacrifice of Christ. For the most part, Faith, at least as it is presently taught, is an end within itself. In other words, it begins and ends within itself, which is grossly unscriptural.

First of all, Jesus must be the *"Author and Finisher of our Faith"* (Heb. 12:2).

What does that mean?

It refers, of course, to everything Jesus is and everything He did; however, more particularly, it refers to His Finished Work.

We are not saved and delivered presently because Jesus is the Son of God. Neither are we saved and delivered because of His Virgin Birth, His perfect Life, His Miracles, and Healings, etc. While all of these things were definitely necessary, and are of extreme importance as it refers to our Salvation experience, still, if Jesus had stopped there, in other words if He had not gone to the Cross, man would have still been unredeemed. Again, all of these other things were and are very important, but if Jesus had not gone to the Cross to bear the sin penalty of mankind, there would have been no way for man to be saved. So, when the Holy Spirit speaks of Jesus being the *"Author and Finisher of our Faith,"* He is speaking primarily of what He did at the Cross and the Resurrection.

Let me give another example.

A Preacher was on our Radio Program some time ago, a Godly man I might quickly add; however, as we were discussing this subject, he quickly retorted by saying, *"When I have a problem of any kind, I go on a three-day fast, and that solves the problem,"* or words to that effect.

While fasting is definitely Scriptural, and definitely will bless the Christian, and is definitely something in which Christians should engage; still, if used in the manner in which our Brother suggested, it will not work. On that particular Program we were discussing sin in the heart and life of the Christian, and how it is to be eliminated. He suggested fasting. That is misplaced Faith!

In that place, one could substitute prayer, the giving of money to the Work of God, confession, manifestations, etc. While all of these things mentioned are very good and actually Scriptural, and will definitely bless the Christian, and something in which we should all be engaged; still, if they are used in this fashion, even as they are almost constantly at the present time, there will be no victory forthcoming because these things have been turned into works, which means we have placed our Faith in the wrong object.

The foundation of our Faith, the object of our Faith, the direction of our Faith, must always be in the Finished Work of Christ. Beginning there, we can go on to spiritual maturity, but only if we begin there.

Paul also said, *"For though we walk in the flesh, we do not war after the flesh"* (II Cor. 10:3). What did he mean by that?

WHAT IS WARRING AFTER THE FLESH?

First of all, we are told not to war after the flesh. Let's first look at the word *"war."*

"War" in the Greek is *"strateuomai,"* and means *"to serve in a military campaign, to contend with carnal inclinations, to soldier."*

The idea is, that Satan will make every attempt to hinder the Child of God, and above all he does so by attempting to hinder our Faith. In fact, I think one could say without any fear of contradiction, that every attack by Satan against the Child of God, and by whatever avenue, is always in one form or the other against our Faith. He wants to destroy our Faith, or at least to weaken our Faith. This is a conflict that is constant, and will not end, at least until the Trump sounds.

So, the question is, how do we face these attacks?

If we try to overcome Satan within our own capabilities or our own strength, we are doomed to failure, because in those modes we are functioning in the flesh. In fact, and as we have stated, anything that is outside of the Finished Work of Christ, constitutes *"warring after the flesh."*

The idea is, that the Holy Spirit do these things within us, which as God, He is very capable of doing. In fact, He is the only One Who can wage this warfare successfully. But the question is, how do we get him to do these things we so desperately need?

As we've already stated, the Believer placing his Faith in the Cross and the Resurrection, insures the help of the Holy Spirit. These are the parameters in which the Spirit works, and the only parameters in which He works. If we *"war"* any other way, we are going to fail, as fail we must. The flesh always brings defeat, which refers to our own efforts or machinations. While *"warring after the Spirit"* so to speak, always brings victory.

In this conflict, Paul says that the flesh *"lusteth against the Spirit"* (Gal. 5:17), and which apart from Christ spells death (Rom. 8:13).

In other words, the flesh wants things which are not appropriate and which opposes the Holy Spirit, hence the struggle. In this context, the Lord has designed it that the Spirit will work and function only according to the Finished Work of Christ, hence that which Paul spoke about in Romans 8:13. Consequently, our Faith must be in the great Sacrifice of Christ, in order for the Holy Spirit to function on our behalf, which will then insure victory over the flesh.

Men are under the Wrath of God on account of their unrighteousness (Rom. 1:18), but God delivers from this. Believers are *"justified by His Blood,"* and thus *"will be saved by Him from the Wrath of God"* (Rom. 5:9).

THE LAW OF MOSES

The Law of Moses which is found in the first five Books of the Bible, actually beginning in Exodus, but actually including the whole of the Old Testament, may be regarded in many ways. But considered as a way of Salvation, and we speak of the Law, etc., it is disastrous.

The Law shows a man his sin (Rom. 7:7), and, men entering into an unholy alliance with sin, slays him (Rom. 7:9-11). The end result is that *"All who rely on works of the Law are under a curse"* (Gal. 3:10), and because they are doomed to failure. But *"Christ redeemed us from the Curse of the Law,"* i.e., *"penalty of the Law"* (Gal. 3:13).

Death to men of antiquity was a grim antagonist against whom none might prevail. But Paul sings a song of triumph in Christ Who gives victory even over death (I Cor 15:55-57). It is abundantly plain that Paul sees in Christ a mighty Deliverer.

The Atonement has many positive aspects. It must suffice simply to mention such things as Redemption, Reconciliation, Justification, Adoption, and Propitiation. These are of course, tremendous concepts, all springing from *"Atonement."*

OUR GREAT HIGH PRIEST

To make it even easier to understand, Paul in Hebrews presents Christ as our great High Priest. He develops thoroughly the thought of the uniqueness and the finality of the Offering made by Christ. Unlike the way established on Jewish Altars and ministered by Priests of the Aaronic line, the way established by Christ in His Death is of permanent validity. It will never be altered. Christ has dealt fully with man's sin.

In the writings of John there is the thought of Christ as the special Revelation of the Father. He is One sent by the Father, and all that He does must be interpreted in the light of this fact. So John sees Christ as winning a conflict against the darkness, as defeating the Evil One. He has much to say about the working out of the purpose of God in Christ. He sees the true Glory in the lowly Cross whereon such a mighty work was done.

From all this it is abundantly apparent that the Atonement is vast and deep. In fact, it is impossible to exhaust its resources. The New Testament writers strive with the inadequacy of language as they seek to present us with what this great Divine act means.

There is more to it by far than we have been able to indicate. But all the points we have made are important, and none are to be neglected. Nor are we to overlook the fact that the Atonement represents more than something negative. We have been concerned to insist on the place of Christ's Sacrifice of Himself in the putting away of sin. That opens up the new way of the new Life in Christ. And that new Life, the Fruit of the Atonement, is not to be thought of as an insignificant detail. It is that to which all the rest leads.

Inasmuch as we are studying the Atonement, perhaps it would be helpful to also address ourselves as well to the *"Great Day of Atonement."*

THE DAY OF ATONEMENT

This Great Day was observed on the 10th day of the seventh month, which would have probably been the very latter part our September or early October. This was Israel's most solemn holy day.

The Day of Atonement served as a reminder that the daily, weekly, and monthly Sacrifices made at the Altar of Burnt-Offering were not sufficient to atone for sin. Even at the Altar of Burnt-Offering the worshiper stood *"afar off,"* unable to approach the Holy Presence of God, Who was manifest between the Cherubim and the Holy of Holies. On this one day in the year, Atoning Blood was brought into the Holy of Holies, the Divine Throne Room, by the High Priest as the representative of the people.

The High Priest made Atonement for *"all the iniquities of the Children of Israel and all their transgressions and all their sins."* Atonement was first made for the High Priest himself, because he as the mediator between God and his people had to be ceremonially clean. The Sanctuary was also cleansed, for it, too, was ceremonially defiled by the presence and ministration of sinful men, as this was the only way it could be.

THE ANCIENT OBSERVANCE

To prepare for the Sacrifices of the day, the High Priest put aside his official robes and dressed in a simple white garment. He then offered a bullock as a Sin-Offering for himself and the Priesthood. After filling his Censor with live coals from the Altar, the High Priest entered the Holy of Holies, where he placed Incense on the coals.

The Incense sent forth a cloud of smoke over the Mercy Seat, which served as a covering for the Ark of the Covenant. The High Priest then took some of the blood of the bullock and sprinkled it on the Mercy Seat and on the ground in front of the Ark. In this way Atonement was made for the Priesthood.

The High Priest next sacrificed a he-goat as a Sin-Offering for the people. Some of this blood was also taken into the Holy of Holies, and it was sprinkled there in the manner in which the Sin-Offering for the Priests had been sprinkled (Lev. 16:11-15).

After purifying the Holy Place and the Altar of Burnt-Offering with the mingled blood of the bullock and the goat (Lev. 16:18-19) the High Priest came out and took a second goat, laid his hands upon its head and confessed over it the sins of Israel.

This Goat commonly called the *"scape goat* (escape goat),"* was then driven into the desert, where it symbolically carried away the sins of the people.

The carcasses of the two Burnt-Offerings — the bullock and the he-goat — were taken outside the city and burnt. The day was concluded with additional Sacrifices.

THE INTERPRETATION

The Epistle to the Hebrews interprets the ritual of the Day of Atonement as a type of the Atoning Work of Christ, emphasizing the perfection of the latter by contrast with the inadequacy of the former (Heb. Chpts. 9-10). Jesus Himself is termed our *"High Priest,"* and the blood shed on Calvary is seen as typified in the blood of bulls and goats. Unlike the Old Testament Priesthood, the sinless Christ did not have to make Sacrifice for any sins of His Own.

As the High Priest of the Old Testament entered the Holy of Holies with the blood of his sacrificial victim, so Jesus entered Heaven itself to appear before the Father on behalf of His people (Heb. 9:11-12).

The High Priest had to offer Sin-Offerings each year for his own sins and the sins of the people. This annual repetition of the Sacrifices served as a reminder that perfect Atonement had not yet been provided. Jesus, however, through His Own Blood effected eternal Redemption for His people (Heb. 9:12), which never again need be done.

A TYPE

The Epistle to the Hebrews notes that the Levitical Offerings could effect only *"the purification of the flesh."* They ceremonially cleansed the sinner, but they could not bring about inward cleansing, the prerequisite for fellowship with God. The Offerings served as a type and a prophecy of Jesus, Who, through His better Sacrifice, cleanses the conscience from dead works (Heb. 9:13-14).

The Old Testament Tabernacle was designed, in part, to teach Israel that sin hindered access to the Presence of God. Only the High Priest, and he only once a year, could enter the Holy of Holies, and then *"not without taking blood"* offered to Atone for sins (Heb. 9:7).

Jesus, through a *"new and living way"* has entered Heaven itself, the true Holy of Holies, where He ever lives to make intercession for His people. The Believer need not stand afar off, as did the Israelites of old, but may now through Christ approach the very Throne of Grace.

In Hebrews 13:11-12, we are reminded that the flesh of the Sin-Offering of the Day of Atonement was burnt outside the camp of Israel. Jesus, also, suffered outside the gate of Jerusalem that He might redeem His people from sin.

(Bibliography: M. Noth, Leviticus; Snaith, The Jewish New Year Festival; R. de Vaux, Ancient Israel; Baillie, God was in Christ; Denney, The Death of Christ; Stewart, A Man in Christ; Morris, The Apostolic Teaching of the Cross; The Cross in the New Testament; Knox, The Death of Christ.)

(9) "WHEREFORE GOD ALSO HATH HIGHLY EXALTED HIM, AND GIVEN HIM A NAME WHICH IS ABOVE EVERY NAME:"

The final movement of thought in this great illustration describes Christ's subsequent Exaltation. The nature of this Exaltation was God's elevating Christ to the highest position and granting Him the Name above all names.

"Exalted . . . to the highest place" in the Greek might be translated *"superexalted."*

The reference is to the Resurrection, Ascension, and Glorification of Jesus following His humiliating death, whereby all that He had laid aside, one might say in a sense was restored to Him, and one might say much more besides, if such words would apply. Implicit in this Exaltation is the coming consummation mentioned in the next two Verses, when His triumph over sin and His Lordship will be acknowledged by every being.

In view of the chronological pattern exhibited in this Passage, the giving of *"the Name"* must have been subsequent to the Cross. This would appear to be sufficient to rule out the identity of the Name in view as being *"Jesus."* A more likely identification of *"the Name"* is *"Lord,"* the equivalent many times of the Old Testament *"Jehovah,"* and supported by the thought of Verse 11. Christ's Exaltation is expressly stated as manifesting His Lordship in Acts 2:33-36 (Kent).

EXALTATION

The phrase, *"Wherefore God also hath highly exalted Him,"* refers as stated, to the highest rank and power, to that of supreme majesty. It refers to a supereminent Exaltation. The word *"wherefore,"* denotes that this was done because of His voluntary act of humility. As God He was infinitely above all possible Exaltation, but as man He was *"highly exalted."*

Jesus taught that Exaltation follows self-humiliation; He also demonstrated it (Mat. 23:12; Lk. 14:11; 18:14).

If Jesus were merely man, there would be no lesson of humility in His Death; if merely God — if we are allowed to use such terminology — there would be no room for reward in His Exaltation. As He was *"lifted up"* on the Cross, so He was lifted up in the Exaltation. It raises Him to the Throne of the Mediatorial Kingdom on which He entered by the Ascension, sitting now at the Right Hand of God till He has put all enemies under His Feet, and which He will then deliver up the Kingdom to the Father, that God may once again be *"all in all"* (I Cor. 15:24-28). Thus, though He was humbled, and appeared in the form of a servant, He is now raised up to the Throne of Glory, and to universal dominion. This Exaltation is spoken of the Redeemer as He was sustaining both a Divine and a human nature. If there was, as the Scriptures indicate, a withdrawing of the symbols of His Glory when He became a Man, then this refers to the restoration of that Glory, and would seem to imply, also, that there was additional honor conferred on Him. There was all the augmented Glory resulting from the work which He had performed in redeeming man.

THE FATHER'S APPROVAL

What is it that attracts so specially the Father's approbation?

What does so is Christ's great act of self-forgetting love. That satisfies and rests the Divine Mind. Doubtless the Son's pure and perfect character, and the perfection of His whole service, were on all accounts approved: but specially the Mind of Christ revealed in His self-forgetting devotion. Therefore, God has highly exalted Him.

In the first place, Christ in this work of His is Himself the Revelation of the Father. All along the Father's heart is seen disclosed. It was in fellowship with the Father, always delighted in Him, that the history was entered on; in harmony with Him it was accomplished. Throughout we have before us not only the Mind of the Son, but the Mind of the Father Who sent Him.

And then, in the next place, as the Son, sent forth into the world, became one of us, and subject to vicissitude, accomplishes His course, it is fitting for the Father to watch, to approve, and to crown the service; and He Who has so given Himself for God and man, must take the place due to such a *"Mind"* and to such an obedience.

Let us observe it then: What was in God's Eye, and ought to be in ours, is not only the dignity of the person, the greatness of the condescension, the perfection of obedience and patience of endurance, but, in the heart of all these, *"the Mind of Christ."* That was the inspiration of the whole marvelous history, carrying it throughout.

THE MIND OF CHRIST

Christ, indeed, was not One Who could so care for us, as to fail in His regard to any interest of His Father's Name or Kingdom; nor could He take any course really unseemingly, because unworthy of Himself.

But carrying with Him all that is due to His Father, and all that befits His Father's Child and Servant, the wonderful thing is how His Heart yearns over men, how His course shapes itself to the necessities of our case, how all that concerns Himself disappears as He looks on the fallen race.

A worthy deliverance for us, consecrating us to God in the blessedness of life eternal — this in His Eye, to be reached by Him through all kinds of lowliness, obedience, and suffering. On this His Heart was set; this gave meaning and character to every step of His history. This was the Mind of the Good Shepherd that laid down His Life for the sheep.

And this is what completes and consecrates all the service, and receives the Father's triumphant approbation. This is the Lamb of God. There never was a Lamb like this (Rainy).

THE NAME

The phrase, *"And given Him a name which is above every name,"* presents by the word *"given"* an act of Grace on the part of God the Father toward the Incarnate Son Who had voluntarily assumed a subordinate position so as to function as the Sin-Bearer on the Cross.

That which was graciously bestowed was not *"a name,"* but rather *"the Name."* The definite article *"the"* appears in the Greek Text and refers to a particular name. It should have been translated accordingly.

The title, *"The Name,"* is a very common Hebrew title, denoting office, rank, and dignity. The expression, *"The Name of God,"* in the Old Testament, denotes the Divine Presence, the Divine Majesty, especially as the object of adoration and praise. The context here dwells upon the honor and worship bestowed on Him upon Whom this Name was conferred.

The conferring of this title *"The Name,"* was upon the Lord Jesus as the Son of Man. A Man, The Man Christ Jesus, Who as Very God had voluntarily laid aside His expression of the Glory of Deity during His Incarnation, now has placed upon His Shoulders all the majesty, dignity, and glory of Deity itself. It is the God-Man Who stooped to the depths of humiliation, Who is raised, not as God now, although He was all that, but as Man, to the infinite height of Exaltation possessed only by Deity.

In fact, it is the answer of our Lord's Prayer: *"And now, O Father, glorify Thou Me with Thine Own Self with the Glory which I had with Thee before the world was"* (Jn. 17:5). It is the Glory of Deity not now seen shining in infinite splendor as in His preincarnate state, but that Glory shining in perfect contrast to and with His glorified humanity raised now to a place of equal dignity with Deity. It is the ideal and beautiful combination of the Exaltation of Deity and the humility of Deity seen in Incarnate Deity (Wuest).

The *"Name"* given Him, even as the 11th Verse proclaims, is *"Lord."*

No other name can be compared with His. It stands alone. He only is Redeemer, Saviour. He only is Christ, the Anointed of God. He only is the Son of God. His rank, His titles, His dignity, are above all others (Barnes).

THE LORD JESUS CHRIST

His birthday is kept around the world. His deathday sets a gallows against every skyline. Who is He? With these words a prominent Preacher stated a question which is of supreme importance and never-failing interest.

The question was put by the Master Himself when, during a crisis in His Ministry, He asked, *"Whom do men say that I the Son of Man am?"*

He listened to the statement of current opinion without comment, but His blessing was pronounced upon the answer which Peter had learned from God: *"Thou art the Christ, the Son of the Living God."*

The question still remains and men still attempt answers. But the true answer must come from the New Testament written by men who knew Him best, and who for that knowledge counted all things but loss.

In view of the all-supreme significance of Christ, and we speak of His Person, perhaps an extended treatment of this question, *"Who is Christ?"* would now be appropriate.

THE NATURE OF CHRIST

The question, *"Who is Christ?"* is best answered by stating and explaining the Names and Titles by which He is known.

This will probably give us an insight as to Who He is, What He is, and Why He is, maybe than anything else. Of course, learning more of Him in any capacity is of extreme benefit and blessing to any Child of God.

THE SON OF GOD

As *"son of man"* means one born of man, so *"Son of God"* means one born of God. Hence, this Title proclaims the Deity of Christ.

Jesus is never called a Son of God, in the general sense in which men and Angels are Children of God (Job 2:1). He is the Son of God in the unique sense. Jesus is described as sustaining toward God a relationship not shared by any other person in the universe.

In explanation and confirmation of this truth let us consider:

THE CONSCIOUSNESS OF CHRIST

What was the content of Jesus' self-consciousness; that is, what did Jesus know about Himself as a child?

Luke, the only writer recording an incident of Jesus' boyhood, tells us that at the age of 12 (at least by that time) Jesus was conscious of two things: a special relationship to God Whom He describes as His Father; second, a special mission on Earth — His *"Father's business."*

Just exactly when and how this self-consciousness came must remain a mystery to us. When we think of God coming to us in the form of a man we must reverently exclaim, *"Great is the mystery of Godliness!"* However, the following illustration may prove helpful.

Hold an infant before a mirror; he will see himself without recognizing himself. But the time will come when he will know that the reflected image represents himself. In other words, the child has become self-conscious of its identity. May it not have been so with the Lord Jesus?

He was always the Son of God; but there came a time when after studying the Scriptures relating to God's Messiah, the consciousness flashed naturally into His Mind that He, the Son of Mary, was none other than the Christ of God. In view of the fact that the Eternal Son of God lived a perfectly natural human life, it is reasonable to think that the self-consciousness of Deity came about in this fashion.

At the River Jordan Jesus heard the Father's voice corroborating and confirming His inner consciousness (Mat. 3:17). Later in His Ministry He commended Peter for the Heaven-inspired testimony to His Deity and Messiahship (Mat. 16:15-17).

When before the Jewish Counsel, He might have escaped death by denying this unique Sonship and simply affirming that He was a Son of God in the same sense that all men are; but put on oath by the High Priest, He declared His consciousness of Deity, even though He knew that it meant the death sentence (Mat. 26:63-65).

THE CLAIMS OF JESUS

He put Himself side by side with the Divine activity. *"My Father worketh hitherto, and I work"* (Jn. 5:17). *"I came forth from the Father"* (Jn. 16:28). *"My Father hath sent Me"* (Jn. 20:21). He claimed a Divine Knowledge and Fellowship (Mat. 11:27; Jn. 17:25). He claimed to unveil the Father's Being in Himself (Jn. 14:9-11). He assumed Divine prerogatives: Omnipresence (Mat. 18:20); power to forgive sins (Mk. 2:5-10); power to raise the dead (Jn. 6:39-40, 54; 10:17-18; 11:25). He proclaimed Himself Judge and Arbiter of man's destiny (Mat. 25:31-46; Jn. 5:22).

He demanded a surrender and an allegiance that only God could rightly claim; He insisted on absolute self-surrender on the part of His followers. They must be ready to sever the dearest and closest of ties, for anyone who preferred even Father or Mother more than Him was not worthy of Him (Mat. 10:37; Lk. 14:25-33).

These tremendous claims were made by One Who lived as the humblest of men, even as we have been studying, and was stated just as simply and naturally as, for example, Paul would say, *"I am a man which am a Jew."*

In order to arrive at the conclusion that Christ was Divine one need make only two concessions: first, that Jesus was not a deceiver; and second, that He was not demented. If He said He was Divine when He knew that He was not, then He could not be good; if He falsely imagined that He was God, when He really wasn't, then He could not be wise.

But no sane or wise person would dream of denying either His perfect character or His superior wisdom. Consequently, one cannot but conclude that He was what He claimed to be — the Son of God in a unique sense.

THE AUTHORITY OF CHRIST

In Christ's teaching one notes a complete absence of such expressions as: *"It is My opinion," "It may be," "I think that . . .," "We may as well suppose,"* etc. A rationalistic Jewish Scholar admitted that Jesus spoke with the authority of God Almighty Himself. Dr. Henry Van Dyke points out, that in the Sermon on the Mount, for example, we have:

"The absolutely overwhelming sight of a believing Hebrew placing himself above the rule of His Own Faith, a humble Teacher asserting supreme authority over all human conduct, a moral reformer discarding all other foundations and saying, 'Whosoever heareth these sayings of Mine and doeth them, I will liken him unto a wise man which built his house upon a rock' (Mat. 7:24). Nine and 40 times, in this brief record of the discourse of Jesus, recurs this solemn phrase with which He authenticates the truth: 'Verily I say unto thee.'"

THE SINLESSNESS OF CHRIST

No teacher who calls men to Repentance and Righteousness can avoid some reference to his own sinfulness or imperfection; indeed, the holier he is, the more will he lament and acknowledge his own limitations.

But in the words and deeds of Jesus there is a complete absence of consciousness or confession of sin. He had the deepest knowledge of the evil of sin, yet no shadow or shame of it fell upon His Own soul.

On the contrary, He, the humblest of men, issues the challenge, *"Which of you convinceth Me of sin?"* (Jn. 8:46).

THE TESTIMONY OF THE DISCIPLES

No Jew ever made the mistake of thinking that Moses was Divine; even his most enthusiastic Disciple would never have dreamed of ascribing to him a statement like, *"Baptizing in the Name of the Father, and of Moses, and of the Holy Spirit"* (Mat. 28:19). And the reason is that Moses neither spoke nor acted as one coming from God and sharing His nature.

On the other hand, the New Testament sets forth this Miracle: Here are a group of men who walked with Jesus and saw Him in all the characteristic aspects of His humanity — and yet who worshiped Him as Divine, preached Him as the power unto Salvation, and invoked His Name in prayer. John, who leaned on Jesus' bosom, has no hesitation in speaking of Him as the Eternal Son of God Who created the universe (Jn. 1:1, 3), and relates without any hesitancy or apology Thomas' act of worship and cry of adoration, *"My Lord and my God"* (Jn. 20:28).

Peter, who had seen his Master eat, drink, and sleep, who had known Him to be hungry and thirsty, who had heard Him pray and watched Him weep — in short, who had witnessed all sides of His humanity, later tells the Jews that Jesus is at the Right Hand of God; that He possesses the Divine prerogative of imparting the Holy Spirit (Acts 2:33, 36); that He is the only Way of Salvation (Acts 4:12), the pardoner of sins (Acts 5:31), and the Judge of the dead (Acts 10:42).

In His second Epistle (II Pet. 3:18) Peter worships Him by ascribing unto Him *"Glory both now and forever."*

OTHER TESTIMONIES

There is no record that Paul the Apostle saw Jesus in the flesh (although he saw Him in glorified form), but he was in direct contact with those who had. And this Paul, who never lost that reverence for God ingrained into him from youth, nevertheless with perfect calmness describes Jesus as *"the great God and our Saviour"* (Titus 2:13), represents Him as embodying the fullness of Deity (Col. 2:9), as being the Creator and Upholder of all things (Col. 1:17). As such His Name is to be invoked in prayer (Acts 7:59; I Cor. 1:2) and His Name coupled with that of the Father and the Holy Spirit in the benediction (II Cor. 13:14).

From the very beginning the primitive Church regarded and worshiped Christ as Divine. Early in the Second Century a Roman official reported that the Christians were accustomed to assemble before daybreak and *"sing a hymn of praise responsively to Christ, as it were to God."* Wrote a pagan author: *"The Christians are still worshiping that great man who was crucified in Palestine."*

Even the ridicule of the pagans is a testimony to Christ's Deity. An inscription was found in an ancient Roman palace (not later than the Third Century) representing a human figure with an ass' head hanging on the Cross, while the man stands before it in the attitude of worship. Underneath is the inscription: *"Alexamenos worships his God."*

Comments Henry Van Dyke:

"Thus the songs and prayers of Believers, the accusations of persecutors, the sneers of skeptics, and the coarse jests of mockers, all join in proving that beyond a doubt the primitive Christians paid Divine honor to the Lord Jesus ... there is no more room for doubt that the early Christians saw in Christ a personal unveiling of God, than that the friends and followers of Abraham Lincoln regarded him as a good and loyal American citizen."

We must not, however, infer that the primitive Church did not worship God the Father, for the contrary is true. Their general practice was to pray to the Father in the Name of Jesus exactly as they should have done (Jn. 16:26), and to thank the Father for the Gift of the Son. But so real to them was the Deity of Christ and the oneness between the two persons, that it came quite natural to them to invoke the Name of Jesus.

It was their firm adherence to the Old Testament teaching of the unity of God, combined with the firm belief in the Deity of Christ, which led them to formulate the Doctrine of the Trinity.

THE NICENE CREED

The following words of the Nicene Creed (Fourth Century) have been, and are still, recited by man in a formal manner, but they nevertheless express faithfully the heartfelt conviction of the Early Church:

"We believe in One Lord Jesus Christ, the Son of God, the only-begotten of the Father, that is, of the substance of the Father, God of God, Light of Light, Very God of Very God, begotten not made, being of one substance with the Father; by Whom all things were made which are in Heaven and Earth: Who, for us men and for our Salvation came down, and was Incarnate and was made man, and suffered, and rose the third day, and ascended into the heavens, and shall come again to judge the quick and the dead."

THE WORD (ETERNAL PREEXISTENCE AND ACTIVITY)

The word of man is that by which he expresses himself, by which he puts himself in communication with others. By his word he makes his thoughts and feelings known, and by his word he issues commands and gives effect to his will.

The word that he speaks carries the impress of his thought and character. By a man's word one could perfectly know him even though one were blind. Sight and information could reveal but little regarding his character if one had not listened to his word. A man's word is his character in expression.

Likewise, the *"Word of God"* is that by which He communicates with other beings, deals with them; it is the means by which He expresses His power, intelligence, and will. Christ is that Word, because through Him God has revealed His activity, will, and purpose, and because by Him God contacts the world. We express ourselves through words; the eternal God expresses Himself through His Son, Who is *"the express Image of His Person"* (Heb. 1:3).

Christ is the Word of God because He reveals God by demonstrating Him in Person. He not only brings God's Message — He is God's Message.

Consider the need of such a Revealer. Try to comprehend the size of the universe, with its untold millions of heavenly bodies, covering distances that stagger the mind; picture the mighty reaches of space beyond the universe of matter; then try to conceive of the mightiness of the One Who is the Source of it all.

Consider, on the other hand, the insignificance of man. It has been calculated that if everybody in this world were six feet tall and a foot and a half wide and a foot thick, the whole six billion of the human race could be packed into a box measuring a mile and a half in each direction. God — how mighty and vast! Man — how infinitesimal! Moreover, this God is a Spirit, and, therefore, not to be apprehended by the eye of flesh and natural senses. The great question arises,

"How can man have communion with such a God? How can he even conceive of His nature and character?"

WHAT IS GOD LIKE?

It is true that God revealed Himself through the prophetic word, through dreams and visions, and through temporary manifestations. But man yearned for a yet plainer answer to the question, *"What is God like?"*

To answer this question there occurred the most stupendous event in history — *"the Word was made flesh"* (Jn. 1:14). The Eternal Word of God took upon Himself human nature and became man, in order to reveal the Eternal God through a human personality.

"God, Who at sundry times and in divers manners spake in time past unto the fathers by the Prophets, hath in these last days spoken to us by His Son" (Heb. 1:1-2).

Therefore, to the question, *"What is God like?"* the Christian answers, *"God is like Christ, because Christ is the Word — the idea that God has of Himself."* That is, He is the *"express Image of His Person"* (Heb. 1:3), *"the Image of the invisible God"* (Col. 1:15).

LORD (SOVEREIGNTY)

A glance through a concordance will reveal the fact that *"Lord"* is one of the most common titles given to Jesus. This title indicates His Deity, Exaltation, and Sovereignty.

As well, the title *"Lord"* indicates *"Covenant,"* which speaks of relationship. Consequently, when a Believer refers to Christ as *"Lord,"* which He certainly is, at the same time, he is implying the New Covenant, which symbol is that which we refer to as *"The Lord's Supper"* (I Cor. 11:23-32).

DEITY

The title *"Lord"* when used before a name, conveyed the thought of Deity to both Jews and Gentiles. The word *"Lord"* in the Greek (*"kurios"*) was the equivalent for Jehovah in the Greek translation of the Old Testament; therefore, to the Jews *"The Lord Jesus"* was clearly an ascription of Deity.

When the Emperor of the Romans referred to himself as *"The Lord Caesar,"* and required his subjects to say *"Caesar is Lord,"* the Gentiles understood that the Emperor was claiming Divinity.

The Christians so understood the term, and chose rather to suffer persecution, even to giving up their lives, rather than ascribing to a man a title which belonged only to One truly Divine. Only to Him Whom God had exalted would they ascribe Lordship and render worship.

EXALTATION

In eternity Christ possesses the title *"Son of God"* by virtue of His relationship to God (Phil. 2:9).

In history He earned the title *"Lord"* by dying and rising from the dead for the Salvation of men (Acts 2:36; 10:36; Rom. 14:9).

He was always Divine by nature; He became Lord by achievement. To illustrate: A young man born into the family of a billionaire is not content with inheriting what others have labored for, but desires to possess only what he has earned by his own achievement. He, therefore, voluntarily relinquishes his privileges, takes his place as a common worker, and by laborious effort wins for himself a place of honor and wealth.

In like manner the Son of God, though He was by nature equal to God, voluntarily subjected Himself to sinless human limitations, by taking man's nature, became a servant to man, and finally died on the Cross for man's Redemption.

As a reward He was exalted to Lordship above all creatures — an appropriate recompense, for what better claim could anyone have to rulership over men than the fact that He loved them, and gave Himself for them! (Rev. 1:5).

This claim has been acknowledged by millions and the Cross has become a steppingstone by which Jesus has ascended to sovereignty over men's hearts.

SOVEREIGNTY

In Egypt, Jehovah revealed Himself to Israel as Redeemer and Saviour; at Sinai as Lord and King. The two go together, for He Who became their Saviour has a right to be their Ruler. That is why the Ten Commandments begin with the declaration, *"I am the Lord thy God, which have brought thee out of the* land of Egypt, out of the house of bondage"* (Ex. 20:2). In other words, *"I the Lord, Who redeemed you, has the right to rule you."*

And so it was with Christ and His people. The early Christians recognized instinctively — as all true Disciples do — that the One Who redeemed them from sin and destruction has a right to be Lord of their lives. Bought with a price we are not our own (I Cor. 6:20), but belong to Him Who died and rose for us (II Cor. 5:15).

Therefore, the title *"Lord"* applied to Jesus by His followers means: *"The One Who by His death has earned the place of sovereign in my heart, to Whom I feel constrained to worship and serve with all my powers."*

When the man who had the infirmity some 38 years, but had been healed by Jesus, was reproved for carrying his bed on the Sabbath Day, he replied, *"He that made me whole, the same said unto me, 'Take up thy bed, and walk'"* (Jn. 5:11). He knew instinctively, with the logic of the heart, that He Who had given him life had a right to tell him how to use that life. If Jesus is our Saviour He must as well be our Lord.

THE SON OF MAN

According to Hebrew usage, *"Son of"* denotes relationship and participation. For example: *"The children of the Kingdom"* (Mat. 8:12) are those who are to share in its truths and blessings. *"The children of the Resurrection"* (Lk. 20:36) are those who partake of the Resurrection Life; a *"Son of peace"* (Lk. 10:6) is one possessing a peaceful disposition; a *"Son of perdition"* (Jn. 17:12) is one destined to taste of doom and ruin.

Therefore, *"Son of man"* means primarily one who shares human nature and human qualities. In this way *"Son of man"* becomes an emphatic designation for man in his characteristic attributes of weakness and helplessness (Num. 23:19; Job 16:21; 25:6).

In this sense the title is applied 80 times to Ezekiel as a reminder of his weakness and mortality, and as an incentive to humility in the fulfillment of his prophetic calling.

CHRIST, THE SON OF MAN

Applied to Christ, *"Son of man"* designates Him as sharing human nature and qualities, and subject to human infirmities. Yet, at the same time, this very title implies His Deity, for, if a person were to declare emphatically, *"I am a son of man,"* people would say, *"Why, everybody knows that."* But on the lips of Jesus the expression meant a Heavenly One Who had definitely identified Himself with humanity as Representative and Saviour. Notice also that it is *"The Son of Man"* and not *"A Son of Man."*

The title is connected with His earthly life (Mat. 8:20; Mk. 2:10; 2:28; Lk. 19:10), with His sufferings on behalf of humanity (Mk. 8:31), and with His Exaltation and rule over humanity (Dan. 7:14; Mat. 25:31; 26:24).

By referring to Himself as *"Son of Man,"* Jesus wished to convey the following Message:

"I, the Son of God, am Man, in weakness, in suffering, even unto death. Yet I am still in touch with Heaven whence I came and hold such relation to the Divine that I can forgive sins, and am superior to religious regulations which have but a temporary and national significance" (Mat. 9:6; 12:8).

"This manhood shall not cease when I have passed through those last stages of suffering and death, which I must endure for man's Salvation and to finish My Work. For I shall arise and take it with Me to Heaven, whence I shall return to rule over those whose nature I have assumed."

The humanity of the Son of God was real and not make-believe; He is portrayed as actually suffering hunger, thirst, weariness, grief, and as being subject in general to the sinless infirmities of human nature.

HOW DID HE BECOME THE SON OF MAN?

By what act, or means, did the Son of God become *"Son of Man"*? What miracle could bring into the world *"The Second Man,"* Who is *"The Lord from Heaven"*? (I Cor. 15:47).

The answer is that the Son of God entered the world as the Son of Man by being conceived in the womb of Mary by the Holy Spirit, which was done by decree, and apart from a human father.

And the quality of the entire life of Jesus is in keeping with the manner of His Birth. He Who came by the Virgin Birth lived the Virgin Life (perfect sinlessness) — the latter as great a miracle as the former. He Who was born miraculously, lived miraculously, rose from the dead miraculously, and left the world miraculously.

Upon the fact of the Virgin Birth is based the Doctrine of the Incarnation (Jn. 1:14). The following statement of this Doctrine is from the pen of Martin J. Scott, an able Scholar:

THE INCARNATION

As all Christians know, the Incarnation means that God became man. This does not mean that God was turned into man, nor that God ceased to be God and began to be man; but that remaining God, He assumed or took a new nature, namely human, uniting this to the Divine nature in the One Being or Person — Jesus Christ, True God and True Man.

"At the marriage feast of Cana, the water became wine at the will of Jesus Christ, the Lord of Creation" (Jn. 2:1-11). Not so did God become man, for at Cana the water ceased to be water when it became wine.

"An example which may help us to understand in what sense God became man, but yet one that does not perfectly illustrate the matter, is that of a king who should of his own will become a beggar. If a mighty king should leave his throne and the luxury of the court, and assume the rags of a beggar, live with beggars, share their hardship, etc., in order to improve their condition, we should say that the king became a beggar, yet was still truly a king. It would be correct to say that what the beggar suffered was the suffering of a king; but when the beggar atoned for something, it was the king that atoned, etc."

GOD AND MAN

"Since Jesus Christ is God and man, it is evident, one might say, that God, in some way, is man also. Now in what way is God man?

"It is clear He was not always man, since man is not eternal and God is. At a certain definite time, therefore, God became man by assuming human nature.

"What do we mean by assuming human nature? We mean that the Son of God remaining God, took another nature, that of man, and so united it with His Own that it constituted One Person, Jesus Christ.

"The Incarnation, therefore, means that the Son of God, True God from all eternity, in the course of time became True Man also, in the One Person, Jesus Christ, consisting of the two natures, the human and the Divine. This, of course, is a mystery. We cannot actually understand it anymore than we can totally understand the Trinity.

"In fact, there are mysteries all about us. We do not understand how the grass and water which cattle live on are converted into their flesh and blood. A chemical analysis of milk shows no ingredient of blood in it, yet the milk which a baby receives from its mother's breasts is changed into the flesh and blood of the child. The mother herself does not know how the milk is produced in her which she gives to the child she suckles.

"As well, all the wise men in the world cannot explain the connection between thought and speech. We should not be surprised, therefore, if we cannot understand the Incarnation. We believe it because He Who has revealed it is God Himself, Who can neither deceive nor be deceived."

THE PURPOSE OF THE INCARNATION

One might ask the question, *"Why did the Son of God become the Son of Man? or, what were the purposes of the Incarnation?"*

1. As we have already seen, the Son of God came into the world to be a Revealer of God. He claimed that His deeds and words were God-guided (Jn. 5:19-20; 10:38); even His evangelistic work was a revelation of the heart of the Heavenly Father, and those who criticized His Work among sinners thereby showed their lack of harmony with the spirit of Heaven (Lk. 15:1-7).

2. He took our human nature in order to glorify it and so fit it for a heavenly destiny. Thus, He fashioned a heavenly pattern, so to speak, by which human nature could be made over into the Divine likeness. He, the Son of God, became the Son of Man in order that the children of men might become the sons of God (Jn. 1:12), and one day we shall be like Him (I Jn. 3:2); even our bodies shall be *"fashioned like unto His Glorious Body"* (Phil. 3:21).

"The first man (Adam) is of the earth, earthy: the Second Man is the Lord from

Heaven" (I Cor. 15:47); therefore, *"as we have borne the image of the earthy* (compare Gen. 5:3), *we shall also bear the Image of the Heavenly"* (I Cor. 15:49), because *"the Last Adam was made a quickening spirit"* (I Cor. 15:45).

3. But the hindrance in the way of the perfection of humanity was sin — which in the beginning deprived Adam of the glory of original Righteousness. In order to deliver us from its guilt and power — the guilt and power of sin — the Son of God died as an Atoning Sacrifice — an Atonement for sin, which was necessary, that is if man was to be redeemed.

THE ANOINTED

"Christ" in the Greek form of the Hebrew word *"Messiah,"* means literally, *"The Anointed One."* In fact, it was Hannah the mother of Samuel who first used this appellative as it regards Christ in what is referred to as the *"Song of Hannah,"* when she said, *"The Lord shall judge the ends of the earth; and He shall give strength unto His King, and exalt the horn of His Anointed"* (I Sam. 2:10). From this point on others take up the theme of God's Anointed One — the Messiah (I Sam. 2:35; Ps. 2:2; 45:7; Isa. 61:1; Dan. 9:25-26; Jn. 1:41; 4:25).

The word is suggested by the practice of anointing with oil as a symbol of Divine consecration to service. While Priests, and sometimes Prophets, were anointed with oil at installation into office, the title *"Anointed"* was applied particularly to the kings of Israel who ruled as Jehovah's representatives (II Sam. 1:14). In some cases the symbol of the anointing was followed by the spiritual reality, so that the person became in a living sense the Anointed of the Lord (I Sam. 10:1, 6; 16:13).

Saul was a failure; but David, who succeeded him, was *"a man after God's Own Heart,"* a king who placed God's Will supreme in his life and who regarded himself as God's representative. But most of the kings departed grievously from the Divine Standard, leading the people into idolatry; and even the Godly kings were not without blemish.

Against this dark background the Prophets displayed the Promise of the coming of a King from the House of David, a King even greater than David. Upon Him should rest the Spirit of the Lord in a power never before known (Isa. 11:1-3; 61:1). Though the Son of David, He would yet be the Son of Jehovah, bearing Divine Names (Isa. 9:6-7; Jer. 23:6).

Unlike that of David His reign would be everlasting, and under His sway should come all nations. This was *"The Anointed,"* or the *"Messiah,"* or the *"Christ,"* and upon Him were centered the hopes of Israel, and the world for that matter.

THE FULFILLMENT

It is the consistent testimony of the New Testament that Jesus claimed to be the Messiah, or Christ, promised in the Old Testament.

Just as the President of this land is first elected and then quickly inaugurated, so Jesus Christ was eternally elected to be the Messiah or Christ, and then publicly inaugurated into His Messianic Office at the Jordan. Just as Samuel first anointed Saul and then explained to him the meaning of the Anointing (I Sam. 10:1), so God the Father anointed His Son with the Spirit of Power and whispered into His Ear the meaning of His Anointing — *"Thou art My beloved Son, in Whom I am well pleased"* (Mk. 1:11).

In other words, *"Thou art the Son of Jehovah, Whose coming was predicted by the Prophets, and I hereby endow Thee with authority and power for Thy mission, and send thee forth with My Blessing."*

The people among whom Jesus was to minister looked forward to the Messiah's coming, but unfortunately their hopes were colored by political stress. They were expecting a *"strong man,"* who should be a combination of soldier and statesman. Would Jesus be that kind of Messiah?

The Spirit led Him into the wilderness to fight the issue out with Satan, who craftily suggested that He adopt the popular platform and so take a short and easy way to power — in other words, a way other than the Cross, which Satan has been attempting to do with all men ever since.

"Meet their material cravings," suggested the tempter (Mat. 4:3-4; Jn. 6:14-15, 26), dazzle them by leaping from the Temple (and incidentally, *"stand in"* well with the Priesthood), set yourself as a champion of the people and lead them to war (Mat. 4:8-9; Rev. 13:2, 4).

THE WAY OF THE CROSS

Jesus knew that Satan was advocating the popular policy which was inspired by his own selfish and violent spirit. That such a course would lead to bloodshed and ruin was certain.

No! He would take God's Way, the Way of the Cross, and rely solely upon spiritual weapons to conquer the hearts of men, even though that path must lead to misunderstanding, suffering, and death. In the wilderness Jesus chose the Cross, and chose it because it was part of God's program for His Life, and in fact, the only means by which unredeemed mankind could be delivered.

From this choice the Master never swerved, although often outwardly tempted to forsake the Way of the Cross (Mat. 16:22).

Jesus scrupulously kept Himself from entanglement in the contemporary political situation. At times He forbade those healed by Him to broadcast His fame lest His Ministry be misunderstood as a stirring of the people against Rome (Mat. 12:15-16; Lk. 23:5), where His success was turned into a charge against Him. He deliberately refused to head a popular movement (Jn. 6:15). He as well forbade the public proclamation of His Messiahship and the testimony to His Transfiguration lest false hopes be raised among the people (Mat. 16:20; 17:9).

With consummate wisdom He escaped a skillful trap to either discredit Him before the people as *"unpatriotic,"* or on the other hand, to involve Him in difficulties with the Roman Government (Mat. 22:15-21).

In all this the Lord Jesus fulfilled the prophecy of Isaiah that God's Anointed should be a proclaimer of Divine Truth, and not a violent agitator and self-seeking rebel-rouser (Mat. 12:16-21) — as were some of the false messiahs who preceded and followed Him (Jn. 10:8; Acts 5:36; 21:38).

He faithfully avoided the carnal and followed the spiritual methods, so that Pilate, Rome's representative, could testify, *"I find no fault in this man."*

A WRONG CONCEPTION

We have seen that Jesus began His Ministry among a people who had the right hope of a Messiah but a wrong conception of His Person and Work. To use a homely illustration: The label was correct but the contents of the bottle did not conform to the label, at least as to that which they thought the contents ought to be. Knowing this, Jesus did not at first publicly proclaim Himself as Messiah (Mat. 16:20), for He knew this would be a signal for rebellion against Rome. He spoke rather about the Kingdom, describing its standards and its spiritual nature, hoping to inspire the people with a hunger for a spiritual kingdom which would in turn lead them to desire a spiritual Messiah.

And His efforts in this direction were not entirely fruitless, for John the Apostle tells us (Chpt. 1) that from the very first there was a spiritual group who recognized Him as the Christ; also, from time to time, He revealed Himself to individuals who were spiritually ready (Jn. 4:25-26; 9:35-37).

But the nation as a whole did not connect His spiritual Ministry with the thought of the Messiah. That He was an able Teacher, a mighty Preacher, and even a Prophet, they freely admitted (Mat. 16:13-14); but certainly not the one to head their economic, military, and political program — as they thought the Messiah should.

WHAT THE BIBLE ACTUALLY TAUGHT

But why blame the people for such an expectation? God had indeed promised to set up an earthly Kingdom (Jer. 23:6-8; Amos 9:11-15; Zech. 14:9-21). True, but preceding that event was to take place a moral cleansing and spiritual regeneration of the nation (Ezek. 36:25-27; Jn. 3:1-3). And both John the Baptist and Jesus made it plain that the nation, in its present condition, was not fit to enter the Kingdom. Hence the exhortation, *"Repent ye: for the Kingdom of Heaven is at hand."*

But while the words, *"Kingdom of Heaven,"* profoundly moved the people, the word *"repent"* made but slight impression. Both the Leaders (Mat. 21:31-32) and the people (Lk. 13:1-3; 19:41-44) refused to meet the conditions of the Kingdom and consequently lost the privileges of the Kingdom (Mat. 21:43).

THE PLAN

But God the all-wise had foreseen Israel's failure (Isa. 6:9-10; 53:1; Jn. 12:37-40), and

God the all-powerful had overruled it for the furtherance of a plan hitherto kept secret. The plan was as follows:

Israel's rejection would offer opportunity for God's taking a chosen People from among the Gentiles (Acts 15:13-14; Rom. 9:25-26; 11:11), who, with Jewish Believers should constitute a company known as *"The Church"* (Eph. 3:4-6). Jesus Himself gave His Disciples a glimpse of this period (the Church Age) which was to intervene between His First and Second Advents, calling these Revelations *"Mysteries"* because they were not revealed to Old Testament Prophets (Mat. 13:11-17).

On one occasion the unwavering Faith of a Gentile Centurion contrasted with the lack of Faith in many Israelites and recalled to the inspired vision of our Lord the spectacle of Gentiles from all lands entering the Kingdom which Israel had rejected (Mat. 8:10-12).

The crisis foreseen in the wilderness had come, and Jesus prepared to break some saddening news to His Disciples. He began tactfully by strengthening their Faith with a Heaven-inspired testimony of His Messiahship, a testimony given by Peter their leader. He then made a remarkable prediction (Mat. 16:18-19), which may be paraphrased as follows: *"The congregation of Israel have rejected Me as their Messiah, and their Leaders will actually excommunicate Me — the very Cornerstone of the nation (Mat. 21:42). But God's Plan will not fail thereby, for I will establish another congregation ('Church'), composed of men like you, Peter (I Pet. 2:4-9), who will believe in My Deity and Messiahship. You shall be a Leader and Minister in this Congregation, and yours will be the privilege of opening its doors with the key of Gospel Truth, and you and your brethren shall administer its affairs"* (Acts Chpt. 10).

THE CROSS

Then Christ made an announcement which the Disciples did not fully understand until after His Resurrection (Lk. 24:25-48); namely, that the Cross was part of God's Program for the Messiah. *"From that time forth began Jesus to shew unto His Disciples, how that He must go unto Jerusalem, and suffer many things of the Elders and Chief Priests and Scribes, and be killed, and be raised again the third day"* (Mat. 16:21).

To be sure, the Cross was God's Plan all along. In fact, Jesus, although presenting the Gospel first of all to the Jews, came for the entirety of the world (Jn. 3:16). All of mankind was lost, and the only way that man could be redeemed was by the Sacrifice of the Cross. Consequently, the Cross was not an accident or incident, but rather the Plan.

As stated, God knew that Israel would reject His Son and their Messiah, actually the Saviour of the world. However, this definitely was not His Plan, but Israel being a free moral agent, could not be forced by God to accept the Saviour; however, there will come a day, and very shortly, when Israel will accept Jesus not only as Messiah, but as well, as Saviour (Zech. Chpts. 12-14).

WHAT IF ISRAEL HAD ACCEPTED CHRIST AT THAT TIME?

The situation would have essentially changed, but only in certain directions. Israel accepting Him or rejecting Him had nothing to do with the original mission of Redemption for the entirety of the world, which required the Cross. That would have to be carried out regardless.

To be sure, even if Israel had then accepted Christ, Rome would never have tolerated Jesus as King, and would have crucified Him anyway. Also, it must be understood, that no one really took the life of Christ from Him, not Israel or Rome, even though God would hold them accountable, because of the condition of their heart. Still, Jesus gave up His Life freely (Jn. 10:18).

So, the fact of the Cross was a necessity irrespective of what Israel would or would not do. Jesus offering up Himself as a perfect Sacrifice, a perfect Sin-Offering, was of absolute necessity in order to satisfy the Heavenly Courts of Justice and to atone for sin — actually the sin of the whole world (Jn. 1:29).

However, if Israel had accepted Him then, even though the Cross would have gone forward as scheduled one might say, still, the terrible delay of the coming Kingdom would have been avoided. It has been nearly 2,000 years now since Jesus first came, and the Kingdom still has not been installed in the world except in the hearts and lives of Believers. In fact, it cannot be installed until Israel finally accepts Him, and because all the Promises were made by God to Israel. This she shall do at the Second Coming, even as Zechariah prophesied, along with others (Zech. Chpts. 12-14).

Had Jesus been accepted by Israel when He first came, the Church then would not have been necessary. In fact, the Church is not mentioned at all in the Old Testament except in shadow, as the word *"Gentiles"* is referred to in a positive sense, mostly by Isaiah. This is what Paul was talking about when he spoke of Israel stumbling and falling (Rom. 11:11), and the wild olive branches of the Gentiles, i.e., *"the Church,"* being grafted in to take their place (Rom. 11:17-24).

The point is, had Israel accepted Him the first time, even though the Cross was a necessity, the Resurrection would have ushered in the coming Millennial Kingdom, with Jesus ruling and reigning, with all its attendant freedom, prosperity, greatness, and glory. In other words, the world at that time will know what it could have been like all along, had the Lord been followed. Instead, with Israel's rejection, the world was submitted to a continued bloodletting, wars and rumors of wars, suffering and sorrow, which has lasted now for nearly 2,000 years. Jesus spoke of this in Matthew Chapter 24.

But of course, all of this is moot for the simple reason that Israel rejected Him, and of course, the Lord knew this would be the case.

JESUS

The Cross came exactly as predicted. When Jesus might have escaped death by denying His Deity, when He might have been acquitted by denying that He was a King, He persisted in His Testimony and died upon a Cross bearing the inscription, *"This Is The King Of The Jews,"* which was a necessity.

But the suffering Messiah (Isa. 53:7-9) rose from the dead (Isa. 53:10-11), and as Daniel had foreseen ascended to the Right Hand of God (Dan. 7:14; Mat. 28:18), whence He shall come to judge the quick (living) and the dead.

After this survey of Old and New Testament Teaching, we are in a position to state our full definition of the title *"Messiah"*; namely, the One Whom God has authorized to save Israel and the nations from sin and death, and to rule over them as the Lord and Master of their lives.

That such a claim implies Deity is understood by thinking Jews, but is a stumblingblock to them. Said Claude Montefiore, noted Jewish Scholar:

"If I could believe that Jesus was God (that is, Divine), then He would obviously be my Master. For my Master — the Master of the modern Jew, is, and can only be, God."

SON OF DAVID

This title is equivalent to *"Messiah,"* for an important qualification of the Messiah was His Davidic descent.

As a reward for his faithfulness David was promised an everlasting dynasty (II Sam. 7:16), and eternal sovereignty over Israel was given to his house. This was the Davidic or Throne Covenant. From that time on dates the expectation that, come what might to the nation, there would surely appear, in God's time, a King belonging to the stock and lineage of David. In times of distress the Prophets reminded the people of this Promise, telling them that the Redemption of Israel and the nations was connected with the coming of a great King from the House of David (Ps. 89:34-37; Isa. 55:3-4; Jer. 23:5; 30:9; Ezek. 34:23).

Notice particularly Isaiah 11:1, which may be translated as follows: *"A shoot shall come forth from the stump of the tree of Jesse* (father of David), *and a green branch shall grow out of his roots* (the Messiah).*"* In Isaiah 10:33-34, Assyria, Israel's cruel oppressor, is compared to a cedar tree, whose stump never puts out any shoots but rots slowly. Once cut down, the tree has no future. And such describes the fate of Assyria, which has long passed off the scene of history.

The House of David, on the other hand, is compared to a tree which will put forth new growth from the stump left in the ground. Isaiah's prophecy is as follows:

"The Jewish nation will be almost destroyed, and the House of David will cease as a royal house — will be hewn down to a stump. Yet from that stump will come a

shoot, from the roots of that stump will come a branch — the King — Messiah."

PROPHECY AND ITS FULFILLMENT

Judah was taken into captivity, and from this captivity they returned, without a king, without independence, to be subjected successively to Persia, Greece, Egypt, Syria, and after a brief period of independence, to Rome.

During these centuries of subjection to Gentiles, there were times of discouragement when the people looked back to the former Glories of David's Kingdom and cried with the Psalmist, *"Lord, where are Thy former lovingkindnesses, which Thou swarest unto David in Thy Truth?"* (Ps. 89:49). But they never lost hope. Gathered around the fire of Messianic Prophecy they warmed their hearts and waited patiently for the Son of David.

They were not disappointed. Hundreds of years after the Royal House of David had ceased, an Angel appeared to a Jewish girl, a virgin, and said, *"And, behold, thou shalt conceive in thy womb, and bring forth a Son, and thou shalt call His Name Jesus. He shall be great, and be called the Son of the Highest: and the Lord God shall give unto Him the Throne of His Father David: and He shall reign over the House of Jacob forever; and of His Kingdom there shall be no end"* (Lk. 1:31-33; Isa. 9:6-7).

A deliverer had arisen from the House of David. At a time when the House of David seemed reduced to its lowest state, when the living heirs were a humble carpenter and a simple maiden, then by God's miraculous agency, the branch sprouted up from the hewn-down stump and grew into a mighty tree that has provided shelter for many people.

THE DAVIDIC COVENANT

The following is the substance of the Davidic Covenant as interpreted by the inspired Prophets: Jehovah would come down for the Salvation of His people, at which time there would be on Earth a living descendant of the Davidic family, through whom Jehovah would deliver and then rule his people. That Jesus was this Son of David is shown by the announcement made at His Birth, by His genealogies (Mat. Chpt. 1; Lk. Chpt. 3), by the fact that He accepted the title when ascribed to Him (Mat. 9:27; 20:30-31; 21:1-11), and by the testimony of New Testament writers (Acts 13:23; Rom. 1:3; II Tim. 2:8; Rev. 5:5; 22:16).

But the title, *"Son of David,"* was not a complete description of the Messiah, for it emphasized mainly His human descent. Therefore, the people, ignoring the Scriptures which spoke of the Divine nature of the Christ, looked for a human Messiah who should be a second David.

On one occasion Jesus attempted to lift the thoughts of the Leaders above this incomplete conception (Mat. 22:42-46). *"What think ye of Christ (that is, the Messiah)?"* He asked, *"Whose Son is He?"*

The Pharisees naturally answered, *"The Son of David."*

Then Jesus, quoting Psalms 110:1, asked, *"If David then called Him Lord, how is He his Son?"*

"How can David's Lord be David's Son?" was the question that baffled the Pharisees.

The answer of course is: the Messiah is both. By the miracle of the Virgin Birth Jesus was born of God and also born of Mary; He was thus the Son of God and Son of Man. As Son of God He is David's Lord; as Son of Mary He is David's Son.

THE OLD TESTAMENT RECORD

The Old Testament records two lines of Messianic Truth. Some portions declare that the Lord Himself will come down from Heaven to deliver His people (Ps. 98:9; Isa. 40:10; 42:13); others state that a Deliverer shall arise from the family of David. Both comings were blended in the appearing of a little baby in Bethlehem, David's city. For then the Son of the Highest was born as the Son of David (Lk. 1:32).

Notice how in Isaiah 9:6-7, the Divine nature and Davidic descent of the coming King are combined. The title mentioned here — *"The Everlasting Father"* — has been misunderstood by some who have deduced therefrom that there is no Trinity but that Jesus is the Father and that the Father is Jesus.

A knowledge of Old Testament language might have saved them from this error. In those days a ruler who governed wisely and righteously was described as a *"father"* to his people. Thus, the Lord speaking through

Isaiah, says of an official: *"He shall be a 'Father' to the inhabitants of Jerusalem, and to the House of Judah. And this key of the House of David will I lay upon His shoulder"* (note the resemblance to Isa. 9:6-7 and compare Rev. 3:7) (Isa. 22:21-22).

This title was applied to David, as shown by the people's acclamation at the Triumphal Entry, *"Blessed be the Kingdom of our father David"* (Mk. 11:10).

They did not mean that David was their ancestor, for they were not all descended from his family; and of course, they had no idea of calling him the Heavenly Father. David is described a *"father"* because as the king after God's Own Heart he was the real founder of the Israelitish Kingdom (Saul was man's choice and not God's, consequently, a failure), extending it from about 6,000 to 60,000 square miles. In like manner Washington is often referred to as the *"Father of our country."*

"Father" David was human, and died; his kingdom was earthly, and in time disintegrated. But, according to Isaiah 9:6-7, David's descendant, the King-Messiah, will be Divine, and His Kingdom will be an everlasting one.

David was a temporary *"father"* to his people; the Messiah will be an *"everlasting (immortal, Divine, unchangeable)"* Father to all people — so appointed by God the Father (Ps. 2:6-8; Lk. 22:29).

THE SAVING GRACE OF CHRIST

The Old Testament teaches that God Himself is the Source of Salvation: He is Israel's Saviour and Deliverer. *"Salvation is of the Lord."* He delivered His people from Egypt's bondage and ever afterwards Israel knew by experience that He was the Saviour (Ps. 106:21; Isa. 43:3, 11; 45:15, 22; Jer. 14:8).

But God acts through agents, therefore, we read of His saving Israel through the mysterious *"Angel of His Presence"* (Isa. 63:9). At times human instruments were used; Moses was sent to deliver Israel from bondage; from time to time Judges were raised up to succor Israel.

"But when the fullness of the time was come, God sent forth His Son, made of a woman, made under the Law, to redeem them that were under the Law (the Law of Moses), *that we might receive the adoption of sons"* (Gal. 4:4-5). On entering the world the Redeemer was given the name expressive of His supreme mission: *"And thou shalt call His Name Jesus: for He shall save His people from their sins"* (Mat. 1:21).

The first Gospel Preachers did not need to explain to the Jews the meaning of *"Saviour"*; they had already learned their lesson from their own history (Acts 3:26; 13:23).

The Jews understood the Gospel Message to mean that just as God sent Moses to deliver Israel from the bondage of Egypt, so He had sent Jesus to deliver His people from their sins. They understood, but refused to believe.

Upon the Cross Christ fulfilled the mission indicated by His Name, for to save people from their sins implies Atonement and Atonement implies death.

But even during His lifetime, He lived up to His Name: He was always a Saviour. All over the land were people who could testify: *"I was bound by sin, but Jesus delivered me"*; Mary Magdalene could say, *"He delivered me from seven devils"*; the former paralytic could testify, *"He forgave my sins."* Jesus Christ is the Saviour, and in fact, there is no other. As well, His Saving Grace came by the way of the Cross and His Resurrection.

THE OFFICES OF CHRIST

In the Old Testament age there were three classes of mediators between God and His people:
1. The Prophet.
2. The Priest.
3. The King.

As the perfect Mediator (I Tim. 2:5) Christ embodies in Himself all three Offices.

Jesus is the Christ-Prophet, to enlighten the nations; the Christ-Priest to offer Himself as a Sacrifice for the nation; and, the Christ-King to rule over the nations.

CHRIST THE PROPHET

The Old Testament Prophet was God's earthly representative or agent, Who revealed His Will in relation to the present and future. That the Messiah should be a Prophet to enlighten Israel and the nations is the testimony of the Prophets (Isa. 42:1; Rom. 15:8), and that Jesus was so regarded is the testimony of the Gospels (Mk. 1:27; 6:4, 15; Jn. 4:19; 6:14; 9:17).

As a Prophet, Jesus preached Salvation. The Prophets of Israel exercised their most important Ministry in times of crisis, when Rulers, Statesmen, and Priests were confused in judgment and impotent to act. It was then that the Prophet stepped forth and with Divine authority pointed the way out of their difficulties, saying, *"This is the way, walk ye in it."*

The Lord Jesus appeared at a time when the Jewish nation was in a state of restlessness caused by a yearning for national deliverance. Through Christ's preaching the nation was confronted with the choice as to a way of deliverance — war with Rome or peace with God. They made the wrong choice and suffered the disastrous consequence of national destruction (Mat. 26:52; Lk. 19:41-44).

As their disobedient and rebellious forefathers once vainly attempted to force their way into Canaan (Num. 14:40-45), so the Jews, in A.D. 68, tried to force their deliverance from Rome. Their rebellion was quenched in blood, Jerusalem and the Temple were destroyed, and the wandering Jew began his painful trek through the centuries.

The Lord Jesus showed the way of escape from sin's guilt and power, not only to the nation, but also to the individual. Those who came with the question, *"What shall I do to be saved?"* received definite instructions, and these always included a command to follow Him. He not only showed, but made the Way of Salvation by His Death upon the Cross.

JESUS ANNOUNCED THE KINGDOM

All the Prophets spoke of a time when mankind should come under the sway of God's Law — a condition of affairs described as the *"Kingdom of God."* This was an outstanding theme of our Lord's preaching. *"Repent: for the Kingdom of Heaven* (or God) *is at hand"* (Mat. 4:17). And He enlarged upon this theme by describing the nature of the Kingdom, its membership, its conditions for entrance, its spiritual history following His Ascension (Mat. Chpt. 13), and the manner of establishment on Earth.

Prophecy is based upon the principle that history does not move with aimless feet but is under the control of God, Who knows the end from the beginning. He reveals the course of history to His Prophets, thus enabling them to predict the future. As a Prophet, Christ foresaw the triumph of His Cause and Kingdom through the fleeting changes of human history (Mat. Chpts. 24-25).

The ascended Christ continues His Prophetic Ministry through His Body, the Church, to whom He has promised inspiration (Jn. 14:26; 16:13), and imparted the Gift of Prophecy (I Cor. 12:10).

This means not that Christians are to add to the Scriptures, which are *"a once for all"* Revelation (Jude vs. 3); but by inspiration of the Spirit they will speak forth messages of *"edification, exhortation, and comfort"* (I Cor. 14:3), all based upon the Word of God.

CHRIST THE PRIEST

A Priest, in the Biblical sense, is a person Divinely consecrated to represent man before God and to offer sacrifices which will secure the Divine favor. *"For every High Priest is ordained to offer gifts and sacrifices: wherefore it is of necessity that this Man should have somewhat also to offer"* (Heb. 8:3).

At Calvary Christ, the Priest, offered Himself, the Sacrifice, in order to secure man's pardon and acceptance before God. His life previous to this was a preparation for His Priestly work. The Son of God partook of our nature (Heb. 2:14-16) and our experiences, for otherwise He could not represent man to God nor offer sacrifices; nor could He succor tempted humanity without knowing by experience what temptation meant. A Priest must, therefore, be human; for example, an Angel could not be a Priest for men.

Compare Leviticus Chapter 16 and Hebrews Chapters 8 to 10. Israel's High Priest was consecrated to represent man before God and to offer sacrifices which would secure Israel's pardon and acceptance. Once a year the High Priest made Atonement for Israel; in a typical sense he was their saviour who appeared in God's Presence to secure their pardon.

The sacrifices of that day were killed in the Outer Court of the Temple; in like manner Christ was crucified on Earth. Then the blood was carried into the Holy of Holies and sprinkled in the very Presence of God; in like manner Jesus ascended into Heaven *"to appear in the Presence of God for us."* God's acceptance of His Blood gives us the confidence of the acceptance of all who trust in His Sacrifice.

Although Christ offered a perfect Sacrifice once and for all, His Priestly work still continues. He ever lives to apply the merits and power of His Atoning Work before God on behalf of sinners.

He Who died for men now lives for them, to save them, and to intercede for them. And when we pray *"in the Name of Jesus,"* we are, in effect, pleading Christ's Sacrificial Work as the basis of our acceptance, for only thus are we assured that we are *"accepted in the Beloved"* (Eph. 1:6).

CHRIST THE KING

The Christ-Priest is also the Christ-King. That both Offices be held by one person was God's Plan for the perfect Ruler. Thus, Melchizedek, because he was both King of Salem and Priest of the Most High God, became a type of God's perfect King, the Messiah (Gen. 14:18-19; Heb. 7:1-3).

There was a period in the history of the Jewish people when this ideal was nearly realized. About a century and a half before the Birth of Christ, the land was ruled by a succession of High Priests who were also Civil Rulers; the Ruler of the land was both Priest and King. Also, during the Middle Ages the Pope claimed and attempted to exercise both spiritual and temporal power over Europe. As Christ's supposed representative he claimed to rule both the Church and the nations. *"Both experiments, the Jewish and the Christian* (Christian so-called), *failed,"* writes Dr. H. B. Swete; *"And so far as can be judged from these examples, neither the temporal nor the spiritual interests of men are promoted by entrusting them to the care of the same representative. The double task is too great for mere man to discharge."*

But the inspired writer spoke of the coming of One Who was worthy to bear the double burden. That One is the coming Messiah, a Ruler, a Priest after the order of Melchizedek (Ps. 110:1-4), and a *"Priest upon His Throne"* (Zech. 6:13). Such an One is the ascended Christ (Ps. 110:1; Heb. 10:13).

According to the Old Testament, the Messiah was to be a great King of the House of David Who should rule Israel and the nations, and usher in the golden age of Righteousness, Peace, and Prosperity (Ps. 72; Isa. 11:1-9).

JESUS CLAIMED TO BE THAT KING

In the presence of Pilate He testified that He was born to be a King, although He explained that His Kingdom was not of this world, that is, not a Kingdom founded by human force and governed according to human standards (Jn. 18:36).

Some time before His death Jesus predicted His Coming in Power and Majesty to judge the nations (Mat. 25:31). Even upon the Cross He looked and spoke as a King, so that the dying thief caught the vision and cried, *"Lord, remember me when Thou comest into Thy Kingdom"* (Lk. 23:42). He dimly perceived that death would usher Jesus into a Heavenly Kingdom, which it did!

After His Resurrection Jesus declared, *"All power is given unto Me in Heaven and in Earth"* (Mat. 28:18). Following His Ascension He was crowned and enthroned with the Father (Eph. 1:20-22; Rev. 3:21).

This means that in the sight of God, Jesus is King; He is not only Head of the Church, but also Lord of all the world and Master of men. The Earth is His and all that is therein. His and His Alone are all the Power and Glory of all those shining kingdoms which Satan the tempter long ago pointed out from the mountaintop. He is Christ the King, Lord of the world, Possessor of its riches, and Master of men.

All this is now true from God's viewpoint; but all men have not yet acknowledged Christ's rule. Though Christ has been anointed King of Israel (Acts 2:30), *"His Own"* (Jn. 1:11) have rejected His Sovereignty (Jn. 19:15) and the nations go their way without knowledge of His rule, and really with no desire for His rule, at least in their present condition.

THE PARABLE OF THE POUNDS

This situation was foreseen and predicted by Christ in the Parable of the Pounds (Lk. 19:12-25).

In those days when a national ruler fell heir to a kingdom he must first go to Rome and receive it from the Emperor, after which he was free to return and rule.

So Christ compares Himself to a certain nobleman who went into a far country to receive for himself a kingdom in return. He came from Heaven to Earth, earned exaltation and sovereignty by His Atoning Death for men, and then ascended to His Father's Throne to receive the Crown and Rulership.

But His citizens hated Him, and sent a message after Him, saying, *"We will not have this man to reign over us"*; Israel likewise rejected Jesus as their King.

Knowing that he would be absent for some time, the nobleman entrusted his servants with certain tasks; in like manner, Christ, foreseeing that a period of time would elapse between His First and Second Advents, has allotted to His servants the task of proclaiming His Kingdom and winning members into it, Baptizing them in the Name of Father, of the Son, and of the Holy Spirit.

Finally, the nobleman, having received his kingdom, returned to reward his servants, assert his sovereignty, and punish his enemies. In like manner will Christ return to reward His servants, assert His sovereignty over the world, and punish the wicked. This is the central theme of the Book of Revelation (Rev. 11:15; 12:10; 19:16).

He will then sit upon the Throne of David, and there will follow the Kingdom of the Son of David, when for a thousand years the Earth shall enjoy a golden reign of peace and plenty. Every sphere of human activity will come under Christ's control, evil-doing will be suppressed with a rod of iron, Satan will be bound, and the Earth shall be filled with the Knowledge and Glory of God *"as the waters cover the Sea"* (Ps. 72:8; Isa. 11:9; Dan. 7:13-14; Mic. 4:1; Hab. 2:14; Rev. 11:18; 20:1-10).

THE WORK OF CHRIST

When we use the term *"Work of Christ,"* we must understand that Christ performed many works. But the work which He accomplished to which we desire to address ourselves, was His Sacrificial Atoning Death on the Cross for the sins of the world (Mat. 1:21; Jn. 1:29).

Included in this Atoning Work are His Death, Resurrection, and Ascension. He must not only die for, but also live for us; He must not only rise from the dead for us, but also ascend to intercede for us (Rom. 4:25; 5:10; 8:34).

THE IMPORTANCE OF THE DEATH OF CHRIST

The outstanding event and central Doctrine of the New Testament may be summed up in the words, *"Christ died* (the event) *for our sins* (the Doctrine)*"* (I Cor. 15:3).

The Atoning Death of Christ is the unique feature of the Christian experience. Martin Luther declared that Christian Doctrine was distinguished from every other kind, and especially from that which seems to be Christian, by the fact that it is the Doctrine of the Cross.

The whole battle of the Reformation was for the right interpretation of the Cross. That he who understands the Cross rightly, understands the Christ and the Bible, was the teaching of the Reformers.

It is this unique feature of the Gospels which makes Christianity *"the Salvation"*; for *"the problem"* is the sin problem, and *"the experience,"* which makes perfect provision for the deliverance from the guilt and power of sin has a Divine finality. Jesus is the Author of *"Eternal Salvation"* (Heb. 5:9), that is, of final Salvation; all that Salvation can mean is secured by Him.

THE MEANING OF THE DEATH OF CHRIST

There is a certain true relationship between man and his Maker. Something has happened to destroy this relationship. Not only is man far from God, and unlike God in character, but there is an obstacle which blocks the way like a great boulder, an obstacle so great that man cannot remove it by his own efforts. That obstacle is sin, or rather guilt, which means sin reckoned by God against the sinner.

Man cannot remove this obstacle; if it is removed, deliverance must come from God's side; God must take the initiative and save man if he is to be saved. That God has done this is the testimony of the Scriptures. He sent His Son from Heaven to Earth to remove that obstacle and so make possible man's reconciliation to God.

By dying for our sins He removed the barrier; He bore what we should have borne; He accomplished for us what we were powerless to do for ourselves; this He did because it was the Will of the Father. This is the essence of the Atonement.

THE RESURRECTION OF CHRIST

The Resurrection of Christ is the miracle of Christianity. Once we establish the reality of this event, discussion of the other miracles of the Gospels become unnecessary. Furthermore, it is the miracle on which the entire Christian Faith stands or falls; for Christianity is a historical experience basing its teachings on definite events that occurred in Israel almost 2,000 years ago.

These events are the Birth and Ministry of Jesus Christ, culminating in His Death, Burial, and Resurrection. Of these, the Resurrection is the capstone, for, if Christ be not risen, then He was not what He claimed to be; His Death was not an Atoning Death; then Christians have been deceived for centuries; Preachers have been declaring error; and, the faithful have been deceived by a false hope of Salvation.

But, thank God, instead of the interrogation point, we may place the exclamation point after this Doctrine: *"But now is Christ risen from the dead, and become the firstfruits of them that slept!"*

THE EVIDENCE FOR THE RESURRECTION

"You Christians live on the fragrance of an empty tomb," said a French skeptic. It is a fact that those who came to embalm Jesus' Body on that memorable Resurrection morning, found His tomb empty. This fact has not been and cannot be explained apart from the truth of the Resurrection of Jesus. How easily the Jews could have refuted the witness of the first Preachers by producing the Body of our Lord. But they did not — and could not!

How explained the existence of the Christian Church, which would surely have remained buried with her Lord — if He had not risen? The living, radiant Church of the Day of Pentecost was not born of a dead Leader!

What shall we do with the testimony of those who saw Jesus after His Resurrection, many of whom spoke with Him, handled Him, ate with Him; hundreds of whom Paul said were still alive in His day; many of whom have given us their inspired testimony in the New Testament.

How shall we receive the testimony of men too honest and sincere to preach a Message they knew to be false, and sacrifice all for it?

How shall we explain the conversion of Paul the Apostle, from a persecutor of Christianity to one of its greatest Missionaries, unless he actually saw Christ on the Damascus Road?

There is only one answer to these questions — Christ arose!

Attempts have been made to evade the fact.

The Jewish Leaders contended that His Disciples had stolen the Body. As if a small band of timid and discouraged Disciples could have mustered up sufficient courage to wrest from hardened Roman soldiers the Body of their Master Whose Death had spelled failure to their hopes!

Modern Scholars have their explanations. *"The Disciples simply experienced a vision,"* they say! As if hundreds would see the same vision and imagine that they were really seeing Christ!

"Jesus did not really die; He simply swooned and was still alive when taken from the Cross," they also say! As if a pale, bloodless, drooping, and weakly Jesus could have persuaded doubting Disciples, and above all a doubting Thomas, that He was the risen Lord of Life!

Would the Centurion who vouched for the death of Christ to Pilate have dared to tell the Governor a lie?

These explanations are so weak that they carry their own refutation. Again we affirm, Christ arose! De Wette, the liberal theologian, affirmed that, *"The Resurrection of Jesus Christ cannot be called into doubt anymore than the historic certainty of the assassination of Caesar."*

THE MEANING OF THE RESURRECTION

It means that Jesus is all that He claimed to be — Son of God, Saviour, Lord (Rom. 1:4). The answer of the world to His claims was — a Cross; God's answer was — the Resurrection.

It means that the Atoning Death of Christ was a reality, and that man may find forgiveness for past sins, and so find peace with God

(Rom. 4:25). The Resurrection is really the completion of the Atoning Death of Christ. In fact, to mention the Cross is at the same time to mention the Resurrection, or vice versa. How do we know that it was not ordinary death — that Faith in it really will take away sin? Because He arose!

It means that we have a sympathetic High Priest in Heaven, Who has lived our life, and known our sorrows and infirmities, and Who is able to give us power to live the Christ-life day-by-day, as we place our Faith in His Finished Work. He Who died for us, now lives for us (Rom. 8:34; Heb. 7:25).

It means that we may know that there is a life to come. *"But no one has ever come back to tell us about the other world,"* is a common objection. But somebody has come back — Jesus Christ.

To the question, *"If a man die shall he live again?"* Science can only say, *"We don't know!"*

Philosophy can say, *"There ought to be a future life."* But Christianity can say, *"Because He lives, we shall live also; because He arose from the dead, so shall all who believe in Him."*

The Resurrection of Christ gives not only proof of the fact of immortality, but also the assurance of personal immortality (Jn. 14:19; II Cor. 4:14; I Thess. 4:14).

It means that there is a certainty of future Judgment. As the inspired Apostle has said, God *"hath appointed a day, in the which He will judge the world in Righteousness by that Man Whom He hath ordained; whereof He hath given assurance unto all men, in that He hath raised Him from the dead"* (Acts 17:31).

As surely as Jesus rose from the dead to be Judge of men, so surely shall men rise from the dead to be judged by Him.

THE ASCENSION OF CHRIST

The fact of the Ascension is witnessed to by the Gospels, Acts, and the Epistles. What is the meaning of this historical fact? What Doctrines are based upon it? What are its practical values?

The Ascension teaches that our Master is the Heavenly Christ.

Jesus left the world because the time had come for Him to return to the Father. His departure was a *"going up"* as His entrance into the world had been a *"coming down."* He Who had descended now ascended where He was before. And as His entrance into the world was supernatural so was His departure.

Consider the manner of his departure. His appearances and disappearances after the Resurrection had been instantaneous, the Ascension was gradual — *"while they beheld"* (Acts 1:9).

It was followed by no fresh appearances in which the Lord appeared in their midst in Person to eat and drink with them; appearances of this kind ended with the Ascension. It was a withdrawal once for all from earthly life which men live on this side of the grave. From now on the Disciples must not think of Him as *"Christ after the flesh,"* that is, living an earthly life, but as the Glorified Christ living a Heavenly Life in the Presence of God and contacting them through the Holy Spirit.

Before the Ascension the Master appeared, disappeared, and reappeared from time to time, in order to gradually wean them from dependence on visible and earthly contact with Him, and to accustom them to invisible, spiritual communion with Him.

Thus, the Ascension becomes the dividing line of two periods of Christ's Life: from Birth to the Resurrection He is the Christ of human history, the One Who lived a perfect human life under earthly conditions. Since the Ascension He is the Christ of spiritual experience, Who lives in Heaven and touches men through the Holy Spirit Whom He sent back to live in the hearts and lives of believing men and women (Jn. 16:7-16).

THE EXALTED CHRIST

In one place Christ is described as *"going up,"* and in another as being *"taken up."* The first represents Christ as entering the Father's Presence in His Own Will and Right; the second lays the emphasis on the Father's act by which He is exalted as the reward of His obedience unto death.

His slow ascent in full view of the Disciples brought to them the realization that He was leaving His earthly life, and also made them eyewitnesses to His departure. But once out of their sight, the journey was completed by an act of will. Comments Dr. Swete:

"That instant all the Glory of God shone about Him, and He was in Heaven. The sight was not altogether new to Him; in the depth of His Divine consciousness the Son of Man had memories of the Glories which in His preincarnate Life He had with the Father 'before the world was' (Jn. 17:5). But the human soul of Christ up to the moment of the Ascension had no experience of the full vision of God which burst upon Him when He was taken up. This was the goal of His human life, the joy set before Him (Heb. 12:2); and in the moment of the Ascension it was attained."

It was in view of His Ascension and Exaltation that Christ declared, *"All power* (authority) *is given unto Me in Heaven and in Earth"* (Mat. 28:18; Eph. 1:20-23; Phil. 2:9-11; I Pet. 3:22; Rev. 5:12).

Quoting again from Dr. Swete:

"Nothing is done in that great unknown world, which we call Heaven, without His initiating, guiding, and determining authority. Processes inconceivable to our minds are being carried forward beyond the veil by agencies equally inconceivable. It is enough for the Church to know that all which is being done there is done by the authority of her Lord."

THE SOVEREIGN CHRIST

Christ ascended to a place of Headship over all creatures. He is the *"Head of every man"* (I Cor. 11:3), the *"Head of all principality and power"* (Col. 2:10); all the authorities of the unseen world as well as the world of men are under His control (Rom. 14:9; Phil. 2:10-11; I Pet. 3:22). He possess this universal sovereignty to be exercised for the good of the Church which is His Body; God *"put all things under His Feet, and gave Him to be the Head over all things to the Church."* In a very special sense, therefore, Christ is the Head of the Church. This Headship is manifested in two ways:

1. By the authority exercised by Him over the members of the Church. Paul uses the marriage relationship as an illustration of the relationship between Christ and the Church (Eph. 5:22-33).

As the Church lives in subjection to Christ, so wives are to be in subjection to their husbands; as Christ loved the Church and gave Himself for it, so husbands are to exercise their authority in the spirit of love and self-sacrifice.

The Church's obedience to Christ is a willing submission; in like manner should the wife be obedient not only for conscience's sake, but out of love and reverence.

For Christians the marriage bond has become a *"mystery (a truth with a Divine meaning),"* for it reveals the spiritual union between Christ and His Church; authority on the part of Christ, subordination on the part of the Church, love on both sides — love answering to love, to be crowned by the fullness of joy, when the union is consummated at the Coming of the Lord (Swete).

A prominent characteristic of the Early Church was the attitude of loving submission to Christ. *"Jesus is Lord"* was not only the statement of a creed but also the rule of life.

2. The Ascended Christ is not only the ruling, directing power of the Church, but also the Source of its life and energy, which He carries out through the Person, Office, Work, and Ministry of the Holy Spirit.

As the vine is to the branches, as the head is to the body, so is the Living Christ to His Church. Although the Head of the Church is in Heaven, He is in the closest union with His Body on Earth, the Holy Spirit being the bond of communication (Eph. 4:15-16; Col. 2:19).

CHRIST THE WAY

The separation between Christ and the earthly Church begun at the Ascension, is not permanent; He ascended as a forerunner to prepare the way for us to follow Him. His Promise was: *"Where I am, there shall also my servants be"* (Jn. 12:26).

The term *"forerunner"* is first applied to John the Baptist as the way-preparer of the Christ (Lk. 1:76). As John prepared the way for Christ, so the ascended Christ prepares the way for the Church. This hope is likened to *"an anchor of the soul, both sure and steadfast, and which entereth into that within the veil; whether the forerunner is for us entered, even Jesus"* (Heb. 6:19-20). Though tossed by the waves of testing and adversity, the soul of the faithful need not fear shipwreck, so long as our hope keeps a firm grip upon the Finished Work of Christ, and our place in that Work. In a spiritual sense the Church has already followed the Glorified Christ; we have been made to *"sit together in heavenly places in Christ Jesus"* (Eph. 2:6).

Through the Spirit Believers ascend in heart and mind to our risen Lord; however, there will be a literal Ascension corresponding to the ascension of Christ (I Cor. 15:52; I Thess. 4:17). This hope of the Believers is no delusion, for already we feel the tug of the anchor chain — we are conscious of the drawing power of the Glorified Christ (I Pet. 1:8).

With this hope Jesus comforted the Disciples before His departure (Jn. 14:1-3). *"Wherefore comfort one another with these words"* (I Thess. 4:18).

THE INTERCEDING CHRIST

By virtue of His assuming our nature and dying for our sins, Jesus is the Mediator between God and man (I Tim. 2:5). But the Mediator is also an Intercessor, and intercession goes a step further than mediation.

A mediator may bring two parties together and leave them to settle their difficulties; but an intercessor goes on to say a word on behalf of the person in whose interest he appears. Intercession is an extremely important Ministry of the ascended Christ (Rom. 8:34).

It forms the climax of His saving activities. He died for us; He rose for us; He ascended for us, and makes intercession for us (Rom. 8:34). Our hope is not in a dead Christ, but in One Who lives; and not merely in One Who lives, but Who lives and reigns with God. Christ's Priesthood is eternal, therefore, His intercession is permanent. Swete says:

"He can, therefore, carry on to completion ('to the uttermost,' Heb. 7:25) every case He undertakes to defend, thus guaranteeing to those who approach God through His mediation entire restoration to the Divine favor and blessing; indeed, to do this is the very purpose of His Life in Heaven; He lives for this end that He may intercede with God on our behalf.

"There can be no suspension of His Intercessory Work as long as the world lasts . . . for the intercession of the ascended Christ is not a prayer but a life. The New Testament does not represent Him as a suppliant standing ever before the Father with outstretched arms, and with strong crying and tears, pleading our cause before the Presence of a reluctant God; but as a throned Priest-King, asking what He will from a Father Who always hears and grants His request."

In fact, to take it a little further than Dr. Swete has stated, Christ really does not have to do anything as it regards intercession. His very Presence guarantees on our behalf whatever is needed. His Work is a Finished Work, meaning that nothing else is to be done. Consequently, His intercession on our behalf, which actually pertains to sin and failure, is a foregone conclusion. His Presence at the Right Hand of the Father guarantees this, because of what He has done and did completely, we might quickly add.

WHAT IS THE INTERCESSORY MINISTRY OF CHRIST?

The prayer in John Chapter 17 will suggest the answer.

Similar to the Office of Mediator is that of Advocate (in the Greek, *"paraclete"*) (I Jn. 2:1). An Advocate or Paraclete is one who is called to the help of a person in distress or necessity, to administer comfort or give advice and protection. Such was the Lord's relation to the Disciples during the days of His flesh.

But the ascended Christ is concerned also with the problem of sin. As Mediator, He gains access for us into God's Presence; as Intercessor, He bears our petitions before God, but actually does that by His mere Presence. As Advocate, He meets the charges laid against us by the *"accuser of the Brethren"* on the score of sin. For true Christians a life of habitual sin is out of the question (I Jn. 3:6); but isolated acts of sin are definitely possible in the best of Christians and such occasions require the advocacy of Christ.

The Bible does not teach sinless perfection, but it does teach victory over sin (Rom. 6:14).

In I John 2:1-2 there are stated three considerations which give force to His Advocacy:

1. He is *"with the Father,"* in God's Presence.

2. He is *"the Righteous,"* and as such may be an Atonement for others.

3. He is *"the propitiation for our sins,"* that is, was a Sacrifice which secured God's favor by atoning for all sin.

THE OMNIPRESENT CHRIST

While on Earth Christ was limited to one place at a time and could not be in contact with each of His Disciples all the time. But by ascending to the Throne of God, He is enabled to broadcast His Power and Divine Personality at all times and in all places and to all His Disciples. Ascension to the Throne of God gave Him not only Omnipotence (Mat. 28:18) but also Omnipresence, making it possible for Him to fulfill the Promise, *"Where two or three are gathered together in My Name, there am I in the midst of them"* (Mat. 18:20).

THE VALUE OF THE DOCTRINE OF THE ASCENSION

These values are many, and that which follows will give us some idea I think of the significance of this all-important Work of Christ:

1. Consciousness of the ascended Christ, Whom we look forward to seeing someday, is an incentive to holiness (Col. 3:1-4). The upward glance will counteract the downward pull.

2. The knowledge of the ascension makes for a right conception of the Church. Belief in a merely human Christ will cause people to regard the Church as merely a human society, useful only for philanthropic and moral purposes, but possessing no supernatural power or authority.

On the other hand, a knowledge of the ascended Christ will result in the recognition of the Church as an organism, a supernatural organism deriving Divine life from its Risen Head.

3. Consciousness of the ascended Christ will produce a right attitude toward the world and worldly things. *"For our conversation* (literally, *'citizenship'*) *is in Heaven; from whence also we look for the Saviour, the Lord Jesus Christ"* (Phil. 3:20).

4. Faith in the ascended Christ will inspire a deep sense of personal responsibility. Belief in the ascended Christ carries with it the knowledge that an account will have to be rendered to Him some day (Rom. 14:7-9; II Cor. 5:9-10).

The sense of a responsibility to a Master in Heaven acts as a deterrent to sin and an incentive to Righteousness (Eph. 6:9).

5. With Faith in the ascended Christ is connected the joyous and blessed hope of His returning. *"And if I go and prepare a place for you, I will come again, and receive you unto Myself; and where I am, there ye may be also"* (Jn. 14:3).

(The above material on Christ was for the most part derived from Myer Pearlman.)

(10) "THAT AT THE NAME OF JESUS EVERY KNEE SHOULD BOW, OF THINGS IN HEAVEN, AND IN THINGS IN EARTH, AND THINGS UNDER THE EARTH;"

At least one of the purposes of Christ's Exaltation is that all things might bow in acknowledgment of the Name that belongs to Jesus, and confess that Jesus Christ is Lord, even as Verse 11 proclaims. Because of what the Name of Jesus represents, a time is coming when every knee shall bow before Him in recognition of His sovereignty. The statement is built on the wording of Isaiah 45:23, a Verse quoted by Paul in Romans 14:11 also. This universal acknowledgment will include Angels and departed Saints in Heaven, people still living on Earth, and the Satanic hosts and lost humanity in Hell (Kent).

THE NAME OF JESUS

The phrase, *"That at the Name of Jesus every knee should bow,"* does not necessarily refer to the Name of *"Jesus"* per se.

"Jesus" was the Name given our Lord at His humiliation. It is at *"The Name"* that belongs to Jesus that every knee will bow. Every knee will bow in recognition of all that Jesus is in *"His Exaltation."* It is *"in"* The Name that every knee will bow. The Name is the spiritual sphere, the holy element as it were, in which every prayer will be offered and every knee will bow.

I think the evidence proclaims, even as it is given in the next Verse, that the Name spoken of here is *"Lord."* Jesus Christ is *"Lord of all."* In the days of Paul a soldier took his oath in the name of Caesar, indicating Caesar's authority. In similar fashion, the new Name of Jesus, i.e., *"Lord,"* indicates His absolute sovereignty.

Even though prayer will be offered in His Name, even as it is now, it is rather the worship here that is to be done to Jesus, which carries the greater strength. The scope of the whole Passage (His Exaltation) requires that He should be set forth here as the Object of Worship rather than merely as the Medium of Prayer, although it certainly does include that. Thus, the meaning is, *"Jesus is manifested by God as Head over all; to Him thus manifested, worship is due by all."*

THE BOWING OF THE KNEE

This doesn't mean merely that at the mention of the Name of *"Jesus"* or *"Lord"* that we should bow; nor is there any evidence that God requires this.

The idea is, as we've already mentioned, that all in Heaven and on Earth should worship Him, and that the time will come when He will be thus everywhere acknowledged as *"Lord."*

Jesus is presently given short shift in the world. In fact, even though He is most revered, respected, and worshiped by some, and I speak of those who truly know Him as Saviour, the facts are, most of the world either ignores Him or bitterly opposes Him. By many He is looked at as a good man but slightly deceived, etc. Others deny His veracity as the Son of God. Much of the world denies that He was actually raised from the dead, consequently, denying His Deity.

The idea that the Father is reached only through Jesus, even as the Word proclaims, is believed by only a few (Jn. 14:6).

However, the day is coming, when all of this will change. It will be after the Second Coming, when Jesus Personally begins to rule and reign over this Earth, even from the city of Jerusalem (Ezek. 48:35).

HEAVEN, EARTH, AND UNDER THE EARTH

The phrase, *"Of things in Heaven, and things in earth, and things under the earth,"* refers to the fact that all creation will render homage, whether animate or inanimate.

"Confess" is from a Greek word which means *"to openly or plainly confess."* It means *"to confess"* in the sense of *"to agree with someone."* Someday, the entire universe will agree with God the Father on the testimony which He has given of His Son.

The word means also, *"to publicly declare."* It contains the idea of *"praise and thanksgiving"* (Wuest).

The meaning in this case is that, though all do not now personally accept the Lordship of Christ, at the final day, because He will be their Judge, they will be unable to deny that He is also Lord, to the Glory of God the Father.

"Every creature which is in Heaven, and on the earth, and under the earth . . . heard I saying, Blessing, and honor, and glory, and power be unto Him that sitteth upon the Throne, and to the Lamb for ever and ever" (Rev. 5:13).

(11) "AND THAT EVERY TONGUE SHOULD CONFESS THAT JESUS CHRIST IS LORD, TO THE GLORY OF GOD THE FATHER."

Submission will be expressed not only by bending the knee, but also by verbal confession. Paul does not imply by this a universal Salvation, but means that every personal being will ultimately confess Christ's Lordship, either with joyful Faith or with resentment and despair.

This ultimate confession that Jesus Christ is Lord is apparently Paul's indication of the *"Name"* granted Jesus at His Exaltation following the Cross. The Name *"Lord"* with all the dignity and Divine prerogatives this implies will eventually be recognized by every creature. Of course, the Son in His *"nature"* was always Deity, but the Exaltation following the Cross granted Him the dignity of station commensurate with His nature and far superior to His humble state while on Earth.

"To the Glory of God the Father" is Paul's closing doxology to this remarkable statement regarding Christ. He has never lost sight of the Divine order and of the grand scheme in which the entire Incarnation of Christ must be viewed. Recognition of Christ's Lordship fulfills the purpose of the Father and so brings Glory to God.

This picture of Christ's humiliation and subsequent Exaltation was intended by Paul to encourage in his readers an attitude of Christlike humility. If we are to be identified as Christ's followers, we must demonstrate His characteristics. The appeal, however, is not only to a life of lowliness and at times even hardship; it also contains the reminder that victory follows humiliation and that God's Glory will ultimately prevail (Kent).

JESUS CHRIST IS LORD

The phrase, *"And that every tongue should confess that Jesus Christ is Lord,"* proclaims *"Lord"* as the *"Name"* of Verse 9.

In any attempt to probe Paul's view of Christ, the term *"Lord"* must be central. It functions in several ways and is enriched by several connotations in Paul.

The term expresses the relationship of Christians to Jesus as subjects and followers to their Master, as in the phrase *"Our Lord Jesus Christ."* For instance, in Philippians 3:8 Paul speaks of this relationship in very personal terms with the reference to *"Christ Jesus my Lord."* As *"Lord,"* Jesus' example and command are unquestionable authorities for Christian behavior in Paul's Letters.

As well, Paul reflects the acclamation of Jesus as *"Lord"* in the worship setting, to which we have already alluded, which is understood by him as the pattern and anticipation of the universal acknowledgment of Jesus as Lord when He comes in Glory.

The Divine Glory of Jesus the Lord, however, has already been revealed to Paul. As a result, Paul views Jesus in incredibly exalted terms, permitting the application to Jesus of Old Testament Passages concerning Jehovah and the portrayal of *"Lord Jesus"* as the ancient of all creation and redemption (I Cor. 8:6).

In short, in some cases at least, Paul's application of *"Lord"* to Jesus connoted the conviction that Jesus had been given to share in the properties and honor of God's *"Name"* (with all that represented in the Old Testament and ancient Jewish tradition) and bore the very Glory of God in such fullness and uniqueness that Jesus could be compared and associated only with God *"the Father"* in the honor and reverence due Him.

GOD THE FATHER

The phrase, *"To the Glory of God the Father,"* refers to the fact that the acknowledgment of the Glory of Christ is the acknowledgment of the Glory of the Father, as the Source of Deity, manifested perfectly in Him. Repeatedly, Jesus professed that His Work on Earth was to manifest the Father (Jn. 17:4).

We learn from all of this that those who do not render proper homage to Jesus Christ, do not in fact, worship the True God. As a matter of fact, it may be added, that they that do not honor the Son, do not worship God at all.

Even though the Holy Spirit is not mentioned here, He in fact, is the One Who is inspiring the Sacred Text, i.e., *"the information concerning Christ as given by Paul."*

All of this tells us that the Father wills that the Son should be honored. He that refuses to do so, disobeys the Father. Actually, They are equal. He that denies the One, denies also the Other. The same feeling that leads us to honor the Father, will also lead us to honor the Son, for He is *"the brightness of His Glory, and the express Image of His Person"* (Heb. 1:3). The evidence of the existence and the Glory of the Son is the same as that of the Father.

Jesus honors the Father, as is evidenced here; consequently, anyone who does not worship and obey the Father — the First Person of the Trinity in truth, is not obeying Christ. This means that if the Father is ignored, one may imagine that he is worshiping God, but one must also realize that there is no God but the God subsisting as the Father, Son, and Holy Spirit. He that withholds proper honor from One, withholds it from all.

(12) "WHEREFORE, MY BELOVED, AS YE HAVE ALWAYS OBEYED, NOT AS IN MY PRESENCE ONLY, BUT NOW MUCH MORE IN MY ABSENCE, WORK OUT YOUR OWN SALVATION WITH FEAR AND TREMBLING."

Paul is not rebuking the Philippians, but exhorting them to pursue their Christian progress without undue dependence on his presence. Perhaps he had noted a weakness along this line. Once before in this Epistle he had mentioned a need to be as diligent in his absence as they were when he was present with them (Phil. 1:27).

The specific exhortation was to work out their own Salvation. The Biblical concept of Salvation needs to be understood in order to comprehend Paul's intent here. Salvation has many aspects, including a present one.

Regeneration initiates the Believer into a life with obligations. Acknowledging Jesus Christ as Lord obligates the Believer to obey Him. Hence, working out Salvation does not mean *"working for"* Salvation, but rather making Salvation operational.

Justification must be followed by the daily living aspects of Sanctification, by which the new life in Christ is consciously appropriated and demonstrated.

"With fear and trembling" is no contradiction of the joyful spirit permeating this Letter. Christian joy is the experience of every Believer in God's Will, but holy fear of God that trembles at the thought of sin is also the attitude of the careful Christian (James 4:8-10) (Kent).

OBEDIENCE

The phrase, *"Wherefore, my beloved, as ye have always obeyed,"* presents by the use of the word *"wherefore"* the Apostle going back to Philippians 1:27 where his presence and absence are referred to as in this Verse.

In Philippians 1:27 we have Paul's exhortation to the Philippian Saints to conduct themselves as citizens of Heaven should. Then the Apostle signals out one of the obligations of a citizen of Heaven, that of living in harmony and unity with his fellow Saints.

In Philippians 2:1-4, he gives four reasons which in themselves are enablements, why they should live in unity together, and further develops the theme of Christian unity.

In Philippians 2:5, he tells them that such unity is one of the constituent elements in the Mind of Christ, and in Philippians 2:6-8, he shows how Christ Jesus exhibited the basic quality of unity, namely, humility and self-abnegation in His Incarnation and vicarious death on the Cross, which act on His part was recognized by God the Father in that He exalted His Son as the Man Christ Jesus, placing Him in the place of highest honor in the universe.

Now, in Philippians 2:12-13, the Apostle exhorts these Saints to make the humility and self-abnegation exhibited by the Lord Jesus, a fact in their own lives. He calls them, *"My beloved ones."*

The distinctive word here for *"love"* refers to the love that God is, to the love produced in the heart by the Holy Spirit, a love that impels one to sacrifice oneself for the benefit of others. This is the heavenly love with which the great Apostle loved the Philippians. He commends them for their constant obedience (Wuest).

MOSES AND THE CHILDREN OF ISRAEL

I do not think that one would be off course to place Paul in the position of thinking of the farewell injunction of Moses to the Children of Israel, whom he had led despite their murmurings, contestings, and disobediences to the very border of the Promised Land (Deut. Chpt. 32). As Moses addressed Israel at that time, Paul is likewise addressing the Philippians, and as well the entirety of the Body of Christ of his day. As we shall see in the next phrase, I think the Apostle has much more in mind than just his not being able to come by the Church as often as he would like. I think he is referring as well to the time when he will be taken permanently.

The Apostle has laid out the Gospel to these Philippians, even as he had all the other Churches, which was done with clarity, conciseness, simplicity, and correctly, of course. It was now to be obeyed.

OBEDIENCE IN THE OLD TESTAMENT

In its simpler Old Testament meaning, the word *"obedience"* signifies *"to hear," "to listen."* It carries with it, however, the ethical significance of hearing with reverence and obedient assent.

Obedience is the supreme test of Faith in God and reverence for Him. The Old Testament conception of obedience was vital. It was the one important relationship which must not be broken.

While sometimes this relation may have been formal and cold, it nevertheless was the one strong tie which held the people close to God, that is if they actually were close to God.

The significant spiritual relation is expressed by Samuel when he asked the question, *"Hath Jehovah as great delight in Burnt-Offerings and Sacrifices, as in obeying the voice of Jehovah? Behold, to obey is better than sacrifice, and to hearken than the fat of rams"* (I Sam. 15:22). In fact, *"obedience"* was the one condition without which no right relation might be sustained to Jehovah. This is most clearly stated in the relation between Abraham and Jehovah when he is assured *"in thy seed all the nations of the earth will be blessed; because thou hast obeyed My Voice"* (Gen. 22:18).

In Prophetic utterances, future blessing and prosperity were conditioned upon obedience: *"If you be willing and obedient, you shall eat the good of the land"* (Isa. 1:19).

After surveying the Glories of the Messianic Kingdom, the Prophet assures the people that *"this shall come to pass, if you will diligently obey the Voice of Jehovah your God"* (Zech. 6:15). On the other hand, misfortune, calamity, distress, and famine are due to their disobedience and distrust of Jehovah.

OBEDIENCE IN THE NEW TESTAMENT

In the New Testament a higher spiritual and moral relation is sustained than in the Old Testament. The importance of obedience is just as greatly emphasized. In fact, Christ Himself is its One great illustration of obedience.

"He humbled Himself, becoming obedient unto death, yea, the death of the Cross" (Phil. 2:8).

By obedience to Him we are through Him made partakers of His Salvation (Heb. 5:9). This act is a supreme test of Faith in Christ. Indeed, it is so vitally related that they are in some cases almost synonymous.

"Obedience of Faith" is a combination used by Paul to express this idea (Rom. 1:5). Peter designates Believers in Christ as *"children of obedience"* (I Pet. 1:14).

Thus, it is seen that the test of fellowship with Jehovah in the Old Testament is obedience. The bond of union with Christ in the New Testament is obedience through Faith, by which we become identified and the Believer becomes a Disciple.

Inasmuch as Paul is using Christ as the great example of humility, which He of course definitely is, the humility of which is spoken here demands obedience. Consequently, I think it will be helpful to us to look at the obedience of Christ, which as well serves as an example for us.

THE OBEDIENCE OF CHRIST

The *"obedience"* of Christ is directly mentioned but three times in the New Testament, although many other Passages describe or allude to it:

1. *"Through the obedience of the One shall the many be made Righteous"* (Rom. 5:19).

2. *"He humbled Himself becoming obedient even unto death, yea, the death of the Cross"* (Phil. 2:8).

3. *"Though He was a Son, yet learned He obedience by the things which He suffered"* (Heb. 5:8).

AN ELEMENT OF CONDUCT AND CHARACTER

Jesus' subjection to His parents (Lk. 2:51) was a necessary manifestation of His loving and sinless character, and of His disposition and power to do right in any situation. His obedience to the moral Law and in every particular is asserted by the New Testament writers: *"without sin"* (Heb. 4:15); *"Who knew no sin"* (II Cor. 5:21); *"holy, guileless, undefiled, separated from sinners"* (Heb. 7:26), etc.; and is affirmed by Himself: *"Which of you convicteth Me of sin?"* (Jn. 8:46); and implicitly conceded by his enemies, since no shadow of accusation against His character appears.

Of His ready, loving, joyful, exact, and eager obedience to the Father, mention will be made later, but obedience was His central and most outstanding characteristic, the filial at its highest reach, limitless *"unto death."*

His usually submissive and law-abiding attitude toward the authorities and the great movements and religious requirements of His day was a part of His loyalty to God, and of the strategy of his campaign, the action of the one who would set an example and wield an influence, as at His Baptism: *"Thus it becometh us to fulfill all Righteousness"* (Mat. 3:15); the Synagogue worship (Lk. 4:16, *"as His custom was"*) the incident of the tribute money: *"Therefore the sons are free. But, lest we cause them to stumble,"* etc. (Mat. 17:24-27).

Early, the necessities of His Mission as Son of God and Institutor of the new dispensation obliged Him frequently to display a judicial antagonism to current prescription and an authoritative superiority to the rulers, and even to important details of the Law, that would in most eyes mark Him as insurgent, and did culminate in the Cross, but in fact, was the sublimest obedience to the Father,

Whose authority alone He, as full-grown man, and Son of Man, could recognize.

HIS FATHER'S WILL

Two Scriptural statements raise an important question as to the inner experience of Jesus.

Hebrews 5:8 states that *"Though He was a Son, yet learned He obedience by the things which He suffered."* This doesn't mean that He learned to be obedient, for that would have meant that He would have been disobedient, which was never the case.

Philippians 2:6-8 says, *"Existing in the form of God . . . He humbled Himself, becoming obedient, even unto death."* As Son of God, His Will was never out of accord with the Father's Will. How then was it necessary to, or could He, learn obedience, or become obedient?

The same question in another form arises from another part of the Passage in Hebrews 5:9: *"And having been made perfect, He became unto all them that obey Him the Author* (cause) *of Eternal Salvation."* Also it says in Hebrews 2:10: *"It became Him* (God) *. . . to make the Captain* (Author) *of their Salvation perfect through sufferings."*

How and why should the perfect be made perfect?

Gethsemane, with which indeed Hebrews 5:8 is directly related, presents the same problem. It finds its solution in the conditions of the Redeemer's Work and Life on Earth in the light of His true humanity.

Both in His Eternal Essence and in His human existence, obedience to His Father was His dominant principle, so declared through the Prophet-Psalmist before His Birth: *"Lo, I am come (in the roll of the Book it is written of Me) to do Thy Will, O God"* (Heb. 10:7; Ps. 40:7).

It was His Law of Life: *"I do always the things that are pleasing to Him. I do nothing of Myself, but as the Father taught Me, I speak these things"* (Jn. 8:28-29); *"I can of Myself do nothing . . . I seek not Mine Own Will, but the Will of Him that sent Me"* (Jn. 5:30).

PERFECT OBEDIENCE

It was the indispensable process of His activity as the *"Image of the invisible God,"* as an expression of both the Deity and the human. He could be a perfect Revelation only by perfect correspondence in every detail, of will, word, and work with the Father's Will (Jn. 5:19).

Obedience was also His life nourishment and satisfaction (Jn. 4:34). It was the guiding principle which directed the details of His Work: *"I have power to lay it* (His Life) *down, and I have power to take it again. This Commandment received I from My Father"* (Jn. 10:18); *"The Father that sent Me, He hath given Me a Commandment, what I should say and what I should speak"* (Jn. 12:49; 14:31).

But in the Incarnation this essential obedience must find expression in human forms according to human demands and process of development. As True Man, obedient disposition on His part must meet the test of voluntary choice under all representative conditions, culminating in that which was supremely hard, and at the limit which should reveal its perfection of extent and strength.

It must become hardened, as it were, and confirmed, through a definite obedient act, into obedient human character. The Son, obedient on the Throne, must exercise the practical virtue of obedience on Earth.

Gethsemane was the culmination of this process, when in full view of the awful, shameful, horrifying meaning of Calvary, the obedient disposition was crowned, and the obedient Divine-human life reached its highest manifestation, in the great ratification: *"Nevertheless not My Will, but Thine, be done."*

But just as Jesus' growth in knowledge was not from error to truth, but from partial knowledge to complete, so His *"learning obedience"* led Him not from disobedience or debate to submission, but from obedience at the present stage to an obedience at ever deeper and deeper cost.

OBEDIENCE THROUGH SUFFERING

The process was necessary for His complete humanity, in which sense He was *"made perfect,"* complete, by suffering. It was also necessary for His perfection as example and sympathetic High Priest. He must fight the human battles under the human conditions. Having translated obedient aspiration and disposition into obedient action in the face of, and in suffering unto, death, even the death of the Cross, He is able to lead the procession of obedient sons of God through every possible trial and surrender.

Without this testing of His obedience He could have had the sympathy of clear and accurate knowledge, for He *"knew what was in man,"* but He would have lacked the sympathy of a kindred experience. Lacking this, He would have been for us, and perhaps also in Himself, but an imperfect *"captain of our Salvation,"* certainly no *"Filial Leader"* going before us in the very paths we have to tread, and tempted in all points like as we are, yet without sin.

It may be worth noting that He *"learned obedience"* and was *"made perfect"* by suffering, not the results of His Own sins, as we do largely, but altogether the results of the sins of others.

HIS LIFE AND HIS DEATH

In Romans 5:19, in the series of contrasts between sin and Salvation (*"Not as the trespass, so also is the free Gift"*), we are told: *"For as through the one man's disobedience the many were made sinners, even so through the obedience of the One shall the many be made righteous."*

Interpreters and Theologians, especially the latter, differ as to whether *"obedience"* here refers to the specific and supreme act of obedience on the Cross, or to the sum total of Christ's Incarnate obedience through His whole life; and they have made the distinction between His *"passive obedience,"* yielded on the Cross, and His *"active obedience"* in carrying out without a flaw the Father's will at all times.

This distinction is hardly tenable, as the whole Scriptural representation, especially His Own, is that He was never more intensely active than in His death: *"I have a baptism to be baptized with; and how am I straitened until it be accomplished"* (Lk. 12:50); *"I lay down My life, that I may take it again. No man taketh it away from Me, but I lay it down of Myself. I have power to lay it down, and I have power to take it again"* (Jn. 10:17-18).

"Who through the Eternal Spirit offered Himself without blemish unto God" (Heb. 9:14), indicates the act of obedience of One Who was both Priest and Sacrifice.

As to the question whether it was the total obedience of Christ or His death on the Cross that constituted the Atonement, and the kindred question whether it was not the spirit of obedience in the act of death, rather than the act itself that furnished the value of His Redemptive work, it might conceivably, though improbably, be said that *"the one act of Righteousness"* through which *"the free Gift came"* was His whole life considered as one act.

But these ideas are out of line with the unmistakable trend of Scripture, which everywhere lays principal stress on the death of Christ itself principle; it is the center and soul of the two Ordinances, Water Baptism and the Lord's Supper; it (His Sacrificial Atoning Death on the Cross) holds first place in the Gospels, not as obedience, but as redemptive suffering and death; it is unmistakably put forth in this light by Christ Himself in His few references to His Death: *"Ransom," "My Blood,"* etc.

THE TEACHING OF PAUL

Paul's teaching everywhere emphasizes the death, and in but two places the obedience; Peter indeed speaks of Christ as an example, but leaves as his characteristic thought that Christ *"suffered for sins once... put to death in the flesh"* (I Pet. 3:18). It is the center and significance of Christ's whole work, that He *"put away sin by the Sacrifice of Himself"* (Heb. 9:26); while John in many places emphasizes the death as an Atonement: *"Unto Him that... loosed us from our sins by His Blood"* (Rev. 1:5), and elsewhere.

PROPITIATION

The Scripture teaching is that *"God set (Him) forth to be a propitiation, through Faith, in His Blood"* (Rom. 3:25).

His lifelong obedience enters in chiefly as making and marking Him the *"Lamb without blemish and without spot,"* Who Alone could be the Atoning Sacrifice. If it enters further, it is as the preparation and anticipation of that death, His Life so dominated and suffused with the consciousness of the coming Sacrifice that it becomes really a part of the death. His obedience at the time of His death could not have been Atonement, for it had always existed and had not atoned; but it was the obedience that turned the possibility of Atonement into the fact of Atonement.

He obediently offered up, not His obedience, but Himself. He is set forth as propitiation, not in His obedience, but in His Blood, His Death, borne as the penalty of sin, in His Own Body on the tree. The distinction is not one of mere academic theological interest. It involves the whole question of the substitutionary and propitiatory in Christ's Redemptive Work, which is central, vital, and formative, shaping the entire conception of Christianity. In other words, if the Believer has a wrong view of the Cross as it refers to his Redemption, he will have a wrong view of everything else as well.

The blessed and helpful part which our Lord's complete and loving obedience plays in the working out of Christian character, by His example and inspiration, must not be underestimated, nor its meaning as indicating the quality of the life which is imparted to the soul which accepts for itself His Mediatorial Death.

These bring the consummation and crown of Salvation; they are not its channel, or instrument, or price, that being the Cross.

(Bibliography: Denney, *"Death of Christ"*; Champion, *"Living Atonement"*; Forsythe, *"Cruciality of the Cross."*)

PRESENCE AND ABSENCE

The phrase, *"Not as in my presence only, but now much more in my absence,"* proclaims the Philippians as adhering to that which Paul had taught them while he was gone just as well as they did when he had been present with them. This had not always been the case with some of the other Churches.

It is notable that this Epistle is the only one which contains no direct rebuke. The Philippian Church has the glory of *"having always obeyed,"* not like the Galatian Churches *"as in his presence only,"* but now much more in his absence.

Inasmuch as there were not nearly as many Jews in Philippi as there had been in some of the other cities where Paul had founded Churches, quite possibly the Judaizers did not target this area. In most Churches then there was a mixture of Jews and Gentiles who had accepted Christ. The Jews would have been fertile territory for the Judaizers, with them already being very familiar with the Law, which also could have, and no doubt did, influence Gentile Christians as well. This particular problem did not seem to appear, although there seemed to be some disunity, which we will study to a greater degree a little later.

The obedience and faithfulness of these Philippians as it regarded Doctrine had to be a great joy to the Apostle, hence him referring to them as *"my beloved,"* and rightly so! A true God-called Preacher, one who is attempting to follow the Lord in all things, can have no greater blessing than to see the Saints of God grow under his or her Ministry. The Holy Spirit has placed in the Church, *"Apostles, Prophets, Evangelists, Pastors, and Teachers,"* for the expressed purpose of *"the perfecting of the Saints, for the work of the Ministry, for the edifying of the Body of Christ"* (Eph. 4:11-12). To see that maturity develop, the work of the Ministry carried forth, and the Body edified, presents the true result of the true Preacher of the Gospel.

I might quickly add, that Preachers who seek to do anything else as it regards the Saints, will answer to God, and the results will not be pleasant. To exploit Believers is a sin of the highest proportion, which regrettably, all false doctrine does. Saints are to be developed, never exploited.

THE EXPLOITATION OF THE SAINTS

I want to make it clear again, that all false doctrine always, and without exception, exploits the Saints of God. It either robs them or keeps them from receiving from God what they could receive, or both!

For instance, the so-called *"Prosperity gospel,"* which in reality is no prosperity or Gospel at all, robs the Saints of their money, always with a dangling carrot of riches held in front of them, while at the same time it keeps them from the true Way of Christ, which stops all true spiritual development. While the Lord definitely *does* bless His people in a material way, such must never be the emphasis but always a by-product.

The false teaching of humanistic psychology also leads Believers away from the help they can receive in Christ, toward that which Jeremiah described as *"broken cisterns, that can hold no water"* (Jer. 2:13).

Actually, the list is endless. Any teaching which does not carry the full weight and power of the Holy Spirit, is false. Consequently, it will lead Saints astray, in effect, exploiting them. Even the Truth taught in many cases has little effect, for the simple reason, that the Spirit of God is little present if at all. In such cases, very little good is actually accomplished.

We must always understand, that not only must the Word of God be preached without compromise, but as well, the bearer of that Word, namely the Preacher of the Gospel, must walk close to God, constantly seeking His Face, providing a suitable temple for the Holy Spirit through which to work and operate, which will then assure the Spirit of God accomplishing His determined task. It is always a combination of Truth and consecration. If the Truth has been compromised, that means the consecration has been compromised as well. However, even if the consecration only has been compromised, the Truth will then be presented with little impact or effect. Unfortunately, Truth and consecration combined are rare.

THE WORKING OUT OF ONE'S SALVATION

The phrase, *"Work out your own Salvation with fear and trembling,"* refers to going on to maturity, to the ultimate conclusion of total Christlikeness.

First of all let's see what this exhortation does *not* mean.

It does not mean to work *for* one's Salvation, and for two reasons: A. Paul was writing to those who were already saved; and, B. Salvation is not a work of man for God, but a work of God for man, a work that was accomplished at the Cross.

The words *"work out"* are the translation of a Greek word which means *"to carry out to the goal, to carry to its ultimate conclusion."* We say, *"The student worked out a problem in arithmetic."* That is, he carried the problem to its ultimate conclusion. This is the way it is used here. The Philippians are exhorted to carry their Salvation to its ultimate conclusion, namely, as stated, to total Christlikeness.

Actually, the Salvation spoken of here is not Justification, that already having been accomplished at conversion, but rather Sanctification, which speaks of victory over sin and a living of a life pleasing to the Lord Jesus. They are to see to it that they continue to make progress in their Christian lives. They are to do this with *"fear and trembling."*

However, this is not a slavish terror, but a wholesome caution. In fact, this fear is self-distrust. It is taking heed lest we leave the Finished Work of Christ, thereby succumbing to our own efforts, which always bring defeat. It is a constant apprehension of the deceitfulness of the heart, and of the insidiousness and power of inward corruption. It is the caution and circumspection which timidly shrinks from whatever would offend and dishonor God and the Saviour. This is a human responsibility (Wuest).

WORK OUT

The Believer must *"work out"* what God in His Grace has *"worked in."*

This powerful inward working of God affects both the will and the work.

To will and to do is the fruit of God's Work in the Believer . . . where He, in executing His good pleasure, it mightily at work in the Believer towards his Sanctification, this at the same time also demands the self-activity of man, in working out that Salvation to God's Honor and Glory.

THE CROSS OF CHRIST

There are many things that one could say as it regards this particular statement by Paul. However, perhaps the most important thing to relate is the fact, the Scriptural fact, that if one is to successfully go toward Christlikeness, ever making this one's goal, that it can only be done by a total dependence on the Finished Work of Christ at the Cross. Any other method, I think, is bound toward failure.

This means that the Cross, which at the same time presupposes the Resurrection and the Exaltation, figures totally and completely not only in the initial Salvation experience of the believing sinner, but also in the Victory and continued growth of the Child of God.

Everything is always *"in Christ,"* which always presupposes the Cross. For one's Faith to end right, or rather to garner the intended and desired results, one's Faith must begin right, and by that I mean the object of Faith must be correct, which always must be the Finished Work of Christ, which of course is *"the Cross."*

CONTROL

Actually, we will find in the next Verse that it is only God, i.e., *"the Holy Spirit,"* Who can bring about this inward work within our lives. So, the battleground falls out to the following:

Either the Holy Spirit controls us, or self-will controls us, which can go in any number of directions, with the ultimate source being Satan.

However, in the efforts of the Evil One to usurp the control desired by the Holy Spirit in our lives, at least one of the strongest tools used by Satan is *"Preachers."* By that I mean the following:

To which we have already alluded, the Godly Preacher desires only to perfect you (bring you to maturity), *"for the Work of the Ministry,"* and your edification. He does not desire to control you, knowing that alone should be done by the Holy Spirit.

Regrettably, there are many Preachers who are not Godly, and in essence desire to control those who sit under their Ministries. While they may be subtle, the desire is *"control."* I do not think I am exaggerating when I say that the far greater majority fall into that category. These evil reasons are varied and many.

With some it is money, while with others it is power. Either direction is evil, because the spiritual welfare of the individual is not the concern, but rather other things.

Using myself as an example, while some Believers belong to Family Worship Center, in reality they belong to God. As their Pastor, I am the undershepherd of this congregation, with the Chief Shepherd being the Lord Jesus Christ (Heb. 13:20; I Pet. 2:25; 5:4).

Untold millions presently are told that unless they belong to the Catholic Church, they will be eternally lost. As well, that goes for many Protestant Churches also. For whatever reason, the individuals who listen to such instruction or rather threats, are being controlled. Control, at least the kind that is designed by men, works from the position of fear or reward. Either way is disastrous for the Believer, simply because such control is originated by man, which means it doesn't come from the Lord.

The Holy Spirit desires to control all Believers; however, the control He desires is that which must be freely given Him, for He will never force the issue Himself.

We as Believers are to freely give Him control of our lives, and continue to do so even on a daily basis, with Him then bringing about the Will of the Father (Rom. 8:26-27).

As Paul mentions Salvation here, perhaps it would be a good time to look at this word as to what it means.

JUSTIFICATION

Inasmuch as Paul is talking about the Finished Work of Salvation, in other words what Salvation means, let us look at this word from this particular angle.

Even though Sanctification is actually the first work which takes place in the heart and life of the believing sinner, and I speak of instant cleansing upon Faith, which must be done before Justification can be effected, we will deal with Justification first (I Cor. 6:11). The believing sinner has to be *"made clean (Sanctified)"* before he can be *"declared clean (Justified)."*

But yet, Sanctification is a somewhat twofold process, with *"positional Sanctification"* taking place immediately at conversion, and *"conditional or progressive Sanctification"* taking place after conversion, and actually continuing for the entirety of the life of the Believer. So, we will address Sanctification later.

Someone has said that Justification is *"Divine Acquittal."* Actually, the word *"justify"* is a judicial term meaning *"to acquit, to declare Righteous, to pronounce sentence of acceptance."*

The illustration is taken from legal relations. The guilty one stands before God the Righteous Judge; but instead of a sentence of condemnation he receives a sentence of acquittal.

The noun *"Justification,"* or *"Righteousness,"* means a state of acceptance into which one enters by Faith. This acceptance is a free Gift of God made available through Faith in Christ, and what He did at the Cross (Rom. 1:17; 3:21-22). It is a state of acceptance in which the Believer stands (Rom. 5:2).

Regardless of his sinful past and of present imperfection, the sinner has a complete and secure position in relation to God upon acceptance of Jesus Christ by Faith; *"Justified"* is God's verdict and none can gainsay it (Rom. 8:34).

The doctrine has been defined as follows: *"Justification is an act of God's free Grace wherein He pardons all our sins and accepts us as righteous in His sight, only because of the Righteousness of Christ imputed to us and received by Faith alone."*

Justification is primarily a change of position on the part of the sinner; once condemned, he is now acquitted; once under Divine condemnation he is now the subject of Divine commendation.

JUSTIFICATION AND RIGHTEOUSNESS

Justification includes even more than pardon of sins and removal of condemnation; in the act of Justification God places the offender in the position of a righteous man. The Governor of a state can pardon a criminal but he cannot reinstate the criminal in the position of one who has not broken the Law. But God can do both.

He blots out the past with its sins and offenses, and then treats the person as if he had never committed a sin in his life! A pardoned criminal is not considered or described as a good or righteous man; but when God justifies the sinner He declares him justified, that is, righteous in His sight. No Judge could justly justify a criminal, that is, declare him to be a good and righteous man. And if God were subject to the same limitations and justified only good people, then there would be no Gospel for sinners, and in fact, none would be justified, because none are good (Rom. 3:10).

Paul assures us that God justifies the ungodly. *"The Miracle of the Gospel"* is that God comes to the ungodly, with a Mercy which is righteous altogether, and enables them through Faith, despite what they are, to enter into a new relationship with Himself in which goodness then becomes possible to them. The whole secret of New Testament Christianity, and of every revival of Salvation and reformation in the Church, is that joyous and marvelous paradox, *"God justifies the ungodly."*

To be sure, all of this is done through Jesus Christ and what He did at the Cross and the Resurrection. Without that Sacrificial, Atoning Work, it would not be possible for anyone to be justified. However, Jesus came as our Substitute, took our place, suffering the penalty of sin which was the curse of the broken Law, which penalty is death, and atoned for all sin, past, present, and future. Simple Faith in Him and more particularly, in what He did, grants the most wicked sinner the Righteousness which Christ purchased with His Own Precious Blood (Jn. 3:16).

Thus, we see that Justification is first subtraction — the cancellation of sin; second, addition — the imputing of Righteousness, all in Christ.

THE NECESSITY FOR JUSTIFICATION

"How should a man be just with God?" asked Job (9:2). *"What shall I do to be saved?"* asked the Philippian Jailor (Acts 16:30-31). Both men voiced one of the greatest questions that can be raised: *"How can a man get right with God and be sure of His approval?"*

The answer to that question is found in the New Testament, especially in the Epistle to the Romans, which presents the Plan of Salvation in a detailed and systematic manner. The theme of the Book is contained in Romans 1:16-17, and may be stated as follows: *"The Gospel is God's Power for men's Salvation, because it tells how sinners can be changed in position and condition so as to be right with God."*

One of the outstanding phrases of Romans is *"the Righteousness of God."* The inspired Apostle describes the kind of Righteousness that is acceptable to God so that the man possessing it is considered *"right"* in God's sight. It is the Righteousness which results from Faith in Christ. Paul shows that all men need the Righteousness of God, in other words *must* have that type of Righteousness, because the entire race has sinned.

The Gentiles are under condemnation. The steps in their downfall were plain: they once knew God (Rom. 1:19-20), but failing to worship and serve Him, their minds became darkened (Rom. 1:21-22). Spiritual blindness led to idolatry (Rom. 1:23) and idolatry led to moral corruption (Rom. 1:24-31).

They are without excuse because they have a Revelation of God in nature, in other words, it is obvious that there is a God simply by looking at creation, and a conscience that approves or disapproves of their deeds (Rom. 1:19-20; 2:14-15).

The Jew also is under condemnation. True, he belongs to the chosen nation, and has known the Law of Moses for hundreds of years, but he has violated that Law in thought, deed, and word (Rom. Chpt. 2). Paul clangs shut the doors of the prison house of condemnation on the human race, with the words: *"Now we know that what things soever the Law saith, it saith to them who are under the Law* (meaning the Jews)*: that every mouth may be stopped, which means that all the world* (both Jews and Gentiles) *may be accounted guilty before God. Therefore by the deeds of the Law shall no flesh be justified in His sight: for by the Law is the knowledge of sin"* (Rom. 3:19-20).

WHAT IS THIS RIGHTEOUSNESS THAT MAN SO NEEDS?

The word *"Righteousness"* means *"rightness, the state of being right."* Sometimes the word describes God's Character, as being free from imperfection and injustice. Applied to man it means the state of being right with God.

The word *"right"* in the original means *"straight,"* that which is conformed to a standard or rule. Therefore, a righteous man is one whose life is lined up with God's Law, i.e., *"His Word."*

But what if he discovers that instead of being *"straight"* he is *"perverse,"* i.e., *"crooked,"* and he cannot straighten himself? Then he needs Justification — which is the Work of God. In fact, all fall into this classification.

Paul has declared that by the deeds of the Law no one can be justified. This is no reflection on the Law of God, which is holy and perfect. It simply means that the Law was not given for the purpose of making people righteous, but for supplying a Standard of Righteousness. As well, inasmuch as Law has no power within itself, but only the stark command, man in his fallen, depraved condition, could not keep the Law irrespective as to how hard he tried.

The Law of Moses (Law of God) may be compared to a measure to which length, breadth, height, and depth are very obvious to man, but a measure to which he cannot attain, as stated, no matter how hard he tries.

"But now the Righteousness of God without the Law is manifested" (Rom. 3:21).

Note the word *"now."* It has been said that *"all time has been divided for Paul into 'now' and 'then.'"* In other words, the coming of Christ made a change in God's dealings with men. It introduced a new dispensation.

For ages men have been sinning and learning the impossibility of putting away or conquering their own sin. But *"now"* God has plainly and openly revealed the way, which of course, is totally and entirely in Jesus and what He did at the Cross.

ISRAEL AND THE LAW

Many Israelites felt that there must be a way of being justified apart from the keeping of the Law; for two reasons:

1. They perceived (at least those Jews who loved God) a wide chasm between God's Standard for Israel and their actual condition. Israel was unrighteous, and Salvation could not come through their own merits and efforts. Salvation must come from God, by His interposition on their behalf.

2. Many Israelites learned from personal experience their inability to keep the Law perfectly. They were led to the conclusion that there must be a Righteousness independent of their own works and efforts. In other words, they longed for Redemption and Grace. And God assured them that such a Righteousness would be revealed.

Paul (Rom. 3:21) speaks about the Righteousness of God without or apart from the Law, *"being witnessed by the Law* (Gen. 3:15; 12:3; Gal. 3:6-8) *and the Prophets* (Jer. 23:6; 31:31-34).*"*

This Righteousness included both pardon of sins and inward Righteousness of heart.

In fact, Paul affirms that Justification by Faith, which God originally showed to Abraham (Gen. 15:6), was God's original method of saving men; the Law was added in order to discipline the Israelites and make them feel their need of Redemption (Gal. 3:19-26).

The Law in itself had no saving power anymore than a thermometer has power to allay the fever which is registers. Jehovah Himself was the Saviour of His people and His Grace their only hope, which Plan was always that Jesus would come and die for sinners.

THE SELF-RIGHTEOUSNESS OF MANY JEWS

Unfortunately the Jews came to exalt the Law as a justifying agent and worked out a scheme of Salvation based on merit for the keeping of its precepts and the added traditions. *"For they being ignorant of God's Righteousness* (refusing to accept God's Plan for Righteousness), *and going about to establish their own righteousness* (self-righteousness), *have not submitted themselves unto the Righteousness of God* (God's Plan for Redemption, which was through the offering of His Only Son, The Lord Jesus Christ)" (Rom. 10:3).

They had plainly misconceived the purpose of the Law. They had come to trust in it as a means of spiritual Salvation; ignoring the innate sinfulness of their own hearts they imagined that they would be saved by the keeping of the Letter of the Law, which incidentally they never were able to do, so that when Christ came offering them Salvation for their sins, they thought they had no need of such a Messiah (Jn. 8:32-34). They thought that He would prescribe some rigid requirements whereby they might attain to Eternal Life.

"What shall we do," they asked, *"that we might work the works of God?"* And they were not willing to follow the way indicated by Jesus: *"This is the Work of God, that you believe"* (Jn. 6:28-29).

They were so busy attempting to establish and work out their own system of Righteousness that they missed God's Plan for justifying sinful man. In going on a journey, a train is a means of an end. We have no intention of making our home on the train; we are concerned simply with reaching our destination, and when we reach the end of our journey we leave the train.

The Law was given to lead Israel to a certain destination, and that end was trust in God's Saving Grace, which was and is in Jesus Christ. But when the Redeemer came, the self-satisfied Jews acted like a man who refuses to leave the train when the destination has been reached, even though the conductor assures him that it is *"the end of the line."*

The Jews refused to move from their seats in the Old Covenant *"train"* although the New Testament assured them that Christ is the *"end of the Law,"* and that the Old Covenant was fulfilled (Rom. 10:4).

THE READER MAY WONDER HOW ALL OF THIS AFFECTS HIM PRESENTLY?

Most modern Christians have been taught wrong as it regards the ancient Law of Moses. They surmise that this was for the Jews only, and has no bearing on them at this present time.

First of all, the Law of Moses, which was really the Law of God, was God's Standard of Righteousness for the entirety of the world and for all time (the moral part), and not merely the Jews. In fact, God raised up a certain group of people called *"Israel,"* for the expressed purpose of giving the world the Word of God, and for bringing the Messiah into the world, i.e., *"serving as the womb for the coming Messiah."*

However, even though these Jews were His special people, raised up by God for a particular purpose, even they couldn't keep the Law. In effect, the Lord was showing the entire world that if the Jews couldn't keep the Law, even though they were His Own special people, how did the Gentile world think they could keep it. In fact, as stated, the Law was not meant to save, because it could not save, but was meant to show man (both Jews and Gentiles) as to how depraved and corrupt they actually were. In other words, because of the fallen nature which resulted from the Fall, man was simply unable to keep the Law, i.e., *"God's Standard of Righteousness."*

Unfortunately, man has tried from the very beginning to institute his own standard, which of course, God cannot accept. Man must come up to God's Standard of Righteousness, which can only be done through Jesus.

The modern Christian must understand that God's requirements for Righteousness, means the keeping of the Law in every respect, never failing even one single time. Of course, no human being has ever reached that Standard, and no human being within his own ability will ever do so. In fact, God demands that Standard presently just as much as He did when the Law was given thousands of years ago. That's how it is important to the modern Christian. Of course, when we speak of the Law of Moses, as it applies to our present situation, we are speaking only of the moral Law, which, in effect, is the Ten Commandments.

The big mistake that Christians presently make is, that they think that because they are now saved, therefore, new creations in Christ Jesus, even baptized with the Holy Spirit, that surely they can now keep the moral Law of God. As Paul found out, even as he describes his own experience in Romans Chapter 7, even the modern Christian cannot keep the Law, and let us explain that.

In fact, if the modern Christian, which of course goes for any Christian for all time, attempts to keep the Law presently, he will fail just as surely as Israel of old failed. And yet, God demands that it be kept, so how is it to be done?

In fact, this is one of the major problems in the Church. It tries to keep the Law, i.e., *"the moral Law,"* and concludes by failing, as fail it must. In fact, Churches think that they can solve this problem by adding more laws, exactly as Israel of old. By the time of Christ, over 600 Laws were added to the original Law of Moses. Ironically enough, they attempted to solve their problem by making it worse. The modern Church too often does the same!

Such efforts always lead to failure and frustration (Gal. 2:20).

What confuses the Christian is, that he thinks that now because he is, in fact, a Christian, having a new nature, that surely he can do these things which he knows he ought to do. And then he tries, and finds that he can't. And yet he knows he must! So what is the answer?

THE ANSWER IS JESUS

Most Christians would very quickly agree that certainly the answer is Jesus, but they don't realize quite how it is Jesus.

In brief, God came to this world and became man, born of the Virgin Mary. He actually came as our Substitute, as our Saviour. As our Representative Man and, in effect, our Substitute, He came to do for us what we could not do for ourselves.

Consequently, He kept the Law in every respect, all the days of His Life, not failing in even one respect, be it thought, word or deed, and as stated, did all of this for us.

He then went to the Cross as a Sacrifice in order to pay for all of our sins, even though He had never sinned Himself. He took the penalty of the broken Law, which is death, actually dying in our place on our behalf. Inasmuch as He had never sinned, He could serve as a perfect Sacrifice which God would accept. When He poured out His Own Precious Blood, He was, in effect, pouring out His Own Life, because the life is in the Blood.

In doing this, He atoned for all sin, past, present, and future, at least for all who will believe (Jn. 3:16; Rom. 10:9-10, 13; Eph. 2:8-9).

Satan's hold upon the human race is sin, and when Jesus paid for all sin, Satan lost his grip on the human race, but once again only for those who will believe.

Inasmuch as Jesus had never Himself sinned, meaning that Satan had no hold on Him, and that He had atoned for all sin, as stated, past, present, and future, death could not hold Him down, meaning that Satan could not keep Him from being raised from the dead. *"The wages of sin is death,"* but if there is no sin, then death is not present and has no sway or hold. That's the reason that Paul also said, *"But the Gift of God* (Jesus Christ is that Gift) *is Eternal Life"* (Rom. 6:23).

Whenever the believing sinner exhibits Faith in this of which we have stated, in effect, in Jesus and what He did, in the Mind of

God, the sinner is automatically placed *"in Christ."* That's what Paul meant by stating that all Believers were *"baptized into His death"* (Rom. 6:3). No, Paul is not speaking here of Water Baptism, but rather the Crucifixion of Christ, as well as His Resurrection. In fact, all Believers are *"in Christ,"* which is, in effect, the key word of all of this (Rom. 8:1), which also includes His Burial and Resurrection (Rom. 6:3-5).

IN CHRIST

The *"in Christ"* principle is, in effect, the principle of all Salvation and all Victory as it regards our victorious, overcoming, Christian experience. In other words, everything that Jesus did at the Cross and the Resurrection becomes ours, because, in effect, and as stated, He did all of this strictly for us and none at all for Himself.

So, if Christ atoned for all sin by His Sacrificial Death, then all sin is eradicated in my heart and life by virtue of my Faith in Him. For that's all that God requires, that we have Faith in Christ and what He did, which anyone can do if they so desire (Jn. 3:16).

This means that I was *"in Him"* also when He was buried, which means all of my old past with all of its sin and failure is buried as well. It also means, that when He was raised from the dead, I also was raised from the dead *"in Him"* in *"newness of life"* (Rom. 6:4-5). Wonder of wonders it also means that even as Christ has now been Exalted, and is seated by the Right Hand of the Father in Heaven, that by Faith I am actually seated there with Him also (Eph. 2:6). So, when one speaks of the Finished Work of Christ, one is actually speaking of the Cross, the Resurrection, and the Exaltation.

Inasmuch as Jesus kept all the Law, and even suffered its penalty on our behalf, my being *"in Him,"* now makes me a *"Law-keeper"* instead of a Lawbreaker, which I had been. As I remain in Him, continuing to trust in what He did at the Cross and the Resurrection, not allowing my Faith to leave this *"Finished Work,"* I am guaranteed the Help of the Holy Spirit, Who guarantees to and for me, all the benefits of the Atonement (Rom. 8:1-2).

So, I'm not a *"Law-keeper"* by actually doing such myself, which I could not do anyway, but because I am *"in Christ,"* consequently, having Faith in what He has already done. The idea is, that He did it for me, which is the only way it could be done, and my Faith in Him as it regards His Sacrifice, makes me a Law-keeper also. In other words, due to Faith in Christ and what He did at the Cross, God imputes to me the Righteousness of Christ, which I never could have attained on my own.

As I stay in Christ, which I do by my constant Faith, even on a daily basis, in His Finished Work, I automatically keep the moral Law, simply because Christ has already done this great and glorious thing. However, the moment that I set about to try to do it myself, through rules and regulations, etc., in effect, I take myself out of Christ, which then brings on failure. The secret is remaining *"in Christ"* with my Faith, which, in effect, speaks of taking up the Cross daily and following Jesus (Lk. 9:23).

TAKING UP THE CROSS DAILY

As we've already stated several times in our commentarial notes, most Christians presently have a total misconception as to what Jesus was speaking about when He demanded that His followers *"deny ourselves, and take up our Cross daily, and follow Him"* (Lk. 9:23).

They think that the denial of self means suffering, and of course, most Christians shy away from that.

That's not what it means at all! To *"deny ourselves"* simply means that we do not trust ourselves or put faith and confidence in our own ability to live this Christian life. That's all that it means. We are to deny self in the sense of attempting to do this which no one has ever been able to do, and which only Christ has done, and only through Him can it be done. Self must be hidden in Christ, and in fact, must remain in Christ.

Also, the taking up of the Cross refers to trusting and believing in what Jesus did at the Cross on our behalf. We are to forever trust in that, forever believe that, forever understand that all of our victory in totality is always in the Cross and never in us.

That's all that He means by *"taking up the Cross"* and not suffering on the part of a Saint, as most have been led to believe.

As well, Jesus said that we must do this on a *"daily"* basis. In other words, it is a renewed Faith every day in the Finished Work of Christ. The Lord has designed it this way in order that we may keep depending on Christ, and never on ourselves.

This is the manner in which the Law is kept, and in fact, the only manner. Jesus has already done this great thing, and for us to attempt to do it all over again, in effect, says that He didn't finish the task, and we must add our efforts to what He has done, which is an insult to Christ of the highest order, as should be obvious.

THE FINISHED WORK

The Believer is to always understand, that everything we have in Christ is totally and completely finished. In other words, the great Work and Plan of Salvation, which includes not only our initial Salvation experience, but as well, our everyday walk before God, has all been completely carried out, and needs nothing added. This is what confuses us many times. We keep trying to be holy, which means to do such by our own machinations, when in fact, we are already holy in Christ, which was given to us automatically when we accepted the Lord as our Saviour.

We keep trying to sanctify ourselves by rules and regulations made up by men, or by ourselves, which again is impossible, for the simple reason, that in Christ we are already Sanctified. We keep trying to gain the victory when, in fact, we already have the victory. We keep trying to overcome particular things within our lives, when in fact, we are already an overcomer. In other words, we are attempting to do by works, which man could never do anyway, which in fact, Christ has already done.

The answer to all Victory in the heart and life of the Believer, is simple trust in Christ. However, what does that mean?

Trust in Christ always means that we are trusting in what He did at the Cross and the Resurrection. Unfortunately, there has been so little preaching and teaching on the Cross in the last half of the 20th Century, that the Church has been moved away from its right foundation. In fact, most of the preaching and teaching in the last 50 years, has been on Faith; however, for the most part, it has not been Faith in the Finished Work of Christ, but rather Faith in ourselves, or so-called Faith in the Word which in reality, at least for the most part, is not really in the Word of God at all. Due to this erroneous teaching, millions of Christians have misplaced Faith, or the object of their Faith is other than Christ and what He did at the Cross and the Resurrection. Remember this:

Jesus came into this world to defeat the powers of darkness, which He did at the Cross and the Resurrection; consequently, if we are not having Faith in what He did at the Cross and the Resurrection on our behalf, we are really not having Faith in Jesus, whatever our claims. To have Faith in Christ, is to have Faith in what He did. To have Faith in the Word of God, is to have Faith in that toward which the Word strains in every capacity, which is the great Sacrifice of Christ. If we try to use the Word of God in any other capacity, we are pulling it out of its rightful setting, in effect, perverting it, which God can never honor.

So, the Message is, *"Jesus Christ and Him crucified"* (I Cor. 2:2). If we stray from that, we stray from the True Gospel. If our Faith is in anything else, no matter how many Scriptures we load on the other efforts, it will bring us no proper fruit. It is only Faith in the Cross and the Resurrection, i.e., *"The Finished Work of Christ,"* which guarantees results in the heart and life of the Believer. That's what it took to get saved, and that's what it takes to stay saved and be victorious.

THE SOURCE OF JUSTIFICATION

Grace, i.e., *"the Grace of God,"* is always the Source of Justification, as such can only be the Source of Justification.

Grace means primarily favor, or the kindly disposition in the Mind of God. It has been called *"pure unrecompensed kindness and favor"*; *"unmerited favor."*

This simply means, that even though no person deserves Salvation, and in fact, can never deserve such on their own, if we will have simple Faith in what Christ did at the Cross on our behalf, God will give us without any strings attached, even though we don't deserve it, all of His great Salvation. That is the meaning of *"Grace."*

As such, Grace cannot incur a debt. This means that if we try to work for what the Lord has freely done for us, we actually nullify or frustrate the Grace of God, which means that God cannot then bestow Grace upon us (Gal. 2:20).

To say it another way, if the sinner wants to be saved, he must come simply by Faith in what Christ did at the Cross, never trying to earn his Salvation. If he attempts to do so, the Grace of God is withheld, and the person remains unsaved.

Also, if the Christian attempts to live a victorious life by works of any nature, he nullifies the Grace of God, which means he is left on his own, which always spells failure. In other words, the surest way to sin, is to try not to sin by our own efforts instead of trusting daily in what Christ did at the Cross.

All Grace comes through the Finished Work of Christ, meaning the Cross and the Sacrifice given there. If we try to obtain Grace any other way, it simply cannot be done. The Grace of God which is a must for every sinner and every Believer, is anchored firmly and totally in the Cross of Christ.

That means that what God bestows, He bestows as a Gift, which is the only way it can be, for man simply and surely cannot earn such. We cannot recompense or pay Him for this great Gift. In fact, if we attempt to do so, we nullify the whole thing.

Salvation is always presented as a Gift, an undeserved and unpayable favor, a pure benefit from God, which is always given freely upon our Faith in Christ (Rom. 6:23).

Christian service, therefore, is not the payment for God's Grace; service is the Christian's way to express devotion and love to God. In other words, we work for Him not in order to obtain His free Gift, but because we have already obtained the Gift. *"We love Him, because He first loved us."*

While the Believer should definitely work for the Lord, should be about His Master's business, such should always be in the form of love and never of merit. In other words, our doing these things, whatever these things might be, and I speak of working for the Lord in any capacity, is never to earn anything from God, but always because we have already been given everything, and we love Him. If in fact, we have been given everything, and we have, then what more are we trying to earn?

Christians have a tendency to get this all mixed up. We tend to think that our working for Him earns us something. It doesn't, and if we think such, we are causing ourselves great difficulties, because we are nullifying the Grace of God. As a Believer, I need the Grace of God every moment within my life, which means this favor and strength coming to me from God unhindered. But the moment I feel that I have earned something from the Lord, or that I merit something, I instantly stop that flow of Grace.

This is a very subtle thing, and has been violated by every single Christian at one time or the other. We must always remember, that Grace comes to us through the Cross and our Faith in the Cross. If we move our Faith from the Cross to our own works of any nature, we have just nullified the Grace of God, which of course, brings upon us untold troubles (Gal. 2:20). The idea is, that if we could do any of this for ourselves, then Christ did not need to come and die on Calvary on our behalf. The truth is, we cannot do any of this for ourselves no matter how hard we try. It can only be done in Christ, and in fact, has already been done in Christ.

THE MANNER OF GOD'S DEALINGS

Grace is God's dealing with the sinner absolutely apart from the question of merit or demerit. *"Grace is neither treating a person as he deserves, nor treating him as better than he deserves."* Writes L. S. Chafer. *"It is treating him graciously without the slightest reference to his deserts, in one way or the other. Grace is infinite love expressing itself in infinite goodness."*

A misunderstanding should be avoided. Grace does not mean that the sinner is forgiven because God is big-hearted enough to remit the penalty or to waive the righteous judgment. As perfect Ruler of the universe God cannot deal leniently with sin, for that would detract from His perfect Holiness and Justice.

God's Grace to sinners is seen in the fact that He Himself, through the Atonement of Christ on the Cross, paid the full penalty of sin; therefore, He can justly pardon sin without regard to the sinner's merit or demerit. Sinners are pardoned, and Grace continues to flow to Believers, not because God is gracious to excuse their sins, but because there is Redemption through the Blood of Christ (Rom. 3:24; Eph. 1:6).

Some Preachers have gone astray at this point: they have thought that God is gracious in pardoning sin, whereas His pardon of sin is actually based on strict justice. In pardoning sin *"He is faithful* (meaning He will do it upon our simple Faith in Christ) *and just* (meaning that His justice has been satisfied by the Death of Christ on the Cross)" (I Jn. 1:9). God's Grace is revealed in His providing an Atonement whereby He could both justify the ungodly and yet vindicate His holy, unchangeable Law.

GRACE IS INDEPENDENT OF MAN'S WORKS OR ACTIVITY

When a person is under Law (meaning that he is attempting to save himself or bring about victory by his own efforts) he cannot be under Grace; when he is under Grace (meaning that he is depending totally on what Christ did at the Cross and the Resurrection), he is not under Law. A person is *"under Law"* when he attempts to secure Salvation or Sanctification as a matter of reward, which refers to the performance of good works and the observance of ceremonies.

This means that millions of people are thinking they are saved because they have been baptized in water, or else they take the Lord's Supper, or else they belong to a certain Church, or else they perform certain good deeds, or don't do certain bad things, etc. Improper Faith in those things strictly stops the Grace of God.

That doesn't mean that these particular things we have named, and many we have not named, are bad or unscriptural. In fact, in their own place they are very good, and should be done by Believers; however, the problem is that in thinking that such merits us something from God, when it doesn't.

A person is *"under Grace"* when he secures Salvation or Victory by trusting in God's Work for him and not in his work for God. The two spheres are mutually exclusive. In other words, they cancel each other out. Grace cancels out works, and works cancels out Grace (Gal. 5:4).

The Law says, even as all Law must say, *"Pay all"*; Grace says, even as Grace must say, *"All is paid."* Law is a work to do, which Jesus, in effect, has already done, and in fact, He was the only One Who could do such a thing; Grace is a work done, which means what He did at the Cross and the Resurrection. Law restrains action; Grace changes the nature. Law condemns; Grace justifies. Under Law a person is a servant working for wages, in other words, attempting to earn something by performance; under Grace he is a Son enjoying an inheritance. As should be obvious, there is a vast difference.

WORKS

Deep-rooted in the human heart is the idea that man must do something to make himself worthy of Salvation, or even the obtaining of Victory in his everyday walk before God. (When we say *"Victory"* we are speaking of victory over sin.)

In the Early Church certain Jewish Christian Teachers insisted that converts are saved by Faith and the observance as well of the Law of Moses. In other words, they taught that one must accept Christ in order to be saved, but as well, must keep the Law of Moses (Acts 15:1).

Among the heathen, and in some sections of the Christian Church, this error has taken the form of self-punishment, the performance of Religious Rites, the making of pilgrimages, the giving of Alms, etc. The idea underlying all this effort is as follows:

God is gracious, man is not righteous, therefore, man must make himself righteous in order to make God gracious.

In fact, this was Luther's error, when by painful self-mortifications he endeavored to work out his own Salvation through works. *"Oh when you become pious enough that you may have a Gracious God,"* he once cried. But he finally discovered the Truth that is at the basis of the Gospel: God is gracious and, therefore, wills to make man righteous. The Grace of a loving Father revealed in the Atoning Death of Christ is an element in Christianity which differentiates from all the religions of the world. Jesus Christ died on the

Cross paying the penalty for man's sins, which satisfied the Justice of God. On that basis, God forgives sin and makes one righteous, as that sinner exhibits Faith in this which the Lord has done.

SALVATION

Salvation is the Imputed Righteousness of God; it is not the imperfect righteousness of man. Salvation is a Divine Reconciliation; it is not a human regulation of any sort.

Salvation is the canceling of all sin; it is not the cessation from *some* sin. Salvation is being delivered from and being dead to the Law; it is not delighting in or doing the Law.

Salvation is Divine Regeneration; it is not human reformation. Salvation is being acceptable to God; it is not becoming exceptionally good. Salvation is completeness in Christ; it is not competency in character. Salvation is always and only of God; it is never of man (Chafer).

GRACE AS IT IS USED

Sometimes the word *"Grace"* is used in an inward sense, to denote the operation of Divine influence (Eph. 4:7), and the effect of the Divine influence (Acts 4:33; 11:23; II Cor. 12:9; James 4:6).

The operations of this aspect of Grace have been classified as follows:

1. *"Preventive Grace"* which literally means *"going before"* is the Divine influence preceding a person's conversion, exciting his efforts to return to God. It is the effect of God's favor in drawing men (Jn. 6:44) and striving with the disobedient (Acts 7:51).

2. It is sometimes called *"Effectual Grace"* in that it is effectual in introducing conversion, if not resisted (Jn. 5:40; Acts 7:51; 13:46).

3. *"Enabling Grace"* enables men to live rightly, to resist temptation and do their duty. Thus, we speak of praying for Grace to perform a difficult task.

4. *"Habitual Grace"* is the effect of the indwelling of the Spirit resulting in a life characterized by the Fruit of the Spirit (Gal. 5:22-23).

THE GROUND OF JUSTIFICATION

How can God treat a sinner as a righteous person?

NOTES

Answer: God provides him with Righteousness through Christ.

But is it just to give the title of *"good"* and *"righteous"* to one who has not earned it?

Answer: The Lord Jesus Christ has earned it for and on behalf of the sinner, that is the sinner who proclaims Faith in the Finished Work of Christ, who is then declared righteous *"through the Redemption that is in Christ Jesus."* Redemption means complete deliverance by a price paid.

Christ earned this Righteousness for us with His Atoning Death; *"Whom God hath set forth to be a propitiation through Faith in His Blood."* A propitiation is that which secures God's favor for the undeserving. Christ died in order to save us from God's righteous wrath and to secure His favor for us.

The Death and Resurrection of Christ represent the outward provision for man's Salvation; the term *"Justification"* has reference to the way in which the saving benefits of Christ's Death are made available for the individual; Faith is the means whereby the sinner lays hold of the benefits, i.e., *"the sinner simply believes in what Christ has done at the Cross and the Resurrection on his behalf."*

THE NEED OF RIGHTEOUSNESS

As the body needs clothing, so the soul needs character. As one must appear, socially speaking, before the world clothed in proper garments, so must man appear before God and Heaven clothed in the garment of a perfectly righteous character, which of course, on his own he cannot do (Rev. 3:4; 7:13-14; 19:8).

The sinner's garment (spiritually speaking) is defiled and tattered (Zech. 3:1-4), and were he to clothe himself in his own goodness and merits, and plead his own good deeds, even as most attempt to do, such are considered in the Eyes of God as *"filthy rags,"* which of course, God cannot accept (Isa. 64:6). It is like trying to pay a million dollar debt at the bank with a handful of waste paper.

Man's only hope is to have a Righteousness which God will accept — in fact, the *"Righteousness of God,"* which can be found only in Jesus Christ. Since man naturally lacks this Righteousness, it must be provided for him; it must be an imputed (freely given) Righteousness.

HOW THIS RIGHTEOUSNESS CAN BE OBTAINED

This Righteousness was purchased by Christ's substitutionary death (Isa. 53:5, 11; Rom. 4:6; 5:18-19; II Cor. 5:21). His Death was a perfect act of Righteousness because it satisfied the Law of God; it was also a perfect act of obedience. And all this was done on our behalf and placed to our credit. *"God accepts us as righteous in His sight only if we have the Righteousness of Christ, which refers to the Righteousness which Christ purchased with His Own Blood, which is imputed or freely given to us by our simply believing and trusting in what He did at the Cross and the Resurrection on our behalf."*

THE DOCTRINE OF IMPUTATION

The act by which God charges or reckons this Righteousness to our account is called *"imputation."*

Imputation is reckoning to a person the consequences of another's act; for example, the consequences of Adam's sin are reckoned to his descendants, which in fact, includes the entirety of the human race, and for all time. In other words, due to the fact that Adam carried in his loins the fountainhead of all humanity, for this was the manner in which God created man, his one sin not only imputed to him death, for the wages of sin is death, this death also was passed on (imputed) to the entirety of the human race who would ever be born.

As well, the consequences of all of this sin, which included every human being, were reckoned or imputed to Christ, and the consequences of Christ's obedience are also reckoned or imputed to the Believer. In effect, one might say that He wore our garment of sin, i.e., suffering the penalty for our sin, that we might wear His garment of Righteousness. He *"is made unto us Righteousness,"* meaning that we can have His Righteousness for which He paid such a price, if we will only have Faith in Him (I Cor. 1:30); He becomes the *"Lord our Righteousness,"* meaning that this is the only manner in which sinful man can find and obtain Righteousness, at least that which God will accept, which is the only kind that matters (Jer. 23:6).

NOTES

Christ expiated (settled our debt by paying its price) our guilt, satisfied the Law (the Law of God — the Ten Commandments), and became our Substitute, so that being united with Him by Faith, His death becomes our death, His Righteousness is our righteousness, His obedience is our obedience, and all because He was our Substitute.

God then accepts us not for anything in us, not for anything so imperfect as works (Rom. 3:28; Gal. 2:16) or merit, which in fact, most of the world attempts to offer to Him in one way or the other, but for the perfect all-sufficient Righteousness of Christ set to our account.

For Christ's sake, God treats the guilty man, when repentant and believing, as if he were righteous. Christ's merit is reckoned to him. That is what we mean by *"Justification by Faith,"* which means that a person is perfectly justified in the sight of God by simply having Faith in what Christ did at the Cross and the Resurrection. Christ's perfect Righteousness it transferred to the believing sinner.

AN EXAMPLE WHICH IS THE OPPOSITE OF THE RIGHTEOUSNESS OF CHRIST

I speak of Mother Teresa, the Catholic Nun who died some time back.

The whole world lauded her righteousness, all because of her *"good works."* She was held up as the perfect example of what ought to be, etc.

Of course, I know nothing of this lady's heart or her Faith in God. However, I do know, that if she depended on those works to save her, as noble as they might be, as sweeping as they might be, as extensive as they might be, that such will afford her, nor anyone else for that matter, no Salvation whatsoever. Such is an attempt to earn Righteousness from God, which of course, cannot be done. It is literally impossible. We might say it this way:

On the day this woman died, there were thousands of other people who died as well. Let's use one of these others as an example. Let's say that at least one of these thousands who died was a wife beater, a child molester, a drunk, etc. In other words, just about as bad as a person could have been. Of course, when we think of the things this individual has done, they are loathing and disgusting, as would be obvious.

However, if that man on his death bed, which incidentally is a very poor time to try to get right with God, but anyway, if in that terrible hour of dying, that man cried out to the Lord asking Him to have mercy on him, and he at that time placed his Faith in the Finished Work of Christ, which of course, he little understood, but still, if that is what happened, that man was instantly saved, and is now with the Lord Jesus Christ in Heaven. On the other hand, if Mother Teresa was, in fact, placing her trust in all the good works that she accomplished, and not in Christ Alone, Mother Teresa died lost, just as every other person has died lost who trusted other than that which Christ did at the Cross.

This which I have just said to be sure is hated by the world. In fact, they will not accept it because they will not admit they are so wicked and sinful, that they cannot save themselves, etc. Sadly and regrettably, much of the Church falls into the same category.

BUT DO NOT GOOD WORKS COUNT AT ALL?

As far as Salvation is concerned, they do not count at all. The Bible plainly says, *"For by Grace are ye saved through Faith* (Faith in what Christ did at the Cross and the Resurrection)*; and that not of yourselves* (meaning that man can do nothing to save himself as far as works are concerned)*: it is the Gift of God* (meaning Salvation is strictly a gift which cannot be earned in any manner)*: not of works* (meaning that anyone who attempts to be saved by works automatically disqualifies themselves)*, lest any man should boast"* (Eph. 2:8-9).

Now good works definitely do count as it regards our after-conversion experience. However, even then, such does not at all earn anything from God, for the simple reason that God has nothing for sale. Good works which should be carried out by all Christians after they are saved, are to be done strictly to glorify the Lord, and not at all to earn anything from God. Jesus plainly said, *"Let your light so shine before men* (the spiritual light we have after conversion)*, that they may see your good works, and glorify your Father which is in Heaven"* (Mat. 5:16). So, we have two sets of problems here:

1. Most in the world attempt to earn their Salvation in some way by their good works. In other words, most in the world keep some type of Brownie point system. They measure their so-called good works up beside their bad deeds, which always come out ahead of the bad deeds. Consequently, they think that because of these things they have done, or certain bad things they have not done, that this qualifies them for Salvation or as many put it, *"for whatever is out there after death."* The world doesn't want to admit that it is so evil, that it took the death of God's Only Son for mankind to be saved (Jn. 3:16). So, it brazenly submits its so-called good works to God, exactly as Cain did so long ago (Gen. 4:1-5). God always rejects this offering, even as He must. It simply is not sufficient to pay the price concerning the terrible debt of sin which man rightly owes to God.

2. Unfortunately, many, if not most, Christians also attempt to earn their Sanctification by works of some nature, after they are saved. While such efforts do not necessarily destroy their Salvation, it definitely does destroy their Sanctification, because once again, God cannot accept works of this nature and in this regard.

In fact, it is just as repugnant, just as sinful in the sight of God, for the Christian to attempt to earn his Sanctification, which all of us have tried to do at one time or the other, as it is for the sinner to try to earn his Salvation. But yet, that's where most Christians are.

Just as Salvation comes to the believing sinner, believing, that is, on the Finished Work of Christ, likewise does Sanctification come to the Believer. The Christian can no more earn his Sanctification than the sinner can earn his Salvation. Both come the same identical way, by our Faith being placed totally and completely, in what Jesus did at the Cross and the Resurrection.

REGENERATION

Back to the subject of Justification by Faith, and its grounds which is the Righteousness of Christ, the following question may arise in the mind of the thoughtful person:

The Justification that saves is something external, which means that it is a legal act carried out in Heaven upon the Faith of the sinner. In other words, it concerns the sinner's position; but is there no change, one might ask, in his spiritual condition?

We know that Justification by Faith affects one's standing before God, but what of his conduct? In other words, one might ask the question, *"Righteousness is imputed but is it also imparted"*? All of this great legal work is done in Heaven upon Faith, but what actually happens to the sinner on Earth? Is there an instant change in his or her life?

One can answer the question in this manner:

In Justification Christ is for us, but at the same time, he also comes into us, which is done through the Person, Office, and Ministry of the Holy Spirit (Jn. 14:16-20). Actually, one could probably say that imputation would dishonor the Law of God if it were not bound up with security for future Righteousness, i.e., *"Righteousness being not only a legal work regarding the sinner, but also a fact which changes the sinner in every way,"* i.e., *"to be Christlike."*

The answer to all of this is that Justifying Faith is the initial act of Christian life (that which happens immediately when one comes to Christ) and this initial act, as one's Faith is now alive, is followed by an inward spiritual change known as *"Regeneration."* Faith unites the Believer to the Living Christ and this union with the Author of Life results in a change of heart, i.e., *"a change in every respect."* The Scripture plainly says, *"If any man be in Christ, he is a new creature: old things are passed away; behold, all things are become new"* (II Cor. 5:17).

Righteousness is imputed in Justification and imparted in Regeneration. The Christ Who is for us becomes the Christ in us.

THE MEANING OF REGENERATION

The Doctrine of Regeneration must be considered in the context of man in sin (Jn. 3:6; Eph. 2:1-3, 5). The effects of sin on human nature are considered to be so serious that, without the New Birth, the sinner cannot see, let alone enter into, the Kingdom of God (Jn. 3:3, 5; I Cor. 2:6-16).

The initiative in Regeneration is ascribed to God, simply because man cannot initiate anything of this nature of himself, meaning that he cannot change himself (Jn. 1:13); this means that Regeneration must originate from above (Jn. 3:3, 7) which is done by the Holy Spirit (Jn. 3:5, 8).

The manner in which the terminology is used in the Scripture indicates that this single, initial act carries with it far-reaching effects, as in I John 2:29; 3:9; 4:7; 5:1, 4, 18.

The abiding results given in these Passages pertain to one doing Righteousness, not committing sin, loving one another, believing that Jesus is the Christ, and overcoming the world, i.e., *"the results of Regeneration."*

These results indicate that in spiritual matters man is not altogether passive. He is passive, in fact, as it regards the New Birth; God acts on him. But the result of such an act is far-reaching activity; he actively repents, and believes in Christ, and henceforth walks in newness of life (Rom. 6:3-5).

John 3:8 serves to warn us that there is much in this subject that is beyond our comprehension. Yet we must inquire what actually happens to the individual in the New Birth.

As it regards the results of Regeneration, the person is now differently controlled. Before the New Birth sin controlled the person and made him a rebel against God; now the Spirit controls him (or should) and directs him towards God. The regenerate man walks after the Spirit, lives in the Spirit, is led by the Spirit, and is commanded to be filled (controlled) with (by) the Spirit (Rom. 8:4, 9, 14; Eph. 5:18).

And yet, the Believer is not perfect; he has to grow and progress in the Lord (I Pet. 2:2), but in every department of his personality he is directed now towards God.

Consequently, we may define Regeneration as a drastic act on fallen human nature by the Holy Spirit, leading to a change in the person's whole outlook. He can now be described as a new man who seeks, finds, and follows God in Christ.

REGENERATION IN THE NATURAL SENSE

Medical science is looking closely at the *"genes"* of man, attempting to ascertain the possibility of wicked aberrations being found in that locality. In other words, they are attempting to ascertain by this method as to what causes individuals to do certain evil things, such as homosexuality, alcoholism, drug addiction, pathological lying, acute dishonesty, stealing, murder, etc. In fact, the list is almost endless.

For instance, they are attempting to find out if a person is a homosexual, or an alcoholic, etc., because they have an abnormal gene along with all the healthy genes. In other words, the alcoholic would have one type of abnormal gene, with the cleptomaniac having another type of abnormal gene, etc.

They are closer to the truth than they realize, but only close! The real question is:

What is it in man that makes the gene abnormal, that is, if in fact it is? Incidentally, *"genes"* are an element of the germ plasm that controls transmission of a hereditary character by specifying the structure of a particular protein or by controlling the function of other genetic material and that consists, therefore, of a specific sequence. In other words, the *"genes"* have to do with the personality, and character direction of an individual. So, the good Doctors think if they can in fact find that an abnormal gene is the cause of particular problems, they can alter the abnormal gene, they think, and, therefore, change the abnormal personality of the individual.

That would be correct if, in fact, man was only a physical being; however, he is also a spiritual being, which means something else altogether. The real question is: *"What is causing the abnormal gene to be the way it is, if in fact that is the case?"* Merely treating the physical part of man will not solve the problem as it regards spiritual direction. As well, denying that man is a spiritual being as well as a physical being, does not at all change the situation either. In fact, denial is one of Satan's greatest forms of deception. Denying that one is blind, however, does not at all alter the fact that he is blind, if in fact, he really is.

Actually, this is what makes the Word of God so different from the world. The Word of God is Truth, and Truth one might say, is reality, i.e., *"reality being as it really is."* Unconverted man has no Truth in him; consequently, he does not actually view things in the realm of reality, but always from the viewpoint of that which is crooked, unreal, hypocritical, a lie, that which is not correct or right.

The problem of humanity is not merely the problem of abnormal genes. The problem is an evil nature which man has as a result of the Fall in the Garden of Eden. In other words, Adam's sinful nature passed onto all his offspring, which includes me and you, and every other individual who has ever lived, with the exception of Jesus Christ, Who was not born by natural procreation (procreation being the sperm of a man being united with the egg of a woman, which produces a human offspring). Jesus was conceived as a result of a decree of the Holy Spirit. In other words, it was a miracle (Mat. 1:20-23).

A SPIRITUAL PROBLEM

Therefore, the problem in man is really not physical but rather spiritual. That's the reason that man must be *"born again"* before he can be straightened out (Jn. 3:3). In fact, there is no other way, despite all of man's efforts otherwise. So, it means that medical science will fail in this regard. In other words, they will not be able to alter man's aberrant condition by addressing themselves to abnormal genes, i.e., *"the physical."* Neither will they get what they desire, by cloning human beings, that is if they ever do so.

In fact, they will only be able to clone the physical appearance, and not at all the spirit and the soul, which really make up the human being. The sum total of man is more than the physical body and even the five senses. Man was originally created by God, *"spirit, soul, and body,"* in fact, in the Image of God (Gen. 1:26-27; I Thess. 5:23).

When a person is *"born again,"* the *"God nature"* or *"Christ nature,"* comes into the person, which is done so by the Power and Person of the Holy Spirit (Jn. 3:3-8). At that time he is *"regenerated"* (Titus 3:5), in other words, *"re-gened."* To be sure, this is the only manner in which a human being can be *"re-gened,"* which actually deals with the root of man's problem, which alone will solve the problem. Hence, upon being *"born again,"* i.e., *"re-gened,"* the former alcoholic is just that, *"a former alcoholic,"* meaning that he or she no longer now is that of which they once were. This applies for every other abnormality, aberration, sin, wickedness, or criminal activity of an individual.

That is the only answer for the human race, and in fact has always been the answer, and testifies to that fact through the conversation and change of untold millions of human beings. But yet, it seems that man, not satisfied with God's solution, Who is Jesus Christ and what He did at the Cross and the Resurrection, keeps attempting to assuage the problem in other ways, which is a fruitless effort, and always doomed to failure. God's Way is the only Way!

A LIVING FAITH

All of this great thing which God does for believing man, which changes his life, in effect, by giving him Eternal Life, is done exclusively through the vehicle of Faith. This is the Faith by which a person is actually justified and must of necessity be a *"Living Faith,"* in other words, a continuing Faith generated by the Holy Spirit, which has always as its object the Finished Work of Christ. Such a Living Faith will produce right living; it will be a *"Faith"* which worketh by Love (Gal. 5:6).

Moreover, wearing the Righteousness of Christ the Believer is called to live a life conformable to that character. *"For the fine linen* (a type) *is the Righteousness* (literally, *'righteous deeds'*) *of the Saints"* (Rev. 19:8). Real Salvation calls for a life of practical holiness. What would we think of a person who always wore white, clean garments but who never washed himself? Inconsistent, to say the least!

No less inconsistent would it be for a person to claim the Righteousness of Christ and yet live in a manner unworthy of that Righteousness. They who wear His Righteousness will be careful to purify themselves, even as He is pure (I Jn. 3:3).

THE MEANS OF JUSTIFICATION: FAITH

Since the Law of Moses cannot justify, man's only hope is for a *"Righteousness without the Law* (not an unlawful unrighteousness, or a religion that permits us to sin, but a change of position and condition)." This is the *"Righteousness of God,"* that is, a Righteousness which God imparts; and it is a gift because man lacks the power to develop it or work it out (Eph. 2:8-10).

But a gift must be accepted; how then is the Gift of Righteousness accepted? Or, in theological language: What is the instrument that appropriates the Righteousness of Christ for the sinner?

Answer: *"By the Faith of Jesus Christ."* Faith is the hand, so to speak, which takes what God offers. That Faith as the instrumental cause of Justification will be seen from the following Scriptures (Rom. 3:22; 4:11; 9:30; Phil. 3:9; Heb. 11:7).

WHAT DO WE MEAN BY FAITH?

To be brief, it refers to having Faith in Jesus Christ, and more particularly what He did at the Cross and the Resurrection on our behalf. In fact, He died on the Cross as a Sacrifice to God, which paid the terrible sin debt owed by man, a debt incidentally, which man could never pay.

This means that Jesus was not executed, but literally gave Himself up for an Offering to God on our behalf. In fact, this was the only Offering which God could accept. The wages of sin is death (Rom. 6:23); consequently, to pay those wages, a life had to be given, but it had to be a life which was perfect.

Man in no way could do this, so God became Man, and did for man what man could not do for himself. In other words, God in the Form of Jesus Christ, offered up His spotless Life and spotless Body as a Sacrifice to God, which God would accept, and, therefore, which paid the terrible sin debt — at least for all who will believe (Jn. 3:16).

In order to be saved, the sinner must believe this which we have stated, in other words that Jesus died for him. He may not understand much about it, and in fact, does not understand much about this great Sacrifice, but he nevertheless, must believe. This is absolutely imperative in what we mean by *"having Faith."*

When a person has Faith in this, the Finished Work of Christ, a work incidentally on behalf of sinners, God awards freely to the believing sinner all that Jesus did, which includes Justification, which means that he is now awarded a perfect Righteousness, and Eternal Life. Inasmuch, as the sinner is now clean, made that way by his Faith in the Precious Shed Blood of Jesus Christ on the Cross, the Holy Spirit now takes up abode in the heart and life of this individual. As stated, all of this is by Faith, as it can only be by Faith.

If God required other things, most of the human race would be left out in the cold. But He only requires Faith in that which He has done for us, and upon the exhibition of such Faith, grants to the person all that Jesus has done.

This goes not only for the sinner coming to Christ, but as well for the Christian in the realm of Sanctification, i.e., *"a life of Holiness and Righteousness."*

FAITH IN THE CROSS

All of this tells us that everything is in Christ and what He did. It means our Faith must be placed strictly in that and that alone. Upon such Faith, Christ's merits are communicated to the believing sinner as well as to the believing Christian. Such a means must be Divinely appointed, since it is to convey what God Himself and He Alone dispenses.

This means Faith — the one principle which God's Grace makes use of for restoring us to His Image and favor. Born in sin, and heir to misery, the soul needs an utter change, both within and without, both in God's sight and its own sight.

The change in God's sight is called *"Justification,"* and the inward spiritual change that follows is as stated, *"Regeneration"* which is done by the Holy Spirit. This Faith which is required, is awakened in man by the influence of the Holy Spirit, generally in connection with the Word of God.

Faith lays hold of God's Promise and appropriates Salvation. It leads the soul to rest on Christ as Saviour and the Sacrifice for sins, imparts peace to the conscience and the consoling hope of Heaven. Being living and spiritual, and filled with gratitude towards Christ, it abounds in good works of every kind — not to earn something from God as stated, but rather to glorify God.

GOD'S METHOD

Man had not a single thing wherewith to purchase His Justification. God could not lower His Standards to what man could offer; man could not measure up to God's Standards. So, God saved him on another basis altogether — the basis of Faith and Faith only, one might quickly add.

When Faith is exhibited in Christ, and more particularly in what Christ did at the Cross and His Resurrection, Grace is then automatically given by God, which means simply *"unmerited favor."* This free Grace is received by Faith, Faith in what Christ did at the Cross. In fact, it can be tendered in no other way. This means that all Grace that comes from God, can be given only through what Christ did at the Cross, and, therefore, if it received by man, can only be received by one's Faith in the Cross.

In fact, Grace is not an automatic thing, but is predicated altogether on the Cross of Christ. In other words, God extends Grace to man, which simply means that He gives all these good things to man, even though man in no way deserves them, all because of what Jesus did at the Cross. Consequently, if it is given in this manner, and it definitely is, then it can only be received in this manner, which means, our Faith in the Cross. This means that if a Believer has an erroneous conception of the Cross and what Christ did there, he will be somewhat confused on just about every other issue as well.

The Cross is always the foundation, the central point, the intersection of all things as it pertains to God and His relationship to man. Actually, there could be no relationship were it not for the Cross of Christ. This is what made everything possible, and if the Christian doesn't understand that, he will have a misunderstanding concerning all other things of the Lord as well.

In fact, Faith within itself has no merit, anymore than a beggar is to be commended for holding out his hand for a gift. This method strikes a blow at man's dignity, but as far as God is concerned, fallen man has no dignity; he has not the power to accumulate enough goodness to buy Salvation. *"By the deeds of the Law* (trying to do good things) *shall no flesh be justified"* (Rom. 3:20).

THE MODERN FAITH MESSAGE

The statement, *"There is no merit in Faith, anymore than a beggar is to be commended for holding out his hand for a gift,"* shoots down Scripturally most of the modern faith message. This message teaches that faith is a merit within itself, which, in effect, makes it the end of all things.

It can be boiled down to the fact, that the modern faith message does not have as its object the Cross of Christ, but something else entirely. In fact, this particular type of faith, which is no faith at all, at least that which God will recognize, is rather faith in oneself, or a faith in faith. In fact, it is no different than the faith the world has, and I might quickly add, has in abundance. But it's not Faith that saves, meaning that it's not Faith in God, irrespective of its claims.

The faith of that erroneous message makes faith itself the object, instead of the Cross of Christ. Anything, that has as its object anything other than the Cross is erroneous, unscriptural, and can never be recognized by God. That's the sin of the modern faith message. It eliminates the Cross, which eliminates Christ, which eliminates God, which eliminates His Plan for dying humanity. It makes man the object which was the prime sin of the Fall. In making man the object, it falls into the trap of Satan concerning superior knowledge.

Satan in his temptation, told Adam and Eve *"that in the day ye eat thereof, then your eyes shall be opened, and ye shall be as gods, knowing good and evil"* (Gen. 3:5). However, the knowledge they received, was not the knowledge they thought they would receive. True knowledge is always in God, and never in disobedience. In fact, due to the Fall, mankind lost the true knowledge of God, and, therefore, had only the *"lie"* on which to stand.

THEONOMY OR AUTONOMY

Theonomy refers to the Government of God, in other words, man looking solely to God for all sustenance, leading, and direction.

Autonomy is self-government meaning *"independent of God,"* which is man's problem.

In the Garden, Adam and Eve opted for self-government instead of God's Government. Consequently, that is the gist of man's problem.

To be sure, this is what the world without God actually does; however, it doesn't stop with the world, actually permeating the Church as well. In fact, Satan's greatest effort one might possibly say, is in the Church. He attempts to get the Believer to look to himself or others, rather than God and His Word.

The modern faith message does this. It is subtle, very subtle; however, if one examines this message closely, it is found that it centers up in self, despite all its Scriptural claims, which is the sin of *"autonomy,"* rather than being centered up in Christ and Him crucified. The Reader must understand this:

Any religion, any effort, any gospel, any theology, any doctrine, which leads man even the slightest away from the Cross, is never of God, but rather Satan's efforts to pervert the True Gospel of Jesus Christ. It is actually what Paul referred to as *"another Jesus,"* . . . *"another spirit,"* . . . and *"another gospel"* (II Cor. 11:4).

The modern faith message, although containing some truth as most error does, does not proclaim the Jesus of the Cross, or the Spirit Who leads men to the Cross, or the Gospel of the Cross, but to something else entirely. In fact, it repudiates the Cross, claiming something else entirely, and can be labeled as none other as Paul said, *"than enemies of the Cross of Christ."*

He then said, *"Whose end is destruction, whose God is their belly, and whose glory is in their shame, who mind earthly things"* (Phil. 3:18-19).

TWO DANGERS REMOVED

All of this means that the Doctrine of Justification by God's Grace, which can only come through the Cross, and can only be received by man's Faith in that Finished Work, removes two dangers:

1. First, the pride of self-righteousness and the pride of self-effort.

2. Second, the fear that one is too weak to *"make the grade."*

If Faith is not meritorious in itself, and it isn't, being simply the holding out of the hand for God's free Grace, then what gives it its power, and what guarantee does it offer that the one who has received the Gift will live a righteous life?

Faith is important and mighty because it unites the soul to Christ, and more particularly what Christ did at the Cross and the

Resurrection, and in that union is found the motive and power for a life of righteousness. Paul said, *"For as many of you as have been baptized into Christ* (baptized into His Death, not Water Baptism) *have put on Christ. And they that are Christ's have crucified the flesh with the affections and lusts"* (Gal. 3:27; 5:24).

Faith not only passively receives but also actively uses what God bestows. It is an affair from the heart (Prov. 4:23; Mat. 15:19; Rom. 10:9-10), which means it is not merely intellectual. To believe with the heart is to enlist all the emotions, affections, and desires in response to God's offer of Salvation.

Through Faith Christ dwells in the heart (Eph. 3:17). As well, Faith works by Love (the work of Faith) (Thess. 1:3); that is, it is an energetic principle as well as a receptive attitude. Faith is, therefore, a powerful motive to obedience and to every other good work.

Faith involves the will and is connected with all good choices and actions, for *"whatsoever is not of Faith is sin"* (Rom. 14:23). It includes the choice and pursuit of the Truth (II Thess. 2:12) and implies subjection to the Righteousness of God, which are all found in Christ and more particularly, in what He did at the Cross (Rom. 10:3).

FAITH AND WORKS

The following is Scriptural teaching concerning the relation between Faith and works. Faith is opposed to works when by works we mean good deeds upon which a person depends for Salvation, or for anything from God for that matter (Gal. 3:11). However, a living Faith will produce works (James 2:26), just as a living tree will produce fruit.

Faith is justified and approved by works (James 2:18) just as the soundness of the roots of a good fruit tree is indicated by its fruit. Faith is perfected in works (James 2:22), just as a flower is completed by its blossom. In brief, works are the result of Faith, the test of Faith, and the consummation of Faith, but never the cause of Faith, that always being the Word of God (Rom. 10:17).

A contradiction has been imagined between the teaching of Paul and that of James, one apparently teaching that a person is justified by Faith and the other that he is justified by works. Compare Romans 3:20 and James 2:14-26.

NOTES

However, there is no contradiction, inasmuch as the Holy Spirit inspired both writers, which means that a contradiction is impossible. An understanding of the sense in which these two men use these terms will quickly dispel the supposed difficulty. Paul is commending a living Faith which trusts God Alone; James is denouncing a dead, formal faith which is merely an intellectual assent.

Paul is rejecting the dead works of the Law, or works without Faith; James is commending the living works which show that Faith is real and vital. In other words, if a person truly has the God kind of Faith, he will also at the same time have proper works to substantiate that Faith. Nevertheless, works are never the cause of Faith, but rather Faith is always the cause of works.

The Justification spoken of by Paul refers to the beginning of the Christian life; while James uses the word in the sense of that life of obedience and holiness which is the outward evidence that a person is saved. Paul is combatting legalism or dependence upon works for Salvation; James is combatting antinomianism, or the teaching that it does not matter so much how one lives so long as he believes. Paul and James are not two soldiers opposed to each other; they are actually standing back to back facing enemies coming from opposite directions.

THE WORK OF THE HOLY SPIRIT

As we have said many times, everything that is done on this Earth by the Godhead, is done through the Work, Purpose, Office, and Ministry of the Holy Spirit. Even though the Godhead — God the Father, God the Son, and God the Holy Spirit — are Omnipresent, which means they are everywhere at the same time, still, in a technical sense, God the Father is in Heaven, with God the Son at His Right Side (Eph. 2:6). It is God the Holy Spirit Who is on Earth carrying out the great Plans of the Godhead, which in fact, has always been the case, with the exception of the time that Jesus was on this Earth regarding His Ministry of the Cross.

In the Work of the Holy Spirit as it regards the sinner, He begins as stated, with Regeneration.

THE NATURE OF REGENERATION

Regeneration is the Divine act which imparts to the penitent Believer the new and higher life in personal union with Christ.

However, this is a several step process, but which happens immediately upon the individual coming to Christ. In other words, the believing sinner thinks of his experience with Christ as simply being *"born again"*; however, several things take place when all of this happens, which comes under the heading of Regeneration.

Let's look at these steps one by one:

A BIRTH

God the Father is He *"Who begat,"* which means that the Believer is *"begotten of God"* (I Jn. 5:1), *"born of the Spirit"* (Jn. 3:8), and *"born from above"* (the literal translation of Jn. 3:7). These terms refer to the act of creative Grace which makes the Believer a Child of God.

In effect, this is what Jesus was talking about when He told Nicodemus, *"Except a man be born again, he cannot see the Kingdom of God"* (Jn. 3:3). This means that the work is totally spiritual, and comes from above. It is not brought about by joining a Church, shaking a Preacher's hand, or becoming religious, etc. It is entered into by Faith, as the believing sinner places his trust in Jesus Christ and what He did at the Cross.

So, Salvation is really wrapped up into a Person, The Lord Jesus Christ, which means that it is not a religion or a philosophy.

A CLEANSING

God saved us by the *"washing* (literally, laver or bath) *of Regeneration"* (Titus 3:5).

To properly understand this *"cleansing"* we have to go back to the Brazen Laver of Old Testament times, which sat immediately in front of the Tabernacle or Temple. In effect, it was a type of the Word of God (Ex. 30:17-21).

The Priests had to wash both their hands and their feet every time they went into the Holy Place of the Tabernacle. As stated, this large vessel filled with water was a type of the Word of God. As the Priests could see their reflection in the water, likewise we see ourselves in the Word of God. As the application of the water cleansed the Priests, likewise we are cleansed by the Word.

This means, that all that God does for the believing sinner and the Christian for that matter, is all done through His Word. In other words, the sinner is saved because in some measure he believes the Word of God, at least the portion he has heard. As well, it will be the same for him as long as he lives, everything will come to him by the Word of God.

At the time of conversion, the soul is completely bathed, one might say, from the defilements of the old life and made to live in newness of life, which continues, as stated, all the days of the Believer's life.

A QUICKENING

We were saved not only by the *"washing of Regeneration"* but also by *"the renewing of the Holy Spirit"* (Ps. 51:10; Rom. 12:2; Eph. 4:23; Col. 3:10; Titus 3:5). This plainly tells us that the Holy Spirit, as stated, is the One Who affects these things.

The essence of Regeneration is a new life imparted by God the Father, which is mediated through Christ, meaning that He acts as the go-between simply because He is the One Who paid the price for man's Redemption, which is all done by the operation of the Holy Spirit.

Consequently, we see the work of the entirety of the Trinity carried out as it regards our Salvation.

A CREATION

He Who created man in the beginning and breathed into his nostrils the breath of life, recreates him by the operation of His Holy Spirit (Gen. 2:7; II Cor. 5:17; Gal. 6:15; Eph. 2:10; 4:24).

The practical results is a radical change in the individual's nature, character, desires, and purposes.

Upon the statement made by Christ to Nicodemus as to how the Born-Again experience takes place in the life of the individual, and done so by the Spirit, it was obvious that the Pharisee did not understand. Jesus then said, *"The wind blows where it desires, and you hear the sound thereof, but cannot tell from where it comes, and where it goes: so is every one who is born of the Spirit"* (Jn. 3:7-8).

The idea is, all of this is a spiritual work, and even though we can certainly feel the effects which evidence themselves in our changed lives, due to the fact that it is spiritual which means that it originates from above, our understanding is naturally limited as to how the Holy Spirit does all of this; however, the miraculous change definitely is obvious which guarantees that it has been done, in other words a creation has taken place, even though our understanding is necessarily limited.

A RESURRECTION

As God quickened the lifeless clay and made it alive to the physical world originally, so He quickens a soul dead in sins and makes it alive to the realities of the spiritual world. One might even say that this is an act of resurrection from spiritual death to Spiritual Life, and is symbolized in Water Baptism (Rom. 6:4-5; Eph. 2:5-6; Col. 2:13; 3:1).

Regeneration is *"that great change which God works in the soul when He brings it into life; when He raises it from the death of sin to the Life of Righteousness."*

It will be noticed that the above terms are simply variants of one great basic thought of Regeneration, namely, the Divine impartation of a new life to the soul of man. And three Scientific facts true of natural life also apply to Spiritual Life, namely, that it comes *suddenly*, appears *mysteriously*, and develops *progressively*.

Regeneration is a unique feature in the New Testament experience. In heathen religions the permanence of character is universally recognized. Though these religions prescribe penances and rituals whereby man may hope to atone for his sins, there is no promise of Life and Grace to transform his nature. The Salvation of Jesus Christ *"is the only Salvation which professes to take man's fallen nature and regenerate it by bringing into it the Life of God."* And it professes to do this because Christianity's Founder is a Living, Divine Person, Who lives to save to the uttermost.

CHRISTIANITY AND THE RELIGIONS OF THE WORLD

There is no analogy between the Christian experience and, say, Buddhism or the religion of Mohammed. There is no true sense in which a man can say, *"He that hath Buddha hath life"* (I Jn. 5:12).

He may have something to do in some minor way with morality. He may stimulate, impress, teach, and guide in a sense, but there is no distinctly new thing added to the souls who profess Buddhism, or any other religion. These religions may be developments of the natural and moral man, but Christianity professes to be more, much more!

It is the mental or moral man plus something else or Some One else, Who is Jesus.

The difference is, Jesus Christ is God, whereas these other individuals are merely human; consequently, as a human and only a human, they are in need of Redemption themselves, so how can they help anyone else?

THE NECESSITY FOR REGENERATION

Our Lord's interview with Nicodemus (Jn. Chpt. 3), to which we have already briefly alluded, provides a fine background for the study of the above topic. Nicodemus' opening words reveal a number of emotions struggling in his heart; and our Lord's abrupt statement, which seems to be a sudden changing of the subject, is explained by the fact He answered the heart rather than the words of the lips of this seeking soul. Nicodemus' opening words reveal the following:

1. His searching reveals spiritual hunger. Had the ruler put into words the desire of his soul, he might have said: *"I am tired of the lifeless services of the Synagogue; I attend, but leave as hungry as I enter. Alas, the glory has departed from Israel; there is no vision and the people perish. Master, my soul is hungry for reality! I know little concerning You Personally, but Your words have touched a deep place in my heart. Your miracles convince me that You are a God-sent Teacher. I would like to join your company."*

2. Despite the spiritual hunger, there is a lack of depth of conviction in this ruler's heart. Nicodemus feels his need, but it is a need of a *Teacher* rather than of a *"Saviour."* Like the Samaritan woman, he wants the Water of Life (Jn. 4:15), but like her, he must realize that he is a sinner needing cleansing and transforming, that is if he is to satisfy the thirst of his heart (Jn. 4:16-18).

3. One detects in his words a touch of self-complacency, natural in a man of his age and position.

If he had spoken the totality of his heart to Christ, he might have said the following: *"I believe that you are sent to restore the Kingdom to Israel, and I am come to advise you on Your plan of operation and to urge upon you certain lines of action."*

Very likely he took it for granted that being an Israelite and a son of Abraham would be sufficient qualifications for becoming a member of the Kingdom of God. In other words, in his mind, he was already a member of that Kingdom.

THE ANSWER AS GIVEN BY CHRIST

"Jesus answered and said unto him, 'Truthfully, truthfully, I say unto you, except a man be born again, he cannot see the Kingdom of God.'"

To paraphrase these words: *"Nicodemus, you cannot join My company as one would join an organization. Whether you belong to My company or not depends on a transformation taking place in your life; My cause is none other than that of the Kingdom of God, and you cannot enter without a spiritual change. The Kingdom of God is quite another thing than you are thinking of, and the way to establish it, enlist citizens in it, is very different from the way upon which you have been thinking."*

Jesus pointed out the deepest and universal need of all men — a radical, out-and-out change of the whole nature and character. Man's entire nature has been warped by sin, the heritage of the Fall, and that warp and twist is reflected in his individual conduct and his various relationships. Before he can live a life pleasing to God, in time and eternity, his nature must undergo a change so radical that it is actually a second birth. Man cannot change himself; the transformation must come from above.

Jesus did not attempt to explain the *how* of the New Birth, but He did explain the *why* of the matter. *"That which is born of the flesh is flesh, and that which is born of the Spirit is spirit."* Flesh and spirit belong to different realms, and one cannot produce the other; human nature can generate human nature, but only the Holy Spirit can generate a spiritual nature.

Human nature can produce only human nature, and no creature can rise beyond its own nature. Spiritual Life does not descend from father to child by way of natural generation; it descends from God to man by way of spiritual generation.

Consequently, Nicodemus being a natural, physical descendant of Abraham effected no spiritual change in him as he erroneously thought.

HUMAN NATURE

Human nature cannot rise above itself. Writes Marcus Dods: *"Every creature has a certain nature according to its kind and determined by its parentage. This nature which the animal receives from its parents determines from the first the capabilities and sphere of the animal's life. The mole cannot soar in the face of the Sun like the Eagle; neither can the bird that comes from the Eagle's egg burrow like the mole. No training can possibly make the tortoise as swift as the antelope, or the antelope as strong as the lion . . . beyond its nature no animal can act."*

The same principle may be applied to man. Man's highest destiny is to live with God forever; but human nature in its present condition does not possess the capacities for living in a Heavenly Kingdom; therefore, heavenly life must come down from above to transform it for membership in that Kingdom.

THE MEANS OF REGENERATION

First of all we must look at the Divine Agency from which Regeneration springs.

The Holy Spirit is the Special Agent in Regeneration, even as we have already said, Who so acts upon a person to produce the change (Jn. 3:6; Titus 3:5). However, each Person of the Trinity is involved. Indeed, the Three Persons are involved in every Divine operation, although each Person has certain Offices which are His in a special sense. Thus, the Father is preeminently the Creator, yet Both the Son and the Spirit are also mentioned as Agents. The Father begets (James 1:18) and throughout the Gospel according to John, the Son is set forth as the Life-Giver

(Jn. Chpts. 5-6), through which the Holy Spirit works.

Note especially Christ's relation to man's Regeneration. He is the Giver of Life. And how does He bring life to men?

By dying for us, so that we by eating His Flesh and drinking His Blood, which actually means to believe in His Atoning Death, may have Eternal Life. How does He actually impart Life to men?

Part of His reward, as it regarded His Atoning Work at the Cross, was the prerogative of imparting the Holy Spirit (Mat. 3:11; Jn. 3:3, 13; Gal. 3:13-14), and He ascended after His Resurrection in order to become the Source of Spiritual Life (Jn. 6:62) and Energy (Acts 2:33).

The Father has Life in Himself (Jn. 5:26); so He gives the Son to have life in Himself; the Father is the Source of the Holy Spirit, but He gives the Son the Power to impart the Spirit; thus the Son is a *"quickening Spirit"* (I Cor. 15:45), having power not only to raise the physically dead (Jn. 5:25-26), but also to quicken the dead souls of men (Gen. 2:7; Jn. 20:22; I Cor. 15:45).

HUMAN PREPARATION

Strictly speaking, man cannot co-operate in the act of Regeneration, which in fact, is the sovereign act of God; but he has part in the *preparation* for the New Birth.

What is that preparation?

It is repentance and faith. Paul plainly said, *"repentance toward God, and faith toward our Lord Jesus Christ"* (Acts 20:21).

Man has sinned against God, and, therefore, he must repent, which means to turn around from his previous way of sin and rebellion.

At the same time, he must exhibit faith toward the Lord Jesus Christ as it regards Salvation or anything else for that matter, because it is Christ Who has paid the price for man's Redemption.

THE EFFECTS OF REGENERATION

We may group them under three heads: *"positional* (adoption)"; *"spiritual* (union with God)"; *"practical* (righteous living)."

The idea that the only difference in the saved and the unsaved is the Blood of Jesus is grossly inaccurate.

NOTES

While the Blood of Jesus spiritually speaking, is definitely applied to the sinner seeking Christ, which cleanses him from all sin, this will play out to a changed life. In fact, the *"changed life"* is the hallmark of Christianity, and what makes Christianity so different than the religions of the world.

These religions can change nothing, because they deal altogether from the external, while Jesus deals first of all with the internal, where He changes the wicked heart of man, which has an outside effect of Righteousness. In fact, if this outside effect is not realized, even though it will be a process, to which we will address ourselves momentarily, the truth is, the individual has really not been saved.

POSITIONAL

The first effect of Regeneration is the new position of the believing sinner upon Faith in Christ.

When a person has undergone the spiritual change known as Regeneration He becomes a Child of God, and does so instantly, and is a beneficiary of all the privileges of that Sonship.

In Truth, the Believer as it regards Regeneration, is adopted into the Family of God (Rom. 8:15). The word *"adoption"* means literally *"the giving of the position of sons"* and refers in ordinary usage to a man's taking into his household children not born to him.

Doctrinally, Adoption and Regeneration should be distinguished: the first is a legal term indicating the imparting of the privilege of Sonship to one who is not a member of a family; the second denotes the inner spiritual change that makes one a Child of God, and a partaker of the Divine nature. However, it is difficult to separate the two in regard to experience, for Regeneration and Adoption represent the twofold experience of Sonship.

In the New Testament the common Sonship is sometimes defined by the term *"sons"* which word lies at the root of the word *"adoption,"* and sometimes by the word *"children,"* which means literally, *"begotten ones,"* and which implies regeneration.

The two ideas are distinguished yet combined in the following Verses:

"But as many as received Him, to them gave He power (implying adoption) *to become*

the Sons of God . . . Which were born . . . of God"* (Jn. 1:12-13).

"Behold, what manner of love the Father hath bestowed upon us, that we should be called (implying adoption) *the Sons of God* (the word used for those born of God)" (I Jn. 3:1).

In Romans 8:15-16, the two ideas are blended:

"For you have not received the spirit of bondage again to fear; but you have received the Spirit of Adoption, whereby we cry, Abba Father. The Spirit Himself bears witness with our spirit, that we are the Children of God."

SPIRITUAL

Because of its very nature Regeneration involves spiritual union with God and with Christ through the Holy Spirit; and this spiritual union involves a Divine indwelling (II Cor. 6:16-18; Gal. 2:20; 4:5-6; I Jn. 3:24; 4:13).

This union results in a new type of life and character, described in various ways:

Newness of life (Rom. 6:4); a new heart (Ezek. 36:26); a new spirit (Ezek. 11:19); the new man (Eph. 4:24); partakers of the Divine nature (II Pet. 1:4). The Believer's duty is to maintain his contact with God through the various means of Grace and so preserve and nourish his spiritual life.

PRACTICAL

The person born of God will demonstrate that fact by his hatred of sin (I Jn. 3:9; 5:18), righteous deeds (I Jn. 2:29), brotherly love (I Jn. 4:7) and victory over the world, the flesh, and the Devil (I Jn. 5:4).

Two extremes should be avoided:

First, making the standard too low so that Regeneration becomes a matter of natural reformation; second, raising the standard too high and failing to make allowance for the frailties of Believers.

Young converts, when learning to walk in Christ may stumble — like a baby learning to walk; older Believers also may be overtaken in a fault.

John declares that it is utterly inconsistent, however, that one born of God and bearing the Divine nature should live habitually in sin (I Jn. 3:9), yet he is careful to write as the Holy Spirit guided him, *"If any man sin,*

we have an Advocate with the Father, Jesus Christ the Righteous" (I Jn. 2:1).

SANCTIFICATION

In studying Sanctification, which of course is a part of Salvation, we must of necessity study the nature of Sanctification.

In studying the meaning of the New Testament Doctrine of Atonement, we have to go to the Old Testament Sacrificial Ritual. In like manner we shall reach the meaning of the New Testament Doctrine of Sanctification by a study of the Old Testament usage of the word *"holy,"* which has to do with Sanctification.

At the outset let it be observed that *"Sanctification,"* *"Holiness,"* *"Consecration"* are synonymous terms; in other words, they all mean the same. This means that *"sanctified"* and *"holy"* have the same meaning; to sanctify is the same as to make holy or to consecrate. The word *"holy"* or *"sanctify"* conveys the following ideas:

SEPARATION

"Holy" is a word descriptive of the Divine nature. Its root meaning is *"separation"*; therefore, Holiness represents that in God which makes Him separate from all that is earthly and human — namely, His absolute moral perfection and Divine Majesty.

When the Holy One wills to use a person or object in His service, He separates him or it from common use, and by virtue of this separation the person or object becomes *"holy."*

DEDICATION

Sanctification includes both a separation *from* and a dedication *to*; it is *"the condition of Believers as they are separated from sin and the world and made partakers of the Divine nature, and consecrated to the fellowship and service of God through the Mediator, the Lord Jesus Christ."*

The word *"holy"* is used mainly in connection with worship. When applied to men or things it expresses the thought that they are used in God's service and dedicated to Him, in a special sense His property. Israel is a holy nation because dedicated to the service of Jehovah; the Levites are holy because specially dedicated to the services of the Tabernacle; the Sabbath and Feast days are holy because they represent the dedication or consecration of time to God.

PURIFICATION

While the primary meaning of holy is that of separation to service, the idea of purification is also involved. Jehovah's character reacted upon whatever was devoted to Him. Hence, men dedicated to Him must share His nature. Things devoted to Him must be clean. Cleanliness, and we speak of spiritual cleanliness, is a condition of holiness, but not the holiness itself, which is primarily separation and dedication.

When Jehovah selects and separates a person or object for His service, He does something or causes it to be done, which constitutes the person or object holy. Inanimate objects (furniture, buildings, or instruments) were consecrated by being anointed with oil (Ex. 40:9-11).

The Israelitish nation was sanctified by the Blood of a Covenant Sacrifice (Ex. 24:8; Heb. 10:29). The Priests were sanctified by Jehovah's representative, Moses, who washed them with water, and anointed them with oil and sprinkled them with the Blood of consecration (Lev. Chpt. 8).

As Old Testament Sacrifices were typical of the One Sacrifice of Jesus Christ, so the various washings and anointings of the Mosaic system were typical of the real Sanctification made possible through the Work of Christ. Thus, as Israel was sanctified by the Blood of the Covenant so *"Jesus also, that He might sanctify the people with His Own Blood, suffered without the gate* (was crucified)*"* (Heb. 13:12).

Jehovah sanctified the sons of Aaron to the Priesthood through the mediation of Moses and by means of water, oil, and blood. God the Father (I Thess. 5:23) sanctifies Believers to spiritual Priesthood (I Pet. 2:5) through the mediation of the Son (I Cor. 1:2, 30; Eph. 5:26; Heb. 2:11), and by means of the Word (Jn. 15:3; 17:17), the Blood (Heb. 10:29; 13:12), and the Spirit (Rom. 15:16; I Cor. 6:11; I Pet. 1:2).

CONSECRATION

What is the difference between Righteousness and Holiness?

Righteousness represents the regenerate life as conformed to the Divine Law;

What does that mean, especially considering that the Christian, due to what Christ did at the Cross and the Resurrection, is now dead to the law? (Rom. 7:4).

The ancient Law of Moses was God's moral Standard of Righteousness. To be sure, that Standard, inasmuch as it deals with morals, cannot change. In other words, the same demands that God made in the Law some 3600 years ago, He requires presently. As well, that Standard is for the entirety of the world, and in fact, always has been.

The manner in which the Christian keeps the Law, is by the Christian's position *"in Christ."* Christ fully kept the Law in every respect, and did so on our behalf. As well, He suffered the penalty of the broken Law, which lifted the sin debt from our hearts and lives, at least to those who will believe (Jn. 3:16). So, in Christ, I am now a Law-keeper, and as such, walk in Righteousness and Holiness.

However, all of this is done, not at all by my own machinations, ability, or personal strength, but rather altogether in Christ. In other words, as long as I understand my position in Christ according to His Death, Resurrection, and Exaltation, and that all of this was done solely and completely for me, and I keep my trust and faith in that and not at all in myself, and do so even on a daily basis (Lk. 9:23), I will continue to be a Law-keeper and walk in Righteousness and Holiness. However, that needs a little more explanation.

I am not all of this because I have the Law before me constantly, and am struggling constantly to keep its precepts. As a Believer such never enters my mind, simply because I am in Christ. Therefore, whatever Christ is, that's what I am.

OVERCOMING VICTORY

The catch is this!

My everyday victory and everyday overcoming strength as it regards the world, the flesh, and the Devil, are not mine because of my personal effort. In fact, the moment I begin to exert personal effort to try to *"keep the Law,"* or *"be holy,"* etc., I am going to fail every time. Actually, the moment I try to have victory, or try to be an overcomer, the results will always be the very opposite of what I am attempting to bring about. The reason is according to the following:

When I try to do these things, I am, in effect, trying to do something that Christ has already done, which can never be sanctioned by the Holy Spirit. In other words, my efforts in this respect, as noble as they might be, deprive me of the help of the Holy Spirit, which guarantees failure on my part. The reason is simple, in that capacity I am *"walking after the flesh,"* which is guaranteed of failure (Rom. 8:1), which means I am not trusting in the Finished Work of Christ.

The Truth is, I am already victorious in Christ, I am already an overcomer in Christ. He has already fought all of these battles and won every one of them in totality. In other words, in this Finished Work of Christ, there is nothing else to be done. It was all done for me, and my being in Christ, and understanding that, acting upon that, continuing to have faith in that on a daily basis, even as we have already said, guarantees me the victory and the overcoming strength which Christ has already brought about on my behalf. The only requirement is for me to continue to have Faith in the Cross and the Resurrection, which will always guarantee the help of the Holy Spirit (Rom. 8:2). That's the way to be *"righteous and holy,"* and in fact, the only way to be Righteous and Holy, and because in Him we are already Righteous and Holy.

WHAT YOU THE BELIEVER SHOULD BEGIN TO DO RIGHT NOW

It is very difficult for us to consider ourselves as *"Righteous and Holy,"* when there is failure in our lives. We can't see the victory for ourselves; however, if the Believer's thinking remains in this capacity, the failure will continue. In fact, it cannot do otherwise.

You as a Believer must begin this walk of victory, by looking away from yourself, away from your failures, away from all the stumblings of the past, and now begin to look to Jesus.

You must do exactly as Paul said about this very thing, *"Likewise reckon* (count) *ye also yourselves to be dead indeed unto sin, but alive unto God through Jesus Christ our Lord"* (Rom. 6:11).

NOTES

I realize it's difficult to consider oneself as *"dead unto sin,"* when it seems like the very opposite is true. However, you as a Believer are never going to get out of this quicksand until you get your eyes off your own failures, and begin looking toward the victories of Christ. In Christ you are right now an overcomer, you are right now victorious. Whether you feel like it or not, whether in fact you are or not as it regards your personal action, you are to look at yourself as being victorious, because in Christ that is really the Truth. I'm trying to say that you'll never get out of this problem of failure until you begin to exercise faith in what Christ has already done, which He did exclusively for you and not at all for Himself, and considering the terrible price He paid, one should certainly realize that He wants us to have all the benefits of this great victory that He purchased with His Own Blood at the Cross.

Once you start seeing yourself in this capacity, a capacity of victory, a capacity of overcoming power and strength, and you start confessing that, having faith in that, believing that, and because it is actually true, you will then start conducting yourself, and in fact, being exactly what you actually are in Christ. In other words, the failure will cease.

THAT WHICH THE LORD SHOWED ME

For about five years I sought the Lord earnestly for the answer to this dilemma. To be sure, I berate myself that the answer did not come sooner, but thank the Lord in God's Grace and Mercy it did come. And when the answer came, I began to see many things in a different way.

First of all, I see the Cross of Christ now in the entirety of the Bible. It fits like it has never fit before. I see the Cross as the center piece of the Word of God, the intersection, the dividing line of all things. I see the entirety of the Old Testament as pointing toward Christ, but more particularly, pointing toward what He did at the Cross and the Resurrection on our behalf. The Reader must understand, that the Cross was not just an incidental thing which happened in the Life and Ministry of Christ.

Peter said in His Message on the Day of Pentecost, *"Him* (Jesus), *being delivered by the determinate counsel and foreknowledge of God,"* means that the Cross was the Plan Of God from the very beginning (Acts 2:23).

Peter further said, *"Forasmuch as ye know that ye were not redeemed with corruptible things, as silver and gold . . . But with the Precious Blood of Christ, as of a Lamb without blemish and without spot: Who verily was foreordained before the foundation of the world"* (I Pet. 1:18-20). This plainly tells us, that the Cross of Christ as it regards the redemption of mankind, was planned in the Mind of God, even before *"the foundation of the world."*

So, as I have stated, the Cross was not an incidental thing, but rather the very centerpiece, the very intersection, the very foundation on which all things are built as it regards the Redemption of mankind.

The Lord showed me that my Faith must be in that Finished Work at all times. To be frank, the great problem with most of Christianity is *"misplaced Faith."* In other words, the object of their Faith is not correct.

In fact, beginning approximately in the 1960's the Church began to be taught the message of Faith perhaps as it had never been taught before; however, for the most part, it was misplaced Faith, and the proof of that is in the fruit that it has brought forth.

MISPLACED FAITH

The modern so-called Faith message has pretty well degenerated into what is presently referred to as the *"prosperity gospel,"* which in reality is no prosperity at all, at least in the Lord. In other words, thousands of pulpits are busy telling their listeners how to get rich. That is a sad spectacle, but that's where the modern faith message is by and large.

The main reason for this is because the proper object of Faith, which at all times must be the Finished Work of Christ, i.e., *"the Cross,"* was not taught, but rather something else altogether. In fact, in all the countless tapes that I have heard in the past regarding this subject and the books read, I do not recall one single time reading or hearing the teachers speak about the correct object of Faith being the Cross, but always something else. In fact, much of the so-called faith message presently denigrates the Cross, concluding it to be nothing more than *"past miseries,"* as I quote one of their bright lights. To be sure, this is close to blasphemy!

People are taught to have Faith in themselves, Faith in their own Faith, but more than all, Faith in the Word. The latter part seems to be right, and in fact, would be right were the Word properly interpreted. However, it is not properly interpreted, but most of the time pulled completely out of context and actually perverted.

The Reader must always understand, that the Word of God in its entirety, every Promise, every statement, every plan, every prophecy, are all anchored totally and completely in the Cross of Christ, i.e., *"The Finished Work of Christ."* In other words, if the Words of the Master, *"Therefore I say unto you, what things soever ye desire, when ye pray, believe that ye receive them, and ye shall have them,"* are not anchored firmly in the Cross, perversion will then result. One of the oldest tricks of Satan there is, is to wrest the Word of God from its proper setting, which was actually the sin of Adam and Eve which resulted in the Fall. In fact, all of the temptation of Christ in the wilderness, had at its base foundation an effort by the Evil One to get Christ to sidestep the Cross.

THE TEMPTATION OF CHRIST

The temptation to turn the stones to bread, was not only a temptation to get Jesus to use His great power solely for Himself, thereby stepping outside of the revealed Will of God, but at its foundation, was an attempt to shift the great Message of Christ into materialism — the exact position that much of the Charismatic Church World is in presently.

The answer, *"Man shall not live by bread alone, but by every word that proceedeth out of the Mouth of God,"* must be understood as to exactly what that Word is (Mat. 4:1-4).

Even though it has many nuances, the entirety of the Word of God can be reduced down to the words of Paul as given to him by the Holy Spirit, *"This is a faithful saying, and worthy of all acceptation, that Christ Jesus came into the world to save sinners; of whom I am chief"* (I Tim. 1:15).

That was and is the great purpose of Christ, in fact, the entirety of the Plan of

God, which addresses the real problem of humanity. So, that *"Word"* is, in effect, *"the Cross!"* Unfortunately, Satan has succeeded in getting much of the Church to make other things the emphasis, such as faith for money, etc. I hope the Reader can see what a travesty is such a direction.

The second temptation of Christ concerned Him jumping from the *"pinnacle of the temple,"* thereby making a grand, miraculous entrance, which would impress the Priesthood, and Israel in general.

Once again, this was an effort by Satan to get Jesus to divert His Message to that of the sensational or spectacular, which in reality would have done no one any good whatsoever.

This means that while God is definitely a miracle worker, definitely able to do all things, the primary Message of the Church is never to be the side issues, but always the salvation of souls and victory over sin in every capacity.

The business of Christ in coming to this world was not to razzle-dazzle mankind with the supernatural, but rather to save sinners. If the mission of the Church deviates from that, it has failed in its mission, and is actually *"tempting God."*

Regrettably at this very moment, giant coliseums are being filled to capacity with Christians who are little there to see souls saved and lives changed, but rather to see something they think is the Power of God, but in reality is not the Power of God, but something else entirely. Sadly, there is so little discernment that most do not know the difference. These things lead people away from the Cross instead of toward the Cross, which is their only answer. In fact, anything in the realm of that which purports to be gospel, but does not center up in the Cross, falls out to *"tempting God"* (Mat. 4:7).

The last temptation concerned Jesus being given the kingdoms of the world by Satan, if He would only fall down and worship the Evil One.

Actually, Satan wasn't really trying to get Jesus to bend His knee to him, but rather to get these kingdoms without going to the Cross. That was the whole plan of Satan (Mat. 4:8-10).

The answer was clear and concise and to the point, *"Thou shall worship the Lord thy God, and Him only shalt thou serve"* (Mat. 4:10).

And last of all, if the Lord is not worshipped in the realm of the Cross, in other words, from the principle of the Cross, it is worship which God cannot accept.

Whenever the Priests of old went into the Holy Place of the Tabernacle or Temple, they were to go in with their Censers containing coals of fire from the Brazen Altar, which was a type of the Cross of Christ, with particular Incense poured over those coals, which filled the Holy Place with smoke. All of this was worship, and all of it was predicated solely on the Cross of Christ, which should be obvious.

The point I am attempting to make is, that it is not possible to properly worship the Lord, unless it's done strictly from the position of what Jesus did at the Cross and the Resurrection. God cannot receive man in any other fashion, only by the principle of the shed blood of the Lamb. We must never forget that, but I am concerned that in fact we are forgetting that.

So, the object of our Faith must always be the Cross, and in that capacity, and in that capacity alone, the Holy Spirit will help us in all things.

The Lord also showed me, that the Holy Spirit will not work in any other manner. In other words, even though the Holy Spirit abides in the heart and life of every Christian, if in fact, our Faith is in directions other than the Cross of Christ, that is faith which He cannot honor. Consequently, failure is going to be the result in our lives. The Believer must have the help of the Holy Spirit in all things, and that help is forthcoming only according to our Faith in the Cross (Rom. 8:2).

CONFORMED TO THE DIVINE NATURE

Holiness is to be the regenerate life as conformed to the Divine Nature and dedicated to the Divine Service; and this calls for the removal of any defilement which would hinder that service.

"But as He which hath called you is holy, so be ye holy in all manner of conversation" (I Pet. 1:15). Thus, Sanctification includes the removal of the spot or defilement which is contrary to the Holiness of the Divine

Nature, which can only be done according to our Faith in the Cross and what Jesus did there.

Following Israel's consecration the question would naturally arise, how should a holy people live?

In order to answer this question, God gave them the code of holiness laws which are found in the Book of Leviticus. Thus, from Israel's consecration followed the obligation to live a holy life. The same is presently true of the Christian.

Those who are declared to be sanctified (Heb. 10:10) are exhorted to follow holiness (Heb. 12:14), in fact, which is the business of the Holy Spirit to bring about in our hearts and lives, which He can do only as we put our Faith in the Cross, and leave our Faith in the Cross.

As well, those who have been cleansed (I Cor. 6:11) are exhorted to cleanse themselves (II Cor. 7:1), which in effect, is done in a sense by our Faith in the Cross, which in essence can be done in no other manner.

SERVICE

The Covenant is a state of relationship with God and men in which He is their God and they are His people, which means His worshipping people. The word *"holy"* expresses this Covenant relationship. To serve God in this relationship in essence is to be a Priest; hence Israel is described as a holy nation and as kingdom of priests (Ex. 19:6). Any defilement that marred this relationship must be washed away with water or with the blood of purification.

In like manner New Testament Believers are *"Saints,"* that is, consecrated holy people. By means of the Blood of the Covenant (the Shed Blood of Christ) we have become *"a royal Priesthood, an holy nation"* (I Pet. 2:9), *"An Holy Priesthood, to offer up spiritual sacrifices, acceptable to God by Jesus Christ"* (I Pet. 2:5); we offer the Sacrifice of Praise (Heb. 13:15) and dedicate ourselves as living sacrifices upon God's Altar (Rom. 12:1).

Thus, we see that service is an essential element of Sanctification or Holiness, because this is the only sense in which men can belong to God, namely as His worshippers doing Him service. Paul expressed perfectly this aspect of Holiness when He spoke of God, *"Whose I am, and Whom I serve"* (Acts 27:23). Sanctification involves *possession* by God and *service* toward God.

THE TIME OF SANCTIFICATION

Sanctification can be described as both positional and, therefore, instantaneous, and second, practical and, therefore, progressive.

This is what confuses many Christians. They simply do not understand the Sanctification process. The truth is, we are sanctified in Jesus, and are being sanctified by the Holy Spirit.

Let us explain:

POSITIONAL AND INSTANTANEOUS

First of all, let me deal with error before we address ourselves to Truth.

The following is a statement regarding Sanctification, made by one who taught this particular doctrine, erroneously we might quickly add, for years:

"Justification is supposed to be a work of Grace by which sinners are made righteous and freed from their sinful habits when they come to Christ. In the merely justified there remains a corrupt principal, an evil tree, 'a root of bitterness,' which continually provokes to sin. If the Believer obeys this impulse and willfully sins, he ceases to be justified; therefore, the desirability of its removal that the likelihood of backsliding be thereby lessened.

"The eradication of this sinful root is Sanctification. It is, therefore, the cleansing of the nature from all inbred sin by the Blood of Christ (applied through Faith) when a full consecration is made, and the refining fire of the Holy Spirit, Who burns out all dross, when all is laid upon the Altar of Sacrifice. This, and this only, is true Sanctification — a distinct second definite work of Grace, subsequent to Justification, and without which that Justification is very likely to be lost."

As stated, this is error pure and simple!

Such a definition teaches that a person may be saved or justified without being Sanctified. This theory, however, is contrary to the New Testament.

The Apostle Paul addresses all Believers as *"Saints"* (literally, *"sanctified ones"*) and as already sanctified, irrespective as to whom they might be (I Cor. 1:2; 6:11); yet this same Epistle was written to the Believers at Corinth to correct them because of carnality and even open sin (I Cor. 3:1; 5:1-2, 7-8).

This means that even those who were weak in the Lord, or even had fallen into sin, were still concluded to be sanctified. They were *"Saints"* and *"Sanctified in Christ,"* but some of them were far from being such in daily conduct. They had been called to be Saints but were not walking worthy of the vocation wherewith they had been called.

The correct doctrine is according to the following:

When the believing sinner comes to Christ, he is immediately sanctified, which means to be cleansed and set apart unto God. In fact, this particular work of Grace must be done before the person can be Justified. Paul plainly said this in his Letter to the Corinthians, *"But ye are washed, ye are sanctified, but ye are justified in the Name of the Lord Jesus, and by the Spirit of our God"* (I Cor. 6:11). In fact, before one can be *"declared clean,"* which is Justification, one must first be *"made clean,"* which is Sanctification. Sanctification is the *"work"* accomplished on the believing sinner by the Lord at the time of conversion, and Justification is the *"position"* in which this *"work"* places the believing sinner. It is all in Christ. Therefore, this means that every single Christian in this world, irrespective of their particular, present state, is in fact, *"sanctified."* It's not possible to be any other way.

To teach that one is sanctified at a later time after conversion, calling it a *"second work of Grace,"* is, in effect, saying, that the Blood of Jesus does not cleanse from all sin. In fact, this teaching brings one into *"works,"* which is outside of the perimeter of the Cross of Christ, and can never be honored by God, because it is actually a reversion to Law. This false doctrine has caused much difficulty and problems for many Christians.

They are told that after they get saved, even as we already quoted above, that they now must be sanctified, which they come by in some particular manner at a later time. Whether the teachers of this erroneous doctrine understand it or not, they are actually saying that the person, even as we've already stated, was not actually cleansed when they were initially saved, which is a direct contradiction of the Word of God (I Cor. 6:11; I Jn. 1:7).

After this second work of Grace is entered into, the Christian is then led to believe that the sin problem is forever eradicated. In one sense, they are teaching sinless perfection, which the Bible does not teach. In fact, when the hapless Saint finds himself in trouble again after his supposed *"Sanctification,"* he becomes more and more confused.

This is another scheme that Satan has perfected in order to draw Believers away from the Cross. Instead of the Believer, as it regards this erroneous doctrine, looking to the Cross on a daily basis for his victory, he is instead, looking to some supposed work which took place when he was supposedly sanctified after being saved. Consequently, he is doomed to the very thing he is trying to avoid, failure as it regards his Christian Life.

AN EXAMPLE

I have given the following in another Volume, so I will be brief.

I think the following illustration portrays the fallacy of what is referred to in some circles as *"entire sanctification,"* perhaps better than all the teaching we could give.

The following was related to me, and I'll do my best to state it as best I can remember.

Finis Jennings Dake was in my opinion, one of the great Bible Scholars of this age and perhaps any age.

For awhile he was a member of a particular organization which believed and taught *"entire Sanctification."*

At a certain meeting, which if I remember correctly was only for Preachers, this subject was broached. How many Preachers were present I'm not sure, but possibly a hundred or so.

As the subject of entire Sanctification began to be discussed, which as stated, was one of the standard doctrines of that Denomination, Dr. Dake opposed the teaching. One of the Preachers took up the cause, who of course, was one of the Believers of this particular doctrine.

In the first place, anyone who would debate Finis Dake had to be somewhat foolish.

In a few minutes time, Dr. Dake had the Brother so tied up with Scriptures, that he was made to look somewhat foolish.

However, if that wasn't bad enough, the man who believed in entire Sanctification, in other words, that a person can reach the place to where they no longer sin, which means the sin nature is completely eradicated — this perfect man lost his perfect temper.

In this situation, the perfect man became so agitated that he had to be restrained by others, or else, I am told, he would have physically attacked Dr. Dake.

With the man's face beet red, and other Preachers restraining him, Dr. Dake calmly spoke up and said, *"I think quite possibly that our Brother has proved my point!"*

PRACTICAL AND PROGRESSIVE SANCTIFICATION

As it is said that *"we are saved, and we are being saved,"* one might also say, *"we are sanctified, and we are being sanctified."*

We have dealt with positional Sanctification, now let us deal with practical or progressive Sanctification.

One might ask the question, *"But does Sanctification consist only of the giving of the position as Saints?"*

No, this initial setting apart is the beginning of a progressive life of Sanctification. In other words, from the moment the Believer comes to Christ, the Holy Spirit immediately sets about to bring the *"condition"* of the Saint up to his actual *"position."*

Paul said, *"And the very God of peace sanctify you wholly; and I pray God your whole spirit and soul and body be preserved blameless until the Coming of Our Lord Jesus Christ"* (I Thess. 5:23).

This passage tells us that Sanctification is progressive, and it also shoots full of holes the erroneous doctrine that states when a person sins that only their body sins and not their spirit and their soul. Paul plainly says here that the entirety of the person is effected, *"spirit and soul and body,"* in all that is done, which includes sin as well as righteousness.

All Christians are separated to God in Jesus Christ; and from this springs the responsibility to live for Him. This separation is to be followed daily, the Believer seeking to become more and more conformed to the Image of Christ.

"Sanctification is the work of God's free Grace, whereby we are renewed in the whole man after the Image of God, and are enabled more and more to die unto sin, and to live unto Righteousness."

This does not mean that we grow into Sanctification, but that we progress in Sanctification.

Sanctification is both absolute and progressive — absolute in the sense that it is a work done once for all (I Cor. 6:11; Heb. 10:14), progressive in the sense that the Christian must follow after Holiness (Heb. 12:14) and perfect his consecration by cleansing himself from all defilement (II Cor. 7:1).

POSITIONAL AND PRACTICAL

Sanctification is positional and practical — positional in that it is primarily a change of position whereby a defiled sinner is changed to a holy worshiper; practical in that it calls for righteous living.

Positional Sanctification is indicated by the fact that all the Corinthians are addressed as *"Sanctified in Christ Jesus, called to be Saints"* (I Cor. 1:2).

Progressive Sanctification is implied in the fact that some of them are described as carnal (I Cor. 3:3), which means that their present condition did not measure up to their God-given position; hence they are exhorted to cleanse themselves from all defilement and so bring their consecration to perfection. The two aspects of Sanctification are implied in the fact that those addressed as sanctified and holy (I Pet. 1:2; 2:5) are exhorted to be holy (I Pet. 1:15); those who are dead to sin (Col. 3:3) are exhorted to mortify (make dead) their sinful members (Col. 3:5); those who have put off the old man (Col. 3:9) are exhorted again to put off the old man (Eph. 4:22; Col. 3:8).

THE DIVINE MEANS FOR SANCTIFICATION

The Divinely appointed means for Sanctification are the Blood of Christ, the Holy Spirit, and the Word of God.

The first (the Blood of Christ) provides primarily and absolute positional Sanctification; it is a finished work which gives the penitent a perfect position in relation to God. This is outlined in Romans Chapter 6. This Chapter more than all proclaims as to how the Believer is *"in Christ,"* and more particularly, *"in Christ"* as it refers to His Death, Burial, and Resurrection. It is this work by Christ on the Cross which satisfied the claims of Heavenly Justice, took the penalty for all sin and, therefore, destroyed the powers of darkness. For the Believer to be what he ought to be, it is absolutely imperative that he understand Romans Chapter 6, and continue to have Faith in this *"Finished Work."*

The second (the Holy Spirit) is internal, affecting the transforming of the Believer's nature. As well, the Holy Spirit does not function automatically in our hearts and lives as it regards the Salvation experience, as many think. He operates totally and completely in the confines of the Finished Work of Christ at the Cross (Rom. 8:2). He will not leave those boundaries, as He does not need to leave those boundaries. Everything that the Believer could ever need, and so much more than we will ever need, was furnished by Christ at the Cross and the Resurrection.

As stated, the Believer is to have Faith in that Finished Work, understanding that his victory totally and completely resides in that, which at the same time guarantees the help of the Holy Spirit.

Many Believers are frustrated. They have the Holy Spirit, with many even baptized with the Spirit with the evidence of speaking with other tongues (Acts 2:4). They have been led to believe that the great work of the Spirit is automatic. Consequently, they have no doubt wondered many times, as to where this great power is which is promised as a result of being Baptized with the Holy Spirit (Acts 1:8).

Their problem is, they have not been taught to evidence Faith in the Cross; therefore, in the words of A. W. Tozer, *"They have clipped the wings of the Holy Spirit."* As stated, He works strictly within the confines of the Sacrifice of Christ; therefore, the Believer must evidence Faith in this exactly as he did when he came to Christ. And this is where many Believers miss out:

They are taught that one must evidence Faith in Christ in order to be saved, but have been taught very little, if anything, as it

NOTES

regards the object of their Faith after they have been saved. That's the key, the *"object of our Faith."* It must always be the Cross of Christ. The idea that we can outgrow the Cross, or leave the Cross behind, is one of the greatest fallacies of false doctrine. To be sure, the Atonement, i.e., *"The Finished Work of Christ,"* is of such magnitude, such height, length, depth, and breadth, that a trillion years from today, we will still not have exhausted all of this that Christ did that memorable day nearly 2,000 years ago. So, the idea that we can outgrow such is facetious indeed!

The third (the Word of God) is external and practical, dealing with the Believer's practical conduct. Thus, God has made provision for both external and internal Sanctification.

THE BLOOD OF CHRIST

Inasmuch as this is so very important for the Child of God, let's look closer at these three Divinely-appointed means.

One might ask the question, *"In what sense is a person sanctified by the Blood of Christ?"*

As a result of the Finished Work of Christ, and Faith in that Finished Work, the believing sinner is changed from a defiled sinner into a holy worshiper. Sanctification is the result of that *"wondrous work accomplished by the Son of God when He offered Himself to put away sin by His Sacrifice on Calvary's Cross. By virtue of that Sacrifice the Believer is forever set apart to God, his conscience is purged, and he himself is transformed from an unclean sinner into, as stated, a holy worshiper, linked up in an abiding fellowship with the Lord Jesus Christ; 'For both He that sanctifieth and they who are sanctified are all of One: for which cause He is not ashamed to call them Brethren'"* (Heb. 2:11).

That there is also a continuous aspect to Sanctification by the Blood is implied in I John 1:7: *"The Blood of Jesus Christ His Son cleanseth us from all sin."*

If there is to be fellowship between a Holy God and man, there must necessarily be some provision for removing the sin of the constant coming short of the Glory of God, that is incumbent even upon the best of Believers, which is a barrier to that fellowship, for even the best of men, the Godliest of Saints, are imperfect. When Isaiah received his vision of the Holiness of God he was smitten with a sense of his own unholiness, and was in no condition to hear God's Message until a coal from the Altar (Representative of the Cross) had cleansed his lips.

Consciousness of sin mars fellowship with God; confession and Faith in the internal Sacrifice of Christ removes the barrier (I Jn. 1:9).

THE HOLY SPIRIT

This pertains to the practical aspect of Sanctification. As stated, we are sanctified (positional) and we are being sanctified (conditional) (Rom. 15:16; I Cor. 6:11; II Thess. 2:13; I Pet. 1:1-2).

In these Passages Sanctification by the Holy Spirit is treated as the beginning of God's Work in the souls of men, leading them to the full knowledge of Justification through Faith in the Blood-sprinkling of Christ. As the Spirit brooded over the primeval chaos (Gen. 1:2), and was followed by the Word of God bringing order, so the Spirit of God broods over the regenerate soul, opening it to receive the Light and Life of God (II Cor. 4:5).

The Tenth Chapter of Acts gives a concrete instance of Sanctification by the Holy Spirit, which in this case is positional.

During the first years of the Church, the evangelization of the Gentiles was delayed, for many of the Jewish Christians considered the Gentiles *"unclean"* and unsanctified because of their nonconformity to the food laws and other Mosaic regulations. It required a Vision to convince Peter that what the Lord had cleansed he must not call common or unclean. This meant that God had made provision for the Sanctification of the Gentiles to be His people.

And when the Spirit of God fell upon the Gentiles assembled in the house of Cornelius, there was no doubt about the matter. Regardless of whether or not they followed the Mosaic Ordinances, they were sanctified by the Holy Spirit (Rom. 15:16), and Peter challenged the Jews who were with him to deny the outward symbol of their spiritual cleansing (Acts 10:47; 15:8).

Actually, when Peter came to the part in his Message where he stated, *"To Him* (Jesus) *give all the Prophets witness, that through His Name whosoever believeth in Him shall receive remission of sins"* (Acts 10:43), God greatly moved.

This spoke totally and completely of Calvary and what Jesus did there in order that the sins of man could be remitted, i.e., *"washed and cleansed by the Blood of Jesus."* At this juncture, the Scripture says, *"While Peter yet spake these words, the Holy Spirit fell on all them which heard the Word"* (Acts 10:44).

The order always is, the Cross first, Faith in the Cross, and then the arrival of the Holy Spirit.

Again we state, the Holy Spirit effects His Work in the heart and live of the Believer in every respect, including Sanctification, and especially Sanctification, according to the Faith of the Believer in this Finished Work of Christ. The Believer is to ever understand that, ever act upon that, ever look to that, or else the Holy Spirit cannot work as He desires to do so.

THE WORD OF GOD

Christians are described as having been *"born of the Word of God"* (I Pet. 1:23; Ps. 119:9; Jn. 15:3; 17:17; Eph. 5:26; James 1:23-25).

The Word of God awakens men to a realization of the folly and wickedness of their lives. When we respond to the Word, repent, and believe in Christ, we are clean through the Word which is spoken unto us. This is the beginning of a cleansing which must continue throughout the Believer's life.

At his consecration the Israelite Priest received a complete priestly bath which was never repeated; it was a work done once for all; but he was required to wash his hands and feet daily. In like manner the Believer has been bathed (Titus 3:5); but there must be a daily putting away of defilements and imperfections as these are revealed by the Word of God, which is the mirror of the soul (James 1:22-25).

He must wash his hands, that is, his deeds must be right; he must wash his feet, that is, keep himself from *"those earth-stains which are so readily contracted by sandaled pilgrim feet pressing along this world's highways."*

In the last several years, the Holy Spirit has prompted me strongly to encourage the people strongly to study the Word of God. Unfortunately, too many Believers little know the Word, and are, therefore, prey for Satan and deception.

The very fact that you are studying this Commentary, tells me that you love the Word. In view of that, and considering the times in which we live, and I'm referring to the great apostasy that has already begun in the Church, which in fact, will lead up to the Antichrist, I admonish you to do your very best to encourage your friends who are Believers to become greater students of the Word. Perhaps you could do so by lending them this Commentary, or better yet, getting a copy for one or more of them as a gift. It could be the greatest favor you ever did for them.

ERRONEOUS VIEWS OF SANCTIFICATION

Many Christians become aware of the fact that the greatest hindrance to Holiness is the *"flesh,"* which thwarts them in their progress toward completion in Christ.

How may one realize deliverance from the *"flesh"*? Three erroneous views have been advanced:

ERADICATION

Eradication of *"inbred sin"* is one view taught.

Writes Lewis Perry Chafer: *"If eradication of the sin-nature were accomplished there would be no physical death; for physical death is the result of that nature* (Rom. 5:12-21).

"As well, parents who had experienced eradication would of necessity generate unfallen children. But even if eradication were secured there would still be the conflict with the world, the flesh (apart from the sin-nature), and the Devil; for eradication of these is obviously unscriptural. In fact, eradication before the Resurrection is unscriptural in totality. In fact, such is contrary to experience."

LEGALISM

Legalism pertains to the keeping of rules and regulations.

Paul teaches that the Law (Law of Moses) cannot sanctify (Rom. Chpt. 6) anymore than it can justify (Rom. Chpt. 3). This Truth is stated and developed in Paul's Epistle to the Galatians. (Please see our Commentary on this all-important Epistle.)

Paul is in nowise depreciating the Law. What he is doing, is defending it against a mistaken conception of its purpose. If a man is to be saved from sin it must be by a power apart from him. Let us use the illustration of a thermometer.

The glass and the red fluid will represent the individual. The record of degrees will represent the Law. Imagine the thermometer saying: *"I am not quite up to the mark today; I ought to be up to 80 degrees."* Could the thermometer raise itself to the required temperature? No, it would have to depend on a condition *outside* of itself. In like manner, a man who perceives he has come short of the Divine Standard cannot raise himself up to the Standard; he must be acted upon by a force apart from him; and that force is the Power of the Spirit.

The Law of Moses served as the barrier in Paul's day, and in fact, is still the problem presently, even though most Christians little understand that fact. However, one of the greatest problems for the modern Saint is not so much the Law of Moses, as it is the laws, rules, and regulations which we make up on our own, or else adhere to those made up by someone else, thinking that such will bring about Sanctification.

In fact, many of these rules or laws which we devise in order to overcome sin, such as prayer and fasting, or manifestations, are all Scriptural and, therefore, extremely helpful within themselves. Nevertheless, if we attempt to use them in the fashion mentioned, we are, in effect, taking them out of their proper context, which means that we are making a *"Law"* out of them, which will bring about no positive effect, at least as far as Victory is concerned.

The Believer should stop and think a moment. If, in fact, such were required, and I speak of all of these laws and rules, etc., then that would mean that the Work of Christ on the Cross was not, in fact, a Finished Work, but rather left something to be desired. We know that is not the case, and our attempting to add things to that which He has already done, only confuses the issue, frustrates the

Grace of God, and in effect, does the very opposite of what we intend, which stops the Sanctification process, and actually makes a bad matter worse.

It is hard for a Christian to swallow that Truth. The idea that these good and noble things could make his situation worse, is somewhat difficult for him to understand. But that's exactly what happens.

The doing of these things, constitutes *"legalism,"* which means that we are attempting to Sanctify ourselves by keeping some rules or laws, etc. The Lord can never bless such efforts, and as we've already stated again and again, the Holy Spirit will have no part of such a process. But yet, that's where most of the Church presently is. These things should be done because we are already victorious, not to gain victory. The victory we seek can only come through the Cross.

TWO DIRECTIONS

In fact, most of the Church world at present, because of not understanding the principle of the Cross and the Resurrection, and how it affects their everyday living and walk before God, in other words their Victory, are either in one of two postures:

1. Many, even as we have just stated, are in the position of *"legalism."* They do not understand this, and probably would deny it, were it suggested to them. In fact, most don't even know what legalism actually is. Nevertheless, when the Christian fails, if that Christian doesn't know God's prescribed order of Victory, which is Faith in the Cross and the Resurrection, then the Believer, especially if he or she is consecrated, will resort to legalism, whether they realize it or not.

Sin is abhorrent to any Believer, and the fact of sin is a tremendous spiritual shock. The Believer does not desire that it happen again, and for all the obvious reasons; however, most of the time, the efforts made to stop this despicable process are unscriptural and wrong, and, therefore, only succeeds in making the matter worse.

There is no victory in legalism; no victory in laws, rules, regulations, etc.

2. Many Christians in addressing the sin question, for whatever reason, and because they do not know or understand their rightful place in Christ, simply do nothing, and just try to live with their particular problem, whatever the problem might be. They do not resort to legalism, for one reason or the other.

Many of these Believers have been led to think that they have to sin, and there is nothing they can do about the situation. In fact, Paul addressed this very situation by asking the question, *"Shall we continue in sin, that Grace may abound?"*

His answer? *"God forbid!"* (Rom. 6:1-2).

He then proceeded to give the key to victory over the world, the flesh, and the Devil. As stated over and over again, it is all found in the Sixth Chapter of Romans.

ASCETICISM

Asceticism represents another way to subdue the flesh and attain to sanctity by means of self-inflicted deprivations and sufferings — a method followed by Roman Catholic and Hindu ascetics.

This method seems based on the ancient heathen belief that all matter, including the body, is evil. The body is, therefore, a clog to the spirit, and the more it is beaten and subdued the quicker will the spirit be released.

This is contrary to Scripture, which teaches that God created everything very good.

In fact, it is actually the soul and not the body that sins in the sense of the seat of the problem. The body is merely the vehicle which within itself is actually neutral (Rom. 6:12-14). Therefore, the sinful impulses, not the material flesh, must be crushed.

Asceticism is an attempt at self-deadening; but self cannot overcome self. That can only be done by the Work of the Holy Spirit.

Unfortunately, many have attempted to follow this erroneous process as it regards their Sanctification. Such is doomed to failure.

AN EXAMPLE

Some time ago I saw a Television Documentary of a Catholic Priest who had prescribed for himself a regimen of asceticism, which was supposed to bring about Holiness, etc. He was interviewed by a reporter, who stated to the Television audience, that the asceticism practiced by this Priest, designed incidentally to make him holy, was in fact, a certain regimen of self-inflicted suffering.

For instance, he was to eat only two meals a day, and only vegetables or fruit at that. He was to sleep on a hard plank with only a thin blanket for a covering and with no pillow. He was to arise at 4 a.m. and engage in prayer, etc. He was not to look at any Television or to listen to any Radio during this self-prescribed time.

As well, he was allowed to go into town only one time a year, and then only for a couple of hours and was not allowed to spend any money whatsoever, etc. Oh yes, he must be alone the rest of the time also.

After describing all of this regimen and showing the audience by Television the spartan room occupied by this Priest, the interview then began.

After discussing some things at length, the interviewer then asked the Priest, *"Do you feel close to God?"*

The man's answer was startling, and totally unexpected by the interviewer.

He sat there a few moments contemplating the question and then said, *"I don't even know that there is a God. In all of this time I've been doing these things, I have never felt Him one single time."*

To be sure, I was somewhat startled myself by his candid response. And yet, I wonder how many of us have somewhat fallen into the same trap? We have tried to sanctify ourselves, when it simply cannot be done. As stated, self cannot improve upon self. Such is literally impossible!

ANOTHER EXAMPLE

Some time later I saw another documentary concerning a Buddhist. He was completing a seven-year regimen which was supposed to make him holy. In fact, this regimen of self-denial and self-imposed suffering, was so stringent, that only two or three other Buddhists in history had ever completed this course.

In view of the fact that he was coming down to the last day of this regimen which was supposed to make him *"holy,"* he was to be met by a battery of Photographers and Television newscasters.

There were several hundred people present, plus all the Media. The moment he crossed the line regarding the finish of his journey and this completion of seven years of self-inflicted torture, of course, the Television cameras were rolling while the flash bulbs were popping. This individual was now a *"holy man!"*

The first question, *"How do you feel?"*

His answer again was not what I think they expected. *"I don't feel anything,"* he said!

There was a look of obvious let-down on his countenance, and the last words he said were, *"I think I will start another seven-year regimen!"*

We may dismiss this immediately as a Buddhist, and, therefore, paganistic, and, therefore, not to be considered. However, even though all of that may be true, how actual different is that, and I speak of this which the Catholic Priest was doing and the Buddhist had done, than we Spirit-filled Believers attempting in some way to do the same identical thing by keeping certain laws, etc.? In fact, I think it's much worse for us, considering that we have the Holy Spirit in us, Who can do all things, if we will only function according to God's prescribed order.

A Buddhist attempting to make himself *"holy,"* by certain self-prescribed tortures, is actually no different than a Believer in Christ attempting to do the same thing, by a regimen of *"fasting,"* etc.

THE TRUE METHOD OF SANCTIFICATION

The Scriptural method of dealing with the flesh must obviously be based upon the objective provision for Salvation, the Blood of Christ, and the subjective provision, the Holy Spirit. Deliverance from the power of the flesh must, therefore, come through Faith in the Atonement and a response to the moving of the Spirit. The first is dealt with in the Sixth Chapter of Romans, and the second in the first section of the Eighth Chapter of that same Epistle.

FAITH IN THE ATONEMENT

Let us imagine that there were Jews present (which was often the case) while Paul was expounding the Doctrine of Purification by Faith. We imagine them saying in protest: *"This is heresy of the most dangerous kind! Telling people that they need only to* believe in Jesus and what He did at the Cross, and that they can do nothing about their Salvation because it is by God's Grace this will result in their becoming careless in their living. They will think that what they do matters little, as long as they believe."

They would continued to have said, *"Your Doctrine of Faith promotes sin. If Justification be by Grace alone without works, why break off sin? Why not continue in it in order to obtain more Grace?"*

Paul's enemies actually accused him of preaching this Doctrine (Rom. 3:8; 6:1). He indignantly repudiates such a perversion.

"God forbid. How shall we, who are dead to sin, live any longer therein?"

Continuance in sin is impossible to a Believer because of his union with Christ in death and life (Mat. 6:24). By virtue of his Faith in Christ and what Christ did at the Cross as it regards the Atonement, the Believer has had an experience which includes such a cleancut break with sin as to be described as death to sin, and a transformation so radical as to be described as a Resurrection. The experience is pictured or rather symbolized by *"Water Baptism."*

The convert's immersion testifies to the fact that because of his union with the Crucified Christ he has died to sin; his being raised from the water testifies that his contact with the Risen Christ means that *"As Christ was raised up from the dead by the Glory of the Father, even so we also are raised, and now walk in newness of life."* Christ died *for sin* in order that we might die *to sin.*

"For he that is dead (in Christ, and, therefore, dead to the world) *is freed from sin."* Death cancels all obligations and breaks all ties (Rom. 6:7).

Through union with Christ the Christian has died to the old life, and the fetters of sin have been broken. As death put an end to the bondage of the literal slave, so the Believer's death to the old life, proclaimed in the Burial of Christ, with the Believer actually *"in Christ,"* at that time, and placed there by Faith — all of this has freed him from the bondage of sin.

To continue the illustration: The Law has no jurisdiction over a dead man; regardless of what crime he may have committed, once dead he is beyond the power of human justice. In like manner, the Law of Moses often violated by the convert cannot *"arrest him,"* for by virtue of his experience with Christ he is *"dead"* (Rom. 7:1-4; II Cor. 5:14).

(The Believer is not to confuse the words *"baptized"* and *"baptism"* in Romans 6:3-4, with Water Baptism. Even though we have used Water Baptism as an illustration of that which is symbolic, and actually meant to be, as it regards the changed life of the Believer; still, Paul is not speaking of Water Baptism in Romans Chapter 6, but rather using these words to describe the Believer's *"in Christ"* experience.)

THE KNOWLEDGE OF THIS GREAT TRUTH

"Knowing that Christ being raised from the dead dieth no more; death hath no more dominion over Him. For in that He died, He died unto sin once (suffered the penalty of the broken Law)*: but in that He liveth* (was Resurrected), *He liveth unto God. Likewise reckon* (consider or account) *ye also yourselves to be dead indeed unto sin, but alive unto God through Jesus Christ our Lord"* (Rom. 6:9-11).

Christ's death ended that earthly state in which He suffered the penalty of sin which was death, and His life is one of unbroken communion with God.

Christians, though still in the world, may share His experience, because we are united to Him.

When Jesus died on the Cross, He died literally as our Substitute. In other words, He did for us what we could not do for ourselves. He became our Representative Man, in effect, the Second or Last Adam. Through sin and disobedience, the First Adam brought death and destruction upon the entirety of the world. Through the Life, Death, and Resurrection of the Second Adam, the Lord Jesus Christ, He purchased back for man the life that was lost, in effect, redeeming us from the powers of darkness.

Our Faith in this which Christ did, actually places us in Him. At least, that's the way that God looks at the situation. As stated, the only requirement is Faith in that Finished Work.

When Faith in the Atonement is tendered by the believing sinner, the Lord actually puts that believing sinner in Christ, becoming one with Him in His Death, Burial, and Resurrection. That's what Paul meant by constantly referring to Believers being *"in Christ"* (Rom. 8:1; Eph. 1:3-4, 6, 10).

In view of all this, considering that the bondage of sin is broken, which means that Satan no more has a hold on us, we should *"Likewise reckon ourselves to be dead indeed unto sin, but alive unto God through Jesus Christ our Lord."*

WHAT DOES THIS MEAN?

God has said that through our Faith in Christ we are dead to sin and alive to Righteousness. There remains one thing to be done, and that is to believe God and reckon or conclude that we *are* dead to sin. God says that when Christ died we died to sin as well; when Christ arose, we arose also to live a new life. We were and are literally *"in Him."*

We are to keep on reckoning these facts as absolutely true, and then, as we reckon them, they will become powerful in our lives, for we become what we reckon ourselves to be.

An important distinction has been pointed out, namely, that between the *"Promises"* and the *"Facts"* of the Bible. But Jesus said: *"If ye abide in Me, and My Words abide in you, ye shall ask what ye will, and it shall be done unto you."* That is a *"Promise,"* because it lies in the future; it is something *"to be done"* (Jn. 15:7).

But when Paul says, *"Christ died for our sins according to the Scriptures,"* he is stating a *"fact,"* something that *"has been done."*

Compare Peter's statement, *"By Whose stripes ye were healed."* And when Paul declares that *"our old man is crucified,"* he is stating a fact — something that has been done.

The question that remains is: *"Are we willing to believe what God declares to be facts about ourselves?"* For Faith is the hand that accepts what God freely offers.

May it not be that the awakening to one's position in Christ constitutes what some persons have described as a *"second definite work of Grace"*?

While in fact, it is not a *"second work of Grace,"* still, it is so revolutionary, this glorious truth of one's position in Christ, that one is hard-put to find the proper definition.

MY PERSONAL EXPERIENCE

When the Lord began to open up to me sometime in 1997 the great Truths of the Cross and the Resurrection, and what it means to my Christian walk, there was a Faith and a joy which filled my heart that words cannot describe. For the first time in my Christian experience all fear was gone, and I might quickly add, an experience which has seen hundreds of thousands brought to a saving knowledge of Jesus Christ. But despite the Lord using me grandly to proclaim His Gospel and on a worldwide basis, and as well seeing results that few human beings have seen in history, I did not properly understand the victorious, Christian walk. As I've said several times, every Christian is a product of what he or she has heard behind the pulpit. And to be sure, despite the fact that I was privileged to sit under some Godly Preachers in my formative years, still, I heard very little about the Cross of Christ, except the part it plays in the Salvation of the soul. To be sure, and regrettably, the approximate last 50 years of the 20th Century have seen such little preaching and teaching on the Cross of Christ, that even the foundational Message of the Cross as it refers to our initial Redemption is close to being lost.

That which I am teaching you concerning the Cross and the Resurrection in this Volume was given to me by the Lord after seeking His Face for some five years concerning this very thing. I had to know the answer to the question of the victorious, overcoming, Christian life. My quest was not one merely of curiosity, but rather of desperation, even to the place, that I told the Lord if He didn't show me the answer, I would rather die than live.

Well, I will say as Paul, *"I thank God through Jesus Christ our Lord,"* He gave me the answer to this all-important question (Rom. 7:25).

As I dictate these notes, it is June 23rd, 1999. These last approximately two years, have been the most joyful, the most rewarding, the most wonderful years of my life. As Peter said, it is truly *"joy unspeakable and full of glory"* (I Pet. 1:8).

To be brief, and even though I have said it scores of times in the last two Volumes of our Commentaries, please allow me the latitude of repeating myself:

1. The Lord showed me that all Victory is in the Cross, regarding all things. He showed me that the Atonement, the Sacrifice of Christ, the Finished Work of Christ, all carried out at the Cross and the Resurrection was and is the basis of everything we receive from God. That refers to Salvation, the Baptism with the Holy Spirit, Divine Healing, Financial Prosperity, Joy, Peace, Hope, and Victory as it pertains to our everyday walk before God. In other words, every single thing we have from the Lord was purchased at the Cross by our Lord and Saviour, Jesus Christ.

2. The object of my Faith, the Holy Spirit related to me, is to always be in the Finished Work of Christ, which of course is the Cross, the Resurrection, and the Exaltation (Rom. 8:2; Eph. 2:6).

If the object of my Faith ceases to be the Cross, then it is Faith which is really not the God kind of Faith, and that which the Holy Spirit cannot bless or honor. He honors only the Faith that is anchored in the Cross of Christ, hence Him saying, *"Looking to Jesus the Author and Finisher of our Faith; Who for the joy that was set before Him endured the Cross, despising the shame, and is set down at the Right Hand of the Throne of God"* (Heb. 12:2).

As should be obvious, the *"Looking unto Jesus"* points to the Jesus of the Cross. Any other Jesus is, *"Another Jesus"* (II Cor. 11:4).

3. The Lord showed me that the Holy Spirit works only in the parameters of the Finished Work of Christ (Rom. 8:2). So, if my Faith is in anything else other than this, the Sacrifice of Christ, even though the Holy Spirit is present within my heart and life, He will not function in these other capacities.

This means that the Holy Spirit will not help me to have greater willpower in order to overcome sin, or as it regards *"works"* of any kind. This is what frustrates many Christians. They know they have the Holy Spirit because the witness is there; however, they find themselves struggling in some particular area, seeming as if the Holy Spirit is not helping. The truth is, He isn't helping, and it's because we are outside of the parameters of the Atonement.

He will not help us as it regards the overcoming of sin, with any type of works. He honors Faith alone, and more particularly, Faith in the Atonement.

RESPONSE TO THE SPIRIT

Romans Chapters 7 and 8, continue the subject of Sanctification; they deal with the Believer's deliverance from the power of sin and his growth in Holiness. In Chapter 6 we saw that victory over sin's power was achieved by Faith — Faith in what Christ did at the Cross and our part in that in which He did. Chapter 8 introduces another ally in the battle of sin — the Holy Spirit, even as we have been discussing.

As a background study the line of thought in Chapter 7, which pictures a man turning to the Law for Sanctification. Here Paul shows that the Law is powerless to save and sanctify, not because the Law is not good, but because of the sinful bias in human nature known as the *"flesh."* He points out that the Law reveals the fact of sin (vs. 7), the occasion of sin (vs. 8), the power of sin (vs. 9), the deceitfulness of sin (vs. 11), the effect of sin (vss. 10-11) and the sinfulness of sin (vss. 12-13).

A PERSONAL EXPERIENCE OF THE APOSTLE

Paul is actually describing in the Seventh Chapter of Romans his own experience in this capacity, which took place immediately after he was saved and baptized with the Holy Spirit. Many Preachers conclude Romans Chapter 7 to be an illustration of Paul's experience before conversion; however, that makes no sense whatsoever. No, Romans Chapter 7, is Paul's experience after he was saved, how he struggled in this capacity, and how the Lord showed him the secret to a victorious, overcoming life, which he gave us in Romans, Chapters 6 and 8. In fact, if the Christian erroneously interprets Chapter 7, which most do, he will have little understanding whatsoever as it regards the single most important thing in his Christian life, his Sanctification. To be frank, most Christians are engaging at this very moment in the same struggle that Paul engaged, but don't know the way out, which is the Cross. (Please see our Commentary on Romans.)

Every Christian faces the struggle with sin after conversion. The problem is, most stay in that struggle simply because they do not understand God's provision for their total victory. As we have stated, Paul was engaged in this same conflict even as all of us, despite the fact that he was saved and baptized with the Holy Spirit. He simply did not know how to function after the Spirit, and rather tried to overcome after the flesh, which always brings defeat, and even makes the situation worse. However, he earnestly sought the Lord, with the Lord giving him the answer to this dilemma, which as stated, he gave to us in Romans Chapter 6.

In that Chapter he explained to us, even as the Holy Spirit had given it to him, as it concerned the Crucifixion of Christ, and our part in that Crucifixion, which of course, included the Burial and Resurrection of our Lord. He explains how that we were and actually are *"in Christ"* (Rom. 8:1).

The idea is, every single human being in this world who had trusted Christ before the Cross, and every human being alive at the time of Christ, and every human being since, were actually *"in Christ"* when He died, was buried and rose from the dead. Now of course, the actual realization of that is brought about only, upon one having Faith in Christ.

This means that the death of Christ did not at all help those who had already died before this particular time, who never evidenced any Faith in the Lord. It also means the same for all who were alive at the time of Christ, and all who have lived thereafter, who did not and do not evidence Faith. Even though Christ died for all of humanity, it is only those who believe in Him and accept Him as their own personal Saviour, who enjoy the benefits of what He did (Jn. 3:16).

To say it in another way, even though Jesus Christ died for all of humanity who has ever lived and who ever will live, it is only those who have Faith in Him, who reap the benefit of the Atonement (Rev. 22:17).

IN CHRIST

In the Mind of God, when Jesus died, you were in Him, and in fact, you are to remain in Him even unto this very hour, and forever. This is the key to your victory in totality, *"in Him!"* What does that mean?

It means that every victory that Jesus purchased with His Own Blood, and to be sure, He purchased all victory in totality, is ours by simple Faith in that which He did. We don't have to work for it, earn it, labor for it, merit it, and that means everything that Christ purchased for us, it is all a free gift. We get it simply by believing Him. This includes our Salvation, our everyday Victory in the Lord, and anything and everything else that one might name. It is all through the Cross, and what He there did.

So, if I attempt to have victory in any other manner except simple Faith in that Finished Work, I will fail, as fail I must. The Apostle learned that, and we must learn it as well. Regrettably, this of which we are teaching, in fact, that which Paul taught, is not taught, or even believed or understood in most Christian circles presently.

The modern Faith Message, has been, I think, the greatest hindrance to the Cross Victory. In this teaching, the Believer is pulled away from the Cross, actually to self, which will never give anyone any help. It is faith in self rather than in the Cross, which the Holy Spirit can never honor.

SIN

The Sanctification process is to help us overcome any and all sin, with Righteousness and Holiness developed within our hearts and lives, which can only be done by the Holy Spirit according to our Faith in the Cross of Christ. What I'm saying is this:

The problem with the Christian is sin. We don't like to admit that, we don't like to think that, but that's what the problem is — sin.

We hide our heads in the sand; we live in a state of denial; we make allowances for ourselves while loudly criticizing others; but irrespective as to what label we put on the situation, or how we address ourselves to this Christian walk, the problem is sin. Satan is trying to pull us down, trying to get us to fail, trying to cause us to lose our way, and he does all of this by trying to get us to fail the Lord in the realm of sin.

Because we do not properly understand Romans Chapter 7, we come up with all type of false scenarios. We Pentecostals think that because we are baptized with the Holy Spirit and speak with other Tongues, and even have Gifts of the Spirit working through and within us, that we are above sin. However, such thinking is foolish!

The Charismatics try to define sin away by claiming that while there are occasions of sin in the life of the Believer, it is only in his body, and not in his soul and spirit. In fact, most Charismatics deny the sin nature that's in the Christian.

Nevertheless, whatever denial we may be involved in, or whatever erroneous thoughts we may have, the struggle with sin continues. We may hide it, deny it, or whatever, but that does not alter the fact.

Anyone who would read Romans Chapters 6, 7, and 8, and not know and realize that the problem in the heart and life of the Christian is sin, then I don't know what they are reading. Sin is the problem, and the Holy Spirit through the Apostle, tells us here how to have victory over this monster. If we follow God's prescribed order, we will have victory, if not, there will not be victory. His prescribed order is Faith in the Cross, i.e., *"The Finished Work of Christ."*

The terrible thing is, when we deny these plain Truths as given to us here in the Word of God, thereby setting about to develop our own righteousness through works, which is the only alternative if we forsake the Cross, the only thing that is truly developed is self-righteousness, which places us in a position of hypocrisy and deceit. The sadness is, most Christians do not want to sin. They do not want to fail God, and in fact, are doing everything within their own personal power not to fail, but still failing. Not only are they failing, but the situation is actually getting worse and worse, even as Law always does. If we operate according to the flesh, there is no alternative, we are going to die, i.e., *"die to the things of God, with sin becoming more and more prominent."* It is only by *"walking after the Spirit"* which always leads us to the Cross and the Resurrection, in which we can then have the *"more abundant life"* of which Jesus spoke (Rom. 8:4-5; Jn. 10:10).

NOTES

PAUL'S EXPERIENCE

The Apostle in describing his own experience, tells us that the very Law, which he earnestly desired to observe, stirred sinful impulses within him. The result was a *"civil war"* in the soul. He is hindered from doing the good that he wants to do, and is impelled to do the thing he hates. Incidentally, these are the words of a Believer not an unbeliever, proving that Romans Chapter 7 pertains to Paul's after-conversion experience and not before his conversion (Rom. 7:15). He said, *"I find then a Law, that, when I would do good, evil is present with me* (the sin nature). *For I delight in the Law of God after the inward man* (which is characteristic of a Believer)*: But I see another law in my members* (the law of the sin nature), *warring against the law of my mind* (the will to obey the Lord) *in bringing me into captivity to the law of sin which is in my members"* (Rom. 7:21-23).

Romans Chapter 7 presents the picture of a man under Law who has discovered the heart-searching spirituality of the Law, but who in every attempt to keep it finds himself thwarted by indwelling sin. In other words, one cannot obey God by one's own efforts, one will fail every time.

Why does Paul describe this conflict? He does so in order to show that the Law (Law of Moses) is just as powerless to sanctify as it is to justify.

MODERN CHRISTIANS

Most modern Saints reading this, automatically dismiss it, thinking. *"I'm not under the Law of Moses, and it has nothing to do with me"*; consequently, they dismiss it out of hand.

First of all, why do you think the Holy Spirit gave all of this information through Paul? The Apostle was not merely reminiscing here for the sake of reminiscing. The truth is, the Moral Law that was given to Moses, which we refer to as the *"Ten Commandments,"* is God's Standard of Righteousness, and demanded of all human beings. In other words, this is what God demands, the keeping of these Commandments, upon all of humanity. However, we have a problem:

Sinful man cannot keep these Commandments, no matter how hard he tries, and because of the fallen nature that's within him. Likewise, the Christian cannot keep them either, if he tries to do so within his own power. As well, they are not automatically kept once one becomes a Christian, as most have been led to believe.

In fact, when we find out that the situation is not automatic, we immediately set about to try to rectify the problem, which Paul did here, and which he failed repeatedly despite all of his efforts, and which you will fail as well.

It is demanded that we live up to this Standard, but we can only do so by trusting in Christ Who has already kept all the Commandments, even satisfying the curse of the broken Law, all on our behalf. So, all of this does matter and matter greatly! God demands a life of Holiness and Righteousness, but it can only be obtained by understanding our place and position in Christ, and that He has already done all of this, and we don't have to do it again — in fact, we can't do it again no matter how hard we try. As we have stated, the Law, even laws of our own making, is just as powerless to sanctify as it is to justify. Only Jesus can do these things, and in fact, has already done these things in His perfect Life and above all His Death on the Cross and His Resurrection. This means that we do not have to perform this work all over again.

If one engages in self-effort as it regards this Christian walk, and I'm speaking of attempting to sanctify ourselves in some way by our own works, we will always come to the same position as Paul, when he said, *"O wretched man that I am! Who shall deliver me from the body of this death?"* (Rom. 7:24).

Paul, who has been describing experience under Law, joyfully testifies now to his experience under Grace: He says, *"I thank God (that deliverance comes) through Jesus Christ our Lord"* (Rom. 7:25).

With this cry of triumph we enter the wonderful Eighth Chapter of Romans, which has as its dominant theme, deliverance from the power of the sinful nature by the Power of the Holy Spirit.

NOTES

THREE DEATHS

There are three deaths in which the Believer must take part:

1. Death in sin, which refers to our condemnation (Eph. 2:1; Col. 2:13):

Sin has brought the soul to that condition the penalty of which is spiritual death or separation from God, which is the basic factor of sin, and which is what God in the Garden of Eden said would happen, if man sinned (Gen. 2:17).

2. Death for sin, which pertains to our Justification: Christ endured upon the Cross the sentence of a violated Law on our behalf as our Substitute and actually our Representative Man, and we, therefore, are accounted as having endured it in Him. God counts us in that capacity as we evidence Faith in what Christ has done (Eph. 2:8-9).

What He did *for* us is reckoned according to our Faith, as having been done *by* us (II Cor. 5:14; Gal. 2:20).

We are held legally or judicially free from the penalty of a violated Law if by personal Faith we consent to this which Jesus has done.

3. Death to sin, which is our Sanctification (Rom. 6:11): What is true *for* us must be made real *in* us; what is judicial (positional in Christ) must be made practical (play out into everyday results of victory); death to the penalty of sin must be followed by death to the power of sin. And this is the work of the Holy Spirit (Rom. 8:13), which He carries out in our hearts and lives according to our Faith in the Finished Work of Christ.

As the Ascending sap in a tree crowds off dead leaves which cling despite frost and storm, so the indwelling Spirit crowds out the imperfections and habits of the old life.

ENTIRE SANCTIFICATION

This truth has often been discussed under the topic of *"Christian Perfection."*

The question could be asked, as to how far can one go in Sanctification? In other words, is it possible to be totally and completely Sanctified in every respect?

Even though we will deal with this, I think really the question is actually moot. Perfection is not really the concern but rather victory. Actually, the Bible does not teach sinless perfection. However, I think it would be good for us to look at the word a little closer.

THE MEANING OF PERFECTION

There are two kinds of perfection, absolute and relative. That is absolutely perfect which cannot be improved upon; this belongs only to God.

On the other hand, that is relatively perfect which fulfills the end for which it was designed; this perfection, as described here, is possible to man.

The word *"perfection"* in the Old Testament has the meaning of *"sincere and upright"* (Gen. 6:9; Job 1:1). In avoiding the sins of the surrounding nations Israel might be *"perfect"* (Deut. 18:13). However, the tragedy is, they did not avoid those sins.

The essence of perfection in the Old Testament is the wholehearted desire and determination to do the Will of God. Regardless of the sins that mar his record, David may be truly called a perfect man or a *"man after God's Own Heart,"* because the supreme aim of his life was to do God's Will.

Explained in this manner, which is correct, it never means sinless perfection, but rather *"finishing the Course."*

THE NEW TESTAMENT

The word *"perfect"* and its derivatives have a variety of applications in the New Testament, and, therefore, must be interpreted according to the sense in which the terms are used. Various Greek words are used to convey the idea of perfection:

1. One word means being complete in the sense of being apt or fit for a certain task or end (II Tim. 3:17).

2. Another Greek word denotes a certain end attained through growth in mental and moral development (Mat. 5:48; 19:21; Col. 1:28; 4:12; Heb. 11:40).

3. The word used in II Corinthians 13:9; Ephesians 4:12, and Hebrews 3:21 means thorough equipment.

4. The word used in II Corinthians 7:1 means to terminate, or to bring to a termination.

5. The Greek word used in Revelation 3:2 signifies to make replete, to fulfill, to cram (as a net), to level (as a hollow).

NOTES

The word is descriptive of the following aspects of the Christian life:

A. Positional perfection in Christ (Heb. 10:14) — the result of Christ's work *for* us.

B. Spiritual maturity and understanding, as opposed to spiritual childhood (I Cor. 2:6; 14:20; II Cor. 13:11; Phil. 3:15; II Tim. 3:17).

C. Progressive Sanctification (Gal. 3:3).

D. Perfection in certain particulars: The Will of God, the love for man, and service (Mat. 5:48; Col. 4:12; Heb. 13:21).

E. The ultimate perfection of the individual in Heaven (Phil. 3:12; Col. 1:22, 28; I Pet. 5:10).

F. The ultimate perfection of the Church, or the corporate Body of Believers (Jn. 17:23; Eph. 4:13).

THE POSSIBILITIES OF PERFECTION

The New Testament presents two general aspects of perfection:

1. Perfection as a Gift of Grace, which is the perfect position or standing given the penitent in response to Faith in Christ. In other words, every Believer is counted by God as perfect because we have a perfect Saviour Who has paid for and given to us His perfect Righteousness, which is our constant standing in Christ.

2. Perfection is actually wrought in the Believer's character. One may overemphasize the first aspect to the neglect of the second, which is practical Christianity.

Such an one was that individual who, after a lecture on the Victorious Life, said to the speaker, *"I have all that in Christ."*

"But do you have it in Glasgow?" was the quiet question.

On the other hand, by overemphasizing the second aspect some have practically denied any perfection apart from that which they find in their own experience.

JOHN WESLEY

Wesley seems to have taken a middle road between the two extremes. He acknowledged that a person was sanctified at conversion, but affirmed the necessity of progressive sanctification, but at times referred to it as *"entire sanctification,"* and concluded it as a second work of Grace.

While our Sanctification whether positional or practical, is definitely a work of Grace, as everything of God actually is; however, the words *"entire Sanctification"* if misunderstood can cause problems. In other words, the statement seems to mean that one can reach a place to where no further progress is possible, which the Scriptures do not teach.

Irrespective, I think all Christians agree to the need of Sanctification because of the power of sin which causes the Christian to be defeated.

Victory in this capacity, and I speak of our everyday walk before God, comes in response to our proper Faith in the Finished Work of Christ. When our Faith is in the Cross and the Cross alone, pure love fills the heart and governs all the work and action, with the result that the power of sin is broken.

It is impossible for one's Faith to be in the Cross, without Love developing from that procedure. The very spirit of the Cross speaks of Love, for the Cross was the greatest exhibition of Love that mankind has ever known and ever will know. To be sure, a love for God, and I speak of the love generated by the Cross, can so fill the Believer's heart, that one strongly desires to do nothing that would offend the Holy Spirit in any manner. Only love can create this type of desire.

A CRISIS EXPERIENCE

The New Testament holds up a high standard of practical holiness and affirms the possibility of deliverance from the power of sin. It is, therefore, the Christian's duty to strive after perfection. That must ever be our goal, even though we fall short (Phil. 3:12; Heb. 6:1).

In this connection it must be acknowledged that progress in Sanctification often involves a crisis experience almost as definite as that of conversion.

A crisis experience can be defined in many ways. But perhaps the Seventh Chapter of Romans is the greatest example of all, and actually that which happened to the Apostle Paul.

I think it is obvious that the Apostle suffered a crisis experience to the extent, that he had to find an answer to this dilemma of the sin problem. How could one have victory over sin and walk in purity and holiness before the Lord?

NOTES

As stated, the Lord gave him the answer to that, but I'm not sure if Paul would have become that earnest before the Lord, had he not reached such a crisis experience as defined in Romans 7:24.

In one way or the other, I think this has happened to all of us, or else will happen sooner or later. The Divine Nature in the Believer which automatically comes as a result of conversion to Christ, demands victory over sin. The two, sin and victory over sin, cannot coexist, as should be obvious. One or the other will go! Of course, the Holy Spirit is laboring from moment one in the life of the Christian, to bring about total victory over all sin, i.e., *"sin not having dominion in any shape, form or fashion over us"* (Rom. 6:14).

Sinful failure on the part of the Child of God is a traumatic thing. When it happens the Believer must seek instant relief by taking the problem to the Lord and seeking His Mercy and Grace, which He has promised to always give, and which He will always give (I Jn. 1:9). However, we must ever understand, that forgiveness, although desperately needed, and thankfully received, at the same time, is not victory or deliverance. We sometimes get the two confused, thinking that forgiveness is victory. It isn't!

FORGIVENESS AND VICTORY

The Christian can have a tendency to confuse the two. Whenever forgiveness is enjoined by the Lord, as He will always do upon proper repentance, relationship is instantly restored, which always brings the joy of restored union. It's done in a moment's time, and can take place anywhere. The moment the Believer asks for forgiveness for whatever has happened, and means it with his heart, forgiveness is instantly given (I Jn. 1:7).

However, we must not mistake forgiveness for victory. As stated, the two are not the same.

It's not God's will, that the Christian sin and repent, sin and repent, sin and repent, even though forgiveness is always available, with no limitation to the number of times. However, that is not the true Christian experience, but rather only the Mercy and Grace of God. As someone has well said, the Lord has not saved us in sin, but rather from sin.

But yet, this business of sinning and repenting, and doing so over and over, is too much the norm for many, if not most, Christians. Pure and simple, that's not the way!

Thank God that forgiveness is always available, but the Holy Spirit is attempting to take us to a greater level in our Christian experience, than this constant repetition. So what we're actually saying is, that the Christian does not need forgiveness nearly so much as he needs victory, or more particularly, the manner of victory.

If the Believer who reads these words will heed the things we have said concerning the Cross, Victory will be his. In fact, the Victory has been his all along, but regrettably, he just simply did not know it. Peter said this:

"As obedient children, not fashioning yourselves according to the former lusts in your ignorance" (I Pet. 1:14).

Notice that the Apostle mentioned *"ignorance!"* The trouble with most Christians is they are ignorant of the provision made by the Lord at the Cross for our Sanctification. Being ignorant of this, in other words, God's prescribed order of Victory, they succumb to *"former lusts."* Please believe me, this is not an isolated thing, but actually pandemic in the Christian community.

Peter also said, *"But as He* (Christ) *which hath called you is Holy, so be ye Holy in all manner of conversation* (citizenship or walk)*"* (I Pet. 1:15).

The great question is, *"How can we obey this command to be holy?"*

We do it in exactly the way that Peter said:

"Forasmuch as ye know that ye were not redeemed with corruptible things, as silver and gold . . . But with the Precious Blood of Christ, as of a lamb without blemish and without spot."

He then said, *"But was manifest in these last times for you"* (I Pet. 1:18-20).

This tells us that all of this was done at the Cross, meaning that we are to put our Faith there and leave it there. Then Victory will be ours, simply because we are trusting totally in Him. Then we can live the life of Holiness which refers to our practical experience, even as we are holy as it concerns our position in Christ.

THE TEMPTATION PROBLEM

Irrespective of the Faith of the individual as it regards the Cross of Calvary and what Christ has done for us, and our being *"in Christ,"* which guarantees victory, there will be temptation from without and from within, hence the need of vigilance (Gal. 6:1; I Cor. 10:12); the flesh is frail and the Christian is still free to yield to the bad or the good, for in essence, all of us are still in a state of probation (Rom. 6:12-16; 7:18; Gal. 5:17; Phil. 3:3); our knowledge is partial and faulty and we may also be subject to sins of ignorance. Nevertheless, we may press on with the following assurance:

In Christ, we can resist and overcome every recognized temptation (Rom. 6:14; I Cor. 10:13; Eph. 6:13-14; James 4:7); we may be always glorifying to God and filled with the Fruits of Righteousness (I Cor. 10:31; Col. 1:10); we may possess the Graces and Power of the Spirit and walk in unbroken fellowship with God (Gal. 5:22-23; Eph. 5:18; Col. 1:10-11; I Jn. 1:7); we may ever have the constant cleansing of the Blood and thus be blameless before God (Phil. 2:15; I Thess. 5:23; I Jn. 1:7).

Were these things not true, then the Scriptures would have said otherwise; nevertheless, this state of victory is not so much a goal which we attain or achieve, but rather a constant experience in living for God, which involves many past failures, with the Grace of God gradually overcoming our frailties and faults. Such is not done quickly or easily, despite our Faith and total dependence on the Lord, and I might quickly add, even having the Cross as the correct object of our Faith. That's why Paul said, *"Fight the good fight of Faith, lay hold on Eternal Life, whereunto thou art also called, and hast professed a good profession before many witnesses"* (I Tim. 6:12).

This Faith walk is exactly that, a *"fight!"* However, it is a *"good fight,"* because if maintained, it will always come out to a victorious conclusion.

JACOB

I think the Patriarch Jacob is perhaps at least one of, if not the greatest example of this of which I speak, found in the entirety of the Word of God.

The name *"Jacob,"* actually means *"supplanter, cheater, deceiver."* That's what Jacob was, but the Lord in a crisis experience, changed his name to *"Israel,"* which means *"Prince with God, a ruling Prince, or Prince who rules"* (Gen. 32:24-32).

Incidentally, the name *"Israel"* which was given to Jacob, was also given to his descendants (Ex. 9:7), and also to Christ (Isa. 49:3).

In fact, the Old Testament is largely a record of the history of Israel and of God's Revelation to them — their beginning as a nation (Gen. 29:21-30:43); their 430 years of sojourn (Gen. 12:1-Ex. 12:40); journeys and wanderings for about 41 years (Ex. Chpt. 12-Deut. Chpt. 34); conquest of Canaan (Josh. 1-24); experiences under 16 judges (Judg. Chpt. 1-I Sam. Chpt. 7); under 42 kings (I Sam. Chpt. 8-II Ki. Chpt. 25; II Chron. Chpt. 36); in the captivities (II Ki. Chpt. 25; Ezra Chpt. 1); the restoration as a nation under Ezra and Nehemiah. Hundreds of the Prophecies recorded in Scripture concern Israel as can be seen from a study of the Old Testament.

Irrespective, and back to our original thought, even after the Lord changed Jacob's name to *"Israel,"* the effects of that change continued until the time of Jacob's death.

Beginning with the 32nd Chapter of Genesis, and on to the end of the Book, we find the names *"Jacob"* and *"Israel"* used interchangeably by the Lord.

We find that God had a controversy with Jacob because of his faulty life; and when as a consequence Jacob found himself in deadly peril and realized that God Himself was behind that peril, and that it was not with Esau his brother that he had to contend, but with the Angel of Jehovah Himself; and when sore broken by that mighty hand he ceased to wrestle and clung with weeping and supplication to the Very God Who wounded him, then it was that he got the victory and the glorious name of *"Israel."*

The great principle that God cannot give victory to *"the flesh,"* appears in this particular scene with the Patriarch. It is the broken heart that begins to experience what Divine Power means. This is the *"crisis experience."*

Going to Genesis Chapter 35, we find the Patriarch is called *"Jacob"* by the Lord some 17 times, except in Verses 10, 21 and 22. Here some four times, the Holy Spirit names him *"Israel."*

The first occasion (vs. 10), referred to a Revelation of God to him, and the second occasion (vss. 21-22), was the time of Rachel's death.

How strange this contradiction appears to human wisdom! Jacob is his name of weakness, Israel, of strength, and yet is he only named Israel in connection with wandering and dishonor! So it is at all times! Bitter earthly sorrows may often closely follow sweet spiritual experiences.

As we go to the close of Genesis, which all along portrays Jacob's life, we find the Holy Spirit referring to him more and more as *"Israel,"* and less and less as *"Jacob."* As stated, Sanctification is a process.

For instance, in Genesis Chapters 48 and 49, the two Chapters which record the end of Jacob's life, he is referred to as *"Jacob"* seven times, and *"Israel"* 14 times. Jacob the supplanter had finally become the Israel of God!

At the end of his life, the Patriarch charges his sons to surely bury him in the land of Canaan. He would not that even his bones should remain in Egypt.

He had now lived in that land for 17 years in ease and splendor. He had the gratification of seeing his son sit, practically, upon his throne; but all the splendor and ease failed to wreck his Faith, it burned brightly to the end, and he says to his sons, *"Bury me with my fathers in the land of Canaan."*

While he was physically in Egypt the last years of his life, his heart was ever in Canaan, because it was to that place that *"Shiloh* (the Messiah) *would come; and unto Him shall the gathering of the people be"* (Gen. 49:10).

In fact, that Scripture has not yet been fulfilled, because it pertains to the Second Coming of the Lord, but which most surely will come to pass.

THE SECURITY OF SALVATION

We have studied the preparations for Salvation and considered the nature of Salvation. In this section we shall consider the question: Is the final Salvation of Christians unconditional, or may it be forfeited because of sin or willful desertion of the Lord?

Experience proves the possibility of a temporary fall from Grace, sometimes referred to as *"backsliding."* Backsliding is not found in the New Testament; it is an Old Testament word. One Hebrew word used means to *"turn back"* or to *"turn away"*; and another word means to *"turn around"* or *"be refractory."*

Israel is compared to a backsliding heifer that refuses to be led and becomes refractory under the yoke; Israel has turned from Jehovah and has stubbornly refused to take upon her the yoke of His Commandments.

The New Testament warns against such an attitude, but uses other terms. A backslider is one who once had zeal for God but who has become cold (Mat. 24:12); he once obeyed the Word but worldliness and sin impeded its growth and prevented fruit (Mat. 13:22); he once put his hand to the plough, but looked back (Lk. 9:62); like Lot's wife he has been delivered from the City of Destruction but his heart has returned there (Lk. 17:32); he was once in vital contact with Christ, but is now out of touch, and is withered and barren and good-for-nothing spiritually (Jn. 15:6); he once heeded the checks of conscience but now has thrown away that guiding compass, and as a result, his ship of Faith has become wrecked on the rocks of sin and worldliness (I Tim. 1:19); he was once happy to call himself a Christian, but is now ashamed to confess his Lord (II Tim. 1:8; 2:12); he was once delivered from the world's defilements, but has returned like *"the sow that was washed to her wallowing in the mire"* (II Pet. 2:22; Lk. 11:21-26).

Lapses from Grace are possible; but may a person who was once saved lapse and be finally lost? Those who follow the Calvinistic system of doctrine answer in the negative; those who follow the Arminian system (named after Arminius, a Dutch Theologian who brought the question to an issue) answer in the affirmative.

CALVINISM

John Calvin's doctrine was not new with him; it was taught by Augustine, a Theologian of the Fourth Century. This is the manner in which Augustine interpreted Paul's doctrine of free Grace.

The Calvinistic doctrine is as follows:

Salvation is entirely of God; man has absolutely nothing to do about it. If he repents and believes and comes to Christ, it is entirely because of the drawing power of God's Spirit. This is due to the fact that man's will has become so corrupt since the Fall that, without God's help, he cannot even repent and believe, or choose rightly.

This was Calvin's starting point — the complete bondage of man's will to evil. Salvation, therefore, can be nothing but the execution of a Divine decree which fixes its extent and conditions.

The question naturally arises: If Salvation is entirely the Work of God, and man has nothing to do about it, and is helpless unless God's Spirit deals with him, why does not God save all men, since all are lost and helpless?

Calvin's answer is: God has predestined some to be saved and others to be lost. *"Predestination is the eternal Decree by God, by which He has decided what is to become of each and every individual. For all are not created in like condition; but Eternal Life is foreordained for some, eternal condemnation for others."*

In so acting God is not unjust for He is under no obligation to save anybody; man's responsibility remains, for Adam's Fall was his own fault and man is always responsible for his own sins.

Since God has predestined certain individuals to Salvation, Christ died only for the *"elect"*; the Atonement would fail were any to be lost for whom Christ died.

From the Doctrine of Predestination follows the teaching *"Once in Grace always in Grace,"* for if God has predestined a man to Salvation, and he can be saved and kept only by God's Grace, which is irresistible, then he can never be lost.

Advocates of the *"Eternal Security Doctrine"* present the following Scriptures in support of their position (Jn. 10:28-29; 17:6; Rom. 8:35; 11:29; Phil. 1:6; I Pet. 1:5).

ARMINIANISM

The Arminian Teaching is as follows:

God's will is that all men be saved because Christ died for all (Jn. 3:16; II Cor. 5:14; I Tim. 2:4-6; Titus 2:11-12; Heb. 2:9).

To that end He offers His Grace to all. While Salvation is the work of God, absolutely free, and independent of our good works or merit, yet man has certain conditions to fulfill.

He can either choose to accept God's Grace or he can resist or reject it. The power of choice ever remains.

In fact, the Scriptures do teach Predestination, but not that God predestines some to Eternal Life and others to eternal suffering. The truth is, He predestines *"whosoever will"* to be saved — and that plan is wide enough to include everybody who really wants to be saved. This Truth has been explained as follows:

Outside the door of Salvation we read the words, *"Whosoever will may come"*; when we enter and are saved, we read the words, *"Elect according to the foreknowledge of God."* God, because of His knowledge, foresaw those persons who would accept the Gospel and stay saved, and predestined such to a heavenly inheritance. He *foreknew* their destiny but did not fix — their destiny. In other words, they chose their destiny, as all men have the power to do.

The Doctrine of Predestination is mentioned not for a speculative, but for a practical purpose. When God called Jeremiah to the Ministry, He knew that he was going to have a very difficult task, and that he might be tempted to give up. In order to encourage him, the Lord assured the Prophet that He had known and called him before he was born (Jer. 1:5).

The Lord as much as says, *"I already know what is ahead of you; but I also know that I can give you Grace to meet every future test and to take you through victoriously."* When the New Testament describes Christians as objects of God's foreknowledge, its purpose is to assure us of the fact that God has foreseen every difficulty that will confront us, and that He can and will keep us from falling.

A COMPARISON

Considering both of these views, is Salvation conditional or unconditional?

Once saved, is a person eternally saved?

The answer will depend on the way we can answer the following *"key questions"*: On whom does Salvation depend? Is Grace irresistible?

1. On whom does Salvation ultimately depend — on God or man? Certainly it must depend on God, for who could be saved if Salvation depended on a person's own strength? We may be sure of this — God will take us through no matter how weak or blundering we are — provided we honestly desire to do His Will. His Grace is ever present to warn, check, encourage, and sustain.

However, is there not a certain sense in which Salvation does depend on man? The Scriptures consistently teach that man has the power of freely choosing between life and death, and that power God will never violate.

2. Can God's Grace be resisted?

One of the fundamental principles of Calvinism is that God's Grace is irresistible. When God decrees the Salvation of a person, His Spirit draws, and that drawing cannot be resisted, they say! Therefore, a True Child of God will certainly persevere to the end and be saved; even though he fall into sin God will chastise him and strive with him. Speaking figuratively: The man may fall on the ship but he cannot fall off the ship.

However, the New Testament does teach that Divine Grace may be resisted, and even resisted to eternal loss (Jn. 6:40; Heb. 2:3; 6:4-6; 10:26-30; II Pet. 1:10; 2:21), and that perseverance is conditional upon keeping in fellowship with God.

HEBREWS

Note especially Hebrews 6:4-6 and 10:26-29. These words were spoken to Christians; Paul's Letters were not addressed to the unregenerate. Those addressed are described as being once enlightened, having tasted of the Heavenly Gift, being made partakers of the Holy Spirit, having tasted the good Word of God and the powers of the world to come. These words certainly describe regenerate persons.

Those addressed were Hebrew Christians, who, discouraged and persecuted (Heb. 10:32-39) were tempted to return to Judaism. Before being received again into the Synagogue they would be publicly required to make the following statements (Heb. 10:29):

"That Jesus was not the Son of God; that His Blood was rightly shed as that of a common malefactor; and that His Miracles were done by the power of the Evil One." All this is implied in Hebrews 10:29.

(That such a repudiation would have been insisted on is illustrated by the case of a Hebrew Christian in Germany who desired to return to the Synagogue, but was refused when he desired to hold onto some of the New Testament Truths.)

Before their conversion they had belonged to a nation which had crucified Christ; to return to the Synagogue would be to crucify to themselves the Son of God afresh and put Him to an open shame; it would be the awful sin of apostasy, a departure from Truth (Heb. 6:6); it does not say that one doing such a thing could not come back to the Lord, if in fact they evidenced Faith, but it does mean, that if they go back into that system, thereby denying the Crucified, Risen Christ, as long as they stay in that state, they cannot be saved. One cannot have both, to accept Christ, repudiates all other systems, and to accept any other system, repudiates Christ.

That is the reason it's not possible for a Catholic to accept Christ as one's Saviour, and then remain in that system, which is totally opposite of the Biblical Christ of Redemption.

The point of all this is, that if the terrible sin of apostasy on the part of saved people were not at least remotely possible, all these warnings would have been meaningless.

THE CORINTHIANS

I Corinthians 10:1-12 gives us another example.

The Corinthians had been boasting of the Christian liberty and the possession of Spiritual Gifts, yet many of them were living on a low plain. They were evidently trusting in their *"standing"* and privileges in the Gospel. But Paul warns them that privileges may be lost by sin and cites the examples of the Israelites. They were supernaturally delivered from the land of Egypt. Their passing through the Red Sea was a sign, or type, if you will, of the Redemption experience (I Cor. 10:1-4).

Overshadowing them was the supernatural symbol of God's guiding Presence. After saving them from Egypt, God sustained them with supernatural food and drink. All this meant that the Israelites were in Grace, that is, in favor and fellowship with God.

But *"once in Grace always in Grace"* was not true in their case; for the route was dotted with the graves of those who had been smitten for their murmurings, rebellion, and idolatries. Sin broke their fellowship with God and as a result they fell from Grace. Paul declares that these events were recorded to warn Christians of the possibility of forfeiting the most exalted privileges through willful sin.

A SCRIPTURAL BALANCE

The respective fundamental positions of both Calvinism and Arminianism are taught in the Scriptures. Calvinism exalts the Grace of God as the only source of Salvation — and so does the Bible; Arminianism emphasizes man's free will and responsibility — and so does the Bible.

The practical solution consists in avoiding the unscriptural extremes of either view, and in refraining from setting one view in antagonism to the other. For when two Scriptural Doctrines are set squarely in opposition to each other the result is a reaction that leads to error. For example: Overemphasis of God's Sovereignty and Grace in Salvation may lead to careless living, for if a person is led to believe that his conduct and attitude have nothing to do with his Salvation, he may become negligent, and in fact, most will.

On the other hand, overemphasis of man's free will and responsibility, in reaction against Calvinism, may bring people under the bondage of legalism and rob them of all assurance. Lawlessness and legalism — these are the two extremes to be avoided.

FINNEY

When Finney ministered in a community where Grace had been overemphasized he bore down heavily on the doctrine of man's responsibility. When he held a meeting in a community where human responsibility and works had been stressed he emphasized the Grace of God. And as we leave the mysteries of predestination and set ourselves to the practical task of getting people saved, we should not be troubled by the matter. Wesley was Arminian in belief and Whitefield was a Calvinist. Yet both led thousands to Christ.

Godly Calvinistic Preachers of the type of Spurgeon and Finney have preached the perseverance of the Saints in such a manner as to discourage carelessness. They were careful to point out that while a True Child of

God was certain to persevere to the end, the fact that he did not so persevere would put in question the fact as to whether he had really been Born-Again! If a person did not follow after Holiness, said Calvin, he would do well to question his election.

We are bound to be confronted with mystery as we set out to relate the mighty Truths of God's foreknowledge and man's free will; but as we keep to the practical exhortations of the Scripture and set ourselves to the definite duties commanded, we shall not go wrong. *"The secret things belong unto the Lord our God: but those things which are revealed belong unto us"* (Deut. 29:29).

In conclusion may we suggest that it is unwise to dwell unduly on the perils of the Christian life. The emphasis should rather be placed upon the means of security — the Power of Christ as Saviour, the faithfulness of the indwelling Spirit, the certainty of the Divine Promises, and the unfailing efficacy of Prayer. The New Testament teaches a true *"eternal security,"* assuring us that regardless of weakness, imperfections, handicaps, or outward troubles, the Christian can be secure and victorious in Christ.

With the Apostle Paul we can cry, *"Who shall separate us from the Love of Christ? Shall tribulation, or distress, or persecution, or famine, or nakedness, or peril, or sword? . . . Nay, in all these things we are more than conquerors through Him that loved us. For I am persuaded that neither death, nor life, nor Angels, nor principalities, nor powers, nor things present, nor things to come, Nor height, nor depth, nor any other creature, shall be able to separate us from the Love of God which is in Christ Jesus our Lord"* (Rom. 8:35-39).

However, we should also consider that of all these things we are told that cannot separate us from the Love of God, self is not mentioned. In fact, that is the only thing which can truly separate a person from the Love of God. God has promised to protect us against all outside influences, but not from ourselves. Man still has the power of choice. It is still *"whosoever will"* (Rev. 22:17).

(Most of the material on Salvation was provided by the scholarship of Myer Pearlman.)

NOTES

(13) "FOR IT IS GOD WHICH WORKETH IN YOU BOTH TO WILL AND TO DO OF HIS GOOD PLEASURE."

Paul describes the enablement to carry out the exhortation as being furnished by God Himself, Who produces in Believers both the desire to live righteously and the effective energy to do so. God does not demand of us what we cannot do. Furthermore, the provision from God takes into account our every need. It is not always enough to *"will"* something, for good intentions are not always carried out. Paul sees Believers having their wills energized by God and then also having the power to work supplied by Him (Kent).

THE WORKING OF GOD

The phrase, *"For it is God which worketh in you,"* speaks of Divine enablement.

The word *"worketh"* in the Greek means *"to energize, to work effectively."*

Salvation must be possessed before it can be worked out, just as a farm must be possessed before it can be developed. The moralist (the religion of ethics) and the sacerdotalist (those who depend on ritual and ceremony for Salvation) work in order to get Salvation; the Christian works because he already possesses it — it is his own; and he does not pursue the religious activities of self-will, but is moved by the Divine Will; and that Will accomplishes what it purposes.

IRRECONCILABLE?

In this famous paradox Paul calls on men to work by their own will, because only God can grant them power both to will and to do. The origination of all in God, and the free action (which is in some sense origination) of man, are both truths recognized by our deepest consciousness, but to our logic irreconcilable. In one Passage only (Rom. 9:14-24) does Paul touch, and that slightly and suggestively, on their reconcilement: Generally the Bible — in this confirming human reason — brings out each vividly and profoundly in turn, and leaves the problem of their reconcilement untouched.

Here the paradoxical form of the sentence forces on the mind the recognition of the co-existence of both — the Will of God and the will of man. If that recognition be accepted, the force of the reasoning is clear.

The only encouragement to work, in a being weak and finite like man, is the conviction that Almighty Power is working in him, both as to will and deed.

The Word *"worketh in you"* is constantly applied to the Divine operation in the soul (I Cor. 12:6, 11; Gal. 2:8; Eph. 1:11, 20; 2:2); rarely, as here (in the word rendered *"to do"*) to the action of men. It must necessarily extend to the will as well as the action; otherwise God would not be sovereign in the inner realm of the mind.

We are familiar with the influence of one created will over another (of one person's will over another) an influence real, though limited. From this experience we may catch a faint glimpse of the inner working of the Spirit of God on the spirit of man. Hence, while we cannot even conceive the existence of freedom under an unbending impersonal law or force, the harmony of our will with a supreme personal Will of God, is mysterious, indeed, but not inconceivable (Ellicott).

TO WILL AND TO DO

The phrase, *"Both to will and to do of His good pleasure,"* refers to God the Holy Spirit Who energizes the Saint, making him not only willing, but actively desirous of doing God's sweet Will. He does not merely leave the Saint with the desire to do His Will, but as well, provides the necessary power to do it.

Actually, the words *"to will"* are the translation of a Greek word meaning *"to desire,"* and refer to a desire that comes from one's emotions rather than from one's reason. It is this desire to do the good pleasure of God that is produced by Divine energy in the heart of the Saint as he definitely subjects himself to the Ministry of the Holy Spirit.

HUMAN RESPONSIBILITY AND DIVINE ENABLEMENT

In Verse 12, we have human responsibility, in Verse 13, Divine enablement, a perfect balance which must be kept if the Christian life is to be lived at its best. It is not a *"let go and let God"* affair. It is a *"take hold with God"* business. It is a mutual cooperation with the Holy Spirit in an interest and an activity in the things of God.

The Saint must not merely rest in the Holy Spirit for victory over sin and the production of a holy life. He must in addition to this dependence upon the Spirit, cooperate fully with the Spirit and even exert himself to the doing of that which is right.

To which we have already addressed, here we have that incomprehensible and mysterious interaction between the free will of man and the sovereign Grace of God, but with God never forcing the will of man.

All of this is for the *"good pleasure"* of God, which means that the Will of God is always a very pleasant, beautiful, and harmonious activity.

THE WILL OF GOD

Many Christians are regrettably fearful of the Will of God. They are afraid to pray or submit themselves to the Will of God, fearing that He will demand that they do something which they do not desire to do. Somehow, people have been led to believe (by Satan I might quickly add) that the Will of God always works out to the sending them to Siberia, or some other undesirable place. None of that is ever true.

In the first place, being in the Will of God is the most beautiful, advantageous, helpful, glorious, fulfilling life that one could ever have. In fact, being in the Will of God is the only life that's worth living.

As well, wherever it is that God would want to send someone, if at all, or whatever the Lord wants one to do, He will give that person a love for that place, or that thing, whatever it might be, that will be absolutely compelling. The Lord never fosters something off on someone, that will make them miserable. It is always *"of His good pleasure,"* which always translates into *"our good pleasure."* In other words, if He does send someone to Siberia, He will fill their heart with such a love for that place, that they will not be happy anywhere else.

So, the Saint must ardently seek the perfect Will of God in all things, knowing and understanding, that this direction, whatever that direction might be, is the most glorious and wonderful life and lifestyle that one could ever have. There is nothing in the world that even remotely compares with this of which I have spoken, and to be sure, Satan doesn't have anything at all in this capacity.

No, our problem is self-will, not God's Will. Self-will is destructive — always — while God's Will is always constructive, and exceedingly so!

In fact, the entirety of this Verse is a Promise that God will do exactly this, a Blessing based on *"His good pleasure"* (Deut. 31:8).

A LIVING SACRIFICE

The greatest deception which Satan, the enemy of our souls, has ever foisted upon humanity is the false but appealing doctrine that man can do something to earn his own Salvation, by keeping the Law of God. The second greatest error is the teaching that we don't have to do anything after we are saved.

The first error says it makes no difference what you believe, just so you live right, and the second error teaches that it makes no difference how you live, just so you believe right. Both are a delusion and a snare of the enemy.

It is ever Faith, followed by works. Faith is the root of Salvation, and more particularly, Faith in the Finished Work of Christ, while works are the fruit of our Salvation. God sees our Faith, without works, and justifies us on the basis of our Faith in His Promise. Men, however, will never recognize our Faith until they can see it evidenced in our works. God looks at our Faith. People can only see our works.

Justification is the Work of God; our works as a result of our Salvation, are the proof to our fellowmen of God's Work in us.

THE WORKING OUT OF OUR SALVATION

He does not say work *for* your Salvation, but rather work *out* what God has already worked *in*. But while Believers are not saved or kept by works, God does expect and claim our complete devotion. Paul makes an impassioned plea to the Christians in Rome that they make a full surrender of their lives on the basis of their great Salvation. He said:

"I beseech you therefore, Brethren, by the Mercies of God, that ye present your bodies a living Sacrifice, holy, acceptable unto God, which is your reasonable service" (Rom. 12:1).

NOTES

Please note the form of the appeal. It is the language of the Grace of God. He says, *"I beseech you."* It is not, I command you.

In other words, this of which Paul says and does, is not on a legal ground, but in the realm of Grace. It must be a voluntary service, motivated by gratitude and love, and not by constraint or fear of punishment. This is implied by the word, *"therefore."* He says, *"I beseech you therefore."*

Whenever you come across the word, *"therefore,"* in the Bible, you should stop and ask, *"What is it there for?"* It always refers us back to a *"wherefore."* It points us back to the reason for the plea, *"I beseech you therefore."* This Verse in Romans 12:1 should logically follow Romans 8:35-39.

A PARENTHESIS

The 9th, 10th, and 11th Chapters of Romans are a parenthesis between Chapters 8 and 12. They are inserted between the closing Verse of Chapter 8 and the opening Verse of Chapter 12, as an illustration of the free Grace of God.

After Paul had shown that we are not only saved by Grace, but kept by Grace, he stops to call attention to the history of the nation of Israel as an illustration of this Truth. The nation had been chosen of God by Grace in the Covenant which God made with Abraham, Isaac, and Jacob. Then they were placed under the Law of Moses with its condemnation; but they failed to keep this Law and fell into idolatry, bringing upon themselves the chastening of the Lord, and even His rejection of them, and were scattered over the face of the whole Earth. They had been in this scattered condition now for over 2500 years.

However, God has not cast them away, or permanently forsaken them, but remembers His Covenant and will restore them again and fulfill every Covenant Promise made to them; however, all of those who forsook the Lord, despite all these Promises, died eternally lost; consequently, the Promises mentioned here, only refer to a future time when Israel will then accept the Lord.

These Three Chapters (Rom. Chpts. 9-11) are inserted here to illustrate the fact that the Grace of God cannot condone open, designed rebellion against God, even as Israel did. Irrespective as to whether it's Israel or a Believer presently, or anyone for that matter and for all time, the Grace of God has always been conditional. God does not require much, only that we believe and that our believing be such that it allow Him to work His Work within our hearts and lives. In fact, Romans Chapters 9, 10 and 11, are the most powerful rebuke of all against the false doctrine of *"once saved always saved, irrespective as to what one might do"* or how one might live.

THE PROMISES OF GOD

Just because Israel failed completely to keep God's Law, and as well rebelled against Him, and ended up rejecting the Messiah, this did not affect God's faithfulness to His Promises. Israel will yet be brought back, and will accept Jesus Christ as Lord and Messiah. This will take place at the Second Coming (Zech. Chpts. 12-14). Nevertheless, even as stated, all of the many million of Jews who rebelled against God in this some 2500 years, died eternally lost. Grace did not save them, as Grace cannot save anyone who refuses to accept God's Offer of Redemption, Which and Who is, The Lord Jesus Christ.

The Promises of God are always conditional as it affects human beings. If it affects only God, it is not conditional. In other words, when He says He will do a certain thing, such as for example, the sending of a Redeemer into this world, it was done, with the Redeemer, The Lord Jesus Christ, going to the Cross exactly as predestined by God, whether men liked it or not. These Promises, and many more of this same nature, were and are unconditional.

Nevertheless, when Promises are made to men, even as it regards these individuals, such Promises are always conditional upon the individual obeying the Lord. For example, Jesus said, *"If ye continue in My Word, then are ye My Disciples indeed"* (Jn. 8:31).

This is just one example of which there are many. In fact, there are 1,522 *"ifs"* in the Bible and all of them express a condition if one of them does. The condition to be met if these new Believers were to remain as true Disciples and have freedom from sin was: *"Continue in My Word."*

BY THE MERCIES OF GOD

Going back to Romans 12:1, the Holy Spirit through Paul said, *"I beseech you therefore, Brethren, by the Mercies of God that ye present your bodies a living Sacrifice, holy, acceptable unto God, which is your reasonable service."*

It is because of the faithfulness of God, that Paul opens Romans Chapter 12 with this impassioned plea. God's faithfulness is to be the incentive and motive of our surrender to Him, and not Law.

We have already pointed out that this is a plea, and not a command. He says, *"I beseech you."* It is the language of *"Grace,"* and not *"Law."* Notice next, he is speaking to Believers. He says *"Brethren."* They were Born-Again Believers but living selfish lives. They were not fully yielded to the Lord. As should be obvious, he is talking to people who had not attained sinless perfection. In fact, there definitely was failure involved, at least in some of these Believers. Nevertheless, Paul asks them to do something, not by threat, but by the *"Mercies of God."*

Consequently, Romans 12:1 could be paraphrased, *"Make Me a present of your body, to be used of Me as an expression of your gratitude for the Mercies I have shown you."*

God wants us to yield our bodies to Him, as well as our souls and our spirits. Notice how the Holy Spirit couches His Words through the Apostle, *"Present these bodies a living Sacrifice,"* or *"a Sacrifice while we are still alive."*

THE PHYSICAL BODY IS THE BATTLEGROUND

While sin originates in the heart, it cannot be carried out to completion without the cooperation of the physical body. It is through the physical members of the body, and the five senses, that sins are carried out. In fact, in its truest sense, the physical body is neutral. Within itself, it does not have a propensity either way, whether toward righteousness or unrighteousness. It is like a tool (Rom. 6:13).

A knife can be used to do many helpful and constructive things. As well, it can also be used to kill someone.

Such is the physical body. The Lord wants it as a *"living sacrifice,"* which means dedicated exclusively to His purpose and service, while Satan wants it for other means. Notice what Paul said:

In dealing with the physical body, and I speak of the physical body of the Christian, he uses the word *"yield,"* implying that the Believer has the means to yield His Body either to Righteousness or unrighteousness (Rom. 6:13), providing the Believer has the Cross of Christ as the proper object of his Faith, which then guarantees the help of the Holy Spirit (Lk. 9:23; Rom. 8:2).

In fact, the unbeliever does not have that privilege. The unbeliever, a slave to his passions, must yield his physical body to whatever those passions dictate, all bad. Hence, the condition of the world at this present time, and in fact, for all time since the Fall.

But when the sinner comes to Christ, he is made a new creature, i.e., *"a new creation"* in Christ, actually given the Divine Nature, which is superintended by the Holy Spirit Who abides in every Believer (Jn. 14:16-17). The Believer is now no longer ruled by the sin nature, at least he shouldn't be; however, it is definitely possible for the Believer to be ruled by the sin nature, with sin having dominion over him, if his Faith is not properly placed (Rom. Chpt. 6). With his Faith properly placed, he has the power to yield his physical body to whatever direction he so desires, but without the proper Faith, and we might quickly add, in the proper object which is the Cross of Christ, he will lose that ability to *"yield,"* and then will be taken over by force as it regards the powers of darkness.

This is a frightful prospect, even as Paul outlined in Romans Chapter 7. That's the reason the Apostle said at that time, *"For that which I do I allow* (understand) *not: for what I would, that do I not; but what I hate, that do I"* (Rom. 7:15).

As should be overly obvious, these are not the words of a man who has the power to yield his physical body as he so desires, but rather the opposite. In fact, this was Paul's experience right after he was initially brought to Christ and baptized with the Holy Spirit. At that time he did not know the Lord's prescribed order of victory, which is the Cross, and he attempted to overcome by means of the Law, which is always doomed to defeat.

No, Romans Chapter 7, even as we've already stated in other Commentary, is not an account of Paul's experience before his conversion, but rather after. Paul earnestly sought the Lord, and the answer to this dilemma was given to him by the Holy Spirit, which he gave to us in Romans Chapters 6 and 8. The victories are all wrapped up in the Cross and the Holy Spirit, and our Faith in that, and not Law.

WHAT DO WE MEAN BY LAW?

So many of God's dear people, who do not yet realize the power of complete yielding of their members to Christ, are still seeking for victory in the strength of the flesh, under the fear of the Law. In other words, they are attempting to overcome by their own efforts, whatever those efforts might be, whether rules or regulations, or even legitimate things such as prayer and fasting, etc.

While some of these things are very legitimate (prayer and fasting), still, if we attempt to use them outside of their prescribed parameters, in other words to try to overcome sin through this means, we will always fail. Stop and think a moment!

If all it took to defeat sin was prayer and fasting, or some such like effort, then why did Jesus have to come down here and die on a Cross?

The idea is, that we get ourselves into a trap when we attempt to do anything, and I mean anything, that takes away from the Finished Work of Christ. What Jesus did at the Cross and the Resurrection, which also includes His Exaltation, addressed this problem of sin in totality. In other words, absolutely nothing was left undone; consequently, when we do anything to try to aid our victory, we are, in effect, saying that Jesus didn't do it all, and He needs our effort added to His Work. Such is preposterous! But yet all of us have fallen into this trap.

The only thing that God requires of us is Faith, and I mean that is all! However, as we've already said, it must be Faith in the proper object, and by that I mean the Cross, i.e., *"The Finished Work of Christ"* (Rom. Chpt. 6).

Most Christians take the position of *"shotgun faith,"* which is faith in everything, but actually faith in nothing. That won't work, for the simple reason, that it actually isn't faith, at least the kind God will recognize and honor.

Your Faith in totality, in completion, in its overall concept in every capacity, is to be totally and solely in the Cross of Christ, for it was there that Jesus satisfied the sin debt, and in effect, broke the stranglehold that Satan had on the human race through sin, at least for those who will believe.

So, your Faith is to anchor there, to hold there, to not be moved from this great principle of Christ.

Do not listen to the false teachers who tell you that we have gone beyond the Cross. In fact, it is impossible to go beyond the Cross. A trillion years from today, even as I've already said, more and greater revelation will continue to be given unto us concerning this of what Jesus did. What He accomplished at the Cross and the Resurrection is absolutely inexhaustible!

When the Believer's Faith is properly enjoined, the Holy Spirit then has the latitude to bring the Believer to the desired place in Christ, which He will not do, and in fact cannot do, if our Faith is in other channels.

YIELDING TO CHRIST

The Christian is to stop his vain struggling and confess before the Lord that he is living a life of failure and then turn to the only One Who Alone can give Victory. Place your Faith in what He did at the Cross and the Resurrection on your behalf — yes, He did it for you — understanding that He did not fail; consequently, our Faith in Him and what He did, means we will not fail. However, His Victory which was actually meant to be our Victory, can be ours only if we have the proper Faith in what He properly did.

Now don't misunderstand these words. It doesn't mean, that you the Believer have to have some superhuman type of Faith. To be frank, the degree is not in question here, but rather the object. If your Faith is in Christ and what He did at the Cross for you, that's all that God requires. Victory will then be yours, because as stated, His Victory was actually our Victory; His overcoming Power actually our overcoming power; His defeat of Satan and all his minions, is actually our defeat of Satan and all his minions. We must understand that, and not think otherwise.

Everything He did, was for you and me. He was our Substitute, our Representative Man, and that means that everything He did, was on our behalf, meaning that we should have the benefits of all that He did. But it all hinges on our Faith in that Finished Work.

Regrettably, Satan has done his best to move the Church away from the Cross, and has by and large succeeded. In fact, the entire direction of modern Pentecostals and Charismatics toward humanistic psychology, stems from unbelief in the Cross of Christ. Also, the modern Faith Ministry, while making Faith within itself its object, has drifted astray. Faith Alone is never to be the object, but rather Jesus. He Alone is the Author and Finisher of our Faith, and more particularly, what He did at the Cross (Heb. 12:2).

Satan doesn't care at all how much we major in Faith, providing the object is Faith alone. In fact, this is what the world does.

FAITH MUST NOT BE WITHIN ITSELF THE OBJECT

Every single day that goes by, somewhere in the world there are literally hundreds of seminars taking place in the business world or in the realm of self-improvement, which teaches faith, and faith as its object. Actually, this is the core of belief of all religions. However, the faith that's being taught is faith for faith's sake, and does not at all have as its object the Lord Jesus Christ, and more particularly, His Finished Work of Redemption. Consequently, it's not faith which God will recognize.

When we speak of Faith, we must always understand that it must be Faith in Christ, and Faith more particularly in His Finished Work, which spells out the Cross and the Resurrection. This is what Redemption is all about. Even though the Miracles of Christ were great and grand, as was His Teaching, and in fact all that He did, still, those things within themselves, as necessary and helpful as they were, could not save anyone. It was what Jesus did at the Cross and the Resurrection, that guaranteed Redemption, i.e., *"all sin being washed away by the Precious Blood of Christ, replaced by the Divine Nature"* (II Cor. 5:16-19).

Actually, Paul plainly said in II Corinthians 5:16, *"Yea, though we have known Christ after the flesh, yet now henceforth know we Him no more."*

What did he mean by that?

He was meaning, that all of these things that Jesus did in His earthly Ministry, as important as they were, did not save anyone. It was only, *"That He died for all . . . and rose again,"* whereby we are saved.

Satan will do everything within his power to shove the Believer away from the Cross. He wants us to major in other things, knowing that these other things, as important as they might be in their own manner, cannot actually save anyone. It was at the Cross where the Evil One was totally and absolutely defeated.

And how was he defeated?

He was defeated by Jesus paying the sin debt which had hung over man, which He did by His Death and Resurrection, which destroyed Satan's hold on humanity. Satan's hold, rather his claim on humanity, is sin, i.e., *"transgressions, iniquity, etc."* With that gone, and to be sure Christ took it away, the Evil One has no more grip, at least on those who will believe. So, as should be understandable, he wants to divert our efforts toward other directions. He really doesn't care what we believe, how much we be immersed in these other ways as religious and even spiritual as they might be, and even Biblical in their own right. If it's not Faith in the Cross, he knows we're not going to get any positive results. So he fights the Cross as he fights nothing else.

Faith in the Cross claims the Supremacy of the Saviour, and the helplessness of the Believer. Faith in the Cross admits the Sacrifice as God's solution, and that man has no solution whatsoever. Faith in the Cross, tells us how good that God is and how evil that man is. Faith in the Cross creates humility, while faith in ourself or other things, creates self-righteousness.

Let the Reader understand, that God has no other way, no other path, no other solution, only the Cross. Consequently, if another way is enjoined, no matter how subtle it might be, how spiritual even it might be, if it's not the Cross it is Satan coming as an angel of light, and is to be avoided at all costs.

God's answer to failing, sinning, dying, lost, wrecked, destroyed humanity, is the Cross of Christ, and nothing else!

A PRAYER TO THE LORD

With your Faith properly placed in the Cross, ask the Lord that the Holy Spirit would help you in the following:

"Here is my body, dear Lord; from now on it shall be wholly Yours."

As well, we must remember that the body is made up of members. We should then say, *"Lord, here are my eyes which have been so enamored by the scenes of this world; take them and open them to the need of seeking out the lost, in reading and studying Thy Word, instead of looking at the silly trash of this age.*

"Lord, take my ears, that have been so given to the listening of the jargon and clamor of a sinful world, so eager to listen to gossip and slander — take these ears and open them to the cry of lost humanity, to listen only for Thy voice, and help me to close them to the things which defile and pollute my mind and my soul.

"Take these lips of mine, and this tongue which has so often been used to cut and wound and hurt, and which has been spent in idle gossip and foolish jesting, and cleanse it by my proper confession of faith in the Cross, that henceforth this tongue shall speak and repeat only the things which are pure and holy, instead of inflicting injury.

"Take these hands which have been so grasping for filthy lucre. Take my feet which have so often walked in self-chosen ways and lead them to some soul for Thee. Take my heart, my mind, my will, yes, my every thought and imagination, and help me to make it subject in totality to Thy Will. In fact, take my stubborn will, my unwillingness to forgive, and teach me true humility."

REASONABLE SERVICE

Again, notice the words that Paul used in Romans 12:1, *"present your bodies a living sacrifice, holy, acceptable to God, which is your reasonable service."* Let me ask this question:

Is it unreasonable of the Lord to ask you for your body as a living sacrifice, when He gave His Body on the Cross for you? Let's ask it another way:

The Lord asks each one, *"In the light of what I have done for you, in saving you from Hell, delivering you from the curse and condemnation of the Law, and setting you free in the liberty of Grace, and doing this by the giving of My Body on the Tree, is it an unreasonable request to ask you to live for Me?"*

In closing this statement, we must again remind you, this service is not on the basis of Law, but Grace. We are not to serve the Lord in order to keep saved, or to escape chastening and punishment, but instead we are to serve Him because we are saved, kept, secure, and above all because we love Him.

I want to say it graciously, but I must say it. I pity those poor professing Christians who behave themselves and live as they do, because of the fear of God's judgment and chastening. That's not *"more abundant life,"* which Jesus promised (Jn. 10:10). As well, that's not the *"rest"* which He said we would have when we came to Him (Mat. 11:28-30).

Paul could say, *"the love of Christ constraineth me,"* not the Law of God threatens me.

I truly pity those sincere souls who live a life of bondage, abstaining from this thing and that thing, and observing this Commandment and that Commandment, keeping this day holy rather than another, because they fear they will be lost again if they don't live a perfect life — perfect we might add, in their eyes, and not God's eyes. They live in fear. Let me repeat this truth:

My heart goes out to those poor souls who must hold themselves in bondage and restraint because they fear losing their Salvation if they should fail. That is a low, mean, unworthy motive for serving the Lord. He wants us to serve Him through love, not fear; from a heart of gratitude which rejoices in doing the things that please Him, Who pleased not Himself but gave His all to redeem us.

Frances and I have one Son, Donnie. Consequently, we have one Daughter-in-law, Debbie, and three grandchildren, Jennifer, Gabriel, and Matthew.

I don't want them obeying and respecting me because they fear a thrashing if they don't; instead, I want their love and gratitude for that which I have tried to do for them. Consequently, how much more we should seek those things which are pleasing to Him, and bring forth . . . the fruit of the Spirit . . . Love, Joy, Peace, Longsuffering, Gentleness, Goodness, Faith, Meekness, Temperance:

"Against such there is no Law" (Gal. 5:22-23).

(14) "DO ALL THINGS WITHOUT MURMURINGS AND DISPUTINGS:"

Compliance with Paul's exhortation should be *"without complaining or arguing."* The first term describes the grumbling discontents among the congregation, and the second depicts the evil reasonings and disputes that usually follow.

Are these directed against God or against each other? Neither alternative is foreign to the context. This Passage influenced by Deuteronomy 32:5, and the example of Israel's complaining, which was chiefly against God, was used elsewhere by Paul to instruct the Church (I Cor. 10:10).

On the other hand, the problem of disunity in the congregation has already been seen in this Letter (Phil. 2:2), and more is to come (Phil. 4:2). Perhaps the command is sufficiently general to cover both.

Emphasis in the command falls on the word *"everything,"* which literally means, *"all things."* It is actually the first word of the Verse in the Greek text.

Most Christians are able to do some things without complaint. It is when we are exhorted to be doing *"all things"* with a joyful spirit that the difficulty comes. Yet the outworking of our Christian faith in daily life lays this responsibility upon us.

DO ALL THINGS

Paul is dealing here with *"murmurings"* and *"disputings"* which we will address momentarily, but first let's look at *"all things"* and the *"doing"* of such.

This is speaking of all things that we may do, whether in our service for the Lord, or in our dealings with each other as Christians. *"All things"* include *"everything."* Consequently, it covers all territory, the good and the bad.

The very nature of the command, even as we shall see, refers to the fact that there will be difficulties along the way. Irrespective of our Faith, everything is not perfect. Satan opposes our work and at times, even Christians oppose our efforts for the Lord.

So, we are told here, that despite being a Christian, and serving God Who is able to do all things, sometimes things will happen, which are adverse, negative, and even hurtful. In the face of that, we are not to complain. To be blunt, the Lord doesn't like such attitudes on the part of those who serve Him.

Paul would later tell Timothy, *"Thou therefore endure hardness, as a good soldier of Jesus Christ"* (II Tim. 2:3).

If any man knew of problems, difficulties, opposition, hindrances, and things which are irritating to say the least, Paul did (II Cor. 11:23-30).

To be frank, *"murmurings"* and *"disputings"* are the great sins of the Church, i.e., *"of the individual Christian."*

MURMURINGS

One of the ways in which this lack of harmony among the Philippian Saints was manifesting itself, was in murmurings and disputings. Paul had somehow gotten that fact out of Epaphroditus whose love for his brethren back home had maybe led him to cover up their sins. Paul exhorts them to be done with these.

The word *"murmurings"* is the translation of a Greek word which means, *"to mutter, to murmur."* It is a word which sound resembles its meaning.

It refers, not so much to a loud outspoken dissatisfaction, but to that undertone murmuring which one sometimes hears in the lobbies of our present day Churches where certain cliques are complaining about something.

The word refers to the act of murmuring against men, but could refer to murmuring as well against God.

The use of this word shows that the divisions among the Philippians had not yet risen to the point of loud dissension, but definitely would, if continued. The word is used of those who confer secretly, those who discontentedly complain.

ISRAEL OF OLD

This sin of murmuring was one of the greatest sins of Israel, probably the sin that brought more judgment on them than any other form of disobedience. Murmuring always shows a lack of gratitude and a lack of faith, both which God abhors, especially considering how good He has been to us.

Israel had been veritable slaves in Egypt, laboring under the taskmaster's whip, in fact, living under horrible conditions. The Lord had delivered them, but their murmuring shows that there was no gratitude.

The Lord said of them, *"How long shall I bear with this evil congregation, which murmur against Me? I have heard the murmurings of the Children of Israel, which they murmur against Me"* (Num. 14:27).

To be sure, God hears our murmurings as well.

Let's look at the record as it concerns Israel:

1. By murmuring and accusing God of deceiving them and deliberately leading them into a trap so the Egyptians could kill them (Ex. 14:11-12).

2. By murmuring at Marah concerning water (Ex. 15:23-26).

3. By murmuring for flesh and bread before reaching Sinai (Ex. 16:1-18).

4. By wilful disobedience in leaving the Manna until morning (Ex. 16:19-22).

5. By murmuring for water at Rephidim (Ex. 17:1-7).

6. By making a golden calf and quickly going back to idolatry (Ex. Chpt. 32).

7. By murmuring at Taberah (Num. 11:1-3).

8. By murmuring for flesh (Num. 11:4-35).

9. By unbelief in God and His Words and asking that spies be sent into the land as if they doubted He told the truth (Num. 13:1-25; Deut. 1:20-25).

10. By rebellion at Kadesh (Num. 13:26-14:37; Deut. 1:26-46).

Six times out of the ten times listed, it says they were murmuring, and no doubt this same sin was committed concerning the other times as well. And the Reader must understand, that this account in no way gives all their history, actually only the beginning.

DISPUTINGS

The word *"disputings"* is the translation of a Greek word that carries the ideas of discussion or debate, with the underthought of suspicion or doubt. Actually, the murmurings led to disputes (Wuest).

The idea of all of this is:

The Lord demands obedience from His people, for the simple reason, that what He desires that we do is always for our good, and the good of all concerned for that matter. The Believer certainly should understand that the Lord has our welfare at heart. He loves us more than we could ever think of understanding or comprehending; consequently, His planned course for us, is always for betterment, for help, for instruction, and for spiritual growth. However, at the same time, He never promised that it would be an uneventful journey, for the simple reason, that we need difficulties along the way as much as they are disliked. We need them in order to strengthen us and test our faith.

At the same time the Lord demands not only obedience, but that obedience be willing and cheerful. So, we have two situations here:

1. Obedience
2. Obedience carried out without murmuring and complaining, but rather willing and cheerful.

The Christian must remember that *"explanations, if they come at all, come after obedience, not before"* (Jn. 7:17). This is a tremendous thought and should be weighed very carefully.

Murmurings and disputations at what displeases us, and multiplying debate about it — is simply one form of the spirit which Paul addresses and deprecates all through this context. It is the sign of the disposition to value unduly one's own ease, one's own will, one's own opinion, one's own party, and to look for opportunities to bring our feelings forth.

The Christian is to be *"salt* (preservative)*"* and *"light* (illumination).*"* Murmuring and disputing are precisely adapted to hinder this impression.

This vice — and yes, murmuring and disputing is a vice — is so suggestive of a man's self being uppermost, in other words, self-will. It so unpleasantly forces itself in as the interpretation of the man, that his real goodness is little accounted of. In other words, the murmuring and complaining destroy the good that is in us.

DIVINE DEALINGS

When the believing sinner comes to Christ, his life changes dramatically. He now belongs to the Lord; consequently, every single thing from then on out, must be looked at as it regards this particular Believer, whomever he may be, as *"Divine dealings."* The Lord has the ability inasmuch as He is God, to deal with each individual Believer, as if He is devoting all His time and attention to that one Person. As a result, the Believer should understand that all things are now from the Lord, or at least the Lord is overlooking the situation concerning our lives in totality.

Considering that, understanding that we are dealing with the Most High, and above all that the Holy Spirit, the Third Person of the Triune Godhead literally lives in us (Jn. 14:16-17), should cause us to be very cognizant of all that we say, do, and even think. One might say that the Believer is *"on duty"* 24 hours a day, seven days a week, 365 days out of the year.

Understanding this total care, total instruction, total leading and guidance, we must ever realize that every single thing we say is, in effect, said to God. If it is praise, well and good; otherwise, if it is murmuring and complaining, we are, in effect, finding fault with God's Leadership. Thankfully, God is patient and longsuffering. If not, where would any of us be. Nevertheless, after awhile He expects us to grow into some type of maturity, thereby leaving off the whining, complaining, murmuring, and disputing.

Remember, He hears the stuff (Num. 14:27).

(15) "THAT YE MAY BE BLAMELESS AND HARMLESS, THE SONS OF GOD, WITHOUT REBUKE, IN THE MIDST OF A CROOKED AND PERVERSE NATION, AMONG WHOM YOU SHINE AS LIGHTS IN THE WORLD;"

The purpose of all of this is that Believers might be pure and uncontaminated Light-givers in the world. By regeneration we have already become Children of God in nature and position. Now as we progress in

Sanctification, we would become *"Children of God without fault,"* particularly as viewed by the world around us.

By faithfully adhering to the Word of God as contained in Scripture, our lives are to be free from anything blameworthy, as well as devoid of matters foreign or improper in the heart. Our nature as God's children is to be clearly evident, with no obvious flaws to disfigure our witness. In fact, the Holy Spirit through the Apostle reminds us of our position within a corrupt society.

In Old Testament language (Deut. 32:5) Paul depicts mankind generally as *"a crooked and depraved generation."* By using the word *"generation"* he was probably thinking of mankind as morally the product of one sinful stock, namely Adam (Jn. 8:44), rather than merely a group of individuals.

Amid this moral blackness, the Children of God are to stand out as stars at midnight. Believers are the possessors of Christ, the Light of the world (Jn. 8:12), and so are now Light-givers to the world (Mat. 5:14).

"You shine" states the present fact. We are not told to shine, but are reminded that we already do. The challenge is to let the light shine unhindered.

BLAMELESS AND HARMLESS

The phrase, *"That you may be blameless and harmless, the sons of God,"* implies by the use of the words *"may be"* that they were not blameless at that time. Actually, it should have been translated *"may become."* As well, the Philippians were not harmless when there were such divisions among them.

The word *"blameless"* has the idea of *"blameless, deserving no censure, free from fault or defect."*

"Harmless" in the Greek text has the idea of *"unmixed, unadulterated."* It was used of juice without water, and metal without alloy.

"Sons of God" is actually *"born ones of God."* This points to the character of God's family, even as we have been illustrating, and thus to a family likeness (Jn. 1:12).

The Apostle is eager, and rightly so, that his converts become blameless. This was the term used in the Septuagint in Genesis 17:1 concerning Abraham, *"walk before Me and be thou perfect."*

NOTES

The word *"perfect or blameless,"* in this instance, and as stated, means *"innocence, freedom from moral defect, sincerity."* This does not mean that Paul expects the Philippians to be sinlessly perfect, for no believer is, but rather that they be free from guile, insincerity, moral blemishes.

This calls for a *"perfection"* not so much of performance as of purpose, of intention. It is a perfection of love one might say (I Jn. 4:18).

A VINDICATED MINISTRY

This constancy and blameless manner of life will be the supreme vindication of the Apostle's life and labors. Even if he loses his life as a Drink-Offering poured out, he will not grieve.

There is no morbid self-pity here on the part of the Apostle but rather the exhilaration of realizing that his investment is justified by the results, that his faith is vindicated.

Every man as he faces his death, likes to consider whether his life has been worthwhile, whether his investment has paid dividends. The values that Paul prized were not money, nor his claim to fame, nor even his writings, but rather these citizens whose membership in the Kingdom it was his privilege to promote.

THE ENCOURAGEMENT OF THE CHILD OF GOD

As we have already stated, the words *"may be"* should have been translated *"may become."* This shows the progressive nature of the experience.

As we look at our lives presently, can we honestly say that we are *"blameless and harmless,"* by God's definition of the terms? If we are honest with ourselves, in looking at the present and the past, I think we would have to say that we are not where we should be; however, the Holy Spirit gave this injunction through the Apostle in such a way as to give us hope for the future.

This Sanctification process, is exactly that, *"a process."* This means that it is not done overnight, but something toward which the Holy Spirit constantly works, and which we as well should constantly work.

Dear Reader, do you presently see in your life that which is not Christlike? Do you grieve at times over this situation, which actually spells out the second Beatitude, *"Blessed are they who mourn: for they shall be comforted"*? (Mat. 5:4).

Every Believer, at least if he is honest with himself, see's these defects. In fact, the first step to victory is properly judging oneself, at least as far as one is able to do so. After seeing and recognizing the defect, which in fact, is as big as an elephant, we should not make allowance for such, but rather earnestly seek the Face of the Lord, that the Holy Spirit would have His way within our lives in removing this thing, whatever it might be. This is practical Christianity. As stated over and over again, the Holy Spirit is attempting to develop Righteousness and Holiness within our lives. He can do so, only with the amount of cooperation He receives from us.

WITHOUT REBUKE

The phrase, *"Without rebuke, in the midst of a crooked and perverse nation,"* in few words tells us what the Holy Spirit expects us to be in this world.

The words *"without rebuke"* which means *"without blemish,"* alludes to a Momus, a carping deity among the Greeks, who did nothing worthwhile himself but find fault with everybody and everything. The idea is, that the Christian is to walk so circumspect that even a Momus himself may have no occasion to find fault with him.

Barclay says that the words translated *"blameless, harmless, and without rebuke"* have to do with the Christian's relation to the world (blameless before the world), (harmless to himself as it regards morality), and without rebuke (a life lived that is pleasing to God).

The *"crooked and perverse nation"* as Paul uses the term, speaks of the entirety of the world without God. The indictment, of course, is 100% correct. It is *"crooked"* in the sense of turning away from the Truth. In other words, it would rather believe the lie of Satan, than the Truth of God.

"Perverse" carries the idea of *"distorted, having a twist"* it is a stronger word than *"crooked."*

This means that the whole world is crooked, twisted, perverse, wicked, truthless, lying, distorted, with no true value of anything. This speaks of the total moral depravity of man, which came instantly as a result of the Fall, and remains with man, despite his repeated attempts to break loose. He tries to do such with money, education, force, politics, psychology, etc., but continues to fail, as fail he must.

There is only one solution for man and that is Christ and more particularly, what Christ did at the Cross; however, man keeps turning away from that Truth, actually with only a few accepting that solution. He keeps thinking he can do for himself, what only God can do.

Man refuses to admit that he is as bad as God says he is, in fact, so bad, that God could not speak man's Redemption into existence as He did all other things, but rather had to become man and die on a Cross, in order that man might be redeemed. Man refuses to believe that he is that bad; consequently, he keeps trying to redeem himself.

In my short lifetime, the Johnson Administration in the United States was going to change things, by creating a *"new society,"* exactly as Kennedy had attempted with his *"new frontier,"* but was cut short by his sudden demise.

Bush was going to solve the problem by his *"thousand points of light,"* in fact, with every President thinking that society can be changed by his particular brand of politics.

Unfortunately, the problem is more severe than that. A changing of the political structure from Democrats to Republicans or vice versa, is not the answer, as Harvard, Yale, Columbia, or Princeton are not the answer as well!

Under the guise of separation of Church and State, which of course, is right, but is rather the separation of *"God and State,"* we have removed God from the classrooms of America; consequently, we now have school massacres, and don't really know the reason why. The children are raised on MTV, with no value system, or if it is a value system, it's that other than God and His Word, and we wonder what's wrong!

LIGHTS

The phrase, *"Among whom you shine as lights in the world,"* refers in the original

Greek structure, not so much to the act of shining, but rather to the fact of appearing. Actually, the word for *"Lights"* is the translation of the Greek word used of the heavenly bodies such as the stars. How appropriate to speak of the Saints as luminaries, since we are heavenly people.

The statement is, that Believers are *"Lights"* and were made so at conversion. The question is, *"how well is the Light shining?"* The idea of all of this, is that we walk clean before the Lord, allowing the Holy Spirit to have His way within our hearts and lives, in order that we might be as we ought to be.

Paul is not telling us here to *"be a Light,"* for this is already the case. The idea is that we shine brilliantly and brightly, unhindered by anything that might lessen the brilliance of this Light.

The Light which we presently are, is actually a reflection from that *"Light, which lighteth every man that cometh into the world"* (Jn. 1:9). Jesus is the True Light, and every Believer is a reflection of Him, or at least we are supposed to be a reflection of Him. Consequently, this refers to two problems which plague the Believer:

1. We have the problem of conduct which is unbecoming to the Child of God, and which hinders the Light.

2. We have the problem of not being a true reflection of Him, but rather ourselves or others. This is sad, considering that we actually have no Light originating within ourselves and neither does any other man.

It has been remarked already that the special way in which we are to manifest to the world the Light of Christ is represented here as the way of blamelessness. That man aright represents the mind of Christ to the world, who in the world keeps himself unspotted from the world, — in whom men recognize a character that traces up to a purer Source elsewhere.

A PERSONAL TESTIMONY

I have given this elsewhere in another of our Volumes, so accordingly I will be brief.

When Frances and I first married, even as I was starting to Preach, I took on a job with a plumbing contractor. If I remember correctly, this was in 1956. It was a small company employing only a few men.

Almost immediately upon beginning work, the men soon found out that I was a Christian. Actually, I suppose all of them claimed to be such, with the exception of the owner. He considered himself to be an Atheist, deriding and demeaning the Faith of any who believed there was a *"God!"*

His words to me were, and even laced with profanity, *"in just a short time you'll be like the rest of us."* I suppose, that he didn't see too very much difference in the other men there and himself, despite their claims. In fact, none of them were actually saved, even though they did claim such. Their lives, even as Paul is proclaiming here, did not measure up at all, which quickly became obvious if one was in their presence any time at all.

The situation did not turn out exactly like the owner of the company thought it would. I did not become like they were, but the Lord helped me to get all the men in Church at least a time or two, with the exception of the owner. Due to this, he grew very angry at me, giving me every dirty job that came along, and blaming me pretty much for whatever happened that went wrong.

To be frank, this was another test, and I did the best I could to let what little Light that I did have shine for the Lord. What type of example I was, only the Lord could answer; nevertheless, that short time I spent in the employ of this particular job, did bring forth eternal dividends.

I only worked there for several months, going very shortly thereafter into full time Evangelistic work.

The years went by and I lost track of the man in question, the owner of this small plumbing company.

If I remember correctly the year was 1986. I received a letter from his sister, telling me that her brother, the man for whom I had originally worked those long years before, never missed my Telecast. And then I received another letter:

She told me that her Brother had just died; however, she said, *"Brother Swaggart, before he died, he prayed with you the sinners prayer, and made Jesus the Lord of his life."*

This professed Atheist had seen Jesus in this poor heart and life of mine, which is the only Salvation for humanity.

I cannot really tell you how I felt as I held that letter in my hands. It had taken many years for that fruit to come forth, but ultimately and eventually it did. As I stood there that day after reading these words written by this dear lady, my mind went back to those years of long ago. I remembered his cursing and profanity, that seemed to be an unending stream. I remember his making fun of my testimony for the Lord, and as stated, giving me about every dirty job that came along. Nevertheless, through all of this, the bluster, the blow, the sarcasm, and the ridicule, there was something way down deep inside this man that saw something which he did not have. He never forgot it, and when the time finally came, the Word of God which cannot return void, came to the fore and performed its intended result. That dear Brother found Christ!

Maybe more than all of our Sermons, all of our profession, all of our philosophy of Christianity, the practical aspect of Christianity is the greatest Light of all. On the job, in the marketplace, rubbing shoulders with the unredeemed, this is where the Light shines best.

That's the reason the Believer must never mistake the outward bluster as the true feelings of the heart of the individual with whom they relate. Many times the unbeliever will respond with arrogance and anger to the Light because that is their natural inclination. They are sons of Satan, so that's really about the only way they can respond.

However, the Light, which in a way is the Word of God as it exemplifies Jesus, has a way of getting through all of that, deep down inside, even as the Scripture says, *"even to the dividing asunder of the soul and spirit, and of the joints and marrow, and is a discerner of the thoughts and intents of the heart"* (Heb. 4:12).

THE LIGHT IS JESUS

There may be many Believers who might complain, that they have very few talents, very few abilities, very little a winsome personality, and they wonder how it is that they can be of service to the Lord? Others complain of their lack of education, of a lack of ability to even speak plainly, even as Moses of old.

However, the Believer must understand, that the Lord is not looking for talent, ability, education, personality, etc. In fact, the Lord needs nothing, being sufficient in all things.

He is merely looking for a vessel, just a vessel. It doesn't have to be pretty, beautiful, talented, smart, clever, etc. It just has to be a vessel, i.e., *"a Believer."*

As Jesus fills such a heart, with such a Believer walking close to Him, the Light will readily shine and do its good work. In other words, the Believer does not so much have to *"do,"* as much as *"be."*

Using a light bulb as an example, they come in all forms, shapes, and sizes. Some are very exquisite, molded and shaped into beautiful designs, while other bulbs are very plain, consequently, inexpensive.

Nevertheless, the light in all is the same. In other words, there is no greater light in the expensive, molded, artistic bulb, than the most plain and simple one. The light all comes from the same source (the powerhouse), and it is the same electricity which goes into the bulb, irrespective of its design.

This means that the least expensive bulb made gives just as good a light, as the most expensive bulb. The light is the same in both cases. When a man is in darkness, he doesn't really care about the shape of the bulb, only the light that it gives. And so it is with Believers.

We spend far too much time trying to dress up the bulb, and not near enough time making sure the bulb is clean, in order that the light may shine forth brightly. Remember this: dust and dirt will cloud the illumination of the most expensive bulb as much as it will the least expensive.

Here, as everywhere, our Lord goes first. The Apostle John, speaking in his Gospel of the Eternal Word, tells us that in Him was Life, and the Life was the Light of men. It was not merely a doctrine of Light; the Life was the Light. As He lived, in His whole Being, in His acting and suffering, in His coming and staying and departing, in His Person and in His discharge of every duty and office, He manifested the Father. Still we find it so; as we contemplate Him, as His Words lead us to Himself, we behold the

Glory, the radiance of Grace and Truth, even more so illuminated by the Cross.

TO BE LIKE HIM

The Scripture everywhere implies that we are made, are being made, and shall be made, like Him (I Jn. 3:2). Through Him, the Word of Life, we become partakers of true life. This life does not dwell in us as it does in our Lord, for He is its original Seat and Source; hence, we are not the Light of the world in the same sense in which He is.

Still, we are luminaries, as stars are in the heavens. By manifesting the genuine influence of the Word of Life which dwells in us, we do make manifest in the world what truth and purity and Salvation actually are. This is our calling; and, in a measure, it is our attainment.

The view of the matter given here may be compared with that of II Corinthians 3:4. Christ, the Father's Word, may also be regarded as the Father's Living Epistle. Then we who behold Him, and drink in the significance of this Message, are also ourselves, in our turn, Epistles of Christ, known and read of all men.

So to shine is the calling of all Believers, not of some only; each, according to his opportunities, may and ought to fulfill it. God designs to be Glorified, and to have His Salvation justified in this form.

Jesus has said in the plainest terms, *"You are the Light of the world."* But to be so implies separateness from the world, in roots and fruits; and that it is for many a hard saying. *"You are a holy nation, a peculiar people, that you should show forth the praises of Him Who called you out of darkness into his marvelous Light"* (I Pet. 2:9).

A LIGHTHOUSE

The image here could very well be taken by Paul, as he is used by the Holy Spirit, from lighthouses on a Seacoast. The image then is, that as those lighthouses are placed on a dangerous coast to apprise vessels of their peril, and to save them from shipwreck, so the Light of the Child of God is to shine on a dark world, and in the dangers of the voyage which all are making.

Let it ever be known, there is no other beacon, no other warning, no other illumination, no other light. All other claims, whether Hinduism, Buddhism, Mormonism, Catholicism, Islam, etc., are but false claims. They have no Light as they can have no Light.

As we have stated, the Source is always in Christ (Jn. 1:4-9).

That means that the Church is not a Light and neither are our good works, or even Believers in the true sense of the word. Jesus is the Light, while we are the reflection of that light, and can be only as He abides in us (Jn. 14:20).

ONE OF THE BIGGEST DANGERS FOR THE CHRISTIAN

The moment that we forget that we are merely the reflection of His Light, of which He is really the Source, that's when we sin against God. While we are privileged to be a reflection and in a sense a reflector of that Light, we must ever understand that in no way are we the Source, or anything close to such.

This is perhaps one of the greatest problems in the Church. Man gets elevated, while Christ is placed in a lessor position. The Christian, and especially the Preacher, have to constantly be on guard regarding this subtle sin of self-will. To be sure, Satan takes advantage of everything, even our consecration, if we're not careful. Consequently, we must go back to the first of this Verse, even as Paul said, *"That we may be blameless and harmless."*

(16) "HOLDING FORTH THE WORD OF LIFE; THAT I MAY REJOICE IN THE DAY OF CHRIST, THAT I HAVE NOT RUN IN VAIN, NEITHER LABORED IN VAIN."

As luminaries in the world of spiritual darkness, they were to *"hold out the Word of Life."* Naturally, the only manner in which this can be done, is that the Believer has first received the Light himself. The Word of Life is, of course, the Gospel, which brings Eternal Life when it is received by Faith (Jn. 6:68).

"The Day of Christ" is the time when Christ will return for His Church, and when Believers will then have their works inspected and rewarded accordingly. Paul wants the content or basis of his boast at that time to be that his labors for the Philippians had not been useless. He desires that all his efforts to win them to Christ and to nurture their Faith will be vindicated at Christ's

Judgment Seat by the victorious presence of the Philippian Believers.

"*Run*" expresses the energetic activity, with "*labor*" depicting its toilsome aspects.

THE WORD OF LIFE

The phrase, "*Holding forth the Word of Life,*" refers to "*holding forth so as to offer.*" This should ever be the attitude of the Saint, offering Salvation to a lost and a dying world.

The "*Word of Life,*" consistent with the Biblical use, must not only refer to a stated message, but to Jesus Christ, the Living Word, Who is Himself both Light and Life (Jn. 1:4; 8:12; I Jn. 1:1). The Word of Life frees from sin and death (Rom. 8:2). It is Christ Himself, the Bread of Life, Whom the Christian offers to a hungry world. Where this is done, and it should be done constantly by all Believers, we who offer such becomes to those who partake "*the savour of Life unto Life*" (II Cor. 2:16).

JESUS CHRIST AND HIM CRUCIFIED

To be more specific, as we offer Jesus to a hurting world, we must at the same time understand that in the words of Paul, we are offering "*Jesus Christ and Him Crucified*" (I Cor. 2:2). Jesus must never be separated from the Cross, and the Cross must never be separated from Christ. Jesus without the Cross, actually presents no Salvation for the sinner, and no victory for the Saint. So, "*the Word of Life*" must ever be "*Christ and Him Crucified.*"

Satan is not too disturbed by the Church presenting Jesus minus the Cross. The Evil One knows that Christ presented in such a fashion, actually constitutes "*another Jesus,*" Who and What the Holy Spirit can never honor (II Cor. 11:4). And yet, the Church is presently filled with this "*other Jesus.*"

THE MODERN CHURCH

Much of the nominal Church world (the Church world which does not believe in the Baptism with the Holy Spirit, with the evidence of speaking with other tongues), mostly presents the philosophy of Christianity. This is Christianity without the Crucified Christ, which basically reduces the message to that of mere "*ethics.*" In other words, we try to "*do good,*" and keep the "*golden rule!*" etc.

That is pretty much the status of most of the nominal Churches, which in effect, delivers no one and effects no Born-Again experience.

Even in that which claims to be "*Spirit-filled,*" the Cross of Christ is given very little latitude. As an example, the "*Word of Life*" which goes forth from what is referred to as the "*Faith Ministry,*" is basically reduced to that which I refer to as the "*prosperity gospel,*" which in effect, addresses man's real problem not at all. In fact, a great part of this philosophy (and a philosophy it is and not the Gospel), actually denigrates the Cross, referring to it as "*past miseries,*" with it having no effect whatsoever in their Message, claiming that man's Redemption was actually brought about by Jesus being Born-Again in Hell, of all places!

And then much of the Pentecostal world even though not going in that particular direction, still, repudiates the Cross by their foray into secular, humanistic psychology. One cannot have it both ways, either man delivers through psychology, or Jesus delivers. The Truth is, psychology holds no answer, which is obvious even to the most casual investigation.

So, the "*Word of Life*" held up at the present time, is little the true Message of Jesus Christ and Him Crucified, which alone can set the captive free. Thank God, there is an exception here and there, but these exceptions are few and far between.

THE LAST DAY APOSTASY

Unfortunately, this problem which we have just mentioned is not going to get better, but rather worse. The Bible teaches that the age will conclude with a great apostasy, which refers to a departure from Truth.

The Holy Spirit through Paul wrote, concerning this particular time: "*Now the Spirit speaketh expressly* (open, to the point), *that in the latter times* (the days in which we now live) *some shall depart from the Faith* (not all but some), *giving heed to seducing spirits, and doctrines of Devils*" (I Tim. 4:1).

He then said, "*This know also that in the last days perilous times shall come.*

"*For men shall be lovers of their own selves, covetous, boasters, proud, blasphemers, disobedient to parents, unthankful, unholy,*

"Without natural affection, trucebreakers, false accusers, incontinent, fierce, despisers of those that are good,

"Traitors, heady, highminded, lovers of pleasures more than lovers of God;

"Having a form of godliness, but denying the power thereof: from such turn away" (II Tim. 3:1-5).

The last Verse of this statement tells us that Paul is speaking here to the Church and not the world. It is not a very pleasant description.

And finally, *"For the time will come* (has already come) *when they will not endure sound doctrine; but after their own lusts* (ungodly desires) *shall they heap to themselves teachers, having itching ears* (trying to find a Bible teacher who will tell them what they want to hear);

"And they shall turn away their ears from the Truth, and shall be turned unto fables" (II Tim. 4:3-4).

The *"Truth"* is the *"Word of Life,"* while everything else is a *"fable!"*

Just today (6-28-99) I was told the following by one of our men in our church (Family Worship Center), who was visited by a Preacher coming through Baton Rouge: In their conversation, the Preacher mentioned, *"I've got to find me a gimmick,"* or words to that effect. The Brother from our Church was appalled, even as he should have been.

Unfortunately, the word *"gimmick"* is the big word in modern ministry, although not so often boldly stated as by the young Preacher.

Those types of Ministries (actually, they are no ministry at all), although supported by many people in some cases, will see no people saved, no Believers baptized with the Holy Spirit, no one truly and honestly healed, and no one truly delivered by the Power of God. The reason is obvious:

The Holy Spirit does not function in the realm of *"gimmicks,"* or anything for that matter, which is not *"Jesus Christ and Him Crucified."* For these things to happen, and I speak of lives being changed, the Holy Spirit is the only One Who can carry forth such things, and to be sure, He will never align Himself with that which is crooked, false, error, dishonest, or unscriptural in any manner.

THE HOLY SPIRIT

Beginning in 1992, I have been seeking the Lord for many things, not the least of these things being a greater Anointing of the Holy Spirit upon my Ministry, coupled as well with the convicting power of the Holy Spirit. During this time, the Lord has opened up to me the Revelation of the Cross of Christ, that has completely revolutionized my life. And as well, the Lord is beginning to answer prayer regarding that of which I have spoken concerning the Holy Spirit.

Just yesterday morning in Service (6-27-99), the Lord gave me an anointing to preach such as I have seldom experienced previously. It resulted in a tremendous response at the Altars.

I believe that this is just the beginning of a moving of the Holy Spirit such as we have not known previously, which means it will eclipse all that which has happened in the past.

It is absolutely impossible for souls to be saved, lives to be changed, bondages of darkness to be broken, without the power of the Holy Spirit. This is all in the realm of His Office, Work, and Ministry. Consequently, if the Preacher does not have the Moving and the Operation of the Holy Spirit within his life and Ministry, there will be nothing done for the Lord. There may be much activity, the working of much religious machinery, with all of this tending to deceive people into thinking that things are happening, when in reality, nothing is happening — at least for the Lord.

Unfortunately, even as we have already quoted the Scripture (II Tim. 4:3-4), many people who call themselves *"Christians,"* actually do not desire to be in Services where the Holy Spirit is moving and working. They do not desire that type of Church. The reason is simple:

They are instantly placed under conviction for their lifestyle, whatever that lifestyle might be, a lifestyle incidentally which they do not want to change; consequently, they seek that which looks like God, acts like God, and purports to be of God, but in reality isn't, and, therefore, they are never made to feel uncomfortable. The Holy Spirit not only makes people glad and happy, but at times, makes a wayward Christian feel like they are hanging over Hell on a rotten stick (Jn. 16:7-11).

However, for those who do want the Moving and Operation of the Holy Spirit, I believe these last days are going to prove to be the greatest example of His Work and Operation that the world has ever known. Joel prophesied, and Peter quoted, *"And it shall come to pass in the last days, saith God, I will pour out of My Spirit upon all flesh"* (Acts 2:17).

Even though the short phrase *"last days,"* refers to the entirety of the time between the Day of Pentecost unto the present, it also has a greater connotation I believe, toward the last of the last days. For the Apostle also said, *"And I will shew wonders in Heaven above, and signs in the Earth beneath; blood, and fire, and vapour of smoke:*

"The Sun shall be turned into darkness, and the moon into blood, before that great and notable Day of the Lord come:

"And it shall come to pass, that whosoever shall call on the Name of the Lord shall be saved" (Acts 2:19-21).

Consequently, this tells us, I believe, that the Latter Rain outpouring will be at its greatest, at its heighth, when the Apostasy is at its worst. To be sure, most will not come in the direction of the Holy Spirit but the very opposite; nevertheless, for those few who do, great things are going to happen!

THE DAY OF CHRIST

The phrase, *"That I may rejoice in the Day of Christ,"* has reference to the Second Coming, or the *"Parousia."* As the Old Testament prophets looked forward to the *"Day of the Lord,"* meaning a day of judgment, of Divine retribution (Joel 2:11), so the New Testament Apostles and Prophets look forward to the Day of Christ's reappearance (I Thess. 5:2).

This *"Day"* will begin with the Rapture of the Church, and will stretch from that time to the rebellion of Satan at the end of that period, a time frame of a little over a thousand years (Rev. 19:11-20:10).

The *"Day of the Lord"* or *"the Day of Christ"* cannot fully come till the Lord comes to reign (Isa. 2:12; 13:6, 9; 34:8; 61:2; 62:1-6; Jer. 46:10; Ezek. 30:3; Dan. 2:44-45;

NOTES

7:13-14; Joel Chpt. 2; Amos 5:18; Obad. vs. 15; Zeph. 1:8, 18; 2:2-3; Zech. Chpt. 14; Mal. Chpt. 4; Mat. 24:29-31; 25:31-46; I Thess. 5:2; II Thess. 1:7-10; 2:1-12; Jude vs. 14; Rev. 19:11-21; 20:1-10).

Paul is moreso speaking here of the Rapture of the Church, which immediately after will be the Judgment Seat of Christ, where all Christians will be judged as it regards works, but not sins, which were taken care of at Calvary (I Cor. 3:8-15).

Paul's rejoicing will be, even as it will every other True Preacher, in the fact that those who sat under his Ministry will be rewarded, and suffer no loss. That will be the final reckoning time, where all things will be judged as it regards every Believer. That's the reason that everything we do here ought to be done in the light of the coming Judgment Seat of Christ. Nothing is more important than that, and if we conducted ourselves accordingly, realizing and understanding that one day we will stand before the Lord to give account, quite possibly we would do some things differently.

LABOR

The phrase, *"That I have not run in vain, neither labored in vain,"* actually means in the Greek *"to labor to the point of exhaustion."*

If the Philippians would continue to hold forth the Word, Paul would have ground for glorying when the Lord Jesus comes for His Saints, for He would not have run his Christian race in vain nor would he have bestowed exhausting labor on the Philippians in vain, for the results of his efforts in Philippi would be apparent in the victorious lives of the Saints there (Wuest).

The idea here is of finishing the race. All who finish will be crowned with glory with no exceptions, even though some reward will be lost because of improper stewardship, etc.

There is much said in this phrase, so much in fact that I'm not certain it is possible to fully grasp it all. The following are only some of the Truths implicated here by the Holy Spirit through the Apostle:

LEADERSHIP

We will look first at the Philippians. These Believers at Philippi had been so blessed by the Lord in being privileged to sit under the Ministry of Paul. Consequently, they had the very best teaching, the benefit of the greatest consecration, all delivered by mighty movings of the Holy Spirit. As a result, they would have no excuse.

How many Believers down through the many centuries and even at present, have the privilege of sitting under a Minister of the Gospel who is totally sold out to the Lord, totally immersed in His Work, totally consecrated to the Ways of the Lord, therefore, used graciously and mightily by the Lord in all aspects of Ministry? To be sure, those are few and far between, and how blessed are the fortunate few who have the privilege of such a Ministry.

CONSECRATION

The problem with many Believers even as with some at Philippi, is that they do not fully know the extent of their Blessing as it regards proper leadership, that is, if they are blessed enough to have such. Jesus said of Israel concerning the coming Judgment and the reason for this judgment, *"Because thou knewest not the time of thy visitation"* (Lk. 19:44).

So, even on the occasion when Believers do, in fact, have proper leadership, they must stay close to the Lord, in order that they may know exactly what they have and not miss this which the Holy Spirit has done on their behalf. Unfortunately, many, if not most, Christians little have the proper *"eyes of understanding"* (Eph. 1:18).

This is always so tragic, because personal consecration is always the privilege of any and every Believer. In other words, the fault is theirs if they do not know.

THE JUDGMENT SEAT OF CHRIST

As we've already stated, the Judgment Seat of Christ is going to reveal every story of every single Believer who has ever lived. This Judgment is for Believers only, and does not at all pertain to one's Salvation, that having been addressed at the Cross; however, it will address itself greatly and grandly to one's works, whatever those works may have been. There the Holy Spirit through Paul said, *"Every man's work shall be made manifest: for the day* (the day of the Judgment Seat of Christ) *shall declare it, because it shall be revealed by fire* (the fire of the Word of God); *and the fire shall try every man's work of what sort it is."*

The Apostle then said, *"If any man's work abide which he hath built thereupon* (built upon the foundation of the Word of God), *he shall receive a reward.*

"If any man's work shall be burned (all will be burned or rather count for nothing that's not built squarely on the Word), *he shall suffer loss* (loss of reward): *but he himself shall be saved; yet so as by fire* (the fire of judgment that fell upon Christ while on the Cross in our place)" (I Cor. 3:13-15). Consequently, every single thing we do, every word we speak, every step we take, every action to which we commit ourselves, every motive, every effort, all must be done in the light of the coming *"Judgment Seat of Christ"* (Rom. 14:10).

TO GIVE ACCOUNT

Not only will every Believer give account at that time for all that he has heard, every Preacher will give account for all that he has said. Paul had preached and taught the Truth to these Philippians, even as he did all others to whom he had the privilege to minister. As well, he preached and taught all the Truth and not just some Truth. He said, and very succinctly, *"I have not shunned to declare unto you all the Counsel of God"* (Acts 20:27).

I'm afraid that on that coming day, many Preachers are going to be found wanting. The question should presently be asked, *"How many Preachers are presently declaring all the Truth as they know and understand that Truth"*?

Of course, only the Lord knows the answer to that question; however, if we observe the condition of most modern Churches, we have to come to the conclusion that Preachers such as Paul are few and far between.

The fundamental desire of the Apostle was to see these people through to total and complete victory. I'm afraid that the agenda for many if not most modern Preachers is something else entirely. In many circles the objective is to get money. With other Preachers, Believers are stepping stones to the advancement of the Preacher's career. (Career?)

Regrettably, many Believers are merely *"used,"* and sadder still, many Believers it seems, enjoy being *"used!"*

RETIREMENT

This Work for God is just that, *"labor!"* It is a 24-hour a day occupation, containing the greatest responsibility on the face of the Earth, the eternal destiny of eternal souls. I speak of the acceptable Ministry of Preachers of the Gospel.

The burden and responsibility never lift, and there is no such thing as retirement, for the Call is without repentance, i.e., *"cannot be rescinded"* (Rom. 11:29).

(17) "YEA, AND IF I BE OFFERED UPON THE SACRIFICE AND SERVICE OF YOUR FAITH, I JOY, AND REJOICE WITH YOU ALL."

The prospect of standing before Christ reminded Paul that it might be soon. By the vivid metaphor of a Drink-Offering, he explained that even though he was presently in a dangerous situation that could lead to a martyr's death, in view of this he was ever more cognizant of his life's work.

Both Jewish and Greek religious practice included the use of wine or even water in some cases, poured out ceremonially in connection with certain Sacrifices (Num. 15:1-10). (The wine was most of the time what we now refer to as grape juice.)

Among all that is to be seen here, what is the most important to see is that Paul regarded his own life as a sacrifice in the interest of the spiritual advancement of such persons as the Philippian Believers. In fact, he used the same metaphor in II Timothy 4:6.

A SACRIFICIAL OFFERING

The phrase, *"Yea, and if I be offered upon the Sacrifice and Service of your faith,"* gives us some insight into the mind and thoughts of the Apostle.

The way in which Paul uses this terminology, I think the Holy Spirit had already informed him that whenever his life did actually end, it would be a violent death as a martyr. It would be his blood poured out.

Concerning a time frame, I don't think the Apostle believed that such would happen presently, with indication given that he felt he would be released, which he was. However, during his second Roman imprisonment, which in fact did see his demise (several years later), knowing that he would shortly be sent to the executioner's block for decapitation, he writes to Timothy, using the same word, *"For I am now ready to be offered,"* or as one could translate, *"For my life's blood is ready to be poured out"* (II Tim. 4:6) (Wuest).

True conversion implies Sacrifice and Service — the Sacrifice of self and self-interests for the Salvation of others, and willing service in confessing Christ and preaching the glad tidings concerning Him.

THE SACRIFICE

Paul had in mind here the Jewish Sacrifices with which he was overly familiar, and which in fact, served as a symbolism of that which God would do through Christ Jesus for dying humanity, and what was expected as well of Believers.

When an animal was about to be slain and Sacrificed, wine at times was poured on it as a solemn act of devoting it to God (Num. 15:5; 28:14). It, in effect, stated, by the pouring out of the liquid, that Jesus would pour out His life for suffering, sinful, humanity, which must be done, if men were to be saved.

It also served as a symbol of the Believer who must live a sacrificial life, in other words, pouring out himself for the Cause of Christ as well. This is actually that of which Paul speaks.

Each Believer in offering this Sacrifice (his poured out life) acts as a Priest, being a member actually of the Holy Priesthood which offers to God spiritual sacrifices, i.e., *"the sacrifice of one's own life"* (I Pet. 2:5).

Such a man is not, indeed, a Priest to make Atonement, that already having been done by Christ, and which it could only be done by Christ, but he is a Priest to present Offerings through Christ his Example.

The Philippians (and all other Believers as well), then, insofar as they were, or were to be, yielding themselves in this manner to God, were Priests who offered to God a spiritual sacrifice. The Master serving as our example, proclaims the fact that the Believer is always to live a sacrificial life.

Here let us notice, as we pass, that no consecration is worth the name that has not its sacrifice through which the worshipper expresses his devotion. In our service for God, the sacrifice is the consecration of the man or woman and of his and her life to God's service in Christ. Let us all see to it what sacrifices we offer.

AN EXAMPLE

While I could give this example many times over, I think presently of three ladies in our Church (Family Worship Center in Baton Rouge, Louisiana), all who I feel have given sacrificially to the Cause of Christ. And yet, I know that many others in the Church have done the same thing, but I speak of these three, simply because I am very much aware of some of their circumstances.

At the beginning of 1999, the Lord spoke to my heart regarding Radio, and the taking of the Gospel by this means to the nation. Of course, this is not new actually being done everyday; however, what I believe the Lord told me to do is somewhat unique.

The Lord instructed me to air the Services of Family Worship Center 24 hours a day over our network of stations, and many which we have taped in the last few years. We were to apply to the F.C.C. for frequencies all over the nation in order to cover as many people as possible. This we set out to do, but not at all having the funds to even begin the task, much less to finish it.

In our appeal for funds, many sacrificed as I have mentioned; however, these three ladies in question, gave to the extent that I feel was and is far and away beyond the call of duty. In other words, it was exactly as Paul stated here, *"a sacrifice."*

They gave of their retirement, and even more. In other words, they really did not give of surplus, but particular significant sums, which as stated, could only be construed as a *"Sacrifice."*

In fact, I wonder how much of our giving as Believers could actually be considered a sacrifice? Of course, only the Lord knows the answer to that, but I suspect, that this particular word does not apply to most of us as it regards our giving. However, the giving of money is only a part of that which the Holy Spirit addresses here.

The first recorded occasion of a *"Drink-Offering being poured out,"* took place in the life of Jacob. It was the time when the Abrahamic Covenant was renewed with him. At this time the Scripture says, *"Jacob set up a pillar in the place where He* (God) *talked with him, even a pillar of stone* (signifying Jesus Christ)*: and he offered a drink offering thereon* (signifying how Christ would pour out His Life), *and he* (Jacob) *poured oil thereon* (signifying the Holy Spirit Who honored this Offering),*"* i.e., *"the Offering of Christ,"* the only offering He will honor (Gen. 35:9-15; Lev. Chpt. 23).

SERVICE

The word *"Service"* is from a Greek word used of the service of the Old Testament Priests. Of course, if anyone knows anything about the Old Testament Priests, one knows that their work consisted of the offering of Sacrifices, in fact, a continual offering of Sacrifices, with other duties inside the Holy Place of the Tabernacle as it regarded the Table of Shewbread, the Golden Lampstand, and the Altar of Incense.

Without going into detail at this time, they were occupied with these items constantly, all symbolizing Christ in His vicarious, Redemptive work on behalf of fallen humanity.

It is interesting to note here, that Paul places the *"Sacrifice"* and the *"Service"* of the Believer on the same level as with himself. In other words, they were to show as much interest in the Work of God, as much diligence and devotion, as much consecration even as him.

Thank the Lord there are definitely a few of the laity who fall into this category, but regrettably not many. With many, if not most, I'm afraid, their life for Christ is secondary to their particular pursuit or occupation, whatever that might be. I'm afraid that many Christians know more about the batting averages of ballplayers, or the accomplishments of other sports figures, etc., than they do that of Matthew, Mark, Luke, and John.

Far too often, one's service for the Lord consists of one hour on Sunday Morning, with Him pretty much forgotten the rest of the time. As stated, there are exceptions, but not many!

What does the Lord actually require of Believers?

Even as a Preacher has a Ministry, every Believer as well has a Ministry, or at least they certainly should have. The Truth is, most don't know what it is.

However, if one will earnestly seek the Lord, the Holy Spirit will quickly lead that Believer into the particular Ministry drawn out for them in the service of God. It might be prayer or even giving, or even hospitality, as Paul outlines in Romans Chapter 12.

At any rate, whatever that Ministry is, the Saint is to pursue it with all diligence, constantly seeking the Face of the Lord that he may carry it forth in a manner which is pleasing to God.

As I've already stated, all of us one day will give an account for our *"Service"* for the Lord.

FAITH

As Faith is spoken of anywhere in the Bible, which at times it goes under the word *"believe"* or *"believing,"* it naturally pertains to the Lord in totality, but in a more particular sense, if traced to its roots, it refers to the Finished Work of Christ.

If it's not Faith in that particular Work, in other words the Cross of Christ, which of course includes the Resurrection, as the object of one's Faith, then it's really not Faith which the Lord will recognize. Millions have Faith in God, but only in a general sort of way, with the Sacrifice of Christ playing but a little part, if any at all. God will not honor such Faith.

As well, millions have Faith in Christ but not really in the correct manner. In other words, they believe in Jesus, but if asked what they believe, some would be hard-put to properly define their feelings.

While Faith in Christ must be in His total Work, the object of that Work whatever it might be, His Virgin Birth, His spotless, sinless life, His Healings and Miracles, His Words of Life, all must be subordinate to the Cross, for this is the reason that Jesus came — to die on a Cross which was demanded in order that man be saved.

If one properly understands this, the Old Testament then opens up to a degree that most have not yet known or understood. To say it another way, everything in the Old Testament points toward the Sacrificial, Atoning Work of Christ on the Cross. This was the symbolism of all the Sacrifices, as is glaringly obvious, as well as the reason for the Sabbath, the Feast Days, etc., in fact, every single thing points to the Cross. This sets the stage for all the happenings of the New Testament.

So, when Paul mentions *"Faith,"* he is speaking of Faith in the Cross of Christ (I Cor. 2:2; Gal. 6:14).

REJOICING

The phrase, *"I joy, and rejoice with you all,"* speaks of several things. Some are as follows:

1. Above all, this rejoicing is in their Faith properly placed, which refers to the Cross of Christ, which alone guarantees Redemption, and a successful conclusion.

2. The *"joy"* and *"rejoicing"* have to do with this wonderful life in Christ, and above all to where it will lead.

3. Paul was so certain of the Victory of Christ over sin at the Cross that his joy did not await the final reckoning, but constantly overflowed. Thus, he seeks to impart to his readers this confidence of triumph. Faith, and more particularly Faith in the Finished Work of Christ, made possible the long-range perspective, and this in turn inspired confidence.

(18) "FOR THE SAME CAUSE ALSO DO YE JOY, AND REJOICE WITH ME."

The idea is that the Philippians should display the same attitude as the Apostle. They must not look at their problems and difficulties, whatever they may have been, but rather to Christ and this great and glorious Salvation afforded them, which will ultimately reach to their presence with the Lord in Glory.

In effect, Paul is saying two things:

1. *"For I reckon that the sufferings of this present time are not worthy to be compared with the glory which shall be revealed in us"* (Rom. 8:18).

2. In view of this, *"Rejoice in the Lord always: and again I say, Rejoice,"* and don't let present circumstances rob you of this joy (Phil. 4:4).

THE SAME CAUSE

The phrase, *"For the same cause also do ye joy,"* refers to the Sacrifice and Service for

Christ, which produces tremendous joy in the heart of the Believer.

In fact, this Epistle lays great stress on joy, not only as a privilege, but in a sense one might say, as a duty, which follows from Christian Faith and proves its reality.

Joy is in itself natural in the first thoughts of childhood and youth; however, it is apt to be checkered or even destroyed by the adverse experiences of life, then darkened by sin, and death. But the greater thought of the Child of God, while at the same time recognizing these darker elements of life, but knowing they shall not be in the end, joy comes back, and is deepened into acute thankfulness. A Christianity which has no power to rejoice, either in flashes of joy amidst tribulation, or, better still, in the calm steady light of cheerfulness, may be true, but is imperfect. It has not yet entered into the promise given by our Lord Himself of the *"joy which no man taketh from you"* (Jn. 16:22).

Beginning with the Greeks, all type of philosophic ideas have been presented as it regards life. In fact, the entirety of the religion of Buddha consists of the individual reaching a place of nirvana, where they are oblivious anymore to feelings, passions, emotions, etc. However, they have no record of any Buddhist who has ever reached such a state.

As stated, Christianity does not deny the problems of life, but in fact meets them head on. It overcomes them through two principles which are:

1. The life we now have in Christ, which gives us joy despite the problems, and furnishes a hope for a glorious tomorrow.

2. The life which shall be in Christ, which is eternal, and which one day will see the elimination of all things which cause sorrow and heartache. That day is coming just as surely as the present day has come (Rev. 21:4-7).

REJOICE WITH ME

The phrase, *"And rejoice with me,"* tells us several things as well:

1. As stated, the Philippians had correct teaching; therefore, inasmuch as they had the same Salvation, provided by the same Christ as did Paul, they could rejoice as well as he.

2. This portrays the fact that the Salvation afforded to those we refer to as *"the laity,"* is identical to that afforded Preachers of the Gospel, which will garner the same results, and meant to do so. I'm trying to say, that in this great Work of God, this great Salvation afforded by Christ, all are equal at the foot of the Cross. Other than particular, distinct callings, the Lord does not treat one Believer differently than the other, and what is available to one is available to all.

So, if Paul was rejoicing, and that despite his present circumstances of being imprisoned, surely, the Philippians could do the same. Why not? They had the same Salvation as stated, afforded by the same Christ.

WHY WOULD A CHRISTIAN NOT HAVE THIS JOY?

Jesus beautifully and wondrously said, *"I am come that they might have life, and that they might have it more abundantly"* (Jn. 10:10).

He also said, *"Come unto Me, all ye that labour and are heavy laden, and I will give you rest.*

"Take My yoke upon you, and learn of Me; for I am meek and lowly in heart: and ye shall find rest *unto your souls.*

"For My yoke is easy, and My burden is light" (Mat. 11:28-30).

In both of these Passages, Jesus spoke of *"more abundant life"* and *"rest."* So, the question I must ask you, Dear Reader, is *"Do you have this of which Jesus has spoken?"*

In fact, there is only one way this of which Jesus spoke can be possessed by the Believer, and that is by our Faith and Confidence on a continued basis, in the Sacrificial, Offering of Christ on the Cross. That means, that it's not enough to merely have Faith in Christ, but more particularly, we must have Faith in what He did. As I have stated repeatedly, Satan endeavors to move us from the Cross moreso than any other attempt made against us. He knows that the Cross is our place of *"Victory,"* and *"more abundant life."*

Most Christians do not know or understand the validity of this of which I have just said. Of course, all Christians, that is if they are truly Christians, believe in the Cross; however, with most, due to a paucity of teaching on the subject, the Cross is just a part of all the mix. They understand somewhat (to a small degree) as to the part the Cross plays in our initial Salvation experience; however, after that, most draw a blank. They have absolutely no idea as to the part the Cross plays in our continued walk with the Lord, and especially as it regards *"more abundant life."*

As a Believer, we are to never leave the principles of the Cross, which speaks of its benefits. If one attempts to go beyond the Cross, one loses one's way entirely.

Every single thing the Believer has in Christ, everything we hope to have in Christ, is all tied in totality to the Cross. It was there that Jesus satisfied the Heavenly Courts of Justice in satisfying the sin debt, which destroyed Satan's hold on the human race, at least for those who will believe (Jn. 3:16).

Of course, all of this is so very important; however, that which is the most important to the Child of God, is the fact that Jesus was in reality our Substitute, in essence, our Representative Man. When he did all of these things which includes His Death, Burial, and Resurrection, as well as His present Exaltation by the Right Hand of the Father (Rom. 6:3-5; Eph. 2:6), they were actually done on our behalf, in other words, totally for us. Upon Faith in Him, one might say, God literally places us in Him in all of these procedures. In fact, that's why Paul constantly used the phrase *"in Christ"* (Rom. 8:1, etc.).

THE ATONEMENT

We must understand, that Jesus in the Atonement, addressed everything which man lost in the Fall. When we say everything, we mean everything. This includes Salvation for the soul, freedom from the guilt of sin, the Baptism with the Holy Spirit, victory over sin in every capacity, victory over all the powers of darkness, Divine Healing, financial prosperity, more abundant life, rest, etc.

This means that the Cross which always presupposes the Resurrection and Exaltation, is actually in a sense, the *"Constitution and Bylaws"* of the Child of God. It is our Magna Carta. It's the only Law which Satan respects (Rom. 8:2).

In the Atonement is every single thing we need, hence our continued looking to this Finished Work of Christ.

Also, the idea that one should leave the Cross after conversion, going on to *"higher things,"* portrays the fact that those who would suggest such, have little understanding as to what the Cross actually is. In fact, the entirety of their concept of Redemption is flawed. It can be no other way. All of history strains toward the Cross. All Blessings come from the Cross, and no other way. In fact, one cannot really and properly understand the Word of God as one should, unless one understands properly the Redemption process as ensconced in the Cross.

Once the Cross is made the center of all things, then the Word of God takes on a brand-new perspective. One then sees the Cross in everything and for the obvious reasons. In fact, the Cross and the Cross alone, is why Jesus came. It is the purpose entirely of the Incarnation, i.e., *"God becoming man."* Everything led to the Cross.

If the Believer doesn't understand that, then of necessity he has an improper view of Redemption, which will seriously hinder and weaken anything and everything else that we receive from the Lord.

In all of this I am saying, that it is impossible to have this more abundant life, this joy of which Paul spoke, unless we have a proper viewpoint of the Cross, in order that our Faith be there properly fixed.

God being God, there is possibly another way that the Lord could have redeemed humanity; however, this is the manner that He chose, and to be sure, it was chosen before the foundation of the world (I Pet. 1:20).

THE APOSTLE PAUL

Being given the New Covenant, Paul had a greater understanding of the Cross than even the original Twelve Apostles. To their credit, every evidence is that they totally followed his example; however, it was Paul who understood the rudiments of Redemption which proclaim the Power of the Cross. That's the reason he told the Corinthians, incidentally, one of the most jaded cities in the world, *"For I determined not to know any thing among you, save Jesus Christ, and Him crucified"* (I Cor. 2:2).

He also said to them, *"For the preaching of the Cross is to them that perish foolishness;*

but unto us which are saved it is the Power of God" (I Cor. 1:18).

He said to the Galatians, *"But God forbid that I should glory, save in the Cross of our Lord Jesus Christ, by Whom the world is crucified unto Me, and I unto the world"* (Gal. 6:14).

That's the reason he explained fully in the Sixth Chapter of Romans the great fundamentals of Justification which also includes our Sanctification, all by the Cross. He then told us in Romans Chapter 8, how that the Holy Spirit functions in regard to the Cross of Christ. In other words, the Holy Spirit will only work for us, through us, and in us, according to our Faith in the Cross (Rom. 8:2). He functions in no other manner and upon no other premise.

To be sure, there was tremendous opposition against Paul regarding this Message of the Cross. That's the reason he said in this Letter to the Philippians, *"For many walk* (attempt to live this Christian life) *of whom I have told you often, and now tell you even weeping, that they are the enemies of the Cross of Christ"* (Phil. 3:18).

Regrettably, the *"enemies"* did not die with the opposers of Paul. They are today alive and well, of whom we will have more to say when we come to Commentary on that particular Scripture.

Irrespective, the Apostle did not allow anyone to push him from the core Message of the Cross. It remained the foundation of his Ministry, which he clung to tenaciously, and rightly so. The Lord evidently made it very clear to the Apostle, that this was the correct path, from which we must not deviate.

(19) "BUT I TRUST IN THE LORD JESUS TO SEND TIMOTHEUS SHORTLY UNTO YOU, THAT I ALSO MAY BE OF GOOD COMFORT, WHEN I KNOW YOUR STATE."

The somewhat somber note of some of the previous Verses is balanced by the more optimistic tone that follows. Paul planned to send Timothy to Philippi with the report and hoped to come shortly himself. His hope was *"in the Lord Jesus."*

Every Believer is *"in Christ,"* and this vital union should influence every thought and activity. Thus, Paul loves in the Lord (Phil. 1:8); grounds his confidence in the Lord (Phil. 2:24); rejoices in the Lord (Phil. 3:3; 4:10); and desires that others rejoice in Christ (Phil. 1:26; 3:1), welcomes Christian leaders in the Lord (Phil. 2:29), and always stands firm in the Lord (Phil. 4:1).

NOTES

Timothy was named in the opening of the Letter (Phil. 1:1), but his mention here in the third person shows that he was not a cowriter. Paul refers to Timothy and his proposed trip to Philippi with graciousness and delicacy.

One might suppose that the Apostle would have explained that the purpose of the trip was to tell the Philippians about his situation. But he only hints at that idea by the word *"also"* and by the phrase *"as soon as I see how things go with me"* (vs. 23), because his main purpose is to hear about the Philippians, though he assumes that his readers will be cheered by a favorable report of him. The spiritual advancement of the Churches was always uppermost in Paul's mind.

Paul must have expected Timothy not to remain at Philippi but to bring him word about the Church immediately. Conceivably, they could have planned to meet at Ephesus after Paul's release. At least, they were presumably together at Ephesus a little after this particular time (I Tim. 1:3).

This would require that before leaving for Philippi, Timothy knew with certainty the date of Paul's release. (Perhaps Phil. 2:23 implies this.) Otherwise, Timothy would have been expected to have returned to Paul before the Apostle left the city (Kent).

TIMOTHY

The phrase, *"But I trust in the Lord Jesus to send Timotheus shortly unto you,"* concerns a young man greatly trusted by Paul. The phrase, *"In the Lord"* as we've already stated, tells us that Paul's every thought, word, and deed proceeded from the Lord as the center of his volition. Paul says in effect, *"My hope is not an idle one, but one that is founded on Faith in the Lord"* (Wuest).

Lightfoot says, *"The Christian is a part of Christ, a member of His Body. Consequently, everything is to center in Christ. Thus, the Believer loves in the Lord, hopes in the Lord, boasts in the Lord, and labors in the Lord. He has one guiding principle in acting and forbearing to act, 'only in the Lord' (I Cor. 7:39)."*

In view of this, the Believer must understand as to exactly how we are *"in the Lord."* Once again, we go back to Romans 6:3-5. Paul tells us there how we are in the Lord, which as stated, concerns His Crucifixion, Burial, and Resurrection. Of course, it extends to His Exaltation (Eph. 2:6).

Even though I'm being repetitive in making these statements, so little has been said about this to the modern Church, that Believers do not really have a true comprehension of what it means to be *"in Christ."* In their minds, most just sort of think it's a particular statement, not really understanding the great significance of what the statement actually says.

Yes, we are *"in the Lord,"* but not by a simple matter of decree. For this to be done, a tremendous price had to be paid, which Paul spells out in Romans Chapter 6. We are *"in Him"* due to what He did at the Cross and as a result of Him being our Substitute and our Representative Man. Our Faith in this, this Finished Work of Christ, this Sacrificial, Atoning, Vicarious (substitutionary), Efficacious (effective) Offering, affords us this privileged *"in Christ"* position.

GOOD COMFORT

The phrase, *"That I also may be of good comfort, when I know your state,"* presents the Apostle seeking to know the spiritual welfare of the Philippians.

It seems that two particular things made up the life of Paul, actually covering the entirety of his work.

First of all, his life was spent as I think is overly obvious, in attempting to carry out exactly what the Lord wanted him to do and in every capacity. He sought to hear from Heaven and then to convey to the people that which he had heard. To be sure, this is not at times, as easy as it might seem. Satan hinders greatly in attempting to confuse the issue, to make someone believe that they've heard from the Lord when they really haven't, or to dilute what they actually have heard. In fact, it takes a life of constant, total consecration in order to be led consistently by the Holy Spirit.

NOTES

That being first, the pleasing of the Lord, the next great phase of Paul's life and Ministry was the care of the Churches. It is obvious as to his concern for them, as any Godly Preacher would have concern. And yet, I think it went much further than that.

Paul having been given the New Covenant, and the responsibility of founding the Church under Christ, actually its Masterbuilder (I Cor. 3:10), he knew the significance of these Gentile Churches. In a sense, they were the foundation of all that would happen in the coming centuries; consequently, this foundation must be sure.

At the same time, I wonder if the people of these various Churches, the Philippians for instance to whom Paul is now writing, fully understood their pivotal role? Did they understand that these Letters sent to them would actually be read by untold millions of people down through the many centuries, and were actually the Word of God? In fact, this which we are now studying, was the single most important thing in the world which was taking place at that particular time. I know that Paul understood the consequences, but I wonder if the people understood it as well!

Bringing it all up to the present time, I continue to wonder if any of us truly understand the significance of all this we do for Christ? Do we really realize how important it actually is? Do we fully comprehend its eternal consequences?

(20) "FOR I HAVE NO MAN LIKEMINDED, WHO WILL NATURALLY CARE FOR YOUR STATE."

Paul's glowing testimony about Timothy was not to introduce his young associate, for he was already well known at Philippi. It did serve, however, to avert possible disappointment that Paul himself could not come at once and indicated that he had the fullest confidence in his younger associate.

"No one else like him" is literally *"no one of equal soul."*

Along with his statement concerning Timothy, the Apostle as well gives us further insight into the Ministry, and the serious lack of consecration even then. His statement, of course, must be limited, even as we will address momentarily; nevertheless, the indictment is strong just the same.

LIKEMINDED

The phrase, *"For I have no man likeminded,"* refers to Preachers of the Gospel under Paul's influence which covered a considerable area as would be obvious, and no doubt, referred also to Preachers from Rome whom he had met during his time of imprisonment there. As stated, this was a severe indictment as we shall see in Paul's further elaboration. First let's look further at Timothy.

This young man's special fitness for this mission, even as sanctioned by the Holy Spirit, was that he had a heart to care for people, especially to care for their true and highest interests in the things of the Lord. So far he resembled Paul himself. He had the true pastoral heart. He had caught the lessons of Paul's own life. That was the main thing.

No doubt, he had intellectual gifts, but his disposition gave him the right use of these gifts. The loving heart, the watchfulness, and thoughtfulness which that inspires, do more to create Godliness than any intellectual superiority.

Timothy had a share of the *"Mind of Christ,"* and that made him meet to be a wise Minister to the Philippians, as well as a trustworthy reporter concerning their state and prospects.

What is most fitted to impress us is the difficulty which Paul experienced in finding a suitable messenger, and the manner in which he describes his difficulty. He was conscious in himself of a self-forgetting love and care for the Churches, which was part, and a great part, of his Christian character.

He was ready (I Cor. 10:33) to please all men in all things, not seeking his own profit, but the profit of many, that they might be saved. He looked out for Preachers among his friends whose hearts might answer to him here, but he did not find them. He had no man likeminded. One indeed was found, Timothy, but no more. As he surveyed the situation, a sense of disappointment settled on him.

GODLY CARE

The phrase, *"Who will naturally care for your state,"* speaks of a heart that has one thing in mind, and that is doing the Will of God, irrespective as to what that will might be. Much is said here:

He was speaking of Preachers whom he could send to Philippi. They claimed the Call of God on their lives. But whoever it is of whom he speaks, which probably covered the city of Rome, and maybe elsewhere, he had learned from some association with them that the burden was lacking. In other words, they had an agenda which was fueled by self-will and not by the Holy Spirit. Consequently, if he sent one of these types of individuals, the actual spiritual state of the Philippians would be of little concern to them. As well, that which Paul desired would be of little concern either.

Their thoughts would be as to how they could take advantage of this situation! How could they fish money from this opportunity? Quite possibly, they could even draw off a group of individuals to follow them, thereby splitting the Church. Unfortunately, this evil did not die with the First Century.

Again, we should make it clear, that the Apostle is speaking only of Preachers in Rome, or others possibly in other places whom he would have in mind. He would not be speaking of Aristarchus, Marcus, Tychicus, or Silas, or others of similar comport. The character he gives to these men in his Epistle to the Colossians and elsewhere, sets them clear respecting the inculcation of this Passage.

(21) "FOR ALL SEEK THEIR OWN, NOT THE THINGS WHICH ARE JESUS CHRIST'S."

These words must be understood in harmony with other statements in the Letter. They must not be denied, therefore, but neither must they be understood with undue harshness.

Paul had already noted that some among his acquaintances at Rome were more concerned with furthering their own interests. As a result, at least one or more among them missed the opportunity of all opportunities. How much more wonderful it would have been, if the Apostle could have recorded here the faithfulness of at least one or a few regarding the need; however, it was not to be. Accordingly, their place in the Sacred Text is positioned in the unfaithful column. How sad!

And yet, I should think we should take a lesson here.

ALL SEEK THEIR OWN

The phrase, *"For all seek their own,"* does not mean that there were no genuine Christians in Rome, but that there were none of the caliber of which he needed. The word *"all"* is strong. It means *"the whole of them, one and all, all without exception."* This should tell us something extremely important.

A person can be saved but yet not measure up to that which they could be, and in fact, ought to be, even as illustrated here. We must remember that it is the Holy Spirit Who is sanctioning Paul's words, which gives them a tremendous significance. Consequently, the same question regarding our consecration should be asked presently of modern Believers. For you the Reader, will the answer be the same as given here by Paul concerning those in Rome, or would it be positive as of Timothy?

To be sure, the Holy Spirit is bringing forth a sure judgment concerning each and every Christian, each and every day, exactly as he did as it regarded those in Rome at that particular time. We should always keep this in mind.

THAT WHICH BELONGS TO CHRIST

The phrase, *"Not the things which are Jesus Christ's,"* pertains to the Will of God in all matters. The Preacher of the Gospel is to ardently seek the Will of God in all things, and then attempt with all of his or her strength to carry out that Will. To which we have already alluded, there must not be any personal agenda, no self-will, in the heart of the Preacher or any Believer for that matter.

What does all of this mean?

It does not necessarily mean that the men in question were openly sinning. It does not mean that they were destitute of the fear of God and love for Christ. But yet, to the Apostle's eye, and which he no doubt strongly felt in his spirit as well, they were too visibly swayed by the eagerness concerning their own doings; they were so swayed that their ordinary course was governed and determined by it, which no doubt quickly showed in their conversation and demeanor.

It might be love of ease, it might be covetousness, it might be pride, it might be party opinion, it might be family interests, it might even be concentration on their own religious comfort — however it might be, to this it came in the end, all seek their own.

You mistake, if you suppose this faulty state implied, in all of these cases, a deliberate, conscious preference of their own things above the things of Jesus Christ. The men concerned might really discern a supreme duty and work in the things of Christ; they might honestly judge that Christ had a supreme claim on their loyalty; and they might have a purpose to adhere to Christ and Christ's Cause at great cost, if the cost must finally be borne. And yet, meanwhile, in their common life, the other principle of faithlessness manifested itself far too much.

The place which their own things held — the degree in which their life was influenced by the bearing of things on themselves, was from Christ occupying a subordinate place in their lives. The things of Jesus Christ did not rise in their minds above other interests, but were jostled, crowded, and thrust aside by a thousand things that were their own.

PAUL'S DECISIONS WERE SPIRIT LED

I'm positive that the Reader would understand that the Apostle was led by the Holy Spirit, and one might even say, led in all that he did. This is not to say that Paul was perfect, for no man is; however, if there was ever anyone who could serve as an example of following after the Spirit, being led by the Spirit, understanding that the Spirit must direct in all things and ardently seeking that course, it would have been Paul.

In this type of situation at least as it regards the present time, far too often, such matters are decided by committees respecting Denominations, who select those who adhere more closely to the denominational line. Consequently, such is not of the Spirit, as such cannot be of the Spirit. But yet, and regrettably, that's the way most of the business of the modern Church is entertained. Once again, the agenda is other than that of the Cause of Christ, even though it may go under the guise of that pretention.

If the Apostle could say this to the Christians of his day, how great must be the danger still!

(22) "BUT YE KNOW THE PROOF OF HIM, THAT, AS A SON WITH THE FATHER, HE HATH SERVED WITH ME IN THE GOSPEL."

The proved character of Timothy put him in a class apart. By the thorough test of his reputed presence and Ministry in Philippi, as well as by his reputation achieved elsewhere, the Philippian Christians knew him as a man of God.

Paul also vouches for him on the basis of many years of personal experience. He and the younger Timothy had a father-son relationship. Together they had served Christ for the furtherance of the Gospel, beginning with Paul's second missionary journey more than some ten years earlier (Kent).

PROOF

The phrase, *"But ye know the proof of him,"* refers to that which has met the test and has been approved. Thus, Timothy's approved character is what the word *"proof of him"* has reference to.

"Ye know" is from the Greek word speaking of knowledge gained by experience. The Philippian Saints knew Timothy personally.

Timothy's record is known to all and is one of absolute faithfulness. Despite an evident timidity (II Tim. 1:6-7) and what might be considered as certain physical infirmities (I Tim. 5:23), this young man faithfully stood by Paul in Philippi (Acts Chpt. 16), in Thessalonica and Berea (Acts 17:1-14), in Corinth and Ephesus (Acts 18:5; 19:21-22), and even now is with Paul in Rome (Phil. 1:1).

He was associated with Paul in the writing of I and II Thessalonians, II Corinthians, Colossians, and now Philippians. He had earlier been sent as a delegate to Jerusalem (Acts 20:4). In it all he had served cooperatively with Paul *"for the furtherance of the Gospel,"* even when it meant occupying a place secondary to the Apostle.

SERVICE

The phrase, *"That, as a son with the father, he hath served with me in the Gospel,"* actually says in the original Greek, *"as a son to a father."*

It is as if Paul was going to speak of Timothy's dutiful ministration and following of his (Paul's) example; but then the sentence changes, in a characteristic humility, and makes Timothy and himself merely fellow-servants — he served with me in the Gospel.

If we may judge of Timothy's character from the general character of Paul's directions to him in the Pastoral Epistles, and especially the significant exhortation, *"Let no man despite thy youth"* (I Tim. 4:12), it would seem to have been gentle and warm-hearted rather than commanding.

What an honor it was for this young Preacher to have it said of him by the great Paul, *"He hath served with me in the Gospel."*

Perhaps more adjectives and superlatives could be piled on, but I think such would serve only to subtract rather than otherwise. There could be no greater honor, and paid by the Holy Spirit at that in having this account placed in the Sacred Text.

As we have previously stated, how much more wonderful it would have been if Paul could have added a name or names of some of the Preachers in Rome, which the great Apostle would grandly have done, if someone, anyone, had fit the bill.

(23) "HIM THEREFORE I HOPE TO SEND PRESENTLY, SO SOON AS I SHALL SEE HOW IT WILL GO WITH ME."

The Greek sentence begins with *"This one,"* which gathers up all that has just been said regarding Timothy and emphasizes that he is the one to be sent to Philippi.

He will not be the bearer of this Letter, however, because Paul wants to retain him until he has more definite information about the outcome of his case. This implies that Paul thinks there will soon be some kind of legal decision regarding him.

This Letter will alert the Philippians to Timothy's coming and will also let them know the reason why he did not come with Epaphroditus. They will also know that when Timothy does come, he will be bringing word about the crucial developments in Paul's legal case (Kent).

THIS ONE I WILL SEND

The phrase, *"Him therefore I hope to send presently,"* refers to a delay, but is hoped it will not be long.

Paul is somewhat anxious concerning the Church at Philippi, wanting as much to hear news from them as to give news to them, i.e., *"the Gospel."* But yet he doesn't want to send Timothy until he knows something definite concerning his own situation.

HOW IT WILL GO WITH ME

The phrase, *"So soon as I shall see how it will go with me,"* lets us know that the Apostle feels that he will have word soon. It is believed that under Roman jurisprudence, a person could be incarcerated only two years without being tried. In fact, Acts 28:30-31, relates that Paul *"dwelt two whole years in his own hired house, and received all that came in unto him, preaching the Kingdom of God, and teaching those things which concerned the Lord Jesus Christ, with all confidence, no man forbidding him."*

The word *"see"* gives us another glimpse into the character of the great Apostle. The Greek word here speaks of the act of turning one's attention from other things and concentrating them upon one's own situation. In fact, Paul was so forgetful of self, yes, so dead to self, too engrossed in the welfare of others, that, even though he was a prisoner, yet he had not taken thought of his own welfare.

He voices the hope that he will be able to send Timothy soon. But his sending Timothy is dependent on his own circumstances which may or may not hinder. As stated, he wants the Philippians to have some solid news about him from Timothy when the young man finally does come.

(24) "BUT I TRUST IN THE LORD THAT I ALSO MYSELF SHALL COME SHORTLY."

As is obvious, Paul is confident that release was in prospect, and he would fulfill his wish to visit the Philippians. Actually, and as previously stated, I think the Apostle had been told by the Lord that he would be released.

TRUST IN THE LORD

The phrase, *"But I trust in the Lord,"* presents the principle that all the acts, thoughts, and attitudes of Christians should spring from the fact that we are *"in the Lord"* and are prompted by the Spirit's energy. Everything we do should be consistent with, and submitted to, the Lord's Will.

The word *"trust"* in the Greek Text is not the usual word for *"trust,"* but one that means *"to persuade."* It means that Paul had come to a settled persuasion. This settled persuasion was in the sphere of the Lord, that is, Paul's convictions in the matter of his release were based on the Lord's faithfulness to him.

Compare Philemon vs. 22, *"Prepare me a lodging, for I trust that through your prayers I shall be given to you,"* where the expectation seems even more immediate. The interval between the Letters is unknown, both being written from Rome.

I SHALL COME SHORTLY

The phrase, *"That I also myself shall come shortly,"* supposes this expectation to have been fulfilled.

The Lord does not tell us all things, demanding Faith on our part, even though He orders every step, every situation, and every circumstance, at least as it regards the Child of God. Nothing is happenchance, luck, or uncertainty with the Lord. He is watching over every one of His Children, even to a minute degree.

Such close introspection may be uncomfortable to those who follow from afar, but to those of us who hunger and thirst for His leading, it provides a comfort unexcelled.

(25) "YET I SUPPOSED IT NECESSARY TO SEND TO YOU EPAPHRODITUS, MY BROTHER, AND COMPANION IN LABOUR, AND FELLOWSOLDIER, BUT YOUR MESSENGER, AND HE THAT MINISTERED TO MY WANTS."

This second of Paul's messengers to Philippi, and the one whose forthcoming trip was the immediate occasion for this Epistle was Epaphroditus. He is mentioned in the New Testament only in this Epistle (Phil. 2:25; 4:18). He should not be confused with Epaphras of Colosse (Col. 1:7; 4:12; Phile. vs. 23), even though the names are similar.

Epaphroditus had brought the Philippians' gift to Paul. He is identified by the Apostle in a series of glowing terms. He is *"my brother,"* a sharer of spiritual life with Paul and so his Brother in Christ.

He is a *"fellow worker,"* a participant with Paul in the labors of the Gospel. Paul said he was also *"my ... fellowsoldier,"* a sharer of the dangers involved in standing firm for Christ and in proclaiming the Gospel.

The next terms tell of Epaphroditus' relation to the Philippians. He had acted as their *"messenger,"* the duly-appointed and commissioned delegate to convey the Philippians' gift to Paul.

In this capacity Epaphroditus had served as their *"Minister,"* functioning officially on their behalf in performing a sacred service to Paul.

The word *"ministered"* as used here, appears five times in the New Testament (Rom. 13:6; 14:15; Phil. 2:25; Heb. 1:7; 8:2) and in several of these a priestly sort of Ministry is in view. It is used of Christ's Priestly Ministry in the Heavenly Tabernacle (Heb. 8:2) and of Paul's sacred service in the evangelizing of Gentiles and presentation of them to God (Rom. 15:16). Hence, the use in Philippians 2:25 has overtones of a Priestly act, that of Epaphroditus' presenting to Paul the Philippians' offering, *"an acceptable sacrifice, pleasing to God"* (Phil. 4:18).

EPAPHRODITUS

The phrase, *"Yet I supposed it necessary to send to you Epaphroditus,"* presents the Brother who had brought the Love-Offering from the Philippians to Paul. After delivering this, it seems he stayed with Paul for some time. During this stay in Rome, Epaphroditus was stricken with an illness so severe that for a time his life was in jeopardy, of which we will have more to say momentarily.

It seems, on all accounts, reasonable to believe that Epaphroditus belonged to the Philippian Church, and could well have been one of its Pastors, although there is no proof of such. Once again, as we can easily see, we have the record as carried out by the Holy Spirit of an individual who sacrificed himself regarding the Work of God, in this case to the help of Paul. His name is forever enshrined in the Sacred Text, read by untold millions, always with a heart of love extended toward this man who tried to make Paul's labors a little easier. How so much we should learn from these examples.

For those who tried to help the Judaizers, the Holy Spirit has no word of commendation, no word at all! In fact, every indication is otherwise! The point I am attempting to make is this:

As is obvious to all, Paul was God's man for this particular time. Consequently, all who helped him, who prayed for him, who helped support him, who stood with him, were greatly blessed and honored by the Lord as the Text amply implies. It is no less at the present time. The Believer should earnestly seek the Will of God as to that which is desired by the Holy Spirit, and then fall in line with that flow. The sadness is, many Christians, lacking discernment, support that too often which actually is not of God, and in many cases is actually opposed to God. Of course, it is obvious that such are not led by the Spirit. Unfortunately, most Christians aren't! They are led rather by impulse, perception, outward appearances, conventional wisdom, etc. All of that is always wrong.

BROTHER, COMPANION, FELLOWSOLDIER, MESSENGER

The phrase, *"My brother, and companion in labour, and fellowsoldier, but your Messenger,"* presents accolades given by the Apostle as it regards this brother, but above all sanctioned by the Holy Spirit. Once again, what a compliment!

The Greek word *"brother,"* means literally, *"from the same womb."* It speaks of a common origin. A common origin speaks of a common level.

The great Apostle puts himself on a common level with this humble brother in Christ who was the Philippians' messenger to Paul.

Thus, it is that Christianity levels off artificial earthly distinctions and places all, rich and poor, nobility and peasantry, wise and unlearned, on the same level, yes, but on what level?

It places all Believers on the highest plain, namely, in Heavenly Places in Christ Jesus. It levels off the distinction between nobility and peasantry, abolishing both so far as our Heavenly Citizenship is concerned, and creates an aristocracy of which all are members, the aristocracy of Heaven (Wuest).

It is strange, men strive for recognition, for place and position, to be recognized, all of which are so fleeting even if such are gained. And yet, the moment the individual comes to Christ, irrespective of their status, place or position, irrespective of their birth, all are placed in a high position regarding the aristocracy of Heaven. What a wonder! What a joy! What a privilege!

Then he calls him his fellow worker. Next he refers to him as his fellowsoldier in the Christian conflict against the powers of darkness. Finally, Paul calls him the Messenger of the Philippians.

The word *"Messenger"* is the translation of a Greek word that is usually translated *"Apostle,"* as in Galatians 1:1. It was used of an Ambassador sent on a commission. However, I think the King James Translators were correct in translating it *"Messenger"* here, instead of Apostle. I think the designation of *"Apostle"* was not intended here by Paul, and because it was not intended by the Holy Spirit.

MINISTERED TO MY WANTS

The phrase, *"And he that ministered to my wants,"* as used by Paul, shows that the Apostle looked upon this service as having such sacredness about it as one would meet with in the ministry of the Priests in the Jewish Temple Services.

Paul supposed it necessary to send Epaphroditus back to the Philippians. The word *"necessary"* in the Greek Text is a very strong word. It means *"indispensable, what one cannot do without."*

"Supposed" is the translation of a word that does not contain a doubt as it seems on the surface, but refers to a decision arrived at after weighing the facts in the case (Wuest).

(26) "FOR HE LONGED AFTER YOU ALL, AND WAS FULL OF HEAVINESS, BECAUSE THAT YE HAD HEARD THAT HE HAD BEEN SICK."

Epaphroditus had become deeply distressed when he learned that the Philippians knew of his illness. One must beware of reading too much between the lines; however, there is inference that more is involved than merely mutual concern.

The strong word *"distressed"* in Paul's emphasis on the point that Epaphroditus had really been seriously ill and should be given a grand welcome may imply that some misunderstanding had arisen in Philippi concerning this dear Brother. Possibly he had stayed longer in Rome than had been previously planned, with those at Philippi not knowing why, with Paul explaining here that all of this was due to his sickness. Whatever the reason, the Apostle went into some length of explanation, which after all may not have meant anymore than just the stating of facts. We must be careful not to read too much into the Text, but we must not rule out the possibility of other reasons as well.

FULL OF HEAVINESS

The phrase, *"For he longed after you all, and was full of heaviness,"* concerns a problem which had arisen, and thereby changing plans in a negative fashion and as well, falling out to a negative fashion.

The words *"full of heaviness"* are from a Greek word used only two other times in the New Testament (Mat. 26:37; Mk. 14:33), both of which refer to our Lord's heaviness of soul in Gethsemane. The Greek word finds its origin in a word that has the idea of *"not at home,"* thus, *"uncomfortable, troubled, distressed."* The word does *not* refer to homesickness, but to the discomfort of not being at home due to some difficulty (Wuest).

SICKNESS

The phrase, *"Because that ye had heard that he had been sick,"* indicates that Epaphroditus is now much improved.

What his sickness was we are not told, even though as the next Verse proclaims, it had been very serious, even to the point that it looked like he might die.

What it was, or its cause really doesn't matter. The point is, we should look at this very brief explanation given here by Paul, in order that we might learn some things concerning Divine Healing, etc. In other words, why did not Paul rebuke this sickness, thereby saving this Brother much grief, for Paul had seen many healings and miracles?

Why didn't Epaphroditus believe for himself, seeing that he was a man of Faith, of which there should be no doubt?

To boil it all down to the bottom line, why is it that this man was sick? Or why did he not get healing immediately?

We definitely need to address the question of sickness here. Many teach presently that all sickness is either because of sin in one's life, or improper Faith. Is that correct?

While it is definitely true that many Christians are sick because of unconfessed sin, and because of not believing the Lord; however, is that true about all? Let's look at it from both the Old and the New Testament perspective. Perhaps we will find some answers.

SICKNESS

The Biblical accounts of Healing can answer many of our questions about this subject; however, much of what we see the Bible saying on this subject is at times colored by our Doctrinal heritage.

Can we be healed from our diseases if only we have Faith enough to believe?

It has been taught very strongly in the last several decades, that Faith is the only ingredient as it regards Healing. In other words, it has been taught that if a Believer does not experience constant health, or at least instant healing upon the advent of sickness, that it is because they do not have the proper Faith. As we have stated, everything, they say, is tied to Faith.

While Faith definitely plays a vital part in all that we do with the Lord, including Healing, is it Scripturally correct that this is the ingredient in any and all situations and circumstances?

We need to look at this very carefully, because it is extremely important as should be obvious. There are millions of Christians (and I think I exaggerate not), who are referred to as *"Faith drop-outs."* In other words, their sickness wasn't healed and so they are dismissed as simply not having enough Faith.

At the outset, that is cruel and definitely not Biblical.

First of all let's see what the Old Testament says about healing and then we'll go to the New.

HEALING IN THE OLD TESTAMENT

The Old Testament Hebrew word for healing is *"rapa,"* and appears 67 times. Its basic meaning is maintained throughout the account which means, *"to heal or make healthy."*

In many Old Testament uses of this word, physical healing of a sickness or disease is in view (Gen. 20:17). But the image of sickness is used in other Passages to portray the ravages of sin. In these contexts, healing speaks of forgiveness and of the restoration of a harmonious relationship with God, as well as of the Blessings that follow such a relationship. Thus, Isaiah cries out to his countrymen, to a people *"loaded with guilt"* (Isa. 1:4).

He describes their condition in their rebellion against God: *"Your whole head is injured, your whole heart afflicted. From the sole of your foot to the top of your head there is no soundness — only wounds and welts and open sores, not cleansed or bandaged or soothed with oil"* (Isa. 1:5-6).

To be healed, God's people must turn to Him and be cleansed (Isa. 1:18). Then, in fellowship again, *"If you are willing and obedient, you will eat the best of the land"* (Isa. 1:19). Thus, spiritual sickness is equated with sin, and healing is equated with forgiveness and relationship with God (II Chron. 7:14-16; Hos. 6:1).

The Prophets announced God's firm intention to heal His sinning people spiritually (Isa. 57:18-19; Jer. 33:6). But it is also clear that God is viewed as the Source of physical healing as well. Both are in view in God's announcement of this distinctive name to His people, recorded in Exodus 15:26: *"I am the Lord Who heals you."*

THE ROLE OF MEDICINE

In view of the radical conviction that both spiritual and physical health come from God, what role was there for medicine and doctors in Old Testament times? In later Judaism, medicines were viewed with considerable suspicion. What do we find in the Old Testament concerning this question?

In fact, there is actually very little evidence concerning this question in the Old Testament to which one can appeal. Genesis Chapter 50 mentions the physicians of Egypt, and II Chronicles 16:12 criticizes King Asa because, *"Though his disease was severe, even in his illness he did not seek help from the Lord, but only from the physicians."*

First of all, the thought here is not that seeking medical help was necessarily wrong. Actually, the wrong came in two ways:

1. First of all, this wicked king did not seek the help of the Lord at all. The Lord was not pleased with that.

2. Also, the physicians mentioned here were mostly soothsayers, in other words, somewhat similar to modern witch doctors, etc. They were not true Doctors as we think of such presently.

The Old Testament does mention medical practices such as the cleansing and binding of wounds and the use of soothing oil (Isa. 1:6). As well, there are references to healing balm (medicine) (II Chron. 28:15; Jer. 51:8).

Isaiah was told by God that a poultice was to be applied to King Hezekiah and he would recover (Isa. 38:21). But although common remedies were in use in Israel, no medical science or practice as such was carried on then as we think of such presently.

HEALING IN THE ATONEMENT

The Old Testament always recognizes God as Healer, irrespective of the manner in which He chooses to carry out this work. As a result, the Godly when in distress always look to the Lord for restoration. In the entirety of the Old Testament, Isaiah in his great 53rd Chapter gives the greatest account of the Atonement found anywhere. However, arguments have raged from then until now as to what the Atonement included?

Did it include healing for the physical body? Victory for the dispossessed soul? Or even prosperity for those in financial and material poverty?

There are many who claim that the Atonement only dealt with sin and nothing else. Their reasoning is, that if physical healing was included in the Atonement, then Christians should never get sick; however, that argument is lame, for Christians still sin at times, even though, as all agree, spiritual deliverance or deliverance from sin is definitely in the Atonement.

The Truth is, Jesus addressed every single thing in the Atonement which man lost at the Fall. That includes deliverance from sin, healing for the physical body, prosperity for the financially depressed, victory over death, and anything else one might think of as it regards all that man lost on that dark day so long ago in the Garden of Eden. The Work of Christ as it regards the Cross and the Resurrection is a *"Finished Work."* Consequently,

NOTES

He either addressed everything, or He addressed nothing.

However, despite all that Christ did there as it regards the Atonement, Believers do not yet have all the benefits there purchased by His Own Precious Blood. The totality of these benefits, which includes a glorified body which will never again know sin or sickness, or aging or death, will not be realized until the Resurrection. In fact, Paul plainly says, *"For the earnest expectation of the creature waiteth for the manifestation of the sons of God."*

He then said, *"Because the creature itself also shall be delivered from the bondage of corruption into the glorious liberty of the Children of God... which have the firstfruits of the Spirit, even we ourselves groan within ourselves, waiting for the adoption, to wit, the redemption of our body"* (Rom. 8:19-23).

So, the idea that Healing is not in the Atonement is foolish as should be obvious. Mostly, those who believe such, do so because they do not believe that the Lord heals at all, or even answers prayer presently, or much of anything else for that matter. They mostly have some type of cold, icebox kind of faith, which in reality, is precious little faith at all.

Yes, Healing is definitely in the Atonement, plus victory over all things with which Satan afflicted the human race at the Fall.

HEALING IN THE NEW TESTAMENT

Healing was a significant part of Jesus' Ministry before the Ascension and in the Ministry of the Apostles in the Early Church. Regarding the Saviour, the Gospels, in straightforward narrative, simply tell what happened, describing Healings that were obvious to Jesus' followers and enemies alike.

In the Gospels and Acts, which of course give the accounts, Healings are often associated with the Faith of the person who was healed (Mat. 8:1-3; 9:21-22; 15:28; Acts 14:9). But the New Testament reports other Miracles of Healing without reference to Faith or even to the conversion of the persons healed (Mat. 9:23-26; Mk. 6:5; Acts 3:1-10; 5:16; 8:7; 28:8).

Concerning the Ministry of Christ, we are to understand that His Works of Healing were an integral part of His primary Ministry: In other words to present Himself to Israel as the Messiah and to demonstrate God's Power and Love. However, His Healing Ministry was also meant to continue as it regards His followers and the Church.

To begin with, He endowed His Disciples with His Own Healing Power (Mat. 10:1, 8; Mk. 6:13; Lk. 9:1, 6). As a result, the Early Church saw this healing power exercised after the Resurrection of Jesus, as the Apostles preached Jesus (Acts 3:16; 4:9-30; 5:16; 8:7; 9:34; 14:9; 28:8).

Some have claimed, that inasmuch as very little is mentioned about Healing in the balance of the New Testament, but only in the Gospels and Acts, then we are not to expect such to be continued presently. However, that is no basis for such thinking.

First of all, the Epistles pertain to Biblical Doctrine as it refers to the foundation of the Faith and discipline, etc. In fact, the Epistles for this very reason, unlike the Gospels and Acts, give very few accounts of particular happenings.

James did address the subject briefly, when he calls on the sick to have the Elders of the Church pray over them and anoint them with oil in the Name of the Lord, and he promises Healing in response to the prayer offered in Faith (James 5:14-16).

In I Corinthians Chapter 12, Paul mentions the Gift of Healing, but really does not say too very much otherwise. However, what *is* said in the entirety of the New Testament lets us know, that it is perfectly proper for Christians to believe the Lord for Healing, and to expect such. However, the following should be noted:

SICKNESS AMONG BELIEVERS

Even as we have already said, despite Jesus addressing everything at the Atonement (His Crucifixion and Resurrection), we still do not have all the benefits of that great Finished Work, and will not have all until the Resurrection. As a result, this takes into account many things.

For instance, and as is obvious, irrespective of the amount of Faith a person may have as it regards the Lord, we still grow older with all of its attendant problems, and ultimately will die unless the Rapture takes us first. As a result of the Fall, this physical body ultimately wears out. Paul addressed this by saying, *"For we know that if our earthly house of this tabernacle were dissolved* (is being dissolved through age), *we have a building of God, an house not made with hands, eternal in the heavens* (the glorified body)" (II Cor. 5:1).

To say it another way, I don't care how much Faith in God a person has, this physical body is still going to get older with age, and as a result of being mortal, it wears out, with all the attendant physical difficulties. No amount of Faith will change that. So that tells us, that even though Faith is definitely required on the part of the Believer as it results Healing, still, we must not claim more than the Lord has promised.

Even with the young, at times, it is not necessarily a lack of Faith which stops Healing, even as with Epaphroditus. We know that Paul had great Faith, and are we going to be so foolish as to think that Epaphroditus was faithless? Surely not! Well then we must ask the question, *"Why wasn't the man healed? Why did he, to use him as an example, not receive Healing, and in fact almost died?"*

QUESTIONS

I don't know the answer to that question, and neither does any other human being. In fact, there are untold millions of Christians who ask the Lord for Healing, Healing I might quickly add which in many cases is desperately needed, but do not receive Healing. Now, one can brush these people aside with the wave of the hand as lacking Faith, or condemn them with some other accusation; however, when this is done, the one doing the accusing must quickly understand, that he is at the same time accusing himself.

We are encouraged to believe the Lord for Healing, even as I think we have already amply demonstrated. As well, the Lord does gloriously and wondrously heal the sick; but at times, Healing is not forthcoming, and there is no satisfactory explanation. The idea is, the Believer is to continue to trust the Lord despite problems and difficulties.

My Faith is not anchored in the fact of whether I receive Healing or not, or anything else of similar nature, but rather on what Jesus did for me at the Cross and the Resurrection. I realize that as a Believer, that even though He addressed everything on that memorable day of so long ago, still, I do not have all the benefits of that which He did, and will not have all of these benefits until the Resurrection. The trouble is, many Preachers tend to get the future mixed up with the present. In other words, they try to pull the coming Millennium into the present. However, all they succeed in doing is to discourage individuals which is the very opposite of which the Lord intends. A great day is coming, when there will be no more sin, sickness, death, aging, or dying. We look forward to that time; however, it has not yet arrived. Until then, even as the song says, I will go on singing despite the difficulties and problems.

Am I to lose all my Faith in the fact that God does heal the sick, simply because He did not heal Epaphroditus, or at least did not heal him immediately?

Of course not!

My Faith is not based on what the Lord might or might not do presently, but in fact, what He has already done, and I speak of the Cross and the Resurrection. That's where my Faith is, and that's where my Faith will remain.

IN CONCLUSION

We can be sure of only a few basic realities. Spiritual and physical health are linked. Spiritual and physical Healing are also linked. God is the Supervisor and Source of it all.

The Believer is expected to bring every need to God in prayer and can be confident that God will hear. However, we must leave the results up to Him. Even though, there is no guarantee of Him performing on cue at our every beck and call; nevertheless, we can definitely be certain that God loves us and will act for our good in every single thing He does, whatever that course of action might be. As a result, we are to love Him, thank Him, worship Him, trust Him, and have Faith in Him, *"that all things work together for good to them who love God, to them who are the called according to His Purpose"* (Rom. 8:28).

(27) "FOR INDEED HE WAS SICK NIGH UNTO DEATH: BUT GOD HAD MERCY ON HIM; AND NOT ON HIM ONLY, BUT ON ME ALSO, LEST I SHOULD HAVE SORROW UPON SORROW."

The precise nature of this man's ailment is not indicated; however, the illness was so severe that Paul regarded the recovery as an intervention of God.

We should learn some things from this brief account given here by the Apostle as it concerns this incident.

SICKNESS AND DEATH

The phrase, *"For indeed he was sick nigh unto death,"* means as is obvious, he almost died.

It should be recognized by the Reader, that Paul had no compunctions about relating this situation as it concerned Epaphroditus. There is no hint in the Text, that he was concerned that the Believers at Philippi, or anywhere else for that matter who would read this, would come away claiming that Paul or Epaphroditus were lacking in Faith. It is obvious from the Text, that Paul had no such thing in mind. However, many of the so-called modern gurus of Faith would immediately brand this as a *"lack of Faith,"* or a *"bad confession."* In fact, it was neither!

This tells us, that this modern presentation of Faith is erroneous. I'm speaking of the so-called modern Faith Ministry. While there is definitely some Truth in this particular teaching, the error embedded therein, which claims that everything hinges on Faith, will always lead one to a wrong conclusion. So, the modern Christian must beware of this false doctrine, and false doctrine it is!

FAITH

While Faith is always a foundation of all that the Believer has and is in Christ, it is the object of Faith which must always be kept in view. If the object of Faith is Faith itself, which promises all types of rewards for its practitioners, it is a false message. The object of Faith must ever be the Will of God, Whose Will is always centered up in the Cross of Christ. If we go beyond that, we will find ourselves in the position of attempting to use God's Word against Himself.

And what do we mean by that?

For instance, Mark 11:24 says, *"Therefore I say unto you, What things soever ye desire, when ye pray, believe that ye receive them, and ye shall have them."*

When Jesus said *"What things soever ye desire,"* did He mean anything?

He meant anything that is in the Will of God. He said this very plainly and clearly when He taught His Disciples to pray. He said, *"Our Father which art in Heaven, Hallowed by Thy Name.*

"Thy Kingdom come, Thy Will be done in earth, as it is in Heaven" (Mat. 6:9-10).

Using this as our foundation, which Jesus definitely meant for us to do, our petitions are always to be in the context of what is His Will on Earth and in Heaven.

But yet, millions of Christians have taken these words, *"What things soever ye desire,"* and have attempted to use them for their own selfish purposes, automatically concluding that they know the Will of God in any and all circumstances. In fact, such is foolishness!

To do such a thing, places the Believer in the position of falling for the lure of Satan, when He tempted Jesus to *"command that these stones be made bread"* (Mat. 4:3).

Unfortunately, millions of Christians heeding this false doctrine of so-called Faith, have succumbed to the materialistic temptation, and have tried to turn the stones to bread. What a travesty!

The Will of God is to always be placed supreme in everything. No Christian dares to presume upon that Will, nor does he dare act outside of that Will. To do such is to invite disaster.

WAS IT THE WILL OF GOD FOR EPAPHRODITUS TO BE SICK AND ALMOST DIE?

In answering that question, we must at first ascertain what the Will of God actually is.

In Truth, it is not the Will of God for anyone to suffer any type of problem, difficulty, failure, sickness, suffering, reverse, etc. However, that is the ideal! Unfortunately, the Lord at this time due to circumstances, and I speak of the Fall, does not work from the privilege and position of the ideal. In fact, nothing is now ideal, and will not be until the Lord ultimately *"delivers up the Kingdom to God, even the Father; when He* (Jesus) *shall have put down all rule and all authority and power* (that of Satan)" (I Cor. 15:24).

First of all, I have every confidence that Paul sought the Lord earnestly as it regarded

NOTES

Healing for Epaphroditus. I am certain that this man also prayed eagerly for himself.

So, taking into consideration that the Lord is in charge of every single thing, and that He minutely guards the life and way of His Own Children, and knowing that He has the power to do even above what we might ask or think, I must come to the conclusion that the situation as it played out with Epaphroditus, had to be the wisdom of God even though I don't think one could Scripturally say that it was the Will of God.

This of which we are discussing is extremely important. Let's look at it for a moment in a little deeper context.

THE WORD, THE WILL, AND THE WISDOM

Paul said, *"Howbeit we speak wisdom among them that are perfect: yet not the wisdom of this world, nor of the princes of this world, that come to nought: But we speak the wisdom of God in a mystery, even the hidden wisdom, which God ordained before the world unto our glory"* (I Cor. 2:6-7).

In this Scripture Paul is careful to specify that he is not discussing wisdom within a worldly context. A little further along in this same Epistle (I Cor. 3:19) he states, *"The Wisdom of this world is foolishness to God."*

Next Paul says, *"We speak the wisdom of God in a mystery."* I believe Paul's use of *"mystery"* infers a situation which God understands perfectly (in His infinite knowledge) but which we, with out limited minds, cannot understand, appreciate, nor even rationalize.

There are a number of situations which hint (to us) that God doesn't always respond to our wishes in the manner in which we would like Him to respond. It is this particular *"mystery"* in our relationship with God which I intend to address in these statements.

There are oftentimes when the Holy Spirit will lay some particular subject heavily on my heart. Whatever else I may be doing, travelling, eating, driving — these thoughts persist until I finally *"see"* the rationale behind the question. I am sure this has happened to other Preachers, and perhaps it has happened to you.

If there is one matter that troubles Christians more than any other, it would no doubt be the question of why prayers are not always answered, or else answered as quickly as we would like, or in the manner we would like.

THE WORD

In order to lay a foundation for what will follow, we must first establish one fact. This is, quite simply, that the Bible is the total, inerrant Word of God.

Of course, you cannot establish this fact to a skeptical world. If you could, the world's problems would totally and dramatically disappear in a short time. The prince of this world is dedicated to keeping men from believing the Bible.

But I believe the Holy Bible is, in fact, the very Word of God. I do not believe the Bible is a series of fables or stories or illustrations. As well, I do not believe the Bible is a compilation of myths and analogies. Our Lord said, *"Not one jot or tittle shall pass away until all be fulfilled"* (Mat. 5:18). Jots and tittles were small marks appended to Hebrew letters. If even the small accent marks of letters were important to God, we can assume that the body of His writing is inviolable.

Our Lord further said, *"Man shall not live by bread alone, but by every Word that proceedeth out of the Mouth of God"* (Mat. 4:4). The Lord Jesus, therefore, held every Word of the Sacred Writings as all-important. I consider anyone who would minimize what the Lord holds important to be foolish indeed.

We should also note in this same Scripture that our Lord did not say *"thought"* or *"concept"* or *"principle."* He said, *"Every word that proceedeth out of the Mouth of God."*

BELIEF WITHOUT BENEFIT

There are literally thousands of Preachers who say they believe every Word of the Bible. Still, these Bible-believing Ministers preach error that leads masses of their followers astray. Though they say they believe every word of the Bible from cover to cover, they teach doctrines and principles which are theologically absurd.

Does this mean they are lying about what they say? Does this then prove they don't believe the Word? No, I don't think it does. I think it just demonstrates how careful we must be in implementing the elements of our relationship with God.

I think their first error lies in their failure to devour the Word. *"Sampling"* just isn't enough. Nutritionists tell us whole grains are good for us. Will we then become healthy if we take a grain of rice, a grain of wheat, and a grain of barley once a month (or even once a day)? Probably not. We should eat a good, solid bowl full of these grains every day and, no doubt, we would then feel the results.

Secondly, I believe Preachers err when they fail to rightly divide the Word (as we are cautioned to do in II Timothy 2:15). God is not a capricious God and His Word is inerrant (without error). But it must be taken within the context of the situation in which it is given. Formulating doctrines from isolated Verses of Scripture can lead to error.

Thirdly, I believe that many Preachers go astray by failing to act upon what they say they believe. Acts without Faith are dead, just as Faith without acts is dead. In order to demonstrate and enjoy a productive, living relationship with God, we must first have the Faith, and then the action based on the Faith — to bring about results.

These three factors are, I believe, a solid foundation upon which to build a real, living relationship with God. Emersion in the Word, right dividing of the Word, and then acting upon the Word are the three components of Christian Life which form a basis upon which we will build the remainder of this statement concerning the Wisdom and Will of God.

THE GREAT PROMISES OF GOD

In recent years the Church, or at least many in the Church, has started to believe and act upon the great mass of Promises given to us by the Living God within His Word. And I am not speaking only of the fundamental truths and promises such as Redemption, Regeneration, and God's essential Plan for man. Many people and even the most unenlightened of Churches understand something about these.

Instead, I am discussing and speaking of those Scriptures which are so expansive, so all-encompassing, that average Christians tend to pass them over when they read their Bibles. Oh, they say, Promises of such magnitude certainly couldn't be for us today. If you will take out your Bible and read Matthew 21:22, Mark 11:23-24, and John 14:14;

15:7, plus others, you will see a collection of astounding Promises that offer us tremendous power relative to receiving from the Lord.

Thankfully, multiplied thousands of Christians have begun to realize that these Promises are for them and they are beginning to stand on them. They are saying, *"God, you told me I can have this and I'm going to stand and claim Your Promise."*

As a result, many Believers have seen great and wonderful things come to pass within their lives.

God, you see, did not put these Promises (and others like them) in His Word to just fill up space. If He didn't mean them He wouldn't have put them there. Since He did put them there He means for us to use them. To be frank, I have believed these great Promises all my life, and continue to believe and stand upon these great Promises up to this very moment, and in fact, ever shall!

Men fail, governments fail, political systems fail. There is only one unfailing element in all of time and eternity and that is the Promises of God. I would rather base my life, my Faith, and my belief on God than on any human entity. With God, nothing can harm us. Without God, nothing can help us.

So the first component in this statement is the very real, the unfailing, the predictable, and trustworthy Word of God. And having established that, we will move on to the second element in this Message.

THE WILL

How many times have you heard the question, *"What is the Will of God?"*

To be sure, there is the stock answer, *"The Will of God is the Word of God."* This statement is correct.

Unfortunately though, stock answers seldom settle controversies. Even with the Word of God as our guide we still hear people attempting to ascertain what the Will of God is in particular situations as it concerns their lives or others. So, we learn from this, and our own experiences, that stock answers aren't quite enough in attempting to ascertain this all-important aspect of our lives, the Will of God.

Despite this I maintain that our own true guide to discerning the Will of God is, in fact, by way of Scripture. There are, however, even within the Will of God, situations where prayers aren't answered. Let's look at some possible reasons.

DO ALL HAVE AUTHORITY?

In Mark 11:23 Jesus said, *"Whosoever shall say to yonder mountain, Be thou removed. . . ."* When our Lord made this statement, was He talking indiscriminately to every person who would ever walk upon the face of the Earth? I don't think He was.

To be sure, He did say *"Whosoever."* Taking that on the surface, many might contend that He meant, therefore, that anyone could move mountains with a simple demonstration of Faith. I can't agree. I believe, when He said *"Whosoever"* that He was addressing the statement to anyone within a particular segment of the population.

If we take *"Whosoever"* out of context and ascribe this potential to anyone within the whole world, we would have to believe that our Lord was giving infinite power to an endless succession of reprobates, perverts, and even Antichrists.

"Well 'whosoever' is 'whosoever,'" you might reply. Yes, and in rebuttal I might offer the account of the seven sons of Sceva in Acts 19:13-16.

These seven sons of this Pharisee took it upon themselves to use the Lord's Name and Power to provide themselves with income by exorcising demons. And what was the end of their venture?

They fled naked from their patient after he fell upon them and beat them severely. Obviously, *"Whosoever"* did *not* extend to the likes of the seven sons of Sceva. I don't believe Mark 11:23 delegates power to *"just anyone"* who chooses to use it.

Going further, we might ask the question whether the Lord would entrust such awesome power even to His Own Children while they are *"yet babes in Christ"*? Proper and judicious use of God's Power, and the insight and maturity to know when, how, and where to utilize this power, is a great responsibility.

Much maturity and Christian development are needed for many situations. Despite this we have Christians today who are exceedingly sketchy in their Scriptures and very shallow in their emotional maturity. They go about asking the Lord for a market-basket of items which, in many cases, are simply not appropriate to their needs. Once again, we go back to Jesus laying the foundation for prayer and petitions, by saying, *"Thy Will be done in earth, as it is in Heaven"* (Mat. 6:10).

This situation is not unlike the Scriptural account in Mark 10:35-40. Here James and John, the sons of Zebedee, came to Jesus and asked if they could sit at His right and left Hands when He came into His Glory.

His answer? *"You know not what you ask!"* Certainly they asked in Faith and they asked believing that their request could and should be granted. It wasn't.

I am convinced that many Christians — all of us at one time or another — are guilty of not knowing what we ask. If the Lord granted our every request, we might often wish He hadn't. I believe this is a definite factor in many situations where prayers aren't answered. We are told very clearly in God's Word that when we pray amiss God may not be able to answer that prayer! (James 4:3).

WHAT IS GOD'S WILL IN PARTICULAR FOR HIS CHILDREN?

As we've already stated, our Lord gave the model prayer in that which we refer to as *"The Lord's Prayer"* (Mat. 6:10-13). I suppose there are few Christians who don't know this prayer by heart. Unfortunately, we sometimes skip through without thinking about the important line: *"Thy Will be done, in earth as it is in Heaven."*

This statement by the Saviour gives us a most important insight into God's Will for us here on Earth. The obvious conclusion is that His Will for us here on Earth is exactly as His Will would be if we were in Heaven at this moment.

What are the conditions in Heaven? Are there financial troubles there? Is there illness in Heaven? Is there death in Heaven? Is there selfishness and bickering and strife in Heaven? Obviously, the answer to all these questions is a resounding *"no!"*

If none of these exist in Heaven, and if it is God's Will for the Earth to be as it is in Heaven, it should be clear that it is *not* God's Will for us to suffer poverty, sickness, death, and other afflictions here. Yet, look around. We do have all these problems with Christians suffering exactly as non-Christians in many cases.

Is something wrong with our reasoning then? Or is there something wrong with God's ability to deliver His Will here on Earth?

To begin with, there's nothing wrong with our reasoning because no long, involved exercise in logic is required to reach this conclusion. We based it on the clear, simple statement of the Lord Jesus Christ, *"Thy Will be done, in earth as it is in Heaven."*

IS GOD ABLE?

So the next matter is whether God's Arm is shortened. Can't He deliver the situations and conditions which are, in fact, His Will?

Turning to Isaiah 50:2 we can make short shift of that question. God Almighty answers it Personally by stating, *"Is My Hand shortened at all, that it cannot redeem? Or have I no power to deliver? Behold, at My rebuke I dry up the Sea, I make the rivers a wilderness: their fish stinketh because there is no water."*

Obviously, that is if we believe in God which we most certainly do, we are not dealing with a handicapped God. The Most High God is completely capable of bringing about anything He wants brought about. Yet, look about us.

There appears to be a contradiction, a paradox. We know from Scripture that there are a number of results God wants brought about, yet they haven't been brought about.

Take for example the statement in II Peter 3:9. It is not God's Will that any should perish but that all should come to repentance. Obviously, all don't come to repentance, many do perish, and God's Will is obviously being thwarted every day of the year.

So an interesting concept is beginning to reveal itself. We know we can't expect answers to prayer if it isn't God's Will, but also we can't be absolutely sure of prayer being answered when something is definitely within God's Will. And if God will not bring about results to satisfy His Will, how can we expect Him to bring about results just because they are our will?

So, finally, we are into the meat of this discussion. The big question raging among questions is: Why do prayers for Healing, financial betterment, family reconciliations and so forth, sometimes go unanswered? This is a most important question and subject. The whole subject of Faith can hinge (especially for those new in Christ) on the answers which evolve. Is God a God we can count on — or isn't He?

That is an awesome question.

THY WILL BE DONE . . .

Let's begin by looking at God's Will, the results God Himself wants brought about. He is an Omnipotent God (all-powerful) a God capable of producing anything conceivable under the Sun (and beyond the Sun). Many Christians believe the universe contains only what God wants and God continually gets exactly what He wants. This is clearly not so.

We have already looked at the Scriptural case of God wanting all to come to repentance. Obviously all don't come to repentance. Then let's look at some other items.

God wants every Christian to be humble. A great many aren't. God wanted the Children of Israel to be obedient and submissive. Most weren't.

Does this mean, then, these aims aren't God's Will? Obviously they are — but they don't necessarily come about. It seems clear that God's Will in many cases (just like ours) is thwarted and frustrated by existing conditions.

ON EARTH . . .

Here on Earth there are many conditions which are obviously not what God would have His Children enjoying. Let's look first, briefly, at the matters of lifestyle, economics, and employment.

Christ came, He said, that we might have life, and that more abundantly (Jn. 10:10). Although He was speaking primarily of spiritual life, it would also somewhat include creature comforts. It is hard to live the abundant life in total poverty, I think all would agree.

Yet, what do we find? We find Christians who are barely getting by, frustrated in dead-end jobs, and living in accommodations that are barely adequate when compared to the wealth of many who don't even know the Lord. They pray, they trust the Lord — and their financial condition at times does not improve dramatically.

Next, let's look at the raging controversy concerning Healing, even as we are discussing. Some say it is God's Will to always heal the sick. Others say it is God's Will to sometimes heal the sick. Still others say it is God's Will to never heal the sick.

I do not believe, nor can I conceive, of a God Who would want to see His Children afflicted with disease. By extension, we can assume that when one of His Children becomes sick, it is His Will that they be healed. Yet what do we see?

We see Christians at times, suffering from illnesses and even dying despite all the praying for them, even as we are now discussing the situation of Epaphroditus.

The situation is obviously one where God's Will is abundantly clear, yet His Will is not necessarily brought about in every case.

I believe, even as I have already stated, that physical healing is as much a part of the Atonement as spiritual healing. Yet, I agree, there are cases where good, devoted, Faith-filled Christians are prayed for and don't receive healing.

"This then," some contend, *"proves that it isn't always God's Will to heal."*

I don't think it proves that at all. I believe the Word of God makes it absolutely clear it *is* His Will that we be healed. But I also believe there are situations which make it impossible at times for God to heal us, or to do other things for which we might ask. Many times there are factors at work we don't understand which stand in God's Way and prevent Him from doing, not only what we want, but also what He wants.

THE WARP AND THE WOOF

In dealing with the human condition — people, events, and circumstances are so irrevocably intertwined that no human mind can conceive of what the ultimate consequences of certain acts and events might be. I might need a piece of yarn to tie up a package but if I try to snatch it from your sleeve as you pass by, I might totally ruin your expensive, hand-knit sweater.

The world is like a piece of fabric with the warp and the woof travelling in so many directions and with so many interactions that no human mind can conceive of the consequences of almost any set of circumstances. In fact, only God can conceive of such. Lives have been changed, for better or for worse, by a decision to take an alternate route home. How many times have you heard people say after an accident, *"If only I hadn't done such and such!"*

These are the influences we can't see when we go before God asking for some prayer result. We think we know exactly what's going on and we think we know precisely what the outcome will be if only God would pay attention and do things our way. And this brings up the third great factor in this question.

THE WISDOM

When we speak of the Wisdom of God, most minds go to the thought of God's infinite capacity for deciding the proper solution to matters of cosmic dimension. This certainly is a factor in God's Wisdom, but it consists of much more than that.

God's Wisdom also involves such matters as the hairs of our heads being counted, how many sparrows have fallen today, and how much thread in a sweater interacts with every other thread in a sweater. Sometimes it is the sweater threads which frustrate our prayer wishes more than the balance of the orbit of Saturn against that of Jupiter.

When I speak in this section of the Wisdom of God, I am not referring to the brilliance of God. I am referring to the nitty-gritty things that He knows lie ahead in the lives of each of us through His foreknowledge.

Without doubt, the matter of Faith enters into the question of answered, or unanswered, prayer. Some, I am sure, are denied answers because they don't have Faith, *"Oh, ye of little Faith,"* our Lord said. He also said, *"If ye have Faith as a grain of mustard seed. . . ."*

But some ascribe *all prayer* disappointments to a lack of Faith. I don't believe this is legitimate, and not just on theoretical and Scriptural grounds. I have personally seen a number of cases where Christians of great Faith have prayed about matters to no avail.

Some preach that sufficient Faith will bring about any result. Again, I don't believe this. If the mustering of great Faith (whatever that is) could bring about any result, we would have in our hands a weapon capable of thwarting the very Will of God. In other words, even as I have already stated, to use the Word of God against God. This cannot be done. God is sovereign and no one will ever usurp His position, no matter their claims!

But the greatest factor in unanswered prayer lies, I believe, in the matter of God's foreknowledge of what awaits us down the road.

Knowing, as He does, all the twists and turns of *every* road which lies over the horizon, there are simply times when stoplights have to be thrown to red lest a road fraught with danger (or even disaster) be opened to us. God's focus must be on the larger picture at all times, never on the *"quick fix"* of the moment.

We can claim Scriptures such as Mark 11:24, Matthew 21:22, or John 15:7 which are our authority to expect God to grant our wishes. But if the things we ask for are not productive in our situation (or in God's long-range Plan), is God still obligated to give us what we ask?

Our problem, when we go before God and request certain things in prayer, is that we are working from an area of limited knowledge. *"Lord, I want to make a lot of money. I want to be rich!"*

Seemingly this is a reasonable and very human ambition. What would it hurt to have the Lord shower a little of His worldly blessings on us?

But the question is: *"What does the Lord see down the road if this were to come about?"* Perhaps something far different from what we envision. Wealth might be the source of great unhappiness in our lives, even as it has been in the lives of many. Perhaps we wouldn't be able to handle the changes which can come about suddenly with the acquisition of great wealth. Perhaps it would topple our outlook and even our very lives. It might be the source of our undoing spiritually, morally, and physically. Such results aren't unknown.

Every action, every alteration in the status quo, has wide-ranging repercussions. We can't begin to picture the effects of the ripples we might produce when we drop a pebble in the pond. God not only sees the ripples, He sometimes prevents us from causing them, by preventing us from dropping our pebble.

FAITH AND DEVELOPMENT

I believe that Faith and personal spiritual development are inseparably intertwined. Many people think they have Faith when they really don't. Others think that if they simply believe God for anything, that this is enough.

I believe Faith is definitely linked to Christian development, and Christian development must be linked to submission to the Wisdom of God.

Have I begun to make the point of this whole presentation clear? People pray and they say, *"If it is in Thy Will, Lord."*

I've preached sermons and written articles a number of times on this subject. I've said repeatedly that we shouldn't pray with an *"if-it's-in-Your-will-Lord"* attitude if He has *already* shown us His Will in His Word. There's no question of what the Lord wants for us. The Lord wants us happy, prosperous, and healthy. He wants us to have all good things. He wants us to have the abundant life (Jn. 10:10; III Jn. vs. 2).

Then why, we might quickly ask, doesn't He just give us these things out of His vast storehouse of good things? Why doesn't He always heal, and why doesn't He always shower riches on His Children? If that is His Will, why doesn't He demonstrate it by giving us all good things since they are in His Will and ours?

TRUST

When you are disappointed in prayer, I would direct your attention to Romans 8:28. This states that all things work together for good to them who love God. This doesn't say *"a few things"* or even *"quite a few things."* It says *all* things work for good for those who love God.

The word *"all"* may include some things we do not like, but irrespective of situations, we must believe God. Despite the storm, Paul said, *"I believe God"* (Acts 27:25).

Trust in God, trust in God's Wisdom. Trust in God's good sense to plan an unbelievably glorious eternity for His chosen. This is the brick and mortar with which we must build our relationship with God and our glorious hope for eternity.

NOTES

We can't take the short view and look at today and next week and be hypnotized by the short-range view. God doesn't work on short-range solutions. God may sorrow (Jn. 11:35) as His Will for a situation is obstructed, but He will not make the human mistake of abandoning the long-range plan because of momentary considerations. Our Heavenly Father knows exactly how everything will be run eternally and He has every dot and comma in place for the events leading up to His grand, final design. And if curing the flu for you or me this February will in some way delay the Grand Plan, is it possible that He might not cure our flu? The crucial thing is to have Faith in God! If we allow ourselves to be diverted from our trust in God by minor matters (like a frustrated prayer request) we are not demonstrating Christian development.

THE WAY TO PRAY

I have discussed my aversion to the habit of prefacing or appending all prayers with the phrase *"If it be in Thy Will, Lord,"* unless His Will is not discernible Scripturally.

We should know the Lord's Will through Scripture whenever possible, and we shouldn't ask for anything if it isn't in His Will. I use to just go before the Lord in prayer and ask (or demand) for what I wished whenever I was sure it was in His Will. Lately, though (I hope I am growing as a Christian, just as I hope you are), I often hesitate before asking something point blank from the Lord.

Today I'm inclined to ask Him to give me answers if it be for my good and for the good of His great Eternal Plan (in His Wisdom).

Of course, when seeking the Salvation of someone, for example, it is never amiss to ask directly for results. But for other things, I feel led in the Spirit to append the phrase, *"If it is for the ultimate good in Your Wisdom, Lord."*

God sees the future, though we can't. If the Millennial Age were here and Satan were chained in the pit, I know what God's Wisdom would reveal and I know we could seek anything within His Will. Sad to say, we aren't at that stage yet. So even though it may be His Will, it may not be His Wisdom regarding certain situations. Consequently, He may not heal immediately, even as with Epaphroditus, or other type of requests may be delayed or not granted.

AN INNOCENT CHILD

Some time ago Frances and I watched friends endure a most tragic incident. The husband was (and is) a Godly Preacher. Both these fine people love the Lord and put their whole Faith in Him.

They had an eight-year-old daughter, a lovely and sweet child. One day while she was playing in the yard at school she slumped unconscious to the ground. There was no apparent reason for this. The parents were called and the child was taken to the hospital, where Doctors were soon gathered about her.

Frances and I, along with many others, visited this little girl and prayed for her. A short time later we were all down in the tiny hospital chapel praying and, as we kept our vigil, the Lord suddenly spoke to my heart, *"The child will not live. However, I cannot at this time tell you the reason. But I do have a reason."*

I will always remember that moment. I related to the parents what I believed God told me. Tears welled in their eyes. *"Oh no,"* the mother sobbed, *"I can't give her up."*

But she did! It rends my heart as I recall the funeral. The mother and father were in shock. It was as though their whole world had ended. It was years before they could even talk about it.

As I said before, the father of this child is a Preacher. He is truly a man of God and his Ministry had gone along quite well up to the point where they lost their daughter. But after the death of the child his Ministry exploded. The congregation grew at a rate never dreamed of before his daughter's death. Hundreds, possibly thousands, have been saved through his Ministry.

Is it possible that the very existence of the taking of their daughter might have caused them to modify the way they reacted to life and God's direction for their lives?

I know, at one time within my own Ministry, I was tempted to give up the Evangelist's life and accept a Church Pastorate. My main reason for wavering was that Donnie's education (I thought) was being adversely affected by our way of life. However, the Lord would not allow me to take that Church, and in retrospect I now see the many reasons why. Incidentally, Donnie's education came out very well after all.

Going back to this beautiful little girl who went home to be with Jesus, I know how this death affected me and especially her family. I know if I were back in that hospital room presently, I would still be praying for her healing. But I can now understand how her death might have brought about changes which were enormously important in God's long-range plan.

Again, of course, this is a matter of God's Will versus His Wisdom. Again, the situation is one where God's Will is for a prayer answer, but where God's long-range Wisdom requires the opposite.

RUNNING FROM GOD

Another incident involving the death of a child illustrates God's foreknowledge in human affairs.

"Son (his nickname)*"* was a simple and basically good man, even though he had never had any *"religious"* training. In fact, he insisted he had never seen a Bible for the first 25 years of his life.

Son had one overriding ambition for his life. That was to become a *"success."* To him, success involved money. With a limited education, and at a time in our nation's history when the great depression was dragging even previously successful people down to poverty, it was a hard road for Son and his ambitions.

But Son had a plan. He had an inborn musical ability and so did his wife. The people of the day, in their desperation to escape the realities of their lives, used to scrape together enough money to go out to *"dance halls"* to listen to music, dance, drink, and push their troubles to the backs of their minds. Son and his wife found that their musical ability made them popular among the dance hall crowd and they were soon playing regularly and beginning to scrape together a small cache of money.

But something unfortunate occurred in Son's plan. A Gospel Preacher named Tom Holcomb brought Son and his wife, Minnie Bell, under his influence. He was pastoring a tiny Church in their hometown and somehow, despite the fact that few found their way to his Church, Son and Minnie Bell did.

Tom Holcomb's preaching zeroed right in on their hearts. There was no question about what he was saying and conviction soon burned in Son's heart. He knew he should throw himself on his knees and accept the Lord as Saviour. But Son's conversion would have to wait until Son and Minnie Bell concluded the first part of their life's plan regarding wealth, or so they thought!

But it wasn't all that easy to ignore God. Son found himself constantly bumping into Brother Holcomb, and his daily errands took him repeatedly past Brother Holcomb's little Church. Every time he endured one of these confrontations, his heart would burn in his chest. Something would have to be done. The only rational solution seemed to be to leave this town and, therefore, this Church. He couldn't stand the constant conviction and the constant reminders, and he thought that a different location would change all of this.

A TURN OF EVENTS

Their road to fame and fortune led them to the tiny town of Rio Honda, Texas, where they ran into the red light God set in their plan. Any normal red light might have been ignored in their desperate flight from God, but there their younger son, Donnie, and soon after, Minnie Bell, came down with pneumonia.

The Doctor gave Son a prescription for medicine for the baby. He took it to the local Druggist in that little town and, while waiting for the Druggist to finish with a prior customer, he meditated on the flight from God which had led to this situation. As he thought about it he was swept with a sudden awareness that his baby son was not going to recover.

Tears welled in his eyes and he could barely see as the Druggist slipped the prescription from his hand.

"Don't worry about it, Brother," the Druggist said. *"I see from the prescription that your child has pneumonia but you don't have to worry. I know your Doctor and he's never lost a pneumonia case. He'll pull him through."*

Despite these encouraging words, Son felt no lift in his heart. He still felt his son wasn't going to live.

NOTES

A few days later, as the first light of dawn began to filter through the uncurtained window of Son's tourist cabin room, there was a knock on the door. Son and his four-year-old boy roused themselves in bed and Son asked who it was. Minnie Bell, also with pneumonia as stated, was in the hospital. *"It's me,"* a voice with a heavy Czech accent answered. A second later the unlocked door swung inward and a large man walked in, his head down and his eyes avoiding Son's.

Son stared at him for a long moment and then tears welled in his eyes. *"It's my baby, isn't it Frank?"* he asked.

Frank nodded without raising his eyes from the floor, *"He died about 30 minutes ago."*

Son was my Dad, and the little boy who had just died was my Brother. Although I was only four-years-old at the time, I still remember the funeral very clearly. My Mother couldn't attend the Service because she wasn't yet recovered. So the only ones at the funeral, for we were away from home and family, were myself, my Dad, and the Pastor of a small Assemblies of God Church, who ministered at the grave side. I have no recollection as to how he knew of the plight of my parents as it regards this situation, but he was there.

As my Dad looked down into the casket, he made a vow to God. He knew full well that probably none of the present problems would have occurred had he not fled cross-country to escape the conviction God had placed on his heart.

I suppose it is forever freeze-framed in my heart. I can still see him looking down into the casket and hearing him say these words.

"Son, I promise I will meet you in Heaven."

That was when his rebellion broke, and a short time later, he gave his heart totally and completely to Jesus, and so did my Mother, both accepting the Lord's Sacrifice as Atonement for their sins. Of course, their Salvation dramatically changed my life and the life of my Sister, who would be born some two years later.

WHY?

Why did my Brother have to be sacrificed to bring about the circumstances required in God's wisdom? I believe I can tell you.

God's Word tells us (Rom. 8:29-30) that we are foreknown, predestinated, called, justified, and glorified. These two Verses hold the entire truth of the Bible and God's Plan in microcosm.

After being called, and freely accepting God's invitation to use the shed Blood as payment for our guilt, we are justified. Our name is then entered into the Lamb's Book of Life. But before that, I believe (based on this Scripture), that due to the foreknowledge of God, we are already on another roll in God's great business office. This is the roll of Ministries awaiting every person whom God calls.

As my Father and I stood over little Donnie's casket on that wind-swept plain outside Rio Honda there is no question in my mind that the entire structure of not only my Dad's future Ministry, but also of my own particular Evangelistic Ministry were already on the blueprint in God's architectural office.

I believe every potential Christian has a Ministry waiting for him from the moment he is conceived in his Mother's womb. I believe there is no one in the world who is not eligible to play a part in God's great Plan for the ages. I also believe, that when some flee to avoid God's call, as many do, God puts a stoplight in their path.

I believe some heed these lights, stopping while God gets their attention, and I believe others run the light to their own destruction. Some may still play important parts in God's Plan after running the light, although their roles will then be negative ones. Even Satan is playing a role in God's Plan although he ran the first and biggest stoplight God ever erected.

I know those many years ago God was looking down on my family as we started out from Ferriday, Louisiana, heading for Texas. He knew if He allowed my father to run his ill-advised course, removing us from the location God had placed us in, that it would interfere with the implementation of His Plan.

He knew I would need the example of my dear Grandmother to lead me to the Lord; He knew I would need the association which would test my resolution to reject the fame and fortune of the music business. He also knew that I would walk into a little Church my Father built in Wisner, Louisiana, and have my eyes fall on the pretty young girl who would later support my sometimes-wavering resolution during the lean, early years.

I fully believe that if we had remained in Texas (or wherever my Father's frantic flight might have taken him) that Jimmy Swaggart Ministries would probably not be in existence today. I have no idea, if that had happened, whether the multiplied thousands coming to Salvation through this Ministry would be saved today. No doubt, if this had happened, maybe God would have raised up someone else for this role, but I am convinced that on that day the Lord looked at me and I was foreknown and predestined. Later, of course, I was called and justified and someday I will be glorified with Christ. But on that day there was a definite future charted for me.

THE WISDOM OF GOD

I know that my Brother, Donnie, would have had a future in the Lord's Plan had it not been necessary to take him home. Today there isn't even a stone to mark his grave as the wind continues to sweep over Rio Honda. But Donnie really isn't residing in the ground in Texas. He's with the Lord Jesus in Heaven and, one of these days when the trump sounds, he will rise. We will all be united again. Our friends and their daughter will, no doubt, be standing nearby.

You see, my Father's rebellion interfered with the Will of God. Then, the *"Wisdom of God"* had to enter and compensate for his rebellion. God will not be mocked. His great Plan will be accomplished, no matter what the degree of rebellion of those choosing to go off on their own.

The problem, of course, is that we are all willful. We say, *"Oh, all I want is the Will of God."* The trouble is, we tend to add an *"except."* We want the Will of God except when it interferes with what we want; we want the Will of God except when it thwarts or inconveniences us; we want the Will of God except when we know better than God what's good for us.

Now when I pray for the sick I almost always say, or else the thought is in my heart, *"God, if it's in your wisdom, I ask this of you."* Some might take issue with this. They might say, *"That's the same as saying 'If it's in Your will.'"*

I don't agree. I believe God is often prevented from seeing His immediate Will carried out, and almost always it is a result of the sinful and rebellious environment man seems to prefer to inhabit. So in His wisdom He charts another course.

Please understand, I am not saying it is sinful to want something. I am saying that we live in an environment of sin brought on by Adam (and every man who followed him) and, because of our sin-saturated environment, there are times when God's Will simply can't be brought forth. God's will is always done in Heaven. But in Heaven there is no sin and that is why it can always be done in Heaven.

We know from Scripture that sin will soon be banished from the Earth. We know that Satan is to be chained and, finally, we will be starting into *"Thy Will be done."* On that day when sin disappears and sickness will be no more, Christians in glorified bodies will have limbs restored, sight returned, and deaf ears open. The basic reason behind God's handling of situations today is to bring that day to fruition. To be frank, it is soon to come.

Momentary frustrations occur when our wishes conflict with what God knows is necessary to create that glorious condition.

I hope I have been able to convey to you some hint of the conclusions God has given me on this question. I believe we are meant to read God's Promises, to believe them, to stand on them, to use them, and to expect answers. I also believe, however, that there will be times when our prayers are not compatible with the end result toward which God is working. When this happens and our requests are delayed, or else are not granted at all, I think we should praise the Lord anyway, knowing that our prayers were heard and that quite possibly they are, in fact, answered. It is just that the answer is larger and further down the road than we can presently realize.

God said He would never forsake us. He doesn't. Our Scriptural prayers will one day all be answered. The only question is, are we viewing the situation through the windowpane of today, or the telescope of tomorrow?

It all boils down to the Word, the Will, and the Wisdom of God.

NOTES

Blessed is the Saint, who learns to trust the Wisdom of God!

MERCY

The phrase, *"But God had mercy on him,"* proclaims the manner in which everything is received from God — all by the Mercy of God.

There is nothing that man can do that would earn or merit the Mercy of God. Mercy is a product of Grace.

Somewhere in eternity past, God freely chose the method of Grace through which He would deal with man. Grace has to be freely chosen, or it is not Grace. However, once Grace was chosen, due to what Grace actually is, God then had no choice but to extend Mercy. However, all of this is thwarted, if the sinner attempts to earn Salvation, or the Believer attempts to earn victory in any capacity.

Grace and Mercy are definitely products of the Cross of Christ. In other words, God cannot grant Grace and, therefore, Mercy to anyone, unless they place their Faith in the Cross of Christ. This Sacrificial, Atoning, Death of Christ on the Cross, is what opens the floodgate of Grace and Mercy to believing sinners, and that alone, we might quickly add! Once again, everything centers around The Finished Work of Christ on the Cross, and if our Faith strays outside of that parameter, it is Faith that God will not honor, and in fact, Faith that God cannot honor.

SORROW UPON SORROW

The phrase, *"And not on Him only, but on me also, lest I should have sorrow upon sorrow,"* proclaims the fact that if the man had died, it would have been a great loss to the Apostle.

Epaphroditus had come to Rome from Philippi, a distance not much short of a thousand miles, to be of service to Paul. In fact, he had brought a Love-Offering from the Church for the Apostle, which was desperately needed. After delivering this offering he remained with the Apostle for sometime. And during this stay in Rome Epaphroditus was stricken with an illness so severe that for a time his life was in jeopardy. However, with his health restored, he would soon be on his way home with this precious document (the

Epistle to the Philippians) expressive of the Apostle's gratitude and love.

What did Paul mean by the statement *"sorrow upon sorrow"*?

Epaphroditus becoming ill and severely so, was a sorrow to Paul, as would be obvious. However, if the man had died, such would have constituted a greatly added sorrow, hence *"sorrow upon sorrow."*

(28) "I SENT HIM THEREFORE THE MORE CAREFULLY, THAT, WHEN YE SEE HIM AGAIN, YE MAY REJOICE, AND THAT I MAY BE THE LESS SORROWFUL."

Communication in those days being totally different than the present, the Apostle is anxious that the Philippians know the truth about all the recent happenings. They had heard, even as Paul had said, that Epaphroditus had been sick and it was possibly related to them, that his sickness was very severe, even with the possibility that he might die.

How this information was relayed to them, we are not told. Evidently, someone came by the place where Paul was incarcerated, and was on their way To Philippi, or else was to go through that city. At any rate, they delivered to the Philippians the information they then had at the time.

With this turn of events, Epaphroditus regaining his health, and other important facts, the Apostle is anxious for the Philippians to have this up-to-date information, and more specifically this Epistle.

So it seems that Epaphroditus is being sent back possibly a little sooner than had been previously anticipated.

THE RETURN

The phrase, *"I sent him therefore the more carefully,"* in the Greek carries the ideas of *"haste and diligence."* As stated, Paul had reason to hasten the departure of Epaphroditus, so the Philippians would know the extent of the situation in Rome, not only as it pertained to this delegate from their Church, but of Paul himself.

I think the idea is expressed here, that having gone through this experience, Epaphroditus was now stronger in the Lord. Whether or not a Christian receives lasting spiritual benefits from the trials of life depends to a great extent on the person's own attitude.

NOTES

No doubt, Paul was able to help Epaphroditus maintain a proper attitude through this total experience. As a result both lives benefitted spiritually.

REJOICING

The phrase, *"That, when ye see him again, ye may rejoice,"* presents the fact of the recovery or the healing of this man.

The idea is also expressed in this statement that Paul wanted the entire Assembly in Philippi to benefit from the experience. Therefore, the fact that God had ultimately healed Epaphroditus brought joy to himself, and ultimately to the entire Assembly at Philippi. The Bible makes it clear that physical healing is not an end in itself. God performs these acts of Mercy because of His love for the individual in question, and that as well people will turn to Him. In other words, God was glorified through the healing of Epaphroditus.

LESS SORROWFUL

The phrase, *"And that I may be the less sorrowful,"* has reference to the fact that the illness of this man had brought sorrow to Paul's heart, but now that sorrow is lessened due to his recovery. The Apostle bears the weight of the concern of the Church at Philippi regarding this situation, and their rejoicing concerning the turn of events, brings joy to Paul's heart also, lessening the sorrow of the entirety of the situation.

(29) "RECEIVE HIM THEREFORE IN THE LORD WITH ALL GLADNESS; AND HOLD SUCH IN REPUTATION:"

Paul's words imply that more was involved in Epaphroditus' disturbed feelings than simple affectionate concern, otherwise no such urging from the Apostle to welcome him would have been necessary. It seems that possibly some sort of alienation had arisen.

Irrespective, the Church was to do more than refrain from criticism of Epaphroditus, they were to give him due recognition for his faithful and sacrificial service to Paul.

RECEIVE HIM

The phrase, *"Receive him therefore in the Lord with all gladness,"* refers as stated, to more than mere reception. The terminology employed by the Apostle lets us know that there had been some type of difficulty it seems between Epaphroditus and the Church in Philippi. What it was we do not know; however, quite possibly some in the Church were unwilling to place total confidence in Epaphroditus as it regards the taking of this Offering to Rome. Maybe some thought he was not up to the task, and had desired that someone else go instead. Of course, that may not have been the case at all; however, from Paul's terminology, it does sound like something like this might have happened. Consequently, the Apostle is telling all concerned that their choice of Epaphroditus, had been an excellent choice. He had acquitted himself with flying colors.

Therefore, they could receive him on two counts:

1. *"In the Lord"* lets us know that Epaphroditus had actually been the choice of the Holy Spirit as it regards this all-important mission. Consequently, this statement carries much weight. In observing this man throughout this entire situation, Paul was fully convinced of his responsibility, dedication, consecration, and Love for God. Trials and tests, which this brother certainly had undergone, will do one of two things:

Draw one closer to the Lord, or push one further away, that is, showing up what is actually there, which tests are meant to do.

2. They were not only to receive him, but to do so with gladness, knowing that their choice in sending him had been right and that he had acquitted himself capably, even putting his life on the line.

REPUTATION

The phrase, *"And hold such in reputation,"* speaks of honor. It seems this man had left Philippi with his personal responsibility somewhat in question, but returns with the accolades of Paul, i.e., *"the Holy Spirit,"* which means that he now has the greatest approval of all. Consequently, the Philippian Church is to treat him accordingly. Whatever doubts or questions they previously had, were to be laid aside and discarded. He was now to be looked at as one of the leaders in the Church.

In this we see several things. Some are as follows:

NOTES

1. Sometimes people are misjudged, even as it seems was Epaphroditus. Events are brought to bear which seems to point in one direction, when the other direction is actually the case. That's what proved to be true in this man's case.

2. This man proved himself faithful, and the Lord honored and rewarded him accordingly.

3. Paul was quick to praise him, as the Apostle was quick to do such with anyone who proved themselves. On the other side of the coin, he could be just as hard on those whom he felt did not measure up, such as Mark. However, the situation with Mark seemed to heal itself, with Paul recommending him highly some years later (II Tim. 4:11).

4. Epaphroditus was faithful and faithfulness is always rewarded by the Lord. In fact, God has not called us to be successful, but He has called us to be faithful (Mat. 25:23; Lk. 16:10; Gal. 3:9; I Tim. 1:12; Rev. 2:10).

(30) "BECAUSE FOR THE WORK OF CHRIST HE WAS NIGH UNTO DEATH, NOT REGARDING HIS LIFE, TO SUPPLY YOUR LACK OF SERVICE TOWARD ME."

It seems somewhat that the ailment of this dear brother was directly due to his Christian labors on behalf of Paul. Perhaps it resulted from the rigors of travel and was compounded by his efforts to continue ministering to Paul despite being sick.

It was not merely an unavoidable circumstance but was a risking of his life in the interest of the Apostle's Ministry. Consequently, Paul strongly commended Epaphroditus to the Church that had sent him. The Church should be grateful, because the man had actually been representing them and was doing for Paul what they could not do.

Inasmuch as Philippians 4:14-18 reveals that the Philippians had done more than other Churches for the Apostle, the *"lack of service"* here must be the lack of their physical presence with him. This Epaphroditus had supplied by his presence and personal care (Kent).

THE WORK OF CHRIST

The phrase, *"Because for the work of Christ he was nigh unto death, not regarding his life,"* refers to this man exposing his life, it seems even recklessly so, in his service on behalf of the Apostle regarding the Work of the Lord in Rome.

The comforts of his own hired house near the barracks of the Praetorian Guard, where Paul was housed for about two years, would not have made necessary such overexertion on the part of Epaphroditus. The probability is that Paul was now confined to a prison, the discomforts of which were somewhat relieved by the strenuous labors of Epaphroditus (Wuest).

In this account is revealed a realm of consolation, comfort, loving fellowship, tender affections, mercies, mutual sympathy, and boundless affection, Christ's love for His people, their love for Him, the Apostle's affection for the Philippians and their affection for the Apostle, the mutual love of Paul, Timothy, and Epaphroditus — the last named lest the Philippians should be grieved — all furnish a picture of mutual sympathy and solicitude that is very beautiful.

God's Own tender love breaks out in the Chapter on every side, forming a precious and beautiful chain, and developing the graciousness of Christian life in His servants. This graciousness, this solicitude, this consideration for others flowed from the Grace of Him Who humbled Himself from the Throne to the Cross (Williams).

LACK OF SERVICE

The phrase, *"To supply your lack of service toward me,"* evidently refers to something the Philippians couldn't do because of circumstances, but which Epaphroditus did do on their behalf. Of course, what it was we have no way of knowing.

"I gave My Life for thee,
"My precious Blood I shed,
"That thou might'st ransomed be,
"And quicken from the dead.
"I gave, I gave My Life for thee, What
   hast thou giv'n for Me?"

"My Father's house of Light,
"My glory circled Throne,
"I left for earthly night,
"For wand'rings sad and lone;
"I left, I left it all for thee, Hast thou
   left aught for Me?"

CHAPTER 3

(1) "FINALLY, MY BRETHREN, REJOICE IN THE LORD. TO WRITE THE SAME THINGS TO YOU, TO ME INDEED IS NOT GRIEVOUS, BUT FOR YOU IT IS SAFE."

By Paul using the word *"finally"* to begin this Verse, doesn't mean at all that he is closing the Letter. He is merely closing the thought of the previous Chapter, and in the same Verse beginning another train of thought.

Some have claimed that several Letters make up this Epistle; however, there is no hint in this Epistle that such thinking is correct. Philippians is one Epistle, and was intended by the Apostle thus to be.

REJOICE IN THE LORD

The phrase, *"Finally, my Brethren, rejoice in the Lord,"* presents the Apostle now turning his attention to the Judaizers. These were Jews who were, one might say, nominal Christians, who accepted the Lord Jesus as the Saviour of Israel only, and who taught that a Gentile had to come through the gate of Judaism in order to be saved. Thus, they refused to accept the fact of the setting aside of Israel at the Cross, and the bringing in of the Church at Pentecost, which was to consist of both Jews and Gentiles. In other words, the distinction, due to the Cross, had been obliterated.

These individuals, and they seem to have been numerous, wished to continue under the Mosaic Law, in other words, adding the Law to Grace, or more particularly, adding Grace to Law. Of course, such is like attempting to mix oil and water. It simply cannot be done.

What had happened in the Galatian Churches, as well as Corinth, Paul was trying to forestall in the Church at Philippi.

His first exhortation was designed as a positive preventive of becoming entangled in this false teaching. *"Go on constantly rejoicing in the Lord."*

The Judaizers were boasting in man and his attainments, i.e., *"the keeping of the Law,"* etc. (Gal. 6:13), but Paul said that he would glory only in the Lord Jesus (Gal. 6:14) (Wuest).

IN THE LORD

Any doctrine, any principle, any teaching, which draws the Believer away from Christ and what was done at the Cross and the Resurrection, falls into the same category as this of which Paul speaks here. We are to rejoice *"in the Lord,"* which refers to what He did at the Cross and the Resurrection on our behalf. That is to be the basis for all rejoicing, all thanksgiving, the foundation of all Doctrine.

Anything outside of this of which we speak, and I refer to the Cross of Christ, draws attention away from the Lord to self, which the Holy Spirit can never condone.

As an example, the so-called modern Faith Ministry falls exactly into this category. The emphasis is on Faith and Faith alone, in other words, Faith in that other than the Finished Work of Christ. This alone is what makes this Doctrine so wrong.

Everything must come through the Cross of Christ, for that is the great Sacrifice which made possible all Redemption, Salvation, Healing, the Baptism with the Holy Spirit, Prosperity, in other words — everything. Actually, that should be obvious. The whole of the Old Testament centered up on the Sacrifices, which of course symbolized the coming Redeemer and the price He would pay for man's Redemption by dying on the Cross. To overlook this, or ignore this, is almost impossible.

As well, the centerpiece of the New Testament, i.e., *"The New Covenant,"* is the Cross of Christ. What Jesus actually did perhaps could be better understood by pointing rather to Who He was and is, rather than What He did!

THE CROSS

To die on a Cross within itself could not save anyone. In fact, the day on which Jesus died, throughout the Roman Empire, there were others who died on crosses as well. Their deaths did not save or help anyone for that matter.

As well, this particular form of execution, although demanded by God concerning Christ, contained no Salvation as well. There is no Redemption in a wooden Cross, as there can be no Redemption in a wooden Cross. So, what made all of this of such value and consequence!

Even though the Cross was definitely necessary, it was Who Jesus actually was, that made it a vicarious (substitutionary), efficacious (effective) Sacrifice — a Sacrifice which God could accept, and which alone would satisfy Heaven's Justice.

While Jesus was definitely Very God (completely God), He at the same time was Very Man (completely man). When He died on the Cross, even though He was God, and continued to be God, actually never losing the possession of His Deity, at the same time He died as a man. The reason is obvious, God cannot die; therefore, God would have to become man, exactly as Isaiah had prophesied (Isa. 7:14).

And yet, becoming a man within itself was not enough. There were millions of men on the Earth at that time, but not one single one of these individuals could redeem fallen humanity.

First of all, the birth of this man had to be different than any birth had ever been. Were He to be born by natural procreation, which refers to the manner in which all others of us are born, He would have been born in original sin exactly as all others, which means He would have been unfit to serve as a Perfect Sacrifice. Consequently, it was of absolute necessity that He be born of a Virgin, meaning that man had no part to play in this birth.

The Hebrew word for Virgin as it was used of the Mother of Christ is *"ha-almah,"* which means *"the Virgin — the only one that ever was, or ever will be a Mother in this way."*

As well, as a man he had to face every onslaught of darkness exactly as all other men, and even more so, and yet without sinning. He must do this as the Second or Last Adam, which means He could not have the help of His Deity to carry out this thing, only the help of the Holy Spirit. And yet, there was one other way, that Jesus was different than any other man, in that He did not have a Sin-nature, which was the result of the Fall, and carried in all of humanity other than Christ. Had He been born by natural procreation, He would have had this Sin-nature.

As a Man, total Man, complete Man, He lived for 33 1/2 years without sin, above sin, a life of absolute perfection. In other words, He kept the Law in every respect, obeying its every command and precept, and disobeying not at all. In fact, this was an absolute necessity. Had He failed in even one point, He would have been a Lawbreaker, subject to the death penalty, and, therefore, unfit to serve as a Sacrifice (Rom. 6:23).

So, What He did was, of course, of vital significance, but yet, Who He was, perfect, spotless, without sin, blameless, without flaw, without stain, without blemish, made it possible for Him to be a Sacrifice which God could accept, and in fact, Alone which God could accept. He was the perfect Man, our Substitute Man, our Representative Man, and Faith in Him and what He did, grants to the believing sinner Eternal Life, and to the Christian, a victorious, overcoming experience.

SATAN'S GREATEST TRUMP CARD

Satan doesn't care much what a person believes, as long as their Faith is not anchored in the Cross. Consequently, he does not mind at all the Faith Message, or any other similar type Message. Actually, he is very happy whenever such a Message, which greatly claims to espouse the Word of God, and thereby deceives many people, is fostered off on a gullible, Christian public. It looks right and sounds right, because it claims to be anchored in the Word of God; however, the Church has been moved so far away from its true foundation, which is the Cross, that it anymore little knows what is right or wrong. It has little anchor, little stability, little foundation, simply because the Cross of Christ *is* the Foundation of Christianity. Of course, when we speak of the Cross we at the same time presuppose the Resurrection and the Exaltation (Eph. 2:6).

The Judaizers did not outright deny the Cross, but neither did they accept the Cross and what Jesus did there, somewhat by their teaching making the Cross merely incidental. The Salvation of man, at least as they taught their error, was wrapped up in keeping the Law of Moses. Paul called them and all others who ignore, minimize, or reject the Cross, *"enemies of the Cross of Christ,"* which we will address moreso at the conclusion of this Chapter.

NOTES

To be frank, there is very little difference in the teaching of the modern Faith Ministry, than the Judaizers of old. The results are the same. The Cross is ignored in either case, and even ridiculed by many of the modern Faith teachers, etc.

The Reader should ask himself or herself as to how many Messages they have heard on the Cross in the last few years? I dare say, in the far greater majority of the cases, not many have been heard. If, in fact, that is the case, and regrettably it is in most circles, that means that the Preacher is trusting something other than the Finished Work of Christ as it regards Salvation, which means that the possibility definitely exists that the man is preaching heresy. In fact, I am concerned that many, if not most, of the so-called Faith Churches fall into this category. What they teach is heresy!

To get back to the original thought, the rejoicing of the Child of God must always be *"in the Lord,"* i.e., *"in what the Lord has done for us as it occasions Salvation, and never in anything else."* Regrettably, there is much rejoicing presently in the Church world; however, most of it is not centered up on that of which we speak.

Christians are rejoicing that God has worked a *"miracle"* for them, in their now being able to drive a luxury car. Money and the things that money can buy, are too often the object of modern Faith.

What blasphemy!

While God definitely does bless His people, and for that we should always be thankful, still, the great rejoicing, the all-consummate rejoicing, the rejoicing that comes from deep down within, always must be directed toward the great Sacrifice of Christ, i.e., *"the Cross."* Paul said to the Galatians, *"But God forbid that I should glory* (boast, rejoice), *save in the Cross of our Lord Jesus Christ, by Whom the world is crucified unto Me, and I unto the world"* (Gal. 6:14).

THE SAME THINGS

The phrase, *"To write the same things to you, to me indeed is not grievous, but for you it is safe,"* refers to former warnings addressed to the Philippian Saints against these dangerous teachers who would lead them astray. In other words, this was not the first time Paul had warned the Philippians of this erroneous teaching. He wanted them to stay *"safe,"* and by constantly bringing this to their attention, could this goal be maintained. We see several things here:

1. The Preacher while preaching Truth, at the same time must point out error. Never take for granted that such is automatically understood. To be frank, most people do not see error until someone strongly spotlights the heresy.

2. This has to be done over and over, even as Paul is doing here. The Fall caused man to be far more susceptible to a lie than to Truth. As someone has quipped, *"A lie can go around the world while Truth is attempting to get on its shoes."*

3. I'm sure that Paul made many enemies by taking this stand, but had he not done so, we quite possibly today would not have the Gospel. It must not be forgotten that inasmuch as Judaism was then being promoted by Satan in an effort to overturn the True Gospel, or at least to seriously weaken it, this effort must then be opposed, and opposed strongly. Most Preachers draw back from doing this simply because it creates enemies — and powerful enemies at that.

That which I have stated concerning the modern Faith Ministry, in no way endears me to those who champion this error. As well, the great similarity in their opposition is that they attack the Preacher exactly as the Judaizers attacked Paul.

In fact, these modern teachers of error, little address themselves to the Message of the True Gospel. If they do so, it is only a somewhat glancing blow. Their major thrust always centers up on the Preacher of the Gospel. In other words, they will attempt to demean the character and person of the individual who opposes them, exactly as did the Judaizers in regard to Paul. They attacked his person vehemently so, trying to undermine his character and his reputation. In fact, they were so successful in their efforts, that the Church at Corinth came very close to being lost. If this had happened, it could have served as a domino effect on all the other Churches, which is exactly what Satan was attempting to do.

I have personally been told several times by Preachers, *"Why don't you just preach, and leave these other things alone!"* By *"other things,"* most of the time they're speaking of that which they harbor, and they take no delight in seeing the error exposed.

I take no delight in the opposition of other Preachers, of whom there seems to be many; however, their opposition is less distasteful to me than lives being wrecked and ruined by their erroneous doctrines. In other words, I like much more the victory which Truth brings, than I dislike the opposition leveled against me as it regards the propagation of that Truth.

I want all people to make Heaven their home. Of course, I realize that will not be the case, but still I am to do my best to get the Gospel to all. As well, I want all Believers to live a victorious, overcoming, Christian life. Consequently, I feel that I must *"earnestly contend for the Faith which was once delivered to the Saints"* (Jude vs. 3).

PAUL AND JUDAISM

As the Apostle will address himself to Judaism in this Third Chapter, perhaps it would be wise if we look further at this subject.

In fact, Paul was, no doubt, the greatest authority on this subject of that day. In other words, he probably knew the Law of Moses moreso than any other human being. So, his addressing the subject as he did, was not from a position of ignorance or lack of knowledge, but rather the very opposite. He knew the true meaning of the Law, the true purpose of the Law, more than anyone else. Therefore, he was imminently qualified to address this subject, and for all the obvious reasons. So, the point I make is this:

When the Judaizers (those who advocated Salvation by Law rather than Grace), took him on, their choice was very unwise.

I was somewhat amused the other day in receiving a letter from a lady, who took exception to something I had said regarding the modern Faith message.

"You say these things," she said, *"because you do not know anything about the Faith Message."*

It was ironical, she stated that she had abandoned this message because of its unscriptural position but evidently was still trying to cling to some of its parts.

I had to smile for the simple reason, that I helped start that message, so I know exactly what this doctrine espouses.

The great difference in the ancient Law of Moses and the modern Faith message is, that the Law of Moses was definitely from God, whereas the modern Faith message isn't.

The trouble was, and that which we will attempt to address, the Jews attempted to make Salvation out of the Law, which God never intended.

Let's look a little further at this subject.

THE ONE COMMANDMENT

"*For when we were in the flesh* (attempting to obey God by personal effort), *the motions* (passions) *of sins, which were by the Law* (which the Law identified), *did work in our members to bring forth fruit unto death* (sin was made evident through our physical body).

"*But now we are delivered from the Law* (meaning that Christ has kept the Law, and our Faith in Him and what He did at the Cross, has satisfied the penalty of the broken Law on our behalf), *that being dead wherein we were held* (we are now dead to the law, due to Jesus having kept the Law in every respect, and as well having suffered its penalty, which means it now has no more hold on us, because it has been satisfied in Jesus); *that we should serve in newness of spirit* (we must put our Faith in the Cross and the Resurrection, which gives the Holy Spirit the latitude to perform His Work within our lives, which guarantees us victory), *and not in the oldness of the letter* (ignoring the Cross and reverting back to the Law, which contains no Salvation nor victory)" (Rom. 7:5-6).

When God gave the Law to Israel, He knew that not one single person would keep the Law perfectly. He demanded obedience to that Law, under penalty of death, even as all Law demands or else it is not Law, knowing beforehand that they were unable to keep it. This does seem, on the surface, an unreasonable demand, unless we understand the purpose for which the Law was given.

It was not given to save, but to show the need of Salvation. It was not given to take away sin, for in fact, it could not take away sin, but to reveal sin, for by the Law is the knowledge of sin (not salvation from sin). We, therefore, ask the question anticipated by Paul in Romans 7:7:

"*What shall we say then? Is the Law sin?* (In other words, is the Law responsible for our sin and failure?) *God forbid. Nay, I had not known sin* (knew what sin was and its awfulness), *but by the Law* (the Law identified sin, and man's helplessness to not succumb to sin): *for I had not known lust* (the desire for unlawful things), *except the Law had said, Thou shalt not covet.* (The Law was not at fault, that being the depraved nature of man, with the Law of Moses only responsible for bringing to the surface what was already there.)"

"*For I was alive without the Law once* (meaning that Paul gave his heart to Christ and experienced Eternal Life, which he did on the road to Damascus, which was obtained without the Law of any nature): *but when the Commandment came* (when Paul attempted to overcome by trying to personally keep the Commandments), *sin revived* (Paul failed and because the Holy Spirit will not help one in such circumstances. In other words, the Holy Spirit will only help us as we anchor our Faith in the Cross and the Resurrection, and not at all in our personal attempts to be an overcomer), *and I died* (Paul failed, meaning that he sinned, despite all of his efforts otherwise)" (Rom. 7:7, 9).

The Law did not and does not produce sin, but instead it revealed the true nature of sin. Paul says, *"When the Commandment came,"* it slew me.

What did Paul mean by the Commandment?

The two Tables of the Law are called the Ten Commandments. They were given by God to Israel in order that His Standard of Righteousness might be known.

Men came up with all types of standards of their own making concerning righteousness, which God could not accept. Consequently, that which He gave as it regards the Ten Commandments, is the Righteousness or Standard of God.

As simple as these Commandments might seem, it is sad when one realizes that not one single Israelite was successful in keeping the Commandments. Everyone failed as failed they must.

Which one of these did Paul refer to when he said, *"The Commandment"*? I believe Paul indicates clearly to which one he referred. It is the last one — *"Thou shalt not covet."*

THE LAST COMMANDMENT

He says, *"I had not known lust, except the Law had said, Thou shalt not covet"* (Rom. 7:7).

That was *the* Commandment which caused sin to revive, *"And I died,"* says Paul. He could claim perfect obedience to the first Nine Commandments as far as outward observance was concerned. He could say honestly:

"If any other man thinketh that he hath whereof he might trust in the flesh (good works), *I more:*

"Circumcised the eighth day, of the stock of Israel, of the Tribe of Benjamin, an Hebrew of the Hebrews; as touching the Law, a Pharisee;

"Concerning zeal, persecuting the Church; touching the Righteousness which is in the Law, blameless" (Phil. 3:4-6).

Paul could claim outward observance to the Law. He had kept everyone of the Commandments and said, *"As touching the Law, I am blameless."*

What did he mean by that?

He could say he had never broken the First Commandment — had never owned any other God.

He could claim the Second — had never worshiped graven images.

He could claim perfect obedience to the Third — he had never taken the Name of the Lord in vain; and so with the Fourth, he had never broken the Law of the Sabbath. And so on with the Fifth, honoring Father and Mother; and the Sixth, thou shalt not kill; and the Seventh, adultery; and the Eighth, stealing; and the Ninth, bearing false witness, lying.

To all these he could say, *"I kept everyone of them. No one can accuse me of not keeping those Laws."* But it applied only to outward observance, and now comes the Tenth Commandment, which Paul calls:

THE COMMANDMENT

It was a new view of sin, and revealed it as a matter of the heart and the mind, and not only the overt act itself. The Commandment said, *"Thou shalt not covet."* Evil desire, covetousness, jealousy, wrong thoughts, sinful motives (even if never carried into action) are sin.

The Commandment now reveals that sin is not only an act, but an attitude. It is a matter of the mind and heart, rather than merely of the body. Actually, the body is rather neutral, serving only as a vehicle through which righteousness or unrighteousness can be carried out (Rom. 6:13).

Before the act of murder is committed, there is the sin of hate which prompted it. Before a person steals, there is first of all the sin of covetousness. Before the act of adultery is committed, there is the sin of lusting.

Jesus emphasized these aspect of sin when He said:

"For out of the heart proceed evil thoughts, murders, adulteries, fornications, thefts, false witness, blasphemies:

"These are the things which defile a man" (Mat. 15:19-20).

When Paul came face-to-face with The Commandment, he had no more boasting of his outward observance of the Law. Up to now Paul could say, I never cursed, broke the Sabbath, worshiped idols, stole, or murdered anyone. He could say as touching those things, I am blameless, but then *"The Commandment"* came, and revealed to Paul the real nature of sin, that even evil desire is sin. This is the meaning of the Verse:

"For I was alive without the Law once (when he accepted Christ and the life that Christ brings)*: but when the Commandment came* (he tried to keep the Commandment within his own ability), *sin revived* (he failed as fail he must), *and I died* (Paul sinned against the Lord, whatever it might have been, which is always the result of personal effort).

"And the Commandment, which was ordained to life (meaning that it was noble and righteous within itself), *I found to be unto death* (meaning he could not obey it no matter how hard he tried, which means he broke it, thereby bringing upon himself the Curse of the Law, which is death — separation from God, which all sin does).

"For sin, taking occasion by the Commandment (Paul tried to overcome sin because

the Commandment said he must, but tried to do it within himself), *deceived me* (sin deceived Paul as it does all others, because he thought he could overcome it), *and by it slew me* (overcame him, as all sin does if addressed by our own personal efforts).

"*Wherefore the Law is holy* (the Law of Moses is not the cause of our problem), *and the Commandment holy, and just, and good* (meaning that it is not unholy because it is a Commandment).

"*Was then that which is good made death unto me?* (Was the Law actually bad?) *God forbid.* (The Law was not and is not the fault.) *But sin, that it might appear sin* (the Law identified sin, thereby bringing the corruption of the sin nature to the surface, which Law always does), *working death in me* (showing me my inability and helplessness) *by that which is good* (the Law which is good, was designed to do this); *that sin by the Commandment* (identified by the Commandment) *might become exceeding sinful* (would show man just how awful that sin is, and how lacking in ability that man is to overcome sin, even the Christian within himself).

"*For we know that the Law is spiritual* (the Law is from God and, therefore, holy): *but I am carnal* (meaning that within myself, even as a Christian I cannot keep the Law), *sold under sin* (the sin nature will triumph even in the Believer, if the Believer's Faith is not properly placed in the Cross)" (Rom. 7:9-14).

THE LAW STIRRED UP SIN

We see then that the Law brought to light the real nature of sin, not as an act but a condition, or an attitude. This is again expressed in Romans 7:5:

"*For when we were in the flesh* (trying to overcome through our own ability, and in which we always failed), *the motions* (movements or passions) *of sins, which were by the Law* (which the Law exposed, as a medicine drawing corruption to the surface), *did work in our members* (our physical bodies) *to bring forth fruit unto death* (which sin always does)" (Rom. 7:5).

Notice carefully the words, "*The motions of sins which were by the Law.*" The motions of sins were caused by the Law. The Law was not sin, but it did set in motion the activities of sin. In other words, it brought to the surface the corruption that was already there.

In Verse 8, Paul says, "*Without the Law sin was dead.*" The meaning is that sin was inactive — it did not appear in its true light as sin. Then the Law came and stirred up sin, so it became apparent and visible. The Law of Moses did not cause or create sin, but it set it in motion — drove it out of hiding, as it were. So in answer to the question, "*Wherefore then serveth the Law?*" Or, "*what was the function of the Law,*" we add the following:

IT WAS REVELATIONAL

First of all, we know that the Law was national in character, meaning that it was for the entirety of Israel. In fact, it actually was for the entire world; however, there was absolutely no point in giving it to the world, considering that the world had no knowledge of God or His Ways whatsoever. In fact, the Lord would use Israel as a test case, showing that even under most favorable circumstances, even Israel could not keep the Law, so if Israel could not keep it, how in the world could the balance of humanity keep the Law considering its gross spiritual ignorance?

Second, the Law was dispensational in its Ministry, meaning that it was to serve only for a period of time, actually until Jesus came and fulfilled all its demands.

Third, it was exemplary in purpose, meaning that it was God's Standard of Righteousness, the only Standard that He could accept.

We now add a fourth dimension, its "*Revelational character.*" That means that it reveals sin as it had not been seen before.

Paul says, "*The motions of sins which were by the Law.*" Before the Law, says Paul, sin was dead; that is, inactive and not visible, at least as it referred to its identification. Before the Law, to be sure, sin was very much in the world, even wreaking its terrible wages, but with no positive identification. In other words, a "*lie*" was not identified as a lie, or "*stealing*" as such, etc., even those these things were carried on constantly.

However, the greater meaning of all this is, that before the Law, man had no way to realize his terrible, desperate, sinful, wicked condition. Having no Standard to serve as a yardstick, or at least a Standard that was reliable, he did not know how bad he was, or how good he wasn't, and above all how absolutely helpless he was to do that which was right.

When the Law was given, sin which was already there, was then made visible, or was *"stirred up"* by the Law, which the Law was meant to do. To be sure, the Law was not the cause of the sin, nor was it the developer of sin, it only brought to the surface that which was already present.

AN ILLUSTRATION

Perhaps the following will be of some help: Imagine that I have on my desk a glass of water. It has stood there for a number of days, quiet and undisturbed. It has not been agitated, and we may call it *"dead water."* It looks clear and sparkling, but it is in reality badly polluted and unsafe to drink!

It contains a large amount of impurities and particles of dirt. These filthy components are not visible to the eye, for they have all been deposited as a layer of sediment at the bottom of the glass. Because the water was quiet, or one might say undisturbed, all the particles had gravitated to the bottom of the glass, laying there quiet and undetected. Now I take a teaspoon and begin to stir the water, and lo, immediately a film of milky, filthy material clouds the glass of water while a repulsive stench issues from the water. Now what have I done?

I have stirred up something I did not know was there before. With the teaspoon I put in motion the pollution and impurities in the glass. Now notice carefully, the teaspoon did not corrupt the water or increase its pollution. As well, neither can the teaspoon purify the water. In order to do that, I remove the spoon and lay it aside. It was not intended to cleanse but to reveal.

You see now what Paul means by the expression, *"The motions of sins, which are by the Law"* — not the sins which were by the Law (the Law did not create the sins), but the *"motions of sins,"* meaning that the Law stirred up the sins that were already there, showing man what he really was. The spoon revealed the filth; but to purify the water, it must be distilled and the pure separated from the impure. This is not the ministry of the Law, for the Law could not do such, the Law actually only brought out the knowledge of sin — showed it was there, identified its source, which is an evil heart, and identified its action.

THE SPOON IS THE LAW

The illustration of the water and the spoon is a picture of the human heart and the ministry of the Law. The glass of water is the human heart. The Law is the spoon which stirred up this sin within the heart. There is nothing wrong with the spoon, and there is nothing wrong with the Law. The Law cannot correct, or remove sin from the heart, just as the spoon cannot remove the impurities in the water. To purify the water takes *"distillation"*; to correct the sin in the human heart requires *"Regeneration."* The Law then, instead of correcting the pollution, which it was not meant to do, and in fact, cannot do, does succeed in stirring it up, which was a part of the function of Law.

WHY WAS THIS NEEDED?

The Fall of man, which instituted the depravity of the human heart has done strange things to man. It has twisted and perverted his nature so that a forbidden thing seems more appealing than the things which are not prohibited. In other words, there is a propensity or desire in the human heart for that which is evil and ungodly, all due to the fallen nature. While unredeemed man may not desire some ungodly things, he definitely will desire other ungodly things. That is his nature. In fact, that's the reason that a person must be *"Born-Again,"* actually making him a new creation, with old things passing away, and all things becoming new (II Cor. 5:17).

As well, the Law was designed to portray the Standard of God, in effect, the Standard of Righteousness demanded by God of man. It was all ensconced in the Ten Commandments.

Man loves to formulate his own standards, which he constantly does even to this very moment; however, the only Standards that God will accept are those He has laid out Himself. In fact, man in his depraved condition cannot formulate correct standards. In other words, it is absolutely impossible for him to do so.

When one looks at these Standards, *"Thou shalt not bear false witness,"* or *"Thou shalt not steal,"* etc., they seem to be very simple, and easy to obey. However, due to man's fallen nature, he finds that it is utterly impossible for him to obey these simple Statutes and Rulings. No matter how hard he tries, he simply cannot do so.

In fact, he might be successful in keeping some of the Commandments, or at least he thinks he does so, simply because he does not overtly break them. In other words, millions would say, *"I haven't killed anyone,"* so I have kept that Commandment, etc.

However, a mere outward observance is not enough. Even as we have already discussed, and which Paul proclaimed, the final Commandment, *"Thou shalt not covet,"* destroys all of man's claims. In other words, in the eyes or God, it is not enough to not overtly commit the act, we must not even want to do so. Looking at it in that light, we realize that every person in the world, has in fact, broken *all* the Commandments.

And yet, man loves to play games with himself, and especially religious man. He makes himself believe that he has kept the Commandments, is keeping the Commandments, when in reality he's not doing any such thing.

SO HOW CAN THE COMMANDMENTS BE KEPT?

First of all, they cannot be kept by man's ability, irrespective as to how hard he might try. And to relate this which is a shocker, even Christians, who in fact are new creations, cannot keep the Commandments. If we as Believers set out to do such, we will fail just as surely as the unredeemed fails constantly.

The Commandments are kept in Christ. And what do we mean by that?

The Law was meant to show man his inability, creating in him a knowledge of his need for a Redeemer, someone who could do for him what he could not do for himself. This is what the Sacrifices were all about.

The Sacrifices being constant, meaning repetitive, were the means by which sinful man could approach a Righteous God. They atoned for his inability resulting in sin and failure.

And yet, the Sacrifices within themselves actually could not take away sin; however, the One Whom they represented, Who was yet to come, namely the Lord Jesus Christ, could, and would in fact take away sin (Jn. 1:29).

The Law was given as the Standard which man could not keep, and the Sacrifices were given to show him the way. Unfortunately, Israel tried to make Salvation out of the Law and out of the Sacrifices, completely perverting their true purpose.

JESUS IS OUR PERFECT SUBSTITUTE AND REPRESENTATIVE MAN

God has never had several types of Salvation, in fact, only one. From the very beginning, the Sacrifices were instituted, hence the account of Cain and Abel (Gen. 4:1-5). The Sacrifices always pointed to Jesus and the death that He would die on the Cross. An innocent victim, whether a lamb or a goat, etc., would take the place of the sinner, even as Christ was an innocent victim.

The animal would be killed, even as Christ offered up Himself on the Cross. The blood of the animal was poured out and actually spilled at the base of the Altar, typifying the Blood that was poured out from the physical body of Christ at the Crucifixion, referring to Him pouring out His Life.

The animal was placed on the Altar, typifying the Cross, which, in effect, was an Altar. The fire on the Altar burned the little animal, typifying the Judgment of God which would fall upon Christ, instead of upon us who rightly deserved it.

In other words, Christ became our Substitute in totality, even our Representative Man. He perfectly kept the Law in every respect. He then offered up Himself on the Cross, suffering the penalty of the broken Law, which He in fact did not break, but nevertheless suffered its penalty in our place. He then rose from the dead on the third day, and some 40 days after the Crucifixion ascended to the Father, where He now sits by the Right Hand of God in an exalted position (Phil. 2:9-11).

Our trust in Him, gives us, and in fact guarantees us, all the victories which He purchased in that great Sacrifice.

BUT HOW DOES THE LAW AFFECT CHRISTIANS PRESENTLY?

Regrettably, most Christians would not even bother to read the things we have just written, simply because they would conclude that the Law has no bearing on us presently. They would say, *"We are Christians, and the Law of Moses was for Israel only, and has no bearing on us presently."*

In a sense that is right, but for the most part, the way that most Christians look at the situation, the statement is totally wrong.

Why do you think Paul gave all this information on the Law? Why do you think he kept speaking about this subject, at least if it has no bearing on us at all presently? If the Law is of no consequence under the New Covenant, why say anything about it at all?

To be sure, the Holy Spirit through the Apostle gave all this information, dealt with this subject extensively, even Chapter after Chapter, because in fact, the Law in a sense, is extremely important presently, and in fact has been ever since it was given, and continues unto this hour.

How?

I am positive that the Christian understands that we as Believers are to live a holy life. To be sure, that *"holy life"* is wrapped up in the Ten Commandments, for that is the part of the Law of which Paul constantly speaks. He is not speaking of the Sacrifices, Sabbath-keeping, Circumcision, Feast Days, etc. All of that was fulfilled and satisfied in Christ. Consequently, those things which were meant to portray His coming, have already been fulfilled, and serve no more purpose, as would be obvious.

As well, He has already fulfilled the moral part of the Law, and by that we refer to the Ten Commandments. But despite Christ having kept and fulfilled the moral law, it still affects us, and we need to know how.

The moment the person accepts Christ, that individual becomes a new creature or a new creation one might better say (II Cor. 5:17). Inasmuch as we are a new creation in Christ, just as instinctively as we once gravitated toward sin, we now gravitate toward Righteousness. We do this because there is a new nature in us and as well we have the Holy Spirit. Truly, all things are changed.

There is something instinctively in us as Believers that wants to obey the moral law in every respect. Of course, this is right and correct, the actual instinct of the Believer.

However, the great question is, how do we obey these instincts, i.e., *"obey the moral law"*?

If asked that question, most Christians would probably draw a blank. *"I'm a Christian now, so I just do the right thing,"* many would say.

Others might say, *"The Lord helps us!"* Others might say, *"I have the Holy Spirit, and He will give me the power to do these things."*

All of these things, plus much we have not said, are right up to a point; however, if that's as far as it goes, most Christians will find themselves living a life of defeat and failure.

THE BIBLICAL WAY

Satan to be sure, takes advantage of our Scriptural ignorance. That's the reason it is so important for the Believer to know and understand the meaning of the Seventh Chapter of Romans. Unfortunately, most Christians have been taught, that is if they've been taught anything at all about this Seventh Chapter, that this is an account of Paul's life before conversion. Consequently, they ignore the things which are said there, but belatedly find themselves falling into the same trap as Paul.

The Seventh Chapter of Romans portrays Paul (yes, the great Paul), trying to obey the moral law *after* he was saved. He was trying to do this even as most Christians continue to try to do it presently. He was trying to obey by his own willpower, his own strength, his own ability, just as most modern Christians. Now that he was a Believer, especially after having had this great experience on the road to Damascus, Paul thinks that surely he can now keep the moral law to perfection. He found he couldn't, just as no Believer can, and that confuses most.

Paul found himself doing the very things he was trying not to do, with him concluding by saying, *"O wretched man that I am! Who shall deliver me from the body of this death?"* (Rom. 7:24).

If most Christians would admit it, they would say the same identical thing that Paul said here. The difference is, Paul cried to the Lord for help, and the Lord gave him the blueprint for victory, which he gave to us in Romans Chapters 6 and 8. However, most Christians don't know anything about that either, and continue to live a life of failure.

Before I further address this issue, please allow me to list some of the efforts made by the Church regarding this tremendous problem.

THE CHURCH AND SIN

Even though I have detailed this in our Commentary on Ephesians, it is so important, and knowing the manner in which most Commentaries are studied, I feel that for the benefit of the Believer I should address the subject again.

If the Believer does not know and understand God's prescribed method for a victorious, overcoming, Christian life, just as surely as there is a God in Heaven, that Christian is going to pretty much live a life of failure. In other words, sin will dominate the Believer in some manner (Rom. 6:14).

It is strange, the Church for the most part refuses to admit this, and yet constantly throws up one effort after the other to try to assuage the problem. In other words, it spends much of its time fighting a problem that it claims does not exist.

That doesn't mean that Believers are unsaved, it just means they are not walking in victory, and for the most part, simply because they don't know the way to Victory.

One so-called spiritual leader, the head of a particular Pentecostal Denomination, boasted that his Denomination had very little problem with sin. He admitted that there might be some few weak Christians who might have such problems, but they were few and far between. That's not hearsay, I read what the man wrote.

The Truth is, Preachers in that particular Denomination, and all others for that matter, are failing by the droves one might say, which includes the laity as well.

Yes, there are some Christians who are walking in victory, but if the truth be known, not many.

If the Believer does not know and understand God's prescribed order of Victory, that Christian, irrespective as to who he might be, is going to be dominated by sin in some manner. There is no other way. Knowing and understanding, that most of the modern Church has little knowledge of God's prescribed order, means that most are not living victorious, Christian lives.

THE WAYS AND MEANS OF THE MODERN CHURCH

Knowing there is a problem, whether admitted or not, and trying to address it, men come up with all type of proposed answers for the sin question. In other words, Christians are fighting the sin problem, they don't really understand why they are failing, and instinctively they know this is not right. So we cast about for particular remedies, which are all the time wrong.

Some of the things we will list here are actually right if used in the way they are intended; however, if used in the wrong way, which they mostly are, we then reduce these great Scriptural attributes to the position of *"works"* which the Lord can never honor. To be sure, we do it with good intentions and even with right motives; nevertheless, there is going to be failure irrespective of our good intentions.

First of all, failure in the life of a Believer, is an extremely hurtful thing. It militates against everything that's within us, against our new nature, against the Holy Spirit, in fact, against what we actually are in Christ. So we know that the problem has to stop, whatever the problem might be. In fact, it can be anything, drinking alcohol secretly, smoking, drugs, immorality in many and varied ways, jealousy, envy, pride, self-righteousness, arrogance, self-will, uncontrollable temper, depression, fear, etc. In fact, the list is long!

None of this is to have dominion over the Believer, but yet with the far greater majority of Believers, even Preachers, even Spirit-filled Believers and Preachers, one or more of these things are ruling in their lives. So we address the problem in many and varied ways, all wrong, at least in these directions.

MANIFESTATIONS

For the last several years, hundreds of thousands of Christians have travelled all over the world to particular places where they have heard the Spirit of God is moving, almost always with some particular type of manifestation. Don't misunderstand, at times the moving of the Spirit is genuine, and the manifestations are real as well.

However, the Christian erroneously thinks, that if they can just get this particular manifestation whatever it is, such as *"being slain in the Spirit,"* or *"holy laughter,"* or any number of other things, they will then solve their problem.

They won't!

While the manifestation may or may not be genuine, and if it is genuine, it will definitely be a blessing to the Believer, but it will not solve the sin and failure problem. Even though the Believer gets the *"Blessing,"* a short time later, the old problem returns, for the simple reason that it has never left.

FASTING

Fasting is definitely a Scriptural principle, meaning that it will help the Believer; however, fasting is not the answer for sin in the flesh despite the fact that many believe that it is.

While the Believer is fasting, the problem may not present itself; however, the Believer is going to have to eat after a while, and to be sure, the problem will be back. The Believer is then left more confused than ever. Consequently, he or she thinks, quite possibly I need to fast for a longer period of time, with some even embarking on such a quest.

Again, the fasting will definitely bless and help, but not in the manner in which the Believer thinks. In other words, the problem of the flesh is going to remain despite the fasting.

THE FAMILY CURSE

As I dictate these notes, this is big at present. Christians are being told, that something happened in their family two or three generations past, and this curse has come on down to the present time causing the Christian great difficulties.

The Scripture used for this error, and error it is, is Exodus 20:5, *"Thou shalt not bow down thyself to them* (idol gods), *nor serve them: for I the Lord thy God am a jealous God, visiting the iniquity of the fathers upon the children unto the third and fourth generation of them that hate Me."*

Consequently, Christians are told that the problem in their lives such as anger, hate, immorality, alcohol, depression, etc., *"is a result of this 'family curse.'"*

However, as stated, that is error. This Passage is qualified by the words *"hate Me."* In

NOTES

other words, if people keep hating the Lord, whatever problems occurred in the past, will definitely continue at the present in some manner; however, Christians don't hate the Lord.

In fact, there is a curse on the entirety of the human race, which would include family curses, generational curses, area curses, etc. But when the person comes to Christ, all of that is handled.

What kind of Salvation would it be, for the Lord to handle only some things and leave other things unhandled? No, everything was addressed at the Cross, and when the Believer accepts Christ, he truly becomes a new creation (II Cor. 5:17). That means that *"old things are passed away,"* referring to curses, sins, problems of the past, etc., *"behold, all things are become new."*

Paul then said, *"And all things are of God,"* meaning that the past has been completely handled and obliterated, including all curses, etc. (II Cor. 5:18). So, Preachers who tell Christians that they need to get in a prayer line and have hands laid on them in order to rebuke this family curse, are not properly interpreting the Scripture, and in fact, are doing the people a terrible disservice. Whatever problem the individual has, after all the rebuking is done, the problem is going to remain, for the simple reason that a so-called *"family curse"* is not the problem at all.

The problem is, that the Christian does not properly understand God's prescribed way of victory, and the Devil takes full advantage of that.

THE BUDDY SYSTEM

Back in the 1980's all Believers were strongly urged to have a confidant, in other words someone they could confide in, with the idea being that two are stronger than one, and, therefore, the problems will be solved.

In fact, this is nothing but a takeoff on modern psychology, actually, a part of the 12-step program, etc.

Should not the Believer understand, that if overcoming sin and Satan was this simple, then these are the instructions that the Lord would have given man. He surely would not have had to have come down here and died on the Cross of Calvary.

No, there is no help in that method whatsoever.

While it's certainly not wrong to have a friend and for both to join together in prayer about certain things, the terrible problem of sin can never be assuaged in this manner.

In fact, all of this tells us that most Christians do not know or understand how bad that sin actually is. In fact, it is so bad, so awful, so powerful, that even God could not speak Redemption into existence. God had to become man and pay a terrible price at the Cross, in order for man to be saved.

PSYCHOLOGY

Unfortunately, almost the entirety of the Church world has opted for humanistic psychology, which in fact, holds no answers whatsoever, but rather harm. The statement, *"You need professional help,"* is big in modern Church circles, but having no Scriptural validity at all. Actually, such a statement says that what Jesus did at the Cross is not enough, and needs something added.

As well, the word *"rehabilitation,"* which incidentally, is not found in the Bible, is big also in Christian circles. It implies that man can rehabilitate man, which is in fact a slap in face of Christ. Once again, if man could rehabilitate man, or if man could rehabilitate himself, then Jesus died needlessly on the Cross.

The Bible tells us exactly what modern psychology is. It says, *"This wisdom descendeth not from above, but is earthly, sensual, devilish"* (James 3:15).

That's a pretty serious indictment!

Either Jesus addressed every single problem at the Cross, or else He didn't. If He didn't, we then need to turn to the likes of Freud, Maslow, and Rodgers, etc. I happen to believe that every single problem of humanity was addressed at the Cross. Peter plainly said:

"According as His Divine Power hath given unto us all things that pertain unto life and Godliness, through the knowledge of Him that hath called us to glory and virtue:

"Whereby are given unto us exceeding great and precious promises: that by these ye might be partakers of the Divine Nature, having escaped the corruption that is in the world through lust" (II Pet. 1:3-4).

Once again, and let me say it very clearly and plainly, either Peter is telling the truth, or else he is lying. One cannot have it both ways.

The foray into modern psychology by the Church is done on the premise of one or two reasons:

1. The Church doesn't know God's prescribed order of victory; therefore, in desperation they turn to something which promises help, even though it in fact gives none.

2. The Church has plunged into psychology simply because of unbelief. In other words, it no longer believes that what Jesus did at the Cross is the answer to the ills, sins, aberrations, and perversions of man. If in fact that is the case, and it definitely is with many, then the death knell has already sounded.

It is my contention that so-called modern spiritual leaders who claim to be Spirit-filled, but have turned to the way of the world, are in greater spiritual danger than all. In other words, there the greater sin is committed.

It is one thing for the nominal Church world to go in the direction of humanistic psychology, and I speak of those who do not believe in the Baptism with the Holy Spirit with the evidence of speaking with other Tongues, but something else altogether for those who claim to have this experience, to rather resort to the wiles of Satan. In fact, this is the most terrible danger sign of all in the modern Pentecostal and Charismatic Denominations and fellowships.

In fact, this is at least one of the reasons that Pentecostal Leaders, once again so-called, dislike Jimmy Swaggart so intently. This of which I have just written I have been preaching for many years. It has not been received very well. In fact, these leaders have done their best to demonize me in every manner possible, in order that people will not listen to what I have to say. Nevertheless, what I'm saying is the truth. Either Jesus is the answer or He isn't. One cannot have it both ways.

Humanistic psychology is Satan's direct attack against the Atonement of Christ. It is another effort by man to try to solve his own problem of sin, which of course, is impossible. Naturally, modern psychology does not even recognize sin as sin. It somehow thinks that by putting a different label on the jar that such will change the contents. It doesn't!

PRAYER

The Reader may be somewhat surprised for me to list prayer in this category.

Actually, prayer is one of the greatest ingredients respecting the Christian's relationship with the Lord. In fact, it is impossible for a Christian to have a proper relationship with Christ without having a proper prayer life. Such is absolutely imperative!

It is through prayer that we establish relationship, receive direction, offer petitions, and exhibit praise to the Lord. Such is an absolute requirement for the Child of God, at least if the Believer desires any relationship with the Lord at all. Sadly, most Christians do not pray at all, and, therefore, have very little personal relationship with the Lord.

And yet, it is possible to turn prayer into *"works."* Let me put it this way:

If the Christian thinks he or she can pray 30 minutes a day, or an hour a day, or whatever, and thereby obtain victory over sin, such will not be brought about. While the Believer will definitely be blessed, strengthened, and encouraged as it regards his habitual prayer life, he will not receive the answer for which he is looking by this method, and I speak of victory over sin.

Once again, if victory could be brought about in this manner, then the Lord did not need to come down and die on the Cross, but rather just teach individuals how to pray.

Again, I surely pray that the Reader does not misunderstand my words, thinking that prayer is insignificant. I pray I have amply addressed this. I am simply meaning, that a certain prayer regimen each day, although greatly helping us in other ways, will not give us victory over sin.

And yet, at the same time prayer can definitely be the vehicle through which Victory can come as far as direction is concerned. In the latter part of 1991 I began to earnestly seek the Lord regarding an answer to this particular problem. In fact, the Lord instructed me to have two prayer meetings a day, which we have done our best to faithfully follow from then until now.

For some five years I earnestly sought the Lord concerning this matter. How can the Child of God walk in perpetual victory? How can we not be dominated by impulses of the flesh, but rather walk in Righteousness and Holiness? How is it that sin will not have dominion over us in any fashion?

With tears I sought the Lord earnestly for these five years, and I mean on a dedicated basis. And then in 1997, the Lord began to answer that prayer. He did it through His Word, showing me the answer to every question, and the key to victory. It wasn't a new way, actually being the very foundation of Christianity which I will address momentarily. In fact, this Revelation of the Cross and the Resurrection has so revolutionized my life, that I stumble respecting words to adequately describe what has happened and what is happening. As stated, it is not new, but actually the very foundation of the Faith.

So, I'm not at all demeaning prayer, but rather putting it in its rightful place.

THE CASTING OUT OF DEMONS

In the 1970's and early 1980's, this particular method was big in many Pentecostal and Charismatic Churches.

Christians having problems, even as we are now discussing, were being told that these things were being caused by demon spirits. Consequently, they should be prayed for by particular Preachers, with these demons being cast out or rebuked, whichever the case, and then their problem would be solved.

In fact, this was big in some Churches, with people lining up by the hundreds to receive this particular help.

It is certainly true that demon spirits definitely get involved in any type of sin or failure. In fact, that is a given. But yet, the method proposed of casting them out, etc., is Scripturally wrong.

In the first place, even though demon spirits definitely do oppress Believers, and do take advantage of the flesh and sinful impulses doing their very best to make matters worse, Christians are not demon possessed. So, it is patently incorrect to lay hands on Believers, claiming to cast out some particular demon which is supposed to be causing them problems. In other words, Christians were being told that if they had an uncontrollable temper, that it was caused by a *"demon of temper,"* etc. It would apply, of course, to anything.

No, these are works of the flesh, and not demon spirits, even though demon spirits as stated, definitely do get involved, as they are involved with all sin and failure (Gal. 5:19-21).

This soon died down simply because it actually offered no relief.

LAYING ON OF HANDS

The laying on of hands is Scriptural. It will definitely help the Child of God. In fact, at Family Worship Center, we call Believers forward every Sunday Morning, and other times as well, regarding particular needs, in order that hands be laid on them (Mk. 16:18; James 5:14).

However, we make a mistake if we think that the Christian can have the sin problem solved by the laying on of hands. Even though it will definitely help, and in fact should be done, if the Believer does not know or understand the true way of Victory, which is the Cross, even though momentarily helped, the problem will return. And yet, *"laying on of hands"* is about all that most Preachers know to do.

Once again, if this is all it took to assuage the sin problem, then Jesus needlessly died on the Cross.

SANCTIFICATION

In fact, what we are actually speaking of regarding the true way of Victory is Sanctification, but not as it is sometimes taught.

In other words, some Preachers claim that after a person is saved, then they need to go on and be sanctified. They are right and they are wrong. In fact, the way they are saying it and believing it, is totally wrong.

They are claiming that Sanctification is a definite work of Grace, and, therefore, once this happens to the Child of God, the sin question is forever settled. Some of these individuals teach sinless perfection, and some don't, but they all claim, at least those who preach this particular doctrine, that the sin question is forever settled at this particular time.

It isn't!

To be brief, the moment the believing sinner comes to Christ, he or she is instantly sanctified. In fact, this must be done (the Believer made clean), before one can be Justified (the Believer declared clean) (I Cor. 6:11).

So, whereas Sanctification definitely is a work of Grace which is given to the Believer automatically at conversion, there is also a progressive Sanctification, which in fact, is ongoing all during the life of the Believer (I Thess. 5:23).

There is no such thing as a Believer receiving some type of spiritual work or blessing, with him then being labeled as *"sanctified,"* and thereby no longer being bothered by the flesh or the sin problem. Such is not taught in the Bible. If it is, where is it?

Sanctification is an instant work, and it is also a progressive work. In other words, our actual *position* in Christ is one of total Sanctification (II Cor. 6:11), but our *condition* in Christ at times leaves something to be desired. In fact, the Holy Spirit goes to work immediately in the life of the Believer in order to bring his *"condition"* up to his *"position."* To be sure, that is a long process, one in fact which never ends (I Thess. 5:23).

The problem is, with these individuals who are told they are *"sanctified,"* as a result of a particular blessing from the Lord, and that they will not have anymore problems with the flesh, they then find that they do continue to have problems with the flesh. Consequently, cover up and hypocrisy then become the rule.

No, there is no such Scriptural doctrine such as *"entire Sanctification,"* as it is sometimes called. If one wants to stretch the statement, such will happen when the Trump sounds, and the Resurrection takes place, but not until them.

COVERING

This absurdity (and absurdity it is) has been taught in one form or fashion all along, that if Christians are under a certain *"covering,"* they are then protected from sin and Satan, etc. This can go in many directions, such as particular Preachers, particular Churches, or particular Denominations.

This is totally unscriptural, and definitely breeds fear. In other words, the people are led to believe that if they get out from under this particular covering, they are inviting disaster for themselves. Consequently, they then begin to look to a Preacher, a Church, or a Denomination, instead of the Finished Work of Christ.

But yet, this is quite often promoted, because religious men love to rule over other people, and unfortunately, many people love to be ruled over. They somehow think that it absolves them of responsibility. It doesn't!

There isn't but one covering and that is the Lord Jesus Christ and what He did at the Cross. Anything else, and no matter how it is religiously labeled, is false and thereby detrimental. Instead of the Believer getting the co-called protection for which they are seeking, they will actually get the very opposite. In other words, the Believer should shun those who teach such, for it is a road to disaster.

DENOMINATIONS

Actually, this would go not only for Denominations but even particular Churches.

The insinuation is offered that affiliation with a certain Denomination or membership in a certain Church, will give one spiritual superiority, and, therefore, aid them in their efforts at victory over sin, etc. In fact, this is very close to the *"covering"* mentioned above.

Denominationalism is very much akin to racism. Racism, of course, claims that if one is not of their particular color, they are inferior, etc. Denominationalism pretty much says the same thing but in a little different way.

Many Believers think that if one is a Christian they must belong to their particular Denomination. Or else they are like some of the leaders with which I was formerly associated. While not coming out and saying that one must belong to that Denomination in order to be saved, they do leave the impression that if one was where they ought to be with God they would be a part of that Denomination. If they were not a part of that Denomination, that means that something is wrong with that particular individual. I think the Reader can get the message.

There is no salvation or victory in Denominations or Churches. While some may certainly be good and be a great blessing, that's about as far as it can go. Whatever is taught behind the pulpit in Churches is what is important, not the Church per se itself, as ought to be obvious.

No earthly institution be it Church or otherwise can give anyone victory over sin. In fact, the Catholic Church openly claims that the Church saves. Unfortunately, many Protestants are not very far behind in their claims as well. Such is a travesty as it regards the Word of God.

No, it is not wrong to belong to a Denomination or Church. In fact, these institutions can be a tremendous help and blessing to the Work of God, if addressed correctly. In other words, these earthly institutions should be tools to help further the Work of God all over the world; however, association with Denominations or Churches contain no saving Grace as ought to be obvious, in fact, no spirituality at all, that being derived solely from the Word of God and one's relationship with Christ.

THE BAPTISM WITH THE HOLY SPIRIT

Unfortunately, many Believers think that the Holy Spirit automatically gives them victory within their lives. This especially refers to those of us who believe in the Baptism with the Holy Spirit with the evidence of speaking with other Tongues. I would suggest that most Spirit-filled Believers think that this work of Grace in their hearts and lives, automatically brings about the victory that is needed. However, it doesn't!

While the Holy Spirit definitely is the key to victory within our lives, even as Paul brings out in Romans Chapter 8, it is not an automatic process at all. In other words, there are millions of Spirit-filled Believers who are at the same time dominated by sin in some way. That's a travesty, but it is the truth.

A short time ago, one of my Associates was speaking with a young Pastor for whom he was conducting a meeting. The young man in referring to this question of victory over sin, said, *"I was taught in Bible School that the infilling of the Holy Spirit automatically took care of all of these things."* Unfortunately, that's what most believe.

He then said, or words to this effect, *"But I'm not finding that to be the case."*

I do not want the Reader to misunderstand. The Holy Spirit is actually the vital implement in the victory we must have; however, He works only according to our Faith in the Cross of Christ. In other words, He will not help us do what we need to do, or be what we ought to be, if we are functioning outside the Finished Work of Christ. In fact, the Believer cannot have victory without the Holy Spirit; however, what most Believers fail to understand is that He functions and works according to prescribed parameters, and I speak of the Great Sacrifice of Christ (Rom. 8:1-2).

So, the Baptism with the Holy Spirit, although vital to the Christian, does not mean an automatic victory in the Christian's life. Not at all! For Him to work as He desires, we must have as the object of our Faith, the Cross of Christ, and that alone.

WILLPOWER

Some Christians think that once they give their hearts to Christ, that the Lord strengthens their willpower, etc. He doesn't! While in fact, the will might be stronger because of our coming to Christ, which addresses itself to many variables, willpower is not the answer to victory.

And yet at the same time, the will of the Believer is always very much involved. The Scripture constantly says in one way or the other, *"whosoever will"* (Rev. 22:17). So, we must will to walk victoriously in the Lord, but that alone cannot bring Victory. In fact, what I'm about to say is going to come as a shock to many Christians, but it just happens to be so, whether believed or not.

If the Christian is depending only on his will, in other words *"willpower,"* Satan can override that will and force the Christian to do things he doesn't want to do. While many deny this, because they simply do not want to face up to the facts, it remains the truth nevertheless.

Paul plainly said, *"For to will is present with me; but how to perform that which is good I find not"* (Rom. 7:18).

This refers to Paul after he had given his heart to Christ on the road to Damascus, and had been Baptized with the Holy Spirit some three days later (Acts Chpt. 9). At that time, and as we've already addressed, the Apostle did not know of God's prescribed way of victory, and was attempting to gain victory in the same manner that most of us have attempted to do such. He failed, as fail he must.

In fact, most don't realize that Paul had to come by victory in the same manner as all of us. Actually, it was to Paul that this great secret of Victory was given, which he gave to us in Romans Chapters 6 and 8, which we will address momentarily. Also, many Believers think that Preachers who are used of the Lord, some in a great way, are above all of these things. That's not so at all. In fact, irrespective that the Lord is using them, and as stated greatly in some cases, if they do not subscribe to God's prescribed order of Victory, they will be dominated by sin exactly as anyone else. This confuses many Christians, although it shouldn't! Unfortunately, however, Preachers are at times put on a pedestal, thinking that such ones are above all of these things of which we speak. As stated, they aren't!

ONE SOURCE OF REDEMPTION

Satan is no respecter of persons, and actually, if one is greatly being used of God, they are, in effect, a greater target for Satan. In other words, Satan zeros in on that person to even a greater degree than others as ought to be obvious. However, if that particular Preacher, and irrespective as to who he might be, does not function according to the Scriptural method of Victory, he will be overcome by Satan the same as the weakest Christian. As stated, many Believers do not understand that; however, God is no respecter of persons, and neither is the Devil.

All Believers, even the greatest, have but one Source of Redemption, and that is Jesus Christ, and what He did at the Cross and the Resurrection. There is no other.

Unfortunately, many Christians build some Preachers up to astronomical heights, even to the place almost of worship, and if that Preacher happens to fail in any manner, they are just as quick to attempt to destroy him as they had been to worship him. Both attitudes are wrong, grossly wrong!

That's the reason many people do not understand Romans Chapter 7. They cannot conceive of Paul ever failing the Lord. The idea of him sinning, despite all of his efforts not to sin, is inconceivable to them. What they are doing is putting him in a category other than themselves.

No, Paul's experience, was and is identical to ours. And if the Reader will understand that correctly, he will go a long way toward solving his own problem.

Paul, after being saved and Baptized with the Holy Spirit, and not knowing God's prescribed order of Victory regarding his everyday walk, the Apostle was living a life of spiritual failure, despite his every effort to do otherwise. Many Preachers not wanting to come to grips with that, relegate Romans Chapter 7, to Paul's before-conversion experience, which is patently wrong.

In fact, every single Believer faces the same thing that Paul faced — how is he to have and to maintain victory in his everyday walk with the Lord? Paul told of his struggle, and to be sure we all have the same struggle in one way or the other; however, Paul's experience is meant to make ours much easier, due to the fact that he has given us the answer.

To be frank, when the Believer first comes to Christ, they are at that time victorious over everything. But of course, Satan pushes in attempting to get the Christian to fail, which I think I can say without fear of contradiction, that he always succeeds in some manner. The Christian then attempts to overcome the situation, most of the time in the wrong way. We fail to understand that the same Faith that got us into Christ, which pertains to believing in what Christ did at the Cross on our behalf, as well, keeps us in. In other words, we are to continue to have Faith in the Cross. Unfortunately, we allow our Faith to drift to other things, which always ensures failure. So we conclude by trying to overcome by *"willpower,"* which of course, is no match for the powers of darkness.

CONFESSION

The great throughway to victory as proclaimed by some, is by the method of *"confession."* In other words, if we confess what we are in Christ, and not lose that confession, this will guarantee victory over sin, etc.

While confession is definitely Scriptural, that is if it's used in the right way; still, a proper confession, although important, does not ensure victory at all.

Unfortunately, untold numbers of Christians are busy trying to confess their way to whatever it is they want or desire. Confession then becomes a *"Law,"* which of course will obtain nothing.

Merely saying something over and over does not spur God to action, as many believe. If reciting the right thing over and over, was the ground for victory, then Jesus died needlessly.

FAITH

There has been more teaching on Faith in the last 40 years I suppose, than all the other 1900 years combined. Some of it has been good, but most I think, has been error. Let me explain:

The Faith that has been taught for the most part, has had as its object the wrong thing. In other words, Faith has been set apart as a principle all to itself. If any object of Faith has been taught it has been that which is called *"the Word of God."* I use the term in that manner, because most of the time it's Faith in the Word which has been perverted, in other words, pulled out of context. So, it is actually Faith for the sake of Faith.

Consequently, Believers are constantly trying to build up their Faith, or to increase their Faith, with Faith made as the throughway of all blessings. In other words, if Believers can muster up enough Faith, they can get anything done. If in fact, whatever it is for which they are seeking is not done, then it is because of a lack of Faith, etc.

Everything is placed in the position of the amount of Faith that one has, which totally disconnects the Will of God in the matter, whether the Believer understands that or not.

We've already explained this, so I will not go into detail again.

For Faith to be the type of Faith which God will honor, it must always be in the Cross, the Finished Work of Christ. Faith must ever have as its object the Cross, for it was there that Jesus paid the price, which guarantees Redemption and victorious living for all Believers. If Faith has as its object anything else, and no matter how religious it might seem, it is Faith that the Holy Spirit will not recognize (I Cor. 1:18; 2:2; Gal. 6:14).

To sum up, the object of Faith must always be the Cross of Christ, which speaks of the Atonement. Faith must begin there, center there, and remain there. Anyone who goes beyond the Cross, has gone beyond the Plan of God, which will obviously never be recognized by the Lord. Unfortunately, many in the modern Faith Movement have done just that — gone beyond the Cross. In fact, they make no bones about the situation.

They claim that if anyone continues to believe in the Cross after Salvation, they will continue to be weak, etc. In fact, the Cross is little addressed even as the focus of Salvation. It is mostly just an incident in the entirety of the Plan of God, at least as these teachers claim.

As a result, they see almost no one brought to Christ in their ranks, or Baptized with the Holy Spirit for that matter. Naturally, there would be some exceptions to this, but not many. They pretty much zero in on *"healing"* and *"prosperity."* However, with some few exceptions, most of the so-called healings are mere claims, with this particular gospel (another gospel), mostly being reduced to mere *"prosperity."* Of course, money always has a powerful appeal. But as Paul also said, and I paraphrase, *"Gain is not Godliness"* (I Tim. 6:5).

So, while Faith definitely plans a tremendously important part in our walk with the Lord, as it does in everything we do with the Lord, still, it must always have as its proper object the Cross of Christ, i.e., *"The Finished Work."*

GOD'S PRESCRIBED ORDER OF VICTORY

There is only one prescribed order, and that is the Cross.

The Believer is to understand, even as we've already stated, that the same Faith that brought him into Christ at his initial conversion, is the same Faith that must continue to be evidenced in the same Cross, regarding his everyday walk before the Lord.

Faith in the Cross, means Faith in the Finished Work of Christ. Faith in that signifies that man knows that he cannot accomplish this task himself, and must depend solely upon Christ. That's our problem, we tend to think that we can get things done, whatever they might be, within our own strength and ability.

Untold millions of unsaved people think they are saved, because they perform good works or something of that nature. They aren't! The only way to Salvation is by trusting in what Jesus did at the Cross on our behalf. As well, when we speak of the Cross we are also at the same time speaking of the Resurrection.

Unfortunately, we have many Christians doing the same identical thing as unbelievers. As unbelievers attempt to find Salvation by their own works, millions of Christians attempt to find victory through their own works. While they are saved, victory to be sure, alludes them completely. In fact, they are dominated by sin in some fashion, despite all of their efforts to do otherwise.

As the sinner placed his trust in Christ and the Cross as it refers to his Salvation, the Believer is to maintain his Faith in the Cross in the same manner.

When Jesus died on the Cross, He died as our Substitute. He was our Representative Man. Our Faith in Him, in the Mind of God, places us actually in Christ. In other words, God looks at us upon our Faith in Christ, as if we paid the price ourselves, which, of course, we could not do.

Nevertheless, the Lord, upon our Faith looks at us, as baptized into Christ at His death. All of this is found in Romans 6:3-5.

It is the same when Christ was buried and raised from the dead. We were literally *"in Him,"* when all of this was done.

Of course, we know that we were not actually in Him. In fact, we did not even exist then; nevertheless, our Faith in Him, and in Him Alone, grants us this position. The secret, even as we've already stated, is being *"in Christ."* Consequently, we are to remain *"in Christ,"* as it regards our everyday walk before the Lord. The Believer may ask as to how that we could not be in Christ, if in fact we are saved?

The Truth is, the Believer does remain in Christ, irrespective of his erroneous directions. But when we try to do things for ourselves, such as trying to gain victory by some machinations of our own, which I've already listed, theoretically we are taking ourselves out of Christ, even though God does not actually do that — remove us from Christ.

FAITH IN THE CROSS

Irrespective, whenever we begin to try to obtain Victory by any one of the methods just mentioned, or others I've not mentioned, the Holy Spirit Who we desperately need in all of this, simply will not help us. He will not help us because we are not functioning in the confines of the Finished Work of Christ, and as such, we tie His Hands (Rom. 8:1-2). So, we fail, as fail we must!

If Christ was victorious at the Cross, and He definitely was, then due to the fact that we *were* in Him, and *are* in Him, we are victorious as well. We must understand that and act upon that.

All of this is done by Faith, in other words, Faith in what He has done, and did it all on our behalf. Faith in that manner will always guarantee the help of the Holy Spirit, which guarantees us victory. That is the only Source of Victory, and in fact, is the only Source that is needed. If we try to pull anything else into the mix, we fail, simply because we then deny ourselves the help of the Holy Spirit, considering that He will work only according to the Finished Work of Christ. Consequently, the Cross must always be the object of our Faith, and never other things, or anything else for that matter, which the Lord will not honor. Victory is always in the Cross, and only in the Cross. It is there where the power is found, i.e., *"the manner in which the Holy Spirit works."*

Paul said, *"For the preaching of the Cross is to them that perish foolishness; but unto us which are saved it is the Power of God"* (I Cor. 1:18).

How is it the Power of God?

It is such because the Cross is the Finished Work of Christ, through which the Holy Spirit works, and only through which the Holy Spirit will work. He has the Power, and He uses that Power on our behalf, according to our Faith in the great Sacrifice of Christ.

Why is it so hard for Believers to see this?

DELIVERANCE

If one is to notice, Jesus said, *"The Spirit of the Lord is upon Me, because He hath anointed Me to preach the Gospel to the poor; He hath sent me to heal the brokenhearted, to preach deliverance to the captives, and recovering of sight to the blind, to set at liberty them that are bruised"* (Lk. 4:18).

If one is to notice, Jesus said *"to preach deliverance."* He didn't say, *"He hath sent me to deliver the captives."* In fact, captives are delivered, but through what He did at the Cross.

We have Preachers running around trying to deliver people, when in fact, everyone has already been delivered. Jesus did all of that at the Cross, and that's what we mean by *"The Finished Work."* In other words, the Lord does not have to do anything else to deliver anyone from anything, simply because it has already been done. It's a matter of one having Faith in that which has already been done, namely the Cross and the Resurrection.

So, the idea that Preachers can lay hands on people and deliver them from particular bondages of darkness, is erroneous. While the laying on of hands and the praying over people are definitely Scriptural, it should always be done in the context of a Work that Christ has already done.

It is the same with Salvation. In the Mind of God, when Jesus died on the Cross, He died for the entirety of the world. So for a person to be saved, the Lord does not have to do anything else, the person simply has to receive it. It is the same with anything and everything that the Lord does for humanity. The Cross paid it all, did it all, finished it all, concluded it all. Every single thing that man lost at the Fall, Jesus addressed in the Atonement. Admittedly, we do not now have all the benefits of what He actually did at the Cross, the totality awaiting the coming Resurrection. But we do have enough at the present to have victory over sin in every capacity.

Let me ask you, Dear Reader, this question:

If you or someone you know needs deliverance or victory as it concerns some problem within your or their life, and you want the Lord to do something for you, what do you think that He is going to do?

If you were to answer this question, you would probably say that He would exert His Power, and remove the problem from your life, whatever it might be.

To be frank, such thinking is not actually Scriptural.

When it comes to sin or bondages of some nature in the life of a Believer, or unbelievers for that matter, there is nothing that the Lord has to do further, than He has already done at the Cross. Every problem of that nature was addressed there.

While it is definitely true that the Lord delivers us from Satan's attacks as it regards particular evil plans formed against us concerning our work for the Lord, that is in fact something different. Paul said:

"Who delivered us from so great a death, and doth deliver: in Whom we trust that He will yet deliver us" (II Cor. 1:10).

However, Paul was not speaking here of victory over sin, but rather something else entirely. When it comes to the sin question, which every Christian has to address, that deliverance has already been effected in totality at the Cross.

CONSTANT FAITH IN THE CROSS

Jesus said, *"If any man will come after Me, let him deny himself* (deny his own abilities and personal strength), *and take up his Cross daily, and follow Me"* (Lk. 9:23).

If one is to notice, Jesus told us that this must be done on a *"daily"* basis. What did He mean by that?

He meant that we are to place our Faith in the Cross, which speaks of what He did there, even doing so on a *daily* basis. Unfortunately, when most Christians read this Scripture, they think the Lord is talking about suffering of some sort, which in reality He is, but in a totally different way than most think.

He is speaking of the suffering that *He* carried out on the Cross, and not some type of suffering that we might have to undergo. In fact, taking up the Cross on a daily basis is the most glorious and wonderful thing that a Christian can ever do. That alone guarantees victory.

Unfortunately, the Devil has caused Christians to have an erroneous view of this which Jesus has spoken, causing Christians to shy away from that which is their actual source of *"more abundant life"* (Jn. 10:10).

WHY DAILY?

By Jesus using the word *"daily,"* it means that we are to renew our Faith in the Cross on a daily basis, and continue to do so in that capacity. He does this for a reason.

If our Faith were a one-time thing, the Believer would soon come to think that it is his power, his strength, his etc., that's bringing about the victory. Having to renew our Faith on a daily basis, understanding that this is necessary, keeps us trusting the Lord, which is the intention of the Holy Spirit.

In some way, this is basically the same thing as the Manna of old. The Children of Israel were to gather only enough to do them and their family for that particular day, trusting that the Lord would send more tomorrow, which He always did. Actually, they were told that if they gathered more than enough and tried to store such, that it would breed worms and stink.

He was teaching the Children of Israel continued Faith, exactly as Jesus did here concerning the Cross (Rom. 1:17).

The Faith that I had yesterday was good for that particular time, but the Lord has so designed this situation that it will not suffice for today. I must have fresh Faith each and every day, which the Lord always gives, that is if we continue to place our Faith and Trust in the Cross of Christ. That's what Jesus meant by *"taking up the Cross daily."* (The daily taking up of the Cross also has to do with *"self,"* of which we will address to a greater extent later.)

MORE ABUNDANT LIFE

Not only is the Cross the way of victory over all sin, it is also the key to *"more abundant life"* and as well, the *"rest"* that Jesus promised (Jn. 10:10; Mat. 11:28-30).

In fact, this is the greatest life, the most joyous life, the most abundant life, that a person could ever have. This is the key to all victory, all successful living, all power, and victory over Satan. In fact, it is impossible for the Believer to fully know, to fully have, to fully enjoy all that Salvation is, without proper Faith in the Cross.

Many, if not most, Christians are presently struggling with sin in some capacity. They may not refer to it as that, or label it as such, but that's what it is. As previously stated, the Church is very good at hiding its head in the sand, in other words living in a state of denial. The problem with the Believer is sin and not something else. If victory can be obtained in that department, victory can be obtained in all things.

How many Christians have looked at Jesus' Words in Matthew 11:28, when He said, *"Come unto Me, all ye that labour and are heavy laden, and I will give you rest,"* and wondered exactly what He was talking about? In fact, most Christians don't really have the *"rest"* of which Jesus spoke.

Why not?

If our Faith is in other than the Cross, we are in a struggle, in fact, a struggle which always places us on the losing side. Consequently, there is no *"rest,"* in that capacity.

The only way in which the Believer can have *"rest,"* exactly as Jesus promised, is to trust what He has already done as it regards the Cross and the Resurrection. This means that the Work is finished, and that there is nothing else for us to do except simply have Faith in what He has already done (Rom. 3:27).

Our lack of rest comes about because we are struggling through our own efforts to overcome the Evil One, and always failing. Consequently, we generally increase the struggle, which means to increase the effort, with failure continuing to come just the same. Much of the Church is in that category at present. They don't know the way to victory, so they keep trying to work themselves out of this morass by their own efforts, with the situation not growing better but rather growing worse.

When our Faith is properly placed, and continued in that capacity, and I speak of the Cross, we are then *"resting"* in what He has already done, and which we don't need to try to do all over again, and in fact, which we cannot do no matter how hard we try. One of the greatest insults to Christ is attempting to add to that which He has already done, and which needs no addition whatsoever.

In fact, I believe at least one of the greatest sins that a Christian commits, is our own personal efforts in attempting to bring about victory through our own machinations, while ignoring the Finished Work of Christ.

Admittedly, we generally don't do this thing intentionally, but nevertheless, that's what it falls out to be. Consequently, it is an insult to Christ, an insult to His great Sacrifice, an insult to the great Plan of God as it regards our Redemption.

THE PREACHING OF THE CROSS

While I am being repetitive, possibly even overly so, this Truth is so significant, so vital as it regards the welfare of the Christian, that I do not feel it is possible to overstate the case. The problem with the Church is, that in the last nearly 50 years, there has been so little preaching on the Cross, that the Church has been moved away from its foundation. Consequently, it is building a house on sand, which the first storm will dislodge, and in fact, is happening constantly.

We've had 40 years of teaching on Faith, most of it wrong, plus other things, but almost no teaching on the Cross of Christ. Consequently, we have a generation of Christians who little know or understand the source of their Victory, the means of their Victory, and the way of their Victory. The Cross to most Christians is little more than a pretty ornament that they can hang around their neck, etc.

In fact, much of the Charismatic community actually degrades the Cross, referring to it as *"past miseries."* They call the Cross, the greatest place of weakness in history.

In one sense that is correct, in that Jesus purposely allowed Himself to die in weakness, but in that weakness the strength and power of Redemption were brought forth, which was accomplished through His Death and Resurrection. In fact, that very so-called weakness translates into Power and Victory for the Child of God. To which we've already quoted, Paul called the preaching of the Cross, *"the Power of God"* (I Cor. 1:18).

If the Church is not a Cross Church, if the Message is not a Cross Message, if the Way is not a Cross Way, then whatever it is will fall out to no victory for the Child of God. From Genesis to Revelation, the Cross is held up as the Source of Victory, and that alone.

THE CROSS WAY

While the Sacrifices of the Old Testament, which were symbolic of the Cross, were the centerpiece of the Old Covenant, the Cross itself is the centerpiece of the New Covenant. If men are to be saved, the Preacher in some way, has to preach the Cross. If Christians are to have Victory, the Preacher in some manner and in some way, has to preach the Cross.

Of course, there are other subjects in the Word of God, but if one inspects these subjects closely, whatever they might be, one will find each and all tie into the Cross in some way. In fact, the Baptism with the Holy Spirit could not be brought about in the hearts and lives of Believers, until the Cross and the Resurrection along with the Ascension. What Jesus did at the Cross satisfied the claims of Heavenly Justice, satisfied the curse of the broken Law, which paid the sin debt and broke Satan's grip on humanity, at least for those who will believe. Consequently, the Holy Spirit can now come and abide in the hearts and lives of Believers, which He does at conversion (Mat. 3:11). However, all of this which we now have, we could not have until the Cross was effected (Jn. 14:17).

Our Sanctification comes through the Cross; our Justification comes through the Cross; our Reconciliation comes totally and completely through the Cross; our Divine Healing comes through the Cross, as well as does our financial prosperity.

If one cannot see that as they read and study the Word of God, then they are not reading the Word of God as it should be read, which means that the Word should mold our thinking, instead of us trying to get the Word to match our thinking.

Satan hates the Cross moreso than he hates anything else, because it was here that He was defeated. He doesn't mind whatever else we project, whatever else we put forth, whatever method we choose, just so it's not the Cross. In fact, he will aid and abet all other methods, while tenaciously fighting the Cross, and for all the obvious reasons. In fact, he uses the Church more than all to oppose the Cross. That is the greatest tragedy of all!

Irrespective, Paul said, *"But we preach Christ crucified* (not just preach Christ, but rather preach Christ and Him crucified, which refers of course to the Cross and what was accomplished there), *unto the Jews a stumblingblock, and unto the Greeks foolishness."*

And then he said, *"But unto them which are called, both Jews and Greeks* (the entirety of the world), *Christ the Power of God* (the power is in the Crucifixion and the Resurrection), *and the Wisdom of God* (the Cross is the Way of God and the Wisdom of God, relative to the Redemption of humanity. Consequently, anyone who attempts to institute another way of Salvation, is, in effect, saying that they are wiser than God, which is a position that no sensible person wants to take)." (I Cor. 1:23-24).

(2) "BEWARE OF DOGS, BEWARE OF EVIL WORKERS, BEWARE OF THE CONCISION."

The Verses which follow warrant the identification of these opponents as the Judaizers — those who dogged the trail of the Apostle and endeavored to compel Gentile converts to submit to Circumcision and other Jewish practices in order to be saved. Three epithets designate them:

1. *"Dogs"*: This denotes the wild, vicious, homeless animals that roam the streets and attack passersby. Used figuratively as it of course is here, it was always a term of reproach (Deut. 23:18; I Sam. 17:43; 24:14; Prov. 26:11; Isa. 56:10-11).

Jesus used it in reference to opponents of God's Truth (Mat. 7:6), and Jews often used it similarly of Gentiles. Paul turns the figure back upon the Judaizing teachers and castigates them with the very term they probably used of others.

2. *"Evil workers"*: If the word *"workers"* is stressed, and it is, the epithet may emphasize the energetic labors of these individuals and perhaps their concentration on performing deeds of Law rather than trusting God's Grace.

In other words, the work they were carrying out, though in the Name of the Lord, and under the guise of the Work of the Lord, was in fact the very opposite, i.e., *"the work of the Devil,"* hence being referred to by Paul as *"evil!"* We will deal with that more fully a little later.

3. *"The concision"*: This is an abbreviated way of saying *"Circumcision,"* i.e.,

"those who circumcise, claiming that such was needed in order to ensure Salvation."

Paul deliberately parodies the Judaizers' insistence on Circumcision by sarcastically calling it mutilation — in other words, just a cutting of the flesh which holds no spiritual connotation at all.

DOGS

The phrase, *"Beware of dogs,"* actually carries two strong particulars which we should investigate:

The first particular is *"beware."* It carries the idea of constantly observing with a view to avoiding, constantly on the lookout for that of which is spoken here, in this case the Judaizers.

Even though this particular danger is not pertinent at this particular time (1999), and I speak of Judaizers; nevertheless, the word *"beware"* is intended by the Holy Spirit to apply to any and all false doctrine.

There is a power about false doctrine and that power is actually evil spirits, who, in effect, are the instigators of all that is error as it pertains to the Gospel. Paul also said, *"Now the Spirit speaketh expressly, that in the latter times* (the times in which we now live, in fact) *some shall depart from the Faith* (depart from the Cross), *giving heed to seducing spirits, and doctrines of Devils"* (I Tim. 4:1).

To be sure, when Satan through *"his ministers"* (II Cor. 11:13-15), presents false doctrine, he always does it as an *"Angel of light,"* i.e., *"by that which looks like it's of the Lord and in fact does contain some truth, which is in fact, 'the hook'"* (II Cor. 11:14).

So, the reason that false doctrine is so powerful is because it's not the mere presentation of a mere philosophy, but rather a lie fabricated by Satan and with his power of deception. As stated, it is almost always accompanied by some Truth which serves as the hook.

Using the Judaizers as an example, there is every evidence that these individuals, whomever they may have been, touted Jesus Christ which served as the hook. The idea was, that after accepting Christ, these Gentiles must go on and then enter into the Law of Moses, by first of all having the boys and men engage in Circumcision. No doubt, the intentions of the Judaizers were to start with that Rite, and then proceed to Sabbath-keeping, etc. (Col. 2:14-17).

As Believers then were told by the Apostle, or actually the Holy Spirit through the Apostle, to *"beware"* of any and all who proclaim any gospel other than that proclaimed by Paul, which, in effect, was *"Jesus Christ and Him crucified,"* as the Way of Salvation, and that alone (I Cor. 2:2), He is saying the same presently. In fact, Paul had said to the Churches in Galatia, *"But though we, or an Angel from Heaven, preach any other gospel unto you than that which we have preached unto you, let him be accursed (damned)"* (Gal. 1:8).

If the Believer does not properly know and understand the Word of God, as regrettably is the case with many, if not most, that Believer is a prime target for false doctrine. That's the reason I plead with Christians over whom I might have some small influence, to study the Word of God, to avail themselves of study helps such as this Commentary, in order to learn more and more about that which is the single most important thing in the world, the Bible. In fact, the study of the Bible ought to be a daily process, a habit if you will, actually continuing if you will, until the Lord calls us home, or the Trump sounds. In the first place, it is impossible to exhaust the Word of God. Inasmuch as it is the Word of God, and, therefore, alive one might say, it is totally unlike anything else in the world in the form of literature, history, or philosophy, etc. It stands alone in its class, but sadly with most Christians little knowing, or at least properly knowing its contents. So, the targets are big, bold, and obvious, of which Satan takes full advantage.

AROUSED ANGER

I have no doubt that the Judaizers and their sympathizers literally hated Paul, especially considering that he called them *"dogs,"* among other things! Consequently, their opposition toward him was fierce indeed, constantly seeking to tear down his character and reputation, by a constant denigration of his person. It is no less at the present time.

I suppose that's the reason that most Preachers back off from taking a stand on much of anything, unless it is *"safe,"* i.e., *"they oppose things which everyone opposes, even the Devil it seems."*

Considering that the Leaders of the largest Pentecostal Denominations in the United States and Canada have opted totally and completely in favor of humanistic psychology, I have taken frightful abuse from this source because of my opposition to this humanistic wisdom which actually is *"earthly, sensual, Devilish"* (James 3:15).

The same can go for music. Most of the music in many Churches can be labelled as none other than *"abominable."* We have individuals attempting to ape the world in copying their ungodly styles, thinking somehow in this demented, spiritual state, that this is going to win the youth. Regrettably, that is so preposterous that it beggars description!

One doesn't win the drunk by drinking with him, or the gambler by gambling with him, etc.

People are won to Christ as the True Gospel is preached, and sang incidentally, with it then being anointed by the Holy Spirit, Who Alone can draw the lost to Christ, and keep the Christians in Christ. Anything else is doomed to failure, and failure of the worst sort.

And yet, many, if not most, Churches presently employ Contemporary Christian music as it regards their youth programs, which constitutes not only the ways of the world, but the actual deployment of Satan himself.

Making these statements in no way endears me to the practitioners of this ungodly medium.

I could say the same for that which I have labelled the *"prosperity gospel,"* which basically incorporates most of that which goes under the heading of the *"Faith Ministry,"* etc. Money is the object there, and not Righteousness and Holiness by any means. Unfortunately, there seems to be enough greed in all of us to make this so-called gospel very appealing.

Some may wonder as to why I *"harp"* on these particular subjects so much. I do so for the same reason that Paul addressed the Judaizers so much. That was the danger then, and these things I have mentioned are the dangers now. Of course, these are not the only dangers, but they are I think presently the most acute.

A GOOD CHURCH

While there certainly are some good Churches which means they are pastored by Godly men, regrettably they are not nearly as numerous as one would like. In fact, they are few and far between. The truth is, false doctrine is taught behind most pulpits, designed to lead people away from Christ, toward whatever agenda the Preacher is promoting.

It is long since gone, and I speak of the privilege of identifying doctrine by the name on the Church door. That may have once been the case at least to a degree, but is not the case whatsoever anymore. In other words, the name on the Church door, gives no indication whatsoever as to what is taught behind that particular pulpit. So, that means if Christians are attending Churches just because it is the Denomination they favor, they have just become a perfect target for Satan. The time has come, that Believers must forget Denominational tags or particular type Churches. One must look exclusively toward the Word of God, and the Preacher who unfailingly preaches that Word without compromise, which alone the Holy Spirit will bless, or else that Believer will be led astray.

But again I come back to the original statement, that so many Believers are so dense regarding the Word, that they have little knowledge as to the veracity of what they are hearing. In other words, they judge what is preached too often not according to what the Bible says, but according to other things entirely, such as popular opinion, conventional wisdom, what things are surface perceived, etc. As I've said many times, Satan is a past master at making Christians believe that which is actually of God, isn't, and that which isn't of God, is!

You need to read those words carefully.

DOGS

The second strong emphasis in this phrase is the epithet which Paul used to describe these Judaizers. He called them *"dogs,"* which was about the worst thing that anyone could be called, at least in the culture of that day.

First of all, Jews hated dogs. It was almost never that they had one has a pet. They were looked at as mongrels, scavengers, filthy, therefore, strongly rejected in any and every capacity. In other words they didn't like dogs!

So, When Paul uses this word, he is insulting these teachers in the most base way that they could be insulted. Of course, these teachers were Jews, and, therefore, the insult all the greater. When we realize that the Holy Spirit sanctioned this insult, and he definitely did, then we begin to realize how serious the entirety of this situation actually is.

The Jews regarded dogs as grossly unclean because they would eat almost anything, showing no distinction between clean and unclean food, etc. So, Paul in using this epithet, is actually saying that the Judaizers do not know the difference in that which is spiritually clean and spiritually unclean, i.e., the *false*, which is anything other than the Crucified Christ, and the *true*, which is the Salvation furnished by Christ Alone by His Death on the Cross and Resurrection. Actually, the term was used at least in one instance by the Saviour (Mat. 7:6).

As someone as said, *"there is nothing worse than a false way of Salvation."* One could also say, there is nothing worse than the Preachers who promote a false way of Salvation.

THE END RESULTS OF A FALSE WAY

If we were speaking here of mere political opinions, or even philosophical ideas, that would be something else altogether; however, we're speaking here of the eternal soul of man and where it will spend eternity. At this very moment, untold millions, even billions, are on their way to a Devil's Hell, even though they in fact think they are saved.

Why do they think they are saved, when in fact they aren't?

They think they are saved because they have believed a lie, a lie incidentally told by a Preacher or a Priest, or someone. These individuals, and as stated they number into the billions, have refused God's Way of Salvation, which is Jesus Christ and Him Crucified, and have rather accepted something else which looks real, and in fact, is very religious, but actually isn't real, i.e., *"not Scriptural."* To be sure, there aren't ten ways of Salvation, or five, or even two. There is only One, and that One Way is Jesus Christ, and even above that, the death He died on the Cross, in which the sinner must believe or he cannot be saved (Jn. 10:1).

Therefore, considering the significance of this of which we say, which pertains to the eternal destiny of the eternal soul, those who would devise a false way, thereby leading untold millions to eternal perdition, can only be described as *"dogs."*

As stated, these words as uttered by Paul in no way endeared him to those who promoted these false doctrines. In fact, they hated him, and sought by every means to hinder or hurt his ministry. Their modern contemporaries to be sure, do no less presently.

THE MODERN CHURCH

Most reading this really do not understand that Satan's greatest effort at spiritual destruction, does not come from outside the Church, but rather from inside the Church. In fact, Jesus said that the Church in the last days, for all practical purposes, and looking at it as a whole, would be totally corrupted. He said the following:

"The Kingdom of Heaven (in this instance the Church) *is like unto leaven* (figurative of sin), *which a woman took* (in this case, the woman represents evil), *and hid in three measures of meal* (the mixture of false and true in the meal, which is a symbol of the Word of God), *till the whole was leavened* (the entirety of the Church corrupted)" (Mat. 13:33).

So, the matter at hand, is not that of isolated situations, but rather that which has settled over the modern Church like a shroud, with but very few exceptions.

Yes, there are some Preachers preaching the Truth, but not many! There are some Believers living for God in a victorious sense, but not many! Most have succumbed or are in the process of succumbing.

Consequently, I will close this thought by saying exactly what Paul said, *"beware of dogs."*

EVIL WORKERS

The phrase, *"Beware of evil workers,"* refers not merely to evil doers, but to those who actually wrought against the Gospel of Grace. In other words, in order to peddle their false message of Law, they at the same time made every effort to denigrate the Gospel of Grace. Consequently, I think it would be obvious as to the terrible evil of such an effort, when one realizes that these individuals were actually denigrating the Cross of Christ and that Salvation is obtained by Faith alone in that Finished Work. That's why it's referred to by the Holy Spirit as *"evil."* Actually, it can be defined in no other terms.

THE PRESENT DAY

For instance, Preachers who ignore the Cross of Christ and the Sacrificial Work accomplished there by our Lord, instead recommending humanistic psychology as the answer to the aberrations of mankind, can be referred to as none other than *"evil."* The same can be said, and in fact must be said, of every other false message.

I would even go so far as to say that Preachers who deny the Baptism with the Holy Spirit with the evidence of speaking with other tongues, fall into the same category. To be sure, that was not always the case, simply due to the fact that up until the Twentieth Century, there was very little teaching on the Holy Spirit, and, therefore, very little understanding as it regards this all-important subject. So, the Preachers of those days and times walked in all the light they had, and God blessed some of them greatly, giving them many souls, etc.

However, in this Century, and especially the latter half of this Century the great Message of the Holy Spirit has been proliferated all over the world. In fact, there are probably at this present time approximately one hundred million people Baptized with the Holy Spirit, with the evidence of speaking with other tongues (Acts 2:4). Actually, in the last half of the Twentieth Century, Preachers and entire Denominations have had to make a choice. They could accept the Baptism with the Holy Spirit as taught in the Scriptures, and demanded by Jesus Christ (Acts 1:4), or they could reject this great Message of the Word of God. Regrettably, even though many Preachers in the denominational world did accept this which is totally Biblical, it was rejected by the far greater majority. As a result, at this particular time, there is almost nothing of any spiritual consequence going on in these particular Churches and Denominations. They are almost totally void of any spiritual results to speak of.

While there may be much religious machinery, and in fact even much activity, still, in those particular circles, very few souls are being saved, and very few lives being changed.

Unfortunately, most of the Denominations which claim to be Pentecostal, have abandoned the Holy Spirit in favor of other things, i.e., *"humanistic psychology."*

Am I being too harsh when I refer to those who have rejected the Holy Spirit as *"evil,"* or even to those who have abandoned the Holy Spirit as *"evil"*?

I don't think I am! I think when we all stand at the Judgment Seat of Christ, we will then see how important all of this actually was and is.

The word *"workers"* insinuates that these Preachers were working this evil, i.e., *"working their false doctrine."*

We have reached the time when the Christian had better look at his situation very minutely and very carefully. As stated, we're not speaking here of mundane things, but rather the consequences of the eternal soul. Is what you are hearing in your Church the True Gospel? You had better look at that question very carefully and do your best to answer it very properly. An awful lot is at stake!

Are you attending a Church simply because of the name on the door, or because of what is being taught and preached behind the pulpit?

Worse yet, are you attending a certain Church because it's popular to attend there, in fact, that's your real reason for your association?

Have you tried to find a Church, and they are easily found, which will agree with your sin, in other words making you feel comfortable in your sin?

Are you attending a Church where there is very little moving, if any, of the Holy Spirit, which means that the Spirit of God never convicts anyone of sin, of Righteousness, and of Judgment? Many people desire these type of Churches, because then they are never made to feel uncomfortable.

Every Believer needs to ask himself some questions, and then try to answer those questions. When we consider that we are speaking of the single most important thing there is, and I'm speaking of your eternal soul, we must give these questions all diligence.

CIRCUMCISION

The phrase, *"Beware of the concision"* presents a Greek word which Paul uses as a play upon the Greek word *"circumcision."* Paul characterizes those who were not of the true circumcision (the circumcision of the heart through acceptance of Jesus Christ), as merely mutilated. In fact, heathen priests mutilated their own bodies.

So, the Apostle is saying that the Judaizers mutilated the Message of the Gospel by attempting to add Law to Grace, and thus their own spiritual lives and those who accepted their false message.

It is not meant here to be understood that Paul intended to throw contempt on Circumcision as originally enjoined by God, and as practiced by Godly Jews of other times, but only as it was held by the false Judaizing teachers.

In fact, as they held it, it was not the true Circumcision. They made Salvation depend on it, instead of it being only a sign of the Covenant with God, which it was originally intended to be, as given originally to Abraham and Moses.

Such a doctrine, as they held it, was a mere cutting off of the flesh, without understanding anything of the true nature of the Rite; and hence the unusual term by which Paul designates it.

Perhaps also, there may be included the idea that a doctrine so held would be, in fact, a cutting off of the soul; that is, that it tended to destruction, that is if total dependence was placed on that instead of Christ, which is exactly what Satan desired.

Considering the seriousness of all this, I think we should look at it a little further.

CAN A TRUE CHRISTIAN LOSE HIS SOUL BY ACCEPTING FALSE DOCTRINE?

It is obvious from the Scriptures that any Believer can cease to trust Christ if he so desires, and if he does, he has left his Salvation, which can only be found in Christ, and if remaining in that condition will be eternally lost.

As well, there are some Christians who want both sin and Salvation at the same time, which in fact cannot be done. In other words, they want to practice some particular sin while at the same time maintaining their Salvation. Unfortunately, they have been told in some Church circles that they can do this and continue to be saved. John plainly said, *"Whosoever is born of God* (saved) *doth not commit* (practice) *sin; for his seed remaineth in him* (the seed of the Gospel)*: and he cannot sin* (cannot continue to practice sin)*, because he is Born of God"* (I Jn. 3:9).

John is not teaching sinless perfection, nor is it taught in the Word of God; however, that the Christian can go on living a life of the perpetual practice of sinning and at the same time maintain Salvation, is anathema to the Word of God. Paul's answer to such a lifestyle is, *"God forbid"* (Rom. 6:2).

As well, Paul perfectly described Believers, in this case Jewish Believers who had accepted Christ as their personal Saviour, but now because of discouragement or whatever reason, were contemplating going back into Judaism.

Of such he said, *"For it is impossible . . . if they shall fall away* (from Christ), *to renew them again unto repentance; seeing they crucify to themselves the Son of God afresh, and put Him to an open shame"* (Heb. 6:1-6).

He wasn't saying that a person couldn't come back to Christ after forsaking Christ, but that if they set aside Christ and His Atoning Work at the Cross, refusing to believe in such any longer, they have forfeited Salvation, because Christ and the Cross and Faith in that, provide the only way of Salvation (Jn. 3:16; Eph. 2:8-9; Rev. 22:17).

He basically said the same thing in the Tenth Chapter of Hebrews. In that Chapter he is speaking of the Shed Blood of Christ, and all that such refers to as it regards Salvation.

He then said, *"For if we sin wilfully* (which means to willfully forsake Christ and what He did at the Cross) *after that we have received the knowledge of the Truth* (after one has been saved)*, there remaineth no more sacrifice for sins."*

He then seals it by saying, that those who would do such a thing, *"Who hath trodden* under foot the Son of God *(denying what Christ did at the Cross), and hath counted the Blood of the Covenant* (the Blood Jesus shed at the Cross), *wherewith he* (the Sinner) *was sanctified* (the sinner was saved by accepting what Christ did at the Cross), *an unholy thing* (regarding not at all the Crucifixion of Christ), *and hath done despite unto the Spirit of Grace* (has repudiated the only means of Salvation which alone the Holy Spirit recognizes)," that person is going to come under *"a certain fearful looking for of judgment and fiery indignation, which shall devour the adversaries* (be eternally lost)" (Heb. 10:26-31).

Some Preachers attempt to pass off these Passages in Hebrews as sinners merely looking into the Gospel but really having not accepted it; however, such interpretation is foolishness. These individuals had accepted Christ, had been saved, and no doubt, Baptized with the Holy Spirit. But as stated, because of discouragement or for whatever reason, they were thinking about going back into Judaism, which would also mean to repudiate Christ and all He did at the Cross — if they did this, and refused again to entertain Faith in Christ and the Cross, they would die eternally lost. It should be obvious, if one does not believe in what Christ did at the Cross, one cannot be saved.

As well, to say that it's not possible for one who has actually been saved to then do such a thing, is to plainly ignore simple Passages which say otherwise.

Therefore, we know from these particular Passages, and many others we could name, that it is possible for a Believer to quit believing, and to, therefore, lose his soul.

What about these Believers at Philippi, who in fact, are warned by Paul.

A DIFFERENCE

The Believers at Philippi, and this would include Corinth and Galatia as well, were not considering repudiating Christ. In fact, the Judaizers were not demanding they do this, but rather just to add Law to Grace.

Could they lose their soul doing this?

Of course, each individual case would have to stand or fall on its own merit or the lack thereof, with God Alone being the Judge.

NOTES

On the surface, no, they would not lose their souls, but they definitely would be seriously weakened, spiritually speaking. Any degree of false doctrine which is accepted by a Believer, to that particular degree will that person be spiritually weakened. Of course, some error is much more lethal than others.

Any error that attacks in some way the Atonement, i.e., *"The Finished Work of Christ,"* is serious indeed, and for the simple reason, that we're speaking of the very foundation of Salvation. This much is guaranteed, to the degree that one has a false understanding of the Finished Work of Christ, to that degree will everything else they believe be somewhat colored as well. Of course, that could be said in some measure about all false doctrine.

For instance, even as we've already addressed, Preachers who do not believe in the Baptism with the Holy Spirit, with the evidence of speaking with other Tongues, can definitely be saved. However, they are greatly shortchanging themselves, as well as their followers.

THE HARM DONE BY FALSE DOCTRINE

Salvation consists solely of one's acceptance of Christ and what He did at the Cross. One can believe that and be saved, even as millions are, and then believe other things which are error. While not hindering their Salvation, such error, whatever it might be, definitely does hinder their spiritual growth, in fact, causing great problems. I suppose I can say without fear of exaggeration, that this has happened to some degree to every single Believer who has ever lived.

There are millions of Christians presently, in fact most, who are not living victorious over sin, simply because they do not properly understand the part the Cross plays in their everyday walk before the Lord, thinking that the Cross pertains only to their initial Salvation experience. Consequently, they depend on other things for victory, which always leaves them in the lurch, so to speak, with the problem continuing to get worse instead of better. They are saved, but their spiritual growth, due to this error, has been seriously hindered.

God is patient, merciful, and kind. He responds to faith. It's quite possible, as stated, for a person to have proper faith in the Cross as it regards Salvation, and then have improper faith as it regards their Sanctification. In fact, this was the reason that Paul wrote the Epistle to the Galatians. He said of them, *"Are ye so foolish? Having begun in the Spirit* (they had been saved the correct, Biblical way by believing in what Christ did at the Cross), *are ye now made perfect by the flesh?* (Do you think you can bring about your Sanctification regarding a holy, righteous life, by resorting to machinations other than the Spirit?)" (Gal. 3:3).

Having listened to the Judaizers, the Galatians were beginning to believe wrong, which of course would hinder their spiritual growth, even as is very obvious. They were saved, but to be sure, they were about to cause themselves untold problems.

So, there are many, if not most, Believers who genuinely know Christ, trusting Him for their Salvation according to the Cross, but at the same time have some erroneous ideas about other things. I think I can say, even to which I have already alluded, that all of us have fallen into this trap at one time or the other.

Consequently, a Believer does not lose his soul because he believes erroneous doctrine as it regards matters other than the Cross. But, if he has an erroneous idea of the true Way of Salvation as it regards being saved, he can definitely be lost.

For instance, if a person truly accepts Christ, and then they are told that the taking of the Lord's Supper constitutes Salvation, and they shift their Faith from the Cross to that particular Ordinance, they can lose their soul, as should be obvious. Even though the Lord's Supper is a very Scriptural Ordinance, in which every Believer ought to participate, the Truth is, there is no Salvation in that Ordinance, the same as there is no Salvation in Circumcision. One cannot have it both ways.

If the Believers at Philippi, had in fact succumbed to Circumcision, and then shifted their faith to Circumcision, thinking they are saved because of that particular physical Rite, if they continue in that vein, they definitely could lose their souls. Proper Faith in Christ must be enjoined at the beginning in order for a person to be saved, and must be maintained throughout one's life in order to continue in

NOTES

Grace. There is no other way! In fact, this is why Paul warned them so severely.

At the same time, it is not my place to judge any person as it regards their Salvation. Only God can do that; however, as a Preacher of the Gospel it is definitely my responsibility to warn of these particular dangers. And to be sure, acute dangers they are!

Once again, that's why it is so very important as to where you attend Church, as to what Preachers to whom you listen, etc.

(3) "FOR WE ARE THE CIRCUMCISION, WHICH WORSHIP GOD IN THE SPIRIT, AND REJOICE IN CHRIST JESUS, AND HAVE NO CONFIDENCE IN THE FLESH."

Paul follows the above warning with an explanation. Christians, and of course, we speak of those who have truly accepted Christ and what He did at Calvary on our behalf, are the real Circumcision, not the Judaizers who insisted on the physical Rite. In fact, he elsewhere refers to those who have received the Circumcision of the heart, whether they be Jew or Gentile (Rom. 2:25-29; Col. 2:11). Actually, this concept was no innovation, for the Old Testament spoke of it frequently (Lev. 26:41; Deut. 10:16; 30:6; Jer. 4:4; Ezek. 44:7).

As should be obvious, Paul was not going outside of Old Testament boundaries regarding his Doctrine, but in fact, staying very much within those boundaries. The Judaizers misunderstood Old Testament Doctrine as well as Christian teaching. The Law of Moses was never meant to be permanent. It was only given to show man how sinful he was and to show him his inability in keeping the Law. In fact, he simply could not keep it, despite it being the Standard of God. As we explained elsewhere, the Law was like a road that led from one place to another destination. In fact, the destination was Christ.

After Paul came to Christ, he then understood the Old Testament, which of course included the great Law of Moses. In other words, the Word of God being spiritually discerned only, could not be understood by the Apostle before his conversion. Therefore, when he came to Christ, he saw the Old Testament now in an entirely different light. In other words, he was able now to properly interpret the Old Covenant, which in fact was given only to point to the New Covenant which was to come, and in fact, had now come.

Paul equates the proper Circumcision as having been performed without hands with the Believer's removal from spiritual death to spiritual life (Col. 2:11-13). Thus, his teaching on this subject, is virtually synonymous with Regeneration.

CHRIST ALONE

Just as Paul characterizes the Judaizing teachers by three terms (epithets) in the previous Verse, so in this Verse he explains the true Circumcision by three descriptive phrases:

1. True Believers worship by the Spirit of God, not by human traditions or some external Rite.

2. We glory in Christ Jesus. Satisfaction comes from recognizing that our hope is found in Christ Alone, not through meticulous conformity to the external demands of the Mosaic Law, or some other law devised by modern men. We have understood that Christ's Sacrifice has Fulfilled the law for us.

Actually, these words of Paul echo Jeremiah 9:23-24, and are used by him also in I Corinthians 1:31 and II Corinthians 10:17.

3. We put no confidence in the flesh. Actually, the way Paul uses flesh here, it refers to what man is outside of Christ. Paul often uses the term in controversy with Judaizers, especially in Romans and Galatians (Rom. 3:20; 7:18, 25; Gal. 2:16; 3:3; 5:19, 24).

He teaches that sinful humanity has no grounds for confidence before God, because man unaided is powerless to achieve Righteousness before God. No matter how many religious rites he may enter into, or religious ceremony, none of this will achieve Righteousness.

The true Believer, however, puts all of his trust in Christ and so removes any grounds for human pride or boasting (Kent).

CIRCUMCISION AS PAUL USES THE TERM

The phrase, *"For we are the Circumcision,"* refers to the true Circumcision which is that of the heart.

The actual idea of ancient Circumcision as it was demanded by God of the Israelites, spoke of separation. The flesh was cut on the man's male member, which of course, caused the shedding of blood, which signified the price that would have to be paid by the coming Redeemer. The separation of the skin referred to Israel being separated from the surrounding nations and unto God. In other words, they were separated from something (the world), to something (God). However, Circumcision of course contained no Salvation, but merely only served as a symbol, pointing to One Who was to come. In fact, even though in a little different way, the Sacrifices of the Old Covenant fell into the same category, even as did the Sabbath.

Now that Jesus had come, in fact, bringing Salvation which He purchased by his Own Shed Blood on the Cross, to which the Rite of Circumcision had long pointed, this Rite was no longer needed, just as the Sabbath was no longer needed, etc. Why have the symbolism, when the reality is present?

The Believer is now saved by trusting Christ and what He did at the Cross, which Salvation separates the Believer from the world unto God, which, as stated, Circumcision symbolized. Consequently, Christians, and I speak of those who have truly accepted Christ, are the true Circumcision, which is actually a fulfillment of all the Old Testament Ritual.

Once again I emphasize, why do we want to go back to the symbolism or the ritual, when we have the reality present with us in the Person of Christ. All of the Old Testament symbolism merely pointed to One Who was to come, and was meant to serve only in that purpose. Unfortunately, Israel attempted to make Salvation out of the signpost instead of that to which the signpost pointed, namely Christ and His Finished Work. Many modern Christians attempt to do the same identical thing, by trying to make Salvation out of the Church, or the Lord's Supper, or Water Baptism, or speaking in Tongues, etc. The problem never ceases it seems! As then so now!

IN THE SPIRIT

The phrase, *"Which worship God in the Spirit,"* probably would have been better translated, *"which worship by the Spirit of God."*

The word *"worship"* is the translation of the Greek word referring to the Service of Jehovah by His peculiar people, the Jews. To be sure, Jews who did not know Christ would be scandalized by the application of this word to a Gentile. However, die to what Jesus did at the Cross, which He did for the entirety of the world (both Jews and Gentiles), the Gospel has now been opened up to the entirety of all mankind. Consequently, due to the advent of the Holy Spirit in the hearts of Believers, all men can now worship God, at least those who are Born-Again.

Actually, the worship of God by the Jews under the Old Testament Economy, was involved moreso in ceremony than actual worship. In fact, the entirety of the Book of Leviticus is the process by which the Jews could worship the Lord, and it is almost entirely made up of ceremony.

The reason is obvious. Due to the sin debt not yet having been paid because Jesus had not yet come, the Holy Spirit could not abide within the hearts and lives of Believers then as He does now (Jn. 14:17); consequently, due to that fact, worship was involved in ceremony far more then than now.

WHAT IS THE TRUE WORSHIP OF GOD?

Worship is what we *are*, praise is what we *do*. In other words, every single thing we are is to speak of worship of God. I speak of our attitude, our spirit, our personality, our thinking, our demeanor, our doing, — everything.

While all praise is worship, all worship is not praise. Praise is the actual proclamation of glorifying God in one way or the other whether through actual words of praise to the Lord, either by saying or singing, or even thinking, etc.

Everything the Believer is and does, is to be placed in the category of *"worship."* Our whole life, and in every capacity, is to be worship of God. Jesus said:

"But the hour cometh, and now is, when the true worshippers shall worship the Father in spirit and in truth: for the Father seeketh such to worship Him.

"God is a Spirit: and they that worship Him must worship him in spirit (by and through the human spirit moved upon by the Holy Spirit) *and in Truth* (the Word of God)*"* (Jn. 4:23-24).

As someone has well said, *"the Lord is not looking for holy worship* (ceremonies, etc.)*, but rather holy worshippers."*

NOTES

The phrase *"in spirit and in truth,"* refers to everything being worship or at least it certainly should be, which can only come about through the regenerated or Born-Again man.

Of course, when the Believer sins and fails the Lord in any manner, naturally that is certainly not worship of God, but rather the very opposite. That's what makes failure such a travesty, it stops the worship of God, which cannot once again be enjoined until Peace with God is made, which speaks of confessing and forsaking the particular sin (I Jn. 1:9). In fact, the only thing that can stop worship is sin. Sin is a lie, therefore, not Truth, therefore, that which God cannot accept.

If the Believer would come to understand this, that every part of his being is worship, or at least is supposed to be, I think that he would think twice before going to some certain places, reading some certain material, or doing some certain things. Anything in the Believer's life which is not worship of God is wrong. I realize that's a bold and strong statement. But it is true. That means we should be careful what we watch over television or any place else for that matter, careful about the thoughts we think, careful about the company we keep, careful about the things we do. The question must always be asked, *"is what we are thinking, is what we are doing, is what we are, conducive to worship of the Lord?"*

THE HOLY SPIRIT IN WORSHIP

Actually it is impossible to worship the Lord without the aid and work of the Holy Spirit. Jesus plainly said, even as stated, that we must *"worship the Father in spirit and in truth"* (Jn. 4:23). While he is speaking of the human spirit here, it is the human spirit regenerated and moved upon by the Holy Spirit. In other words, it is literally impossible for the human spirit which has not been regenerated to worship God. Such cannot be, for the simple reason that unregenerate man (those not Born-Again), is spiritually dead, which means to be dead to any and all things pertaining to God (Gen. 2:17; Rom. 6:23). To be sure, dead is dead, which means to have no life whatsoever, in this case no life of God.

As we have stated, worship of God before Christ did not have near the potential as presently, because the Holy Spirit now abides literally in the heart and life of the Believer, thereby rejuvenating every single fibre and particle of the being. Before the Cross, the Holy Spirit was only able to come upon Believers, and if within them, only for a short time to enable them to perform a certain task (Jn. 14:17). Due to the Cross, all of that has changed dramatically, with even the weakest Believer now having access to God on a far higher level than even the great Prophets of old. That's the reason Jesus said the following words:

"Verily I say unto you, among them that are born of women there hath not risen a greater than John the Baptist: notwithstanding he that is least in the Kingdom of Heaven is greater than he" (Mat. 11:11).

Jesus wasn't speaking of the greatness of the individuals as it regarded their personal selves, but rather the time in which they lived. John the Baptist was the last Prophet who functioned under the Old Covenant which was not nearly as great a Covenant as the New. Consequently, Jesus is saying that all in the New Covenant which speaks of the Cross forward, even the least, have greater privileges than the greatest Prophets of old under the former Covenant.

This referred to many things, but perhaps most of all it referred to the Holy Spirit being able now to come into the heart and life of the Believer and abide there forever, which He could not do before Pentecost (Jn. 14:16-17).

SALVATION

The moment the believing sinner accepts Christ, the Holy Spirit comes into the heart of that Believer. When we use this phraseology concerning the Holy Spirit, we are not speaking of bodily entrance into, for the simple reason that the Holy Spirit does not have a physical body. What we do mean, is that the Presence of the Holy Spirit is incorporated literally into the Believer. The Holy Spirit being God, means that He is everywhere, and as such, can be in as many Believers as have come to Faith in Christ.

One might say that the Bible Doctrine of interpenetration means the union of two or more persons together for the same end.

However, the work of the Holy Spirit as it regards regeneration in the heart and life of the Believer is a far cry from the Baptism with the Holy Spirit. While all Believers have the Holy Spirit, all Believers are not Baptized with the Holy Spirit, although they certainly should be. They are not baptized with the Holy Spirit, either because of apathy on their part, or because they have been taught wrong. In other words, they have been taught that they received everything at conversion, and there is nothing else to receive. This teaching completely denies great parts of the Word of God.

It should be obvious to all concerned, at least if they are honest with themselves and the Scripture, that the people in Samaria where Philip preached had given their hearts to Christ and were definitely saved, but had not yet been baptized with the Holy Spirit. In fact, if one receives all of which we speak at Salvation, why did Peter and John later go to Samaria, and *"prayed for them* (prayed for these Samaritans who had been saved), *that they might receive the Holy Spirit"*?

The Scripture plainly says, *"For as yet He* (the Holy Spirit) *was fallen upon none of them."*

The Scripture then says, *"Then laid they their hands on them, and they received the Holy Spirit"* (Acts 8:14-17).

As well, why did Paul ask the Ephesian Believers, *"Have ye received the Holy Spirit since ye believed?"* (Acts 19:2).

These men were already saved, but the truth is they did not know anything about the Baptism with the Holy Spirit, until Paul taught this extremely valuable subject to them, and then they received (Acts 19:1-7).

Again I make the point, that if everything is received at conversion as many teach, there is no logical explanation for these particular passages in the Word of God.

The truth is, the Baptism with the Holy Spirit is an experience different from Salvation, actually following Salvation (Acts 2:4). It is given for power and many other things as well, and is possible now of receiving because of one having been Born-Again.

As well, the Scripture plainly says that any and all who are Baptized with the Holy Spirit, with no exceptions I might quickly add, will speak with other Tongues (Acts 2:4; 10:46,47; 11:17; 19:6). In other words, if one has not spoken with other Tongues, one has not been

Baptized with the Holy Spirit, and if one has been Baptized with the Holy Spirit, one spoke with other tongues at the time of their initial Baptism (Acts 2:4).

I do not mean to belabor the point; however, inasmuch as there is much controversy concerning this subject, I feel constrained to explain the situation periodically.

THE LIFE AND MINISTRY OF THE LORD JESUS CHRIST

Let's look at the Lord for a moment, Who is without a doubt, the greatest example of all. In fact, Jesus was not only the True Israel (is the True Israel), but as well, He is the True Church and the True Man. In other words, He is the perfect example of all and for all.

I think it should be obvious that the Holy Spirit was present and working in every single thing that Jesus did, beginning with His conception (Lk. 1:35). In fact, every single thing done on the Earth by the Godhead, is done through the Person, Agency, Office, Work, and Ministry of the Holy Spirit (Gen. 1:2; Rom. 8:26-27). The Holy Spirit is mentioned over fifty times in the Book of Acts alone, signifying His work and activity in the Early Church, which is supposed to be a pattern for the Church for all time. Unfortunately, the Holy Spirit is given little latitude in many, if not most, Churches presently.

Jesus from the time of His Birth, through the first thirty years of His Life, entered into no Ministry whatsoever; however, the Holy Spirit was with the Lord all of this time, actually teaching Him.

The Bible says, and that which was inspired by the Holy Spirit, *"And the Child (Jesus) grew, and waxed strong in spirit, filled with wisdom: and the Grace of God was upon Him"* (Lk. 2:40). This refers to the Holy Spirit Who was working with Him, for all of these attributes are Works of the Spirit.

Actually, Jesus knew even when He was twelve years old, that He was the Messiah of Israel, the Son of God, the Saviour of the world. He made the statement, *"I must be about My Father's Business"* (Lk. 2:49).

How long He knew before this, we are not told. But I suspect this knowledge came quite early.

NOTES

The Psalmist said of Him: *"I have more understanding than all My teachers: for Thy Testimonies are My meditation.*

"I understand more than the ancients, because I keep Thy precepts.

"I have refrained My feet from every evil way, that I might keep Thy word.

"I have not departed from Thy Judgments: for Thou hast taught Me" (Ps. 119:99-102).

We are plainly told here that the Holy Spirit taught Christ the Word of God, and no doubt, beginning very early in His life. In fact, all little Jewish boys were taught to read and write in the Synagogue, beginning at about five years old. It is even thought that they were required to memorize the entirety of the Book of Leviticus.

So, after He had learned to read and write, which He had to do exactly as other little boys, He began to pore over the ancient Scrolls of the Old Testament, with the Holy Spirit teaching Him, which means that He knew more about the subject than His teachers, as no doubt quickly became obvious in the classes.

At any rate, the Holy Spirit was definitely with Him as I think we have made clear from the time of His conception; however, His Ministry was not to begin until the Spirit descended upon Him and remained, which in the Greek actually means that the Spirit came into Him for a particular purpose (Jn. 1:33).

Even though Jesus was Very Man, the Holy Spirit could come into Him to abide before the Cross, even though He could not do so with any other human being. Whereas, all other men, even Believers before the Cross, had a sin debt hanging over their head, for the simple reason that the blood of bulls and goats could not take away sin, Jesus had no sin nature and no sin debt, because He was not born of natural procreation, i.e., *"Not born as all other human beings, conceived in sin, as a result of the Fall."*

So, one could say that Jesus, while having the Holy Spirit since He was born, was Baptized with the Holy Spirit at the river Jordan, even as described by John (Jn. 1:31-32).

As the True Man, the Spirit of God was with Jesus, and of course, in Him from the time of His conception; however, He did not begin His Ministry until He was Baptized with the Holy Spirit, one might say.

From this example, we certainly should see the necessity of the Believer being Baptized with the Holy Spirit after conversion (Acts 1:4). Now I have said all of that to say the following:

THE HOLY SPIRIT IS THE KEY IN ALL OF THIS

I maintain that one cannot properly worship God, cannot properly minister for the Lord, cannot properly witness for the Lord, cannot properly see the growth of the Fruit of the Spirit, cannot have the Gifts of the Spirit, in fact, cannot properly experience any type of spiritual growth, unless one is Baptized with the Holy Spirit with the evidence of speaking with other Tongues (Acts 1:4).

The Baptism with the Holy Spirit is the *"help"* which Jesus promised as it regards this experience (Jn. 14:16). This refers to *"help"* in every capacity, and in every avenue of life, for this is what the word *"Comforter"* means, i.e., *"Paraclete, one called along side to help."* I realize what I've said is strong, and covers a lot of territory, but I cannot see anything else in the Word of God.

Again I emphasize, that all Believers have the Holy Spirit, for it's not possible for one to be saved without the Holy Spirit doing His Office Work within our lives. But that is far different than being Baptized with the Holy Spirit, which opens up the Believer to total and complete access by the Holy Spirit, or at least it should!

Unfortunately, there are millions of Spirit-filled people, who do not cooperate with the Holy Spirit very much, and in fact, allow Him very little latitude within their lives, with very little fruit being produced. Nevertheless, I maintain that this is the fault of the person and not the experience.

That which we must say and say strongly, is, *"If Jesus Who was perfect, Who was and is the Son of God, — if He needed the Holy Spirit, and if He experienced a genuine Baptism of the Spirit, how much more do we need the work and help of the Holy Spirit!"*

Jesus as the *"True Man,"* and the *"True Church,"* gave us and showed us the example. We are to follow that example, which is so obvious and so plain. If we deviate from that example, nothing is going to be done for God.

Now let me make another statement:

For the Churches, Denominations, and Preachers who do not believe in the Baptism with the Holy Spirit with the evidence of speaking with other Tongues, and that it is a separate and distinct Work of Grace subsequent to Salvation, I maintain that even though there may be much religious machinery involved with these Churches and individuals, there will actually be very little done for God. The reason is simple, if the Holy Spirit does not birth the effort, empower the effort, and lead the effort to its successful conclusion, it is not of God, irrespective as to how religious it might be; consequently, very little is going to be done for the Lord.

A LITTLE DONE OR NOTHING DONE?

I am not saying that nothing will be done by Preachers who do not believe as I have stated, but I am saying that little will be done.

Of course, the question must be asked, that if the Holy Spirit is disavowed, at least as He is given in the Scripture, how can anything be done?

First of all, people can be saved in the most strange of circumstances. In other words, a soul coming to Christ, which some few do in the Churches which do not believe as I have stated, they are saved because of the Faith in their own individual hearts, and not because of who or what the Preacher is, or necessarily what he believes. If a soul is hungry for the Lord, and the Word of God even in some way is preached, even though it is without the power of the Holy Spirit, the Holy Spirit working on that particular heart can definitely bring that person to a place of Salvation, as is often done. But the truth is, most people in Churches, I think, who do not subscribe to the Baptism with the Holy Spirit, are not actually saved. Regrettably and sadly, I'm afraid that would go for the far greater majority.

Sadder still, even in the Churches which claim to believe in the Baptism with the Holy Spirit, if dependence on the Spirit is not constantly generated, and if He is not looked to constantly, precious little is going to be done for the Lord even in those circles. Being initially Baptized with the Holy Spirit with the evidence of speaking with other Tongues, does not guarantee anything. To be sure, the potential is there, but whether that potential is realized or not, is dependent upon many things, the consecration of the individual certainly not being the least.

SPIRIT CONTROL

Once again we use our Lord as the example. He was controlled by the Holy Spirit as no other human being has been controlled. That's the secret! We are to be controlled by the Holy Spirit at all times; however, this is control which we must freely give Him, because He will never take it by force. There must be a *"hunger and thirst after Righteousness"* at all times by the Believer, for the Holy Spirit to properly work within our lives (Mat. 5:6).

Do not misunderstand, one cannot earn anything that the Holy Spirit does. In fact, the Lord has nothing for sale, all being a gift. Nevertheless, what the Believer can do, and definitely is required to do, is to always have *"a willing mind and an obedient heart."* That's all the Believer can do, but the Lord definitely does require that.

To which I have already addressed, but will mention it again briefly: The Prophet Joel prophesied as it regards the outpouring of the Holy Spirit, that there would be a *"former rain"* and *"latter rain"* (Joel 2:23). The *"former rain"* constituted the Early Church, which account is given to us in the Book of Acts. The *"latter rain"* began at about the turn of the 20th Century.

To be sure, there were individuals Baptized with the Holy Spirit during the time between the former rain and the latter rain; however, not many!

Whenever the Word of God is not taught, it is impossible for people to receive that which they do not know or hear. Actually, during the Dark Ages, not many people were saved, as the Catholic Church completely cut the Word of God off from most of the people. So, during these times, due to the apostasy of the Church, not only were there not many people Baptized with the Holy Spirit, there were not many people saved as well. The hearing of the Word of God generates Faith, and when the Word of God is not heard, no Faith is generated, which means whatever is being promised cannot be received.

NOTES

But at the turn of the 20th Century, in response to the fulfillment of the prophecy of Joel, hungry hearts began to cry out to God, and Believers began to be Baptized with the Holy Spirit, with the evidence of speaking with other Tongues, exactly as they had been in Early Church times (Acts 2:4). From that humble beginning until presently, untold millions have been Baptized with the Holy Spirit.

Inasmuch, as there wasn't much Light on the subject before the turn of the 20th Century, many Preachers during those times, walked in all the Light they had, and God greatly blessed by giving them many souls. I speak of men such as Finney, Moody, Whitefield, etc. However, when the Light on the Spirit was given, as it began to be so at the turn of the 20th Century, the Lord expected more as a result of that Light. Therefore, when the Light was plainly shown on this vital subject, even as it was, for those who have rejected that Light, even as most did and do, and I speak of the nominal Church world, they have not only lost that which they could have had, but what little they did have. Light which is rejected, is always Light withdrawn (Mat. 25:29).

NOW LET'S LOOK AGAIN AT WORSHIP

Due to Television, it is now possible to observe Church Services in operation, and from various different religious persuasions. As one observes the Catholics, one observes that it is almost all ceremony, which, in effect, is no worship at all. (Under the Old Covenant some ceremony was looked at as worship, but not under the New, at least if it is mere ceremony.)

As one observes the nominal Protestant Churches, one observes that there is never any Praise. As we have stated, *"worship is what we are, while praise is what we do."* If in fact there is true worship, there will as well be some praise. Actually, it is impossible for such not to be. As we have stated, praise is simply acknowledging Who God is and What He is, which is done by our thanksgiving, which must come from the heart. It doesn't have to be loud, and can definitely be silent in the heart; however, there will be at least some times that the Praise is to be vocal. The Scripture plainly says, *"Let the Redeemed of the Lord say so"* (Ps. 107:2).

While one certainly can *"say so"* as it involves the singing of songs unto the Lord in public Services (or wherever), it definitely is not guaranteed that such is so just because the words are uttered from the mouth. They have to come from the heart as well, as should be obvious.

What I'm saying is this: While I'm certain that some small amount of the effort in such Church Services is constituted by the Lord as true Praise from the heart, I do venture to say that the percentage is small. These people do not believe in the Baptism with the Holy Spirit, and while I do not question their love for God, I do say they have greatly shortchanged themselves, making it almost impossible to worship the Lord, as well as to do much of anything else for the Lord for that matter. As previously stated, there may be much motion and much religious machinery at work, which fools a lot of people, but that in no way means that a work is being done for God.

Now on the other side of that coin, as we look at the Pentecostal and Charismatic varieties, we see some true Worship and Praise, but we also see a lot of absurd foolishness, to be blunt and plain.

For instance, much from that source, which comes over Television presently in the Name of the Lord, is no more than efforts of the flesh, even though it goes under the guise of the Spirit. In my opinion, it is far worse than the *"deadness"* of the non-Pentecostals, etc.

All type of wild claims are being made concerning supposed miracles, when in fact precious few, if any, miracles are being performed. This does not hold true for all, but it does for most, I fear!

Also, all types of wild manifestations are claimed to be of the Holy Spirit, when in reality, most are not of the Spirit. And how do I know?

First of all, much of it is not Scriptural, and then a lot of it which is Scriptural, is induced by the power of suggestion instead of a true moving of the Spirit.

For instance, I believe the Lord definitely *"slays people in the Spirit,"* to use that for an example, but I don't believe that it happens on cue as it does with many Preachers and people, etc. As well, I don't think the Holy Spirit induces people to bark like dogs and crow like roosters, etc. That is not only unbiblical, but rather downright stupid!

It is bad enough to function outside of the Holy Spirit, but to do stupid things, and then to claim that it is the Lord, is adding insult to injury!

Some of the *"stuff"* that comes over Television under the guise of *"Christian,"* and worse than that, under the guise of the *"Anointing of the Holy Spirit,"* can be labeled as none other than an *"abomination."* I maintain that there are many in the so-called Pentecostal world and the Charismatics, who are bordering on blasphemy of the Holy Spirit, especially the acts of chicanery and dishonesty carried out, claiming that it's of the Spirit. These are dangerous grounds indeed!

Too often and too much, poor people who desperately need healing, or desperately need financial help, are exploited, which within itself is a grievous sin. But when we bring the Holy Spirit into the act, and an *"act"* it is, we are on dangerous ground! Telling people they are healed of cancer when they aren't, is a terrible sin. Telling people they're going to receive a thousand dollars back for every hundred dollars they give to God, is a grievous sin as well. While it is true that the Lord definitely does heal and definitely does perform miracles, and definitely does bless as it regards our giving to Him, and abundantly so I might quickly add, once again, He does not do these things on cue, and people are never to be exploited in their giving, by promises which are not backed up by the Word of God.

At this moment (1999), as I dictate these words, there is so little true Moving and Operation of the Holy Spirit evidenced in Churches and over what is referred to as Christian Television and Radio, as to be almost non-existent. There is some small amount, and for that we thank God, but not much!

Most is an effort which is religious and carries the covering of dignity, but is dead, while the other claims the life of the Spirit, but too often is no more than the machinations of the flesh. Again, there is very little true Moving and Operation of the Holy Spirit, but thank God for what little there is.

The point I am attempting to make is, that we must have the Holy Spirit in all that we do, and I speak of His Leading, Guidance, Operation, and Manifestations in every manner. Without Him we cannot worship, or do anything for that matter! However, the fake is an abomination.

REJOICING IN CHRIST JESUS

The phrase, *"And rejoice in Christ Jesus,"* refers to not only Who Christ actually is, but also to what He has done, which refers to the Cross and the Resurrection. We can properly rejoice in the Lord Jesus only in that capacity, which refers to our Faith in His Finished Work. *"Rejoicing"* constitutes Praise. In the Greek Text it carries the idea of *"glorying"* or *"exulting."*

So, in the previous phrase we have *"worship,"* which constitutes what a Believer *is*, while in this phrase we have *"praise,"* which constitutes what a Believer *does*. If the life of a Believer is that truly of worship, as it certainly must be, then one will definitely have some *"glorying"* and *"exulting"* as it refers to Christ Jesus. How could we help but not do so, considering all that He has done for us.

WHAT HAS HE DONE FOR US?

He has redeemed us from the kingdom of darkness, bringing us over into the Kingdom of Light. He has cleansed every sin of our past, taken away the guilt and making us one with the Lord. He has given us Eternal Life, which comes from the Lord Jesus Christ, its Source. He has baptized us with the Holy Spirit, Who abides within our hearts and lives constantly, giving us help in every respect, which is a blessing of unprecedented proportions. He has made provision for us to live with Him forever and forever, which speaks of the coming New Jerusalem and, as well, a coming renewed Earth. He has filled our heart with love, joy, and peace. He has given us *"more abundant life,"* and a *"rest"* of which the world cannot give and, in fact, has no knowledge. He has made us a part of this great Family of God, which in effect, makes us a part of *"heavenly aristocracy."* He has taken us from spiritual death into spiritual life, all through Christ Jesus.

NOTES

I could keep making statement after statement for, in fact, what the Lord has done for us, is literally unending.

HOW DID HE DO ALL OF THESE THINGS FOR US?

To be sure, this of which I speak was not done quickly neither was it done easily. Actually, the Plan of Redemption carried out by Jesus Christ, is the most comprehensive, the most all-inclusive, the most wide-sweeping, the most profound, of anything that man could even begin to think or imagine.

God had to literally become man which, in effect, means that the Creator became the creature. That is beyond comprehension to our minds, but that's exactly what He did.

He then had to live a perfect life as the Second Man (the Second Adam), in effect, accomplishing what the first Adam did not accomplish and doing what the first Adam did not do. Jesus had to live a perfect life, obeying the Law of God in every respect, and in the doing of this face every single onslaught of Satan that could be thrown His way in order to get Him to fail. In fact, God lowered the entirety of the Godhead to the lowest, possible, common denominator, that of man. Consequently, this was Satan's great opportunity.

As God, sin was not possible, nor any form of failure or transgression; however, as man, which Jesus became in totality although never ceasing to be God, sin was definitely possible, meaning that failure was definitely possible. It is absolutely impossible for anyone to even begin to imagine or conceive as to what would have happened in the entirety of the Kingdom of God if Jesus had failed in any way.

We can pass all of this off by saying that it was not possible for Him to fail, but that is patently incorrect and unscriptural. Had it not been possible for Him to fail He could not have been the Second Adam. He had to *be* the True Man in every respect, exactly as He *was* the True Man. Consequently, that included temptation with the possibility of failure. But of course, He did not fail, not even one time, not even in the slightest way, not even in the slightest impure thought, etc.

As a result, when He went to the Cross, which was His destination all along, in other words, that for which He originally came, He could offer up His Body as a perfect Sacrifice, in fact, a Sacrifice which God could readily accept, which He did!

In the offering up of that Sacrifice, which means He readily and freely poured out His Own life, and that means that the Romans or the Jews did not take it from Him, He by doing this, satisfied the claims of Heavenly Justice. In other words, the terrible sin debt owed by man to God, which man could not pay, had no means to pay, was not possible to pay, was paid in totality by Jesus Christ, by the pouring out of His Life's Blood, which satisfied the curse of the broken Law which was Death.

When He did this, which atoned for every single sin that had ever been committed or would ever be committed by all who had ever lived or would ever live, this broke the grip of Satan on the human race, because his claim on man was always sin, i.e., *"iniquity, transgression, disobedience,"* etc.

Inasmuch as all sin along with its death wages were taken away (Jn. 1:29), Satan then had no right or no power to hold Jesus in the tomb. Sin being atoned for, death which is the wages of sin now had no power; consequently, Jesus could come from the dead, i.e., *"be resurrected,"* and there was nothing that Satan could do about the situation. As well, His Resurrection not only guaranteed our Justification, but it also guaranteed a future Resurrection for every Saint who would ever live (I Cor. 15:51-57).

WHAT DOES ALL OF THIS MEAN?

It means that Satan has now been totally and completely defeated, along with every fallen angel and every demon spirit. Their claim on mankind has been totally and completely destroyed, for Jesus has totally *"destroyed the works of the Devil"* (I Jn. 3:8).

ISRAEL

So, that being the case, why is Satan still allowed certain freedom? Why are demon spirits still active? And why does sin still take its deadly toll on the human race?

Due to the failure of Israel to accept Christ when He first came, the world was submitted to a continued period of Satanic oppression and darkness, even though these evil forces had been completely defeated, which was done at the Cross. Jesus dealt with this in Matthew Chapter 24.

In other words, if Israel had accepted Christ in the manner and way they should have accepted Him when He first came, the Crucifixion would still have taken place, for Rome would not have tolerated another king whatsoever not of their choosing. Of course, God in His power could easily have stopped this; however, Jesus had to go to the Cross in order to redeem mankind. There was no other way!

Irrespective, if Israel had accepted Him then, even though He would have gone to the Cross anyway, upon His Resurrection, the Kingdom Age would then have commenced, exactly as it will at the Second Coming.

However, all of this I have stated presents a moot point, for the simple reason that God through foreknowledge knew that Israel would reject their own Messiah, thereby submitting the world to continued destruction and darkness. Nevertheless, during this period of time, which has lasted now nearly 2,000 years, the Lord has taken out of the Gentile world a Church, a people for His Name, which in effect, took the place of Israel even as Paul outlined in Romans Chapter 11. Consequently, because of the foreknowledge of God, the Prophets would predict many things concerning the future.

Even though the Second Coming was outlined graphically by the Prophets, it was Isaiah who more than any other Prophet, spoke of the coming Kingdom Age, which will commence with the Second Coming, ushering the world into a golden age, a golden age incidentally that it could have had all along.

If one is to notice, the Church is not mentioned at all in the Old Testament accept in shadow. Gentiles are referred to by Isaiah and Malachi as coming to the Lord, but that's as close as it comes to speaking of the Church. The reason being, is because the Church was really not in the original Plan of God.

While it was definitely the Plan of God that the Gospel go to the entirety of the world, Israel was meant to be the Evangelists who would bring the Gentiles to Christ. This of course, they failed to do, and failed miserably. However, even as Isaiah also prophesied, Israel will yet fill this role in the coming

Kingdom Age, when Jewish Evangelists will travel the length and the breadth of the world at that time, extolling the glory and grandeur of their Messiah and also their Savior and our Savior, the Lord Jesus Christ (Isa. 66:18-21).

So, this means that those in the modern Church who claim that Israel has no future, simply do not know what they are talking about. Every single Promise made to Abraham, Isaac, and Jacob, along with David, etc., must be fulfilled in totality, which of course has to do with the Jewish people, and to be sure, which will definitely be fulfilled. In fact, it is impossible to read the Bible without seeing this, as it screams on almost every page.

Consequently, to say that we *"rejoice in Christ Jesus,"* is an understatement of unparalleled proportions. He is the One Who has paid the price, redeemed humanity, set the captive free, defeated Satan, and made possible for all to come who will come (Rev. 22:17). The Gospel is for all, as His Death and Resurrection were for all (Jn. 3:16).

WHY DOES MOST OF THE WORLD REJECT JESUS CHRIST?

In fact, most of the world does reject the Lord, despite this great and glorious Salvation afforded to those who will believe Him.

The reason goes back to the Fall of man in the Garden of Eden. Man still suffers from the very thing that brought about the Fall — deception, self-will, and lying.

Satan lied to Adam and Eve and they believed that lie. In other words, they were deceived, because they did not gain from the Fall what they were told they would gain — to be like God (Gen. 3:4-5).

In fact, they became totally unlike God in that the Fall lowered man to the far lower level of self-consciousness, whereas he had previously possessed total God-consciousness. He gained nothing and actually lost everything.

As a result of what happened there, man became a child of Satan with the very nature of Satan within his heart and life, which is the cause of all the bloodshed, hatred, and destruction in the world. That's the reason that man must be *"born again,"* or else he cannot even *"see the Kingdom of God,"* stated Christ! (Jn. 3:3)

NOTES

God told man that if he disobeyed (partook of the tree of the knowledge of good and evil, which he was forbidden to do), that he would die, which referred to spiritual death, which meant *"separation from God"* (Gen. 2:17). To be sure, when man did this thing spiritual death was the result. In other words, man was left with no recognition of God, no touch with God, no inclination toward God, in other words, totally sinful and depraved, i.e., *"the nature of Satan."*

So from that time, man has been plagued with deception (he is deceived), lowered to the level of self-will, with the entirety of his fabric and being literally existing on the *"lie."*

That's the reason that most of the world does not accept Christ!

NO CONFIDENCE IN THE FLESH

The phrase, *"And have no confidence in the flesh,"* speaks volumes, and that which every Child of God should understand minutely.

In fact, what actually did Paul mean by that statement?

The word *"confidence"* has the idea of *"coming to a settled persuasion regarding something."*

To start at the beginning, the implication is that the Judaizers had come to a settled confidence in the flesh, while Paul disclaims such a thing in relation to himself. The Apostle had used this word before in this Epistle (Phil. 1:25). It shows that Paul did not arrive at his decisions or convictions hastily, but only after mature consideration. In fact, the Seventh Chapter of Romans proclaims Paul's efforts to find consecration and victory through the flesh, which of course left him a total failure (Rom. 7:24). Thankfully, the Lord gave the Apostle the answer to this dilemma, which he gave to us in Romans Chapter 6, which details the manner of one's Salvation, as well as one's victorious walk in Christ. It is all centered up in the Cross (Rom. 6:3-5). So, the Apostle puts Christ Jesus as was proclaimed in the previous phrase, in juxtaposition to the flesh in this last phrase. This means that the Believer, can either trust Christ or the flesh. He cannot have it both ways. The idea is, one can glory in Christ Jesus or one can glory in the flesh, he cannot glory in both (I Cor. 1:31; II Cor. 10:17; Gal. 6:14).

To glory in Christ is something more than even to believe and to trust in Him; it expresses a deep sense of privilege, both in present thankfulness and in future hope.

WHAT DOES PAUL MEAN BY THE TERM *"THE FLESH"*?

First of all he is speaking of Believers here. He is actually speaking of the attempt to attain Righteousness, which one can do in Christ or attempt to do in the flesh, which of course is impossible.

The term for *"flesh"* here does not refer to the physical body, but rather one's own efforts outside of Christ — efforts to attain Righteousness, etc.

The Judaizers were claiming that all Believers along with accepting Christ, must as well be physically circumcised (the boys and the men). Paul is saying that this act of Circumcision, plus anything else of this nature cannot bring about Righteousness of any kind, such being brought about only by Christ.

FIRST OF ALL, LET'S LOOK AS TO HOW RIGHTEOUSNESS IS ACTUALLY OBTAINED

It is obtained totally and completely in Jesus Christ, even as Paul addresses in the previous phrase.

And what do we mean by that?

There was no way that man could obtain any type of Righteousness within himself, but yet which God demanded. In other words, God demanded that man attain to a certain Righteousness which, in fact, was given in the Ten Commandments. This was God's Standard of Righteousness, but as simple as it might seem, due to the fallen nature, it was a Standard to which man could not attain irrespective of his efforts.

So, even as we've already stated, God became Man, i.e., *"the Lord Jesus Christ."* He did for man what man could not do for himself, and did so by going to the Cross, paying the price, thereby redeeming humanity, at least all those who will believe (Jn. 3:16; Eph. 2:8-9).

The idea is, a perfect, spotless Righteousness is given to every believing sinner who accepts Christ, no matter how evil and wicked they have previously been. This Righteousness is not earned by man and, in fact, cannot be earned by man. It is obtained only by Faith, and by that, we mean Faith in what Jesus did at the Cross and the Resurrection. When the sinner believes that, even though he understands little about what has happened, God imparts to him the Righteousness of Christ, which now becomes his (the sinners), all by Faith.

Actually, at conversion, the believing sinner receives a spotless Righteousness, as stated, the Righteousness of Christ, which cannot be improved upon, and greatly insults God if we try (Rom. 5:1).

In other words, when the Judaizers came along saying that the Believers must be circumcised as well as accepting Christ, this was a gross insult to God and to Christ, because it said in its action, that what Christ did was not enough, and something has to be added to that which we know was His Finished Work. In fact, this is probably the greatest sin that man can commit, other than blaspheming the Holy Spirit (Jn. 16:7-11).

Irrespective as to what the Believer does after he comes to the Lord, no matter how consecrated he might be, no matter how much he may work for the Lord, no matter how close to God he may strive to be, none of this, as important as it might be in its own way, adds anything to the spotless Righteousness of Christ which was given to the sinner at conversion. As stated, we sin greatly, when we think that any of our actions make us more righteous, for nothing can make one more righteous than the Shed Blood of Christ, and Faith in that atoning Sacrifice.

That's why the Apostle said that he had no confidence in the flesh, meaning that all of the religious efforts other than Christ are totally unnecessary and, in fact, greatly hinder the Grace of God in our lives (Gal. 2:21).

SO HOW DOES ALL OF THIS AFFECT MODERN CHRISTIANS?

Many would read this and dismiss it out of hand, simply because there are no Judaizers presently demanding Circumcision, etc.

While that is correct, the entire principle of this of which Paul speaks, is extremely important to the modern Saint. In fact, it is just as important now as it was then. Right here is where the Christian either has victory or no victory at all. In fact, most modern Christians have little victory, and it's because they do not understand these things of which Paul speaks.

To be sure, the Holy Spirit would not have devoted all of this space and attention to something that applied only to those of Paul's day and had no bearing on the present time.

Almost all Christians understand this as it refers to the sinner being saved. In other words, they know that the sinner must trust Christ and Christ Alone in order to be saved, which means they cannot trust in their good works, etc. Most every Christian is well versed in that great Truth. However, after that is where the trouble begins.

The Christian readily understands that the sinner cannot trust in the flesh, i.e., *"good works, merit,"* in order to be saved. But then, the Christian too often turns right around, and does the same thing (trust in the flesh), in order to obtain Righteousness when he actually already has Righteousness, or overcome sin, or be victorious over the Devil, etc., which he knows the sinner must *not* do in order to be saved. It amounts to the same thing as trying to add Circumcision, although it can be any number of other types of things.

All of this is so very subtle, that it deceives the Christian. The truth is, most Christians (and I exaggerate not) are trusting in the flesh, whether they realize it or not!

IN WHAT WAYS CAN A CHRISTIAN TRUST IN THE FLESH?

One might answer that question in this manner: anything that anyone does other than trust in the Finished Work of Christ, which speaks of His Death on the Cross and the Resurrection, constitutes the flesh, and irrespective as to what it might be, even scriptural, legitimate things.

Every Christian wants to walk close to the Lord, or at least they certainly should. Of course, we know that there are many who do not have much consecration; nevertheless, the true heart after God wants to draw closer to the Lord.

How do we do this?

All of this which really refers to our Sanctification, does not come about by *"works,"* or any effort on our part of this nature. This means that one cannot pray oneself into Sanctification, even though prayer is one of the most vital principles in the life of the Christian. It also means that one cannot *"fast"* their way to Sanctification, or pay their way into Sanctification, by the giving of money to the Work of the Lord. As should be obvious, these three things I've just named are very legitimate, very Scriptural, and very necessary, especially prayer and our giving to God. However, if we attempt to do these things in order to be Sanctified, or to overcome sin, etc., we have in fact turned these things into works, which God cannot bless.

This is what fools the Christian! Because these things are so right within themselves, we tend to think that they will help us to overcome the Devil, etc. They won't!

I don't want the Reader to misunderstand this, thinking that we're denigrating prayer and other such type things. Actually, it's impossible for a Christian to have a proper relationship with the Lord as we have already stated, without having a proper prayer life, and other things we could mention. But when we turn these things into *"works,"* we, in effect, are doing the same identical thing that the Judaizers were doing, which means that we are attempting to add something to the Finished Work of Christ, which, in effect, is a great sin, even as we've already stated. And yet, I'm concerned that all of us have attempted to do this at one time or the other. In fact, *"works"* are just as prominent in the lives of Christians, and I speak of works which we carry out attempting to make ourselves holy, etc., as works are prominent in the lives of the unsaved, attempting to make themselves acceptable unto God in some way.

So, when Paul mentions *"confidence in the flesh,"* this was a road that he had himself traveled as is outlined in Romans Chapter 7, which gives his own personal experience, and which brought him to a dead-end, even as it will all other Believers. And yet, we keep trying in this capacity, and keep failing.

HOW CAN THE CHRISTIAN BE VICTORIOUS?

When we speak of being *"victorious,"* we are referring to the world, the flesh, and the

Devil. It means to be victorious over sin, victorious over self-will, victorious in every capacity with the Lord, which surely every Christian desires to be, or certainly should!

The answer is simple: The Christian *is* victorious, which means it's already done, which means it was accomplished in Christ. The moment that the believing sinner accepts the Lord as his personal Saviour, at that moment he obtains all that Salvation is, which speaks of victory over Satan in every capacity. This means that the Christian is victorious and, in fact, can do nothing to make himself more victorious.

The Christian upon reading this might say, *"Well I'm not victorious, because I'm failing the Lord as it regards some particular sin."* Regrettably, that is true with most Christians.

So, what is wrong?

Satan never ceases to attack the Child of God. Peter said, *"Think it not strange concerning the fiery trial which is to try you, as though some strange thing happened unto you."*

He then said, *"But rejoice, inasmuch as ye are partakers of Christ's sufferings"* (I Pet. 4:12-13).

In a sense, these words by Peter have a double meaning:

First of all, it speaks of Satan hating Christ and, therefore, hating those who follow Christ, which entails some sufferings, as would be obvious. In other words, it's the problem which we are now discussing.

However, the greater meaning as it regards *"being partakers of Christ's Sufferings,"* is that He suffered on the Cross for us, and we are to reap the benefits of those Sufferings, which in a sense means to be a *"partaker of them."* Our partaking of them has to do with our Faith in what He did, even as Paul describes in Romans 6:3-5.

The Believer is to place his Faith in what Christ did at the Cross, and the Resurrection, understanding that in this is his entire Salvation, which includes victory over sin in every capacity, even until he dies or the Trump sounds. In other words, exactly as the believing sinner had to have Faith in Christ for Salvation, he has to continue to have Faith in Christ, i.e., *"in what was done at the Cross,"* as it regards his daily walk before the Lord. In fact, every single thing is wrapped up in this, victory over sin, an overcoming life, more abundant life, a victorious walk, etc.

The problem is, the Faith we exercised in Christ to be saved, is too often abandoned after we come to Him. We don't realize we're doing this, but it's exactly what happens.

We tend to think that all the things we do as a Christian, such as Church attendance, or working in the Church, witnessing to souls, giving of money to the Cause of Christ, or our prayer life, or whatever, somehow adds to our Righteousness, or our walk with the Lord.

To be sure, we should do these things, but as a result of what we are in Christ, instead of thinking that they help us to attain something in Christ.

IT IS ALL BY FAITH

Christians hear that term over and over, *"It is all by Faith."* So what does it really mean?

Actually, it means exactly what it says.

As the sinner had to have Faith in Christ to be saved, and in fact could be saved in no other way, which most Christians understand even as we have stated, everything else is on the same basis.

By *"everything else,"* we mean exactly that, our walk with the Lord, our consecration in Christ, our overcoming victory, etc.

It means, that we understand that what Jesus did at the Cross actually paid it all. We were in Him when He died, as well as being in Him when He was buried and raised from the dead (Rom. 6:3-5).

Of course, we were not literally there as would be obvious, but our Faith in that, places us there, at least in the Mind of God. Jesus was our Substitute, and as well our Representative Man. Faith in Him, gives us, all the great victories which He purchased at the Cross and the Resurrection, which was done actually on our behalf.

So, the Christian is to understand, that there is absolutely nothing else that needs to be done, or in fact can be done, in order to make one more righteous or more holy or more sanctified. The whole thing was accomplished in totality at the Cross, which means that we are to have Faith in that, and continue to have Faith in that. Instead, too often we begin to have faith in our own efforts, our own good works, our own labors for Christ, etc., which is what Paul meant by *"confidence in the flesh."* It is an effort that God can in no way honor, because whether we understand it or not, whether we realize it or not, these efforts on behalf of the Christian, is, in effect, stating that Christ didn't do it all, and we must add something to that which He has already done. We may not think of it in that way, but that's exactly what is happening.

I am victorious, not because I have a strong prayer life (which I do). I am victorious not because I'm a Preacher of the Gospel, which I am. I am victorious not because I give so much money to the Work of the Lord, etc. I am victorious simply because of what Christ did at the Cross and the Resurrection, and my Faith in that. I must never forget that, because if I do, I will fall into failure every single time.

NOW ENTERS THE HOLY SPIRIT

Of course, the Holy Spirit has been there all the time, having come into the heart and life of the person immediately at conversion. Also, with many Christians, they have been baptized with the Holy Spirit, which presents even greater operation. But yet, most Christians don't get much help from the Holy Spirit, at least in the capacity of overcoming sin, simply because He will only function in one sphere of operation, and that is the Finished Work of Christ.

In other words, He demands, which is actually the Message of the entirety of the Bible, that we have Faith in that Finished Work, and maintain Faith in that Finished Work. He then works on our behalf, but only then. Of course, with Him doing the things which only He can do, Satan is easily driven back, etc.

Most Christians understand that they had to have Faith in the Cross as it regarded their initial Salvation experience, but have little or no teaching whatsoever as it regards their continued Faith, respecting their everyday walk before God. Not having teaching on this subject, many fall prey to the *"flesh,"* which refers to trying to carry out this task within their own ability and strength, which is an impossible situation.

In fact, many Christians despite their trying so hard, not only continue to fail, but the situation actually gets worse, because that's what Law is designed to do. Consequently, the Christian becomes very confused not understanding what is happening, especially considering that they are trying so hard, if in fact that is the case.

Unfortunately, the Church has had so little teaching on the Cross in the last nearly 50 years, that it is almost devoid of the greatest teaching of all as it regards Christians, actually the Foundation of the very Gospel of Christ.

I realize that everything I've said, I have given it several times in the last two Commentaries, and actually even in this one as well. However, understanding that Paul dealt with this very situation over and over again, and because it is the place of the Christian's greatest failure, which refers to a lack of understanding, I feel compelled in my spirit, to present this truth in every capacity that I know how, which I am attempting to do. I do not mean to be overly repetitive or above all, redundant; however, knowing how important all of this is, and knowing it is the greatest area of misunderstanding, I have felt compelled to state this truth in every manner I know how, praying that the Reader will get the totality of what is being said.

Once again, if the Holy Spirit through the Apostle dealt with this so very much in Paul's Epistles, He certainly did all of this for a specific reason. He did so, because this is the greatest conflict with the Child of God, and again, the place of the greatest misunderstanding.

It is tragic, but there are many Christians laboring with everything within them to walk holy before the Lord, actually loving Him with all their heart, but at the same time failing. In fact, there are untold numbers who have simply given up and quit. If they were questioned closely, and would totally relate all that's in their heart, I am persuaded that many would say, *"I tried my best to live it, and I can't!"*

The terrible truth is, they are right, at least in the way they were trying to live for the

Lord. No Believer, can live a life of victory by depending on his own strength, whether he does so ignorantly or otherwise. Even Paul could not do such, even as Romans Chapter 7 outlines. It is all by Faith in Christ and what He did at the Cross.

A PERSONAL EXAMPLE

Just this morning, in addressing our prayer meeting group, I used our prayer meetings as an example.

In fact, we have been having these prayer meetings since the latter part of 1991, actually some two a day, with the exception of service nights and Saturday mornings.

Doing all of this, it is very easy for one to think that the carrying out of such earns one an added degree of Righteousness, etc. However, it doesn't!

These prayer meetings are very important, at least if we keep them in the manner in which they are intended, which is to worship the Lord and seek His Leading and Guidance regarding all that we do. But the moment, that we think such earns us something from God, at that moment we have turned the prayer meetings into *"works"* which God cannot honor.

I am no more righteous presently for attending these prayer meetings twice a day for about seven and a half years, than I was when the prayer meetings began. In fact, the Lord gave me instructions, I believe, to start the prayer meetings. Nevertheless, my Righteousness has nothing to do with those things, as helpful as they may be in other ways. My Righteousness comes exclusively from what Christ did at the Cross and the Resurrection, and my Faith in that and that alone.

However, it is so easy to fall into the trap of thinking that things we do for the Lord, money we give, efforts we make, etc., earns us something in some capacity. As we've already stated, these things are very important, and should be done, but only as a result of our Righteousness, and never as a cause of our Righteousness.

(4) "THOUGH I MIGHT ALSO HAVE CONFIDENCE IN THE FLESH. IF ANY OTHER MAN THINKETH THAT HE HATH WHEREOF HE MIGHT TRUST IN THE FLESH, I MORE:"

NOTES

Paul's personal testimony shows that he is not reacting against the Judaizers because he is jealous of their supposed strengths and heritage. In stating that true Believers put no confidence in the flesh, he has in mind the contrary teaching of those opponents who stress the importance of conformity to Jewish practices.

For the sake of argument, therefore, he temporarily adopts one of their attitudes (*"confidence in the flesh"*) and shows that his rejection of certain Jewish *"advantages"* was not because he did not possess them. He merely wanted it known, that he could stand on equal footing with any Judaizer, and even more so.

He disavowed such as reasons for confidence before God, not because he did not possess them, but because he had found them inadequate to provide the Righteousness God requires. That's the gist of it all!

THE WAYS OF MAN

The phrase, *"Though I might also have confidence in the flesh,"* refers to human attainments, in this situation, the superiority of Judaism, or rather as the Jews supposed it to be. One might explain it this way:

Theirs was not a supernatural system in which Salvation was a work of God for man, but a natural system in which Salvation was a work of man for God. In other words, they did not believe in a supernatural Judaism, which God originally intended, in which He had given Salvation to the offerer of the symbolic Sacrifice by virtue of the merits of the coming True Sacrifice for sin, the Lord Jesus. Over against this dependence of the Judaizers upon human attainment and merit, Paul sets his own human attainments and merits, saying that he had more to boast of than they, and yet he had discarded all these and any dependence on them that he might appropriate the Salvation which is in Christ Jesus Alone. Thus, Paul uses himself as an example to warn the Philippians, and all others for that matter, against the seductive snares of the Judaizers.

Even though we have said this many times, the manner in which Paul uses the word *"flesh,"* falls out to referring to trust in anything which is not Faith in the Finished Work of Christ. It actually doesn't matter what it is, whether religious or otherwise. If it's not Faith in what Christ did on the Cross as it regards the Salvation of humanity, then it is looked at as *"flesh,"* i.e., *"the works of man."*

Paul had once trusted in these things totally and completely. In fact, his entire relationship with God, which in fact, was no relationship at all, for the man was not even saved, was wrapped up in his Jewish heritage. He had lived by the fact that the Jews were God's chosen people, the recipients of the great Law of Moses, consequently the only people on Earth who had such a thing, in fact, the only people on Earth who truly knew God, at least until the Gospel was given to the Gentiles. In fact, much of Israel had built up a prideful, arrogant attitude in respect to their supposed Spiritual superiority. This is what Paul batters so hard in the first few Chapters of Romans.

THE PRESENT SITUATION

That which had been the problem of Paul before his conversion, and the problem of most of Israel, is in fact, the problem with untold millions presently. Even though the difficulty does not pertain to any type of Jewish heritage, it does play out to the same negative result in other ways.

For instance, untold millions think they are saved simply because they are a member of the Catholic Church. In other words, they think that association with that institution brings about some type of Salvation. At least that's what they are told by their superiors, and hundreds of millions believe this lie.

The same could be said for many Baptists, as well as others, even some Pentecostals.

Others, while not involved in any religious activity, are extremely active relative to particular *"works,"* such as charity, etc. They think that all of this provides some type of Salvation, and if the truth be known, they are relying on these things totally and completely. This means, that they are not relying upon the Finished Work of Christ.

It should be obvious to the world, but it seems it isn't, that if these things could bring about Salvation in the heart of unredeemed man, then Jesus needlessly died a cruel death on the Cross. That being the case, the world does not give any credence to the Cross whatsoever, and regrettably, neither does much of the Church.

THE CROSS

The Cross tells us how good, how noble, how wonderful, how loving that God really is, and at the same time, how evil, how wicked, how awful, that man actually is. Man does not like that, as should be obvious.

If one wants to know the true heart of man, and even above that, the true heart of religion, one only has to look at the Cross. The world nailed Jesus to a Cross, and religion was the prime foundation from which this terrible sin sprang. In fact, the greatest hindrance to the Work of God in the world, is not the world per se, but rather, the world of religion.

For the most part, it is religion which has spilled the blood of untold numbers of the Saints of God, and opposed the Prophets of old, and the Apostles of the present.

Unfortunately, this *"world of religion,"* which is so insidious, so wicked, so evil, in fact, the most evil thing on the face of the Earth, is not found in that which we would commonly refer to as the *"modernist,"* etc., for those things are obvious. Instead, it comes from the ranks of those who claim nearness to God, such as the Fundamentalists and the Evangelicals. I speak of those who claim to believe all the Bible, which would include most Baptists, many Methodists, the Holiness, the Pentecostals, and the Charismatics.

In all of this, there are found wonderful and Godly Christians, and as well, Godly Preachers; but at the same time, that's where the greatest evil comes from and, therefore, the greatest hindrance to the Work of God.

As stated, the pattern for all of this was set with Christ, as the pattern for all things is found in Christ.

It was not Rome who crucified Christ, even though they were *"used"* in this horrible travesty. It was the Religious Hierarchy of Israel, and more particularly, the Pharisees, who were the Fundamentalists of that day. In fact, the two greatest parties in Israel at that time, were the Pharisees and Sadducees. The Sadducees, would fall under the heading of present-day *"modernists,"* which mean they had very little belief in anything. It was the

Pharisees who claimed to believe all the Bible and to be sticklers for the Law of Moses, which would seem to make them Godly and holy. It had the exact opposite effect.

No! That doesn't mean that all people who believe the Bible are unholy, it just means that claims are not always the facts of the situation. Sometimes, the very opposite is the case.

It should make sense, that Satan would perform his greatest work, or one should say, his most devious work, in this sector. Everyone knows who and what modernists are and all of their stripe; however, almost everyone thinks of Fundamentalists and Evangelicals as being Godly people, just exactly as much of Israel thought of the Pharisees of Jesus' day.

I'm trying to say the following:

A LESSON WE SHOULD LEARN

Even though the Pharisees claimed to studiously follow the Word of God, in fact, they knew the Word of God not at all and, therefore, followed it not at all. Their entire existence was that of facade and sham. But it fooled many people, because very few in Israel of that day actually knew the Word.

It is the same presently: The Word of God is to be the example, the criteria, the plumb line if you will, for all things. If it doesn't measure up to the Word, it must be discarded at all costs, even as the Judaizers did not measure up to the Word.

The sad fact is, even as before, modern Christians know the Word very little as well. So, it's possible for all type of people to make all types of claims, because most don't know if it is truly Scriptural or not!

Even though there are no more Judaizers, the truth is, their modern counterparts are very numerous, although cloaked in different garb. Now it is Baptist garb, Pentecostal garb, Holiness garb, or Charismatic garb.

None of these things are wrong within themselves and, in fact, can be very right. It is just that, the greatest danger to the Work of God is going to come and, in fact, is already coming from these sources. That doesn't mean that the sources themselves are evil, but that evil men within these particular institutions use these things as a cloak for their own devious purposes. Consequently, millions (yes, I said millions), are eternally lost, because they are deceived by this cloak.

Paul is saying here, and I am trying to say, that our confidence must not be in anything, not the Church, not men, not religious offices, etc., but only in the Finished Work of Christ. This is absolutely imperative.

This doesn't mean that all of these things are evil, for they aren't. It just means, that from these sources come the greatest evil, always as angels of light, against which the true Saint of God must always be on guard.

Regrettably, most go with the tide, and very seldom think for themselves. In other words, most do not measure the things which are done in the world of religion against the Word of God. They just accept what they perceive things to be, which most of the time is wrong.

THAT IN WHICH WE TRUST

The phrase, *"If any other man thinketh that he hath whereof he might trust in the flesh, I more,"* drives to the very heart of the matter.

For generations, the pious Jews, those who were determined to keep the Covenant, had come to place great reliance upon purity of ancestry. This helps explain the elaborate genealogies of Chronicles and of Matthew, even though the Holy Spirit gave these for an entirely different reason, namely as it referred to the proper lineage of Christ concerning Abraham and David. It also helps to explain the horror that Ezra and Nehemiah had of mixed marriages and the stern prohibition against such, and rightly so!

Concern at this point was justified historically, because as stated, all of this had to do with Israel's purpose, her bringing the Messiah into the world, Who would be the Redeemer and Saviour of all humanity.

As time went on, however, a false importance began to be attached to these externals. To conservative people who are careful about such things in keeping with the best traditions of the past, Paul could speak man-to-man, for he too could point with pride to the purity of his ancestry. Actually, in this respect, the Apostle was second to none. Consequently, the Judaizers chose very unwisely in attempting to come up against Paul with their false way.

Paul is about to say, that if there was any advantage for Salvation to be derived from birth, blood, and external conformity to the Law, he possessed all of this. He had more to rely on than most other men; nay, he could have boasted of advantages of this sort which could not be found united in possibly many other individuals. What these advantages were he proceeds to specify, which, incidentally, would have meant little to Gentiles, but very much to Jews.

MODERN CHRISTIANITY

The truth is that a remiss Christianity always becomes very much a Judaism. Such Christianity assumes that a life of respectable conventions, carried on within sacred institutions, will please God and save our souls. Consequently, what the Apostle has said against Judaism may very well be said against that in all its forms, even as we have been discussing.

For any full statement of the grounds of the Apostle's indignation at the Judaizing propaganda, the Reader must be referred to the expository writings on other Epistles, especially on those to the Corinthians and to the Galatians. Here a few words must suffice.

Judaizing made the highest pretensions to spiritual security and success; it proposed to expound the only worthy and genuine view of man's relation to God. But in reality the Judaizers wholly misrepresented Christianity, for they had missed the main meaning of it.

Judaizing turned men's minds away from what was highest to what was lowest — from love to law, from God's great gift of His Son, The Lord Jesus, to man's merits, from inward life and power, to outward ceremonial performance, from the spiritual and eternal to the material and the temporary. It was a huge, sad mistake; and yet it pressed upon Christians as the true Salvation, which availed with God, and could alone bring blessing to men.

Hence, as our Lord denounced the Pharisees with special energy — sometimes with withering sarcasm (Lk. 11:47) — so, and for the same reasons, does Paul attack the Judaizers. The Pharisees, to which we have already briefly alluded, applied themselves to turn the true spirituality of Israel into a soul-withering business of formalism and pride; and Paul's opponents strove to pervert to like effect even the gracious and life-given Gospel of Christ. To such he would not give place, no, not for an hour.

PREACHERS OF THE GOSPEL

Two things may be suggested here: one is the responsibility incurred by those who claim to be Preachers, and in that character endeavor to exert influence upon others. Such men, who claim to be called of God, take that which is highest and most sacred in the soul's capacities, and if they misdirect the soul's life here, if consciously or unconsciously they betray interests so sacred, if they successfully teach men to take that which is false for the true, and of course we're speaking of things which pertain to God, their responsibility is of the heaviest.

Another point we must make, is the energy with which the Apostle denounces these evil workers. Unfortunately, this is a distasteful business, and only draws the ire of those who are ensconced in such false directions. In other words, no Preacher who stands up for what is right, will receive accolades, but rather the very opposite.

While we should at the same time, warn those who would become judgmental and, therefore, self-righteous; still, even though such Preachers exist, they are few and far between, at least as it regards taking a stand against that which is false. While we must be very careful that we do not engage in a wrath which worketh not the Righteousness of God, at the same time we must not be so timid as to be fearful of taking a stand on anything. Tragically, the latter is the great problem and danger in most cases.

THE APOSTLE

At this point the Apostle cannot but emphasize his own right to speak. He appeals to his remarkable history. He knows all about this Judaic religion, which glories in the flesh, and he knows also the better way. The experience which had transformed his life entitled him to a hearing; for, indeed, he, as no man, had searched out the worth of both the ways of it.

So he is led into a remarkable testimony regarding the nature and the working forces of true Christian Salvation. And this, while it serves the purpose of throwing deserved disgrace on this *"religion of the flesh,"* serves at the same time a higher and more durable purpose. It sets the glory of the life of Faith, Love, and Worship, against the meanness of all fleshly life whatever; thus it vividly impresses on all hearers and readers the alternatives with which we have to deal, and the greatness of the choice which we are called to make.

Now comes this remarkable catalog of things one might have a tendency to glory in, especially were he Jewish:

(5) "CIRCUMCISED THE EIGHTH DAY, OF THE STOCK OF ISRAEL, OF THE TRIBE OF BENJAMIN, AN HEBREW OF THE HEBREWS; AS TOUCHING THE LAW, A PHARISEE;"

Now he enumerates some of those reasons for confidence in the flesh. First on the list is physical circumcision, perhaps because the Judaizers so greatly stressed it. Proselytes received this rite at the time they adopted Judaism. (Were some of the Judaizing teachers of this sort?) Others perhaps, submitted to this rite in adulthood for other reasons (Acts 16:3).

But Paul had been circumcised as a Jewish boy in accord with the instruction given to Abraham (Gen. 17:12) and in accord with what the Law later prescribed (Lev. 12:3). Furthermore, he was born of Israelite stock. He was no proselyte; the blood of Jacob flowed in him.

As well, he belonged to the Tribe of Benjamin, a fact he proudly acknowledged on more than one occasion (Acts 13:21; Rom. 11:1). This Tribe alone had been faithful to the Davidic Throne along with Judah, at the time of the division of the Kingdom. In fact, it had given the nation its first king, after whom Paul had been named by his parents.

By calling himself a *"Hebrew of Hebrews,"* he may have meant he had no mixed parentage but was of pure Jewish ancestry from both parents. The phrase probably also referred to his linguistic and cultural upbringing, which involved the Hebrew and Aramaic languages (in distinction from that of the Hellenistic Jews), even though he had been born outside of Israel (Acts 6:1; 22:2-3).

NOTES

BENJAMIN

It is often averred that Paul mentions his connection with Benjamin because that Tribe was especially honored among the tribes of Israel. In addition to the distinctions of Benjamin mentioned in the exposition, this Patriarch (Benjamin) was the only one born in the Promised Land, his brothers being born in Syria. As well, he was the offspring of Jacob's favorite wife, and the Feast of Purim commemorated the national deliverance by Mordecai, a Benjamite.

Furthermore, some suggest that this Tribe held the post of honor in the armies of Israel (*"following you, Benjamin,"* Judg. 5:14).

We must recognize, however, that the Tribe of Benjamin had its share of disappointing episodes, King Saul left much to be desired as a spiritual leader. As well, the shameful episode of the Levite and his concubine (Judg. Chpts. 19-20), the kidnapping of women at Shiloh (Judg. Chpt. 21), and the cursing of David by Shimei (II Sam. 16:5-14), are blots upon the name of Benjamin and should caution us against elevating this tribe unduly. Paul's point may simply have been that he was an Israelite by birth — a Benjamite as a matter of fact — and thus was certainly a genuine Jew.

In addition, it had been his own choice to belong to the most orthodox of the Jewish parties, the Pharisees. This party contained the most zealous supporters and interpreters of Old Testament Law, and also, Paul had studied under Gamaliel, its most celebrated teacher (Acts 5:34; 22:3) (Kent).

THE STOCK OF ISRAEL

The phrase, *"Circumcised the eighth day, of the stock of Israel,"* means very little to Gentiles, but was very important as it regarded the Jews.

He says literally, *"Eight days old in circumcision."* Converts to Judaism were circumcised at the time of their conversion. Ishmaelites in their thirteenth year. But Paul was neither. He was a pure-blooded Jew. He was *"of the stock of Israel."*

"Of" is literally *"out of,"* and is the word used to denote origin, the class or country of a man.

The word *"stock"* also speaks of origin. Paul came, not from Esau but from Jacob. So, regarding ancestry, there was no blemish on this part of Paul's life. Consequently, and as stated, the Judaizers did not choose wisely when they picked Paul to argue the point of Grace and Law. He knew both sides of the argument as possibly no other human being on Earth at that time.

THE TRIBE OF BENJAMIN

The phrase, *"Of the Tribe of Benjamin,"* as stated, was worn with some pride as it regarded the affiliation of Israel. Judah was the kingly Tribe, but as stated, Benjamin was the only Tribe which stayed with Judah at the time of the division of the nation, which took place a little over 40 years after the death of David.

THE HEBREWS

The phrase, *"An Hebrew of the Hebrews,"* actually goes all the way back to Abraham.

This title containing allusion of the *"passing over of Abraham"* from the other side of Euphrates; who was, therefore, in the language of the Phoenician tribes among whom he came, *"Abraham the Hebrew,"* or *"Ho perates (the one who is from beyond)"* as it is well given in the Septuagint (Gen. 14:13). The name, as thus explained, is not one by which the chosen people know themselves, but by which others know them; not one which they have taken, but which others have imposed on them; and we find the use of *"Hebraios"* through all the Old Testament, entirely consistent with this explanation of its origin. In every case it is either a title by which foreigners designate the Chosen Race (Gen. 39:14, 17; 41:12; Ex. 1:16, 19; I Sam. 4:6; 13:19; 29:3); or by which they designate themselves to foreigners (Gen. 40:15; Ex. 2:7; 3:18; 5:3; 9:9; Jonah 1:9); or by which they speak of themselves in tacit opposition to other nations (Gen. 43:32; Deut. 15:12; I Sam. 13:3; Jer. 34:9, 14); never, that is, it seems, without such national antagonism, either latent or expressed.

THE SIGNIFICANCE OF ALL THIS

Some may wonder as to why the understanding of these things carries significance, or the history of the Old Testament for that matter.

While the Old Testament is definitely history, it is far more than that as it regards the Child of God, and even the entirety of the world for that matter.

When one reads the Old Testament, one should understand that he is reading more than mere accounts of happenings which took place thousands of years ago, and which at first thought would seem to have little bearing upon the individual at present. If one would read these accounts, no matter how trivial that some of them may seem, with the understanding that each of these happenings is in fact a step toward our Redemption, which is the single most important thing in the world, then all of a sudden, everything in the Old Testament takes on a brand-new perspective. In fact, all of this is the story of God's dealings with the human race, and the bringing of a Redeemer into the world which was of absolute necessity, that is if man was to be saved. Whereas Israel figured so prominently in all of this, simply because they were raised up for the particular purpose of giving to the world the Word of God and as well, to serve as the womb of the Messiah so to speak, understanding this, Israel takes on a brand-new perspective as well.

That means that nothing in the Bible, and we mean absolutely nothing, is insignificant. Every part and particle of each and every account serves its purpose in portraying the greatest event in human history, proclaims to us what the Bible is all about, i.e., *"the coming of The Lord Jesus Christ as our Redeemer."* Consequently, that's why it is so very, very important!

HEBREWS AND JEWS

The word *"Hebrews"* is a much rarer word than the word *"Jews."* This word is employed when it is intended to designate the people on the side of their language. Consequently, we speak to this present day of the *"Jewish Nation,"* but of the *"Hebrew Tongue."*

In fact, the name *"Jew"* is of much later origin. It does not carry us back to the very birth and cradle of the chosen people, to the day when the Father of the faithful passed over the river, and entered into the land of inheritance; but keeps rather a lasting record of the period of national disruption and decline.

It is easy to see how the name *"Jew"* extended to the whole nation. When the Ten Tribes were carried into Assyria, and were absorbed among the nations, that smaller section of the people (Judah and Benjamin) which remained henceforth represented the whole; and thus it was only natural that the word *"Jew"* should express, as it now came to do, not only the Kingdom of Judah as distinguished from that of Israel, but any member of the nation, a *"Jew"* in this wider sense, as opposed to a Gentile. Consequently, the Eastern Wise Men inquired, *"Where is He that is born King of the Jews?"* (Mat. 2:2). In fact, the manner in which they posed this question, testified to the fact that they were themselves Gentiles, for they would certainly have asked for the King of Israel, had they meant to claim any nearer share in Him. So, too, the Roman soldiers and the Roman Governor give to Jesus the mocking title, *"King of the Jews"* (Mat. 27:29, 37), while His Own countrymen, the High Priests, challenge Him to prove by coming down from the Cross that He is *"King of Israel"* (Mat. 27:42).

They were using the title *"Israel,"* in this case, because they wanted to stir up more indignation against Jesus by Rome, who did not take kindly to people declaring themselves kings, etc.

Indeed, the absolute name, that which expressed the whole dignity and glory of a member of the theocratic nation, of the people and peculiar Covenant with God, was *"Israelites."*

This name was for the Jew his special badge and title of honor. To be descendants of Abraham, this honor they must share with the Ishmaelites (Gen. 16:15); or Abraham and Isaac with the Edomites (Gen. 24:25); but none except themselves were the seed of Jacob, such as in this name of *"Israelite"* they were declared to be.

Nor was this all, but more gloriously still, their decent was herein traced up to him, not as he was Jacob, but as he was Israel, who as a Prince had power with God and with men, and prevailed (Gen. 32:28). Thus, this title (Israelite) was accounted the noblest, we have ample proof. Thus, as we have seen, when the Ten Tribes threw off their allegiance to the House of David, they claimed in their pride and pretention the name of *"the Kingdom of Israel"* for the new kingdom which they set up — the kingdom, as the name was intended to imply, and which the line of the Promises, the true succession of the early Patriarchs, ran. So, too, there is no nobler title with which the Lord can adorn Nathanael than that of *"an Israelite indeed"* (Jn. 1:47), one in whom all which that name involved might indeed be found.

And when Peter, and again when Paul, would obtain a hearing from the men of their own nation, they, therefore, addressed them with the name most welcome to their ears, *"Israelites"* (Acts 2:22; 3:12; 13:16; Rom. 9:4; II Cor. 11:22; Phil. 3:5).

THE THREE TITLES

When we use the three titles, *"Hebrews, Jews, and Israelites,"* we should remember the following:

The word *"Hebrews"* speaks rather of the language as contrasted with Gentile languages.

When using the title *"Jew,"* it is his national distinction from a Gentile.

When using the word *"Israelite,"* we are actually using the most august title of all. It refers to a Jew as he is a member of the theocracy, meaning of the nation of Israel, and thus an heir of the Promises given to the Patriarchs and Prophets of old.

In the first word or title is predominately noted his language; the second his nationality; and the third his theocratic privileges and glorious vocation (Trench).

A PHARISEE

The phrase, *"As touching the Law, a Pharisee,"* referred to those who were the successors of the *"men of the great Synagogue."* These were the Covenanters who would agree to keep the Law no matter what happened. They were descendants of the Hasidim, or the devout ones whose main concern was adherence to the Covenant.

During the Second Century B.C. the Pharisees were prominent in the Maccabean revolt against heathenism. They were the hard core of resistance to the move to abandon the faith of their fathers. They were the righteous remnant within the nation whose main concern was keeping the Law of God pure.

Thereafter, Pharisaism, which began so right, became a synonym for Righteousness, for Holiness, for the Faith. In fact, the Pharisees during the time of Jesus were the largest and most influential of the several sects of the Jews. It was they who kept alive worship in the Synagogues throughout Israel. Tragically, they had deteriorated so much from their original position of Righteousness, that when the True Righteousness came, The Lord Jesus Christ, they opposed Him greatly, actually becoming bitter enemies of our Lord, playing the greatest part of all in His crucifixion.

But Paul was more than just another Pharisee, as we shall see.

(6) "CONCERNING ZEAL, PERSECUTING THE CHURCH; TOUCHING THE RIGHTEOUSNESS WHICH IS IN THE LAW, BLAMELESS."

When measured for its zeal, Paul's pre-Christian life had been noted for promoting Judaism and condemning followers of Christ. In fact, he had become the arch-persecutor of the Church, and his reputation had gone far beyond Jerusalem (Acts 9:13, 21).

He had been no half-hearted Judaist. When judged by men in accord with the Righteousness the Law demands, at least as it was presumed to be, he had been blameless. As an earnest Pharisee, he had paid meticulous attention to the requirements of the Mosaic Law, and no one could have charged him with failure to keep it, at least as they saw such according to the externals.

Of course, a distinction must be drawn between external conformity to the Law in areas where men can judge and inflict legal penalties, and the perfect spiritual conformity to it that God Alone can truly assess, and by which *"no man will be justified,"* i.e., *"by which no man can measure up"* (Gal. 2:16; 3:11).

PERSECUTING THE CHURCH

The phrase, *"Concerning zeal, persecuting the Church,"* portrays the fact that Paul at that particular time frame in his life, of course before his conversion, considered then his persecution of the Church a meritorious work. That's how spiritually blind religion actually is.

Zeal was supposed to be, as it is, an important part of religion. Paul says that he had shown the highest degree of zeal that was possible. He had gone so far in his attachment for the religion of his fathers, or at least what he thought that religion was to be, as to pursue, with purposes of death, those who he claimed had departed from it, and who had embraced a different form of belief. If any, therefore, could hope for Salvation on the ground of extraordinary devotedness to religion, then he would have qualified. He honestly believed that the New Testament Church should be wiped from the face of the Earth, and he did his worst to accomplish that purpose (Acts 7:58; 9:1-2).

It is believed by some, that Paul was being groomed to be the shining light of Pharisaism. In other words, Pharisaism had penned its hopes on him. Consequently, his zeal was demonstrated by the ardor by which he sought to defeat the early Christian witness to Christ. As the chief heresy-hunter, his name was feared above that of all others as he labored to stop by force an idea and a faith with which force could not cope. This shows how in this he departed from the teaching of Gamaliel, when he was *"exceedingly mad against"* the Christians, and *"persecuted them even unto strange cities."* He thought he was doing God service by persecuting those whom he counted as heretics.

WHY HAS THIS BEEN THE PATTERN OF SO MUCH OF RELIGION?

I think it stems from self-righteousness.

In fact, even at this present time, there are many Preachers in the United States, some of them recognizable names, who would go to any length to stop those who do not agree with their brand of religion, or for whatever reason, even to the point of murder, exactly as had been the life of Paul then known as Saul, were it not for the law of the land. In fact, that is the only thing that stops their efforts. Most of the Church world doesn't know that; nevertheless, it is true!

In fact, some of the heads of Denominations would do the same, in other words, go to any length to stop the Ministries of those of whom they do not approve.

And what is it of which they do not approve?

Self-righteousness can come up with many things which it labels as reasons, but in reality are excuses. With some it is doctrine, but with most it is control, and I speak especially of denominational heads. Self-righteousness always thinks that it's doing God a service by its actions, and it legitimizes those actions irrespective as to what they might be. This is how the Pharisees could kill the Lord in the Name of the Lord. To those who truly know the Lord, the actions of such are so obviously wrong that they beggar description, and yet, such is not obvious at all to the self-righteous. The more brutal they can be, the more hurtful, the more pain they inflict, all seems to add up to them as a *"work for God."*

As we've already stated, Satan's greatest opposition to the True Work of God always comes from this sector. With these people, and they are numerous, the Word of God has no bearing on anything. They make up their own rules as they go along and change them according to their whim or fancy. As Paul before his conversion, they have no idea that they are actually fighting against God, but rather think they are doing the Work of God.

WHY DOES SELF-RIGHTEOUSNESS AFFECT PEOPLE IN THIS MANNER?

Of course, self-righteousness is any and all so-called righteousness, which is not of Christ. At all times, even as with Paul, it is very religious, and because it is very religious, it serves as a self-deceiving power.

Those who truly have the Righteousness of Christ, let the Lord take care of situations which seem to be negative. They do not take matters into their own hands and never seek vengeance, and never seek to punish people, etc. As stated, they leave all of that up to the Lord. He is the Head of their Church, and they look to Him, while the self-righteous look to themselves or other men.

Inasmuch as self-righteousness is that which is concocted by men, it has to be protected by men. Inasmuch as it's all done in the Name of the Lord, it seems to feel justified in anything it does, any act carried out, with no limitations on anything. In other words, the end justifies the means, whatever those means might be, and ever how diabolical those means might be. The Pharisees will join with the Sadducees against Christ, even though they normally hated the Sadducees. Self-righteousness, draws up its own rules, and feels free to change them as it so desires.

So, Paul could apprehend followers of Christ, drag them from their homes, cause them to be thrown into prison, and for some even to their deaths. He could do this before his conversion, without a twinge of conscience, without one single grief of heart, but rather the very opposite — all the time, thinking he was doing the Work of the Lord. That's how deceived the man was, and that's how deceived millions are presently!

Strangely enough, Paul was to suffer the same persecution after his conversion, as he had meted out to others before his conversion.

THE RIGHTEOUSNESS IN THE LAW

The phrase, *"Touching the Righteousness which is in the Law, blameless,"* speaks of how ardent Paul was before his conversion, thinking all the time that doing all of this, even to the killing of followers of Christ, that such was earning merit with God. Consequently, it was not sins so much that Paul surrendered in order to win Christ, but righteousness, i.e., *"self-righteousness."* Christ died not only to expiate and abolish Paul's sins, along with all of ours, but also to expiate and abolish his righteousnesses, and ours as well.

The Righteousness which is from God is offered to the sinner in Christ, and secured by him freely by Faith as opposed to works.

I think we can see from this that *"righteousness"* was an important word with Paul. In fact, it is probably the most important single word in the Epistle to the Romans. Paul constantly contrasts the righteousness in the Law with the Righteousness in Christ.

When Paul speaks of the righteousness in the Law, he means a conformity to the letter of legislation, i.e., *"the keeping of rules."* He has reference to performance, to obedience.

The Old Covenant stressed the importance of performance — *"this do and thou shalt live."* Adherence to the Covenant, therefore, meant obedience, conformity, performance. In this Covenant, the faithful placed chief stress upon *"duty, that stern daughter of the voice of God."*

This was excellent as far as it went. Theoretically, every Jew could keep the Commandments; actually, none did. Irrespective, they tried to make Salvation out of their efforts, becoming more and more tedious, even adding over a hundred laws of their own making to the original Law of Moses.

When Paul used the word *"blameless,"* he was not speaking of sinless perfection, not at all! He was speaking of meeting every requirement of Judaism, being of pure stock, and of fanatical zeal in protecting Judaism (II Cor. 11:22; Gal. 1:13-14).

The truth was, Paul did not know God, despite all his claims, was not doing the Work of God as he thought, but rather the very opposite, was not making himself righteous, but actually making himself very unrighteous. But yet he was so blinded to all of this, that he did not see it and, in fact, could not see it until Christ appeared to him on the road to Damascus.

AFTER HIS CONVERSION WAS PAUL THEN OPPOSED TO THE LAW OF MOSES?

No, not at all! The Law of Moses was actually from God and, in fact, the greatest and only perfectly righteous legislation the world ever knew. Actually, it was the Standard of God, the Standard to which man must attain, if God was to be pleased.

The situation is, after his conversion, Paul then was able to properly understand the Law of Moses, whereas previously, he did not understand it at all, completely misinterpreting its precepts.

How does the Law of Moses affect Christians presently, and I speak primarily of the moral Law, which we refer to as the Ten Commandments?

The Scripture plainly tells us, actually the words of Paul, that Believers are delivered from the Law (Rom. 7:6); dead to the Law (Gal. 2:19); free from the Law (Rom. 8:2); and redeemed from the Law (Gal. 3:13; 4:5; 5:18); and that Christ is the end of the Law (Rom. 10:4).

Does this mean that we Christians can do as we please, ignore the Ten Commandments, and actually live any way we like?

This is a question which is repeatedly raised by those who do not understand either

NOTES

the nature, purpose, or the Ministry of the Law. Consequently, the Church vacillates from one extreme to the other, from ignoring the Law altogether, to the extreme opposite of legalism.

Some claim that Grace covers all things, and that sin is insignificant as it regards a Christian. Others attempt to be holy by trying to keep the Law, actually even making more laws, even as the Pharisees of old.

Which is correct?

Of course, neither way is God's way, with both leading oddly enough to the same end, self-righteousness.

The truth is, when Paul introduced the great Gospel of Grace under the New Covenant, exactly as it was given to him by the Holy Spirit, he was accused of giving people a license to sin, in other words, that the sin of the Christian was merely a stepping stone to demonstrate God's goodness. Paul called these critics, *"slanderers."* Consequently, we can tell anyone who claims that Grace gives a license to sin, that they are merely slandering the True Gospel. No one who understands the tenants of Grace ever teaches that Grace permits sin. In fact, Paul emphatically denies the charge. He says:

"What shall we say then? Shall we continue in sin, that Grace may abound?

"God forbid. How shall we, who are dead to sin, live any longer therein?" (Rom. 6:1-2).

PAUL'S APPRAISAL OF LEGALISM

Paul taught that love is the fulfilling of the Law, springing from a purified heart and unfeigned faith.

In fact, Paul never downgraded the Law, or deny its perfection and holiness in justice. He says:

"But we know that the Law is good, if a man use it lawfully" (I Tim. 1:8).

This means that there is nothing wrong with the Law, but rather those who are trying to keep it. And now follow closely Paul's argument.

Before we read it, remember he has said that the Believer is not under the Law. To whom then does it apply? Pay close attention to I Timothy 1:9-11:

"Knowing this, that the Law is not made for a righteous man, but for the lawless and

disobedient, for the ungodly and for sinners, for unholy and profane, for murderers of fathers and murderers of mothers, for manslayers.

"For whoremongers, for them that defile themselves with mankind, for menstealers, for liars, for perjured persons, and if there be any other thing that is contrary to sound doctrine;

"According to the Glorious Gospel of the Blessed God, which was committed to my trust" (I Tim. 1:9-11).

NOT FOR THE RIGHTEOUS

Note carefully the opening words of the Passage we have just quoted, *"Knowing that the Law is not made for a righteous man."* A righteous man who has never broken the Law in any manner at any time has nothing to fear from the Law. It has no claim upon him if he is not guilty.

The Law does not punish the innocent or the righteous. It only punishes transgressors. If there had ever lived a man who kept God's Law perfectly, he would be totally free from any obligation or fear of punishment. But such a man never lived, for David said:

"The Lord looked down from Heaven . . . to see if there were any (one) *who did understand, and seek God"* (Ps. 14:2).

And what did God find? Did He find any righteous men? Listen:

"They are all gone aside, they are all together become filthy: there is none that doeth good, no, not one" (Ps. 14:3).

And Paul under inspiration echoes the same verdict in Romans. He says it is a proven fact that all men are under sin:

"As it is written, there is none righteous, no, not one:

"There is none that understandeth, there is none that seeketh after God.

"They are all gone out of the way . . . there is none that doeth good, no, not one" (Rom. 3:10-12).

The condemnation of the Law, therefore, is universal, without a single exception. Now let us go back to Paul's Letter to Timothy:

"Knowing this, that the Law is not made for a righteous man . . ." (I Tim. 1:9).

But there is none righteous, so who is it then for? The answer is devastating.

NOTES

It is for sinners, profane, murderers, whoremongers, thieves, liars, and the like. If you are guilty of any of these, plus many sins we have not named, you have reason to fear the Law, and we speak of the Law of God, for it condemns you. Consequently, those who say they are under the Law, thereby admit (although they may not know it) that they are in the category of the sinners enumerated by Paul: lawless, disobedient, profane, filthy, murderers, whoremongers, and liars. The only way to escape the Curse of the Law upon these sins is to be a righteous man — holy and sinless, but there aren't any!

WHO IS RIGHTEOUS?

We have seen that there is not a single Adam's son, which covers the entirety of the human race and for all time, who is righteous. What a hopeless situation!

But wait!

While man does not possess a Righteousness of his own, there is Another Who has provided a Righteousness which can be imputed to the guilty sinner. This One Who can provide the Righteousness of the Law is the Lord Jesus Christ, the only One Who ever kept God's Law perfectly, and then, in addition, paid the penalty of the broken Law for unrighteous, guilty sinners. By His Death on Calvary He atoned for the broken Law; by His Resurrection He provided His Righteousness to all who believe.

And now see the result in those who believe. God accepts the payment of the penalty for sin which Jesus made when He died on the Cross, and reckons it to the account of those who receive His offer of Salvation by Faith. The penalty for sin is paid, and there is no condemnation. And then that pardoned sinner is clothed in the sinless Righteousness of the Lord Jesus Christ, and stands in God's sight, as though he had never sinned, but is as holy in Christ as the Law demanded. The sinner has by imputation (something freely given to him) of Jesus' Righteousness become a justified Saint.

Regrettably, we are still imperfect in our old nature, we still fail at times in our walk, but in our position in the Sight of God, which is by Faith, we are perfect and complete, because we are in Christ Jesus, and He is perfect.

A SUBSTITUTE AND A REPRESENTATIVE MAN

Christ was both our Substitute and our Representative Man. As our Substitute He did for us what we could not do for ourselves, in effect, taking our place. That means that as our Substitute, He was born of the Virgin Mary, so He was born sinless, the only One Who ever was after Adam. As our Substitute He walked perfect before God, perfectly keeping the Law, in effect, walking perfect before the Father.

As our Substitute He hung on the Cross, paying the penalty which we rightly owed, but could not pay. He gave his life as our Substitute, was buried as our Substitute, and raised from the dead as our Substitute. Also, as our Substitute He is now seated by the Right Hand of the Father.

However, He is more than our Substitute, in that He is also our Representative Man. The latter means that as such, whatever it is that He gained in all of this, is looked at by God as being mine, that is if I evidence Faith in Him and His Sacrificial Work. Being a Substitute is one thing, but being a Representative Man is something else altogether.

As a Substitute He did for me what I could not do for myself; however, as my Representative Man, whatever He did, whatever victory He purchased, in fact, whatever He is, I am. That's why Paul kept using the phrase over and over *"in Christ!"*

This is a powerful Truth, actually the bedrock of Christianity, which is the Source of all Salvation and all Victory in our everyday walk. And yet, sadly and regrettably, most Christians little know or understand these things of which we speak. And the truth is, if one does not properly understand these things, one simply cannot walk in Victory. One can be saved, because Salvation comes strictly by simple Faith in what Christ did at the Cross; however, our everyday walk before God as it concerns our Victory, actually our Sanctification, comes in the very same manner that our Salvation came, simple Faith in Christ and what He did at the Cross and the Resurrection. But regrettably, we little maintain that simple Faith in that great Work, but rather start to put our Faith in other things, and it doesn't really matter what the other things are. If our Faith is not squarely in the Finished Work of Christ, sin will dominate us in some way (Rom. 6:14).

While it may not be one of the common vices such as immorality or alcohol, etc., it will be something else such as jealousy, envy, malice, unforgiveness, covetousness, depression, etc. I'll say it again, *"It is impossible to live a life of Victory, without knowing and understanding these things of which I say."*

THE RIGHTEOUSNESS OF CHRIST

Such a justified sinner, one who has placed his Faith totally in Christ and what Christ has done for us, is called righteous before God because of the merits of the Lord Jesus Christ and that alone. God will judge him if he sins as a Believer and fails to confess, but condemnation is forever past, that is, if Faith remains in the Cross.

Let's go back to our Scripture in I Timothy:

"Knowing this, that the Law is not made for a righteous man . . ." (I Tim. 1:9).

The man or woman who has been declared righteous through God's Grace by Faith in Christ is, therefore, free from the condemnation of the Law, for all its demands have been satisfied in Christ. That's why he is free from those demands, not because he has kept the Law, because none have other than Christ.

Actually, the Law is still condemning sin and sinners all over the world and for all time, at least ever since it was given. It continues to be God's requirement, and stands to condemn and even damn everyone who is not in Christ. Listen again to Paul:

"Who was before a blasphemer, and a persecutor, and injurious: but I obtained mercy, because I did it ignorantly in unbelief.

"And (but) *the Grace of our Lord was exceeding abundant with Faith and Love* (toward me) *which is in Christ Jesus"* (I Tim. 1:13-14).

Despite what Paul had been before coming to Christ, due to the Grace of God, which was extended to Paul as it is every seeking soul, upon Faith in Christ, all of these past terrible sins, have been stricken from the record and no longer hang over the head of the Apostle, or anyone else who has trusted Christ. That's what it means to not now have any condemnation.

DOES THE LAW OF MOSES HAVE ANY MINISTRY PRESENTLY?

The ceremonial and civil parts of the Law have no ministry at present, all having been fulfilled in Christ. I speak of the Sabbath, Circumcision, Feast Days, Sacrifices, etc. They were types, and when Jesus came, the types were of no more necessity, as should be obvious.

However, the moral part of the Law, which is the Ten Commandments, actually minus the fourth concerning the keeping of the Sabbath, is very much incumbent upon the entirety of the world, and simply because moral laws cannot change.

In fact, Sabbath-keeping was the only one of the Ten Commandments which had no moral content. Consequently, we do not find in the Book of Acts where the Church kept the Sabbath at all. In fact, it met and worshiped on Sunday, labeled the *"first day of the week"* (Acts 20:7; Mat. 28:1; Mk. 16:9; Jn. 20:1, 19, 26; I Cor. 16:2; Rev. 1:10). However, all the other Commandments are still incumbent upon the entirety of the world.

So, is the Christian to try to keep the Commandments? Instinctively we know in our hearts, due to the fact that we are new creations in Christ Jesus, that we must no longer steal, or lie, etc. And yet, even though these things must be kept, the secret is, they have already been kept in Christ. As long as the Believer rests in Christ, the Commandments, the moral Law, will automatically be kept. But when the Christian sets out to try to keep them in any other way except through Christ, he will fail every single time.

So, what is the ministry of the Law today, since Christ fulfilled its demands on Calvary?

Its ministry is still the same in condemning the sinner who rejects Christ. While the Believer is free from the Law, delivered and redeemed, those who refuse the Righteousness Jesus provided, are still under its threatenings, whether they are unbelievers or Believers.

But to the Believer who is totally trusting Christ, the Law holds no threat anymore, for he is in God's sight, righteous, but only because of the Righteousness of Christ, and such Righteousness which has come to the Believer through Faith in Christ, and in no other way.

RIGHTEOUSNESS OUTSIDE OF THE LAW

Paul plainly said, *"But now the Righteousness of God without the Law is manifested...*

"Even the Righteousness of God which is by Faith of (in) *Jesus Christ unto all and upon all them that believe"* (Rom. 3:21-22).

What a Glorious Gospel of Grace. For all who reject God's Righteousness, the Law stands as the minister of judgment and wrath. Paul says:

"For the Wrath of God is revealed from Heaven against all ungodliness and unrighteousness of men" (Rom. 1:18).

And then, *"Because the Law worketh wrath"* (Rom. 4:15), in other words, it has a penalty, even as all Law does or should!

In Colossians Chapter 3, Paul gives a list of sins which are condemned by the Law, and says:

"For which things' sake the Wrath of God cometh on the children of disobedience" (Col. 3:6).

But the Believer is counted righteous in the sight of God. Abraham, the example of saving Faith, *"believed God, and it was counted unto him for Righteousness"* (Rom. 4:3). In other words, Abraham did not earn this Righteousness, but it was rather freely imputed to him according to his Faith in God, and more particularly, what the Son of God would do on the Cross in order to provide this Righteousness.

IN SUMMARY

The Law of God as it refers to the moral Law (the Ten Commandments), is still incumbent on the entirety of the human race. In other words, this is what God demands of all humanity.

However, there is no way, due to man's fallen nature, that he can come up to this Standard, no matter how hard he tries. As well, he can devise his own laws, set up his own religions, even as most of the world does, but that does not make things right with God whatsoever, only worse. God still demands that mankind come up to the Standard which He gave us in Exodus Chapter 20.

Of course, man cannot do this, so God provided a way that it could be done. He became man, kept the Law in every respect, and even took its penalty and curse upon Himself through His Death on the Cross, even though He never failed Himself, doing all of this on our behalf.

If man will exercise simple Faith in that which Jesus did, the great Righteousness which belongs to Christ, which He won by totally keeping the Law, and which penalty was handled by His Death, the perfect, pure, spotless Righteousness which belongs to Christ will be instantly given to the believing sinner, making him in the Eyes of God, just as pure as is Christ.

Again we emphasize it was not sins so much that Paul surrendered in order to win Christ, but rather his own self-concocted righteousnesses, of which the entirety of the world is guilty as well. In fact, and as stated, Christ died not only to expiate and abolish sins, but also to expiate and abolish man's phoney righteousnesses (plural), which are only a facade and nothing more, and in fact, that which God can never recognize.

So, the entirety of the world, which includes the Church, has a choice: It can try to be acceptable to God by its own works of righteousness, or at least what it calls righteousness but which God calls something else entirely, or it can accept the Righteousness provided by God through Jesus Christ. There is no other alternative, it is either one or the other.

Without the Righteousness of Christ man will die eternally lost. With the Righteousness of Christ, man will be eternally saved.

(7) "BUT WHAT THINGS WERE GAIN TO ME, THOSE I COUNTED LOSS FOR CHRIST."

Through his conversion on the Damascus road, Paul had learned to count all these things which he had once considered as *"advantages"* rather as liabilities because of Christ. *"Whatever"* or *"what things"* indicate that the previous listing was not exhaustive but illustrative. He once had regarded such things as place and position in the form of profit or gain toward his goal of achieving Righteousness by the Law. But now he has come to the settled conviction that they were actually a detriment.

They had not provided him with true Righteousness, even as they could not do so. By trusting falsely in human performance, he had not only failed to make any progress toward the righteousness God requires, but had also let his Jewish *"advantages"* drive him to persecute the Church — the Church incidentally, which proclaimed the Message of the Righteousness of God received by Faith, the only kind of Righteousness which God will accept.

GAIN TO ME

The phrase, *"But what things were gain to me,"* needs to be looked at very closely. As we've already brought out, Paul was speaking of his privileges as a Jew, which were illustrative of anything of this nature.

How does that affect us presently?

Repentance, includes not only a forsaking of sins, but as well, a forsaking of all good things which we have tried to use to bring about Righteousness. Consequently, man, and especially religious man, needs to repent not only of bad things, but as well of good things. That comes as very confusing to many Christians, because they hold these works of the flesh very dear to their heart.

What do we mean by that?

I speak of our Church affiliation, our work in the Church, all the religious things we do, the fact that our parents and grandparents possibly, belong to this or that particular Church, our Church heritage, etc.

All of these things are *"good,"* at least in our sight. And don't misunderstand, there's nothing wrong with belonging to a Church and being active in a Church. The point I'm attempting to make is this:

If we think these things earn us anything with God, they don't! If we think these things, and a whole lot we have not named, make us more holy or righteous, they don't! And we have to repent of our leaning in that direction, which means to repent of our good things, etc.

Everything must be thrown aside in order that we may win Christ. Every hope must be placed in Him and on Him. Everything we possess in the realm of Spiritual Blessings has come totally and completely through what Jesus did at the Cross. Consequently, our Faith, our confidence, our trust, our past, present, and future, all must reside in that, the Finished Work of Christ.

Everything else is out, and we mean everything! However, and as stated, this is very grievous to the flesh, because all of these things are very dear to our heart. Exactly as Abraham did not desire to give up Ishmael, simply because Ishmael was a fair work of his flesh; likewise, Christians do not like to give up these things which we think are so spiritual and religious, but in fact aren't (Gen. 21:9-12).

The problem with the Christian is, that we tend to turn good things, legitimate things, into works, which God cannot accept. Church is good, but if we think that attending a certain Church makes us holy before God, then we have perverted the true meaning of what Church ought to be.

Prayer is wonderful, without which a Christian cannot have a proper relationship with the Lord; however, we can turn prayer into works, which nullifies its effect. The same can be said for fasting, winning souls, giving money to the Work of the Lord, or doing any number of things in this capacity.

These things are good and right in their own way, but we are to never think of them as something that earns Righteousness for us. They don't, even as they can't. If kept in their proper perspective, they provide tremendous blessings, but only in their proper perspective.

The problem is, even as we've already said, we tend to make an idol out of things we do, which greatly frustrates the Grace of God.

LOSS FOR CHRIST

The phrase, *"Those I counted loss for Christ,"* presents *"loss"* in the singular. The various gains are all counted as one loss.

The circumstances under which Paul turned from these assumed assets and counted them loss for Christ is reported in three of the Chapters of Acts: 9, 22, and 26. So drastic was the sudden change in Paul's life that it seemed incredible to his contemporaries. In fact, had it not been for the intercession of Barnabas, Paul (rejected it seems from the Jerusalem Church) may well have turned back to Tarsus a broken man.

In fact, the suddenness of Paul's conversion has been compared many times to that of Augustine, Luther, and Wesley. In each of these cases there was determination and mistaken zeal that had to be turned into entirely new channels. The conversion of men like these was the more difficult because they had so much to unlearn and reject.

Paul counted his assets as *"refuse"* not because they were so bad, but because Christ was so good by contrast; he was speaking relatively. The result, however, was that Paul became more negative than he probably would have been otherwise.

THE PROBLEM OF MAN

What we're dealing with here, is actually the very essence of sin. Man is so full of himself that he has no openness of spirit which can be filled with God. He trusts his intellectual acumen, his humanistic ideals, his personal virtues, his disciplined life, his honesty, even his religious exercises — and holds them up to God as though they merit some type of Salvation. However, when one truly sees Christ, truly finds Christ, truly trusts Christ, one becomes horrified at his former trust in these past good things. Paul on the Damascus road saw that this native trust in his own achievements merited such horror; it was more of a hindrance than a help.

Consequently, when the Apostle found Christ, he transferred these former works from the credit side of the ledger to the debit side, considering all of them together as one great loss (Mat. 16:26). As a seaman throws everything overboard in a storm to save his life, so Paul discarded every vestige of personal merit *"on account of Christ."*

THE CAUSE FOR THE ANIMOSITY

As one sees Paul's insistence upon Christ and Christ Alone, which necessitates the abandoning of all trust in all good things other than Christ, for those who place some type of worth in things such as this, the animosity toward the Apostle would be great from those sources. It is the same presently!

It is very hard for the Church to understand, how a person can be unrighteous one moment and totally righteous the next. While most accept that as it regards a sinner initially coming to Christ, it is little accepted at all as it regards a Christian. In other words, if a Christian does something wrong, the spirit of the Church as it operates in the flesh, is to punish that Christian. That's what the flesh demands, and that's what the flesh does. Consequently, it has great difficulty in understanding how that Believer can simply ask the Lord's forgiveness with such being instantly done.

If any instruction is needed, it is that the Cross is to be explained to the failing brother or sister, which will show them how they went wrong to start with, even as Paul explains in Galatians 6:1. Instead, not accepting the Righteousness of Christ, the Church resorts to psychology, or to punishment in some form, or fashion.

All of this shows that the Church, at least the segment that falls into this category, which is the majority, is operating outside of the Spirit of God, in fact, in its own self-righteousness. The tell-tale signs are everywhere!

It all amounts to the Righteousness of Christ being totally rejected, and in its place, the so-called righteousness of man proposed. Of course, the Church would deny this, but that's actually what is happening.

Self-righteousness always hates, always despises, the pure, Righteousness of Christ. Please allow me to deal with this again, and because it is so very important.

If a Christian does wrong and all have at one time or the other, the Biblical remedy is repentance (I Jn. 1:9). Quite possibly the Christian may not really understand how he has been overcome, which will definitely be the case if he's not trusting in the Cross. Consequently, the Victory of the Cross is to be explained to that Christian, showing him that his failure is because that his trust and dependence was in something else instead of the Finished Work of Christ. That's why he failed. That is the extent as to what should be done.

Instead, what does much of the Church attempt to do?

It attempts to exert some type of punishment, which of course is an insult to Christ.

NOTES

First of all, it is hypocritical, because oftentimes, the ones doing the punishing, are in worse shape spiritually than the ones they are punishing. As well, there is no Christian qualified to punish another, even as James pointedly said (James 4:12).

However, such foolishness is carried out simply because the Righteousness of Christ has been rejected in favor of man's own contrived righteousness. Sadly and regrettably, this is rife in the present Church.

BUT DON'T WE NEED DISCIPLINE?

Most definitely we need discipline; however, the type of discipline we need can only be supplied by the Lord. Man cannot supply discipline for the simple reason, that man is not worthy to do so.

Now that statement will come as a great offense to the self-righteous. But it just happens to be true.

The truth is, when we attempt to punish a Christian for some failure they have had, we add insult to injury. We are, in effect, saying, whether we realize it or not, that what Christ did at the Cross was not enough. In other words, Christ did not suffer enough, and we must add some suffering to that which He has already done.

Does the Reader realize how crass that such thinking actually is? Do we realize how sinful and abominable that such is in the sight of God? Do we realize what an insult to Christ that such action is?

The problem is, the self-righteous cannot see this of which I say, for the simple reason that self-righteousness blinds them.

If we go any way but God's Way, we will reap the bitter results of the flesh which are always corruption. In fact, the great sin of the Church, is the rejection of the Righteousness of Christ, attempting to replace it with something else. The tragedy is, most do not believe they are doing such a thing, when they are doing it all the time.

Every single thing we do as a Believer, and especially as Preachers, must be evaluated in the light of the Word of God. Is it Scriptural? Does it line up completely with the Bible?

If it doesn't, we must abandon what is being done, and line it up with what the Word says, doing our very best to follow as close as possible to that which is laid down by the Holy Spirit. To do anything else will always lead to trouble and big trouble at that!

(8) "YEA DOUBTLESS, AND I COUNT ALL THINGS BUT LOSS FOR THE EXCELLENCY OF THE KNOWLEDGE OF CHRIST JESUS MY LORD: FOR WHOM I HAVE SUFFERED THE LOSS OF ALL THINGS, AND DO COUNT THEM BUT DUNG, THAT I MAY WIN CHRIST,"

Paul's thought broadens from his Jewish advantages just mentioned to include everything that might conceivably be a rival to his total trust in Christ. Christ is far superior to all of this in every respect, so much so that Paul had cast them away as nothing but rubbish.

For Paul, the knowledge of Christ Jesus as his Lord meant the intimate communion with Christ that began at his conversion and had been his experience all the years since then. It was not limited to the past, but was a growing relationship in which there was blessed enjoyment in the present and the challenge and excitement of increasing comprehension of Christ in personal fellowship.

Although at Regeneration a person receives Christ, this is only the beginning of his discovery of what riches this entails. In Christ all the treasures of wisdom and knowledge are hidden (Col. 2:3), but to search them out and appropriate them personally requires a lifetime (Kent).

THE EXCELLENCY OF THE KNOWLEDGE OF CHRIST JESUS MY LORD

The phrase, *"Yea doubtless, and I count all things but loss for the excellency of the knowledge of Christ Jesus my Lord,"* refers not merely to the knowledge which the Lord Jesus possesses, but the knowledge of the Lord Jesus which Paul gained through the experience of intimate companionship and communion with Him. Paul came to know the heart of the Lord, His Will, as one comes to know another through intimate fellowship and close association with that person. The distinctive Greek word for *"knowledge"* used here, leads us to this interpretation (Wuest).

Paul had come to a settled conviction with reference to the liability of what he had previously termed gains, that is, when failure to appropriate Christ would be the price he would have to pay should he hold onto those things. And he still held this conviction tenaciously as an habitual attitude of his mind towards anything which would come between him and his Lord. He sets everything down as a loss if he by retaining them, would deprive Himself in any way, of Christ.

The word *"excellency"* proclaims the fact that the knowledge of Christ so surpasses all other knowledge, and, indeed, all other blessings whatever, as to make them less than nothing.

As Chrysostom says, *"When the Sun has appeared, it is loss to sit by a candle."*

How that knowledge is gained we learn in Ephesians 3:17-19, *"That Christ may dwell in your hearts by Faith; that ye, being rooted and grounded in love, may ... know the Love of Christ, which passeth knowledge."*

THE WORDS OF JESUS

As it regards life, Jesus plainly said, *"Come unto Me, all ye that labour and are heavy laden, and I will give you rest.*

"Take My yoke upon you, and learn of Me" (Mat. 11:28-29).

To learn of Jesus, and about Jesus, is a lifelong project simply because He is inexhaustible in every capacity. Being God and especially considering that He became man, makes the situation in a sense even more grand. Considering this, it is so sad, that most Christians little avail themselves of the opportunity of the greatest fountain of wisdom available to mankind. But the manner in which Paul states these things, and which we know the Holy Spirit inspired him to do so, lets us know that this is a pursuit which must be put above everything else. And anything which would hinder that pursuit, be a blockage to its fulfillment, must be laid aside, irrespective as to what it might be. And to be sure, this is not just for Preachers, but for any and all Believers. That's what makes this so wonderful.

Any Believer, the least Believer, whomever that might be, has the same access to Christ as the greatest Apostle or Prophet in the world today. So, if we do not avail ourselves of this privilege, it is our fault and our fault alone.

HOW EXACTLY DO WE LEARN CHRIST?

We do so first of all, by stating that as our objective, our goal, our priority. Once that is established, and it must be established, other things tend to fall into place.

Second, if the Church we attend does not lift up Jesus and Jesus exclusively, but rather other things, in other words Jesus is a mere by-product, then we need to seriously consider finding another Church. As well, the Jesus Who is presented, must not be merely a philosophical Jesus, an intellectual Jesus, or even a miracle-working Jesus, but rather Jesus of the Cross and the Resurrection. How Jesus is presented to a great deal determines as to how we will learn Him, i.e., *"the excellency of the knowledge of Christ Jesus."*

The Christ held up by Paul, as we will see in the following Verses, is the Christ of the Cross and the Resurrection. If the foundation of our knowledge of Christ is not built on that, then it is a false foundation.

The idea is, Who and What Christ actually is must without fail include the Cross and the Resurrection. Christ has always been God, and those things as important as they are to us, actually add nothing to Him. However, the Cross and the Resurrection, i.e., *"the Finished Work of Christ,"* just happens to be the means by which and through which we learn Christ. Other than through the Cross, Christ really cannot be approached. In other words, unless we accept what He did for us as it regards Salvation, we cannot have anything to do with Him and the Eternal Life He offers, or if we do not understand the part the Cross plays in our everyday victory in living for Christ after we are saved, there simply will be no victory. So, the prerequisite is always the slain Lamb, which gives access. Regrettably, this particular foundation of the Cross is little known or understood at the present time in the Church, at least as it ought to be. The Cross is pretty much relegated to the sinner initially coming to Christ. As to the part it plays in everything else the Christian is and does, is little understood presently. Consequently, it is very difficult for one to properly learn Christ, with a skewed understanding of the single most important thing there is.

THE INSPIRATION OF PAUL

The difficulty for us here is to estimate worthily the elevation of that regard to Christ which had become the inspiration of the life of Paul.

At the time when he was arrested on the road to Damascus, God revealed His Son to him and in him. Paul then became aware of Jesus as the Messiah of his people, against whom his utmost energies had bent themselves — against Whom he had sinned with his utmost determination. That discovery came home to him with a sense of great darkness and horror; and, no doubt, at the same time, his whole previous conceptions of life, and his judgments of his own life, were subverted, and fell in ruins around him.

He had his scheme of life, of success, of welfare; it had seemed to him a lofty and well-accredited one; and, with whatever misgivings he might occasionally be visited, on the whole he thought of himself as working it out hopefully and well.

Now on every side were written only defeat, perplexity, and despair. However, the Son of God was revealed in his heart (Gal. 1:16) as the Bearer of Righteousness and life to sinners — as the embodiment of Divine Reconciliation and Divine Hope. In this light a new conception of the world, a new scheme of worthy and victorious life, opened itself to Paul — new and wonderful.

But the reason of it, the hopefulness of it, the endless worth of it, lay chiefly here, that God in Christ had come into his life. The true relation of moral life to God, and the ends of human life as judged by that standard, were opening before him; but, if that had stood alone, it might only have completed the dismay of the paralyzed and stricken man.

THE CROSS MADE IT REAL

What made all new was the vision of Christ victoriously treading the path in which we fail to go, and of Christ dying for the unrighteous. So God came into view in His Love, redeeming, reconciling, adopting, giving the Holy Spirit — and He came into view *"in Christ Jesus."* God was in Christ. The manifold relation of the living God to His creature man began to be felt and verified in the manifold relation of Christ the Son of God, the Mediator, and Saviour, to the broken man who had defied and hated Him.

Christ henceforth became the ground, the meaning, and the aim of Paul's life. Life found its explanation, its worth, its loving imperative here. All things that once had value in his eyes fell away. If not entirely dismissed, they were now to have only such place and use as Christ assigned to them, only such as could fit the genius of life in Christ. All new prerogatives and attainments that might yet accrue to Paul, and might seem entitled to assume value in his eyes, could only have the same subordinate place: Christ first, Whose Light and Love, Whose Power to fix, fill, and attract the soul, made all things new; Christ first, so that all the rest was comparatively nowhere; Christ first, so that all the rest, if at any time it came into competition with Him, if it offered itself to Paul as a source of individual confidence and boasting, is recognized as mere loss, and in that character resolutely cast away.

THE LOSS OF ALL THINGS

The phrase, *"For Whom I have suffered the loss of all things,"* speaks of what Paul gave up when he received the Lord Jesus as his Saviour on the road to Damascus.

The words *"have suffered"* are in the Greek Text a business term meaning, *"to punish by exacting a forfeit."* One could translate *"for Whose sake I have been caused to forfeit."*

Paul was a citizen of Tarsus. At the time he lived there, only families of wealth and reputation were allowed to retain their Tarsian citizenship. This throws a flood of light upon Paul's early life. It seems that he was born into a home of wealth and culture. His family were wealthy Jews living in one of the most progressive of oriental cities. All this Paul left to become a poor itinerant Evangelist.

But not only did he forfeit all this when he was saved, but his parents would have nothing to do with a Son who had in their estimation dishonored them by becoming one of those hated, despised Christians. They had reared him in the lap of luxury, had sent him to the Jewish School of Theology in Jerusalem to sit at the feet of the great Gamaliel, and had given him an excellent training in Greek culture at the University of Tarsus, a Greek school of learning, it is believed. But they had now cast him off. He was still forfeiting all that he had held dear, what for?

THAT I MAY WIN CHRIST

The phrase, *"And do count them but dung, that I may win Christ,"* tells us what for!

Up beside Christ all the things the world holds so dear, such as place, position, power, riches, etc., *"seemed as nothing,"* actually as *"garbage."*

This must be understood, if we do not lay everything on the Altar, and I mean everything, then we will stumble as well over even the small things. Christ cannot take second place, and for all the obvious reasons.

He is the Lord of Glory, the Creator of all things, the King of kings, and Lord of lords. Up beside Him, everything else is exactly as Paul pictured it, as *"dung,"* i.e., *"garbage, refuse!"*

Many Christians know Jesus but in a philosophical way, or even an intellectual way, and even though redeemed by Him, still have very little relationship with Him; consequently, most Christians simply do not know Jesus Christ, except in a most elementary way. And the sadness, none of us know Him as well as we could know Him, which is a travesty.

GARBAGE

The word *"dung"* used here occurs nowhere else in the New Testament. It means, properly, *"dregs, refuse"*; what is thrown away as worthless, chaff, offal, or the refuse of a table or of slaughtered animals; and then filth of any kind.

No language could express a more deep sense of the utter worthlessness of all that eternal advantages could confer in the matter of Salvation. In the question of Justification before God, all reliance on birth, blood, external morality, and forms of religion, are to be renounced, and, in comparison with the merits of the great Redeemer, to be esteemed as vile.

Such were Paul's views; and we may remark, that if this was so in his case, it should be in ours.

(9) "AND BE FOUND IN HIM, NOT HAVING MINE OWN RIGHTEOUSNESS, WHICH IS OF THE LAW, BUT THAT WHICH IS THROUGH THE FAITH OF CHRIST, THE RIGHTEOUSNESS WHICH IS OF GOD BY FAITH:"

The Righteousness of God provided in Christ is received by man *"through Faith"* and thus man acquires it *"by Faith"* or *"on the basis of Faith."* It is not man's achievement as accomplished by doing the Law's requirements but is God's provision freely offered men in Christ (Rom. 3:20-22). *"Faith"* is the very opposite of human works; it is the reception of God's Work which has already been accomplished by those who acknowledge the futility of their own efforts to attain Righteousness.

FOUND IN HIM

The phrase, *"And be found in Him,"* refers to being united to Christ by a living Faith.

The idea is, that when the investigation of the great day should take place in regard to the ground of Salvation, it might be found that he was united to the Redeemer, and depended solely on His merits for Salvation.

The short phrase, *"in Him,"* goes back to Romans 6:3. Actually, if any two words could properly describe the entirety of the great Plan of God for the human race as it regards Salvation, those two words would be *"in Christ."* This has to do with Christ as our Representative Man.

As such, all that He did at the Cross and the Resurrection and as well the Exaltation, was done on our behalf, actually for us, with God treating this work exactly as if we would have done such, even though it was impossible for us to have done such. Our Faith in what He did, places us actually, in Him, at least in the Mind of God.

So, the Apostle is saying that whatever happens in the future, the only Salvation that God will recognize is that which is *"in Christ."*

The word *"found"* carries the idea of a testing of metals to ascertain if it is what it claims to be. All who are not *"in Him,"* but rather in a Church, a Denomination, any other particular religion, etc., will be *"found wanting."* It is only that which is *"in Him"* which God will recognize.

The words just stated are not to mean that something is wrong with Church, etc. The idea is, that untold millions are trusting in the Church to save them, which of course it cannot do.

Many are fond of saying that they are *"in the Church,"* which in a sense means that they are trusting in the Church to save them which, if correct, means that they are not *"in Christ."* Consequently, they are unsaved!

A FALSE RIGHTEOUSNESS

The phrase, *"Not having mine own righteousness,"* is not meant to assume that Paul had a personal righteousness. The idea is *"not having any righteousness which can be called his own."*

The words *"my own righteousness,"* are some of the most lethal words in any language. Sadly, it includes almost all of the human race.

Man has a choice: He can trust in the Righteousness provided by God through Jesus Christ, and Jesus Christ Alone, and more particularly, what He did at the Cross and the Resurrection, or he can trust in a concocted, devised, righteousness of his own making, which regrettably includes most of the world.

This type of righteousness comes in many hues, colors, and prisms. Some of it is very crass and some is very subtle.

For instance, untold millions attempt to provide a cushion for the *"afterlife"* as it is referred to, by the giving of large sums of money. Unfortunately, most people don't have large sums to give, so this would include only a favored few. Others simply tally what I refer to as the *"Brownie point system,"* meaning that they place their good deeds up beside their bad deeds, and of course, the good deeds, at least in their eyes, always outweigh the bad.

The world almost always looks to good deeds, merit, or at least what they think is merit, and good works as some type of passport or ticket to Heaven, that is if they believe in Heaven. Most of the time, when the eulogy is given, they will recall these particular *"good deeds,"* and say something like this: *"If there is a Heaven, John* (or Sally, or whatever the name), *is surely there."*

That's one of the reasons that much of the world buys into the Catholic Church so much. The Catholic Church operates solely on a basis of *"works"*; consequently, these things look good to the unregenerate heart, because they speak of *"merit."*

To the world, the idea that God will not accept such arouses anger and hostility.

RELIGION

In all of this mix is the world of religion. Religion is that which is devised by man which is supposed to help one reach God, or to help one better oneself in some way or manner. It is always self-improvement in some fashion, and it seldom makes an effort to curtail man's involvement in sin. Or if it does do so, it is only in the realm of particular restrictions such as *"stealing,"* etc. Consequently, the *"doing"* of these religions makes man feel good, while at the same time allowing him to maintain his particular lifestyle, whatever that might be.

All of this is of man and is, therefore, unacceptable to God which should be obvious.

THE CHURCH

The type of righteousness we have mentioned is rife in the world, and easily recognizable by the Church; however, as bad as that is, the false righteousness in the Church is even worse.

Even though I've given the following in other Volumes of our Commentaries, I think a brief perusal of that given by Jesus would be of great benefit.

Jesus told the story of two men who went to the Temple to pray; *"the one a Pharisee, and the other a Publican."*

The Publican was a tax-collector, not so very bad in our eyes presently, but then was the worst form of low-life in Israel, or at least was looked at as such by the Jews. Actually, there was nothing wrong with this particular occupation, with Jesus even choosing a Publican, Matthew, to be one of His Disciples. Irrespective, the Religious Hierarchy of Israel, looked at Publicans as traitors to the nation, having sold out to Rome, etc. Even though much more could be said, I think that will suffice for that which we desire to explain.

At any rate, the Pharisees were looked at as the Religious Leaders of Israel, the holiest, most righteous group in the nation. They were supposed to be sticklers for the Law of Moses, in essence the spiritual guides of the people. They hated Christ!

Some three types of righteousness are presented in this illustration. They are as follows:

RELATIVE RIGHTEOUSNESS

Relative righteousness: Jesus said, *"The Pharisee stood and prayed thus with himself, God, I thank Thee, that I am not as other men are, extortioners, unjust, adulterers, or even as this Publican"* (Lk. 18:11).

This man was measuring his so-called righteousness by other men. As stated, it's called *"relative righteousness."*

Unfortunately, the Church is very fond of this type of righteousness as well. Self-righteousness always works in this capacity. It compares its righteousness with someone else, always with someone it thinks is worse. It is a righteousness that God cannot accept!

WORKS RIGHTEOUSNESS

Works righteousness: The Pharisee then said, *"I fast twice in the week, I give tithes of all that I possess"* (Lk. 18:12).

This is *"works righteousness"* which thinks that such activity merits us something with God. As the Church is full of *"relative righteousness,"* it is also full of *"works righteousness."* Once again, this is a type of righteousness that God will not accept.

IMPUTED RIGHTEOUSNESS

Imputed righteousness: Jesus then said, *"And the Publican, standing afar off, would not lift up so much as his eyes to Heaven* (knew he was unworthy), *but smote upon his breast* (knowing his undone condition) *saying, God be merciful to me a sinner"* (Lk. 18:13).

Of this man Jesus said, *"I tell you, this man went down to his house justified* (saved) *rather than the other: for every one who exalteth himself shall be abased* (lost); *and he who humbleth himself shall be exalted* (saved)*"* (Lk. 18:14).

Imputed righteousness, which we have discussed in commentary on the previous Chapter, is that which is freely given to the undeserving sinner by God, simply because of that person's Faith in Christ and what He did at the Cross.

The idea is, that there is no way that sinful man can attain Righteousness on his own; therefore, if he is to obtain such, it has to come from a source outside himself, and that Source is the Lord Jesus Christ.

Christ offered up Himself on the Cross as a Sacrifice, which satisfied the claims of the Law, i.e., *"its Curse,"* which atoned for all sin, thereby securing for man, at least for those who will believe, a perfect, pure, spotless Righteousness. As our Representative Man, this spotless Righteousness is given strictly upon one's Faith in Christ.

It has somewhat of a strange twist: Before one can qualify for this Righteousness, one has to be disqualified and know it. Upon such admittance, and having Faith in what Jesus has done on his behalf, a perfect Righteousness is imputed to him. This is the only Righteousness which God will recognize. In fact, this is the great battleground in the Church, and in fact, always has been.

Men love to make rules and to force other men to obey them, and religious men most of all. So, the Church is very fond of making rules which have no bearing whatsoever on the Word of God, which is supposed to be the Standard for all things. Unfortunately, the Constitution and Bylaws of some Denominations are drawn up with no regard whatsoever for the Word of God. In other words, they form their own government without knowing what the Word says, and I suppose not really caring what it says.

If this is done, and in fact it is done constantly, I'm afraid as the old song says, *"There's going to be trouble with a capital 'T' in river city."*

THE MANNER IN WHICH THE CHURCH IMPUGNS THE RIGHTEOUSNESS OF CHRIST

1. Anytime man adds anything to the Finished Work of Christ, claiming that such is needed in order to be saved, such as the Lord's Supper, Water Baptism, or Water Baptism according to a particular formula, or joining a certain Church, etc.

2. Whenever repentance is not accepted, but rather other things demanded such as probationary periods, etc.

3. Religious superiority, which claims that certain Churches are superior to others. While that certainly is true, if the idea that belonging to such Churches gives one certain spiritual superiority, that is an insult to the Righteousness of Christ.

4. The use of anything to gain victory over sin other than Faith in the Finished Work of Christ.

We've only touched on a few, but those things we have named should give pause for thought. In fact, the Church sadly and regrettably, is eaten up with either these things said, or nuances springing from such direction. In fact, this is the area of Satan's greatest effort. He wants the individual to lean on his own righteousness, or that provided by someone else other than Christ. He is very subtle in his approach to this effort, making the Believer think all the time, that what he is doing is Biblical and, therefore, correct.

The things we've mentioned, plus many we have not mentioned, present the telltale signs of self-righteousness. The Reader should take a look at all of these things mentioned, and, in fact, should observe them very carefully. He should then look at himself and at the Church he attends. The reason is simple, that which we are speaking of here is the single most important thing in the world. In other words, your soul is at stake!

THE LAW

The phrase, *"Which is of the Law,"* pertains to Law-keeping. He was done with that. He wanted men to see in his life, the Righteousness which the Holy Spirit would produce in answer to his Faith in Christ.

Paul is actually speaking here of both personal righteousness, which can be seen by men, and Justifying Righteousness, which pertains to one's position in Christ.

When he speaks here of the Righteousness of the Law, he is speaking of righteousness which is dependent upon one's performance.

In fact, the Law of Moses, and we speak of the part of that Law called the Ten Commandments, did possess Righteousness, in other words, a Righteousness which could be obtained if the Law was kept perfectly. However, such was impossible simply because of man's fallen nature. This feat simply lay beyond man's power of performance, so much so in fact, that not one single person ever kept the Law except Christ.

Nevertheless, Israel developed her own brand of righteousness, which of course God would not accept, by her great efforts in trying to keep the Law. In other words, she made a religion, which attempted to make Salvation out of the mechanics of Law involvement. Of course, religion is always wrapped up in the matter of *"doing,"* which, in fact, is the greatest narcotic there is.

Due to all of this, Paul knew that the Righteousness of the Law, to which man really could not attain, consequently fell out to self-righteousness. When the factor of pride entered in, which it always does in the matter of attempted Law-keeping, the asset became a liability. This was the fault that Jesus found in the Pharisees of His day. Their righteousness became perverted and, therefore, inverted. Instead of being meritorious, it was actually a hindrance to finding the Righteousness that is of God.

Paul is telling the Philippians what he told the Galatians, that the only Righteousness that one can experience comes as a Gift from God and not as a reward of effort (Gal. 3:3). This Gift God mediates through His Son Jesus Christ; it comes by no other means. *"There is no other name given among men whereby we must be saved,"* declared Peter (Acts 4:12).

CHRIST, THE WAY

This *"narrow-mindedness"* helped to make the early Christians zealous Evangelists. They did not think of Christ as a way, but as *"The Way."*

This meant that Paul's entire religious perspective was shifted from pride in performance to gratitude for unmerited favor. It meant that he had no merit that was earned or deserved. The Righteousness he possessed was a completely unmerited Gift of God through Christ, giving no grounds for pride or self-esteem.

This is what Augustine insisted upon so strenuously in his arguments of his day. Augustine followed Paul in the insistence that Salvation comes by Grace alone and not by human effort or merit. This is what Luther insisted upon in the 16th Century. This is the major theme of Wesley's Evangelistic preaching in the 18th Century, and which sparked both the reformation and revival.

When he preached at St. Mary's, Oxford, England, on *"The Circumcision of the Heart,"* he bore down hard on this great truth; this is the central affirmation of the Christian experience.

He accused the learned professors of religion that theirs was an outward righteousness rather than an inward Grace. So incisive were his words that he was denied an opportunity ever to preach there again. But, in the providence of God, *"the common people heard him gladly."*

THE ISSUE PRESENTLY AS WELL!

The issue between inward and outward Righteousness is a live issue today. The constant temptation is to prefer Salvation by works, by code, by committees, by something external. There are those who prefer something tangible and precise, to whom Faith alone seems rather vague, elusive, and precarious. This dualism between true and false security runs throughout the Scriptures.

The ancient Israelites preferred to trust a Temple, and a Priest, rather than obedience, rather than in God Himself. Repeatedly, the Israelites learned the hard way that trust in the Ark, or the Temple, or genealogy, or the city is a false trust, if it is a substitute for obedience, love, and adherence to the Covenant.

THE RIGHTEOUSNESS OF GOD

The Righteousness of God, therefore, comes as a Gift following submission and trust. In the light of Hebrews, Faith was a conviction of unseen reality and perseverance toward the end (Heb. 11:1).

To Paul, Faith was trust and commitment that brings peace. In Hebrews, Faith is that confidence in God's faithfulness that undergirds the Believer and enables him to persevere. With Paul, on the other hand, Faith involves a relinquishment of all self-effort, a deliberate abandonment and commitment.

This gives rise to a completely new basis for Righteousness, a Righteousness not of self but of God Alone, mediated through Christ. Thus, Paul could say, *"When I am weak, then am I strong."* The emphasis in Paul, therefore, is upon the *"new creature"* that emerges after this drastic reorientation, i.e., *"the Bible way of thinking"* (II Cor. 5:17) (Turner).

To sum up, the Righteousness which is from God is offered to the sinner in Christ, and secured by him by Faith as opposed to works.

THE FAITH OF CHRIST

The phrase, *"But that which is through the Faith of Christ,"* refers to the Faith which Christ kindles, of which He is the Author, which also He nourishes and maintains. It is, therefore, the Faith which is furnished the Believer by God and with which he appropriates the Blessings of Grace (Wuest).

One might say that *"God's Righteousness comes through Christ"* (I Cor. 1:30) and by Faith (Gen. 15:6; Rom. 3:22-26; 4:1-25; 9:30-31; 10:1-13).

RIGHTEOUSNESS BY FAITH

The phrase, *"The Righteousness which is of God by Faith,"* sums up the whole of Christianity. This Righteousness proceeds from God, which means that God is the Source and Alone the Source, which means it is not at all of man, even as it cannot be of man.

So, if man is to obtain Righteousness, he must look outside of himself, and that means all men everywhere. That's at least one of the reasons that all the religions of the world such as Buddhism, Hinduism, Islam, Confucianism, etc., are bogus. These were all begun by men, in fact, men who needed Redemption themselves, making it impossible for them to impart Righteousness to anyone else, especially considering that they did not even have such themselves.

Christianity being totally different, comes from God Who became man, The Man Christ Jesus. As God, He has the power to change men, and as Man, He paid the price on the Cross, in order that man could be changed without defiling the Justice of God.

WHAT DO WE MEAN BY THE PHRASE, *"BY FAITH"*?

In God's dealings with man, He chose Faith as the vehicle or medium one might say, by which contact could be made, and relationship established.

Had He chosen anything else such as money, education, good works, etc., such a choice would have left out the majority of mankind in one way or the other. Faith on the other hand, is the most fair medium of all, simply because it is the same for all, includes all, and can be had by all.

WHAT IS FAITH?

The Scripture plainly says, *"Now Faith is the substance of things hoped for, the evidence of things not seen"* (Heb. 11:1).

In effect, it means for one simply to believe. In fact, the entirety of the world, and we speak of both the redeemed and the unredeemed, have faith in something. It is by faith that fortunes are made in the business world, inventions come about, and great things happen. Even though this is faith, it is not necessarily Faith in God. In fact, the only type of faith the world can have, is that which is in themselves. In other words, they have faith in themselves, in their ability, in their talents, in their acumen, etc. The world's system operates on this type of faith. But as stated, it is seldom Faith in God!

THE OBJECT OF OUR FAITH

When it comes to Christians, Faith of course is extremely important, but more than all, it is the object of our Faith which is important. Many Christians are attempting to build their Faith, when they would do much better by simply making certain that the object of their Faith is what it ought to be. To be frank, even as previously stated, I think one could say without fear of contradiction, that the Faith of most Christians is misdirected, in other words, it has the wrong object in view.

When the Scripture says, *"Faith cometh by hearing, and hearing by the Word of God,"* it is more so than anything speaking of the correct object of Faith (Rom. 10:17).

Unfortunately, in the past few decades, the Church has majored in Faith, but I'm afraid it's been Faith for the most part, in the wrong object. Consequently, it is more akin to the world than it is to the Word of God, even though it quotes the Word of God extensively.

If Faith is not tendered toward the proper object, namely the Finished Work of Christ, in some way it will always center up on self, which breeds self-righteousness and arrogance. Of course, inasmuch as this is the same type of faith which spurs the world, even though it is faith, it is not faith that God can recognize.

As stated, the object of Faith must always be the Cross of Christ. If it is not that, it is wrong whatever its other directions.

Every single thing that man receives from God, all relationship with God, all Salvation, the Baptism with the Holy Spirit, Divine Healing, financial prosperity, the knowledge of the Word of God — all, comes through the Blood Atonement of Christ. In other words, everything that man lost in the Fall, Christ addressed in the Atonement. So, Preachers arguing whether Divine Healing is in the Atonement, simply don't know what they're talking about.

Not only is Divine Healing in the Atonement, everything is in the Atonement, at least everything that was lost at the Fall. If Jesus didn't address every part and parcel of the sin question at the Atonement, then it could not have been a Finished Work. But we know that it is a Finished Work, because He presently is *"sat down on the Right Hand of the Majesty on High"* (Heb. 1:3).

The Priests under the Old Economy of God did not sit down in the Tabernacle or Temple, simply because there were no chairs among the holy vessels, and because the work of the Priests was never finished. However, that which Jesus did is finished, meaning that He can now *"sit down,"* also meaning, that He in the Atonement addressed every single thing lost in the Fall.

While it is true that we do not now have all the benefits of the Atonement, that coming only in the Resurrection, still, and to be sure, the Atonement handled everything.

So, for whatever it is, we are to exhibit Faith in the Cross, meaning that this must always be the object of our Faith. Of course, when we speak of the Cross, we are at the same time speaking of the Resurrection and the Exaltation (Eph. 2:6).

THAT WHICH GOD DEMANDS

When the Holy Spirit through the Apostle said *"By Faith,"* he is meaning that the only thing that man must have and must exercise in order to receive Righteousness from God, is Faith. This means Faith in what Jesus did there. Man is not to trust whatsoever in his own efforts or machinations, but altogether in what Christ did on the Cross.

Our Faith is to rest in that and to remain in that. God requires nothing else, and in fact, will accept nothing else. The Lord simply asks that sinful man *"believe,"* and rather believe in that which Jesus did at the Cross, and God will respond by awarding that man a perfect, pure, spotless Righteousness.

Seeing how simple all of this is, it would seem that man could do this very easily, doesn't it?

WHY IS IT SO HARD FOR MAN TO HAVE FAITH IN WHAT JESUS DID AT THE CROSS?

Due to the Fall, which actually speaks of the way man fell, man wants to do something himself in order to earn his Salvation, in effect, refusing to admit that such a work cannot be done.

We like to think that we can contribute something, can atone for something, can furnish at least a part of what is needed to bring about our Redemption. Of course, such is impossible! But yet, man keeps trying because of this deception in which he lives.

We love to think of ourselves as a *"self-made man,"* or *"I did it my way,"* or *"I'm able to pull myself up by my own bootstraps."* Of course, there are many other sayings of this nature, which only shows man's stubbornness in refusing to go God's Way, rather trying to carve out a way of his own, which is literally impossible.

WHAT PAUL SOUGHT

In earlier days Paul sought Righteousness — an approved and accepted standing with God — by the works of the Law. That project failed when the great discovery on the road to Damascus showed him to himself as all astray; in particular, when the Law itself, coming home to him in the fullness of its meaning, both revealed to him the beggarliness of his own performance, and, at the same time, stung into appalling activity ungodly elements within him.

Then he saw before him the Law rising from its deep foundations in eternal strength and majesty, imperative, unalterable, inexorable; and over against it his own works lay withered and unclean. But another vision came.

He saw the Son of God in His Life, Death, and Resurrection. Mere love and pity were the inspiration of His Coming: obedience and sacrifice were the form of it. So in that great vision one element or aspect that rose into view was Righteousness, — Righteousness grounded as deep as the Law itself, as magnificent in its great proportions, as little subject to change or decay, radiant with surpassing glory. As he sought, and bowed, and trusted, he became conscious of a new access and nearness to God Himself; he passed into the fellowship of God's dear Son; he found acceptance in the Beloved.

THE ANSWER

Here was the answer to that woeful problem of the Law: Righteousness in Christ for a world of sinners, coming to them as a free gift to Faith. Here was the strong foundation on which Faith found itself set to learn its lessons, and perform its service, and fight its battles. In Christ he received the reconciliation — merciful, and also righteous. As Paul thought of the ground on which he once had stood, and of the standing granted to him now, *"in Him,"* it was with a *"yea, doubtless"* he declared that he counted all to be loss for the gain of Christ, in Whom he was found, not having his own righteousness, which was of the Law, but that which is by Faith in Christ.

WHAT RIGHTEOUSNESS MEANS

Righteousness by Faith in Christ, and more particularly in what Christ did at the Cross, opened what seemed to Paul the prosperous way into the Righteousness of daily living. In the very hour when he first believed for Righteousness, he felt himself entering a kingdom of light, love, and power, in which all things were possible; and ever after the same order of experience verified itself for him afresh. The Righteousness of Faith being the relation in which, through Christ, he found himself standing to God, fixed at the same time his relation to all Christian benefits, including, as a principal element, conformity to the likeness of Christ, which is the greatest thing of all.

To the man in Christ all these benefits pertained; in Christ he could claim them all; in Christ he found himself before doors that opened of their own accord to let him in; in Christ it proved to be a fit thing, grounded deep in the recesses of God's Administration, that God should be for him; therefore, also, the pathway of Holiness lay open before him.

The fullness of Blessing had not yet come into possession and experience. But in the Righteousness of Faith he apprehended all Blessings as stretching out their hands to him, because through Christ they ought to be his.

That he should find himself in a relation to God so simple and so satisfying was wonderful; all the more, when it was contrasted with the condemnation belonging to him as a sinner. This was the Righteousness from God by Faith, in the strength of which he could call all things his own — all things in Christ.

THAT FOR WHICH HE HAD SO LONG SOUGHT

For the sake of argument, let's say that Paul had succeeded in the enterprise of his earlier days, when he sought Righteousness by the Law. He would, as he hoped, have found acceptance in the end; and various blessings would have followed. He would have emerged from his task a man stamped as righteous, one might say, and fit to be treated accordingly. However, that would have been the end.

But now, in reference to his present situation, he has found, in Christ, acceptance at the very beginning. So often as Faith lifts him into the Heavenly Places where Christ is, he finds all things to be his; not because he has achieved Righteousness, but because Christ has died and risen, and because God justifies him who believes in Jesus.

The platform he hoped to reach by the efforts of a lifetime is already under his feet. Paul faces each arduous step in his new enterprise, strong in the conviction that his standing before God is rooted, not in his doings nor in his feelings, but in his Saviour in Whom he holds the Righteousness which comes by Faith. One must shout, *"Hallelujah!"*

THE MANNER OF FAITH

The Christian experience roots itself in the confession of sin, and, therefore, of ill-desert; it signalizes itself by a deepening sense of the seriousness of the situation in this respect. With this it comes face-to-face before God.

"I will confess my transgressions unto the Lord. God be merciful to me a sinner."

We have nothing that is not sinful to bring before Him; so, at length, we come with that. It is all we have. Our prayer rises not merely out of the sense of weakness, but out of the consciousness of demerit.

That's quite a thought! And I want the Reader to dwell on it. Consequently, I will say it again:

We have nothing that is not sinful to bring before Him. Once we think about that, it is a sobering thought!

We cannot bring before Him Righteousness, for we have none! We cannot bring before Him goodness, for we have none! We cannot bring before Him merit, for we have none! We can only bring before Him transgression, disobedience, rebellion, failure, and sin. Never has a human being brought anything else, because he has nothing else to bring.

Considering this, that is the reason we should constantly praise Him. In fact, it is inconceivable to a human being, to our way of thinking, that God has only received sinful men, because that's the only kind there is. And yet, He has never turned one away, never closed the door in our faces, never said *"no"* to an honest, seeking heart.

Instead of rejection, instead of the way being closed, instead we find the very opposite.

We hear that clarion call as it comes through the ages, *"Come unto Me, all ye that labour and are heavy laden, and I will give you rest"* (Mat. 11:28).

As well, when we could not go where He was, He came where we are, and what a step down for Him that was. But He came anyway!

And why did He come?

He came to give us life, to give us hope, to give us forgiveness for sins, to regenerate us, to make us new creations, to do all of these wonderful things for us which we could never do for ourselves; He came to make us Righteous.

However, He had to pay a terrible price in order for that Righteousness to be given to us, a Righteousness which we should think of in such wonderful terms, should consider with such utter awe, should treasure to the very highest — a Righteousness incidentally, which drips with Blood, His Blood!

NOTES

THE FORGIVENESS OF SINS

However, in all of this, all because of Christ, we are aware, as of strength which can remedy our weakness, so of forgiveness which can put away our sins. *"There is forgiveness with Thee." "Through this Man is preached to us the forgiveness of sins."* It is clear also that this forgiveness comes, wherever it comes, as full and free forgiveness, *"forgiving you all trespasses."* So that in this great Christian Testimony we listen at Christ's Feet to the word directed to all penitent Believers, that instead of reckoning in part or whole about the guilt of sins committed, we are to find God in Christ to be One Who simply puts away our sin. That should hold us apart from God no more. Rather the putting of it away brings with it the strangest, lowliest access to God. *"O God, Thou art my God. Who is a God like unto Thee?"*

As well, forgiveness is by no means mere immunity. Punishment, certainly, in the sense of the separation and evil which sin deserves, passes away.

Isn't that beautiful?

No punishment is required, because Jesus has already been punished in our place and on our behalf.

Therefore, forgiveness in this Christian Faith, is forgiveness with the Forgiver in it. We meet God in the forgiveness of sins. We abide with God in the forgiveness of sins, all because of Christ and what He did on a Cross so long ago.

CALLED TO GO FORWARD

Forgiveness, too, is but the foundation and beginning of a history in which we are called to go forward. This history may have sad passages in it, as it in fact does for all of us. In other words, there are failures along the way. But in going forward in it in Faith we are assured that on God's part it is a history of most painstaking and most sublime benefaction: all of it ordered so as to be a part of all that it means, with His sending of His Son; all of it instinct with the Grace of our Lord Jesus Christ.

Faith looking to Christ believes this, and receives it. And to Faith upheld by Him on Whom we trust all this is more and more made good, and comes true. It is a history of progress in true goodness. And the end is Life Everlasting.

From the base upwards, this Christian Faith is an experience of Grace; and *"it is of Faith, that it might be by Grace."*

Whatever activities, whatever successes may fall into the Christian's struggle, whatever long possession of accustomed good may eventually mark his experience, all is to be informed and inspired by this initial and perpetual conviction, *"Not having mine own righteousness, which is of the Law."*

It is rather the Righteousness of Christ, freely given to sinners who dare to have Faith in what Jesus did on a bloody Cross.

When God gave us Christ, He gave us, in a sense, *"all things,"* and indeed all things ordering themselves into an eternal expression of fatherly love and care. In Christ comes into view not goodness only, but goodness allying itself for us with Wisdom, Power, and Right. It makes its way by Incarnation and Atonement and Resurrection to a Kingdom which, being first Christ's, appointed to Him, is also His people's, appointed to them, and I should say *"to us."*

Now a relation to God which looks forward to all this, which is the basis for it and the entrance to it, descends on the believing man through Christ. It is due to Christ that it should come so. It is the Father's loving Will that it should be so.

All is needful to ground and vindicate that most gracious relation found in Christ, Who of God is made unto us Righteousness; in Whom we hold the Righteousness which is of God on Faith.

THE WAY OF FAITH

The only way of entering on new relations with God or ourselves becoming new men, is the way of Faith. This Christian way is the only way. Every other is simply impossible. Let any man seriously try it, and I speak of ways other than Faith, and all have found and all will find that what I'm saying is so.

But the question, *"What kind of faith?"* is best answered by saying, such faith as is called for by the object of Faith that is set before us. In other words, just to have Faith is not enough. In fact, as stated, every single person in the world has faith, but very little of it is in God, but rather other things. As well, to merely have Faith in God, which a Believer certainly should have, does not really tell the whole story. In other words, we ought to know what having Faith in God actually means.

Some would hear that question and would just simply say, *"It means to believe God."* That is correct, but believe God for what? Believe God on what basis?

When the Scripture says that *"Abraham believed God, and it was counted unto him for Righteousness,"* what does that exactly mean? (Rom. 4:3).

It meant far more than the mere fact that Abraham simply believed that there was a God, or that he believed in God. While of course all of that was true, the real meaning is actually the secret of all that we are in Christ.

Abraham believed God according to what God had said respecting the sending of a Redeemer into this world to save lost humanity. In other words, his Faith rested not only in God, but more particularly in what God would do, and more particular still in Christ going to the Cross to redeem lost humanity. In other words, the object of his Faith was in the Cross of Christ. That's what it means by *"believing God."*

Many Christians presently, when they speak of believing God, it's sort of a nebulous statement that really doesn't quite have an object in view.

The idea must always be, that the object of our Faith is in what Christ did at the Cross and the Resurrection. If we veer from that, while it may still be Faith, it's not Faith that God will recognize. Every single thing that the Believer receives from God, and I mean everything from Salvation to Divine Healing, to the Baptism with the Holy Spirit, to financial prosperity, to leading and guidance, etc., and I'll say it again, everything, comes through what Jesus did at the Cross and the Resurrection. Even though I've said these things several times before, I will continue to say them and for the reason, that the Church has been so far moved away from the Cross that it has by and large lost the understanding of what all this means. Consequently, it flounders from one quicksand to the next, not really knowing where it is or where it's going.

As the Gospel is, Faith must be, and the Gospel is that Jesus Christ came into this world to save sinners, and did so by dying on the Cross. This is the instrument by which Faith is evoked, sustained, and guided. The great object of Faith is God, of course, but more particularly how He revealed Himself through Christ, and what Christ did at the Cross and the Resurrection.

Every genuine aspect of this Revelation takes its significance from its disclosure of God, as it relates to Jesus Christ. The so-called Faith which misses this, is wrong faith; the faith which marks and welcomes this, is right Faith. And such faith is already, even its earliest life, breaking forth into repentance and love and obedience. It must be for God is in it.

THAT WHICH FAITH IS TO RECEIVE

To confine ourselves to the aspect of things which occupy this Chapter, the Faith which meets God in the forgiveness of sins through Christ, and genuinely accepts from Him the wonderful position of holding fellowship with God, comes strictly through the Atoning Work of Christ. The man who so meets with God, is therein agreed with God about his own sins: he feels God to be in the right and himself to be wholly in the wrong; he feels, in particular, God to be most sublimely and conclusively in the right as it regards man's need, which is Mercy, Grace, and cleansing from sin.

The real problem with the Child of God and consequently, with the Church, is sin. Nobody likes to admit that, no one wants to say that, rather hiding our heads in the sand, somehow claiming that we are superheroes, and thereby sin is no problem for us; however, sin is the greatest problem for the Child of God. Satan wants to drag the Christian down to such an extent that through discouragement he will quit. In fact, untold numbers have quit. They did so because they simply said, *"I tried to live it, and I can't!"*

If Satan cannot do that, he at least wants to dominate the Christian with some type of sin, which makes life miserable to say the least.

Now the Church can deny that! It can take the position of one Pentecostal Leader of a certain Denomination and say, *"We have almost no problem with sin in our ranks,"* or words to that effect. This is not hearsay, because I read what the man said. However, I happen to know better as it concerns his Denomination.

Sin is destroying Preacher after Preacher, and making mockery out of the laity. In other words, they are having a problem with sin, just as all Christians will have problems with sin, if they do not function according to God's prescribed order.

So what am I saying?

I'm saying, that the problem in the Church is not a lack of Faith as it concerns material things. In fact, the Church has gone overboard on that foolishness. In other words, it is trying to have Faith for bigger cars, bigger houses, bigger paychecks, etc., which is foolishness indeed! While the Lord definitely does bless His people, material things are not the problem in the modern Church. The problem is sin.

Unfortunately, this of which I've said has no priority whatsoever, but rather other things. In other words, the Church has made a fatter paycheck its priority, which is exactly what Satan desires.

What good does it do, even if a Christian is blessed greatly in a financial sense, if his personal life is a shambles? What good does it do, irrespective of what kind of *"things"* we might obtain with our Faith, if in fact, we are being dominated by sin in some way?

IT IS THE CROSS OR ELSE!

Of course, the Church is mostly in a state of denial claiming that it's not being bothered and troubled by sin. However, I maintain this:

If the Church doesn't have its Faith anchored squarely in the Cross, which ensures the help of the Holy Spirit, then pure and simple, the Church is going to be dominated by sin, and I don't care what Church it is.

You see, almost every particular Denomination or Church for that matter, likes to think that it has a corner on the market, and that it is something special and, therefore, not bothered by these things. In other words, it is so perfect with the Lord, that sin is no more problem, nor much of anything else for that matter.

All of that foolishness, and foolishness it is, comes from pride, which is ugly before God. The truth is, and I'll say it again, that if the Believer does not have his or her Faith anchored squarely in the Cross, understanding that all of our Victory is in Christ, and Christ Alone, which as stated, will then bring us the help of the Holy Spirit, that Christian, and I don't care who the person is, is going to live a life of spiritual failure. It is just that simple!

God's prescribed order is the Cross and the Resurrection. If we veer from that, we can make our boasts, we can hide our head in the sand, we can live in a state of denial, but none of that changes things. The facts are, that person is being dominated by sin in some way, in some fashion. And to be sure, that is a miserable life!

The Church has tried to compensate for this by making all type of rules — rules incidentally, which are supposed to make one holy and righteous. How absurd!

How in the world can some words written down on a piece of paper make anyone holy or righteous? Even the great Law of God given to Moses, which was light years ahead of any little puny laws that we formulate, could not make one holy. In fact, Law, even the Law of God, has the very opposite effect. Even though the Law of Moses actually did contain Righteousness, still, it demanded a perfect performance on the part of the Lawkeeper in order for this Righteousness to be accrued. With man's fallen nature, such performance was and is impossible. But yet, it seems that we keep trying, and keep trying, and keep failing, and keep failing.

RIGHTEOUSNESS AND HOLINESS

There is absolutely no way that an individual can be righteous and holy in the Lord, except by Faith in what Christ did at the Cross and the Resurrection. Oh, dear Reader, can't you feel what I am saying! Can't you sense the rightness of these words I have just put down on paper.

There is no Righteousness or Holiness in man's laws, rules, machinations, efforts, works of the flesh, etc. Such is impossible as it regards a successful conclusion. The Believer will not come to Righteousness and Holiness in this manner, but only succeed in doing the very opposite, i.e., *"actually becoming more unrighteous and more unholy!"*

All is in Jesus! All is in what He did at the Cross and the Resurrection! He defeated every demon, every fallen angel, even Satan himself at the Cross. He atoned for every sin. He satisfied the curse of the broken Law. He satisfied the claims of Heavenly Justice. He left nothing undone, in effect, it being a Finished Work.

Why do we want to try to add something to this to which He has already done? Why do we conduct ourselves in this fashion? Why do we think that we have something to add to the great Victory purchased by Christ with His Own Blood at the Cross? Who do we think we are?

I have Righteousness and Holiness, and I'm not ashamed to utter those words. Neither do I draw back from saying them, and I have this attitude because of not trusting in myself whatsoever, but totally in Christ. I have been down that road, and I speak of the road of self-effort. I know what it is to try to make myself righteous and holy by religious machinations. I know what it is to try to work for these things, and fail miserably. In fact, the whole world knows what I'm talking about.

However, I also know what it is to seek the Lord earnestly for the answer to this question, and for Him to give me that answer. I know what it is for Him to show me the Revelation of the Cross and the Resurrection and what Jesus did there. To be sure, it has been in the Word of God all the time. It is not new, but actually the very foundation of the Faith.

However, we are so prone to try to help the Lord, that it seems we are not satisfied until we've tried and failed. Yes, I know what failure is in that respect; however, I also know what Victory is in the Lord. A Victory that is so wonderful, so glorious, so far-reaching, so all-inclusive, that I find difficulty in expressing myself.

However, I can gladly say, that all of this Victory came totally from what Jesus did at the Cross, and as the Lord showed me that my Faith must be anchored there completely and not at all in myself.

He also showed me, that the Holy Spirit would then give me power, work through me, exhibit His greatness and strength on my behalf, which He has done and does do. To be sure, there is no demon spirit that can overcome the Holy Spirit. There is no power of darkness that can overcome the Holy Spirit.

THE WORKING OF THE HOLY SPIRIT IN OUR LIVES

Paul brings it out very clearly in Romans Chapter 8 that it is only the Holy Spirit Who can do these things, bring about these things, and I speak of Righteousness and Holiness, as it regards our personal experience. To be sure, He does this according to *"the Law of the Spirit of Life which is in Christ Jesus"* (Rom. 8:2). In other words, this of which I speak is a *"Law,"* but it's not the Law of Moses. It is the *"Law of the Spirit of Life in Christ Jesus."*

What does that mean?

It means that all that the Holy Spirit does within us and for us, is done strictly according to the parameters of the Finished Work of Christ, i.e., *"in Christ Jesus,"* meaning what He did at the Cross and the Resurrection. The Holy Spirit confines Himself to this and for all the right reasons. This is the Law, but yet it's a Law that's totally different than the Law of Moses, or any type of law that man might devise. This is the *"Law of Life,"* and not the law of death.

The Believer does not have to concern himself with this *"Law of Life,"* only to the extent that he believes it, and wants it appropriated within his own heart and life. The only thing that can stop it from being brought about, and I'm speaking of course of the heart and life of the Christian, is whenever we try to exert the flesh, which refers to our own self-efforts in this regard, which frustrates the Grace of God, and stops this *"Law of Life"* (Gal. 2:21).

If we simply exercise Faith in this which Jesus has done on our behalf, we don't have to worry about this great Law, it will kick in and the Victory will be experienced within our heart and life. This Law is activated strictly by our Faith, which means that it's a very simple thing.

In other words, all I have to do as a Believer, is to understand that my Victory is totally and completely in the Cross and the Resurrection, and quit trying to bring it about by my own religious machinations of some type. When my Faith is exercised accordingly, the Holy Spirit functions according to this Law, and He will give us what we need, and I speak of Righteousness and Holiness.

Now, don't let the word *"Law"* confuse you, as Paul uses it in Romans 8:2. One might say that this is a good Law, and not a Law that will cause us problems. This is the *"Law of Life,"* which every Believer wants activated within his heart and life. We can only have it one way, and that is by placing our Faith in the Cross and leaving our Faith in the Cross.

There is just one difficulty in Faith — the difficulty of being real, and by that I mean real Faith in the real thing, which is the Cross of Christ. But when it is real, it makes all things new.

(10) "THAT I MAY KNOW HIM, AND THE POWER OF HIS RESURRECTION, AND THE FELLOWSHIP OF HIS SUFFERINGS, BEING MADE CONFORMABLE UNTO HIS DEATH;"

This Scripture is one of the most glorious in the Word of God, but yet mostly misunderstood by most Christians.

While all certainly want *"the Power of His Resurrection,"* the next two phrases, *"the fellowship of His sufferings,"* and *"being made conformable unto His Death,"* leaves most Christians cold. They just read over that very hurriedly, because most people don't desire to suffer, and that's what they think it means. It doesn't!

Paul wants to know experientially the Power of Christ's Resurrection. He is not thinking only of the Divine Power that raised Christ from the dead, but of the Power of the Resurrected Christ now operating in the Believer's life. This Power enables Believers to *"live a new life"* (Rom. 6:4) because we have been *"raised with Christ"* (Eph. 2:5-6; Col. 3:1).

So far so good! However, this next phrase makes most Believers want to jump ship. As stated, they think the Apostle is talking about suffering and suffering greatly on behalf of Christ, etc. That's not what he is saying!

We'll deal with it at length, but Paul is merely saying that we receive the benefits of all the things His suffering provided. If we don't receive these benefits, whatever they might be, in effect, His suffering is in vain.

As well, *"being made conformable unto His Death,"* refers to our complete identification with Him as it regards His Crucifixion and Resurrection, and what these things accomplished. This is the process of Sanctification and is intended to bring the Believer's present state into ever-increasing conformity to Christ (Rom. 8:29; II Cor. 3:18; Phil. 3:21).

Therefore, those who died with Him and rose with Him (Col. 2:20; 3:1-3) must exhibit this Truth by a separation from their old life and a continual walking in the Power supplied by Christ's Resurrection Life. That's what it means!

We are to conform ourselves, to what His Death did on our behalf, and draw the benefits from that Death.

What a power this Scripture holds, when we understand what Paul is saying.

TO KNOW HIM

The phrase, *"That I may know Him,"* refers to Paul knowing and understanding, that all things which pertain to life and Godliness, all things which pertain to happiness and fulfillment, all things which really count, which really matter, all the true blessings of Life, everything that one might think, is all found in Christ, and Christ Alone.

It may seem somewhat strange that Paul would utter this statement, especially considering that he wrote almost half the New Testament, and was given the great New Covenant, which in effect, made him the Moses of the New Testament. If any man knew Christ, one would certainly think that Paul knew Him.

In fact, He did, and perhaps as few men have ever known Him. The idea is this:

Irrespective as to how much Paul might already know Christ, he at the same time knows and understands that Christ cannot be exhausted. In other words, we have only scratched the surface.

A trillion years from today, and I exaggerate not, we will still be learning about Christ, finding out things about Him that we did not know which greatly enriches us to the better, in fact, which will continue forever. I'll say it again, Christ is utterly and absolutely inexhaustible.

As well, the Apostle knew and understood that the constant learning of Christ, was, in effect, the learning of more abundant life. This is what Jesus was speaking of when He said, *"Come unto Me all ye who labour and are heavy laden, and I will give you rest. Take My yoke upon you, and learn of Me"* (Mat. 11:28-30).

RELATIONSHIP WITH CHRIST

All of this of which we speak, in fact, is relationship with Christ — in fact, a relationship which should never stop growing.

The secret is this: The world makes its bid for the Christian. It holds up its enticements and to be sure, they do have a certain allurement about them. Those allurements have trapped many Christians, actually causing many to be lost. So what is the answer to this problem?

The Church has attempted to counter this by making up rules and regulations as to what Believers can do and cannot do. That's the road to disaster! It holds no answers whatsoever, and in fact, if that course is maintained, it will bring about the very opposite result, which means entrapment by the world. Laws will never do this, and that's what rules and regulations are — laws.

The answer is relationship with Christ. The closer one gets to Christ, the less allurement the world has.

It's somewhat like an old dog that's holding onto a bone. If that's all he has, he'll fight you for that bone even though there's not a scrap of meat on it. However, you can throw a T-bone steak before him, and he will more than likely let go of the bone in favor of the steak.

It's the same with the Christian. Once we see Christ, we learn Christ, we understand Christ, and as He begins to fill our lives as only He can do, the world simply loses its attraction. That's the answer, and in fact the only answer to worldliness.

HOW DOES ONE HAVE A RELATIONSHIP WITH CHRIST?

Of course, the moment the person comes to Christ, a relationship is then established; however, that relationship must grow, that is if it is to be proper. The sadness is, it does not grow in the hearts and lives of many Christians.

First of all, the Christian has to have a prayer life and as well, must have an habitual study of the Word. These two (prayer and the Word) go hand in hand.

How can anyone have a relationship with someone, if they don't talk to that person! It's not that we earn something by prayer, not at all! It's that we talk to the Lord, thereby establishing relationship with Him, which will grow as time goes on.

To be frank, Paul used the illustration of a husband and wife as it regards relationship. The marriage bonds and the relationship between a husband and wife are supposed to epitomize the Lord and His Church. To be sure, a husband and wife cannot have any type of relationship if they do not talk to each other. It's the same with Believers and the Lord. Why not?

We are Christians! We serve the Lord! Jesus Christ is our heart and life, so why would we not want to talk to Him? (Eph. 5:22-33).

To have a relationship with Christ, one must work at this, as should be obvious. The desire for that relationship must first of all be paramount in one's heart and life. And then we must take the necessary steps to ensure such a relationship, and even that it will grow. As stated, this comes about by prayer and the study of the Word.

I'll use another analogy: One has to work at this for it to grow, but he has to simply do nothing for it to languish and diminish. It is somewhat like one being in a river. If one does nothing, he will simply float downstream. To go upstream, he must work at that effort, as would be obvious.

To grow closer to the Lord, we have to specifically make that effort. To lose contact with Him, we simply have to do nothing, and that's why it's so easy to become lukewarm. Paul also addressed this by saying, *"And that, knowing the time, that now it is high time to awake out of sleep"* (Rom. 13:11). He was speaking of spiritual apathy, which is just as much a problem now as then.

"Sleep" speaks of inactivity, which means that the person sort of drifts with the tide. As stated, to draw closer to the Lord, which means to increase the relationship with Christ, takes some effort on our part, but effort which will be rewarded greatly. To lose what little relationship we do have, we simply have to do nothing, i.e., *"sleep."*

THE KNOWLEDGE OF CHRIST

The words *"to know"* are again, *"to know by experience."* The tense causes us to translate, *"to come to know by experience."* Paul wants to come to know the Lord Jesus in that fullness of experimental knowledge which is only wrought by being like Him.

The knowledge of which Paul speaks, is not something which relies on past experience, but that which he desires to grow constantly. As well, the knowledge of which he speaks is not of mere information, though that is included; it refers primarily to a deeper insight, a greater participation in the mind and purpose of the Master.

It is what one might call Paul's *"Christ-mysticism."* It recalls the great Verse of Galatians 2:20 — *"I am crucified with Christ."*

Paul desired nothing less than that Christ might think through his mind, speak through his lips, completely dominate his mode of living, his intellectual life, his volition.

All of this of which Paul speaks, is not merely an acquaintance with facts, nor an intellectual conviction of their reality, but an appropriation of this knowledge of Christ (so to speak) as an influencing power into the very being of him who knows them.

In order to fully know Him, we must be found in Christ. We must have that Righteousness which is through the Faith of Christ, for we can know Him only by being made like unto Him — this we must remember, for it is very important.

John said, *"When He shall appear, we shall be like Him; for we shall see Him as He is"* (I Jn. 3:2).

Now, all who see Him by Faith, which is the only way it can be done, are in a measure being transformed into the same Image. For the knowledge spoken of here is a personal knowledge, gained, not by hearing or reading, but by direct personal communion with the Lord; in other words, it is not theoretical, but experimental.

THE OPEN DOOR

All that Paul has found in Christ, has not at all exhausted that knowledge, but rather only opened the door of progress, and brought near the most stirring possibilities. For, indeed, to be found in Christ having that Righteousness, meant that God in Christ was His, and had begun to communicate Himself in Eternal Life. Now this must still reveal itself in further and fuller knowledge of Christ.

According to the Apostle's conception, that which Christ means to be to us, that which we may attain to be by Christ, opens progressively to the soul, showing us that we have walked through a door into a treasure house which actually has no end. In fact, one could explain this as an eternal quest, with each glorious room in this treasure house only making one desire further exploration.

We must not forget, what has more than once been said, that this earthly life of ours in Christ is only the beginning. In fact, one might say that this is where the discipline begins, goes on, with us understanding, that if it is this glorious now, what will it be a thousand years from today?

Capacity for such a life is not something superhuman; it is actually common to man, or at least it should be, because man is made in the Image of God. The problem is, due to the Fall, man seeks this life in all the wrong places, in fact, in places where there is no life. As someone has said, *"The soul of man is so large, that only God can fill it up."* Let's say it another way:

The two Books of the Bible, *"Ecclesiastes"* and the *"Song of Solomon,"* epitomize this of which we speak.

In Ecclesiastes, which is the description of man trying to find what his soul longs for outside of God, we find that all is emptiness. In the Song of Solomon which is the very opposite, all is fullness. Christ and the world are contrasted.

In the one Book the heart is too large for the portion; in the other, the portion is too large for the heart.

The world and all that it has, can never fill the heart of man, but by contrast, Christ is so large, that He can not only fill the heart, but He can keep it overflowing forever and forever.

THE POWER OF HIS RESURRECTION

The phrase, *"And the power of His Resurrection,"* refers to experiencing the same power which raised Christ from the dead. This power, is to be used to overcome sin in the life, and to produce Christian graces.

The Greek word for *"power"* used here is the same one that is used in Romans 1:16, and means *"that which overcomes resistance."*

This is what Paul was speaking of when he said, *"But if the Spirit of Him* (God the Father) *that raised up Jesus from the dead dwell in you, He that raised up Christ from the dead shall also quicken your mortal bodies by His Spirit that dwelleth in you"* (Rom. 8:11).

Paul is talking about the Holy Spirit Who dwells in the Child of God, and stands ready and willing to use the same power to help the Christian overcome sin, as He did in raising Christ from the dead. Consequently, what we're speaking of here, is something awesome to say the least!

Therefore, the Reader is to understand that Paul is not speaking here of the coming Resurrection of all Saints. He is speaking of living an overcoming, victorious Christian life, which the Holy Spirit stands ready to help the Believer do, but which He does according to our Faith in the Cross and the Resurrection of Christ.

Understanding that we as Christians have this power at our disposal, the Power of the Holy Spirit which raised Jesus from the dead, then there is really no excuse for failure on our part. However, the problem is, most Christians don't know how the Holy Spirit works. They think, that is if they think about it at all, that He just works automatically. None of that is correct, thereby leaving the Believer oftentimes without any power whatsoever.

I'll say it again. The Power of the Holy Spirit is available to every Child of God, but it is not an automatic thing as most believe. The display of His Power on our behalf, is tied to Faith; however, it must be Faith that's anchored in the Cross on our part. This is where the victory was won, where Satan was defeated, and actually which made it possible for the Holy Spirit to take up abode within our hearts and lives (Jn. 14:12-21).

THE FELLOWSHIP OF HIS SUFFERINGS

The phrase, *"And the fellowship of His sufferings,"* means the exact opposite of what most Christians think it means. Most think that it refers to Christians suffering, and the more we suffer, the more Christlike we are, or something to that effect. That's not what it means at all!

The word *"fellowship"* here in the Greek means *"a joint participation."* Now how do we have that joint participation? Once again, most would interpret this as saying we have such a participation by suffering with Christ, etc. Again, no! That's not what Paul is saying.

The *"joint participation"* in the sufferings of Christ, refer to us being *"Baptized into . . . His Death,"* and of course, refers to the Cross (Rom. 6:3).

Of course, we were not actually there when all of this happened; however, whenever the believing sinner comes to Christ, and has Faith in what Jesus did at the Cross, his Faith, at least in the Mind of God, places the sinner actually in Christ, simply because Jesus was our Representative Man. At that moment, the new convert is literally placed *"in Christ."* However, it doesn't stop there:

The Believer is to remain there all the days of his life, and I speak of being *"in Christ,"* which includes not only His Death, but as well, His Burial, Resurrection, and Exaltation (Rom. 6:3-5; Eph. 2:6).

We are a *"joint participant"* in this which Christ did, by having Faith in this great work. As we've stated repeatedly, our Faith is to remain in the Cross, and in fact, never leave the Cross.

It is not the idea of trying to put Jesus back on the Cross, or us trying to suffer in some way to be similar to the Cross, but rather that every benefit we have from Christ, has come about due to what He did at the Cross. In fact, and as should be obvious, Jesus is no longer on the Cross, no longer in the Tomb, but rather is seated presently by the Right Hand of the Father in Heaven. In fact, due to being *"in Christ,"* which means to be a joint participant in all that He did, we are able to have all the things for which He suffered. This is what Paul is saying. He's not trying to get Christians to suffer.

It's a terrible thing for Jesus to pay the price that He paid, to suffer as He suffered, all on our behalf, all to purchase for us Redemption, plus a host of other things, and then us still not have these things. How would you feel if you paid a terrible price for something, which actually came out of your own blood, doing it all for a group of people, and then them not availing themselves of this great thing? That would be a terrible thing! And yet, that's where most of the Church presently is.

Most probably know what Jesus has done, but they don't know how to obtain it, or else they think they know when in reality they don't, which is worse still!

CONFORMABLE UNTO HIS DEATH

The phrase, *"Being made conformable unto His Death,"* actually means in the Greek, *"to bring to the same form with some other person."* It actually means to conform to what Jesus did at the Cross and the Resurrection, which at the same time means not to try to do these things ourselves, which are impossible anyway.

We are to conform to why He died, for whom He died, and for what He died. We are to accept the fact, that we could not save ourselves, and at the same time we cannot make ourselves holy and righteous. Neither can we contribute anything toward this which is so very, very important. So, we are to stop trying and rather conform to what He has already done, thereby reaping its glorious and wonderful benefits.

Once again, this goes back to Paul, and everyone else as well, literally being Baptized into the death of Christ, in effect, *"crucified with Christ"* (Gal. 2:20; Rom. 6:3).

VICTORY IN CHRIST

The Church readily understands the believing sinner conforming to the death of Christ in order to be saved. This is preached widely and rightly so, that the sinner must believe that Jesus died on the Cross, and died for him, or words to that effect. In fact, the sinner doesn't have to understand much about all of this, just simply to believe. When he does so, Salvation is instant and wonderful (Jn. 3:16).

But that's about as far as most of the Church goes. It little understands how conforming to the Death of Christ also has to do with our everyday walk before the Lord, in other words, living a victorious, overcoming

Christian life. To be sure, not understanding this, brings about a host of problems.

If one is to notice, Paul is not really speaking here to the lost, but rather Believers. He is actually talking about himself, and if Paul wanted this, needed this, and sought for this, how much more should we fall in line in the same manner as well.

The problem with Christians, and I have fallen into this trap myself as I guess has every other Believer at one time or the other, we try to add to what Jesus has already done. In other words, we do not properly *"conform unto His Death."* We do so partially, but then we try to add our own little efforts which we think will help us to overcome sin, etc. It not only does not help us to overcome sin, but it actually makes a bad matter worse.

THE TRUE INTERPRETATION

To properly understand what His Death actually means, we must understand that everything we have received from Christ, everything we hope to be in Christ, is all wrapped up in the Crucifixion.

It is unfortunate, that many in the Charismatic community claim that while the Cross may have been necessary as it regards conversion, it plays no more part, they say, in what follows thereafter. In effect, they are going beyond the Cross, or attempting to do so, which means they're really not going anywhere. Beyond the benefits of the Cross there is nothing, as there needs to be nothing. There is no victory in that direction, no overcoming power in that direction.

So, the Believer is to understand that all is in the Cross, and ever will be in the Cross. As we've said several times, in the last two Chapters of the Bible (Rev. Chpts. 21-22), which speak of the New Jerusalem and the coming Perfect Age, Jesus as the *"Lamb"* is mentioned seven times. The word *"Lamb"* is used all of these times, in order that we never forget, that our place and position in this coming New Jerusalem, was brought about and is brought about, totally and entirely, as a result of what Jesus did on the Cross, actually being offered up as the *"Lamb of God"* (Jn. 1:29). So, for anyone to think they can go beyond the Cross, or rather the benefits of the Cross, is simply going in a direction which leads to nowhere.

NOTES

Understanding what we've said, the word *"conform"* simply means to believe what has been said, and receive its benefits.

(11) "IF BY ANY MEANS I MIGHT ATTAIN UNTO THE RESURRECTION OF THE DEAD."

As well, most Christians read this particular Verse wrong, thinking that Paul is speaking of the coming Resurrection which will include all the Saints, etc. He isn't!

If one is to notice, the way this sentence is structured, presents Paul as being hopeful. To be sure, the coming Resurrection is not a merely hopeful thought, but rather something which is guaranteed (I Cor. 15:1-34). So, what is the Apostle saying?

He has in mind the spiritual resurrection of the believing sinner spoken of in Ephesians 2:4-8, a Resurrection out from a state in which one is dead in trespasses and sins, to one in which one is alive with the Divine Life of God motivating his being. Paul desires the full operation of this life to surge through his Christian experience in such a manner that the fragrance of the Life of his Lord may permeate his life. This is the goal to which he is striving and the goal to which he has not yet attained, at least in totality.

ATTAINMENT

The phrase, *"If by any means I might attain,"* does not as stated, refer to the coming Resurrection. There is nothing that the Believer has to do to attain that, such being guaranteed to all who are in Christ. So, as stated, Paul is speaking of something else entirely.

The word *"attain"* means *"to know, to take hold, to be found, to reach or overtake, to rest, to grasp."* It can also mean, *"to do or to accomplish."*

There are actually six different Greek words which can be translated *"attain."* But there is a theological consistency in each of these New Testament Passages where the idea of attaining is found. In looking at these Passages, we discover how we cannot attain spirituality — and how we can!

THE EXPLANATION

In two of the following examples we will give, the word *"attain"* is not actually used; however, even though another word was chosen by the King James translators, it actually means the same thing as *"attain"* or *"attainment."*

Romans 9:30-32 gives us Paul's explanation of why Old Testament Israel failed to attain righteousness. It was because they approached righteousness as if it were to be won by works rather than received by Faith.

In Galatians Chapter 3, the Greek word is used again, but translated something else, but it means, as stated, the same.

Paul warns the young Church that they are making this same mistake (Gal. 3:1-14, especially vs. 3). These believers have accepted Salvation by Faith, but now they want to try to go on in the Christian life as if growth were a matter of keeping the Law. Paul shows that the Law cannot help. Faith is the key after Salvation as well as for Salvation. Keep in mind, we are speaking of attaining something, in this case a Victorious Life.

In Ephesians 4:13-16, Paul examines Christian growth. We attain maturity by growing up into Christ. Our growth comes in the context of warm, loving relationships with other Believers in the Body of Christ — those who support us by caring and ministering.

In Philippians 3:11-16, the Passage of our present study, Paul looks again at the idea of spiritual attainment. He himself has turned his back on his own considerable accomplishments under Law. He has tossed them aside and considers them worthless.

His goal now is simply to be found in Christ and so to *"attain to the Resurrection from the dead."* As stated, this expression does not refer to the coming physical resurrection, but to Paul's present experience concerning a power for righteous living that can be found only by Faith and only as Jesus shares His Own Resurrection Life with the Believer (Rom. 6:8, 13; Phil. 3:9).

This experience of power comes as we seek to follow Jesus and put into daily practice whatever level of understanding and maturity we may arrive at.

The picture that emerges as we connect these Passages is an exciting one. God does have a high calling for Christians. But we attain it, not by self-reliant attempts to live by the Law, but rather by humble commitment of ourselves to Jesus, asking and believing by Faith that He will give us the power to follow Him, which He does through the Holy Spirit, and according to our Faith in His Death and Resurrection.

RESURRECTION

The phrase, *"Unto the Resurrection of the dead,"* refers to Romans 6:3-5. As we have repeatedly stated, it has nothing to do with the coming Resurrection of all Saints, but rather the practical attainment of a victorious life, which is already our position in Christ, according to what He has done for us.

As we have stated, Paul gives the actual meaning of all this in Romans Chapter 6. We are baptized into the Death of Christ, buried with Him, and raised with Him in *"newness of life"* (Rom. 6:4-5).

However, even as we shall see in Philippians 3:12, fully experiencing all of these wonderful things in our everyday walk, which of course the Holy Spirit intends, does not come about easily or quickly. And yet, the Reader must understand, that irrespective of the complications involved, there is simply no other way to this path of Victory. What Jesus did at the Cross provides the only way, the only manner, the only solution.

Even Paul will say, as we will read in the next Verse of our study, that he had not attained to all the benefits provided by Christ. Consequently, I suppose that one would ask the question as to why it is this difficult, if in fact it is difficult? The next Verse I think will shed some light on this subject.

(12) "NOT AS THOUGH I HAD ALREADY ATTAINED, EITHER WERE ALREADY PERFECT: BUT I FOLLOW AFTER, IF THAT I MAY APPREHEND THAT FOR WHICH ALSO I AM APPREHENDED OF CHRIST JESUS."

Paul is explaining here how his present life is a pursuit ever after Jesus. And in this he does not want to be misunderstood. He is not claiming that his maturity in Christ has already brought him to his final goal. In fact, he states here that he has not already received all he longs for nor has he been brought to that perfect completeness to which he has aspired.

In this Verse of Scripture, hopefully, we will learn several things.

ATTAINMENT AND PERFECTION

The phrase, *"Not as though I had already attained, either were already perfect,"* presents the growth process of the Apostle.

The word *"attained"* in this Verse is from a different Greek word than in the preceding Verse. In the previous Verse, we found that it meant *"to arrive at, as at a goal."* Here the Greek verb speaks of an appropriation.

That which Paul says he has not yet appropriated in an absolute sense, he mentions in Verse 10. In fact, he has definitely come to experience the Power of God surging through his being, helping him in his joint-participation in that which Christ did at the Cross and the Resurrection. He has definitely been brought to the place in his experience where he radiates to some degree the selflessness, his self-abnegation to the Lord Jesus, which is actually what this is all about — self. But he has not appropriated these, laid hold upon these, in the fullest measure. There is room for much improvement and advance in these respects.

Regarding the word *"perfection,"* the Greek word used here does not mean *"sinless perfection,"* but rather, *"spiritually mature."*

The Apostle is stating, that he has not come to the place in his Christian life where growth in spiritual maturity has been completed, beyond which there is no room for further development, and that as a result he is now in a state of absolute spiritual maturity. He has not reached this place to where there is no more room for development. In fact, the truth is, due to the fact that Christ cannot be exhausted, consequently, there is actually no end to the degree of development that one may attain. Therefore, this is an unending process, which actually will continue for all of eternity.

THE LESSON OF *"SELF"*

To sum up what the Apostle is saying in these Passages, I think the word *"self,"* would probably come to the heart of the matter quicker than any other word.

The idea regarding what the Holy Spirit is doing with us, or rather trying to do according to our cooperation, is to bring *"self"* into proper Christlikeness. This is not an easy process, neither is it a simple process. The Holy Spirit struggles for control within our lives, while self, and that speaks of the wants, passions, and desires of the flesh, seeks to go its own direction, which is always wrong. Without the Holy Spirit constantly leading, guiding, empowering, and teaching, self will automatically go astray. And to be frank, religious self is the worse self of all.

We tend to think that we know how to get this thing done. Inasmuch, as the religious man does religious things, he automatically thinks of himself as being spiritual. The truth is, anything that's not birthed completely by the Holy Spirit, which will always be according to the Word of God in totality, is of self, i.e., *"the flesh."*

When the person comes to Christ, the Lord does not destroy the self in us. That's not the idea of the Holy Spirit. The idea is to bring self into total Christlikeness, which of necessity demands the crucifixion process. As someone has well said, *"Jesus died on the Cross not only to deliver us from sin, but as well from self."*

Due to the nature of self, and the problems of the Fall which still cling to the Child of God, the victory we had yesterday will not suffice for today. That's the reason Jesus told us to *"deny ourselves, and take up our Cross daily."*

He then said, *"For whosoever will save his life* (allow self to direct his life), *shall lose it but whosoever will lose his life* (lose it in Christ, as self is placed in Christ), *for My sake, the same shall save it"* (Lk. 9:23-24).

However, the losing of the life or self in Christ is not a one-time process, but rather a continuing, even a daily process. This is what makes it so difficult. It is this way because we are human; consequently, the Lord must work within the concept of humanity. That's the reason that consecration must be renewed even on a daily basis.

AT THE CROSS

It is literally impossible for the Believer to be what he ought to be, to be brought to the place to where the Holy Spirit is seeking to bring us, without the Believer fully understanding the Cross, fully knowing his place in all of this which Christ did on our behalf, and how to appropriate its benefits by Faith. The Cross breeds humility, and the Cross alone breeds humility. Inasmuch, as humility is the very opposite of unsanctified self, we are now dealing with the heart of the problem. Arrogance and pride characterize all of us. We may like to think that such is not the case, but irrespective of our thoughts, it is the case with all of us. Admittedly, it's worse with some than others, and every once in a while we might have the privilege of meeting someone who has properly hidden self in Christ; regrettably, that person is rare.

I realize that my statements are strong when I state that it is impossible for the Believer, and irrespective as to how much God may be using him or her, to be what one ought to be in Christ, to fully mature and develop in Christ, without a proper understanding of the Cross, but it just happens to be true. Paul plainly said, *"But God forbid that I should glory, save in the Cross of our Lord Jesus Christ, by Whom the world is crucified unto me, and I unto the world"* (Gal. 6:14). This is the only way that this Christ-filled life can be brought about.

The Church has attempted to *"confess"* its way there, *"fast"* its way there, *"pray"* its way there, *"witness"* its way there, arrive at this goal by spiritual *"manifestations"* of different sorts, with not one person ever having succeeded by these ways. While these things are very good within their own way and manner, they will not accomplish that of which Paul speaks — spiritual maturity. That can only come by one's understanding of the Cross, and thereby properly living the crucified life, all in Christ.

SELF AND THE INEXHAUSTIBLE CHRIST

There are two major factors in all of this which causes Paul to say that he has not yet attained to all that is possible.

The first is the difficulties of the flesh, the impossibility actually of making it do on a constant basis all that we want and desire in Christ. This is a constant, never-ending struggle. We have this monster caged, we think, and then the next day he is out again. The point is, even as Paul succinctly brings it out, if one, even such as Paul, who fully understands the Cross, at least as much as is humanly possible, thereby exacting all its benefits, still has these problems with the flesh, where does that leave one who is trying to reach this goal by other methods? I think it is obvious to where it leads those individuals.

The other factor, even that to which we have already alluded, is the absolute impossibility of exhausting Christ in any measure. Irrespective as to how close one comes to Him, there is still much further to go. Irrespective as to how much we obtain of Him, we cannot exhaust Him, and, in fact, will never exhaust Him. Inasmuch as He is God, how is it possible for the creature to exhaust the potential of the Creator!

The idea is, the more we attain of Him, to know Him, to understand Him, to be like He is, to have His life flowing through us through the Person of the Holy Spirit, instead of reaching a saturation point, or even a satisfaction point, this wonder of Christ only makes us hunger and thirst for more. Thank God there is always more to be had!

I FOLLOW

The phrase, *"I follow after,"* means *"to pursue."*

Concerning this journey, a journey incidentally which will never end, we hear Jesus saying to His proposed Disciples, *"Follow Me"* (Mat. 4:19).

At that moment on that memorable day, when Peter and others heard that clarion call, they little dreamed to where it would lead. Actually, and as stated, there is no end to this.

When one begins to follow Christ, the probationary time comes first as it regards this earthly life. And now soon the Rapture will take place, with Jesus calling all of His people away, in effect, still saying, *"Follow Me."*

This second stage will lead to the portals of Glory. It's called the *"Rapture of the Church"* (I Thess. 4:16-17).

Then Revelation Chapter 19 signals the Second Coming, where every Saint of God who has ever lived, even up unto the time of the First Resurrection, will again follow Jesus back to this Earth to rule and reign with Him for a thousand years.

The last two Chapters of Revelation proclaim the New Jerusalem coming down from

God out of Heaven, with God literally changing His headquarters from Heaven to Earth. Once again, every Saint of God will follow Jesus into that New Jerusalem (Rev. 22:14).

However, this is not the end, only the end of the beginning. This Perfect Age will last forever and forever, with every Saint of God living forever and forever, and continuing to follow Christ. As the following will never end, neither will the wonder, beauty, glory, and joy of His Person.

THE APPREHENDING

The phrase, *"If that I may apprehend that for which also I am apprehended of Christ Jesus,"* presents this which Paul is pursuing, which is absolute Christlikeness.

The word *"apprehend"* is from the same Greek word translated *"attained,"* but with a preposition prefixed which means in its local force *"down."* He wants to catch hold of it and pull it down, like a football player who not only wants to catch his man, but wants to pull him down and in a sense, make him his own. Paul wants to appropriate and make his own that for which Christ caught Paul and made him His Own.

Paul speaks of the latter in Galatians 1:16, where God's purpose of calling Paul into Salvation and the Office of Apostle was that He might reveal His Son in Paul. And that is exactly what Paul is talking about in the expression, *"being made conformable to His Death."* As stated, it was Christlikeness that Paul was pursuing after. It is absolute Christlikeness that he says that he has not yet captured and pulled down so as to make his own (Wuest).

The idea is, that Jesus Christ saved Paul (apprehended him) for a purpose. That purpose is to develop Christlikeness in the realm of Righteousness and Holiness in the Apostle, which of course, the Holy Spirit desires to do as well in all of us.

We were not saved to just merely miss Hell and go to Heaven. We were saved in order to be made into the Image of Christ.

A SPIRITUAL INSTINCT

Inasmuch as we are saved, in fact, new creations in Christ, we instinctively know that these qualities, these attributes, these Graces of Righteousness and Holiness must be developed in us. But our problem is, we most of the time go about the task in all the wrong ways. We attempt to do by the flesh, even as we have been discussing here, what only the Spirit of God can do. In fact, Paul deals with this in Romans Chapter 8. If one studies Paul very much, one will find him saying the same thing over and over again, but in slightly different ways. The Spirit of God does it this way in order for us to ultimately grasp what is being said and understand.

All of these things must be understood spiritually. In other words, they are all spiritually discerned, and only spiritually discerned (I Cor. 2:14). That's the reason we have to hear some of these things several times before they begin to catch hold within our hearts.

Paul said in Romans, *"But ye are not in the flesh* (we are not to subdue sin and evil passions merely by the flesh, which is impossible) *but in the Spirit* (as Saints, we have the Spirit of God) *... And if Christ be in you* (if you are saved), *the body is dead because of sin* (ruined because of the Fall, which means we cannot gain victory by our own machinations); *but the Spirit is Life because of Righteousness* (the Spirit of God Alone can bring about victory within our lives.)" (Rom. 8:9-10).

We know that we need to *"apprehend"* or *"attain"* this Christlikeness, but our problem is, we often deal with the subject in all the wrong ways, actually trying to bring it about within our own efforts, and because these efforts are spiritual, we are fooled at times into thinking that it's the Spirit of God when it isn't.

THE HOLY SPIRIT

Romans Chapter 8 declares that which we need to be in Christ, in fact, what we must be in Christ, can only be brought about by the Holy Spirit. He Alone can perform this task, can make us into that which we instinctively know we ought to be. As stated, Christ has apprehended us, which means that He has saved us, and He has done this for a purpose. It is ever to become more and more Christlike!

All that the Believer needs, is to be understood as having been done and brought about at the Cross of Christ, even as Paul will bring out in Verse 18. As we have said over and over, we are to put our Faith in that, knowing that our Victory is tied to the Cross and the Resurrection, and then the Holy Spirit will do this great work within our lives, but only then!

THE FAITH WALK

To be sure, once the Believer begins to walk this Faith walk, which is always centered up in the Cross, Satan will test such Faith, and test it greatly at times. In fact, this is a given. In other words, there is nothing one can do to stop the difficulties and problems which will come our way. Jesus in giving us the illustration of the house built upon the Rock or upon the sand, didn't say that the storms would possibly come, but rather, *"The rain descended, and the floods came, and the winds blew"* (Mat. 7:24-29).

If one's Faith is properly placed in the Cross, and it remains there, even though Satan will do his very best to try to dislodge it, victory is assured. Otherwise, there can be no victory whatsoever.

I want everything that the Lord has for me. I want nothing of this world, nor any of its doings to hold sway over my life. I want only Christ, for Christ Alone can satisfy the hunger and thirst of the soul. The more of Jesus one gets, the more he attains, the more that one wants, with each application drawing one closer and closer, thereby giving this *"more abundant life"* (Jn. 10:10).

This is the greatest life there is, in fact, the only life there is. But if it's lived wrong, meaning if we do not have as the proper object of our Faith, the Cross of Christ, it will in fact be wrong, and cause us much difficulty and problems. But if it's right, and it definitely can be right, it will be exactly as Simon Peter said, *"Joy unspeakable and full of glory"* (I Pet. 1:8).

(13) "BRETHREN, I COUNT NOT MYSELF TO HAVE APPREHENDED: BUT THIS ONE THING I DO, FORGETTING THOSE THINGS WHICH ARE BEHIND, AND REACHING FORTH UNTO THOSE THINGS WHICH ARE BEFORE,"

In this statement Paul addresses the Philippians by the endearing title *"Brothers,"* as he repeats the thought of Verse 12.

NOTES

Some may claim that Paul was being accused by some at Philippi of claiming perfection regarding his Christian experience; however, absence of any other indication along this line, makes it more likely that his emphasis was in contrast with what some Philippians were claiming about themselves. In other words, it seems as if some in that particular Church were in fact claiming perfection.

Paul did not regard himself as having obtained the final knowledge of Christ which is impossible anyway, and the fullest conformity to Him, which no Believer will have in totality until the Resurrection.

As well, the possibility definitely existed that some may have been teaching that performance of Jewish Rites attached to Christ could in fact bring such perfection; consequently, the Apostle hits this hard in Verse 2 of this Chapter.

Teaching that which is correct, and using the metaphor of a footrace, Paul describes his Christian life as involving the continual forgetting of *"what is behind,"* and the relentless centering of his energies and interests on the course that is ahead of him.

"Forgetting" does not mean obliterating the memory of the past (Paul has just recalled some of these things in Verses 5-7, and did so graphically in Romans Chapter 7), but a conscious refusal to let them absorb his attention and impede his progress.

This should be a tremendous lesson for us all, because the past of every Christian is checkered with failure. To deny such, is to deny reality. The idea is, that we learn from our mistakes, and press forward toward total victory in all things, not allowing the past to hinder that progress.

BRETHREN

The phrase, *"Brethren, I count not myself to have apprehended,"* in effect, repeats what he had said in the previous Verse.

As stated, Paul is speaking here to Believers, and why do we need to say this?

Some Believers have such a warped idea of the Christian life, that they cannot admit to any failure of any nature, which, of course, puts them into a category of hypocrisy. I suppose their theology doesn't include failure, therefore, they have to live in a state of denial or else refusing to admit the truth. And then again, some Christians have the mistaken idea that if other people do not know of the struggle in which they are involved, concerning their own Christian experience of living Righteous and Holy, then somehow it doesn't count. That is silly indeed! The Believer should always understand that it's what God knows that counts.

Paul faced all these questions of life very openly. Romans Chapter 7 proclaims him speaking candidly of his failures, and how that God helped him over these things, in fact, giving him the great Truths which he in turn gave to us in Romans, Chapters 6 and 8.

The truth is, the Christian experience is one of trial and error. Perhaps one could say that it shouldn't be that, but it is! This problem of the flesh is so volatile, and at the same time so subtle, that we do not come to the place of victory easily or quickly. And then again, Satan does everything within his power to steer the Believer away from the Cross, where alone he can find the answer, and through alone which the Holy Spirit will work.

The Reader should apply all of these things given to us by Paul to his or her own life. In fact, and as should be obvious, this is what the Holy Spirit intends.

COUNT

The word *"count"* is from a Greek word which has the force of looking back upon the process of a discussion and calmly drawing a conclusion. One might say that Paul had after much deliberation and consideration, arrived at certain conclusions concerning this struggle, which he stated in Verse 12.

It is evident that some of the Philippian Saints had arrived at the opposite conclusion regarding themselves. The manner in which Paul says these things proves that.

The erroneous teaching of sinless perfection is not new. In fact, it seems, as stated, to have been held by some in the Philippian Church. So Paul is addressing this subject.

The words *"attained"* and *"apprehended"* in Verse 12 merely refer to a past fact, with the word *"apprehend"* referring to a present process. But the word *"apprehended"* in this Verse (vs. 13) speaks of a past completed process with present results, the strongest way Paul had of stating the fact. That settled the question.

He meant that he had not completely grasped that for which the Lord Jesus had grasped him. In other words, he was still growing, and if he was still growing, it would certainly stand to reason that Christians at Philippi were still growing as well, and had not reached any type of sinless perfection. I wonder how in the world anyone could come to such a conclusion as *"sinless perfection!"*

In the first place, all one has to do is to question for a few moments the friends and loved ones of the individual in question, and I think it will become quickly obvious that sinless perfection doesn't exist. How silly can we be! How foolish can we be! To claim something which is so obviously not, presents the height of spiritual ignorance, or to say it in another way, *"presents the height of ignorance in any manner."*

PAUL AS AN EXAMPLE

In all of this, Paul is addressing several errors.

First of all, he is addressing the argument contained in the false teaching that sin doesn't really matter that much. In other words, *"Let us sin that Grace may abound."* Nothing could be more abhorrent to Paul, as the Sixth Chapter of Romans makes clear.

Paul's striving for a greater Christlikeness is the corrective for those who say that being in Christ makes sin irrelevant. Instead, Paul strenuously asserts that Grace, far from making one tolerant of sin, makes sin all the more intolerable and incompatible with true Christianity.

The second error, is the allusion of false security, i.e., *"sinless perfection."* Of course, the false security can play out in either direction, with Christians thinking they can sin all they want to and still be secure, with others thinking they have reached perfection, and are, therefore, secure. The error comes full circle, whatever the case. The Apostle is on guard against allusions of false security in any capacity.

He wants to know *"more about Jesus."* He is praying, *"Lord, plant my feet on higher ground."*

It would have been very easy for the Apostle to rest from his labors and to relax. Many who have borne the *"burden in the heat of the day"* feel justified in taking it easy in retirement. Such was never the case with Paul, with, in fact, the word *"retirement"* not even in his vocabulary.

His eagerness to do his best for Christ, his strenuous endeavors for a greater degree of Christlikeness, continued until his death. Since Christ had laid hold on him, he also wishes to lay hold of Christ and follow closely behind, ever closer! Ever closer!

THIS ONE THING

The phrase, *"But this one thing I do,"* should have been translated from the literal Greek, *"But one thing."* This sums up his Christian conduct and purpose.

The Apostle had one great aim and purpose of life. He did not attempt to mingle the world and Salvation, and thereby, hope to gain both. This is very important, and the Reader should study those words very carefully.

As well, he did not seek to obtain wealth and Salvation too, of which many Charismatics should take note. Neither did he look for honor here and the Crown of Glory hereafter. As stated, he had one object, one aim, one great purpose of soul, and that was to *"win Christ."*

I think, to this singleness of purpose he owed his extraordinary attainments regarding his personal life and his Ministry.

From that, I think we can say that a Christian will accomplish nothing who has not a single great aim and purpose of soul. That purpose should be to secure the prize, and to renounce everything that would be in the way to its attainment. Let us, then, so live that we may be able to say, that there is one great object which we always have in view, and that we mean to avoid everything which would interfere with that.

FORGETTING PAST FAILURES

The phrase, *"Forgetting those things which are behind,"* refers to things the Apostle had depended upon to find favor with God, and the failure that type of effort brought about (Phil. 3:5-6).

NOTES

"Forgetting" is stronger in the Greek, meaning, *"completely forgetting."*

Paul is using an illustration here of a Greek runner completely forgetting his opponents whom he is leading in the race. Just as a runner's speed is slackened should he think of those behind him, and the thud, thud of their pounding feet, so the Christian's onward progress is hindered should he dwell on the past full of failures and sins, full of heartaches and discouragements, full of disappointments and thwarted hopes and plans.

As long as a Christian has made things right with God and man, he should completely forget the past, at least as it regards hindering his present and future. What a person is, is what they are presently in Christ.

To be sure, we certainly should learn from our mistakes, and to learn we have to try to figure out where we have gone wrong, which definitely necessitates us looking at the situation of the past in a rightful light. As we've already said, the idea is, that we not allow those things to hinder us, or to slow us from our rightful objective, which is to *"win Christ."*

THE TRUE NATURE OF THE PAST

Someone has well said, *"The Christian has no past, and the Devil has no future."* That is certainly correct!

"Justification by Faith" is brought to bear as it concerns our Living for God. Many Christians do not know that, thinking that this great work of Grace only applies to our initial Salvation experience. While Justification by Faith definitely does apply to the initial experience, which at that time places the Believer in a right standing with God; in other words, Justification by Faith is the act of God in declaring a guilty sinner *"not guilty."* He can do that, because Jesus has acted as the Substitute for the guilty sinner, actually even as his Representative Man, which means that the believing sinner can have the Righteousness of Christ by simply believing on Him (Jn. 3:16).

However, Justification by Faith does not end there. It affects, as stated, the life of the Believer in totality until he dies or Jesus comes.

What do I mean by that?

Whenever the Christian does something wrong, whatever it might be, and then asks the Lord to forgive him (I Jn. 1:9), John said that the Lord will be *"faithful and just in forgiving us our sins, and cleansing us from all unrighteousness."*

We are so very thankful that He is *"faithful,"* meaning that He will never turn down the seeking soul; however, the word *"just"* means that He does not do this on the ground of injustice in any nature. In other words, God is not overlooking sin in any fashion, just because it is in the life of one of His Children. In fact, He cannot treat sin in any manner except by demanding the full penalty, irrespective as to whom it might affect.

However, He can be *"just"* in forgiving sin in the heart and life of the Christian, at least upon proper seeking of such, because Jesus has paid the price for all sin, which includes not only the past, but as well, the present and the future. So, He forgives on the basis of the Finished Work of Christ on the Cross and the Resurrection, and our Faith in that Work.

This means that when the Lord forgives sin in the life of the Christian, that sin is forgotten by Him, with God then looking at the Christian as if the sin was never committed. That actually is *"Justification by Faith."* The guilty are no longer guilty; the sinner is no longer a sinner; the sin is no longer a factor.

Consequently, for the Christian to allow past sin, which in fact has already been washed, cleansed, forgiven, and forgotten, to be held over his head by Satan, does a terrible injustice to Christ. The truth is, *"There is therefore now no condemnation to them who are in Christ Jesus"* (Rom. 8:1).

Unfortunately, Satan is not the only one who seeks to drag up past failures. Unfortunately, many Christians seem to enjoy doing the same thing regarding others as well. They do not too very much enjoy such being done to them, but they seem to feel very free in doing it to other Believers.

How sinful, how wicked it is, to drag up something which a fellow Believer has done in the past, but yet has been totally forgiven, cleansed, and washed by the Blood of Jesus.

This comes under the heading of the Words of Jesus, *"For if ye forgive men their trespasses, your Heavenly Father will also forgive you:*

NOTES

"But if you forgive not men their trespasses, neither will your Father forgive your trespasses" (Mat. 6:14-15).

This is a serious indictment indeed!

PROBATION

Unfortunately, much of the Church operates according to the system of the world and not according to the Word of God. Consequently, the Church very easily puts Christians on probation. The idea is, these people have done something wrong, whatever it might have been, therefore, they are to be punished. Probation is just one of those punishments, with other things added as well. As stated, this is the system of the world and not the Word of God!

In the first place, these individuals who are doing the punishing, are worse off spiritually than the ones they are punishing. And how do I know that?

For a person to do such a thing, it means that in his own mind he thinks he is morally qualified to do such a thing. However, James plainly said, *"There is one Lawgiver* (the Lord), *Who is able to save and to destroy: who art thou that judgest another?"* (James 4:12).

In other words, James is saying, *"Who do you think you are, thinking you are qualified to judge and punish someone else?"*

Of course, James is speaking here of Believers and not the world.

As well, whether they realize it or not, such action shows that the ones doing the punishing, do not believe that Jesus was punished on the Cross for this very thing, and I speak of our sins. They are, in effect, saying that Jesus was not punished enough, He did not suffer enough, in other words He did not fully pay the price, therefore, more price has to be paid.

What a travesty! What an insult to the Finished Work of Christ! What an insult to Christ Himself! In fact, what an insult to the entirety of the Plan of God as it regards Redemption!

There is no such thing as *"punishment"* as it regards a Child of God, which means there's no such thing as *"probation."* Whenever a Believer puts another Believer on probation for any reason, that Believer has placed himself on probation as well, at least in the Eyes of God. Jesus addressed this also when He said, *"For with what judgment ye judge, ye shall be judged: and with what measure ye mete, it shall be measured to you again"* (Mat. 7:2).

In fact, if this type of *"punishment"* is carried out equally and fairly over the entirety of the Christian Family, every single Christian would have to be brought under the same judgment and suffer punishment, for the simple reason, that there is no sinless perfection, even as we are studying here. No, that doesn't mean that sin is to be overlooked or condoned in any manner.

It does mean, that whenever a Believer sins and repents, which validity can easily be ascertained, the matter is to drop then and there. Paul said it beautifully, *"forgetting those things which are behind!"*

WHAT ABOUT ENTIRE DENOMINATIONS WHO ENGAGE IN SUCH PRACTICES?

Unfortunately, much of the Church operates on the principle of the world, which functions on the premise of judging, punishment, etc. While the world must conduct itself in this manner and for all the obvious reasons, it is a travesty when the Church follows suit.

The things I'm about to say will not readily be understood too very much by most of the laity, and because it does not directly affect them; however, it definitely does affect them indirectly, with the fallout actually being severe. Because most of the laity are not directly involved, they tend to not take a stand, mostly doing whatever their so-called Leaders suggest. That is unfortunate, because it means they are following men and not the Word of God.

There are all type of different rules in different Denominations regarding the discipline of Preachers, etc. This within itself tells us that something is wrong. How can rules be different, if in fact the Word of God is being followed?

If a Preacher of the Gospel has some type of problem, most Denominations little consider repentance and the manner laid down in the Word of God concerning such situations. As stated, they just make up their own rules, which they feel free to change from time to time. Again, if it's right to begin with, how can it be changed? An entire Church body voting on something does not make it right. The Word of God addresses all of these matters which means its already been settled, and is meant by the Holy Spirit to be followed. Unfortunately, most of the Church simply ignores what the Word says regarding these matters, and most other things as well.

Even though these rules vary with Denominations, let me state just a few:

STOP PREACHING?

In one particular Pentecostal Denomination, if there is failure on the part of a Preacher, he cannot preach for two years. The ruling once was that he could not ever preach again, and then was shortened to five years, and then to two years. Once again we ask the question, *"if it was right to start with, how could it be changed?"*

As well, if God has called someone to preach, what man has the right to tell him he can't preach? Also, what does not preaching for two years have to do with forgiveness, restoration, etc.?

Again, if these so-called leaders, are going to insist upon this system, which incidentally is grossly unscriptural, to be fair and right, they will have to stop preaching themselves as well!

Oh yes, I forgot to mention, they will allow him to preach on a street corner, or to kids, or in a nursing home, or mission, etc. But not behind the pulpit in a Church. What type of rationale is that?

If it's wrong to preach under such circumstances, it's wrong to preach anywhere. How silly can we be!

Much of the time, the individual is told that he must move to another city. This is not for any particular reason, just some type of rule somebody made up. Again I ask, how will that help?

All Preachers in that particular Denomination are required to shun this Brother for two years. They are to treat him with no respect and with disdain. Other similar Denominations are strongly encouraged to conduct themselves toward the individual in the same manner, with most complying.

FAIR GAME

The idea is, the man has become *"fair game,"* and just about anything anyone would desire to say about him, or do to him, is sanctioned.

If the Reader noting these things I have said, has little knowledge of the Word of God, he or she might think that these particular rulings of punishment are what ought to be. The idea is, *"we've got to be hard on sin."* However, what they do not realize is, the Bible way is that the Lord is extremely hard on sin, so hard that His Only Son had to die on a Cross in order to atone for sin; however, the Lord is not hard on sinners at all, and all had better be thankful for that. Because if He was, none of us would be around.

No, this Denomination in question is not hard on sin at all, actually being very lenient on this terrible matter of iniquity. They are hard on sinners, as all self-righteousness is. As stated, and I can say this without exception, *"those who do such things, and I speak of so-called Spiritual Leaders, are in worse shape spiritually than the ones they are punishing."* Beside their own personal problems, they are violating the Word of God to a terrible degree, actually making a mockery out of the Grace of God.

Preachers who are in these particular Denominations, and who yield to this foolishness, as well, are sinning. I realize that's quite a statement, but it is true. Anything that's opposed to the Word of God is sin.

To be frank, if a Preacher wants to fully obey the Lord, considering the condition that most of these Denominations are presently in, and I speak of going astray from the Word of God, the best course would be to disassociate themselves. Unfortunately, the matter is not going to get better, but rather worse. This is the age of Apostasy, which means a departure from Truth, in fact, the last great Apostasy, which will be the worst of all! This *"leaven"* which has permeated most of these Denominations for years, has now spread until it almost engulfs the whole, which is exactly what leaven does, if it's not rooted out. I have only scratched the surface, with the situation being far more evil than one could ever even begin to think. As stated, it will not get better.

BIBLE EXAMPLES

Considering that Peter failed the Lord shortly before the Crucifixion, if he had belonged to the Denomination of which I have just spoken, he would not have been able to preach on the Day of Pentecost, and in fact, would probably have not been heard of again. Considering Romans Chapter 7, Paul would not have been able to have written any of his Epistles, which means that about half the New Testament would be missing. Jonah would never have gone to Nineveh, and David would have been forced to step down as King of Israel.

Abraham after lying to Pharaoh about Sarah, would have never been given the great Covenant of Justification by Grace. To think that Jacob would have made it, would have been a joke! Moses would have been forced to have stepped down from being the Leader of Israel. Several years before he died, considering that he disobeyed the Lord and committed a grievous sin in striking the Rock which was a type of Christ, when he was told by the Lord to speak to it only, he would have been disqualified.

I remember the great Preacher, C.M. Ward saying that most of the Bible Greats could not have belonged to his Denomination. They would not have been worthy, or words to that effect!

We might pass this off by claiming that these things mentioned were in Bible times, and this is now, which is different. No, it's not different!

The problem is sin, and God has always dealt with sin in the same manner and the same way. He did it all through His Son, the Lord Jesus Christ.

The problem is, men forsake the Ways of God, thereby devising their own ways, which always leads to death.

Once again, the Reader may think that these things do not concern him; however, they concern him very much. Ministers whose Ministries the Church desperately needs are denied, just as the Ministries of Peter and Paul would have been denied, had their situations been transferred to the present. One cannot have it both ways, it is either according to the Word of God and, therefore, legitimate and right, or else it's not according to the Word of God, and is, therefore, very wrong, and desperately needs to be corrected. However, it's very difficult for men to admit they are wrong, and religious men most of all. In fact, there's never been a case in history of which I am aware, that a religious Denomination has ever repented. In fact, almost all of them lose their way after the third generation.

A PRESENT ILLUSTRATION

Donnie was preaching a meeting in a particular Church a short time back, actually a Church associated with the Denomination of which I have just mentioned. The Pastor related the following to him:

They were in a certain Denominational meeting held in a particular Church, with one of its Leaders ministering that night. At the close of the Message, the Speaker, as I stated, a Leader in that Denomination, gave an utterance in Tongues.

The Congregation grew quiet for a moment, and then an Interpretation was given, which was followed by worship.

The next day, the Pastor for whom Donnie was preaching, said that he called the District Superintendent about a particular matter, and was discussing the service. He asked this District Leader, *"did you know who gave the Interpretation to that Utterance last night?"*

After a few moments, the District Official said, *"Yes, I do!"*

The one who Interpreted the Utterance happened to be a Preacher who had some type of difficulty some months back, and had been excommunicated. He was forced to resign his Church, and as stated above, could not preach for two years, etc.

The Pastor asked the District Official, *"If this man was worthy enough to be used by the Holy Spirit to give this Interpretation, why isn't he worthy enough to Preach the Gospel, and more particularly, worthy enough to Preach in our Churches?"*

There was a long silence, with the District Official finally answering and saying, *"I see what you mean!"*

The Truth is, whatever problem this dear Brother had, he had repented of the situation, with it being washed clean by the Blood of Jesus, with the Holy Spirit continuing to use him, as the Holy Spirit always does. When a person is forgiven, the thing is cleansed and washed, and as stated, forgotten by the Lord.

At that time, the man should have resumed his Ministry, as ought to be obvious. But in that particular Denomination, that was not the case, and in fact could not be the case.

It would seem that such an example which we have just given, would be enough to cause some of these men to begin to think a little bit. However, the following should be noted:

Most of these Leaders (thankfully, there are a few exceptions), have little interest in the Word of God, the Moving and Operation of the Holy Spirit, the Blessings of God, or the Anointing of the Holy Spirit. Even though those things are the true signs of approval by the Lord, they are completely ignored by these individuals.

The idea is, the Ways of God are completely ignored, with the words of men given preeminence. Untold millions have died and gone to Hell because of this very thing, and I speak now of the laity.

They listened to men instead of God. Irrespective as to what the cost might be, the Word of God is to always be the criteria. It must come before religious Denominations, even family and friends.

GOD WORKS FROM WHAT IS, NOT FROM WHAT MIGHT HAVE BEEN

Too many Christians live in a state of *"what might have been,"* or *"if only,"* etc. The Lord never works from such a premise. If He did there would be absolutely nothing done. Without exception, He always works from *"what is,"* irrespective as to what it might be.

Yes, it is definitely true that failure of any sort hurts and hurts greatly. Sin has a terrible price tag attached. So if anyone thinks, that anyone gets by with sin, even though the Lord does graciously forgive and cleanse, they simply don't know what their talking about. Irrespective, the Lord still works from *"what is!"*

God being God, He can do things that men cannot do. He is able to put the pieces back together again. He is able, to use a favorite saying, *"to unscramble scrambled eggs."* To be sure, only God can do such a thing, He definitely can perform miracles.

In fact, that's the story of the Gospel. When the Lord came down to this world, He came to a world in chaos, even as the First Chapter of Genesis proclaims. The entire warp and woof of Redemption proclaims God working from *"what is"* instead of *"if only."* In fact, there is no *"if only"* with God! There is only a *"what is!"*

The great sins of the age are not the terrible vices of this world, as wicked and ungodly as they might be. The great sin of the age is religious leaders departing from the Word of God, in effect, devising their own plan of Salvation.

They should take a look at their results! The situation is not turning out too very well.

The business of the Gospel is the proclamation of this *"Good News."* A part of that Good News is, that the Lord forgives sinners. Where would any of us be were that not the case?

Many may claim that it's not a matter of forgiveness.

It really doesn't matter what it is, forgiveness or otherwise. We must adhere to the Word of God regardless. If it's not a matter of forgiveness, that makes it even worse. That being the case, we have a Denomination attempting to devise another way of Salvation. That is the greatest sin of all, and in fact, that's exactly what is happening.

When anyone who calls themselves a Christian, and especially those who call themselves Preachers or Spiritual Leaders, will not accept those accepted of the Lord, they have placed themselves in a position, where God will not accept them. That is a sober thought, and should be thought out very carefully.

If we do what the Lord does, we will do exactly as Paul said, *"forget those things which are behind."* If not, those things behind us will not be forgotten by the Lord (Mat. 6:14-15).

The Believer must not fall prey to the *"if only,"* or *"what might have been,"* facade. He must not allow other Christians or anyone for that matter, to wrap such a noose around him. Instead, he must believe God!

Again we emphasize, while all sin and wrongdoing takes a deadly toll, still, we must not allow what has happened in the recent or distant past to destroy us. We must do our very best to forget those things. We must understand, that whatever there is presently, as distasteful as it might be, as hurtful as it might be, as wrecked as it might seem, if we'll give it to the Lord, trust in Him, believe in Him, and totally consecrate to Him, He still performs miracles.

To Naomi it might have seemed that all was lost. Her husband had died along with her two sons. She was left with nothing but a Gentile daughter-in-law, and still in this land of Moab. If anything ever looked bleak, that did!

However, where sin abounded, Grace did much more abound. Naomi went back to the land of Covenant, the land of Blessing, the little town of Bethlehem. You can go back as well!

Also, this Gentile daughter-in-law Ruth, even cursed by God unto the tenth generation as were all Moabites, still, because of Faith, would turn out to be the Great-Grandmother of David, from whom would come the Greater Son of David, the Lord Jesus Christ (Ruth 4:21-22).

The modern Church would little have allowed her to enter into such glory and wonder, but God did!

He will do the same for you, if you will only believe Him, regardless of the circumstances!

REACHING FORTH

The phrase, *"And reaching forth unto those things which are before,"* tells us several things:

Reaching forth: One cannot reach forth while at the same time looking behind. All our attention must be on that which is ahead, and not that which is past.

THOSE THINGS

Those things: What are those things?

They are victory in Jesus, power with God, Christlikeness, our life being what it ought to be and amounting to something for Christ. Irrespective of the past, it can be done.

The idea is, that irrespective of what has happened in the past, *"those things"* are still available, still there, still within the reach. Oh yes, the world will tell you the opposite, and most of the Church; therefore, you can listen to the doubters, the naysayers, the gainsayers, or whomever, or you can listen to the Word of God. The Book says *"those things"* are still available, are still attainable, are still apprehendable.

There were things behind Paul, things of which he was ashamed, as should be obvious. But he did not allow those things to stop him, and you must not allow those things to stop you as well. You must understand the following:

Man does not have the final say in these things. Oh to be sure, religious man will do almost anything he can to stop your progress. That is sad, but it is true. Consequently, you must not look to men, you must not listen to men, you must look to the Word of God, and listen to men and women who adhere to the Word, such as you are reading right here.

Millions who once had a close walk with God, and I think I exaggerate not, are sitting down presently doing nothing, because some off-the-wall Preacher, some Denominational Leader who probably needed to get saved himself, told you that you could not preach anymore, or could not do anything anymore. To whom are you going to listen? To what are you going to look?

The Word of God is plain and simple, and placed right before you. Believe the Word. The goal is still attainable; you just must reach for it. To be sure, it will not be easy, but it can be done.

WHICH ARE BEFORE

Which are before: While failure may be in your past, exactly as it is every single Christian who has ever lived, victory is before you. That's what the Scripture is saying.

All of these grand and glorious things promised by the Lord are still there. Just because you failed, those things did not go away, and they will not go away. As well, there's nothing in the Word of God that says you can no longer have them.

The Word says instead, that if you will look to the Lord, believe in Him, trust Him, humble yourself before Him, pick yourself up out of the dirt, and to be sure when you begin to do this, He will help you up. Others may push you down, but Jesus is in the business of picking people up. He's picked up millions, and He can pick you up as well. Also, He has never lost one who has put their trust in Him.

I'll say it again: don't listen to doubters and unbelievers. Don't listen to the Church or Preachers who says you can't. The Word of God says you can. As I've stated several times already, this is actually what the Word of God is all about — the picking up of failures out of the dirt and dust, putting them back on their feet, and starting them toward victory. It's all in Christ, and He is ready and waiting!

It's not what others say, it's what He says! It's not what others do, it's what He does! It's not what others think, it's what He knows!

You see, the Devil, and he works through the Church, will try to draw up rules which are not in the Book. Don't play by those rules, play by the ones laid down by the Lord.

It's all a matter of your Faith, and you believing in what Jesus did at the Cross and the Resurrection. He either Atoned for all sin or He didn't! I believe He did, and that's what I act upon. I'm saved, not because some man says I'm saved, but because the Word of God says I'm saved. I'm a Preacher of the Gospel not because some man says I am, but because God called me, and He says I am. I am washed and cleansed from all sin, not because some man says so, but because the Word of God says so, and I believe the Word. I am what God says I am, not what people say I am. Unfortunately, too many Christians listen to what people say, instead of what God says.

He doesn't say *"look behind,"* but rather *"reach forth."* What are you going to do? Keep looking behind, or begin reaching forth? It's up to you!

(14) "I PRESS TOWARD THE MARK FOR THE PRIZE OF THE HIGH CALLING OF GOD IN CHRIST JESUS."

Continuing the metaphor, Paul likens his Christian life to pressing onward to the goal so as to win the prize. In applying the figure, the goal and the prize are virtually identical, though viewed perhaps from different aspects.

Paul's goal was the complete knowledge of Christ, at least such knowledge as is appropriate at our level of maturity, both in the Power of His Resurrection and the fellowship of His sufferings. When the goal was reached, the prize would be fully his.

"Goal" rivets attention on the race that is being run, whereas *"prize"* centers the thought on the glory that follows (Hendriksen).

THE MARK

The phrase, *"I press toward the mark,"* actually means *"to pursue the hitting of a bull's-eye on the target."* Here, it is a moral and spiritual target.

Paul likens himself to a runner with one objective, that of winning the race.

Paul has in mind the runners of the Grecian games. In fact, these games began long before Paul. Whether in competition with other athletes or to better his own effort, Paul classifies himself with those who are determined to excel.

The Apostle does not seek to be versatile, a man with many varied interests. It is difficult, if not impossible, to be both broad and intensive. Paul chose to be narrow and intensive. The wedge that has the greatest driving power is that which has the narrowest angle.

Did Salvation depend upon Paul's effort or upon God's Grace? How can Paul's strenuousness harmonize with his Doctrine of free Grace, of unmerited favor?

It is clear in these passages that Paul does not at all think of himself as achieving his own Salvation, or of meriting God's favor. That is not the idea whatsoever. This he has sufficiently disposed of in the earlier Verses of this Chapter.

What he does say is that whereas once he laboriously sought self-justification by good works and by his zeal, now this same driving energy, instead of working for his own Salvation, is devoted to being Christlike. They are two different things. As a love slave, Paul's sole concern is to be closer to his Master and to be more like Him.

Thus, he disproves any assumption that free Grace, which Grace naturally is, would make one indolent, complacent, and stagnant.

Paul wanted to be more Christlike, ever more Christlike! Consequently, he sets himself to this task, not meaning that one can earn such, but definitely meaning that one can certainly supply a *"willing mind and obedient heart."*

THE PRIZE

The phrase, *"For the prize of the High Calling of God,"* presents a goal of unprecedented proportions. The *"mark"* and the *"prize"* are *"Christlikeness."* What a goal for the Christian!

Contrast this with Omar Khayyam, *"The stars are setting and the caravan starts for the dawn of nothing."* And that's exactly the condition of hopelessness of all who do not know Jesus Christ.

If one is to notice, unconverted men are constantly looking back toward their *"roots."* Somehow they seem to think that they can find the answer to life here. They can't, only its failure!

These *"roots"* which men so ardently seek, hold nothing but shame, sorrow, heartache, crime, and sin. There is no help from that source, only the opposite. I have no interest in my *"roots,"* because I know they are filled with sin and shame.

Paul is saying that the answer is not behind us, i.e., *"the Fall in the Garden of Eden,"* but rather ahead of us, Who and What is Christ Jesus.

This *"prize"* is the *"High Calling of God,"* which means it is worthy of pursuit, in fact, worthy of anything we might have to do to attain this goal.

"High Calling" is literally the *"upward calling."* The Christian is summoned from above (Heb. 12:2). This means that it is the highest, the most noble, the most grand, the most glorious of any Calling. From this Calling, one would have to step down as far as place and position are concerned, to be the President of the United States.

As well, this is the only *"High Calling"* there is in this world — that which comes from God. How so awful, how so foolish, to turn that down for the weak, tawdry, foolish, ill-conceived, absolutely empty allurements of the world.

I realize that the world understands not at all how that Jesus Christ could be worth so much, could be of such desire! They say that, because they do not know Him.

In Him is all life, all Salvation, all Redemption, all leading and guidance, all fulfillment, all development, in fact, so much more than we could ever think of wanting or desiring, so much more in fact, that we will never exhaust the potential. That's why Paul gave up everything in order to *"win Christ."* He got the best of the trade!

IN CHRIST JESUS

The phrase, *"In Christ Jesus,"* proclaims the manner and means in which all of this is done, which speaks of the Cross and Resurrection of Christ, plus His Exaltation. All that God gives to dying humanity comes only through Jesus Christ. As Paul said it is all *"in Christ."* I speak of Salvation, which was purchased at the cost of His Shed Blood; I speak of Eternal Life with Christ as the Source; I speak of the mighty Baptism with the Holy Spirit, which literally places God in man; I speak of Divine Healing, for by His stripes we are healed; I speak even of financial prosperity, for all good things comes from above; I speak of leading, guidance, and direction, which He Alone can give, which He does through the Office, Ministry, Power, and Person of the Holy Spirit; I speak of the privilege of living in the New Jerusalem forever and forever; I speak of more abundant life; I speak of this *"glorious rest"* which only Jesus can give; I speak of the Manna from Heaven.

As I've said previously, if there are any two words in any language which describes Redemption more so than any others, it would be the two words *"In Christ!"* All of this is in virtue of the unity with Him, in which we were at once Sanctified and Justified (I Cor. 6:11).

This Heavenly Calling is from God. He calls us in the Person of Christ, by the Voice of Christ, *"Come unto Me."* It was His Will that we should run the race below; He then gives the Crown.

THE RACE TO BE RUN

Even though Paul uses the analogy of an athlete running a race, still, the conclusion is somewhat different.

For instance, in an athletic race only one wins, and all the rest are defeated and disappointed. However, this is not so in the Christian race. It is different!

In order to run well this spiritual race, the runners submit to preparation in which everything is done to bring out their utmost energy. Now here is the difference:

In this race each competitor may possibly win: in order to win he must put forth his utmost power; he must do so all the days of his life; and during that time nothing must distract him from the one aim of winning. He does this for a benefit embodied in, or symbolized by, the prize which rewards and commemorates his victory.

This prize can be nothing less than Life Eternal (I Tim. 6:12) which comes, as we have seen, into full possession which will take place at the coming Resurrection. Then we will hear the words, *"Well done, good and faithful servant; enter thou into the joy of thy Lord."*

The prize stands in strict connection with the perfecting of the Believer: the time of receiving the prize is also the time of being presented faultless (Jude vs. 24).

Neither prize nor perfectness is attained here; however, neither is ultimately attained unless sought here.

On all these accounts the prize is spoken of as a Crown; a Crown of Glory, for it is very honorable; a Crown of Life, incorruptible, that fadeth not away, for it shall never wither on the brow as the wreaths of those earthly champions did.

CHRIST

We read the words as uttered by Paul *"in Christ,"* and they seem to roll off our tongues very easily. But yet, behind that short phrase is all the great Plan of God for the Redemption of humanity, which began even before the world was created (I Pet. 1:20).

Even after the creation of man, it took some four thousand years for Jesus to ultimately come. Man was in such a state, and I speak of such a state of unbelief, of degradation, of spiritual depravity, that there was actually no Faith in the Earth — no Faith in God. So, step by step, with the Work of God being carried out a little at a time, it all ultimately fell into place when the *"fullness of time"* finally arrived.

And then, His Coming, which was not at all like the Jews had contemplated, was in fact centered up in one purpose, and that was the Cross. If man was to be Redeemed, the Cross was of absolute necessity. He came to die on the Cross, for in this manner man would be redeemed and Eternal Life dispensed. The only requirement would be Faith on the part of the lost sinner.

This is something so grand, so glorious, that it is even beyond the Angels.

Peter said, *"Of which Salvation the Prophets have enquired and searched diligently* (they prophesied that it was coming), *who prophesied of the Grace that should come unto you* (they said it would be by Grace):

"Searching what, or what manner of time the Spirit of Christ which was in them did signify (it was the Holy Spirit Who did inspire them to prophesy), *when it* (He) *testified beforehand the Sufferings of Christ* (of the Crucifixion), *and the Glory that should follow* (the Resurrection and the Exaltation)."

"Unto whom it was revealed, that not unto themselves (even the Prophets of old did not understand all that they prophesied), *but unto us* (the Apostles) *they did minister the things, which are now reported unto you by them that have preached the Gospel unto you* (preached by the Apostles) *with the Holy Spirit sent down from Heaven* (because of what Jesus did at the Cross and the Resurrection, the Holy Spirit can now abide in the heart and life of every Believer); *which things the angels desire to look into* (angels are amazed at the wonderful plan of Redemption and of the eternal exaltation of the redeemed. Even now they are being taught by the Church the manifold Wisdom of God)" (I Pet. 1:10-12).

(15) "LET US THEREFORE, AS MANY AS BE PERFECT, BE THUS MINDED: AND IF IN ANY THING YE BE OTHERWISE MINDED, GOD SHALL REVEAL EVEN THIS UNTO YOU."

In concluding this section, Paul exhorts those who are mature to think in harmony with what he has just said, and promises that those who think differently about minor points will be enlightened by God if their attitude is right.

The word *"perfect"* here means *"mature."* He does not mean *"sinless perfection,"* but is referring to a certain level of spiritual growth and stability in contrast to the opposite.

By using the Greek word *"teleioi* (perfect)" Paul, I think, just might be using a tiny bit of sarcasm toward those who had claimed sinless perfection. He is calling on them to recognize the Truth he has just voiced.

MATURITY

The phrase, *"Let us therefore, as many as be perfect,"* speaks of spiritual maturity. He asserts that some of the Philippian Saints and also he himself were perfect, i.e., *"Spiritually Mature."* But in Verse 12 he denies the fact that he is yet perfect. How are we to correlate this Verse with his use of the word *"perfect"* in Verse 15?

Is there a contradiction?

The answer is found in the fact that in Verse 12 Paul is speaking of a finished process and absolute spiritual maturity beyond which there is no room for improvement, whereas in Verse 15 he is speaking of relative spiritual maturity where there is room for development and growth. This is clear from the fact that in the former Verse he uses a verb in the perfect tense, whereas in the latter, he uses a noun.

Therefore, Paul exhorts the Philippian Saints who are spiritually mature to consider themselves so only in a relative sense, and to remember that there is much room for spiritual growth in their lives.

The spiritual maturity spoken of here is as we have seen, not a state of sinlessness or flawlessness, but one of completeness, of a well-rounded Christian character, a state opposite to spiritual infancy (Wuest).

A TOUCH OF SARCASM?

To which we have alluded, Paul may have been speaking here with a touch of sarcasm as in I Corinthians 2:6. There were those in many congregations at that time, influenced by contemporary gnosticism, which we will study to a greater degree in our commentary on Colossians. These persons thought of themselves as more sophisticated than their Brethren.

In effect, therefore, Paul is saying to those who are inclined to be self-satisfied and complacent, by claiming some type of spiritual perfection, *"if you are as perfect as you profess to be, you will be as eager for growth in Grace as I am."* Of course, if this indeed were the case, we can note the sarcasm. How can one grow in Grace, if one is already perfect regarding growth?

The lesson we learn from all of this is that Christian maturity properly understood, does not cut the nerve for aspiration, for a greater degree of Christlikeness. Instead, it will whet one's appetite to be more like Jesus.

In other words, proper spiritual growth into proper spiritual maturity, only makes one desire more of Christ, in effect, instilling even a greater hunger and thirst for more of the Lord.

As well, there is a sense, therefore, in which the one experiencing the Grace of perfect love has the witness of the Spirit that in Christ he is victorious over indwelling sin. At the same time he feels no less dependent upon the only Source of grace and goodness that he has. He knows from where he has come, and I speak of trial and error and even much failure, and the Grace of God in bringing him through this. Therefore, there is no pride only thanksgiving, no criticism of others who have not reached that maturity but only encouragement, no self-dependency, but total dependency on Christ.

Since there will be no longer any lingering desire for sin, the whole ardor of his soul will be focused upon Christ Alone.

MATURITY, IN CHRIST, IN THE CROSS

I want to again emphasize the patience, love, and compassion which one has when coming to true spiritual maturity, even as Paul evidences here. Paul used himself here as an example, so I suppose it would not be displeasing to the Holy Spirit for me to do the same in a limited way.

I empathize with all this the Apostle is saying to such a degree, that I hardly know where to begin. I know what it is to be immature and I know what it is to be mature. My heart grieves as it regards the immaturity, and I speak of the failure that such brings about, and all because of a lack of understanding of the Cross, but which was no doubt caused by much self-will.

Even as Paul will bring out in Verse 18, it is impossible for spiritual maturity to be realized outside of the Cross. The Cross of Christ is the great humbling factor which plays such a part in one's spiritual growth, even as the Apostle outlines in the Second Chapter of this Epistle. If the Believer does not understand the Cross, the vicarious, atoning Work carried out there by the Christ of Glory, and all that it means to the Believer, then I think spiritual maturity is impossible of realization. This is the one great key!

NOTES

If this key is realized, this knowledge of the Cross, everything begins to fall into place, without which nothing falls into place. This is a life that I have lived, a life of hurt, disappointment, failure, and then of Victory, Power, and the true Work and Operation of the Holy Spirit. However, I did not find the latter until the veracity of the Cross was revealed unto me by the Spirit of God.

How can one walk in spiritual victory, and I mean being victorious over the world, the flesh, and the Devil? How can one overcome all manner of sin and iniquity? How can one have this *"more abundant life"* which Jesus promised? (Jn. 10:10). How can one enjoy the *"rest"* which Jesus said He would give to those who came unto Him? (Mat. 11:28-30). How can one live a life that's not dominated in any way by sin? (Rom. 6:14). With those questions burning in my heart, I sought the Lord earnestly, even to the point of acute desperation.

I wish I could say that the answer came quickly, but it didn't! In fact, I sought His face earnestly for some five years regarding these questions I have just asked, and to an extent, all my life. And yet, looking back over the entirety of a life spent in attempting to serve God, I suspect as stated, that the entirety of this experience plays into this of which I say. In other words, quite possibly it was not merely the five years I have just mentioned, but rather the entirety of the experience which covers the entirety of my life.

Perhaps it was only in that particular five years that I really understood enough about this great Christian experience to even properly ask the right questions. As I have said repeatedly, we do not come to this place quickly or easily. That means that there are no shortcuts. It means that no Preacher can lay his hands on you and impart this of which I speak.

DEATH AND RESURRECTION

Many years ago, I heard the great Preacher A.N. Trotter preached a message on *"Death and Resurrection."* It moved me greatly, but yet in looking back, I think that I only partially understood that of which he said.

He was speaking of the Cross and what Jesus did and our part in that process, even as is recorded in Romans Chapter 6; however, he was moreso speaking of our experience in Christ after conversion. Even though every person is *"in Christ"* from the time of conversion, why is it so difficult and hard to properly realize our place and position in Christ which was given to us by the Grace of God? Why do we almost immediately resort to the flesh? Why is there such a great dependency on self instead of the Lord? Why do we have to learn these things the hard way? And I am persuaded that all must come this way in one manner or the other. Why do we learn so slowly?

I still don't have the answer to all of these questions, but I believe I do have some answers, and the fact of understanding the questions moreso than ever. That may not seem like much, but to be sure, properly understanding the question is of far greater worth than most realize.

Death of course, even as brother Trotter brought it out so long ago, speaks of death to self, to personal ambition, to the attempts of bringing about Righteousness and Holiness by our own machinations. Let me again touch on the question:

Many, if not most, Christians do not even understand their doing this, much less why they are doing it! In other words, they don't even understand that their failure is caused by their own efforts, much less why those efforts are wrong. This is what Paul was speaking about when he used the phrase *"For to be carnally minded is death"* (Rom. 8:6). The point is, it's bad enough to be *"carnally minded,"* but to not even know you are carnally minded is that of which I speak.

To be *"carnally minded,"* to which we have previously alluded, refers to the attempt to be holy and righteous by means other than the Holy Spirit.

Once the Believer is brought to the place that he knows why he is failing, which speaks of dependence on the flesh, then the problem can begin to be corrected. He then understands that the Spirit of God must do these things within our lives, and that He functions and works in our lives according to our Faith in the Cross and proper understanding of the Cross. Actually, it is virtually impossible for one to have faith in something of which he

NOTES

has no understanding. Even the sinner coming to Christ must have some elementary understanding that Jesus died for him, etc. God does not require much, but He does require some understanding, which comes about through the Word of God.

As *"death"* speaks of the dying of all the carnal efforts, all the ability of self, all the machinations of personal efforts, *"Resurrection"* speaks of one coming forth into the new life in Christ, generated by the Holy Spirit.

I think the following would provide an excellent illustration.

GOD'S PLAN FOR YOU

A man found a cocoon of a butterfly. One day he saw a small opening in the cocoon. He sat and watched the butterfly for several hours as it struggled to force its body through that little hole. Then it seemed to stop making any progress. It appeared as if it had gotten as far as it could and could go no further.

So, the man decided to help the butterfly. He took a pair of scissors and snipped off the remaining bit of the cocoon. The butterfly then emerged easily.

But, it had a swollen body, and small shrivelled wings. He continued to watch the butterfly, because he expected that, at any moment, the wings would enlarge and expand to support the body, which would contract in time.

Neither happened! In fact, the butterfly spent the rest of its life crawling around with a swollen body and shrivelled wings. It was never able to fly.

What he had done, in his well-intentioned kindness and haste, that he did not understand, was that the restricting cocoon and the struggle required to get through the tiny opening were God's way of forcing fluid from the body of the butterfly into its wings so that it would be ready for flight once it achieved its freedom from the cocoon.

Sometimes, struggles are exactly what we need in our life. If God allowed us to go through life without any obstacles it would cripple us. We would not be as strong as we could have been . . . and we could never fly.

Remember, God wants you to fly, but such a state is not achieved without struggle.

The Resurrection will come, which speaks of new life, a new beginning, a maturity, actually the type of maturity of which Paul speaks here, but there must be death first — death to self; death to personal effort; death to the flesh; death to the carnal mind!

DEATH IS NOT PRETTY

No one likes death, and no one likes to see one die. Consequently, the dying process of the Child of God is never pretty, but is absolutely necessary. Unfortunately, there are many Christians who have not yet even arrived at the dying process — dying to self — and, therefore, ridicule such in those who are in that process. What a shame! Regrettably and sadly, I think that most will never reach the stage of maturity. They will do as the butterfly who tried to short circuit the process. They will never fly, but rather slide around at a much lower level never knowing the freedom and the power and the joy which full maturity brings — the leaving of the boundaries of the confines of restrictions, and soaring to the rarified heights of God's intentions.

Nevertheless, the dying process is absolutely necessary, for there can be no Resurrection without a death. It's not pleasant, and we like it not at all! We wish there were other ways, and to be sure, many have come up with other ways, but all to no avail. They have thought that one could confess their way through, or positive think their way through, or self-esteem their way through, or come to this place through some type of spiritual manifestation such as *"holy laughter,"* or being *"slain in the Spirit,"* etc. However, such cannot be done!

Jesus spelled this out very succinctly in Luke 9:23-24. He spoke of taking up the Cross daily and following Him, and losing one's life in order to find one's life. As stated, many Christians have attempted to short circuit that process, evidently thinking they had a better way than that announced by the Lord. They have been sadly disappointed, as they always will be sadly disappointed.

It is the way of the Cross, there is no other way as there can be no other way.

THUS MINDED

The phrase, *"Be thus minded,"* refers to the things Paul has just said. In other words, this which he has said was given to him by the Holy Spirit, is, therefore, without error, and should be heeded accordingly by every Believer. Those who would think otherwise, who would put forth another thought such as sinless perfection, or its opposite, are in error, which will always lead to extremely negative results. The reason for the negative results is twofold:

1. Any way other than that of the Lord means that it is devised of man, and as such, can lead to no positive results. All of Salvation, which includes all of its rudiments, come in totality from God and not at all from man. Man's efforts, which we have been studying, only lead to ruin, and especially his religious efforts. It is the story of Abraham, Sarah, and Ishmael, all over again.

2. Error is likened as *"leaven,"* which always spreads. In other words, a little error will steadily enlarge until it totally engulfs the whole. So, when Paul said, *"be thus minded,"* even though the phrase is short, it carries with it a wealth of meaning, which I would hope by now is obvious.

REVELATION

The phrase, *"And if in any thing ye be otherwise minded, God shall reveal even this unto you,"* means that some were actually otherwise minded.

The word *"if"* presents, not an hypothetical case but a fulfilled condition. Some of the Philippians were otherwise minded. Epaphroditus evidently had told Paul of those in the Church who were teaching sinless perfection. Paul turns these over to God.

The idea is, God will reveal the truth about the matter to them if they are willing to be taught.

The word *"otherwise"* speaks of diversity in a bad sense, and refers to the *"otherwise thinking"* of some of these Philippian Saints who thought that they had reached the place beyond which there could be no spiritual development or progress. In other words, *"sinless perfection."*

This statement as given by Paul is extremely important, and deserves close attention.

We find that Christians can be wrong about some things, even as Paul describes here. It doesn't mean they aren't saved, but it does mean that there is error contained in their thinking, and if continued, even as stated, will cause great difficulties.

His statement also proclaims to us, that if the heart is honest, earnest, and sincere, that the Lord will reveal the Truth to the individual in question. This is extremely important, and actually applies to every single Believer, because all have contained some error at one time or the other. Even Paul falls into this category, even as he describes the situation to us in his account given in Romans Chapter 7. But again I emphasize, if the heart is honest before God, sincerely seeking Truth, sincerely wanting Truth, the Holy Spirit will ultimately reveal that Truth to the individual. It is only when our minds are closed, when we think we know all things, that the Holy Spirit is shut off from giving us that which we desperately need.

Also, prejudice and bias play a great part in all of this. There are many Christians who will not hear the Truth if it comes from someone they do not like. This is a serious matter indeed, simply because the Lord may not send someone else with that particular Truth. So our hearts must remain open at all times, which means to be pliable to the movings and operations of the Holy Spirit.

HINDERING THE HOLY SPIRIT IN THIS VITAL OPERATION

Due to the vast significance of which we speak, actually that which Paul has said, let us state again, that no Christian is immune from wrong thinking in some manner. No one has all the light on all Biblical Subjects, so that means that there is room for growth in all of us, even the strongest, whomever they may be. So, in understanding this, we must at all times realize that we still have things to learn, and that these things we need to learn are very important. So our hearts must remain open to the administration of the Holy Spirit.

To which I have alluded often, in 1997 the Lord began to open up to me a Revelation on the Cross and the Resurrection of Christ. As stated, it has been the answer to many questions through the years, and has been the most revolutionary thing that has ever happened to me.

However, in receiving this Revelation, and enjoying the fruits thereof, it has only made me realize how much yet I do not know. Actually, in my heart it seems the Holy Spirit has placed great emphasis on this fact, which of course is obvious, at least it is to me. And I speak of so much more I need to learn. The awareness of this, the knowledge of this, is more pronounced than ever. What I have learned, makes me so eager to learn more, and I speak of learning Christ. It's like a consuming desire, a thirst that anticipates being slaked, a hunger which anticipates being satisfied. I know the Holy Spirit has placed this consuming desire for more of Christ within my heart. However, I have said all of that to say this:

I know what this great Revelation has done for me. And as stated, I know it's only the beginning so to speak. But yet I fear that many Christians will not receive this Revelation simply because it comes from me.

Why?

I once again go back to *"prejudice"* and *"bias."* We Christians carry these twin evils within our hearts far more than any of us realize. Consequently, these twin evils, and they are evil when carried in this capacity, act as a barrier to the Holy Spirit.

In fact, this problem is acute in almost all religious circles. For instance, there are millions of Christians I think, who would receive the truth on the Baptism with the Holy Spirit, with the evidence of speaking with other Tongues, if it came through their particular Denomination, i.e., *"Church!"*

They are biased and prejudiced toward others, so this hinders them from receiving. The same could be said for Divine Healing, and many other Truths as it pertains to the Word of God.

Prejudice and bias against other particular Denominations or Churches keep us from receiving Truths which other Believers have which we just might not have.

PREJUDICE AGAINST PAUL

With the great stand that Paul took against the Judaizers, there was tremendous prejudice against him from the Jewish sector of the Church. This is not to say that all Jews in the Church felt in a negative way toward Paul, for such was not the case; however, I think it should be obvious that some definitely were prejudiced against the Apostle. I think the Book of Hebrews is an excellent example.

Of course, there has been much argument over who actually wrote the Epistle to the Hebrews. Even though there is no concrete evidence, I personally feel that there is enough evidence to warrant the suggestion that Paul was the author. As far as I am personally concerned, I think that evidence is irrefutable.

If one is to notice, this particular Book does not begin at all as any other Epistle in the New Testament. It actually carries no salutation, such being omitted entirely.

I think it is this way because Paul didn't want the Jews to whom it was addressed, and I speak of Christian Jews, to know that he was the author. He felt upon that knowing this, many of them would be prejudiced and would, therefore, fail to heed the great Truths given therein.

I think from this that we can see how lethal all of this actually is. Imagine some Christians not wanting to receive instruction from Paul, especially considering that what he wrote, at least in these capacities, was the Word of God! The great Truths given to this man by the Holy Spirit, and intended for the entirety of the Church, would be lost on some and for the reasons mentioned. What a travesty! And yet, I wonder how many of us have fallen into the same trap.

I want to receive from the Lord, and I want to receive from Him irrespective as to the direction from whence it comes, or the one whom He chooses to use. Therefore, my heart must be open at all times, and even at times to the most unlikeliest of sources. Now that certainly doesn't mean that we are to accept all Preachers and Teachers as being from the Lord. The truth is, all aren't! So we must be very, very careful about what we hear, and from whom it is heard. So, don't misunderstand my words.

Preachers who are preaching and teaching error, have no Truth to impart. So there will be no Truth from that Source; however, there definitely can be Revelation and Truth given by Preachers who are walking in all the light they know and have, even though they are remiss in other areas. In other words, what they actually do know, they know it to a great extent, and they can be a great blessing to all who will listen to them in these particular categories. Let me give another example:

There are many Preachers who do not believe in the Baptism with the Holy Spirit with the evidence of speaking with other Tongues, which I feel is error on their part. However, they are not opposed to this Grace of which I speak, they just don't have much understanding on the subject, and, consequently, have not yet received. But yet, in the area regarding Salvation in which they are well versed, they certainly are capable of bringing forth excellent Truths in this regard, Truths I might quickly add, which will be of tremendous benefit to those who hear them.

However, at the same time, for those who reject the Baptism with the Holy Spirit, and I mean reject it with anger, even as many do, I personally feel that their attitude in this respect has shut them off from even what Truths they presently may hold. I don't think these particular individuals can help anyone with anything. I trust I'm making myself clear.

For instance, a short time ago I was looking at a pamphlet which outlined the purposes and intentions of a particular Christian College. In the section on the Baptism with the Holy Spirit, the founder wrote that anyone who believed in the Baptism with the Holy Spirit with the evidence of speaking with other Tongues, was of the Devil. His statement basically was, that they were of the Devil, or else mentally unbalanced. He then went on to say, that no one would be allowed in this particular school who believed such, and if found to entertain such after they had enrolled in the School, would be summarily dismissed.

I don't think that man has anything to say to me about anything as it pertains to God. That's what I'm trying to say!

AN OPEN HEART TO GOD

Receiving from the Lord is totally different than receiving from anyone else. There are several requirements, the first, of course, being *"Born-Again."*

The entire fact of living for God, of being a Christian, of having a relationship with the Lord, is all tied up and played out, by being led by the Spirit. To be sure, the Spirit of God does this in many and varied ways, but whatever the way might be, everything must coincide with the Word of God. In fact, the Word is always the primary manner in which the Holy Spirit reveals Himself to the Saint. Of course, the more that one knows the Word, the easier it is for us to be led by the Holy Spirit.

However, in all of this, even taking into account everything I've just said, we must have, as previously stated, an open heart, in other words, a responsive heart toward God if we are to receive from the Lord and be led by the Spirit. Of course, sin stops any type of relationship with the Lord and especially being led by the Spirit. Unconfessed, unrepentant sin, is the greatest barrier there is. The Scripture plainly tells us that sin *"hardens the heart"* (Heb. 3:13). And sin comes in many shapes, forms, and sizes.

Unforgiveness is sin! A bad attitude is sin! As we've already stated, bias and prejudice, at least in the manner we are discussing it here, is sin!

That's the reason the Lord plainly says, *"But to this man will I look, even to him that is poor and of a contrite spirit, and trembleth at My Word"* (Isa. 66:2).

The word *"poor"* here refers to *"poor in spirit"* exactly as it does in the Beatitudes (Mat. 5:3).

It means that the Believer is to know and understand that within himself, he is spiritually and morally bankrupt, i.e., *"poor in spirit."*

"Contrite" speaks of that which is broken and in a sense *"crushed."*

The whole thing speaks of humility, which can only be gained at the Cross. This is at least one of the reasons we are demanded to take up the Cross daily and follow Christ (Lk. 9:23).

Only with such a spirit, can a person be led by the Spirit of God.

(16) "NEVERTHELESS, WHERETO WE HAVE ALREADY ATTAINED, LET US WALK BY THE SAME RULE, LET US MIND THE SAME THING."

Paul is saying here that we must not wait for God to reveal all the truth on all points before we begin to give ourselves to spiritual growth. Each Believer should exercise fully the degree of maturity he already possesses, whatever that might be.

The words *"live up to"* which actually mean *"to keep in line with"* calls for Christians to maintain a constant life in harmony with the understanding of God's Truth we already have, at whatever level that might be. The Holy Spirit through the Apostle tells us that Christians proceeding along the same path, may be at different stages of progress and should be faithful to as much of God's Truth as they understand. This is the only way to continued spiritual growth, for this Christian life is a process of growth, and as all should know, growth in any capacity is never instantaneous, but is always a process.

PRESENT ATTAINMENT

The phrase, *"Nevertheless, whereto we have already attained,"* presents a different word regarding *"attained"* than the word translated *"attained"* in Philippians 3:12. The word there meant *"to take or appropriate."* This word in Verse 16 means *"to arrive at, to reach."* It speaks of progress along a road to a certain point.

Paul is thinking of the Philippians along the Christian path. His idea is, *"So far as we have come,"* meaning of course, that there is still another distance to go. In other words, I think one is safe to say that no Christian has all the Light on any Biblical subject; nevertheless, we are to walk according to the Light we presently have.

I think the idea of all of this is, that we who have entered on the race, may trust God to set us right if we err in anything, provided only that we are persevering in the course. The assurance of Light from Him does not supersede the duty of perpetual and watchful effort.

There is another meaning to this as well. Though there might be different degrees of attainment among Christians, and different views on many subjects, yet there are points on which all can agree; there are attainments which all have made, and in reference to the agreement, we should walk in harmony and love.

In fact, it might be and no doubt is, that some have made much greater advances than others. They have a greater degree of the Light on a particular subject, which means they have a higher knowledge, with all of its attendant blessings. However, they did not get to this place automatically or easily, and if they are truly at an advanced level, always remembering how this place and position were attained, which means through and by the Grace of God, they will be overly patient and kind with others who are walking the same road, but yet have not attained the same level.

THE TRUE LIGHT OF THE GOSPEL

True light if followed truthfully, will always bring about humility. The reason follows along this line.

This of which we speak is not attained by study, education, intellectualism, or human ability. It is always given by the Spirit; however, the manner in which He gives this of which we speak, and on whatever subject, usually comes about (and possibly always comes about), as a result of trial and error on our part — trial and error incidentally, which at times have brought great difficulty and problems. In other words, most of us I think have attempted to develop ourselves, or to go into maturity, by means of the flesh, which Paul addresses greatly so in Romans Chapter 8. True attainments in the Lord can never be reached in this manner, irrespective of our efforts. All of these things can only be brought about through and by the Holy Spirit.

HOW DOES THE HOLY SPIRIT BRING SUCH ATTAINMENTS ABOUT?

Spiritual growth could probably be summed up in the realm of Righteousness and Holiness, with the word *"Christlikeness"* described being everything more than all. This is the direction of the Holy Spirit. The Scripture says, *"For whom He did foreknow* (knew that they would be saved), *He also did predestinate to be conformed to the image of His Son, that He* (Jesus) *might be the firstborn among many Brethren* (Christ as the True Church)" (Rom. 8:29).

"Conformed to the image of His Son," sums it all up! Even though the growth and attainment of which we speak covers many areas, possibly it can be summed up in the words just given.

But the great question is: *"How does the Holy Spirit bring this about in our lives?"*

First of all, it's not an automatic process. In other words, the Holy Spirit doesn't just automatically do these things because we are a Christian. If that were the case, every Christian would be spiritually mature, but we know that all aren't, and in fact, only a few actually are. So, what is the problem?

Assuming that every true Christian wants to be more and more Christlike, wants to grow in Grace and the Knowledge of the Lord, let us look at the main hindrance to this effort.

The main hindrance is the *"flesh"* which Paul very succinctly dealt with in Romans Chapter 8. This hinders our progress more than all, but the truth is, most Christians simply don't know what the flesh actually is, etc. Let me give this example!

ABRAHAM AND SARAH

Almost anything we can think of as it regards spiritual things, we can find a counterpart in the Old Testament who lived out this situation in graphic detail. In other words, their life experiences provided an excellent example of this of which we speak. In this case, Abraham and Sarah provide the perfect example.

It was some time in early 1998 if I remember correctly. I was listening to a particular Christian Radio Broadcast. The Preacher in question is now with the Lord; however, he made a statement at that time, which I knew was from the Lord and greatly ministered to me, even though at the time I did not really understand exactly what he meant. For some reason I didn't hear the balance of the Program, or else he never fully explained his statement, but I knew what he said was of tremendous significance.

He said, *"Abraham and Sarah had to deal with their sin before Isaac could be born."*

When he said those words, the Spirit of God came all over me. Actually it was to such a degree, that I had no doubt that it was the Lord, even as I began to weep because of the Presence of God.

Some may ask the question as to why this statement would affect me to such a degree?

It affected me because of my quest for an answer to the very things we are discussing here. I knew what the man said was right, even though I did not exactly know why it was right, at least at that particular time.

After that I thought about this many times, knowing that the Holy Spirit was telling me something, but I had not then grasped the Truth. I sought the Lord about the matter, asking Him to reveal this to me, knowing that it would contain a valuable Truth.

When I attempted to analyze the statement, *"Abraham and Sarah had to deal with their sin before Isaac could be born,"* I kept trying to figure out what sin?

In my mind and spirit I dealt with Abraham's life trying to come to an answer. Was it the Hagar situation?

I felt in my heart that this played a part in the scenario, but I did not feel this was what the Holy Spirit was saying. Then the Lord revealed this thing to me.

It was not so much these acts of wrongdoing which the Spirit of God was talking about such as Hagar. While it was truly wrong, that was more the result of the real wrong than anything else.

The sin of Abraham and Sarah was their dependence on the flesh, their self-efforts, their own machinations in attempting to bring about the great Promise of God, instead of allowing it to be done by the Holy Spirit. That was their sin, and that is our sin as well.

Only when Abraham and Sarah quit trying to bring this about by their own machinations, was Isaac finally born, because only then could the Spirit of God work as He desired. In other words, all the hope of the flesh had to die, before the Holy Spirit could bring about the miracle birth of this child. This is exactly what happens to us as well.

Whenever we attempt to become Christlike in our own way and manner, irrespective that we think it's very spiritual, we seek in doing nothing but frustrating the Grace of God (Gal. 2:20-21).

Abraham and Sarah were frustrating the Grace of God by their own personal efforts in trying to bring about the Promise of God, just like we frustrate the Grace of God by our own efforts to bring about Holiness and Righteousness.

HOW DO WE FRUSTRATE THE GRACE OF GOD?

First of all, the Grace of God is the Goodness of God in freely giving the Saint all that we need in respect to being what we ought to be in Christ. However, the Grace of God, just as the work of the Holy Spirit, is not automatic. The Grace of God always functions through, by, of, and within the Cross of Christ, i.e., *"the Finished Work of Christ on the Cross."* That is the only manner in which God can extend to anyone His Grace.

When the sinner comes to Christ, he does so because he puts his Faith in Christ and the Cross, even though he understands very little about what was done there. Even so, God honors his Faith simply because the object of his Faith is correct, and gives the sinner Grace, which is his Salvation.

After Salvation, the Grace of God continues to work in the same capacity. God gives good things to us, and without merit, without payment on our part, or earning such in any way, which is impossible to do in any case. However, this Grace comes to us as Christians, not because we are Christians, but because of Christ and what He did on the Cross. It is all tied to the Cross!

That means that the Believer must place his Faith in the Cross, leave his Faith in the Cross, understanding that all the things we receive from God comes through what Jesus did on the Cross. The Grace of God can then flow unhindered, with the Holy Spirit helping us to be what we must be, in the realm of Righteousness and Holiness — but only by this method. Our problem is, we often frustrate this method:

The manner in which the Grace of God is frustrated is varied and many. Please allow me to use personal examples.

THE MEANS OF FRUSTRATION

Any time any Believer does anything in the realm of spirituality, such as attending Church, giving money, etc., as a means of making one holy or righteous, in other words, one does these things in order to be holy, the only thing one will succeed in actually doing is to frustrate the Grace of God.

We have two prayer meetings a day here at the Ministry. I attend each and everyone of them unless I'm out of town, or something comes up at the last moment which seldom happens; however, we do not conduct these prayer meetings thinking they will make us holy or Christlike, but we conduct them for entirely different reasons. Frances and I also give well above the ten percent of our income to the Work of the Lord, but not in order to be righteous. I could go on and on with such type scenarios, but the emphasis I wish to make is that none of these things, as spiritual as they may be in their own right, have anything to do with Righteousness, Holiness, or Christlikeness.

The same can be said for the type of clothing one wears. Some think that wearing certain types of clothing makes them holy, or cutting their hair in a certain way makes them holy. All of that is facetious to say the least.

Whatever it is we do for the Lord, such as the giving of money, attending Church, prayer, etc., are all done because we love the Lord. None of these things have anything to do whatsoever with Righteousness and Holiness. But yet, most of the Church world thinks in some way that they do. They don't, and they never will.

In fact, such efforts are constituted by the Lord as *"flesh,"* and the Scripture plainly says, *"So then they that are in the flesh cannot please God"* (Rom. 8:8).

Does it mean that these things we've mentioned are wrong?

No! Not at all! In fact, they are very right, but in their own way. In Truth, if one neglects to go to Church, neglects to give anything as it regards money to the Work of the Lord, or any other thing we could name in this category, one will be severely hindered in a spiritual sense. So, we are not knocking these things, but only putting them in their rightful place.

THE DOING OF RELIGION

Someone has said that the *"doing of religion,"* is the greatest narcotic there is. Because its good things or religious things, the very *"doing"* of these things, whatever they might be, tends to make one feel that one has earned something from the Lord, etc. Believers must know, that the Lord has nothing for sale! He is not in the merchandise business.

Everything He has is in the form of a gift, but it all comes through what Jesus did at the Cross and the Resurrection.

That means that one cannot earn anything from God in any capacity, so we should quit trying.

We must understand that everything we receive from the Lord is a free gift, but always based upon our Faith, but yet, it must be Faith in the Finished Work of Christ.

When we place our Faith in the Cross and the Cross exclusively, knowing that everything we receive from the Lord comes from this Source, the Holy Spirit can then help us and bring us to the place that He wants us to be, i.e., *"Christlikeness!"* He cannot, and in fact, will not do it any other way.

This means that whatever He does, it is entirely a work of the Spirit, and not a mixture of the flesh and the Spirit which God cannot accept. Salvation, and everything that goes with this glorious Grace, is all of God and not whatsoever of man.

The whole thing confuses us at times, simply because the things we do are spiritual and because they are spiritual, we tend to think of them as of the Spirit. And to be sure they are, if they're kept in their right perspective. I've mentioned the following before, but please allow me to say it again:

A PERFECT EXAMPLE

A young Minister was on our Radio Program some time ago. I think that there was no doubt that he loved the Lord very much, which was evident in his spirit. Even though I did not really know him, one could tell in just a few moments by speaking with him, that he was consecrated to the Lord. However, his knowledge of the Cross and the provision made there, were not as strong as it should have been.

During the course of our conversation which was going out over our daily Radio Program, he made this statement, or words to this effect:

"When I have a problem with sin or evil passions, I go on a three-day fast, and that takes care of the situation."

No it won't!

I was not that blunt with him, but I pray that I did say enough to let him know that what he was saying was not exactly right.

While fasting is definitely Scriptural, definitely helpful, if we attempt to use it in that manner, and I speak of trying to overcome sin, in effect, we are saying that what Jesus did at the Cross was not necessary, or else He didn't complete the task; therefore, we have to add fasting to His Work in order to have victory.

While fasting will definitely help any Believer, that is if it's done in the right way, it is not a means of overcoming sin. Once again I emphasize, were this the case, then Jesus died in vain exactly as Paul said (Gal. 2:21).

As a Believer, I want to grow in Grace and the Knowledge of the Lord. I want to be what He wants me to be. I want to be Christlike, and furthermore I want to be more and more Christlike all the time; however, I have learned that I cannot bring this thing about, and please believe me, I have tried. It can only be brought about by the Spirit of God, and the only part I am to play is to exhibit Faith in the Cross of Christ, understanding that my Victory is in the Cross, and then the Spirit of God can bring about the work all of us so desperately need.

OUR WALK BEFORE GOD

The phrase, *"Let us walk by the same rule, let us mind the same thing,"* refers in the Greek to *"direct one's life, to live."*

Actually, the word *"rule"* is not in the original Greek, but has been supplied by the translators. The literal Greek is, *"walk by the same."* The context speaks of a path, and could be translated, *"Let us walk the same path. . . ."*

Most of the time when the word *"walk"* is used in Scripture, it concerns itself with our conduct, our manner of life, the way we live, the things we do. In its truest sense it refers to following the Lord.

TWO WAYS TO WALK

One is the following of Jesus, which is the only true way, and speaks of what Jesus did at the Cross and the Resurrection.

All other ways, irrespective as to how many they might be, are enemies of the Cross of Christ, which Paul will deal with in the next Verse.

The Early Church was constantly beset by two temptations, which, in effect, are the same presently: the tendency to swerve to the right and end in legalism, and the tendency to swerve to the left and end in lawlessness. As stated, such is the current trend today.

The thing that such people glory in is actually their shame and disgrace. Paul will actually say in Verse 19 that their end is destruction. Even in his present continued state of imprisonment Paul was very much aware that tensions existed in the Churches under his care.

In the above phrase, the Apostle used two words *"walk"* and *"mind."* Consequently, in this Passage there seems to be the same double reference which has pervaded all of Paul's practical teaching. He is anxious for two things — that they should keep on in one course (walk), and that all should keep on together (mind).

In both senses he addresses the *"perfect,"* or *"maturity"*; he will have them understand that they have attained only one thing — to be on the right path, and that it is for them to continue in it; second, he also bids them refrain from setting themselves up above *"the imperfect"*; for the very fact of division would mark them as still *"carnal,"* mere *"babes in Christ"* (I Cor. 3:1-4).

(17) **"BRETHREN, BE FOLLOWERS TOGETHER OF ME, AND MARK THEM WHICH WALK SO AS YE HAVE US FOR AN ENSAMPLE."**

In the early years of the Church, which actually continues unto this moment, Believers needed examples. So Paul urged the Philippians to join together in imitating his conduct, just as he had done in his exhortation to the Church at Corinth — *"Follow my example, as I follow the example of Christ"* (I Cor. 11:1).

Such advice was not egotism, for Paul's emphasis was always strongly that of Christ. Furthermore, Paul includes others in this model as he urges his readers to take note of those who were living in conformity with *"the pattern we gave you,"* i.e., *"the high standard"* (outlined in Philippians 3:7-16).

Literally, Paul wrote, *"You have us as a pattern,"* and the *"us"* includes not only himself but Timothy and perhaps Epaphroditus also. Hence, he was not claiming a unique superiority.

FOLLOWERS OF ME

The phrase, *"Brethren, be followers together of me,"* means to be *"fellow-imitators."* Paul is compelled to make his own example a norm or standard of the new life, even as every Christian ought to seek to do the same.

Paul has far more here in mind than merely trying to get Christians to follow him. The direction he's going has nothing to do with his ego, or even the localized situation. The Holy Spirit is impressing this through him for the following reasons:

Under Christ, Paul was the Masterbuilder of the Church (I Cor. 3:10). As it should be understood, the Church was and is altogether different from the Israel of old, through whom and which the Lord previously worked. In fact, there were many in the Jewish segment of the Church who were attempting to pull the Church into Judaism, which Paul vigorously opposed. So, the Apostle had much more in mind than merely his conduct. He was speaking of Doctrine as well, and I think more particularly of Doctrine. As we shall see in the next Verse, the Cross is the central point of Christianity. It is actually the foundation of Christianity, i.e., *"what Christ did on the Cross and in the Resurrection."* Consequently, to have what Jesus did there, one must follow a prescribed order. This is what Paul is speaking of moreso than anything else.

MARK THEM

The phrase, *"And mark them which walk so as ye have us for an example,"* means *"to fix the attention upon with the desire for or interest in."* It means *"to observe intently."*

The idea is, that the Philippians and all others for that matter, observe his life attentively and become imitators of him, and to do the same also with reference to those other Christians in whose lives they find an example of Paul's own manner of life (Wuest). Two things are said here:

First was the new way of living, which in effect was after Christ, and produced a walk, i.e., *"lifestyle,"* totally unlike anything else in the world. In effect, the Standard of Righteousness demanded by God in the Ten Commandments, was now kept; however, they were kept by a different means than anyone had ever known. Jesus Christ had kept the Law perfectly, which of course includes the Ten Commandments, had never failed even one single time, and as our Representative Man, God gives us the perfection of Christ, upon Faith on our part registered in Him, and what He did at the Cross and the Resurrection. Then in our daily walk before God, and the world for that matter, Christ Who continues to live in us through the Power and Person of the Holy Spirit, literally lives this life in and through us. He does for us what we cannot do for ourselves. This great victorious walk comes to us and remains with us, as we exhibit Faith in the Finished Work of Christ, i.e., *"The Cross,"* by which principle the Holy Spirit works, and by which principle only He works. This is the only manner and way of Victory (Rom. 8:1-2).

THE GREAT MISTAKE MADE BY MANY CHRISTIANS

When we think of Jesus saving us and then Baptizing us with the Holy Spirit, we come to realize how privileged and fortunate we actually are. But then, too often we make the mistake of thinking that because we are now saved and Spirit-filled, that we can now live this life as it ought to be lived; consequently, we set out to do just that and we always fail. It confuses us because we really don't understand why we fail. We have the Holy Spirit, and I'm speaking of those who have been baptized with the Holy Spirit with the evidence of speaking with other Tongues (Acts 2:4), and we know that there is Almighty Power registered in the Holy Spirit (Acts 1:8). So, with this power to help us, we think surely we can do all the things we need to do, and live the kind of life we need to live.

The first failure which comes our way, we sort of think of as a fluke, somewhat brushing it aside as we ask the Lord to forgive us — whatever that failure might be. Then it happens again with a repetition of repentance and forgiveness. We then discover that the same thing has happened quite a number of times, and we resolve within our hearts that it must stop and for all the obvious reasons. We are now a Child of God, and sin is repugnant to us. Actually, to fail the Lord is a terrible thing, which registers greatly in the heart and life of the Believer, with them actually not able to rest until the thing is washed and cleansed by the Blood (I Jn. 1:9).

In this scenario, we resolve to *"try harder,"* whatever that means! We must read the Bible more! We must pray more! We must check our lives to see if there is some fault or difficulty that is allowing Satan access with which to overcome us.

In regard to all of this, we do try harder, and harder, and harder, but regrettably, the situation is not getting better but rather worse.

WHAT IS ACTUALLY HAPPENING?

At this stage, we do not realize it, but we have resorted to law. While it's not the Law of Moses, it definitely is a law of our own making. And because these things we are doing are very right in their own way, actually very Scriptural, it fools us. And again, we at times mistake forgiveness for Victory. It isn't!

Forgiveness is that which God has promised to all who would seek such (I Jn. 1:9), which restores the relationship between Himself and the sinning Believer. But again, it is not Victory, and even though we sense and feel the joy of restored fellowship, that doesn't mean we are free from this dominion of sin of some nature with which Satan has ensnared us.

As we've already stated, we have to be very careful here, because many Christians think if they're not snared by the big five (gambling, drugs, alcohol, nicotine, immorality), that they are home free. We must never forget that there are other sins as well, such as greed, covetousness, uncontrollable temper, malice, pride, etc. Satan doesn't care with which he ensnares us, just so we are snared.

This may come as a shock, but if the Christian has to be snared by something, it would probably be better were it one of the big five, as we humorously say, because it's much easier to bring such to repentance, than it is sins of pride. Jesus said as much (Mat. 21:31).

At any rate, the reason we are failing is because we are not looking to the Cross, but rather to law whether we understand it or not. Law has only one effect, it just makes matters worse. That doesn't mean that the law itself is wrong; in fact, the law is right, whether the ancient Law of Moses, or laws of our own devising. What is wrong, is our attempting to bring about Victory through these Laws, i.e., *"efforts."* Again I state, we may not think we are attempting to do this within our own strength, but that's exactly what's happening. We think because we are Baptized with the Holy Spirit, that He automatically exerts His great Power on our behalf. The truth is, He does no such thing.

WHAT IS THE PATH TO VICTORY?

There is only one path or way of victory and that is Jesus. Now let's see what that means.

It means what Jesus did at the Cross and the Resurrection. Our Faith is to be in that exclusively, understanding that this is where Satan was totally defeated, with all sin addressed and atoned, which destroyed the power of Satan, at least for those who will believe. Whenever the Saint expresses Faith in the Cross, which he should do on a daily basis (Lk. 9:23; Gal. 6:14), the Holy Spirit will then exert His great power of which we speak, and do so on our behalf (Rom. 8:2). And to be sure, there is no power of darkness which can overcome the Holy Spirit. But if we try to have the Victory for which we seek by our own machinations of any kind, no matter how holy they may be in their own right, we are going to fail every single time.

THE TRAGEDY!

What is so bad about all of this is, that in the last nearly fifty years there has been so little preaching and teaching on the Cross of Christ, that the Church little knows its way of victory; consequently, it casts about in every conceivable way possible attempting to find the answer to its problems. It does so through humanistic psychology, which is tantamount to saying that what Jesus did on the Cross was not sufficient. Or else it resorts to means and ways of its own devisings.

The great fad at the moment (1999), is to seek manifestations of the Holy Spirit. If some Preacher can lay hands on us with the Power of God accompanying his petition, and especially if we are *"slain in the Spirit,"* we think that will solve all of our problems. While in many cases, that which we have just mentioned is right, proper, and Scriptural, and will definitely bless the Believer, it will not bring about victory in our hearts and lives for which we seek. Then we're more confused than ever.

Part of the Church tells Believers that if their *"confession"* is proper, that this is the means of victory. While confession is very important, there is no victory in this capacity.

Others claim that Christians who are having problems of some nature, are having these problems because of Demon Spirits. They admonish them to have these Demons cast out, and then their problems will be solved. While Demon Spirits definitely are involved in every manner of sin and failure, that's not what the Christian needs.

In the first place, no Believer can be demon possessed. While we might definitely be oppressed by Demon Spirits, possession is not possible for a Believer, as should be obvious.

Back in the 1970's this was all the rage. Christians were lining up in Churches all over the world, with some Preacher laying hands on them, and supposedly casting out the demon of fear, immorality, lust, alcohol, etc., etc.

While the laying on of hands is definitely Scriptural, as are many of these things mentioned, at least in their own right and way, when we misuse them, we then take them out of their proper Scriptural context, which the Lord will not honor.

We should stop and think a moment. If any of these things could bring about Victory in the hearts and lives of Believers, plus a lot of things we haven't mentioned, then Jesus did not need to come down here and die on the Cross (Gal. 2:21). The Lord could have just instituted whatever particular fad being presently promoted. Unfortunately, the problem is much worse than that. It took Jesus coming down and dying on a Cross in order to set captives free. Nothing else will suffice but that.

THE REAL PROBLEM OF THE CHURCH IS SIN

The heading I have just given is not easily admitted. In fact, most of the modern Church world denies this. We are now Christians and we are little bothered by sin, many believe!

One Leader of a major Pentecostal Denomination made the statement that those in his particular Denomination were seldom bothered by these type of things, etc. He admitted that once in a while it might happen, but seldom.

I happened to have been very much acquainted with his Denomination, and I knew that what he was saying was totally off the wall. The truth was and regrettably is, that Preachers in that particular Denomination were and are failing right and left. I don't say that with any joy, but regrettably it is the truth.

In fact, the majority of the modern Church is in a state of denial. It hides its head in the sand refusing to look at the real problem which is sin, all the time claiming it is something else.

"Our Faith is not strong enough," many claim! Others say, as we've already mentioned, *"The confession is wrong!"*

Others claim, that if we'll just go to a certain meeting and have Brother so and so pray for us, our problems will then be solved. Others claim that the problem is a *"family curse,"* and that this particular curse must be rebuked, etc.

No, the real problem in the hearts and lives of Believers is sin. Satan is trying to drag the Christian down, and he does so by sin in some way or the other. We can deny that fact if we want to, but it doesn't make it any less true.

Now there is only one answer for sin, and that is what Christ did at the Cross. Nothing else will address itself to this terrible malady of darkness! Nothing else will suffice! It is only what Jesus did at the Cross and the Resurrection, that addressed this terrible problem, and addressed it totally and completely. In other words, Christ left nothing undone, which means that His Work was and is a Finished Work.

This means that this thing is so bad, and I speak of the problem of sin, that even though God could speak worlds into existence, He in fact, could not speak Redemption into existence. That's a startling statement, but it happens to be true! God had to become man, literally becoming the Second Adam, serving as our Substitute and Representative Man, paying a terrible price on the Cross of Calvary in order that this horrible problem of sin may be conquered. He did it in a most expensive manner, with the giving of His Own Life.

This means that the Cross was not an accident or an incident. The Cross of Christ was planned even before the foundation of the world (I Pet. 1:20). In other words, Jesus came down here to die on the Cross. That was His objective. Many other things were necessary, such as His Virgin Birth; His spotless, sinless, perfect life; His perfect keeping of the Law, but it was the Cross which broke the back of Satan so to speak.

Therefore, the Victory is in the Cross and the Cross alone. I speak of the Atonement, where Jesus addressed every single thing that was lost in the Fall. While we do not have all the benefits of the Atonement presently, and will not do so until the Resurrection of all Saints, still, the benefits we do have presently are so astounding that there is no reason that any Believer should be overcome by sin. The Victory is ours, all purchased by Christ.

Our problem is, the modern Church little understands the veracity of the Cross, and what it means for the Child of God.

THE CROSS OF CHRIST IS THE ONLY WAY OF SALVATION FOR THE SINNER AND THE ONLY WAY OF VICTORY FOR THE SAINT

Most Christians, as we have repeatedly stated, know and understand the part the Cross plays as it regards their initial Salvation experience; however, most have no idea whatsoever as to the part it plays in our continued life as lived for the Lord. The Truth is, the Cross of Christ plays just as much part in our Victorious, daily walk before God, as it did when we initially gave our heart to Christ. Just as you as a sinner had to believe the Lord and what He did at the Cross in order to be saved, such Faith must continue even on a daily basis and for the entirety of our lives, that is if we are to walk in Victory (Lk. 9:23-24).

FAITH

We've heard more teaching on Faith in the last several decades than possibly all the remainder of the centuries of the Church put together. Some of the teaching has been very good; however, most of it I think has not been good at all. It has led the Church away from the Cross.

When we speak of Faith, exactly what do we mean?

We talk about having *"Faith in God,"* or having *"Faith in Christ,"* or having *"Faith in the Word,"* etc. All of these statements are correct, but if left there they leave some things to be desired.

The Reader should read the next phrases very carefully, even several times, for the significance of what is being said.

It is the object of Faith that is important. By that I mean that when we talk about having Faith in Christ, we must understand that it's Faith in what He did at the Cross which guarantees my Salvation and Victory. In other words, *"Christ and Him Crucified,"* must ever be the object of our Faith (I Cor. 2:2). It is not just Jesus, as grand and glorious as that would be, but rather Jesus and what He did at the Cross. That's where our Victory resides, and only where our Victory resides.

So, when we say that we're having Faith in the Lord, it must always register within our heart that we're speaking of the great price which He paid on the Cross of Calvary. That is where Satan was defeated, where every sin was atoned, where death was defeated, where the claims of Heavenly Justice were satisfied, where the Curse of the Law was also satisfied.

However, most Christians are running around trying to increase their Faith, because they've been taught that the more Faith they have the more great things they will receive; however, it is not the amount of Faith which causes one to receive from God, but rather the object of one's Faith (Rom. 6:3-5; 8:1-2).

Actually, Faith in God is not difficult to have. All we have to do is simply believe Him, i.e., *"His Word,"* and that is Faith. It's nothing hard or complicated about the subject. We either believe or we don't.

And if we do believe, we must make sure the object of our Faith is correct, which means that we are to have Faith at all times in the Cross of Christ. Salvation comes through the Cross; the Baptism with the Holy Spirit comes through the Cross; our economic prosperity comes through the Cross; our Victory in every capacity comes through the Cross; our mental well-being comes through the Cross; our answer to prayer comes through the Cross; the Grace of God comes through the Cross; in other words, every single thing we receive from the Lord comes to us because of what Jesus did at the Cross and the Resurrection. Consequently, our Faith must be in that great Finished Work, must stay in that great Finished Work, and must do so, even as we have repeatedly stated, on a daily basis (Lk. 9:23).

Basically, this is what Paul was speaking about, even as the next Verse will proclaim.

WHO WILL YOU FOLLOW?

Second, the Saints of God were admonished by Paul to follow those who believed and taught exactly as he is here proclaiming — the Message of the Cross. If the Preacher or the Layman was not living the Cross life, they were not to be followed.

Where does that leave the modern Church?

People are following Denominations, so-called great Faith Teachers, fads, particular Churches, and about everything one could think, most all leading nowhere.

Paul is saying that you must follow the Preacher who is preaching the Cross, who is living the Cross, who understands the Cross and holds it up as the foundation of Christianity, and the throughway of all Blessing.

The Apostle used the word *"mark"* which in the Greek is *"skopos,"* and means *"look at, look on, take heed and consider."* These are the ones to follow and no one else!

That means that if the Church is not a Cross Church, one should not attend there. If the Preacher is not a Cross Preacher, he should not be heeded.

That is blunt, but the best way I know to say the words. Please remember, we are speaking of the single most important thing in the world, your soul and your victory. The Cross of Christ is the only answer for that!

(18) "(FOR MANY WALK, OF WHOM I HAVE TOLD YOU OFTEN, AND NOW TELL YOU EVEN WEEPING, THAT THEY ARE THE ENEMIES OF THE CROSS OF CHRIST:"

Who were these *"enemies of the Cross of Christ"*?

They are anyone, and for all time, who attempt to substitute something else in place of the Cross, who does not recognize the rightful place of the Cross as the foundation of Christianity.

To attempt to pinpoint of whom exactly Paul was speaking, begs the issue, and misses the point. It didn't really matter who he had in mind at that particular time, it refers to all who build structures other than the Cross of Christ. Consequently, it covers a great many people, Churches, Denominations, Preachers, etc.

In Paul's day it would have covered the Judaizers who were attempting to add Law to Christ, and who little understood the Cross, and who little believed in what the Cross represented. It would have also referred to those who had taken liberty into license, claiming that sin little mattered. They little realized, if at all, that Jesus died on the Cross in order to deliver us from sin. In fact, that was at least one of His great purposes in this great Sacrifice. So, Paul's statement cuts a wide swath.

MANY WALK THE WRONG ROAD

The phrase, *"For many walk,"* speaks of those, even as we have stated, who were attempting to live for God outside of the victory and rudiments of the Cross of Christ. In other words, their ways and means were a crossless Christianity, i.e., *"a crossless Christ!"* Even though they admitted that the Cross happened, in their thinking it was only incidental and played little or no part in one's Salvation and relationship with God. Even then, there were *"many"* who walked these erroneous paths.

If it was many then, and it definitely was, what is the percentage presently especially considering that the modern Church is entering into the last day apostasy? Of course, only the Lord knows the answer to that question; however, I think it should be obvious, that the *"many"* as used by Paul then, would now be changed to *"most!"*

For instance, the entirety of the Catholic Church teaches other than the Cross of Christ. While the Cross is pictured in Catholic dogma, what Jesus did there is not held up at all as the way of Salvation. It is rather the Church itself, and obedience to its principles and precepts, whatever they might be, that is held up as the Salvation process. In other words, if they will be faithful to the Church, and pray to Mary, they will be saved. Nothing could be further from the truth. One can only say, albeit regrettably, that the entirety of the Catholic Church is an enemy of the Cross of Christ.

The modern prosperity gospel falls into the same category. The Cross of Christ is not the object at all in this teaching, but rather material things, i.e., *"money!"* In fact, in these circles the Cross of Christ is actually repudiated. Many of their particular Churches will not sing songs concerning the Cross or the Blood, because that refers, they say, to weakness and not strength. They actually refer to the Cross as *"past miseries,"* which has no place in the life of the modern Christian.

These blasphemers, for that's what they are, claim that we are Resurrection people, etc. They seem to forget, that one cannot have Resurrection Life, unless one properly accepts the Cross Life. Paul plainly said, *"For if* (since) *we have been planted together in the likeness of His Death* (this is the Cross Life), *we shall be also in the likeness of His Resurrection* (Resurrection Life)" (Rom. 6:5).

As is clearly stated here, it is impossible to have Resurrection Life, without first understanding and accepting the *"Cross Life."* In fact, Paul used the word *"planted,"* which means that we must literally be planted in the Cross, which refers to all that was there accomplished, before we can have this glorious *"Resurrection Life."* Unfortunately, those who teach and preach the so-called prosperity gospel have tried to ignore the *"Cross Life,"* jumping instead to the *"Resurrection Life."* Of course, such cannot be done.

This is the same thing as Adam and Eve not being allowed to remain in the Garden to partake of the Tree of Life. To have done so in their sinful state, would have resulted in monsters instead of the opposite. It is the same presently!

Embracing the Cross Life, which refers to placing one's Faith in what Jesus did at the Cross, and understanding its veracity, qualifies one then for *"Resurrection Life."* There is no other way to God except through Christ, and there is no other way to Christ than through His Cross.

THE BLOODY DOOR

He said, *"Verily* (truthfully), *verily* (truthfully), *I say unto you, he that entereth not by the Door into the sheepfold, but climbeth up some other way, the same is a thief and a robber"* (Jn. 10:1).

Jesus then said, *"Verily, verily, I say unto you, I am the Door of the sheep"* (Jn. 10:7).

I must remind the Reader, that this Door is a bloody Door. In using this as an example, Jesus was going all the way back to the deliverance of the Children of Israel from Egyptian bondage, all a type of our present Salvation.

Each family was to slay a Lamb in Sacrifice to God, which of course represented the coming Christ, and then apply its blood to the doorpost of each house. The Lord then said, *"And the blood shall be to you for a token* (a symbol of the Blood which would be shed by Christ when He ultimately came) *upon the houses where ye are: and when I see the blood, I will pass over you, and the plague shall not be upon you to destroy you, when I smite the land of Egypt"* (Ex. 12:13).

Again I say, if we try to go in through another door we are a thief and a robber, which of course God can never accept. The True Door is Jesus Christ, but more particularly, it is a bloody door, which speaks of His Death and Resurrection on our behalf.

THE CHURCH HAS NEVER BEEN IN GREATER TROUBLE THAN PRESENTLY

I realize that's quite a statement I've just made, but I believe it to be true. I believe it is true simply because the Cross is little preached or taught anymore. Of course, there are exceptions here and there, but they are few and far between. As I've stated over and over again, the Church has been moved so far away from the Cross, that most modern Believers have little understanding of its veracity, its power, and what it all means as it regards Christianity. In other words, most Christians little know and understand that the Cross of Christ is the very foundation of Christianity. All must be built on that premise, the premise of the Cross, or else it is a house built on sand (Mat. 7:24-27).

In 1997 the Lord began to open up to me the Revelation of the Cross of Christ and how it pertains to our everyday walk before the Lord. I had always known of the veracity of the Cross as it refers to our initial Salvation, and preached strongly this great Truth, which resulted in hundreds of thousands all around the world being brought to a saving knowledge of Jesus Christ. But as stated, I little knew or understood the part the Cross plays in our daily living.

This lack of knowledge, caused me tremendous problems to say the least. But thank the Lord, after some five years of soul-searching and seeking the face of the Lord, imploring Him to open up the answers to me as it regards the living of a victorious, Christian life, the Lord answered my prayer.

This Revelation didn't come all at once. In fact, it is still coming, and I believe this Revelation will ever continue to expand. The Truth is, that what Jesus did at the Cross is of such moment, such portend, that it's absolutely impossible to exhaust its resources and treasures.

This which has happened to me, is the most revolutionary thing I've ever experienced other than my Salvation and Baptism with the Holy Spirit. It's almost like I've been *"Born-Again!"* The Bible has become brand-new to me. In fact, I see everything in an entirely different light — the light of the Cross. And Oh yes, I have found there the victory for which I had so long sought. A victory so total, so complete, so absolute, so all-encompassing, that I hardly know how to define or explain this of which I feel and have experienced, even with this experience continuing to expand.

As I have said previously, I do not know why it took so long for me to receive this from the Lord, but thank God I did receive.

And what was it that I did receive?

THE CROSS, OUR FAITH, AND THE HOLY SPIRIT

Even though I've said it repeatedly, please allow me to say it again.

The Lord showed me that all Salvation, and all Victory, is found totally and completely in the Cross (Rom. 6:3-5).

He then showed me that my Faith in totality and continuously, must rest in the Cross of Christ. I must not allow my Faith to be pulled aside to other things, but must anchor it in the Cross and keep it there for all time (Gal. 6:14).

He then showed me that once I understand that all Victory is in the Cross, and then place my Faith in the Cross, understanding its veracity, the Holy Spirit will then help me be what I ought to be and do what I ought to do, for the simple reason that He works only within the confines of the Finished Work of Christ (Rom. 8:1-2).

Now, I've given this in few words, but what it all means would take volumes to tell. As well, these great Truths are understood totally and only in the spiritual sense. In other words, they are spiritually discerned (I Cor. 2:14). That's the reason I keep saying these truths in many and varied ways, knowing that if you the Reader will keep reading what I have to say, that ultimately the Spirit of God will reveal this to you, and you will understand clearly what I am saying, that is if your heart is open. That means to receive this great Truth, you are going to have to want and desire it greatly, which the Holy Spirit will always honor. Otherwise, you'll read the words that I say, with little understanding or meaning.

I TELL YOU OFTEN

The phrase, *"Of whom I have told you often, and now tell you even weeping,"* proclaims to us two things:

1. Due to the extreme seriousness of this matter, Paul related these great truths to the Philippians and all others as well, over and over again, exactly as I am doing here. He did it in this manner because of all the obvious reasons.

2. What he was saying was of such moment, such consequence, that if the Readers fail to properly hear what he was saying, they could bring upon themselves great trouble. As well, those who tried to bypass the Cross, could only lead themselves to ultimate perdition, which means the loss of their souls.

I think one can say without fear of contradiction, that this of which Paul speaks is the single most important thing. If we have an improper viewpoint of the Cross, everything else will be improper also. Always, the results will be disastrous and in a disastrous way.

The Apostle knew this, knew the consequences, knew the seriousness of the matter, actually that this was the single most important thing there is, which filled his heart with great emotion. He wept, and literally, because he knew the end result of forsaking the Cross, or refusing to accept the Cross, would be disaster. There is only one way of Victory, and that's Jesus Christ and what He did at the Cross. If we try to divorce Christ from the Cross, which these individuals were trying to do whomever they may have been, and which men are attempting to do today, then we have *"another Jesus," "another gospel," "another Spirit"* (II Cor. 11:4). That's the reason the Apostle wept, and the reason we should weep also!

ENEMIES OF THE CROSS OF CHRIST

The phrase, *"That they are the enemies of the Cross of Christ,"* refers to the results of such a course which the next Verse proclaims, but more than all refers to correct Doctrine.

The *"Cross"* was the instrument of death on which the Redeemer died to make Atonement for sin. As the Atonement made by Christ for sin is that which peculiarly distinguishes His Way from all others, the *"Cross"* comes to be used to denote His Way.

It is His Way, because it is there that He defeated all the powers of darkness and actually made a show of them openly. He satisfied the claims of Heavenly Justice, because the Cross was demanded by God and definitely not by the Devil. There was only one way that man's sins could be addressed, that the penalty of the broken law could be satisfied, and that was by Christ dying on the Cross. As I've said over and over again, the Cross was not an accident or an incident, it was rather the very purpose and reason for which He came.

By the manner in which Jesus had to die in order to save man from sin, we learn and realize just how bad, how awful, how terrible, or how devastating that sin actually is. In fact, it is the cause of all the sorrow, heartache, pain, loneliness, suffering, and death on this planet. It has filled the world with blood, with graves, with death! It is the one great cause of all heartache — sin!

NOTES

WHAT IS SIN?

Sin is defined as *"missing the mark,"* but more particularly, missing God's Mark. And what is that Mark?

Of all that one might say, I think that it could be summed up in the Ten Commandments. This was and is God's Standard, in other words, what God required of man as it regarded Righteousness.

When we read these Commandments they seem simple enough; however, due to man's depraved, fallen nature, it was and is impossible for him within himself to keep these Commandments. It simply cannot be done! So, because of that fallen nature, man substitutes other gods in place of his Creator, other saviors in place of Jesus, keeps on stealing, murdering, lying, and engaging in immorality and covetousness. This is the cause of all the trouble and heartache in the world, even though man refuses to recognize such.

THE PROBLEM!

Man knows that something is wrong, but he refuses to admit how wrong it actually is. In other words, he refuses to admit that he is totally wrong, completely wrong, going in the wrong direction, and in no way can find the right way by his own machinations. In fact, he doesn't even recognize the right way, i.e., Jesus Christ, when he sees it. It takes a Revelation of the Spirit by the Word on his soul for his eyes to be opened.

This means that man's problem is not merely a maladjustment, or improper environment or improper education. It means that his problem is far deeper, far greater, far more widespread than all of that. As stated, he is altogether wrong, not just slightly so.

So, man refusing to admit how wrong he actually is, thinks he can solve his problem in various different ways. One of the greatest ways of all is humanistic psychology. This false way claims that man's problem is outward of himself instead of inward. In other words, that man is actually good, and if he is not good, it is because of outside forces of some nature. Control those forces, change those forces, whatever they might be, and then man can be good.

The Bible teaches the very opposite. It teaches that man is inwardly evil, inwardly corrupt, inwardly depraved; consequently there is absolutely nothing he can do to change his situation from a personal viewpoint. In other words, he is beyond rehabilitation. In fact, not only is he beyond a cure, at least from his own resources, but as well, everything he touches he corrupts, kills, steals, destroys, etc. (Rom. Chpt. 3).

THE CROSS IS THE ONLY ANSWER

Knowing that man could not save himself, and yet with love refusing to let him go, God would save man, but at a fearful price. As stated, the price paid, which was the Cross, tells us just how bad is sin.

Man doesn't like to admit this — how bad he is, or how good God is. He refuses to believe that he cannot save himself, so he keeps trying, even as he keeps failing.

THE CHRISTIAN AND THE CROSS

These things we have said of the world are fairly understandable as it regards the Church. Unregenerate man will not admit that he is unregenerate, even though he is. But the sadness is, that the Church little realizes as well, even as Paul is addressing here, that the Cross is needed for the Child of God after coming to Christ, as much as it is needed for the sinner coming to Christ. More than likely, that is the greater problem of all — the Church not understanding the veracity of the Cross as it applies to our everyday living and life.

The manner in which Paul uses this statement, *"enemies of the Cross of Christ,"* falls out to two directions. One asks, *"Does he mean enemies of the Doctrine of the Cross, or of its practical influence and efficiency?"* The two are naturally connected. But here perhaps the latter is principally intended, even as the former is intended in I Corinthians Chapter 1. The context, especially what follows in the Apostle's description, seem to point that way.

When Christ's Cross is rightly apprehended, and when the place it claims in the mind has been cordially yielded, it becomes, as we see in the case of Paul himself, a renovating principle, the fountain of a new view and a new course.

That immense Sacrifice for our Redemption from sin decides that we are no more to live the rest of our time in the flesh to the lust of men (I Pet 4:1).

So Christ's Cross teaches us the slender worth, or the mere worthlessness, of much that we otherwise would idolize — in other words, it takes the luster in totality from the world.

On the other hand it assures us of Redemption into His likeness, as a prospect to be realized in the renunciation of the *"old man,"* which refers to victory over sin, which can only be achieved in this manner.

As well, it embodies an incomparable wealth of motive to persuade us to comply, for we find ourselves in fellowship with Love unspeakable, which the Cross portrays.

SELF-DENIAL

Under this influence we take up our Cross, even as Jesus demanded (Lk. 9:23-24); which is substantially the same as renouncing or denying ourselves (Mat. 16:24). It is self-denial for Christ's sake and after Christ's example, accepted as a principle, and carried out in the forms in which God calls us to it.

However, exactly what does the Lord mean by demanding that we deny ourselves or enter into a life of self-denial?

First, let's see what it doesn't mean:

It doesn't refer to a life of denial of all pleasure or good things as much of the Church down through the ages has thought. In the Middle Ages many in the Church took denial of the flesh or self to the place of fine art. In other words, a regimen of suffering of some nature they thought, was what Christ meant by bearing the Cross. Then certain ones began to equate such denial with holiness, etc. The more one suffered or put himself through some type of stringent, physical torture of some nature, the more holy was one supposed to be, etc. None of that is what Jesus was speaking of as it regards self-denial, i.e., *"bearing the Cross"* (Lk. 9:23-24).

Actually, the Lord was saying the very opposite. He, in effect, was saying that one cannot attain Holiness or Righteousness by this method. In other words, self and all of its machinations, cannot bring about the desired spiritual results.

He was actually saying, that we must stop all of this self-effort in this respect, quit trying to bring about this great work within our lives, which can only be done by the Holy Spirit (Rom. 8:1).

The denial of self, refers to taking self out of the picture as far as self-effort is concerned, and allowing the Holy Spirit to do this which only He can do. And how do we do that?

The taking up of the Cross, does not mean suffering as many think (Lk. 9:23-24). It means that we are to look to the Cross as it regards what Jesus did there on our behalf and for us, and receive its benefits. It is all done by Faith — Faith in the Cross, which means Faith in the Finished Work of Christ. That is what bearing the Cross actually means, not suffering as many have thought!

The biggest problem for the Christian is self. And by that I mean trying to do that which only the Holy Spirit can do. There is no way that a Christian can make himself Holy or Righteous, irrespective of the religious work he may engage. One cannot make themselves Holy and Righteous by fasting, by prayer, by the study of the Word of God, by giving of money to the Work of the Lord, by witnessing to souls, by depriving ourselves, etc. Now as I've already stated, don't mistake what I've said. I'm not demeaning prayer and fasting, etc. Most of these things I've mentioned are very needful and desirable in their own right, actually which without the Christian cannot have a proper relationship with the Lord; however, they must never be used as *"works"* in order to bring about some desired result of Righteousness and Holiness.

LOOK TO THE CROSS

The Child of God is to look to the Cross, or more particularly to what the Cross afforded as it regards the great Sacrifice of Christ. He is to understand that every single thing we are, we need, we have, or ever will have, was brought about as a result of what Jesus did at the Cross and His Resurrection. We are to look to that, understand that, place our Faith in that, and that's the key word — Faith. However, and as I have repeatedly stated, the object of our Faith must always be the Cross.

The Holy Spirit can then bring about in our lives these things which we so desperately need, but only then. That's what denying self actually means. We simply quit trying within ourselves to do this thing, as stated, which only the Holy Spirit can do. And as well, He does all His Work within our hearts and lives according to what Jesus did at the Cross and our Faith in that Finished Work (Rom. 8:2).

Actually, the Holy Spirit is so absolutely regimented to the Sacrifice of Christ, that it is referred to as a *"Law."* Let's look at what Paul actually said:

THE LAW OF THE SPIRIT

"For the Law of the Spirit (the only manner in which the Spirit will work) *of life* (this is where our life and victory comes from) *in Christ Jesus* (meaning that this which the Spirit does is predicated entirely on what Jesus did at the Cross and the Resurrection. In other words, it is all in Him, meaning what He did) **hath made me free from the law of sin and death** (gives the Saint victory over the world, the flesh, and the Devil)" (Rom. 8:2).

And I might quickly add, the only way that the Saint is going to have victory over the *"law of sin and death,"* is by allowing the Holy Spirit to bring about this victory, which He always does through our Faith in the Finished Work of Christ. The *"law of sin and death"* is so strong, so powerful, that it is not possible to be defeated in any other manner.

WHAT DOES IT ALL EXACTLY MEAN?

I do not want to leave the impression that the Holy Spirit carries out an added work regarding what Christ did at the Cross. That's not the idea at all.

The idea is, Jesus in His Sacrificial Work on the Cross, combined with His Resurrection, carried out a completed Work. Nothing must be added, as nothing needs to be added. It is all done in Christ.

The Holy Spirit comes into our heart and life at conversion, and is there to guarantee all that Christ did. In other words, He will not allow Satan to usurp authority over the Saint of God in any regard, forcing him to obey in every respect all that Jesus did at the Cross.

However, all of this, or none of this I should say, is an automatic process as it regards the Holy Spirit, even as we have already stated. He demands of us that we have Faith in what Jesus did at the Cross. He demands that we keep our Faith in that, understanding that all of our victory, all of our success, all of our overcoming power, all of our Blessings, come entirely from this Source and from no other source. When our Faith is properly anchored there, the Holy Spirit then can perform His Work within our lives, which guarantees us victory over the *"law of sin and death."*

As well, it is not a one-time thing, but actually that which we must renew on a daily basis. This is what Jesus meant by telling us that we must *"take up our Cross daily, and follow Him"* (Lk. 9:23). Again, he is not speaking of us suffering some type of spiritual regimen, etc.

The greatest problem of the Saint, and that which we have all faced, is that of trying to do within our lives, trying to bring about within our lives, that which only the Holy Spirit can do. As a Saint of God I want to be Righteous and I want to be Holy. Actually, that spirit, attitude, feeling, and desire, are in the heart of every true Saint. We want to be Christlike, and in fact, more and more Christlike. But these things cannot be brought about by our own religious machinations or efforts. But these things fool us because within their own right many of them are spiritual, and because of that, when they don't bring about the desired results, but actually the very opposite, it confuses us. The actual Truth is, that we've turned these things such as prayer, fasting, etc., into works, which God can never honor, and on which the Holy Spirit cannot function.

By our doing these things, and whatever they might be, and thinking they bring about some type of Righteousness or Holiness, whether we realize it or not, we are actually saying that Jesus did not finish the Work at the Cross, and that which He did needs something added. As we've already stated, such only seeks to frustrate the Grace of God (Gal. 2:21).

I realize that we in no way are claiming that what we are doing is adding to the Finished Work of Christ; however, whatever we think, that's the way it comes out to the Lord.

IT IS ALL BY FAITH

As the unsaved man cannot save himself by his works, but can be saved only by having Faith in what Jesus did at the Cross on his behalf (Jn. 3:16), likewise, the Christian cannot bring about a life of holiness or any other desired result for that matter, by his works, but only by Faith.

However, what do we mean when we say *"by Faith"*?

We are speaking of Faith in Christ, but more particularly, what He did at the Cross and the Resurrection. Our Faith is always in Jesus, but it's not merely in Jesus, but rather in what He did for us. We must not forget that.

Millions of Christians have Faith in Christ, but they do not properly understand what their Faith actually is. It's sort of a nebulous Faith, sort of a shadowy Faith. In other words, they do not properly understand what the true object of their Faith should be.

Were this question to be posed to them, what the true object of their Faith should be, most would just simply say *"Jesus."* While that is correct, at least as far as it goes, it leaves much to be desired.

To be sure, Paul had great Faith in Jesus immediately after his conversion. But yet, even as the Seventh Chapter of Romans proclaims, Paul found himself failing and failing miserably, even though he definitely had Faith in Christ. Unfortunately, millions of Christians right now are in the same situation. That's what confuses them.

They have Faith in Christ but yet they are failing. In other words, sin is claiming dominion over them in some manner (Rom. 6:14).

If they confide in a Preacher, they are more than likely told that they must have greater Faith in the Lord. So they set about to do that by reading the Scriptures more, or being more faithful to Church, etc. Or some of them think if they can just get to a certain Preacher who is supposed to have a great touch with God, have him lay his hands on them, then their problem will be solved. If the Lord at that time slays them in the Spirit, then it's even better.

However, they find that even though these things may bless them and even bless them greatly, they will not walk away with the Victory which they desire. In other words, the same old problem will be there.

While these people definitely have Faith in Christ, even as Paul did, it is not the type of Faith that's going to bring them victory.

Paul was told by the Lord that his Victory, his overcoming strength, his more abundant life, were all found in what Jesus did at the Cross and the Resurrection, which the Apostle gave to us in graphic detail in Romans Chapter 6. Now, the object of Paul's Faith is in the Cross of Christ, through which the Holy Spirit can work, which brought the Apostle tremendous victory, even as he records in Romans Chapter 8.

To be sure this was given for Paul, but it was also given for every other Believer. In other words the Lord showed us through Paul's example, how that we can walk in victory as well. But instead, too many of us attempt other things, other methods, which never bring satisfactory results, and for all the obvious reasons — obvious when one begins to understand Romans Chapter 6.

DOES PROPER FAITH IN THE CROSS MEAN THAT SATAN WILL NEVER BOTHER THE SAINT AGAIN?

To be sure, Satan will test your Faith every single day of your life or until Jesus comes. That's what Paul meant by telling us that we must *"fight the good fight of Faith"* (I Tim. 6:12).

Until Jesus calls you home or else He comes to rapture us away, this *"fight"* will continue. However, it is to always be the proper fight. And what do we mean by that?

You as a Believer are not to fight the Devil per se. He has already been defeated. Neither are you to fight Demon Spirits in the same manner. Satan and all his cohorts were totally defeated at the Cross and in every manner. So, we don't want to find ourselves trying to fight a battle that's already been fought and won.

While we definitely are engaged in a fight, and a fight which will continue, it is to always be remembered that it is a fight of *"Faith."* This means, that every attack that Satan levels at us, whether it's in the physical, financial, domestic, or spiritual sense, is always but for one purpose, and that is to weaken or hopefully destroy our Faith. That's what his attacks are all about. It's all against our Faith in Christ.

The Saint is to believe, regardless of circumstances, that Jesus handled every single thing at the Cross, defeated every power of darkness, and made it possible for us to live the life we ought to live, i.e., *"to be Christlike!"* No matter what happens, we are to believe that, understand that, and act upon that constantly. We are not to allow circumstances, difficulties, problems, hindrances, or whatever, to dislodge our Faith in Christ and what He did for us at the Cross and the Resurrection. That's the fight we are in!

As well, even as Paul said, while it is definitely a fight, it is at the same time a *"good fight!"*

This means that we are assured of victory, if we will only maintain our Faith, and maintain it in the proper object — the Cross. This fight will always lead to a successful conclusion, a victorious ending, irrespective as to what it may seem to be at the moment.

Hallelujah! I can sense the Presence of the Lord even as I say these words. Yes, at times the struggle is great! At times the conflict is severe! At times we may even wonder if we're going to make it! However, take heart! This fight of Faith will not be lost, simply because it cannot be lost. The end result is going to be victory! victory! victory! — that is, if you as a Saint of God will just keep believing.

FAILURE!

In this age of so-called super Faith, but I might quickly add, most of the time Faith in the wrong thing, it's not popular to admit failure. However, the truth is, every single Christian who has ever lived and who will ever live, has failed many times in his or her Faith. It means that Satan overcame them for a short period of time and they sinned. What the sin was or is, doesn't really matter at the moment. Now we can deny this, but the truth is what I've just said.

However, we are not to allow our failures to stop us. We are to ask the Lord to forgive us (I Jn. 1:9), and then seek His Face as to the reason we have failed.

I realize that many might read these words with astonishment, saying, *"You mean if I put my Faith in the Cross even as I should, that I still might fail?"*

That's exactly what I'm saying!

Even though you read all of these things which I am saying, and even though the Holy Spirit quickens them to your heart, meaning that you know what I'm saying is right, and that you are engaging upon this life of victory, regrettably, there will still be some failures in your life.

Why? How?

The reason is simple and which all of us learn by experience. Our Faith is not perfect. In other words, even though we embark as we should upon this road of Faith in Christ, and more particularly what He did for us at the Cross and the Resurrection, determined to have all the Victory which the great Finished Work of Christ guarantees, which as well brings the Holy Spirit to our side, our Faith is by no means perfect. To be sure, Satan will test our Faith. In fact, he will test it every day, and the Lord will allow him to do such.

It is by this method, the method of the Lord allowing temptation, test and trial, which proves our Faith. As someone has said, *"Faith must be tested, and great Faith must be tested greatly."*

By this method we find that our Faith is not perfect, and needs growth. Failure, as hurtful as it is, as debilitating as it is, as wrong as it is, has a tendency to pull us up short in order that we inspect ourselves to see where we went wrong. We are then to seek the Lord asking Him to show us, which He always will.

This is the struggle and the battle between the flesh and the Holy Spirit. It is all a struggle of Faith, but it's played out in our lives. The Holy Spirit wants dominance, even as He must have dominance, but self-will keeps cropping up, of which Satan takes full advantage, which commences the battle. This it the *"fight"* of which Paul spoke.

It is not a fight that is won easily or quickly. In fact, this struggle as stated, will continue until the Lord comes.

Nevertheless, as the Saint continues to evidence Faith, little by little he will find his Faith growing, with failures less and less, and further and further between.

The following little poem I have quoted several times in our Commentaries, but I believe that it should be quoted again here:

"I can see far down the mountain, where I have wandered many years,

"Often hindered on my journey by the ghosts of doubts and fears.

"Broken vows and disappointments, thickly strewn along the way,

"But the Spirit has led unerring to the land I hold today."

WHY WOULD ANYONE WHO PROFESSES CHRIST, BE AN ENEMY OF THE CROSS OF CHRIST?

Satan fights the Cross as he fights nothing else, and for all the obvious Scriptural reasons. He knows that if he can get the Believer to look elsewhere for victory or whatever, he has succeeded. He knows in these other areas whatever they might be, the Christian will not find victory, will not find Christlikeness. In fact, he will dress up these other things in great religious garb, so they will be enticing, and make the Believer think that these things are the right way. So, the enemies of the Cross are many times, the most religious of all.

But notice, I said *"religious!"*

Religion in any form, is always that which is devised by man. In fact, Christianity is not a Religion, but rather a Relationship, and more particularly, a Relationship with Christ and all that He did to save lost humanity. So, anything other than Faith in Christ and the Cross, can be labeled as *"religion."*

If the Cross is not properly taught and preached behind pulpits, the people will not know or understand this great Truth, actually the central Truth of all Christianity. And the sadness is, there have been very little teaching and preaching on the Cross in Christendom in the last nearly half century. Satan has been very successful at pushing in other things to take the place of the Cross.

Strangely enough the two things that he used, which of course has proved to be very subtle and very effective, are *"Faith"* and the *"Holy Spirit."* Now that may seem strange. Faith and the Holy Spirit are the two stanchions of the Child of God.

That is very true, but if we misinterpret Faith or the Holy Spirit, which we have in many circles, and which Satan has designed, the end result will be error and great error at that.

First let's look at the Holy Spirit: How can we go wrong regarding the Holy Spirit? To be sure, the fault is not the Holy Spirit at all, but of the Saint.

At about the turn of the century, the great Latter Rain prophesied by Joel, began to take place in the world. I speak of the great outpouring of the Holy Spirit which has resulted in hundreds of millions being baptized with the Holy Spirit with the evidence of speaking with other Tongues (Acts 2:4, 16-21).

This was a mighty turning point for the Church, as men, women, boys, and girls began to be baptized with the Holy Spirit, which ensured great power to do things for the Lord, which evidence is obvious as it regards the Work of God (Acts 1:4, 8).

So far so good! However, because of improper teaching, Satan I think, was able to maneuver Christians into certain thinking which was really not Scriptural. And what do I mean by that?

Christians thought, and I speak of those who were baptized with the Holy Spirit, that because they were filled with the Spirit and spoke with other Tongues, and even had Gifts of the Spirit functioning through them, that victory over sin, etc., was just automatic. In other words, they were looking to the Spirit in a wrong manner, a wrong way. They thought that His Presence just automatically guaranteed Victory in all respects. Consequently, we told the non-Pentecostal world, that if they would only be baptized with the Holy Spirit with the evidence of speaking with other Tongues, their problems would be solved.

However, we found that in our personal lives, and I speak of walking in victory before the Lord, that we were having just about as many problems as our non-Pentecostal friends. This was very confusing, so what did we do?

Most of us refused to admit our problems, hiding them, all the time trying to find Victory in the wrong way, and all the time failing, with the situation steadily getting worse. No, all Spirit-filled Believers did not fall into that category, but I think most did and most do. Some few thank the Lord, did and do have their Faith properly in the Cross of Christ. But most didn't and most don't!

WRONG THINKING CONCERNING THE HOLY SPIRIT

Looking to the Holy Spirit to do all these things for us, while most of us ignored the Cross of Christ, mostly from a lack of knowledge and not willful rebellion, still, the results were the same — failure.

In effect, whether we realized it or not, we were wanting the Holy Spirit to do for us, what Jesus had actually already done at the Cross. We did not properly understand the manner in which the Holy Spirit worked. So, we had and have, Preachers doing great things for God and because of the Holy Spirit, but at the same time failing in their own lives. I'll say it again. All did not fall into that category, but I think most did and most do.

A short time ago, one of my Associates was ministering in a particular Church, whose Pastor had graduated from one of the Charismatic Schools. They were discussing these very things, with the young Pastor admitting that something was missing. As my Associate began to explain the Cross to him, the light suddenly came on.

He then said, *"We were taught that the Holy Spirit just automatically did all of these things for us."*

Yes, he was taught that, as were most of us. Actually, the Holy Spirit *is* the One Who does all of these things within our lives, even as we have been repeatedly stating; however, He does these things only according to our Faith in the Cross of Christ, even as Paul explains in Romans Chapters 6 and 8. But that's where we missed it!

THE HOLY SPIRIT AND THE CROSS

We were taught little or nothing about the Cross, depending on the Holy Spirit to do all of these things without our Faith properly placed, which He will not do.

A. W. Tozer said, or words to this effect, *"We clip the wings of the Holy Spirit, if we do not properly understand, and thereby place our Faith in the Finished Work of Christ."*

That's one of the reasons that many in the great Pentecostal World have resorted to humanistic psychology. They do not properly understand the Work of the Holy Spirit in this capacity, in other words how He works, which is always according to our Faith in the Finished Work of Christ. I would like to believe that their resorting to this broken cistern (Jer. 2:13), is because of a lack of knowledge concerning the Scriptures rather than rank unbelief. If it is unbelief, then the situation is critical indeed!

When I say *"unbelief,"* I'm speaking of the terrible sin of not believing that what Jesus did at the Cross handled all the problems of mankind and in every capacity.

So, what am I saying as it regards the Baptism with the Holy Spirit and the Pentecostal Way?

I am saying that too many of us have expected the Holy Spirit to give us victory in our lives without our having proper Faith in the Cross, which He will not do. Satan promoted this error which has reaped bitter results.

NOW LET'S LOOK AT FAITH

Just as the Holy Spirit is the mainstay of the Child of God, Faith is likewise. So, Satan has taken advantage of our improper understanding of the two greatest foundations of the Christian Way, *"The Holy Spirit and Faith."*

Now the Believer may ask as to how Faith has been turned into that which is wrong?

I speak primarily of the *"Faith Ministry"* per se. While some things taught in this regard are good, most have not been good.

At the present time, there are tens of thousands of *"Faith Churches,"* all over the world. I'm not meaning in my statements, that all fall into the category of which I will address, but I think almost all do.

This particular way began approximately in the 1960's one might say. Faith is the main object as it regards this teaching, which on the surface seems to be good. All Christians must have Faith, and all Christians need more Faith. As well, it is by Faith through which the Lord does all things. So, one can see how subtle this can be.

The great wrong that has been done in this particular teaching pertains to the object of Faith. In other words, the object of Faith has not been the Cross of Christ, but something else altogether. In fact, Faith has been held up as a power or strength within itself. This means, that if Believers could have enough Faith, they could do anything.

Such teaching completely disregards the Will of God, making God subject to the whims of men, which of course is ridiculous.

In this teaching, people are told that if they have enough Faith they will never be sick a day in their lives, they will all be wealthy, etc., etc. Consequently, the individual or Faith itself, becomes the primary objective instead of Christ. If a person is prayed for and they are not healed, it is because they don't have enough Faith, or so they claim! Consequently, the barometer of Faith is the criteria for all things.

As a result, the devotees to this teaching are ever trying to increase their Faith. This means that their Faith is merely in their Faith. In other words, Faith within itself is the objective, which is totally wrong.

Faith must always be subjected to the Will of God (Rom. 8:27).

They call themselves *"Word people,"* which means that they go strictly by the Word of God. The Truth is, most of them are pulling the Word out of its rightful context, attempting to force it into the position of bringing about their will instead of the Will of God. In fact, this is the highest sin of all, the very sin that Adam and Eve committed, and the very sin which Satan attempted to get Jesus to commit regarding the temptations in the wilderness (Mat. Chpt. 4).

In these circles, Faith is the foundation principle, but the foundation principle of Faith alone. In other words, it is divorced from the true Word of God and the Will of God, which makes it a work of the flesh and thereby *"sin."*

In these circles, Faith in the Cross is repudiated, actually, the Cross is repudiated in totality. It is referred to as *"weakness,"* or *"past miseries,"* in which the Christian is to ignore or worse yet, deny.

If one will look at all the Faith teaching, most everything said about the Cross will be in a denigrating way, placing it in a subordinate position, if any position at all. Consequently, in these respective Churches, there are few songs sung regarding the Blood or the Cross. In fact, songs regarding the *"Cross"* are forbidden in many of these Churches. It doesn't fit with their stereotype of supermen, etc. As stated, they refer to the Cross as weakness, to which these super Faith men do not subscribe, because weakness does not fit into their category.

In fact, Jesus *"was crucified through weakness"* (II Cor. 13:4), but it was a weakness which He purposely contrived, but which actually demonstrated His Power. He died in weakness in order that men might be saved; however, He was raised *"by the Power of God,"* having completed that task.

As well, Paul also said, *"For we also are weak in Him, but we shall live with Him by the Power of God"* (II Cor. 13:4).

Actually, this weakness, which is actually the state of all humans, even the Godliest, turns into our strength. When we understand that we are weak, and must rely totally upon Him, then Victory is ours.

This *"weakness"* of Christ one might say, completely destroyed the power of sin and the power of death. The Death of Christ on the Cross completely defeated every Demon Spirit, because it atoned for all sin, and sin is Satan's strength. With the sin removed, which Jesus did, and did it through the weakness of dying one might say, Satan was totally and completely defeated. Satan was defeated by the Death of Christ, and Saints are justified by His Resurrection (Rom. 4:25; Jn. 1:29).

Consequently, Faith in the Cross is not the type of Faith taught by the *"Faith Ministry"* or *"Word People,"* which type is spurious.

By this means, Satan has been very successful in polluting or perverting the Faith of the Saints. Hundreds of thousands have bought into this teaching, because on the surface it seems very good. But actually, it isn't!

I'll say it again. Anything which is the object of Faith other than the Cross, is error. Everything the Saint has from God, and I mean everything, comes through the Finished Work of Christ. This means, that our Faith must rest in that Finished Work, and nothing else!

(19) "WHOSE END IS DESTRUCTION, WHOSE GOD IS THEIR BELLY, AND WHOSE GLORY IS IN THEIR SHAME, WHO MIND EARTHLY THINGS.)"

As this Scripture so plainly brings out, the ultimate end for all who attempt to travel ways of supposed Salvation and/or victory, other than the Cross of Christ, can only be destruction.

The idea behind the word *"belly"* or *"stomach"* is that their whole attention is fixed on physical and material interests. In other words, they attempt to use the Word of God, i.e., *"Christ,"* for material gain other than that which is spiritual.

DESTRUCTION

The phrase, *"Whose end is destruction,"* proclaims plainly the fact, even as stated, that if the Cross of Christ is ignored which is the only means of Salvation, the loss of the soul is the only ultimate conclusion.

Some Commentators have attempted to place Paul's statement into narrow confines of some particular groups who lived during his day. That is not the case at all.

If one properly understands that the only manner of Salvation is one's Faith in the Cross of Christ, in other words what He did there, then we must conclude that all other ways can only lead to perdition. The Lord does not have five or four or even two ways of Salvation. He has only one, and that is *"Jesus Christ and Him Crucified"* (I Cor. 2:2). In fact, this is what Paul dealt with so stringently in I Corinthians. He said, *"For Christ sent me not to baptize* (not to make Water Baptism the criteria for Salvation), *but to preach the Gospel* (the Gospel is the Cross of Christ): *not with wisdom of words* (Salvation is not through the route of intellectualism), *lest the Cross of Christ should be made of none effect* (Faith in what Jesus did on the Cross is the only manner of Salvation)" (I Cor. 1:17).

He then said, *"For the preaching of the Cross is to them that perish foolishness* (all who reject the Cross); *but unto us which are saved* (we were saved by having Faith in what Jesus did on the Cross) *it is the Power of God.* (Faith in the Cross of Christ produces a power from God which sets captives free, and is alone that which sets captives free.)" (I Cor. 1:18)

And then he said, *"For after that in the Wisdom of God* (which is the Cross) *the world by wisdom knew not God* (cannot find out or know God by the intellect alone), *it pleased God by the foolishness of preaching* (the preaching of the Cross) *to save them that believe* (who believe in the Cross and what Jesus there did)" (I Cor. 1:21).

Paul then plainly said, *"But we preach Christ crucified* (the foundation Message of the Gospel), *unto the Jews a stumblingblock* (they refused to believe), *and unto the Greeks foolishness* (they cannot see how a Peasant hanging on a Cross can save anyone): *But unto them which are called* (who accept the Call of God), *both Jews and Greeks* (the entirety of the world), *Christ the Power of God* (what Jesus did on the Cross produces the Power of God, and that alone produces the Power of God), *and the Wisdom of God* (The Cross of Christ is God's Way of Salvation, and there is no other.)" (I Cor. 1:23-24).

And finally, *"For I determined not to know any thing among you* (would not preach philosophy and such type things), *save Jesus Christ, and Him Crucified.* (This is the Message of Redemption, and it carries the Power of God, and there is no Redemption or Power otherwise.)" (I Cor. 2:2)

As we've already stated, Satan has been very successful in the latter half of the 20th Century in pushing the Church away from the Cross. He has used *"other gospels,"* even as we have already enumerated, to carry out this task. In fact, Paul referred to these as no gospel at all (Gal. 1:6-7). He, in effect, labeled them as *"perversions of the Gospel of Christ."* However, they are always very clever versions, almost always carrying some Truth which serves as the hook. The Church is presently inundated with this, and regrettably, the situation will not get better but rather worse. As we've already stated, the Church has already entered into the last great Apostasy which Paul also described in I Timothy 4:1 when he said, *"Now the Spirit speaketh expressly* (the Spirit of God revealed this to Paul even in his day), *that in the latter times* (the times in which we now live) *some shall depart from the Faith* (the Message of the Cross), *giving heed to seducing spirits, and doctrines of devils* (meaning that evil spirits are the true originators of false doctrine, using Preachers merely as pawns)."

PERSONAL WELFARE

The phrase, *"Whose God is their belly,"* refers to those who attempt to pervert the Gospel into their own personal gain. In fact, this is a perfect example of the modern prosperity gospel.

Jesus Christ is spoken of constantly, the Word is used constantly, but all in an attempt to bring about physical or material gain in some manner. As stated, there is some Truth in all these perversions.

The Lord is our Healer. He definitely does bless His people in the realm of financial and material prosperity. However, to make that the primary objective of the Child of God, is to grossly misinterpret the Scriptures, actually, as stated, perverting them.

The end in view for all Believers, must ever be Christlikeness. The Holy Spirit is attempting to bring about the Fruit of the Spirit within our hearts and lives. He ever works toward this end, which of course, will make us more and more like Christ. While the other things do definitely carry significance, and I speak of prosperity, etc., they are to never be the overriding factor by any means. If this is done, and in fact it is done in a wholesale manner by those who promote the *"money gospel,"* it can be summed up as an engrossment in self-indulgence instead of Christlikeness.

AN EXAMPLE

In the Summer of 1988, Frances and I were in England where we ministered in a particular Church in the city of Norwich. We were in London a couple of days before the meeting, and received a call from a friend who also happened to be in that particular city. He desired that we have a meal with he and his wife and other friends who were with them, which we did.

In asking him his reason for being in London, he informed me that a larger convention was being conducted in the city, pertaining to World Missions. Of course, when he mentioned World Missions I was immediately interested.

I asked him as to how the meeting was going, etc.?

His answer was somewhat revealing.

He said a Preacher's name, and asked me if I was acquainted with him? I knew his name, but I had never met him or heard him minister, but knew he was a part and parcel of the so-called prosperity message.

The Brother went on to relate the extent of this man's message which was preached the night before. The title was *"Money Cometh!"*

There were some 3,000 to 4,000 people present, he said, and he had them on their feet shouting constantly, *"Money cometh!"*

Unfortunately, there is enough greed I suppose in the hearts of all of us to make such a message alluring; however, this is not the Gospel, nor anything close to the Gospel.

Man's problem is not money, but rather sin. The only answer for the sin question is the Cross of Christ, which these people incidentally, repudiate.

Only one conclusion can be reached regarding such a message, *"Their belly is their God!"* i.e., *"personal gain."*

SHAME

The phrase, *"And whose glory is in their shame,"* refers to the fact that this for which they seek, and I speak of material things, is looked at by God as *"shame."*

It is ironical, they *"glory (boast)"* in supposed blessings which they claim to be from God, but which God rather labels as *"shame."* It is a *"shame"* because they have perverted the Gospel of Christ. It is a *"shame"* because they have withheld the true Message of Redemption from searching, seeking souls. It is a *"shame"* because they have placed the word *"glory"* onto that which God by no means refers to as *"glory."* Let me explain further:

The true *"glory,"* in other words that for which the Church ought to exult or glory, is the Salvation of souls, Believers being baptized with the Holy Spirit, sick bodies truly being healed and not just wild claims, bondages of darkness being broken, etc. Instead, they are *"glorying"* in material things exclusively.

AN EXAMPLE

A Seminar on Faith was conducted some time back, of which there are many of this nature, with several hundreds of Preachers present. The host was one of the gurus of the prosperity message.

As an example of his Faith, he took all of these Preachers over to a large building near the Church where the meeting was being conducted. In this building (actually a hangar) was a Jet airplane. He took the Preachers through this plane, explaining to them how much it cost, and that this was an example of Faith. In other words, if they had his kind of Faith, they could themselves ultimately secure an airplane of this nature. This was their Faith model — this particular Preacher and the accoutrements mentioned.

The Holy Spirit refers to this as *"shame!"*

This Preacher could not boast of souls being saved, for none are saved in his meetings, I suppose with very little effort, if any, even made to get people saved. As well, there are precious few baptized with the Holy Spirit. As well, there are almost no healings, despite all the wild claims. And last but not least, no bondages of darkness are broken.

So what is such a Ministry? That is if it could even be referred to as Ministry!

Pure and simple, it is *"another gospel"* (II Cor. 11:4), but which millions are following. As stated, I suppose there is some greed in all of us to which such a message can appeal. God help us!

EARTHLY THINGS

The phrase, *"Who mind earthly things,"* fits to a *"T"* this of which we have just described.

Now I suppose you know and understand why most of the Church world doesn't like Jimmy Swaggart too very much. I don't think they would have liked the Apostle Paul very much either! As a true Preacher of the Gospel, it is my responsibility to serve as a *"watchman"* exactly as God spoke of the Prophet Ezekiel. He said, *"Son of man, I have made Thee a watchman unto the house of Israel: therefore hear the Word at My mouth, and give them warning from me"* (Ezek. 3:17).

As a true Preacher of the Gospel, is less required of us presently? I think not!

Even though many presently claim to be friends of Christ, the facts are, they are not crucified with Him, and thus are enemies of His Cross, which is the symbol of death to self and sin. And in fact, the Cross is the only place where self can be conquered and sin can be eradicated. God has provided no other solution.

(20) "FOR OUR CONVERSATION IS IN HEAVEN; FROM WHENCE ALSO WE LOOK FOR THE SAVIOUR, THE LORD JESUS CHRIST:"

The *"our"* is emphatic and stresses the distinction between true Believers whose essential relationships belong to the heavenly sphere, and the *"materialists"* just discussed, who are exclusively concerned with earthly things.

The Christian's *"commonwealth"* is in Heaven, and for him earthly things must at best be secondary.

The Philippians would understand very well Paul's symbolism, for in a political sense they knew what it was to be citizens of a far-off city (even though most of them had probably never been to Rome) and they were somewhat proud of that status (Acts 16:12, 21). However, on an immeasurably higher plane, Believers belong to the *"City ... Whose Architect and Builder is God"* (Heb. 11:10), the *"Jerusalem that is above"* (Gal. 4:26), and are ourselves *"foreigners and strangers on Earth"* (Heb. 11:13; I Pet. 2:11). As such, our eyes should be Heavenward, anticipating the coming of our Saviour, Who is not a mere earthly emperor but the Lord Jesus Christ. An eager expectation of His return does much to protect the Believer from earthly, sensual enticements (Kent).

CITIZENSHIP

The phrase, *"For our conversation is in Heaven,"* refers actually to our *"citizenship."* The Greek word is *"polipeuma,"* and means *"citizenship, city, civil rights, state, society, or government."* In other words, the true citizenship and government of the Believer is above.

To which we have already briefly alluded, the stability and security of the citizen under Roman Law fill the thoughts of the time with high conceptions of citizenship and its value. Philippi, being a Roman Colony, and its citizens, therefore, Roman citizens, thought in terms of citizenship, which was then a great privilege.

Paul seizes this fact as a good opportunity to illustrate to the Saints their Heavenly Citizenship with its privileges and responsibilities.

What a contrast between those mentioned in Philippians 3:18-19, who were citizens of this Earth and thought only of earthly ways, although claiming Christ, and those spoken of in Philippians 3:20-21, who are citizens of Heaven! (Wuest).

NOTES

By Paul using the pronoun *"our"* he is, in effect, saying, *"Follow us, not those earthly-minded guides."*

Or perhaps it could be said better in this manner, *"Let us hold to our course, you following me, though many follow earthly and sensual ways."*

THE KINGDOM OF HEAVEN

The Christian, and I speak of the true Christian, although a part of the system of this world as is obvious, still, has his actual citizenship in Heaven. We belong to the Kingdom of Heaven, and we long for that Kingdom to become a present reality (Mat. 6:10; Eph. 2:19).

The Church is actually a *"Colony of Heaven"* such as Philippi was a Roman Colony. As a member of this *"Colony of Heaven"* and thereby a part of the *"Kingdom of Heaven"* it is my responsibility as a Believer to conduct myself accordingly. My ways are not to be the ways of this world. My thoughts are not to be the thoughts of this world. My preparation is not to be as the preparation of those who *"mind earthly things."*

As a Believer, every single thing I do is to always be done with the *"heavenly thought"* in mind. Every action, every word, every direction, and as stated, every thought, is to come under the scrutiny of the King of this Kingdom, The Lord Jesus Christ. As well, the Holy Spirit resides in our hearts, to help us to ever look away from this Earth toward the Heavenly Kingdom.

Consequently, the Church is to never ape the things of this world, but rather be led by the Spirit. We are to use the things of this world, but never abuse the things of this world, which means to become attached to such. We are *in* the world, but are never to be *of* the world, which refers to being of its system, attached to its system, immersed in its system, etc.

The more Christlike that one becomes, the more this world loses its lustre. Regrettably, the less Christlike, the more attractive becomes the world.

The old song is right, and should be heeded:

"This world is not my home, I'm just a travelling through,

> "My treasures are laid up, somewhere beyond the blue,
> "The Saviour beckons me to Heaven's open door,
> "And I can't feel at home in this world anymore."

All men draw much from the spirit and laws of the commonwealth to which they belong; and in antiquity this influence was even stronger than we commonly find it to be in our day. The individual was conscious of himself as a member of his own city or state. Its life enfolded his. Its institutions set for him the conditions under which life was accepted and carried on. Its laws determined for him his duties and his rights. The ancient and customary methods of the society developed a common spirit, under the influence of which each citizen unfolded his own personal peculiarities. When he went forth elsewhere he felt himself, and was felt to be, a stranger.

Now in the Heavenly Kingdom which had claimed them and had opened to them through Christ, Believers had found their own city; and finding it, had become, comparatively strangers in every other.

THIS WORLD

A way of thinking and acting prevails throughout the world, as if Earth and its interests were the whole sphere of man; and being pervaded by this spirit, the whole world may be said to be a commonwealth with a spirit and with a maxims of its own. We, who live in it, feel it natural to comply with the drift of things in this respect, and difficult to stand against it; so that separation and singularity seem unreasonable and hard. But yet, that is what is demanded of us.

It was urged against the Christians of the early ages that their experience with the Lord made them unsocial — it broke the ties by which men held together; and doubtless many a Christian, in hours of trial and tests, felt with pain that much in Christian life offered a foundation for such reproach.

On the other hand, those who, like the enemies of the Cross, refer their lives to the world's standard, rather than to Christ's, are immersed in this present comfort, this tangible city. This is because the world, so to speak, is their city, therefore, also the prince of it is their king. But the Apostle, for himself and his fellows, sets against this the True City or State — with its far more pervading and mighty Spirit, for the Spirit of God Himself is the life which binds this Heavenly City all together; with its glorious and gracious King.

This Commonwealth has its seat in Heaven; for there it reveals its nature, and thence its power descends. We recognize this whenever we pray, *"Thy Will be done in Earth as it is in Heaven."* This, says the Apostle, is our citizenship.

Our state, and the life which as members of that state we claim and use, is celestial. Its life and strength, its glory and victory, are in Heaven. But it is ours, though we are here on Earth.

OUR CONDUCT

Therefore, according to the Holy Spirit through the Apostle, the standard of our living and its sanctions, and its way of thinking and proceeding, and, in a word, our city, with its interests and its objects, being in Heaven, the earnest business of our life is there as well.

While we have to do with Earth constantly and in ways most various; but, as Christians, our way of having to do with the Earth itself must be heavenly, and is to be conversant with Heaven. What we mainly love and seek is in Heaven; what we listen most to hear is the voice that comes from Heaven; what we most earnestly speak is the voice we send to Heaven; what lies next to our heart is the treasure and the hope which are secure in Heaven; we are most intent upon that which we have laid up in Heaven, and how we are getting ready for Heaven; there is One in Heaven Whom we love above all others; we are children of the Kingdom of Heaven; it is our country and our home; and something in us refuses to settle on those things here that reject the stamp of Heaven.

THE STANDARD!

Does this of which we have said seem too high? Does someone say, *"Something in this direction of Heaven attracts me and I reach out to it, but ah! how feebly"*? Then how strongly does the principle of the Apostle's admonition apply?

If we own that this city rightfully claims us, if we are deeply conscious of shortcomings and our response to that claim, then how much does it concern us to allow no earthly thing that by its own nature drags us down from our Citizenship in Heaven.

We must guard against all things that would hinder in any manner our citizenship there. Yes, the standard is high, because Heaven is high, and the Lord is high. He is preparing a people who are high, and as a result, the standard must be high as well!

The King of this Kingdom demands total allegiance, even to a degree not known in this world's system. He must come before everything else, Father, Mother, Brother, Sister, Son, Daughter, or any earthly affections. Jesus Christ is that King, is that Lord, is that Emperor, is that Potentate!

Not long after Paul's day, untold thousands died because they would not simply say *"Caesar is Lord!"* They gave up their lives rather than place an earthly king above their Heavenly King, so as not to mar their Citizenship of Heaven.

Yes, it is a high standard, but it is a high calling as well. How wonderful, how glorious, to be a part of that Heavenly Calling.

LOOKING FOR OUR SAVIOUR, THE LORD JESUS CHRIST

The phrase, *"From whence also we look for the Saviour, the Lord Jesus Christ,"* speaks of an attitude of intense yearning and eager waiting for the Coming of the Lord Jesus into the air to take His Church to Heaven with Him, the attention being withdrawn from all else and concentrated Alone on the Lord Jesus (Wuest).

The idea is this:

To those who properly look and look properly to the Cross of Christ, understanding that the great Sacrifice there offered contains the whole of our Redemption, this sanctified group also yearns for the Coming of the Lord. The idea is, when the Cross is ignored, the Coming is ignored as well! We should read those words again and very carefully, because they are very important. So important in fact, that I feel they must be repeated:

"No 'Cross' no 'Coming!'"

The idea is, and it is obvious according to observation, that those who little look to the Cross, as well little look for the imminent return of the Lord. It is as if the *"Cross"* and the *"Coming"* are tied together. Of course, we are speaking of the Rapture (Resurrection) of the Church (I Thess. 4:13-18).

Concerning the Rapture of the Church, which Verses 20 and 21 graphically proclaim, I think I can say without fear of contradiction that this particular Doctrine is believed less at the present time than ever before.

Very few who subscribe to the prosperity message, believe in the Rapture of the Church. Some few do, but that number is small. As well, those who I refer to as the *"kingdom now,"* believe in the Rapture not at all. They believe the world is going to gradually become better and better by political means mostly, thereby ushering in the Millennium. This Doctrine repudiates Israel as having any part in last day events, as well as the coming Rapture, great tribulation period, rise of the Antichrist, Battle of Armageddon, etc. Even though there are various interpretations of this Doctrine, what I've said pretty much sums it up. They claim that the Prophecies of Daniel and John as it regards the Book of Revelation, have all been fulfilled. How in the world they can fit the Book of Revelation into some past fulfillment I have no idea, but they do!

As well, all of these, plus many I have not mentioned, little look to the Cross of Christ. Of course, there are possibly some exceptions, but not many.

THAT WHICH JESUS HAS DONE

The Lord of Heaven is our Lord. He, in effect, has made this city ours, caring for us, calling us to the present fellowship with Him that is attainable in a life of Faith, and He is especially the one for Whom we look to come forth from Heaven for us. He has done wonders already to set up for us the Grace of the Kingdom of Heaven, and He has brought us into it; He is doing much for us daily in Grace and in providence, upholding His Church on Earth from age to age; and this *"working"* is proceeding to a final victory. He is *"able to subject all things to Himself."* And the emphatic proof of it which awaits all Believers, is that the Body itself, reconstituted in the likeness of Christ's Own, shall at last be in full harmony with a destiny of immortal purity and glory. So shall the manifestation of His Power and Grace at last sweep through our whole being, within and without.

This is the final triumph of Salvation, with which the long history finds all its results attained. For this we await the Coming of the Saviour from Heaven. Well, therefore, may we say that the state to which we pertain, and the life which we hold as members of that state, is in Heaven.

THE EXPECTATION OF HIS COMING

The expectation of the Coming of Christ out of the world of supreme truth and purity, where God is known and served aright, to fulfill all His Promises, — this is the Church's and the Believer's great hope. It is set before us in the New Testament as a motive to every duty, as giving weight to every warning, as determining the attitude and character of all Christian life.

In particular, we cannot deal aright with any of the earthly things committed to us, unless we deal with them in the light of Christ's expected Coming. This expectation is to enter into the heart of every Believer, and no one is warranted to overlook or make light of it. His Coming, His appearing, the revelation of Him, the revelation of His Glory, the Coming of His day, and so forth, are pressed on us continually. In a true waiting for the Day of Christ is gathered up the right regard to what He did and bore when He came first and died on a Cross, and also a right regard to Him as He is now the Pledge and the Sustainer of our soul's life: the one and the other are to pass onward to the hope of His appearing.

THE TIME OF OUR LORD'S RETURN

Some harm has been done, perhaps, by the degree in which attention has been concentrated on debateable points about the time of the Rapture of the Church, or the order of events in relation to it; but more by the measure in which Christians have allowed the world's unbelieving temper to affect on this point the habit of their own minds.

It must be most seriously said that our Lord Himself expected no man to succeed in escaping the corruption of the world and enduring to the end, otherwise than in the way of watching for his Lord (Lk. 12:35-40 — but the passages are too numerous to be quoted).

Actually, the statement we have just made is the core of that given by Paul. The Rapture of the Church is to ever be paramount in the thinking of the Believer. We are to live as if we expect the Lord to come at any moment and conduct our lives accordingly.

The thought of His immanent return, the presence of mind regarding this all-important event, the expectation which every Believer should have, presents an effect, no doubt orchestrated by the Holy Spirit, which tells us several things:

1. The Rapture of the Church is the hope of the Church, even as the Second Coming of the Lord is the hope of the world.

2. If Christians are properly attuned to the Lord, His immanent return will be the foundation thinking of all our motives.

3. The knowledge that He is coming soon, and that we must be ready, tends toward a Godly life. John said, *"And every man that hath this hope* (His immanent return) *in him purifieth himself* (is watchful and waiting), *even as He* (Jesus) *is pure"* (I Jn. 3:3).

SAVIOUR

The Apostle lays great emphasis on the character in which we may expect Him. The word *"Saviour"* is emphatic. We look for a Saviour; not merely One Who saved us once, but One Who brings Salvation with Him when He comes.

It is the great good, in its completeness, that the Church sees coming to her with her Lord. Now she has the faith of it, — and with the faith an earnest and a foretaste, — but then the Hope of all things will be realized.

Therefore, the coming is spoken of as Redemption drawing nigh, as the time of the Redemption of the purchased possession. So also in the Epistle to the Galatians the end of Christ's Sacrifice is said to be to *"deliver us from this present evil world."*

Doubtless it is unwise to lay down extreme positions as to the spirit in which we are to deal with temporal things, and especially with their winning and attractive aspects. Beyond all of that, the Christian's hope is to be saved out of this world, and out of life as we know it here, into one far better — saved out of the best and brightest state to which this present state of things can bring us.

Whatever involvement we have in the world, is always to be with the knowledge that such is temporal and must be treated accordingly. Our affections are above, and must ever remain above. That means that we are not to become entangled in the things of this world as to weaken that heavenly affection. This can so easily happen, because the world does have its allurements.

Regarding those allurements, it is sometimes easy for their attraction to dim our affection for heavenly things; consequently, we must always understand, that which we cannot now presently see, is so far ahead of anything the world might have, as to be no contest. Therefore, we are to always walk by faith rather than by sight.

PAUL'S DAY

In the days of the Apostle, general history was simply discouraging to spiritual minds. It led men to think of all creation groaning together. Civilization certainly had at that time made advances; civil government had conferred some of its benefits on men; and lately, the strong hand of Rome, however heavily it might press, had averted or abridged some of the evils that afflicted nations.

Still, on the whole, darkness, corruption, and social wrong continued to mark the scene, and there was little to suggest that prolonged effort might gradually work much improvement. Consequently, it must have seemed to most Christian minds that Jesus must soon appear. So Paul addressed that thinking at that particular time by saying, *"Let no man deceive you by any means: for that day shall not come, except there come a falling away first, and that man of sin be revealed, the son of perdition"* (II Thess. 2:3).

Paul knew that the Church then in its infancy, must rather cover the entirety of the world. Regrettably, and because of spiritual declension, the building of the Church throughout the entirety of the world, at least in a measure, has taken longer than it should.

Irrespective, all the predictions made by Paul concerning the end times, as well as Christ in Matthew Chapter 24, along with the prophecies of Daniel and John in the writing of the Book of Revelation, tells us that the Rapture of the Church must be very, very close. Actually, Israel is the greatest prophetic sign of all. Her becoming a state in 1948 was the beginning of the fulfillment of the end-time prophecies. To fulfill all the predictions of the Prophets of the Old Testament, Israel will play the major part in these coming days, which will extend into the Great Tribulation. Actually, that terrible time which will immediately follow the Rapture, is called by Jeremiah *"the time of Jacob's trouble."* However, the Prophet also said, *"But he shall be saved out of it"* (Jer. 30:7).

Actually, Israel at that dark time, the darkest time she will have ever known, will be saved by the Second Coming of the Lord, when Christ shall come back to this Earth with all the Saints which He had raptured away at least seven years earlier (Rev. Chpt. 19).

If Paul was telling Believers in the Early Church to live a life of expectancy even then, how much more should it apply now!

(21) "WHO SHALL CHANGE OUR VILE BODY, THAT IT MAY BE FASHIONED LIKE UNTO HIS GLORIOUS BODY, ACCORDING TO THE WORKING WHEREBY HE IS ABLE EVEN TO SUBDUE ALL THINGS UNTO HIMSELF."

The Rapture of the Church, i.e., *"the Resurrection,"* for this is what Paul is speaking of, will proclaim the change of the outward form of Believer's mortal bodies, so that we will conform to the character of His Resurrection Body. In other words, even as John said, we will be like Him (I Jn. 3:2).

This present body is described literally as *"the body of lowliness,"* a description calling attention to its weakness and susceptibility to persecution, disease, sinful appetites, and death. At Christ's Coming, however, this earthly, transient appearance will be changed, whether by resurrection of those dead or by the Rapture of the living, and all Believers will be transformed and will receive glorified bodies which will more adequately display our essential character as Children of God and sharers of Divine Life in Christ. This will be accomplished by the same effective operation that will ultimately bring all things in the universe under the authority of Christ.

THE CHANGE

The phrase, *"Who shall change our vile body,"* refers to what is sometimes called the *"out-Resurrection,"* when the Believers' body of humiliation will in a moment be fashioned like unto Christ's body of glory by that Almighty Power which can subdue everything to Himself.

The word *"change"* is the translation of a Greek word which speaks of an expression which is assumed from the outside, which act brings about a change of outward expression. It is the change which will occur in our physical bodies at the rapture of the Church.

These mortal bodies will then become immortal. These bodies which are now dominated by the soul and adjusted to its control, will be changed so as to be dominated by the human spirit, which in turn will be dominated by the Holy Spirit, and adjusted to His control.

Now the life principle is in the blood, then the body then be devoid of blood and will have a new life principle, the Holy Spirit. Whereas now our physical bodies are flesh, blood, and bone, they will then be bodies of flesh and bones only (Lk. 24:39).

Our present bodies, although saved, still contain the sin principle (sin nature) (Rom. 7:17-18). They will then be devoid of such in their new condition (I Cor. 15:51-57).

This change has to do with the body, the house or outer casing in which the person dwells. The individual himself is not changed at glorification, only his body. That is why the particular Greek word was used which denotes an outward change (Wuest).

VILE

The word *"vile"* is the translation of the Greek word rendered *"low estate"* in Luke 1:48, *"humiliation"* in Acts 8:33, and *"made low"* in James 1:10. The root of the word is also found in words meaning *"humble"* and *"humility"* (Phil. 2:8; I Pet. 5:6).

The word *"vile"* presently means *"unclean, filthy, repulsive"*; however, that is not what Paul means here by the use of the word *"vile."*

Our present physical bodies have death in them, and, therefore, sickness and weakness. As stated, the principle of sin, sometimes called the sin nature, dwells in its members. The body has been humiliated by the Fall of Adam. The enswathement of glory (Light) which proceeded out from within the inmost being of Adam before he sinned, and provided a covering of glory for his body, was taken away in the Fall of man. In other words, Adam dwelt in a covering of light before the Fall, which was lost at that dark time. Thus, we now wear clothes.

As well, the mind of Adam, functioning perfectly before the Fall was wrecked by sin. The sense functions operating perfectly before the Fall, became debilitated after he sinned. As such, our present bodies are imperfect mediums through which the regenerated Spirit-filled life of the Believer seeks unsuccessfully to express itself in the fullest measure. The Greek word speaks of the unfitness of our present bodies to fulfill the claims of the spiritual life, which will be rectified at the Rapture (Wuest).

HIS GLORIOUS BODY

The phrase, *"That it may be fashioned like unto His Glorious Body,"* means that the enswathement of Glory which Adam lost at the Fall, will return. Our minds will again function perfectly. Our bodies will be immortal, perfect, free from all the effects of sin that have accumulated in six thousand years of human history.

This new body, this Glorified Body, made like unto that of Christ, will be like His Body not only in substance and nature, but made so that it will be a perfect medium through which our inner spiritual lives can express themselves.

Paul had seen Christ in the Glory, and that Glory had dimmed for him all the glamour and glitter of Earth; it dethroned self and self-righteousness; it effected a radical change in his whole moral being; he ceased to be the center of his own importance and Another, worthy of being so, became the Center of his life — a Divine Person, a Man in the Glory, i.e., *"the Lord Jesus Christ."*

This doesn't mean that the Saints will become gods or be Divine, for such will not be the case. We will still be human. Hence, the change of the body is only an outward change, but there will also be an inner spiritual transformation. All this will be a result of God's Grace, which will complete the benefits of the Atonement. In other words, all that Jesus did at the Atonement are not possible to us yet in totality. It is being made possible, and I speak of the coming Glorified Body, etc.

In the final outcome God will be Lord of all. Nothing will be excluded from His jurisdiction.

As Paul describes here the change that will come in the physical body, he describes the change that will come to the mind in I Corinthians 13:11.

He said, *"When I was a child, I spake as a child, I understood as a child, I thought as a child* (likening our present existence mentally as no more than that of a child)*: but when I became a man, I put away childish things* (meaning that the intelligence level of the Glorified State will be the difference in that of a little child presently and an adult)." As should be understood, that is quite a change!

THE WORKING OF HIS POWER

The phrase, *"According to the working whereby He is able even to subdue all things unto Himself,"* is centered up in the word *"working,"* which is from a Greek word meaning *"power in exercise, energy,"* and is only used of superhuman power.

The word *"subdue"* is the translation of a Greek military term meaning *"to arrange under one's authority,"* as a General arranges his regiments in orderly array before himself.

Thus, it means here, *"to bring all things within His Divine economy, to marshall all things under Himself"* (Wuest).

This of which must be done, can only be done by the Almighty Power of God. To be sure, He definitely can do exactly what He has promised to do. He will change our vile bodies, and will fashion them like unto His Glorious Body.

Even nature itself looks forward to this coming change. The Holy Spirit through Paul said, *"For we know that the whole creation groaneth and travaileth in pain together until now."*

He then said, *"And not only they, but ourselves also, which have the Firstfruits of the Spirit* (the down payment of the Atonement), *even we ourselves groan within ourselves, waiting for the adoption, to wit, the Redemption of our body* (the coming Resurrection)" (Rom. 8:22-23).

Due to the terrible effects of sin which came about at the Fall, nothing works correctly. That means that everything of God's creation is somewhat out of kilter, and brought about by this dread corruption which took place in the Garden of Eden. This means that the Fall was of far greater dimension, far worse, than we can comprehend. Actually, man has really never seen God's original creation, only that which has been marred by sin. The Resurrection will cure most of that, and in fact, is due at any time.

Concerning this, and that it is very close, Peter said, *"Wherefore, beloved, seeing that you look for such things, be diligent that ye may be found of Him in Peace, without spot, and blameless"* (II Pet. 3:14).

"Guide me Oh Thou great Jehovah,
"Pilgrim through this barren land;
"I am weak, but Thou art mighty,
"Hold me with Thy powerful hand.

"Open now the crystal fountain,
"Whence the healing waters flow;
"Let the fire and cloudy pillar
"Lead me all my journey through;

"When I tread the verge of Jordan,
"Bid my anxious fears subside;
"Bear me through the swelling current,
"Land me safe on Canaan's side."

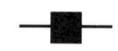

CHAPTER 4

(1) "THEREFORE, MY BRETHREN DEARLY BELOVED AND LONGED FOR, MY JOY AND CROWN, SO STAND FAST IN THE LORD, MY DEARLY BELOVED."

The reference to the Philippians as *"brothers, you whom I love and long for,"* shows the strong feeling of intimacy the Apostle felt toward these Readers. Their description as Paul's *"joy and crown"* echoes his earlier words to another Macedonian Church (I Thess. 2:19).

The Philippians were his present joy as he received favorable reports of their spiritual growth, and their presence with Christ at the Rapture would be his future crown when Christ comes to reward his servants. The *"crown"* mentioned here is the wreath of victory or celebration (Kent).

MY BRETHREN

The phrase, *"Therefore, my Brethren dearly beloved and longed for,"* proclaims the love of this Apostle for the Philippians. Having founded the Church, and at great price (Acts Chpt. 16), these Philippian Saints were indeed his children, i.e., *"converts,"* whether directly or indirectly.

The word *"therefore"* harks back to previous Verses concerning Saints of God living as citizens of a Heavenly Commonwealth, and having a hope of a coming Saviour.

Paul calls them *"dearly beloved."* The expression is one word in the Greek, the word which is used for God's Divine and Self-Sacrificial love. It is plural in number. Paul loves all of these Saints individually, and with a love produced in his heart by the Holy Spirit.

The word *"longed for"* is also plural. It is *"Divinely loved ones and longed-for ones"* (Wuest). *"Longed for"* does not occur elsewhere in the New Testament and indicates the special fellowship which existed between Paul and the Philippians.

As well, the Church at Philippi registered the first converts on European soil. Consequently, this was actually the beginning of what we now refer to as *"Western Civilization,"* although Paul would not have known such at that time. Nevertheless, I think it is obvious as to the extreme significance of all of this, especially as a play out in world events.

The Gospel would eventually go from there to other parts of Greece, and then ultimately to Spain, and finally to Great Britain and other Western European Countries. Ultimately, it would come to the *"New World,"* i.e., *"the Americas."* In fact, the first Pilgrims coming to America did so to escape the tyranny of the Church of England, and that they may worship God as they saw fit. Hence, the birth of the United States demanded the separation of Church and State, and as well the freedom of Religion.

So, the greatness and glory of the present United States with its economic prosperity, its military might, and above all its envied freedom for its people, all had its birth in a Jew by the name of Paul and his obedience to the Lord in taking the Gospel to Europe.

THE LOVE OF PAUL FOR THESE CONVERTS

I think it should be obvious that Paul serves as an excellent example of what the Preacher of the Gospel ought to be as it regards the Saints of God. Such love for these people, which of course was the God kind of love, guarantees that they will never be exploited but always developed. In fact, love cannot exploit, it can only develop.

As is obvious in all of Paul's writings, he was not hesitant to correct when correction was needed, even strongly so, but at the same time, it was always done with love, even as is plainly obvious here.

Unfortunately, there aren't many Preachers who have the love which Paul expresses here. There are a few, but only a few!

First of all, there must be a total dedication to the Lord, a total commitment to His Cause, all referring to being totally sold out to Christ. If this is done, then the love for people and especially the Saints of God will be automatic.

That is one of the reasons that Paul couldn't find a Preacher in Rome (or wherever) to send to Philippi. Even though they were Preachers, and no doubt Paul knew quite a few, they were not completely committed to the Lord. As such, their love for the Brethren would have been weak, if at all. Such an environment breeds exploitation (Phil. 2:19-21).

JOY AND CROWN

The phrase, *"My joy and crown,"* presents the feelings of the Apostle with him regarding it as a high honor to have been the means of founding such a Church. He looked upon it with the same interest with which a Monarch looks upon the diadem which he wears.

Concerning Preachers of the Gospel, and irrespective of the type of Calling they may have, the end result is to be this of which Paul speaks — people saved and then growing in Grace and the knowledge of the Lord. That's what the whole thing is all about.

It's not about money, prestige, place, position, fame, popularity, or anything else of that nature. The Work of God in its totality is strictly about people being saved and then nurtured in the Lord, as we see these Philippians being nurtured.

Some Preachers have great success in getting people saved, while others have great success in developing those who have already come to Christ. Paul was proficient in both, as should be obvious.

If we lose sight of this — souls and their sustenance — this for which Jesus died, then our Ministry is of no more consequence, irrespective as to how large it might be.

A PROBLEM IN THE MODERN CHURCH

Perhaps there are many problems, but I think the greatest one of all is what I refer to as the *"Religion business."* Denominations become top-heavy with religious bureaucracy — Preachers incidentally who for the most part I think, forget their true purpose — souls and their development.

The people become pawns, just something to be used, in other words, incidental! Multimillion dollar Church Buildings become the goal, with money too often as the object. Preachers vie for acceptance by other Preachers. The Gospel becomes a business, with the people only being incidental, almost a necessary evil.

Other things become the *"joy and crown!"*

There is a vast difference between the Sheep and the Shepherds. God help the Shepherds who lead the Sheep wrong!

STAND FAST

The phrase, *"So stand fast in the Lord, my dearly beloved,"* presents another military expression. In the preceding Chapter the Apostle uses the metaphor of running. Here he uses a military expression, *"stand,"* as of a soldier in the midst of battle (Eph. 6:10-18). Regarding their love and labors the Philippians must ever be advancing. As to faith and fidelity, they must stand immoveable.

To stand fast in the Lord in a time of almost universal departure from God is difficult, and also painful, for it necessitates solitude. But all is easy when the heart is set upon Christ seen in Glory.

Communion with Him gives light and certainty; it more than compensates for friendships which must be lost. This life of fidelity to the Word of God and of separation from evil, is displayed by the Holy Spirit in this Epistle. He gives very plainly its example, its principle, its character, and its strength.

IN THE LORD

To *"stand fast,"* which means to stand against all the powers of darkness which come against us and not be moved from our place and position in Christ, can only be done *"in the Lord!"* Those three words are short, but they carry a weight all out of proportion to the brevity of the statement. This is where the rubber meets the road, where the pedal meets the metal, so to speak!

How do we stand fast in the Lord?

As stated, Paul tells us how to do this in Ephesians 6:10-17. (Please see our Commentary on this all-important Chapter.)

To give a brief synopsis here, I would urge upon the Reader that Paul's admonition given to the Philippians extends to us as well. In other words, we are admonished also to *"stand fast in the Lord,"* for the simple reason that the battle is also the same, even as the foe is the same.

It is *"the good fight of Faith,"* as it is always *"the good fight of Faith"* (I Tim. 6:12).

WHAT DO WE MEAN BY FAITH?

When we use the word *"Faith"* as it applies to Christians, almost all think they understand exactly what is meant; however, even though a few definitely do, most don't!

All Faith must always have as its object, the Cross of Christ. This is where Jesus defeated every power of darkness, atoned for all sin, and satisfied the claims and demands of Heavenly Justice. In other words, at the Cross, considering the great price that Jesus paid by the shedding of His Own Precious Blood, the honor and justice of God were completely satisfied. The satisfying of the sin debt atoned for all sin, which as well destroyed Satan's claims on humanity, for his claim has always been made on the basis of sin. But for those who believe (Jn. 3:16), Satan now has no claim, simply because all the sin has been washed and cleansed by the Blood of Jesus.

Consequently, he is a defeated foe, and defeated in every capacity. As well, this includes all demon spirits and fallen Angels. Jesus has literally destroyed the works of the Devil, actually triumphing over him in every respect (Col. 2:15).

The point I'm making is that all of this was done at the Cross and the Resurrection. This means that this great work, which Christ accomplished, is the bedrock, the foundation of Christianity. Actually, the Cross is the very reason that God became man, coming down to this forsaken world. The Cross was not incidental, but the very purpose of Christ, actually the fulfillment of the totality of the Plan of God. Everything centers up on the Cross (I Cor. 1:18). So this means that all Faith must center up on the Cross, which, of course, includes the Resurrection and the Exaltation of Christ (Eph. 2:6). If this is not the object of Faith, the intention of Faith, the anchor of one's Faith, then it is not Faith which God will recognize.

Consequently, whenever the Saint places his Faith in the Finished Work of Christ, the great Atonement, the great Sacrifice, the Holy Spirit will then issue forth all the necessary power that is needed in order that the Child of God may *"stand fast"* (Rom. 8:1-2). There is no Victory outside of one's Faith in what Christ did at the Cross. There is no *"more abundant life"* outside of our Faith anchored in the Cross (Jn. 10:10).

Due to this which Jesus has done, this Finished Work, which actually made it possible for the Holy Spirit to abide within the hearts and lives of all Believers, which has only been done since the Cross (Jn. 14:17), the Spirit demands that the Faith of the Child of God always rest in this which Christ has accomplished on our behalf. In reality, when *"Faith"* is mentioned in the Bible, whether in the form of *"Believe"* or *"Believing,"* it must always have as its object the Cross, or it is Faith which God will not recognize.

Only in this manner can the Believer stand and *"stand fast."*

CROWNS AS SPOKEN OF BY PAUL, PETER, JAMES, AND JOHN

Inasmuch as Paul mentioned *"crowns"* several times, along with mention made by other of the Apostles, perhaps a short study on this word would be beneficial to the Bible student.

It surprises one to see how much of the life and speech expressions of the First Century are reflected in the statements found in the Greek Manuscripts of the New Testament. The writers under the guidance of the Holy Spirit (I Cor. 2:13) constantly draw from contemporary life as they seek to bring to man the message of God.

To understand something of First Century life and its use of words, is to have a clearer understanding of the message they bring. That is why a knowledge of the Greek language, and a study of the early secular Manuscripts, is of great help in the explanation of the New Testament.

The one English word *"crown"* is used to translate two Greek words, each of which speaks of a different kind of crown, both of them being in common use in the First Century in connection with the daily life of the people. To understand their difference and significance as they are related to the local customs, is to come into a fuller, clearer appreciation of those passages in the New Testament which contained them.

STEPHANOS

One of the Greek words for crown is *"stephanos."* It was the crown given to the victor in the Greek athletic games, the runner who first crossed the goal, the athlete who hurled the discus farthest, the wrestler who pinned his opponent to the mat. It was given to the servant of the State whose work deserved to be honored.

It was worn at marriage feasts. A *"Stephanos"* was, therefore, a symbol of victory, of deserved honor, and of festal gladness. The crown was woven of oak leaves, of ivy, of parsley, of myrtle, of olive, of violets, or of roses.

The inscriptions give us concrete instances of its use. The Emperor Claudius acknowledges the golden *"Stephanos"* sent him by the Worshipful Gymnastic Club of Nomads on the occasion of his victory over the Britons. An inscription of A.D. 138-161 may refer to this club, where *"allowances"* are made to an athlete on account of his *"athletic stephanos."*

The word was used in the sense of a reward other than a crown. An inscription of

2 B.C., speaks of Peteuris, who promises a reward (stephanos) of five talents of copper, on account of some special service. The verb form of the noun *"stephanos"* is found in the Manuscript of 257 B.C., in which a certain Hierokles writes to Zemon regarding a boy who is Zemon's nominee in the athletic games, *"I hope that you will be crowned* (i.e., be victorious) *through him."*

To us today, a crown is just a crown. The English word usually brings to our minds the picture of a large golden crown set with jewels, such as is or was worn by the crowned heads of Europe. But to impose this conception upon the Passages in the New Testament where the word *"stephanos"* is found, is to misconstrue and at the same time lose some precious truth.

But when the First Century reader found that word in the Holy Scriptures, he recognized it as a word familiar to him by reason of its association in the ordinary secular life by which he was always surrounded. Thus, he understood the full implication of this secular word brought over into the Sacred Text of the new Faith that was sweeping the Roman Empire. And this ability to understand a word like this was not confined merely to the native Greek speaking population of the Empire, for the Roman world was as to is culture, predominantly Grecian. The Greek language was the international language. There was more Greek spoken actually than Latin.

DIADEMA

The other word translated *"crown"* is *"diadema,"* from which we get our word *"diadem."* This Greek word is derived from a verb meaning *"to bind around."* It referred to a blue band of ribbon marked with white which the Persian kings used to bind on a turban or a tiara. It was the kingly ornament for the head, and signified royalty.

A *"stephanos"* is, therefore, a victor's crown, whereas a *"diadema"* is a royal crown. We will study those passages in which each one is found.

STEPHANOS, A REWARD FOR SERVICE

Paul in I Corinthians 9:24-27 is speaking of Christian service in a context that takes in the entire Chapter. In Verse 24, he is using the footraces held in the Greek athletic games as an illustration of the activity of a Christian in his work for the Lord. He uses the same illustration borrowed from contemporary life in Philippians 3:7-14, where he speaks, not of Christian service but of progress in the living of a Christlike life.

He says that the Greek athletes run a race in order to obtain a corruptible *"stephanos* (crown)"* of oak leaves that soon will wither and fade. But he speaks of a *"stephanos"* which a Christian receives as a reward for his services, as an incorruptible crown. Then he tells us that he buffets his body and makes it his slave in order that after preaching to others he might not be a castaway.

The word *"castaway"* comes from a Greek word which means, *"to be put to the test and after being tested, to be rejected because of not meeting that test."* Paul draws this word from the Greek games where it was a technical expression meaning *"to disqualify a runner from competing for the 'stephanos' because he broke the training rules."*

If Paul did not practice what he preached, he would be disqualified, not allowed to compete for the crown given to those who rendered Christian service.

The First Century reader, having the historical background of the Greek games in his mind, would interpret this Passage correctly. He would understand that Paul is not speaking necessarily of his eternal Salvation here, for rewards are in view, and Salvation is a gift. The same can be said of Philippians 3:7-14, where Sanctification is referred to, not Justification. It is the victor's crown won through Christian service which Paul wants to win.

HIS CROWN

In Philippians 4:1, the Verse of our study, Paul calls the Philippian Saints *"his crown."* As oak leaves were woven together to form a *"stephanos* (crown),"* a chaplet or garland of victory of civic worth, so Paul says in effect, *"You Philippians are woven together into my crown of victory, an eternal symbol of my victory over the hosts of Satan at Philippi, and my reward for service in that place."*

He speaks of the Thessalonian Saints whom he also won to the Lord as his *"stephanos"* of rejoicing. He will wear a victor's crown at the coming of the Lord Jesus for the Saints, his converts composing a more beautiful festal garland than ever graced the brow of a Greek athlete, even though that *"stephanos"* was made of roses or violets (I Thess. 2:19).

THE CROWN OF RIGHTEOUSNESS

In II Timothy 4:8 we have the Crown of Righteousness. The imagery is again that of the Greek games.

"I have fought" not *"a good fight,"* but *"the good fight."* The indefinite article would indicate egotism on the part of the Apostle. The definite article (the) is used in the Greek, pointing to *the* good fight which each Christian is expected to wage.

The picture here is taken from the Greek stadium where a huge crowd of spectators is keenly watching two Greek athletes as they engage perhaps in a wrestling contest. Here is not a race, but a tremendous contest of strength competing with strength. The words *"fought"* and *"fight"* come from the same Greek root. We get our word *"agony"* from this word.

It refers to a contest in which the participants exert their strength to the point of agony.

What for?

For a *"stephanos"* of oak leaves that will shortly fade away, and for the plaudits of a fickle crowd that may the next moment turn thumbs down. How this should convict us of laziness, indolence, and laxness in Christian service.

The word *"good"* is from the Greek word meaning *"goodness as seen from the outside by a spectator,"* in contrast to another word which speaks of internal intrinsic goodness.

The Greek spectators would say, *"That was a beautiful display of skill and strength."* Paul says that the Christian life as it is related to the antagonism of the powers of evil, should display a beauty of skill and spiritual strength that will glorify the Lord Jesus. Such a battle he waged.

Notice in passing, if you will, the composition of that word, *"antagonism,"* from our word *"agony,"* and *"anti"* which comes from the Greek, meaning *"against."* That is, an antagonist is one who fights against one to the point of agony.

THE FINISHING OF THE COURSE

Paul also says, *"I have finished my course."*

The word *"course"* is from the Greek word meaning *"a racecourse,"* used here in connection with footraces. It is the *"cinder-path"* of college athletic fields. The word *"finished"* means *"to come to the end."* It is in the perfect tense in the Greek which speaks of a past completed action with present existing results.

Paul, awaiting martyrdom in Rome, looks back upon his life as a runner who, having won his race, is resting at the goal and is looking back down the cinder-path over which he sped to victory, and sees the race as over, and its result, the *"stephanos (crown)"* of Righteousness awaiting him.

The crowds leave the Greek Stadium after the games are over, and the victors crowned with a garland of oak-leaves, are carried on the shoulders of rejoicing friends. So someday, the Saints will leave the Stadium of this life's battles, and in Heaven will rejoice with each other over the crowns they have won through the wonderful grace of God.

THE CROWN OF LIFE

"Blessed is the man that endureth temptation: for when he is tried, he shall receive the crown of life, which the Lord hath promised to them that love Him" (James 1:12).

In this Verse as given by James we have the *"stephanos (crown)"* of life.

"Blessed" is literally in this context, *"spiritually prosperous."*

"Temptation" is from a Greek word which has two meanings, to be used according to the context in which the word may be found. It means either *"to put one to a test"* as in Genesis 22:1 where God tested Abraham, that is, tested him to see whether he would be obedient in relation to the request that he sacrifice his son. Or it can mean *"to solicit one to do evil,"* as in our text in James. Of course, God never solicits one or tempts one to do evil, that coming only from Satan; however, God will definitely test someone in respect to their obedience, even as we have given the example of Abraham.

The word *"endureth"* is literally *"to remain under,"* and must be interpreted in its context, namely, the word *"tried."*

The word *"tried"* is from a technical Greek expression found in an early Manuscript, where it referred to the action of an examining board putting its approval upon those who had successfully passed the examinations for the degree of Doctor of Medicine. The verb means *"to test for the purpose of approving."* The noun, *"the approved character of the one who has successfully met the test."*

ENDURING TEMPTATION

Here is a Child of God who has been solicited by Satan to do evil. He has successfully met the test by refusing to sin. That is what James means by *"enduring temptation."* The *"stephanos* (crown) *of the life"* is his reward.

This is not eternal life. He has that already, or he could not have overcome temptation. Furthermore, this is a reward given in recognition of what the Believer has done, whereas Salvation is a free gift given in view of what Christ has done on the Cross. The article in the Greek before *"life,"* (the) points to a particular kind of life, the eternal life which is in Christ Jesus which enabled the Believer to overcome temptation. Thus, this crown is a *"stephanos"* given in recognition of the Believer's victory over sin, that victory having been procured by means of the eternal life he has in Christ, and which energizes his being.

A CROWN OF GLORY

"And when the Chief Shepherd shall appear, you shall receive a Crown of Glory that fadeth not away" (I Pet. 5:4).

We come here to Peter's use of *"stephanos"* in his First Epistle, and have another illustration of how Greek culture had stamped itself upon the life of the Roman world.

Peter knew Greek, but he had not lived in a Greek city such as Tarsus, the home of the Apostle Paul. He was not schooled in Greek learning as was Paul. Yet this fisherman, reared in a Jewish environment, engaged in the fishing trade around the Sea of Galilee, was conversant enough with the life about and beyond his little world, that he used a typical illustration from a phase of First Century life of which he as a Jew was not a part.

The same can be said of John, and also of James the brother of our Lord, for they also use the Greek word for Crown *"stephanos."*

NOTES

THE CROWN OF LIFE

"Fear none of those things which thou shall suffer: behold the Devil shall cast some of you into prison, that ye may be tried: and ye shall have tribulation ten days: be thou faithful unto death, and I will give thee a Crown of Life" (Rev. 2:10).

John, writing from the Island of Patmos in the Aegean Sea to the Church at Smyrna, a city which was in a region where Greek culture predominated, exhorts the Christians there who were undergoing severe persecutions, *"be thou faithful unto death, and I will give thee the stephanos* (crown) *of Life."*

The word *"unto"* does not mean *"until."* The same Greek word is used in Philippians 2:8, where our Lord was obedient *"up to the point"* or *"to the extent"* of death.

This Smyrna Church represents the *"Martyr Period"* of Church history, from A.D. 100 to about A.D. 316 when some ten bloody persecutions, some think, were hurled at the Church by Rome. This is the victor's crown given to those who are martyrs to the Faith once for all delivered to the Saints.

The word *"martyr"* comes from the Greek word meaning *"to bear witness to."* These Christians bore witness to the Christian Faith by death (Rev. 2:10). It is touching to know that the name of the first recorded Christian martyr was Stephen, which comes from *"stephanos."*

THE LOSS OF THE CROWN

"Behold, I come quickly: hold that fast which thou hast, that no man take thy crown" (Rev. 3:11).

The Philadelphian Church Saints are exhorted to hold fast the little spiritual strength which they have, lest they lose their *"stephanos,"* namely, their victor's crown, a reward for service. The Elders (Rev. 4:4, 10) representing the Redeemed in Heaven, are seen, each with a golden *"stephanos* (crown)*"* on their heads. Sometimes a *"stephanos"* of gold, made in the form of an oak leaf garland for instance, was used in the First Century. We saw that in the case of the golden stephanos given to the Emperor Claudius. Here the glorified Saints wear such a victor's crown, but not for long, for, overcome with gratitude, they cast their victor's crowns at the feet of the One who through His victory at Calvary gave them the Grace to overcome in their own lives.

VARIOUS CROWNS

There are two riders on white horses in the Book of Revelation, one found in Chapter 6, Verse 2, who is the Antichrist, and the other found in Chapter 19, Verse 11, Who is Jesus Christ.

To the Antichrist there is given a *"stephanos,"* the victor's crown, but of course, this has nothing to do with a righteous crown but rather the very opposite. He goes forth conquering and to conquer.

The Demon locusts of Revelation 9:7 have victor's crowns on their heads, but again, these are not righteous crowns by any means.

The woman clothed with the Sun, representing Israel, has a *"stephanos"* made of stars, indicative of Israel's final victory over Satan and the Antichrist, which victory will be brought about by Jesus Christ when He comes to Israel's Rescue, which is the Second Coming (Rev. Chpt. 19).

Then in Revelation 14:14, we have the Lord Jesus with a victor's crown on His Head, coming in His Second Advent to conquer the Antichrist and set up His Kingdom.

THE VICTOR'S CROWN

"And if a man also strive for masteries, yet is he not crowned, except he strive lawfully" (II Tim. 2:5).

In this Verse, the words *"strive for masteries"* is from a word which comes into our language in the word *"athlete."* It means *"to exert one's self in a contest as an athlete, for a prize or reward."*

"Is crowned" is from our word *"stephanos," "is crowned with a victor's crown."*

The same verb is used in Hebrews 2:7, 9, where we see the Son of Man, made for a short time lower than the Angels, now in His Glorified State, crowned with a garland of victory.

What shall we say when we come to the *"stephanos"* of thorns which the soldiers placed on the Head of our Lord (Mat. 27:29; Mk. 15:17; Jn. 19:2, 5)? While there is an instance where the word *"stephanos"* is used to signify royalty, as in *"the crown-tax,"* yet its predominant usage was that of a victor's crown.

NOTES

The other word *"diadema"* which refers to a royal crown, could hardly be used here, for it referred to a narrow ribbon-like band worn around the head. The crown of thorns was of interwoven material like the *"stephanos"* of oak leaves or ivy, and this word was probably chosen for that reason. But what the soldiers meant in mockery for a royal crown, became for our Lord in the hour of seeming defeat, the victor's crown, for Paul could write (I Cor. 15:55) *"Where, O death is your victory? Where, O death is your sting?"*

A SURE VICTORY

The victor's crown was placed on His brow before the victory was complete, in other words, before He died on the Cross. This meant that so sure was the victory of the Cross, that this could be done.

As well, so sure is the victory procured at the Cross for you and for me who are trusting in the Savior's Precious Blood poured out at Calvary as the God-appointed substitutionary Atonement for sin.

So, when we read in the Gospels of the crown of thorns placed on Jesus' brow, even though the soldiers meant it for mockery, the Holy Spirit allowed it to be done with an entirely different meaning in mind. The Holy Spirit meant it as a *"Victor's Crown,"* signifying what the Cross would do respecting the Redemption of lost humanity, and the defeat of all the powers of darkness.

For the simple reason that we were in Christ when He died on the Cross, in essence, that Crown which He wore, was our crown, signifying total and complete victory in our hearts and lives, all because of what He did at the Cross. We must shout, *"Hallelujah!"* We must shout, *"Praise the Lord!"* We must shout, *"Glory to God!"*

That crown which He wore at that time, was my crown, because He did it all for me. Because I wear the *"Victor's Crown,"* due to what Jesus did there, I as well have the *"Victor's shout!"*

BACK TO THE *"DIADEMA,"* THE ROYAL CROWN

This was the kingly ornament or crown worn by kings or heads of State.

Sometimes more than one *"diadema"* was worn at the same time. When Ptolemy, king of Egypt entered Antioch in triumph, he set two crowns on his head, the *"diadema"* showing his sovereignty over Asia, and the *"diadema"* speaking of his kingly authority over Egypt.

Revelation 12:3 portrays Satan as having seven *"diadema (crowns)"* on his head, showing his close connection with the empires which persecuted Israel. Those Empires were and are *"Egypt, Assyria, Babylon, Greece and Rome."* Two more are yet to come, which are *"ten nations which will arise shortly and will persecute Israel, and then the Antichrist, who will control many of the nations of the world."* The latter two are directly ahead of us, with the ten nations possibly being formed for this purpose, at this very moment. This tells us that we are very close to the Rapture.

These are royal crowns worn by Satan, indicating imperial authority over the Revived (Revised) Roman Empire, which is in the making now. And yet, in Revelation 13:1, we see the Antichrist having ten kingly crowns upon his head, showing his sovereignty over the ten kings or nations we have just mentioned (Rev. 17:12-13).

The Lord Jesus (Rev. 19:12), when He comes to bring in the Messianic Kingdom which will be worldwide will wear many Crowns. To one whose conception of a crown is limited to that of a large golden crown studded with jewels, this statement is unintelligible. But when one understands that these Crowns consist of narrow bands of ribbon encircling the forehead, one can appreciate the description.

These *"diadema"* represent all the kingdoms of the world over which the Lord Jesus will rule as supreme Sovereign when He comes back. He will truly be King of kings and Lord of lords.

(The article on crowns was devised from the Greek Scholar, Kenneth Wuest.)

(2) "I BESEECH EUODIAS, AND BESEECH SYNTYCHE, THAT THEY BE OF THE SAME MIND IN THE LORD."

The Apostle turns from his general exhortation to an application of it.

Two women, Euodias and Syntyche, are instructed to bring their attitudes into harmony.

Paul does not indicate which one was in the wrong but knows that if the attitude of each would be formed *"in the Lord,"* the disharmony would vanish.

The manner in which he makes his statement indicates that the rift between them had become quite severe. Paul's method of handling the problem suggests that it was not a doctrinal issue, but a clash of personalities.

TWO WOMEN OF PROMINENCE

The phrase, *"I beseech Euodias, and beseech Syntyche,"* should have been translated *"Euodia,"* because *"Euodias"* is a man's name. Her name means *"prosperous journey."*

This woman in modern language could be spoken of as *"one who has arrived."* Actually both were of prominence, with leadership capabilities, even as their names indicate.

"Syntyche" means *"pleasant acquaintance, happy person."* Her name indicates that she was one of those pleasant people who are what we call today *"good mixers,"* one of these valuable people in the local Church who is the first to greet strangers and who makes everybody feel welcome and at home.

BESEECH

The Greek order of words in the original text is *"Euodia I beseech, and Syntyche I beseech."* The word *"beseech"* in the Greek is a strong word. It means *"I exhort, I beg, please."*

Paul sends an individual message to each. Observe the humility and lovingkindness of the great Apostle when he writes from his prison in Rome to these two women and says *"please"* to them, and begs them to become reconciled.

He could have used his Apostolic authority had he chosen to do so. Instead, in meekness and humility he beseeches. He begs them to be of the same mind in the Lord.

However, this was no abrupt request. Paul had prepared these women for this exhortation in Philippians 1:27-30 where he exhorts the Philippian Saints to stand fast in one spirit, and in Philippians 2:1-4, where he exhorts them all in lowliness of mind to esteem others better than themselves, and to be likeminded, in Philippians 2:5-8, where he brings to their attention the humility of the Lord Jesus, of which we will say more momentarily, and in Philippians 2:19-30 where he speaks of the selflessness of both Timothy and Epaphroditus (Wuest).

The manner which Paul used, and which was his manner constantly, is really the only manner that has a potential for any type of positive results. When we start ordering people to do certain things, the results almost always are not positive. If people cannot be reached with kindness, they generally cannot be reached. As well, when leaders take the position that they are to be obeyed because they are leaders, in the mind of God, they have just lost their position of leadership, that is if they ever had such a position to begin with. Unfortunately, the Church has taken on so many of the ways of the world, that we little know anymore, the true ways of God. In other words, we have strayed so far from the Word of God, which tells us how to do things, rather adopting our own methods, which again are the ways of the world, that we little do things God's way.

For instance, regarding one large Pentecostal Denomination of which I am well acquainted, at any given time they have any number of suits (legal action) going on against Churches, etc. That is totally unscriptural (I Cor. 6:1-8). While legal action is permissible as it regards the world, and even the dealings of Christians with the world, if such is absolutely necessary, it is not permissible between Christians.

However, this entire scenario has come about because improper, unscriptural Church government has been enjoined, with the leaven steadily getting worse.

The Lord's way is always the best way, and by far!

THE SAME MIND IN THE LORD

The phrase, *"That they be of the same mind in the Lord,"* harks back to Philippians 2:5 where the Apostle wrote, *"Let this mind be in you, which was also in Christ Jesus."* In fact, this little situation between Euodia and Syntyche, plus some other particulars in the Church at Philippi, seems to inspire one of, if not the greatest, Christological Passages in the New Testament. In Philippians 2:3-4, the Apostle is exhorting humility among Believers, and then in Philippians 2:5-8, he presents our blessed Lord as the example. Inasmuch as this is so very important as it regards the Believer, I think it would be proper for us to look into these Passages concerning Christ to a greater extent, even though we have dealt with them in our Commentary on that Chapter. Humility of life is that of which these Verses speak, and is, therefore, the key which will unlock the treasures of these great statements given by Paul.

THE MIND OF CHRIST

The words *"Let this mind be in you which was also in Christ Jesus,"* could be variously translated: *"Be thinking this in yourselves which was also in Christ Jesus. Be having this mind in you which was also in Christ Jesus. Reflect in your own mind that which was also in Christ Jesus. Let the same purpose inspire you as was in Christ Jesus."*

Putting all these together, we have what the Apostle means. He describes the Mind of Christ in Philippians 2:5-8, presenting the controlling factor, humility, that made His mind what it was.

FORM

The phrase, *"Who (speaking of Jesus), being in the form of God,"* presents the word *"form"* which comes from a Greek word which refers to the outward expression one gives of his inner being. It is used here as one would use it in the sentence, *"The tennis player's form was excellent."*

We mean that the expression he gave in action of his ability to play tennis was excellent. The word carries no idea of physical form or shape. Here the word refers to that expression of the Glory and Majesty of His Deity which our Lord portrayed to the Angels before He came to Earth in His Incarnation. By that statement we mean that this expression was through a spiritual medium, discernible only to the spiritual faculties of the Angels.

The same Greek word is found in Matthew 17:2 with a preposition prefixed which when in composition signifies a change. It is translated there, *"transfigured,"* but the sentence could be rendered, *"His mode of expression was changed before them."* That is, our Lord's usual mode of expression in His days of humiliation on Earth was that of a servant (bond slave), which is the same word translated *"servant"* in Romans 1:1.

That was an expression which came from His innermost Being as the One Who *"came not to be ministered unto but to minister."* But now for a moment, at the Transfiguration, the mode of His expression was changed.

He gave expression to the essence of Deity in which He is a co-participant with God the Father and God the Holy Spirit. The splendor and majesty of His Deity shone through the clay walls of His humanity in the transfiguration, and by means of a medium discernible to the physical eyes of the spectators.

However, the Philippian Passage, which we are now studying, speaks of an expression of glory not discernible to our physical vision, but only to the spiritual capacities of Angels. However, this expression of Glory which the Angels saw, will be discernible to we Saints when we receive our Glorified Bodies, for then we will be spiritual intelligences with spiritual capacities like the Angels.

This is what John had in mind when he wrote (I Jn. 3:2), *"When He shall appear, we shall be like Him, for we shall see Him just as He is."* But in the meanwhile, it is (I Pet. 1:8), *"Of whom not* (yet) *having had a glimpse, yet Whom we love."*

Thus, our Lord in His preincarnate state manifested the Glory of His Deity to the Holy Angels in an outward mode of expression discernible only to their spiritual intelligences. This is what is meant by the phrase, *"Being in the form of God."*

BEING

The word *"being"* is not the usual word of *"being"* in the Greek, but is from a word which refers to a previous condition which is protracted into the present. That is, our Lord's being in the Form of God was true of Him before He became Man and was true of Him at the time of the writing of this Epistle, which tells us that in taking upon Himself humanity with its limitations yet without its sin, He lost nothing of His intrinsic Deity, its attributes or its prerogatives.

We could translate, *"Who subsisting, being constitutionally by nature, in that mode of existence in which he gave outward expression of the essence of His Deity."*

ROBBERY

The word *"thought"* in the original, refers to a judgment based upon facts.

The word *"robbery"* is from a Greek word which has two meanings:
1. *"A thing unlawfully seized."*
2. *"A prize or treasure to be retained at all hazards."*

Knowing that the Holy Spirit gave Paul the word *"robbery"* to be used here in this context, the meaning is as follows:

First of all, the Lord would not do anything unlawfully. So the first meaning does not apply to Christ.

As well, the second meaning does not apply to Christ, for if He had asserted His rights to the expression of Deity, He would be claiming this as His rightful prerogative. But to assert one's rights does not partake of humility.

Therefore, if He did not consider this expression of His Deity a prize or treasure to be retained at all hazards, He would be showing a willingness to relinquish His Divine rights, which is the essence of humility. Paul is setting forth our Lord as an example of humility. Therefore, our Lord is not guilty of *"robbery"* in any capacity.

Perhaps we could say it better in the following manner:

That is, when He was marked out as the Lamb for Sacrifice in the eternal ages before the universe was created (I Pet. 1:20), which at that time He exercised all His Divine expression of Glory of His Deity, He did not then consider that equality with God was such a treasure that its exercise would keep Him from setting aside that activity for the time being, so as to change His mode of expression from that of the Glory of Deity to the humiliation of Deity Incarnate in humanity. It was the King of Glory willing to step down to the place of a bond slave.

THE EMPTYING OF SELF

The phrase, *"He made Himself of no reputation,"* in the Greek means either *"to empty"* or *"to make void."*

Of what did He empty Himself?
What did He make void?

He emptied Himself of self-will, which is the essence of humility. He made self void, which again is the essence of humility. He set self-will aside when He set His legitimate desires aside.

His rightful natural desire as Deity was to be glorified, to give expression of His Glory to the Angels. But to go to the Cross, He had to set that desire aside. Setting that desire aside, He set self-will aside, He emptied Himself of self-will, He made self void. The very Person Who had the right to assert self, which is the prerogative of Deity alone, He laid aside. Here is the supreme example of the self-emptied life.

THE CROSS, SIN, AND SELF

Jesus died on the Cross to save humanity from sin and self. The first part is understandable to most who serve the Lord, but Salvation from *"self"* is not too very well understood.

This is at least one of the reasons that the Cross is an absolute imperative for all Believers. It is why Jesus said that we must deny self, taking up the Cross daily to follow Him (Lk. 9:23).

As horrible as sin is, it was handled readily at the Cross, and is handled in the same manner in the life of the Believer. However, there is still another problem: That problem is *"self,"* which is where the struggle commences with the Believer after coming to Christ. Sin finds its expression in unsanctified self.

The Believer does not become selfless after coming to Christ. Actually, a person is a *"self,"* and to continue to be a person one has to continue to be a *"self."* What we actually are saying about Christ and the individual Christian is:

When we speak of Christ emptying Himself of Self, we are not meaning that He ceased to be a Person, but rather of all personal desires, etc. In other words, He totally hid Himself, i.e., *"self,"* in the Will of the Father. Likewise, we as Believers are to totally hide our *"selves"* into Christ (Gal. 2:20).

Actually, this is done at conversion when the sinner accepts Christ. This is what Paul was speaking about in Romans 6:3-5, when he spoke of the believing sinner being baptized into Christ's Death. Consequently, He constantly uses the phrase *"In Christ,"* describing Salvation, or one of its derivatives (Rom. 8:1).

However, even though *"self"* was placed totally into Christ at conversion, which is accomplished by the believing sinner evidencing Faith in Christ, which is actually demanded if one is to be saved (Jn. 3:16), self seemingly has a way of slipping its moorings so to speak, which means that we attempt to function in a sense outside of Christ, one might say *"on our own."* Consequently, this is where the battle between self (the flesh) and the Holy Spirit commences. It is a struggle which will remain with the Believer until he dies, or the Trump sounds. As the Cross is the only remedy for sin, it is also the only remedy for *"self."*

SUBSTITUTION AND THE REPRESENTATIVE MAN

As our Substitute, Jesus died *for* us. As our Representative Man, Jesus died *as* us.

Him serving as our Substitute took care of the sin question. Him dying as our Representative Man addressed the *"self"* question. As stated, He died to save us from sin and self.

The sinner only has to believe in Christ and what He did at the Cross in order to be saved, even though he understands very little about what he believes. Unfortunately, most Christians have no more knowledge about the Cross than that which we have just stated. In other words, they believed in Christ when they were saved, knowing that He died for them, and that's about the extent of their understanding of the Cross. Most have absolutely no knowledge as to how the Cross affects their continued life and living before the Lord.

The Truth is, the Believer must maintain continued Faith in the Cross on a daily basis, even as Jesus stated, in order for *"self"* to properly maintain victory in Christ (Lk. 9:23-24). Just as one had to believe in what Jesus did at the Cross to be saved, likewise one has to continue to believe in what Jesus did at the Cross in order to be Sanctified. Even then, it is a growth process.

As we have stated, Jesus emptied Himself of His own personal desires, making such totally subject to the Father. He did this even unto *"the death of the Cross,"* which Paul will say in Philippians 2:8. With Jesus as our example, we are to follow suit, in placing ourself, which refers to our passions, desires, and feelings, totally into Christ.

In effect, victory over sin is a one-time affair. This happens when we are saved. All sin is washed and cleansed. That doesn't mean we cannot sin again, but it does mean the debt of sin has been totally cleared from the believing sinner.

With *"self"* it is somewhat different. The sanctification of self, for that's what we are talking about, is an ongoing, daily affair, which as we have stated, will never end, at least until we die or the Lord comes. Whereas the sin question was settled once and for all, the self question is a daily affair, hence, Jesus demanding that we take up the Cross *"daily"* (Lk. 9:23).

VICTORY

As we live this Christian life, we will sooner or later come to the place that we understand that *"self"* is actually our real problem, which is probably the greater subject of the entirety of the Epistle of Paul to the Philippians. Sin occurs when self is not properly in Christ. And if self stays in that position very long, outside of Christ one might say, sin will then begin to dominate us (Rom. 6:14). It is all because of unsanctified self. Unfortunately, we often attempt to solve our problem by making self bigger and greater, which only tends to have the opposite effect. In other words, the more that self is involved in trying to overcome sin, the worse that sin gets. If one can find victory over self, then one has victory over sin.

HOW CAN ONE HAVE VICTORY OVER SELF?

This is where the great conflict is, where we fight the *"good fight of Faith."*

Self can only be brought under control by the work and administration of the Holy Spirit, which Paul graphically outlines in Romans Chapter 8.

It is literally impossible for *"self"* to sanctify *"self."* It just cannot be done! But yet, this is where many Believers run aground. They cover self with spiritual things, which makes them think their effort is legitimate, but it always fails. This has to be a work totally and completely of and by the Holy Spirit.

Let's see how He works.

The Spirit of God demands that we as Christians know and understand that all of our victory, and in every capacity, comes strictly through and by the Cross of Christ. This means that every single thing we receive from the Lord, comes through the Cross, and I mean everything (I Cor. 2:2). The Believer is to understand that totally, believe that totally, anchor his Faith in that totally, and never move his Faith from that great principle. To the unsaved world, such is foolishness, but to we who are saved, it is the *"Power of God"* (I Cor. 1:18).

Understanding this, we are to place our Faith in the Cross entirely. Not only must it be placed there, but in effect, our Faith must be renewed even on a daily basis as it regards the Cross. Again, this is what Jesus said in Luke 9:23. The renewal of Faith even on a daily basis is required, simply because self is a continuing, ongoing situation, which is obvious, because that's what we are — a self. But the secret is, that this self be in Christ, and more particularly, the Christ of the Cross. This is absolutely essential! It is not merely that self is in Christ, but is in the crucified Christ, which was done on our behalf, totally for us.

Concerning the *"daily"* situation, this means that the victory we possessed yesterday, is not necessarily the victory we have today. While we certainly can have victory each and every day, which is the ideal, and which the Holy Spirit intends, it can only be done as we understand the Cross on a daily basis, literally placing ourself there by Faith each and every day. This is the only remedy for self.

When we do this, the Holy Spirit will then perform the work within our hearts and lives regarding self which we so desperately need. Now don't misunderstand:

The Holy Spirit is involved in every single thing that we do as it regards the Lord. In other words, our understanding of the Cross is supplied by the Holy Spirit. As well, our Faith in that great Finished Work of Christ, is also a work of the Holy Spirit, as He makes the Word of God real to our hearts and lives in this respect, and in fact, in every respect (Rom. 6:3-5).

When we do this, and I speak of exercising Faith in the Cross of Christ on a daily basis, the Holy Spirit Who abides within us, exerts His mighty power on our behalf, actually the same power that raised Christ from the dead (Rom. 8:11).

Victory is then won over self, and only by this method. The Holy Spirit will not function in any other manner. He restricts His activities totally and completely to the parameters of the Finished Work of Christ (Rom. 8:2). Whenever the Believer steps outside of those parameters, which we always do when we attempt to sanctify self by self, the Holy Spirit lets us go alone, which means we are doomed to defeat, and not only defeat, but a bad situation steadily getting worse. In fact, that's where most Christians are presently.

HUMILITY

All of this great work which the Holy Spirit does within our hearts and lives, and does on the basis of the Finished Work of Christ, can probably be summed up in one word *"humility."* This is what Paul is explaining in this Second Chapter of Philippians. In fact, the Cross of Christ is the essence of humility. As well, it is impossible for the Believer to know, understand, or to be humble or have humility, outside of the Cross. In fact, one does not have humility so much as one *is* humility.

I think one can say that the *"Cross"* and *"Humility"* are synonymous.

In fact, the world has a type of humility, but it is not based on the Cross, and is quickly exposed for what it really is — a form of pride. True humility is gained only at the Cross of Christ, which probably explains why there is so little of this very precious commodity, so to speak.

Let's continue now with our study as it regards the great self-emptying of Christ, as Paul explains in Philippians 2:3-8.

BOND SLAVE

The word *"took"* as from *"and took upon Him the form of a servant,"* indicates the means by which our Lord set Himself aside by taking upon Himself the form of a servant.

The word *"form"* has the same content of meaning as the word *"form"* in Verse 6, *"which refers to the outward expression one gives of his inner being."*

The word *"servant"* is literally *"bond slave."* He changed His mode of expression from that of the Glory of Deity to that of the humiliation of a bond slave, and in doing that, He set aside His legitimate desire of being glorified, thus setting *"self"* aside, at least as it refers to one's own personal passions and desires, in order to express Himself as a bond slave, receiving instead of the worship of the Angels, the curses and hatred of mankind.

It was the Lord of Glory at the Passover Feast (Jn. Chpt. 13), Who laid aside His outer garments to wrap a towel about Himself and perform the duties of a slave. Those garments speak of the expression of Glory which He had before His preincarnate state (before becoming man). That towel, symbol of His position as a bond slave, speaks of the humility with which He clothed Himself. One had to be laid aside if the other was to be taken up.

While He was kneeling on the floor washing the Disciples' feet, He was still the Lord of Glory although He looked like a bond slave. The travel-stained, weary, homeless, itinerant Preacher of Galilee looked like a man, even like a peasant, yet He was the Lord from Heaven.

When He had finished the duties of a bond slave, He laid aside the towel and took His robes again. When He had finished His Work of Salvation wrought out on Calvary's Cross, He took His robes of Glory again, resuming the expression of the Glory of Deity which He had previously possessed.

IN THE LIKENESS OF MEN

Paul said, as the Holy Spirit inspired his words, *"He* (Jesus) *was made in the likeness of men."* The Greek for *"likeness"* refers to *"that which has been made after the likeness of something else."*

Our Lord's humanity was a real likeness, not a mere phantom. But this likeness did not express the whole of Christ's nature. His mode of manifestation resembled what men are. But His humanity was not all that there was of Him. While He was a man, He was not merely a man, but rather the Son of God manifest in the flesh and nature of man.

FASHION

Paul also said, *"He was found in fashion as a man."* The Greek word for *"fashion"* refers to that which is purely outward and appeals to the senses.

The contrast here is between what He was in Himself, God, and what He appeared to be in the eyes of man. *"Likeness"* states the fact of His real resemblance to men in mode of existence. *"Fashion"* defines the outward mode and expression.

While on Earth, He did not give expression to the glory of His Deity except on the Mount of Transfiguration. He appeared as the Man Christ Jesus to the world around Him. He was in His humiliation.

HE HUMBLED HIMSELF

In this lowly estate, Paul said *"He humbled Himself,"* which speaks of His self-emptying.

Probably the best way to describe humility, at least as it's used in the Greek language, is of a river *"that runs low."* This means that it runs low and slow.

A river which runs high and fast destroys much, if not all, that's in its path. A river that *"runs low and slow,"* hurts no one, but rather provides great service in respect to many things.

The only words that Jesus ever said personally of Himself were, *"I am meek and lowly in heart"* (Mat. 11:28-30).

He became obedient, not to death per se, but obedient to the Father up to the point of death, even the death of the Cross.

THE TRANSLATION

The translation could read: *"This mind be constantly having in you which also was in Christ Jesus, Who has always been and at present still continues to be by nature in that mode of Being in which He gives outward expression of His inmost nature, that of Deity, and Who did not after weighing the facts, consider it a treasure to be clutched and retained at all hazards, to be equal with God* (in the expression of His essential nature), *but emptied Himself, having taken upon Himself that mode of Being in which He gave outward expression of Himself as a bond slave, doing this by entering into a new state of existence, that of likeness to mankind. And being found to be in outward guise as a man, He brought Himself to a lowly place by having become obedient to the extent of death, even the death of the Cross"* (Phil. 2:5-8).

This is the self-emptied life, ever an example and a challenge to us as servants of the One Who came not to be ministered unto but to minister, and give His Life a ransom for many.

(Many of the thoughts on the Incarnation, i.e., *"the self-emptying"* of Christ were derived from Kenneth S. Wuest).

(3) "AND I INTREAT THEE ALSO, TRUE YOKEFELLOW, HELP THOSE WOMEN WHICH LABOURED WITH ME IN THE GOSPEL, WITH CLEMENT ALSO, AND WITH OTHER MY FELLOWLABOURERS, WHOSE NAMES ARE IN THE BOOK OF LIFE."

At this point it seems that Paul seeks to enlist the aid of a third party (yokefellow), whom he challenges to live up to his name and be a *"loyal yokefellow,"* by bringing these women together.

Inasmuch as Euodia and Syntyche had once labored with Paul, they should be able to do so again. Perhaps they had been among the original group of converts at Philippi, for women had been Paul's first hearers there (Acts 16:13-15).

Their Christian labors had been in conjunction with Clement and others of Paul's coworkers.

This *"Clement"* is not otherwise known to us with certainty.

Even though some of these people are not recorded by name in this Letter, Paul knows that their service is not forgotten, for their names are recorded in the Book of Life. The references to the Register in Heaven is of those who are saved (Lk. 10:20; Heb. 12:23; Rev. 3:5; 17:8; 20:12, 15; 21:27; 22:19).

YOKEFELLOW

The phrase, *"And I intreat thee also, true yokefellow,"* does not tell us exactly who he is. The English spelling of the Greek word meaning *"yokefellow,"* is *"Syzygus"*; however, it is not known for certain if that is a proper name. Some even think that Paul might even be referring to Epaphroditus.

The word *"and"* which begins this Third Verse, is a translation of a Greek word which assumes the granting of the request just made (vs. 2), and pursues the matter further. Thus, Paul does suggest to these women his confidence in their willingness to comply with his request.

The word *"entreat"* is from a word that implies a request that has back of it the authority of the Apostle. When dealing with these two Saints who were out of fellowship with each other because of some difference, which as well insinuates that because of this, they were also out of fellowship with their Lord, Paul uses a very tender word, pleading with them in all humility, for one must deal very carefully with a Saint out of fellowship with his Lord.

Witness the *"You which are spiritual restore such"* of Galatians 6:1. It requires all the tact, love, and gentleness of a Spirit-filled Saint to deal with such as Euodia and Syntyche.

But when Paul makes a request of the *"true yokefellow,"* he uses his authority, for *"true yokefellow,"* in fellowship with the Lord, is like an obedient soldier who expects just such orders given with a military curtness, and is willing to snap right into the action demanded and obey the order.

TRUE YOKEFELLOW

This man designated by the Apostle as *"true yokefellow,"* was a particular associate of Paul in the labor of the Gospel. The word *"true"* refers to that which is true in the sense of genuine as contrasted to that which is counterfeit. He was *"all wool and a yard wide,"* so to speak!

The word *"yokefellow"* is made up of a word referring to the yoke or crossbar tied to the end of a pole and having collars or loops at each end by which two oxen were put to the plough, and a preposition meaning *"with."*

It was a practice among these First Century Greeks at their Christian Baptism, to discard their pagan name, and be given a new name descriptive of their new characters as molded by their new Lord and Master, the Lord Jesus Christ.

This was not so in the case of *"Diotrephes"* of John's Third Letter, whose name means *"nourished by Zeus."* Zeus was the principal god of the Greeks. This probably indicates that the man never was actually saved.

NOTES

But *"Syzygus,"* for that is the English spelling of our Greek word meaning *"yokefellow,"* was truly born from above, as his character and name indicated.

His name referred to one who pulled well in double harness. How we need such today in our Churches. What troublemakers the *"diotrephes"* kind are, and how helpful are those like *"Syzygus."*

To this man Paul appealed, enlisting his aid in helping these women make up their differences. He could not have appealed to a better one, for Syzygus knew how to pull well in harness with someone else, and these women evidently did not.

STRIFE BETWEEN CHRISTIANS

What the difference was between these two ladies we do not know. Actually, what the difference was really does not matter. Their attitude in respect to whatever it was, and more particularly toward each other, is really what matters, and which caused the problem then, and which continues to cause problems presently.

If one is to notice, Paul does not address himself to the problem, whatever it was — the actual difference. I think this should tell us something.

When we try to deal specifically with whatever the problem is, in other words the difference between two parties, we are actually operating on the same basis as the system of the world. It really doesn't matter what the problem is, Christians are to conduct themselves in such a manner, and with humility, that unless the situation is a matter of conscience, we should give over. Consequently, Paul holds both parties to be in the wrong, and, equally in the wrong. Consequently, he addresses entreaty to both, in exactly the same terms, that they are to agree in Christ and be done with the situation, whatever it might be. They must no longer allow this thing to mar their own edification and hinder the Cause of Christ.

Yet, while he is sure that this is the right way, he does not conceal from himself how difficult human nature finds it to come happily out of such a complication. So he appeals to one with whom he is evidently well acquainted, his *"genuine yokefellow,"* to lend a hand.

These good women had little idea, probably, that their names should come down through the ages in connection with their disagreement. Had they realized this, they might have taken greater steps themselves to stop the situation before it got out of hand.

We should take a lesson from this. If the Holy Spirit deemed it necessary to record this squabble for all time, one can be certain that the same thing is done in Heaven as it regards all other such like activity among Christians.

Once again, the Holy Spirit through the Apostle proclaims the reason for this problem between these two women, as being a lack of humility, which is stressed throughout the entirety of the Epistle, even using Christ as the great example of humility. In other words, it was pride on the part of both of these women which caused their difference, whatever the particular circumstance was. It is no less the same presently. It is the old problem of *"self"* constantly rearing its ugly head, which has to be crucified each and every day, hence the demand by Christ that we take up the Cross daily, which refers to denying *"self"* (Lk. 9:23-24).

MY WAY OR GOD'S WAY

This whole thing boils down to *"my way"* versus *"God's Way."*

What is God's Way?

God's Way is the way of humility, which refers to one giving over to another even to the loss on his own part. It also refers to one not defending himself, unless it pertains to defending the Gospel.

Those who constantly demand their *"rights,"* do not understand humility, do not have humility, and, in fact, are functioning in *"their own way,"* and not *"God's Way."*

When a person comes to Christ, they give up their rights in all respects, and in every manner, rather looking to Christ to handle the situation, whatever the situation might be.

I suppose the question must be asked, *"Are we willing to do that? Are we willing to allow Christ to defend us, to take our part?"*

A PERSONAL EXPERIENCE

Even though I have related this briefly in another Volume, please allow me to briefly restate the following.

NOTES

It was in 1997 if I remember correctly. CNN did a story on this Ministry, that was very debilitating to say the least.

There was a particular reporter at CNN, who incidentally once worked at one of the Television Stations in Baton Rouge, who dislikes Jimmy Swaggart intently, and that's a gross understatement.

At any rate, he did a one-hour story, which went into about 150 nations of the world. These people know how to take something that is innocent, and make it into something that is totally sinister, in other words making it portray basically whatever they want it to say. As I told this man once, *"You could take the Sermon on the Mount, and make it seem like a plot to overthrow the Government."*

At any rate, when this was done it hurt to say the least. It is not very pleasant for one to see oneself pilloried, threatened, lambasted, demeaned, and in every debasing manner one can imagine, before a worldwide audience. The very first thing you want to do is to defend yourself. And of course, the Television Networks enjoy something of this nature, because it increases their ratings. Consequently, the Larry King Show, plus I think every other similar show on every network was calling almost hour by hour, trying to get me to appear and tell my side of the story, etc. As stated, they couldn't care less about me, they just wanted to boost ratings.

My natural inclination is to do exactly that, in other words, to pick up the spear and throw it back.

Going home from the Office the day after they had aired this thing the night before, naturally all of this was heavily on my mind. I had been asking the Lord what to do, and had pretty well thought in my mind to go on these particular talk shows and tell my side of the story.

About a mile before I reached our home that evening, the Spirit of the Lord came all over me and began to deal with my heart.

"Are you willing to allow Me to defend you?" the Lord asked! *"Are you willing to let others say what they want to say and think what they want to think, and place yourself completely in My Hands?"*

I remember remonstrating, *"But Lord, good Christians will believe some of this* stuff! *Some who are supporting the Ministry, which we desperately need, will stop their support; therefore, it seems that they should know the Truth about the matter!"* These were my thoughts.

The Lord again spoke and said, *"I can handle that as well!"*

In my heart at that moment, I turned the whole thing over to the Lord, leaving everything totally to Him, whatever people might think or say — and from experience, I knew that many Christians would have plenty to say and in the negative sense.

However, when I made that commitment in my heart, there was a Peace which came over me like I think I have never experienced before. It literally filled my heart, flowing all through my very being, which made me know that I was doing the right thing.

What happened?

Yes, this particular effort by CNN which went all over the world, did hurt somewhat. Yes, many people thought many debilitating things. Many Christians did the same thing. However, in looking back, I know I heard from the Lord, and I know my decision was right. I fully believe, had I set out to defend myself, that the situation would have been much worse and the hurt would have been much worse.

THE MAIN ISSUE AT STAKE

However, I don't really think those things I've just mentioned, and I speak of how the Ministry was hurt or not hurt, was or is the real issue here. I think the real issue is us allowing the Lord to defend us, to take our part, whatever that might be. Are we willing to trust the Lord, whatever happens?

We always like to think in terms of plus or minus, of profit and loss; however, I don't really think the Holy Spirit is looking at it in quite that way. While those things definitely do count, and while the Lord will always ultimately bring it out to a plus and profit, still, at times, He does these things in a totally different way than we at first can understand.

Again, the question was not how much the Ministry would be hurt by what this Network did, or even how much I would be hurt personally. Even though those things were primary in my mind, I think that which was in the Mind of the Spirit was something else entirely — the degree of trust on my part.

The Lord's Ways aren't our ways, and we have to learn to trust His Ways, irrespective as to what it looks like on the surface, or what seems to be happening at the present. Too oftentimes we have only the present circumstances in mind, when the Lord always has in mind the big picture.

HELP THOSE WOMEN

The phrase, *"Help those women which laboured with me in the Gospel, with Clement also, and with other my fellowlabourers,"* tells us several things:

The word *"help"* implies that Euodia and Syntyche were already trying to lay aside their difficulties. The word means *"to take hold with another"* in a task. This same word is used where Martha asked Jesus to bid Mary lend her a helping hand (Lk. 10:40). Paul asked Syzygus to lend a hand with these women in their efforts at settling their differences.

How much does the Holy Spirit ask all of us to involve ourselves accordingly, but always in the realm of *"help,"* instead of the opposite.

HOW CAN ONE HELP IN SUCH SITUATIONS?

Taking sides in the situation, whatever the situation might be, cannot help at all.

As well, serving as a judge in the matter, and I speak of judging one right and the other wrong, is not called for either. That will really settle nothing.

The only thing one can do in such circumstances, is to tell both parties that it really doesn't matter who is right or wrong. If what is done is creating a difference to the degree that a difference has actually been created, then both parties are wrong. It's not so much the situation at hand, whatever it might be, but again, it's the attitude toward the situation.

The only true *"help"* which can be rendered is to advise both parties, that whether right or wrong, it is to be placed in Christ and left there. Then as Christians, both parties should go their way loving each other, knowing that the situation is in Christ, and

He will attend to it as He so desires. It comes down to that which I've just mentioned, of trusting Christ and not ourselves.

Are we as Christians willing to do that? Are we willing to let Christ handle the thing? Are we willing to take loss if that's what the situation calls for, which means we will trust Christ to make it up in His Way?

Such advice and counsel, is the only thing that can be done as it regards *"help."* That is the Christlike Way, with all other efforts being the ways of the world.

LABORED WITH ME IN THE GOSPEL

Paul describes Euodia and Syntyche as *"those women which laboured with me in the Gospel."*

The word *"which"* has a qualitative character. They were women who were of such a character as to have labored with Paul.

The word *"labored"* is the translation of a Greek word used of a group of athletes who played on a team together, cooperating with one another in perfect harmony to attain a certain end, the word having in it also the ideas of strenuous and agonizing effort. This is the way Euodia and Syntyche had once worked in perfect cooperation with Paul in the great task of spreading the knowledge of the Word of God. But now they were causing trouble in the Philippian Church, leading rival factions.

Who *"Clement"* was, is not certain. Some say that he was the same one who was afterwards the Pastor of the Church at Rome and who wrote an Epistle to the Corinthians, which still exists. But that is speculation only!

FELLOWLABORERS

I think we should not slide over these statements by Paul quickly. The Holy Spirit desired that they be included, and for a reason.

The Lord told Paul to go to Philippi and to plant this Church. Actually, the Philippian Church was the result, or at least the beginning of the results of the Macedonian Call (Acts 16:9-12). Of course, let it be understood that anything the Lord does is of great significance, irrespective as to how small it may seem at the beginning.

Nevertheless, one can well imagine how pleased the Lord was regarding those who helped Paul in whatever capacity they were able to help as it regards this Church, and anything else the Apostle did for that matter.

Believers should take a cue from this, and I speak of the following:

God calls men and women to do His Work. He does not call Denominations, committees, boards, groups, etc. As stated, He calls individuals, which has always been His Way, and will always be His Way.

Much of the Denominational world insists upon their members supporting the Denomination per se, with them parcelling out the funds to various Missionaries, etc. That is not Biblical, and I'll tell you why:

First of all, there is no Scriptural precedent for such action. One will look in vain in the Book of Acts or the Epistles for such procedure. The reason for the Lord doing it His way should be obvious.

God calls an individual for a specific work, and He as well calls individuals to support that particular person whom He has called (Rom. 10:14-15).

Too often, Denominational Boards and Committees seek to place themselves between the individual who is called, and the ones who support this particular individual and his calling. This is where problems begin to arise.

While there certainly may be men and women on such particular boards who are attempting to ascertain the Will of God, and to follow the Lord regarding those whom He has called, the Truth is, those individuals are, few and far between. Most of the time, these Missions Boards little care or regard those who claim to be called of God to certain particular places in the world and for particular Ministries. Instead, they choose the ones they desire, almost all the time with the choosing based upon secular principles and not at all concerning that which pertains to the Lord and His Word. Consequently, we now have a mediator other than Christ Himself, which is one of the biggest sins of the Church.

Millions of Christians give their money to Denominations regarding the taking of the Gospel to the world, thinking that this organization can handle their money better, etc.

While that certainly might be true in some few cases, the far greater majority of the time it isn't true. Most of the time the money is wasted, and what do I mean by that?

Missionaries are supported who really do not have the Call of God on their lives. Some few do, most don't! I know of that of which I speak, because I've been there. So, money is wasted in such circumstances, as should be obvious.

The millions of Christians who give money in this manner, are trusting a Board somewhere whom they have never seen, to handle these funds responsibly. As stated, some few do, most don't! Just because it is a Denomination means nothing, even though the people giving the money think it means everything.

Regarding support of the Work of God, we must do two things:

1. We must seek to be Scriptural at all times and in all things.

2. We should earnestly seek the Lord about that, or whom we support.

The sad Truth is, that the far greater majority of money given to that which claims to be of God, and claims to be for God, is in fact, carrying out the very opposite. Too often, people give because they believe something someone has said, which is not the Truth.

If Samuel the great Prophet of God had gone by appearance, he would have chosen another one of Jesse's sons to have been king, instead of the one chosen by God, who was David. In other words, even the great Samuel had to have the leading of the Holy Spirit to make the right choice. Appearances can be very deceiving. And to be sure, they are just as deceiving now, if not more so, than they were in the days of Samuel (I Sam. 16:1-13).

To be sure, every Believer will have to answer to the Lord for every dime and dollar given to the Work of God, or that which claimed to be God's Work, when we stand at the Judgment Seat of Christ. Were we responsible stewards?

It is a question we need to answer now, so we won't have to answer it then with shock and surprise.

Every Believer is a *"fellowlaborer,"* whether he realizes it or not. The question is, *"With whom are you a fellowlaborer?"*

You need to check that out and come up with a responsible, Scriptural answer.

THE BOOK OF LIFE

The phrase, *"Whose names are in the Book of Life,"* refers to the roster of Believers kept in Heaven. It is sometimes referred to as the *"Lamb's Book of Life,"* taken from Revelation 13:8 which says, *"And all that dwell upon the earth shall worship him* (the Antichrist), *whose names are not written in the Book of Life of the Lamb slain from the foundation of the world."*

This tells us that admittance into this Book is gained only by accepting the Lord Jesus Christ, and more particularly *"Jesus Christ and Him crucified"* (I Cor. 2:2). Acceptance of Him and what He did at the Cross, is the only means of acceptance. That means that belonging to a certain Church does not gain one acceptance, or participation in any of the Ordinances of the Church, such as the Lord's Supper, or Water Baptism, etc. While these things, plus others not named, have their own place and significance, the only means of Eternal Life, is the acceptance of Jesus Christ and what He did at the Cross on our behalf. That's the reason the Holy Spirit so strongly, even dogmatically, emphasized that this *"Book of Life,"* is *"of the Lamb slain from the foundation of the world."* This tells us two things:

1. The slain Lamb, i.e., *"the Crucified Christ,"* and Faith in that, is the only means of Salvation.

2. This is no hastily contrived plan, but rather formulated by God *"from the foundation of the world,"* with the Holy Spirit through Peter saying this very thing (I Pet. 1:20).

CAN NAMES BE BLOTTED OUT OF THE BOOK OF LIFE?

The Holy Spirit through David said, *"Let them be blotted out of the Book of the living, and not be written with the Righteous"* (Ps. 69:28).

This tells us that names can be blotted out of the Book of Life.

God said the same thing in Exodus 32:33, as did Moses in Exodus 32:32. The Lord Jesus Christ said the same thing in Revelation 3:5; 22:19.

This means that a Believer can stop believing, and if they do stop believing, and of course, we're speaking of believing in Christ and what He did at the Cross, that person reverts to a lost state (Heb. 6:4-6; 10:26-31).

Now we have a choice! We can accept what the Word tells us, or we can accept that which man says.

This *"Book of Remembrance"* is mentioned in Malachi 3:16. It includes the names of the Saints. Perhaps the clearest meaning of such a Book is seen in Daniel 7:10 and Revelation 13:8. In these Apocalyptic contexts the Book contains the names of those who have Eternal Life. The concept of the Book of Life underscores the worth of the individual in Christian theology. It implies that people are not saved en masse but one by one.

Salvation and the final judgment are thus vividly personal matters. Each person will be judged on one fact alone, and that is their Faith in Jesus Christ and what He did on the Cross on our behalf. That alone is the criteria.

(4) "REJOICE IN THE LORD ALWAY: AND AGAIN I SAY, REJOICE."

Paul places a double emphasis on rejoicing here and, no doubt, with reason.

It may imply that a single injunction might prompt the question, *"How can we rejoice, in view of our difficulties?"* So he repeats the command, because in all the vicissitudes of the Christian Life, whether in attacks from Satan, personality clashes among Believers, persecution from the world, or even the threat of imminent death — all of which Paul himself was experiencing at this very time — the Christian is to maintain a spirit of joy in the Lord. We are not immune to sorrow nor should we be insensitive to the troubles of others; yet we should count the Will of God the highest joy and so be capable of knowing inner peace and joy in every circumstance.

I realize that what we have just said is a tall order; however, this great Salvation afforded by Christ, also affords this of which we have just mentioned, of which cannot be boasted by any religion or philosophy on Earth.

REJOICE IN THE LORD ALWAYS

The phrase, *"Rejoice in the Lord always,"* means as we have just stated, in every circumstance, every situation, whether it be negative or positive.

If the Apostle wept over many (Phil. 3:18) yet he always rejoiced in the Lord, for in Him nothing alters. It was not indifference that caused Paul to rejoice always, but it was an unfailing spring of joy which becomes more abundant in distress. The heart that drinks daily and deeply of that spring, will warmly and unfailingly love others and be concerned regarding their welfare. As Christ never changes, this fount never changes; and the joy which the Christian feels and manifests is a testimony to the existence of that Source of Joy.

Years in prison chained to a soldier, failed to destroy that Source for Paul or to hinder him from urging others more at ease than himself to drink of its fullness (Williams).

In both the Old Testament and the New Testament joy is consistently the mark both individually of the Believer and corporately of the Church. It is a quality, and not simply an emotion, grounded upon God Himself and indeed derived from Him (Ps. 16:11; Rom. 15:13; Phil. 4:4), which characterizes the Christian's life on Earth (I Pet. 1:8), and also anticipates eschatologically (future events) the joy of being with Christ forever in the coming Kingdom of Heaven (Rev. 19:7).

JOY IN THE OLD TESTAMENT

Joy was related to the total national and spiritual life of Israel, and was particularly expressed in terms of noisy, tumultuous excitement at the Festivals, Sacrifices, and Enthronements (Deut. 12:6; I Sam. 18:6; I Ki. 1:39).

Spontaneous joy is a prevailing feature of the Psalter, where it is a mark both of corporate worship (largely centered in the Temple, Ps. 42:4; 81:41) and of personal adoration (Ps. 16:8; 43:4).

Isaiah conceives a joy in other than simply ritual terms (Ps. 126), and he associates it with the fullness of God's Salvation, and, therefore, with the anticipation of a future state (Isa. 49:13; 61:10). Of course, Isaiah was seeing into the future as it regards what Jesus would do on the Cross, which would make possible the Advent of the Holy Spirit, even as He came on the Day of Pentecost, Who is the great instigator of Joy.

JOY IN THE NEW TESTAMENT

Matthew, Mark, and Luke, record the note of joy in connection with the proclamation, in its varied forms, of the Good News of the Kingdom: For example, at the Saviour's Birth

(Lk. 2:10), at the Triumphal Entry (Mk. 11:9; Lk. 19:37), and after the Resurrection (Mat. 28:8). In John it is Jesus Himself Who communicates this joy (Jn. 15:11; 16:24), and it now becomes the result of a deep fellowship between the Church and Himself (Jn. 16:22).

In Acts joy marks the life of the Early Church. It accompanies the Gift of the Holy Spirit to the Disciples (Acts 13:52), the miracles performed in the Name of Christ (Acts 8:8), and the fact and report of the conversion of the Gentiles (Acts 15:3); it also characterizes the taking of the Lord's Supper (Acts 2:46).

PAUL AND HIS DESCRIPTION OF JOY

Among the several Greek words typifying *"joy,"* Paul used *"chara"* the most. He used it in three distinct ways:

1. First, progress in the Faith on the part of the members of the Body of Christ, and particularly those he has led to Christ, is a cause for joy — he describes them, indeed, as *"he chara hemon," "our joy"* (Phil. 2:2; I Thess. 2:19).

2. Christian joy may paradoxically be the outcome of suffering and even sorrow for Christ's sake (II Cor. 6:10; Col. 1:24; Heb. 10:34; I Pet. 4:13, etc.), since it is produced by the Lord and not by ourselves.

3. Joy is in fact, a Fruit of the Holy Spirit (Gal. 5:22), and is, therefore, something dynamic and not static. Moreover, it derives from love — God's and ours — and is, therefore, closely associated with love in Paul's list of the Fruit of the Spirit.

But since it is a Fruit which may be interrupted by sin, every Believer is called upon to share in the joy of Christ by a daily walk with Him and a daily practice of rejoicing in the knowledge of Him and His Salvation, made possible by the Cross and our Faith placed there (Phil. 3:1; 4:4; I Thess. 5:16; I Pet. 1:8).

AGAIN . . . REJOICE

The phrase, *"And again I say, Rejoice,"* emphasizes the necessity by the double portrayal. This double exhortation, is not without meaning.

The idea is, that the Christian life is not uneventful. We have sorrows, problems, and difficulties like all others; however, we are not to allow these things to rob us of our joy, for the *"joy of the Lord is our strength"* (Neh. 8:10). So, the Christian is to rejoice and constantly rejoice for two reasons:

1. We are to rejoice because the Lord has been so good to us, which speaks of Eternal Life, the mighty Baptism with the Holy Spirit, as well as all His many Blessings in the physical and material sense, plus every other way. So, there is no reason that the Child of God should not rejoice constantly as it regards these things, which have absolutely nothing to do with circumstances, events, reverses, etc.

In view of what the Lord is to us, we also know what the future will bring, at least as it regards the Promises of God. There is no leap into the dark for the Child of God, but rather the very opposite. He has gone away to prepare a place for us, that where He is we may be also (Jn. 14:1-4).

2. We are to rejoice, and of course we speak of rejoicing in the Lord, because this is the source of our strength, as already stated. A rejoicing Believer is a strong Believer. Of necessity, one who does not rejoice, is not strong in the Lord.

HOW DOES ONE REJOICE IN THE LORD?

As stated, most of the joy expressed in the Old Testament was more ritualistic than anything else. While these people definitely knew the Lord, still, due to the fact that Jesus had not yet gone to the Cross, the Holy Spirit, Who is the originator of joy, could not abide within their hearts and lives as He does presently with Believers. Consequently, the joy, of necessity, although real, did not have the depth that it does presently. As stated, Isaiah by the Holy Spirit, saw this glad day coming. With the Advent of the Holy Spirit on the Day of Pentecost, the very Origin of joy came to live within the hearts and lives of Believers (Acts Chpt. 2). Actually, the joy was so pronounced on that glad day that Peter said concerning this outpouring and the reaction of those who were filled, *"For these are not drunken, as ye suppose, seeing it is but the third hour of the day.*

"But this is that which was spoken by the Prophet Joel" (Acts 2:15-16).

Consequently, I think I can say without fear of exaggeration, that even though joy definitely comes to the Believer upon coming to Christ, it is with the Advent of the Baptism with the Holy Spirit, which is always accompanied by the speaking with other Tongues, that joy or at least it's potential, was brought into full flower. As stated, Isaiah saw this coming day (Isa. 28:10-12).

The Advent of the Spirit Baptism automatically elicits praise in the heart and life of the Believer. This is always, I think I can say, an accompanying factor. The Spirit Baptized Saint automatically desires to Praise the Lord, which within itself produces Joy. It has to do with the *"River of Water of Life"* which flows like an artisan spring from the heart of the Believer (Jn. 7:37-39).

True life always elicits joy, and the Holy Spirit is referred to as *"The Law of the Spirit of Life"* (Rom. 8:23). Of course, all of this is made possible by what Jesus did at the Cross, hence Paul saying, *"The Law of the Spirit of Life in Christ Jesus."*

Rejoicing in the Lord is always characterized by Praise, and Praise of the Lord should be a continuous fountain in the heart of the Believer. Actually, the more Christlike one becomes, I think one can say, a constant praise will be coming from the heart of the Believer, even though there may not be an audible sound. This means that rejoicing is not reserved only for Church, but should be a characteristic at all times, even constant.

Admittedly, the unsaved person would have no idea whatsoever of this of which we speak, and regrettably, neither will many Christians. Even many so-called Spirit-filled Christians have little knowledge of true praise and rejoicing in the Lord, simply because they little cooperate with the Holy Spirit.

Last of all, if rejoicing is to be constant, it must be a state of the heart, which automatically springs from a heart of thanksgiving. If we really understand what He has done for us, is doing for us, and yet shall do for us, such cannot help but be the occasion for rejoicing, and even constant rejoicing.

THE BEGINNING OF MORE ABUNDANT LIFE

Paul's admonition regarding rejoicing, is followed by the greatest formula found in the Word of God, and thereby the only legitimate formula in the world, as it regards more abundant life, which we will now study. It must begin with rejoicing. This is the key to victory over fear, doubt, unbelief, worry, consternation, depression, and all the cares of life. In other words, the Holy Spirit through the Apostle beginning with Verse 4 and continuing through Verse 8, is giving us the key to that which the world strives for and never finds, but which the Child of God readily has, that is, if we obey the Word of God.

As we have stated, but which I again must emphasize, to have this which the Holy Spirit promises, which concerns a true peace of mind, we must begin with *"rejoicing."* It is so important, that the Holy Spirit repeats it again, signifying its importance.

Beginning with rejoicing, I would pray that the Believer would carefully read the following commentary, for I believe it will hold the answer through the Word of God for many things, especially freedom from worry, etc. This is God's solution, and in reality, the only solution which works.

(5) "LET YOUR MODERATION BE KNOWN UNTO ALL MEN. THE LORD IS AT HAND."

Second, Believers are to be gentle to all. The Greek term *"epieikes"* (*"gentleness"*) is difficult to translate with its full connotation. Such words as *"gentle, yielding, kind, forbearing, and lenient"* are among the best English attempts, but no single word is adequate.

Involved is the willingness to yield one's personal rights and to show consideration and gentleness to others. It is easy to display this quality toward some persons, but Paul commands it be shown toward all. That would seem to include Christian friends, unsaved persecutors, false teachers — anyone at all. Of course, Truth is never to be sacrificed, but a gentle spirit will do much to disarm the adversary.

As an encouragement, Paul now reminds his Readers the Lord is near. This, in effect, has a double meaning:

1. First of all, his reference is to the Parousia — the Rapture of the Church. This seems clear from the context of the Letter, where Philippians 3:20-21 focused attention on the glorious prospect in view for Believers at Christ's return. A similar connection

between a longsuffering spirit and the Lord's coming occurs in James 5:8.

The statement is a reminder that at His arrival the Judge will settle all differences, which will take place at the Judgment Seat of Christ.

2. The Passage as given by Paul refers to the continuing presence of the Lord with Believers. He is with us constantly; therefore, we should be ever reminded that all that we say, think and do, are observed by Him constantly. This should cause us to desire to do all things at all times, that He would want.

Also, whether we have the kindness, thoughtfulness, or help of other Christians, is not really that important as far as we are concerned. We have the Lord, He is near, and, therefore, nothing else really matters.

Of course, at all times we should have the kindness and help of other Believers, exactly as we should give the same to others on our own part, but whether we have such or not, should have little to do with our disposition, place, or position. We have Christ and that's enough.

I'VE HAD TO LEARN THIS THE HARD WAY

These Passages are very dear to me personally, for the simple reason that I have lived them. Since 1988, I have had to learn to trust the Lord completely and to depend on Him completely, understanding that whatever other Christians may do or not do, the Lord will have the final say. When one has almost all the Church world attempting to put one out of business, attempting to destroy one's Ministry, using any legal means at their disposal and even means which are illegal, one will then learn to lean on the Lord, trust in the Lord, look to the Lord exclusively, or the simple matter is, one will perish.

It is heartbreaking that the situation exists as it does, with one wondering how that people can be saved and still do such things. One simply has to learn to leave it all to the Lord and not make judgments.

It is very difficult to grasp and understand, that God has called you to do certain things, in this case the airing of the Gospel by Television for example, by which many souls are saved and lives changed, and at the same time see fellow Christians do everything within their power to keep the Program from being aired. You wonder how that one can be of God and at the same time oppose God!

In all of this, one realizes that most Christians, even most Preachers, little think or do for themselves, rather following the lead of others. In other words, if a certain Denomination or certain Preachers take the lead in their efforts of hindrance and even destruction, most other Preachers and Christians seem to think that such is the proper thing to be done, and consequently, follow without question. To be sure, that in no way excuses them for their wrongdoing, but it is the sad fact of unconsecrated human nature.

So, on a scale that few have ever had to address, I have had to ask the Lord to help me that I not think hard of these people, whomever they may be, and whatever they might do, leaving the situation with the Lord.

That is not easy when one considers that what we are speaking of here, happens constantly, and on a worldwide basis. But the Lord is equal to the task, whatever the task might be. He is able to place love in one's heart for such people, wishing them well, and praying God's Blessings upon them; however, it is not something to which one consecrates one time and then it's done. It is something that one must address on a daily basis, asking the Lord for strength to do what must be done without allowing malice in one's heart. That's the greatest secret of all! The heart must remain pure and clean before God.

And then on the other side of the ledger, in all of this, one learns to trust the Lord, knowing and understanding, that He is the only One Who can see us through.

And, I have watched Him do exactly that, over and over again. I have watched men rule, even rule with an evil intent, and then I've watched God overrule. I've watched religious men close one door after the other and do so with devilish intent, and watch the Lord open another door even greater than the one that was closed.

The Reader must ever understand, that our conflict is never between us and other people, irrespective as to whom those other people might be, but rather between ourselves and the Lord. Jacob found that out in his wrestling with the Lord. This very wrestling match as recorded in Genesis Chapter 32, was not really between him and his father Isaac, or his brother Esau, or his relative Laban, but rather with the Lord Himself. It is the same with us presently. Our problem is always ourselves and our relationship with the Lord. While other people certainly figure into the situation, the only way in which they actually matter, is our reaction to them. How do we react?

I'll say it again, and because it's so very important; our problem is really not with others irrespective as to what they might do, hence the Lord telling us to always be *"gentle with them."* Our problem is always with ourselves and how we relate to the Lord, in other words, how do we conduct ourselves?

MODERATION

The phrase, *"Let your moderation be known unto all men,"* means exactly what it says, *"all men,"* which takes in our enemies, even our worst enemies.

Of all the meanings of *"moderation"* which we have already addressed, perhaps the more or most important meaning is: *"Being satisfied with less than one's due."*

The word *"known"* refers to knowledge gained by experience. The exhortation is, therefore, *"Do not keep this reasonableness in your heart. Let it find expression in your conduct toward others. Thus, others will experience this blessing also, whether it causes them to feel any better toward you or not."* Again we emphasize, whatever others do or don't do, and we speak of those who would harm you, is not really the point in all of this. The point is our reaction. Do we react with kindness and gentleness or the opposite? As stated, this wrestling bout is not really with others, but with ourself and the Lord.

This of which we speak, is what we often associate with Christlikeness. It means an attitude that will *"pardon human feelings and look solely to the Lord."* To be sure, it is not an easy thing to do, and, in fact, can only be done as the Believer knows and understands that it must be done, thereby asking the Lord for help, which He intends for us to do, and which He will always answer.

Directly Paul's admonition is to Euodias and Syntyche, but indirectly to all other Believers. He bids them *"Shew forth in the eyes of all men"* a spirit such as he attributes to Christ Himself, of *"yielding gentleness, willing to suffer wrong, that all men may see and glorify God in them"* (II Cor. 10:1).

As well, he means that this spirit is to be *"exercised towards all men impartially,"* even towards the enemies of the Cross.

Once again, this does not mean that we are to compromise Truth in any way or to slack in our defense of the Gospel. That is not the idea. The idea is, that while defending the Gospel with all of our strength, which means standing up for true Doctrine, at the same time we must not allow our feelings to become personal toward these individuals who bear this error or ill will even personally toward us, and because such will affect us in a very negative sense a whole lot more than it will affect them. In fact, almost all of the negative effect will carry out itself in our own hearts, which will play out to anger, pride, arrogance, vengeance, bitterness, etc. So, our attitude is definitely meant by the Lord to be a blessing to others, but more particularly, it is for our own good.

THE LORD

The phrase, *"The Lord is at hand,"* literally means *"near."*

As stated, it refers to the nearness of the Lord's return (Rapture), and, as well, His nearness to us at all times, which among other things, even as we have already addressed, cures worry, or certainly should do so.

So here, we have the second admonition by the Holy Spirit through the Apostle as it regards well-being in life. It is as follows:

First, we are to rejoice in the Lord always, and irrespective of the circumstances and situations. This means that we are to rejoice not only as it regards the good things which happen to us, but also those things which do not seem to be so good. This shows that we believe that the Lord will ultimately bring out the situation to our good, irrespective as to how it presently looks. This speaks of Faith, Trust, and dependence on the Lord.

Second, we are to be moderate or gentle toward others in all things, again, realizing that the Lord has the final say and not others.

As well, if one is to notice, Paul is admonishing the Believers at Philippi to always be cognizant of the Lord's soon return, even though he had said to the Thessalonians that the Day of Christ was not then at hand (II Thess. 2:1-2).

Is there a contradiction?

No, the idea is, that the Believer is to always live and to conduct himself as if the Lord was coming immediately. Concerning all admonitions of this nature, this is the tenor of what the Holy Spirit means.

The actual date of the Lord's return is not to be the thought or concern of the Believer even as Jesus said immediately before His Ascension (Acts 1:6-7). The business of the Church, which refers to every Believer, is to take the Gospel to the world, in other words to occupy until He comes, and to live as though He might come today (Acts 1:8; I Jn. 3:3).

(6) "BE CAREFUL FOR NOTHING: BUT IN EVERY THING BY PRAYER AND SUPPLICATION WITH THANKSGIVING LET YOUR REQUESTS BE MADE KNOWN UNTO GOD."

Third, Believers should be prayerful instead of anxious. The meaning of all this is that of anxiety, fretfulness, or undue concern. Paul is not calling for apathy or inaction, for as we make plans in the light of our circumstances, it is our Christian privilege to do so in full trust that our Father hears our prayers for what we need.

In other words, the answer to anxiety is prayer. *"Prayer"* denotes the petitioner's attitude of mind as worshipful. *"Petition"* denotes prayers as expressions of need. *"Thanksgiving"* should accompany all Christian praying, as the supplicant acknowledges that whatever God sends is for his good.

"Requests" refer to things for which we ask (Kent).

DON'T WORRY ABOUT ANYTHING

The phrase, *"Be careful for nothing,"* means, *"Don't worry about anything."* The word *"nothing"* is literally *"not even one thing."*

Paul is not speaking here of stoicism, which was a philosophy of Zeno of Citium which he formulated in about 300 B.C. It held that one should not show passion or feeling toward anything, i.e., *"indifference."*

NOTES

Christianity does not deny problems or the severity of problems. It just denies that the problem, whatever it might be, is the ruling factor, that being the Lord. It is foolish to deny problems, when they are obvious, and as well it is foolish to think that we as human beings can be indifferent to such problems. Irrespective as to what philosophy one might embrace, when we are cut, we bleed.

No, the idea of all of this, and a wonderful idea it is, circumstances and situations do not decide our destiny. As Believers we are never at the whim of chance, circumstances, situations, or forces beyond our control. The Lord is able to change things, and if He doesn't see fit to change it now, He will give us Grace to go through the situation, which will bring us out stronger and better, that is if we react properly.

Actually, Paul's statement is an exact repetition of our Lord's Command, *"Take no thought"* (Mat. 6:25, 34). One might say that the prohibition is of that painful anxiety which is inevitable in all who feel themselves alone in mere self-dependence amidst the difficulties and dangers of life. It is possible to sink below this anxiety in mere levity and thoughtlessness, which of course is foolish, and not what the Apostle intends. The idea is, that we rise above these things by *"casting our care on Him Who careth for us"* (I Pet. 5:7).

GOD'S CURE FOR WORRY

First of all, let me say that anything that is promised in the Word of God (and I am referring to life and living) can only be obtained by one properly understanding the Message of the Cross and how that Message is applied to one's life. In other words, irrespective of what blessings we are speaking of, if we attempt to have any of them by trying to obtain them in any manner except by Faith in Christ and the Cross, the proper end result never will be realized.

The following ever must be understood:

Christ is the *"Source"* of all things, while the Cross is the *"Means."*

Most Christians do not have much of a problem with Christ being the total and complete Source, but they have great problems with the Cross being the Means. That's why we have every type of advice and counsel being given as to how to obtain things from the Lord, which, incidentally, really aren't Scriptural.

It is not God's Will for one to worry. It shows a lack of faith, a lack of trust, and a lack of confidence in the Lord. There isn't any special provision for one to have victory over worry and another type of special provision for one to have answer to prayer in other capacities. Everything we receive from the Lord, and I mean everything, is derived, as stated, from Christ as the Source and the Cross as the Means.

Let me say it again:

This includes every single, solitary thing that we receive from the Lord, irrespective as to what it is.

FAITH

If one evidences Faith in the Cross, thereby doing what we are told to do in Philippians 4:6, we will find the Peace of God given to us, and in a remarkable way. But we must remember, we obtain every blessing (including victory over worry) by evidencing a constant faith (never-ending) in Christ and what He has done for us at the Cross.

The Cross is ever the Means by which God gives us all things; we speak of those things paid for by the Lord Jesus Christ. The greater problem with the Church is its ignorance of the Cross or ignoring the Cross, which shuts the door to the Blessings of God. That's the reason that Christians have all types of problems. They simply do not understand the Cross, at least as it refers to our Sanctification (Rom. 6:1-14; 8:1-2, 11; Gal. 6:14).

PRAYER AND SUPPLICATION

The phrase, *"But in every thing by prayer and supplication,"* presents the cure for worry, which is believing prayer. The word *"prayer"* as used here, is the translation of a Greek word which speaks of prayer addressed to God as an act of worship and devotion.

"Supplication" is from a word that speaks of supplicating for one's personal needs, i.e., *"making petition."*

The exhortation to prayer is based on the admonition not to be anxious. Jesus laid great emphasis upon anxiety. According to Jesus this attitude of mind feeds upon fear. It is basically a lack of trust, of confidence in God. Consequently, *"Be anxious about nothing"* is a better translation than *"Be careful for nothing."* The meaning is, *"In no case should you permit yourself to be full of care."*

The corrective for undue worry is not to resort to indifference, even as we've already addressed as it regards stoicism, but rather to prayer and to trust. Commitment frees one from anxiety. Faith is the chief corrective of worry, as love is the chief corrective of fear.

Anxiety debilitates; it is abrasive. It renders one less efficient. Thus, anxiety feeds upon itself. The more anxiety one has, the less efficient he becomes and the greater the reason for his anxiety. The remedy then is positive.

It is to commit all things to God in confidence. In this, Paul encourages specific praying, which speaks of being deliberate concerning one's petitions before God, believing that He is able to do all things, but at the same time always desiring His Will.

EVERYTHING

Here the Holy Spirit, through the Apostle, tells us that we are to pray about *"everything,"* and that means *"everything."* Considering, as we've already stated, that God has the final say regarding everything as it pertains to the Child of God, most definitely we should desire to take everything before Him.

When we speak of everything, we are speaking of the small things as well as the large things, the significant things as well as those things which we think to be insignificant. We must always remember, it is the seemingly insignificant things which lead to significant things, which, therefore, must be committed to prayer.

The Holy Spirit wants it this way for a variety of reasons. First of all, we must understand that we as Believers are to be led exclusively by the Holy Spirit, and that means in all things. As human beings, we do not know the way through these spiritual minefields; however, the Lord does know the way. Understanding that there are dangers on every hand and that Satan is planning constantly our hurt, at the same time, we should season everything in prayer, seeking the Will of the Lord in all things, and His direction and help in all things.

So, when the Holy Spirit said *"every thing,"* he meant exactly that.

Now I suppose I should ask the question as to how many Christians follow this admonition? The Truth is, most Christians sadly and regrettably, don't pray about anything, much less everything. This is perhaps at least one of the greatest sins of the Christian, and one of the most foolish sins I might quickly add. To have the opportunity to speak to someone Who can do all things, Who has the power to do anything, Who is able irrespective of the difficulty, and Who desires to help us, and desires to do so strongly, and not take advantage of that, has to be foolishness or ignorance of the highest order; however, if it is ignorance and foolishness, and it definitely is, it is willful ignorance and foolishness on the part of the Believer, because there is no reason that any Christian should not know better.

WHAT IS PRAYER?

Prayer is not so much an action of the individual, as it is a state of the heart. In other words, prayer is the privilege of being able to take all things to our Heavenly Father. It is being able to petition Him for our needs, for direction, for leading, and guidance.

Every religion in the world incorporates prayer or meditation in some fashion, but all to no avail other than that which is offered to God in the name of Jesus (Jn. 16:23). Everything from Islam to Hinduism is all a waste of time, and for all the obvious reasons. It is only to God as our Heavenly Father that prayer can be said to be true.

As I have said quite a few times in these Volumes, in October of 1991, the Lord told me to begin two Prayer Meetings a day, which we have done our very best to faithfully follow from then until now. To be frank, that has been at least one of the greatest things that's ever happened to me and this Ministry.

In these Prayer Meetings, I do my best to do exactly what the Holy Spirit, through Paul, said here to do. I bring everything to the Lord, and I mean everything. I ask His leading, His guidance, and His help, and He never fails to give that help. He has performed miracle after miracle on behalf of this Ministry and on behalf of my person as well, even with the enemy attempting to steal, kill, and destroy with all of his might.

At the outset, the Lord spoke to my heart and said to me, *"Do not seek Me so much for what I can do, but rather for Who I am."* I found out through this, that prayer is the greatest way I think, that one can get to know the Lord. It establishes relationship and communion. One gets to know the Lord, what He wants and desires, with the Word of God then becoming more and more prominent. In fact, the Word and Prayer go hand in hand. The Believer really cannot pray properly unless he has an understanding of the Word, for the simple reason that everything we do in prayer must be based squarely on the Word. So how can we profitably pray, if we do not know the Word?

Paul also told us to *"pray without ceasing"* (I Thess. 5:17).

What did he mean by that?

He wasn't speaking of the posture of prayer, in other words one getting on his or her knees constantly, but rather an attitude of prayer. In one's heart, the Believer should stay in an attitude of prayer, constantly praising the Lord, seeking the Lord and petitioning the Lord. It should become second nature, in other words, even as the Scripture says here, pray about everything.

So, prayer one might say, is the attitude of one's heart toward God, which will result in one seeking the Lord constantly. However, it is imperative that one set aside a certain amount of time each day to get alone with the Lord, spending a concentrated time in prayer. This should be in addition to one's constant state of prayer.

WHY PRAYER?

There are two basic reasons for prayer. They are:

1. God is the Creator and we are the creatures. As such, we are to depend exclusively upon Him for all things. Prayer says that I know and understand Who God is, and recognize Him as such. In other words, He is my Creator, and prayer acknowledges that fact. It also acknowledges the fact that inasmuch as He is the Creator, I am to look to Him for all things. I am to draw all things from Him,

believe Him for all things, and expect all things from Him. In other words, we are speaking here of creaturely dependence.

The Fall in the Garden of Eden destroyed that creaturely dependence, which in effect, set man adrift with no moorings, no direction, and no help, with basically him having to help himself out of difficulty and great problems to which the Fall has driven him, all to no avail. The first thing that happens to a person when they come to Christ, is that they recognize their creaturely dependence on God. He now becomes the Source of all things, even as He desires to be. In the Garden of Eden, our original parents stupidly thought they could exist without the Creator, having ability to function better without Him. This was the lie fed to them by Satan, and regrettably the lie they believed. However, man cannot function without God, and for all the obvious reasons. As everything God has created must depend upon Him for sustenance and survival, the highest creation of all, mankind, definitely falls into the same category. So, as stated, when man comes back to God, this is the first thing that happens in his heart and life, he feels his need of God, and he begins to lean upon Him and look to Him. To be frank, it is the greatest feeling, the greatest life, the greatest experience that one could ever have — the looking to God for all things.

So, prayer is a natural part of all of this, as ought to be obvious.

2. God has given all Believers the privilege of sharing with Him all things. Now I realize that's quite a statement but it happens to be true. Paul said, *"The Spirit Himself beareth witness with our spirit, that we are the Children of God:*

"And if children, then heirs; heirs of God, and joint-heirs with Christ; if so be that we suffer with Him, that we may be also glorified together" (Rom. 8:16-17).

In other words, every single thing the Lord does, all of His plans, all that He has formulated, He allows us as sons and daughters of God, to have a great part in all of this. Even though this covers every aspect of our life and living, prayer is definitely the greatest medium through which proper direction is ascertained in this great privilege.

NOTES

In prayer, I find out what the Lord wants, what He desires, and my part in this great Work and Plan of God. Actually, it is impossible to ascertain one's position otherwise.

To be more succinct, even dogmatic, the Lord makes plans, but if we do not play our part, consecrate ourselves accordingly, find out our place and disposition in those plans, the Truth is, those plans will not come to proper fruition.

That means, that God does not treat us as little children, even as we do our own children. At times, a parent will allow a little son or daughter to climb up on his or her lap and place their hands on the steering wheel of a car. For a few moments they think they are driving, but, in effect, the parents' hands are guiding the car all the time. The Lord does not function in this capacity toward us.

He literally allows us to drive the car so to speak. He makes us a part of His Plans, treating us with responsibility and maturity. Unfortunately, we do not all the time respond accordingly.

If the Believer properly understood what all of this means, how important all of it actually is, and how much is dependent on us, quite possibly we would take steps to conduct ourselves in a more forthright manner.

So, *"prayer"* amounts to creaturely dependence and participation in all that God does.

HOW DO WE PRAY?

The Disciples asked Jesus this same question.

The Scripture says that *"He (Jesus) was praying in a certain place, (and) when He ceased, one of His Disciples said unto Him, Lord, 'Teach us to pray, as John also taught his Disciples'"* (Lk. 11:1).

Jesus then followed by giving them what we refer to as the *"model prayer"* or *"Lord's Prayer."* (For a more detailed treatment of this very important subject, please see our Commentary on Matthew.)

In brief I will give the following:

1. Our Father which art in Heaven: We are to recognize, even as stated, that God is the Author of all good things; therefore, we pray to Him. As well, we must understand, that He is not merely God, but to us who believe, He is our *"Heavenly Father,"* which

opens up all type of possibilities. As well, our help comes from Heaven and not from men. We should always understand this.

Due to the Cross and what Jesus has now done for us, we should address all of our prayers to the Father in the Name of Jesus, which the Saviour did not mention at the time He gave the Lord's Prayer (Jn. 16:23).

2. Hallowed be Thy Name: We are to begin our prayer with Praise and Thanksgiving, exactly as Paul mentioned in the Verse of our study.

3. Thy Kingdom come: Even though we now have the Kingdom of God within our hearts, we long for it to cover the entirety of all things, which it soon shall. We are to ever look forward to this, realizing that everything is pushing toward a successful conclusion, and of course we speak of all that is in the Lord.

4. Thy Will be done on Earth as it is in Heaven: The way to pray involves strongly that we understand that everything must be according to the Will of God. We must want His Will, ardently seek His Will and desire His Will, which always forgoes our will.

All of this is to be with understanding that the total Will of God will not be done on this Earth until ultimately the Kingdom comes. But come it shall!

5. Give us this day our daily bread: This speaks of our daily sustenance and also of Jesus, for He is the True Bread of Life. As well, we are told in this part of the Lord's Prayer, that the Lord is the One Who supplies all things.

6. And forgive us our debts (trespasses), as we forgive our debtors (those who trespass against us): As someone has well said, and which we quoted in commentary on the last Chapter, *"We have nothing that is not sinful to bring before Him."* If we properly understand that, we now know and understand as to why Jesus said that we are to always come before the Lord in a state of contrition, or one might even say repentance. The Believer, and irrespective as to how close he walks with the Lord, is still *"coming short of the Glory of God"* (Rom. 3:23). As such, we always need forgiveness, and as such we must be very quick to forgive others who trespass against us. The reasons should be obvious.

NOTES

7. And lead us not into temptation, but deliver us from evil: The first part actually says, *"Do not permit us to be overcome with evil."* The latter part tells us that God is the only One Who can deliver us from evil. This means that if we look to any other source, such as psychology or to man in any form, we simply will not be delivered.

8. For Thine is the Kingdom, and the Power, and the Glory, forever, Amen: This tells us that the Kingdom belongs to God, and we are privileged to be a part of this Kingdom, which comes about by the *"New Birth"* (Jn. 3:3). As well, the Power belongs to God, *"and the Glory."* We must never forget that, for it will never change.

This means that man must never encroach upon the Glory of God, and again, for all the obvious reasons.

"Amen" seals all of this, in effect, saying that it will not change. In brief form, we have given the Lord's prescription as to how we ought to pray (Mat. 6:9-13).

THE FOUNDATION OF PRAYER

God can approach sinful man only on one basis, and that is through the Sacrifice of Christ. At the same time, sinful man as well can approach God only on the basis of the Sacrifice of Christ. Of course, we speak of the Cross!

Everything and we mean everything, is predicated on what Jesus did at the Cross and the Resurrection. This speaks of all contact with God, all fellowship with God, all communion with God. Everything goes through Jesus, but more particularly, through *"Jesus and Him Crucified"* (I Cor. 2:2).

This means that the Word of God in its entirety has as its foundation the Cross of Christ. Even though Faith cometh by hearing the Word, the Word must be anchored in the Cross, or else it ceases to be the Word (Jn. 1:1-5, 29). It doesn't matter how much Faith a person may have, if it is not Faith in the Finished Work of Christ, in His Atoning Sacrifice, in His Vicarious Offering, in Jesus as the Lamb of God, then it is not Faith that God will recognize (Rom. 8:1-2). Everything is always *"in Christ,"* which always refers to the Cross and the Resurrection, and the part the Believer has in that great Sacrifice (Rom. 6:3-5).

So, when we speak of prayer, or anything else for that matter as it pertains to the Lord, we must always begin with the Cross as our Foundation. If we begin otherwise, we sin! It is just that simple!

The Scripture plainly says, *"Whatsoever is not of* (the) *Faith is sin"* (Rom. 14:23). Considering that all Faith must have as its foundation the Cross of Christ, this means that any type of prayer which does not have as its foundation the Cross of Christ, and Faith in that Atoning Work, cannot be heard by God, at least in the sense of it being answered. This doesn't mean that the Believer has to have perfect understanding of all of these things, but just that he knows and understands at least in some way, that the Cross is the reason for our access to God in any capacity.

In fact, once the Believer properly understands the Cross and the Resurrection of Christ, and what it all means, and that everything that God does for us, to us, through us, and of us, is all tied to that Finished Work, then everything takes on a totally different complexion. The Word of God reads different, at least than before this was understood. Our life becomes different, our Faith is different, in fact, everything is different, and for the good. The reason is simple:

We are now trusting not at all in our performance, but totally in His performance, which is the basic story of the Gospel.

THANKSGIVING

The phrase, *"With thanksgiving,"* takes in all that God has done for us in the past, and what He will do in the future. This means that we are always to enter into the Presence of the Lord with thanksgiving. It is not proper to immediately begin to petition the Lord for all types of things, without first properly thanking Him for all He has done. We are speaking here of good manners, which to say the least, every Believer ought to have.

In fact, if one is to notice, the closer to the Lord one gets, his prayer time will be made up moreso of *"thanksgiving"* than anything else. What God has done for us stands out so big, so great, so wonderful, that we just want to thank Him over and over, actually never stopping. This shows gratitude and creaturely dependence, which are an absolute necessity if the Believer is to be what he ought to be in the Lord.

Actually, the manner in which the Holy Spirit gives us this Sixth Verse is that a listing of petitions should always be preceded and accompanied by thanksgiving. Thanksgiving is appropriate both in view of past answers to prayer and in view of anticipated answers. It is especially appropriate when one is giving thanks to God apart from His specific Gifts.

REQUESTS

The phrase, *"Let your requests be made known unto God,"* speaks of all things, material, physical, and spiritual — everything that concerns us in life along any line.

Concerning requests, God does not need to be informed of our needs for He knows what needs we have before we ask Him, but it is important that we voice these requests so that Faith can operate to bring the desired answer.

"Requests" is the translation of a word which emphasizes the objects asked for, namely, the things requested.

The preposition *"unto"* in the Greek Text suggests the translation, *"in the Presence of God,"* and is a delicate and suggestive way of hinting that God's Presence is always there, that it is the atmosphere surrounding the Christian.

As well, the word *"requests"* carries the idea that such for which we are asking, might not necessarily be in the Will of God; consequently, we are to always make all requests with the idea in mind, that we want His Will in all matters. In other words, if it is His Wisdom that we have these things, whatever the things might be, then we are to believe the request will be granted. If it is not in His Wisdom for such to be, then we are readily to accept that direction.

No, such an attitude does not hinder Faith; in fact, it increases Faith, for the simple reason that Faith for certain things cannot be proper, if those things are not in the Will of God. And any Christian who would demand such things, whatever they might be, is only conducting himself like a child, which God cannot honor.

There are many things spoken to us in the Word of God which tells us the Lord's direct Will; therefore, I do not have to seek the Will of God in those matters, because I already know what His Will actually is. For instance, I don't have to ask the Lord to save someone if it is His Will, because I already know His Will in those matters. He wills that everybody be saved.

But if I ask Him for a certain amount of money, which I certainly should do if I feel the need is there, I should leave it in His Hands after the petition is made, as to how that prayer will be answered and in the manner it will be answered. In respect to such a request, maybe the timing is not quite right, or the Lord wants to do something else which is always better for us than we at first realized. So this type of *"request"* must always be predicated on the Will of God, and the mature Saint will definitely always want it to be predicated on the Will of God.

DIVINE PROMISE

Anxieties as well as passions cannot stay when the Lord has His place at one's hand. Events do not disturb Him, so He is the Believer's confidence and refuge. Events shake neither His Throne nor His Heart; they only accomplish His Purposes.

He loves His people, and we are the objects of His tender care. He listens to our petitions and they are sure of the answer, be what they may, that is if we always have the Will of God in mind.

Prayer is request based upon Divine Promise. Supplication is a petition addressed to the Mercy of God. A man prays for the forgiveness of his sins, for that is promised; he supplicates for the recovery of his child for that lies in the Mercy and Counsels (Wisdom) of God.

The Apostle does not say that all asked for will be received, but he does say, even as we will study in the next Verse, that the Peace of God will garrison the heart.

(7) "AND THE PEACE OF GOD, WHICH PASSETH ALL UNDERSTANDING, SHALL KEEP YOUR HEARTS AND MINDS THROUGH CHRIST JESUS."

Having just given us a classic exhortation to pray, Paul attaches to it the beautiful promise that when we turn from anxiety to prayer and thanksgiving, God will give us His Own Peace. This Peace is for those who are already at Peace with God through Justification by Faith in Christ (Rom. 5:8). It speaks of sanctifying Peace, God's Peace, which is far more than any human forethought or plan might devise. It passes all understanding. It acts as a sentry to guard the Believer's heart (a Biblical symbol for the personality in which the mind resides) and the Believer's thoughts from all anxiety and despair.

THE PEACE OF GOD

The phrase, *"And the Peace of God,"* speaks of Sanctifying Peace and not Justifying Peace. They are two different things altogether!

Justifying Peace is that which a person instantly receives when he comes to Christ. It means that all enmity between the sinner and God is removed, because the sinner has evidenced Faith in Christ and what He did at the Cross. However, Sanctifying Peace is something else altogether, actually a process. The Christian may have it or may not have it, according to one's Faith and Trust in the Lord.

The words used here by Paul *"shall keep,"* refer to Sanctifying Peace, and are from a military word, meaning *"shall mount guard."* God's Peace, like a sentinel, mounts guard and patrols before the heart's door, keeping worry out; however, this is only if we commit all things to prayer seeking the Face of the Lord, sincerely wanting and desiring His help, leading, and guidance. Again, we emphasize that the two are linked together. Without a proper *"prayer life,"* one cannot have proper *"Peace."*

Guarding the heart is the consequence or the result of one's proper prayer life. Prayer is the condition, Peace the consequence.

There is a paradoxical quality in this Peace, in the sense that it exceeds our capacity for understanding it. We can experience it and know its ingredients in part, but we cannot encompass the total.

The word *"guard"* means *"to garrison."* The picture is that of a fortress with guards on duty (I Thess. 4:11). This Peace will serve to act as a rudder and a compass. It acts like a gyroscope in a battleship, giving poise under pressure. It helps to maintain one's spiritual and mental equilibrium under all conditions.

Since it is internal it is relatively unaffected by outward circumstances.

This is Faith; the heart does not keep the Peace of God, but the Peace of God keeps the heart, that is, when all burdens are cast upon Him Whose Peace nothing can disturb. How matchless the Grace that uses even anxiety as a means of ministering this marvelous Peace if the anxiety is brought to God.

So in anxieties the Believer may have the Peace of God, and in his ordinary life of Christian Testimony, he may have the God of Peace. Paul in his painful prison at Philippi rejoiced in the Lord, and at midnight sang praises to Him.

NOT AN ABSENCE OF PROBLEMS, BUT RATHER A POSSESSION OF PEACE

In the so-called confession principle some have claimed that if the right confession is maintained all or at least most problems will disappear. The Scriptures do not teach such. In fact, Satan is going to always oppose the Child of God, and especially one who truly trusts the Lord, in every way he can. However, at the same time, he can only do what he is allowed by the Lord to do. In other words, he does not have free access or free run one might say (Job Chpt. 1).

While Satan, of course, desires to destroy us, or at least, severely hinder us, the Lord naturally has something else in mind altogether.

The Faith of the Child of God must be tested constantly, but if the Believer will follow the admonition of the Scripture as given here by Paul, keep his Faith anchored in the Finished Work of Christ, without fail, he will have the Peace which God promises here. To be sure, it will be of such magnitude, that it will *"pass all understanding,"* i.e., *"be beyond the pale of comprehension, and because it is from above."*

This means that the Lord doesn't promise an absence of problems, but He does promise a plentiful supply of Sanctifying Peace, which means we've done several things, which we will outline after commentary on the next Verse.

THROUGH CHRIST JESUS

When Paul makes such statements as *"In Christ,"* or *"In Him,"* or such as made here, *"Through Christ Jesus,"* he always has in the mind the Finished Work of Christ, which has made all of this possible. Of course, we're speaking of the Cross and the Resurrection. The Reader must never misunderstand this or forget this.

In fact, a frightful price was paid that we might have this great Peace which Paul specifies here, and every other thing for that matter that comes to us from the Lord. The Cross is responsible for all things. I speak of access, blessings, the great Baptism with the Holy Spirit, etc. In fact, it is the Holy Spirit Who brings about all of these things, but He could not do so for Believers until the Cross, at least in the magnitude of this of which we speak (Jn. 16:17).

As well, the Holy Spirit demands that the Faith of the Believer be always anchored in the Cross, the Finished Work of Christ (Rom. 8:1-2).

The Reader may think I am overly repetitive respecting this all-important principle; however, due to the fact that the Church has had so little teaching on this in the last half of the 20th Century, I feel compelled to address this subject in every way I can, using every opportunity which presents itself. The problem with the modern Church is, that it thinks all of this is automatic. It isn't! In fact, Spirit-filled Believers probably fall into this trap more than anyone else.

Because they have been baptized with the Holy Spirit with the evidence of speaking with other Tongues, they somehow tend to think that this is all that is necessary, with all the great and good things automatically following. Then they learn to their dismay that all of these great and good things do not automatically follow and they are very confused. Unfortunately, instead of attempting to address the problem, the Church pretty much is in a state of denial. I think it takes a crisis before an individual will face up to his theology and admit that something isn't right, that is if such is actually the case, which it is with most.

There are millions of Christians who read these words as given by Paul, understanding them perfectly and clearly, but not at all enjoying their benefits. They wonder what is wrong? They search their hearts, but do not actually know what they're doing wrong, but just know that they don't have this Peace which Paul specifies here.

Or else, they claim to have it, when in reality they have actually never had it, and, therefore, don't really know what it actually is. We Christians are very bad about claiming things we don't have, because we feel like to not do so makes us less than others. And in this superman type of Christianity, this Hollywood version if you will, each one of us has to have all type of miracles daily. It's almost a one upmanship! It's the age of the rabbit out of the hat, and if we don't have our rabbit, we have to manufacture one somehow. Our miracle cannot be less than the miracle of the testimony we've just heard. So we deny reality and claim things oftentimes which aren't there.

A DISHONEST SPIRITUAL CLIMATE

We disguise our dishonesty by calling it *"Faith,"* and even try to make ourselves believe it is Faith, because that's what we've been taught. However, it isn't Faith! It isn't anything which resembles Faith! It is just plain dishonesty if one wants to know the truth about the matter, and I speak of claiming things we really don't have.

If the Believer does not understand the Cross and what it all means, which is certainly possible for even the least of us to understand, that is if we are given the proper teaching, the Believer is simply not going to have victory within his or her life. I don't care whatever else they do, whatever other confession they make, whatever other direction they take, there will be no victory. Victory is found only in the Cross, only in what Christ there did, only in His Finished Work.

For the most part, the so-called modern faith teaching is responsible for most of this dishonesty. It pictures a climate that is actually not true, and in fact, cannot be true as it is approached in that manner. In those circles, Faith is held up as a means to an end, the pipeline through which all good things come. All of this is very subtle, because Faith certainly does, of course, play such an important part in all that we are in Christ.

THE OBJECT OF FAITH

However, if one studies the Scriptures carefully, one notes that the greater emphasis is always placed on the object of Faith instead of Faith itself. The object of Faith must always be the Cross of Christ, which of course, includes the Resurrection and the Exaltation (Eph. 2:6).

Millions of Christians are busy trying to increase their Faith, when the Truth is they don't have a proper object of Faith. Of course, they claim the Word of God as the object; however, the Word they read, not properly in their minds being anchored in the Cross, turns out to be a perverted word. In other words, even as we've said several times, most attempt to use God's Word against Himself (against His Will). In other words, they think they can take the Word of God in any capacity, and make it do for them whatever they want. That is blatantly wrong!

The Word of God is always predicated on the Will of God (what He wants), which has its foundation in the Wisdom of God, with all having its foundation in the Finished Work of Christ.

Just as it was impossible for those in Judaism during the time of Paul to rightly understand the Scriptures, it is the same today with those who attempt to understand the Word of God apart from the Finished Work of Christ. It simply cannot be done!

So, when Paul says *"Through Christ Jesus,"* he is referring solely and completely, to what Christ did at the Cross, in order to make all of this possible promised to us in the New Covenant. We must never forget, that every bit of it is based on the Shed Blood and the broken Body of our Saviour.

Paul told us we must never forget this, and if we do improperly discern the Body of Christ, we can bring to ourselves very unfortunate circumstances (I Cor. 11:23-30).

(8) "FINALLY, BRETHREN, WHATSOEVER THINGS ARE TRUE, WHATSOEVER THINGS ARE HONEST, WHATSOEVER THINGS ARE JUST, WHATSOEVER THINGS ARE PURE, WHATSOEVER THINGS ARE LOVELY, WHATSOEVER THINGS ARE OF GOOD REPORT; IF THERE BE ANY VIRTUE, AND IF THERE BE ANY PRAISE, THINK ON THESE THINGS."

As we read this beautiful Passage, we must always understand, that it is impossible to do this of which the Apostle proclaims that we should do, if we have not first of all engaged that which he has previously said.

Believers should keep on thinking and doing what is morally and spiritually excellent. This involves centering our minds on exalted things and then putting into practice what we have learned.

Here Paul has set forth in memorable words a veritable charter for Christian thought. Although this beautiful list of virtues is not exclusively Christian, we need not suppose that Paul has borrowed it from pagan moralists, for such in real terms do not exist. Such are found only in Christ.

BRETHREN

The phrase, *"Finally, Brethren,"* tells us, that only Believers can enjoy these things given to us by the Holy Spirit. In fact, the world denies these qualities in Christians, or else think they can obtain such by their own ingenuity, etc. Despite the claims, all are doomed to failure, because all of this is a work exclusively of the Lord and from the Lord. These qualities can only be had by those who truly serve the Lord and are truly Born-Again. Sadly and regrettably, many, if not most, Christians little enjoy all of these great qualities we can have. Unfortunately, too many of us attempt to have them in all the wrong ways, which, of course, God can never honor.

However, the gist of all this is, that whatever is promised in the Word of God, can be ours. We just have to know the way and the manner in which the Lord deals with people, and the results will be ours. In fact, that way is simple, but we tend to confuse the issue, and very quickly.

The following is the manner in which we are able to have all of the great things promised to us in the Word of God:

1. We must always understand, that all blessings, and in every capacity, flow strictly from the Finished Work of Christ. By that we speak of the Cross and the Resurrection. The Believer must know and understand that.

2. God works on the principle of Faith. Some have tried to make Faith very difficult, very hard to obtain. It isn't! To have Faith simply means that we believe what God has said. We may not understand it all, but we do believe it. That's what Faith actually is; however, we must not stop there.

We must always understand, that this commodity called Faith, this great principle called Faith, must always rest within the Cross. This is absolutely imperative if we are to have all the things God has promised.

3. When we exhibit Faith in the right object, which is the Finished Work of Christ, the Holy Spirit then helps us to do all of these things and have all of these things promised; however, He will not work for us unless our Faith is properly anchored and in the correct object which is the Cross (Rom. 8:1-2).

TRUE

The phrase, *"Whatsoever things are true,"* in the Greek Text, refers to that which is true in character in the widest sense. The term implies integrity and sincerity with no falsehood or hypocrisy.

This virtue was greatly prized among the best of the Greeks. It is a Persian ideal as well. However, that which those particular cultures deemed as *"true,"* pretty well changed with the climate. It is only with Christianity, and that which pertains to the Lord, can anything actually be termed or labeled as *"true."*

There is a difference, however, in that which is *"true,"* and in the principle of *"Truth"* itself. In effect, Truth is actually a Person, and I speak of the Lord Jesus Christ (Jn. 14:6). So, the *"true"* of which Paul speaks here, does not pertain to that which is merely true, but only that which is anchored in Christ. In other words, for it to be *"true"* as the Apostle speaks here, it must at the same time be *"Truth."*

It is true that Heroin will give one a *"high,"* so to speak; however, that is merely a fact, and has no resemblance to *"Truth."* So, the *"true"* of which Paul speaks, must in every capacity be tied to *"Truth,"* which of course is only in Christ Jesus and, in fact, can only be in Christ Jesus.

HONEST

The phrase, *"Whatsoever things are honest,"* refers to that which is venerable, inviting reverence, worthy of reverence. The word exhorts us here to a due appreciation of such things as produce a noble seriousness.

Actually, the Greek word used can be translated in a variety of ways, with the word *"honorable"* probably being the nearest to the true meaning. The word points to a Christian decorum, a Christian self-respect, which is quite consistent with true humility, for it is a reverence for the Temple of God, which in essence is ourselves, but understanding that we house the Holy Spirit, so to speak.

This means that the word, therefore, does not express precisely what the word honest does with us, as confined to dealings or business transactions, but rather has reference to what was regarded as worthy of reputation or honor; what there was in the customs of society, and the respect due to age and rank, and in the intercourse of the world, that which deserves respect or esteem.

It includes indeed what is right in the transaction of business, but it embraces also much more, and means that the Christian is to show respect to all the venerable and proper customs of society, when they do not violate conscience or interfere with the Law of God.

JUST

The phrase, *"Whatsoever things are just,"* is from the Greek word meaning both *"just"* and also *"righteous."*

In a non-Christian world it was the Romans who made the chief contributions to the world's concept of justice. Roman Law acquired a worldwide and well-deserved reputation. Paul wants his readers to appreciate these qualities and not reject them out of hand simply because they are found in a pagan context.

The wisdom of such exhortations is illustrated by the action of an early Methodist Preacher who, in his zeal for separation from the world, destroyed all his volumes of Shakespeare. Wesley did not approve of this because he wanted his men to appreciate any merit they found in this great English Poet. The Christian should be both discriminating and selective, not withholding appreciation where it is due.

However, from a fact, the world has precious little to offer as it regards these qualities which, in effect, are the product of the Holy Spirit.

NOTES

PURE

The phrase, *"Whatsoever things are pure,"* speaks of purity in all things.

This term is relatively rare in the New Testament. It comes from the same root as the word *"holy"* and has the meaning of *"purity"* as in I John 3:3. It means *"moral purity"* and has the connotation of Holiness.

It calls for a freedom from defilement and from all that is unwholesome. The devout Christian who is filled with the Spirit and who has the Mind of Christ will instinctively shrink from anything he reads or hears that is not noble and pure. To take part in a joke or story that lacks purity is inconsistent with the profession of Christ.

A secret admiration for such type of thinking in a person indicates a need for purity of heart. A person who feels this secret satisfaction in impurity needs to be Crucified with Christ and purged from every vestige of defilement.

That's the reason that most Television, as well as the Movies, is an offense to Christians. In fact, most of that which is produced by the world falls into this category, which means that the Child of God must be very discriminating in what he watches, reads, observes, etc., or with whom he associates.

LOVELY

The phrase, *"Whatsoever things are lovely,"* employs the term, meaning amiable or attractive. The term occurs nowhere else in the New Testament. It means *"winsome, attractive, affectionate, and beloved."*

This adjective was common on pagan epitaphs. Thus, the deceased were described as *"pleasing"* and *"agreeable."* We learn from this that everyone who possesses Grace should also be gracious.

It is often an embarrassment to an earnest Christian to realize that there are some non-Christians who have more gracious ways than some Christians. Along with some rugged Christian virtues, every Believer in Christ should also possess the milk of human kindness and the traits of courtesy and agreeableness that are so universally admired and desirable.

A little girl once prayed, *"Lord, make all the bad people good, and make all the good people nice."* How wonderful it would be if this prayer would be answered!

To be practical, it speaks of being nice and kind to the waiter or waitress. They appreciate kind words as well! Let's put it this way:

What you as a Christian are when you are alone with a person who has the lowest station in life, is what you actually are. Unfortunately, some Christians are one thing to some people and another to others. I think you know what I mean!

A Christian should not be sour, crabbed, and irritable in his temper — for nothing almost tends so much to injure the Cause of Christ as a temper always chafed; a brow morose and stern; an eye that is severe and unkind; or, a disposition to find fault with everything.

And yet, as stated, it is to be regretted that there are many persons, who make no pretensions to Christ, who far surpass many professors of the Lord in the virtue commended here. A sour and crabbed temper in a professor of Salvation will undo all the good that he attempts to do.

GOOD REPORT

The phrase, *"Whatsoever things are of good report,"* refers to that which is *"of good repute, well thought of, generally commendable."*

Unfortunately, far too many Christians enjoy hearing a *"bad report,"* and I speak of something morally bad as it concerns someone else, than they do that which is good. What does that say?

It says that those who conduct themselves accordingly are not actually saved, or else they have strayed so far from the Lord, that they have completely extended themselves beyond the great Christian Graces. In other words, they are on the trembling edge of spiritual oblivion. But regrettably, the *"bad report"* problem is altogether too desirable in many so-called Christian circles. We speak of gossip!

VIRTUE

The phrase, *"If there be any virtue,"* in classical Greek stands for any mental excellence, moral quality, or physical power. Paul elsewhere studiously avoids using this word. Only here does he use it.

It seems that the Apostle includes it in order that he may not omit any possible ground of appeal.

As it is obvious according to the manner Paul uses these phrases, he tells the Christian, I think, that even though we are not of this world's system, we should do our best to appreciate any and all things which, in fact, stand the test of scrutiny and are, therefore, commendable. Of course, these are few and far between, but they do exist. I guess what we are trying to say here, is that true Christianity doesn't put one above the crowd, even though, in fact, one is above the crowd. The idea is, that humility be the foundation of all that we are and all that we do.

If someone in the world, and of course I speak of those who do not know the Lord, has an excellent voice for singing, it is not wrong for me as a Christian to express appreciation for such a voice, even though I may be totally opposed to the material which comes from the voice, etc. Talent and ability can be admired, and, in fact, I think that Paul is saying here, that as Christians it is demanded that we properly admire that which can be properly admired.

This curtails the *"holier than thou"* attitude which is so prevalent in some circles. This spirit never characterized our Saviour, and it should not characterize us.

PRAISE

The phrase, *"And if there be any Praise,"* refers to whatever excellence, which we have just stated, that there might be which can be a fit object of Praise. It is not referring to spiritual things only, but to anything which can be judged accordingly in a proper sense.

The term actually carries the idea of anything worthy of praise or that ought to be praised. Let's say it another way:

As it is proper to praise that in the world which is commendable of praise, we certainly should not do less concerning those who are in Christ. If a Preacher preaches a good Message, it's not wrong to praise that which is done, providing we keep it within proper bounds. The same can be said, for anything done by any Believer. To be frank, such at times is very encouraging.

We little know what is going on in the hearts and lives of our Christian Brothers and Sisters. Sometimes, even though they may not show it on their countenance or by their demeanor, discouragement may actually be the case. A word of praise at the right time, can go a long way toward dispelling such.

While it is not to be overdone, and while we as Christians are to never take such too seriously, still, these admonitions given here by the Apostle are sanctioned by the Holy Spirit. As such, it is far more than mere advice, but rather that which should be characteristic of the Child of God.

THE WAY WE THINK

The phrase, *"Think on these things,"* speaks of the act of careful reflection. How scarce a commodity this is in our mechanized age (Wuest).

It follows from these exhortations that we should not occupy our minds, or at least feed our minds, on anything to which any of these adjectives could not be applied. Not only do unedifying subjects bring moral pollution, they also usurp the place of something better.

There are so many good things in the world, that it will more than occupy one's attention if he follows Paul's admonition to meditate upon these things.

Since the mind is one of the most important parts of the personality, it is of the utmost importance to make the best use of it, which in fact, can only truly be done in Christ.

This which Paul tells us, implies that we can, and, therefore, are bound to, control our thoughts. But to *"think on"* is not to contemplate merely, not such speculation apart from action, such merely *"going over the theory of virtue in one's thoughts and drawing fine pictures of it,"* instead what the Holy Spirit is saying here, is that these should be looked at as principles for the guidance of life.

Thus, we have in the Word not so much *"those things do"* but the thought which precedes, suggests and directs action, which will decide what type of action it will be. In other words, to carry out that which is right in our daily living, we must first have reflected on the Truth of what must be done. Consequently,

NOTES

I hope we now see just how important all of this actually is.

GOD'S FORMULA FOR MENTAL AND SPIRITUAL HEALTH

There are seven steps which the Holy Spirit has outlined here which constitute the key or even the formula one might say, of a balanced, healthy, victorious, Christian Life. However, if one is to notice, even though all these things are spiritual, the Holy Spirit is dealing with the mental moreso than anything else. At the same time, it is impossible to deal with the mental, at least as it ought to be, unless we first deal with the spiritual. That means one has to know the Lord, and be faithfully following the Lord, before this which is given will have effect in one's life. And yet, I fear that even most Christians little take advantage of that which is given, which means that we greatly shortchange ourselves. Considering how important all of this is to our mental equilibrium and health, I should think the Christian ought to make these admonitions priority. It would seem to me that would be an absolute necessity.

In abbreviated form, let's look at what the Holy Spirit through Paul has given us:

1. Rejoice in the Lord always, irrespective as to what might be happening.

2. Be gentle with all people, even one's enemies, thereby allowing the Lord to defend us.

3. The Lord is at hand, which means that we as Believers are not subject to circumstances and situations, knowing and understanding that it is the Lord Who always has the final say in our lives concerning everything. In other words, nothing can happen without Him giving His approval one might say.

4. Don't worry about anything.

5. Commit everything to the Lord in prayer.

6. Always be thankful to the Lord for all the wonderful things He has done, and is doing, for us.

7. Think constantly on things of the Lord, which of course are always positive, and not on the opposite.

I think the Lord gave seven admonitions to us for a purpose, seven being God's perfect number. In other words, I think He is telling us, that if we will faithfully adhere to these simple admonitions as given by the Holy Spirit through Paul, that we will without fail guarantee to ourselves the benefits thereof. As well, there are several other things which we should mention in conjunction with this which are so very important. They are:

THE CROSS

We have the privilege of this mental health as outlined by the Holy Spirit, all because of what Jesus did at the Cross. He is the One Who has made all of this possible, and which He did so at great price. This must never be forgotten, the price He has paid, and that He paid it on a Cross. So, once again we go back to the Foundation of all Blessings, which is the Cross of Christ. It is very important that the Believer know this, grasp this, comprehend this, understand this, and never allow it to be pulled from our grasp.

PROPER OBJECT OF FAITH

Our Faith must always anchor itself in the Cross as it regards these many and even multitudinous Blessings which flow from the Finished Work of Christ. In other words, I must have Faith that what the Lord has said here, will in fact, come to pass. Faith is so very, very important, but more particularly, the proper object of one's Faith is the single most important thing. There are many Christians who are laboring trying to increase their Faith; however, if the object of Faith is not right, they will only come to frustration. Our Faith at all times must be in the Cross and for each benefit, and in this case our mental health, which we are now discussing.

THE HOLY SPIRIT

As our Faith is properly registered in the Cross, the Holy Spirit will then help us to do these things which He alone can do. In other words what I'm trying to say is, that even though we see these things, and even though they are afforded to us through the great Price that Jesus paid at the Cross, still, it is the Holy Spirit Who Alone can make all of these great things real within our hearts and lives. In fact, that's the reason that most Christians little have all the benefits of which Jesus has purchased with His Own Blood. All of these things, and irrespective as to what they might be as it regards the Lord, are spiritually discerned and only spiritually discerned, which means that only the Holy Spirit can perform the task. Regrettably, many Christians approach the Word of God exactly as they approach instructions given concerning secular things. It doesn't work that way. God's prescribed Order for all that we receive from Him is laid out in detail. It is very simple, but yet the Holy Spirit demands that we follow these instructions.

They are exactly that which we have just given you, *"The Cross, from which all Blessings flow, our Faith in the Cross, which every Believer must have, and which then allows the Holy Spirit to do His Work, making real to us that which Jesus has purchased for us."* To be even more simple, it is *"The Cross, our Faith, and the Holy Spirit."* If we take any other route, and irrespective as to how religious it might be, or how much effort we make, the end result will not be that promised by the Lord. We must go His Way!

(9) "THOSE THINGS, WHICH YE HAVE BOTH LEARNED, AND RECEIVED, AND HEARD, AND SEEN IN ME, DO: AND THE GOD OF PEACE SHALL BE WITH YOU."

Since Paul himself had been their teacher and example, what they had learned from him they were to keep on practicing.

The four verbs in this Verse form two pairs. The first pair, *"learned"* and *"received,"* describes the Philippians' instruction by Paul, from whom they had been taught Christian Doctrine and Christian living.

The next pair, *"heard"* and *"saw,"* depicts their personal observation of the Apostle — both his speech and his conduct. Consequently, several things are said here, which we will attempt to address:

THOSE THINGS

The short phrase, *"Those things,"* in fact, pertains to the entirety of the New Covenant. Even though said politely and in abbreviation, *"those things"* are the single most important thing there could ever be, pertaining to our Salvation as it regards our serving the Lord.

But yet, Paul is more particularly speaking in this part of the Epistle of *"Peace"* than he is anything else. As stated, this is *"Sanctifying Peace,"* which has to do with our spiritual and mental welfare.

Even though the world offers all type of solutions, in fact, they have no solution whatsoever. This as it concerns our Peace, which of course is extremely important to the Child of God, is strictly a spiritual principle, and can be entered upon in no other manner.

What we are addressing here, is that which the world of humanistic psychology addresses as well, but with no success whatsoever. In fact, psychology is expert as it regards symptoms, which fools many people. In other words, people think because Psychologists understand the principle of Pavlov's dog, meaning that if certain things are repetitively done, the dog will act the same way every time, they have proper knowledge. Nevertheless, even though psychology is a master at symptoms, it knows nothing of the real origin of problems or of their cure. In fact, it only majors in symptoms, with proposed solutions worthy of a Roman Circus. And yet, most of the Church world falls for this foolishness, and foolishness it is!

THE MANNER OF PSYCHOLOGY

Psychology basically falls into three directions. They are:

1. Behavioristic psychology: this states that behavior is brought about through one's environment, therefore, it can be changed by changing the environment.

2. Humanistic psychology: this teaches that man is an animal and can thereby be trained to do whatever needs to be done — exactly as most animals can be trained. As environment is the key word in behavioristic psychology, education is the key word in humanistic psychology.

3. Freudistic psychology: Freud taught that every single problem that besets humanity is sexual in some nature; consequently, human beings go through various sexual stages, and if things are not presently going well, it is because they have not addressed one of these stages correctly, or else they are still in that particular stage, never having advanced, etc. However, it is known that Freud had particular sexual hangups, which no doubt colored his thinking along these particular lines.

While man is a physical being, and a mental being, he is also a spiritual being. Psychology completely ignores the spiritual, at least in the manner in which the Bible addresses the subject, so of necessity, it is impossible for their proposals to be of any service. In fact, the Word of God holds the answer, actually the only answer, for the ills of man in every spiritual and mental capacity. Therefore, if our help is not derived solely from that Source, and I speak of the Word of God, then in reality we can find no help. Peter plainly said:

"According as His Divine Power hath given unto us all things that pertain unto Life and Godliness, through the knowledge of Him (Jesus) *that hath called us to glory and virtue."*

He then said, *"Whereby are given unto us exceeding great and precious promises: that by these ye might be partakers of the Divine Nature, having escaped the corruption that is in the world through lust"* (II Pet. 1:3-4).

No, environment is not man's problem, and neither is it education. As well, the problem is not sexual hangups either.

While all of these things, and even others we have not named, may definitely play a part in the hurdles of life, it is a part only, of which the solution will not greatly alleviate the situation. Man can only find what he is looking for in Christ. It is all and total in what Jesus did at the Cross on our behalf. That and that alone is the solution.

LEARNED AND RECEIVED

The phrase, *"Which ye have both learned, and received,"* tells us several things:

1. All things we receive from the Lord have to be learned. Two things are required in the learning process.

First of all, we have to make the effort, and second, we have to understand that the Holy Spirit on top of our effort, is the only One Who can reveal the truth of all this to us, but He demands the effort on our part.

It's not that we earn anything by our effort, but that we show desire to learn the things of God, which if such desire is present, will always fall out to effort on our part.

What do we mean by effort?

First of all, we speak of every Christian setting himself to the task of learning and understanding the Word of God. This means setting aside some time each day to study the Word, and be habitual about this time, and not allow anything to rob us of this all-important effort.

We live in a very busy time, and Satan uses all of this to crowd out the things which are very important. The truth is, we have time for ball games, recreational activities, hobbies, and a hundred and one other things, but we little make time for that which is a million times more important than anything else we might do — the learning and understanding of the Word of God.

Unfortunately, most laymen take the position that such study and effort to learn applies only to Preachers. While it definitely does apply to Preachers, in fact, it applies to all Believers. And yet, most Believers, and I think I can say without exaggeration, allow someone else to do their thinking for them, which always leads to tremendous trouble. In other words, they simply believe what they hear, without really knowing if it is Scriptural or not! As stated, this is the blueprint for disaster. Any Christian who is too busy for the Word of God, is busier than he ought to be.

2. We are not only to learn this of which the Word of God tells us, but as well we are to receive it. By that, the Holy Spirit means that we are to make it a practicing part of our lives.

Satan does not want you to receive the Truth, so he clouds the Truth, shades the Truth, or else surrounds error with Truth, which in fact, is his most subtle effort of all.

Every Christian *"receives"* the Word of God in some manner. As should be obvious, if what we receive is wrong, the results will play out in our lives in the realm of trouble and problems and of every description.

These Philippians heard Paul teach and preach the Gospel, and received it. As we will see momentarily, he is urging them to not allow anything else to come in which will hinder that which they have received.

The Truth is, all Believers are continually receiving; however, we should ask ourselves the question as to what it is we are receiving?

NOTES

If in fact, you the Reader have received the Truth, then Satan will do all within his power to feed you error. He will do it in many and varied ways, but almost always all together using Preachers as his instruments. If so, the Holy Spirit refers to them as Satan's ministers (II Cor. 11:12-15).

THE CHURCH ALWAYS RECEIVES FROM THE LORD WHAT IT ACTUALLY IS

And what do we mean by that statement?

If the Church wants foolishness, chicanery, dishonesty, false apostles, false prophets, false doctrine, etc., the Lord will see to it that that's what the Church receives. And tragically that's exactly what the Church is mostly now receiving.

The Church little wants and desires the True Gospel of Jesus Christ, so the Lord allows the Church to have what it wants. And what does it have?

It has Preachers who have denied the veracity of the Holy Spirit, and so the Church has spiritual deadness. It has Preachers who have perverted the Holy Spirit and the Word of God, claiming that gain is godliness (I Tim. 6:5), which tends only to exploit the Saints. It has Preachers promoting every type of manifestation which one can think, all claiming to be of God. It has false prophets claiming that Christians should stock up on dried beans, or some other type foolishness as it regards the coming new Millennium, and false apostles promoting every weird doctrine which can be conceived in the perverted minds of men.

I'll say it again, *"what the Church has, is what the Church is!"*

The ministry as a whole (with some few exceptions), is busy telling the Church that the Book of Acts is not for this present time, or else it is going to the other extreme and blowing on them, making them think they have just received some type of miracle. The modern Church either denies the miracles, or puts forth false miracles. Either way is disaster. Christians are crawling on their all fours barking like dogs or crowing like roosters, claiming such to be a manifestation of the Spirit. While it is definitely a manifestation of a spirit, it is definitely not the manifestation of the Holy Spirit.

Again, what the Church has, is what the Church is!

Why?

Addressing myself only to the present, I will answer accordingly:

In the 1980's the Church was presented with the True Gospel. It basically stated that it did not want that Gospel, so it was removed. It now has what it wanted. It received the Gospel but would not accept the Gospel, so now it is receiving at least for the most part, a false message.

HEARD AND SEEN

The phrase, *"And heard, and seen in me, do,"* refers to the fact that Believers are to be living Epistles and especially Preachers.

One might boil all of this down to the actual fact that the Philippians had heard Paul preach and teach the Truth of the Gospel. The word *"heard"* as given here needs to be looked at a little more closely.

There are two particulars as it concerns the Gospel of Christ. First of all, the Word of God has to be preached and taught correctly, and as well, it has to be seen and heard correctly. As we're dealing here with the *"seeing and hearing,"* we will limit ourselves to that.

Hearing the Gospel correctly, goes back to what Jesus said over and over again, *"Who hath ears to hear let him hear"* (Mat. 11:15; 13:9; Mk. 4:9; etc.). He also said, *"see not; and hearing they hear not"* (Mat. 13:13).

What did he mean by having ears to hear?

First of all, He wasn't speaking of the physical aspect of their hearing but rather the spiritual. In fact, they could hear the Words He was saying very clearly, and as well, at least in most cases, the words were easy to understand referring to their meaning. But due to the fact that we have to *"hear spiritually,"* as well as hear physically, they could not hear, because they did not have the spiritual capacity to do so. Consequently, they did not know or understand what He was talking about, at least most of them. It is the same presently.

For a Believer to properly *"hear"* the Gospel, several things must be involved. First of all, we must have a desire to hear the Word of God, and I mean to hear it properly to where we properly understand what is being said and done. This also means that we should not be willing to let others hear for us, but rather that we are to hear for ourselves, which God certainly intends. There's only One Mediator between God and men, the Man Christ Jesus. Unfortunately, much of the Church world, whether they realize it or not, are actually looking to mediators other that Christ.

To be sure, the Lord has set in the Church, *"Apostles, Prophets, Evangelists, Pastors, and Teachers."* He has done all of this *"For the perfecting of the Saints, for the work of the Ministry, for the edifying of the Body of Christ;*

"Till we all come in the unity of the Faith, and of the knowledge of the Son of God, and to a perfect (mature) *man, unto the measure of the stature of the fullness of Christ"* (Eph. 4:11-13).

But at the same time, just because the individuals in question are definitely called of God, doesn't mean they are to be obeyed without question. In fact, all, even God called Preachers, are human and thereby, prone to mistakes. This means that the Believer is to know the Word of God himself, that he might know that what he is hearing is in fact Scripturally correct.

Also, the Believer should keep his mind open constantly as it regards the Word of God, never having the attitude that he has all the light on any given subject. In fact, it is impossible to exhaust the Word, meaning that whatever we know about the Word, there is still more to be learned. But at the same time, Satan is ever attempting to insert the false along with the true, so we have to be careful as to what we hear.

THE ANOINTING

Every Believer has the Holy Spirit, and some Believers also are baptized with the Holy Spirit, which gives greater latitude to the Spirit. One of the works of the Holy Spirit in our hearts and lives is the *"anointing"* which helps us to understand if what we are hearing is in fact, correct, and, of course, we're speaking of the Word of God (I Jn. 2:27).

For this *"anointing"* to properly function, the Believer must be humble before the Lord, always desiring to learn the Word, and earnestly seeking the Face of the Lord that we be in such spiritual condition that we can properly hear the Word. None of this is automatic! It is all predicated on our submission to the Lord with an humble and contrite spirit, knowing and realizing that we must have His help, if we are to function properly as a Believer. All of this is extremely important as should be obvious, and prayerfully the Reader will take it all to heart. Considering that we are speaking of that which is the single most important thing in the world, one's Salvation and thereby one's victory in the Lord, we should want to know all that is possible to know about this very important subject.

It is very easy for the Believer to get into the place spiritually speaking, that Israel was when Jesus came. Only a small number actually heard what He said, and simply because they did not have spiritual ears to hear. He was speaking, but they did not know what He was saying, even though the words were very clear and plain. It is the same no less with many modern Christians.

Inasmuch as all of this is so very important, let's look more fully at what the Word says about hearing.

TO HEAR AND TO LISTEN

At times the two words in our heading are used in the Bible in their simplest descriptive sense: Adam and Eve *"heard the sound of the Lord God as He was walking in the Garden"* (Gen. 3:8). But the text goes on to report that they immediately tried to hide.

Because we human beings have been shaped as we are by God and have been given minds that process the data of our senses, we go beyond the simple act of hearing to interpret what we hear and to act on it. In both Testaments the word *"hear"* and *"listen"* recognize this fact and thus have special significance.

THE OLD TESTAMENT CONCEPT

The root word of both *"hear"* and *"listen"* in the Hebrew is *"sama."* It occurs many times in the Old Testament, either in the words mentioned, or many of its derivatives. The basic thought is that of effective hearing.

In most contexts the act of hearing is extended beyond:

1. The physical act of hearing to suggest . . .

NOTES

2. Processing what we have heard . . .
3. Responding to what is heard.

The emphasis of *"hear"* or *"listen"* may be on any of these three aspects. The statement that Adam and Eve *"heard the sound of the Lord"* focuses on the act of hearing. In Genesis 3:17 God introduced an announcement of judgment on the fallen pair by saying to Adam, *"Because you listened to your wife."*

Here there is an emphasis on the response: Adam listened, considered, and paid attention to what Eve said. He let her view shape his action, rather than paying attention to the command of God.

In Genesis 11:7 the emphasis is on processing. God acted on the minds of the people at Babel *"so they* (would) *not understand each other."* Usually the context will make the focus of the word (on the act, the processing, or the response) clear. Often the translators choose a word that gives one of those specific meanings.

HEARING GOD

The Christian experience is a revealed experience. The Creator of the universe, Who has acted to redeem mankind, has spoken in a clear and decisive Word. Man is called upon to perceive, process, and respond appropriately to God's Word. Because God is Lord, the appropriate response to His Word is obedience.

This stress in the Old Testament is so deeply established that in most cases where we read the word *"obey"* the actual Hebrew word used before translated was *"sami,"* which actually means to *"hear or listen."*

Wherever the words *"hear"* and *"listen"* are used of human relationship with God, obedient response is implied. Response is not only appropriate but essential to truly *"hearing the Lord."* Consequently, I think one could say that the reason that Israel did not properly hear what Jesus was saying, is because they did not want to obey. It is the same presently.

Pharaoh, for instance, who did not recognize God, reacted understandably to Moses' demand that he let Israel go. *"Who is the Lord, that I should obey* (sama, 'hear') *Him and let Israel go?"* (Ex. 5:2). But even after a series of Divine Judgments demonstrated to all Egypt who Israel's God actually was, Pharaoh still would neither listen nor respond.

As God's chosen people, Israel knew God. It was on their behalf that the Lord did all His wonderful works. Thus, Israel would be responsible to hear, grasp, and respond to God's Word. This call was basic to the relationship between God's people and the Lord.

"Now if you obey Me fully (sama, *'hear'*) *and keep My Covenant, then out of all nations you will be My treasured possession"* (Ex. 19:5).

Much later in history the disasters that struck the nation were explained by Jeremiah as happening because of Israel's failure to hear, in the sense of responding appropriately to the Lord: *"They did not obey* (sama) *You or follow Your Law; they did not do what You commanded them to do. So You brought all this disaster upon them"* (Jer. 32:23).

So we remember as we read. The call to hear God, which runs as a bright thread through the Old Testament, is a call to know what He said, to grasp the meaning of what He said, to respond by putting God's Word into practice.

ASKING GOD TO HEAR

The Old Testament presents a Living God, Who can and does act in the world of people. Thus, God's people can pray to God and expect His intervention. Often in the prayers recorded in the Bible this expectation is expressed in cries to God to hear the worshippers.

The link between hearing and action is clearly seen in Solomon's prayer at the dedication of the Temple. Hearing is extended in this prayer and is defined in context as *forgiving* (II Chron. 6:21, 25, 27, 30), as *repaying* the guilty and *establishing* innocence (II Chron. 6:23), as *bringing* Israel back to the land (II Chron. 6:25), as *teaching* the right way to live and *sending* rain on the land (II Chron. 6:27), as *dealing* with each person according to all he does (II Chron. 6:30), as *doing* whatever the petitioner asks (II Chron. 6:33), and as *upholding* the worshipers' cause (II Chron. 6:35-39).

The Psalmist finds it impossible to believe that *"He* (God) *Who implanted the ear cannot hear or that He Who formed the eye cannot see"* (Ps. 94:9). As Judge, God is aware of all that happens on Earth, and He is not only able to intervene, but, in fact, Satan has to have His permission for whatever is done (Job Chpt. 1). Thus, we can pray to Him with confidence, expecting Him to *"hear,"* to understand our need, and to respond by giving us the help we require.

HEARING AND LISTENING IN THE NEW TESTAMENT

The Greek word for *"hear"* or *"listen"* is *"akouo,"* and is not quite as inclusive as the Hebrew *"sama."* In Greek culture, *"akouo"* involved the act of hearing and was extended to include processing what was heard. But the further extension to response is expressed in Greek by another word *"hypakouo,"* which means *"to listen," "to obey."*

This means that in the New Testament, the word *"hear"* in the Greek sense rather than carrying over the Hebrew sense in which response is implied and included in hearing, there is a different meaning given. As we have learned, the words *"hear"* or *"listen"* in the Hebrew, meant not only would the person hear, but they were also expected to obey. It is not quite that way in the Greek, with another emphasis placed on *"obedience."* Let's look at it closer:

HEARING AS PERCEPTION

Several incidents in the Gospels help us to explore the relationship between hearing and perception. Exploring the unresponsiveness of Israel, Jesus related the Parable of the Sower (Mat. 13:1-23; Mk. 4:1-20; Lk. 8:4-15).

He linked His use of Parables to Isaiah's prophetic picture of an unresponsive Israel: *"This people's heart has become calloused; they hardly hear with their ears, they have closed their eyes"* (Mat. 13:15). In Jesus' Parable, He likens the Word to seed spread by a Sower. It falls on different soils, representing the way different hearers process the message.

Some (the rocky ground) are unable to perceive or grasp anything of the meaning of the Message (Mat. 13:19). Some readily receive the Word; but, then when persecution comes on account of the Word, they cease living by the Word (Mat. 13:20-21).

Others receive the Word but soon become unfruitful because of the *"worries of this life and the deceitfulness of wealth"* (Mat. 13:22). The good soil represents the *"man who hears the word and understands it"* (Mat. 13:23). Understanding involves reshaping one's whole perception of the meaning of life.

Only when the Word is allowed to reshape perception will it produce a crop over an extended period of time in the hearers life.

John's Gospel reports another confrontation of Jesus with those who refuse to hear. *"Why is My language not clear to you?"* Jesus asked. *"Because you are unable to hear what I say"* (Jn. 8:43).

He explained that these men who rejected and resisted Him were in the family line of Satan, who is committed to lies and cannot comprehend Truth. Jesus concluded, *"He who belongs to God hears what God says. The reason you do not hear is that you do not belong to God"* (Jn. 8:47).

A person's perceptual feel — how one views life and attends to the multiple messages that each of us hears — is ultimately shaped by one's attitude toward God and His Word. If God has the central place that is rightly His, all other things fall into place as well. But if God is not given His rightful place in our lives and recognized for Who He is, the Message of the Word of God cannot be heard, in the sense of truly being understood.

HEARING AND FAITH

The New Testament makes it clear that hearing God's Word also necessarily involves responding to it, just as the Hebrew *"sama"* implies. In other words, the person is going to respond in some manner, whether right or wrong.

Jesus emphasizes response in His story of the two builders (Mat. 7:24-27). The wise builder builds on rock and pictures *"everyone who hears these words of Mine and puts them into practice"* (Mat. 7:24).

The foolish builder builds on sand; he represents *"everyone who hears these words of Mine and does not put them into practice"* (Mat. 7:26). James puts it in terms of self-deceit: only the one who looks into the Word *"and continues to do this* (i.e., maintains the perception that the Word shapes), *not forgetting what he has heard, but doing it* (acting in harmony with the new perception) *he will be blessed in what he does"* (James 1:25).

But with this emphasis, the New Testament adds in Hebrews Chapters 3 and 4 an analysis of what it is that moves the individual beyond a mere understanding to response. Looking back in history, the writer describes the Exodus generation. They heard God's voice but hardened their hearts and did not obey. The writer who was probably Paul, explains, *"We see that they were not able to enter* (the Promised Land), *because of their unbelief"* (Heb. 3:19).

Continuing, the writer points out that *"we also have had the Gospel preached to us, just as they did; but the Message they heard was of no value to them because those who heard it did not combine it with Faith"* (Heb. 4:2).

It is Faith, a settled confidence that God's spoken Word is reliable and can be trusted, that is a necessary attitude as we approach God. We hear, we understand the implications as the Word reshapes our perceptions, and then we express trust in God by acting on the Word and putting it into practice.

IN SUMMARY

Both the Old Testament and the New Testament place great theological significance on *"hearing."* In the Old Testament the physical act, the mental process of grasping meaning, and the appropriate response of obedience are all included when hearing or listening to God is mentioned.

The New Testament uses a Greek word that focuses on the first two of these aspects — hearing and responding. The mental process is pictured as a shaping of perspective, so that the Word determines the way the hearer views all the issues of life. The goal of hearing is to have our outlook completely reshaped, so that God's Word will determine our values and attitudes.

But the New Testament also focuses on the third aspect of hearing, which is obedience. It does so by pressing us to put into practice what was heard. The first two are considered to be futile unless they issue in appropriate action — in doing God's Word.

The key to response is a believing heart. When we hear what God says, see its meaning, and trust His outlook as being in fullest harmony with reality, we will put His Word into practice. Then, in the doing of the Word we have heard, which refers to obedience, we will be blessed.

The idea of all of this is, that what God has said is true and right and because it corresponds with reality. Conversely, what Satan says and does, which in effect, is the spirit of the world, because it is the spirit of fallen man, is not reality. In other words, it is not right and neither is it true. So, if we want reality, that which actually is, and we speak of the correct way of things, we must hear God, and more particularly hear His Word. Along with that, we must respond accordingly in respect to obeying correctly. Consequently, I would certainly think that the Reader can see as to how important all of this is.

DOES BEING A CHRISTIAN MEAN THAT ONE AUTOMATICALLY HEARS CORRECTLY?

Of course not! While every Believer definitely has the capacity to hear God and His Word correctly, which the world incidentally does not have, in no way means, however, that the Believer does in fact hear correctly, hence Paul giving these admonitions. We have the potential to do so, but not necessarily the actual fact of doing so.

The failure to hear correctly in no way lies with God or His Word, or the moving and operation of the Holy Spirit upon our hearts and lives, which should be obvious. The fault is always with us (II Cor. 13:5).

There are many problems still in the heart and life of the Believer. I speak of stubbornness, self-will, the tendency to lean on the arm of flesh, our own prejudice and bias, along with the frightful propensity to do wrong. However, the Holy Spirit can get through all of this, if we will but do several things:

THE BAPTISM WITH THE HOLY SPIRIT

Even though every Believer has the Holy Spirit as stated, I feel it is imperative that every Believer also be baptized with the Holy Spirit, which will always be accompanied by the speaking with other Tongues (Acts 2:4). I believe this gives the Holy Spirit greater latitude in the Believer's life, hence Jesus commanding this infilling and reception (Acts 1:4). This doesn't mean that the Believer is more saved, for one cannot be more saved than by trusting Christ, which refers to what He did at the Cross; however, it does refer to greater access by the Holy Spirit to the Child of God.

Unfortunately, none of this is automatic, and many Spirit-filled Believers little realize the full potential of the Holy Spirit which can be ours; however, that's not the fault of the Spirit, but ours alone.

THE CROSS

Once again we go back to the Cross of Christ. The Cross breeds humility, without which the Believer cannot be what he or she ought to be. So, I'm saying that every Believer should understand the Cross and the part that the Cross and the Resurrection of Christ plays, not only in our initial Salvation experience, but as well, in our every day walk before God. In other words, the Cross is just as viable for our continued experience with the Lord, as it was our initial experience of Salvation.

It is only through the Cross that humility is available to the Child of God, and the Cross alone. I personally feel that humility is impossible in any other way. The Believer must have a correct viewpoint on the Cross and a correct response to the Cross.

Of course, there must be a willingness and desire to properly hear the Word, just as we've already described, but I believe if the Christian will look to the Cross for all things, which of course epitomizes the Finished Work of Christ, then these other things will really take care of themselves. We will then properly listen, properly hear, properly respond, and thereby, properly obey.

ITCHING EARS AND THE AGE OF APOSTASY

I think one more word would be appropriate before we close our comments respecting this statement as given by Paul.

People who do not desire to *"hear"* the Word of God correctly, eagerly search out Churches where the Preacher tells them what they desire to *"hear."* In other words, they have *"itching ears,"* even as Paul said. His words were cryptic and to the point:

"For the time will come (it has already come) *when they will not endure sound doctrine; but after their own lusts shall they heap to themselves teachers, having itching ears;*

"And they shall turn away their ears from the Truth, and shall be turned unto fables" (II Tim. 4:3-4).

As stated, this time has already come, the time of apostasy.

In fact, there are very few modern Christians who really want the Truth of the Word of God. Most desire to make up their own religion, which will appease their conscience toward their wrongdoing, whatever that might be. Of course, there are always Churches, plenty of them, which will accommodate about anything anyone wants. However, anytime the Word of God is abrogated, curtailed, hindered, weakened, or compromised, it always falls out to the hurt of the individual who is involved.

During this time of apostasy, in fact, which will be the last great apostasy, people had better be trying to find Churches where the Word of God is preached in all of its power and purity. Unfortunately, those are few and far between, but there are some.

OBSERVED IN PAUL

The Philippians not only heard Paul preach and teach the Truth, but they as well saw it in action in his life, which is the greatest proof of all. This tells us something:

The Gospel of Jesus Christ changes lives. If the proper doctrine is known and followed, the proper results will always accrue, for that's what the Gospel is all about. That which does not change one's life, is really not the Gospel.

What was it exactly that the Philippians saw in the life of Paul?

They saw victory over sin in any and every capacity. They saw a joyful, even rejoicing attitude, irrespective as to what the circumstances were. They saw him exhibiting gentleness toward all people, and even his enemies, because he knew that the Lord had the final say in all things, and his trust was in the Lord.

They saw no anxiety or fear about Paul, and observed that he had a strong prayer life. They noted as well that he took everything to the Lord in prayer, and did so constantly thanking Him for all the things He had done and was doing.

Of course, they could not read his thoughts, but knowing the counsel that he had given them concerning *"think on these things,"* they knew that this was Paul's lifestyle. So what is actually being said here is, everything he had told the Philippians to do, it was this which he did himself, and which of course the Holy Spirit gave him, and which had proved so effective. Consequently, he is telling the Philippians to *"do"* the same things he has done.

In a similar manner, the Lord has opened up to me the Revelation of the Cross, which in effect, I also received from Paul, i.e., *"Romans Chapters 6, 7, and 8."* However, even though reading these Chapters all of my life, I did not actually know what they meant until some time in 1996.

Irrespective, this great teaching which was given to the Apostle by the Holy Spirit, has proved to be so revolutionary in my heart and life that in fact it has changed my life, and changed it totally. Consequently, I want every other Christian to observe this Evangelist, and hopefully to *"do"* exactly as I am doing, even as Paul concerning himself.

EXAMPLE

A number of different Greek words are found where the Scripture reads *"example."* However, the basic meaning of the most significant words is that of a figure or pattern which can serve as a model. In the New Testament the pattern is nearly always established by a person whose words and actions provide a living expression of that for which Scripture calls from all Believers.

At times the example found in the Bible is negative (Heb. Chpt. 4). But the concept of example is essentially positive.

Jesus set His followers an example of humility and love (Jn. 13:1-17). Christians are urged to follow the example of their leaders. In fact, providing an example is a primary task of leaders (I Tim. 4:12; I Pet. 5:3). The truths leaders teach must be given living expression so that the truths taught may be fully understood.

But Jesus remains the Believer's prime example (Jn. 13:15; II Pet. 2:8). Leaders can call on others to imitate them only as they themselves imitate the Lord (I Cor. 11:1).

Thus, Paul also served as an excellent example.

THE GOD OF PEACE

The phrase, *"And the God of Peace shall be with you,"* presents the assurance of God's Presence, which is the greatest possible Source of Security. That spoken is Sanctifying Peace.

To have the *"Peace of God"* with us is much; to have *"the God of Peace"* Himself with us is more. With this Promise the Letter in a way itself ends. What follows is but postscript.

If a person will take seriously the seven conditions which we have listed, given by the Apostle Paul and put them into practice, God will prove Himself faithful to His Promise. Of that, one can be certain!

In these ways which Paul gave unto us, (for they are God's Ways) God walks with men, exactly as He did with Adam and Eve before the Fall. What a privilege! What an honor! How valuable and how profitable!

(10) "BUT I REJOICED IN THE LORD GREATLY, THAT NOW AT THE LAST YOUR CARE OF ME HATH FLOURISHED AGAIN; WHEREIN YE WERE ALSO CAREFUL, BUT YE LACKED OPPORTUNITY."

As Paul begins to conclude his letter, he voices his joy over the Philippians' recent contribution to him. This is probably not his first note of thanks to them, for considerable time had probably elapsed since Epaphroditus had brought the gift and several contacts with the Church at Philippi had already been made.

The words *"at the last"* should not be regarded as a rebuke, but merely as showing that communication had again occurred after a period of no contact. Paul makes it clear that the fault was not theirs but came from a lack of opportunity. Perhaps no messenger had been available.

In addition, the Apostle's own circumstances had been highly irregular in recent years, in part, at least, because of imprisonment and shipwreck. Now the demonstration of concern had bloomed again, like plants in the spring (Kent).

REJOICING IN THE LORD

The phrase, *"But I rejoiced in the Lord greatly,"* concerns, as stated, the gift which the Philippians had sent to him. More than likely this was money, which was so desperately needed. However, we should not get the impression that Peace results from doing something; it results rather from relationship. Please notice the progression in this Passage. It begins with joy, then leads to Peace which is the cause of Joy. In turn, it leads to relationship which is the cause of Peace. Without a genuine relationship with Christ, the other two blessings cannot be realities.

As well, even though it was the Philippians who sent this gift, it was the Lord who moved upon the Philippians to do so, and who should rightly be looked at as the true Source. Actually, the Lord is the Source of all Blessings. James said, *"Every good gift and every perfect gift is from above, and cometh down from the Father of lights, with Whom is no variableness, neither shadow of turning"* (James 1:17).

YOUR CARE OF ME

The phrase, *"That now at the last your care of me hath flourished again,"* proclaims the fact that for a period of time the Philippians had ceased to help the Apostle.

The figure as used by Paul is of a plant which revives in the spring. Though it was *"at the last,"* once again the Philippians demonstrated their love for Paul. No clue is given as to why they had not done so sooner. Perhaps they had no one by whom to send the gift, or maybe they simply had been financially unable to do so.

And then again, it could well have been the fact that the squabble which had arisen in the Church between Euodias and Syntyche, had diverted their attention to other things, which is exactly what Satan would have wanted. Of course, we cannot be certain that this was the case, but I do personally know, as do all Christians, that Satan uses such a method very successfully. If he can get the Church fighting and squabbling over something, most of the time over very insignificant things, then the true and great Plan of God always meant to go forward, instead lapses by the wayside. From the manner in which Paul makes statements concerning their support, it seems that something rather peculiar had happened, which well could have been the case we have just mentioned.

If such a thing actually did happen, some evidently did remember their obligation and responsibility to the great Apostle and now attempted to get back on line. I do not at all mean to place the Philippians in an embarrassing posture; however, something there had not been quite right, but is now hopefully back on track, or at least partially so.

OPPORTUNITY

The phrase, *"Wherein ye were also careful, but ye lacked opportunity,"* could simply mean, as we have previously stated, that the Philippians simply had not had an opportunity to send anything to the Apostle because of no one whom they could trust going in that particular direction. Consequently, they would ultimately send Epaphroditus with the gift.

The words *"were also careful,"* are from a Greek word speaking of the act of taking thought, not from the Greek word translated *"be careful"* of Verse 6. The idea is, that some in the Church were thinking of these things as it regards Paul, but simply lacked opportunity to do so.

The word *"opportunity"* could refer to that which we have just said, or to Church difficulties which had arisen. Either way, there had been a delay in the support for Paul, which evidently he very much needed.

Satan will do anything and everything he can to stop support for the true work of God. And of course when this happens, the work suffers as would be obvious. So, Believers should take careful note of this example given, and not allow Satan to have his way in these matters. Too much is at stake, which we should always remember.

(11) "NOT THAT I SPEAK IN RESPECT OF WANT: FOR I HAVE LEARNED, IN WHATSOEVER STATE I AM, THEREWITH TO BE CONTENT."

The Apostle hastens to make clear that though he undoubtedly had a need, it was not relief of this need that primarily concerned him. He had learned to be content with what God provided, irrespective of circumstances.

NOTES

It is significant that Paul had to *"learn"* this virtue. Contentment is not natural to most of mankind.

In stoic philosophy, to which we have already briefly alluded, the word *"content"* describes a person who accepts impassively whatever comes. Circumstances that he could not change were regarded as the will of God, and fretting was useless. Because this philosophy is similar to that which is Biblical, it is often advocated by some Believers. However, this philosophy fosters a self-sufficiency in which all the resources for coping with life are located within man himself. By contrast, Paul locates his sufficiency in Christ Who provides strength for Believers, which is quite different from Stoicism.

IN RESPECT OF WANT

The phrase, *"Not that I speak in respect of want,"* proclaims the Apostle declaring his independence from creature comforts. This does not mean that he opposes them, but rather that his life and happiness does not depend on them, but rather Christ.

How so much modern Believers should take these words to heart. They should be all the more important when we consider that much of the modern Gospel in fact, concerns itself with *"creature comforts."* I speak of the *"prosperity message."*

Once again I emphasize, that the Apostle is not teaching against these things, even as we shall see, but rather that they do not in any form control his life. If he has them well and good; if not, well and good anyway. His sufficiency was in Christ, not things (Lk. 12:15).

I HAVE LEARNED

The phrase, *"For I have learned, in whatsoever state I am, therewith to be content,"* simply means to be independent of external circumstances. While it does speak of self-sufficiency and competency, it is not the Stoic kind, but rather *"Christ-sufficiency."* His dependence totally was in Christ. He found his sufficiency in Christ. He was independent of circumstances because he was dependent upon Christ.

The words *"have learned"* are in a construction form in the Greek which speaks of entrance into a new condition. It is, *"I have *come to learn."* It means that Paul had not always known that.

In fact, the Apostle had been reared in the lap of luxury, and had never known want as a young man. The *"I"* is emphatic, meaning that he had learned this in his living for Christ.

At some particular point in his life, Paul had made a commitment to serve the Lord faithfully no matter what circumstances he had to face. To be sure, those circumstances, at times, were very disagreeable (Acts Chpt. 16).

The word *"content"* tells us that in earthly things he is satisfied to be as he is; in spiritual things, however, he presses ever onward for higher attainment (Phil 3:13-14).

As well, when he asserts for himself such self-sufficing, it is to be understood as absolute towards men only, — not towards Him who said to him *"My Grace is sufficient for thee"* (II Cor. 12:9). To be sufficient in the things of this world is one thing, to be sufficient in the things of God is something else altogether. Unfortunately, the modern Church all too often, seems to strive for the former instead of the latter. Perhaps then this is a lesson that all of us should learn, and learn greatly.

The things of this world are relatively insignificant, and yet we seem to make them very significant. The things of God are significant beyond compare, and yet, I wonder if we fully understand that as we should!

Incidentally, the Greek word *"autarkes"* which is translated here *"content,"* has no equivalent in English, but should be taken in the sense of *"competency."* It means that the Apostle is adequate for every situation, having learned that circumstances as such neither add to nor detract from his higher calling and happiness.

THE MANNER IN WHICH THESE THINGS WERE LEARNED

Paul says, even as we have stated, that he had *"learned"* this. Probably by nature he had a mind as prone to impatience as others, but he has been in circumstances fitted to produce a different state of feeling. He had ample experience (II Cor. 11:26) and, in his life of trials, he had acquired invaluable lessons on this subject.

He had abundant time for reflection, and he had found that there was Grace enough in the Gospel to enable him to bear trials with resignation. The considerations by which he had been taught, this he does not state; but they were probably such as the following:

It is wrong to murmur at the allotments of Providence; that a spirit of impatience does no good, remedies no evil and supplies no want; that God could provide for him in a way which he could not foresee, and that the Saviour was able abundantly to sustain him.

Contentment, at least as Paul uses it here, arises from the belief that God is right in all His ways. Why should we be impatient, restless, or discontented, knowing that the Lord is able to remedy any situation, and if we must go through some difficulties, it is that which He designs because He knows they are needed.

Consequently, blessed is the man who comes to this *"state."* I suppose the question should be further asked:

Can you the Reader say the same as Paul? Does your state either mar your happiness or add to it? If it does, and in either direction, it means that our self-sufficiency is not quite in Christ as it ought to be. Far too often, our contentment is tied to our *"state,"* which Satan plays like a yo-yo.

When we can come to this place, this place of victory, no matter our circumstances, no matter our state, then we know what real Christianity actually is.

What a lesson!

(12) "I KNOW BOTH HOW TO BE ABASED, AND I KNOW HOW TO ABOUND: EVERY WHERE AND IN ALL THINGS I AM INSTRUCTED BOTH TO BE FULL AND TO BE HUNGRY, BOTH TO ABOUND AND TO SUFFER NEED."

Paul understood what it was to be *"in want"* as well as *"to have plenty."* Exactly as to what times he is referring are not clear. In fact, the expression is probably relative.

It may be that Paul considered the times he was not suffering privation to be times of plenty (Acts 9:19, 28; 16:15, 33-34; 18:3; 21:8). He had learned the secret of trusting God *"in every particular situation"* and in all situations as a whole.

LITTLE AND PLENTY

The phrase, *"I know both how to be abased, and I know how to abound,"* proclaims the fact that Paul's life was not in *"things."* His life was in Christ, and Christ totally, which means that Satan could not get at him respecting material, domestic, or physical situations. If he had nice things, wonderful! If he didn't, it had no effect upon the inner man respecting his joy and his more abundant life, because all was in Christ. This is where the Saint of God is to be — spiritually independent of situations and circumstances.

I think one can gage this by one asking oneself questions. If you lose your health, have you lost your *"life"*? If you lose your finances, have you lost your *"life"*? If you lose one of your loved ones, as hurtful as that is, have you lost your *"life"*?

Jesus addressed himself to this when He said, *"Take heed, and beware of covetousness: for a man's life consisteth not in the abundance of the things which he possesseth"* (Lk. 12:15).

He then said, *"Take no thought for your life, what ye shall eat; neither for the body, what ye shall put on.*

"The life is more than meat, and the body is more than raiment" (Lk. 12:22-23).

And finally He said, *"For all these things do the nations of the world seek after: and your Father knoweth that ye have need of these things.*

"But rather seek ye the kingdom of God; and all these things shall be added unto you" (Lk. 12:30-31).

The Lord does not deny the need of these things, only that they should not make up our life, which they certainly do for the world which does not know God.

If one studies Paul's statements enough, one will find that almost all of them in someway go back to what Jesus said.

Men keep trying to come up with philosophies which will help them meet the difficulties of life, such as Stoicism, but all without Christ. They fail to realize that Christ is the Centerpiece of all things, actually the Source of true Life, and in fact, the only Source of true Life. Consequently, when He is ignored, as He is by most, irrespective of their nimble minds in formulating particular philosophies, the end result they seek will not be reached. Whether admitted or not, they will come to the same conclusion as Solomon, *"all is vanity and vexation of spirit"* (Eccl. 1:14).

As someone has said concerning the two books of Ecclesiastes and Song of Solomon, in Ecclesiastes, all is emptiness, as in the Song of Songs all is fullness. Christ and the world are contrasted. In one Book the heart is too large for the portion; in the other, the portion is too large for the heart.

INSTRUCTION

The phrase, *"Every where and in all things I am instructed both to be full and to be hungry, both to abound and suffer need,"* presents in a fashion the advanced Christian life as a mystery, the secrets of which are taught by God the Holy Spirit to the soul that longs to prove its own personal experience *"what is that good and acceptable and perfect will of God."*

"Instructed" comes from a Greek word which means *"I have been initiated."* It is a word adapted from the old Greek mysteries.

In effect, it says that God has mapped out each particular life according to the needs which He knows are present, and we speak of spiritual needs, all for one purpose, and that is to make the person into the Image of the Heavenly, i.e., *"into the Image of Christ Jesus."* That means that what is needed for one Believer might not be needed for another. Each Christian has his own blueprint outlined by the Holy Spirit, a particular course which must be travelled, that is if the desired conclusion is to be reached. It's a *"mystery"* for several reasons:

First of all, each is different. Second, as human beings, we have scant knowledge as to how or what the Lord is doing with us, which is intended to garner trust and dependence in the Lord on our part.

Now this *"mystery,"* can be a source of irritation to some, or a source of great blessing, which the latter is meant by the Lord for all, and which the former is entertained only because of self-will.

It should be a great blessing to know and understand that the Lord loves us so much, that He would map out a diagram specifically for our own lives and experiences. As well, this *"mystery"* includes surprises which come constantly, all in the growth process, and which opens new vistas of experience and learning. In fact, this *"mystery"* of life as led by the Lord, is the most exciting life that one could ever live. To be sure, there is absolutely nothing in it that is boring, because we are always in the training program with all of its various colors, mysteries, directions, and blessings, all designed by the Lord.

THE MANNER IN WHICH PAUL LOOKED AT ALL OF THIS

After thanking the Philippian Saints for their gift in Philippians 4:10, Paul, in view of the slanders to the effect that he was making the Gospel a means of his livelihood, in other words preaching for money, informs them in Philippians 4:11 that he has come to learn, in the circumstances in which he is placed, to be independent of this, rather finding total sufficiency in Christ. That being the case, he certainly is *not* bending any efforts at making money in Gospel preaching, therefore, attempting to meet the requirements of a certain standard of life.

In Philippians 4:12, the Scripture of our present study, he tells them that he knows how to suffer hunger and how to enjoy affluence. The words *"to be abased"* are the translation of the Greek word which is rendered *"humbled"* in Philippians 2:8, and *"vile"* in Philippians 3:21, and means *"to make low, to humble, to humiliate."*

The expression refers to Paul's ability to keep himself low respecting the needs of the daily life. Thus, the Apostle assured the Saints that he knew how to live on a very small income. The words *"to abound"* are the rendering of a Greek word which means *"to overflow"* thus, Paul knew what it was to live on a little, and also to have more than he could use.

The words *"I am instructed"* are from a technical word, as we have already stated, used in the initiation rites of the pagan mystery religions, literally, *"I have been initiated,"* or, *"I have learned the secret."*

The word is used in the New Testament of something which, while it may be obscure in nature or kept hidden in the past, is now revealed.

The words *"to be full"* are from a strong word in the original. It was used of the feeding of animals. It means in this connection, *"to be filled,"* and so *"to fatten like an animal."* It means *"to be satiated"* (Wuest).

THIS MANNER OF TRAINING

If we would know by what discipline the Lord trained Paul to this mind, we may listen to what Paul himself says of it (I Cor. 4:9-13): *"I think God hath set forth us the Apostles last of all, as men doomed to death: for we are made a spectacle unto the world . . . even unto this present hour we both hunger, and thirst, and are naked, and are buffeted, and have no certain dwellingplace; and we toil, working with our own hands: being reviled, we bless; being persecuted, we endure; being defamed, we entreat: we are made as the filth of the world, the offscouring of all things, unto this day"* (see also II Cor. 6:4; 11:23).

If, again, we would know the manner of his training and such experiences, take II Corinthians 12:8-9: *"Concerning this thing I besought thrice that it might depart from me. And He said unto me, 'My Grace is sufficient for thee; for My strength is made perfect in weakness.' Most gladly therefore will I rather glory in my infirmities."*

Also how his faith wrought and gathered strength in all these, we may see from Romans 8:24-28: *"We are saved by hope . . . if we hope for that which we see not, then do we with patience wait for it. Also the Spirit helpeth our infirmities: for we know not how to pray as we ought: but the Spirit Himself maketh intercession for us . . . And we know that all things work together for good to them that love God."*

So *"being strengthened with all might, according to His glorious power, in all patience and long suffering with joyfulness"* (Col. 1:11), he was able to say, *"I can do all things through Christ which strengtheneth me"* (Phil. 4:13).

This was the course, and this the fruit, of Paul's biography. But each Christian has his own life, the tenor and the upshot of which might be totally different than that of Paul, even as we've already stated.

But yet, even though the direction may be different, the goal is the same for all, *"the Christlike Image."*

The Christian makes a mistake if he looks at another Christian thinking that such is the course of life, be it good or bad, etc. As stated, the Lord has a blueprint designed carefully and especially for each individual, but all designed to come out to the same conclusion.

(13) "I CAN DO ALL THINGS THROUGH CHRIST WHICH STRENGTHENETH ME."

Paul did not trace his resources to some inner fortitude that would enable him to take with equanimity whatever life brought him. Instead, his strength for *"everything"* lay in the One Who continually empowered him (Kent).

ALL THINGS

The phrase, *"I can do all things,"* refers as is obvious from the previous Scriptures, to either that which is abasing or abounding. Unfortunately, the *"all things"* mentioned here are normally placed in the category by modern Disciples, of only great and powerful things, etc. In their vocabulary and thinking *"all things"* does not include the difficult assignment, which of course, is blatantly unscriptural.

Why does most of the Church think in this vein?

THE MODERN FAITH MESSAGE

This particular message has made great inroads into the Body of Christ in the last half of the Twentieth Century, influencing I suspect every particular Denomination in one way or the other. As well, my knowledge of this particular message would possibly be a little greater than most, due to the fact that in some ways I actually helped start this message. This was in the early 1970's. We were then on Radio with our daily program, *"The Campmeeting Hour,"* being broadcast over some six hundred stations.

I began to teach this particular Doctrine on a daily basis, I suppose continuing to do so for the better part of two years. The Holy Spirit then began to show me some things in the message which was not right, in fact, gross error. He demanded that I straighten up the situation, which we did, actually discontinuing our efforts in that particular direction.

By that statement, I do not mean to cast reflection on any of the principal Teachers of that particular time. In fact, I think some few of them were definitely of God and were used of God. Without going into detail, I think, however, the emphasis was wrong and then some of their Disciples took the message into heresy.

Be that as it may, it has pretty well degenerated presently into little more than the *"prosperity message,"* which makes money the object instead of Christlikeness.

This erroneous doctrine pretty much teaches that if one has proper faith and maintains a proper confession, that one can forego any type of difficulties and problems. Hence, some of them foolishly teach that had Paul been in possession of the knowledge that these modern teachers have, he would never have had to undergo the terrible problems he encountered. In other words, they basically deny all difficulties and problems, claiming that such comes because of a lack of faith or proper confession, etc.

While this is blatantly unscriptural even grossly so, it still garners a large following, for the simple reason that there seems to reside in all of us an ample supply of pride and greed.

In these circles the Cross is mostly repudiated, even ridiculed as being a place of weakness, etc. The wrong emphasis on Faith is bad enough, but when one begins to denigrate the Cross, one is tampering with the very foundation of Salvation which is the Atonement, which presents dangerous grounds indeed!

At any rate, this teaching has so permeated Christian thinking, that Paul's statement concerning *"doing all things through Christ . . ."* automatically presupposes, at least in their thinking, the positive, even though the Scriptures plainly label his statement as meaning otherwise.

He is plainly stating that he can do without (be abased) if forced to do so, or he can enjoy plenty (abound), should the Lord provide such. Either way, his victory is not affected, simply because his victory is not in those things, but rather in Christ, Who never leaves nor forsakes him. At the same time he is saying that irrespective of the validity of our Faith, both the abasement and abundance will come.

PAUL

In Paul this declaration was not a vain self-reliance, nor was it the mere result of his former experience. He knew very well where the strength was to be obtained by which to do all things, and on that Arm that was able to uphold him, he confidently relied. He could bear any trial, perform any duty, subdue any evil propensity of his nature, and meet all the temptations incident to any condition of prosperity or adversity.

To be sure, this knowledge did not come easily or quickly, but rather as the song says *"through many dangers, toils, and snares."*

As well, we must understand that what the Apostle says here is sanctioned by the Holy Spirit, and even above that, inspired; consequently, we must definitely understand that his statements are not merely his opinion or the dividend of his thinking. He is actually saying that which the Holy Spirit desires that he say, and saying it in the way and manner the Holy Spirit wants it said, even down to the very words. In other words, this is Gospel, and that which we must surely understand as such, and be, therefore, guided. Anything that contradicts what is said and done here, simply means that it is a deviation from the Gospel, and should be rejected out of hand.

To which we've already discussed, while Paul's life does serve as an example, it is the principle which is the example and not the actual activity. As far as activity is concerned, the Lord has His Own special blueprint for each particular life, which does not necessarily coincide with others.

THROUGH CHRIST

The phrase, *"Through Christ,"* proclaims the source of the Apostle's sufficiency. It is Christ who continuously infuses power into him. He can be grateful for any and all circumstances, one might say, because they are the occasion for the Revelation of Christ's power. That is a tremendous statement and should be enlarged upon.

It's not that we want or desire adverse circumstances, not at all! In fact, we should do everything we legitimately can to avoid such; however, whatever the circumstances, they do provide an opportunity for the Lord to reveal His care and His power. It is that for which we are thankful, and not actually the adverse circumstance itself.

As we've said repeatedly, everything that happens to the Child of God is actually orchestrated by the Lord. In other words, He either causes or allows the situation.

Naturally, He does not cause sin or failure of any nature, but even in those circumstances He does allow certain things to happen. The point I'm endeavoring to make is that the Lord minutely watches over every one of His children. While Satan certainly desires to cause us great harm and even our destruction, still, his latitude as it regards each Believer is decided totally by the Lord, with the Evil One not able to go any further than the boundaries allowed. The Lord allows such, in order that our Faith might be strengthened. I think one can say without fear of Scriptural contradiction, that Faith is always the object, at least on the part of the Lord, hence Him looking at situations as *"training."*

FAITH

The short phrase *"through Christ,"* rests squarely on the principle of Faith. Due to its great significance, let's look at this situation in greater detail.

As it regards the Child of God, and our dealings with the Lord and His dealings with us, I think one can say that *"Faith"* is the prime ingredient in everything. This is the means by which the Lord has chosen to deal with the human race.

Even though Faith is one of the most often taught subjects from the Word of God, actually the most often taught, I think most Christians still have an incomplete understanding as it regards Faith — despite all the teaching.

Three things have to be considered here:
1. Faith and what it actually is.
2. The object of Faith.
3. The maturing process of Faith.

Let's look at them one by one:

THE PRINCIPLE OF FAITH

Christians are very quick to talk about *"Faith in God,"* or *"Faith in the Word of God,"* etc. While these are correct statements, they leave something to be desired.

While *"Faith definitely comes by hearing, and hearing by the Word of God,"* for the statement to be understood, certain things must be explained (Rom. 10:17).

Most Christians believe that for one to increase their Faith, in other words to have stronger Faith, that one must read the Bible, because it is there that Faith is generated. That is correct; however, as well, that answer also leaves something to be desired.

The entirety of the principle of Faith, which speaks of our belief in God and His Word, is all based on the principle of the Cross of Christ. Actually, the entirety of the Word of God strains toward this great Work. This is so blatantly obvious, that to give Chapter and Verse, one would probably be safer to just say *"the Old Testament and the New Testament."*

The story of the Bible in its entirety is the story of the Fall and the Redemption of man. The story of the Fall takes place in the first three Chapters of Genesis, with the remainder of the entirety of the Bible addressing itself to man's Redemption, which was and is brought about exclusively by what Jesus did at the Cross. As we have said previously, Paul identified the Cross as being so much the Gospel, that he actually uses the word in place of the Gospel at times (I Cor. 1:18; 2:2; Gal. 6:14).

So, everything strains toward the Cross, because the Gospel in its entirety springs from what Jesus did on the Cross. So the point I'm making is this:

When we say Faith, if it's not Faith in the Cross of Christ, which acts as its very foundation, as its very principle, then really we're not speaking of the type of Faith which the Holy Spirit is proclaiming.

When Paul said, *"Abraham believed God, and it was counted unto him for Righteousness,"* what exactly did he mean by that? (Rom. 4:3).

It did not merely mean that Paul believed there was a God in Heaven, but rather something else altogether. It actually meant that Abraham believed that God would send a Redeemer into this world to save lost humanity, in which he (Abraham) would actually be a part of the process. In other words, one might say in an abbreviated manner, that *"Abraham believed in the Cross, for that was the way in which mankind would be redeemed."*

So if we attempt to understand the Word of God apart from the Cross, then we will have a skewed understanding of the Word. We must at all times understand that the Word is embedded totally and completely in the Cross of Christ (Jn. 1:1-5, 29).

The principle of Faith must rest upon the principle of the Cross or else we have a faith which is of man and not of God. The problem is, the Church has pretty much divorced Faith from the Cross, almost making it an entity within itself. While in that context it might be referred to by the Church as Faith, but it is not Faith which God will recognize. The very principle of Faith must be understood to be embedded in the principle of the Cross (Gen. 4:1-5).

THE OBJECT OF FAITH

Inasmuch as the Cross must be *"the principle of Faith,"* meaning that our Faith must be tied to the Cross, understanding that everything we receive from the Lord comes by means of the Sacrifice He offered at Calvary, then the Cross must always by *"the object of Faith."* To try to go any other way, to devise any other method, to institute any other means, is a repudiation of God's Plan of Salvation; consequently, irrespective of what label we put on our thinking, it all amounts to Faith. So it's Faith in the principle of the Cross, which demands that the object of our Faith be the Cross.

If it's *"through Christ,"* then it's through *"the Cross,"* for it cannot be any other way. The very purpose for which Jesus came was to die on the Cross, for such was demanded in order for man to be saved. Actually, this was planned in the mind of God even before the foundation of the world (I Pet. 1:20). This means that the Cross was not step four in a ten step process. It is the culminating step, and of course, to speak of the Cross we automatically as well speak of the Resurrection and, in fact, the Exaltation of Christ also (Eph. 2:6).

Regarding the fact that most Christians do not understand that the principle of faith is the Cross, likewise they do not understand that the object of Faith must be the Cross.

As we've stated repeatedly, there has been more teaching on Faith in the last half of the Twentieth Century, than perhaps the entire former timespan of Christianity put together, but most of the teaching I think, has been wrong.

The faith which has been taught, for the most part, has had as its object things other than the Cross. By that I speak of Faith in ourselves, faith in our faith, and probably the most often used phrase, *"Faith in the Word."* However, much of the time, the faith which is spoken of as being in the Word, is not in the Word at all, but rather in oneself. In fact, far too often, the Word is pulled out of its rightful place, waved around like some magic talisman, which is supposed to stir God into action. God will never allow His Word to be used against Himself, which means, against His Will. But this is where most of the Church is.

Without the Cross as the proper object of Faith, the so-called faith being promoted is not faith at all, at least that which God will recognize.

With the Cross as one's object of Faith, which means that we understand that everything we have received from the Lord or shall receive from the Lord, has come about because of what Jesus did at the Cross and the Resurrection. Everything is built upon that particular basis, which means that our Faith must always be in the Cross, for this is where the price was paid, the sin debt settled, and the Atonement made. Faith in anything else totally misses the point.

THE GROWTH OF ONE'S FAITH

Even with one's Faith properly placed, which of course refers to the Cross which is the Finished Work of Christ, our Faith must be constantly tested. As someone has well said, *"Faith must always be tested, and great faith must be tested greatly."*

This testing comes about in various and different ways, but most of the time through difficulties which the Lord allows to come our way. Also, Satan is allowed a certain latitude of temptation, which most find ourselves failing from time to time. Considering that our Faith is properly in the Cross, that is if it is, we may wonder as to why the failure?

Even though our Faith might be properly placed, it by no means is as strong as it ought to be, or we think it might be, which is proven by our failure, if in fact there is failure of some sort. What exactly we mean by failure, I will address momentarily in a more particular way.

I personally had to learn this the hard way, as I'm sure most others do as well! For approximately five years I sought the Lord earnestly as it regards the answer to several questions.

How can a Believer walk victorious in the Lord, and do so constantly? How do we have victory over the flesh and self-will? How can we live a life of Righteousness and Holiness?

After those years of earnestly seeking the face of the Lord, actually crying unto Him even in desperation, the Lord answered my prayer.

He showed me that the Cross contains all the answers, because it was there that Jesus paid all the price. He showed me that my Faith must be in that Finished Work, and then the Holy Spirit would help me, in fact, will guarantee that for which Christ paid at the Cross and the Resurrection (Rom. 8:1-2).

I cannot even begin to relate to you the Reader how I felt upon the advent of this Revelation. As I have previously stated, it was as if I had been Born-Again. The entirety of my life has changed and in every capacity. I see things in an entirely different way, and again in every capacity. It's like the prison bars have fallen off, with the door swinging wide, and the Lord saying *"walk out and enjoy your freedom."* To be frank, I have never sensed anything like this or felt anything like this in all of my years of living for God.

And the beautiful thing about all of this is, I know that this is just the beginning. In fact, there is no limit to what one can have in Christ, and simply because it is impossible to exhaust the potential of Christ in any capacity.

NOW WHAT DO WE MEAN BY FAILURE?

As a Believer, I want to do everything perfect before the Lord. I want to be perfect in every capacity, and by that I mean mature in every way, which means to address all things in maturity. No, I'm not speaking of sinless perfection, because the Bible does not teach such.

However, situations come our way, and then we find, despite this great Revelation of the Cross, that we don't meet all things with maturity, in other words, we fail by getting into the flesh, etc. Let me give a very brief example:

A short time back, Frances related to me as to how a certain Preacher had attempted to get our Telecast taken off the air in a particular place. It was stopped with him not being successful, but not for lack of trying.

I did not know the man very well, and had never had any dealings with him in any capacity, so of course, I had to wonder as to why he would do such a thing. But knowing that he had tried this same thing before, I became very irritated, so much so in fact, that I don't have the proper words to explain my feelings. No, I did not do anything, but I sure thought a lot of things, and in my discussion with Frances, my statements were quite heated.

I did not meet this situation right, and what I did could only be described as *"failure."* Knowing what I know about the Lord and His Work, I know that men cannot do anything in a negative sense to any Believer, no matter how hard they try, unless the Lord would allow such. In other words, the Lord has the final say in all things concerning His Children. Of course, it hurts to see a fellow Preacher attempt such a thing, especially when he should be trying to help rather than hurt. However, I've had my share of this in the last few years, and should not have been taken off guard as I was.

The situation was really not what the Preacher had done, and thousands of others just like him, but rather my reaction to the situation, which was not Christlike.

In asking the Lord as to the why of the failure, of which I had to repent, I feel the Holy Spirit instructed me that it was my Faith. In other words, my Faith was not nearly as strong as I thought it was.

Even though the Lord had given me this great Revelation on the Cross, and in fact had advanced me tremendously as far as Spiritual and Scriptural depth were concerned, there were still flaws in my Faith, which the test showed up, as tests are meant to do.

The Believer is to not think that because he has his Faith properly placed, that the Devil will cease all operations. That is not correct at all! In fact, Satan will never quit, constantly seeking permission from the Lord to do varied things as it results in his efforts to hinder and hurt us.

Years ago I heard A.N. Trotter say, *"every attack against us by Satan, and irrespective as to what direction it takes, be it physical, spiritual, mental, or material, is all for one purpose, and that is to destroy or at least weaken our Faith."* In other words, every attack is against our faith.

I knew then what he said was right, but I didn't exactly know why it was right. I know now!

THE PRECIOUS COMMODITY OF FAITH

Faith is the most precious thing that a person actually has (Heb. Chpt. 11). In fact, it is actually the only commodity one might say, that a person can take with him when he dies. That's the reason that Satan fights so hard in this regard. It is all because of and about our Faith.

I've had Believers to say to me words to this effect, *"Brother Swaggart I don't quite understand, I know that your teaching on the Cross is right. It has helped me immeasurably and for the first time in my life, I feel like I'm really growing in the Lord and seeing victories. And yet, at times when Satan attacks, I will fail, even though I know my Faith is now properly placed. Why is this?"*

At first I did not know how to answer such questions. But the Lord then instructed me as to the reason why.

Even though the Faith of these individuals, as previously stated, is now properly placed and now properly held; still, such Faith is not nearly as mature, not nearly as strong, not nearly as advanced as they think it is. Consequently, even as we have stated, these tests and even temptations from the Evil One, show up the weaknesses in our Faith, whatever those weaknesses might be. In fact, we may not even actually know what the weaknesses are, but little by little the Holy Spirit will bring us to that knowledge, as we begin to properly see ourselves. Actually, one can only properly see oneself as one looks at the Cross. Need I say more!

I think we will find, that when the introspection becomes deep enough, as the Holy Spirit will always bring it about, we will find that self-will is the major hinderance and problem. Even as we've previously addressed, this can only be handled by a daily dying, which has to do with taking up the Cross daily (Lk. 9:23-24).

Incidentally, the Cross also humbles one, and that means that it humbles our Faith. It's a sobering feeling, a humiliating feeling, to fail the Lord in any capacity, which means to not properly address situations as they are brought to bear upon us. In other words, we do not address them or react toward them with Faith, but rather with our feelings, etc. This is what failure actually is!

So, when we say *"through Christ,"* we must understand that this is not an automatic process, but rather a lived-out process. It is all by Faith, and more particularly Faith in the Cross, which we hope we have adequately explained.

STRENGTH

The phrase, *"which strengtheneth me,"* tells us several things:

1. We need not sink under any trial, for there is One Who can strengthen us.

2. That we need not yield to temptation: there is One Who is able to make a way for our escape.

3. That we need not be harassed, and vexed, and tortured with improper thoughts and unholy desires: there is One Who can enable us to banish such thoughts from the mind, and restore the right balance to the affections of the soul.

4. That we need not dread what is to come. Trials, temptations, poverty, want, persecution, may await us; but we need not sink into despondency. At every step of life Christ is able to strengthen us, and can bring us triumphantly through.

What a privilege it is, therefore, to be a Christian — to feel in the trials of life, that we have one Friend, unchanging and most mighty, Who can always help us! Considering this, how cheerfully should we engage our duties, and meet the trials that are before us, leaning on the arm of our Almighty Redeemer! Consequently, let us not shrink from duty; let us not dread persecution; let us not fear the bed of death. In all circumstances, Christ, our unchanging Friend, can uphold us.

Let the eye and the affections of the heart be fixed on Him; let the simple, fervent, believing prayer be directed always to Him when trials come, when temptations assail, when duty presses hard upon us, and when a crowd of unholy and forbidden thoughts rush into the soul, and we shall be safe (Barnes).

However, we must not forget, never forget, that Christ does all of this for us, strictly on the basis of His Finished Work on the Cross, and our Faith in that Work. In other words, none of this came cheaply, but actually at great price, but a price already paid by Him. That means, that the only price which the Lord requires of us, is that we simply believe Him, trust Him, have Faith in Him, etc. And by that, we mean to have Faith in that which He did for us at the Cross of Calvary, which benefits never end, because in fact they cannot end.

Faith taps this great Reservoir, but it must be Faith which has as its principal the Cross of Christ, and of necessity, which object is the Cross. Even then, the process, for it is a process, is slow, with the Believer actually going from Faith to Faith (Rom. 1:17), which means that we go from weaker faith to stronger faith as light is revealed and received (I Jn. 1:7).

(14) "NOTWITHSTANDING YE HAVE WELL DONE, THAT YE DID COMMUNICATE WITH MY AFFLICTION."

Paul does not want to leave the impression that he is not thankful for the gift sent by the Philippians. In fact, they had responded properly to his need, and he was truly grateful — not so much for what the gift did for him as for the willingness of the Philippians to share with him. They had accepted, in effect, his affliction as their own and had done something about it.

WELL DONE

The phrase, *"Notwithstanding ye have well done,"* he includes lest in declaring his independence of human aid, he should seem to disparage the gift of the Philip-pian Church.

The word *"well"* is the translation of the Greek word for *"good"* which refers to a beautiful goodness.

The phrase *"ye have done well"* is in the Greek the equivalent of our present day *"'You did a beautiful thing' when you did that"* (Wuest).

In all of this we see something extremely important. While Paul was very thankful for the gift sent by the Philippians, which he no doubt desperately needed, and who God used to meet this need; still, Paul's dependence, as is amply illustrated in these Passages, was not at all in the Church at Philippi, but rather in the Lord. This is the great secret! Even though God uses individuals even as He used those at Philippi to carry out His wishes, still, it is the Lord who does the doing, and it is the Lord to whom we must look, even though not for a moment ceasing to be greatly thankful for those and to those, whom He uses.

A PERSONAL ILLUSTRATION

In 1991 this Ministry (Jimmy Swaggart Ministries) was completely cut off from any type of financial and material support as it regards Churches or people. Of course, the fault of the far greater majority of that must be laid at my personal door; nevertheless, and irrespective of fault or blame, this was the case.

My Calling is World Evangelism, and to be carried out in many and varied ways, but especially by mass communication such as Television, Radio, and Evangelistic Crusades. Television and Radio reaches vast numbers of people, and according to the number reached is inexpensive as far as per capita is concerned; nevertheless, the amount of money needed each day is large to say the least.

With funds cut off from almost every source, how in the world could we survive? What were we to do?

Without going into detail, at a given point and time, I went before the Lord, even when the situation looked darkest, imploring Him as to what He wanted us to do! Were we to cease all efforts regarding the mass communication of the Gospel? Of course, this is exactly what our enemies, which seemed to be many, were trying to bring about all along. They wanted to silence my voice, and would do anything within their power to bring this about, for which I had provided ample ammunition. Irrespective of the tremendous number of souls being saved, of lives being changed, of Believers being baptized with the Holy Spirit, and all over the world at that, they didn't like what I preached, and would use any means to silence my efforts.

Unmistakably, the Lord informed me, and in no uncertain terms, that I was not to cancel the Telecast or any efforts respecting Evangelism, but which efforts would be somewhat reduced. As to how this was to be financed, and considering that all avenues respecting the Church in general were closed, and I mean closed tightly, the Lord spelled out to me the most unorthodox means of finance that I had ever known.

In prayer that October morning in 1991, as I along with others was seeking His Face, He drew my attention to the miracle of the tribute money found in Matthew 17:24-27.

Concerning taxes that were to be paid, and with no money to pay those taxes, Jesus told Peter to *"go thou to the Sea* (Sea of Galilee)*, and cast an hook, and take up the fish that first cometh up; and when thou hast opened his mouth, thou shalt find a piece of money: that take, and give unto them for Me and thee"* (Mat. 17:27). Thus was the need met!

The Lord then spoke to my heart, telling me that he would meet the needs of the Ministry in this fashion. And for these years that's exactly what He has done. As stated, it has been most unorthodox, and at times we have come to cliff-hangers; however, the Lord in one mysterious way after the other, has always met the need. In other words, it has been a miracle each and everyday, for the simple reason, if the Lord did not supply the need, there was no way the need could be met.

While we're operating presently on a reduced scale, at least from that of the 1980's, still, the Lord is helping us to reach a large number of people. The Telecast is still aired in over 30 countries of the world, translated into several languages. Souls are still being saved, Believers are still being baptized with the Holy Spirit, sick bodies are still being healed, and bondages of darkness are still being broken — all by the Power of God.

A MIGHTY WORK WHICH THE LORD HAS DONE

As I dictate these notes on August 8, 1999, these last years have not been wasted at all.

Actually, they have been the most productive and fruitful years of my life, at least as it regards a personal basis. The Lord has drawn me immeasurably closer to Him. He has dealt with my heart regarding many and varied things, but more than all, to be drawn closer and closer to Him, i.e., *"to become more and more Christlike."* As I have mentioned a number of times, in October of 1991, He instructed me to begin two prayer meetings a day. He told me at the outset, *"do not seek me so much for what I can do, but rather for Who I am."* In other words, I was to seek more and more to know Him, and not so much the things He can do.

There has been a lot of work to do on Jimmy Swaggart, much flesh to be eradicated, much Vision to be imparted and many changes to be made.

Even though there is still much to be done, thankfully I can say, much has been done.

In seeking His Face incessantly regarding particular questions, *"how can one walk in perpetual victory? how can one overcome the flesh? how can one be an overcomer?"* After several years of earnestly seeking His face, in 1996 the Lord began to open up to me the great Truths of the Cross and the Resurrection of Christ. This Revelation which continues to expand even unto this hour, has completely revolutionized my life. The *"Message of the Cross"* has helped me to see myself as never before, and above all, to see Christ as I've never known Him previously. It has been, even as I have previously stated, the most revolutionary thing I have ever experienced, other than my initial Salvation experience and Baptism with the Holy Spirit.

This Message has changed me, and changed me completely. Whether others realize such or not, I am not the same person I once was, and of course, I give the Lord all the Praise and Glory for that.

So, these last years have not at all been wasted, but have been the most fruitful time of my life. Of course, I grieve and mourn over many things; however, these years at the backside of the desert have been most productive and most fruitful.

The crucifixion of the flesh is not an easy process, and because it is a process, it is tedious, long, and at times very painful, but

NOTES

altogether necessary. Irrespective, even as Paul said, *"that I may know Him and the Power of His Resurrection, and the Fellowship of His sufferings, being made conformable unto His death,"* must ever be the overriding goal.

THAT WHICH THE LORD IS PRESENTLY DOING

As we come now to the beginning of a new Millennium, I can say with all honesty of heart, and as never before, *"I can hear the sound of an abundance of rain."* In other words, I sense great and tremendous things which the Lord is about to do.

Just last night in Prayer meeting (August 7, 1999) the Lord moved mightily. He spoke to my heart saying to me, *"as I spoke to Samuel telling him to fill his horn with oil and go, thereby planning great things for Israel, I am planning great things for this Ministry as well"* (I Sam. 16:1).

In the first part of 1999 the Lord began to move upon my heart concerning Radio, and I'm speaking of a different type of programming than has ever been aired, at least on this scale, of which I am aware. He instructed me to air the services from Family Worship Center, which we immediately began to do. I speak of all the music and worship, and, of course, the Messages. From the outset, the response has been absolutely tremendous. People are being saved and lives are being changed, and for the simple reason that the Gospel is being preached in all of its power.

As well, it's all of the same spirit, which is totally unlike most Gospel Radio programming. Let me explain:

There are a few Preachers who are truly preaching the Word, and who are truly anointed by the Holy Spirit, but if the truth be known, that number is few and far between. However, even when the Spirit of God does move through an individual, he always works in conjunction with that person's spirit. In other words, it's the Holy Spirit working with the human spirit of the individual in question. In conjunction with the Holy Spirit, whatever type of spirit the person has comes through as well. Sometimes it's not quite what it ought to be.

I realize a lot of folk may not understand that, but the answer is simple. The Lord doesn't wait until any of us are perfect before he begins to use us. If he did, He would use no one, as should be plainly obvious. Of course, being God, He knows all things, and above all, He knows our hearts. So, even though we might even be wrong about some things, still, if we are attempting to move in the right direction, the Holy Spirit will use us and help us, and that's the case with all Preachers, or anyone for that matter, used of the Lord.

However, the Reader should understand, that being the case, there can be conflicting spirits, which hinders what is being said and done to a certain extent, even though the Holy Spirit is present and working in that person's heart and life.

To try to eliminate these conflicting spirits, is the reason I believe the Holy Spirit instructed me to air programming only from the Church, which we immediately began to do. As stated, the results have been and are absolutely tremendous, for which we give the Lord all the Praise and the Glory.

As well, the Lord showed me how to take this programming all over the nation by the securing of Radio frequencies wherever they are available, which we immediately set out to do, and will do so until we have covered every part of this nation.

Also, the Lord has instructed me to change the Television programming to the same format, which at the time of this writing we are just beginning. In other words, as we air programming for Radio 24 hours a day, 7 days a week over the same station, we are setting out to do the same thing with Television.

THE REASON I BELIEVE THE LORD IS OPENING THESE DOORS

First of all, the Lord has performed a tremendous work in my own heart and life and in this Ministry, of which I will have more to say in a moment. To say we are thankful would be a gross understatement. As I have stated, it has been the most life changing experience I've ever known other than when the Lord saved me as a child and Baptized me with the Holy Spirit.

I have sought from the time of a child, to walk as close to the Lord as I know how, to be a proper vessel which He might be able to use. In this I have failed miserably, but at the same time, my heart by the Grace of God has always been exactly in that capacity. I believe I can say that without fear of contradiction from the One Who is the only One Who actually counts, my Lord. And I will say as Paul said so long ago, *"For I am the least of the Apostles, that am not meet to be called an Apostle, because I persecuted* (failed) *the Church of God.*

"But by the Grace of God I am what I am: and His Grace which was bestowed upon me was not in vain; but I labored more abundantly than they all: yet not I, but the Grace of God which was with me" (I Cor. 15:9-10).

THE ANOINTING

First of all, the reason I believe the Lord has opened these doors is because of the Anointing of the Holy Spirit which is upon this Ministry. To be sure, if the Spirit of God does not move and work upon the Message and the Minister, whomever they might be, there will be no results, at least for the Lord. There may be much religious machinery, much activity, and many people may be fooled, but unless the Spirit of God is truly moving and working, there will not be anything done for the Lord. In fact, there cannot be anything done for the Lord. Anything and everything done for God, must be birthed by the Spirit, or else it cannot be of God.

That's the reason that we seek the Lord incessantly, crying to Him, imploring Him, to help us to live such a life, that we might be a fit vessel in order that the Holy Spirit may use us to perform His Work. Because of that, the Lord has helped us to see hundreds of thousands all over the world brought to a saving knowledge of Jesus Christ, as well as untold thousands baptized with the Holy Spirit, which translates into untold thousands of lives changed by the Power of God. All of this is because of the moving and operation of the Holy Spirit upon the Word of God, as Jesus Christ is lifted up as the only hope of this world.

SOUND DOCTRINE

The second reason is I think, because of Sound Doctrine. What we preach is true. Now I realize that any Preacher can make that statement, and in fact, I suppose that all do. So, those words within themselves do not really mean anything.

However, that which I say concerning Sound Doctrine is not an idle word, because the fruit is there to back up these things which I have said. When I speak of fruit I am speaking of that which I have just mentioned in the previous statement concerning souls being saved and lives being changed. To be sure, God does not anoint error, and neither does He anoint sin. In fact, Jesus plainly said that the mark of a true Prophet would be *"good fruit"* (Mat. 7:15-20).

Now I realize that anyone can claim such; however, if anyone is honest and wants to know that which is actually the case, they cannot deny the hundreds of thousands of souls who have been brought to Christ as a result of the Spirit of God moving upon this particular Ministry. There are people in untold thousands of Churches all around the world, who are now serving God, because they were brought to Christ through the Telecast or in the Crusades. That is undeniable. As stated, the fruit is obvious for all to see.

Consequently, I can say as Paul said concerning those of you who support this Ministry, *"you have well done"* (Phil. 4:14). Your money and your prayers have not been wasted, but have gone to reach souls for Christ, which results will bring dividends forever and forever.

IT'S ALL BECAUSE OF THE MESSAGE OF THE CROSS

I have always preached the Cross as the only answer to dying, lost, Hell-bound humanity. As a result, and as stated, we have seen hundreds of thousands brought to a saving knowledge of Jesus Christ. However, during that period of time, even though I understood what the Cross meant for the Salvation of the lost, I little understood its veracity or its power, as it pertains to our living for the Lord after coming to Christ. I did not know that the Cross plays just as important a part in our living for the Lord after conversion, as it did in our being converted. To be frank, almost no one else knew as well, the Cross being so little preached in the last half of the Twentieth Century. Had I known this great Truth, it would have saved me untold heartache and humiliation, but I had to go through exactly what Paul went through at least in some measure, as he records in the Seventh Chapter of Romans.

The Lord gave Paul the answer to the victorious, overcoming, Christian life, which he gave to us in Romans Chapters 6 and 8. When the Lord opened up to me those Chapters, even after seeking His Face for some five years over this one thing, as stated, it completely revolutionized my life.

Why did I not see it earlier?

As I have already stated, I really do not have the answer to that. But this one answer I do have.

I didn't stop until the answer came, even though at times I will admit I grew very discouraged. And when it came, it so changed my life, so changed my thinking, so revolutionized my experience, that I really do not have the vocabulary to properly explain what has happened. As Peter said, *"it is joy unspeakable and full of glory"* (I Pet. 1:8).

As well, the Lord has commissioned me to preach, to teach, to proclaim this Message of the Cross, not only to lost sinners which I've always done, but as well now to the Body of Christ which I might prayerfully help in some small way to be brought back to its proper foundation. To be sure, the Cross is not just a part of Christianity, in fact, it is the very foundation of all that we are and all that we believe. It covers every aspect of our Christian experience, every nuance of our serving the Lord, every Blessing that we receive from the Lord, all and without exception, coming through the Finished Work of Christ. If one leaves that, one leaves the Gospel, it is just that simple! If one ignores that, one does so to one's own peril!

Actually, the *"Cross"* and the *"Gospel"* are so synonymous, so identical, that when one says *"the Cross"* he has at the same time said *"the Gospel,"* and when one says *"the Gospel"* he has at the same time said *"the Cross."*

AFFLICTION

The phrase, *"That ye did communicate with my affliction,"* refers to the Philippians becoming fellow-partakers with Paul in his needs.

Actually, the word *"communicate"* means *"to make one's self a fellow partaker in common with."* They made themselves responsible for the satisfying of his needs.

The words *"with my affliction,"* tell us that it was not the actual gift so much as the sympathy and fellowship of the Philippian Saints in his sorrow, which the great Apostle valued (Wuest).

"Affliction" in the Greek is *"thlipsis,"* and is not a disease as many think, but rather *"tribulation."* The word is translated *"tribulation"* some twenty times and *"affliction"* in the sense of tribulation eighteen times in the New Testament. It is translated *"burden"* (II Cor. 8:13); *"anguish"* (Jn. 16:21); *"persecution"* (Acts 11:19); and *"trouble"* (I Cor. 7:28; II Cor. 1:4, 8). Not once is it used of physical sickness or disease.

What the Philippians did as it regards the gift sent to Paul, which evidently they had done several times in the past, meant very much even as the gift itself was concerned, but much more because of what the act itself stated. It stated that they recognized the extreme significance of Paul's Calling and Work, and that they were laboring with him in spirit, as well as furnishing these material gifts, whatever they may have been.

GIVING TO THE WORK OF GOD

In fact, this is one of the things that makes giving to the Work of God so very important. When one gives to something, one in essence becomes a part of that to which one gives. In other words, one becomes a part of the Call of God on that respective Preacher's heart and life, as it regards all the Lord has designed to be done. That's the reason that when Christians give to that which is really not of God, they then actually become a part of the falsehood, chicanery, evil doings, and wrong direction. In a sense, *Christians actually support what they are* — what they actually are themselves in a spiritual sense. As I have previously said, the Lord is presently giving the Church what the Church is, and that's not a pretty picture. Most of the non-Pentecostals have plainly said that they do not want the Holy Spirit, so the Lord has seen to it that that's exactly what they have — no Holy Spirit.

Unfortunately, many, if not most, Pentecostals and Charismatics have, in effect, stated that they have little desire for Righteousness and Holiness, but rather desire money and manifestations. Consequently, the Lord has seen to it that this is the message they have received and are receiving; however, it won't be money they receive nor true manifestations of the Lord, but rather the opposite. The Scripture plainly tells us to *"seek first the Kingdom of God, and His Righteousness; and all these things shall be added unto you"* (Mat 6:33).

This should be clear that if the Kingdom of God and Righteousness are not sought first of all, that the other things will not be added, no matter what covetous Preachers might say.

The Holy Spirit through all of this is telling us something very important. We should take it to heart. The Philippians should serve as an example. We support what we are, so we better be careful what we actually do support.

These people shared Paul's burden, his love for souls, his defense of the Gospel and, therefore, shared his Calling, and will, therefore, share his reward. This principle holds no less true for the Work of God down through the ages. The Believer should seek the Lord earnestly about where his money goes. To be sure, the Lord surely would not have blessed those during Paul's time, who were supporting the Judaizers, even as some actually did. It is the same presently.

WHY DO PEOPLE ACTUALLY GIVE TO GOD?

Some few give to the Lord for all the right reasons. They are close to God and, therefore, seek the Face of the Lord earnestly about what they should support. These people would fall into the same category of the Philippians, and no doubt others of Paul's day who helped him in the greatest undertaking that one could ever imagine, the actual founding of the Church.

However, having said that, I think it also should be said that the percentage of the ones just mentioned would be very small. Many Christians have the mistaken idea, that if they just give, that is the end of their responsibility. A little thinking will prove the fallacy of such direction.

The Lord expects each and every Believer to walk close to Him. Consequently, He expects all to be led by the Holy Spirit in all that they do, and that speaks especially for their giving.

Does anyone in their right spiritual mind actually believe that the millions of people in particular Churches which are modernists in belief, could actually be blessed by the Lord regarding their giving? Of course they can't. In fact, irrespective as to what they think, they are actually not giving to the Lord. Their money is going to support that which is the very opposite of God, i.e., *"the work of the Devil."*

But how about Preachers and Churches which claim to believe all the Bible, etc.?

Just because people claim something doesn't mean it's true. In fact, as I've said many times, Satan is a master at making people believe that what is of God, isn't, and what isn't of God, is!

Once again, we go back to the fruit of which Jesus spoke in Matthew 7:15-29.

Christians need to investigate carefully what is being preached behind their pulpits, what is being taught and practiced by their particular Church or Denomination. Unfortunately, there are untold millions of so-called Christians who support their Denomination, just because it's the Denomination they like. They really don't care too very much what is preached, just so it's in that Denomination. Consequently, anything outside of that Denomination they will not support, and the real reason is, they are actually serving the Denomination instead of the Lord.

It's not wrong to belong to a Denomination or to support a Denomination, providing it's preaching the Gospel. But once it ceases to do that, and in any capacity, it should not be supported in any manner, as ought to be overly obvious.

Others respond from the premise of greed. In other words, the message is that if one will give so much money to that which purports to be the Work of God, then one will receive so much money in return from the Lord. In fact, such *"pitches"* have become so common in that which claims to be the Gospel, that it's hardly even shaded or disguised anymore. Unfortunately, there seems to be enough greed in all of us, that such messages have a ready audience. Once again, we go back to what we said previously, unless one is seeking first the Kingdom of God and His Righteousness, they can forget the *"other things."* The Lord will not respond to greed, as ought to be obvious, irrespective as to how much we dress it up with Scriptures.

SPIRITUAL IGNORANCE?

Millions of Christians give to that which they think is the Work of God, but which actually isn't. No matter how sincere they may be in their efforts, such ignorance is inexcusable.

Each Believer plainly has the Word of God at his disposal. Each Believer has the capacity to seek the Lord as to the leading of the Holy Spirit in these areas. Unfortunately, many, if not most, Christians let somebody else do their thinking for them, and to be sure, there are Preachers and others, who are ready and willing to do just that. In other words, they will gladly think for you, and thereby, empty your pockets.

Yes, it's much easier to be led by someone else, allowing them to do your thinking for you, than it is for you to personally seek the Lord, and personally ascertain His Mind as it regards your consecration. The latter takes a little work, while the former requires nothing. So, it's no excuse for Believers to give to that which is not of God, and if they do so, it shows what they actually are. Please allow me to say it again:

Christians give to what they are. That word is so very important, that I would pray the Reader would look at it several times. In fact, Jesus said more about money then he did anything else, and not always in the positive sense. He did this simply because of that which I have just said.

What Christians support, what they give their money to, what they finance, is what they really are, which says within itself, that *"giving"* is a great barometer of spirituality.

Giving constitutes in a sense, the giving of one's self, of one's labor, of one's very being. While it is expressed in money, the money was earned in various ways. So, in effect, when the Christian gives, he is giving of himself, and that to which he gives, is what he actually is. We should think about that very carefully.

(15) "NOW YE PHILIPPIANS KNOW ALSO, THAT IN THE BEGINNING OF THE GOSPEL, WHEN I DEPARTED FROM MACEDONIA, NO CHURCH COMMUNICATED WITH ME AS CONCERNING GIVING AND RECEIVING, BUT YE ONLY."

In order to make it clear the he is not minimizing the Philippians generosity toward him, Paul recalls some earlier demonstrations of their love for him. When the Gospel was first preached to them — approximately ten years before (Acts Chpt. 16) — they were the only Church to contribute to him when he left Macedonia.

Paul does not mean that no other Church had ever assisted him (II Cor. 11:8), but that on the specific occasion referred to here no other Church had come to his aid.

THE BEGINNING OF THE GOSPEL

The phrase, *"Now ye Philippians know also, that in the beginning of the Gospel,"* refers to the time when Paul first preached the Word to them about ten years previously, as stated.

This *"beginning of the Gospel"* has a far greater meaning than meets the eye. Paul went into Macedonia where Philippi was located as a result of the *"Macedonian Call,"* given to him by the Lord (Acts 16:9-10). This of course, was extremely important within itself, but the fact that this was the very first presentation of the Gospel in Europe, gives it a significance all out of proportion to Paul's short statement here. In fact, this set the stage for the Evangelization of the Western World, which in effect, was the beginning of what we now refer to as *"Western Civilization."*

This which is presently the envy of the world, owes its blessings in totality to the Gospel of Jesus Christ as preached by Paul. Truly, it was the *"beginning of the Gospel,"* not only for the Philippians, and the Macedonians, but as well for Western Europe as a whole, and ultimately for the United States of America.

WHY WAS THE THRUST OF THE GOSPEL GREATER TOWARD THE WEST THAN THE EAST?

First of all we know that God is no respecter of Persons, and as well, when Jesus died on the Cross, He died for the entirety of the world (Jn. 3:16). So, God does not favor the West over the East, or anyone over any other for that matter. The Lord loves all alike and, therefore, Redemption is for all alike.

Nevertheless, in the foreknowledge of God, He obviously knew that the Gospel would be better received in the West than it was the East. In fact, Paul later did go into the East and with some success; however, the seed there planted did not bring forth the fruit that it did toward the West. The fault was not in the seed of the Gospel and certainly not in the Lord, but rather in unreceptive hearts. Even though the Gospel of Jesus Christ has definitely had some success in the East, for the most part, however, it has not been successful. Hence, the East is muchly dominated by Islam, Hinduism, Buddhism, Confucianism, Shintoism, etc.

The Truth is, a nation is guided much by its religion. If it worships Demons and Devils, the results are obvious. There will be less freedom, less prosperity, with human life looked at as cheap. The great values which make a people great, a nation great, can only come from the Word of God. Consequently, the more that the Gospel is given latitude and leeway in any nation, the more blessings will follow, and blessings in every capacity — material, domestic, sociological, mental, and above all spiritual.

"Let us hear the conclusion of the whole matter: Fear God and keep His Commandments: for this is the whole duty of man" (Eccl. 12:13).

MACEDONIA

The phrase, *"When I departed from Macedonia,"* pertains to the account given in Acts 17:14. The last place that Paul visited in Macedonia, at that time, was Berea. There a tumult was excited by the Jews, and it was necessary for him to leave. He left Macedonia to go to Athens; and left it in haste, amidst scenes of persecution, at a time incidentally, when he needed sympathizing aid.

At that time, as well as when he was in Thessalonica (Acts 17:1-10), he needed the assistance of others to supply those needs; and he says that aid was not withheld.

The meaning here is, that this aid was sent to him *"as he was departing from Macedonia"*; that is, the Philippians sent aid to him when he was in Thessalonica and afterwards.

Paul is reaching back, reminding the Philippians of their kindness to him in the past, which of course he did not forget, and which meant very much to him, as should be obvious. As well, by Paul treating this in this fashion, we know how important it was to the Holy Spirit, hence it being recorded. Once again, I emphasize, that we should take a lesson from all of this.

GIVING AND RECEIVING

The phrase, *"No Church communicated with me as concerning giving and receiving, but ye only,"* proclaims the fact the Philippians had always been generous. Once again, the Holy Spirit desires strongly that we note all of this.

The Philippians made themselves a fellow-partaker with Paul in his efforts to evangelize the lost and to plant Churches. They made themselves fellow-partakers with him in the responsibility of spreading the Gospel.

The words *"giving and receiving"* are a business term referring to the credit and debit side of a ledger. The Philippian Saints owed Paul much since he was the one who won them to the Lord and nurtured them in the Faith. Thus, in a sense, one might say, Paul had certain credits on their ledger which they were obligated to honor. The Apostle referred to a like thing in I Corinthians 9:11, *"If we have sown unto you spiritual things, is it a great thing if we shall reap your carnal things?"* Meaning by carnal things, material things, i.e., money.

Paul prized all of this, not only because of the intrinsic merit and worth of the gift, but even more because it symbolized their affection, love, and loyalty.

It seems from this said by Paul, that of all the Churches planted by the Apostle, which referred to possibly thousands of people brought to Christ, which of course placed them eternally in his debt, only Philippi considered keeping an account with him, i.e., *"helping to habitually support him in his continued labors for the Lord."*

NOTES

Why other Churches did not at that time, Paul does not intimate. However, I think their lack of sensitivity in this area was a disappointment to him, or he would not have mentioned it here. I think as well, that the Holy Spirit was not at all pleased with the attitude of the other Churches regarding this very important matter.

Paul did not necessarily stay long in any one place. He was always being led by the Lord to go to other areas, areas which incidentally did not have the Gospel, in order to plant another Church; consequently, he was totally dependent upon the Spirit of God speaking to people who had been brought to Christ under his Ministry, in order that they might support him. Sometimes he received support, sometimes he didn't.

Again, we must understand that the Apostle is speaking only of the time when he left Macedonia and not necessarily of other times. As we have previously stated, the Philippians helped him then when the need was acute, but no other Churches then seemed to have done so. What these other Churches had done earlier, or what they did later, we are not told.

We don't want to make more of this then we should, but neither should we make less. This situation carries great significance, and I speak of the time Paul left Macedonia with even his life at stake, when it seems that help was desperately needed. It is very important, because the Holy Spirit notes all of this, which means we are to learn from what is being said here.

THE LESSON I THINK THE HOLY SPIRIT WANTS TAUGHT

Certainly at this particular time, other work for God was being carried on by other of the Apostles, and we speak of the original Twelve, plus others. And of course, all of that work was very important, as all the work of God is important. However, I think one would have to say, that this of which Paul was doing, was the most important of all, for the simple reason that Paul was the Masterbuilder of the Church, which responsibility the Lord had laid upon him. Consequently, we see the account given here by the Holy Spirit of his efforts, and not the accounts of others, as important as those efforts may have been.

So, any and all help given to the Apostle, which no doubt the Spirit of God greatly encouraged, would have been totally in the Will of God, and greatly blessed by God, and for all the obvious reasons.

We are taught here that we should be sensitive to the Holy Spirit. Is it possible that the Spirit dealt with many hearts and lives in certain respective Churches at that particular time, but for whatever reasons they did not heed? I personally think that definitely was the case, or else it would not have been mentioned here in this fashion by Paul. Understanding that every word written here was inspired by the Holy Spirit, should tell us something.

How many times does the Work of God suffer, because Christians are not sensitive to the leading of the Spirit? How many times does the Work of God suffer because Christians have been wrongfully influenced by others and, consequently, cannot properly hear the Voice of the Spirit?

If it is to be noticed, Paul mentioned both *"giving"* and *"receiving."*

He is speaking, I believe, of the manner of Christian giving, and how that the Lord gives back to us, hence, *"receiving."* All of this is a part and parcel of the Christian Faith. Christians who are not taught the value of giving to God, and even how that He gives back to us, of which the Scripture amply proclaims, are not being properly taught the Gospel. As we've already stated, *"giving"* is very, very important, inasmuch, as it is actually a barometer of our Love for God (II Cor. 8:8).

As well, we must be taught the rudiments of *"receiving."* The Truth is, that God does not return our gifts to Him only in the form of money. He as well blesses us in the realm of good health, of accidents we did not have because He prevented them, of equipment which lasted longer, simply because He caused it to do so, of problems and difficulties experienced by those who do not know the Lord, but are kept from the Child of God, etc. In fact, the Lord is constantly giving blessings of this nature, which we are constantly receiving, and which we are to be also constantly thankful. In fact, the *"receiving"* part of this, is not only to be a blessing to us, not only to meet our needs, which our Heavenly Father knows that we always have need of, but is also done on our behalf to teach us gratitude and thankfulness. We are to thank the Lord constantly, which means to not murmur and complain. *"Receiving"* enters into all of this. Christians who *"murmur and complain"* really do not know how to receive from the Lord, consequently, cutting themselves off from the Blessings of God.

It really doesn't matter whether we have much of this world's goods or not, even as Paul has amply stated. What does matter, is that we are saved, we are washed in the Blood, our names are written down in Heaven, which alone should give us cause for thanksgiving forever and forever. Considering what the Lord has done for us, we ought to be constantly thanking Him, with everything coming from our mouth being that of praises to Him.

(16) "FOR EVEN IN THESSALONICA YE SENT ONCE AND AGAIN UNTO MY NECESSITY."

Not only had the Philippians sent him a gift when he left Macedonia, but even when he was in Thessalonica, which was shortly after his departure from Philippi (Acts 17:1), they had made a contribution to him on more than one occasion.

Presumably these earlier gifts were small and so were in a different category from the one mentioned in Verse 15. This is also implied by references in the Thessalonian Epistles showing that Paul earned his living there by repairing tents (I Thess. 2:9; II Thess. 3:7-8) (Kent).

THESSALONICA

The phrase, *"For even in Thessalonica,"* speaks of the planting of the Church in that particular city.

After leaving Philippi, Paul went to Thessalonica, where a Church was there founded, but in the midst of great persecution (Acts 17:1-10).

Thessalonica was about eighty miles southwest of Philippi, situated in modern day Greece. Situated at the junction of the main land route from Italy to the East with the main route from the Aegean to the Danube, her position under the Romans was assured. Thessalonica was the first place where Paul's preaching achieved, it seems, a numerous and socially prominent following (Acts 17:4).

His opponents, lacking there hitherto customary influence in high places, resorted to mob agitation to force the Government's hand. The authorities, neatly trapped by the imputation of disloyalty towards the imperial power, took the minimum action to move Paul on without hardship to him.

It seems in Thessalonica that Paul supported himself, despite the fact that the Church there was wealthier than the Church at Philippi, etc. He was apparently afraid that the flourishing condition of the Church would encourage parasites unless he himself set the strictest example of self-support (II Thess. 3:8-12). The two Epistles to the Thessalonians, written soon after his departure, reflect also his anxiety to conserve his gains from rival teachers (II Thess. 2:2) and from disillusionment in the face of further agitation (I Thess. 3:3). He need not have feared. Thessalonica remained a triumphant crown to his efforts (I Thess. 1:8).

In all of this, we see the Apostle striving to obey the Spirit in all things in respect to the founding of the New Testament Church. While he received very few offerings it seems for himself, he did receive financial help for other particular needs, even as II Corinthians Chapters 8 and 9 proclaim. In fact, he praised the Churches of Macedonia for their example regarding giving to a particular effort.

In his Second Letter to the Corinthians he actually said, *"Have I committed an offence in abasing myself that ye might be exalted, because I preached to you the Gospel of God freely? I robbed other Churches, taking wages of them, to do you service"* (II Cor. 11:7-8).

He is actually saying that he's not sure if he did right in not receiving offerings for himself at Corinth, where it seems he followed the same pattern in Thessalonica, and possibly other places as well.

The Priests of the heathen temples in these particular localities, leaned heavily upon their devotees for money, and did so in about every capacity. Among other things, Paul probably desired strongly to show his converts that the Lord's Work was not carried on in similar fashion. Whatever his reasons for conducting the

NOTES

money situation as he did, of this we can be assured, he was doing his very best to follow the leading of the Holy Spirit.

I might quickly add, that this which I have just described, is a far cry from the prosperity teachers who claim they are proclaiming the Word of God.

The Truth is, they are proclaiming no such thing. It's just another scam under a religious cloak.

NECESSITY

The phrase, *"Ye sent once and again unto my necessity,"* proclaims the faithfulness of the Philippians.

One might say that the manner in which something is born, somewhat sets the course for the direction thereafter. The earliest convert at Philippi, Lydia, struck the keynote, *"If ye judge me faithful in the Lord, come into my house"* (Acts 16:15). Both in individuals and in Churches, the style of feeling and action embraced at the outset of Christianity, under the first impressions, often continues to prevail long after.

It is beautiful, the manner in which the Apostle proclaims his appreciation to the Philippians for their kindness, but at the same time, always stating that his dependence is totally in the Lord. Of course, the Holy Spirit is guiding him totally in these things which he writes, and, as well, which proclaim his principle and manner of Doctrine.

(17) "NOT BECAUSE I DESIRE A GIFT: BUT I DESIRE FRUIT THAT MAY ABOUND TO YOUR ACCOUNT."

The Apostle plainly states here that although the gift is very much needed and very much appreciated; still it is only a part of the bigger picture, which speaks of the development of the grace of giving among them. Continuing to use business terminology, he says that he regards such displays as interests accruing (credited) to their account. Their spiritual growth was the fruit Paul desired, and to this end he directed his remarks and his Ministry.

DESIRE

The phrase, *"Not because I desire a gift,"* presents the Apostle in a sense defending himself against the slanderous assertion that he is using the Gospel as a means to make money. The word *"desire"* is in the present tense which usually indicates habitual action. Consequently, it could be translated, *"Not that it is my character or habit to seek."* He shrinks sensitively from the danger of being mistaken; his words are not to be understood as a hint for further gifts.

The word *"desire"* is the key word in all of this. What did Paul desire? Of course, the answer is obvious in the next phrase; however, the great question should be, as we search our hearts as Preachers, *"What do we desire?"*

To be sure, God knows exactly what the desire is in our hearts, irrespective as to what we might say. Man may look upon the external and listen to the external, but it is God Who knows the heart. If greed is there, He full well knows that. If our motives are right, He knows that as well.

Even though we are discussing Paul's motives here, at the same time we should address ourselves to the motives of the Philippians. Of course, both serve as an example for Preachers and the laity.

Does the Preacher actually desire blessing upon the people, as it regards their spiritual growth concerning their giving, or does he in fact have greed in his heart? At the same time, do those who give, as they listen to the appeal of the Preacher, whomever he may be, give out of a true motive to be of blessing to the Work of God, or out of greed?

Beyond the shadow of a doubt we know what Paul's desire actually was, and as well we know the desire of the Philippians. All were in the boundaries of the Grace of God.

What about ourselves?

Are we Preachers appealing for money, to truly further the work of God, or to enrich ourselves?

As Laity, are we giving to that which purports to be the Work of God, because we truly have a burden to see souls brought to Christ, or are we responding to a scam thinking that we will get much more money back?

FRUIT

The phrase, *"But I desire fruit that may abound to your account,"* tells us several things:

NOTES

1. Paul's desire for these people, even as much as he needed and appreciated the gift, as stated, was their spiritual growth.

2. This tells us that all giving which is truly to God, actually gathers interest in Heaven, that is if we are allowed to use such terminology.

3. It also tells us, that if we do not give to that which is truly of God, it is the same as a bad investment which not only earns no interest, but the investment will be lost as well.

4. All of this, even as the next Verse describes, is very holy to the Lord, and should be looked at in the same manner by ourselves as well. That's at least one of the reasons why the present *"greed motive"* is so ungodly!

5. The *"fruit abounding to one's account"* as it regards one's giving, is the Apostle's way of saying with Jesus, *"It is more blessed to give than to receive"* (Acts 20:35).

(18) "BUT I HAVE ALL, AND ABOUND: I AM FULL, HAVING RECEIVED OF EPAPHRODITUS THE THINGS WHICH WERE SENT FROM YOU, AN ODOUR OF A SWEET SMELL, A SACRIFICE ACCEPTABLE, WELL-PLEASING TO GOD."

The Apostle considers this contribution a Sacrificial Offering to God, made to further the Lord's Work by helping His servant (Mat. 25:40).

"A Fragrant Offering" is used in Ephesians 5:2 of Christ's Sacrificial Offering of Himself to God on man's behalf. It also reflects the Levitical Ritual (Lev. 1:9, 13, 17; 2:12).

Such Offerings please God, because they come from obedient hearts.

ABOUNDING AND FULL

The phrase, *"But I have all, and abound: I am full,"* proclaims the fact that the Philippian gift must have been generous.

The words *"I have"* are a rubber-stamp of the First Century for, *"I give you a receipt for what you sent me,"* or *"I have received in full."* What a demonstration of the work of the Holy Spirit is seen in this act of generosity on the part of these former pagans, performed for one (Paul) who in origin, training, and religion had been and in some ways was still so different from them, different in a sense which would naturally militate against Paul, Gentiles of the proudest and most exclusive race of antiquity, the intelligentsia of the world, loving one who belonged to a race (Hebrews) that was looked down upon and despised.

Then Paul says, *"I am full."* The verb is in that wonderfully descriptive Greek tense, which says in this one Greek word, *"I have been filled full and at present am well supplied."* How the Greek language is able to compress so much into one word (Wuest).

Because the Philippians were truly sensitive to the Holy Spirit, truly understood the Work of God at that time, truly understood Paul's place in this great work, which many Christians at that time, even many of Paul's converts did not seem to understand, the Apostle for a change can say *"I am full,"* instead of (I) *"hunger and thirst"* (II Cor. 11:27). Thank God for the Philippians, but this of which Paul says, should have been the case altogether and for the entirety of his Ministry. Thank the Lord, in the midst of so much spiritual insensitivity, in the midst of so much carnal thinking, in the midst of so many so little led by the Holy Spirit, there are the Philippians. How they stand out! How the Holy Spirit records their generosity for time and eternity! They stood with Paul. They helped Paul. And above all, they were led by the Lord in the doing of this, which receives accolades of the highest order.

No, they did not do such for praise or glory, little realizing that what they did would be forever enshrined in the Word of God, captioned by the Holy Spirit, made forever to serve as an example of generosity and liberality, which has such approval by the Spirit of God. These Philippians should be an example to all of us, and in fact, are meant to be an example.

EPAPHRODITUS

The phrase, *"Having received of Epaphroditus the things that were sent from you,"* presents this dear brother as we have previously stated, as having the distinct privilege of sharing in this which was so pleasing to the Lord. What an honor!

It was almost a thousand miles from Philippi to Rome, which in those days was definitely not an easy journey, and which took several weeks. Little did Epaphroditus know

NOTES

when preparing for this journey, or the people of the Church in Philippi who contributed so generously to this offering for Paul, know or understand I think, the significance of all of this. How could they know? But yet God knew!

Could they even begin to think or understand, that 2,000 years later people would still be reading about their kindness, commenting on it, even writing Books about this which they carried out! Had such a thing been related to them, they probably would have looked aghast, wondering what all the fuss was about!

However, the lesson learned here, or at least should be learned, is that the Holy Spirit notes all things, and for time and eternity. Think about the following for a moment.

There were Christians at that very moment, even many who had been saved under the Ministry of Paul, who were being led astray by the Judaizers, even strongly encouraged to repudiate the Apostle, their father in the Lord. They were giving money to these individuals, even as Paul mentions in his two Letters to the Church at Corinth. To be sure, there were no grand words spoken by the Holy Spirit in regard to these acts of spiritual high treason. It is alluded to only in passing, and then in extremely negative terms. So again, what am I saying?

I'm saying that we need to understand that all that we do as Believers is being marked down by the Holy Spirit, and for an eternal record. Consequently, we should do all within our power to be led by the Spirit instead of other things. Regrettably, and I think I exaggerate not, most of the Church is in fact, led by other things.

A SWEET SMELL

The phrase, *"An odour of a sweet smell,"* presents the Old Testament odors of the Levitical Sacrifices, all typifying Christ.

Going back as far as Noah, the Scripture says, *"And Noah builded an Altar unto the Lord . . . and offered Burnt Offerings on the Altar."*

It then says, *"And the Lord smelled a sweet savour* (a sweet odor)*"* (Gen. 8:20-21).

Concerning the Levitical Offerings, it says, *"It is a Burnt Offering unto the Lord: it is a sweet savour"* (Ex. 29:18).

How could the burning of a little animal on an Altar, with the greasy smoke winding upwards, and even with the smell of burning flesh filling the air, be a sweet odor, a sweet smell unto the Lord?

It was such because it represented the Plan of Redemption, in essence, the dying of Christ upon the Cross, offered up as a Sacrifice, which for all of its horror, still, would set the captives free, at least for those who will believe (Jn. 3:16). Anything else offered to God as a means of Salvation, comes up as a foul odor unto Him, which should be obvious. It is only the Sacrifice of His Son and nothing else, which pleases Him.

At the same time, this which the Philippians did, the giving of an Offering to the Work of God, in this case to Paul, affected the Lord in the same manner.

HOW COULD AN OFFERING OF MONEY BE EQUATED WITH THE SACRIFICE OF CHRIST?

This is a very important question and should be looked at very closely.

Paul's Message was the Message of the Cross, the only Message in fact, which will set men free. Consequently, anything done for Paul, or any Preacher of the Gospel with the same Message, will be looked at by the Lord exactly as the Offering of the Philippians.

If an Offering is given to help take the great Message of the Cross to a lost and dying world, and the Preacher uses the Offering in that fashion, in the mind of God, exactly as the Holy Spirit says through the Apostle, it is equated with the Cross which pertains to the Redemption of mankind; therefore, it comes up into the nostrils of God as a sweet fragrance.

At the same time, this means that all the money given, plus any other type of effort made, which does not pertain to the Cross, irrespective of how religious it might be, is not at all looked at by God in the same fashion as should be obvious. This speaks volumes, and should tell us something.

This means that most of the money given in today's religious climate, is not at all looked at by God as furthering His Work, but rather something else altogether. We should understand, that the terminology used here by Paul was given to him by the Holy Spirit,

therefore, sanctioned by the Holy Spirit, which tells us how important it actually is.

This means that anyone who gives money strictly with the idea in mind of God giving them much more in return, is not sanctioned at all by God. It means as well, that Christians who are supporting Churches and Denominations which espouse the psychological way, instead of the Cross of Christ, are, in fact, not supporting the Work of God, but rather that of the Evil One. That's a strong statement, but it is true!

We cannot have it both ways. It is either God's Way, which is the Cross, or else it is another way, which can never be sanctioned by the Lord, i.e., *"have the odour of a sweet smell."*

A SACRIFICE ACCEPTABLE

The phrase, *"A Sacrifice acceptable,"* carries the same meaning as the Sacrifices of the Old Testament, but more particularly, of the Sacrifice of Christ, which every Sacrifice represented, at least if appropriately offered.

The word *"acceptable"* should be noted. Inasmuch as this Offering was given by the Philippians to help Paul take this great Message of the Cross to a hurting world, even though he was then still imprisoned, lets us know how special was this action. The terminology employed by the Holy Spirit through the Apostle puts all of this on a far higher plane than a mere gift. It tells us that the only thing acceptable unto God is the Message of the Cross, and nothing is acceptable to God if it omits the Cross. It is just that simple!

Did these Philippians know and understand all of this when they sent their Offering to Paul?

I seriously doubt they understood it to that degree; however, they were definitely led by the Lord as to whom they supported; therefore, in giving to God's man, and not to someone who merely claimed to be God's man but actually wasn't, they entered into all the blessings of such an effort.

We have more light at the present even than the Philippians had, for the simple reason that we have the entirety of the New Testament completed, which they then only had in part. And yet I'm afraid, that most modern Believers little function in the Will of God as it regards this of which we speak.

In fact, and as I've stated many times, the Cross has been so little preached and taught the last half of the 20th Century, that the Church has almost lost her moorings. The Cross of Christ is the foundation of all that we are, actually the foundation of the great Christian Faith. Everything is built around the Cross of Christ. If that be neglected, everything else is then colored and skewed, which means it is understood imperfectly. If that is true, and it is, then it means the Church has little knowledge of true Faith, and because of a serious lack of knowledge of the Cross.

WELL-PLEASING TO GOD

The phrase, *"Well-pleasing to God,"* tells us that which is so very, very important.

Paul told us in Romans 8:8, *"So then they that are in the flesh cannot please God."* So, we know and understand, that the only thing that pleases God as it regards Redemption, is the Sacrifice of His Only Son, The Lord Jesus Christ. Isaiah said, *"Yet it pleased the Lord to bruise Him"* (Isa. 53:10). This means that nothing pleases him that is divorced from the Cross.

It means the psychological way does not please Him!

It means the so-called prosperity gospel does not please Him!

It means the modernistic way does not please Him!

It means that works righteousness doesn't please Him!

It means that anything and everything that's not squarely tied to the Cross sorely displeases Him!

The Reader should understand, if the Lord used a simple offering of money to illustrate the single most important thing in the world as it pertains to mankind, the Salvation of the soul, with the Holy Spirit even using the holiest of terms, we certainly should get the Message which He is attempting to portray.

The next time that you the Reader give an offering to what is purported to be the Work of God, you should ask yourself some questions as to what your money is really supporting. If it's not supporting the Message of the Cross, then it's not only wasted, but I think extremely displeasing to the Lord.

NOTES

Unfortunately, there is an awful lot which displeases Him in these particular times.

The Reader should well understand as to why the Cross is so very, very important. The Cross was not accidental or incidental, but rather the destination of Christ. In other words, He came to this world to die on a Cross, because that was what was demanded by God, that is if mankind was to be delivered from the terrible bondages of sin. The Cross as well, addresses the terrible problem of *"self."* As sin could be conquered by the Cross alone, likewise, self is handled in the same manner.

(19) "BUT MY GOD SHALL SUPPLY ALL YOUR NEED ACCORDING TO HIS RICHES IN GLORY BY CHRIST JESUS."

In words that countless Christians have relied on as one of the great Scripture Promises, Paul now reminds his benefactors that God will do what He Himself is in no position to do; namely, reimburse his benefactors.

This assurance of the Divine supply implies that the Philippians possibly had given so liberally that they actually left themselves in some real *"need."* Consequently, it is true that those who share generously with others, especially to advance the Work of the Lord as we have mentioned, are promised a Divine supply of anything they might lack because of their generosity (Prov. 11:25; 19:17; Mat. 5:7).

THE SUPPLY OF ALL YOUR NEED

The phrase, *"But my God shall supply all your need,"* presents the Apostle assuring the Philippians, and all other Believes as well, that they have not impoverished themselves in giving so liberally to the Cause of the Gospel. The word *"supply"* is the translation of the same Greek word translated *"I am full."* That is, *God's treatment of these Saints will correspond to their treatment of Paul.* They filled full Paul's every need to overflowing. God will do the same for them (Wuest).

The idea is, that God accepts these gifts to Paul as oblations (gifts) to Himself, and consequently, will take it upon Himself to recompense, and that in superabundant measure.

In II Corinthians 8:2, we learn that Macedonia had been in deep poverty, due to particular political problems with Rome;

however, whether that was the case presently is not known. Irrespective, the Philippians gave abundantly even in that deep poverty, with, no doubt, conditions having improved from then until now. It had been about four years time between the writing of II Corinthians and Philippians. Irrespective of the situation politically, none of this deters the Lord from meeting the needs of His people. He is not limited by resources, situations, circumstances, etc. In fact, we limit Him only by our doubt and unbelief.

One might say that the Philippians responded to the Work of God out of their need, and God will likewise, but out of His riches.

It should be remembered, that God's treatment of the Philippians would correspond to their treatment of Paul. It is the same presently regarding those who are truly God-called!

In this, we learn that we must not shrink from the doctrine of reward because it has been perverted by some. We are plainly told here what the Lord will do, but of course, there are conditions attached. Many Christians are fond of quoting this particular Scripture, and rightly so; however, He will not supply all of our need if we are supporting the wrong thing, on the wrong track, or have impure motives. Many people loosely throw this Passage around, little understanding that there definitely are conditions attached. In fact, these conditions should be obvious.

God cannot bless that which is opposed to Him, even though it claims to be of Him. It is up to the Believer to know what he is supporting, whom he is supporting, and why he is supporting that person, or Church. The reasons had better be Scriptural, and the Preacher that is being supported had better measure up to the Word of God. Otherwise, God's abundant supply will definitely not be forthcoming.

ACCORDING TO HIS RICHES IN GLORY

The phrase, *"According to His riches in Glory,"* presents the fact that the measure of the supply which God the Father has, is determined by His wealth in Glory, which wealth in Glory is in Christ Jesus, at least as it corresponds to the Saints. It is an infinite supply.

NOTES

One might say that Verse 19 is a note upon the Bank of Faith, but please remember, it must be the proper Faith, which we will address momentarily.

"My God" — the Name of the Banker.
"Shall supply" — the promised pay.
"All your need" — the value of the note.
"According to His riches" — the capital of the Bank.
"In Glory" — the address of the Bank.
"By Christ Jesus" — the signature without which the note is worthless.

The Holy Spirit through the Apostle does not say that God will supply every want. He does say that God will supply every need. Since God knows our needs better than we know our own, the supplying of these needs may not always in line with our petitions.

This inner expression of assurance is consistent with II Corinthians 9:8, *"God is able to make all Grace abound unto you; that ye, having always all sufficiency in every thing, may abound unto every good work."*

In both cases, these Promises are in the context of proper stewardship. When we seek first the Kingdom of God, and His Righteousness, all these things are added for good measure.

When Solomon gave priority to wisdom, God gave him wealth and honor as a *"fringe benefit."* All of these things are a *"fringe benefit"* to Redemption.

BY CHRIST JESUS

The phrase, *"By Christ Jesus,"* should have been translated *"In Christ Jesus."*

Whenever Christ is mentioned in this capacity, it is always referring to the Christ of the Cross. The price Jesus paid at the Cross and the Resurrection, made it possible for us to have all of these great and wonderful things. In other words, God could not give us anything, other than by or in Christ Jesus, which refers to His Sacrificial, Atoning, Vicarious Offering of Himself, on the Cross. Everything comes through the Cross. All blessings stream from the Cross, for it was there that the price was paid. As the song says:

"Jesus opened up the way, the way to Heaven's Gate."

That Way was opened by Christ shedding His Own Precious Blood, which satisfied the claims of Heavenly Justice and atoned for all sin. The wages of sin is death, and Jesus died in order to pay those wages.

He died as our Substitute, and our Representative Man. As we have previously stated, as our Substitute He died for us, as our Representative Man, He died as us.

As our Substitute, He died for sinners. As our Representative Man, He died as a sinner, even though He wasn't a sinner (II Cor. 5:21).

Consequently, this was all done for us, and not at all for Himself.

Even as God, Jesus could not give us all of these great things of which we speak. As well, even as a Man, The Man, Christ Jesus, He could not bring these things about by His Miracles, His Healings, His Words of Eternal Life, His Virgin Birth, His perfect Life, even though all of these things were necessary. He had to go to the Cross, if the price was to be paid and all sin atoned.

Only that is a *"sweet smell, a Sacrifice acceptable, well-pleasing to God."* Consequently, our Faith must always be in the Finished Work of Christ, and for everything. This means the Cross must ever be the object of our Faith.

(20) "NOW UNTO GOD AND OUR FATHER BE GLORY FOR EVER AND EVER. AMEN."

Small wonder that Paul closes this beautiful Passage in this manner. The Glory of God's providential care must always be recognized by His Children. Even the Eternal Ages yet to come will not be sufficient to exhaust the praises that belong to Him (Kent).

GOD OUR FATHER

The phrase, *"Now unto God and our Father,"* suggests the most beautiful privilege that any human being could ever have, the privilege of referring to God as *"Our Father."* This can only come about as a result of the *"Born-Again"* experience, which is brought about totally by the Grace of God, as the believing sinner exhibits Faith in what Jesus did at the Cross on his behalf. Then the believing sinner, who had nothing, who could obtain nothing at least on his own, and was worthy of nothing good, now is given everything because of the Grace of God, and is adopted into the great family of God. As such,

NOTES

"And if children, then heirs; heirs of God, and joint-heirs with Christ" (Rom. 8:17). The Believer is now made a part of the aristocracy of Heaven, which benefit accrues to all who accept Christ. As a result, all type of privileges open up to the Child of God.

With the Creator of the Ages now our Heavenly Father, with the door always open, incidentally opened in totality by what Jesus did at the Cross and the Resurrection, there is absolutely no end to what can now be accomplished.

The following was given to me by a friend, and although hypothetical perhaps will be of some blessing.

THE INTERVIEW

I dreamed I had an interview with God.
"Come in," God said.
"So, you would like to interview Me?"
"If you have the time," I said. God smiled and responded:
"My time is eternity and is enough to do everything; what questions do you have in mind to ask Me?"
"What surprises you most about mankind?" I posed!
God answered: *"That they get bored of being children, are in a rush to grow up, and then long to be children again.*
"That they lose their health to make money and then lose their money to restore their health.
"That by thinking anxiously about the future, they forget the present, so that they live neither for the present or the future.
"That they live as if they will never die, and they die as if they have never lived."
God's Hands took mine and we were silent for a while and then I asked . . . *"As a Parent, what are some of life's lessons You want Your Children to learn?"*
God replied with a smile: *"To learn that they cannot make anyone love them. What they can do is to let themselves be loved.*
"To learn that what is most valuable, is not what they have in their lives, but who they have in their lives.
"To learn that it is not good to compare themselves to others. All will be judged individually on their own merits, not as a group on a comparison basis!

"To learn that a rich person is not the one who has the most, but is one who needs the least.

"To learn that it only takes a few seconds to open profound wounds in persons we love, and that it takes many years to heal them.

"To learn to forgive by practicing forgiveness. To learn that there are persons who love them dearly, but simply do not know how to express or show their feelings.

"To learn that money can buy many things but cannot buy happiness.

"To learn that two people can look at the same thing and see it totally different.

"To learn that a true friend is someone who knows everything about them . . . and loves them anyway. To learn that it is not always enough that they be forgiven by others, but that they have to themselves, forgive."

I sat there for awhile enjoying the moment. I thanked Him for His time and for all that He had done for me and my family, and He replied, *"Anytime. I'm here 24 hours a day. All you have to do is ask for Me, and I'll answer."*

He then said in closing: *"People will forget what you said. People will forget what you did, but people will never forget how you made them feel."*

THE GLORY FOREVER

The phrase, *"Be Glory for ever and ever. Amen."* represents a Truth we must never forget.

All the *"Glory"* belongs totally and completely to God. Man is worthy of no glory whatsoever, and if he in fact does have some, it is only that which is given freely to him by the Lord. In other words, he did not earn such glory, cannot earn such glory, and must ever understand that he is not worthy of such glory.

The word *"Amen,"* actually means *"Truth,"* and means that what has been said is right, and will not change.

What is Glory?

Glory, whether pertaining to man or God, is splendor, fame, power, wonder, grandeur, excellence, magnificence, honor, etc. Of course, there is no comparison whatsoever to the glory of man, at least that which we refer to as glory, and the Glory of God. The magnificence of God is of such wonder, such power, such splendor, that vocabulary could never begin to express such. In fact, we only know in part at present concerning the Glory of God, or anything for that matter about God. But yet, the Word of God does give us enough clue to let us know something of the splendor of His Majesty. Revelation Chapters 21 and 22 are an excellent case in point. What is there described, is so far beyond our comprehension, that superlatives fail us.

To which we have briefly alluded, all Glory belongs to God, hence Paul making the statement as he did. That's why Saints are constantly saying in one way or the other, *"Glory to God!"*

It means that all that God has done for the human race, all that He has given to the human race, all that He means to the human race, is totally and strictly of Him and none of man. Unfortunately, man has a tendency to attempt to rob God of the Glory. This stems from the Fall in the Garden of Eden.

Adam traded the Glory of God which freely and wondrously rested upon him, for his own contrived glory, in effect, trying to be like God, but in an unlawful way. As a result, he became totally unlike God, in that God is able only to do good, while unredeemed man is able only to do bad. So from then until now, man has been attempting to build for himself, to make for himself, a contrived glory, whether in the realm of dictatorial powers, or in his own contrived manner through money, power, etc. He fails on all counts, as fail he must!

When the believing sinner comes to Christ and is *"Born-Again,"* at that moment some of the Glory of God rests upon his person and remains with him. We refer to it as the Presence of God, which although in minute quantities only, still gives us an idea as to the wonder and Glory of God.

At the Baptism with the Holy Spirit, more Glory is infused into the Saint, but all from God, and never from the individual. This we must never forget: No matter how much God may use us, or what He may do through us, at best, we are only a reflection of His Glory, having none of our own.

(21) "SALUTE EVERY SAINT IN CHRIST JESUS. THE BRETHREN WHICH ARE WITH ME GREET YOU."

Paul now sends greetings to every Believer at Philippi, to be conveyed to them, no doubt, by the leadership of the Church to whom the Letter was initially delivered.

Paul's associates also send their greetings. They are to be distinguished from the resident Roman Christians who are mentioned in the next Verse. These *"Brothers who are with me,"* include Timothy, and possibly even some of those mentioned in Philippians 1:14.

As well, the inclusion of these greetings is a caution against interpreting Philippians 2:21 as an indictment of all Paul's associates except Timothy.

IN CHRIST JESUS

The phrase, *"Salute every Saint in Christ Jesus,"* proclaims Paul's normal manner of ending his Letters. Perhaps the most notable of these examples is found in the 16th Chapter of Romans. Such greetings were common in Letters of that time. However, the felicitations in Paul's Letters were more cordial than in most.

"Salute" means to greet.

Everyone who is a Believer is a *"Saint."* The word simply means, *"To be sanctified or to be set apart unto the Lord."* This happens instantaneously and immediately at the New Birth. Consequently, the Catholic practice of making certain people *"Saints"* after their death, has no Scriptural validity whatsoever, which practice is totally opposed in the Word of God. Only Jesus Christ can make one a Saint, and He does so by imputing His Righteousness to the believing sinner.

The words *"In Christ Jesus,"* portray the foundation of Christianity as perhaps no other words. It has a wealth of meaning.

When the individual accepts Christ, in the Mind of God, that person was literally in Christ when Christ died on the Cross, was buried, and raised from the dead (Rom. 6:3-5).

Of course, it is obvious that the sinner was not there when Jesus died, but the sinner's Faith in what Jesus did there, places that sinner literally in Christ, at least in the Mind of God. That's what we mean by Jesus being our *"Representative Man."* When He died and rose from the dead, He did it on our behalf as our Substitute, but more particularly, He did it as us, which means as our Representative Man. He did *for* us, and *as* us, what we could not do for ourselves.

NOTES

FAITH

The only thing required for all of this to happen, is Faith on the part of the believing sinner. The Lord does not require works of any nature, and in fact, if such are offered, frustration of the effort immediately occurs (Gal. 2:21).

On the basis of Faith, and we mean Faith in what Jesus did at the Cross and the Resurrection, God is able to justify the believing sinner. In fact, He can do so on no other basis. Consequently, the moment the person accepts Christ, they are in effect, *"in Christ,"* and are to remain in Christ for eternity.

The things we have said are not complicated at all, but yet in another sense of the word, are extremely complicated. The simplicity of it all is that we only have to exhibit Faith to be the beneficiary of all that Jesus did at the Cross. But on the other side of that coin, at least as God sees the situation, and which the Believer most certainly must learn and, therefore, understand after conversion, is a complicated process.

Even as the initial Salvation process stands solely on our Faith in Christ, our continued life of victory stands on the same basis. Unfortunately, we do not learn the lesson easily of staying in Christ. Actually, the process is basically the same as it regards the sinner coming to Christ. Most do not come easily, generally as the result of a crisis.

As it regards the Believer, many times we do not come fully to the Cross, and I speak of the Victory which can be obtained only in that capacity, until we come to some type of crisis in our lives. Of course, that's not true of all, but is definitely true of some.

BRETHREN

The phrase, *"The Brethren which are with me greet you,"* no doubt, as we have stated, included Timothy, and several others. Just who all of them were, we are not told.

Paul stayed in prison, actually in a hired house in Rome, for at least two years. During this time, even as recorded in the last two Verses of Acts, he pretty much had complete latitude and freedom regarding the Preaching and Teaching of the Gospel. No doubt, there were people coming and going constantly, which necessitates the Apostle having some help.

I am confident, that the Apostle would have been Preaching and Teaching almost constantly, whether to several people, or as many as could crowd into the small dwelling. I have every confidence as well, that not only was the Church in Rome greatly strengthened by his teaching, but most likely there were many saved and baptized with the Holy Spirit also. During all of this, Paul was chained constantly to a Roman soldier.

(22) "ALL THE SAINTS SALUTE YOU, CHIEFLY THEY THAT ARE OF CAESAR'S HOUSEHOLD."

"*All the Saints*" refers to members of the Church at Rome. Paul also extends special greetings from *"those who belong to Caesar's household."*

This expression denotes those engaged in imperial service, whether as slaves or freedmen. Among them may have been the Palace Guard (Phil. 1:13). It is most unlikely that Nero's immediate family is meant, but the expression could refer to persons of considerable importance on the Emperor's staff.

Paul does not say why they were singled out for special mention. Presumably the Philippians would understand. Perhaps some of these Government Servants had come from Philippi or had once been stationed at that Roman Colony (Kent).

ALL THE SAINTS

The phrase, *"All the Saints salute you,"* refers as stated, to those in the Church at Rome. This tells us that many of them had been coming to hear Paul, and had no doubt benefitted greatly by his Preaching and Teaching.

To be frank, by this time Paul was famous. This means that many wanted to visit with the Apostle, whether out of curiosity or whatever the reason. Irrespective, it would have been an opportunity for Paul to proclaim the Gospel.

Rome being the capital of the world of that day, saw visitors coming constantly from all over the Empire. Of these individuals, whomever they may have been, no doubt some of them had heard of Paul, with others possibly even having been saved under his Ministry.

NOTES

At any rate, I am confident that the house where he was incarcerated, which was probably very close to the Palace, was filled with people on a daily basis, coming and going, but with all having heard the Gospel in some fashion.

CAESAR

The phrase, *"Chiefly they that are of Caesar's household,"* presents the fact that Paul's work had operated notably to produce results, even in the most unlikely of places.

It is believed that Caesar's household was an immense establishment, comprehending thousands of persons, employed in all sorts of functions, and composed chiefly, either of slaves, or of those who had emerged from slavery into the condition of freedmen.

One might say, that it was somewhat like the Capitol in the U.S.A. and the White House all rolled into one, etc. It was where at least some of the Government of the Empire was carried on.

Indications have been gathered from ancient mortuary inscriptions tending to show that a notable proportion of Christians, whose names are preserved in this way, had probably been connected with this particular household. At the end of the First Century, a whole branch of the Flavian imperial family became Christians; and it is possible, as indicated earlier, that they may have done so under the influence of Christian servants. However, this came over thirty years after Paul.

The Apostle wrote in Nero's days, that it is certain at this time singularly profligate persons exercised great sway in the household. It is also certain that powerful Jewish influences had secured a footing; and these would in all likelihood act against the Gospel.

Yet there were also Christian Brethren. We may believe that Paul's own work had served to bring many to Christ, with some of these individuals undoubtedly a member of the household in question.

At any event, there they were, amid all that was vile and unscrupulous. The Word of God had its great effect, with individuals accepting Christ by Faith.

Then, as now, the Lord gathered His Elect from unlikely quarters: *"How secure soever the strong man's goods seemed to be, his defenses went down before the might of a Stronger than he."* Probably the Christians in the household belonged chiefly or exclusively to the lower grades of the service, and might be partly protected by their obscurity. But yet, there definitely could have been some who had accepted Christ who held higher or even high positions.

This glimpse lets us see the process going on which by-and-by made so strange a revolution in the heathen world. It reminds us also for what peculiarities of trial God's Grace has been found sufficient.

(23) "THE GRACE OF OUR LORD JESUS CHRIST BE WITH YOU ALL. AMEN."

The concluding benediction is exactly the same as Philemon Verse 25 and similar to Galatians 6:18. It evokes on the Philippian Church the continuing favor of Christ to be with their spirits.

The realization of this benediction would increase the harmony of the congregation by causing the spirit of each Believer to cherish the Grace of the Lord Jesus Christ and by bringing a joyous peace among them, fulfilling the Apostle's opening wish (Phil. 1:2) (Kent).

GRACE

The phrase, *"The Grace of our Lord Jesus Christ,"* presents the parting benediction. Actually, the whole Epistle breathes the atmosphere of Grace.

Paul is referred to as the great Apostle of Grace, and because it was to him the great New Covenant was given, actually to which the Old Covenant had all the time pointed.

As we have explained several times, Grace is merely the favor of God, the blessings of God, the good things of God, bestowed upon undeserving individuals, who evidence Faith in the Finished Work of Christ. Inasmuch as this subject is so very, very important, please allow me to say it again.

God has always had Grace, i.e., *"has always been the God of Grace."* Grace is not something which He acquired at some point in time. He has always possessed this most wonderful commodity, if one might use such terminology. However, at a point in time, He chose the instrument of Grace as the vehicle through which He would deal with man. In fact, Grace has to be a choice, or else it isn't Grace.

However, Grace could not be simply administered to wicked, depraved man. It just was not possible in that manner. In fact, Grace can only come to sinful man through the Cross of Christ, and man's Faith in that Cross.

If one is to notice, while Grace was extended in Old Testament times, it was not nearly on the basis as it is now, and because the Cross was yet future. However, even then, it was given on the premise of this coming work, and man's Faith in that which was to come.

Of course, presently, inasmuch as the Cross is an historical fact, the Grace of God is given much more abundantly, for all the obvious reasons. And yet, Faith in the Cross of Christ continues to be demanded for Grace to abundantly flow to undeserving sinners.

In fact, the bestowal of Grace is somewhat akin to the Holy Spirit. As the Holy Spirit only works, at least in the capacity of which we speak, according to one's Faith in the Cross of Christ, Grace is extended to one and all strictly on the basis of the same thing — one's Faith in the Cross. Consequently, there are many Christians who do not have the help very much of the Holy Spirit, simply because of a lack of Faith in the Cross, and there are many Christians who do not experience near as much of the Grace of God as they could, because of improper Faith in the Cross. Everything is tied to the Cross. By Faith in the wrong object, we frustrate the Grace of God (Gal. 2:21).

WITH YOU ALL

The phrase, *"Be with you all. Amen,"* actually records the great Promise that *"The Grace of our Lord Jesus Christ"* is absolutely indiscriminate. It is *"for all,"* at least *"all who will believe"* (Jn. 3:16).

Once again, *"Amen,"* is included, which means *"Truth,"* and as well means that what is said here will not change.

IN CONCLUSION

It is August 11, 1999, 1:30 p.m., as I finish the work on the Commentary of the Epistle of Paul to the Philippians. As usual, the privilege of being able to do this overwhelms me.

I thank the Lord daily for His Grace in allowing me such an opportunity.

Again, if you the Reader are half as blessed in studying this material, as I was in putting it together, then you will be blessed indeed! Time and time again, the Spirit of God would move upon me as the Holy Spirit would enlighten my heart and my mind relative to the Word of God. We give Him all the Praise and the Glory!

If you have been encouraged in the Word, and have learned more about the Word, of which there could be nothing greater, as a result of this effort, then our labors have been well worthwhile. As always, it is our intention to glorify Christ, and this can be done by hopefully shedding a little more light on this, the most important of all subjects, the God Breathed Word.

"I am trusting Thee, Lord Jesus
"Trusting only Thee;
"Trusting Thee for full Salvation,
"Great and Free."

"I am trusting Thee to guide me,
"Thou Alone shalt lead,
"Every day and hour supplying
"All my need."

"I am trusting Thee for power,
"Thine can never fail;
*"Words which Thou Thyself shall
   give me,*
"Must prevail."

"I am trusting Thee, Lord Jesus,
"Never let me fall;
"I am trusting Thee forever,
"And for all."

BIBLIOGRAPHY

W. T. Armstrong *"Chronology of the New Testament."*

Kenneth Grayston *"The Epistles to the Galatians and to the Philippians."*

Maurice Jones *"The Epistle to the Philippians."*

J. B. Lightfoot *"Saint Paul's Epistle to the Philippians."*

M. R. Vincent *"Word Studies in the New Testament."*

Kenneth S. Wuest *"Philippians In The Greek New Testament."*

W. E. Vine *"Vine's Expository Dictionary of New Testament Words."*

Dr. Bernard Rossier *"A Study in Philippians."*

Henry Alford *"The Greek Testament."*

H. G. G. Moule *"The Epistle to the Philippians."*

W. M. Ramsay *"Saint Paul the Traveller and the Roman Citizen."*

John F. Walvoord *"The Humiliation of the Son of God."*

Charles John Ellicott *"Commentary on the Whole Bible."*

Robert Rainey, D. D. *"The Epistle to the Philippians."*

Albert Barnes *"Notes on the New Testament."*

George Williams *"The Student's Commentary on the Holy Scriptures."*

E. F. Scott *"The Epistle to the Philippians."*

M. R. Vincent *"Studies in the New Testament."*

D. D. Whedon *"Commentary on the New Testament."*

James Hastings *"The Great Text of the Bible."*

INDEX

The index is listed according to subjects. The treatment may include a complete dissertation or no more than a paragraph. But hopefully it will provide some help.

As well, even though extended treatment of a subject may not be carried in this Commentary, one of the other Commentaries may well include the desired material.

ABRAHAM, 366
ABUNDANT LIFE, 416
ACCEPTABLE, 464
ADVANTAGES, 66
ADVERSARIES, 84
AFFLICTION, 48, 455
ANCIENT, 135
ANGELS, 113
ANGER, 287
ANIMOSITY, 322
ANOINTED, 145, 435, 454
ANSWER, 333
APOSTASY, 59, 230, 439
APOSTLE, 5, 41, 204, 311
APPROVAL, 28
ARMINIANISM, 212
ASCENSION, 155, 158
ASCETICISM, 200
ATMOSPHERE, 79
ATONEMENT, 61, 127, 128, 135, 201, 238, 248
ATTAINMENT, 343, 345, 365, 366
AUTHORITY, 140
AUTONOMY, 183
BAPTISM, 279, 439
BATTLEGROUND, 218
BELIEVER, 10, 11, 12, 62, 96
BENJAMIN, 312, 313
BIBLE, 146
BIRTH, 185
BISHOPS, 5
BLAMELESS, 225
BLOOD, 51, 127, 197
BODY, 393
BOLDNESS, 44, 65
BOND SLAVE, 407

BONDS, 20, 42
BOOK, 413
BOWELS, 101, 102
BRETHREN, 348, 395, 428, 469
BUDDY SYSTEM, 275
CAESAR, 470
CALVINISM, 212
CHANGE, 393
CHARACTER, 162
CHOICE, 70
CHRIST, 138, 139, 140, 143, 147, 150, 151, 152, 153, 154, 155
CHRISTIANITY, 311
CHRISTLIKENESS, 96, 101
CHURCH, 5, 26, 29, 34, 46, 63, 73, 89, 230, 274, 288, 289, 315, 328, 329, 372, 375, 396, 434
CIRCUMCISION, 291, 294
CITIZENSHIP, 388
CLAIMS, 139
CLEANSING, 185
CLIMATE, 427
COMFORT, 99
COMMANDMENT, 268, 269
COMPARISON, 213
COMPASSION, 23
CONCEPTION, 146
CONDITION, 94
CONDUCT, 162, 389
CONFESSION, 281
CONFIDENCE, 44, 73
CONFIRMATION, 21
CONFLICT, 93, 94
CONSECRATION, 19, 190, 233
CONTENTION, 47
CONTROL, 167

CONVERSATION, 79
CONVERTS, 395
CORINTHIANS, 214
COUNT, 349
COURSE, 399
COVERING, 278
CREATION, 185
CRISIS, 209
CROSS, 7, 8, 26, 33, 63, 86, 91, 97, 106, 126, 129, 146, 147, 166, 172, 182, 265, 283, 284, 309, 325, 332, 336, 345, 360, 373, 376, 377, 378, 379, 381, 382, 383, 405, 432, 439, 455
CROWN, 395, 397, 398, 400, 401
CRUELTY, 48
DANGERS, 229
DAVIDIC COVENANT, 149
DEACONS, 5, 6
DEATH, 66, 115, 126, 128, 153, 164, 207, 250, 342, 360, 362
DEDICATION, 189
DEFENSE, 20, 49
DEITY, 142
DELIVERANCE, 60, 130, 283
DEMONS, 277
DENOMINATIONS, 279, 352
DEPRAVITY, 106
DESCRIPTION, 123
DESIRE, 461
DESTRUCTION, 385
DIRECTION, 32
DISCERNMENT, 27
DISCIPLES, 140
DISCIPLINE, 323
DISPUTINGS, 223
DIVINE ENABLEMENT, 216
DIVINE NATURE, 193
DOGS, 287, 288
DOMINATION, 35
DOOR, 340, 375
EARTH, 159
ENEMIES, 377, 382
ENVY, 45
EPAPHRODITUS, 245, 251, 463
EQUALITY, 114, 116
ERADICATION, 199
ERROR, 58
EVIDENCE, 154
EVIL WORKERS, 289
EXALTATION, 116, 137, 142
EXAMPLE, 36, 114, 195, 200, 201, 235, 308, 349, 353, 368, 386, 387, 440
EXCELLENT, 28

EXPECTATION, 64, 391
EXPLANATION, 343
EXPLOITATION, 165
FAILURE, 89, 350, 381, 449
FAIR GAME, 352
FAITH, 39, 62, 63, 74, 82, 97, 106, 181, 182, 184, 192, 201, 220, 236, 250, 281, 283, 306, 331, 333, 335, 336, 348, 373, 376, 380, 381, 384, 396, 427, 432, 438, 446, 447, 448, 449, 450, 469
FALSE DOCTRINE, 291, 292
FAMILY CURSE, 275
FASHION, 122, 408
FASTING, 275
FELLOWLABORERS, 412
FELLOWSHIP, 13, 100, 341
FINISHED WORK OF CHRIST, 4, 8, 173
FINNEY, 214
FLESH, 67, 72, 131, 132, 134, 303, 304, 305
FOLLOWERS, 370
FORGIVENESS, 209, 334
FORM, 112, 403
FORMULA, 431
FOUND, 327
FRUIT, 31, 68, 462
FRUSTRATION, 32, 367
FULFILLMENT, 145, 149
GARBAGE, 326
GENTLENESS, 108, 109
GIVING, 13, 14, 456, 459
GLORY, 36, 400, 466, 468
GOD, 113
GOOD REPORT, 430
GOOD WILL, 46
GOSPEL, 13, 21, 40, 41, 49, 82, 311, 366, 412, 458
GOVERNMENT, 6
GRACE, 6, 7, 8, 22, 106, 150, 175, 176, 367, 471
GROWTH, 24
HARMLESS, 225
HEAD, 6
HEALING, 247, 248
HEALTH, 431
HEART, 20, 364
HEAVEN, 80, 159, 388
HEAVINESS, 246
HEBREWS, 213, 313
HELL, 54, 56
HIGH PRIEST, 135
HOLINESS, 18, 337
HOLY SPIRIT, 31, 34, 38, 61, 298, 307, 376, 383
HOME, 40
HONEST, 428
HUMAN, 121

HUMAN NATURE, 115, 187
HUMILIATION, 120
HUMILITY, 106, 107, 109, 115, 123, 407
IDENTIFICATION, 51
IGNORANCE, 457
ILLUSTRATION, 271, 354, 452
IMPUTED RIGHTEOUSNESS, 177, 328
IN CHRIST, 172, 205, 358
INCARNATION, 144
INSPIRATION, 325
INSTRUCTION, 444
INTERCESSION, 12
INTERPRETATION, 136, 343
INTERVIEW, 467
ISRAEL, 147, 302, 312
ITCHING EARS, 439
JACOB, 210
JESUS, 55, 56
JESUS DIED SPIRITUALLY DOCTRINE, 50
JEWS, 43, 313
JOHN WESLEY, 208
JOY, 13, 74, 102, 237, 395, 414, 415
JUDAISM, 267
JUDGMENT, 26
JUDGMENT SEAT, 233
JUST, 429
JUSTIFICATION, 167, 168, 173, 176, 181
KEY, 298
KING, 152
KINGDOM, 151, 388
KNEE, 159
KNOWLEDGE, 25, 26, 202, 324, 340
LABOR, 68, 232
LAMB, 129
LAW, 134, 169, 219, 270, 272, 316, 317, 320, 329
LAW OF THE SPIRIT, 133, 379
LAYING ON OF HANDS, 278
LEADERSHIP, 232
LEGALISM, 199, 317
LESSON, 310, 459
LIFE, 164, 230, 284, 399, 413
LIGHT, 226, 228
LIGHTHOUSE, 229
LIKEMINDED, 103, 241
LIKENESS, 407
LIMITATION, 121
LOVE, 23, 25, 49, 99, 101, 104
LOVELY, 429
LOWLINESS, 105
MACEDONIA, 458
MAN, 322
MANIFEST, 42

MANIFESTATIONS, 274
MARK, 357
MATURITY, 92, 359, 360
MEDICINE, 247
MEEKNESS, 107, 109
MERCIES, 101, 102, 261
MIND, 81, 105, 110, 137, 403
MINISTRY, 12, 157, 225
MIRACLE, 123
MISPLACED FAITH, 133
MODERATION, 416, 418
MONARCHICAL EPISCOPACY, 5
MONEY, 464
MOSES, 161, 317, 320
MURMURINGS, 223
MYSTERY, 121
NAME, 138
NATURE, 129, 138, 350
NECESSITY, 461
NICENE CREED, 141
OBEDIENCE, 125, 161, 162, 163
OFFENCE, 29
OFFERING, 234
OPERATION, 363
OPPORTUNITY, 442
OPPOSITION, 14
PARABLE, 152
PAUL, 39, 43, 46, 57, 108, 267, 325
PEACE, 9, 425, 426, 441
PERCEPTION, 17, 437
PERFECTION, 92, 208, 345
PHARISEE, 124, 314
PLAN, 146
POSITIONAL, 188, 194, 196
POUNDS, 152
POWER, 394
PRACTICAL, 189, 196
PRAISE, 36, 430
PRAYER, 12, 13, 221, 277, 420, 421, 423
PREACHER, 16, 36, 46, 311
PREACHING, 125, 352
PREJUDICE, 363
PREPARATION, 188
PRIEST, 151
PRIZE, 357
PROBATION, 351
PROBLEM, 47, 377, 426
PROMISE, 218, 252, 425
PROOF, 243
PROPHECY, 149
PROPHET, 150
PROPITIATION, 164

PSYCHOLOGY, 276, 433
PURE, 29, 429
PURIFICATION, 190
QUESTION, 50, 78, 249
QUICKENING, 185
RACE, 358
REALITY, 15
REBUKE, 226
RECEIVING, 459
REDEMPTION, 130, 280
REGENERATION, 178, 179, 185, 186, 187, 188
REJOICING, 57, 76, 236, 237, 262, 264, 301, 414, 415, 441
RELATIONSHIP, 339
RELIGION, 48, 186, 315, 368
REMEMBRANCE, 11
REPRESENTATIVE MAN, 272, 319, 405
REPUTATION, 116, 263
REQUESTS, 424
RESPONSIBILITY, 216
RESURRECTION, 154, 186, 341, 344, 360
RETIREMENT, 234
REVELATION, 25, 362
RICHES, 466
RIGHTEOUSNESS, 18, 31, 168, 169, 176, 177, 304, 316, 318, 319, 327, 329, 330, 331, 333, 337, 399
ROBBERY, 114, 404
SACRIFICE, 52, 234, 464
SADDUCEES, 124
SAINTS, 3, 470
SALVATION, 176, 211, 296
SANCTIFICATION, 189, 194, 196, 199, 201, 207, 278
SARAH, 366
SARCASM, 359
SATAN, 53
SAVIOUR, 390, 391
SECURITY, 211
SELF, 345, 346, 404, 405, 406
SELF HELP, 27
SELF-DENIAL, 97, 378
SELF-EMPTYING, 118
SELF-RIGHTEOUSNESS, 170, 316
SELF-WILL, 103
SEPARATION, 189
SERPENT, 53
SERVANT, 2, 117, 120
SERVICE, 115, 194, 235, 243, 264
SHAME, 64, 387
SICKNESS, 246, 247, 249, 250
SIN, 3, 35, 52, 205, 270, 274, 372, 377, 405
SIN-OFFERING, 52
SINCERITY, 28

SINNER, 53
SLAVE, 2
SMELL, 463
SON OF DAVID, 148
SON OF MAN, 143
SORROW, 261
SOUND DOCTRINE, 454
SOVEREIGNTY, 142, 156
SPIRIT CONTROL, 299
SPIRITUAL, 189
STANDARD, 389
STRENGTH, 451
STRIFE, 45, 105, 409
SUBSTITUTE, 51, 129, 272, 319, 405
SUFFERING, 87, 163, 341
SUPPLICATION, 420
SUPPLY, 465
SUPPORT, 15
TEACHING, 125
TEMPTATION, 192, 210, 400
TESTIMONY, 43, 140, 227
THANKSGIVING, 424
THEONOMY, 183
THESSALONICA, 460
TIMOTHY, 239
TITLES, 10
TOKEN, 84
TRAGEDY, 371
TRAINING, 445
TRUST, 244, 257, 310
TRUTH, 58, 77, 202
TYPE, 136
VAINGLORY, 105
VICTORY, 190, 209, 282, 342, 371, 373, 401, 406
VILE, 393
VIRTUE, 110, 430
WALK, 131, 369, 374
WAY, 330
WEIGHT, 81, 118
WELFARE, 386
WILLPOWER, 280
WISDOM, 251, 256, 260
WITNESS, 22
WORD, 141
WORKS, 175, 184
WORKS RIGHTEOUSNESS, 328
WORLD, 34, 389
WORRY, 419
WORSHIP, 295, 299
YOKEFELLOW, 408, 409

For all information concerning the *Jimmy Swaggart Bible Commentary*, please request a Gift Catalog.

You may inquire by using Books of the Bible.

- Genesis (639 pages) (11-201)
- Exodus (639 pages) (11-202)
- Leviticus (435 pages) (11-203)
- Numbers
  Deuteronomy (493 pages) (11-204)
- Joshua
  Judges
  Ruth (329 pages) (11-205)
- I Samuel
  II Samuel (528 pages) (11-206)
- I Kings
  II Kings (560 pages) (11-207)
- I Chronicles
  II Chronicles (528 pages) (11-226)
- Ezra
  Nehemiah
  Esther (288 pages) (11-208)
- Job (320 pages) (11-225)
- Psalms (688 pages) (11-216)
- Proverbs (320 pages) (11-227)
- Ecclesiastes
  Song Of Solomon (245 pages) (11-228)
- Isaiah (688 pages) (11-220)
- Jeremiah
  Lamentations (688 pages) (11-070)
- Ezekiel (508 pages) (11-223)
- Daniel (403 pages) (11-224)
- Hosea
  Joel
  Amos (496 pages) (11-229)
- Obadiah
  Jonah
  Micah
  Nahum
  Habakkuk
  Zephaniah *(will be ready Spring 2013)* (11-230)

- Matthew (625 pages) (11-073)
- Mark (606 pages) (11-074)
- Luke (626 pages) (11-075)
- John (532 pages) (11-076)
- Acts (697 pages) (11-077)
- Romans (536 pages) (11-078)
- I Corinthians (632 pages) (11-079)
- II Corinthians (589 pages) (11-080)
- Galatians (478 pages) (11-081)
- Ephesians (550 pages) (11-082)
- Philippians (476 pages) (11-083)
- Colossians (374 pages) (11-084)
- I Thessalonians
  II Thessalonians (498 pages) (11-085)
- I Timothy
  II Timothy
  Titus
  Philemon (687 pages) (11-086)
- Hebrews (831 pages) (11-087)
- James
  I Peter
  II Peter (730 pages) (11-088)
- I John
  II John
  III John
  Jude (377 pages) (11-089)
- Revelation (602 pages) (11-090)

For telephone orders you may call 1-800-288-8350 with bankcard information. All Baton Rouge residents please use (225) 768-7000. For mail orders send to:

Jimmy Swaggart Ministries
P.O. Box 262550 • Baton Rouge, LA 70826-2550
Visit our website: www.jsm.org

NOTES

NOTES

NOTES

NOTES

NOTES

NOTES

NOTES

NOTES

NOTES